METRIC AND ENGLISH EQUIVALENTS

MEASURE	EQUIVALENTS

LENGTH

1 millimeter = 0.0394 inches
1 centimeter = 0.3937 inches or 0.0328 feet or 0.0109 yards
1 meter = 39.37 inches or 3.28 feet or 1.094 yards
1 kilometer = 3,280.8 feet or 1,093.6 yards or 0.621 miles
1 inch = 2.54 centimeters or 25.4 millimeters
1 foot = 30.48 centimeters or 0.305 meters
1 yard = 91.44 centimeters or 0.9144 meters
1 mile = 1,609.35 meters or 1.609 kilometers

LIQUID VOLUME

1 milliliter = 0.0338 ounces
1 liter = 33.82 ounces or 1.06 quarts or 0.264 gallons
1 ounce = 29.57 milliters or 0.0296 liters
1 pint = 473 milliliters or 0.473 liters
1 quart = 946 milliliters or 0.946 liters
1 gallon = 3,785 milliliters or 3.785 liters

DRY VOLUME

1 cubic centimeter = 0.061 cubic inches
1 cubic meter = 35.31 cubic feet or 1.308 cubic yards
1 cubic foot = 0.0283 cubic meters
1 cubic yard = 0.765 cubic meters

WEIGHT

1 gram = 0.035 ounces or 0.0022 pounds
1 kilogram = 2.205 pounds
1 metric ton = 1.102 tons
1 ounce = 28.35 grams or 0.0284 kilograms
1 pound = 453.6 grams or 0.454 kilograms
1 ton = 0.907 metric tons

TABLES OF WEIGHTS AND MEASURES

METRIC UNITS	ENGLISH UNITS

LENGTH

10 millimeters (mm) = 1 centimeter (cm)
100 centimeters (cm) = 1 meter (m)
1,000 millimeters (mm) = 1 meter (m)
1,000 meters (m) = 1 kilometer (km)

12 inches (in) = 1 foot (ft)
3 feet (ft) = 1 yard (yd)
1,760 yards (yd) = 1 mile (mi)
5,280 feet (ft) = 1 mile (mi)

LIQUID VOLUME

1,000 millimeters (ml) = 1 liter (l)
1,000 liters (l) = 1 kilometer (kl)

16 ounces (oz) = 1 pint (pt)
2 pints (pt) = 1 quart (qt)
4 quarts (qt) = 1 gallon (gal)
2 pints pt) = 1 quart (qt)
128 ounces = 1 gallon (gal)
8 pints pt) = 1 gallon (gal)

DRY VOLUME

1,000 cubic millimeters (mm^3) = 1 cubic centimter (cm^3)
1,000,000 cubic centimeters (cm$^{3)}$ = 1 cubic meter (m^3)

1,728 cubic inches (cu in) = 1 cubic foot (cu ft)
27 cubic feet (cu ft = 1 cubic yard (cu yd)
46,656 cubic inches (cu in) = 1 cubic yard (cu yd)

WEIGHT

1,000 milligrams (mg) = 1 gram (g)
1,000 grams (g) = 1 kilogram (kg)
1,000 kilograms (kg) = 1 metric ton

16 ounces (oz) = 1 pound (lb)
2,000 pounds (lb) = 1 ton

METRIC PREFIX MEANINGS

kilo- = one thousand
deci- = one tenth
centi- = one hundredth
milli- = one thousandth
micro- = one millionth

SCIENCE K–8

An Integrated Approach

Edward Victor
Emeritus Professor
Northwestern University

Richard D. Kellough
Emeritus Professor
California State University at Sacramento

Robert H. Tai
Associate Professor
University of Virginia

Upper Saddle River, New Jersey
Columbus, Ohio

Library of Congress Cataloging-in-Publication Data

Victor, Edward,
Science K-8 : an integrated approach / Edward Victor, Richard D. Kellough, Robert H. Tai. — 11th ed.
p. cm.
Includes bibliographical references and index.
ISBN-13: 978-0-13-199210-8
1. Science—Study and teaching (Elementary) 2. Science—Study and teaching (Middle school) I. Kellough, Richard D. (Richard Dean) II. Tai, Robert H. III. Title.
LB1585.V46 2008
372.3'5—dc22

2007019359

Vice President and Executive Publisher: Jeffery W. Johnston
Executive Editor: Meredith D. Fossel
Editorial Assistant: Kathleen S. Burk
Production Editor: Alexandrina Benedicto Wolf
Production Coordination: Kelli Jauron, Carlisle Publishing Services
Design Coordinator: Diane C. Lorenzo
Cover Designer: Jeff Vanik
Cover Image: Jupiter Images
Production Manager: Susan Hannahs
Director of Marketing: David Gesell
Marketing Coordinator: Brian Mounts

This book was set in Berkeley by Carlisle Publishing Services. It was printed by Edwards Brothers. The cover was printed by Coral Graphics.

Pearson Education Ltd.
Pearson Education Australia Pty. Limited
Pearson Education Singapore Pte. Ltd.
Pearson Education North Asia Ltd.
Pearson Education Canada, Ltd.
Pearson Educación de Mexico, S.A. de C.V.
Pearson Education—Japan
Pearson Education Malaysia Pte. Ltd.

10 9 8 7 6 5 4 3 2
ISBN-13: 978-0-13-199210-8
ISBN-10: 0-13-199210-4

Preface

Our intent for *Science K–8: An Integrated Approach* is to provide a contemporary source of appropriate and relevant pedagogy, subject-matter content, learning activities, and resources for people preparing to teach science to children in Grades K–8. Experienced teachers, administrators, and science curriculum specialists will also find it a useful reference.

Exemplary K–8 educational programs are rooted in celebrating and building upon the diverse characteristics and needs of young people. To become and to remain exemplary, teachers in such programs must be in a continual mode of inquiry, reflection, and change. It is no different for us as the authors of this book. In a continuing effort to prepare a comprehensive and exemplary book on teaching science to children in Grades K–8, we are in a *continual mode of inquiry* into the latest findings in research and practice, in *constant reflection* as we listen to and assess the comments from practitioners in the field and from users and reviewers of the book, and in *steady change* as we respond to the challenge of providing new coverage for integrating methods and resources.

Organization of This Edition

Competent teaching is a kaleidoscopic, multifaceted, eclectic process. When preparing and writing a book for use in one segment of a program for teacher preparation, by necessity one must separate that kaleidoscopic process into separate parts, which is probably impossible to do in a way that makes the most sense to everyone using the book.

This book is divided into four parts. Part One focuses on pedagogy, and Parts Two, Three, and Four focus on science content. For the sake of clarity and sensible organization for this eleventh edition, Part One addresses what we consider to be the four developmental components of teaching and learning:

- *Why*—the rationale to support the components that follow
- *What*—the content, processes, and skills you will be helping children learn
- *How*—how you will do it
- *How well*—how well you are doing it

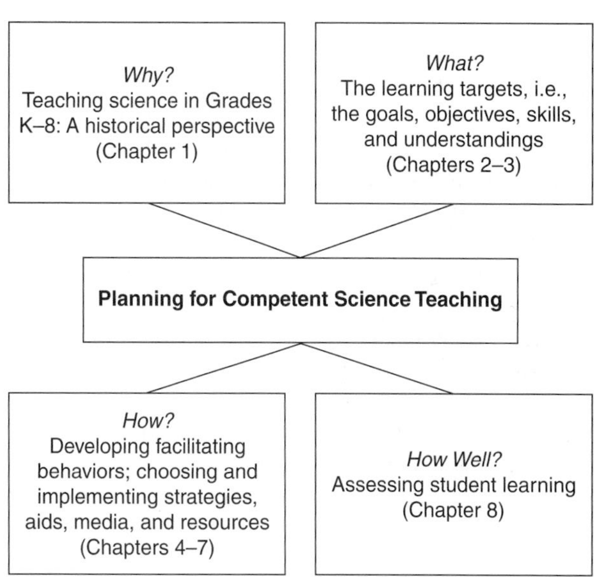

Together, these four components constitute the essentials of effective instruction. The visual map above illustrates how these four components are divided.

It is neither likely nor advisable that one should or could effectively learn about one component exclusive of the others. The four components are inextricably intertwined, with each affected by and dependent upon the others. Indeed, teaching and learning are reciprocal processes that depend on and affect one another. For the sensible organization of this book, assessment is addressed as the fourth and final component of competent instruction even though it is really an integral part of an ongoing process in the total educational arena. For example, one cannot thoroughly plan for instruction (Chapter 7) without considering the learning objectives (Chapter 2) and the assessment strategies (Chapter 8).

Our Beliefs: How and Where They Are Reflected in This Book

As a teacher, your greatest resources are the children you teach and the adults with whom you work. This is not a book of recipes; we are preparing teachers, not chefs. We cannot tell you what will always succeed best with your students; you will know them better than we do. In this book we do share the best practices, the most useful research findings, and the richest experiences.

Integrated learning by inquiry is the cornerstone of effective science instruction for the twenty-first century. We present strategies that integrate learning and provide illustrations of how they may be used. Active learning by student inquiry and teaching for thinking are emphasized in this book. You are probably well aware that professional education is rampant with its own special jargon, which can be confusing to the neophyte. The use of the term *direct teaching* (or its synonym, *direct instruction*), and its antonym, *direct experiences,* are examples of how confusing the jargon can be. The term *direct teaching* (or *direct instruction, expository teaching, teacher-centered instruction*) can also have a variety of definitions, depending on who is doing the defining. In this book, we try to keep our use of terminology simple and succinct. For example, what we mean by *integrated approach to learning* is addressed in Chapter 1; *inquiry* is addressed in Chapter 5 in greater depth than previous editions.

Effective science teaching doesn't just happen. Certain understandings and behaviors are absolutely fundamental for the most effective teaching and learning to occur. Fundamental understandings include the nature of science and how children learn science (Chapter 3). Fundamental teacher behaviors (Chapter 4) create the conditions needed to enable students to think and to learn, whether the learning is a further understanding of a science concept, the internalization of attitudes and values, the development of cognitive processes, or the actuating of the most complex behaviors (all addressed in Chapter 2). Clearly, at least some of the fundamental teacher behaviors are also instructional strategies. Questioning is one example. The difference is that the behaviors must be in place for the most effective teaching to occur, but strategies (Chapter 5) are more or less discretionary; that is, they are pedagogical techniques from which you may select but are not obligated to use. For example, questioning and the use of silence are fundamental teaching behaviors (discussed in Chapter 4), whereas lecturing (Chapter 5) and taking children on a field trip (Chapter 6) are not. Therefore, your task is two-fold: (1) develop your awareness of and skills in using the fundamental teaching behaviors, and (2) develop your repertoire and skills in selecting and using appropriate instructional strategies for facilitating children's learning of science. Starting now, your understanding and development of these skills will continue throughout your teaching career.

To be most effective, a teacher must use an eclectic style in teaching. Rather than focus your attention on particular models of science instruction, we emphasize the importance of an eclectic model—that is, one in which you select and integrate the best from various instructional approaches. For example, while most of the time you will want to use an indirect, social-interactive, student-centered approach that features process-based, cooperative learning and project-based learning, there are times when you will want to use a direct, expository, and content-centered approach. More often the exemplary teacher is doing both at the same time, that is, using what we refer to as *multilevel instruction* (see Chapter 5). Our desire is to present information and guidelines that will help you develop the skills necessary for selecting and using a specific approach. Practice, experience, time, and reflection are your best allies for increasing your effectiveness in implementing multilevel instruction.

Acknowledgments

Teaching and learning in Grades K–8 has become increasingly complex—with many new and exciting things happening as schools continue to restructure their efforts to provide the best learning for today's children. While wanting to be as thorough as possible, we struggle to keep the text at a reasonable length and to make it user friendly. We thank all the persons who helped in its development. We thank those who contributed and who are acknowledged at appropriate places throughout and our friends and highly competent professionals at Merrill/Prentice Hall, who have maintained their belief in and support for this book. We also wish to thank Scott S. Lloyd for his assistance.

While preparing this eleventh edition, we carefully heeded the recommendations by users and reviewers of the previous edition. We acknowledge and offer a sincere thank you for the cogent reviews and recommendations made by Andrew Kemp, University of Louisville; Jose Rios, University of Washington-Tacoma; Paul Prell, Concordia University; and Norman Thomson, University of Georgia.

Although this book is the result of the contributions of many professionals, we, as always, assume full responsibility for any shortcomings. Our aspiration for this eleventh edition is that it will spark reflective thinking about your teaching and that you will find it stimulating and professionally rewarding now and for several years to come.

A Note to Readers

You may have noticed the addition of a third author to this eleventh edition of *Science K–8: An Integrated Approach*. When Dr. Kellough asked me to take on the role of helping shape the next edition, I approached this task with a healthy respect for the existing work. I use this textbook with my own classes and though it is not a perfect fit, I have come to adapt it to the needs of my students. This I believe will be the case for many if not all teacher educators. There are distinct elements in this text that distinguishes it from other elementary/middle school teacher education textbooks. The inclusion of a content resource (Chapters 9–21) offers students a fingertip option for lesson planning. The in-depth discussion of Bloom's Taxonomy offers a clear overview of constructs that remain valuable to those just entering the teaching profession.

In this new edition, rather than making a move to break away from the past, I chose to keep much of the existing text and make some additions with respect to the area of teaching with an inquiry-based approach. While the "standard and accountability" movement continues to press classroom teachers to focus on student achievement and standardized test performance, the role of science education at the K–8 grade levels as a means of igniting children's interest and creativity cannot be ignored. In an educational research article published in the journal *Science*, my research team and I offered some empirical evidence in support of the notion that generating interest in science is an essential function for K–8 science.[1] For this reason, a thoughtful and well-designed approach to helping students become more proficient in making their own scientific inquiries seems a reasonable pedagogical tactic. Readers will find these additions in Chapter 5.

While accountability through standardized testing may currently dominate the educational landscape, we should not lose sight of our ultimate goal as educators—the goal of making the act of learning a source of interest and delight to our students. Science has long held an important place in the imagination of young children, and while good test scores may be important in the short run, deep and abiding interest in science and the exploration of ideas about the natural world is the outcome that will have lasting impact.

I thank Dick Kellough for placing his trust in me. I am humbled by this task. I hope that my efforts in this and any successive editions will bear out his decision to include me.

Robert H. Tai.
Curry School of Education, University of Virginia

[1] Tai, R. H., Liu, C. Q., Maltese, A. V., & Fan, X. (2006). Planning early for careers in science. *Science, 312, 1143–1144.*

Contents

Chapter 7

Chapter 8

Basic Science Information, Learning Activities, and Other Resources: An Introduction to Inquiry

PART TWO

Chapter 9

Part ONE

Teaching Science K–8

All teachers of science need to

- Understand the nature of scientific inquiry, its central role in science, and how to use the skills and processes of scientific inquiry
- Understand the fundamental facts and concepts in the major science disciplines
- Be able to make conceptual connections within and across science disciplines, and to mathematics and technology
- Use scientific understanding and ability when dealing with personal and societal issues[1]

[1]Reprinted from National Research Council, *National Science Education Standards,* © 1996 by the National Academy of Sciences, 59. Courtesy of National Academy Press, Washington, DC.

Chapter 1

Teaching Science in Grades K–8: Then and Now

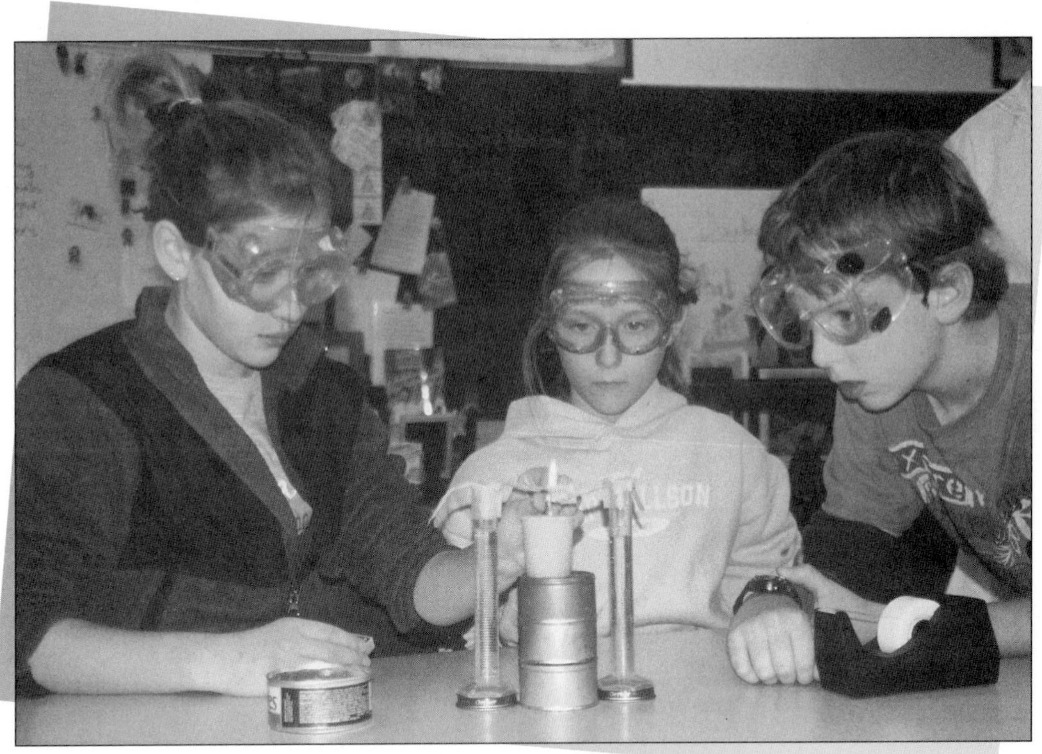

Lori Whitley/Merrill

Teachers of **grades K–4** usually are generalists who teach most, if not all, school subjects. A primary task for these teachers is to lay the experiential, conceptual, and attitudinal foundation for future learning in science by guiding students through a range of inquiry activities. To achieve this, elementary teachers of science need to have the opportunity to develop a broad knowledge of science content in addition to some in depth experiences in at least one science subject. Such in depth experiences will allow teachers to develop an understanding of inquiry and the structure and production of science knowledge.

Science curricula are organized in many different ways in the **middle grades.** Science experiences go into greater depth, are more quantitative, require more sophisticated reasoning skills, and use more sophisticated apparatus and technology. These requirements of the science courses change the character of the conceptual background required of middle level teachers of science. While maintaining a breadth of science knowledge, they need to develop greater depth of understanding than their colleagues teaching grades K–4. An intensive, thorough study of at least one scientific discipline will help them meet the demands of their teaching and gain appreciation for how scientific knowledge is produced and how disciplines are structured.[2]

Welcome to the exciting, ever-changing world of K–8 science teaching. Whether or not you will ever be responsible for teaching science, you need to know why learning science is so important for children. Regardless of the grade level and designation of the school in which you teach,[3] if you are teaching science now or will be in the future, you need to know what to teach and how to teach it well. This book of methods, activities, and resources is designed to help you make decisions and gain appropriate understandings and skills, and then to implement those understandings and skills effectively.

The quest begins in this chapter as you learn why science is taught in grades K–8. To understand the reasons, it is helpful to have some knowledge of the history of 20th century K–8 science. Science has not always been an esteemed subject of the K–8 curriculum. During the final years of the 20th century, however, there was renewed emphasis, both nationally and locally, on the importance of children's having early and continued experiences in science. For the K–8 curriculum, science at last is recognized as a basic discipline. As stated in *Educating Americans for the 21st Century*, "The basics of the twenty-first century are not only reading, writing and arithmetic . . . [but also] communication and higher problem-solving skills, and scientific and technological literacy."[4] Furthermore, as stated in a 1990 publication of the American Association for the Advancement of Science (AAAS), a leading federation of scientific societies, "Human survival and the quality of life depend on liberally educated citizens who are able to make informed assessments of the opportunities and risks inherent in the scientific enterprise. . . . Science must be taught as one of the liberal arts, which it unquestionably is."[5]

The number and variety of effective techniques for teaching science are steadily increasing. These advances result from (a) a recognition of the importance of science as a basic discipline in the school curriculum, (b) the continuing rapid development of new technologies, and (c) a growing body of research about thinking and how children learn. Each of these areas is presented

[2]Reprinted from National Research Council, *National Science Education Standards*, © 1996 by the National Academy of Sciences, 60. Courtesy of National Academy Press, Washington, DC.

[3]For example, what is referred to as the *elementary school* sometimes includes students from kindergarten through grade 8, although often it stops with grade 5 or 6. An *intermediate school* commonly houses children of grades 4–6. *Middle level schools* most often house children of grades 6–8.

[4]National Science Board Commission on Precollege Education in Mathematics, Science, and Technology, *Educating Americans for the 21st Century* (Washington, DC: National Science Board, 1983), v.

[5]American Association for the Advancement of Science, *The Liberal Art of Science: An Agenda for Action* (Washington, DC: Author, 1990), xi.

and discussed in this book, complemented by a broad array of exciting teaching ideas and ways of integrating science learning into the K–8 curriculum.

Reasons for Science in the K–8 Curriculum

In the United States, science was the last of the major disciplines to be included in the K–8 curriculum. Today it is taught in those grades because (a) learning science can build attitudes that are important, (b) science learning attends to and nourishes the child's natural curiosity about the environment, (c) science learning builds a base for important understanding, and (d) learning science develops skills necessary for survival in the adult world. As stated in *Project 2061: Science Literacy for a Changing Future,* "K–12 education . . . should be reformed so that all American high school graduates are science literate—that is, equipped with the knowledge and skills they need to make sense of how the world works, to think critically and independently, and to lead interesting, responsible, and productive lives in a culture increasingly shaped by science and technology. . . . The common core of learning in science, mathematics, and technology should center on science literacy . . . [and] should emphasize connections among the natural and social sciences, mathematics, and technology and between those areas and the arts, humanities, and vocational subjects."[6]

To help you understand the role of science in the K–8 curriculum today, let's review how the science curriculum has evolved.

In the Beginning

The history of science in the school curriculum is a reflection of economic and political events in our society. Until the economic depression of the 1870s, practically no science was taught in the elementary schools; the emphasis was on reading, writing, spelling, and arithmetic. Only children of well-to-do parents who could afford private tutors learned science. Their tutoring in science involved the use of didactic reading materials about natural phenomena that were brought from abroad, primarily from England. In 1857, the National Education Association helped to make some of that literature available for use in school classrooms in the United States.

Pestalozzi and Object Teaching

In the 1870s, science taught in schools was based on the writings of the Swiss educator Johann Pestalozzi (1746–1827). Pestalozzi believed that the emphasis in teaching should be on training the mind and that students should learn by observing and experimenting, using all their senses, rather than by merely memorizing facts from books. However, at the time of the U.S. Industrial Revolution in the late 19th century, Pestalozzi's "object-centered" approach lost its appeal because of its lack of emphasis on content and sequential organization. As a direct result of the Industrial Revolution, which precipitated an exodus of people from rural areas into cities and mass migrations of people to the United States, elementary science programs were developed that emphasized content and vocational technology—utilitarian science.

The Nature Study Movement

In the final decade of the 19th century, nature study was introduced into the vocational-oriented science curriculum in a few schools, mostly in New York state. Its purpose was to help children develop a more balanced life by getting to know the natural environment through firsthand observation, classification, and measurement of objects and organisms—for example, birds, flowers, and rocks—in natural habitats.

Almost from its beginning, however, the nature study movement met obstacles and criticism, and resistance to it only increased with time. The people who introduced the movement were both specialists in science and master teachers. They were able to make the study of nature a dynamic and unforgettable experience for the children. However, once entrusted to other teachers with little or no background in science and with varying degrees of teaching effectiveness, the study of nature in the elementary schools deteriorated. Undue emphasis was placed on incidental items. Identification and classification assumed increasing importance and eventually became the end, rather than the means. Learning activities involving firsthand observations gave way to reading about nature in books, where much of the science content was only partially correct, and fable and fancy were often interspersed with fact. By 1920 it was clear that nature study, as it was being taught in the schools, was not successful. Nature study was dead; utilitarian science was alive.

Landmarks in the Development of the K–8 Science Curriculum

As we reset our compass for a voyage into science education for the 21st century, it seems most appropriate to

[6]American Association for the Advancement of Science, *Project 2061: Science Literacy for a Changing Future: Update 1994* (Washington, DC: Author, 1994), 6.

Scott Cunningham/Merrill

The goals of K–8 science require programs that emphasize experiences designed to further the intellectual, emotional, physical, and social development of children. Firsthand observation and learning by doing have nearly always been recognized as important in achieving those goals.

reflect on and to learn from the history of the past century of K–8 science education in the United States. There have been significant and important landmarks indeed.

John Dewey

A century ago, John Dewey demonstrated in his laboratory school in Chicago the importance of giving children responsibility for their own learning and of allowing them to pursue their natural curiosity. He further posited that children learn best through direct experience. Shortly thereafter, in his 1910 publication *How We Think,* Dewey spoke of the importance of *science as inquiry* and argued for curriculum integration.[7]

School Restructuring

During those early years of the 20th century, the nation's population increased markedly. Schools were undergoing reorganization. One of the changes was the development of the junior high school, with an initiation of courses in general science. Because of pressure from colleges and universities and because of the change from an 8–4 pattern of organization (eight years of elementary school and four years of high school) to a 6–3–3 pattern (six years of elementary school, three years of junior high school, and three years of high school), the science curriculum at each level changed.

Gerald S. Craig

In 1927 while a graduate student at Columbia University, Gerald S. Craig wrote a doctoral dissertation that became another landmark in the historical development of science curriculum. Written in response to economic and political situations, his thesis titled "Certain Techniques Used in Developing a Course of Study in Science for the Horace Mann Elementary School," led to the development of a science curriculum that dominated elementary school science for more than three decades. Strongly favoring teaching science through hands-on investigations by the children, Craig organized the existing chaos of science instruction into a sequence of what and how.

Yearbooks of the National Society for the Study of Education

In 1932, shortly after the publication of Craig's thesis and while the nation started to recover from economic depression, yet another landmark appeared—the *Thirty-first Yearbook* by the National Society for the Study of Education (NSSE).[8] The yearbook, which dealt exclusively with science in public schools, recommended a continuous science program from kindergarten through 12th grade. Further, it proposed that the objectives of science teaching be to develop an understanding of (a) the major generalizations of science, and (b) associated scientific attitudes. Emphasizing scientific understandings, science as a body of factual information, and the applications of science and technology, the *Thirty-first Yearbook* had profound influence on the direction of textbooks, course syllabi, and curriculum development. The importance of problem-solving strategies and the development of certain attitudes and appreciations, however, were neglected.

In 1947, following the end of World War II, the NSSE published a second yearbook devoted to science education. Recognizing the impact of science on society, the *Forty-sixth Yearbook* reaffirmed NSSE's earlier recommendation for a continuous K–12 science program.[9] Further, it stressed that the learning outcomes should be functional and proposed the following general goals: (a) The functional understanding of facts, principles, and concepts, and (b) the development of functional scientific skills, attitudes, appreciations, and interests. Although facts and

[7] J. Dewey, *How We Think* (Boston: Heath, 1910).

[8] G.W. Whipple, ed., *Thirty-first Yearbook, Part I* (Bloomington, IL: National Society for the Study of Education, Public School Publishing, 1932).

[9] N. B. Henry, ed., *Forty-sixth Yearbook, Part I* (Chicago: National Society for the Study of Education, University of Chicago Press, 1947).

understanding of science remained the major focus of science instruction, problem-solving skills and development of attitudes and appreciations were also addressed.

In 1960, in its *Fifty-ninth Yearbook*—the third to be devoted to science education—the NSSE expressed awareness of the increasing dependence of society on science.[10] It now took for granted that schools had a continuous and articulated K–12 science program. It repeated the basic goals stated in the *Forty-sixth Yearbook,* deleting the word "functional," adding critical thinking and emphasis on problem solving, and stressing the importance of teaching science as a process of inquiry. By the early 1960s, it had become clear to science educators that what scientists do is to invent and use conceptual schemes, which are gradually modified and occasionally even discarded.[11] Conceptual schemes, then, became the framework for an articulated kindergarten through 12th grade science program.

In the early 1960s, children's learning of science became a national concern, which was triggered by several factors. In 1957, the Soviet Union had sent up the world's first manufactured orbiting space satellite, Sputnik I. In the world race for technological superiority that ensued, the United States, experiencing a critical shortage of scientists and technicians, was not winning. And scientists and science educators around the country were deploring the insufficient attention being given to teaching science as a process of inquiry.

The National Curriculum Development Projects of the 1960s

Out of this national concern came many new programs, sponsored mostly by the National Science Foundation (NSF), to improve the teaching and learning of science in public schools. The first NSF-sponsored projects were developed to upgrade science teaching at the high school level. Projects were then created for improving middle level science programs. Attention eventually focused on elementary school science, and several projects were developed at that level.

The national curriculum projects were the most exciting events that had happened in science education. They were publicized extensively because their heavy financial support made possible the large-scale involvement of scientists, science educators, teachers, psychologists, and children. For guidance and direction in developing the programs, the creators of the projects turned to theories and research by child development psychologists on how children develop intellectually and how they learn. The projects were actively concerned with teaching science as a process of inquiry—*teaching science as it is practiced.* After several years of testing, scientific supply houses packaged, advertised, and sold the materials needed for the learning activities that were an integral part of the projects.

Although the NSF-sponsored projects did not agree on the role, quantity, and emphasis of content or on the degree of freedom for student exploration, they did agree that science should be taught as a *process of inquiry.* A major contribution of the projects was to ensure a place in the school science program for an inquiry approach to teaching science. The emphasis on this approach continues today. For example, "Teaching Standard A" of the *National Science Education Standards,* published in 1996, suggests that "teachers of science plan an inquiry-based science program for their students."[12] Since the release of the standards, at least two major books have been published to explain the meaning of that statement.[13]

A second major contribution of the NSF-sponsored projects was the change from the teacher telling about science to the teacher facilitating students' doing hands-on science—another emphasis that continues today.

A third contribution was the movement from a textbook-centered curriculum to a materials-centered one that presented fewer areas of content studied in greater detail. Covering fewer topics but learning fundamental science concepts well is an emphasis that continues today.[14]

Of the elementary science curriculum projects developed in the 1960s, three emerged as the most popular: the Elementary Science Study (ESS), the Science Curriculum Improvement Study (SCIS), and Science—A Process Approach (SAPA). Although the NSF-sponsored inquiry-based, activities-oriented programs were more effective in raising student performance and attitudes about science than were traditional reading-based programs,[15] in the 1970s their popularity began to wane for several reasons. (SAPA is no longer available but versions of ESS and SCIS are available from Delta Education, Inc., phone 1-800-258-1302 [http://www.delta-ed.com].) School systems found it difficult to adapt the prepackaged materials to local curricula. Schools'

[10]N.B. Henry, ed., *Fifty-ninth Yearbook of the National Society for the Study of Education* (Chicago: National Society for the Study of Education, University of Chicago Press, 1960.)

[11]J.D. Novak, "Application of Advances in Learning Theory and Philosophy of Science to the Improvement of Chemistry Teaching," *Journal of Chemistry Education* 61(7):607–612 (July 1984).

[12]Reprinted from National Research Council, *National Science Education Standards,* © 1996 by the National Academy of Sciences, 30. Courtesy of National Academy Press, Washington, DC.

[13]See National Research Council, *Inquiry and the National Science Education Standards: A Guide for Teaching and Learning* (Washington, DC: National Academy Press, 2000) and J. Minstrell and E.H. van Zee, eds., *Inquiring into Inquiry Learning and Teaching in Science* (Washington, DC: American Association for the Advancement of Science, 2000).

[14]See, for example, page 3 of American Association for the Advancement of Science, *Science for All Americans: Project 2061 Summary* (Washington, DC: Author, 1995) and *National Science Education Standards,* 6.

[15]J.A. Shymansky, "A Reassessment of the Inquiry-Based Science Curricula of the 60s on Student Performance," *Journal of Research in Science Teaching* 27(2):127–144 (February 1990).

finances diminished as a long inflationary period steadily eroded their budgets. For many teachers, the activities were too complex and required too much preparation time in an already busy school day. So the trend again was for schools to develop their own science programs, adapted to their own needs and conditions.

In the 1970s, there also was concern about the decreasing verbal and mathematical scores of children on national examinations. A growing movement to get back to the basics undoubtedly distracted schools from the interest in science generated during the previous decade.

Back to the Basics

In the 1970s and throughout much of the 1980s, schools were accused of relaxing their demands for children to thoroughly learn the basics of reading, spelling, grammar, composition, and mathematics. Consequently, a strong back-to-basics movement arose. Simultaneously, a steadily increasing shortage of well-trained science and mathematics teachers made it difficult to find teachers capable of teaching science as inquiry. During the 1970s and 1980s the original NSF-sponsored projects underwent revision and new projects emerged, but by 1990 a preoccupation with learning scientific facts was accompanied by an increased emphasis on textbook learning of the fundamentals.

> As stated by Bruce Watson and Richard Konicek, today's texts, which have the greatest influence on how science is taught in American schools, have come almost full circle, and teachers who rely primarily on them are little closer to teaching science as inquiry than were their counterparts in the 1920s. In too many classrooms across the U.S., science is still taught as a cohesive set of facts to be absorbed, and children are viewed as blank slates on which teachers are to write.[16]

During this period, science teaching stressed acquisition of science knowledge, with little or no attention given to application or to the reforms offered by the science curriculum projects of the 1960s. In 1982, the National Science Teachers Association (NSTA) published a position statement urging that new goals be developed for science teaching that emphasized the education of students for scientific literacy.[17]

Decade of the Reports

Certainly no facet of education receives more attention from the media, causes more concern among parents and teachers, or gets larger headlines than a reported decline in students' achievement in the public schools. Reports are issued, polls taken, debates organized, and blue-ribbon panels formed. Community members write letters to local editors about this trend, news editors devote editorial space to it, television anchors comment about it, and documentaries and specials focus on it. Headlines proclaim, for example, "America's Children Study and Know Less Science Than Do Children of Most Other Countries."

Never were there so many reports about education published in such a short time as there were in 1983 and 1984. More than 120 national studies were published during just those two years. The interest continues today. Consider the brief sample of influential publications listed in Figure 1.1.

Anderson, R. C., et al. *Becoming a Nation of Readers: The Report of the Commission on Reading.* Washington, DC: National Institute of Education, 1985.
Applebee, A. N., et al. *The Writing Report Card: Writing Achievement in American Schools.* Princeton, NJ: National Assessment of Educational Progress at Educational Testing Service, 1986.
Berliner, D. C., and B. J. Biddle. *The Manufactured Crisis: Myth, Fraud, and the Attack on America's Public Schools.* New York: Addison-Wesley, 1995.
Carnegie Council on Adolescent Development. *Turning Points: Preparing Youth for the 21st Century.* New York: The Carnegie Corporation, 1989.
The Continuing Crisis in Science Education: The AAAS Responds. A Report to the Board of Directors. Washington, DC: American Association for the Advancement of Science, 1986.
Criteria for Excellence. Washington, DC: National Science Teachers Association, 1987.
Educating Americans for the 21st Century. Washington, DC: National Science Board, 1983.
Glasser, W. *The Quality School.* New York: Harper & Row, 1990.
Goodlad, J. I. *A Place Called School.* New York: McGraw-Hill, 1984.
Jacobson, W., and R. Doran. *Science Achievement in Western Countries.* Elmsford, NY: Pergamon Press, 1989.
The Liberal Art of Science: Agenda for Action. Washington, DC: American Association for the Advancement of Science, 1990.
National Commission on Excellence in Education. *A Nation at Risk.* Washington, DC: United States Office of Education, 1983.
A Nation Prepared: Teachers for the 21st Century. Washington, DC: Carnegie Forum on Education and the Economy, 1986.
Project Synthesis. Washington, DC: National Science Foundation, 1981.

FIGURE 1.1 Sample of the influential publications that began in the 1980s.

---

[16]B. Watson and R. Konicek, "Teaching for Conceptual Change: Confronting Children's Experience," *Phi Delta Kappan* 71(9):680–685 (May 1990), 681. For added historical perspectives, see also N.C. Harms, *Project Synthesis* (Boulder: School of Education, University of Colorado, 1979); N.C. Harms and R.E. Yager, eds., *What Research Says to the Science Teacher,* vol. 3 (Washington, DC: National Science Teachers Association, 1982); and D. Freedman, "Science Education: How Curriculum and Instruction Are Evolving," ASCD's *Curriculum Update* (fall 1998), 1–3, 6–8.

[17]National Science Teachers Association, *Science–Technology–Society: Science Education for the 1980s* (Washington, DC: Author, 1982).

The Final Decade of the 20th Century

In response to the reports, educators and politicians acted. Across the country, their actions resulted in changes in standards for teacher certification. For example, model standards describing what prospective teachers should know and be able to do to receive a teaching license were prepared and released in 1992 by the Interstate New Teacher Assessment and Support Consortium (INTASC), a project of the Council of Chief State School Officers (CCSSO), in a document titled *Model Standards for Beginning Teacher Licensing and Development.* INTASC is made up of representatives from at least 36 states and professional associations, including the National Education Association (NEA), the American Federation of Teachers (AFT), the American Association of Colleges for Teacher Education (AACTE), and the National Council for the Accreditation of Teacher Education (NCATE). The standards are performance-based and revolve around a common core of principles of knowledge and skills that cut across disciplines. The INTASC standards are compatible with the National Board for Professional Teaching Standards (NBPTS). Specifically addressing middle level instruction, in 1997 the NBPTS released 11 categories of standards for certification of Middle Childhood/Generalist.[18]

In addition to new standards for teacher certification, actions by educators and politicians responding to the flood of reports in the 1980s also resulted in

- Emphasis on education for cultural diversity and ways of teaching language minority students
- Emphasis on helping students make effective transitions from one level of schooling to the next and from school to life, with an increased focus on helping them to make connections between what is being learned and real life, and to make connections between subjects in the curriculum and between academics and vocations
- Emphasis on raising test scores, reducing dropout rates (that is, the number of students who do not complete high school or receive the equivalent degree), increasing instructional time, and changing curricula
- Federal enactment of *Goals 2000: Educate America Act* and the development of national curriculum standards for all major subject areas
- Formation of school–home–community connections
- New "basics" required for a high school diploma
- School restructuring to provide more curriculum options

[18]For information about NBPTS, see the Website at http://www.NBPTS.org. For information about the INTASC standards, go to http://www.ccsso.org/.

 Key Trends and Practices Today

Key trends and practices today include

- Deemphasizing traditional curriculum tracking and instead providing meaningful curriculum options with multiple pathways for academic success
- Dividing the student body and faculty into smaller cohorts—that is, the school-within-a-school concept—and using nontraditional scheduling
- Encouraging the practices of reflective thinking and self-discipline
- Facilitating students' social skills as they interact, relate to one another, solve meaningful problems, develop skills in conflict resolution, and foster peaceful relationships and friendships
- Facilitating the development of students' values relating to their families, the community, and schools
- Holding high expectations, although not necessarily the same expectations, for every student by establishing benchmark academic standards and assessing student achievement against those standards
- Integrating the curriculum
- Involving parents/guardians and communities in the schools
- Involving students in self-assessment
- Moving away from the traditional agrarian school calendar to a 45/15 year-round calendar to reduce the effect of the so-called summer regression—the loss of skills and content knowledge during the summer layoff
- Providing students with the time and the opportunity to think and be creative, rather than simply memorizing and repeating information
- Redefining giftedness to include nonacademic as well as traditional academic abilities
- Teaching and assessing for higher-order thinking skills
- Using heterogeneous small-group learning, peer coaching, and cross-age tutoring as instructional strategies
- Using the Internet in the classroom as a communication tool and learning resource

Focus on Science and Technology Literacy

In *The Liberal Art of Science: Agenda for Action,* the AAAS emphasized that science is fundamental to a liberal education and that people need to understand

- The nature of the scientific endeavor, concepts, principles, and theories that describe the natural world
- Unifying concepts that integrate the sciences with other disciplines

- How scientific knowledge influences and is influenced by the intellectual tradition of the culture in which that knowledge is embedded[19]

Nearly a decade before that publication, however, the AAAS began its Project 2061, a long-term multiphase project to work in collaboration with school-district teams to "radically improve science, mathematics, and technology education for the 21st century." The approach to Earth of Halley's comet in 1985 prompted the project's originators to imagine all the scientific and technological changes that a child entering school in 1985 would likely live to witness before the return of the comet in 2061—hence the name Project 2061.[20]

Initially, Project 2061 focused on the substance of science literacy. Publication of *Science for All Americans (SFAA)* was the major product of that effort. It proposes the dimensions of scientific literacy—the knowledge, skills, and attitudes—that students should have as a result of their K–12 science experiences. As defined by that publication, the dimensions of scientific literacy are

- Being familiar with the natural world and recognizing both its diversity and its unity
- Understanding key concepts and principles of science
- Being aware of some of the important ways in which science, mathematics, and technology depend on one another
- Knowing that science, mathematics, and technology are human enterprises and knowing what that implies about their strengths and limitations
- Having a capacity for scientific ways of thinking
- Using scientific knowledge and ways of thinking for individual and social purposes[21]

Emphasizing the connectedness of knowledge from various disciplines, *SFAA* recommends softening the boundaries to make better connections between and among traditional subject disciplines. It also recommends reducing the amount of detail that students are required to remember.

Project 2061 involves teams of educators and scientists transforming the recommendations of *SFAA* into a number of alternative curriculum models. A product of that effort, and the second major tool developed by Project 2061, is *Benchmarks for Science Literacy.*[22] *Benchmarks* elaborates on the *SFAA* recommendations in terms of students' progress toward each of the learning goals it outlines—specifically, what students should be able to do by the end of grades 2, 5, 8, and 12.

Project 2061 teams continue to work on identifying useful current materials, units of instruction and curriculum models, a resource database for curriculum and instruction, and blueprints for reforming other aspects of the educational system to accommodate new curriculum models.[23]

Focus on Curriculum Standards

Curriculum standards define what students should know (content) and be able to do (process and performance). At the national level, curriculum standards did not exist until the National Council of Teachers of Mathematics developed and released standards for mathematics education in 1989 (revised in 2000). Shortly thereafter, support for national goals in education was endorsed by the National Governors Association. The National Council on Education Standards and Testing then recommended that in addition to those for mathematics, national standards for subject matter content in K–12 education be developed for the arts, civics/social studies, English/language arts/reading, geography, history, and science. The U.S. Department of Education provided initial funding for the development of national standards. In 1994, the U.S. Congress passed the *Goals 2000: Educate America Act*, which was amended in 1996 with an Appropriations Act that encouraged states to set curriculum standards. Long before that however, national organizations devoted to various disciplines were already defining standards, as had been done for mathematics.

The national standards represent the best thinking by expert panels, which includes teachers from the field, about the essential elements of a basic subject knowledge that all K–12 students should acquire. They serve not as national mandates but rather as voluntary guidelines to encourage curriculum development to promote higher student achievement. It is left to the discretion of state and local curriculum developers to decide the extent to which the standards are used.

In 1991, the National Research Council (NRC), operating arm of the National Academy of Science, began coordinating work on national standards for science curriculum, teaching, and assessment. They were published in their final form in 1996 and are available on the Internet.[24]

The National Science Education Standards draws extensively from, and makes independent use and interpretation of, the statements concerning what students should know and be able to do that were published earlier in the AAAS publications *Science for All Americans* and *Benchmarks for Science Literacy.*

Strongly influenced by the national standards, nearly all states have completed and are implementing

[19]American Association for the Advancement of Science, *Liberal Art of Science,* 16.
[20]American Association for the Advancement of Science, *Project 2061,* 6.
[21]American Association for the Advancement of Science, *Science for All Americans,* 4.
[22]American Association for the Advancement of Science, *Benchmarks for Science Literacy* (New York: Oxford University Press, 1993).

[23] See the Project 2061 home page at http://project2061.aaas.org.
[24] See http://www.nap.edu/readingroom/books/nses/html and NSTA at http://www.nsta.org.

at least some of their own standards for science and for the various disciplines. For example

- For the state of Massachusetts, standards are found in seven Curriculum Frameworks: Arts, English/Language Arts, Health, Mathematics, Science and Technology, Social Studies, and World Languages.
- For the state of Montana, Content and Performance Standards are found in documents for Reading, Mathematics, Speaking and Listening, Media Literacy, Writing, Literature, Health Enhancement, Science, Technology, World Languages, Arts, Library Media, Social Studies, and Work Place Competencies.
- The North Carolina Standard Course of Study presents curriculum in Arts Education, Computer/Technology Skills, English/Language Arts, Healthful Living, Mathematics, Science, Second-Language Studies, Social Studies, and Work-Force Development (which includes sections on Planning, the Middle Grades, Agricultural Education, Business Education, Family and Consumer Sciences, Health Occupations, Marketing Education, Career Development, Technical Education, and Trade and Industrial Education).
- For the state of Texas, the Texas Essential Knowledge and Skills (TEKS) are in the foundation areas of English Language Arts and Reading, Mathematics, Science, Social Studies, and Spanish Language Arts and English as a Second Language, and in the enrichment areas of Languages Other Than English, Fine Arts, Health, Physical Education, and Technology Applications (which includes Agricultural Science and Technology, Business Education, Health Science Technologies, Home Economics Education, Technology Education/Industrial Technology Education, Marketing Education, Trade and Industrial Education, and Career Orientation).

Both national and state standards provide guidance to the developers of the standardized tests used in what is referred to today as high-stakes testing—that is, the tests being used at various grade levels to determine student achievement; promotion; financial rewards to schools and even to individual teachers, principals, and students; and in about half the 50 states as a requirement for graduation from high school.

Preparing Students for High-Stakes Testing: When All Students Are Expected to Do Well on a Mandated Assessment, Then All Should Be Given Equal Opportunity to Prepare for It

The adoption of tougher K–12 learning standards throughout the United States, coupled with an emphasis on increased high-stakes testing to assess how schools and teachers are helping their students meet those standards, has provoked considerable debate, action, and reaction among educators, parents, and politicians, and from the world of business. Some argue that this renewed emphasis on testing means too much "teaching to the test" at the expense of more meaningful learning and that it ignores the leverage that home, community, and larger societal influences have over the education of children and young people today. For example, in the words of Lauren Sosniak,[25]

> We need to find ways to ask what our communities, corporations, media, and all of our organizations and institutions are doing to promote the development of readers, writers, historians, scientists, artists, musicians, designers and craftspersons. Schools cannot do this work alone, in the 9% of [a child's K–12 lifetime in school] allotted to them. If this is only "school work," it is hard to imagine that our students will see it as a meaningful part of their lives and their futures. . . . For too long our schools have been held accountable for too much, with too little acknowledgement of the responsibilities of the rest of society.

Nevertheless, responding to the call for increased accountability, especially, although certainly not exclusively, when state and federal funding may be withheld and/or jobs are on the line for schools, teachers, and administrators where students do not score well, teachers in some schools put aside the regular curriculum for several weeks in advance of the testing date and concentrate on the direct preparation of their students for the test.

Although interest has been rekindled in recent years, this oft-called "drill and kill" practice is certainly not new. Today's interest in annual statewide testing has caused us to consider how it compares with past practices when we were classroom teachers. Comparing standardized testing of today with that of about a half century ago, it is probably safe to conclude that (a) the purpose of statewide standardized testing remains unchanged—fundamentally it is to determine how well children are learning, at least to the extent determined by the particular test instrument, and to encourage improved learning, (b) test design is accomplished today with much greater precision and accuracy, but (c) today's focus on testing is taking precious time away from the most creative aspects of teaching and learning, and (d) the way test results are being used today and the long-term results of that use may have ramifications considerably more serious than at any time in the past.[26]

---

[25] L. Sosniak, "The 9% Challenge: Education in School and Society," *Teachers College Record* [Online only, 2001, http://www.tcrecord.org ID Number: 10756, Date Accessed: 5/7/01].

[26] See, for example, W.J. Popham, "Right Task, Wrong Tool," *American School Board Journal 189*(2):18–22 (February 2002).

Schools with the required computer technology can subscribe to software programs such as *eduTest* (http://www.eduTest.com) and *Homeroom.com* (http://www.homeroom.com). If enough computers are available to provide access time to individual students, they can practice and prepare for the mandated tests online. Proponents of such online preparation argue that a major advantage is the immediate scoring of practice tests with feedback about each student's areas of weakness, which provides the teacher with information necessary for immediate remediation. If the arguments are accurate, then it would seem axiomatic that children in such technology-rich schools would clearly be at an advantage over children in schools where this technology is not available. It would only follow that district and government agencies that mandate the standards and specific assessment practices should provide avenues and tools to assure equity and success for all children in reaching the expected learning outcomes within the designated time.

Problems and Issues That Affect the School Science Program

Improvement in the teaching and learning of science in grades K–8 does not occur just because influential individuals and organizations say it should. As someone once remarked, reorganizing and restructuring schools is like trying to rebuild a 747 jetliner while it is in flight. Changing tradition and people's minds is like trying to stop an onrushing tank with only your hands. Changing what people do and think is often a slow process, which may be one reason that Project 2061 is designed to be long-term. As a new teacher, you will become an important agent in this change process.

As Good and Brophy (below) imply, improvement in K–8 science teaching and learning does not occur in a vacuum. All the problems and issues that affect the total school and society, such as those listed in Figure 1.2, affect what science is taught, how it is taught, and the effectiveness with which it is taught.

Consideration of these complex issues, along with recent research on how children learn concepts, have helped correct some of the imbalances produced by the earlier science curriculum projects. For example, the preoccupation of earlier projects with the key processes of science led schools and teachers to discourage reading in science and often to eliminate it completely from the science program. New knowledge about learning and a renewed emphasis on human issues and the fundamentals needed to live a useful and meaningful life has now led to efforts to integrate subjects in the curriculum. Today's science teacher is no longer isolated from the rest of the school curriculum. Dewey recommended synthesis of the curriculum with children's life experiences. Today there is a concerted national effort to develop a curriculum that focuses on helping children make connections between disciplines and real-life experiences and that emphasizes ideas and thinking, rather than preserving the traditional boundaries between academic disciplines. (See Chapter 5, "Problem Solving and Decision Making in the Real World Is an Integrated and Interdisciplinary Inquiry Activity" and "Unit Planning" in Chapter 7).

In the earlier science curriculum projects, emphasis on the key operations of science resulted in a tendency to assign the learning of concepts to a position of secondary importance in the program. Now concepts, processes, the internalization of values, and the human aspects of the scientific enterprise are recognized as equal in importance. They are interdependent and interrelated, not only among themselves but also with the entire curriculum. Science has become a vital, balanced, integrated school activity. Exemplary science teaching today is concerned with teaching science and integrating it into the curriculum in a way that is meaningful to the everyday lives of all students and helpful to each child's developing self-esteem. That, as we said in the preface, is the basic premise of this edition of our textbook.

A Continuing Dilemma for the Classroom Teacher

Breadth versus Depth of Content Coverage Many more things are worth teaching than we have time to teach in school, so breadth of topic coverage must be balanced against depth of development of each topic. This is an enduring dilemma that can only be managed in sensible ways, not a problem that can be solved once and for all. In recent decades we have drifted into addressing far too many topics and including too many trite or pointless details. Curriculum analyses in all of the subject areas suggest the need for teacher decision-making about how to reduce breadth of coverage, structure the content around powerful ideas, and develop these ideas in depth.

[*Source:* T. L. Good and J. E. Brophy, *Looking in Classrooms*, 8th Edition (New York: Addison Wesley Longman, 2000), p. 418.]

- Bias, prejudice, harassment, and violence on school campuses.[27]
- Buildings and facilities that are outdated, old, and in need of repair and upgrading.[28]
- Controversy created by mandatory high-stakes testing.[29]
- Controversy over the use, extent, and legality of school dress codes.[30]
- Debate regarding the value of the child-centered middle school concept versus a rigorous curriculum-centered approach.[31]
- Inadequate funding to classroom teachers for equipment and supplies.[32]
- Lack of materials for individualizing the instruction.[33]
- Recruiting and retaining school administrators.[34]
- Retention in grade and the search for alternatives to grade retention.[35]
- Using standardized test scores and statistics to judge and reward the performance of schools and classroom teachers, thereby creating a disincentive for teachers to teach particular groups of children.[36]
- Scarcity of minority teachers to serve as role models for students.[37]
- Schools that are too large.[38]
- Shortage of computers and software.[39]
- Shortage of qualified teachers.[40]
- The education of teachers to work effectively with children who may be too overwhelmed by personal problems to focus on learning and to succeed in school.
- The number of youth at risk of dropping out of school.[41]

FIGURE 1.2 Problems and issues that plague our nation's schools.

The Integrated Approach

The term **integrated approach** refers to both a way of teaching and a way of planning and organizing the instructional program so the discrete disciplines of subject matter are related to one another in a design that (a) matches the developmental needs of the learners and (b) helps to connect their learning in ways that are meaningful to their current and past experiences. In that respect, it is the antithesis of traditional disparate subject-matter-oriented teaching and curriculum designations. It is antagonistic to the tradition of science being taught as a disparate subject at the same time each school day or every few days of the school week.

Today's interest in an integrated approach has risen from a variety of resources, especially recent research in cognitive science and neuroscience. This research has demonstrated the necessity of helping students establish bridges between school and life, knowing and doing, content and context. Interest in constructivism as opposed to a strictly behaviorist philosophical approach to teaching and learning has also been rekindled (a topic that is discussed in Chapter 2).

Just as you will learn in later chapters about using inquiry teaching, using an integrated approach is not necessarily how every teacher should or must always plan and teach. As evidenced by practice, the truth of this statement becomes obvious. There are, for example, times in facilitating children's learning that they must simply memorize science facts, practice skills, and read about what others have already discovered. But more about that in subsequent chapters.

Attempts to connect students' learning with their experiences fall at various places on a spectrum or continuum, from the least integrated instruction (level 1) to the most integrated (level 5), as illustrated

[27]See, for example, S. L. Wessler, "Sticks and Stones," *Educational Leadership 58*(4):28–33 (December 2000/January 2001).
[28]See, for example, "National Survey Provides Snapshot of K–12 Science Classrooms," *NSTA Reports! 13*(4):1, 6–7, 15 (February/March 2002).
[29]See, for example, S. Ohanian, "News from the Test Resistance Trail," *Phi Delta Kappan 82*(5):363–366 (January 2001).
[30]See, for example, B. Dowling-Sendor, "A Question of Rights vs. Authority," *American School Board Journal, 188*(7):38–39, 44 (July 2001) and R. Trerise and C. Johnson, "Are You Going to School in *That*?" *Principal 81*(4):60–61 (March 2002).
[31]See, for example, V. A. Anfara, Jr. and L. Waks, "Resolving the Tension Between Academic Rigor and Developmental Appropriateness," *Middle School Journal 32*(2):46–51 (November 2000) and R. M. Offenberg, "The Efficacy of Philadelphia's K–8 Schools Compared to Middle Grades Schools," *Middle School Journal 32*(4):23–29 (March 2001).
[32]"National Survey Provides Snapshot of K–12 Science Classrooms," *NSTA Reports! 13*(4):1, 6–7, 15 (February/March 2002).
[33]"National Survey Provides Snapshot of K–12 Science Classrooms," *NSTA Reports! 13*(4):1, 6–7, 15 (February/March 2002).
[34]See, for example, D. A. Gilman and B. Lanman-Givens, "Where Have All the Principals Gone?" *Educational Leadership 58*(8):72–74 (May 2001).
[35]See, for example, W. A. Owings and L. S. Kaplan, *Alternatives to Retention and Social Promotion* (Bloomington, IN: Fastback 481, Phi Delta Kappa Educational Foundation, 2001).
[36]See, for example, A. Goodnough, "Strain of Fourth-Grade Tests Drives Off Veteran Teachers," *New York Times,* June 14, 2001.
[37]See, for example, O. Jorgenson, "Supporting a Diverse Teacher Corps," *Educational Leadership 58*(8):64–67 (May 2001).
[38]See, for example, the entire theme issue, "class size, school size," of *Educational Leadership,* vol. 59, no. 5 (February 2002).
[39]"National Survey Provides Snapshot of K–12 Science Classrooms," *NSTA Reports! 13*(4):1, 6–7, 15 (February/March 2002).
[40]See, for example, L. Darling-Hammond, "The Challenge of Staffing Our Schools," *Educational Leadership 58*(8):12–17 (May 2001).
[41]See, for example, P. Kaufman, et al., *Dropout Rates in the United States, 1998.* Statistical Analysis Report (Washington, DC: ED438381, National Center for Education Statistics, 2000).

Least Integrated Level 1	*Level 2*	*Level 3*	*Level 4*	*Most Integrated Level 5*
Subject-specific topic outline	Subject-specific	Multidisciplinary	Interdisciplinary thematic	Integrated thematic
No student collaboration in planning	Minimal student input	Some student input	Considerable student input in selecting themes and in planning	Maximum student and teacher collaboration
Teacher solo	Solo or teams	Solo or teams	Solo or teams	Solo or teams
Student input into decision making is low.		Student input into decision making is high.		Student input into decision making is very high.

FIGURE 1.3 Levels of curriculum integration. *Source:* The concept of "levels of curriculum integration," as presented here, was developed by R. D. Kellough and appeared first in several books published simultaneously in 1996 by Prentice Hall, including Kellough, et al., *Integrating Mathematics and Science for Kindergarten and Primary Children,* and Kellough et al., *Integrating Mathematics and Science for Intermediate and Middle School Students.*

in Figure 1.3. This illustration should not be interpreted as going from "worst case scenario" (far left) to "best case scenario" (far right), although some people may interpret it in exactly that way. The fact is that there are various interpretations of curriculum integration and each teacher must make his or her own decisions about its use. Being able to suspend judgment while gathering data, to consider their own unique circumstances, and then to make such decisions is what defines teachers as *professionals*. Figure 1.3 is meant solely to show how efforts to integrate science instruction and learning fall on a continuum of sophistication and complexity. The following is a description of each level of the continuum.

Level 1 Curriculum Integration

Level 1 curriculum integration is the traditional organization of curriculum and classroom instruction, where teachers plan and arrange the subject-specific scope and sequence in the format of topic outlines. Any attempt to help students connect their experiences and their learning is up to individual classroom teachers. A student in a school and classroom that has subject-specific instruction at varying times of the day (e.g., language arts at 8:00, mathematics at 9:00, social studies at 10:30, and so on) from one or more teachers is likely learning at a level 1 instructional environment, especially when what is being learned in one subject has little or no connection with content being learned in another. The same applies for a student, as found in many middle level schools, who moves from classroom to classroom, teacher to teacher, subject to subject, and one topic to another. A topic in science, for example, might be earthquakes. A related topic in social studies might be the social consequences of natural disasters. These two topics may or may not be studied by a student at the same time.

Level 2 Curriculum Integration

If the same students are learning English/language arts, or social studies/history, or mathematics, or science using a thematic approach rather than a topic outline, then they are learning at level 2. (See Chapter 7, "Select a Suitable Topic or Theme," for a discussion about what a topic is and what a theme is.) At this level, themes for one discipline are not necessarily planned and coordinated to correspond or integrate with themes of another or to be taught simultaneously. At Level 2, the students may have some input into the decision-making involved in planning themes and content from various disciplines.

Some educators say that the curriculum of the future will be based on broad, unchanging, and unifying concepts; that is, on conceptual themes.[42] If so, it would be a recycling of an approach of the 1960s, as supported by the writings of Jerome Bruner[43] and implemented in some of the NSF-sponsored curriculum projects of that era, such as *Elementary Science Study* (ESS).[44] In fact, there is already action in that direction. For example, the National Science Education Standards are centered on unifying conceptual and procedural schemes, such as "systems,

[42]See, for example, E. M. Lolli, "Creating a Concept-Based Curriculum," *Principal* 76(1):26–27 (September 1996) and T. L. Riley, "Tools for Discovery: Conceptual Themes in the Classroom," *Gifted Child Today Magazine* 20(1):30–33, 50 (January/February 1997).

[43]See, for example, J. S. Bruner, *Process of Education* (Cambridge, MA: Harvard University Press, 1960).

[44]Information and materials about ESS are available from Delta Education http://www.deltaed.com.

order, and organization," "evidence, models, and explanation," "change, constancy, and measurement," "evolution and equilibrium," and "form and function."[45] And forming the basis for the national standards for social studies are 10 "thematic strands," including "people, places, and environment" and "science, technology, and society."[46]

Level 3 Curriculum Integration

When the same students are learning two or more of their core subjects (English/language arts, social studies/history, mathematics, and science) around a common theme such as "natural disasters" from one or more teachers, they are then learning at level 3 integration. At this level, teachers agree on a common theme and then deal with it *separately* in their individual subject areas, usually at the same time during the school year. So what the student is learning from a teacher in one class is related to and coordinated with what the student is concurrently learning in another class or several others. At level 3, students may have some input into the decision-making involved in selecting and planning themes and content. Some authors may refer to levels 2 or 3 as *coordinated* or *parallel curriculum*.

Level 4 Curriculum Integration

When teachers and students collaborate on a common theme and its content, and when discipline boundaries begin to disappear as teachers teach about this common theme, either solo or as an interdisciplinary teaching team, level 4 integration is achieved.

Level 5 Curriculum Integration

When teachers and their students have collaborated on a common theme and its content, when discipline boundaries are truly blurred during instruction, and when teachers of several grade levels and various subjects teach toward student understanding of aspects of the common theme, this is level 5, an *integrated thematic approach*.

Guidelines for integrating topics and for planning and developing an interdisciplinary thematic unit are presented in Chapter 7.

Integrated Curriculum in a Standards-Based Environment

It is still too early to obtain reliable data on how students in programs using an integrated approach fare on mandatory statewide standardized proficiency tests. It should be reassuring to today's classroom teacher, however, to know that from their analysis of recent data, Vars and Beane conclude that "almost without exception, students in any type of interdisciplinary or integrative curriculum do as well as, and often better than, students in a conventional departmentalized program. These results hold whether the combined curriculum is taught by one teacher in a self-contained or block-time class or by an interdisciplinary team."[47]

Key Reasons for Science in Grades K–8

The words of Herbert Smith, written in 1963, are no less appropriate today.

> One may summarize the historical overview [of K–8 science] by pointing out that the past century has been a century of unprecedented social, economic, scientific, and technological change. The schools are to a very large degree a mirror of the ambient culture, and they are probably more sensitive to social change than any other educational level. They are always, to a degree, consonant with the prevailing philosophies and state of knowledge in existence at any particular time. Fundamental changes in philosophy, in theories of child rearing and educability, in the need for universal and extended educational training for all children and adolescents of our society with capacity to learn, have been accepted within this century. Science, itself, has progressed from the dilettantism of the leisured intellectual to a basic and fundamental activity of a substantial percentage of [all humankind].[48]

Everything considered, the key reasons science is taught in grades K–8 today are summarized in the paragraphs that follow.

Building Positive Attitudes Is Important

Dogmatic teaching is lethal to effective learning in science, whereas unrestrained thought enhances a child's natural curiosity. You should teach your class as if it were a think tank, encouraging skepticism, suspension of judgment, guessing, and intuitive thought. As the teacher, you must model these behaviors yourself.

Values and attitudes begin forming at an early age. Therefore, there are attitudinal objectives for science learning for the earliest grades that should be

[45]National Research Council, *National Science Education Standards* (Washington, DC: National Academy Press, 1996), 104.

[46]National Council for the Social Studies, "Curriculum Standards for Social Studies," 1994, available: http://www.ncss.org/standards/toc.html (2002, October 30).

[47]G. F. Vars and J. A. Beane, *Integrative Curriculum in a Standards-Based World* (Champaign, IL: ED441618, ERIC Clearinghouse on Elementary and Early Childhood Education, 2000).

[48]H.A. Smith, "Historical Background of Elementary Science," *Journal of Research in Science Teaching 1*(3):200–205 (1963), 203.

Scott Cunningham/Merrill

Through science learning, children develop their language skills, communicate with others, and learn by direct observation through listening, investigating, and sharing their experiences.

incorporated into the science curriculum starting in kindergarten. Sound learning objectives for all grades, beginning in kindergarten, include the following:

- The child demonstrates curiosity about the natural world.
- The child demonstrates respect for humans and other living things.
- The child demonstrates conservation practices.

Children must learn that science and scientific ways of thinking are important to their daily living and that careers in science and technology are open to all. The teacher can and should help dispel myths, superstitions, and stereotypes about science, sciencing,[49] and scientists.

Through science, children can develop intellectual and communication skills that improve their ability to get along with one another and to understand the natural world. Our environment is a rich "classroom" in which to teach science to children. We should strive always to leave it a better place. This includes avoiding unnecessary collecting and general "ripping off" of the outdoors. It means encouraging practices of preservation and enhancement of the environment. Such practice should begin with the child's inner environment (the child's own self), then proceed to the child's immediate environment (the child's own "turf"), which includes the classroom and other places where the child lives. When these environmental aspects of the child's world have been nourished and cared for, the global environment can be considered. A child cannot be expected to show concern for the future of an endangered species in a faraway place if the world of the child's own inner self is being inadequately tended. For example, a child from an urban environment in the Southeast who comes to school hungry cannot be expected to show much concern for the depletion rate of aquifers in the Midwest.

A skillful teacher strives for a balance between objective behaviors and intuitive thinking and creates a classroom climate where all children are welcomed and feel free to learn within a rich environment of shared responsibilities and decision-making.

Building Foundations for Understandings

In science, children should practice inquiry skills that lead to higher-order thinking. For example, kindergarten children can be taught the importance of listening fully to the ideas of others—a step toward the development of a critical, questioning attitude. They can be helped in their learning of impulse control, and they can be taught skills needed to generate data, such as observing, recalling, identifying, and measuring. Children should also be taught how to handle and care for plants, for animals, and for one another.

Children should learn cognitions in science that build as they progress from one level of schooling to the next. Kindergarten children learn to identify objects with similar characteristics, to compare and match pictures of animals and their offspring, to predict what will happen in some particular case, and to experiment to discover whether their predictions were correct. These are but a few of the intellectual skills that lead to a child's developing understanding of the larger conceptual organizations around which the K–12 science curriculum is built.

Science is taught in the earliest grades, not only because that is where we must begin laying the foundation for conceptual understandings, process skills, and positive attitudes and feelings about science and technology, but also because it is when we must begin stimulating and developing the child's innate curiosity about the natural environment. By doing science and learning science, children can

- Develop and apply values that contribute to their affective development
- Develop positive attitudes about science and technology
- Develop an awareness of the relationship and interdependence of science, technology, and society
- Develop an awareness of careers in science and technology
- Develop higher-order thinking skills

[49] "Sciencing" is a word used to emphasize the importance of process when talking about what it is a scientist does.

- Develop knowledge, understandings, and skills that contribute to their intellectual growth
- Develop their psychomotor skills

The development of students' interest in science also appears to have a real influence on their career decisions later in life. In 2006, a study appearing in *Science* offered evidence suggesting that students who reported an interest in science-related careers in eighth grade were two to three times more likely to graduate with a baccalaureate in a science discipline than their peers who were interested in nonscience careers.[50] This study also showed that standardized test performance was related to earning degrees in the physical sciences, but was not significant in determining who earned degrees in the life sciences. In the end, it appears that what we do as teachers to promote interest in science, may have far-reaching influence in our students' lives.

Summary

In this beginning chapter we have briefly surveyed the history of science education in this country, specifically how it has developed for K–8 science teaching. You gained knowledge of why science learning is so important for children today. In essence, you acquired an overview of why science is taught in grades K–8.

As is true for our schools in general, science teaching today may still need improvement, but science itself has undoubtedly become a basic subject for the K–8 grades. As a new teacher, you may understand this well. However, some experienced teachers and school administrators might not. Part of your task as a teacher might be to convince your colleagues of the importance and value of science in the school curriculum.

In Chapter 2, we begin addressing the *what* of science teaching and learning, with a focus on the specific goals and objectives of K–8 science.

Questions for Class Discussion

1. Select a grade range, such as K–2, 3–5, or 6–8, and give a rationale for why science should or should not be taught in those grades.
2. Name and describe the contributions of at least five major landmarks in the history of science teaching in this country.
3. Explain why some people consider science to be a basic subject. Explain why you agree or disagree that science is a basic.
4. Two teachers were asked, "What do you teach?" One teacher responded, "Children." The other teacher responded, "Science." From their responses, what tentative conclusions might we draw about these two teachers? In small groups, discuss your conclusions; then give a summary of your group's discussion to the entire class.
5. Explain the differences and similarities between science and technology. Is it important for children to understand the differences? Explain your answer and, if you think it is important, describe some ways you could help their understanding. What achievements in science and technology can you think of that have affected the social, economic, or cultural aspects of people's existence? Explain the effects.
6. What questions do you have about the content of this chapter? Where do you think the answers might be found?
7. Thinking back to your own experiences as students learning science in school, what was the single most exciting experience you had learning science as a student? What made it exciting for you? Did your classmates share your excitement?

[50] R. H. Tai, C. Q. Liu, A. V. Maltese, and X. Fan, "Planning Early for Careers in Science," *Science* 312(5777): 1143–1144 (2006).

Chapter 2

Goals and Objectives for K–8 Science

David Mager/Pearson Learning Photo Studio

During planning, goals are translated into a curriculum of specific topics, units, and sequenced activities that help students make sense of their world and understand the fundamental ideas of science. The content standards, as well as state, district, and school frameworks, provide guides for teachers as they select specific science topics. Some frameworks allow teachers choices in determining topics, sequences, activities, and materials. Others mandate goals, objectives, content, and materials. In either case, teachers examine the extent to which a curriculum includes inquiry and direct experimentation as methods for developing understanding. In planning and choosing curricula, teachers strive to balance breadth of topics with depth of understanding.[1]

As a teacher, you will often encounter the compound structure "goals and objectives." There is a distinction, however, and the easiest way to understand the difference between goals and objectives is to look at your intent.

Goals are ideals that you intend to reach; that is, ideals that you would like to have accomplished. Goals may be stated as teacher goals, as student goals, as course goals, or even more broadly, as goals of K–8 science (the broadest goals are sometimes referred to as "aims"). Ideally, however stated the goal is the same. If, for example, the broad goal (aim) is to improve students' scientific literacy, it can be stated two ways:

To help students become scientifically literate
= *teacher or course goal*
To improve my literacy in science = *student goal*

Goals are general statements of intent and are prepared by others or by teachers early in curriculum planning. (Note: Some writers use the phrase *general goals and objectives*, but that is redundant and incorrect. Goals are general; objectives are specific.) From goals, objectives are prepared and written, preferably in measurable (i.e., behavioral) terms so that assessment strategies can be prepared that best align with the objectives. Objectives are not intentions; they are the actual behaviors teachers intend to cause students to display. In short, objectives are what students do—their performance. Objectives represent the most detailed aspect of the "what" component of instruction (see the Preface), and they are integrally connected to the "how well" component (the focus of Chapter 8).

As implied in the preceding paragraphs, goals guide the curriculum and instructional methods; objectives drive student performance. Instructional goals are general statements, usually not even complete sentences, that often begin with the infinitive *to*. They identify what the teacher intends for the students to learn. Objectives, stated in performance (behavioral) terms, are specific, anticipated student actions. Objectives are complete sentences that include the verb *will* to indicate what each student is expected to be able to do as a result of the instructional experience. Objectives that are written in behavioral terms are more clearly measurable. Goals may not always be quantifiable; that is, readily measurable. However objectives, when correctly written, are always measurable.

Goals for K–8 Science

An articulated science curriculum is held together by at least six broad goals that have evolved during the past century or more of science education in the United States. The broad goals are to help students

- To become scientifically literate
- To solve problems by thinking critically and creatively
- To understand our environment and the problems of preserving it and making it better
- To understand how science, technology, and society are inextricably interconnected
- To live successfully and productively in a constantly changing world
- To grow intellectually, emotionally, and socially according to individual abilities, interests, and needs

Indeed, a strong argument could be made that these are not the exclusive goals of K–8 science but goals of formal K–12 education in general, to which each discipline may and should contribute. However true that might be, they are still the broad goals of K–8 science.

[1]Reprinted from National Research Council, *National Science Education Standards*, © 1996 by the National Academy of Sciences, 30. Courtesy of National Academy Press, Washington, DC.

To further your understanding, let's now consider each of these goals.

To Become Scientifically Literate

One goal of science education is to develop scientifically literate and personally concerned citizens who think and act rationally and productively. The K–8 science programs play an important role in getting children off to a good start toward achieving this goal.

The *scientifically literate person* understands the products and processes of science and uses them daily in making decisions while interacting with other people and the environment. The products of science include facts, concepts, principles, and theories. The processes include specific skills, attitudes, and values.

Important to scientific literacy is an understanding of the specialized vocabulary of science.[2] As a teacher of science, you must understand this concept and model correct usage; to do that, you, too, must understand terms. A teacher's use of the precise language of science helps children develop their science-process skills (the process skills are presented and discussed in Chapter 3).[3] The concept of using precise language with children is addressed later in Chapter 4 (see, for example, "Preparing Questions").

Terms That Are Basic to Understanding Science and Attaining the Goal of Scientific Literacy

◆ **Fact**. A fact is something known by observation or experience to be true or to have happened. Generally, two criteria are used to identify a scientific fact: (a) It is directly observable, and (b) it can be readily demonstrated. Facts, such as the fact that you are reading these lines now, have little meaning by themselves. However, they provide the foundation for the development and understanding of concepts, principles, and theories. Thoughtful reasoning is necessary to make sense from a fact.

◆ **Concept**. A concept is an abstraction that organizes the world of objects and events into a smaller number of categories.[4] Examples of concepts are combine, human, plant, star, acid, water, and electron flow. A concept results from the accumulation of facts with a common attribute. To comprehend the full meaning of a concept, we must understand its definition, its attributes, and its value.

◆ **Principle** (or **generalization** or **law**). Principles can be concepts or rules, but they involve some sort of relationship between two or more concepts. An example of a principle is "An acid and a base will combine to form water." Within this principle are four separate concepts—acid, base, combine, and water.

◆ **Theory** and **hypothesis.** To understand the term *theory*, as used in science, you must understand the term *hypothesis*. In ordinary usage outside science, the terms are used interchangeably. In science, however, they are not; they mean different things.

A *hypothesis* is a speculation—a guess that remains untested. In everyday usage, when someone says, "I have a theory about, . . ." that person actually has a hypothesis. Theories have more empirical support than do hypotheses—even more than so-called educated guesses. (Note: We see no reason to differentiate between wild guesses and educated guesses. In reality, a hypothesis could be either a wild guess or an educated one. It is simply an idea that is yet to be tested. What for one person might be a wild guess, for another might be an educated one. It doesn't matter.) A major activity for children in learning science is coming up with ideas that they can test. That is hypothesizing! (See "Understanding That the Process of Sciencing Is Cyclic" in Chapter 3.) Rather than thinking of a hypothesis as a guess, educated or otherwise, some science educators encourage thinking of a hypothesis in terms of a cause and effect relationship; that is, as an *if-then* statement that can be used to guide a student investigation or inquiry. For example, "*If* the source of light is removed, *then* the plant will lose its green color." Or "*If* the incline is made steeper while the force acting on an object remains constant, *then* the object will move more slowly up the incline."

A *theory* is a speculation about a rather large idea that has been experimentally supported. Examples of scientific theories include molecular structure, biological evolution, and cell structure.

The person who is scientifically literate knows the difference between facts and theories. Whereas facts are accepted truths—that is, realities that are directly observable and consistently demonstrated—theories are in a constant state of revision. The scientific name for humans is *Homo sapiens*, and that is a fact. That the Sun consists of helium, however, is neither a fact nor a theory, but rather a conclusion.

◆ **Conclusion**. A conclusion is not a fact but an inference based on fact. In contrast to a fact, a conclusion has not been directly observed.

◆ **Model**. In science, a model is a visual or mental image of something we cannot see. It is a representation

[2] See, for example, American Association for the Advancement of Science, *The Liberal Art of Science: An Agenda for Action* (Washington, DC: Author, 1990), xiii.

[3] See, for example, F. L. Misiti, Jr., "Standardizing the Language of Inquiry," *Science and Children 38*(5):38–40 (February 2001).

[4] P. L. Dressel, "How the Individual Learns Science: Rethinking Science Education," in N. B. Henry, ed. *Fifty-ninth Yearbook of the National Society for the Study of Education* (Chicago: University of Chicago Press, 1960), 60.

of either a phenomenon or an abstract idea. For example, in the planetary model of atoms, electrons are imagined as miniature planets circling in precisely defined orbits around a sun—the nucleus that contains protons and neutrons. Although not strictly accurate, planetary models are easy to visualize and to understand, and they provide a useful working model from which investigations can ensue.

Of course, terms and their definitions are words invented by people for ease and efficiency in communication. Natural phenomena do not always fit textbook definitions. Sometimes the distinctions between hypotheses, theories, and models are obscure. Nonetheless, to be scientifically literate requires that we understand the language so that we can communicate effectively. To help students increase their literacy in science, the teacher must model scientific literacy.

As well as being able to communicate articulately, being scientifically literate also includes being able to self-reflect.

◆ **Self-reflection**. Self-reflection means being conscious of one's own opinions and judgments and the role of humans in the natural world. Self-reflection derives from an ability to analyze one's own arguments, to determine the factual basis for information, to evaluate the quality of evidence, and to identify and assess one's premises and values. The ability to self-reflect frees an individual from egocentrism, intellectual provincialism, and an anthropocentric worldview.[5]

◆ **Scientifically literate**. The scientifically literate person (SLP) knows the social implications of science and recognizes the role of rational thinking in arriving at value judgments and solving social problems. The SLP knows how to learn, to inquire, to gain knowledge, and to solve new problems. In short, the SLP exhibits behaviors of intelligence (the focus of "Teaching Thinking for Intelligent Behavior" in Chapter 3). Throughout life, SLPs continue to inquire and to increase their knowledge base and use that knowledge to self-reflect and to promote the development of people as rational human beings.

To Solve Problems by Thinking Critically and Creatively

Children are natural problem identifiers and solvers. The school science program should help them develop their skills in identifying and solving problems. The methods of problem solving should not be presented to students so rigidly that they are discouraged from trying to do things their own way. Creative problem solving must allow for serendipity and intuitive thought. Like scientists, children can and do learn from their own mistakes. When given latitude, children sometimes devise surprisingly interesting, creative, and satisfactory solutions.

A good science program takes advantage of the fact that children have naturally inquiring minds and encourages students to inquire into the cause and effect of things that are happening to them. It raises problems that will allow meaningful learning, not just rote memorization. A good science program also whets the students' natural curiosity and enthusiasm. It is designed to help students think about their own thinking (metacognition) and develop their thinking skills (discussed further in Chapter 3). Each time a student uses a rational and reflective thinking approach in trying to solve a problem, that student is one step closer to being a scientifically literate person.

Anthony Magnacca/Merrill

Good science teaching allows for, provides for, and indeed encourages coincidental learning.

To Understand Our Environment and the Problems of Preserving It and Making It Better

Children are interested in and curious about almost everything. They are interested in themselves, the sky,

[5]American Association for the Advancement of Science, *Liberal Art of Science*, 11.

the Earth, the air, matter and energy, and living things. Therefore, the science program should be designed to help students learn concepts that enable them to understand and interpret objects and events in their environment. Facts should be used primarily for building students' understandings of concepts rather than as ends to their learning.

The program should provide opportunities to reinforce the students' understanding of concepts and their relationships. It must help students realize that scientific knowledge is cumulative and that often, not just when sciencing but in all walks of life, it is necessary to use prior knowledge to gain new knowledge. In the process, students become familiar with historical incidents in science and thus assimilate the historical flavor of science. Finally, in learning science, children develop a vocabulary that they will find useful for years to come.

Today our environment is faced with many complex problems, such as air and water pollution, global warming and ozone depletion, solid and nuclear waste disposal, depletion of natural resources, and ecological imbalances. It is aphoristic that science, society, and technology must play collaborative roles to solve these problems. The science program, then, must be vitally concerned with helping students learn how to work collaboratively and to understand the delicate balance of nature and ways of preserving and enhancing what remains of it.

To Understand How Science, Technology, and Society Are Inextricably Interconnected

The science program must consider the relationship and interdependency of science, technology, and society. Although science and technology are interrelated and interdependent, they are not the same, and their goals are sometimes quite different. *Science* is the knowledge gathered through systematic inquiry about the natural world. *Technology* is the translation of scientific knowledge into the development of products and processes that satisfy personal and societal needs and wants. The statements shown in Figure 2.1 illustrate the difference between technology and science.

Technology	*Science*
Concerned with "how to."	Concerned with "what is."
Knowledge is created.	Knowledge is discovered.
Guided by trial and error.	Guided by theory.
Oriented toward action.	Oriented toward research.

FIGURE 2.1 Differentiation of science and technology. *Source:* W. Dugger, Jr. and J. E. Yung, *Technology Education Today,* Fastback 380 (Bloomington, IN: Phi Delta Kappa Educational Foundation, 1995), 9.

Science usually has a long-range effect on humans and on the course of civilization, whereas technology has an immediate effect on the physical, economic, social, and cultural aspects of our existence. The achievements of science and technology often call for social and economic innovations if such achievements are to be used for the benefit of humans and without detrimental effects to the environment. Consequently, a science program must be designed to help students develop an awareness and understanding of the social and economic aspects of science and technology, and the values derived from them. We want our children to become informed citizens who understand these relationships and can make intelligent decisions when called upon.

To Live Successfully and Productively in a Constantly Changing World

It is human nature to be comfortable and secure with the known and familiar, but it is also true that we live in a world of ongoing change. Scientific knowledge is rapidly changing, and societies of people are forever changing. The science program must help students understand that scientific knowledge is tentative and continues to change as evidence accumulates. Understanding the tentative and cumulative nature of scientific knowledge and of the thinking skills used in sciencing can help students better deal with ambiguity, with the tentative nature of knowledge, and with the problems that result from the continued changes in society and in their own lives.

To Grow Intellectually, Emotionally, and Socially According to Individual Abilities, Interests, and Needs

The science program must provide for the individual and emotional growth of all children. You must be prepared to not only teach science but to do so effectively to students with various cultural backgrounds, diverse linguistic abilities, different learning styles, and special needs. The science program should offer a wide range of learning activities for students to provide for their varied abilities, interests, and needs. An exemplary educational program helps each child grow to the utmost of his or her ability.

These six broad goals should guide the K–8 science program. They are compatible with the four goals for school science outlined in the National Science Education Standards (see Figure 2.2). The principles that underlie those standards are shown in Figure 2.3. From such goals, teachers derive specific objectives.

School science should educate students who are able to:

- Experience the richness and excitement of knowing about and understanding the natural world.
- Use appropriate scientific processes and principles in making personal decisions.
- Engage intelligently in public discourse and debate about matters of scientific and technological concern.
- Increase their economic productivity through the use of the knowledge, understanding, and skills of the scientifically literate person in their careers.

FIGURE 2.2 Goals for school science outlined in the National Science Education Standards. *Source:* National Research Council, *National Science Education Standards,* © 1996 by the National Academy of Sciences, 13. Courtesy of National Academy Press, Washington, DC.

- Science is for all students.
- Learning science is an active process.
- School science reflects the intellectual and cultural traditions that characterize the practice of contemporary science.
- Improving science education is part of systemic education reform.

FIGURE 2.3 Principles underlying the National Science Education Standards. *Source:* National Research Council, *National Science Education Standards,* © 1996 by the National Academy of Sciences, 19. Courtesy of National Academy Press, Washington, DC.

Objectives for K–8 Science

Whereas goals and their underlying principles guide the science curriculum, objectives drive student performance. Objectives provide the basis for the selection of specific content and activities, and they are the criteria by which student achievement is assessed. (Assessing student achievement is the focus of Chapter 8.)

Objectives for teaching science, most often derived from content standards mandated by the school district's curriculum, may be found in various textbooks and in the teacher's manual and curriculum documents for specific programs. At first glance, objectives from various sources may seem to differ and some may appear to be more complete than others. On closer scrutiny, however, objectives from various lists will be found to be in close agreement, differing only in how they are written. (Understanding, preparing, and writing objectives will be discussed next.) The consensus is that the objectives of K–8 science programs fall into three broad areas: understanding science concepts; process skills; and attitudes, appreciations, and values. Learning in these three areas helps students grow in scientific literacy and become proficient problem solvers and critical thinkers. It helps them understand the differences and relationships between science and technology, and the interrelationship of both those enterprises with society. Finally, the feeling of accomplishment in these areas leads to improvement in a student's self-esteem, which in turn leads to further achievement.

Aims, Goals, and Objectives and Their Roles in Planning for Science Instruction

As discussed at the start of this chapter, goals are general statements of intent, which are prepared early in course planning. Goals are useful when planned cooperatively with students or when shared with students as advance mental organizers. The students then know what to expect and can begin to prepare mentally to learn the subject matter. From the goals, specific objectives are prepared and written in terms that are measurable (i.e., behavioral terms). Objectives are not intentions. They are the actual behaviors teachers intend to cause students to display. In short, objectives are what students do.

No standardized terminology is used for designating the various types of objectives. In the literature, the most general educational objectives are often called *aims;* the general objectives of schools, curricula, and courses are called *goals;* and the objectives of units and lessons are called *instructional objectives.* Aims are more general than goals, goals are more general than objectives. Instructional (behavioral) objectives are quite specific.

As implied in the preceding paragraphs, goals guide the instructional methods; objectives drive student performance. Assessment (i.e., evaluation) of student achievement in learning should be an assessment of that performance. When the assessment procedure does match the instructional objectives, it is sometimes referred to as assessment that is aligned or authentic (discussed in Chapter 8).

Although instructional goals may not always be quantifiable—that is, readily measurable—instructional objectives should be measurable. Furthermore, those objectives then become the essence of what is measured with instruments designed to authentically assess student learning.

Consider the following examples of goals and objectives.

Goals
1. To learn about the properties of sound
2. To provide opportunities for student inquiry

Objectives 1. The student will demonstrate that the pitch of the sound can be varied by changing the rate of vibration.
2. The student will follow his or her own inquiry by asking a question, designing and completing an investigation about it, answering the question, and presenting the results to others.

Learning Targets and Goal Indicators

One purpose for writing objectives in performance terms is to be able to assess with precision whether the instruction has resulted in the desired behavior. In many schools, the educational goals are established as *learning targets,* competencies that the students are expected to achieve that were derived from the district and state curriculum standards. These learning targets are then divided into performance objectives, sometimes referred to as *goal indicators.* Instruction is designed to teach toward those objectives. When students perform the competencies called for by these objectives, their education is considered successful. This is known variously as *criterion-referenced, competency-based, performance-based, results-driven,* or *outcome-based education.* When the objectives are aligned with specific curriculum standards, as they usually are or should be, then it can also be referred to as *standards-based education.* Expecting students to achieve one set of competencies before moving on to the next set is called *mastery learning.* The success of the student achievement, the teacher performance, and the school may each be assessed according to these criteria.

Overt and Covert Performance Outcomes

Assessment is not difficult to accomplish when the desired performance outcome is overt behavior, which can be observed directly. Each of the sample objectives of the preceding section is an example of an overt objective. Assessment is more difficult to accomplish when the desired behavior is *covert,* that is, when it is not directly observable. Although certainly no less important, behaviors that call for appreciation, discovery, or understanding, for example, are not directly observable because they occur within a person, and so are covert behaviors. Since covert behavior cannot be observed directly, the only way to tell whether the objective has been achieved is to observe behavior that may be indicative of that achievement. The objective, then, is written in overt language, and evaluators can only assume or trust that the observed behavior is, in fact, reasonably close to being indicative of the expected learning outcome.

Furthermore, when assessing whether an objective has been achieved—that learning has occurred—the assessment device must be consistent with the desired learning outcome. Otherwise, the assessment is not aligned; it is invalid. When the measuring device and the learning objective are compatible, we say that the assessment is authentic. For example, a person's competency to teach specific science process skills to fifth graders is best (i.e., with highest reliability) measured by directly observing that person *doing* that very thing—teaching specific science process skills to fifth graders. Using a standardized paper-and-pencil test of multiple-choice items to determine a person's ability to teach specific science process skills to fifth grade children is *not* authentic assessment. Although the particular multiple-choice item assessment device might indeed be valid, it is not authentic. (See Chapter 8 for additional discussion on test validity and authentic assessment.)

Balance of Behaviorism and Constructivism

Although behaviorists (behaviorism) assume a definition of learning that deals only with changes in overt behavior, constructivists argue that learning entails the construction or reshaping of organizational or conceptual mental models or patterns (often referred to as schemata) and that these mental processes mediate learning. Thus, people who adhere to constructivism or cognitivism are concerned with both overt and covert behaviors.[6] Does this mean that you must be one or the other—a behaviorist or a constructivist? Probably not. For now, the point is that when writing instructional objectives, you should write most or all of your basic expectations (minimal competency expectations) in overt terms (the topic of the next section). However, you cannot be expected to foresee all learning that occurs nor to translate all that is learned into performance terms—most certainly not before it occurs.

Teaching Toward Multiple Objectives, Understandings, and Appreciations

Any effort to write all learning objectives in performance terms is, in effect, to neglect the individual learner for whom it purports to be concerned; such an approach does not allow for diversity among learners. Learning that is most meaningful to children is not so neatly or easily predicted or isolated. Rather than teaching one objective at a time, much of the time you should direct your teaching toward the simultaneous learning of multiple objectives, understandings, and appreciations. However, when you assess for learning, assessment is cleaner when objectives are assessed one at a time. Let's now review how objectives are prepared.

---

[6]See, for example, D. R. Geelan, "Epistemological Anarchy and the Many Forms of Constructivism," *Science and Education* 6(1–2):15–28 (January 1997).

 Preparing Instructional Objectives

When preparing instructional objectives, you must ask yourself, "How is the student to demonstrate that the objective has been reached?" The objective must include an action that demonstrates that the objective has been achieved. Inherited from behaviorism, this portion of the objective is sometimes called the *anticipated measurable performance.*

Components: The ABCDs of Writing Objectives

When written completely in performance terms, an instructional objective has four components, although in practice you are unlikely to use all four. To aid your understanding and as a mnemonic for remembering, you can refer to these components as the ABCDs of writing objectives.

One component is the *audience*. The *A* of the ABCDs refers to the student for whom the objective is intended. To address this, sometimes teachers begin their objectives with the phrase "The student will be able to. . ." or, to personalize the objective, "You will be able to. . . ." (Note: To conserve space and to eliminate useless language, in examples that follow we eliminate "be able to," and write simply "The student will. . . ." As a matter of fact, we prefer eliminating the use of "be able to" and simply use "will." For brevity, writers of objectives sometimes use the abbreviation "TSWBAT. . ." for "The student will be able to. . ." or more simply "TSW. . ." for "The student will. . . .")

The second component is the expected *behavior,* the *B* of the ABCDs. It is this second component that represents the learning target. The expected behavior (or performance) should be written with verbs that are measurable—that is, with action verbs—so that it is directly observable that the objective, or target, has been reached. Some verbs are too vague, ambiguous, and not clearly measurable. When writing overt objectives, you should avoid covert verbs such as *appreciate, comprehend, and understand* (see Figure 2.4).

When writing objectives for your unit and lesson plans, usually you will not bother to include the next two components. However, as you will learn, they are important considerations for assessment.

appreciate	enjoy	indicate	like
believe	familiarize	know	realize
comprehend	grasp	learn	understand

FIGURE 2.4 Verbs to avoid when writing overt objectives.

The third component is the *conditions,* the *C* of the ABCDs. This is the setting in which the behavior will be demonstrated by the student and observed by the teacher. Conditions are forever changing; although the learning target should be clearly recognizable long before the actual instruction occurs, the conditions may not be. Therefore, in curriculum documents in particular, conditions are not often included in the objectives. However, when preparing to assess student learning toward specific objectives, you must consider the conditions in which the performance will be displayed.

The fourth component, again, is not always included in objectives found in curriculum documents. It is the *degree (or level) of expected performance*—the *D* of the ABCDs. This is the ingredient that allows for the assessment of student learning. When mastery learning is expected, the level of expected performance is usually omitted (because it is understood). In teaching for mastery learning, the performance-level expectation is 100%. In reality, however, the performance level will most likely be 85% to 95% particularly when working with a group of students, rather than with an individual student. The 5% to 15% difference allows for human error that can occur when using written and oral communication. Like conditions, the level of performance will vary depending on the situation and purpose. Therefore, it is not normally included in the unit and lessons that teachers prepare.

Performance level is used to assess student achievement and sometimes to evaluate the effectiveness of the teaching. Student grades might be based on performance levels; evaluation of teacher effectiveness might be based on the level of student performance. Indeed, with today's use of state-mandated standardized testing, schools, administrators, and teachers are evaluated on the basis of student performance on those tests.

Classification of Learning Objectives

Useful in planning and assessing student learning are three domains for classifying learning objectives:

- **Cognitive:** the domain of learning that involves mental operations from the lowest level of simple recall of information to high-level and complex evaluative processes
- **Affective:** the domain of learning that involves feelings, attitudes, and values, from lower levels of acquisition to the highest level of internalization and action
- **Psychomotor:** the domain of learning that ranges from the low-level, simple manipulation of materials, to the higher level of communication of ideas, and finally to the highest level of creative performance

The student will identify the correct definition of the term *osmosis.* (knowledge)

The student will identify examples of the principle of osmosis. (comprehension)

The student will identify the osmotic effect when a cell is immersed into a hypotonic solution. (application)

The student will identify the osmotic effect on turgor pressure when the cell is placed in a hypotonic solution. (analysis)

FIGURE 2.5 Sometimes the same action verb may be used appropriately in objectives at different cognitive levels. For example here the verb *identify* is used in objectives at four levels (identified in parentheses) within the cognitive domain.

The Domains of Learning and the Developmental Needs of Children

Educators attempt to design learning experiences to meet the five areas of developmental needs of children: intellectual, physical, emotional/psychological, social, and moral/ethical. As a teacher, you must include objectives that address learning within each of these categories of needs. While the intellectual needs are primarily within the cognitive domain and the physical are within the psychomotor, the other three categories of needs mostly are within the affective domain.

Too frequently, teachers focus on the cognitive domain, assuming that the psychomotor and affective will take care of themselves. If the current nationwide focus on standardized achievement testing sustains, this may become even more true. Many experts argue, however, that teachers should do just the opposite. They maintain that when the affective is directly attended to, the psychomotor and cognitive naturally develop. They argue that unless the social and emotional needs of students are adequately addressed, little happens cognitively.[7] Whether the domains are attended to separately or simultaneously, you should plan your teaching so your students are guided from the lowest to highest levels of operation within each domain.

The three developmental hierarchies are discussed next to guide your understanding of each of the five areas of needs. Notice the illustrative verbs within each hierarchy. These verbs help you fashion objectives when you are developing unit plans and lesson plans. (To see how goals and objectives are fit into one lesson plan, see Figure 7.3, Chapter 7, "Multiple-Day, Project-Centered, Interdisciplinary and Transcultural Lesson Using World-Wide Communication via the Internet.") However, caution is urged, for there can be considerable overlap among the levels at which some action verbs may appropriately be used. For example, as shown in Figure 2.5, the verb *identifies* is appropriate in each of the objectives at different levels (identified in parentheses) within the cognitive domain.

Scott Cunningham/Merrill

While learning science content, children can also develop their gross and fine motor skills.

Cognitive Domain Hierarchies

In a widely accepted taxonomy of objectives, Bloom and his associates arranged cognitive objectives into classifications according to the complexity of the skills and the abilities they embodied.[8] The result was a ladder ranging from the simplest to the most complex intellectual processes. Within each domain, prerequisite to a student's ability to function at one particular level of the

[7]See, for example, L. Hopping, "Multi-Age Teaming: A Real-Life Approach to the Middle School," *Phi Delta Kappan* 82(4):270–272, 292 (December 2000).

[8]B. S. Bloom, ed., *Taxonomy of Educational Objectives, Book 1, Cognitive Domain* (White Plains, NY: Longman, 1984).

hierarchy, is his or her ability to function at the preceding level or levels. In other words, when a student is functioning at the third level of the cognitive domain, that student is automatically also functioning at the first and second levels. Rather than an orderly progression from simple to complex mental operations as illustrated by Bloom's taxonomy, some researchers prefer an organization of cognitive abilities that ranges from simple information storage and retrieval, through a higher level of discrimination and concept attainment, to the highest cognitive ability to recognize and solve problems.[9]

The six major categories (or levels) in Bloom's taxonomy of cognitive objectives are (a) *knowledge*—recognizing and recalling information, (b) *comprehension*—understanding the meaning of information, (c) *application*—using information, (d) *analysis*—dissecting information into its component parts to comprehend their relationships, (e) *synthesis*—putting components together to generate new ideas, and (f) *evaluation*—judging the worth of an idea, notion, theory, thesis, proposition, information, or opinion. In this taxonomy, the top four categories or levels—application, analysis, synthesis, and evaluation—represent what are called *higher-order cognitive thinking skills.*[10]

While space limitation prohibits elaboration here, Bloom's taxonomy includes various subcategories within each of these six major categories. It is probably less important to absolutely classify an objective than it is to be aware of hierarchies in thinking and doing and to understand the importance of attending to your students' intellectual behaviors from lower to higher operational levels in all three domains. A discussion of each of Bloom's six categories follows.

Knowledge. The basic element in Bloom's taxonomy concerns the acquisition of knowledge; that is, the ability to recognize and recall information. (As discussed in Chapter 4, this is similar to the *input level* of thinking and questioning.) Although this is the lowest of the six categories, the information to be learned may not itself be of a low level. In fact, it may be of an extremely high level. Bloom includes here knowledge of principles, generalizations, theories, structures, and methodology, as well as knowledge of facts and ways of dealing with facts.

Action verbs appropriate for this category include *choose, complete, define, describe, identify, indicate, list, locate, match, name, outline, recall, recognize, select,* and *state.* (Note that some verbs may be appropriately used at more than one cognitive level.)

A sample objective at this cognitive level is, "The student will state the chemical symbols for the elements hydrogen, oxygen, sulfur, and nitrogen."

The five remaining categories of Bloom's taxonomy of the cognitive domain deal with the *use* of knowledge. They encompass the educational objectives aimed at developing cognitive skills and abilities, including comprehension, application, analysis, synthesis, and evaluation of knowledge.

Comprehension. Comprehension includes the ability to translate or explain knowledge, to interpret that knowledge, and to extrapolate from it to address new situations.

Action verbs appropriate for this category include *change, classify, convert, defend, derive, describe, estimate, expand, explain, generalize, infer, interpret, paraphrase, predict, recognize, summarize,* and *translate.*

A sample objective at this cognitive level is, "When given the temperature in degrees Celsius, the student will correctly convert it to degrees Fahrenheit."

Application. Once students understand information, they should be able to apply it. This is the category of operation above comprehension. Action verbs include *apply, compute, demonstrate, develop, discover, discuss, modify, operate, participate, perform, plan, predict, relate, show, solve,* and *use.*

A sample objective at this cognitive level is, "When given a choice between two coats on a cold winter day—a light-colored one and a dark-colored one—the student will correctly predict which would be warmest (assuming they are alike in all other respects)."

Analysis. This category includes objectives that require students to use the skills of analysis.

Action verbs appropriate for this category include *analyze, break down, categorize, classify, compare, contrast, debate, deduce, diagram, differentiate, discriminate, identify, illustrate, infer, outline, relate, separate,* and *subdivide.*

A sample objective at this cognitive level is, "The student will detect discrepancies between advertising claims and actual nutritional quality of certain processed food products."

Synthesis. This category includes objectives that involve such skills as designing a plan, proposing a set of operations, and deriving a series of abstract relations.

Action verbs appropriate for this category include *arrange, categorize, classify, combine, compile, constitute,*

---

[9]See R. M. Gagné, L. J. Briggs, and W. W. Wager, *Principles of Instructional Design,* 4th ed. (New York: Holt, Rinehart and Winston, 1994).

[10]Compare Bloom's higher-order cognitive thinking skills with R. H. Ennis's, "A Taxonomy of Critical Thinking Dispositions and Abilities," and Quellmalz's "Developing Reasoning Skills," both in J. B. Barron and R. J. Sternberg, eds., *Teaching Thinking Skills: Theory and Practice* (New York: W. H. Freeman, 1987), and with Marzano's "complex thinking strategies" in R. J. Marzano, *A Different Kind of Classroom: Teaching With Dimensions of Learning* (Alexandria, VA: Association for Supervision and Curriculum Development, 1992).

create, design, develop, devise, document, explain, formulate, generate, modify, organize, originate, plan, produce, rearrange, reconstruct, revise, rewrite, summarize, synthesize, tell, transmit, and *write.*

A sample objective at this cognitive level is, "From facts generated during a discussion of the controversy about the spotted owl and the cutting of forest trees in the Pacific Northwest, the student will summarize the environmental concerns raised by the issue."

Evaluation. The highest cognitive category of Bloom's taxonomy of cognitive objectives is evaluation. This includes offering opinions and making value judgments.

Action verbs appropriate for this category include *appraise, argue, assess, compare, conclude, consider, contrast, criticize, decide, discriminate, evaluate, explain, interpret, judge, justify, rank, rate, relate, standardize, support,* and *validate.*

A sample objective at this cognitive level is, "The student will write a critical appraisal about the use of nuclear-power-generating plants."

Affective Domain Hierarchies

Krathwohl, Bloom, and Masia developed a useful taxonomy of the affective domain.[11] Following are their major levels (or categories), from least internalized to most internalized: (a) *receiving*—being aware of the affective stimulus and beginning to have favorable feelings toward it, (b) *responding*—taking an interest in the stimulus and viewing it favorably, (c) *valuing*—showing a tentative belief in the value of the affective stimulus and becoming committed to it, (d) *organizing*—placing values into a system of dominant and supporting values, and (e) *internalizing*—demonstrating consistent beliefs and behavior that have become a way of life. Although there is considerable overlap from one category to another within the affective domain, these categories do provide a basis by which to judge the quality of objectives and the nature of learning within this area. A discussion of each of the five categories follows.

Receiving. At this level, which is the least internalized, the student exhibits willingness to give attention to particular phenomena or stimuli, and the teacher is able to arouse, sustain, and direct that attention.

Action verbs appropriate for this category include *ask, choose, describe, differentiate, distinguish, hold, identify, locate, name, point to, recall, recognize, reply, select,* and *use.*

A sample objective at this level is, "The student pays close attention to the directions for the exploratory activities."

[11] D. R. Krathwohl, B. S. Bloom, and B. B. Masia, *Taxonomy of Educational Goals, Handbook 2, Affective Domain* (New York: David McKay, 1964).

Responding. Students respond to the stimulus they have received. They may do so because of some external pressure, or they may do so voluntarily because they find it interesting or because responding gives them satisfaction.

Action verbs appropriate for this category include *answer, applaud, approve, assist, comply, command, discuss, greet, help, label, perform, play, practice, present, read, recite, report, select, spend (leisure time in), tell,* and *write.*

A sample objective at this level is, "The student discusses what others have said."

Valuing. Objectives at the valuing level have to do with students' beliefs, attitudes, and appreciations. The simplest objectives concern a student's acceptance of beliefs and values. Higher-level objectives concern a student's learning to prefer certain values and finally becoming committed to them.

Action verbs appropriate for this level include *argue, assist, complete, describe, differentiate, explain, follow, form, initiate, invite, join, justify, propose, protest, read, report, select, share, study, support,* and *work.*

A sample objective at this level is, "The student supports actions against gender discrimination."

Organizing. This fourth level in the affective domain concerns building a personal value system. At this level the student is conceptualizing values and arranging them to a value system that recognizes priorities and relative importance of various values faced in life.

Action verbs appropriate for this level include *adhere, alter, arrange, balance, combine, compare, defend, define, discuss, explain, form, generalize, identify, integrate, modify, order, organize, prepare, relate,* and *synthesize.*

A sample objective at this level is, "The student forms judgments concerning responsible ecological behavior in the classroom, school, and community."

Internalizing Values. This is the highest level within the affective domain. At this level the student's behaviors are consistent with his or her beliefs.

Action verbs appropriate for this level include *act, complete, display, influence, listen, modify, perform, practice, propose, qualify, question, revise, serve, solve,* and *verify.*

A sample objective at this level is, "The student works independently and diligently."

Psychomotor Domain Hierarchies

Whereas identification and classification within the cognitive and affective domains are generally agreed upon, there is less agreement on the classification within the psychomotor domain. Originally, the goal of this domain was simply to develop and categorize proficiency in skills, particularly those dealing with gross and fine muscle control. The classification of the domain presented here follows this lead, but includes at its highest level the most creative and inventive behaviors, thus coordinating skills and knowledge from all three domains. Consequently, the objectives are in a hierarchy ranging from simple gross locomotor control to the most creative and complex skills requiring originality and fine locomotor control—for example, from simply threading a needle to designing and making an article of clothing.

From Harrow is the following taxonomy of the psychomotor domain: (a) *Moving,* (b) *manipulating,* (c) *communicating,* and (d) *creating.*[12] Included here are sample objectives, as well as a list of possible action verbs for each level of the psychomotor domain.

Movement. This level involves gross motor coordination.

Action verbs appropriate for this level include *adjust, carry, clean, locate,* and *obtain.*

A sample objective at this level is, "The student correctly grasps and carries the microscope to the workstation."

Manipulating. This second level involves fine motor coordination.

Action verbs appropriate for this level include *assemble, build, calibrate, connect,* and *thread.*

A sample objective at this level is, "The student will adjust the microscope so that the object is in focus under high power."

Communicating. This third level involves the communication of ideas and feelings.

Action verbs appropriate for this level include *analyze, ask, describe, draw, explain,* and *write.*

A sample objective at this level is, "The student will demonstrate the ability to listen to the ideas of others about an environmental issue."

Creating. This is the highest level of the psychomotor domain, and of all other domains, and represents the student's coordination of thinking, learning, and behaving in all three domains.

Action verbs appropriate for this level include *create, design,* and *invent.*

A sample objective at this level is, "From his or her own data collecting and calculations, the student will design a more time-efficient and learning-effective way of moving people from one place to another on the school campus."

Using the Taxonomies

Theoretically, the taxonomies are constructed so that students achieve each lower level before they are ready to move to the higher levels. But because categories and behaviors overlap, as they should, this theory does not always hold in practice. Furthermore, as explained by others, feelings and thoughts are inextricably interconnected; they cannot be neatly separated as the taxonomies might seem to imply.[13]

The taxonomies are important in that they emphasize the various levels to which instruction and learning must aspire. For learning to be worthwhile, you must formulate and teach to objectives from the higher levels of the taxonomies as well as from the lower ones. Student thinking and behaving must be moved from the lowest to the highest levels of thinking and behavior. When all is said and done, perhaps we aspire to the highest level of the psychomotor domain—creating.

In using the taxonomies, remember that the point is to formulate the best objectives for the job to be done. Standards-based and results-driven education models used in today's schools describe levels of mastery standards *(rubrics)* for each outcome. The taxonomies provide the mechanism for assuring that you do not spend a disproportionate amount of time on facts and other low-level learning. They can be of tremendous help where teachers are expected to correlate learning activities to learning outcome standards (see Figure 2.6).

Preparing objectives is essential to the preparation of good assessments of student learning. Clearly communicating your performance expectations to students and then specifically assessing student learning against those expectations makes your teaching most efficient and effective. It also makes the assessment of the learning more authentic. This does not mean that you will always write performance objectives for everything taught, nor will you always be able to accurately measure what students have learned. As stated earlier, learning that is meaningful to students is not as easily compartmentalized as the taxonomies of educational objectives would imply.

[12]A. J. Harrow, *Taxonomy of the Psychomotor Domain* (New York: Longman, 1977). A similar taxonomy for the psychomotor domain is that of E. J. Simpson, *The Classification of Educational Objectives in the Psychomotor Domain. The Psychomotor Domain: Volume 3* (Washington, DC: Gryphon House, 1972).

[13]R. N. Caine and G. Caine, *Education on the Edge of Possibility* (Alexandria, VA: Association for Supervision and Curriculum Development, 1997), 104–105.

Results-driven education helps produce people who are life-long learners, who are effective communicators, and who have high self-esteem. They are problem solvers, self-directed learners, high-quality producers, collaborative workers, and community contributors.

Problem Solvers

- are able to solve problems in their academic and personal lives
- demonstrate higher level analytical thinking skills when they evaluate or make decisions
- are able to set personal and career goals
- can use knowledge, not just display it
- are innovative thinkers

Self-Directed Learners

- are independent workers
- can read, comprehend, and interact with text
- have self-respect with an accurate view of themselves and their abilities

Quality Producers

- can communicate effectively in a variety of situations (oral, aesthetic/artistic, nonverbal)
- are able to use their knowledge to create intelligent, artistic products that reflect originality
- have high standards

Collaborative Workers

- are able to work interdependently
- show respect for others and their points of view
- have their own values and moral conduct
- have an appreciation of cultural diversity

Community Contributors

- have an awareness of civic, individual, national, and international responsibilities
- have an understanding of basic health issues
- have an appreciation of diversity

FIGURE 2.6 Sample school district-expected learning outcome standards.

Learning That Is Not Immediately Observable

As you undoubtedly learned in your educational psychology class, unlike behaviorists, constructivists do not limit the definition of learning to that which is observable behavior, and neither should you. Bits and pieces of new information (science facts, for example) are stored in short-term memory, where the new information is "rehearsed" until it becomes part of long-term memory. If the information is not rehearsed, it eventually fades from short-term memory. If it is rehearsed and made meaningful through connections with other stored knowledge, it is transferred to and stored in long-term memory, either by building on existing schemata or by forming new schemata. As a teacher, regardless of the discipline or grade level, your responsibility is to provide learning experiences that will result in the creation of new schemata as well as the modification of existing schemata.

Summary

To be an effective teacher, your challenge is to use performance-based criteria with a teaching style that encourages the development of intrinsic sources of student motivation. It should allow, provide, and encourage coincidental learning that goes beyond what might be considered predictable, immediately measurable, and representative of minimal expectations.

Many teachers realize that to be most effective in helping students develop meaningful understandings, much of the learning in each subject area can be made more effective and longer lasting by integrating it with the whole curriculum and making it meaningful to the lives of the students, rather than simply teaching it as an unrelated and separate discipline at the same time each day.

If learning is defined only as being the accumulation of bits and pieces of information, then we already know how that is learned and how to teach it. However, the accumulation of pieces of information is at the lowest end of a spectrum of types of learning. For higher levels of thinking and for learning that is most meaningful and longest lasting, research findings support using (a) a curriculum where disciplines are integrated, and (b) instructional techniques that involve the learners in social interactive learning. This might include well-designed, project-centered learning; cooperative learning; peer tutoring; and cross-age teaching. We address these topics specifically in Chapters 4 through 7 of this text. But before we go to those topics, we have one other aspect to discuss regarding *what* is to be taught. This has to do with the nature of science and sciencing—the focus of Chapter 3.

Questions for Class Discussion

1. Do you think students should be encouraged to make guesses about explanations of scientific phenomena? Explain your answer.
2. During a lesson, topics are sometimes raised that may deviate from the lesson plan. Do you believe a teacher should or can encourage this kind of incidental learning? If not, explain how it should be avoided. If so, explain how it might be done.
3. Select one important science objective for children at a particular grade level (K–8). Describe briefly how you might teach to that objective and how you would determine if the objective had been successfully achieved.
4. Using the objective that you identified for question three, write the objective in complete ABCD terms as described in this chapter.
5. Increasingly, we hear both new and experienced teachers complaining about lack of time. They say that there is not enough time to cover all the curriculum content they are supposed to teach, and little or no time to teach topics of their choice. We hear that teachers are losing the freedom to decide what is important for their students to learn and to do, and the freedom to create activities for that learning. Teachers complain that there is less time for students to reflect on what is being learned and that interdisciplinary thematic instruction takes too much time. Teachers say that they are told they must spend more time on direct instruction and less on student-centered instruction. There is not enough time for student-initiated exploratory learning, because more time is being devoted to testing and test preparation. Do any of these comments sound familiar to you? If so, what do you believe may be at the root of these concerns? Is there any danger to the profession if the act of teaching becomes so highly prescriptive? Is there an analogous danger if a child's learning also becomes highly prescriptive?
6. What questions do you have about the content of this chapter? Where might answers be found?

Chapter 3

Understanding the Nature of Science and Sciencing

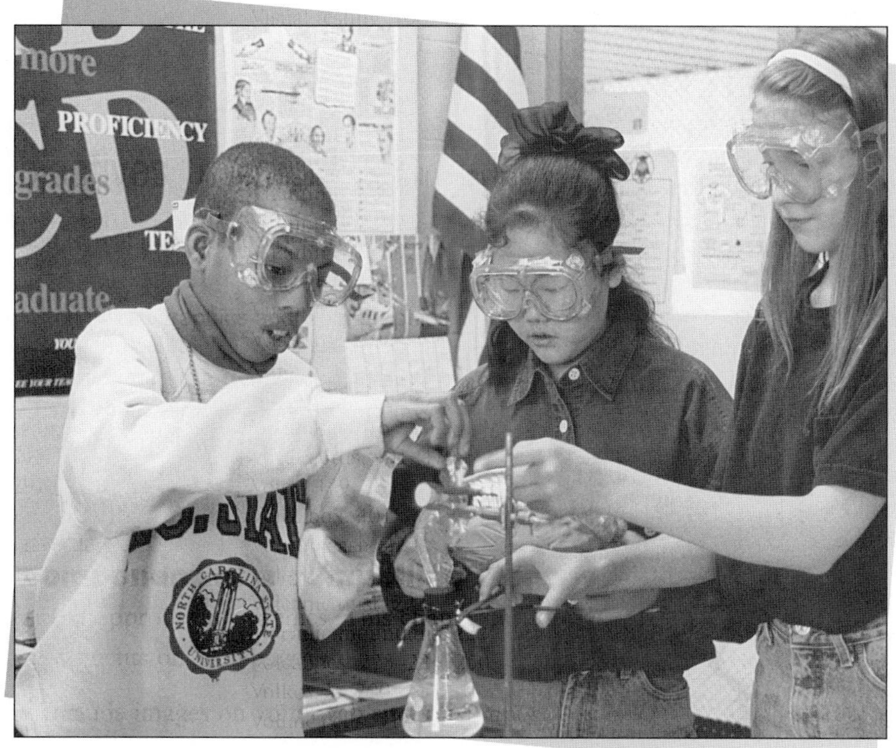

Anne Vega/Merrill

Effective science teaching is more than merely knowing science content and applying some teaching strategies. Skilled teachers of science have special understandings and abilities that integrate their knowledge of science content, curriculum, learning, teaching, and students. Be aware that this knowledge was accumulated over time, learning from mistakes and missteps. Such knowledge allows teachers to tailor learning situations to the needs of both individuals and groups. This knowledge of teaching, called "pedagogical content knowledge," distinguishes the knowledge of science teachers from that of scientists. It is one element that defines a professional teacher of science.[1]

While knowledge of science content is important, you should not expect to have a comprehensive knowledge of all the areas of K–8 science that you are likely to teach—for example, earth and space science, life science, and physical science. Because of the sheer breadth of science covered in K–8 classrooms, it is not uncommon for K–8 teachers to learn science content as they teach. Therefore, having a strong, broad base of scientific understanding in each of the eight content standards shown in Figures 3.1 and 3.2 is very important. Learning more science as you learn to teach is a key to being a good science teacher. (Part Two of this book provides current and useful content references and instructional ideas for these areas.)

All teachers of science need to understand science and sciencing. Furthermore, because science is a useful vehicle for *interdisciplinary teaching,* you need to know how to use science in thematic teaching. Chapter 7 and some of the "exploratory activities" in Part Two illustrate how that can be done.

Teachers have found thematic teaching to be an effective curriculum approach. For example, a second-grade teacher might select a theme, such as transportation or dinosaurs or plants. A teaching unit is then built around that theme during which the children learn not only science but also language arts, mathematics, social studies, and all the other subject areas expected to be learned at that grade level. Because two or more disciplines are involved, we refer to it as an *interdisciplinary thematic unit.* Thematic teaching units are important components of many state science frameworks. (For an interdisciplinary thematic unit, see "Opening the Ocean" in Chapter 11.)

Schools are advised to increase their emphasis on dropout prevention at early grade levels. Making learning meaningful for students at school and in their lives outside school is an imperative responsibility of K–8 teachers, who, for many students, are their last hope for receiving formal schooling and becoming scientifically literate. One way to make learning meaningful for students is by using interdisciplinary thematic instruction.[2] *Science for All Americans* identifies common abstract themes that cut across many scientific disciplines, including systems, models, scale, constancy, and patterns of change. These themes have been used as the basis for current development of science curriculum frameworks, but they were not intended for designing units of study for elementary or middle school students. These students do not yet have the experiences and intellectual maturity necessary to understand such abstract conceptual schemes. Like the "Opening the Ocean" unit in Chapter 11, the interdisciplinary thematic units of most use in teaching K–8 science are much less abstract. Moreover, they are designed to integrate subject disciplines; that is, the core subjects of language arts/English/reading, mathematics, social studies/history, and science, as well as the various disciplines of science.

The specific uses of interdisciplinary thematic units are presented in Chapter 7, but here it is important to understand that the purpose of the approach is to integrate content from various subject areas to show the interconnectedness of life and learning. Students need to know that the information they are learning will be practical, not only in school but also in the workplace and throughout life.

[1]Reprinted from National Research Council, *National Science Education Standards,* © 1996 by the National Academy of Sciences, 62. Courtesy of National Academy Press, Washington, DC.

[2]See, for example, "Improving Learning Through Thematic Instruction" in R. H. McBee and J. Moss, "PDS Partnerships Come of Age," *Educational Leadership* 59(6):61–64 (March 2002).

Science as Inquiry	Physical Science	Life Science	Earth and Space Science	Science and Technology	Science in Personal and Social Perspectives	History and Nature of Science	Unifying Concepts and Processes
Abilities necessary to do scientific inquiry Understandings about scientific inquiry	Properties of objects and materials Position and motion of objects Light, heat, electricity, and magnetism	Characteristics of organisms Life cycles of organisms Organisms and environments	Properties of Earth materials Objects in the sky Changes in Earth and sky	Abilities to distinguish between natural objects and objects made by humans Abilities of technological design Understandings about science and technology	Personal health Characteristics and changes in populations Types of resources Changes in environments Science and technology in local challenges	Science as a human endeavor	Systems, order, and organization Evidence, models, and explanation Change, constancy, and measurement Evolution and equilibrium Form and function

FIGURE 3.1 Content standards, grades K–4. *Source:* Reprinted from National Research Council, *National Science Education Standards,* © 1996 by the National Academy of Sciences, 109. Courtesy of National Academy Press, Washington, DC.

Science as Inquiry	Physical Science	Life Science	Earth and Space Science	Science and Technology	Science in Personal and Social Perspectives	History and Nature of Science	Unifying Concepts and Processes
Abilities necessary to do scientific inquiry Understandings about scientific inquiry	Properties and changes of properties in matter Motions and forces Transfer of energy	Structure and function in living systems Reproduction and heredity Regulation and behavior Populations and ecosystems Diversity and adaptations of organisms	Structure of the Earth system Earth's history Earth in the solar system	Abilities of technological design Understanding about science and technology	Personal health Populations, resources, and environments Natural hazards Risks and benefits Science and technology in society	Science as a human endeavor Nature of science History of science	Systems, order, and organization Evidence, models, and explanation Change, constancy, and measurement Evolution and equilibrium Form and function

FIGURE 3.2 Content standards, grades 5–8. *Source:* Reprinted from National Research Council, *National Science Education Standards,* © 1996 by the National Academy of Sciences, 110. Courtesy of National Academy Press, Washington, DC.

Understanding the Nature of Science

If you are apprehensive about teaching science because you think that you lack sufficient knowledge of content, please understand that there is a difference between knowing the science content before teaching and possessing the confidence and skills to find out what you need to know before teaching. For example, a teacher may have many scientific facts stored in long-term memory. If he or she presents these facts to the students and requires them to memorize the facts and tell them back through tests or projects, this teacher may be dangerous indeed. That is not science teaching but merely a series of exercises in short-term recall. Teachers who approach unfamiliar science content with a sense of curiosity and excitement, and a willingness to learn and to seek resources to help themselves understand have a great deal of insight to offer their students from their own personal learning experiences.

There is perhaps no quicker way to discourage student interest in science than to teach it as though it were *only* "an organized body of knowledge to be learned." Teachers who teach as if everything scientific is already known, and students must simply memorize a certain number of facts, are misguided in their approach—and herein lies the danger. A serious consequence of such teaching is that it risks perpetuating the myth that science is knowledge, when in fact, science is less about the knowledge than it is about learning. Although students must learn the information that has been developed through scientific investigations, rote memorization is not science! A teacher who does nothing more than transmit information is merely an orchestrator of factual-recall memory tests.

Science is a continuing process and a human endeavor to discover order in nature. The products of that endeavor are human knowledge. Facts, which are building blocks, are reference points for understanding bigger ideas, the principles and concepts. These products of science are tentative and cumulative. The tentative and cumulative nature of science is exceedingly important for teachers and their students to understand.

In science teaching, attention must be given to the processes of science as well as the products, and intuitive thought and guessing must be valued. Guesses, wild or otherwise (see Chapter 2), are hypotheses—possible explanations for recognized problems and discrepancies. Hypotheses are then tested, data are collected and analyzed, and tentative conclusions reached. These conclusions may lead to further understanding of concepts, which in turn provide further comprehension of the major themes that make up the structural framework for the K–12 science curriculum.

A curriculum based on a thematic structure unites the facts and activities of the daily content of lessons. Examples of major themes, sometimes called conceptual schemes, are order and organization, form and function, evolution and equilibrium, matter-energy relationships, and systems and interaction. Students build their understandings of concepts and develop their skills in science as they engage in and practice the processes, thereby learning that they can science and that science is a human activity.

Anthony Magnacca/Merrill

Beginning in the primary grades, children are taught how to order, sequence, and classify important data-organizing processes.

Understanding Children and How They Learn

In your preparation to become a teacher, you are probably learning much about children through direct observation and experience, through theory classes in child development and other courses in psychology, or both. You have learned that children in grades K–8 differ in their abilities to learn, their readiness to learn, their learning skills, and how they learn. In recent years, a wealth of information has been developed about children and their intellectual development, about how they learn, and about how they are taught. It may sometimes seem to you that you are expected to know it all!

From educational psychology, you have learned how children develop intellectually and emotionally. You have also learned about the contributions of David Ausubel (cognitive theory of meaningful learning; advance organizers), Benjamin Bloom (cognitive taxonomy; mastery learning), Jerome Bruner (concept learning; guided discovery), Abraham Maslow (hierarchy of needs), Joseph Novak (concept mapping), Jean Piaget (stages of intellectual development; cognitive disequilibrium), Lev Vygotsky (cooperative learning in a supportive environment), and other cognitive psychologists and researchers. Although it is beyond the scope or purpose of this book, you need to understand the importance of their contributions.

Styles of Learning and Implications for Science Teaching

Exemplary teachers are those who customize or adapt their teaching styles and methods to their students. They use approaches that interest the students, that are neither too easy nor too difficult, that match the students' learning styles and learning capacities, and that are relevant to the students' lives. This adaptation process is further complicated because each student is different from every other one. Not all students have the same interests, abilities, backgrounds, or learning styles and capacities. As a matter of fact, not only do students differ from one another, each student can change over time. A student who struggles with some materials may later in the semester exhibit a powerful facility with other learning materials. What appeals to a student today may not have the same appeal tomorrow. Therefore, you need to consider both the nature of young people in general and each student in particular. The following is a brief synopsis of knowledge about learning and the psychology of learning.

Learning Modalities and Their Implications for Science Teaching

Learning modality refers to the *sensory portal* (or input channel) by which a student prefers to receive sensory experiences (modality preference). It is often the way a student learns best (modality adeptness). Some K–8 children prefer learning by seeing, a *visual modality;* some by listening to others, an *auditory modality;* some by doing and being physically involved, the *kinesthetic modality*; and still others by touching objects, the *tactile modality.* A student's modality preference is not always that student's modality strength.

Primary modality strength can be determined by observing students. However, it can be mixed, and it can change as the result of experience and intellectual maturity. As one might suspect, modality integration (i.e., engaging more of the sensory input channels by using several modalities at once or by staggering modalities) has been found to contribute to better achievement in student learning.

Because many children in grades K–8 have neither a preference nor a strength for auditory reception, teachers of those grades should carefully limit their use of the lecture method of instruction; that is, too much reliance on formal teacher talk. (Specific guidelines for using teacher talk are presented in Chapter 5.) Furthermore, instruction using a singular approach, such as lecturing, cheats students who learn better in other ways. This difference can affect student achievement. For example, a teacher who only talks to his or her students, whether through lectures or discussions, day after day is shortchanging the education of learners who learn better another way—for example, primarily kinesthetic or visual learners.

Finally, keep in mind that teachers also communicate to their students through their actions. For example, a teacher who teachers a lesson on energy conservation but does not turn off the lights when the class leaves for recess or lunch sets a bad example and erodes his or her own credibility with the students. Another common example is a teacher who asks students not to interrupt others when they are on task but repeatedly does so him or herself, thereby confusing children with contradictory words and behavior. To avoid pitfalls, think through what you really expect from your students and then think through your own verbal and nonverbal behaviors, ensuring that they are consistent with those expectations.[3]

As a general rule, most young people prefer and learn best by touching objects, by feeling shapes and textures, by interacting with each other, and by moving things around. In contrast, learning by sitting and listening is difficult for many of them.

Learning Styles

Related to learning modality is learning style, which can be defined as independent forms of knowing and processing information. While some students may be comfortable with beginning their learning of a new idea in the abstract (e.g., visual or verbal symbolization), most need to begin with the concrete (e.g., learning by actually doing it). Many students prosper while working in groups, but others prefer working alone. Some are quick in their studies, whereas others are slow, methodical, cautious, and meticulous. Some can sustain attention on a single topic for a long time, becoming more absorbed in their study as time passes. Others are slower starters and more casual in their pursuits but are capable of shifting with ease from topic to topic, subject to subject. Some can study in the midst of music, noise, or movement; others need quiet, solitude, and a desk or table. The point is this: People vary not only in their skills and their preferences in how knowledge is received, but also in how they mentally process information once it has been received. The latter is a person's style of learning.

It is important to note that learning style is *not* an indicator of intelligence, but rather an indicator of how a person learns. Although there are probably as many types of learning styles as there are individuals, David Kolb describes two major differences in how people learn: how they perceive situations and how they process information.[4] On the basis of perceiving and processing and earlier work by Carl Jung on psychological types,[5] Bernice McCarthy has described four major learning styles, presented in the following paragraphs.[6]

The *imaginative learner* perceives information concretely and processes it reflectively. Imaginative learners learn well by listening and sharing with others, integrating the ideas of others with their own experiences. They often have difficulty adjusting to traditional teaching, which depends less on classroom interactions and on students' sharing and connecting

[3]T. L. Good and J. E. Brophy, *Looking in Classrooms,* 8th ed. (New York: Addison Wesley Longman, 2000), 127.

[4]D. A. Kolb, *Experiential Learning: Experience as the Source of Learning and Development* (Upper Saddle River, NJ: Prentice Hall, 1984).

[5]C. G. Jung, *Psychological Types* (New York: Harcourt Brace, 1923).

[6]See B. McCarthy, "A Tale of Four Learners: 4MAT's Learning Styles," *Educational Leadership* 54(6):47–51 (March 1997).

their prior experiences. In a traditional classroom, the imaginative learner is likely an at-risk student.

The *analytic learner* perceives information abstractly and processes it reflectively. They prefer sequential thinking, need details, and value what experts have to offer. Analytic learners do well in traditional classrooms.

The *common sense learner* perceives information abstractly and processes it actively. Common sense learners are pragmatic and enjoy hands-on learning. They sometimes find school frustrating unless they can see an immediate use for what is being learned. In the traditional classroom, the common sense learner is likely to be at risk of not completing school, of dropping out.

The *dynamic learner* perceives information concretely and processes it actively. Dynamic learners also prefer hands-on learning and are excited by anything new. They are risk takers and are frustrated by learning if they see it as being tedious and sequential. In a traditional classroom, the dynamic learner also is likely to be an at-risk student.

Learning Capacities: The Theory of Multiple Intelligences

In contrast to learning styles, Gardner introduced what he calls *learning capacities* exhibited by individuals in differing ways.[7] Originally, and sometimes still, referred to as *multiple intelligences*, or *ways of knowing*, capacities identified thus far are

- *Bodily/kinesthetic:* ability to use the body skillfully and to handle objects skillfully
- *Existentialist:* ability to understand and pursue the ultimate philosophical questions, meanings, and mysteries of life
- *Interpersonal:* ability to understand people and relationships
- *Intrapersonal:* ability to assess one's emotional life as a means to understand oneself and others
- *Logical/mathematical:* ability to handle chains of reasoning and to recognize patterns and orders
- *Musical/rhythmic:* sensitivity to pitch, melody, rhythm, and tone
- *Naturalist:* ability to draw on materials and features of the natural environment to solve problems or fashion products
- *Verbal/linguistic:* sensitivity to the meaning and order of words
- *Visual/spatial:* ability to perceive the world accurately and to manipulate the nature of space, such as through architecture, mime, or sculpture

As discussed earlier, and as implied in the presentation of McCarthy's four types of learners, many educators believe that many of the students who are at risk of not completing school may be dominant in a cognitive learning style not in synch with traditional teaching methods. Traditional methods of instruction are largely of McCarthy's analytic style: Information is presented in a logical, linear, sequential fashion. Traditional methods also reflect three of the Gardner types: verbal/linguistic, logical/mathematical, and intrapersonal. Consequently, to better synchronize methods of instruction with learning styles, some teachers and schools have restructured the curriculum and instruction around Gardner's learning capacities,[8] or around Sternberg's Triarchic Theory.[9]

CLASSROOM VIGNETTE

Using the Theory of Learning Capacities (Multiple Intelligences) and Multilevel Instruction

In a fifth-grade classroom, during one week of a six-week thematic unit on weather, students were concentrating on learning about the water cycle. For this study of the water cycle, with the students' help the teacher divided the class into several groups of three to five students. While working on six projects simultaneously to learn about the water cycle (1) one group of students designed, conducted, and repeated an experiment to discover the number of drops of water that can be held on one side of a new one-cent coin versus the number that can be held on the side of a worn one-cent coin, (2) working in part with the first group, a second group designed and prepared graphs to illustrate the results of the experiments of the first group, (3) a third group of students created and composed the words and music for a song about the water cycle, (4) a fourth group incorporated their combined interests in mathematics and art to design, collect the necessary materials, and create a colorful and interactive bulletin board about the water cycle, (5) a fifth group read about the water cycle in materials they researched from the Internet and various libraries, and (6) a sixth group created a puppet show about the water cycle. On Friday, after each group had finished, the groups shared their projects with the whole class.

---

[7]For Gardner's distinction between "learning style" and "intelligences," see H. Gardner, "Multiple Intelligences: Myths and Messages," *International Schools Journal 15*(2):8–22 (April 1996) and the many articles in the "Teaching for Multiple Intelligences" theme issue of *Educational Leadership* 55(1) (September 1997).

[8]See, for example, L. Campbell and B. Campbell, *Multiple Intelligences and Student Achievement: Success Stories from Six Schools* (Alexandria, VA: Association for Supervision and Curriculum Development, 1999).

[9]See R. J. Sternberg, "Teaching and Assessing for Successful Intelligence," *School Administrator* 55(1):26–27, 30–31 (January 1998). See also R. J. Sternberg, E. L. Grigorenko, and L. Jarvin, "Improving Reading Instruction: The Triarchic Model," *Educational Leadership 58*(6):48–51 (March 2001).

Sternberg identifies seven metaphors for the mind and intelligence (geographic, computational, biological, epistemological, anthropological, sociological, and systems) and proposes a theory of intelligence consisting of three elements—analytical, practical, and creative.

See the sample classroom vignette, "Using the Theory of Learning Capacities (Multiple Intelligences) and Multilevel Instruction."

From the preceding information about children and their learning you must understand at least two important facts:

1. *Intelligence is not a fixed or static reality, but can be learned, taught, and developed.* This concept is important for students to understand, too. When students understand that intelligence is incremental, that it is developed through use over time, they tend to be more motivated to work at learning than when they believe intelligence is a fixed entity.[10]
2. *Not all students learn and respond to learning situations in the same way.* A student may learn differently according to the situation or according to the student's ethnicity, cultural background, or socioeconomic status.[11] A teacher who uses only one style of teaching for all students, or who teaches to only one or a few styles of learning day after day is short-changing those students who learn better another way.

Anne Vega/Merrill

Thinking skills are the skills of sciencing. Rather than assume that students have developed these skills, direct instruction must be given to students on how to think through the analysis of a problem.

 Understanding Sciencing

As we said in Chapter 1, *sciencing* is a word that is useful in emphasizing the importance of process when talking about what a scientist does. The word *science* can and should be used not only as a noun that describes the product of scientific exploration, but also as a verb that considers the process of scientific exploration. We make this point only to emphasize the process as well as the product of scientific work. Sciencing is not only what a scientist does; it is what students should do when they study science. Children should learn the processes of science as well as the product (the content).

We do not believe children should be taught that there are steps to the scientific method. To ask children to learn and memorize steps in the scientific method implies that the process of sciencing is linear. It is not (see "Understanding That the Process of Sciencing Is Cyclic" that follows). It implies that there is a beginning and an end that is final. That is misleading. It further implies to students that, for them, science is a repetition of experiments or the memorization of facts—of learning what is already known. That is dull.

By the time children reach the middle level grades, those taught in such a dogmatic fashion are bored. This kind of teaching is lethal to a child's natural interest in science. We can all recall teachers who taught us in such a dreary fashion. They required that we memorize such "facts" as "Pluto is the outer planet of our solar system" (not always); "Saturn has nine rings" (it has hundreds); "human cells have 48 chromosomes" (they don't); "roots of trees grow down, and stems grow up" (some do); "plants produce oxygen for animals" (plants need oxygen, too).

As professed by Dewey a century ago and observed by Pestalozzi even before that, children should learn science by observing and investigating, using all their senses, rather than by merely memorizing facts they read in books or hear from a teacher. A teacher who does nothing more than have students memorize and repeat "facts" is not teaching science; that teacher is simply orchestrating memorization.

 Understanding That the Process of Sciencing Is Cyclic

The process of sciencing progresses through cycles (see Figure 3.3), not in a straight line sequence of orderly steps with a clear beginning or end. A learner enters a cycle whenever a discrepancy or problem is observed. Furthermore, discrepancy or problem recognition can occur at any point in the cycle.

[10]See, for example, R. J. Marzano, "20th Century Advances in Instruction," in R. S. Brandt, ed., *Education in a New Era,* Chapter 4 (Alexandria, VA: ASCD Yearbook, Association for Supervision and Curriculum Development, 2000), 76.

[11]See P. Guild, "The Culture/Learning Style Connection," *Educational Leadership 51*(8):16–21 (May 1994).

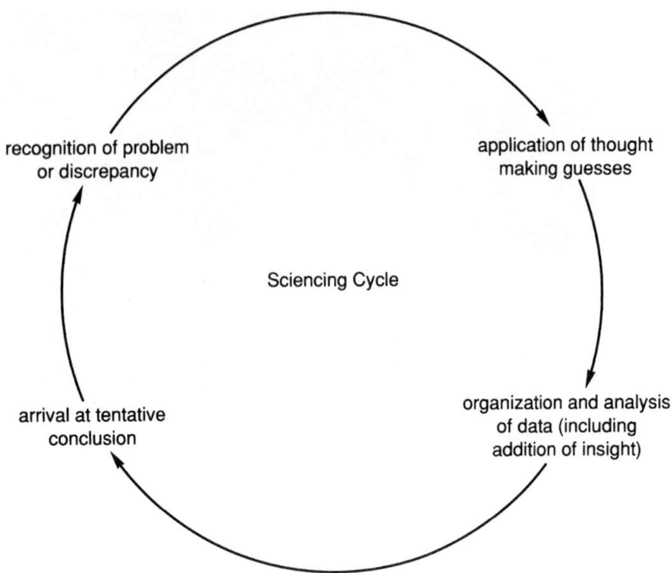

FIGURE 3.3 The sciencing cycle.

When a person is sciencing, the cycle progresses through a series of states where the person

- recognizes a problem or discrepancy
- hypothesizes an explanation
- designs a controlled (that is, with only one variable) experiment to test the hypothesis
- collects data from the experiment
- analyzes the data
- arrives at a tentative conclusion

Consider the following illustration. When a biochemist believes she has discovered a new enzyme, there is no textbook or teacher expert to whom she can go to find out whether she is right. She arrives at a tentative conclusion that is confusing and counterintuitive, and upon reviewing her work discovers an incorrect measurement. She returns to the experiment with a strong sense of self-confidence and collects a new set of data, which appears to fit better with her hypothesis, but still leaves a few questions unanswered. She draws a set of conclusions based on her best analysis. Later, new data may cause her to revise that conclusion. The process of sciencing may begin with the recognition of a problem but move from state to state as a researcher looks for answers and explanations.

In everyday living, problems are resolved in the same fashion by any scientifically literate person. For example, most of us have probably been faced with the daunting task of choosing the fastest checkout line at the grocery store. We begin by quickly assessing the facts. First, which line has the fewest people? Next, which line has the people with the fewest groceries? Quickly, we make a decision and pull in, just ahead of the next person jockeying for the same spot. Remember, however, that the conclusion is tentative. The process does not end with the conclusion. The process is cyclic. At first, it may seem like things are going along really well, but further data may show a need for a revision of the earlier conclusion—like when you realize that the cashier is a trainee and has lots of questions for his supervisor that slow him down. "Rats." Now you have more data to base your decision the next time you go shopping. That is, if you can keep this in mind.

In sciencing, as in real-world problem-solving, we do not think in terms of absolute truths. Data support ideas; data never prove conclusively. (Note of explanation: Scientific research relies on the statistical analysis of data that are obtained. Because of that statistical treatment, there is always a possibility of variation. Therefore, the researcher can be only fairly certain about the conclusion, not absolutely certain. In addition, data are usually collected by means that are indirect and dependent on reliability of instruments.) What your students will do while learning science, then, is generate their own ideas and test them. That is sciencing. The processes involved are varied: Some are concerned with generating and organizing data, others are concerned with building and using ideas. Figure 3.4 illustrates processes in each of these operations.

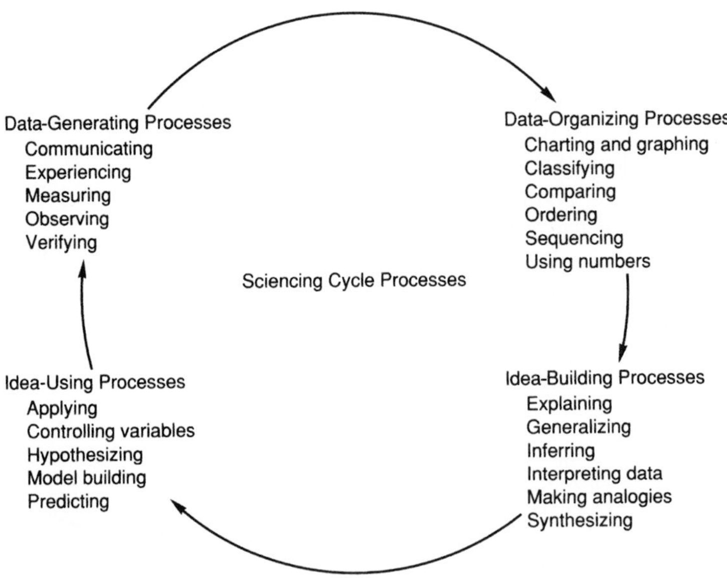

FIGURE 3.4 Sciencing cycle processes.

Pedagogy for Sciencing: The Learning Cycle

To understand conceptual development and change, researchers in the 1960s developed a Piaget-based theory of learning where students are guided from concrete, hands-on learning experiences to the abstract formulations of concepts and their formal applications. This theory became known as the *three-phase learning cycle.*[12] Long a popular strategy for teaching science, the learning cycle can be useful in other disciplines as well.[13] The three phases are (a) the *exploratory hands-on phase,* where students can explore ideas and experience assimilation and disequilibrium that lead to their own questions and tentative answers, (b) the *invention* or *concept development phase,* where, under the guidance of the teacher, students invent concepts and principles that help them answer their questions and reorganize their ideas (that is, the students revise their thinking to allow the new information to fit), and (c) the *expansion* or *concept application phase,* another hands-on phase in which students try out their new ideas by applying them to situations that are relevant and meaningful to them.[14] During application of a concept, the learner may discover new information that causes a change in the learner's understanding of the concept being applied. Thus, the process of learning is cyclical.

Recent interpretations or modifications of the three-phase cycle include McCarthy's 4MAT. With the 4MAT system, teachers employ a learning cycle of instructional strategies to try to reach each student's learning style. As stated by McCarthy, in the cycle learners "sense and feel, they experience, then they watch, they reflect, then they think, they develop theories, then they try out theories, they experiment. Finally, they evaluate and synthesize what they have learned in order to apply it to their next similar experience. They get smarter. They apply experience to experiences."[15]

In this process they are likely using all four learning modalities.

Constructivist learning theory suggests that learning is a process involving the active engagement of learners who adapt the educative event to fit and expand their individual worldview (as opposed to the behaviorist pedagogical assumption that learning is something done to learners)[16] and to accentuate the importance of student self-assessment. In support of that theory, some variations of the learning cycle include a fourth phase of assessment. However, because we believe assessment of what students know or think they know should be a continual process permeating all three phases of the learning cycle, we reject any treatment of assessment as a self-standing phase.

 Understanding the Sciencing Cycle Processes

As a teacher of science to children, you need to understand and know how to use the processes of sciencing, and you must be able to help your students develop their skills. These processing skills are also important in language arts, mathematics, and social science.

Sciencing Cycle and the Learning Cycle

We illustrate the sciencing cycle processes (Figure 3.4) by clustering them into four groups: data generating, data organizing, idea building, and idea using.

Generally, students perform the data-generating processes during the exploration phase of the learning cycle, the data-organizing and idea-building processes during the concept introduction phase, and the idea-using processes during the concept application phase. As emphasized earlier, discrepancy recognition can occur at any time and at any place within the cycle.

Some processes in the sciencing cycle are discovery processes; others are inquiry. (Additional explanations about discovery and inquiry appear in Chapter 5.) Inquiry processes are more complex intellectual operations (all the idea-using processes) sometimes referred to as *integrated processes.* Early grades should concentrate on discovery skills. By the time children are young adolescents, many are in the process of developing formal operational thought and should be provided experiences requiring the integrated processes of inquiry. Teachers of grades 4 and up should introduce integrated processes and begin the process of aiding students in developing those skills, thus facilitating their readiness

[12]See R. Karplus, *Science Curriculum Improvement Study,* Teacher's Handbook (Berkeley: University of California, 1974).

[13]See, for example: M. M. Bevevino, J. Dengel, and K. Adams, "Constructivist Theory in the Classroom: Internalizing Concepts through Inquiry Learning," *Clearing House* 72(5):275–278 (May/June 1999); A. C. Rule, *Using the Learning Cycle to Teach Acronyms, a Language Arts Lesson* (ED383000, 1995); and J. E. Sowell, "Approach to Art History in the Classroom," *Art Education* 46(2):19–24 (March 1993).

[14]The three phases of the learning cycle are comparable to the three levels of thinking, described variously by others. For example, in Elliot Eisner's *The Educational Imagination* (Macmillan, 1979), the levels are referred to as "descriptive," "interpretive," and "evaluative." For a comparison of thinking models, see A. L. Costa, "Toward a Model of Human Intellectual Functioning," Chapter 12 of A. L. Costa, ed., *Developing Minds: A Resource Book for Teaching Thinking* (Alexandria, VA: Association for Supervision and Curriculum Development, 1985), 62–65.

[15]B. McCarthy, "Using the 4MAT System to Bring Learning Styles to Schools," *Educational Leadership* 48(2):33 (October 1990).

[16]R. DeLay, "Forming Knowledge: Constructivist Learning and Experiential Education," *Journal of Experiential Education* 19(2):76–81 (August/September 1996).

for formal-operation thinking. For example, all K–8 children can be expected to (a) ask a question about something they observe, (b) plan an investigation about that event, (c) use simple equipment and tools to gather data and extend the senses, (d) use data they collect to construct a reasonable explanation regarding the event, and (e) communicate to others about their investigation; but, in addition, children of grades 5–8 should be able to (f) recognize and analyze alternative explanations and procedures and (g) use mathematics in various aspects of their inquiry.[17]

The Processes: Thinking Skills

The processes of sciencing are thinking skills. As students develop maturity in the use of these skills, they will be able to do more sophisticated work in science, in other subjects, and in real-life problem solving. The descriptions that follow show how the processes of the sciencing cycle relate to the learning cycle. Assessment, including student self-assessment, should be built into each of the four phases of the sciencing cycle and should not appear just at the completion of a study.

Data-Generating Processes (The Exploratory Phase of the Learning Cycle)

These are the processes needed to produce data, a major product of student investigation during the exploratory phase of the learning cycle. Teachers help children develop their skills in these processes beginning in kindergarten. Children produce data by developing their language skills, by communicating with others, by listening and sharing their experiences. The test of a child's developing skill in communication is whether others understand the child's written and spoken communication. Communication skill development is enhanced as children are provided a variety of exciting, carefully planned opportunities to experience their environment. As they experience their natural environment, they are taught skills in measuring; in observing with all their senses; and in verifying by looking, touching, perhaps tasting, listening, or smelling again. Beginning in kindergarten, the planned development of skills in these data-generating processes continues throughout schooling.

Data-Organizing Processes (The Beginning of the Concept Introduction Phase of the Learning Cycle)

For data to make sense, they must be organized. The planned development of skills in organizing data also starts in kindergarten. Beginning in the primary grades, children are taught how to order ("Arrange these objects from smallest to largest"), to sequence ("Which duck do you suppose came first, and which came last—the mother, the young duckling, or the baby?"), and to classify ("If each of us places a shoe into the center of the room, how do you suppose we could arrange the shoes?"). They are taught how to chart and graph data and to use numbers so that comparisons can be made. From the things they do and make, children may recognize discrepancies and, if so, they may begin the cycle all over again. While doing these things, the children are also integrating their learning of mathematics and science and perhaps other disciplines as well.

Idea-Building Processes (A Continuation of Concept Introduction, and the Concept Building Phase of the Learning Cycle)

As data are collected and organized, students can begin to make sense out of the data, to build ideas, to develop concepts, and to arrive at tentative decisions about the information. As they bring together ideas generated by the data (synthesizing) and try to interpret or make sense of their data, they arrive at tentative conclusions about the data (generalizing) and test their conclusions by explaining to others. As they are reasoning or thinking through their explanations, they are developing the skill of inferring (a more sophisticated form of drawing a conclusion). During the explaining and inferring processes, children may think of analogies, and they may recognize discrepancies that might cause them to start the learning cycle all over again.

Interpreting data, making analogies, and synthesizing, which are higher thinking skills than explaining, inferring, and generalizing, are not usually emphasized until the late primary or early intermediate grades.

Idea-Using Processes (The Concept Application Phase of the Learning Cycle)

When a person gets an idea, he or she usually wants to try it out, to test it, to put it to work, to apply it. After getting an idea, *wanting to test it is a nearly unavoidable impulse.* Various skills are involved in using ideas. Predicting "what will happen if" is a skill that should be encouraged and practiced from the earliest grades. From ideas generated, children can predict "what will happen if" and then test their hypotheses by designing experiments in which all variables but one are controlled. Sometimes the experiment is one of designing, building, and testing a model. Skill in concept application can be demonstrated by testing one's ideas through experimenting or by applying a fully tested idea, as Jonas Salk did once his polio vaccine had been fully tested in a controlled environment. Although most of the skills in the idea-using category are complex mental operations, at some degree of sophistication all children can be helped in their development of these skills.

---

[17]National Research Council, *Inquiry and the National Science Education Standards: A Guide for Teaching and Learning* (Washington, DC: National Academy Press, 2000).

These are the skills that intelligent people put to use. They are skills that are used not just in science but in all disciplines and that help one to live productively and intelligently throughout life.

Teachers should encourage and model the skills of scientific inquiry, as well as the curiosity, openness to new ideas, and skepticism that characterize science.[18]

Teaching Thinking for Intelligent Behavior: Developing a Sense of "I Can" and the Feeling of "I Enjoy"

Pulling together what has been learned about learning and brain functioning, teachers are encouraged to integrate explicit thinking instruction into daily lessons. In other words, teachers should help students develop their thinking skills. As their thinking skills develop, students develop a sense of "I can," with an accompanying feeling of "I enjoy." Art Costa expresses it this way:

> In teaching for thinking, we are interested not only in what students know but also in how students behave when they don't know. . . . Gathering evidence of the performance and growth of intelligent behavior . . . requires "kid-watching": observing students as they try to solve the day-to-day academic and real-life problems they encounter. . . . By collecting anecdotes and examples of written, oral, and visual expressions, we can see students' increasingly voluntary and spontaneous performance of these intelligent behaviors.[19]

Characteristics of Intelligent Behavior

Characteristics of intelligent behavior that you should model, teach for, and observe developing in your students, as identified by Costa and Kallick,[20] are described in the following paragraphs.

Drawing on knowledge and applying it to new situations. A major goal of formal education is for students to apply school-learned knowledge to real-life situations. To develop skills in drawing on past knowledge and applying that knowledge to new situations, students must be given opportunity to practice doing that very thing. Problem recognition, problem solving, and project-based learning are significantly important ways of providing that opportunity to students.

Finding humor. The positive effects of humor on the body's physiological functions are well established: a drop in the pulse rate, an increase of oxygen in the blood, the activation of antibodies that fight against harmful microorganisms, and the release of gamma interferon, a hormone that fights viruses and regulates cell growth. Humor liberates creativity and provides high-level thinking skills, such as anticipation, finding novel relationships, and visual imagery. The acquisition of a sense of humor follows a developmental sequence similar to that described by Piaget[21] and Kohlberg.[22] Initially, young children and immature youth may find humor in all the wrong things—human frailty, ethnic humor, sacrilegious riddles, and ribald profanities. Later, creative young people thrive on finding incongruity, and will demonstrate a whimsical frame of mind during problem solving.

Creating, imagining, innovating. All students must be encouraged to do, and discouraged from saying "I can't." Students must be taught in such a way as to encourage intrinsic motivation rather than reliance on extrinsic sources. Teachers must be able to offer criticism so the student understands that the criticism is not a criticism of self. In exemplary educational programs, students learn the value of feedback. They learn the value of their own intuition, of guessing—they learn "I can."

Listening with understanding and empathy. Some psychologists believe that the ability to listen to others, to empathize with and understand their point of view, is one of the highest forms of intelligent behavior. Empathic behavior is considered an important skill for conflict resolution. Piaget refers to this behavior as *overcoming egocentrism*. In class meetings, brainstorming sessions, think tanks, town meetings, advisory councils, board meetings, and legislative bodies, people from various walks of life convene to share their thinking, to explore their ideas, and to broaden their perspectives by listening to the ideas and reactions of others.

Managing impulsivity. When students develop impulse control, they think before acting. Impulsive behavior can worsen conflict and can inhibit effective problem solving.[23] Students can be taught to think

[18]National Research Council, *National Science Education Standards* (Washington, DC: National Academy Press, 1996), 3.

[19]A. L. Costa, *The School as a Home for the Mind* (Palatine, IL: Skylight Publishing, 1991), 19. From original in A. L. Costa, ed., *Developing Minds*, 2nd ed. (Reston, VA: Association for Supervision and Curriculum Development, 1991).

[20]A. L. Costa and B. Kallick, *Discovering and Exploring Habits of Mind*, Book 1 of *Habits of Mind: A Developmental Series* (Alexandria, VA: Association for Supervision and Curriculum Development, 2000). See also Armstrong's 12 qualities of genius—curiosity, playfulness, imagination, creativity, wonderment, wisdom, inventiveness, vitality, sensitivity, flexibility, humor, and joy—in T. Armstrong, *Awakening Genius in the Classroom* (Alexandria, VA: Association for Supervision and Curriculum Development, 1998), 2–15.

[21]J. Piaget, *The Psychology of Intelligence* (Totowa, NJ: Littlefield Adams, 1972).

[22]I. Kohlberg, *The Meaning and Measurement of Moral Development* (Worcester, MA: Clark University Press, 1981).

[23]See, for example, M. Goos and P. Galbraith, "Do It This Way! Metacognitive Strategies in Collaborative Mathematics Problem Solving," *Educational Studies in Mathematics 30*(3):229–260 (April 1996).

before shouting out an answer, before beginning a project or task, and before arriving at conclusions with insufficient data. One of several reasons that teachers should routinely expect a show of student hands before a student is acknowledged to respond or to question is to help students develop control over the impulsive behavior of shouting out in class.[24]

Persisting. Persistence is sticking to a task until it is completed. Consider the following examples.

◆ **Clara Barton.** Nearly single-handedly and against formidable odds, Clara Barton persevered to form the American Red Cross in 1882.

◆ **Rachel Carson.** Refusing to be intimidated by the chemical industry, powerful politicians, and the media, Carson was persistent in her pursuit to educate society about the ill effects of pesticides on humans and the natural world. She refused to accept the premise that damage to nature was the inevitable cost of technological and scientific progress. Her book *Silent Spring,* published in 1962, was the seed for the beginning of the development of a more responsible ecological attitude.

◆ **Thomas Edison.** Edison tested nearly 3,000 materials before finding one that worked to his satisfaction as a lightbulb filament.

◆ **Wilma Rudolf.** As the result of childhood diseases, Wilma Rudolf, at the age of 10, could not walk without the aid of leg braces. Just 10 years later, at the age of 20, she was declared to be the fastest running woman in the world, having won three gold medals in the 1960 World Olympics.

Questioning and posing problems. Young people are usually full of questions, and, unless discouraged, they do ask them. As educators, we want students to be alert to and to recognize discrepancies and phenomena in their environment and to freely inquire about their causes. In exemplary science programs, students are encouraged to ask questions (see Chapter 4) and then from those questions to develop a problem-solving strategy to investigate their questions. That, as discussed in Chapter 2, is hypothesizing, the essence of sciencing.

Remaining open to continuous learning. Intelligent people are in a continuous learning mode, always eager to learn and find new ways.

Responding with wonderment and awe. Young children express wonderment, an expression that should never be stifled. Through effective teaching, students can retain or recapture that sense of wonderment as they are guided by an effective teacher into a sense of "I can" and express a feeling of "I enjoy."

Striving for accuracy. Teachers can observe students growing in this behavior when students take time to check over their work, review the procedures, and refuse to draw conclusions about their sciencing with only limited data.

Taking responsible risks: venture forth and explore ideas beyond the usual zone of comfort. Such exploration, of course, must be done with thoughtfulness; it must not be done in ways that could put the student at risk psychologically or physically. Using the analogy of a turtle going nowhere until it sticks its neck out, classroom teachers should model this behavior. They should also provide opportunities for students to develop this intelligent behavior by using techniques such as brainstorming strategies, divergent-thinking questioning, think-pair-share, cooperative learning, inquiry, and project-based learning (all discussed in Chapter 5). As stated so clearly elsewhere, "no coward ever got the Great Teacher Award."[25]

Thinking and communicating with clarity and precision. Strive for clarity and accurate communication in both written and oral form.

Thinking about thinking (metacognition). Learning to plan, monitor, assess, and reflect on one's own thinking is another characteristic of intelligent behavior. Cooperative learning groups, journals, student-led portfolio conferences, self-assessment, and thinking aloud in dyads are strategies that can be used to help students develop this intelligent behavior. Thinking aloud is good modeling for your students, helping them to develop their own cognitive skills of thinking, learning, and reasoning.[26]

Thinking flexibly. Sometimes referred to as *lateral thinking,* flexibility in thinking is the ability to approach a problem from a new angle, using a novel approach. With modeling by the teacher, students can develop this behavior as they learn to consider alternative points of view and to deal with several sources of information simultaneously.

Thinking interdependently. Real-world problem solving has become so complex that seldom can any person go it alone. As stated by Elias, "We live in an interdependent world; there is no such thing, in any practical sense, as independence and autonomy. We live lives of synergy and linkage."[27] Not all students come to school knowing how to work effectively in groups. They may exhibit competitiveness, narrow-mindedness, egocentrism, ethnocentrism, or criticism of others' values, emotions, and beliefs. Listening, consensus seeking, giving up an idea to work on someone else's, empathy, compassion, group leadership, cooperative learning, knowing how to support group efforts, altruism—those are behaviors

[24]For further reading about the relation of impulse control to intelligence, see D. Goleman, *Emotional Intelligence: Why It Can Matter More Than IQ* (New York: Bantam Books, 1995) and D. Harrington-Lueker, "Emotional Intelligence," *High Strides* 9(4):1, 4–5 (March/April 1997).

[25]S. Wassermann, "Shazam! You're a Teacher," *Phi Delta Kappan* *80*(6):464, 466–468 (February 1999).

[26]See, for example, J. W. Astington, "Theory of Mind Goes to School," *Educational Leadership* *56*(3):46–48 (November 1998).

[27]M. J. Elias, "Easing Transitions With Social-Emotional Learning," *Principal Leadership* *1*(7) [Online 4/1/01 http://www.nassp.org/news/pl_soc_emo_lrng_301.htm].

indicative of intelligent human beings, and they can be learned by students at school and in the classroom.

Using all the senses. As often as is appropriate and feasible, students should be encouraged to learn to use and develop all their sensory input channels to learn (i.e., verbal, visual, tactile, and kinesthetic).

We should strive to help children develop these characteristics of intelligent behavior. In Chapter 4, we focus on particular teacher behaviors and instructional strategies that facilitate this development. Now, let's review additional research findings that offer important considerations in the facilitation of student learning and intelligent behaving.

Direct Teaching for Thinking and Intelligent Behavior

The science curriculum of any school includes the development of skills that are used in thinking, such as *classifying, comparing and contrasting, concluding, generalizing, inferring,* and others. Because the academic achievement of students increases when they are taught thinking skills directly, many researchers and educators concur that direct instruction should be given to all students on how to think and to behave intelligently. We believe the exemplary teacher concentrates on helping children develop these skills—while learning science or some other subject.

Rather than assuming students have developed thinking skills, teachers should devote classroom time to teaching them directly.[28] When teaching a thinking skill directly, the subject content becomes the vehicle for thinking. For example, a lesson can teach students how to distinguish fact and opinion, a lesson can instruct students how to compare and analyze, and a lesson can teach students how to set up a problem for their inquiry. Inquiry teaching and discovery learning, discussed in Chapter 4, are both useful tools for learning and for teaching thinking skills.

Understanding the Origin and Nature of Misconceptions

While teaching science, you will discover that children sometimes have false notions or understandings, or misconceptions (also called *naïve views*) about certain science concepts. It is difficult enough to teach science concepts to children; it is even more difficult to reverse their understandings. Children, like human beings in general, tend to tenaciously hold onto their beliefs, accurate or not. One thing you should try to avoid is teaching misconceptions. Here are guidelines to follow to *avoid* this.

[28]See, for example, A. Zohar, "Inquiry Learning as Higher Order Thinking: Overcoming Cognitive Obstacles," in J. Minstrell and E. H. van Zee, eds., *Inquiring into Inquiry Learning and Teaching in Science* (Washington, DC: American Association for the Advancement of Science, 2000), 405–424.

Avoid Prejudices about the Natural World

Artificialism is the term used by Piaget to represent the natural tendency for young children to believe that everything in the world is for the benefit of humans; more specifically, for the individual. Although natural for children in early grades, artificialism does represent a selfish, prejudiced, nonobjective attitude, which a science teacher has an obligation, and an opportunity, to correct. Unfortunately, as evidenced along highways and city streets, many adults have yet to learn that the world is not their own private trash can.

Avoid Prejudices about Human Beings

Good science teaching can help dispel attitudes and superstitions that are detrimental to humanity. For example, we have observed teachers requiring students to learn the differences between racial groups. When speaking in terms of science, more specifically genetics, differences between racial groups are so insignificant that they are of no consequence. Differences based on race stem almost entirely from social and cultural variations. Ascribing a genetic basis for these differences is misleading and overemphasizes them, placing a lesser importance on similarities or likenesses spanning peoples of the world. Historically, science has been misused to perpetuate attitudes that justify social stratification and the oppression of groups of people. As a teacher of science, there is no greater good that you can do than to dispel these prejudices among the children you teach.

Use Caution when Simplifying Science Concepts

While trying to simplify concepts for students, teachers sometimes unintentionally teach misconceptions. For example, in grades 6–8, the science program considers the concept of photosynthesis. With the intention of simplifying what occurs in photosynthesis, teachers and textbooks may use the following equation: $CO_2 + H_2O +$ chlorophyll $\rightarrow$ sugar + energy. If this equation were accurate, any student should be able to perform photosynthesis simply by shaking carbon dioxide with water and chlorophyll in a jar. Of course it will not happen, because in photosynthesis water and carbon dioxide do not combine to form sugar, or anything else. Nonetheless, perhaps because of a combination of tradition and lack of knowledge, textbook writers continue to perpetuate the misconception by putting the equation in science books, and many teachers continue to teach it. In this instance, the damage is only minor. In another example to follow, however, the danger is greater. The point is this: *To avoid teaching misconceptions, and, most certainly, to correct children's misconceptions about science, teachers themselves must understand the concepts they are trying to teach and must be aware that, in their effort to simplify a concept for student understanding, they may, in fact, teach a misconception.*

The exact explanation of photosynthesis is quite complex; however, it is possible to offer a simplified explanation for middle level students that does not foster misconceptions. The simplified explanation goes like this. In the presence of chlorophyll, the water molecule is split into hydrogen and oxygen. This is the *light reaction;* it can be shown as $H_2O \rightarrow [H] + O_2$. While the oxygen is released into the environment, the hydrogen is combined with carbon dioxide to form a carbohydrate. Sometimes that carbohydrate is a sugar; at other times it is a more complex carbohydrate. This reaction is the carbon-fixing reaction, sometimes called *dark reaction* because it continues in the absence of light. This reaction can be illustrated as $[H] + CO_2 \rightarrow (CH_2O)_x$. The brackets around the hydrogen atom indicate that it is never freed. Instead, it is attached to other molecules in transport to carbon dioxide. For elementary grades, words can be substituted for the chemical symbols. Light (such as sunlight) is necessary to start photosynthesis, but the process continues in the absence of light. Water and carbon dioxide do not combine. So, when teaching about photosynthesis, rather than perpetuate a misconception, it is just as easy to summarize the concept correctly as involving two processes—the light reaction, in which hydrogen is released from water, and the carbon-fixing or dark reaction, in which the hydrogen is combined with carbon dioxide to form a carbohydrate. The oxygen released from the water is released into the air unless the plant uses it for its own cellular respiration.

We have observed many teachers and books, as a result of their misconception about photosynthesis, emphasizing or implying inaccurately that *cellular respiration* (the breakdown of sugar into water and carbon dioxide and the release of energy) is the opposite of photosynthesis. Although both reactions involve water and carbon dioxide, cellular respiration and photosynthesis are *not* opposites.

This brings us to our second example, involving a concept that is more important for K–8 children to understand. When we asked science teachers and their students where the oxygen comes from that is in water, that fish need in order to breathe, we found that a significant number of children *and their teachers* held a misconception. They thought the oxygen that fish needed to breathe came from the oxygen in the water molecule, rather than from oxygen dissolved in the water. Holding that misconception, students (and their teachers) will never comprehend that water pollution results from bacteria and other organisms consuming the dissolved oxygen, or from oil or detergents on the surface of a polluted stream keeping oxygen in the air from dissolving in the water. In both cases, fish and other organisms in the stream will die from lack of oxygen.

Summary

As we teach toward an understanding of science concepts, let's not teach misconceptions. To avoid teaching misconceptions about science, the teacher must be aware of his or her own lack of understanding of certain concepts. Please be assured that there is absolutely nothing wrong with you if you don't know everything there is to know about the science content you are supposed to teach. There are plenty of resources available to help you teach the expected content. However, it is important to be open-minded, to avoid dogmatic teaching, and to help children develop their personal skills of thinking and doing. That leads us into the next chapter where we begin to focus attention on the *how* component of exemplary instruction. Chapter 4 focuses on specific teacher behaviors necessary to most effectively facilitate student learning.

Questions for Class Discussion

1. For a specific age or grade level, research and describe the students' common misconceptions or naïve theories in science. Discuss your findings with your colleagues. Describe how you would go about helping students change their misconceptions in science.
2. Explain why you agree or disagree that knowledge of student learning styles is important for a science teacher.
3. Ms. Lee, a science teacher, has a class of 33 seventh graders who, during her lectures, teacher-led discussions, and recitation lessons, are restless and inattentive, creating a major problem for her in classroom management. At Ms. Lee's invitation, the school psychologist tests the children for learning modality and finds that of the 33, 29 children are predominately kinesthetic learners. Of what use is this information to Ms. Lee? Describe what changes, if any, she should make in her teaching style as a result of having this information.
4. Identify any concepts you held previously that changed as a result of your experiences with this chapter. Describe the concepts and the changes.
5. From your recent observations and fieldwork related to this teacher preparation program, identify one specific example of educational practice that seems contradictory to exemplary practice or theory as presented in this chapter. Explain the discrepancy.
6. What questions do you have about the content of this chapter? Where might answers be found?

Chapter 4

Questioning and Other Behaviors That Provide the Foundation for Active Science Learning

Tom Watson/Merrill

Teachers of science guide and facilitate learning. In doing this, teachers

- Focus and support inquiries while interacting with students
- Orchestrate discourse among students about scientific ideas
- Challenge students to take responsibility for their own learning
- Recognize and respond to student diversity and encourage all students to participate fully in science learning
- Encourage and model the skills of scientific inquiry, as well as the curiosity, openness to new ideas and data, and skepticism that characterize science.[1]

Chapter 1 provides an historical perspective of school science curriculum and instruction. Chapter 2 provides an overview about the goals and objectives of today's K–8 science curriculum, and Chapter 3 provides an overview of the knowledge and skills needed by a teacher to most effectively teach science. Pulling together concepts from those three chapters, this chapter begins to focus on the *how* component of instruction—how best to facilitate student learning, specifically focusing on the practical application of fundamental behaviors necessary to facilitate student learning in science.

Throughout your career as a teacher, you will continue to build a repertoire of behaviors and strategies, and to hone the skills to use those strategies. To be most effective, you need a large repertoire from which to select a specific strategy for a particular goal with a distinctive group of students. This chapter and the two that follow will help you build your repertoire and begin developing your skills in the use of specific strategies.

Your ability to perform your instructional responsibilities effectively is directly dependent upon your knowledge of students and how they learn best and on your knowledge of and the quality of your teaching skills. Development of your strategy repertoire along with your skills in using specific strategies should be ongoing throughout your teaching career. This chapter is designed to help you begin to build those strategies and skills. Like intelligences, teaching style is neither absolutely inherited nor fixed, but continues to develop and emerge throughout one's professional career.

First, you must know why you have selected a particular strategy. An unknowing teacher is likely to use the teaching strategy that is most common in college classes—the lecture. However, as many beginning teachers have discovered the hard way, the traditional lecture is seldom, if ever, an effective or appropriate way to instruct children in grades K–8. (See more on this topic under "Teacher Talk" in Chapter 5). As a rule, as was emphasized in Chapter 3, not many children are strong auditory learners by preference and by adeptness. For most children in grades K–8, learning by sitting and listening is difficult. Instead, they learn best when they are physically (hands-on) and intellectually (minds-on) active—that is, when using tactile and kinesthetic experiences, touching objects, feeling shapes and textures, and moving objects, and when together they are able to talk about and share what they are learning.

Second, basic teacher behaviors create the conditions needed to enable students to think and to learn, whether the learning is a further understanding of a science concept, the internalization of attitudes and values, the development of cognitive processes, or the actuating of the most complex behaviors. The basic teacher behaviors are those that produce the following results: (a) students are physically and mentally engaged in the learning activities, (b) instructional time is efficiently used, and (c) classroom distractions and interruptions are minimal.

Third, the effectiveness with which a teacher carries out the basic behaviors can be measured by how well the students learn. Teachers have a choice of whether to assume full responsibility for the instructional outcomes or whether to assume responsibility for only the positive outcomes of the planned instruction and place the blame for the negative outcomes on outside forces (e.g., parents and guardians or society in general, peers, other teachers, administrators, textbooks).

[1]Reprinted from National Research Council, *National Science Education Standards,* © 1996 by the National Academy of Sciences, 32. Courtesy of National Academy Press, Washington, DC.

Where the responsibility for outcomes is placed is referred to as *locus of control*.

Just because a teacher thinks he or she is a competent teacher doesn't mean it is so. If many students are not learning, then their teacher is not competent. In the words of the late Madeline Hunter, "To say that I am an effective teacher, and acknowledge that my students may not be learning is the same as saying I am a great surgeon, but most of my patients die."[2] Teachers who are intrinsically motivated and competent tend to assume full responsibility for instructional outcomes, regardless of whether or not the outcomes are as intended.

Of course every teacher realizes there are factors that he or she cannot control, such as the negative effects on children from poverty, gangs, alcohol, and drug abuse, so they must do what they can within the confines of the classroom and resources of the school and district. History brims with examples of how even a few positive moments with a truly caring and knowledgeable adult drastically changed for the better the life of a young person who, until then, had a history of mostly negative experiences. So, in this first chapter dealing with the *how* component of exemplary instruction, your attention is focused on those teacher behaviors that facilitate student learning.

Teacher Behaviors That Facilitate Student Learning

The fundamental teacher behaviors that facilitate student learning are structuring the learning environment, accepting and sharing instructional accountability, demonstrating withitness and overlapping, providing a variety of motivating and challenging lessons, modeling appropriate behaviors, facilitating student acquisition of data, creating a psychologically safe environment, clarifying whenever necessary, using periods of silence, and questioning thoughtfully.

Teachers of science design and manage learning environments that provide students with the time, space, and resources needed for learning science. In doing this, teachers

- Structure the time available so that students are able to engage in extended investigations
- Create a setting for student work that is flexible and supportive of science inquiry
- Ensure a safe working environment
- Make the available science tools, materials, media, and technological resources accessible to students.
- Identify and use resources outside the school
- Engage students in designing the learning environment[3]

Facilitating Behaviors and Instructional Strategies: A Clarification

Clearly, at least some of the fundamental teacher behaviors are also instructional strategies. Questioning is one example. The difference is that the behaviors must be in place for the most effective teaching to occur, but strategies—discussed in Chapter 5—are more or less discretionary. They are pedagogical techniques from which you may select but that you may not be obligated to use. For example, questioning and the use of silence are fundamental teaching behaviors, whereas lecturing and using a CD-ROM for instruction are not. Therefore, your task is two-fold: (a) Develop your awareness of and skills in using the fundamental teaching behaviors, and (b) develop your repertoire and skills in selecting and using appropriate instructional strategies. Fundamental teaching behaviors are the focus of this chapter, and instructional strategies are the topic of the chapter that follows.

Starting now and continuing throughout your teaching career, you will want to evaluate your developing competency for each of the fundamental facilitating behaviors and improve in areas where you need help. Consider the following descriptions and examples, and discuss them with your classmates.

Structuring the Learning Environment

Structuring the learning environment means establishing an intellectual, psychological, and physical environment that enables all students to act and react productively. It is the way teachers provide clarity and control classroom environmental resources, such as time, space, human energy, equipment, and materials.[4] Specifically, you

- Attend to the organization of the classroom as a learning laboratory to establish a positive, safe, and efficient environment for student learning.
- Establish and maintain clearly understood classroom procedures, definitions, instructions, and expectations.
- Help students to clarify the learning expectations and to establish clearly understood learning objectives (as was discussed in Chapter 2).

---

[2]In R. A. Villa and J. S. Thousands, eds., *Creating an Inclusive School* (Alexandria, VA: Association for Supervision and Curriculum Development, 1995), 36.

[3]Reprinted from National Research Council, *National Science Education Standards*, © 1996 by the National Academy of Sciences, 43. Courtesy of National Academy Press, Washington, DC.

[4]T. L. Good and J. E. Brophy, *Looking in Classrooms*, 8th ed. (New York: Addison Wesley Longman, 2000), 382; and A. L. Costa, ed., *Developing Minds: A Resource Book for Teaching Thinking* (Alexandria, VA: Association for Supervision and Curriculum Development, 1985), 129.

Valerie Schultz/Merrill

The teacher structures a learning environment that physically and mentally engages the children in the learning process.

◆ Help students assume tasks and responsibilities, thereby empowering them in their learning.

◆ Organize the students, helping them to organize their learning. Help students in the identification and understanding of time and resource constraints. Provide instructional scaffolds, such as building bridges to student learning by helping students connect that which is being learned with what they already know or think they know and have experienced.

◆ Plan and implement techniques for schema building, such as providing content and process outlines, visual diagrams, and opportunities for thinking (topics discussed in Chapters 3 and 5).

◆ Use techniques for students' metacognitive development, such as *think-pair-share* (see also in Chapter 5), in which students are asked to think about an idea, share thoughts about it with a partner, and then share the pair's thoughts with the entire class; *think-write-pair-share,* in which each student writes his or her ideas about the new word and then shares in pairs before sharing with the entire class; and *jigsaw,* in which individuals or small groups of students are given responsibilities for separate tasks that lead to a bigger task or understanding, thereby putting together parts to make a whole.

◆ Plan units and lessons that have clear and concise beginnings and endings with at least some of the planning done collaboratively with the students. (Planning units and lessons are the focus of Chapter 7.)

◆ Provide frequent summary reviews, often by using student self-assessment of what is being learned. Structure and facilitate ongoing formal and informal discussion based on a shared understanding of rules of discourse. (Assessment is the topic of Chapter 8.)

Accepting and Sharing Instructional Accountability

While holding students accountable for their learning, the teacher is willing to be held accountable for the effectiveness of the learning process and outcomes. Specifically, you

◆ Assume a responsibility for professional decision making and for the risks associated with that responsibility. Share some responsibility for decision-making and risk-taking with the students. A primary goal in the students' education must be to see that students become accountable for themselves as learners and as citizens. Teachers are advised to work with their students as *partners* in their learning and development. One dimension of the partnership is shared accountability. One effective way of doing that is using student portfolios that show their work and progress (discussed in Chapter 8).

◆ Communicate clearly to parents/guardians, administrators, and colleagues.

◆ Communicate to the students that accomplishment of learning goals and objectives is a responsibility they share with you.

◆ Plan science exploratory activities that engage students mentally and physically in their learning.

◆ Provide continuous cues for desired learning behaviors and incentives contingent upon desired performance, such as grades, points, rewards, and privileges. Establish a clearly understood and continuous program of assessment that includes reflection and self-assessment. (Assessment is the topic of Chapter 8.)

◆ Provide opportunities for the students to demonstrate their learning, to refine and explore their questions, to inquire, and to share their thinking and results. (These topics are discussed fully in Chapter 5.)

Teachers of science develop communities of science learners that reflect the intellectual vigor of scientific inquiry and the attitudes and social values conducive to science learning. In doing this, teachers

- Display and demand respect for the ideas, skills, and experiences of all students.
- Enable students to have a significant voice in decisions about the content and context of their work, and require students to take responsibility for the learning of all members of the community.
- Nurture collaboration among students.

- Structure and facilitate ongoing formal and informal discussion based on a shared understanding of rules of scientific discourse.
- Model and emphasize the skills, attitudes, and values of scientific inquiry.[5]

Demonstrating Withitness and Overlapping

Withitness and overlapping, first described by Jacob Kounin, are separate but closely related behaviors.[6] *Withitness* is the teacher's awareness of the whole group (i.e., the ability to remain alert in the classroom, to quickly spot and redirect potential student misbehavior, which is analogous to having "eyes in the back of your head"). *Overlapping* is the ability to attend to several matters simultaneously. Specifically, you

- Attend to the entire class while working with one student or with a small group of students, communicating this awareness with eye contact, hand gestures, body position and language, and understated but clear verbal cues.
- Continually and simultaneously monitor all classroom activities to keep students at their tasks and to provide students with assistance and resources.
- Continue monitoring the class during any distraction, such as when a visitor enters the classroom or while the students are on a field trip.
- Demonstrate an understanding of when comprehension checks and instructional transitions are appropriate or needed.
- Dwell on one topic only as long as necessary for the students' understandings.
- Quickly intervene and redirect potential undesirable student behavior.
- Refocus or shift activities for a student when that student's attention begins to fade.

Guidelines for Developing Withitness

Consider the following guidelines for developing withitness.

- Avoid spending too much time with any one student or group; longer than 30 seconds may be approaching "too much time."
- Avoid turning your back to all or a portion of the students, such as when writing on the writing board.
- If two or more errant behaviors are occurring simultaneously in different locations, attend to the most serious first, while giving the other(s) a nonverbal gesture showing your awareness (such as eye contact) and displeasure (such as a frown).
- Involve all students in the act, not just any one student or group. Avoid concentrating on only those who appear most interested or responsive, sometimes referred to as the "chosen few."
- Keep students alert by calling on them randomly, asking questions and calling on an answerer, circulating from group to group during team learning activities, and frequently checking on the progress of individual students.
- Maintain constant visual surveillance of the entire class, even when talking to or working with an individual or small group of students and when meeting a classroom visitor at the door.
- Move around the room. Be on top of potential misbehavior and quietly redirect student attention before the misbehavior occurs or gets out of control.
- Try during whole-class direct instruction to establish eye contact with each student about once every minute. It initially may sound impossible to do, but it is not; it is a skill that can be developed with practice.

Examples of Overlapping Ability

A prerequisite to being withit is the skill to attend to more than one matter at a time. This is referred to as *overlapping ability.* The teacher with overlapping skills uses body language, body position, and hand signals to communicate with students. Consider the following examples of overlapping ability.

- Rather than bringing their papers and problems to her desk, the teacher expects students to remain seated and to raise their hands as she circulates in the room monitoring and attending to individual students.
- The teacher takes care of attendance while visually and/or verbally monitoring the students during their warm-up activity.
- While attending to a messenger who has walked into the room, the teacher demonstrates verbally or by gestures that he expects the students to continue their work.
- While working in a small group, a student raises his hand to get the teacher's attention. The teacher, while continuing to work with another group of students, signals with her hand to tell the student that she is aware that he wants her attention and will get to him quickly, which she does.
- Without missing a beat in her talk, the teacher aborts the potentially disruptive behavior of a student by gesturing, by making eye contact, or by moving closer to the student (applying what is called *proximity control*).

---

[5]Reprinted from National Research Council, *National Science Education Standards,* © 1996 by the National Academy of Sciences, 45–46. Courtesy of National Academy Press, Washington, DC.

[6]J. S. Kounin, *Discipline and Group Management in Classrooms* (New York: Holt, Rinehart and Winston, 1970).

Providing a Variety of Motivating and Challenging Activities

The effective teacher uses a variety of activities that motivate and challenge all students to work to the utmost of their abilities, and that engage and challenge the preferred learning styles and learning capacities (as discussed in Chapter 3) of more of the students more of the time. Specifically, you

- Demonstrate optimism toward each student's ability.
- Demonstrate an unwavering expectation that each student will work to the best of his or her ability.
- Show pride, optimism, and enthusiasm in learning, thinking, and teaching.
- View teaching and learning as an organic and reciprocal process that extends well beyond that which can be referred to as the traditional 2 by 4 by 6 curriculum—that is, a curriculum that is bound by the two covers of the textbook, the four walls of the classroom, and the six hours of the school day.
- Collaborate with the students to plan exciting and interesting learning activities, including those that engage the students' natural interest in the mysterious and the novel.

Modeling Appropriate Behaviors

Effective teachers model the very behaviors expected of their students. Specifically, you

- Are prompt in returning student papers and offer comments that provide instructive and encouraging feedback.
- Arrive promptly in the classroom and demonstrate on-task behaviors for the entire class meeting just as is expected of the students.
- Demonstrate respect for all students. For example, you do not interrupt when a student is showing rational thinking, even though you may disagree with or frown upon the words used or the direction of the students' thinking.
- Demonstrate that making errors is a natural event in learning and during problem-solving, and readily admit and correct any mistake that you make.
- Model and emphasize the skills, attitudes, and values of higher-order intellectual processes.[7] Demonstrate rational problem-solving skills and explain to the students the processes being engaged while problem-solving.[8]
- Model professionalism by spelling correctly, using proper grammar, and writing clearly and legibly.
- Practice communication that is clear, precise, and to the point. For example, use *I* when referring to yourself, *we* when *we* is meant. Rather than responding to student contributions with simply "good" or "okay," tell specifically what about the response was good, or what made it okay.
- Practice moments of silence (see "Using Periods of Silence" that follows), thus modeling thoughtfulness, reflectiveness, and restraint of impulsiveness.
- Realizing that students are also models for other students, reinforce appropriate student behaviors, and intervene when behaviors are not appropriate.

Facilitating Student Acquisition of Data

The teacher makes sure data are accessible to students as input they can process. Children can't use what is not available to them. Specifically, you

- Create a responsive classroom environment with frequent direct learning experiences.
- Ensure that major ideas receive proper attention and emphasis.
- Ensure that sources of information are readily available to students for their use. Select books, media, and materials that facilitate student learning. Make sure that equipment and materials for science learning are readily available for students to use. Identify and use resources beyond the walls of the classroom and the boundaries of the school campus. (Resources are the focus of Chapter 6.)
- Provide clear and specific instructions.
- Provide feedback and feedback mechanisms about each student's performance and progress (discussed in Chapter 8). Encourage students to organize and maintain devices (such as portfolios) to self-monitor their progress in learning and thinking.
- Select anchoring (also called model or benchmark) examples of student work that help students bridge what is being learned with what they already know and have experienced.
- Serve as a resource person and use cooperative learning (Chapter 5), thus regarding students as resources too.

Creating a Psychologically Safe Environment

To encourage the positive development of student self-esteem, to provide a psychologically safe learning environment, and to encourage the most creative thought and behavior, the teacher provides an attractive and stimulating classroom environment and appropriate nonjudgmental responses. Specifically, you

[7]See T. L. Good and J. E. Brophy, *Looking in Classrooms*, 8th ed. (New York: Addison Wesley Longman, 2000), 244–246.

[8]See, for example, J. W. Astington, "Theory of Mind Goes to School," *Educational Leadership* 56(3):46–48 (November 1998).

Scott Cunningham/Merrill

To be effective as an environment for learning science, the school classroom must be adequately supplied with a variety of materials and resources.

◆ Avoid negative criticism. Criticism is often a negative value judgment, and "when a teacher responds to a student's ideas or actions with such negative words as 'poor,' 'incorrect,' or 'wrong,' the response tends to signal inadequacy or disapproval and ends the student's thinking about the task."[9]

◆ Frequently use minimal reinforcement (that is, nonjudgmental acceptance behaviors, such as nodding head, writing a student's response on the board, or saying "I understand"). Whereas elaborate or strong praise is generally unrelated to student achievement, minimal reinforcement, using words like "right," "okay," "good," "uh-huh," and "thank you," does correlate with achievement.

However, as implied earlier in the discussion about modeling, be careful with a too frequent and thereby ineffective and even damaging use of the single word *good* following student contributions during a class discussion. Use the word only when the contribution was truly that—good—and better yet, say not only "good" but tell what specifically was good about the student's contribution. That provides a more powerful reinforcement by demonstrating that you truly heard the student's contribution and you, indeed, thought it was good.

◆ Infrequently use elaborate or strong praise. By the time students are in the intermediate grades, teacher praise—a positive value judgment—has little or no value as a form of positive reinforcement. When praise is used for young adolescents it should be mild, private, and for student accomplishment, rather than for effort. For each child, the frequency of using praise should be gradually reduced. When praise is reduced, a more diffused sociometric pattern develops; that is, more of the children become directly and productively involved in the learning. Praise should be simple and direct, delivered in a natural voice without dramatizing.[10] Children beyond primary years especially see overly done theatrics as insincere.

Let us take pause to consider this point. Probably no statement in this chapter raises more eyebrows than the statement that praise for most children beyond primary years especially has little or no value as a form of positive reinforcement. After all, praise may well motivate some people. However, at what cost? Praise and encouragement are often confused and considered to be the same (see Figure 4.1), but they are not, and they do not have the same long-term effects. This is explained as follows:

> For many years there has been a great campaign for the virtues of praise in helping children gain a positive self-concept and improve their behavior. This is another time when we must "beware of what works." Praise may inspire some children to improve their behavior. The problem is that they become pleasers and approval "junkies." These children (and later these adults) develop self-concepts that are totally dependent on the opinions of others. Other children resent and rebel against praise, either because they don't want to live up to the expectations of others or because they fear they can't compete with those who seem to get praise so easily. The alternative that considers long-range effects is

[9] A. L. Costa, *The School as a Home for the Mind* (Palatine, IL: Skylight Publishing, 1991), 54.

[10] T. L. Good and J. E. Brophy, *Looking in Classrooms,* 8th ed. (New York: Addison Wesley Longman, 2000), 142.

Statement of Praise	Statement of Encouragement
1. I am delighted that you behaved so well on our class field trip.	1. I am so delighted that we all enjoyed the field trip.
2. You did a good job on that experiment.	2. I can tell that you got really interested in that experiment.
3. Your oral report on your project was well done.	3. I can tell that you have been working and are enjoying science.
4. Great answer, Fatana!	4. Fatana, your answer indicates that you gave a lot of thought to the question.
5. Great hypothesis, Sage!	5. Okay, let's record Sage's hypothesis as one possibility to test.

FIGURE 4.1 Examples of statements of praise versus encouragement.

encouragement. The long-range effect of encouragement is self-confidence. The long-range effect of praise is dependence on others.[11]

In summary, then, our advice to you is, while being cautious with the use of praise, do reinforce student efforts by recognizing specific personal accomplishments.[12]

- Perceive your classroom as the place where you work and students learn, and make it and the tools available a place of pride—as stimulating and practical as possible.
- Within the lessons, plan behaviors that show respect for the cultures, experiences, and ideas of individual children.
- Provide positive individual student attention as often as possible. Write sincere reinforcing personalized comments on student papers. Provide incentives and rewards for student accomplishments.
- Use nonverbal cues to show awareness and acceptance of individual students.
- Use paraphrasing and reflective listening. Use empathic acceptance of a student's expression of feelings; demonstrate by words and gestures that you understand the student's position.

Clarifying Whenever Necessary

Your responding behavior seeks further elaboration from a student about that student's idea or comprehension.[13] Specifically, you

- Help students to connect new content to that previously learned. Help students relate content of a lesson to students' other school and nonschool experiences. Help students make learning connections between and among disciplines.
- Politely invite a student to be more specific, to elaborate on or rephrase an idea, or to provide a concrete illustration of an idea.
- Provide frequent opportunity for summary reviews.
- Repeat or paraphrase a student's response, allowing the student to correct any other person's misinterpretation of what he or she said or implied.
- Select instructional strategies that help students correct their prior notions (misconceptions as discussed in Chapter 3) about a topic.

Anthony Magnacca/Merrill

The teacher seeks further elaboration from a student about the child's idea.

Using Periods of Silence

Use periods of silence in the classroom. Specifically, you

- Actively listen when a student is talking.
- Allow sufficient think time, sometimes as long as 9 seconds, after asking a question or posing a problem. (See "wait time" later in this chapter.)

---

[11] J. Nelsen, *Positive Discipline* (New York: Ballantine Books, 1987), 103. See also L. A. Froyen, *Classroom Management: The Reflective Teacher-Leader,* 2nd ed. (Upper Saddle River, NJ: Prentice Hall, 1993), 294–298.

[12] See the discussion titled "Research and theory on providing recognition," in R. J. Marzano, et al., *Classroom Instruction That Works* (Alexandria, VA: Association for Supervision and Curriculum Development, 2001), 53–59.

[13] A. L. Costa, ed., *Developing Minds: A Resource Book for Teaching Thinking* (Alexandria, VA: Association for Supervision and Curriculum Development, 1985), 134.

- Keep silent when students are working quietly or are attending to a visual display, and maintain classroom control by using nonverbal signals and indirect intervention strategies. (See the classroom scenario, "Jennifer's Teaching Episode.")
- Pause while talking to allow for thinking and reflection.
- Use teacher silence, supported by body language and nonverbal gesturing (i.e., a nod of the head, a thumbs up), to stimulate group discussion.

Questioning Thoughtfully

Use thoughtfully worded questions to induce learning and to stimulate thinking and the development of students' thinking skills. (Questioning is the topic of the section that follows.) Specifically, you

- Encourage student questioning without judging the quality or relevancy of a student's question. Attend to student questions, and respond and encourage other students to respond, often by building upon the content of a student's questions and student responses.
- Help students develop their own questioning skills and provide opportunities for students to explore their own ideas, to obtain data, and to find answers to their own questions and solutions to their problems.
- Plan questioning sequences that elicit a variety of thinking skills, and that maneuver students to higher levels of thinking and doing.

Classroom Scenario

Jennifer's Teaching Episode

1. Instructions: From your class ask for three volunteers. One volunteer will read the lines of Jennifer, the second will read the one line of the student, while the third volunteer uses a stopwatch with a hundredths designation to direct Jennifer and the student to speak their lines at the specified times. The rest of your class can pretend to be students in Jennifer's fifth-grade class.

   1:00: *Jennifer:* "Think of a mammal you admire and write a three-sentence paragraph describing that animal." Students begin their writing.
   1:00:05: *Jennifer:* "Only three sentences about a mammal you like."
   1:00:07: *Student:* "Does it have to be about a mammal?"
   Jennifer: "No, it can be any animal, but one you admire."
   1:01: Jennifer works the rows, seeing that students are on task.
   1:01:10: *Jennifer:* "Three sentences are all you need to write."
   1:01:15: *Jennifer:* "Think of an animal you really admire, and write three sentences in a paragraph that describes that animal."
   1:01:30: *Jennifer:* "One you would like to be were you an animal."
   1:02: Jennifer continues walking around helping students who are having difficulty. All students are on task.
   1:04: *Jennifer:* "Now I want you to exchange papers with the person behind or beside you, read that person's description of the animal they admire, and describe an environment that you see that animal in. Write a paragraph that describes the environment."
   1:04–1:05: Students exchange papers; Jennifer walks around seeing that everyone has received another student's paper.
   1:05: *Jennifer:* "Where do you see that animal being? Below the paragraph I want you to write a new paragraph describing where you see this animal, perhaps in a stream, the ocean, the air, underground, or in a forest."
   1:05:10: *Jennifer:* "Describe the habitat you see this animal in."
   1:05:15: *Jennifer:* "After you read the description I want you to create a habitat for the animal described."
   1:05:18: Students seem confused either about what they are reading (e.g., asking the writer what a word is or means) or what they are supposed to do.
   1:05:19: *Jennifer:* "Anything is fine. Use your imagination to describe the habitat."
   1:05:22: *Jennifer:* "Describe a habitat for this animal."
   1:09: *Jennifer:* "Now I want you to exchange papers with yet someone else, and after reading the previous two paragraphs written by two other students, write a third paragraph describing this animal's place in the food chain."

2. Following the role play simulation, hold a whole-class or small-group discussion and use the following as a springboard for your discussion: Describe what you believe are the good points and weak points of this portion of Jennifer's lesson and her implementation of it.

- Use a variety of types of questions.
- Use questions to help students explore their knowledge, to develop new understandings, and to discover ways of applying their new understandings.

This section about fundamental teacher behaviors undoubtedly has caused you to think about how you will manage a classroom for instruction. In this chapter, you are being offered advice for setting up and maintaining a classroom environment and responding to children in a way that is favorable to their learning. To become an accomplished classroom manager takes thoughtful and thorough planning, consistent and confident application, and reflective experience. Be patient with yourself as you accumulate the prerequisite knowledge and practice and hone the necessary skills that in this book we can only begin to address.

Questioning: The Foundation for Sciencing

In the preceding list of basic behaviors needed to facilitate student learning, questioning is last, but not because it is of lesser importance. Rather, it is so important in teaching and is so frequently used—and misused—that we want to expand our discussion of it. Questioning is the foundation for the most effective science teaching and learning. You will use questioning for so many purposes that there is no way you can teach effectively unless you are skilled in its use.

Purposes for Using Questions

Effective teachers adapt the type and form of each question to the purpose for which it is asked. Encourage your students to question and then build the science curriculum around the students' questions.

The purposes for which you might use questioning can be separated into five types.

To give instructions (as in a rhetorical question). For example, "Caesar, will you please get the magnets out of the cupboard for us?" Teachers sometimes also use rhetorical questions to regain student attention and maintain classroom control, but this strategy can backfire and is not recommended. The teacher might say, for example, "Adan, would you like to go back to your seat?" If Adan says, "No," the teacher will have a problem that perhaps could have been avoided had he or she been more direct and simply told Adan to return to his seat.

To review and remind students of classroom procedures. For example, if students continue to talk without first raising their hands and being recognized by you, you can stop the lesson and say, "Class, I think we need to review the procedure for answering my questions. For talking, what is the procedure that we agreed upon?"

To gather information. For example, "How many of you have been to a tide pool?" Teachers can also use questions as a preassessment to find out what students already know or think they know. For example, "Gretchen, can you please tell us what is meant by the greenhouse effect?"

To discover student interests. For example, "How many would be interested in going to the marine aquarium?"

To guide student thinking and learning. This category of questioning is the focus here. Teachers use questions in this category to

- *Develop appreciation.* For example, "Do you now understand the ecological relationship between that particular root fungus, voles, and the survival of the large conifers of the forests of the Pacific Northwest?"
- *Develop student thinking.* For example, "What do you suppose the effects to the ecology are when standing water is sprayed with an insecticide that is designed to kill all mosquito larvae?"
- *Diagnose learning difficulty.* For example, "What part of the formula are you finding difficult to understand, Sally?"
- *Emphasize major points.* For example, "If we have never been to the sun, how do we know what it is made of?"
- *Encourage students.* For example, "Okay, so you didn't remember the formula for water. Do you know what part impressed me? What really impressed me about your essay is what you did understand about photosynthesis."
- *Establish rapport.* For example, "We have a problem here, but I think we can solve it if we put our heads together. What do you think ought to be our first step?"
- *Evaluate learning.* For example, "Sean, what do you think happens when two rough surfaces are rubbed together?"
- *Give practice in expression.* For example, "Yvonne, what examples of magnetism did you find in your home?"
- *Help students in their own metacognition.* For example, "Yes, something did go wrong in the experiment. Do you still think your original hypothesis is correct? If not, then where was the error in your thinking? Or, if you still think your hypothesis is correct, then where might the error have been in the design of your experiment? How might we find out?"
- *Help students interpret materials.* For example, "Something seems to be wrong with this compass. How do you suppose we can find out what is wrong with it? For example, if the needle is marked N and S in reverse, how can we find out if that is the problem?"
- *Help students organize materials.* For example, "If you really want to carry out your proposed experiment, then we are going to need certain materials. We are going to have to deal with some strategic questions here,

such as: What do you think we will need? Where can we find those things? Who will be responsible for getting them? and How will we store and arrange them once we are ready to start the investigation?"

◆ *Provide drill and practice.* For example, "Team A has prepared some questions that they would like to use as practice questions for our unit exam, and they are suggesting that we use them to play the game of Jeopardy on Friday. Is everyone in agreement with their idea?"

◆ *Provide review.* For example, "Today, in your groups, you are going to study the unit review questions I have prepared. After each group has studied and prepared its answers to these written questions, your group will pick another group and ask them your set of review questions. Each group has a different set of questions. Members of Team A are going to keep score, and the group that has the highest score from this review session will receive free pizza at tomorrow's lunch. Ready?"

◆ *Show agreement or disagreement.* For example, "Some scientists fear that the Antarctic ice shelf is breaking up and melting, which would lead to worldwide flooding. With evidence that you have collected from recent articles, would you agree with this conclusion? Explain why or why not."

◆ *Show relationships, such as cause and effect.* For example, "What do you think would be the global effect if just one inch of the total Antarctic ice shelf were to suddenly melt?"

◆ *Build the curriculum.* Students' questions provide the basis for learning that occurs in an effective inquiry-based and project-centered program of science. More on this subject follows later in this chapter.

It is important to note at this point a common characteristic of many of the questions in these examples—the use of the phrase "do you think" in the questions. The questions we offer as examples have structure that open themselves up to be answered by school children. Questions asking children "what do you think" cannot be answered incorrectly and because of this, alleviate a great deal of the burden on students who may wish to share their ideas but are afraid of being told that they are wrong. A critical step in teaching comes from understanding your students' ideas. Questioning that helps your students to share their ideas is essential for effective teaching.

Questions to Avoid Asking

It is important to avoid asking rhetorical questions; that is, questions for which you do not want a response. You should also avoid asking questions that call for little or no student thinking, such as those that can be answered with a simple yes or no or some other sort of deadend response. Unless followed with clarifying questions (see next section), questions that call for simple responses such as yes or no have little or no diagnostic value; they encourage guessing and inappropriate student responses.

When teaching science you should also avoid "why" questions or questions dealing with "purpose," asked either by yourself or by the children. Although frequently asked by children (and adults, too), these questions tend to be teleological and cannot be answered via scientific investigation. When confronted with "why" or "purpose" questions, turn the question into a "what" or "function" question; that is, one dealing with cause and effect. For example, the questions "Why do we have an appendix?" and "What is the purpose of the appendix?" cannot be answered via scientific inquiry. Acceptable, although often tentative answers to questions such as "Does the human appendix have a function?" or "What, if any, function does the appendix have in humans?" can be answered by scientific investigation.[14] We should take care to distinguish this form of a "why" question from a "why do you think" question, which asks students to reason, think logically, and offer an evaluation, which is also acceptable. This is a probing question, which we discuss in the next section.

You must avoid using questions that embarrass a student, punish a student, or in any way deny the student's dignity. Questions that embarrass or punish tend to damage the student's developing self-esteem and serve no useful academic or instructional purpose. Questioning is an important instructional tool that should be used by the teacher only for academic reasons. Although it is not always possible to predict when a student might be embarrassed by a question, a teacher should *never* deliberately ask questions for the purpose of embarrassment or punishment. When done deliberately, such action borders on abuse.

Types of Cognitive Questions

This section defines, describes, and provides examples for each type of cognitive question that you will use in teaching. The following section describes the levels of cognitive questions.

Analytic Question

The analytic question is used to encourage students to analyze and even critique information before them. Some examples are, "In what way was that science news headline misleading?" and "How might we solve this problem?" and "How could we limit the variables?"

Clarifying Question

The clarifying question is used to gain more information from a student to help the teacher better understand the student's ideas, feelings, and thought processes. When asked to elaborate on an initial response, a student will

[14]See, for example, the discussion in National Research Council, *Inquiry and the National Science Education Standards*, 24–25.

Classroom Scenario

Kindergarten Teacher Asks a Rhetorical Question

At the completion of the class opener, Sarah, a kindergarten teacher, asked, "Shall we do our science lesson now?" One of the children in the class, Mario, answered, "I don't want to, I don't like science." Ignoring Mario's response, Sarah began the science lesson. It is likely that the lesson learned here by Mario was not the lesson intended by Sarah, if indeed she intended one at all. The lesson learned by Mario probably is that the teacher didn't really care what his answer to her question was. The next time Sarah asks a question, Mario may be reluctant to answer at all. What are your thoughts about this scenario? Explain why you believe that Sarah should or should not have acted differently.

often think more deeply, restructuring his thinking, and while doing so, will discover a fallacy in the original response. An example of a clarifying question is, "What I hear you saying is that you would rather work alone than in your group. Is that correct?" Research has shown a strong positive correlation between student learning and the development of metacognitive skills (that is, their thinking about thinking) and the teacher's use of questions that ask for clarification.[15] In addition, by seeking clarification, the teacher is likely to be demonstrating an interest in the student and her thinking.

Convergent-Thinking Question

Convergent-thinking questions (also called narrow questions) are low-order-thinking questions that have a single answer (such as the recall question exemplified in the next section). An example of a convergent question is, "What are the products of photosynthesis?"

Cueing Question

If you ask a question to which, after sufficient wait time (longer than 2 seconds and as long as 9 seconds), no students respond or their inadequate responses indicate they need more information, then you can ask a question that cues the answer or response you are seeking. In essence, you are going backward in your questioning sequence to cue the students. For example, as an introduction to a lesson on the study of arthropods, a teacher asks her students a recall question such as, "How many legs do crayfish, lobsters, and shrimp have?" If there is no accurate response, she might cue the answer with the following information and question, "The class to which those animals belong is Decapoda. Does that give you a clue about the number of legs they have?"

Divergent-Thinking Question

Divergent-thinking questions (also known as broad, reflective, or thought questions) are open-ended (i.e., usually having no single correct answer), high-order-thinking questions (requiring analysis, synthesis, or evaluation), that require students to think creatively, to leave the comfortable confines of the known and reach out into the unknown. An example of a question that requires divergent thinking is, "What measures could be taken to improve the habitats of the animals at our city zoo?"

Evaluative Question

Some types of questions, whether convergent or divergent, require students to place a value on something. These are referred to as evaluative questions. If the teacher and the students all agree on certain premises, then the evaluative question would also be a convergent question. If original assumptions differ, then the response to the evaluative question would be more subjective and the question would be divergent. An example of an evaluative question is, "Should the United States allow clear-cutting in its national forests?"

Focus Question

A focus question is any question that is designed to focus student thinking. For example, the sample question in the preceding paragraph is a focus question when the teacher asking it is attempting to focus student attention on the ecological issues involved in clear-cutting.

Probing Question

Like a clarifying question, a probing question requires student thinking to go beyond superficial first-answer or single-word responses. An example of a probing question is, "Why do you think that each state should have total control over its wetlands?"

Levels of Cognitive Questions and the Relationship to Student Thinking

Questions posed by the teacher are cues to the students about the level of thinking expected by the teacher, ranging from the lowest level of mental operation, requiring simple recall of knowledge (convergent thinking), to the highest, requiring divergent thought and application of

[15] Costa, *School as a Home,* 63.

that thought. It is not crucial that a question be absolutely classified. However, you must (a) be aware of the levels of thinking, (b) understand the importance of attending to student thinking, from low to higher levels of operation, and (c) understand that what for one child may be a matter of simple recall of information, for another may require a higher-order mental activity, such as figuring something out by deduction.

You need to structure questions in a way that is designed to guide students' thinking to higher levels. For example, when students respond to questions in complete sentences that provide supportive evidence for their ideas, it is reasonably safe to assume that their thinking is at a higher level than if the response were an imprecise and nondescriptive single-word answer.

To help your understanding, three levels of questioning and thinking are described in the following paragraphs. You should recognize a similarity among these three levels of questions, the three phases of the learning cycle (Chapter 3), and the six levels of thinking presented in Bloom's taxonomy of cognitive objectives in Chapter 2. When preparing lesson plans (Chapter 7) and assessment items (Chapter 8), you might want to refer to the key words illustrated in the descriptions of these three levels of questioning.

Lowest Level (The Data Input Phase): Gathering and Recalling Information

At this level, questions are designed to solicit concepts, information, feelings, or experiences that students gained in the past and stored in memory. Sample key words and desired behaviors are *complete, count, define, describe, identify, list, match, name, observe, recall, recite,* and *select.*

Thinking involves receiving data through the senses, followed by the processing of those data. (Inputting data without processing those data is brain dysfunctional.) Information that has not been processed is stored only in short-term memory.

Intermediate Level (The Data Processing Phase): Processing Information

At this level, questions are designed to draw relationships of cause and effect, to synthesize, analyze, summarize, compare, contrast, or classify data. Sample key words and desired behaviors are *analyze, classify, compare, contrast, distinguish, explain, group, infer, make an analogy, organize, plan,* and *synthesize.*

Thinking and questioning that involve processing of information can be conscious or unconscious. When students observe the teacher thinking aloud, and when they are urged to think aloud—to think about their thinking and to analyze it as it occurs—they are developing their intellectual skills.

At the processing level, this internal analysis of new data may challenge a learner's preconceptions (and misconceptions) about a scientific phenomenon. The learner's brain will naturally resist this challenge to existing beliefs. The greater the mental challenge, the greater will be the brain's effort to draw upon data already in storage. With increasing data, the mind will gradually examine existing concepts and ultimately, as necessary, develop new mental concepts.

If there is a match between new input and existing mental concepts, no problem exists. Jean Piaget called this process *assimilation.* If, however, in processing new data there is no match with existing mental concepts, then the situation is what Piaget called *cognitive disequilibrium.* The brain does not like this disequilibrium and will drive the learner to search for an explanation for the discrepancy. Piaget called this process *accommodation.* Although learning is enhanced by challenge, in situations that are threatening, the brain is less flexible in accommodating new ideas. That is why each student must feel welcome in the classroom and must perceive the classroom environment as challenging but nonthreatening—what researchers refer to as an environment of *relaxed alertness.*[16]

Questions and experiences must be designed to elicit more than just memory responses (assimilation). One technique many teachers have found effective is to use discrepant events to introduce science concepts.[17] *Discrepant events* are phenomena that cause cognitive disequilibrium, thus stimulating higher-level mental functioning. However, merely exposing students to a discrepant event will not, in itself, cause them to develop new conceptual understandings. It simply stirs the mind into processing, without which mental development does not occur. (See Figure 4.2.)

Balloon Will Not Pop

Practice this first. Partially blow up a balloon, tie it off. Take a large but sharp sewing needle and slowly push it into the balloon. Because the needle immediately plugs the hole, the balloon remains filled. Sure, you say, students have seen this done by magicians or birthday party clowns. But wait. Now for the real discrepant event: Slowly remove the needle and—voilà! The balloon does not collapse. The balloon material expands to plug the hole. Make several holes. Take a long needle (the kind used in doll making) and push it through the balloon and out through the other side, keeping the needle in both holes. The balloon stays filled. (Hint: Push the needle into the thickest portion of the balloon, opposite the opening.) If students believe you are using a fake balloon, take the same needle and quickly puncture the balloon, popping it.

FIGURE 4.2 An example of a discrepant event demonstration.

---

[16] R. N. Caine and G. Caine, *Education on the Edge of Possibility* (Alexandria, VA: Association for Supervision and Curriculum Development, 199), 107.

[17] See, for example, T. O'Brien et al., "Baker's Dozen of Discrepantly Dense Demos," *Science Scope 18*(2):35–38 (October 1994); and F. L. Misiti, Jr., "The Pressure's On," *Science Scope 24*(1):34–38 (September 2000).

Highest Level (The Data Output Phase): Applying and Evaluating in New Situations

Questions at the highest level encourage learners to think intuitively, creatively, and hypothetically; to use their imagination; to expose a value system; or to make a judgment. Sample key words and desired behaviors are *apply a principle, build a model, evaluate, extrapolate, forecast, generalize, hypothesize, imagine, judge, predict,* and *speculate.*

Instead of	*Say*
"How else might it be done?"	"How could you *apply* . . . ?"
"Are you going to get quiet?"	"If we are going to hear what Joan has to say, what do you need to do?"
"How do you know that is so?"	"What evidence do you have?"

FIGURE 4.3 Examples of questions that use appropriate cognitive terminology.

You must use questions at the level best suited for the purpose, use questions from a variety of different levels, and structure questions in a way that is intended to move student thinking to higher levels. When teachers use higher-level questions, their students tend to score higher on tests of critical thinking and on standardized tests of achievement.[18]

With the use of questions as a strategy to move student thinking to higher levels, the teacher is facilitating the students' intellectual development. Developing your skill in the use of questioning requires attention to detail. The guidelines that follow will be useful as you develop your skill in using this important instructional strategy.

Guidelines for Using Questioning

Your goals are to help your students learn how to identify and to solve problems; to make decisions and value judgments; to think creatively and critically; and to feel good about themselves, their schools, and their learning—rather than simply to fill their minds with bits and pieces of information that will likely last only a brief time in their short-term memory. How you construe your questions and how you carry out your questioning strategy is important to the realization of these goals.

Preparing Questions

When preparing questions, consider the following guidelines.

Key cognitive questions should be planned, thoughtfully worded, and written into your lesson plan. Thoughtful preparation of questions helps to ensure that they are clear, specific, not ambiguous; that the vocabulary is appropriate; and that each question matches its purpose. Incorporate questions into your lessons as instructional devices, and welcome pauses, attention grabbers, and checks for student comprehension. Thoughtful teachers even plan questions that they intend to ask specific students, targeting questions to the readiness level, interest, or learning profile of the students in their classes.

Match questions with their target purposes. Carefully planned questions allow them to be sequenced and worded to match the levels of cognitive thinking expected of students. To help students develop their thinking skills, you need to demonstrate how to do this. To demonstrate, you must use terminology that is specific and that provides students with examples of experiences consonant with the meanings of the cognitive words. You should demonstrate this every day so students learn the cognitive terminology. As stated by J. G. Brooks and M. G. Brooks, "framing tasks around cognitive activities such as analysis, interpretation, and prediction—and explicitly using those terms with students—fosters the construction of new understandings."[19] See the three examples in Figure 4.3.

Implementing Questioning

Careful preparation of questions is one part of the skill in questioning. Implementation is the other part. Here are guidelines for effective implementation.

Ask your well-worded question before calling on a student for a response. An error teachers often make is to call on a student and then ask the question, such as "Dylan, would you please describe for us the differences between cellular respiration and photosynthesis?" Although probably not intended by the teacher, as soon as he or she calls on Dylan, the rest of the class feels that they are released from having to think about the question. The preferred strategy is to phrase the question, "What do you think are the differences between cellular respiration and photosynthesis?", allow time for all students to think, and then call on Dylan and other students for their understandings of the similarities and differences.

Avoid bombarding students with too much teacher talk. Teachers sometimes talk too much, especially teachers who are nervous, as many are during the initial weeks of their student teaching. Knowing the guidelines presented here will help you avoid that syndrome.

[18]See, for example, B. Newton, "Theoretical Basis for Higher Cognitive Questioning: An Avenue to Critical Thinking," *Education 98*(3): 286–290 (March/April 1978); and D. Redfield and E. Rousseau, "A Meta-Analysis of Experimental Research on Teacher Questioning Behavior," *Review of Educational Research 51*(2):237–245 (Summer 1981).

[19]J. G. Brooks and M. G. Brooks, *In Search of Understanding: The Case for Constructivist Classrooms* (Alexandria, VA: Association for Supervision and Curriculum Development, 1993), 105.

Remind yourself to be quiet after you ask a question that you have carefully formulated. Sometimes, because of lack of confidence, and especially when a question has not been carefully planned, the teacher asks the question and then, with a slight change in wording, asks it again or asks several questions, one after another. That is too much verbiage. It is called shotgun questioning and only confuses students, allowing too little time for them to think.

After asking a question, provide students with adequate time to think. The pause after asking a question is called *wait time* (or *think time*).[20] Knowing the subject better than the students know it and having given prior thought to the subject, too many teachers fail to allow students sufficient time to think after asking a question. In addition, by the time they have reached the intermediate grades, students have learned pretty well how to play the game—that is, they know that if they remain silent long enough the teacher will probably answer his or her own question. After asking a well-worded question, you should remain quiet for a while, allowing students time to think and to respond. If you wait long enough, they usually will. You may need to rehearse this procedure with your students.

After asking a question, how long should you wait before you do something? You should wait at least 2 seconds, and as long as 9. Stop reading now and look at your watch or a clock to get a feeling for how long 2 seconds is. Then observe how long 9 seconds is. Did 9 seconds seem a long time? Because most of us are not used to silence in the classroom, 2 seconds of silence can seem quite long, while 9 seconds may seem eternal. If, for some reason, students have not responded after a period of 2 to 9 seconds of wait time, then you can ask the question again. Do not reword an already carefully worded question, or students are likely to think it is a new question. Pause for several seconds; then if you still have not received a response you can call on a student, then another, if necessary, after sufficient wait time. Soon you will get a response that can be built upon. Avoid answering your own question!

Practice gender equity. To practice gender equity, follow these four rules when using questioning: (a) Avoid going to a boy to bail out a girl who fails to answer a question. (b) Avoid going to a boy to improve upon a girl's answer. For the first, without seeming to badger, try to give the student clues until she can answer with success. For the second, hold and demonstrate high expectations for all students. (c) Allow equal wait time regardless of student gender. (d) Call on boys and girls equally.

Practice calling on all students. Along with observing Rule d of the preceding paragraph, you must not only call on a subset of your students. For example, many times teachers will call on the quickest students to raise their hands. These tend to be the same students every day. As the teacher, you must teach all students and this usually requires that you call on all of them to answer questions appropriate for their learning levels. To do these things takes concentrated effort on your part, but it is important. To ensure that students are called on equally, some teachers carry laminated copies of their seating charts, perhaps on bright neon-colored clipboards, which gives students a visual focus. With a wax pencil or water-soluble marker, they make a mark next to the name of a student each time he or she is called on. If the seating chart is laminated and erasable markers are used, the marks can be erased at the end of the day and the seating chart used over and over. Photocopying this record at the end of each day will help you keep track of your progress. Calling on students is a way to reinforce each student's place as a member of your class. Making each question appropriate for each student will help them gain confidence and look forward to their turn to answer.

Give the same minimum amount of wait time (think time) to all students. This, too, will require concentrated effort on your part, but it is important to do. A teacher who waits for less time when calling on a slow-responding student or students of one gender is showing prejudice or a lack of confidence in certain students. Both behaviors are detrimental when a teacher is striving to establish for all students a positive, equal, and safe environment for classroom learning. Show confidence in all your students. Some students may take longer to respond but not necessarily because they are not thinking or have less ability. There may be cultural differences to think about; some cultures simply allow for longer wait time than others. The important point here is to individualize to allow students who need more time to have it. Variation in wait time allowed should not be used to single out some students and lead to lower expectations but instead to allow for higher expectations.

Require students to raise their hands and be called on. When you ask questions, instead of allowing students to randomly shout out their answers, require them to raise their hands and be called on before they respond. Establish that procedure and stick with it. This helps to ensure both that you call on all students equally, fairly distributing your interactions with the students, and that you do not interact less with girls because boys tend to be more obstreperous. Even in college classrooms, male students as a group tend to be more vocal than female students and, when allowed by the instructor, tend to outtalk and to interrupt their female peers. Every teacher has the

[20] For wait-time studies, now classics in science education, see M. B. Rowe, "Wait-Time and Rewards as Instructional Variables, Their Influence on Language, Logic, and Fate Control: Part One—Wait-Time," *Journal of Research in Science Teaching 11*(2):81–94 (June 1974); and M. B. Rowe, "Wait-Time: Slow Down May Be a Way of Speeding Up," *American Educator 11*(1):38–47 (Spring 1987).

responsibility to guarantee a nonbiased classroom and an equal distribution of interaction time in the classroom.

Another important reason for students to raise their hands is to help them learn to control their impulsivity. Controlling one's impulsivity is one of the characteristics of intelligent behavior presented and discussed in Chapter 3. One of your many instructional responsibilities is to help students develop this skill.

To keep all students mentally engaged, you will want to call on students who are sitting quietly and have not raised their hands, but avoid badgering or humiliating an unwilling participant. When a student has no response, you might suggest he or she think about it and you will come back to the student to ensure that the student eventually understands or has an answer to the original question.

Use strong praise sparingly. A teacher's use of strong praise is sometimes okay, especially with kindergarten and early primary grade children. But for older students and when you want students to think divergently and creatively, you should be stingy with your use of strong praise of student responses. Strong praise from a teacher tends to terminate divergent and creative thinking.

One of your goals is to help students find intrinsic sources for motivation; that is, an inner drive of intent or desire that causes them to want to learn. Use of strong praise tends to build conformity, causing students to depend on outside forces—the giver of praise—rather than themselves for their worth. An example of a strong praise response is "That's right! Very good." In contrast, passive acceptance responses, such as "Yes, that is one possibility," keep the door open for further thinking, particularly for higher-level, divergent thinking.

Another example of a passive acceptance response is one used in brainstorming sessions, when the teacher says, "After asking the question and giving you time to think about it, I will hear your ideas and record them on the board." Only after all student responses have been heard and recorded does the class begin its consideration of each. That kind of nonjudgmental acceptance of all ideas in the classroom has the potential to generate the expression of high-level thought.[21]

Avoid bluffing an answer to a question for which you do not have an answer. Nothing will cause you to lose credibility with students faster than faking an answer. There is nothing wrong with admitting that you do not know; in fact, it helps students recognize that you are human. Your willingness to show your humanness makes it acceptable for them to be more human as well. What *is* important is that you know where and how to find possible answers and that you help students develop that same knowledge and those same process skills. This having been said, you should take great care *not* to dump an assignment on a student when he or she asks a question you cannot answer. Turning a student's question into an assignment for him or her or the class will in all likelihood dissuade students from asking questions in the future.

Questions from Students: The Question-Driven Science Classroom

As emphasized by the U.S. Department of Education in *Tried and True,* question asking often indicates that the inquirer is curious, puzzled, and uncertain; it is a sign of being engaged in thinking about a topic. And, yet, in too many classrooms, too few students ask questions.[22] Students should be encouraged to ask questions. From students, there is no such thing as a dumb question. Sometimes students, like everyone else, ask questions that could just as easily have been looked up or are irrelevant or show lack of thought or sensitivity. Those questions can consume precious class time. For a teacher, they can be frustrating. A teacher's initial reaction might be to quickly and mistakenly brush off that type of question with sarcasm, while assuming that the student is too lazy to look up an answer. In such instances, you are advised to think before responding and to respond kindly and professionally, although in the busy life of a classroom teacher that may not always be easy to remember to do. However, be assured, there is a reason for a student's question. Perhaps the student is signaling a need for recognition or simply demanding attention.

Should you ever give answers to student questions in science? Sure you should! Understanding requires knowledge, and not all the knowledge that is needed by children can or should be acquired by inquiry or direct experiencing (see the Learning Experiences Ladder in Figure 5.4, Chapter 5). But then, student questions often can and should be used as springboards for further questioning, discussions, and investigations. Decisions about how to respond to students' questions depend on your goals and the context of the lesson, and represent one of the many kinds of professional decisions that must be made in the daily work of a classroom teacher.[23]

Students should be encouraged to refine their questions and then to seek tentative or satisfactory answers from reliable sources of scientific information and from their own investigations.[24] Encouraging your students to rely on their ability to find answers for themselves is

---

[21]For further discussion of the use of praise and rewards in teaching, see C. H. Edwards, *Classroom Discipline and Management,* 2nd ed. (Upper Saddle River, NJ: Prentice Hall, 1997).

[22]United States Department of Education, *Tried and True: Tested Ideas for Teaching and Learning from the Regional Educational Laboratories* (Washington, DC: Office of Educational Research and Improvement, U.S. Department of Education, 1997), 53.

[23]National Research Council, *Inquiry and the National Science Education Standards,* 131.

[24]National Research Council, *National Science Education Standards,* 122, 145.

an often overlooked and under-used aspect of teaching in most classrooms. Indeed, in a constructivist learning environment, student questions often drive content. Developing a classroom environment where your students ask and take the first stab at answering their own questions before they come to you for guidance nurtures their self-confidence and self-reliance.

Being able to ask questions may be more important than having the right answers. Knowledge is derived from asking questions. Being able to recognize problems and to formulate questions is a skill and the key to developing the further skills of problem-solving and critical thinking. You have a responsibility to encourage students to formulate questions and to help them word their questions in such a way that tentative answers can be sought. That is the process necessary to build a base of knowledge that can be drawn upon time and again to comprehend new data in new situations.

Summary

In this chapter, we have discussed and presented guidelines for the use of fundamental teacher behaviors that facilitate student learning. In the chapter that follows we focus on instructional strategies in particular. Some of the fundamental behaviors, such as questioning, are also instructional strategies. As you learned, the difference is that while the behaviors must be in place for the most effective teaching to occur, strategies—discussed in Chapter 5—are more or less discretionary; that is, they are pedagogical techniques from which you may select but that you may not be obligated to use. Those pedagogical techniques are the focus of Chapter 5.

Questions for Class Discussion

1. Identify which of the fundamental teacher behaviors you feel most comfortable with and which you feel might give you the most trouble initially. Share your lists with your classmates. Identify classmates with the same concerns as you and discuss ways you might work on ameliorating your concerns.
2. Explain each of the following two concepts and why you agree or disagree with each. The classroom teacher should (a) hold high, although not necessarily identical, expectations for all children and never waver from those expectations, and (b) not be controlled by a concern to cover the contents of the mandated science curriculum by the end of the school term.
3. Compare the teacher's use of praise and of encouragement for student work; describe specific classroom situations in which each is more appropriate.
4. Identify any concepts you held that changed as a result of your experiences with this chapter. Describe the concepts and changes.
5. From your recent observations and fieldwork related to this teacher preparation program, identify one specific example of educational practice that seems contradictory to exemplary practice or theory as presented in this chapter. Explain the discrepancy.
6. Do you have questions about the content of this chapter? Where might answers be found?

Chapter 5

Strategies for Helping Children Learn Science

KS Studios/Merrill

Teachers of science must decide when and for what purposes to use whole-class instruction, small-group collaboration, and individual work.[1]

In selecting an instructional strategy, there are two distinct choices: whether as teacher you should deliver information to the students (teacher-centered teaching), or whether you should provide students with access to information (student-centered teaching). The strengths and weaknesses of each of these two approaches are discussed next.

 Modes of Instruction

The traditional mode of science instruction is to deliver information; that is, knowledge is transmitted from those who know (the teacher and the textbook) to those who do not (the students). Within the delivery mode, traditional and time-honored strategies include textbook reading, formal teacher talk (the lecture and questioning), and informal teacher talk (the discussion and recitation). For the classroom teacher, teacher talk is an important and unavoidable teaching tool, and it can be valuable when used judiciously. However, being told about science without being allowed to do science is like learning the alphabet without being encouraged to put letters together to make words.

With the second approach, the access mode, rather than provide direct delivery of information and maintain direct control of what is learned, the teacher provides access to information by collaboratively designing experiences with the students that facilitate their obtaining new knowledge and skills. Within this mode, an important instructional strategy is inquiry, which most certainly will use questioning, although the questions more often should originate with the students. Discussions and other strategies, too, may be involved in inquiry.

It is likely that you are more experienced with the delivery mode (sometimes referred to as direct instruction), and although this chapter provides guidelines for the use of strategies within that mode, to be most effective as a science teacher you must become knowledgeable and skillful with the use of access strategies. Although our intent is not to imply that one mode is unquestionably better in all instances, strategies within the access mode do facilitate learning in a more consistently positive manner. As mentioned earlier, we believe that to be most effective, teachers should be eclectic in selecting strategies; that is, they should appropriately select and effectively use strategies from both modes, but with a strong focus on access, or facilitating, strategies. Therefore, our goal in this section is to help you become knowledgeable about the use of techniques within each mode in order to make intelligent decisions in choosing the best strategy for particular goals and objectives for your unique group of students. Figures 5.1 and 5.2 present a review of specific strengths and weaknesses of each mode.

The strengths of the delivery (traditional) mode are:

- Much content can be covered within a short span of time, usually by formal teacher talk and guided discussions, which may be followed by an activity.
- The teacher is in control of what content is covered.
- The teacher is in control of time allotted to specific content coverage.
- Strategies within the delivery mode are consistent with performance-based teaching.
- Student achievement of specific content is predictable and manageable.

The potential weaknesses of delivery strategies are:

- The sources of student motivation are mostly extrinsic.
- Students have little control over the pacing of their learning.
- Students make few important decisions about their learning.
- There may be little opportunity for divergent or creative thinking.
- Student self-esteem may be inadequately attended.

FIGURE 5.1 Delivery mode: its strengths and weaknesses.

[1]Reprinted from National Research Council, *National Science Education Standards,* © 1996 by the National Academy of Sciences, 32. Courtesy of National Academy Press, Washington, DC.

The strengths of access strategies are:

- Students learn content, and in greater depth.
- The sources of student motivation are more likely intrinsic.
- Students make important decisions about their own learning.
- Students have more control over the pacing of their learning.
- Students develop a sense of personal self-worth.

The potential weaknesses of access strategies are:

- Content coverage may be more limited.
- Access strategies are time-consuming.
- The teacher has less control over content and time.
- The specific results of student learning are less predictable.
- The teacher may have less control over class procedures.

FIGURE 5.2 Access mode: its strengths and weaknesses.

Anthony Magnacca/Merrill

Children love to participate in hands-on science learning.

As you can see from these figures, the strengths and weaknesses of one mode are nearly mirror opposites of those of the other. For most novice teachers, the delivery mode appears to offer the most classroom control. However, most effective teachers find that the access mode offers instructional strategies reaching beyond the delivery mode—strategies that include more student-centered, hands-on, and direct student interaction. And in the end, familiarity with these instructional strategies offer teachers options where students are actually physically and mentally engaged in sciencing without a reduction in classroom control.

Multilevel Teaching: A Blend of Modes

Many teachers arrange their classrooms so that various groups of students can be learning in different ways (and sometimes even different content) at the same time. While some may be receiving direct instruction (delivery mode), others can be learning by discovery activities (access mode). Direct instruction can be given either by the teacher or at a self-paced learning activity center. Simultaneously, in other areas of the classroom, other groups of students may be doing laboratory investigations, creating bulletin board displays, or brainstorming how they are going to investigate a problem.

When the class is divided into groups of children doing different things—that is, learning in different ways at the same time—the process is called multilevel (or multitask) teaching. Multilevel teaching demands careful planning to ensure that materials are ready and that the needs of individual students are being carefully considered. Multilevel teaching is very appropriate for teaching science in today's classroom of mixed-ability students. It allows the teacher to attend to individual learning styles, learning capacities, language proficiencies, and levels of understanding and doing.

In addition, your students may also need to become familiar with your expectations in this classroom environment. Many times, students are not accustomed to such a degree of autonomy and lack the judgment to monitor their own behavior and the behavior of those they are working with. Therefore, as the teacher, you must be clear about the expectations, the behavioral boundaries, and the consequences students must face when they misbehave.

When several groups of students are doing different kinds of tasks, you must plan carefully. You must also exercise well-developed with-it-ness and overlapping skills; otherwise, classroom management can become a nightmare. While the initial stages of planning and implementing these strategies may be time-consuming, the rewards of having thoughtful, responsible, self-directed, and highly engaged students are immense.

Inquiry Teaching and Discovery Learning

Inquiry and *discovery* are common terms describing important science teaching tools. However, there is sometimes confusion about what exactly inquiry teaching is and how it differs from discovery learning. The distinction should become clear as you study their descriptions.

Problem Solving

Perhaps a major reason that inquiry and discovery are sometimes confused is that in both, students are actively engaged in problem solving. Problem solving is *the ability to define or describe a problem, determine the desired outcome, select possible solutions, choose strategies, test*

TABLE 5.1 Level of Inquiry

Learner Behaviors		Level I	Level II (Transition from Level I)	Level II (Transition to Level III)	Level III
Problem identification	Learner engages with scientifically oriented questions	Learner engages with a question provided to them	Learner sharpens or clarifies a question provided to them	Learner selects among questions, poses new questions	Learner poses a question
Process of solving the problem	Learner gives priority to evidence in responding to questions	Learner given data and told how to analyze it	Learner given data asked to analyze it	Learner given direction on to the data to collect	Learner Determines what constitue evidence and collects it
Identification of tentative solution to problem	Learner formulates explanation after summarizing evidence	Learner provided with evidence	Learner given possible ways to use evidence to formulate explanation	Learner guided in process of formulating explanations from evidence	Learner formulates explanation after summarizing data
	Learner connects explanations to scientific knowledge		Learner given possible connections	Learner directed toward areas and sources of scientific knowledge	Learner independently examines other resources and forms links to explanations
	Learner communicates and justifies explanations	Learner given steps and procedures for communication	Learner provided broad guidelines to sharpen communication	Learner coached in development of communication	Learner forms reasonable and logical argument to communicate explanations

trial solutions, evaluate outcomes, and revise these steps where necessary.[2] It is the central tool of scientific inquiry.

Inquiry versus Discovery

Problem solving is not a teaching strategy but a high-order intellectual behavior that facilitates learning. *When teaching science, a teacher can and should provide opportunities for students to identify and tentatively solve problems.* We say tentatively because science is based on an ever-growing and changing body of evidence. At times, what is considered scientific knowledge must be revised as we learn. Your students and you as their teacher should accept that problems solved in science may need to be solved again if new evidence is revealed through additional investigation. *Experiences in inquiry and discovery represent the processes for provision of those opportunities.* With the processes involved in inquiry and discovery, teachers can help students develop the skills necessary for effective problem solving. Table 5.1 shows the various levels of inquiry, each defined according to its degree of student self-direction versus teacher or material-based guidance.[3]

[2]A. L. Costa, ed., *Developing Minds: A Resource Book for Teaching Thinking* (Alexandria, VA: Association for Supervision and Curriculum Development, 1985). 312.

[3]The concept of three levels of inquiry is adapted from J. J. Schwab, *The Teaching of Science as Enquiry* (Cambridge, MA: Harvard University Press, 1962), 55. Table 5.1 is adapted from "Essential Features of Classroom Inquiry and Their Variations," with an accompanying discussion in the National Research Council's *Inquiry and the National Science Education Standards: A Guide for Teaching and Learning* (Washington, DC: National Academy Press, 2000). 29.

Level I is a mode of teaching that relies heavily on guidance from the teacher and/or the learning materials. This may be considered a starting point for most students, since students often do not have a great deal of experience at the K–8 level with a high degree of autonomy. As students begin to develop an understanding of what they will be asked to produce from their work, you may begin to transition them through Level II, which may be considered two stages.

In the first stage of Level II, students transition from Level I. Students progress from answering questions provided by the teacher to focusing or clarifying a broad question proposed by the teacher. For example, a broad question might be, "what do wild animals in our state eat during the winter?" The students may be asked to choose a specific animal to investigate. Some may choose white-tailed deer, ground squirrels, beavers, field mice, snowy owls, or red-tailed hawks. Students will also be asked to analyze data provided by the teacher on their own using the skills developed in Level I. Also, students will be offered various options for communicating what they have found as they explore ways to share their ideas and results of their work.

In the second stage of Level II, students transition into Level III. Students progress to selecting questions from a list and are given the option of posing new questions of their own. As more responsibility is shifted to the learner, students collect data for themselves using guidelines established by the teacher or the learning materials. In addition, students are directed to resources and given coaching rather than given data and told what to do. The primary difference between the first and second stage within Level II is the shift from *teacher as the center of the activity* to *teacher as facilitator of activity*.

Finally, Level III represents highly autonomous student-centered learning where students may be asked to pursue topics within a general category, but are allowed to choose both the topics and their mode of inquiry for learning. At Level III, the teacher monitors student activity and redirects student work only when he or she sees possible pitfalls that are beyond the skills and knowledge of the students to overcome.

A major difference between discovery and inquiry is *who* identifies the problem. Another important difference lies in the decisions that are made by the students. Level I inquiry is actually traditional, didactic, cookbook teaching, whereby both the problem and the process for resolving it are defined *for* the student. If the activity is well designed, the result is inevitable, because the student "discovers" what was intended by the writers of the lesson. This level of learning is also called *guided inquiry* or *discovery*, because the students are carefully guided through the investigation to (the predictable) discovery.

Students who never experience learning beyond Level I are missing an opportunity to engage their highest mental operations, and may come away with the false notion that problem solving (and sciencing) is a linear process. As illustrated in Figure 3.3 (in Chapter 3), true inquiry is cyclic rather than linear. Level I inquiry is ultimately misleading because it suggests that sciencing is a linear process, which it is not. In science (and social science) and in the real world, problem solving is a cyclic process that one may enter at any point.

Students at all levels of science instruction should be provided experiences for inquiry, which begins with Level II. Students, under the guidance of their teacher, actually decide and design processes for inquiry. In true inquiry, teachers emphasize the tentative nature of conclusions, which makes the activity more like real-life problem solving in which decisions are always subject to revision if and when new data are found.

Anthony Magnacca/Merrill

The science teacher encourages children to solve problems. Problem solving is not a teaching strategy but a high intellectual behavior that facilitates learning. The development of a child's problem-solving skills is a major goal in school science teaching.

Anthony Magnacca/Merrill

In guided discovery, children are carefully escorted through an investigatory activity to discovery.

Presentation of the Problem. In groups of three or four, students receive the following information.

Background. You (your group is considered as one person) are one of 120 passengers on the ship, the *Prince Charles.* You left England 12 weeks ago. You have experienced many hardships, including a stormy passage, limited rations, sickness, cold and damp weather, and hot, foul air below deck. Ten of your fellow immigrants to the New World, including three children, have died and been buried at sea. You are now anchored at an uncertain place, off the coast of the New World, which your captain believes to be somewhere north of the Virginia Grants. Seas are so rough and food so scarce that you and your fellow passengers have decided to settle here. A landing party has returned with a map they made of the area. You, as one of the elders, must decide at once where the settlement is to be located. The tradesmen want to settle along the river, which is deep, even though this seems to be the season of low water levels. Within 10 months they expect deep-water ships from England with more colonists and merchants. Those within your group who are farmers say they must have fertile, workable land. The officer in charge of the landing party reported seeing a group of armed natives who fled when approached. He feels the settlement must be located so that it can be defended from the natives and from the sea.

Directions, step one: You (your group) are to select a site on the attached map that you feel is best suited for a colony. Your site must satisfy the different factions aboard the ship. A number of possible sites are already marked on the map (letters *A–G*). You may select one of these locations or use them as reference points to show the location of your colony. When your group has selected its site, list and explain the reasons for your choice. When each group has arrived at its tentative decision, these will be shared with the whole class.

Directions, step two: After each group has made its presentation and argument, a class debate is held about where the colony should be located.

Notes to teacher: For the debate, have a large map drawn on the writing board or on an overhead transparency, where each group's mark can be made for all to see and discuss. After each group has presented its argument for its location and against the others, we suggest that you then mark on the large map the two, three, or more hypothetical locations (assuming that, as a class, there is no single favorite location yet). Then take a straw vote of the students, allowing each to vote independently rather than as members of groups. At this time you can terminate the activity by saying that if the majority of students favor one location, then that, in fact, is the solution to the problem—that is, the colony is located wherever the majority of class members believe it should be. No sooner will that statement be made by you than someone will ask, "Are we correct?" or "What is the right answer?" They will ask such questions because, as students in school, they are used to solving problems that have right answers (Level I inquiry teaching). In real-world problems, however, there are no "right" answers, though some answers may seem better than others. It is the process of problem solving that is important. You want your students to develop confidence in their ability to solve problems and understand the tentativeness of "answers" to real-life problems.

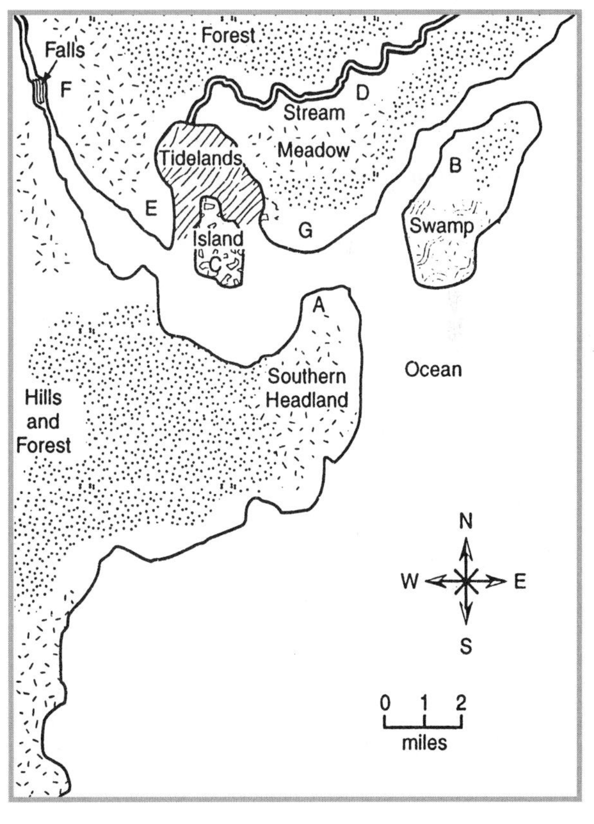

FIGURE 5.3 Locating a colony: a Level II inquiry. *Source:* Adapted by permission from unpublished material provided by Jennifer Devine and Dennis Devine.

Figure 5.3 presents a Level II activity that we suggest you perform with your classmates.

At Level III inquiry, students recognize and identify a problem, decide the processes, and reach a conclusion. Levels II and III inquiry should be a major strategy for K–8 science instruction. And, in many exemplary schools that use cross-age teaching and interdisciplinary thematic instruction, it often is.

Classroom Scenario

Problem Solving and Decision Making in the Real World Is an Integrated and Interdisciplinary Inquiry Activity

Public officials in Colorado were confronted with the task of making decisions about projects proposed for watersheds for their state. While gathering information, they brought in a state hydrologist. The hydrologist led the officials into the field to demonstrate specific ways by which he helped control erosion and rehabilitate damaged streams. He took the officials to Wolf Creek, where they donned high waders. He led the group down the creek to examine various features of that complex natural water habitat. He pointed out evidence of the creek's past meanders, patterns that he had incorporated into his rehabilitation projects. In addition to listening to this scientist's point of view, the public officials listened to other experts to consider related economic and political issues before making final decisions about projects that had been proposed for watersheds in the state.

Problem Solving and Decision Making in the Real World Is an Integrated and Interdisciplinary Inquiry Activity

As evidenced by the inquiry shown in Figure 5.3, real-world problem solving is an integrated and interdisciplinary inquiry activity. Although not many of your children are likely to find careers in science, they all will find it necessary to identify and solve problems in their lives, and they need to learn to do this well. Just as in real life, you and your students can look at a problem or topic of study from the perspective of disciplines other than science. Such an interdisciplinary approach to some degree has been adopted not only by teachers but by other professionals as well. It is *the* mode of meaningful learning and real-life problem solving. See the real-life scenario "Problem Solving and Decision Making in the Real World Is an Integrated and Interdisciplinary Inquiry Activity."

During an inquiry, students study a topic or theme and its underlying ideas as well as related knowledge from various disciplines. Just as the hydrologist introduced information from hydrology to the state officials, you can (with the help of students and other teachers and adults) introduce experiences designed to foster ideas and skills from various disciplines. During an inquiry II or III study, for example, some of the knowledge and skills may actually evolve from direct instruction, that is, from level one inquiry activities. As with real-life learning, throughout an inquiry you can guide your students in exploring ideas related to different disciplines to integrate their learning.

The program of study must emphasize student understanding through inquiry. Inquiry is a set of interrelated processes by which scientists and students pose questions about the natural world and investigate phenomena. . . . Inquiry is a critical component of a science program at all grade levels and in every domain of science. Designers of curricula and programs must be sure that the approach to content, as well as the teaching and assessment strategies, reflect the acquisition of scientific understandings through inquiry.[4]

As a result of learning activities, all students should develop abilities necessary to do scientific inquiry. Abilities that underlie this standard include the following:

- Identify questions that can be answered through scientific investigations.
- Design and conduct a scientific investigation.
- Use appropriate tools and techniques to gather, analyze, and interpret data.
- Develop descriptions, explanations, predictions, and models using evidence.
- Think critically and logically to make the relationships between evidence and explanations.
- Recognize and analyze alternative explanations and predictions.
- Communicate scientific procedures and explanations by communicating experimental methods, following instructions, describing observations, summarizing the results of other groups, and telling other students about investigations and explanations.[5]

The Critical Thinking Skills (Processes) of Discovery and Inquiry

In Level II and III inquiry, students generate ideas and then design ways to test those ideas. The various processes used represent the many critical thinking

[4]Reprinted from National Research Council, *National Science Education Standards,* © 1996 by the National Academy of Science, 214. Courtesy of National Academy Press, Washington, DC.

[5]Reprinted from National Research Council, *National Science Education Standards,* © 1996 by the National Academy of Science, 145, 148. Courtesy of National Academy Press, Washington, DC.

Meryl Joseph/PH College

Direct learning is likely to engage more of the senses, thus to better effect learning.

skills. Some of these skills are concerned with generating and organizing data; others are concerned with building and using ideas. Figure 3.4 provides four main categories of these thinking processes and illustrates the place of each within the inquiry cycle. Some processes in the cycle are discovery processes and others are inquiry processes. Inquiry processes include the more complex mental operations, including all of those in the idea-using category. Because they are likely to be in the process of developing their higher-level thinking capabilities, students from grades 5 and up should be provided experiences that require these more complex, higher-level inquiry skills.

Inquiry learning is a higher-level mental operation that introduces the concept of the discrepant event, something that establishes cognitive disequilibrium (using the element of surprise) to help students develop skills in observing and being alert for discrepancies. Such a strategy provides opportunities for students to investigate their own ideas about explanations. Inquiry, like discovery, depends on skill in problem solving; the difference between the two is in the amount of decision-making responsibility given to students. Experiences in inquiry help students understand the importance of suspending judgment, as well as the tentativeness of answers and solutions. With these understandings, students eventually are better able to deal with life's problems and ambiguities.

General Rule in Selecting Learning Activities

In planning and selecting science learning activities, an important rule is to select activities that are as concrete as possible. When students are involved in concrete experiences, they are using more of their sensory modalities (e.g., auditory, visual, tactile, kinesthetic), and when all the senses are engaged, learning is most effective and longest lasting. This is learning by doing or, as it is commonly called today, hands-on learning—one end of the spectrum on the learning experiences ladder (see Figure 5.4).

At the other end of the spectrum are abstract experiences through which the learner is exposed only to symbols (i.e., words and numbers), using only one or two senses. Visual and verbal symbolic experiences, although impossible to avoid in teaching, are less effective in ensuring that the planned learning occurs. So, to reiterate, when planning experiences and selecting materials, you are urged to select activities that engage the students in the most direct experiences possible. Hands-on, or firsthand experience, learning has to be very potent when combined with reflection and discussion. Learning is more than just seeing; it is more than just doing. Learning must include reflecting on one's own ideas and comparing them with ideas others may have.

The learning experiences ladder in Figure 5.4 depicts this range of experiences, from direct to abstract. As the example indicates, when teaching about tidal pools, the most effective strategy is to take the students to a tidal pool (bottom of ladder; most direct, or concrete, experience) where students can see, hear, touch, smell, and perhaps even taste the tidal pool. The least effective strategy is for the teacher simply to talk about the tidal pool (top of the ladder; most abstract, symbolic experience), engaging only one sense—the auditory.

Of course, for various reasons—such as matters of safety, lack of resources for a field trip, location of your school—you may not be able to take students to a tidal pool. Because it is not always possible to use the most direct experience, sometimes you must select an experience higher on the ladder. In addition, self-discovery teaching is not always appropriate. Sometimes it is more appropriate to build on what others have discovered and learned, rather than to "reinvent the wheel." However, the most effective and longest-lasting learning is that which engages most or all of the learner's senses. In the learning experiences ladder, those are the experiences that fall within the bottom three rungs—the direct, simulated, and vicarious categories.

Of particular significance is that direct, simulated, and vicarious experiences are usually interdisciplinary; that is, they frequently cross subject content boundaries. That makes these experiences especially useful for integrated learning. Direct, simulated, and vicarious experiences are more like real life, thereby providing an important benefit to students' learning. See the classroom scenario, "Students Write and Stage a One-Act Play."

ABSTRACT ↕ CONCRETE

Verbal Experiences
Teacher talk, written words; engaging only one sense; using the most abstract symbolization; students physically inactive. *Examples:* (1) Listening to the teacher talk about tidal pools. (2) Listening to a student report about the Grand Canyon.

Visual Experiences
Still pictures, diagrams, charts; engaging only one sense; typically symbolic; students physically inactive. *Examples:* (1) Viewing slide photographs of tidal pools. (2) Viewing drawings and photographs of the Grand Canyon.

Vicarious Experiences
Computer programs; video programs; engaging more than one sense; learner indirectly "doing"; may be some limited physical activity. *Examples:* (1) Interacting with a computer program about wave action and life in tidal pools. (2) Viewing and listening to a video program about the Grand Canyon.

Simulated Experiences
Role-playing; experimenting; simulations; mock-up; working models; all or nearly all senses engaged; activity often integrating disciplines; closest to the real thing. *Examples:* (1) Building a classroom working model of a tidal pool. (2) Building a classroom working model of the Grand Canyon.

Direct Experiences
Learner actually doing what is being learned: true inquiry; all senses engaged; usually integrates disciplines; the real thing. *Examples:* (1) Visiting and experiencing a tidal pool. (2) Visiting and experiencing the Grand Canyon.

FIGURE 5.4 The learning experiences ladder. *Source:* Earlier versions of this concept can be found in C. F. Hoban, Sr., et al., *Visualizing the Curriculum* (New York: Dryden, 1937), 39; J. S. Bruner, *Toward a Theory of Instruction* (Cambridge: Harvard University Press, 1966), 49; E. Dale, *Audio-Visual Methods in Teaching* (New York: Holt, Rinehart & Winston, 1969), 108; E. C. Kim and R. D. Kellough, *A Resource Guide for Secondary School Teaching,* 2nd ed. (Upper Saddle River, NJ: Prentice Hall, 1978), 136; and R. D. Kellough, *A Resource Guide for Teaching: K–12,* 2nd ed. (Upper Saddle River, NJ: Prentice Hall, 1997), 300.

The Classroom as a Learning Laboratory

The classroom should be a learning laboratory where students can explore scientific phenomena. Exploring is the heart and soul of science teaching and learning. Of all the methods used specifically to teach science, the use of investigations with hands-on/minds-on learning is the one that evokes the greatest curiosity, interest, excitement, and satisfaction among students. It is the means by which students develop proficiency in many process skills while they are developing their understanding of concepts. Other teaching strategies are valuable for teaching and learning science, but they are usually most effective when used either with or as a result of exploratory investigations.

Anthony Magnacca/Merrill

The science classroom is designed as a learning laboratory where children are motivated to explore phenomena.

Guidelines for Doing Exploratory Investigations

If you adhere to the following guidelines for doing exploratory investigations, your students will be motivated and will learn, and your instruction should run more smoothly.

The investigation should have a purpose. The purpose should be clearly understood by the students. An investigation can be designed for any one or more of the

Classroom Scenario

Students Write and Stage a One-Act Play

Early in the year in preparation for a unit on the study of oxygen and other gases, Maurice told the 28 students in his seventh-grade physical science class that if they were interested he would like for them to plan, write, and stage a one-act play about the life of Joseph Priestley. Priestley was a theologian and scientist who in 1774 discovered what he called "dephlogisticated air," later named *oxygen* by Lavoisier. Furthermore, the students would be given one week to plan. The play would be presented and videotaped in class. The students accepted Maurice's idea with enthusiasm and immediately went about the task of organizing and putting their ideas into motion. They took on the challenging task with such vigor and seriousness that they asked Maurice for an additional three days to prepare. Sean, a bright student who was really more interested in theatre than science, was selected by the students to play the role of Priestley and to also be the producer. Other students played lesser rolls. Students with special interest in writing wrote the play. Others with interest in art and stagecraft assumed the task of designing and preparing the set, while another acted as the sound stage manager. The resulting 60-minute presentation was more successful than Maurice, and perhaps the students, had anticipated—so much so that by request of the school principal the students performed the play twice again, once for the entire student body, a second time for the school's parent-teacher-student organization. Both performances resulted in standing ovations. During the performance before the PTO, the student production was recorded by the local cable television network and later played several times over the community cable channel. Maurice later said that during this experience the students learned far more content than they ever would have via his traditional approach to the topic, plus these students were highly motivated in science class for the entire rest of the year. Sean, 10 years later, graduated with honors from the University of California with a degree major in theatre and a minor in chemistry.

following purposes: to give students an opportunity to participate in active sciencing; to actively pursue a student-stated problem or observational interest; to provide a mind-capturing introduction to, a review of, or closure to a lesson or unit of study; to provide for discrepancy recognition; to assist in the recognition of a solution to an existing problem; to establish problem recognition; and to illustrate a concept.

Students should understand procedures, expected behavior, and the consequences for not following established procedures. Two important points must be made. First, the science classroom should be a learning laboratory where students are actively learning and multitasking, where there are different things happening simultaneously, some of which will cause excitement, curiosity, and purposeful movement about the classroom. Second, the science classroom is a place where, without enforcement of procedural expectations, serious injuries to students can result.

Unfortunately, some teachers, because of their fear of liability or their fear that the class will get out of control, do not allow students to actively science, or they allow it only in rare instances, perhaps to reward students for their sustained good behavior. To prevent this unfortunate situation, your students must understand classroom procedures and from the first day you must consistently enforce those procedures.

In addition, you should ensure that students understand basic safety guidelines (see Figure 5.5) and the consequences for not following procedures. These consequences should be fair and consistent, and appropriate for the grade level you teach.

Teachers ensure a safe working environment. Safety is a fundamental concern in all experimental science. Teachers of science must know and apply the necessary safety regulations in the storage, use, and care of the materials used by students. They adhere to safety rules and guidelines that are established by national organizations and local regulatory agencies.[6]

Planning is important and should involve the students. The necessary materials must be collected and prepared in advance, and be ready for assembling or distribution so there is no delay or "dead time" during class. Try to do the experiments yourself in advance, remembering the adage "If anything can go wrong, it probably will." Students should be involved in various phases of planning their exploratory investigations. Aim for thinking and discussion about the investigation. Talk about it before you begin and again after it is completed. Keep investigations as simple as possible. If an investigation is too complex for the intellectual maturity level of your students, they may never know what it was all about.

[6]Reprinted from National Research Council, *National Science Education Standards*, © 1996 by the National Academy of Science, 44. Courtesy of National Academy Press, Washington, DC.

1. Teachers are responsible for preventing accidents and ensuring that the science classroom is as safe as possible. Whenever an accident happens, notify the school office immediately by telephoning or sending a pair of runners to the office.
2. Rules for investigatory work should be taught to the students, posted in a conspicuous place, and reviewed continually. Instruct and rehearse the students in the procedures for classroom behavior and the consequences for misbehavior.
3. When taking students on a field trip, solicit adult help, even when the trip is only a short distance from the school. A recommended guideline is one adult for every 10 students.
4. Maintain a neat classroom, with aisles kept clear and books and coats in designated storage areas. Students should not be allowed to wear coats while doing laboratory investigations. Loose-fitting clothing can too easily knock over equipment.
5. Be aware of eye safety precautions and regulations regarding eye protection.
6. Avoid using flammable materials and alcohol burners, and use lighted candles and hot plates with caution.
7. Keep a well-supplied first aid kit available in the classroom.
8. Know exactly what to do in case of emergencies, and have emergency procedures posted conspicuously in your classroom.
9. Have an ABC-type fire extinguisher available always, and be sure it is adequately charged.
10. Use proper waste disposal methods. Learn from your school district the regulations for disposing of various kinds of waste materials.
11. Maintain accurate labels on all drawers, cupboards, and containers.
12. Never allow students to taste unknown substances.
13. Avoid using dangerous plants, animals, chemicals, and apparatus in the classroom.
14. Handle pets with care and caution. For example, birds can carry psittacosis, and turtles and other animals can carry salmonellosis. Dogs, rabbits, and other animals may have parasites. Some children may be allergic to animal dander.
15. Do not allow students to handle or to bring dead animals into the classroom.
16. Do not store heavy items above the heads of the students.
17. Do not allow students to climb or to be in positions where they may fall.
18. Do not leave dangerously sharp objects or those that may shatter where students can obtain them without approval and supervision.
19. Avoid allowing students to overheat or to overexert themselves.
20. Never leave students unattended for any reason.
21. Inspect electrical equipment for frayed cords and, if frayed, do not use.
22. Avoid overloading an electrical circuit.
23. Employ caution in the use of any mechanical equipment with moving parts.
24. Under no circumstances allow blood or any other body fluids to be extracted from your students.
25. Be alert for students who have allergies or other medical problems, and be aware of what to do if a student is having a medical problem while in your classroom. Remember, however, unless you are a licensed medical professional, you must never give medication to students, whether prescription or over-the-counter.
26. Be aware of what to do in an emergency situation. Accidents to students at school do occur. While doing a laboratory experiment, a student may be cut by glass or burned by a hot item. A student may fall and be hurt during an excursion outside the classroom. Do you know what to do if a student is injured while under your supervision?

    First, you should give first aid only when necessary to save a child's limb or life. When life or limb is not threatened, you should follow school policy in referring the student to immediate professional care. When immediate care is not available but you believe it is necessary, you may take prudent action as if you were the child's parent or legal guardian. However, you must be cautious and knowledgeable about what you are doing so that you do not cause further injury.

    For activities involving electricity and magnetism additional safety guidelines are found in Part Two of this book.

    The National Science Teachers Association (NSTA) publishes safety guidelines (see Suggested Readings at the end of this chapter) and your local school and state department of education may have a publication about safety in the science classroom.

FIGURE 5.5 Safety guidelines for the science classroom.

Scott Cunningham/Merrill

To test their hypotheses, children understand the importance of repeated trials and careful observations.

Help students connect what is learned to their own world. To be most meaningful, exploratory investigations should have relevance to the students' real world of everyday living, which is one of the reasons students should be involved in the planning phase of their investigations.

Use controls and repeated trials whenever possible. The use of controls in investigations is one of the key operations in sciencing. Students are able to understand very early the need for, as well as the nature of, a controlled experiment. In an experiment using a control, all the conditions are duplicated except one. This single condition—the variable—is the one that is being tested. For example, when studying the effect of heat on the rate of evaporation, a control helps to prove conclusively that heat makes liquids evaporate more quickly. The same measured quantity of water is poured into each of two identical pie pans. One pan is placed on a warm radiator, and the other pan is placed on a table on the other side of the room. The windows and door are kept closed to prevent any effect caused by wind or air circulation. Now all conditions are the same except one—namely, the heat to which the water is exposed. As a result of the control, the results of the investigation are clear.

After students have learned the nature and value of control, they should sometimes be exposed to the necessity of performing repeated trials to secure results that are both reliable and valid. The consistency with which a technique measures what it is meant to measure is called its reliability. The accuracy with which it makes the measurement is called its validity. If, for example, a scale consistently records 10 grams when we place a 10-gram weight on it, we can say the scale has reliability. However, if a scale consistently records 5 grams when we place a 10-gram weight on it, we can still say the scale has reliability. Through this example, it should be clear that an experiment can be reliable without being valid—that is, accurate. In addition, students need to understand the concept of instrument calibration.

Students are quick to understand the need for repeated trials. If a teacher were to suggest that the class conduct an experiment to see which is the faster runner, a right-handed or a left-handed student, the students would be quick to object to an experiment involving just one right-handed and one left-handed student. The need for testing several students to make the experiment reliable would be obvious to all. (To make an experiment valid, all variables but one, handedness in this instance, would have to be controlled.)

Similarly, when you are finding the dew point (the temperature at which water vapor in the air will condense back into water), it will be so difficult to note the exact temperature at which the dew point is reached that the students will recognize the need to repeat the experiment several times and perhaps take an average to obtain satisfactory results. Consequently, experiments requiring several repetitions can help prevent students from making broad generalizations from just one test. Not making broad generalizations from limited data is an important habit for life whether or not the student becomes a scientist.

Aim for quantitative as well as qualitative results. Students are exposed to the *why* and the *what* of science but should also be exposed to the *how much*. Dealing with quantitative aspects gives students an opportunity to practice measurement, a key process of science.

Take, for example, investigations designed to show how the strength of an electromagnet may be increased. It is customary to prove this either by increasing the number of turns of wire around the piece of iron or by using more dry cells. However, consider how much more effective this learning situation becomes if we make the experiments quantitative as well. When first making the electromagnet, the students wrap 30 turns of wire around the iron nail or bolt. They count the number of tacks the electromagnet will pick up. Then, when the students wrap 60 turns of wire around the iron nail, they find that this electromagnet will pick up twice as many tacks. There should be little difficulty in realizing that if they double the number of turns of wire, they double the number of tacks that will be picked up. Consequently, the electromagnet has been made twice as strong. If the experiment is repeated, however, this time using the same number of turns of wire in each case and using first one and then two dry cells (connected in series), the results will be the same as when the number of turns of wire was doubled. That is, if the students double the number of dry cells, using the same number of turns, they double the number of tacks that will be picked up, and again they have made the electromagnet twice as strong. The students could then be asked to find out what would happen if they doubled both the number of dry cells and the number of turns.

In this investigation, not only do the students learn a science concept but they are also given an opportunity to discover mathematical ratios and relationships. There are many opportunities in the teaching of science to include the teaching of measurement, numbers, size, and simple ratios.[7]

The science program should be coordinated with the mathematics program to enhance student use and understanding of mathematics in the study of science and to improve student understanding of mathematics.[8]

Adhere to the philosophy that "no experiment fails." Sometimes experiments fail to work as expected. Recall Thomas Edison and his trial of some 3,000 filaments before finding one that worked satisfactorily. When an experiment is unsuccessful, grab that opportunity to model problem solving and creative thinking. Involve the students in proposing and testing hypotheses about why it didn't work.

Teacher Talk: Formal and Informal

Teacher talk encompasses both lecturing *to* students and talking *with* students. A lecture is considered formal teacher talk, whereas a discussion with students is considered informal teacher talk.

[7]See, for example, R. D. Kellough et al., *Integrating Mathematics and Science for Kindergarten and Primary Children* and *Integrating Mathematics and Science for Intermediate and Middle School Students* (both Columbus, OH: Merrill/Prentice Hall, 1996).

[8]Reprinted from National Research Council, *National Science Education Standards,* © 1996 by the National Academy of Science, 214. Courtesy of National Academy Press, Washington, DC.

Teacher Talk: Cautions and General Guidelines

Whether your talk is formal or informal, you need to be mindful of the following cautions.

Avoid talking too much. This is the most important caution. If a teacher talks too much, the significance of the teacher's words may be lost because some students will tune the teacher out.

Avoid talking too fast. Children can hear faster than they can understand what they hear. It is a good idea to remind yourself to talk slowly and to check frequently for student comprehension of what you are talking about. It is also important to remember that your one brain is communicating with many student brains, each of which responds to sensory input (primarily auditory in this instance) at different rates. For this reason, you will need to pause to let words sink in and you will need to pause during transitions from one point or activity to the next.

Be sure you are being heard and understood. Sometimes teachers talk in too low a pitch, use words that are not understood by many of the students, or both. You should vary the pitch of your voice, and you should stop and help students with their understanding of vocabulary that may be new to them. If you have children in your class who have only limited English-language proficiency, you will need to help them learn what is essentially two new vocabularies—the vocabulary of the English language in general and the new science vocabulary.

Remember that just because students have heard something before does not necessarily mean that they understand it or have learned it. From our discussion of the learning experiences ladder, remember that although verbal communication is an important form of communication, because of its reliance on the use of abstract symbolization it is not a very reliable form of communication. Teacher talk relies on words and on skill in listening, a skill that is not mastered by many children (or for that matter, even many adults). For that and other reasons, to ensure student understanding, it is good to reinforce your teacher talk with either direct or simulated learning experiences.

Resist believing that students have attained a skill or have learned something that was taught previously by you or by another teacher. During any discussion—formal or informal—rather than assuming that your students know something, you should *ensure* that they know it. For example, if the discussion and a student activity involve a particular skill, such as weighing an item, make sure that students know how to do that.

Avoid talking in a humdrum monotone. Students need teachers whose voices exude enthusiasm and excitement (although not to be overdone) about science and about teaching and learning. Such enthusiasm and excitement are contagious. A voice that demonstrates enthusiasm for teaching and learning is more likely to motivate children to learn.

Begin the talk with an advance organizer. Advance organizers are introductions that mentally prepare students for a study by helping them make connections with material already learned or experienced—a *comparative organizer*—or by providing students with a conceptual arrangement of what is to be learned—an *expository organizer.*[9] The value of using advance organizers is well documented by research.[10] An advance organizer can be a brief introduction or statement about the main idea you intend to convey and how it is related to other aspects of the students' learning—an expository organizer. It can also be a presentation of a discrepancy to arouse curiosity—a comparative organizer, in this instance causing students to compare what they have observed with what they already knew or thought they knew. Preparing an organizer helps you plan and organize the sequence of ideas, and its presentation helps students organize their own learning and become motivated about it. An advance organizer can also make their learning meaningful by providing important connections between what they already know and what is being learned.

Plan your talk so that it has a beginning and an end, with a logical order in between. During your talk, you should reinforce your words with visuals (discussed in the specific guidelines that follow). These visuals may include writing unfamiliar terms on the board to help students learn new vocabulary; visual organizers; and prepared graphs, charts, photographs, and various audiovisuals.

Pacing is important. Your talk should move briskly but not too fast. Knowing how to pace the instruction is a difficult skill for many beginning teachers, who tend to talk too fast and too much, but one that will improve with experience. Until you have developed your skill in pacing lessons, you probably will need to constantly remind yourself during lessons to slow down and provide silent pauses to allow for think time and frequent checks for student comprehension. Observe the following guidelines in pacing instruction.

- Make your talk brisk, though not too fast, and with occasional slowdowns to change the pace and to check for student comprehension.
- Pause often enough to allow students time to think, ask questions, and make notes.
- Have a time plan. A talk planned for 10 minutes, if it is interesting to students, will probably take

[9] D. P. Ausubel, *The Psychology of Meaningful Verbal Learning* (New York: Grune & Stratton, 1963).
[10] T. L. Good and J. E. Brophy, *Looking in Classrooms,* 8th ed. (New York: Addison Wesley Longman, 2000), 252–253.

longer. If it is not interesting to them, it will probably take less time.

- Always plan with careful consideration to the characteristics of the students. For example, if you have a fairly high percentage of students with limited proficiency in English or with special needs, then your teacher talk may be less brisk and sprinkled with even more visuals, and use more frequent checks for student comprehension.

Encourage student participation. Students' active participation enhances their learning. This encouragement can be planned as questions that you ask, as time allowed for students to comment and ask questions, or as some sort of a visual and conceptual outline that students complete during the talk.

Plan a clear ending (closure). Be sure your talk has a clear ending, followed by another activity during the same or the next class period that will help secure the learning. As for all lessons, you should strive to plan a clear and mesmerizing beginning, an involving lesson body, and a firm and meaningful closure.

Teacher Talk: Specific Guidelines

Keep in mind the following specific guidelines for using teacher talk.

Understand the various purposes for using teacher talk. Teacher talk, formal or informal, can be useful to discuss the progress of a unit of study, explain an inquiry, introduce a unit of study, present a problem, promote student inquiry or critical thinking, provide a transition from one unit of study to the next, provide information otherwise unobtainable to students, share the teacher's experiences, share the teacher's thinking, summarize a problem, summarize a unit of study, and teach a thinking skill by modeling that skill.

Clarify the objectives of the talk. Your talk should center on one idea. The learning objectives, which should not be too numerous for one talk, should be clearly understood by the students.

Choose between informal and formal talk. Although an occasional formal, cutting-edge lecture may be appropriate for some classes, spontaneous interactive informal talks of 5 to 12 minutes are preferred for most classes of young learners. You should *never* give long lectures with no teacher-student interaction. Remember also that today's children are of the *media,* or *light,* generation and are used to video interactions as well as commercial breaks. For many lessons, especially those that are teacher-centered, student attention is likely to begin to stray after about 10 minutes. When that happens, you need to have elements planned that will recapture their attention. These planned elements can include analogies to help connect the topic to students' experiences; verbal cues, such as voice inflections; pauses to allow information to sink in; humor; visual cues, such as slides, overhead transparencies, charts, board drawings, video clips (excerpts from videotapes or DVDs), real objects (realia), or body gestures; and, sensory cues, such as eye contact and proximity (as in moving around the room or casually and gently touching a student on the shoulder without interrupting your talk).

Vary strategies and activities frequently. Perhaps most useful as a strategy for recapturing student attention is changing to an entirely different strategy or learning modality. For example, from teacher talk (a teacher-centered strategy) you would change to a student activity (a student-centered strategy). Notice that changing from a lecture (mostly teacher talk) to a teacher-led discussion (mostly more teacher talk) would not be changing to an entirely different modality.

In general, when using teacher-centered direct instruction, with most groups of students whether teaching kindergarten or any higher grade, you will want to change the learning activities about every 10 to 15 minutes. This means that for a 60-minute time block, for example, you should probably plan three or four *sequenced* learning activities, some of which are teacher-centered and many others that are more student-centered. For a 90-minute block, five or six learning activities will be needed. At all age levels, in exemplary classrooms, teachers often have several activities being performed *concurrently* by individuals, dyads, and small groups of students (that is, using multitasking or multilevel instruction).

Prepare and use notes as a guide for your talk. Planning your talk and preparing notes to be used during formal and informal teacher talk is important—just as important as implementing the talk with visuals. There is absolutely nothing wrong with using notes during your teaching. You can carry them on a clipboard, perhaps a brightly colored one that gives students a visual focus as you move around the room. Your notes for a formal talk can first be prepared in narrative form; for class use, though, they should be reduced to an outline form. *Talks to students should always be from an outline, never read from prose.* The only time it is appropriate for a teacher to read aloud from prose is when it is from a brief published article or portions of a story or a poem.

In your outline, use color coding with abbreviated visual cues to yourself. You will eventually develop your own coding system—but keep whatever coding system you use simple lest you forget what the codes are for. Consider these examples of coding: Where a transition of ideas occurs and where you want to allow silent moments for ideas to sink in, mark *P* for *pause, T* for a *transition,* and *S* for moments of *silence;* where you want to show a slide or other visual aid, mark *M* for *media;* where you intend to stop and ask a question, mark *TQ* for *teacher question,* and where you want to stop and allow time for *student questions,* mark *?* or *SQ;* where you plan to have a *discussion*, mark *D;* where you plan *small-group work*, mark *SG;* where you plan to switch to a *laboratory* investigation, mark *L;* where you plan *reviews* and *comprehension checks*, mark *R* and *CS*.

Share your note organization with your students. Teach the students how to take notes and what kinds of things they should write down. Use various colors to outline and highlight your talk; have your students use colored pencils for notetaking so their notes can be color-coded to match your writing board notes.

Rehearse your talk. Rehearsing your planned talk is important. Using your lesson plan as your guide, rehearse your talk using a camcorder or an audio recorder, or while talking into a mirror or to a housemate. You may want to include a time plan for each subtopic to allow you to gauge your timing during implementation of the talk.

Avoid racing through the talk solely to complete it by a certain time. It is more important for students to understand some of what you say than for you to cover everything and have them understand nothing. If you do not finish your talk, continue it later.

Augment your talk with multisensory stimulation and allow for thinktime. Your verbal presentation should be interspersed with visuals, comments from students, or simply a few moments of silence. When using visuals, such as video excerpts or overhead transparencies, do not think that you must be constantly talking. After clearly explaining the purpose of a visual, give students sufficient time to look at it, to think about it, and to ask questions about it. The visual is new to the students, so give them time to take it in.

Carefully plan the content of your talk. The content of your talk should supplement and enhance that found in the student textbook rather than simply rehash content from the textbook. Students may never read their book if you tell them in an interesting and condensed fashion everything that they need to know from it.

Monitor your delivery. Your voice should be pleasant and interesting to listen to and should not come across in a steady, boring monotone or a constantly shrieking, irritating, high pitch. Your voice should, however, show enthusiasm for what you are talking about, for teaching and learning. Occasionally, then, use dramatic voice inflections to emphasize important points and meaningful body language to give students a visual focus. To avoid appearing phony, practice these skills so they become second nature.

Avoid standing for long periods in the same spot. As for all forms of teaching, even during direct instruction, you need to monitor student behavior and to use proximity as one way of preventing student misbehavior.

View the vocabulary of the talk as an opportunity to help students with their word morphology. Words you use should be easily understood by the students, though you should still model professionalism and help students develop their vocabulary—both the specialized vocabulary of science and the more general vocabulary of the English language. During your lesson planning, predict when you are likely to use a word that is new to most students, and plan to stop to ask a student to help explain its meaning and perhaps demonstrate its derivation. Help students with word meaning. Regardless of subject or grade level, *all teachers are language arts teachers*. Knowledge of word morphology is an important component of skilled reading and includes the ability to generate new words from prefixes, roots, and suffixes. For some students, nearly every subject in the curriculum is like a foreign language. That is certainly true for students who have limited or no proficiency in English, for whom teacher talk, especially formal teacher talk, should be used sparingly, if at all. Every teacher has the responsibility of helping students learn how to learn, and that includes helping students develop their word comprehension skills, reading skills, and thinking and memory skills, and their motivation for learning.

Use familiar examples and analogies to help students make relevant connections, or bridges. Although this sometimes takes a great deal of creative thinking during the planning phase of your instruction, it is important that you attempt to connect the talk with ideas and events with which the students are already familiar. The most effective talk is one that makes frequent connections between what students already know and what they are learning, thereby bridging what they are learning with what they have experienced in their lives.

Consider student diversity. While preparing your talk, consider students in your classroom who are culturally and linguistically different and those who have special needs. Personalize the talk for them by planning appropriate analogies and examples and relevant visual displays.

Establish eye contact frequently. We cannot overemphasize the importance of this point: Your primary eye contact should be with your students— always! Only momentarily should you look at your notes, your visuals, the projection screen, the writing board, or other adults or objects in the classroom. Although you will probably not believe this when you read it, it is true and it is important that with practice you can learn to scan a classroom of 30 students, establishing eye contact with each student, about once a minute. To establish eye contact means that the student is aware that you are looking at him or her. Frequent eye contact can have two major benefits. First, as you read a student's body posture and facial expressions, you obtain clues about that student's attentiveness and comprehension. Second, eye contact helps to establish rapport between you and a student. Be alert, though, for students who are from cultures where eye contact is infrequent or unwanted, and could have negative consequences. In other words, don't push it!

Frequent eye contact is easier when using an overhead projector than when using the writing board. When using a writing board, you have to turn at least partially away from your audience, and you may also have to pace back and forth from the board to the students to retain that important proximity to them.

Remember our earlier discussions of overlapping as an important teaching skill? Well, this is one of those times when its importance really comes into play. While talking on a topic, you must remain aware and attentive to everything that is happening in the classroom; that is, to student behavior as well as to the content of your talk. No one who knew what he or she was talking about ever said that good teaching is easy. But do not dismay; with the knowledge of the preceding guidelines and with practice, experience, and intelligent reflection, you will develop the necessary skills.

Grouping Children for Instruction

Rather than watering down standards and expectations, exemplary schools and teachers who believe in the learning potential of every child, modify the three key variables of time, grouping, and methodology to help individual students achieve mastery of the curriculum. In the most effective instructional environments, during any given week—or even day—of school, a student might experience a succession of group settings. Ways of grouping children for instruction is the initial topic of this next section, from individualized instruction to working with dyads, small groups, and large groups.

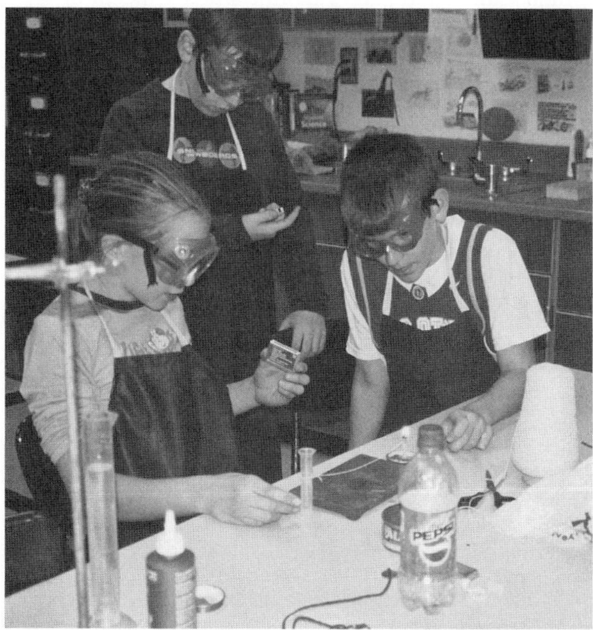

Valerie Schultz/Merrill

For children to work cooperatively and productively in groups requires the development of certain social skills, and these skills are not innate, they are learned.

Mastery Learning and Personalized Instruction

Learning is an individual or personal experience. Yet as a classroom teacher you will be expected to work effectively with students on other than an individual basis—perhaps 30 or more at a time. Much has been written on the importance of individualizing the instruction for learners. Virtually all the research concerning effective instructional practice emphasizes greater individualization, or personalization, of instruction.[11] We know about the individuality of the learning experience. And we know that while some students are primarily verbal learners, many more are primarily visual, tactile, or kinesthetic learners. As the classroom teacher, though, you find yourself in the difficult position of simultaneously treating many separate and individual learners with individual learning capacities, styles, and preferences.

To individualize the instruction, exemplary schools and teachers use a variety of strategies—exploratory programs, cooperative learning groups, project-based learning, personalized learning plans, and independent study—to respond to individual student competencies, interests, needs, and abilities. They also use non-conventional scheduling so that teaching teams can vary the length of time in periods, the size of instructional groups, and the learning strategies within a given time period.

Common sense tells us that student achievement in learning is related to both the quality of attention and the length of time given to learning tasks. In 1968, Benjamin Bloom, building upon a model developed earlier by John Carroll, developed the concept of individualized instruction called **mastery learning**, saying that students need sufficient time on task (i.e., engaged time) to master content before moving on to new content.[12] The instruction is mastery oriented; that is, the student demonstrates mastery of the content of one module before proceeding to the next.

Today's Emphasis: Quality Learning for Each Child

Emphasis today is on mastery of content, or quality learning, for every student. By mastery of content, we mean that the student demonstrates his or her use of what has been learned. Because of that emphasis and

[11]J. M. Carroll, "The Copernican Plan Evaluated," *Phi Delta Kappan* 76(2):105–113 (October 1994).

[12]See B. Bloom, *Human Characteristics and School Learning* (New York: McGraw-Hill, 1987); and J. Carroll, "A Model of School Learning," *Teachers College Record* 64(8):723–733 (May 1963).

research that indicates that quality learning programs positively affect achievement, the importance of the concept of mastery learning has resurfaced and is becoming firmly entrenched. For example, the general nationwide approach of standards-based instruction and two specific approaches—*Results-Driven Education* (RDE), also known as *Outcome-Based Education* (OBE), and *the Coalition of Essential Schools* (CES)—use a goal-driven curriculum model with instruction that focuses on the construction of individual knowledge through mastery and assessment of student learning against the anticipated outcomes. In some instances, unfortunately, attention may be on the mastery of only minimum competencies; therefore, students are not encouraged to work and learn to the maximum of their talents and abilities.

Any instructional model designed to teach toward mastery (quality) learning will contain the following components: (a) clearly defined learning targets (objectives); (b) a pre-assessment of the learner's present knowledge, (c) an instructional component, with a rich variety of choices and options for students; (d) frequent practice, reinforcement, and comprehension checks, with corrective instruction at each step to keep the learner on track; and (e) a post-assessment to determine the extent of student mastery of the learning objectives.

You can immediately provide personalized instruction by (a) starting study of a topic from where the children are in terms of what they know (or think they know) and what they want to know about the topic (see "think-pair-share" discussed in the following section titled "Learning in Pairs"); (b) providing students with choices from a rich variety of pathways and hands-on experiences to learn more about the topic; (c) providing multiple instructional approaches (that is, using multilevel instruction in a variety of settings from learning alone to whole-class instruction); and (d) empowering students with responsibility for decision making, reflection, and self-assessment.

Learning Alone

Although some students learn well in pairs (dyads); some with their peers in groups—collaboratively, cooperatively, or competitively—or collaboratively with adults; and others in combinations of these patterns, some children learn best alone. Learning-alone students often are gifted, nonconforming, able to work at their own pace successfully, comfortable using media, or seemingly underachieving but potentially able students for whom unconventional instructional strategies work best. For them, *contract learning packages*—that is, agreements between the teacher and individual students to proceed with tasks appropriate to their readiness, interests, or learning profiles in a sequence and at a pace each student selects—or multisensory instructional packages, encourage academic success.[13]

Learning in Pairs

It is sometimes advantageous to pair students (dyads) for learning. Four types of dyads are described as follows:

Peer tutoring, mentoring, and cross-age coaching. Peer mentoring, tutoring, or peer-assisted learning (PAL) is a strategy whereby one classmate tutors another. This activity is based on the notion that one rarely learns something as well as when one needs to explain it to someone else. It is also useful when one student helps another who has limited proficiency in English or when a student skilled in math helps another who is less skilled. For many years, it has been demonstrated repeatedly that peer teaching is a significant strategy for promoting active learning.[14] Cross-age coaching is a strategy whereby one student coaches another from a different, and sometimes lower, grade level. This is similar to peer tutoring, except that the coach is from a different age/grade level than the student being coached.[15]

Paired team learning. Paired team learning is a strategy whereby students study and learn in teams of two. Students identified as gifted work and learn especially well when paired. Specific uses for paired team learning include drill partners, reading buddies, book report pairs, summary pairs, homework partners, project assignment pairs, and elaborating and relating pairs.

Think-pair-share. Think-pair-share is a strategy in which students in pairs examine a new concept or topic about to be studied. After the students of each dyad discuss what they already know or think they know about the concept, they present their perceptions to the whole group. This is an excellent technique for discovering student's misconceptions (also called *naïve theories*) about a topic. A modification called *think-write-pair-share* introduces a writing step. The dyad thinks and writes their ideas or conclusions before sharing them with the larger group.

---

[13]R. Dunn, *Strategies for Diverse Learners,* Fastback 384 (Bloomington, IN: Phi Delta Kappa Educational Foundation, 1995), 15.

[14]See, for example: R. B. Schneider and D. Barone, "Cross-Age Tutoring," *Childhood Education 73*(3):136–143 (Spring 1997); J. Wagmeister and B. Shifrin, "Thinking Differently, Learning Differently," *Educational Leadership 58*(3):45–48 (November 2000); L. Thrope and K. Wood, "Cross-Age Tutoring for Young Adolescents," *Clearing House* 73(4):239–242 (March/April 2000); and P. Wolfe, "Peer Teaching," in *Brain Matters: Translating Research into Classroom Practice* (Alexandria, VA: Association for Supervision and Curriculum Development, 2001), 185–186.

[15]See, for example, R. Bombaugh, "Blast Off into Space Science with Fuses," *Science Scope 23*(5):28–30 (February 2000).

The Learning Center

Another significantly beneficial way of pairing students for instruction (as well as individualizing the instruction, learning alone, and integrating the learning) is by using the learning center (LC) or learning station. (Note: Whereas each *learning center* is distinct and unrelated to others, *learning stations* are sequenced or in some way linked to one another.) The LC is a special station located in the classroom where one student (or two, if student interaction is necessary or preferred at the center, or as many as four or five students in the case of learning stations) can quietly work to learn more, at his or her own pace, about a special topic or to improve specific skills. All materials needed are provided at the center, including clear instructions for operation of the center.

The value of learning centers as instructional devices undoubtedly lies in the following facts. LCs can provide instructional diversity. While working at a center, the student is giving time and quality attention to the learning task (learning toward mastery) and is likely to be engaging his or her most effective learning modality, or integrating several modalities or all of them.

LCs are of three types. In the *direct-learning center,* performance expectations for cognitive learning are quite specific, and the focus is on mastery of content. In the *open-learning center,* the goal is to provide opportunity for exploration, enrichment, motivation, and creative discovery. In the *skill center,* as in a direct-learning center, performance expectations are quite specific but the focus is on the development of a particular skill or process.

Anthony Magnacca/Merrill

Learning centers are the focal point of many active science classrooms.

In all instances, the primary reason for using an LC is to individualize—that is, to provide collections of materials and activities adjusted to the various readiness levels, interests, and learning profiles of students. Other reasons to use an LC are to provide (a) a mechanism for learning that crosses discipline boundaries; (b) a special place for a student with exceptional needs; (c) opportunities for creative work, enrichment experiences, multisensory experiences; and (d) opportunity to learn from learning packages that use special equipment or media of which only one or a limited supply may be available for use in your classroom (e.g., science materials, a microscope, a computer, or a videodisc player, or some combination of these). LCs should always be used for educational purposes, *never* for punishment.

To adapt instruction to the curriculum and to students' individual needs and preferences, it is possible to design a learning environment that includes several learning stations, each of which uses a different medium and modality or focuses on a special aspect of the curriculum. Students then rotate through the various stations according to their needs and preferences.

In constructing an LC, you can be as elaborate and as creative as your time, imagination, and resources allow. Students can even help you plan and set up LCs, which will relieve some of the burden from your busy schedule. The following paragraphs present guidelines for setting up and using this valuable instructional tool.

The center should be designed with a theme in mind, preferably one that integrates the student's learning by providing activities that cross discipline boundaries. Decide the purpose of the center and give the center a name, such as "the center for microscopic studies," "the center for the study of wetlands," "structure and function," "patterns in nature," "our science exploratory reading center," and so on. The purpose of the center should be clearly understood by the students.

The center should be designed so it is attractive, purposeful, and uncluttered, and should be identified with an attractive sign. LCs should be activity-oriented (i.e., dependent on the student's manipulation of materials, not just paper-and-pencil tasks).

Topics for the center should be related to the instructional program—for review and reinforcement, remediation, or enrichment. The center should be self-directing (i.e., specific instructional objectives and procedures for using the center should be clearly posted and understandable to the student user). An audio- or videocassette or a computer program is sometimes used for this purpose. The center should also be self-correcting (i.e., student users should be able to tell by the way they have completed the task whether or not they have done it correctly and have learned).

The center should contain a variety of activities geared to the varying abilities and interest levels of the students. A choice of two or more activities at a center is one way to provide for this.

Materials to be used at the center should be maintained at the center, with descriptions for their use provided to the students. Materials should be safe for student use, and you or another adult should easily supervise the center. Some centers may become more or less permanent centers—that is, remain for the school term or longer—whereas others may change according to what is being studied at the time.

Learning in Small Groups

Small groups are those involving three to five students, in either a teacher- or a student-directed setting. Using small groups for instruction, including the cooperative learning group (CLG), enhances the opportunities for students to assume greater control over their own learning, sometimes referred to as *empowerment*.

Small groups can be formed to serve a number of purposes. They might be useful for a specific learning activity (e.g., *reciprocal reading groups*, where students take turns asking questions, summarizing, making predictions about, and clarifying a story). Or they might be formed to complete an activity that requires materials that are in short supply, or to complete a science experiment or project and only last as long as the project does. Teachers have various rationales for assigning students to groups. Groups can be formed by grouping students according to (a) personality type (e.g., a teacher may want to team less-assertive students together to give them the opportunity for greater management of their own learning), (b) social pattern (e.g., it may be necessary to break up a group of rowdy friends, or it may be desirable to broaden the association among students), (c) common interest, (d) learning styles (e.g., forming groups of either mixed styles or of styles in common, or (e) their abilities in a particular skill or their knowledge in a particular area. One specific type of small group instruction is the cooperative learning group.

Anthony Magnacca/Merrill

The theory of cooperative learning is that when a small group of children of diverse backgrounds and capabilities work together toward a common goal they increase their liking and respect for each other. The result is an increase in each child's self-esteem and academic achievement.

 Cooperative Learning

Lev Vygotsky (1896–1934) studied the importance of a learner's social interactions in learning situations. Vygotsky argued that learning is most effective when learners cooperate with one another in a supportive learning environment under the careful guidance of a teacher. Cooperative learning, group problem solving, problem-based learning, and cross-age tutoring are instructional strategies that teachers use that have grown in popularity as a result of research evolving from the work of Vygotsky.

The Cooperative Learning Group

The *cooperative learning group* (CLG) is a heterogeneous group (i.e., mixed according to one or more criteria, such as ability or skill level, ethnicity, learning style, learning capacity, gender, and language proficiency) of three to five students who work together in a teacher- or student-directed setting, emphasizing support for one another. Often times, a CLG consists of four students of mixed ability, learning styles, gender, and ethnicity, with each member of the group assuming a particular role. Teachers usually change the membership of each group several to many times during the year.

The theory of cooperative learning is that when small groups of students of mixed backgrounds and capabilities work together toward a common goal, members of the group increase their friendship and respect for one another. As a consequence, each individual's self-esteem is enhanced, students are more motivated to participate in higher-order thinking, and academic achievement is accomplished. In short, the effective use of heterogeneous cooperative learning helps students grow academically, socially, and emotionally.[16]

---

[16]See, for example, J. D. Laney et al., "The Effect of Cooperative and Mastery Learning Methods on Primary Grade Students' Learning and Retention of Economic Concepts," *Early Education and Development* 7(3):253–274 (July 1996); and N. Schniedewind and E. Davidson, "Differentiating Cooperative Learning," *Educational Leadership* 58(1):24–27 (September 2000).

There are several techniques for using cooperative learning.[17] Regardless of the technique, the primary purpose of each is for the groups to learn, which means, of course, that each individual within a group must learn. Group achievement in learning, then, is dependent upon the learning of each individual within the group. Rather than competing for rewards for achievement, members of the group cooperate with one another by helping one another learn, so that the group will earn the reward. Normally, the group is rewarded on the basis of group achievement, though individual members within the group can later be rewarded for individual contributions.

It is advisable to assign roles (specific functions) to each member of the CLG. (The lesson plan shown in Figure 7.4, Chapter 7, shows a CLG activity using assigned roles for a lesson in science.) These roles should be rotated, either during the activity or from one time to the next. Although titles may vary, five typical roles are

- *Group facilitator*—role is to keep the group on task.
- *Materials manager*—role is to obtain, maintain, and return materials needed for the group to function.
- *Recorder*—role is to record all group activities and processes, and perhaps to periodically assess how the group is doing.
- *Reporter*—role is to report group processes and accomplishments to the teacher and/or to the entire class. When using groups of four members, the roles of recorder and reporter can easily be combined.
- *Thinking monitor*—role is to identify and record the sequence and processes of the group's thinking. This role encourages metacognition and the development of thinking skills.

It is important that students understand and perform their individual roles, and that each member of the CLG performs her or his tasks as expected. No student should be allowed to ride on the coattails of the group. To give significance to and to reinforce the importance of each role, and to be able to readily recognize the role any student is playing during CLG activity, one teacher went to an office supplier and had permanent badges made for the various CLG roles. During CLGs, each student attaches the appropriate badge to her or his clothing.

Actually, for learning by CLGs to work, each member of the CLG must understand and assume two roles or responsibilities—the role that he or she is assigned as a member of the group, and the responsibility of seeing that all others in the group are performing their roles. Sometimes this requires interpersonal skills that students have yet to learn or to learn well. This is where the teacher must assume some responsibility, too. Simply placing students into CLGs and expecting each member and each group to function and to learn the expected outcomes may not work. In other words, cooperation skills must be taught, and if all your students have not yet learned them, then you will have to teach them. This doesn't mean that if a group is not functioning, you immediately break up the group and reassign members to new groups. Part of group learning is learning the process for working out conflict, which may require your assistance. With your guidance, the group should be able to discover what the problem is that is causing the conflict, then identify some options and mediate at least a temporary solution. If a particular skill is needed, then with your guidance students identify and learn that skill.

CLGs can be used for problem solving, investigations, opinion surveys, experiments, review, project work, test making, or almost any other instructional purpose. Just as you would for small group work in general, you can use CLGs for most any purpose at any time, but as with any other type of instructional strategy, they should not be overused.

When the process is well planned and managed, the outcomes of cooperative learning include (a) improved communication and relationships of acceptance among students of differences, (b) quality learning with fewer off-task behaviors, and (c) increased academic achievement.

Cooperative Group Learning, Assessment, and Grading

Normally, the CLG is rewarded on the basis of group achievement, though individual members within the group can later be rewarded for individual contributions (see Figure 5.6). Because of peer pressure, when using CLGs you must be cautious about using group grading.[18] Some teachers give bonus points to all members of a group to add to their individual scores when everyone in the group has reached preset criteria. In establishing preset standards, the standards can be different for individuals within a group, depending on each member's ability and past performance. It is important that each member of a group feel rewarded and successful. For determination of students' report card grades, individual student achievement is measured later through individual results on tests and other sources of data.

---

[17]See, for example, R. E. Slavin, *Student Team Learning: A Practical Guide for Cooperative Learning,* 3rd ed. (Washington, DC: National Education Association, 1991); and Y. Sharan and S. Sharan, *Expanding Cooperative Learning through Group Investigation* (New York: Teachers College Press, 1992).

[18]See S. Kagan, "Group Grades Miss the Mark," *Educational Leadership* 52(8):68–71 (May 1995); and D. W. Johnson and R. T. Johnson, "The Role of Cooperative Learning in Assessing and Communicating Student Learning," Chapter 4 in T. R. Guskey, ed., *Communicating Student Learning,* ASCD Yearbook (Alexandria, VA: Association for Supervision and Curriculum Development, 1996).

Goals	9–10 Consistently and actively helps identify group goals; works effectively to meet goals.	8 Consistently communicates commitment to group goals; carries out assigned roles.	7 Sporadically communicates commitment to group goals; carries out assigned role.	1–6 Rarely, if ever, works toward group goals or may work against them.
Interpersonal Skills	9–10 Cooperates with group members by encouraging, compromising, and/or taking a leadership role without dominating; shows sensitivity to feelings and knowledge of others.	8 Cooperates with group members by encouraging, compromising, and/or taking a leadership role.	7 Participates with group but has own agenda; may not be willing to compromise or to make significant contributions.	1–6 May discourage others, harass group members, or encourage off-task behavior. Makes significant changes to others' work without their knowledge or permission.
Quality Producer	9–10 Contributes significant information, ideas, time, and/or talent to produce a high-quality product.	8 Contributes information, ideas, time, and/or talent to produce a high-quality product.	7 Contributes some ideas, though not significant; may be more supportive than contributive; shows willingness to complete assignment but has no desire to go beyond average expectations.	1–6 Does little or no work toward the completion of group product; shows little or no interest in contributing to the task; produces work that fails to meet minimum standards for quality.
Participation	9–10 Attends daily; consistently and actively utilizes class time by working on the task.	8 Attends consistently; sends in work to group if absent; utilizes class time by working on the task.	7 Attends sporadically; absences/tardies may hinder group involvement; may send in work when absent; utilizes some time; may be off task by talking to others, interrupting other groups, or watching others do the majority of the work.	1–6 Frequent absences or tardies hinder group involvement; fails to send in work when absent; wastes class time by talking, doing other work, or avoiding tasks; group has asked that member be reproved by teacher or removed from the group.
Commitment	9–10 Consistently contributes time out of class to produce a high-quality product; attends all group meetings as evidenced by the group meeting log.	8 Contributes time out of class to produce a high-quality product; attends a majority of group meetings as evidenced by the group meeting log.	7 Willing to work toward completion of task during class time; attends some of the group meetings; may arrive late or leave early; may keep inconsistent meeting log.	1–6 Rarely, if ever, attends group meetings outside of class or may attend and hinder progress of the group; fails to keep meeting log.

FIGURE 5.6 Scoring rubric for assessing individual students in cooperative learning group projects. Explanation for use: Possible score = 50; scorer marks a relevant square in each of the five categories (horizontal rows), and student's score for that category is the small number in the top right corner within that square. For ranges 1–6 or 9–10 the teacher makes a single number selection based on his or her judgment. *Source:* Courtesy of Susan Abbott and Pam Benedetti, Elk Grove School District, Elk Grove, California.

Some Teachers Have Difficulty Using Cooperative Learning Groups.

Sometimes teachers have difficulty using CLGs and either give up trying to use the strategy or simply tell students to divide into groups for an activity and call it cooperative learning. As emphasized earlier, for the strategy to work, each student must be given training in and have acquired basic skills in interaction and group processing and must realize that individual achievement rests with that of their group. And, as is true for any other strategy, CLGs must not be overused—teachers must vary their strategies.

For CLGs to work well, advanced planning and effective management are a must. Students must be instructed in the necessary skills for group learning. Each student must be assigned a responsible role within the group and be held accountable for fulfilling that responsibility. And, when a CLG activity is in process, groups must be continually monitored by the teacher for possible breakdown of this process within a group. In other words, while students are working in groups, the teacher must exercise skills of with-it-ness. When a potential breakdown is noticed, the teacher quickly intervenes to help the group get back on track.

With practice and careful implementation of the guidelines as presented here, you will find that CLGs are very appropriate for assisting children in their learning of science, from discussing science to actually doing investigations.

 Whole-Class Discussion

Whole-class discussion is a technique frequently used in teaching. In deciding to use this strategy, there are certain questions you will want to ask yourself. Some of these are as follows.

For what reasons would I hold a whole-class discussion? When using a whole-class discussion, as opposed to small-group discussions or CLGs, a teacher has more precise control over the direction of the discussion, its content and outcome, and the time needed for completion. In addition, the teacher has greater assurance of involvement by certain students.

Patrick Whitley/Merrill

While learning science, children are encouraged to develop their research skills.

How can I arrange student seating in a classroom with movable seats? For a discussion that will last long enough to justify moving seats, you will probably want to arrange the students in a circle so each student can see every other student's face.

What ground rules should be established before starting the discussion? The first ground rule is that each student is to be listened to while talking. Talking is expected only when students are recognized by the teacher. An effort will be made to allow every student to speak to ensure that the discussion is not dominated by a few students. Adequate think time and response time will be allowed, but each speaker has a limited amount of time. When relevant, students are expected to have done their homework on the discussion topic.

Should student participation be forced? To maintain a nonthreatening classroom environment, student participation should not be forced.

How can I handle digression from the topic? Regardless of how thoroughly you plan your lessons, you can never predict with certainty where the lesson will go, nor should you expect to. A teacher must make many on-the-spot decisions, one of which is whether to allow a digression to continue. Sometimes you will want to allow digression; other times not. That is a professional decision that you are expected to be able to make. And remember, a good science teacher allows for serendipity but cannot plan for it.

Another consideration is your own role during a class discussion. For example, there may be a time during a whole-class discussion when you will want to turn the discussion leadership over to a student while you step aside to monitor it. Brainstorming can be a form of whole-class discussion, and your role during part of a brainstorming session might simply be that of recorder and monitor.

You will also have to decide on the sorts of activities that should precede a class discussion, and the activities that would be appropriate as follow-up to a whole-class discussion session. For example, an exploratory investigation might precede a discussion; student investigations, motivated by the discussion, might follow. Sometimes discussions follow or precede achievement testing.

Another decision that teachers invariably must make is whether students should be graded for their participation in class discussion. Why or why not? If so, how? On what basis? By whom? Our answer to this general question may not be entirely satisfactory to you, but here it is. Over the long term, we think, yes, students should be evaluated by the teacher on the basis of their participation in class discussions; but, no, they should not be given grades for every discussion. Knowing that they are being evaluated can create an artificial and less productive atmosphere.

 Equality in the Classroom: Ensuring Equity

Especially when conducting direct whole-group discussions, it is easy for a teacher to fall into the trap of interacting with only "the stars," or only those in the front of the room or on one side, or only the most vocal and assertive. You must exercise caution and avoid falling into that trap. To ensure a psychologically safe and effective environment for learning for every person in your classroom, you must attend to all students and try to involve all students equally in all class activities. You must avoid any biased expectations about certain students, and you must avoid discriminating against students according to their gender or some other personal characteristic.

You must avoid the unintentional tendency of teachers of *both* sexes to discriminate on the basis of gender. For example, teachers, along with the rest of society, tend to have lower expectations for girls than for boys in mathematics and science. They tend to call on and encourage boys more than girls. They often let boys interrupt girls but praise girls for being polite and waiting their turn. To avoid such discrimination may take special effort on your part, no matter how aware of the problem you may be.

To strive for equity in interaction with students, many teachers have found it helpful to ask a colleague or one of the students to secretly tally classroom interactions between the teacher and students during a class discussion. After an analysis of the results, the teacher arrives at decisions about his or her own attending and facilitating behaviors. The interaction analysis can be modified to include responses and their frequencies according to other teacher-student interactions, such as your calling on all students equally for responses to your questions, calling on students equally to assist you with classroom helping jobs, chastising students for their inappropriate behavior, or asking questions to assume classroom leadership roles.

In addition to the advice given in Chapter 4 about questioning, there are many other ways of ensuring that students are treated fairly in the classroom, including the following:

- Encourage students to demonstrate an appreciation for one another by applauding all individual and group presentations.
- Have and maintain high expectations, although not necessarily identical expectations, for all students.
- Insist on politeness in the classroom. For example, a student can be shown appreciation—such as with a sincere "Thank you" or "I appreciate your contribution," a whole-class applause, or a genuine smile—for her or his contribution to the learning process.
- Insist that students be allowed to finish what they are saying without being interrupted by others. Be certain that you model this behavior yourself.
- During large group instruction, insist that students raise their hands and be called on by you before they are allowed to speak.
- Keep a stopwatch handy to unobtrusively control the wait time given for each student. Although at first this idea may sound impractical, it works.
- Using a seating chart attached to a clipboard, make a tally for each interaction you have with a student next to his or her name. This is also a good way to maintain records to reward students for their contributions to class discussion. Again, it is workable at any grade level. The seating chart can be laminated so it can be used day after day simply by erasing the marks of the previous day.

 Demonstrations

Children like science demonstrations, both when performed by other children and when performed by the teacher, because the demonstrator is modeling scientific behavior and is actively engaged in a learning activity, rather than merely verbalizing about it. (Many demonstrations for science teaching are presented in the content section of Part Two of this book.) A demonstration can be designed to serve any of the following purposes: as a mind-capturing introduction to a lesson or unit of study, for a review, as an unusual closure to a lesson or unit of study, to assist in the recognition of a solution to an existing problem, to establish problem recognition, to give students opportunity for vicarious participation in active learning, to illustrate a particular point of content, to reduce potential safety hazards (in which the teacher demonstrates, using materials too dangerous for student use), to save time and resources (as opposed to the entire class doing that which is demonstrated), or to set up a discrepancy recognition.

Guidelines for Using a Demonstration

When planning a demonstration, consider the following guidelines.

1. Decide which is the most effective way to conduct the demonstration; that is, as a verbal or a silent demonstration, by a student (as a kind of science show and tell), by the teacher, by the teacher with a student helper, to the entire class or to small groups, or by a guest. An inquiry-based demonstration is usually much more effective than a teacher-centered procedure. Involve the students in the demonstration by asking them questions and allowing them to ask questions before, during, and after the demonstration.
2. Be sure that the demonstration is visible to all students.
3. Practice with the materials and procedure before demonstrating to the students; consider what

Alternate 1 Teachers often demonstrate static electricity by using plastic and glass rods with fur and silk cloths to move balloons and bits of paper. Students in upper-level elementary classrooms may already be familiar with this activity. The following demonstration, however, is one they may not have experienced. Suspend a large piece of lumber (an 8-foot 2-by-4 works well) on a string from the classroom ceiling, or balance the board on a large watch glass using a few drops of oil at the pivot point. Make sure the board is balanced and that it freely rotates. Hold a charged plastic rod (or a comb) near the end of the board. Voilà! The board moves toward the rod.

Alternate 2 Rub a rubber comb (or rubber rod), then hold the comb close to water running slowly from a faucet (or poured from a pitcher). The charge on the comb will cause the column of running water to bend toward the comb.

FIGURE 5.7 Alternate static electricity investigations.

might go wrong, because if anything can, it probably will.

4. Sometimes your students may have already experienced the demonstration that you had planned to do, and to prepare for that possibility, it is good to have an alternative demonstration ready. For example, see Figure 5.7 for an alternative demonstration dealing with static electricity.
5. Consider your pacing of the demonstration, allowing for enough wait-see and think time.
6. At the start of the demonstration, explain its purpose and the learning objectives. Remember the adage: Tell them what you are going to do, show them, then tell them what they saw. As with any lesson, plan your demonstration closure and allow time for questions and discussion.
7. During the demonstration, as in other types of teacher talk, stop frequently to check for student understanding and to allow time for student questions.
8. Consider the use of special lighting to highlight the demonstration. For example, a slide projector can be used as a spotlight.
9. Be sure that the demonstration table and area are free of unnecessary objects that could distract, be in the way, or pose a safety hazard.
10. With potentially hazardous demonstrations, consider using plastic containers, wearing safety goggles, having fire safety equipment at hand, or placing a protective shield between the demonstration table and nearby students.[19]

Learning from Assignments and Homework

An assignment is a statement of *what* the student is to accomplish and is tied to a specific instructional objective. Assignments, whether completed at home or at school, can ease student learning in many ways, but when poorly planned they can discourage the student and upset an entire family. *Homework* can be defined as any out-of-class task that a student is assigned as an extension of classroom learning. Like all else that you do as a teacher, it is your professional responsibility to think about and plan carefully any and all homework assignments you give to students.

Before giving students any assignment, consider how you would feel were you given the assignment, how you would feel were your own child given the assignment, about how much out-of-class time you expect the assignment to take, and to what extent, if any, parents and guardians should or could be involved in assisting the child in doing the assignment.

The time a student needs to complete assignments beyond school time will vary according to grade level and school policy. For elementary grades in particular, there seems to be ongoing debate about the value of homework.[20] Perhaps the issue is, or should be, not with the value of homework per se but with the quality of the homework that is assigned. Having said that, very generally, children in grades K–3 may be expected to spend from none to about 15 minutes each school night on homework, while children in grades 4–8 may spend an hour or more.

Purposes for Assignments

Purposes for giving homework assignments can be any of the following: to constructively extend the time that students are engaged in learning; to help students develop personal learning skills; to help students develop their research skills; to help students develop their study skills; to help students organize their learning; to individualize the learning; to involve parents, guardians, or other family members in the children's learning; to provide a mechanism by which students receive constructive feedback; to provide students with opportunity to review and

[19]For additional guidelines and an assessment rubric, see M. P. Freedman, "Using Effective Demonstrations for Motivation," *Science and Children 38*(1):52–55 (September 2000).

[20]See, for example, S. Black, "The Truth about Homework," *American School Board Journal 183*(10):48–51 (October 1996).

practice what has been learned; to reinforce classroom experiences; or to teach new content.

Guidelines for Using Assignments

To use assignments, consider the guidelines in the following paragraphs. While an assignment is a statement of *what* the student is to accomplish, procedures are statements of *how* to do something. Although students may need some procedural guidelines, especially with respect to your expectations on an assignment, generally you will want to avoid supplying too much detail on how to accomplish an assignment.

Plan early and thoughtfully the types of assignments you will give (e.g., daily and long-range; minor and major; in class, at home, or both; individual, paired, or group), and prepare assignment specifications. Assignments must correlate with specific instructional objectives and should *never* be given as busywork or as punishment. For each assignment, let students know what the objectives are; for example, whether the assignment is to prepare the student for what is to come in class, to practice what has been learned in class, or to extend the learning of class activities.

Use caution in giving assignments that could be controversial or that could pose a hazard to the safety of students. In such cases (especially if you are new to the community), before giving the assignment it is probably a good idea to talk it over with members of your teaching team, the grade-level or departmental chair, or an administrator. Also, for a particular assignment, you may need to have parental or guardian permission and even support, or be prepared to give an alternate assignment for some students.

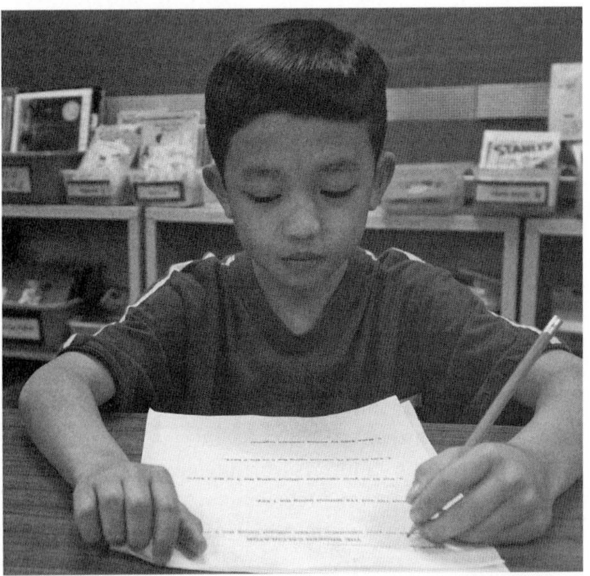

Patrick White/Merrill

Written work reinforces the learning process and helps children develop their skills in written expression.

Provide differentiated, tiered, or optional assignments—assignment variations given to students or selected by them on the basis of their interests and learning capacities.[21] Students can select or be assigned different activities to accomplish the same objective, such as reading and discussing, or participating with others in a more direct learning experience. After their study, as a portion of the assignment, students share what they have learned. This is an example of using multilevel teaching.

Teachers have found it beneficial to prepare individualized study guides with questions to be answered and activities to be done by the student while reading textbook chapters as homework. One advantage of a study guide is that it can make the reading more than a visual experience. A study guide can help to organize student learning by accenting instructional objectives, emphasizing important points to be learned, providing a guide for studying for tests, and encouraging the student to read the homework assignment.

Beginning teachers need to understand that not only can homework help students learn factual information, develop study skills, and involve parents or guardians as facilitators in their child's education, but it can also overwhelm students and cause them to dislike learning, encourage them to take shortcuts such as copying others' work, and prevent them from participating in extracurricular activities. Teachers sometimes underestimate just how long it will take a student to complete a homework assignment or how a particular assignment can disrupt the relationships in the child's home. With these considerations in mind, think carefully about all homework assignments before you make them.

Some students find homework and assignments very difficult, especially those students who have limited English proficiency or special needs, and those who have little to no support from home. It is important to consider differences between your cultural background and the cultural background of your students with any lesson, but since homework is intended to be taken home with a child, it is especially important. Many teachers use student volunteers to serve as homework helpers to assist other students both during class and after school by exchanging telephone numbers. In some schools, teachers also use older students and even paid college students and adults as mentors.

As a general rule, homework assignments should stimulate thinking by arousing a student's curiosity, raising questions for further study, and encouraging and supporting the self-discipline required for independent study. Homework should also offer the opportunity for parents and students to connect through school work.

---

[21]See, for example, M. H. Sullivan and P. V. Sequeira, "The Impact of Purposeful Homework on Learning," *Clearing House* 69(6):346–348 (July/August 1996).

Determine the resources that students will need to complete assignments, and check the availability of these resources. This is important; students can't be expected to use resources that are unavailable to them or not readily available.

Avoid yelling out assignments as students are leaving your classroom. When giving assignments in class, you should write them on a special place on the writing board, give a copy to each student, require that each student write the assignment into his or her assignment folder (an expectation in many schools), or include them in the course syllabus, taking extra care to be sure that assignment specifications are clear to students and allowing time for students to ask questions about an assignment. It's important that your procedure for giving and collecting assignments be consistent throughout the school year.

Students should be given sufficient time to complete their assignments. In other words, avoid announcing a new assignment that is due the very next day. As a general rule, all assignments should be given much longer than the day before they are due.

Although not always possible, try to avoid changing assignment specifications after they are given. Especially avoid changing them at the last minute. Changing specifications at the last minute can be very frustrating to students who have already completed the assignment, and it shows little respect for those students.

It is our opinion that time in class should be provided for students to begin work on homework assignments, so the teacher can give them individual attention (guided or coached practice). Your ability to coach students is *the reason* for in-class time to begin work on assignments. The benefits of this coached practice include being able to (a) monitor student work so that a student does not go too far in a wrong direction, (b) help students reflect on their thinking, (c) assess the progress of individual students, and (d) discover or create a teachable moment. For example, while monitoring students doing their work, you might discover a commonly shared student misconception. Then, taking advantage of this teachable moment, you stop and talk about it and attempt to clarify the misconception.

Timely, constructive, and corrective feedback on the homework from the teacher—and giving grades for completed homework—increases the positive contributions of homework. If the assignment is important for students to do, then you must give your full and immediate attention to the product of their efforts. Read almost everything that students write. Students are much more willing to do homework when they believe it is useful, when it is treated as an integral part of instruction, when it is read and evaluated by the teacher, and when it counts as part of the grade.

Provide feedback about each student's work, and be positive and constructive in your comments. Always think about the written comments that you make to be relatively certain they will convey your intended message to the student. When writing comments on student papers, consider using a color other than red, such as green or blue. Although to you this may sound trite, to many people, red brings with it a host of negative connotations (e.g., blood, hurt, danger, stop), and children often perceive it as punitive.

Most routine homework assignments should not be graded for accuracy, only for completion. Rather than giving a percentage or numerical grade, with its negative connotations, teachers often prefer to mark assignment papers with constructive and reinforcing comments and symbols they have created for this purpose.

When teaching science, or any other subject, you must still give attention to the development of students' reading, listening, speaking, and writing skills. Attention to these skills must also be obvious in your assignment specifications and your assignment grading policy. Reading is crucial to the development of a person's ability to write. For example, to foster high-order thinking, students should be encouraged to write (in their journals, as discussed later in this chapter) or draw representations of their thoughts and feelings about the material they have read.

Opportunities for Recovery

Using the concept of mastery (quality) learning would seem to us to necessitate a policy whereby students are able to revise and resubmit assignments for reassessment and grading. Although it is important to encourage good initial efforts by students, sometimes, for a variety of reasons, a student's first effort is inadequate or is lacking entirely. Perhaps the student is absent from school without a legitimate excuse, or the student does poorly on an assignment or turns it in late, or not at all. Although accepting late work from students is extra work for the teacher, and although allowing the resubmission of a marked or tentative-graded paper increases the amount of paperwork, many teachers report that it is worthwhile to give students an opportunity for recovery and a day or so to make corrections and resubmit an assignment for an improved score. However, out of regard for students who do well from the start, you are advised against allowing a resubmitted paper to receive an *A* grade (unless, of course, it was an *A* paper originally).

Some teachers and schools provide recovery methods that encourage students by recognizing both achievement and improvement on report cards and by providing students with second opportunities for success on assignments, although at some cost to encourage a good first effort.

Students sometimes have legitimate reasons for not completing an assignment by the due date. It is our opinion that the teacher should listen and exercise professional judgment in each instance. As someone once said, there is nothing democratic about treating unequals as equals. The provision of recovery options seems a sensible and scholastic tactic.

 Project-Centered Learning

When students have been well-prepared to direct their own study, the most meaningful learning occurs through independent study, individual writing, student-centered projects, and oral reports. There will be times when the students are interested in an in-depth inquiry of a topic and will want to pursue an independent study on that particular topic. This undertaking of a learning project can be flexible—an individual student, a team of two, a small group, or the entire class may carry out an investigation. The *project* is a relatively long-term investigative study from which students produce something called the culminating presentation. It is a way for students to apply what they are learning. The *culminating presentation* usually includes an oral and written report accompanied by a hands-on item of some kind (e.g., a display, play, or skit; book, song, or poem; multimedia presentation; diorama; poster; maps; or charts.

The values and purposes of encouraging project-centered learning are to develop individual skills in cooperation and social-interaction; develop student skills in writing, communication, and higher-level thinking and doing; foster student engagement, independent learning, and thinking skills; optimize personal meaning of the learning to each student by considering, valuing, and accommodating individual interests, learning styles, learning capacities, and life experiences; provide opportunity for each student to become especially knowledgeable and experienced in one area of subject content or in one process skill, thus adding to the student's knowledge and experience base and sense of importance and self-worth; provide opportunity for students to become intrinsically motivated to learn because they are working on topics of personal meaning, with outcomes and even time lines that are relatively open ended; provide opportunity for students to make decisions about their own learning and develop their skills in managing time and materials; and provide opportunity for students to make some sort of real contribution. As has been demonstrated time and again, when students choose their own projects, integrating knowledge as the need arises, motivation and learning follow naturally.[22]

Guiding Students in Project-Centered Learning

In collaboration with the teacher, students select a topic for the project. You can stimulate ideas and provide anchor studies—also called model or benchmark examples. You can stimulate ideas by providing lists of things students might do; by mentioning each time an idea comes up in class that this would be a good idea for an independent, small group, or class project; by having former students tell about their projects; by showing the results of other students' projects; by suggesting Internet resources and readings that are likely to give students ideas; and by using class discussions to brainstorm ideas.

Sometimes a teacher will write the general problem or topic in the center of a graphic web and ask the students to brainstorm some questions. The questions will lead to ways for students to investigate, draw sketches, construct models, record findings, predict items, compare and contrast, and discuss understandings. In essence, brainstorming such as this is the technique often used by teachers in collaboration with students for the selection of an interdisciplinary thematic unit of study.

Allow students to individually choose whether they will work alone, in pairs, or in small groups. If they choose to work in groups, then help them delineate job descriptions for each member of the group. For project work, groups of four or fewer students usually work better than groups of more than four. Even if the project is one the whole class is pursuing, the project should be broken down into parts with individuals or small groups of students undertaking independent study of these parts.

It is important to keep track of students' progress by reviewing a weekly update of their work, setting deadlines with the groups, or meeting with groups daily to discuss any questions or problems they have. Based on their investigations, the students prepare and present their findings in culminating presentations. One important thing to keep in mind is that students must be well-prepared before undertaking such a project. The variations from Level I to Level III described in Table 5.1 are an indication of how such preparation may be accomplished.

Provide coaching and guidance. Work with each student or student team in topic selection, as well as in the processes of written and oral reporting. Allow students to develop their own procedures, but guide their preparation of work outlines and preliminary drafts, giving them constructive feedback and encouragement along the way. Aid students in their identification of potential resources and in the techniques of research. Your coordination with the library and other resource centers is central to the success of project-centered teaching. Frequent drafts and progress reports from the students are a must. With each of these stages, provide students with constructive feedback and encouragement. Provide

---

[22]See, for example, D. K. Meyer et al., "Challenge in a Mathematics Classroom: Students' Motivation and Strategies in Project-Based Learning," *Elementary School Journal* 97(5):501–521 (May 1997); and C. McCullen, "In Project-Based Learning, Technology Adds a New Twist to an Old Idea," *Middle Ground* 3(5):7–9 (April 2000).

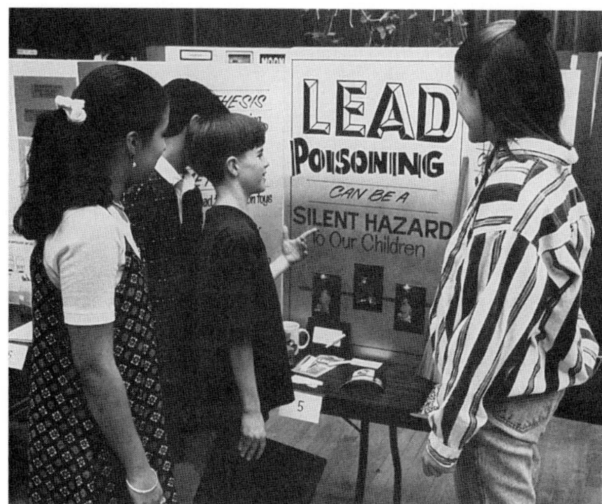

Scott Cunningham/Merrill

Children should be given ample opportunity to present their ideas, opinions, and knowledge gained from their own individual and small-group investigations.

written guidelines and negotiate time lines for the outlines, the drafts, and the completed project.

Promote sharing. Insist that students share both the progress and the results of their study with the rest of the class. The amount of time allowed for this sharing will, of course, depend upon many variables. The value of this type of instructional strategy comes not only from individual contributions but also from the learning that results from the experience, and the communication of that experience with others. For project work and student sharing of the outcomes of their study, some teachers have their students use the KWHLS strategy, which is a modified version of the well-known KWL strategy (see Chapter 6). Using the KWHLS strategy, the student identifies what he or she already *K*nows about the topic of study, *W*hat he or she wants to learn, *H*ow the student plans to learn it, what he or she *L*earned from the study, and how the student will *S*hare with others what he or she has learned from the study.

Without careful planning, and unless students are given steady guidance, project-based teaching can be a frustrating experience for both the teacher and the students, and especially for a beginning teacher who is inexperienced in such an undertaking. Students should do projects because they want to and because the project seems meaningful. Therefore, students should decide with guidance from you *what* project to do and *how* to do it. Your role is to advise and guide students so they experience success. If the teacher lays out a project in too much detail, that project is a procedure rather than a student-centered project. There must be a balance between structure and opportunities for student choices and decision making. Without frequent progress reporting by the student, and guidance and reinforcement from the teacher, a student can get frustrated and quickly lose interest in the project.

Provide options but insist that writing (or drawing) be a part of each student's work. Research examining the links among writing, thinking, and learning has helped emphasize the importance of writing. Writing is a complex intellectual behavior and process that helps the learner create and record his or her understanding—that is, to construct meaning.

When teachers use project-centered teaching, a paper and an oral presentation are usually required of all students. It is recommended that you use the *I-Search paper* instead of the traditional research paper. Under your careful guidance, the student (a) lists things he or she would like to know and, from the list, selects one that becomes the research topic; (b) conducts the study while maintaining a log of activities and findings, which, in fact, becomes a process journal; (c) prepares a booklet that presents his or her findings and that consists of paragraphs and visual representations; (d) prepares a summary of the findings including the significance of the study and his or her personal feelings; and (e) shares the project as a final oral report with the teacher and classmates.

At least for children of grades 4 and up, the final product of the project, including papers, oral reports, and presentations, should be graded. The method of determining the grade should be clear to students from the beginning, as well as the weight of the project grade toward each student's term grade. Provide students with clear descriptions (rubrics) of how evaluation and grading will be done. Evaluation should include meeting deadlines for drafts and progress reports. The final grade for the study should be based on four criteria: (a) how well it was organized, including meeting draft deadlines; (b) the quality and quantity of both content and procedural knowledge gained from the experience; (c) the quality of the student's sharing of that learning experience with the rest of the class; and (d) the quality of the student's final written or oral report. (See Figures 8.5 and 8.12, in Chapter 8, for a checklist form and rubric, respectively, for use in assessing a student's oral presentation.)

Sometimes what began as a science project can become an ongoing permanent endeavor with many spin-off projects of shorter duration. For example, what began as a science classroom project at W.H. English Middle School (Scottsburg, IN) has become the largest animal refuge shelter in the Midwest. While nursing animals back to health, the students study them and learn about environmental policies. Over the years, students in the program have shared their work by making presentations in 10 states and as guests of the International Animal Rights Convention in Russia.[23]

---

[23]J. Arnold, "High Expectations For All: Perspective and Practice," *Middle School Journal* 28(3):52 (January 1997).

Student Journals

Many teachers have their students maintain journals in which the students keep a log of their activities, findings, and thoughts (i.e., *process journal,* as discussed previously) and write and draw their thoughts about what they are studying (*response journal*). Actually, two types of response journals are commonly used: dialogue journals and reading-response journals. *Dialogue journals* are used for students to write anything that is on their minds, usually on the right side of a page. Peers, teachers, and parents or guardians respond on the left side, thereby "talking with" the journal writer. *Response journals* are used for students to write (and perhaps draw—a visual learning log) their reactions to whatever is being studied.

Normally, academic journals are *not* the personal diaries of the writer's recollection of daily events and the writer's thoughts about the events. Rather, the purpose of journal writing is to encourage students to write, to think about their writing, to record their creative thoughts about *what they are learning,* and to share their written thoughts with an audience—all of which helps in the development of their thinking skills, in their learning, and in their development as writers. Students are encouraged to write about experiences, both in school and out, that are related to the topics being studied. They should be encouraged to record their feelings about what and how they are learning.

Journal writing provides practice in expression and should *not* be graded by the teacher. Negative comments and evaluations from the teacher will discourage creative and spontaneous expression by students. Teachers should read the journal writing and then offer constructive and positive feedback, but teachers should avoid negative comments or grading the journals. For grading purposes, most teachers simply record whether or not a student does, in fact, maintain the required journal.

Integrating Strategies for Integrated Learning

In today's exemplary K–8 classrooms, instructional strategies are combined to establish the most effective teaching-learning experience. For example, in an integrated language arts program, teachers are interested in their students' speaking, reading, listening, thinking, study, and writing skills. These skills (and not textbooks) form a holistic process that is the primary aspect of integrated language arts.

In the area of speaking skills, oral discourse (discussion) in the classroom has a growing research base that promotes methods of teaching and learning through oral language. These methods include cooperative learning, instructional scaffolding, and inquiry teaching.

In cooperative learning groups, students discuss and use language for learning that benefits both their content learning and their skills in social interaction. Working in heterogeneous groups, students participate in their own learning and can extend their knowledge base and cultural awareness with students of different backgrounds. When students share information and ideas, they are completing difficult learning tasks, using divergent thinking and decision making, and developing their understanding of concepts. As issues are presented and responses are challenged, student thinking is clarified. Students assume the responsibility for planning within the group and for carrying out their assignments. When needed, the teacher models an activity with one group in front of the class; when integrated with student questions, the modeling can become inquiry teaching. Activities can include any of a variety of heuristics (a heuristic is a tool used in solving a problem or understanding an idea), such as the following, some of which you will recognize from Chapter 3 as science process skills:

Brainstorming. Members generate ideas related to a key word and record them. Clustering or chunking, mapping, and the Venn diagram (all discussed in this section) are variations of brainstorming.

Chunking or clustering. Groups of students apply mental organizers by clustering information into chunks for easier manipulation and remembering.

Comparing and contrasting. Similarities and differences between items are found and recorded.

Inferring. For instance, students assume the roles of people (real or fictional) and infer their motives, personalities, and thoughts.

Memory strategies. The teacher and students model the use of acronyms, mnemonics, rhymes, or clustering of information into categories to promote learning. Sometimes, such as in memorizing one's social security number, one must learn by rote information that is not connected to any prior knowledge. To do that, it is helpful to break the information to be learned into smaller chunks, such as dividing the nine-digit social security number into smaller chunks of information that are separated by hyphens. Learning by rote is also easier if you can connect that which is to be memorized to some prior knowledge. Strategies such as these are used to bridge the gap between rote learning and meaningful learning and are known as *mnemonics.* Sample mnemonics are

- The periods of the Paleozoic era are *C*ave *d*wellers *o*bject *s*trenuously *d*uring *m*ost *p*olite *p*arties (Cambrian, Ordovician, Silurian, Devonian, Mississippian, Pennsylvanian, and Permian).
- The hierarchy of the biological classification system is *K*indly *p*rofessors—or *d*octors—*c*an *o*nly *f*ail *g*reedy *s*tudents (kingdom, phylum—or division—class, order, family, genus, and species).

Outlining. Each group completes an outline that contains some of the main ideas but with subtopics omitted.

Paraphrasing. In a brief summary, each student restates a short selection of what was read or heard.

Reciprocal teaching. In classroom dialogue, students take turns at summarizing, questioning, clarifying, and predicting.[24]

Review. While frequent review of material being learned is essential, it is most effective when the students are actively involved in planning and implementing the review as opposed to their being passive respondents to a review conducted by the teacher.[25]

Study strategies. Important strategies that should be taught explicitly include vocabulary expansion; reading and interpreting graphic information; locating resources; using advance organizers; adjusting one's reading rate; and skimming, scanning, and study reading.[26]

Think-pair-share. The teacher presents a concept, and students are paired to discuss the concept. They share what they already know or have experienced about the concept, and then share that information with the rest of the class. This strategy is an excellent technique for preassessing and discovering students' prior notions and *naïve views* (i.e., misconceptions) in science.

Visual tools. A variety of terms have been invented for the visual tools useful for learning (some of which are synonymous) such as brainstorming web, cluster, cognitive map, conflict map, graphic organizer, mindmapping web, semantic map, spider map, thinking process map, Venn diagram, and visual scaffold. Visual tools are separated into three categories according to purpose: (a) *brainstorming tools* (such as mindmapping, webbing, and clustering) for the purpose of developing one's knowledge and creativity; (b) *task-specific organizers* (such as life-cycle diagrams used in biology, decision trees used in mathematics, and text structures used in reading); and (c) *thinking process maps* for encouraging cognitive development across disciplines.[27] It is the latter in which we are interested here.

Based on Ausubel's theory of meaningful learning,[28] thinking process mapping has been found useful for helping students to change prior notions—their naïve views. It can help students in their ability to organize and to represent their thoughts, as well as to connect new knowledge to their past experiences and precepts.[29] Simply put, and as we said in Chapter 2, concepts can be thought of as classifications that organize the world of objects and events into a smaller number of categories. In everyday usage, the term *concept* means idea, as when someone says, "My concept of love is not the same as yours." Concepts embody a meaning that develops in complexity with experience and learning over time. For example, the concept of love that is held by a second grader is unlikely to be as complex as that held by an eleventh grader. Thinking process mapping is a graphical way of demonstrating the relationship between and among concepts.

Typically, a thinking process map refers to a visual or graphic representation of concepts with bridges (connections) that show relationships. Figure 5.8 shows a partially complete thinking process map where students have made connections of concept relationships related to fruit farming and marketing. The general procedure for thinking process mapping is to have the students (a) identify important concepts in materials being studied, often by circling those concepts; (b) rank order the concepts from the most general to the most specific; and (c) arrange the concepts on a sheet of paper, connect related ideas with lines, and define the connections among the related ideas.

Vee mapping. A kind of V-shaped road map is completed by students as they learn, showing the route they follow from prior knowledge to new and future knowledge.

Venn diagramming. This is a technique for comparing two concepts or, for example, two stories, to show similarities and differences. Using stories as an example, a student is asked to draw two circles that intersect and to mark the circles one and two and the area where they intersect three. In circle one, the student lists characteristics of one story, and in circle two she or he lists the characteristics of the second story. In the area of the intersection, marked three, the student lists characteristics common to both stories.

---

[24]See A. S. Palincsar and A. L. Brown, "Reciprocal Teaching: Activities to Promote Reading with Your Mind," in T. L. Harris and E. J. Cooper, eds., *Reading, Thinking and Concept Development: Strategies for the Classroom* (New York: The College Board, 1985); C. J. Carter, "Why Reciprocal Teaching?" *Educational Leadership 54*(6):64–68 (March 1997); and R. J. Marzano, D. J. Pickering, and J. E. Pollock, *Classroom Instruction That Works* (Alexandria, VA: Association for Supervision and Curriculum Development, 2001).

[25]P. Wolfe, *Brain Matters: Translating Research into Classroom Practice* (Alexandria, VA: Association for Supervision and Curriculum Development, 2001), 187–188.

[26]J. S. Choate and T. A. Rakes, *Inclusive Instruction for Struggling Readers*, Fastback 434 (Bloomington, IN: Phi Delta Kappa Educational Foundation, 1998.

[27]D. Hyerle, *Visual Tools for Constructing Knowledge* (Alexandria, VA: Association for Supervision and Curriculum Development, 1996).

[28]D. P. Ausubel, *The Psychology of Meaningful Learning* (New York: Grune & Stratton, 1963).

[29]About thinking process mapping, see J. D. Novak, "Concept Maps and Vee Diagrams: Two Metacognitive Tools to Facilitate Meaningful Learning," *Instructional Science 19*(1):29–52 (1990); and E. Plotnick, *Concept Mapping: A Graphical System for Understanding the Relationship Between Concepts*, ED407938, 1997.

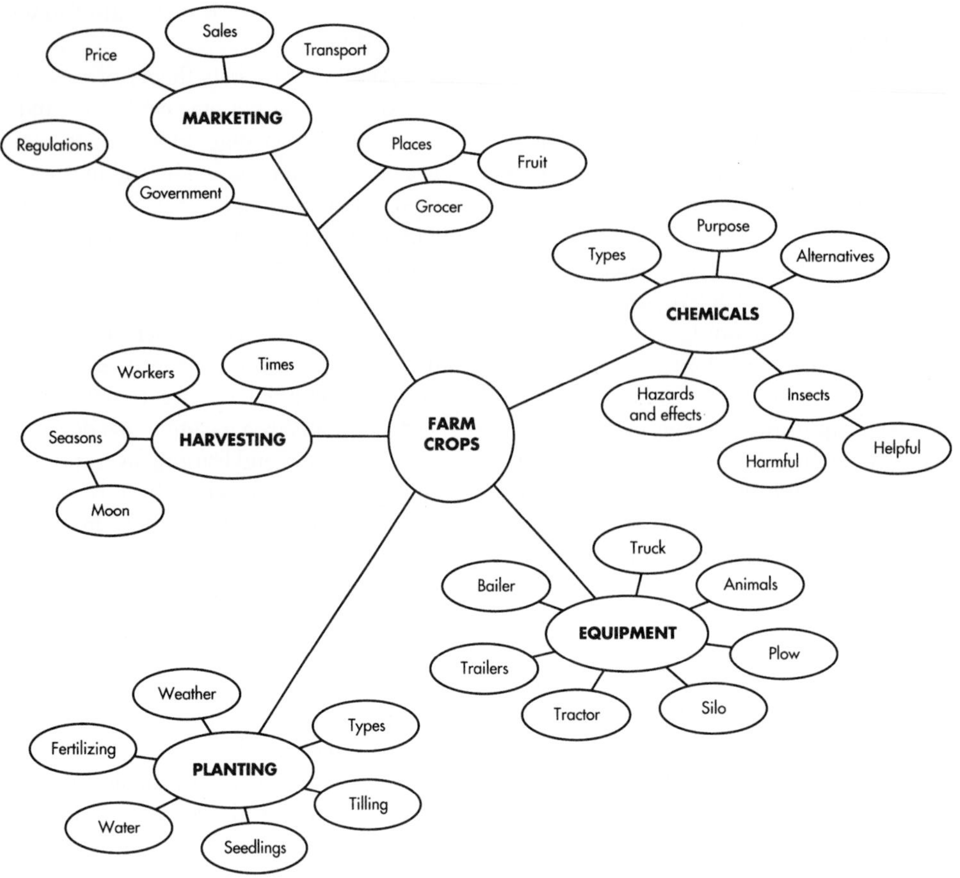

FIGURE 5.8 Sample of partially completed thinking process map.

Visual learning log (VLL). This is another kind of road map completed by students showing the route they follow from prior knowledge to new and future knowledge, except that the VLL consists of pictograms (free-form drawings) that each student makes and that are maintained in a journal.

Summary

In this chapter we have completed our presentation of specific strategies for teaching. However, methods in the absence of media and other resources would be bland and boring indeed. For teaching science, there are a large variety of aids and resources from which you can select. Before completing plans for instruction (Chapter 7), you must consider the resources that are available to you and to the children for the content and processes to be learned by the children. Those resources are the topic of the next chapter.

Questions for Class Discussion

1. Recall your own K–8 schooling. What do you really remember? Most likely you remember projects, your presentations, the lengthy research you did and your extra effort doing art work to accompany your presentation. Maybe you remember a compliment by a teacher or a pat on the back by peers. Most likely you do *not* remember the massive amount of factual content that was covered. Discuss this and your feelings about it with your classmates.
2. Divide into teams and have each team build a working learning center for teaching science at a particular grade level. Share your centers with the rest of the class.

3. When facilitating students' understanding of a particular science concept, should the teacher first assess what the students already know or think they know about it? Explain why or why not. If so, explain how you would do it. Identify a specific science concept and demonstrate how you would teach toward an understanding of that concept to students in the first, fourth, and sixth grades.
4. Describe any reservations you have about teaching science via inquiry. Share those reservations with your classmates.
5. Explain the concept of multilevel teaching. Describe a situation in which you would use it in teaching science for a particular group of children.
6. Identify any concepts you held that changed as a result of your experiences with this chapter. Describe the concepts and changes.

Chapter 6

Selecting and Using Media and Other Instructional Aids and Resources

Patrick White/Merrill

Teachers make the available science tools, materials, media, and technological resources accessible to students.[1]

Tools for helping students construct their understandings are available and exist in a large variety of useful and effective media, aids, and resources. However, the sheer quantity of different materials available can be overwhelming—textbooks, supplementary texts, pamphlets, anthologies, paperbacks, encyclopedias, tests, programmed instructional systems, dictionaries, reference books, classroom periodicals, newspapers, films, records and cassettes, computer software, transparencies, realia, games, filmstrips, audio- and videotapes, slides, globes, manipulatives, CD-ROMs, DVDs, and graphics. You could spend a great deal of time reviewing, sorting, selecting, and practicing with these materials and tools to pick what works best for you. Although nobody can make the job easier for you, information in this chapter may expedite the process.

Additionally, in January of each year the National Science Teachers Association (NSTA) publishes *NSTA Science Education Suppliers*, a supplement to *Science and Children, Science Scope,* and *The Science Teacher.* The supplement provides a current list of publishers and descriptions of their products, including textbooks, program and resource materials, and trade books, as well as equipment, software, and other media. You can browse the supplement online via the Internet at http://www.nsta.org/scisupp, and you can purchase it directly from the NSTA.

Printed Materials, The Internet, and Visual Displays

Historically, of all the materials available for science instruction, the printed textbook has had, and still has, the most influence on teaching and learning. In addition to the student textbook and perhaps an accompanying workbook, there is a vast array of other printed materials available for teaching science—many without cost. Printed materials might be books, workbooks, pamphlets, magazines, brochures, newspapers, professional journals, periodicals, and duplicated materials, including those copied from Internet sources.

In reviewing printed materials, be alert for (a) appropriateness of the material in both content (for example, the material should show no bias toward gender, race, ethnicity, socioeconomic status, or disabilities) and in reading level; (b) articles in newspapers, magazines, and periodicals related to the content that your students will be studying or to the skills they will be learning; (c) workbooks from tradebook publishers that emphasize thinking and problem solving rather than rote memorization—with an assortment of workbooks available so you can have students working on similar but different assignments depending upon their interests and abilities—an example of multilevel teaching; (d) pamphlets, brochures, and other duplicated materials that students can read for specific information and viewpoints about particular topics; and (e) inexpensive paperback books that would provide multiple book readings for your class and that make it possible for students to read primary sources.

Student Textbooks

For several reasons—recognition of the diversity of learning styles, capacities, and modalities of students; changing concepts about literacy and habits of thought; enhanced graphics capabilities; economic pressures in the publishing industry; and the availability of electronic and other nonprinted materials—textbook appearance, content, and use has changed in recent years and in all likelihood will continue to change.

Within the span of your teaching career, you will likely witness and even be a part of a revolution in the continuing redesign of school textbooks. Some schools already allow teachers in certain disciplines to choose between traditional printed textbooks and interactive

[1]Reprinted from National Research Council, *National Science Education Standards*, © 1996 by the National Academy of Sciences, 44. Courtesy of National Academy Press, Washington, DC.

David Mager/Pearson Learning Photo Studio

While learning science, children use a variety of printed material and other resources. Reading materials that are carefully selected and used appropriately can inspire students to read and facilitate student learning.

computer programs. With the continuing developments in electronics and microcomputer chip technology, textbooks may take on a whole new appearance. With that will come dramatic changes in the importance and use of text as well as new problems for the teacher—some that are predictable, others that we can't even imagine. On the positive side, it is probable that the classroom teacher will have a variety of textbooks available to better address the reading levels, interests, abilities, and perhaps even the primary language of individual students. With these changes, the distribution and maintenance of reading materials could create a greater demand on the teacher's time. Regardless, dramatic and exciting events have begun to affect the teaching tool that had not changed much throughout the 20th century. The textbook of the future may become a palm-size, hand-held, multimedia, interactive, personal tool that encompasses digitized text, sound, and video and allows for global communications.

Still, today, printed textbooks may regulate as much as 90% of all science learning activity in the classroom. School districts periodically adopt new textbooks (usually every 5 to 8 years). If you are a student teacher or a first-year teacher, this will most likely mean that someone will tell you, "Here are the books you will be using."

It is unlikely that anyone could rationally argue that textbooks are of no benefit to student learning in science. Textbooks can provide (a) an organization of basic or important content for the students, (b) a basis for deciding content emphasis, (c) previously tested activities and suggestions for learning, (d) information about other readings and resources to enhance student learning, and (e) a foundation for building higher-order thinking activities (e.g., inquiry discussions and student research) that help develop critical thinking skills. The textbook, however, should not be the "be all and end all" of instructional experiences.

The student textbook is only one of many teaching tools, and not the ultimate word. Of the many ways textbooks can be used for student learning, the *least* acceptable is to show a complete dependence on a single book and require students simply to memorize material from it. This is the lowest level of textbook use and learning; furthermore, it implies that these teachers are unaware of other significant resources and have nothing more to contribute to student learning.

Another potential problem brought about by reliance upon a single textbook is that because textbook publishers prepare books for use in a larger market—that is, for national or statewide use—a state- and district-adopted book may not adequately address issues of special interest and importance to the community in which you teach. That is one reason some teachers and schools provide supplementary printed and electronic resources.

Still another problem brought about by reliance upon a single source is that the adopted textbook may not be at the appropriate reading level for many of the students.[2] In today's heterogeneous classrooms, the level of student reading can easily vary by as much as two-thirds of the chronological age of the students. This means that if the chronological age is 9 years (typical for fourth-graders), then the reading-level range would be 6 years. Some students might be reading at the first-grade level and others at the seventh-grade level.

Generally speaking, students benefit by having their own copies of a textbook in the current edition. However, because of budget constraints, this may not always be possible. The book may be outdated; quantities may be limited. When the latter is the case, students may not be allowed to take the books home or may only be allowed to do so occasionally. In some high-poverty-area schools, in particular, students are not allowed to take textbooks from the classroom. In other classrooms, because of inadequate funding there may be no textbook at all.

Encourage students to respect books by covering and protecting them and not marking in them. In many schools this is a rule; at the end of the term, students who have damaged or lost their books are charged a fee. This is why books are not issued at all in some high-poverty areas. If students lose or damage their books and are charged a fee, neither the students nor their parents/guardians can afford to pay it.

In some school districts, there are *two* sets of textbooks—one set for use in the classroom and another set

---

[2]See, for example, I. Chavkin, "Readability and Reading Ease Revisited: State-Adopted Science Textbooks," *Clearing House 70*(3): 151–154 (January–February 1997).

Maria B. Vonada/Merrill

Science textbooks can provide children with important content organization and resources in learning science.

that is assigned to students for studying at home. With that arrangement, students don't have to carry heavy books around in their backpacks. The paragraphs that follow offer general guidelines for using the textbook as a learning tool.

Progressing through a textbook from the front cover to the back in one school term is not necessarily an indicator of good teaching. The textbook is one resource; to enhance their learning, students should be encouraged to use a variety of resources. Encourage students to search additional sources to update the content of the textbook. This is especially important in certain disciplines such as the sciences and social sciences, where the amount of new information is growing rapidly and students may have textbooks that are several years old. Students should use the library and Internet to research the latest information on certain subjects, always keeping in mind, however, that just because something is found in print or on the Internet doesn't mean that the information is accurate or even true. Maintain supplementary reading materials for student use in the classroom. School and community librarians and resource specialists are usually delighted to cooperate with teachers in the selection and provision of such resources.

Individualize the learning for students of various reading abilities. Consider differentiated reading and workbook assignments in the textbook and several supplementary sources (see multitext and multireadings approaches). Except to make life simpler for the teacher, there is no advantage in having all students working out of the same book and exercises. Some students benefit from the drill, practice, and reinforcement afforded by workbooks or software programs that accompany textbooks, but this is not true for all students, nor do all benefit from the same activity. In fact, traditional printed workbooks may eventually be

- ***KWL:*** Students recall what they already know (K) about a topic, determine what they want to learn (W), and later assess what they have learned (L).
- ***KWLQ:*** Students record what they already know about a topic (K), formulate questions about what they want to learn about the topic (W), search for answers to their questions to learn (L), and ask questions for further study (Q).
- ***POSSE:*** *Predict* ideas, *organize* ideas, *search* for structure, *summarize* main ideas, and *evaluate* understanding.
- ***PQRST:*** *Preview, question, read, state* the main idea, *test* yourself by answering the questions you posed earlier.
- ***RAP:*** *Read* paragraphs, *ask* questions about what was read, and *put* in your own words.
- ***Reciprocal teaching:*** Students are taught and then practice the reading skills of summarizing, questioning, clarifying, and predicting.
- ***SQ3R:*** *Survey* the chapter, ask *questions* about what was read, *read, recite,* and *review.*
- ***SQ4R:*** *Survey* the chapter, ask *questions* about what was read, *read* to answer the questions, *recite* the answers, *record* important items from the chapter into their notebooks, then *review* it all.
- ***SRQ2R:*** *Survey, read, question, recite,* and *review.*

FIGURE 6.1 Methods for helping students develop their higher-level thinking skills and their comprehension of expository material.[3]

replaced by software-based workbooks. Computers and other interactive media provide students with a psychologically safer learning environment where they have greater control over the pace of the instruction. Students can repeat instruction parts of lessons and ask questions without the fear of having to do so publicly.

Teachers have invented several methods to help students develop their higher level thinking skills and their comprehension of expository material. Some of these methods are shown in Figure 6.1.

[3]Source of KWL: D. M. Ogle, "K-W-L: A Teaching Model That Develops Active Reading of Expository Text," *Reading Teacher 39*(6):564–570 (February 1986). Source of POSSE: C. S. Englert and T. V. Mariage, "Making Students Partners in the Comprehension Process: Organizing the Reading 'POSSE'," *Learning Disability Quarterly 14*(1):23–138 (September 1991). Source of PQRST: E. B. Kelly, *Memory Enhancement for Educators*, Fastback 365 (Bloomington, IN: Phi Delta Kappa Educational Foundation, 1994), 18. Source of RAP: J. B. Schumaker et al., *The Paraphrasing Strategy* (Lawrence, KS: Edge Enterprises, 1984). Source of SQ3R: F. P. Robinson, *Effective Study*, rev. ed. (New York: Harper & Brothers, 1961). The original source of SQ4R is unknown. For SRQ2R, see M. L. Walker, "Help for the 'Fourth-Grade Plump'—SRQ2R Plus Instruction in Text Structure or Main Idea," *Reading Horizons* 36(1):38–58 (1995). About reciprocal teaching, T. L. Good and J. E. Brophy, *Looking in Classrooms*, 8th ed. (New York: Addison Wesley Longman, 2000), 431–433.

Encourage students to be alert for errors in the textbook, both in content and in printing—perhaps giving them some sort of credit reward, such as points, when they bring an error to your attention. This helps students develop the skills of critical reading, critical thinking, and healthy skepticism.

The Internet

Originating from a Department of Defense project in 1969 (called ARPANET) to establish a computer network of military researchers, its successor, the federally funded Internet, has become an enormous, steadily expanding, worldwide system of interconnected computer networks. The Internet provides literally millions of resources to explore, with thousands more added nearly every day. Today you can surf the Net and find a variety of resources in an instant. You can walk into almost any bookstore and find hundreds of recent titles, most of which give their authors' favorite Websites. New technologies are steadily emerging, and the Internet changes every day. Some sites and resources disappear or are not kept current; others change their locations or undergo reconstruction, as new ones appear. Therefore, in this book, which will be around for a few years, it would be superfluous for us to make too much of sites that we personally have viewed and can recommend as teacher resources. Nevertheless, the listing at the end of this chapter shows Internet resources that we have recently accessed and can recommend. Perhaps you have found others that you can share with your classmates.

If you have yet to learn to use the Internet, we leave the mechanics of that to the many resources and people available to you. Learning how to use the Internet starts with trying. The remaining pages of this section address the *how* of using the Internet from an academic perspective. Let's begin with the fictitious although feasible "Natural Disasters" scenario illustrated in the accompanying box.

To the natural disasters scenario, there are both a desirable aspect and a not-so-desirable aspect. It was good that the students used a worthy technological tool (the Internet) to research a variety of sources, including many primary ones. But when they published their document on the Internet and made copies of their guide to be sold, without obtaining permission from original copyright holders, they were infringing on copyright law. Although it would take an attorney to say for sure, it is probable that the students, teacher, school, and school district would be liable. As is true for other documents (such as published photos, graphics, and text), unless there is a clear statement that materials taken from the Internet are public domain, it

Classroom Scenario

Natural Disasters

Let us suppose that the students from your "house" have been working most of the year on an interdisciplinary thematic unit titled "Surviving Natural Disasters." As a culmination of their study they published a document titled *Natural Disaster Preparation and Survival Guide for (name of their community)* and proudly distributed the guide to their parents and members of the community.

Long before preparing the guide, however, the students had to do research. To learn about the history of various kinds of natural disasters that had occurred or might occur locally and about the preparations a community should make for each kind of disaster, students searched sources on the Internet such as federal documents, scientific articles, and articles from newspapers from around the world where natural disasters had occurred. They also searched in the local library and the local newspaper's archives to learn about floods, tornadoes, and fires that had occurred during the past 200 years. Much to their surprise, they also learned that their community is located very near the New Madrid Fault and did, in fact, experience a serious earthquake in 1811, but none since. As a result of that earthquake, two nearby towns completely disappeared. In addition, the Mississippi River flowed in reverse, and its course changed and even caused the formation of a new lake.

From published and copyrighted sources, including Websites, the students found many useful photographs, graphics, and articles, which they included in whole or in part in their *Natural Disaster Preparation and Survival Guide*. They did so without obtaining permission from the original copyright holders or even citing those sources.

You, the other members of your teaching team, and other people were so impressed with the students' work that the students were encouraged to offer the document for publication on the school's Website. In addition, because the document was received with so much acclaim, the students decided to place it for sale in local retail outlets. This would help defray the original cost of duplication and enable them to continue to supply the guides.

is advisable to assume that they are copyrighted and therefore should not be republished for profit or placed on another Website without adhering to copyright laws.

There is a proliferation of information today, from both printed materials and the Internet. Except for obviously reliable sites such as the *New York Times* (http://www.nytimes.com) and the Library of Congress (http://www.loc.gov), how can a person determine the validity and currency of a particular piece of information? When searching for useful and reliable information on a particular topic, how can one avoid wasting valuable time sifting through all the information? People need to know that just because information is found on a printed page or is published on the Internet doesn't necessarily mean that the information is accurate or current. Using a checklist, such as the one found at http://lib.nmsu.edu/instruction/eval.html, and using examples of materials that meet and do not meet the criteria of the checklist, students can learn how to assess materials and information found on the Internet.

Teaching students how to access and assess Websites adds to their repertoire of skills for lifelong learning. Consider allowing each student or team of students to become experts on specific sites during particular units of study. It might be useful to start a chronicle of student-recorded log entries about particular Websites to provide comprehensive long-term data about those sites.

When students use information from the Internet, require that they print copies of sources of citations and materials so you can check for accuracy. These copies may be maintained in their portfolios.

Student work published on the Internet should be considered intellectual material and be protected from plagiarism by others. You might also be interested in knowing that the prevention of student plagiarism of materials found on the Internet is a service offered to teachers by several Internet providers.[4]

Most school districts post a copyright notice on their home page. Usually, someone at the school or from the district office is assigned to supervise the school Website to see that district and school policy and legal requirements are observed.

Professional Journals and Periodicals

Figure 6.2 lists examples of the many professional periodicals and journals that can provide useful teaching ideas and Website information and that carry information about instructional materials and how to get them. Some of these may be in your university or college library and be accessible through Internet sources. Check there for these and other titles of interest to you.

AIMS Magazine
Air & Space/Smithsonian
The American Biology Teacher
American Teacher
Audubon
Childhood Education
Connect
The Earth Scientist
Education in Science
Issues in Science and Technology
Journal of Geoscience Education
National Geographic
National Wildlife
Natural History
Nature Magazine
Odyssey
Popular Science
Primary Science Review
Ranger Rick
School Science and Mathematics
School Science Review
Science
Science Activities
Science and Children
Science Is Elementary
Science Scope
The Science Teacher
Scientific American
Sky and Telescope
Smithsonian
Weatherwise
Young Children

FIGURE 6.2 Selected professional journals and periodicals for science teachers.

- *Assessment and Evaluation.* University of Maryland, College Park, Department of Measurement, Statistics, and Evaluation, 1129 Shriver Laboratory, College Park, MD 20742. URL: http://ericae.net
- *Disabilities and Gifted Education.* The Council for Exceptional Children (CEC), 1920 Association Drive, Reston, VA 20191-1589. URL: http://ericec.org
- *Reading, English, and Communication.* Indiana University, Smith Research Center, 2805 East 10th Street, Suite 140, Bloomington, IN 47408-2698. URL: http://reading.Indiana.edu?
- *Science, Mathematics, and Environmental Education.* Ohio State University, 1929 Kenny Road, Columbus, Ohio 43210-1080. URL: http://www.ericse.org

FIGURE 6.3 Selected ERIC addresses.

The ERIC Information Network

The Educational Resources Information Center (ERIC) system, established by the United States Office of Education, is a widely used network providing access to information and research in education. Selected clearinghouses and their addresses are shown in Figure 6.3.

Copying Printed Materials

As a teacher, you must be familiar with the laws about the use of copyrighted materials, both printed and non-printed, including those obtained from sources on the Internet. Even though there is no notice on many Web pages, the material is still copyrighted. Copyright law

[4]See, for example, L. Renard, "Cut and Paste 101: Plagiarism and the Net," *Educational Leadership* 57(4):38–42 (December 1999/January 2000).

Permitted Uses—You May:

1. Make single copies of:
   A chapter of a book
   An article from a periodical, magazine, or newspaper
   A short story, short essay, or short poem whether or not from a collected work
   A chart, graph, diagram, drawing, cartoon
   An illustration from a book, magazine, or newspaper
2. Make multiple copies for classroom use (not to exceed one copy per student in a course) of:
   A complete poem of fewer than 250 words
   An excerpt from a longer poem, but not to exceed 250 words
   A complete article, story, or essay of fewer than 2,500 words
   An excerpt from a larger printed work (not to exceed 10 percent of the whole or 1,000 words)
   One chart, graph, diagram, cartoon, or picture per book or magazine issue

Prohibited Uses—You May Not:

1. Copy more than one work or two excerpts from a single author during one class term (semester or year)
2. Copy more than three works from a collective work or periodical volume during one class term
3. Reproduce more than nine sets of multiple copies for distribution to students in one class term
4. Copy to create, replace, or substitute for anthologies or collective works
5. Copy "consumable" works (e. g., workbooks, standardized tests, or answer sheets)
6. Copy the same work year after year

FIGURE 6.4 Guidelines for copying printed materials that are copyrighted. *Source:* Section 107 of the 1976 Federal Omnibus Copyright Revision Act.

protects original material; that is just as true for the intellectual property created by a minor as it is for that of an adult.

Although space here prohibits full inclusion of U.S. legal guidelines, your local school district should be able to provide a copy of current district policies for compliance with copyright laws. District policies should include guidelines for teachers and students on publishing materials on the Internet. If no district guidelines are available, adhere to the guidelines concerning printed materials shown in Figure 6.4.[5]

When preparing to make a copy, you must find out whether the law permits the copying under the category of "permitted use." If not, you must obtain written permission from the holder of the copyright to reproduce the material. If the address of the source is not given on the material, it might be obtained from various references, such as *Literary Market Place, Audio-Visual Market Place,* and *Ulrich's International Periodicals Directory.*

[5]See also the Copyright and Fair Use Website of Stanford University, at http://fairuse.stanford.edu.

The Classroom Writing Board

As is true for an auto mechanic or a brain surgeon or any other professional, a teacher needs to know when and how to use the tools of the trade. One of the tools available to almost every classroom teacher is the writing board.

Writing boards were, and in some schools still are, slate blackboards (slate is a type of metamorphic rock). In today's classroom, the writing board might be a painted plywood board (chalkboard); however, these too, are becoming obsolete, at least in part because of concern about the dust created from using chalk. Most common are white or colored (light green and light blue are common) *multipurpose dry-erase boards* on which you write with special marking pens and erase with any soft dry cloth. In addition to providing a surface where you can write and draw, the multipurpose board can be used as a projection screen and as a surface where figures cut from colored transparency film will stick. It may also have a magnetic backing.

An *electronic whiteboard* can transfer information written on it to a connected computer monitor, which in turn can save the material as a computer file. The electronic whiteboard uses special electronic *markers* and *erasers* with optically encoded sleeves that enable the device to track their position on the board. The data are then converted into a display for the computer monitor that can be printed, cut and pasted into other applications, sent as an e-mail or fax message, or networked to other sites.

Each day, each class, and even each new idea should begin with a clean board, except for announcements that have been placed there by you or another teacher. At the end of each class, clean the board, especially if another teacher follows you in that room, which is simple professional courtesy. It may seem trivial at first, but a stray mark left behind from previously written material can cause a great deal of confusion among students.

The use of colored chalk or marking pens to highlight your board talk is very effective. This is especially helpful for students with learning difficulties. Beginning at the top left of the board, print or write neatly and clearly, with the writing intentionally positioned to indicate content relationships (e.g., causal, oppositional, numerical, comparative, or categorical).

Use the writing board to acknowledge acceptance and to record student contributions. Print instructions for an activity on the board, in addition to giving them orally. At the top of the board frame you may find clips for hanging posters, maps, and charts.

It is important to be aware of your board presence. Are you blocking your students' view of what you are writing on the board? Are you saying what you are saying for students to hear what they may not be able to see? Learn to use the board without turning your back entirely on students and without blocking their view of the board. When you have a lot of material to put on the board, do it before class and then cover it. Better yet, put the material on transparencies and use the overhead projector rather than the board, or use both. Be careful not to write too much information. Most importantly, take your time going over the writing on the board. Many times, students are copying furiously and paying no attention to what you are saying, when what you are saying is actually more important that the notes on the board. Keep in mind that the purpose of writing board is to focus students' attention; it is not designed to replace a teacher's words or a class discussion.

The Classroom Bulletin Board

Bulletin boards also are found in nearly every classroom, and, although sometimes poorly used or not used at all, they can be relatively inexpensively transformed into attractive and valuable instructional tools. Among other uses, the bulletin board is a convenient location for posting reminders, assignments, schedules, and commercially produced materials, and to celebrate and display model student work and anchor papers.

Some teachers use student assistants or committees, giving them guidance and responsibility for planning, preparing, and maintaining bulletin board displays. When preparing a bulletin board display, keep these guidelines in mind: The display should be simple, emphasizing one main idea, concept, topic, or theme; captions should be short and concise; illustrations can accent learning topics; verbs can vitalize the captions; phrases can punctuate a student's thoughts; and alliteration can announce anything you wish on the board. Finally, as in all other aspects of the classroom learning environment, remember to ensure that the board display reflects gender and ethnic equity.

 The Community as a Resource

One of the richest resources for learning is the local community and the people and places in it. You will want to build your own file of community resources—speakers, sources for free materials, and field trip locations. Your school may already have a community resource file available for your use. However, it may need updating. A community resource file (see Figure 6.5) should contain information about (a) possible field trip locations, (b) community resource people who could serve as guest speakers or mentors, and (c) local agencies that can provide information and instructional materials.

Airport
Apiary
Aquarium
Archeological site
Bakery
Bird and wildlife sanctuary
Bookstore
Broadcasting and TV station
Canal lock
Chemical plant
Dairy
Dam and floodplain
Dock and harbor
Farm
Fire department
Fish hatchery
Forest and forest preserve
Gas company
Geological site
Health department and hospital
Historical sites and monuments
Industrial plant
Levee and water reservoir
Library and archive
Mine
Museum
Native American Indian reservation
Observatory
Oil refinery
Park
Recycling center
Sanitation department
Sawmill or lumber company
Shoreline (stream, lake, wetland, ocean)
Telecommunications center
Utility company
Water reservoir and treatment plant
Weather bureau and storm center
Wetlands area
Wildlife park and preserve
Zoo

FIGURE 6.5 Community resources for speakers, materials, and field trips related to science.

There are many ways to use community resources to aid children in learning science. Here, the discussion is limited to three often used, although sometimes abused, instructional tools: (a) home-school-community connections, (b) guest speakers, and (c) out-of-classroom and off-campus excursions, commonly called *field trips*.

Home and School Connections

It is well known that parental and family involvement in a child's education can have a positive impact on the student's achievement at school. For example, when parents or guardians of at-risk students get involved, the student benefits with more consistent attendance at school, more positive attitudes and actions, better grades, and higher test scores. Recognizing the positive effect parent and family involvement has on student achievement and success, the National PTA published National Standards for Parent/Family Involvement Programs.[6]

Although not all schools have a parent organization, many schools have adopted formal policies about home

[6]See P. Sullivan, "The PTA's National Standards," *Educational Leadership* 55(8):43–44 (May 1998).

and community connections. These policies usually emphasize that parents/guardians should be included as partners in the educational program, and that teachers and administrators will inform parents/guardians about their child's progress, about the school's family involvement policy, and about any programs in which family members can participate. Some schools are members of the National Network of Partnership 2000 Schools. Schools' efforts to foster parent/guardian and community involvement are as varied as the people who participate. They include (a) student-teacher-parent contracts and assignment calendars sometimes available via the school's Web page on the Internet, (b) home visitor programs, (c) involvement of community leaders in the classroom as mentors, aides, and role models, (d) newsletters, workshops, and electronic hardware and software for parents/guardians to help facilitate their children's learning, (e) homework hotlines, (f) regular phone calls and personal notes home about a student's progress, (g) enrollment of not only students but of entire families as members of a learning team, and (h) involvement of students in community service learning.

Service Learning

With service learning, students learn and develop through active participation in thoughtfully organized and curriculum-connected experiences that meet community needs.

For example, elementary school children of the Powder River County School District (Broadus, MT) adopted community flower gardens and conduct an annual food drive for the needy. At Great Falls Middle School (Montague, MA), students research and produce television documentaries on subjects related to energy. The documentaries are broadcast on the local cable channel to promote energy literacy in the school and community. Students at Baldwyn Middle School (Baldwyn, MS) plan and care for the landscaping of the local battlefield/museum.

Professional Resources File

Community members, geographic features, buildings, monuments, historic sites, and other places in a school's geographic area constitute some of the richest instructional laboratories that can be imagined. To take advantage of this accumulated wealth of resources, as well as to build school-community partnerships, once hired by a school you should start a file of community resources. For instance, you might include files about the skills of the students' parents and other family members, noting those that could be resources for the study occurring in your classroom. You might also include files on various resource people who could speak to the class, on free and inexpensive materials, on sites for field trips, and on what other communities of teachers, students, and adult helpers have done. It is a good idea to start your professional resources file now, and to maintain it throughout your professional career; for that, see Figure 6.6.

Telecommunications Networks

To guide their students toward becoming autonomous thinkers, effective decision makers, and life-long learners, and to make their classrooms more student-centered, collaborative, interdisciplinary, and interactive, teachers are increasingly turning to telecommunications networks and to the community. See, for example, the vignette, "Interdisciplinary Thematic Instruction at West Salem Middle School." Webs of connected computers allow teachers and students from around the world to reach each other directly and gain access to quantities of information previously unimaginable. Students using networks learn and develop new inquiry and analytical skills in a stimulating environment, and gain an increased appreciation of their role as world citizens. For a sample lesson plan illustrating student use of the Internet, see Figure 7.3 (Chapter 7).

A professional resources file is a project you could begin now and continue throughout your professional career. Begin your resources file either on a computer database program or on color-coded file cards listing (1) name of resource, (2) how and where to obtain the resource, (3) how to use the resource, and (4) evaluative comments about the resource.

Organize the file in a way that makes the most sense to you now. Cross-reference or color-code your system to accommodate the following categories of instructional aids and resources.

- Articles from print sources
- Compact disc titles
- Computer software titles
- Games
- Guest speakers and other community resources
- Internet resources
- Media catalogs
- Motivational ideas
- Pictures, posters, graphs
- Resources to order
- Sources of free and inexpensive materials
- Student worksheets
- Test items
- Thematic units and ideas
- Unit and lesson plans and ideas
- Videocassette titles
- Videodisc titles
- Miscellaneous

FIGURE 6.6 Beginning my professional resources file.

CLASSROOM VIGNETTE

Interdisciplinary Thematic Instruction at West Salem Middle School*

What began as an isolated, single-grade, telecommunications-dependent project for students at West Salem Middle School (Wisconsin) eventually developed into a longer-term, cross-grade interdisciplinary program of students and adults working together to design and develop a local nature preserve. Students began their adventure by interacting with explorer Will Steger as he led the International Arctic Project's first training expedition. Electronic online messages via the Internet allowed students to receive and send messages to Will and his team in real time. Students delved into the Arctic world, researching the physical environment and the intriguing wildlife, reading native stories and novels about survival, keeping their own imaginary expedition journals, learning about the impact of industrialized society on the Arctic, and conversing with students from around the world. But something very important was missing—a connection between the students' immediate environment and the faraway Arctic.

West Salem Middle School's focus became the local 700-acre Lake Neshonoc, an impoundment of the LaCrosse River, a tributary of the Mississippi. Although many students had enjoyed its recreational opportunities, they had never formally studied the lake. The Neshonoc Partners, a committee of parents, community leaders, teachers, students, and environmentalists, was established to assist in setting goals, brainstorming ideas, and developing the program for a year's study of the lake. Right from the start, students showed keen interest in active involvement in the project. A second committee, involving parents, students, and the classroom teacher, met during lunch time on a weekly basis to allow for more intensive discussions about the lake and the overall project.

The team of teachers brainstormed ideas to further develop an interdisciplinary approach to the study of Lake Neshonoc. Special activities, including an all-day winter survival adventure, gave students a sense of what the real explorers experienced. Students learned about hypothermia, winter trekking by cross-country skiing, and building their own snow caves.

For several weeks, students learned about the ecosystem of Lake Neshonoc through field experiences led by local environmentalists and community leaders. Guest speakers told their stories about life on the lake and their observations about the lake's health. Student sketchbooks provided a place to document personal observations about the shoreline, water testing, animal and plant life, and value of the lake. From these sketchbooks, the best student creations were compiled to create books to share electronically with students who had similar interests in Russia, Canada, Missouri, South Carolina, Nevada, Wisconsin, and Washington, DC. The opportunity to share findings about their local watershed sparked discussions about how students can make a difference in their own community. Comparative studies gave students a chance to consider how humans and nature impact other watersheds.

West Salem students worked with the local County Parks and Recreation Department to assist in developing a sign marking the new County Park where the nature sanctuary would reside. Students brainstormed design ideas and then constructed a beautiful redwood sign with the help of a local technical educational teacher. Today the sign is a symbol of the partnership that has been established between the students and the community. It is a concrete reminder that together we can work for the common good of the community and the environment. Students celebrated the study of the lake with a closure. Will Steger, along with community leaders, parents, school board members, and staff, commended the students for what is sure to be the start of a long and enduring relationship—a partnership created out of common respect and appreciation for the value of our ecosystem.

**Source:* J. Wee, "The Neshonoc Project: Profiles in Partnership," *World School for Adventure Learning Bulletin* (Fall 1993):2–3. Adapted by permission.

Guest Speakers

Bringing outside speakers into your classroom can be a valuable educational experience for students, but not automatically so. In essence, guest speakers can be classified within a spectrum of four types, two of which should not be used: (a) the speaker is both informative and inspiring; (b) the speaker is inspiring but with nothing substantive to offer, except for the possible diversion it might offer from the usual rigors of classroom work; (c) the speaker is informative but boring to students; or (d) at the worst end of the spectrum, the speaker is both boring and uninformative. So, just like any other instructional experience, to make a guest speaker experience most effective takes careful planning on your part. To make sure that the experience is beneficial to student learning, consider the following guidelines.

- If at all possible, meet and talk with the guest speaker in advance to inform the speaker about your students and your expectations for the presentation, and to gauge how motivational and informative the speaker might be. If you believe the speaker might be informative but boring, then perhaps you can help structure the presentation in some way to make the presentation a bit more inspiring. For example, stop the speaker every few minutes and involve the students in questioning and discussions of points made.
- Prepare students in advance with key points of information that you expect students to obtain.

◆ Prepare students in advance with questions to ask the speaker, things the students want to find out, and information you want them to inquire about.

◆ Follow up the presentation with a thank-you letter to the guest speaker and perhaps further questions that developed during class discussions subsequent to the speaker's presentation.

Field Trips

What is the most memorable field trip that you were ever on as a student? What made it memorable? You might want to discuss these questions and others like them with your colleagues.

Today's schools often have very limited funds for the transportation and liability costs for field trips. In some cases, there are no funds at all. Sometimes parent-teacher groups, businesses, and civic organizations provide financial resources so students can get the valuable first-hand experiences that field trips so often provide.

To prepare for and implement a successful field trip, there are three important stages of planning—before, during, and after—and critical decisions to be made at each stage. Consider the following guidelines.

Before the Field Trip

When the field trip is your idea (and not the students') discuss the idea with your teaching team, principal, or department chair (especially when transportation will be needed) *before* mentioning the idea to your students. There is no cause served by getting students excited about a trip before you know if it is feasible.

Once you have obtained the necessary, but tentative, approval from school officials, take the trip yourself (or with team members), if possible. A previsit allows you to determine how to make the field trip most productive and what arrangements will be necessary. You might consider taking a couple of your students along on this previsit for their ideas and help. If a previsit is not possible, you still will need to arrange for travel directions; arrival and departure times; parking; briefing by the host, if there is one; storage of students' personal items, such as coats and lunches; provisions for eating and rest rooms; and fees, if any.

If there are fees, you need to talk with your administration about who will pay the fees. If the trip is worth taking, the school should cover the costs. If that is not possible, perhaps students can plan a fundraising activity, or financial assistance can be obtained from some other source. If this does not work, you might consider an alternative experience that does not involve costs.

Arrange for official permission from the school administration. This usually requires a form for requesting, planning, and reporting field trips. After permission has been obtained, you can discuss the field trip with your students and arrange for permissions from their parents or guardians. Although parents or guardians sign official permission forms allowing their children to participate in the trip, these only show that the parents or guardians are aware of what will take place and give their permission for their child to participate. The permission form should include a statement that the parent or guardian absolves the teacher and the school from liability should an accident occur, but that *does not* lessen the teacher's and the school's responsibilities should there be negligence by a teacher, driver, or chaperone.

Arrange for students to be excused from their other classes while on the field trip. Using an information form prepared and signed by you and perhaps by the appropriate administrator, the students should then assume responsibility for notifying their other teachers of the planned absence from classes or other school activities and assure them that they will make up whatever work is missed. In addition, you will need to make arrangements for your own teaching duties to be covered. In some schools, teachers cooperate by filling in for those who will be gone. In other schools, substitute teachers are hired. Sometimes teachers have to hire their own substitutes.

Arrange for whatever transportation is needed. Your principal, or the principal's designee, will help you with the details. In many schools, someone else does this. In any case, the use of private automobiles is ill-advised, because you and the school could be liable for the acts of the drivers.

Arrange to collect money for fees. If there are out-of-pocket costs to be paid by students, this information needs to be included on the permission form. No students should ever be excluded from the field trip because of a lack of money. This can be a tricky issue, because there may be students who would rather steal the money for a field trip than say they don't have it. Try to anticipate problems; perhaps the school or some organization could pay for the trip so that fees need not be collected from students and, thus, potential problems of this sort are avoided.

Plan details for monitoring student safety from departure to return. Included should be a first-aid kit and a system of student control, such as a buddy system whereby students must remain paired throughout the trip. The pairs sometimes are given numbers that are recorded and kept by the teacher and the chaperones, checked at departure time, periodically during the trip, at the time of return, and again upon return. Use adult chaperones. As a very general rule, there should be one adult chaperone for every 10 students. Some districts have a policy regarding this. While on a field trip, all students should at all times be under the direct supervision of a responsible and trustworthy adult.

Plan the complete route and schedule, including any stops along the way. If transportation is being provided, you will need to discuss the plans with the provider.

Plan on taking a fully charged cell phone. Given the ubiquity of cell phones, this is not likely to be an issue for most teachers. Cell phones are no longer considered a luxury item by many.

Establish and discuss, to the extent you believe necessary, the rules of behavior your students should follow. Included in this might be details of the trip, its purpose, directions, what they should wear and bring, academic expectations of them (consider, for example, giving each student a study guide), and follow-up activities. Also include information about what to do if anything should go awry; for example, if a student is late for the departure or return, loses a personal possession along the way, gets lost, is injured, becomes sick, or misbehaves. *Never* send a misbehaving student back to school alone, for example, via the city's transit system or a taxi.

Involve the adult chaperones in the previsit discussion. All of this information should also be included on the parental permission form.

If a field trip is meant to promote some kind of learning, as is probably the case, the learning expectations need to be clearly defined to avoid leaving the learning to chance. The students should be given an explanation of how and where they may encounter the learning experience. Before the field trip, students should be asked questions such as, "What do we already know about ______ ?" "What do we want to find out about ______ ?" "How can we find out?" and then, with their assistance, an appropriate guide can be prepared for the students to use during the field trip.

To further ensure learning and individual student responsibility for that learning, you may want to assign different roles and responsibilities to students, just as you would in cooperative learning, assuring that each student has a role with responsibility.

You may want to take recorders and cameras, so the field trip experience can be relived and shared in class upon return. If so, roles and responsibilities for the equipment and its care and use can be assigned to students as well.

During the Field Trip

If your field trip has been carefully planned according to the preceding guidelines, it should be a valuable and safe experience for all. En route, while at the trip location, and on the return to school, you and the adult chaperones should monitor student behavior and learning, just as you would in a classroom setting.

After the Field Trip

Plan the follow-up activities. As with any other lesson plan, the field trip lesson is complete only when there is both a proper introduction and a well-planned closure. All sorts of follow-up activities can be planned as an educational wrap-up to this educational experience. For example, a bulletin board committee can plan and prepare an attractive display summarizing the trip. Students can write about their experiences in their journals or as papers. Small groups can give oral reports sharing what they did and learned. Their reports can then serve as springboards for further class discussion, and perhaps further investigations. Finally, for future planning, all who were involved should contribute to an assessment of the experience.

 Media Tools

A whole category of instructional tools depends upon electricity to project light and sound and to focus images on screens. Included are projectors of various sorts, computers, CD-ROMs, sound recorders, video recorders, and DVDs. The aim here is *not* to provide instruction on how to operate modern equipment but to help you develop a philosophy for using it and to provide strategies for using media tools in your teaching. Consequently, to conserve space in this book, other than the overhead projector, we devote no attention to traditional AV equipment, such as film, opaque, and slide projectors. There are staff members on any school faculty who will gladly assist you in locating and using those tools.

It is important to remember that the role of media tools is to aid student learning, not to teach *for* you. You must still select the objectives, orchestrate the instructional plan, tweak the instruction according to the needs of individual students, assess the results, and follow up the lessons, just as you have learned to do with various other instructional strategies. If you use media tools prudently, your teaching and the students' learning will benefit. Like a competent brain surgeon or a competent auto mechanic, a competent teacher knows when and how to select and use the right tools at the right time. Would you want your child operated on by a surgeon who was unfamiliar with the tools used in surgery? The education of youth should be no less important.

When Equipment Malfunctions

When using media equipment, it is usually best to set up the equipment and have it ready to go before students arrive. That helps avoid problems in classroom management that can occur when there is a delay because the equipment is not ready. After all, if you were a surgeon ready to begin an operation and your tools and equipment weren't ready, your patient's life would likely be placed in extra danger. Like any other competent professional, a competent teacher is ready when the work is to begin.

Of course, delays may be unavoidable when equipment breaks down or a videotape breaks. Remember "Murphy's law" that says if anything can go wrong, it will? It is particularly relevant when using audiovisual equipment. You want to be prepared for such emergencies. Effectively planning for and responding to this eventuality is part of your system of movement management and takes place during the preactive stage of your planning (see Chapter 7). That preparation includes consideration of a number of factors.

When equipment malfunctions, three principles should be kept in mind: (a) you want to avoid dead time in the classroom, (b) you want to avoid causing permanent damage to equipment, and (c) you want to avoid losing content continuity of a lesson. So, what do you do when equipment breaks down? Again, the answer is: Be prepared for the eventuality.

If a projector bulb goes out, quickly insert another. That means that you should have an extra bulb on hand. As simplistic as this seems, when the bulb goes, unless you have a replacement bulb, so goes an effective part of the lesson. If a tape breaks, you can do a quick temporary splice with cellophane tape. That means that tape should be readily available. If you must do a temporary splice, do it on the film or videotape that has already run through the machine rather than on the end yet to go through, so as not to mess up the machine or the film. Then, after class or after school, be sure to notify the person in charge of the tape that a temporary splice was made, so it can be permanently repaired before its next use. If the computer screen freezes during direct, whole-class instruction, you should probably quickly move to an alternate activity. If it is during multilevel instruction, you can probably take the time to treat this as a teachable moment. While maintaining your classroom with-it-ness, show the student who is working on the computer what to do, which probably would be simply how to restart the computer.

If, during surgery, a patient's cerebral artery suddenly and unexpectedly breaks, the surgeon and the surgical team are ready for that eventuality and make the necessary repair. If while working on an automobile a part breaks, the mechanic gets a replacement part. If, while teaching, a computer program freezes or aborts, a fuse blows, or for some other reason you lose power, and you think there will be too much dead time before the equipment is working again, go to an alternate lesson plan. You have probably heard the expression "go to Plan B." It is a useful phrase meaning that without missing a beat in the lesson and to accomplish the same instructional objective or another objective, you immediately and smoothly switch to an alternate learning activity. For you, the beginning teacher, it does not mean that you must plan *two* lessons for every one, but that when planning a lesson that uses media equipment, you should plan an alternative activity, just in case. Then, you can move your students into the planned activity quickly and smoothly.

Anthony Magnacca/Merrill

The overhead projector is an important teaching tool.

The Overhead Projector

In addition to a writing board and a bulletin board, nearly every classroom is equipped with an overhead projector. The overhead projector is a versatile, effective, and reliable teaching tool, especially for teaching and learning science. Except for the bulb burning out, not much else can go wrong with an overhead projector. There is no film to break or program to crash.

The overhead projector projects light through objects that are transparent (see Figure 6.7). A properly functioning overhead projector usually works quite well in a fully lit room. Truly portable overhead projectors are available that can be carried easily from place to place in their compact cases.

Other types of overhead projectors include rear-projection systems that allow the teacher to stand off to the side rather than between students and the screen, and overhead video projectors that use video cameras to send images that are projected by television monitors. Some schools use overhead video camera technology that focuses on an object, pages of a book, or a demonstration, while sending a clear image to a video monitor with a screen large enough for an entire class to clearly see.

In some respects, the overhead projector is more practical than the writing board, particularly for a beginning teacher who is nervous. Using the overhead projector rather than the writing board can help avoid tension by decreasing the need to pace back and forth to the board. And by using an overhead projector rather than a writing board, you can maintain both eye contact and physical proximity with students, both of which are important for maintaining classroom control.

As with any projector, find the best place in your classroom to position it. If there is no classroom

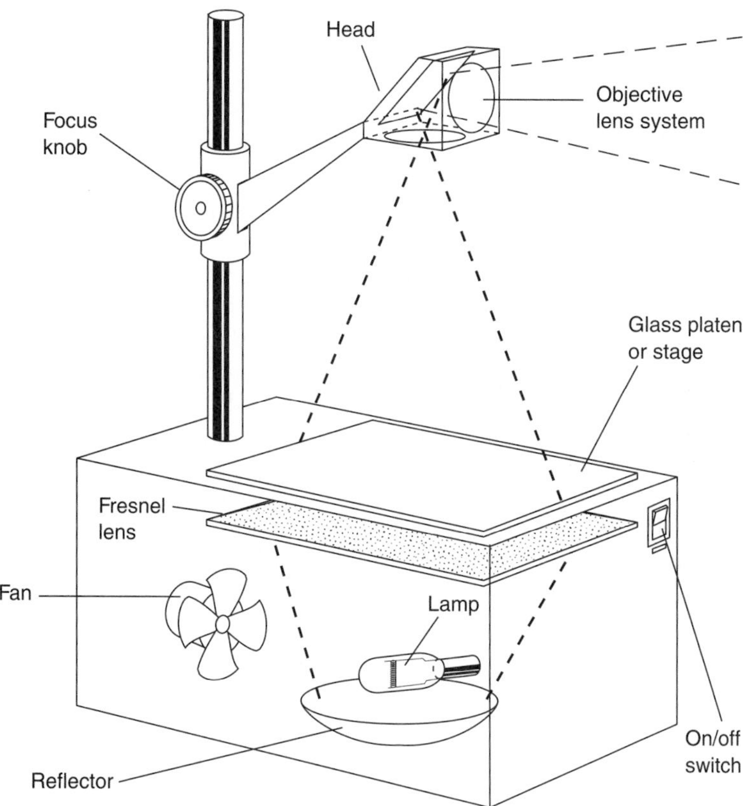

FIGURE 6.7 Overhead projector, cutaway view.

To preserve the life of the projector's bulb, it is best not to move the projector until the bulb has cooled. In addition, bulbs will last longer if you avoid touching them with your fingers.

For writing on overhead projector transparencies, ordinary felt-tip pens are not satisfactory. Select a transparency-marking pen available at office supply stores. The ink of these pens is water-soluble, so be careful that your hand does not rest on the transparency or you will have ink smudges on your transparency and on your hand. Non-water-soluble pens—permanent markers—can be used, but the transparency must be cleaned with an alcohol solvent or a plastic eraser. When using a cleaning solvent, you can clean and dry with paper toweling or a soft rag. To highlight the writing on a transparency and to organize student learning, use pens in a variety of colors. Transparency pens tend to dry out quickly, and they are relatively expensive, so the caps must be taken on and off frequently, which is something of a nuisance when working with several colors. Practice writing on a transparency, and also practice making overlays. You can use an acetate transparency roll or single sheets of flat transparencies. Flat sheets of transparency come in different colors—clear, red, blue, yellow, and green—which can be useful in making overlays; for example, to illustrate parts of a flower.

Some teachers prepare lesson outlines in advance on transparencies, which allows more careful preparation of the transparencies and means that they are then ready for reuse at another time. Some teachers use an opaque material, such as a three-by-five notecard, to block out prewritten material and then uncover it at the moment it is being discussed. For permanent transparencies, you will probably want to use permanent marker pens, rather than water-soluble ones that smudge easily. Heavy paper frames are available for permanent transparencies. Marginal notes can be written on the frames. Personal computers with laser printers and thermal processing (copy) machines, probably located in the teacher's workroom or in the school's main office, can also be used to make permanent transparencies.

Other transparent objects can be shown on an overhead projector, such as Petri dishes, transparent rulers, protractors, and clear glass dishes; even opaque objects can be used if you want simply to show silhouette. Calculators, too, are available specifically for use on the overhead projector, as is a screen that fits onto the platform and is circuited to a computer, so whatever is displayed on the computer monitor is also projected onto the classroom screen.

projection screen, you can hang white paper or a sheet, or use a white multipurpose board or a white or near-white wall.

Have you ever attended a presentation by someone who was not using an overhead projector properly? It can be frustrating to members of an audience when the image is too small, out of focus, partially off the screen, or partially blocked from view by the presenter. To use this teaching tool in a professional manner

◆ *Turn on the projector (the switch is probably on the front) and place it so that the projected white light covers the entire screen and hits the screen at a 90-degree angle, then focus the image to be projected.*

◆ *Face the students while using the projector.* The fact that you do not lose eye contact with your audience is a major advantage of using the overhead projector rather than a writing board. What you write as you face your students will show up perfectly (unless it is out of focus or off the screen).

◆ *Lay the pencil flat onto the transparency with the tip of the pencil pointing to the detail being emphasized* rather than tilting the pencil, using your finger to point to detail, or pointing directly to the screen (thereby turning away from your students).

◆ *To lessen distraction, turn the overhead projector off when you want the students to shift attention back to you.*

Commercial transparencies are available from a variety of school supply houses. For sources, check the catalogs in your school office or at the audiovisual and resources centers in your school district.

The overhead projector can also be used to trace transparent charts or drawings into larger drawings on paper or on the writing board. The image projected onto the screen can be made smaller or larger by moving the projector closer or farther away, respectively, and then traced when you have the size you want. Also, an overhead projector (or a filmstrip projector) can be used as a light source (spotlight) to highlight demonstrations or presentations by you or by students.

Multimedia Program

A multimedia program is a collection of teaching/learning materials involving more than one type of medium and organized around a single theme or topic. The types of media involved vary from rather simple kits—perhaps a videotape, a game, activity cards, student worksheets, and a manual of instructions for the teacher—to very sophisticated packages involving building-level site licensed computer software, student handbooks, reproducible activity worksheets, classroom wall hangings, and an online subscription to a telecommunication network. Some kits are designed for teachers, others for individual or small groups of students, and many more for the collaborative use of students and teachers. Teachers sometimes incorporate multimedia programs with learning activity centers.

Many multimedia programs are available on CD-ROM; they are designed principally as reference resources for students and teachers but include other uses as well. One example is National Geographic's *Mammals: A Multimedia Encyclopedia,* which provides a lesson-planning guide, facts on more than 200 animals, 700 still color photos, range maps, animal vocalizations, full-motion movie clips, an animal classification game, glossary, and a printing capability. Selected sources of programs are shown in Figure 6.8.

- **Apex Learning Inc:** http://www.apexlearning.com
- **Boxer Learning:** http://www.boxerlearning.com
- **Cognitive Concepts:** http://www.earobics.com
- **Educational Insights:** http://www.educationalinsights.com
- **Maris Technologies:** http://www.maris.com
- **Pitsco, Inc:** http://www.pitsco.com
- **Riverdeep Interactive Learning:** http://www.riverdeep.net
- **SVE & Churchill Media:** http://www.SVEmedia.com
- **Tom Snyder Productions:** http://www.tomsnyder.com

FIGURE 6.8 Selected Internet resources for computer software, CD-ROMs, DVDs, and interactive multimedia.

Everyone knows that television, videos, and DVDs represent a powerful medium. Their use as teaching aids, however, may present scheduling, curriculum, and physical problems that some school systems are not yet able to handle adequately.

For purposes of professional discussion, television programming can be divided into three categories: instructional television, educational television, and general commercial television. Instructional television refers to programs specifically designed as classroom instruction. Educational television refers to cable television and public broadcasting programs designed to educate in general, but not aimed at classroom instruction. Commercial television programs include the entertainment and public service programs of the television networks and local stations.

Watch for announcements for special educational programs in professional journals. And, of course, television program listings can be obtained from your local commercial, educational, or cable companies or by writing directly to network stations. Some networks sponsor Internet Websites.

Combined with a television monitor, the VCR (videocassette recorder) is one of the most popular and frequently used tools in today's classroom. Videotaped programs can do nearly everything that the former 16-mm films could do. In addition, the VCR, combined with a video camera, makes it possible to record student activities, practice, projects, and demonstrations, as well as yourself when teaching. It gives students a marvelous opportunity to self-assess as they see and hear themselves in action.

Entire instructional packages, as well as supplements, are now available on videocassettes or on computer discs. The schools where you student teach and where you eventually are employed may have a collection of such programs. Some teachers make their own.

Carefully selected programs, tapes, discs, films, and slides enhance student learning. For example, DVDs and CD-ROMs offer quick and efficient accessibility to thousands of visuals, thus providing an appreciated boost to teachers of students with limited language proficiency. With the use of frame control, students can observe phenomena in detail that, in the past, they only read about. Check the January NSTA supplement, school supply catalogs, and Internet resources for titles and sources of media programs. Figure 6.8 provides sample Web addresses where you can obtain information.

Computers and Computer-Based Instructional Tools

As a teacher, you must be computer literate—you must understand and be able to use computers as well as you can read and write. The computer can be valuable to

Patrick White/Merrill

Combined with a television monitor, the VCR is a frequently used audiovisual tool in today's science classroom.

you in several ways. For example, it can help you manage instruction by obtaining information, storing and preparing test materials, maintaining attendance and grade records, and preparing programs to aid in the academic development of individual students. This category of uses of the computer is referred to as *computer-managed instruction* (CMI).

The computer can also be used for instruction by employing various instructional software programs, and it can be used to teach about computers and to help students develop their metacognitive skills as well as their skills in computer use. When it is used to assist students in their learning, it is called *computer-assisted instruction* (CAI) or *computer-assisted learning* (CAL).

The Placement and Use of Computers

Teachers who want to make their classrooms more student-centered, collaborative, and interactive increasingly turn to telecommunications networks. Webs of connected computers allow teachers and students from around the world to reach each other directly and to gain access to quantities of information previously unimaginable. Students using networks learn new inquiry and analytical skills in a stimulating environment, and they can also gain an increased awareness of their role as world citizens.

How you use the computer for instruction is determined by several factors, including your knowledge of and skills in its use, the number of computers that you have available for instructional use, where computers are placed in the school, the software that is available, printer availability, and telecommunication capabilities (that is, wiring and phone lines, modems, and servers).

Schools continue to purchase or lease computers and to upgrade their telecommunication capabilities. Some school districts are beginning to purchase hand-held computers and others have invested heavily in outfitting their students with laptop computers. This option offers a great deal of flexibility, but requires a strong commitment on part of teachers to make their classrooms paperless. Regarding the more traditional desktop computer placement and equipment available, following are some possible scenarios and how classroom teachers work within each.

Scenario 1. With the assistance of a computer lab and the lab technician, computers are integrated into the whole curriculum. In collaboration with members of interdisciplinary teaching teams, students use computers, software, and sources on the Internet as tools to build their knowledge, to write stories with word processors, to illustrate diagrams with paint utilities, to create interactive reports with hypermedia, and to graph data they have gathered using spreadsheets.

Scenario 2. In some schools, students take a computer class as an elective or exploratory. You might give students in your classes who are simultaneously enrolled in such a course special computer assignments that they can then share with the rest of the class.

Scenario 3. Some classrooms have a computer connected to a large-screen video monitor. The teacher or a student works the computer, and the entire class can see the monitor screen. As they view the screen, students can verbally respond to and interact with what is happening on the computer.

Presentation software, such as Microsoft's *Power Point*™, can help teachers, and students, create powerful on-screen presentations. First developed for use in the world of business for reports at sales meetings and with clients, educators quickly became aware of the power provided by presentation software to display, illustrate, and elucidate information. It quickly made its way into university classrooms and then into K–12 classrooms. Today it is not uncommon for it to be used by kindergarten children in their own presentations. When students are using modern presentation software, teachers must ensure that students don't give more attention to fonts and formats and other aspects of the technology than to the content of their presentations. Of course, that is no more a concern for electronic presentations than for students using any other format to display their work, such as an interactive student-created bulletin board display.

Scenario 4. You may be fortunate enough to have one or more computers in your classroom for all or part of the school year with Internet connections, CD-ROM playing capabilities, a DVD player, an overhead projector, and a LCD (liquid crystal display) projection system. Coupled with the overhead projector, the LCD projection system

Patrick White/Merrill

In teaching science, computers can be used for practice and reinforcement, tutoring, simulations, games, and problem solving. With the computer, children can explore certain science phenomena in more accurate and graphic ways than are possible in traditional science teaching.

allows you to project onto your large wall screen (and TV monitor at the same time) any image from computer software or a videodisc. With this system, all students can see and verbally interact with the multimedia instruction.

Scenario 5. Many classrooms have at least one computer with telecommunications capability, and some have many. When this is the case in your classroom, you most likely will have one or two students working at the computer while others are doing other learning activities (multilevel teaching). Computers can be an integral part of a learning center and an important aid in your overall effort to personalize the instruction within your classroom.

Programs are continually being developed and enhanced to meet the new and more powerful computers being made available. (DVDs, computer software, and CD-ROMs are usually available from the same companies, addresses of which are listed in Figure 6.8.) For evaluating computer software programs and testing them for their compatibility with your instructional objectives, many forms are usually available from the local school district or from the state department of education.

 Using Copyrighted Video, Computer, and Multimedia Programs

You must be knowledgeable about laws regarding the use of copyrighted videos and computer software materials. Although space here prohibits full inclusion of U.S. legal guidelines, your local school district undoubtedly can provide a copy of current district policies to ensure your compliance with all copyright laws.

Permitted Uses—You May:

1. Request your media center or audiovisual coordinator to record a program for you if you cannot or if you lack the equipment.
2. Keep a videotaped copy of a broadcast (including cable transmission) for 45 calendar days, after which the program must be erased.
3. Use the program in class once during the first 10 school days of the 45 calendar days, and a second time if instruction needs to be reinforced.
4. Have professional staff view the program several times for evaluation purposes during the full 45 day period.
5. Make a few copies to meet legitimate needs, but these copies must be erased when the original videotape is erased.
6. Use only a part of the program if instructional needs warrant.
7. Enter into a licensing agreement with the copyright holder to continue use of the program.

Prohibited Uses—You May Not:

1. Videotape premium cable services such as HBO without express permission.
2. Alter the original content of the program.
3. Exclude the copyright notice on the program.
4. Videorecord before a request for use is granted—the request to record must come from an instructor.
5. Keep the program, and any copies, after 45 days.

FIGURE 6.9 Copyright law for off-air videotaping. *Source:* R. Heinich, M. Molenda, J. D. Russell, and S. E. Smaldino, *Instructional Media and Technologies for Learning,* 6th ed. (Upper Saddle River, NJ: Merrill/Prentice Hall, 1999), 389. © 1999. Reprinted by permission of Prentice Hall, Inc., Upper Saddle River, NJ.

Permitted Uses—You May:

1. Make a single back-up or archival copy of the computer program.
2. Adapt the computer program to another language if the program is unavailable in the target language.
3. Add features to make better use of the computer program.

Prohibited Uses—You May Not:

1. Make multiple copies.
2. Make replacement copies from an archival or back-up copy.
3. Make copies of copyrighted programs to be sold, leased, loaned, transmitted, or given away.

FIGURE 6.10 Copyright law for use of computer software. *Source:* December, 1980, Congressional amendment to the 1976 Copyright Act.

As discussed earlier, when preparing to make any copy you must find out whether it is permitted by law under the category of "permitted use." If it is not, you must get written permission to reproduce the material from the holder of the copyright. Figures 6.9 and 6.10

1. For portions of copyrighted works used in your own multimedia production for use in teaching, follow normal copyright guidelines (e.g., the limitations on the amount of material used, whether it be motion media, text, music, illustrations, photographs, or computer software).
2. You may display your own multimedia work using copyrighted works to other teachers, such as in workshops. However, you may *not* make and distribute copies to colleagues without obtaining permission from copyright holders.
3. You may use your own multimedia production for instruction over an electronic network (e.g., distance learning) provided there are limits to access and to the number of students enrolled. You may *not* distribute such work over any electronic network (local area or wide area) without expressed permission from copyright holders.
4. You must obtain permissions from copyright holders before using any copyrighted materials in educational multimedia productions for commercial reproduction and distribution or before replicating more than one copy, distributing copies to others, or using beyond your own classroom.

FIGURE 6.11 Fair use guidelines for using multimedia programs.

present guidelines for copying videotapes and computer software.

Usually, when purchasing CD-ROMs and other multimedia software packages intended for use by schools, you are also paying for a license to modify and use its contents for instructional purposes. However, not all CD-ROMs include copyright permission, so always check the copyright notice on any disc you purchase and use. Whenever in doubt, don't use it until you have asked your district media specialists about copyrights or have obtained necessary permissions from the original source.

As yet, there are no guidelines for fair use of films, filmstrips, slides, and multimedia programs. A general rule of thumb for using of any copyrighted material is to treat the work of others as you would want your own material treated were it protected by a copyright (see Figure 6.11).

Summary

You have learned of the variety of tools available to supplement your science instruction. When used wisely, these tools will help you reach more of your students more of the time and aid in the children's learning. As you know, teachers must meet the needs of diverse students—many who are linguistically and culturally different. The material selected and presented in this chapter should be of help in doing that. The future will undoubtedly continue bringing technological innovations that will be even more helpful—compact discs, computers, online textbooks, presentation software, and telecommunications equipment have only marked the beginning of a revolution for teaching. In the near future, new instructional delivery systems made possible by microcomputers and multimedia workstations will likely fundamentally alter what had become the traditional role of the classroom teacher during the last century.

You should remain alert to developing technologies, especially for your science teaching. Digital videodiscs (DVDs), CD-ROMs interfaced with computers (i.e., the use of multimedia), telecommunications, digitized textbooks, and portable hand-held computers offer exciting technologies for learning. New instructional technologies are advancing at an increasingly rapid rate. You and your colleagues must maintain vigilance over new developments, constantly looking for those that will not only help make student learning meaningful and interesting, and your teaching effective, but that are cost effective as well.

Questions for Class Discussion

1. Explain how your effective use of the writing board and bulletin board can help students see relationships among verbal concepts or information.
2. Identify ways that a field trip can be planned to incorporate the three phases of learning—input of data, processing of data, and application of data—or the three stages of the learning cycle—exploration, invention, and discovery.
3. In 1922, Thomas Edison predicted that "the motion picture is destined to revolutionize our educational system and . . . in a few years it will supplant largely, if not entirely, the use of textbooks." In 1945, William Levenson of the Cleveland public schools' radio station claimed that "the time may come when a portable radio receiver will be as common in the classroom as is the blackboard." In the early 1960s, B. F. Skinner believed that with the help of the new teaching machines and programmed instruction, students could learn twice as much in the same time and with the same effort as in a standard classroom. Did motion pictures, radio, programmed instruction, and television revolutionize education? Will computers become as much a part of the classroom as writing boards?

What do you predict the public school classroom of the year 2050 will be like? Will the role of a teacher be different in any way than it is today?

4. Select and identify one instructional tool for teaching science in particular that is *not* discussed in this chapter and explain to your classmates its advantages and disadvantages for use in teaching.
5. Has the purchase of new textbooks and library books become stagnated as schools use their available funds for leading-edge technology? Have music and art programs suffered as a result of expenditures on technology? How are school districts finding the funds necessary for the cost of technology, such as for wiring classrooms for networking and for updated computers, for the planning, installation, and maintenance of complex computer networks? Or are districts finding the necessary funds? In this respect, are some districts worse off or better off than others? Is this an issue?
6. Do you have questions generated by the content of this chapter? If you do, list them along with ways answers might be found.

Chapter 7

Planning the Instruction

Anthony Magnacca/Merrill

An effective program of science is planned to include these elements:

- A set of clear goals and expectations for students
- A curriculum framework that is used to guide the selection and development of units and courses of study
- Curriculum patterns that are developmentally appropriate, interesting, and relevant to students' lives
- An emphasis on inquiry as a tool for learning
- A curriculum that connects to other school subjects[1]

In Chapter 1 you learned about *why* science is taught in grades K–8 and about what we mean by the term *integrated approach*. In Chapter 2, you learned about the significance of science standards and curriculum frameworks; that is, about *what* science is taught. In Chapter 3, you learned about important *understandings* needed to teach science, and in Chapter 4, about *teacher* behaviors important in facilitating children's science learning. Then, in Chapter 5 you learned how to select and implement important instructional *strategies*. With Chapter 6, you became knowledgeable about important *instructional aids and resources* that enhance instruction and children's learning. With that background, we now guide you through the process of *planning* your instruction.

As a science teacher, your instructional task is twofold: (a) to plan for and provide developmentally appropriate hands-on experiences, with useful materials and the supportive environment necessary for students' meaningful scientific exploration; and (b) to know how to facilitate the most meaningful and long-lasting learning possible once the child's mind has been activated by the hands-on experience. This chapter, specifically, is designed to help you complete these tasks.

Planning for instruction is a very large and important part of a teacher's job. With responsibility for planning at three levels, you will participate in planning long-range for a semester or academic year, planning units of instruction, and planning short-range, or preparing lessons. Throughout your career you will be engaged almost continuously in planning at each of these three levels; planning for instruction is a steady and cyclic process that involves preactive and reflective thought processing. The importance of mastering the process at the very beginning of your career cannot be overemphasized. The process of planning and preparing for instruction involves a number of important skills.

> Teachers develop a framework of year-long and short-term goals for students.
> Teachers select science content and adapt and design curricula to meet the particular interests, knowledge, skills, and experiences of students.
> Teachers work together as colleagues within and across disciplines and grade levels.[2]

 Unit Planning

The teacher's edition of the student textbook and other resource materials will expedite your planning but should not substitute for it. You must know how to create a good instructional plan. In this section, you will learn how it is done.

Documents produced at the national level, state department of education curriculum frameworks, district courses of study, and school-adopted printed and nonprinted materials are the sources you will examine to obtain guidance for content selection. Many of these documents may be viewed via the Internet.

Organizing the entire year's content into recognizable chunks of learning, called units, makes the teaching process manageable. Whether you are teaching in a

[1] Adapted from National Research Council, *National Science Education Standards*, © 1996 by the National Academy of Sciences, 210–214. Courtesy of National Academy Press, Washington, DC.

[2] Reprinted from National Research Council, *National Science Education Standards*, © 1996 by the National Academy of Sciences, 30. Courtesy of National Academy Press, Washington, DC.

self-contained classroom or in some other model, the content you intend to present to students must be organized and carefully planned well in advance. The teaching unit is a major subdivision of a course (for one course or one self-contained classroom there are several or many units of instruction) containing instruction planned around a central theme, topic, issue, or problem.

Whether an interdisciplinary thematic unit, or a stand-alone, the standard (also known as conventional or traditional) science teaching unit is like a chapter in a book, an act or scene in a play, or a phase of work in a project such as building a house. Breaking down information or actions into component parts and then grouping the related parts into a unit brings a sense of cohesiveness and structure to student learning and avoids the piecemeal approach that might otherwise unfold. You can learn to articulate lessons within, between, and among unit plans and focus on important elements without ignoring significant tangential information. Students remember chunks of information, especially when those chunks are related to specific units.

Although the steps for developing any type of instructional unit are basically the same, units can be organized in several different ways. In this book, we consider two basic types: the standard unit and the integrated unit.

A *standard unit* consists of a series of lessons centered on a topic, theme, major concept, or block of subject matter. Each lesson builds on the previous lesson by contributing additional subject matter, providing further illustrations, and supplying more practice or instruction, all of which are aimed at bringing about mastery of the knowledge and skills on which the unit is centered.

When a standard unit is centered on a theme, the unit may be referred to as a **thematic unit.** When, as discussed in Chapter 1, the thematic unit integrates disciplines, such as combining science and mathematics, social studies and English/language arts, or all four core disciplines, it is called an *integrated* (or *interdisciplinary*) thematic unit (ITU).

Steps for Planning and Developing a Unit of Instruction

The steps described in the following paragraphs are appropriate for planning and developing any unit, whether it is a standard unit or an interdisciplinary (or multidisciplinary) thematic unit (ITU). (A sample standard unit that integrates mathematics with a topic in science is shown in Figure 7.4 of this chapter, and a sample ITU, "Opening the Ocean," appears in Chapter 11.)[3]

[3] See also M. Lee, M. Lostoski, and K. Williams, "Diving Into a Schoolwide Science Theme: Interdisciplinary Lessons for an All-School Theme in Science, Art, and Music Classes," *Science and Children* 38(1):31–35 (September 2000).

Select a Suitable Topic or Theme

The topic or theme might already be laid out in your course of study or textbook or might already have been agreed to by members of the teaching team. The primary responsibility for the development of units of instruction can fall to a single teacher or several teachers. A teaching team may develop from one to several units a year. Eventually, then, a team will have several units available for implementation, but the most effective units are often those that are the most current. This means that teaching teams must be constantly alert to new global, national, and local topics so they can update old units and develop new and exciting ones. Before going further, let's stop and consider the difference between a *theme* and a *topic.* As you may already suspect, the difference is not always clear.

"Earthquakes" and "social consequences of natural disasters" are examples of topics, whereas "a survival guide to local natural disasters" could be the theme or umbrella under which these two topics fall. A *theme is the point, the message, or the idea that organizes a study.* It is likely to be based on a problem statement or questions, and to result in a product. A theme is more dynamic than a topic and usually lasts longer. The theme explains the significance of the study; it communicates to the student what the experience means. Many topics organized around one theme make up an interdisciplinary thematic unit. Often the theme of a study becomes clearer to students when an overall guiding question is presented and discussed, such as "What could we do to improve our environment?" or "What happens in our community after natural disasters?"

Sometimes the teacher or teaching team selects themes or topics before meeting the students for the first time. Other times the teachers select themes in collaboration with students. But even when the theme is preselected, students still should be given major responsibility, with guidance from the teacher, for deciding the final theme title, topics, and corresponding learning activities. Instruction works best when students have ownership in the study, when they have been empowered with major decision-making responsibility.

Every unit topic or theme should satisfy two criteria: (a) it should fit within the expected scope and sequence of mandated content, and (b) it should be of interest to the students. Regarding the first criterion, many teachers have said that when they and their students embarked on an interdisciplinary thematic study they did so without truly knowing where the study would go or what the learning outcomes would be—and they were somewhat frightened by the unknowns. But when the study was completed, their students had learned everything (or nearly everything) that the teacher would have expected them to learn had the teacher used a more traditional content-centered approach. And, it was more fun!

- Is the theme within the realm of understanding and experience of the teachers involved?
- Will the theme interest all members of the teaching team?
- Do we have sufficient materials and resources to supply information we might need?
- Does the theme lend itself to active learning experiences?
- Can this theme lead to a unit that is of the proper duration, not too short and not too long?
- Is the theme helpful, worthwhile, and pertinent to the instructional objectives?
- Will the theme be of interest to students and will it motivate them to do their best?
- Is the theme one with which teachers are not already so familiar that they cannot share in the excitement of the learning?

FIGURE 7.1 Questions to ask when selecting a theme.

When selecting a theme, consider the questions shown in Figure 7.1.

The second criterion is easy to satisfy, as it will most assuredly be of interest to the students when they are truly empowered with major decision-making responsibility for what and how they learn. So, once a general theme or topic is selected (one that satisfies the first criterion), its final title, subtopics, and corresponding procedural activities should be finalized in collaboration with the students.

Select the Goals of the Unit and Prepare the Overview

The goals are written as an overview or rationale, covering what the unit is about and what the students are to learn. In planning the goals, you should (a) thoroughly study the topic and materials used; (b) consult curriculum documents (such as courses of study), state frameworks, and resource units for ideas; (c) decide the content and procedures (i.e., what the students should learn about the topic and how); (d) write the rationale or overview, in which you summarize what you expect the students to learn about the topic; and (e) confirm that your goals are consistent with those of the course or grade level program.

Select the Instructional Objectives

In doing this, you should (a) include skills, ideals, attitudes, appreciations, and understandings; (b) be specific, avoiding vagueness and generalizations; (c) write the objectives in performance terms; and (d) be as certain as possible that the objectives will contribute to the major learning described in the overview.

Detail the Instructional Procedures

These procedures include the subject content and the learning activities, established as a series of lessons. Proceed with the following steps in your initial planning of the instructional procedures.

1. Gather ideas for learning activities that might be suitable for the unit. Refer to state and local standards, curriculum documents, resource units, colleagues, and even students as resources.
2. Check the learning activities to make sure that they will contribute to the learning designated in your objectives, discarding ideas that do not.
3. Confirm that the learning activities are feasible. Can you afford the time, effort, or expense? Do you have the necessary materials and equipment? If not, can they be obtained? Are the activities suited to the intellectual and maturity levels of your students?
4. Check available resources to be certain that they support the content and learning activities.
5. Decide how to introduce the unit. Provide *introductory activities* that will arouse student interest and tell students what the unit is about; that will help you learn about your students' interests, abilities, experiences, and present knowledge of the topic; that will provide transitions that bridge this topic with others that students have already learned; and that involve the students in the planning.
6. Plan *developmental activities* that will sustain student interest, provide for individual student differences, promote the learning as cited in the specific objectives, and promote a project.
7. Plan *culminating activities* that will summarize what has been learned, bring together loose ends, apply what has been learned to new situations, provide students with opportunity to demonstrate their learning, and provide transition to the unit that follows.

Plan for Preassessment and Assessment of Student Learning

Preassess students by determining what they already know or think they know. Assessment of student progress in achievement of the learning objectives (formative evaluation) should permeate the entire unit (that is, as often as possible, assessment should be a daily component of lessons). Plan to gather information in several ways, including informal observations, checklist observations of student performance and their portfolios, and paper and pencil tests. Assessment must be congruent with the instructional objectives. Assessment is the focus of Chapter 8.

Provide for the Materials and Tools of Instruction

A unit in science cannot function without materials. Therefore, you must plan long before the unit begins for special science materials, media equipment, references, reading materials, reproduced materials, and community resources.

Unit Format, Inclusive Elements, and Duration

Follow the preceding steps to develop any type of unit. In addition, keep in mind two general points. First, although there is no single best format for a teaching unit, there are minimum inclusions. The format depends on grade level, topic, and type of activities. During your student teaching, your college or university's teacher preparation program and your cooperating teacher or teachers might have a format that you will be expected to follow. Regardless of the format, every unit plan should include the following elements: (a) identification of grade level, subject, topic or theme, and time allotted for the unit; (b) statement of rationale and general goals for the unit; (c) statement of major objectives of the unit; (d) materials and resources needed; (e) lesson plans; (f) assessment strategies; and (g) a statement of how the unit will attend to variations in students' reading levels, experiential backgrounds, and special needs.

Second, there is no set duration for a unit plan, although curriculum guides will recommend certain time spans for specific units. Units may extend for a minimum of several days or, for some integrated thematic unit (ITU), for several weeks or even an entire school year.[4] Be aware, however, that when standard units last more than two or three weeks, they tend to lose the character of clearly identifiable units. For any unit of instruction, the exact amount of time it takes for implementation will be dictated by several factors, including the topic, problem, or theme; the age, interests, and maturity of the students; and the scope of the learning activities. Sometimes, for example, the study involves the entire school.[5]

The steps just outlined are essential for planning any type of teaching unit, including the ITU and the smaller, subject-specific standard units that might make it up.

Developing the Learning Activities: The Heart and Spirit of Any Unit Plan

Central to the most successful selection, development, and implementation of learning activities for a unit of instruction is a common thread of four tightly interwoven components: (a) the instruction is centered on a big and meaningful idea (topic or theme) rather than on factitious subject areas; (b) the students and the teacher share in the decision making and responsibility for learning; (c) the learning activities are selected so each student is actively engaged in learning—that is, students are physically active (hands-on learning) and mentally active (minds-on learning); and (d) there is steady reflection on and frequent sharing of what is being done and what is being learned.

Activities that engage the students in meaningful learning constitute the heart and spirit of any unit plan. These include *initiating activities, ongoing developmental activities,* and *culminating activities.*

Initiating Activities

A unit can be initiated in a limitless variety of ways. You must decide which are appropriate for your educational goals and objectives, the amount of time you intend to spend, and your unique group of students, considering their interests, abilities, and skills. You might start with a student question, a current event, a community problem, an artifact, a book,[6] a demonstration of a discrepant event, or something interesting found on the Internet.

Ongoing Developmental Activities

Once the unit has been initiated, students become occupied with a variety of ongoing learning activities. When working with students in selecting and planning these activities, you will want to keep in mind the concept represented by the Learning Experiences Ladder (Chapter 5) as well as the predetermined goals and objectives.

Culminating Activity

A unit of instruction is brought to a close with a culminating activity, which often includes sharing the product of the students' study. A culminating activity that brings closure to a unit can give the students an opportunity for synthesis (by assembling, constructing, creating, inventing, producing, or incorporating something) and even an opportunity to present that synthesis to an audience, such as by presenting the work on the school's Website.

With a culminating activity, students can move from recording information to reporting on their learning. For example, students might take field trips (discussed in Chapter 6) to study something related to the theme or topic and then synthesize their learning after the trip in a way that culminates the study.

On field trips, students can be given notepads similar to the ones reporters use and asked to take notes and make sketches of what they learn. They can discuss what questions they have on the ride to the site. They can discuss what they liked and did not like on the ride back to school. After the trip, each student can choose something he or she saw on the trip and then build it to scale, so each student can have a scale model of some thing that caught her or his interest. Teacher and students might devote one full afternoon, or more, to working with

[4]See, for example, the introduction of the natural world to kindergarten children through a yearlong study of birds in P. Whitin, "First Flight," *Science and Children* 39(4):16–21 (January 2002).

[5]See, for example, M. Lee, M. Lostoski, and K. Williams, "Diving Into a Schoolwide Science Theme: Interdisciplinary Lessons for an All-School Theme in Science, Art, and Music Classes," *Science and Children* 38(1):31–35 (September 2000).

[6]See, for example, A. G. Terrell, "Leaders, Readers, & Science," *Science and Children* 39(1):28–33 (September 2001).

Colleen Schneider/USDA/NRCS/Natural Resources Conservation Service

Effective science teachers plan activities that challenge and excite students. When planning science units, teachers should include many hands-on activities in which children actively participate. Investigations, field trips, and inquiry sessions can provide firsthand experiences for learning science content, developing process skills, and developing healthy attitudes about science, technology, and society.

rulers, yardsticks, cardboard, clay, and other materials. The students could then invite other classes in to examine the scale models and listen to student reports about why an object caught their interest. Students might also present an art show of drawings about the unit's theme, with a narration that informs others about their study. You might also schedule a culminating activity that asks students to report on individual projects—the aspect each student formerly reserved for individual study.

Examples of actual culminating activities and products of a unit of instruction are endless. Culminating activities are opportunities for students to proudly demonstrate and share their learning in different and individual ways.

 Lesson Planning

The process of designing a lesson is important in planning class meetings that provide the most efficient use of valuable and limited instructional time and the most effective learning for the students to meet the unit goals.

As you may have noticed, this section is not titled "*daily* lesson plans," but rather "lesson planning." You will learn how to prepare a lesson plan that might or might not be a daily plan. In some instances, a lesson plan might extend for more than one class period or day—perhaps two or three. In other instances, it is a daily plan that might run for an entire class period. In block scheduling, one lesson plan might run for part or all of a 2-hour block of time. See "The Problem of Time" later in this chapter.

Effective teachers are always planning for their classes. For the long range, they plan the scope and sequence, and develop content. Within this long-range planning, they develop units and, within units, they design the activities to be used and the assessments of learning to be done. They familiarize themselves with books, materials, media, and innovations in their fields of interest. Yet, despite all this planning activity, the lesson plan remains pivotal to the planning process.

Assumptions about Lesson Planning

Not all teachers need elaborate written plans for every lesson. Sometimes effective and skilled veteran teachers need only an outline. Sometimes they may not need written plans at all. Teachers who have taught the topic many times in the past may need only the presence of a class of students to stimulate a pattern of presentation that has often been successful (though there are some pitfalls—frequent use of old patterns may lead one into the rut of unimaginative and uninspiring teaching). In addition, you probably do not need to be reminded that the obsolescence of many past classroom practices has been substantiated repeatedly by those researchers who have made serious and recent studies of exemplary educational practices.

Considering the diversity among teachers in their instructional styles and their students, and what research has shown, certain assumptions can be made about lesson planning: (a) Not *all* teachers need elaborate written plans for all lessons; (b) beginning teachers need to prepare detailed written lesson plans—failing to prepare is preparing to fail; (c) some subject-matter fields, topics, or learning activities require more detailed planning than others do; (d) exemplary veteran teachers have clearly defined goals and objectives in mind even though they have not written them into lesson plans; (e) the depth of knowledge a teacher has about a subject or topic influences the amount of planning necessary for the lessons; (f) the skill a teacher has in remaining calm and in following a trend of thought in the presence of distraction will influence the amount of detail necessary when planning activities and writing the lesson plan; (g) a plan is more likely to be carefully and thoughtfully plotted when it is written out; (h) the diversity of students within today's public school classroom necessitates careful and thoughtful consideration about individualizing the instruction—these considerations are best implemented when they have been thoughtfully written into lesson plans; (i) there is no particular pattern or format that all teachers need to follow when writing out plans—some teacher-preparation programs have agreed on certain lesson-plan formats for their teacher candidates, and you need to know if this is true for your program; and (j) all effective teachers have a planned pattern of instruction for every lesson, whether that plan is written out or not.

In summary, then, well-written lesson plans provide many advantages. They give a teacher an agenda or outline to follow in teaching a lesson; they give a substitute teacher a basis for presenting appropriate lessons to a class—thereby retaining lesson continuity in the regular teacher's absence; they are certainly very useful when a teacher is planning to use the same lesson again in the future; they provide the teacher with something to fall back on in case of a memory lapse, an interruption, or some distraction such as a call from the office or a fire drill; they demonstrate to students that the teacher cares about them and is working for them; and, above all, they provide beginners with security because, with a carefully prepared plan, a beginning teacher can walk into a classroom with confidence gained from having developed a sensible framework for that day's instruction.

Therefore, as a beginning teacher, you should make considerably detailed lesson plans. Naturally, this will require a great deal of work for at least the first year or two, but the reward of knowing that you have prepared and presented effective lessons will compensate for that effort. You can expect a busy first year or two of teaching.

A Continual Process

Lesson planning is a continual process even for experienced teachers, for there is always a need to keep materials and plans current and relevant. Because no two classes of students are ever identical, today's lesson plan will probably need to be tailored to the needs of each classroom of students. Also, because the content of instruction and learning will change with each group of students and their distinct needs and interests, and as new thematic units are developed and new theories are introduced, your objectives and the objectives of the students, school, and faculty will change.

For these reasons, lesson plans should be in a constant state of revision. Once the basic framework is developed, however, the task of updating and modifying becomes minimal. If you maintain your plans on a computer, making changes from time to time is even easier.

Well Planned but Subject to Change

The lesson plan should provide a tentative outline of the amount of time given for the lesson but should always remain flexible. A carefully worked out plan may have to be set aside because of the unpredictable, serendipitous effect of a "teachable moment" or because of unforeseen circumstances, such as a delayed school bus, an impromptu school assembly program, an emergency drill, or the cancellation of school because of inclement weather. Student teachers often are appalled at the frequency of interruptions during a school day and the disruptions to their lesson planning that occur. A daily lesson planned to cover six aspects of a given topic may end with only three of the points having been considered. Although far more frequent than necessary in many schools, these occurrences are natural in a school setting and the teacher and the plans must be flexible enough to accommodate this reality.

Implementation of Today's Lesson May Necessitate Changes in Tomorrow's Plan

Although you may have your lesson plans completed for several consecutive lessons, what actually transpires during the implementation of one day's lesson may necessitate last minute adjustments to the lesson you had planned for the following day. Consequently, during student teaching in particular, it is not uncommon or unwanted to have last-minute changes penciled in your lesson plan. If, however, penciled-in modifications are substantial and might be confusing to you during implementation of the lesson, then you should rewrite the lesson plan.

The Problem of Time

A lesson plan should provide enough materials and activities to consume the entire period or time allotted. As mentioned earlier, it should be well understood that, in your planning for teaching, you need to plan for every minute of every class period. The lesson plan, then, is more than a plan for a lesson to be taught; it is a plan that accounts for the entire class period or time that you and your students are together in the classroom.

Planning is a skill that takes years of experience to master, especially when teaching a block of time that may extend for 90 or more minutes and that involves more than one discipline, and perhaps more than one teacher. Therefore, as a beginning teacher you should overplan rather than run the risk of having too few activities to occupy the time the students are in your classroom. One way of ensuring that you overplan is to include "if time remains" activities in your lesson plan.

When a lesson plan does not provide sufficient activity to occupy the entire class period or the time that students are available for the lesson, a beginning teacher often loses control of the class as behavior problems mount. Therefore, it is best to prepare more than you likely can accomplish in a given period. This is not to imply that you should involve the students in meaningless busywork. Students can be very perceptive when it comes to a teacher who has finished the plan and is attempting to bluff through the minutes that remain before dismissal. And, they are not usually favorably responsive to meaningless busywork.

If you ever do get caught short—as most teachers do at one time or another—one way to avoid embarrassment is to have students work on what is known as an *anchor assignment,* one that is ongoing and understood by students that whenever they have spare time in class they should be working on it. In other words, the anchor activity, such as journal writing or portfolio organization, is an ongoing "if time remains" activity. Alternative "if time remains" activities are to spend the time in a review of material that has been covered that day or in the past several days, or allow students the time to work on a homework assignment or project. Regardless of how you handle time remaining, it works best when you plan for it and write it into your lesson plan, and when the procedures for doing it are well understood by the students.

Format, Components, and Samples

Each teacher develops a personal system of lesson planning. But a beginning teacher needs a more substantial framework from which to work. For that reason, this section provides a preferred lesson plan format (Figure 7.2). Nothing is hallowed about this format, however. Review the preferred format and samples, determine which appeals to your situation and style of presentation, and, unless your program of teacher preparation insists otherwise, use it with your own modifications until you find or develop a better model. All else being equal, however, you are encouraged, to begin your teaching following as closely as possible this preferred format.

A written lesson plan should contain the following basic elements: (a) descriptive data, (b) goals and objectives, (c) rationale, (d) procedure, (e) assignments and assignment reminders, (f) materials and equipment needed, and (g) a section for assessment of student learning, reflection on the lesson, and ideas for lesson revision.

Those seven components need not be present in every written lesson plan or be presented in any particular order; nor are they inclusive or exclusive. You might choose to include additional components or subsections. Figure 7.3 illustrates a completed format that includes the seven components and sample subsections of those components. Figure 7.4 displays a completed multiple-day lesson that incorporates a number of developmentally appropriate learning activities. Following are descriptions of the seven major components of the preferred format, with examples and explanations of why each is important.

Descriptive Data

A lesson plan's descriptive data is the demographic and logistical information that identifies details about the class. Anyone reading this information should be able to identify when and where the class meets, who is teaching it, and what is being taught. Although as the teacher you know this information, someone else may not. Members of the teaching team, administrators, and substitute teachers (and, if you are the student teacher, your university supervisor and cooperating teacher) appreciate this information, especially when asked to fill in for you, even if only for a few minutes during a class session. Most teachers find out which items of descriptive data are most beneficial in their situation and then develop their own identifiers. Remember this: The mark of a well-prepared, clearly written lesson plan is the ease with which someone else (such as another member of your teaching team or a substitute teacher) could implement it.

As shown in the sample plans in Figures 7.3 (language arts/science) and 7.4 (science), the descriptive data include

1. *Name of course or class.* These serve as headings for the plan and facilitate orderly filing of plans.

   Language Arts/Science (integrated block course)
   Science

2. *Name of the unit.* Inclusion of this facilitates the orderly control of the hundreds of lesson plans a teacher constructs. For example:

   Language Arts/Science
   Unit: ***Investigative Research and Generative Writing***

   Science
   Unit: ***What's the Matter***

3. *Topic to be considered within the unit.* This is also useful for control and identification. For example:

   Language Arts/Science
   Unit: Investigative Research and Generative Writing
   Topic: ***Writing Response and Peer Assessment via the Internet***

   Science
   Unit: What's the Matter
   Topic: ***Density of Solids***

Anticipated Noise Level. Although not included in the sample lesson plans in this book, the teacher might include in the descriptive data the category of "anticipated classroom noise level," such as "high," "moderate," or "low." Including it, or at least considering the idea, is useful during the planning phase of instruction because it allows you to think about how active and noisy the students might become during the lesson, how you might prepare for that, and whether you should warn supervisors and teachers in neighboring classrooms.

Goals and Objectives

The instructional goals are general statements of intended accomplishments from a lesson. Teachers and students need to know what the lesson is designed to accomplish. In clear, understandable language, the general goal statement provides that information. In the sample in Figure 7.3, the goals are

1. **Descriptive Data**

   Teacher ________________________________ Class __________ Date ______________ Grade level __________

   Room number ______________ Period or Time ________________ Unit ____________________________________

   Lesson Number _____________ Topic ____

   Anticipated noise level (high, moderate, low) [optional]

2. **Goals and Objectives**

   Instructional goals:

   Specific objectives: [All three domains are not always present in every lesson.]

   Cognitive:

   Affective:

   Psychomotor:

3. **Rationale** [Rationale is not always present in every lesson.]

4. **Procedure** [Procedure includes modeling examples, planned transitions, etc., and should usually take up most of the lesson plan space, often a full page.]

   Content:

   ____________ minutes. Activity 1: (introduction)

   ____________ minutes. Activity 2:

   ____________ minutes. Activity 3: [The exact number of activities in the procedures will vary.]

   ____________ minutes. Final Activity: (lesson conclusion or closure)

   If time remains:

5. **Assignments and Assignment Reminders**

   Special notes and reminders to myself:

6. **Materials and Equipment Needed**

   Audiovisual:

   Other:

7. **Assessment, Reflection, and Revision**

   Assessment of student learning, how it will be done:

   Reflective thoughts about lesson after taught:

   Suggestions for revision if used again:

FIGURE 7.2 Preferred lesson plan format with seven components.

1. **Descriptive Data**

Teacher ______________________ Class Language Arts/Science Date __________ Grade level 5–8

Title of unit Investigative Research and Generative Writing

Lesson Topic Writing Response and Peer Assessment via Internet

Time duration: several days

2. **Goals and Objectives**

Instructional Goals:

2.1. One goal for this lesson is for students to collaborate and prepare response papers to peers from around the world who have shared the results of their own experimental research findings and research paper about ozone concentrations in the atmosphere.

2.2. The ultimate goal of this unit is for students around the world to prepare and publish, for worldwide dissemination, a final paper about global ozone levels in the atmosphere.

Specific Objectives:

COGNITIVE:

a. Through cooperative group action students will conduct experimental research to collect data about the ozone level of air in their environment. (application)
b. In cooperative groups, students analyze the results of their experiments. (analyze)
c. Students will collect data and infer from their experimental data. (synthesis and evaluation)
d. Through collaborative writing groups, the students will prepare a final paper that summarizes their research study of local atmospheric ozone levels. (evaluation)
e. Through the Internet students will write response papers to their peers from other locations in the world. (evaluation)
f. From their own collaborative research and worldwide communications with their peers, the students will draw conclusions about global atmospheric ozone levels. (evaluation)

AFFECTIVE:

a. Students will respond attentively to the presentations of their peers. (attending)
b. Students will cooperate with others during the group activities. (responding)
c. Students will offer opinions about the atmospheric level of ozone. (valuing)
d. Students will form judgments about local, regional, and worldwide ozone levels. (organizing)
e. Students will communicate their findings and attend to the work of their worldwide peers. (internalizing)

PSYCHOMOTOR:

a. Students will manipulate the computer so that their e-mail communications are transmitted accurately. (manipulating)
b. Students will describe their feelings about atmospheric ozone concentrations in a summary to the study. (communicating)
c. Students will create a proposal for worldwide dissemination. (creating)

3. **Rationale**

3.1. Important to improvement in one's writing and communication skills are the processes of selecting a topic, decision making, arranging, drafting, proofing, peer review, commenting, revising, editing, rewriting, and publishing the results—processes that are focused on in the writing aspect of this unit.

3.2. Student writers need many readers to respond to their work. Through worldwide communication with peers and dissemination of their final product, this need can be satisfied.

3.3. Students learn best when they are actively pursuing a topic of interest and meaning to them. Brainstorming potential problems and arriving at their own topic for this unit provides that opportunity.

3.4. Real-world problems are interdisciplinary and transcultural. This unit is an interdisciplinary transcultural unit because it involves writing (English), science, mathematics (data collecting, graphing, etc.), and intercultural communication.

4. **Procedure**

CONTENT:

At the start of this unit, collaborative groups were established via Intercultural E-mail Classroom Connections (IECC) (http://www.stolaf.edu/network/iecc) with other classes from schools around the world. These groups of students from

FIGURE 7.3 Lesson plan sample: multiple-day, project-centered, interdisciplinary, and transcultural lesson using worldwide communication via the Internet.

around the world conducted several scientific research experiments on the ozone level of their local atmospheric air. To obtain relative measurements of ozone concentrations in the air, students set up experiments that involved stretching rubber bands on a board, then observing the number of days until the bands broke. Students maintained daily journal logs of the temperature, barometric pressure, and wind speed/direction, and of the number of days that it took for bands to break. [The information here about the science experiment is from Randall James Ryder and Tom Hughes, *Internet for Educators* (Upper Saddle River, NJ: Merrill/Prentice Hall, 1997), p. 98; the Internet address for IECC is from the same source, p. 96.] After compiling their data and preparing single-page summaries of their results, via the Internet, students exchanged data with other groups. From data collected worldwide, students wrote a one-page summary as to what conditions may account for the difference in levels of ozone. Following the exchange of students' written responses and their subsequent revisions based on feedback from the worldwide peers, students are now preparing a final summary report about the world's atmospheric ozone level. The intention is to disseminate worldwide (to newspapers and via Internet) this final report.

Activity 1: Introduction (_10_ minutes)
Today, in think-share-pairs, you will prepare initial responses to the e-mail responses we have received from other groups from around the world. (Teacher lists the places from which e-mail has been received.) Any questions before we get started?

As we discussed earlier, here are the instructions: in your think-share-pairs (each pair is given one response received via e-mail), prepare written responses according to the following outline: (a) note points or information you would like to incorporate in the final paper to be forwarded via Internet, (b) comment on one aspect of the written response you like best, and (c) provide questions to the sender to seek clarification or elaboration. I think you should be able to finish this in about 30 minutes, so let's try for that.

Activity 2: (_30_ minutes, if needed)
Preparation of dyad responses

Activity 3: (open)
Let's now hear from each response pair.
Dyad responses are shared with the whole class for discussion of inclusion in response paper to be sent via Internet.

Activity 4: (open)
Discussion, conclusion, and preparation of final drafts to be sent to each e-mail corresponder to be done by cooperative groups (the number of groups needed to be decided by the number of e-mail corresponders at this time).

Activity 5: (open)
Later, as students receive e-mail responses from other groups, the responses will be printed and reviewed. The class then responds to each using the same criteria as before and returns this response to the e-mail sender.

CLOSURE:
The process continues until all groups (from around the world) have agreed upon and prepared the final report for dissemination.

5. **Assignments and Assignment Reminders**

   Remind students of important dates and decisions to be made.

6. **Materials and Equipment Needed**

   School computers with Internet access; printers; copies of e-mail responses.

7. **Assessment, Reflection, and Revision**

   Assessment of student learning for this lesson is formative: journals, daily checklist of student participation in groups; writing drafts.

   Reflective thoughts about lesson and suggestions for revision:

FIGURE 7.3 *Continued*

- To collaborate and prepare response papers to peers from around the world who have shared the results of their own experimental research findings and research papers about ozone concentrations in the atmosphere.
- For students around the world to prepare and publish for worldwide dissemination a final paper about global ozone levels in the atmosphere.

And, from the sample unit of Figure 7.4, two of the goals are

- To understand that all matter is made of atoms.
- To develop a positive attitude about science.

Because the goals are also included in the unit plan, sometimes a teacher may include only the objectives in the daily lesson plan (as in the one shown in Figure 7.4), but not the goals. As a beginning teacher, it may be a good idea to include both (as in Figure 7.3).

Setting the Objectives. Setting the objectives is a crucial step in the development of any lesson plan. This is the point at which many lessons go wrong, and at which many beginning teachers seem to have problems.

In setting the learning objectives, teachers sometimes confuse learning activity (*how* the students will learn it) with the learning objective (*what* the student will learn as a result of the learning activity). For example, teachers sometimes mistakenly list what *they* intend to do—such as "lecture on photosynthesis" or "lead a discussion on the causes of the loss of the global rain forests." They fail to focus on just what the learning objectives in these activities truly are—that is, what the students will be able to do (performance) as a result of the instructional activity. Or, rather than specifying what the student will be able to do as a result of the learning activities, the teacher mistakenly writes what the students will do in class (the learning activity)—such as, "in pairs the students will answer the 10 questions on page 72"—as if that were the learning objective.

When you approach this step in your lesson planning, to avoid this error, ask yourself, "What should

Sample Unit Plan

Course: Science *Teacher:* ______________________

Title of unit: What's the Matter *Duration of unit:* 2 weeks

Purpose of unit: This unit is designed for sixth-grade science students to develop their understanding of matter. At the completion of this unit, students should have a better understanding of properties and changes of properties in matter.

Rationale of unit: This unit is important in continuing to build a physical science foundation of knowledge for future science classes. This foundation can increase students' chances of success in later science courses, thereby increasing students' self-confidence and self-esteem. A basic understanding of matter and its properties is necessary for the sixth-grade student because of daily decisions that affect the manipulation of matter. It is more likely that students will make correct and safe decisions when they understand what matter is, how it changes form, and how its properties determine its use.

Goals of unit:
1. To understand that all matter is made of atoms
2. To understand that matter stays constant; it is neither created nor destroyed
3. To develop basic chemistry lab skills
4. To develop a positive attitude about science

Objectives of unit: Upon completion of this unit of study, students should be able to:
1. List at least 10 examples of matter
2. List the three states of matter with one example of each
3. Calculate the density of an object when given mass and volume
4. Describe the properties of solid, liquid, and gas
5. Demonstrate an understanding that matter is made of elements, and elements are made of atoms

Overview of unit: Throughout this unit of study, students will be developing a concept map of matter. Information for the map will come from class and lab work, class discussions, lectures, and student readings and research. The overall instructional model is that of concept attainment.
1. What is matter and what are its properties? Students will develop the concept of matter by discovering the properties common to all matter (has mass and takes up space). Students will develop this concept through use of the concept attainment model.

FIGURE 7.4 Sample integrated unit plan with one daily lesson. Note that the unit topic is consistent with Content Standard B as recommended for grades 5–8 in *National Science Education Standards.* (See Figure 3.2.)
Source: Courtesy of Will Hightower.

2. Students will continue to build on their concept of matter by organizing matter into its four major states (solid, liquid, gas, plasma). The concept development will be used to define the attributes of each state of matter, and students will gather information by participating in laboratory activities and discussions.
3. What are some of the physical properties of matter that make certain kinds of matter unique? Students will experiment with properties of matter such as elasticity, brittleness, and density. Lab activities will allow students to contribute their observations and information to the further development of their concept of matter. Density activities will enable students to practice lab and math skills.
4. What are the basic units of matter and where did matter come from? Students will continue to develop their concept of matter by dissecting matter into mixtures, compounds, elements, and atoms.

Assessment of student achievement: Assessment of student achievement will be based on

1. Student participation as evidenced by completion of homework, classwork, lab activities, and class discussions
2. Weekly quizzes
3. Unit test

Sample Lesson Plan

Lesson number: ____________________ *Duration of lesson:* 1–2 hours

Unit title: What's the Matter *Teacher:* ____________________

Lesson title: Mission Impossible

Lesson topic: Density of Solids

Objectives of lesson: Upon completion of this lesson, students should be able to:

1. Determine the density of a solid cube
2. Based on data gathered in class, develop their own definition of density
3. Communicate the results of their experiments to others in the class

Materials needed:

1. Two large boxes of cereal and two snack-size boxes of the same cereal
2. Four brownies (two whole and two cut in halves)
3. Four sandboxes (two large plastic boxes and two small boxes, each filled with sand)
4. Two scales or balances
5. Several rulers
6. Six hand-held calculators
7. Eighteen colored pencils (six sets with three different colors per set)
8. Copies of lab instructions, one for each student

Procedure with approximate time line

1. ***Anticipatory set (10–15 minutes).*** Begin class by brainstorming (preassessment) what students already know about density. Place the word *density* on the board or overhead, and ask students (using think-write-pair-share) to describe what the word means to them. As each pair shares what they have come up with, write down their definitions and examples.
   Hold up a large box of cereal in one hand and a snack-size box in the other. Ask students which is more dense. Allow them to explain their predictions. Then tell them that by the end of the lesson they will know the answer to the question. They will develop their own definition of density.

2. ***Laboratory investigation (30–60 minutes).*** Students are divided into teams of three or four students per team. Each team has 8 minutes before switching stations. Each team completes three stations and then meets to do its graphs and discuss results. Each student has a role:

FIGURE 7.4 *Continued*

Measure master: In charge of group's ruler and ruler measurements
Weight master: Responsible for all weighing
Engineer: In charge of the group's calculator and calculations
Graph master: In charge of plotting data on graph paper

STATION 1: *Cereal box density*
Students calculate the density of large and small boxes of cereal brand A to determine whether a larger and heavier object is more dense. The densities of the two boxes are plotted on graph paper (using one of the pencil colors).

STATION 1: *Instructions*

a. The density of any object is determined by dividing its mass (weight) by its volume. Mass is expressed in grams divided by volume (cubic centimeters). Example: 20 g/10 cm^3 = 2 g/cm^3
b. Measure the volume of the small cereal box (length × width × height), and use the balance to determine its mass in grams. The engineer can do the calculations on the calculator. The graph master should graph the results of each and connect the two points with a straight line.
c. Repeat the procedure using the large box of cereal.
d. The engineer computes the density of the cereal box with the calculator for both cereal boxes. Fill in the density spaces below the graph.

Object	*Density (g/cm³)*
1. Large box of cereal	
2. Small box of cereal	
3. Large brownie	
4. Small brownie	
5. Large sandbox	
6. Small sandbox	

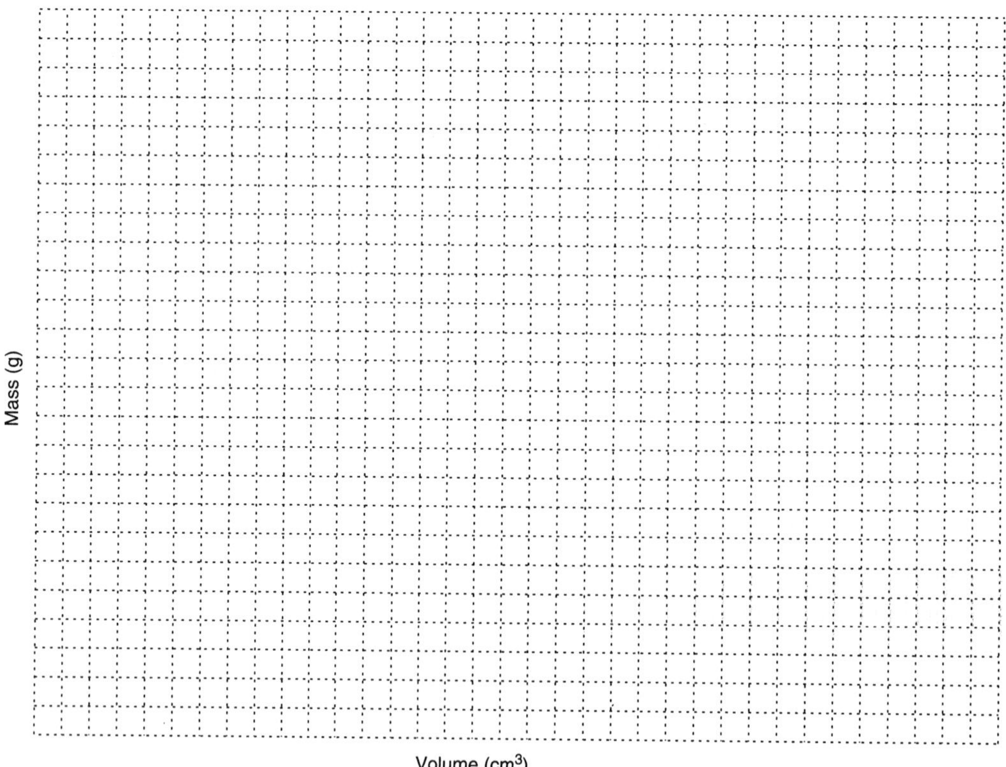

FIGURE 7.4 *Continued*

STATION 2: *Brownie density*
Students calculate the density of a full-size brownie and of a half-size brownie. Results are plotted on the same graph as in Station 1 (with a second color).

STATION 2: *Instructions*
a. The density of any object is determined by dividing its mass (weight) by its volume. Mass is expressed in grams divided by volume (cubic centimeters). Example: 20 g/10 cm^3 = 2 g/cm^3.
b. Measure the volume of the small brownie (length × width × height), and use the balance to determine its mass in grams. The engineer can do the calculations on the calculator. The graph master should graph the results of each and connect the two points with a straight line.
c. Repeat the procedure using the large brownie.
d. The engineer computes the density of the brownie with the calculator for both sizes. Fill in the density spaces below the graph.

STATION 3: *Sandbox density*
Students calculate the density of a large and a small box of sand, each filled half full with sand. Results are plotted on the same graph as in Stations 1 and 2 (with a third color).

STATION 3: *Instructions*
a. The density of any object is determined by dividing its mass (weight) by its volume. Mass is expressed in grams divided by volume (cubic centimeters). Example: 20 g/10 cm^3 = 2 g/cm^3.
b. Measure the volume of the small sandbox (length × width × height), and use the balance to determine its mass in grams. The engineer can do the calculations on the calculator. The graph master should graph the results of each and connect the two points with a straight line.
c. Repeat the procedure using the large sandbox.
d. The engineer computes the density of the boxes with the calculator for both sizes. Fill in the density spaces below the graph.

Lab work sheet
Teams return to their seats to do their graphing, to analyze their results, and to answer the following questions from their lab sheet.
a. Is a larger, heavier object always more dense than its smaller counterpart? Explain your evidence.
b. What is your definition of density?
c. Which is more dense, a pound of feathers or a pound of gold? Explain your answer.

3. Closure. When all teams are finished, teams should display their graphs, then share and discuss their results.

Reminder of week's assignments:
Concepts:
Density is one of the properties of matter.
Mass and volume are related.
Density is determined by dividing mass by volume.

Extension activities:
Use a density graph to calculate the mass and volume of a smaller piece of a brownie. Explore the story of Archimedes and the King's Crown.

Assessment, reflection, and revision:
Upon completion of this lesson and of the unit, on the basis of teacher observations and student achievement, this lesson may be revised.

FIGURE 7.4 *Continued*

students learn *as a result* of the activities of this lesson?" Your answer to that question is your objective! Objectives of the lesson are included then as specific statements of performance expectations, detailing precisely what students will be able to do as a result of the instructional activities. Teachers and students need to know what is expected from a lesson.

More recently, the national emphasis on educational content standards has resulted in statewide learning standards from which lesson objectives may be directly taken. Commonly, state standards in science consist of specific content areas that teachers are expected to teach at each grade level.

All three domains (cognitive, affective, and psychomotor) are not necessarily represented in every lesson plan. Any given lesson plan may be directed to only one or two, or a few, specific objectives. Over the course of a unit of instruction, however, all domains, and levels within each, should be addressed.

The following sample objectives are drawn from the lesson in Figure 7.3, with the domain and the level within that domain given in parentheses:

- Through cooperative group action, students will conduct experimental research to collect data about the ozone level of the air in their environment. (cognitive, application)
- Through the Internet, students will write response papers to their peers from other locations in the world. (cognitive, evaluation)
- Students will form judgments about local, regional, and worldwide ozone levels. (affective, organizing)
- Students will create a proposal for worldwide dissemination. (psychomotor, creating)

And, from the lesson illustrated in Figure 7.4, sample objectives are as follows:

- Determine the density of a solid cube. (cognitive, application)
- Communicate the results of their experiments to others in the class. (psychomotor, communicating)

Rationale

The rationale is an explanation of why the lesson is important and why the instructional methods chosen will achieve the objectives. Parents, students, teachers, administrators, and others have the right to know why specific content is being taught and why the methods employed are being used. Prepare yourself well by setting a goal for yourself of always being prepared with intelligent answers to those two questions.

Teachers become reflective decision makers when they challenge themselves to think about *what* (the content) they are teaching, *how* (the learning activities) they are teaching it, and *why* (the rationale) it must be taught. As illustrated in the sample unit in Figure 7.4, sometimes the rationale is included within the unit introduction, but not in every lesson plan of the unit. Some lessons are carryovers or continuations of a lesson; in these instances there is no reason to repeat the rationale for a continuing lesson.

Procedure

The procedure consists of the instructional activities for a scheduled amount of time. The substance of the lesson—the information to be presented, obtained, and learned—is the *content*. Appropriate information is selected to meet the learning objectives, the level of competence of the students, and the grade level or course requirements. To be sure your lesson actually covers what it should, you should write down exactly what minimum content you intend to cover. This material may be placed in a separate section or combined with the procedure section. The important thing is to be sure that your information is written down so you can refer to it quickly and easily when you need to.

If, for instance, you intend to conduct the lesson using discussion, you should write out the key discussion questions. Or, if you are going to introduce new material using a 12-minute lecture, then you need to outline the content of that lecture. The word *outline* is not used casually—you need not have pages of notes to sift through; nor should you ever read declarative statements to your students. You should be familiar enough with the content so that an outline (in as much detail as you believe necessary) will be sufficient to carry on the lesson.

The procedure or procedures to be used, sometimes referred to as the *instructional components,* comprise the *procedure* component of the lesson plan. This is the section that outlines what you and your students will do during the lesson. Appropriate instructional activities are chosen to meet the objectives, to match the students' learning styles and special needs, and to ensure that all students have an equal opportunity to learn. Ordinarily, you should plan this section of your lesson as an organized entity having a beginning (an introduction or set), a middle, and an end (called the closure) to be completed during the lesson. This structure is not always needed, because some lessons are simply parts of units or long-term plans and merely carry on activities spelled out in those long-term plans. Still, most lessons need to include in the procedure: (a) an *introduction,* the process used to prepare the students mentally for the lesson, sometimes referred to as the *set,* or *initiating activity;* (b) *lesson development,* the detailing of *activities* that occur between the beginning and the end of the lesson, including the transitions that connect activities; (c) plans for *practice,* sometimes referred to as the *follow-up,* that is, ways that you intend to have students interact in the classroom—working alone, in dyads, or in small groups—while receiving guidance or coaching from one another and from you; (d) the *lesson conclusion,* or *closure,* the planned process of bringing the lesson to an end, thereby providing students with a sense of completeness and, with effective teaching, accomplishment and comprehension by helping students to synthesize the information learned from the lesson; (e) a *timetable* to use as a planning and implementation guide; (f) a plan for what to do if you finish the lesson and time remains; and (g) *assignments,* that is, what students are instructed to do as follow-up to the lesson, either as homework or as in-class work, providing students an opportunity to practice and enhance what is being learned. Let's now consider some of those elements in detail.

Introduction to the Lesson. Like any good performance, a lesson needs an effective beginning. The introduction sets the tone for the rest of the lesson by alerting the students that the business of learning is to begin, and a thoughtful introduction makes clear that you are well prepared. The introduction should be an attention-getter. If it is exciting, interesting, or innovative, it can create a favorable mood for the lesson. Although developing an exciting introduction to every lesson taught each day is difficult, there are many ways to spice up the launching of a lesson. You might, for instance, begin by briefly reviewing the previous lesson, thereby helping students connect the learning. Another possibility is to review vocabulary words from previous lessons and to introduce new ones. Still another possibility is to use the key point of the day's lesson as an introduction and then again as the conclusion. Sometimes teachers begin a lesson by demonstrating a discrepant event (i.e., an event that is contrary to what one might expect, sometimes referred to as a *hook*). Yet another possibility is to begin the lesson with a writing activity on some controversial aspect of the ensuing lesson. For a lesson on adhesion and cohesion, a sample introduction might be as follows:

> The teacher takes a glass filled to the brim with colored water (colored so it is more visible) and asks students (in dyads) to discuss and predict how many pennies can be added to the glass before any water spills over the edge of the glass.

In short, you can use the introduction of the lesson to review past learning, tie the new lesson to the previous lesson, introduce new material, point out the objectives of the new lesson, or help students connect their learning with other disciplines or with real life. Showing what will be learned and why the learning is important will help motivate students and put them in a mindset favorable to the new lesson.

Lesson Development. The developmental activities or specifics by which you intend to achieve your lesson objectives, comprise the bulk of the plan. They include activities that present information, demonstrate skills, provide reinforcement of previously learned material, and provide other opportunities to develop understanding and skill. Furthermore, by actions and words during lesson development, the teacher models the behaviors expected of the students. Students need such modeling. Through effective modeling, the teacher can exemplify the anticipated learning outcomes. Activities of this section of the lesson plan should be described in some detail so (a) you will know exactly what you plan to do and (b) during the stress of the class meeting, you do not forget important details and content. For this reason you should consider, for example, noting answers (if known) to questions you intend to ask and solutions (if known) to problems you intend to have students solve.

Lesson Conclusion. Having a clear-cut closure to the lesson is as important as having a strong introduction. The closure complements the introduction. The concluding activity should summarize and bind together what has ensued in the developmental stage and should reinforce the principal points of the lesson. One way to accomplish these ends is to restate or briefly outline the key points of the lesson. Another is to repeat the major concept. Sometimes the closure is a review of what was learned as well as a summary of a question left unanswered that signals a change in your plan of activities for the next day. In other words, it becomes a transition to the next lesson. No matter what the concluding activity involves, it is usually brief and to the point.

Timetable. Try to gauge the amount of time needed for each learning activity and note it alongside the activity and strategy in your plan, as shown in the preferred sample lesson plan format. But be flexible. Placing too much faith in your time estimate may be foolish—an estimate is more for your guidance during the preactive phase of instruction than for anything else. Furthermore, estimating the time needed for a lesson can be very difficult, especially for beginning teachers, who frequently find that their planned discussions and presentations do not last as long as was expected. To avoid being embarrassed by running out of material, try to make sure you have planned enough meaningful work to consume the entire class period. (See "The Problem of Time" discussed earlier in this chapter.) Another important reason for including a time plan in your lesson is to give information to students about how much time they have for a particular activity, such as a quiz or a group activity.

Assignments and Assignment Reminders

Note in your lesson plan where an assignment is to be given. You can present an assignment to the students at any time—except, to repeat, it should never be called out as an afterthought as the students are exiting the classroom at the end of the period. Whether an assignment is to be started or started and completed during class time, or done entirely out of school, always write assignments on the writing board, in a special place on the bulletin board, in each student's assignment log maintained in a binder, or on a handout, taking extra care to be sure that assignment specifications are clear to the students. Many teachers give assignments to their students once a week. When given periodically, rather than daily, assignments should still show in your daily lesson plans as reminders to yourself to remind students of them.

Once assignment specifications and due dates are given, avoid making major modifications to them and, especially, do not change assignment specifications several days after an assignment has been given. Last-minute changes in assignment specifications can be very frustrating to students who have already begun or completed the assignment; it shows little respect for those students.

Special Notes and Reminders

Many teachers provide a place in their lesson plan format for special notes and reminders. Most of the time you will not need such reminders, but when you do, it helps to have them in a regular location in your lesson plan so you can refer to them quickly. In that special section, you can place reminders about such things as announcements to be made, school programs, long-term assignment due dates, and makeup work for certain students.

Materials and Equipment Needed

Materials of instruction include books, media, handouts, science supplies, and other materials necessary to accomplish the lesson objectives. Teachers must be *certain* that the proper and necessary materials and equipment are available for the lesson; to be certain requires planning. Teachers who, for one reason or another, have to busy themselves during class looking for materials or equip-

Anthony Magnacca/Merrill

Unit planning should include activities that allow children to work alone, in dyads, and in small groups. Grouping children and assigning roles facilitates science learning. When students have specific and understood tasks and responsibilities, they have more direction and will demonstrate a greater interest in learning.

ment that should have been readied before class began are likely to experience classroom control problems.

Assessment, Reflection, and Revision

Details of how you will assess how well students *are* learning (formative assessment) and how well they *have learned* (summative assessment) should be included in your lesson plan. This does not mean that both types of assessment will be in every daily plan. Comprehension checks for formative assessment can be in the form of questions that you ask and that the students ask during the lesson, as well as various kinds of checklists. Questions you intend to ask (and possible answers) should be built into the developmental section.

For summative assessment, teachers typically use review questions at the end of a lesson (as a closure) or at the beginning of the next lesson (as a review or transfer introduction); independent practice or summary activities at the completion of a lesson; and tests. Assessment is discussed fully in Chapter 8.

In most lesson plan formats, a section is reserved for the teacher to make notes or reflective comments about the lesson. Many student teachers seem to prefer to write their reflections at the end or on the reverse page of their lesson plans. As well as being useful to yourself, reflections about the lesson are useful for those who are supervising you if you are a student teacher or a teacher being mentored or considered for tenure. Sample reflective questions you might ask yourself are shown in Figure 7.5.

Writing and later reading your reflections can provide ideas that might be useful if you plan to use the lesson again at some later date, but writing also offers catharsis, easing the stress from teaching. To continue working effectively at a challenging task (that is, to prevent intellectual downshifting, or reverting to earlier learned, lower cognitive level behaviors) requires significant amounts of reflection.

- What is my overall feeling about today's lesson—good, fair, or bad? What made me feel this way?
- Did students seem to enjoy the lesson? What makes me think so?
- Did the objectives seem to be met? What evidence do I have?
- What aspects of the lesson went well? What makes me believe so?
- Were I to repeat the lesson, what changes might I make?
- Which students seemed to do well? Which ones should I give more attention to? Why and how?
- To what extent was this lesson individualized according to student learning styles, abilities, interests, talents, and needs? Could I do more in this regard? Why or why not?
- Did the students seem to have sufficient time to think and apply? Why or why not?
- Would I have been proud had the school superintendent been present to observe this lesson? Why or why not?

FIGURE 7.5 Questions for lesson self-reflection.

Personalizing the Unit and Lessons: Celebrating, Planning for, and Teaching with Student Diversity

It is well known, as emphasized in Chapter 3, that not all students learn and respond to learning situations in the same way. We know that students learn differently according to various elements of the situation, such as the time of day, the brightness of the classroom lighting, the amount of mobility allowed during their learning, whether the student is allowed to chew gum or take in food or drink while learning, the amount of peer interaction allowed and encouraged during the learning experience, and the student's ethnicity or socioeconomic status. Indeed, learning is an individual experience. You have learned about the individuality of the learning experience, the cognitive differences in learning, the differences in learning styles, and the learning strengths of individuals within a group. In addition, you must know about students' differences according to their socioeconomic backgrounds, ethnic and cultural backgrounds, and physical or learning disabilities. As a classroom teacher, you are placed in the difficult position of teaching 20 or more students as individuals, all at the same time. It seems like an impossible expectation, and it is important that its difficulties are understood. The rest of this chapter is designed to help you minimize failures and maximize successes. The information provided will help you tweak your unit and lesson plans in ways that best meet the needs of your unique group of children. Specifically, you must understand

1. The challenges of teaching posed by the diversity in students' backgrounds and instructional needs
2. General practices that are developmentally appropriate in meeting the needs of students in the classroom
3. Developmentally appropriate practice for teaching science to specific learners

Developmentally Appropriate Practice

Teachers must develop unit and lesson plans that provide instruction that is developmentally appropriate to meet the needs of their students. For teaching science to children of grades K–8, developmentally appropriate practice includes the use of thematic units and interdisciplinary team teaching, with the students simultaneously involved in a variety of tasks at several levels of skill involvement (i.e., multilevel teaching). There are other developmentally appropriate practices, and guidelines for using them to meet the diversity of students in the classroom are offered in the discussions that follow.

The Challenge

To help you meet the challenge in today's classroom teaching, a wealth of information is available. As a licensed teacher, you are expected to know it all, or at least know where you can find all the necessary information—and review it when needed. Certain information you have stored in memory will surface and become useful at the most unexpected times. In addition to being concerned about each student's safety and physical well-being, you will want to remain sensitive to each student's attitudes, values, social adjustment, emotional well-being, and cognitive development. You must be prepared not only to teach one or more subjects but to do it effectively with students of different cultural backgrounds, diverse linguistic abilities, and different learning styles, as well as with students who have been identified as having exceptionalities or special needs. It is, indeed, a challenge! The following statistics make even clearer this challenge.

Approximately one-half of the children in the United States will spend some years being raised by a single parent. Nationwide, it is estimated that as many as a quarter million children have no place at all to call home. Even with all the nation's resources and wealth, about one out of every ten children in the United States has a mental illness[7] and about one out of every five children live in poverty. This is inexcusable in these United States, the wealthiest nation on earth.[8]

By the year 2050, the nation's population is predicted to reach 400 million (from the approximately 283 million in 2001). This population boom is led by Hispanics and Asian Americans. Although non-white youths in the school-age population throughout the United States will average nearly 40% by 2050, a steady increase in interracial marriages and interracial babies may challenge today's conceptions of multiculturalism and race.[9]

The United States truly is a multilingual, multiethnic, multicultural nation. Of children ages five to seven, approximately one out of every six speaks a language other than English at home. Many of those children have only limited proficiency in the English language (i.e., conversational speaking ability only). In many large school districts, as many as 100 languages are represented, with as many as 20 or more different primary languages found in some classrooms. An increasing ethnic, cultural, and linguistic diversity is quickly and strongly affecting schools all across the country, not only in the large urban areas but also in traditionally homogeneous suburbs and small rural communities.

The overall picture that emerges is a diverse student population that challenges teaching skills. Teachers who traditionally have used direct instruction as the dominant mode of instruction, especially for science, have done so with the assumption that their students were relatively homogeneous in terms of experience, background, knowledge, motivation, and facility with the English language. However, no such assumption can be made in today's diverse classrooms. *As a classroom teacher today, you must be knowledgeable and skilled in using teaching strategies that recognize, celebrate, and build upon that diversity.* In a nutshell, that is your challenge.[10] As teachers, we must focus our efforts on our immediate realities. For our students, we can only control their educational experiences for the time they are in our classrooms. It is here that we must do our work.

---

[7] N. Shute, "Children in Anguish: A Call for Better Treatment of Kids' Mental Ills" [Online 1/8/01] http://www.usnews.com/usnews/issue/010115/kids.htm.

[8] H. Hodgkinson, "Educational Demographics: What Teachers Should Know," *Educational Leadership* 58(4):9 (December 2000/January 2001).

[9] See "race facts," pp. 8–9 in H. Hodgkinson, "Educational Demographics: What Teachers Should Know."

[10] There may be another recently occurring dimension to this challenge. As we prepare this edition of the book we read of elementary school teachers being instructed by their supervisors to do more, rather than less, direct instruction in order to help their children score well on the state's proficiency tests. Although increasing the amount of direct instruction may or may not help children score well on proficiency tests, it is inconsistent with what is known about instilling meaningful, longest-lasting learning.

From research and practical experience have come a variety of instructional techniques that do make a difference. The discussion that follows begins with general guidelines.

Instructional Practices That Provide for Student Differences: General Guidelines

To provide learning experiences that are consistent with what is known about ways of learning and knowing, consider the recommendations that follow (many of which are repeated from previous chapters of this book) and refer to them during your instructional planning.

- As frequently as is appropriate, and especially for science skills development, plan the learning activities so they follow a step-by-step sequence from concrete to abstract.
- Collaboratively plan, with students, challenging and engaging classroom learning activities and assignments.
- Concentrate on student-centered instruction by using project-centered learning, discovery and inquiry strategies, and simulations and role play.
- Establish multiple learning centers within the classroom.
- Maintain high, although not necessarily identical, expectations for each child; establish high standards and teach toward them without wavering. Contrary to most people's predisposition for equal treatment, children are very well aware that not everyone can be held to identical standards. Our focus should not be identical standards for all our students, but high standards for all our students.
- Make learning meaningful by integrating learning with life, helping each student successfully make the transitions from one level of learning to the next, from one level of schooling to the next, and from school to life.
- Provide a structured learning environment with regular and understood procedures.
- Provide ongoing and frequent monitoring of individual student learning (formative assessment).
- Provide variations in meaningful assignments.
- Use direct instruction to teach to the development of observation, generalization, and other thinking and learning skills.
- Use reciprocal peer coaching and cross-age tutoring.
- Use multilevel instruction.
- Use interactive computer programs and multimedia.
- Use small-group and cooperative learning strategies.

Because social awareness is such an important and integral part of a student's experience, many exemplary K–8 school programs and practices are geared toward some type of social interaction. Indeed, learning is a social enterprise among learners and their teachers. Although many of today's successful instructional practices rely heavily on social learning activities and interpersonal relationships, each teacher must be aware of and sensitive to individual student differences. For working with specific learners, consider the guidelines that follow and refer back to these guidelines during the preactive phase of your instruction.

Recognizing and Working with Students with Special Needs

Students with disabilities (referred to also as students with *special needs* or *exceptionalities*) include those with disabling conditions or impairments in any one or more of the following categories: mental retardation, hearing, speech or language, visual, emotional, orthopedic, autism, traumatic brain injury, other health impairment, or specific learning disabilities. To receive special education services, a child must have a disability in one or more of these categories and by reason thereof need special education and related services. In other words, not all children who have a disability need services available via special education. For example, children with hearing impairments would be entitled to special services when the impairment was so severe that they could not understand what was being said even when equipped with a hearing aid.

To the extent possible, students with special needs must be educated with their peers in the regular classroom. Public Law 94–142, the Education for All Handicapped Children Act (EAHCA) of 1975, mandates all children have the right to a free and appropriate education, as well as to nondiscriminatory assessment. (Public Law 94–142 was amended in 1986 by P.L. 99–457, and in 1990 by P.L. 101–476 at which time its name was

Scott Cunningham/Merrill

When planning, it is important to select content that lends itself to manageable learning activities. A well-planned, activity-based program of study benefits all types of learners and learning styles.

changed to Individuals with Disabilities Education Act—IDEA, and in 1997 by P.L. 105–17.) Emphasizing normalizing the educational environment for students with disabilities, this legislation requires provision of the least-restrictive environment (LRE) for these students. An LRE is an environment that is as normal as possible.

Teachers today know students with disabilities fall along a continuum of learner differences rather than in a separate category of student.[11] Because of their wide differences, students identified as having special needs might be placed in the regular classroom for the entire school day, called *full inclusion*. Students may also be in a regular classroom for the greater part of the school day, called *partial inclusion*, or only for designated periods. Although there is no single, universally accepted definition of the term, *inclusion* is the concept that students with disabilities should be integrated into general education classrooms regardless of whether they can meet traditional academic standards.[12] (The term *inclusion* has largely replaced the use of an earlier and similar term, *mainstreaming*.) As a classroom teacher, you will need information and skills that are specific to teaching the learners with special needs who are included in your classes.

Generally speaking, teaching students who have special needs requires more care, better diagnosis, greater skill, more attention to individual needs, and an even greater understanding of the students. The challenges of teaching students with special needs in the regular classroom are great enough that to do it well you need specialized training beyond the general guidelines presented here. At some point in your teacher preparation, you should take one or more courses in working with special-needs learners in the regular classroom.

When a student with special needs is placed in your classroom, your task is to deal directly with the differences between this student and other students in your classroom. To do this, you should develop an understanding of the general characteristics of different types of special-needs learners, identify the student's unique needs relative to your classroom, and design lessons that teach to different needs at the same time, called multilevel teaching, or multitasking.

Remember that just because a student has been identified as having one or more special needs does not preclude that person from being gifted or talented. Gifted students with disabling conditions remain a major group of poorly recognized and underattended-to youth, perhaps because focus on accommodations for their disabilities precludes adequate recognition and development of their gifts and talents.[13]

Congress stipulated in P.L. 94–142 that an Individualized Educational Program (IEP) be devised annually for each special-needs child. According to that law, an IEP is developed for each student each year by a team that includes special education teachers, the child's parents or guardians, and the classroom teachers. The IEP contains a statement of the student's present educational levels, the educational goals for the year, specifications for the services to be provided and the extent to which the student should be expected to take part in the regular education program, and the evaluative criteria for the services to be provided. Consultation by special and skilled support personnel is essential in all IEP models. A consultant works directly with teachers or with students and parents. As a classroom teacher, you may play an active role in preparing the specifications for the special-needs students assigned to your classroom and assume a major responsibility for implementing the program.

Guidelines for Working with Special-Needs Children in the Regular Classroom

Although the guidelines represented by the paragraphs that follow are important for teaching all students, they are especially important for working with special-needs children.

Familiarize yourself with exactly what the special needs of each learner are. Privately ask the special-needs student whether there is anything that you specifically can do to facilitate his or her learning.

Adapt and modify materials and procedures to the special needs of each student. For example, a student who has extreme difficulty sitting still for more than a few minutes will need planned changes in learning activities. When establishing seating arrangements in the classroom, give preference to students according to their special needs. Try to incorporate activities into lessons that engage all learning modalities—visual, auditory, tactile, and kinesthetic. Be flexible in your classroom procedures. For example, allow the use of electronic tools for note taking and test taking when students have trouble with the written language.

Look for science programs designed especially for special-needs learners such as "Science Activities for the Visually Impaired" and "Science Enrichment for Learners with Physical Handicaps," both developed at the Lawrence Hall of Science at the Berkeley campus of the University of California—http://www.lhs.berkeley.edu.

---

[11]A. Meyer and D. H. Rose, "Universal Design for Individual Differences," *Educational Leadership* 58(3):39–43 (November 2000), 40.

[12]E. Tiegerman-Farber and C. Radziewicz, *Collaborative Decision Making: The Pathway to Inclusion* (Upper Saddle River, NJ: Merrill/Prentice Hall, 1998), 12–13.

[13]C. Willard-Holt, *Dual Exceptionalities* (Reston, VA: ERIC Digest E574, ERIC Clearinghouse on Disabilities and Gifted Education, 1999).

Provide high structure and clear expectations by defining the learning objectives in behavioral terms. Teach students the correct procedures for everything. Break complex learning into simpler components, moving from the most concrete to the abstract, rather than the other way around. Check frequently for student understanding of instructions and procedures, and for comprehension of content. Use computers and other self-correcting materials for drill and practice and for providing immediate, constructive, and private feedback to the student.

Develop your with-it-ness (see Chapter 4), monitoring students for signs of restlessness, frustration, anxiety, and off-task behaviors. Be ready to reassign individual learners to different activities as the situation warrants. Classroom learning centers (discussed in Chapter 5) can be a big help.

Have all students maintain assignments for the week or some other period of time in an assignment book or in a folder kept in their notebooks. Post assignments in a special place in the classroom (and perhaps on the school's Website) and frequently remind students of assignments and deadlines.

Maintain consistency in your expectations and in your responses. Special-needs learners, particularly, can become frustrated when they do not understand a teacher's expectations and when they cannot depend on a teacher's reactions.

Plan interesting activities to bridge learning, and activities that help the students connect what is being learned with their real world. This helps motivate students and keep them on task.

Plan questions and questioning sequences and write them into your lesson plans. Plan the questions you ask special-needs learners so they are likely to answer them with confidence. Use signals to let students know you are likely to call on them in class (e.g., prolonged eye contact or mentioning your intention to the student before class begins). After asking a question, give the student adequate time to think and respond. Then, after the student responds, build upon the student's response to indicate the student's contribution was accepted as being important.

Provide for and teach toward student success. Offer activities and experiences that ensure each individual student's success and mastery at some level. Use of student portfolios (discussed in Chapter 8) can give evidence of progress and help build student confidence and self-esteem.

Provide scaffolded instruction; that is, give each child as much guided or coached practice as time allows. Provide time in class for students to work on assignments and projects. During this time, you can monitor the work of each student while looking for misconceptions, thus ensuring students get started on the right track.

Provide help in organizing of students' learning. For example, give instruction in the organization of notes and notebooks. Have a three-hole punch available in the classroom so students can put papers into their notebooks immediately, thus avoiding disorganization and loss of papers. During class presentations, use an overhead projector with transparencies; students who need more time can then copy material from the transparencies. Ask students to read their notes aloud to each other in small groups, thereby aiding their recall and understanding, and encouraging them to take notes for meaning rather than for rote learning. Encourage and provide for peer support, peer tutoring or coaching, and cross-age teaching. Ensure that the special-needs learner is included in all class activities to the fullest extent possible.

Recognizing and Working with Students of Diversity and Differences

Quickly determine the language and ethnic groups represented by the children in your classroom. A major problem for newcomers, as well as some ethnic groups, is learning a second (or third or fourth) language. Although in many schools it is not uncommon for more than half the students to come from homes where the spoken language is not English, using standard English is a necessity in most communities if a person is to become vocationally successful and enjoy a full life. Learning to communicate reasonably well in English can take an immigrant student at least a year and probably longer; some authorities say 3 to 7 years. By default, then, an increasing percentage of teachers are teachers of English language learning. It is helpful to the success of teaching students who are English Language Learners (ELLs) (those who have limited proficiency in English language usage) to demonstrate respect for the students' cultural backgrounds, to employ long-term, teacher-student cohorts (such as in looping where a teacher progresses with the same groups of students through a number of grade levels), and to use active and cooperative learning.[14]

There are numerous programs specially designed for English language learners. Most use the acronym LEP (limited English proficiency) with five number levels. LEP 1 designates non-English-speaking, although the student may understand single sentences and speak simple words or phrases in English. At the other end of the spectrum is LEP 5, sometimes designated FEP (fluent English proficiency), which means the student is fully fluent in English; however, his or her overall academic achievement may still be less than desired because of language or cultural differences.

Some schools use a pullout approach, where part of the student's school time is spent in special bilingual

---

[14] See P. Berman et al., *School Reform and Student Diversity, Volume II: Case Studies of Exemplary Practices for LEP Students* (Berkeley, CA: National Center for Research on Cultural Diversity and Second Language Learning, 1995).

classes and the rest of the time in regular classrooms. In some schools, LEP students are placed in academic classrooms that use a simplified or sheltered English approach. Regardless of the program, specific techniques recommended for teaching ELL students include the following:

- Allowing more time for learning activities than one normally would
- Allowing time for translation by a classroom aide or by a classmate and allowing time for discussion to clarify meaning, encouraging the students to transfer into English what they already know in their native language
- Avoiding jargon or idioms that might be misunderstood (See the scenario that follows.)
- Dividing complex or extended language discourse into smaller, more manageable units
- Giving directions in a variety of ways
- Giving special attention to key words that convey meaning, and writing them on the board
- Maintaining high expectations for each learner
- Reading written directions aloud, and then writing the directions on the board
- Speaking clearly and naturally but at a slower than normal pace
- Using a variety of examples and observable models
- Using simplified vocabulary but without talking down to students.[15]

Anthony Magnacca/Merrill

Social interaction is an important component for learning science. While learning science, children can also learn reading and language arts, social studies, mathematics, and how to cooperate with and respect others.

Additional Guidelines for Working with Language-Minority Students

While they are becoming literate in English language usage, LEP students can learn the same curriculum in the various disciplines as native English-speaking students. Although the guidelines presented in the following paragraphs are important for teaching all students, they are especially important when working with language-minority students.

Present instruction that is concrete and includes the most direct learning experiences possible. Use the most concrete (least abstract) forms of instruction.

Build upon, or connect with, what the students already have experienced and know. Building upon what students already know, or think they know, helps them connect their knowledge and construct their understandings.

Encourage student writing. One way is by using student journals. Two kinds of journals that are appropriate when working with LEP students are dialogue journals and response journals (see Chapter 5).

Help ELL students learn two vocabulary sets: the regular English vocabulary needed for learning and the new vocabulary introduced by the science content. While learning science, a student is dealing with both the regular English language vocabulary and the special vocabulary of science.

To the extent possible, involve parents guardians or older siblings. Students whose primary language is not English may have other differences that you should know about. These differences are related to culture, customs, family life, and expectations. To be most successful in working with language minority students, you should learn as much as possible about each student. Parents and guardians of new immigrant children are usually truly concerned about the education of their children and may be very interested in cooperating with you in any way possible. In a study of schools recognized for their exemplary practices with language-minority students, the schools were recognized for being "parent friendly," that is, for welcoming parents in a variety of innovative ways.[16]

Plan for and use all learning modalities. As with teaching young people in general, when working with language-minority students in particular you need to use multisensory approaches—learning activities that involve students in auditory, visual, tactile, and kinesthetic learning activities.

Use small group cooperative learning. Cooperative learning strategies are particularly effective with language-minority students because they provide opportunities for students to produce language in a setting that is less threatening than speaking before the entire class.

---

[15] D. R. Walling, *English as a Second Language: 25 Questions and Answers,* Fastback 347 (Bloomington, IN: Phi Delta Kappa Educational Foundation, 1993), 26. Adapted by permission.

[16] C. Minicucci et al., "School Reform and Student Diversity," *Phi Delta Kappan* 77(1):77–80 (September 1995), 78.

Classroom Scenario

A Humorous Scenario Related to Idioms: A Teachable Moment

While Elina was reciting, she had a little difficulty with her throat (due to a cold) and stumbled over some words. The teacher jokingly commented, "That's okay Elina, you must have a horse in your throat." Quickly, Fatana, a recent immigrant from Afghanistan, asked, "How could she have a horse in her throat?" The teacher ignored Fatana's question. Missing this teachable moment, he continued with his planned lesson.

Use the benefits afforded by modern technology. For example, computer networking allows the language-minority students to write and communicate with peers from around the world and to participate in "publishing" their classroom work.

Additional Guidelines for Working with Students of Diverse Backgrounds

To be compatible with and to be able to teach students who come from backgrounds different from yours, you need to believe that, given adequate support, all students *can* learn—regardless of gender, social class, physical characteristics, language, and ethnic or cultural backgrounds. You also need to develop special skills that include those in the following guidelines, each of which is discussed in detail in other chapters. To work successfully and most effectively with students of diverse backgrounds, you should

- Build the learning around students' individual learning styles. Personalize learning for each student, much like using the IEP with special-needs learners. Involve students in understanding and in making important decisions about their own learning, so they feel ownership (i.e., a sense of empowerment and connectedness) of that learning. As was stated previously, some schools report success using personalized learning plans for all students, not only those with special needs.
- Communicate positively with every student and with the student's parents or guardians, learning as much as you can about the student and the student's culture, and encouraging family members to participate in the student's learning. Involve parents guardians and other members of the community in the educational program so all have a sense of ownership and responsibility and feel positive about the school program.
- Establish and maintain high expectations, although not necessarily the same expectations, for each student. Both you and your students must understand that intelligence is not a fixed entity, but a set of characteristics that—through a feeling of "I can" and with proper coaching—can be developed.
- Teach to individuals by using a variety of strategies to achieve an objective or by using a number of different objectives at the same time.
- Use techniques that emphasize collaborative and cooperative learning—that de-emphasize competitive learning.

Recognizing and Working with Students Who Are Gifted

Historically, educators have used the term *gifted* when referring to a person with identified exceptional ability in one or more academic subjects, and *talented* when referring to a person with exceptional ability in one or more of the visual or performing arts.[17] Today, however, the terms more often are used interchangeably which is how they are used here; that is, as if they are synonymous.

Sometimes, unfortunately, in the regular classroom gifted students are neglected.[18] At least part of the time, it is probably because there is no singularly accepted method for identification of these students. In other words, students who are gifted in some way or another may go unidentified as such. For placement in special classes or programs for the gifted and talented, school districts traditionally have used grade point averages and standard intelligence quotient (IQ) scores. However, IQ testing measures linguistic and logical/mathematical aspects of giftedness (refer to earlier discussion in Chapter 3—Learning Capacities: The Theory of Multiple Intelligences), but it does not account for other giftedness, so gifted students sometimes are unrecognized. They also are sometimes among the students most at risk of dropping out of school.[19] It is estimated that between 10% and 20% of school dropouts are students who are in the range of being intellectually gifted.[20]

To work most effectively with gifted children, their talents first must be identified. This can be done not only

---

[17] See the discussion in G. Clark and E. Zimmerman, "Nurturing the Arts in Programs for Gifted and Talented Students," *Phi Delta Kappan* 79(10):747–751 (June 1998).

[18] See, for example, J. F. Feldhusen, "Programs for the Gifted Few or Talent Development for the Many?" *Phi Delta Kappan* 79(10):735–738 (June 1998).

[19] C. Dixon, L. Mains, and M. J. Reeves, *Gifted and At Risk,* Fastback 398 (Bloomington, IN: Phi Delta Kappa Educational Foundation, 1996), 7.

[20] S. B. Rimm, "Underachievement Syndrome: A National Epidemic," in N. Colangelo and G. A. Davis, eds., *Handbook of Gifted Education,* 2nd ed. (Needham Heights, MA: Allyn & Bacon, 1997), 416.

by using tests, rating scales, and auditions but also by observations in the classroom and out of the classroom, and from knowledge about the student's personal life. With those information sources in mind, indicators of superior intelligence include ability to assume adult roles and responsibilities at home or at school; ability to cope with school while living in poverty; ability to cope with school while living with dysfunctional families; ability to extrapolate knowledge to different circumstances; ability to lead others; ability to manipulate a symbol system; ability to reason by analogy; ability to retrieve and use stored knowledge to solve problems; ability to think and act independently; ability to think logically; creativity and artistic ability; a strong sense of self, pride, and worth; and understanding of one's cultural heritage.[21]

Every student, not only those identified as being gifted, needs a challenging academic environment. Although grouping and tracking students into classes based on interest and demonstrated ability is still widely practiced (such as reading groups, grade level retention, accelerated groups, and special education placement), an overwhelming abundance of sources in the literature adamantly opposes the homogeneous grouping of students according to ability, or *curriculum tracking*, as it has long been known. Grouping and tracking do not seem to increase overall achievement of learning, but they do promote inequity.[22]

Although many, perhaps most, research studies lead one to conclude that tracking as has been traditionally practiced should be discontinued because of its discriminatory and damaging effects on students, many schools continue using it. Direct examples are counseling students into classes according to evidence of ability and the degree of academic rigor of the program. Tracking also happens indirectly when certain classes and programs are designated as "academic" or "accelerated" and others as "non-academic" or "standard" and students are allowed some degree of latitude to choose, either partly or wholly, from one or the other.

Meaningful Curriculum Options: Multiple Pathways to Success

Because of what is now known about learning and intelligence, the trend today is to assume each student, to some degree and in some area of learning and doing, has the potential for giftedness, and to provide sufficient curriculum options, or multiple pathway, so each student can reach those potentials. Clearly, achievement in school increases when instruction is developmentally appropriate for the needs of particular students. Students learn more, enjoy learning, and remember more of what they have learned when individual learning capacities, styles, and modalities are identified and accommodated.

To provide relevant curriculum options, a trend in exemplary schools is to eliminate what have traditionally been the lower and general curriculum tracks and to instead provide curriculum options to try to assure success for each student. Educators are attempting to diminish the discriminatory and damaging effects on students that are believed to be caused by tracking and homogeneous ability grouping. They have devised and are refining numerous other seemingly more productive ways of attending to student differences, of providing a more challenging but supportive learning environment, and of stimulating the talents and motivation of each child. Using a combination of responsive practices concurrently is generally more effective than using any singular practice, so practices often overlap and are used simultaneously. These practices are shown in Figure 7.6.

- Adult advocacy relationships for each student
- Allowing a student to attend a high school class while still in middle grades
- Allowing a student to skip a traditional grade level, thereby accelerating the time in which a student passes through the K-12 grades
- Assuring bilingual programs are intellectually stimulating and designed for integration with mainstream education
- Community service learning that is connected to some portion of the academic program
- Cooperative learning in the classroom
- Curriculum compacting
- Extra effort to provide academic help
- Flexible block scheduling
- High expectation for each student
- Individualized educational plans and instruction for each child
- Integrating appropriate, relevant, and modern technologies into the curriculum
- Interdisciplinary teaming and thematic instruction
- Mastery learning with instructional scaffolding
- Peer and cross-age teaching
- Providing assistance with personal problems at school
- Second opportunity recovery strategies
- Specialized and/or smaller schools or schools within a school
- Ungraded or multiage grouping (looping)
- Within class and across discipline student-centered projects

FIGURE 7.6 Multiple pathways to success: Productive ways of attending to student differences, of providing a more challenging learning environment, and of stimulating the talents and motivation of each and every student.

[21]S. Schwartz, Strategies for Identifying the Talents of Diverse Students, ERIC/CUE Digest, Number 122 (New York: ED410323, ERIC Clearinghouse on Urban Education, May 1997).

[22]See J. Oakes et al., "Equity Lessons from Detracking Schools," Chapter 3 of A. Hargreaves, ed., *Rethinking Educational Change with Heart and Mind* (Alexandria, VA: ASCD 1997 Yearbook, Association for Supervision and Curriculum Development, 1997), 43–72.

Additional Guidelines for Working with Gifted Learners

When working in the regular classroom with a student who has special gifts and talents, you are advised to

- Collaborate with students in some planning of their personal objectives and activities for learning.
- Emphasize skills in critical thinking, problem solving, and inquiry.
- Identify and showcase the student's special gift or talent.
- Involve the student in selecting and planning activities, encouraging the development of the student's leadership skills.
- Plan assignments and activities that challenge the students to the fullest of their abilities. This does *not* mean overloading them with homework or giving identical assignments to all students. Rather, carefully plan so students' time spent on assignments and activities is quality time on meaningful learning.
- Provide in-class seminars for students to discuss topics and problems they are pursuing individually or as members of a learning team.
- Provide independent and dyad learning opportunities. Gifted and talented students often prefer working alone or with another gifted student.
- Use curriculum compacting, a process that allows a student who already knows the material to pursue enriched or accelerated study.[23] Plan and provide optional and voluntary enrichment activities. Learning centers, special projects, and computer and multimedia activities are excellent tools for providing enriched learning activities.
- Use preassessments (diagnostic evaluation) for reading level and subject content achievement so you are better able to prescribe objectives and activities for each student.

Summary

Theories about the intellectual, physical, and social-emotional development of young people directly affect the school science program. Teachers must be aware of the developmental level of each student and plan developmentally appropriate content and instruction to meet their students' diverse needs. Because learning is both a social and an individual process, teachers must be prepared to develop interactive and individual instruction for the students.

A concern to many elementary school teachers is how to find time to teach all of the required content areas of the curriculum. A very real problem in elementary schools is that many teachers give less attention to science and social science than they give to English/language arts/reading and mathematics instruction. Many teachers use an integrated approach, effectively combining the teaching of English/language arts/reading with the teaching of mathematics, science, social science, or art, or with some combination of these, often by using interdisciplinary thematic units. When planned and implemented effectively, interdisciplinary thematic instruction can provide both interactive and individual instruction for the students.

As has been emphasized several times in this book, all children in today's classrooms can do higher levels of thinking and gain understandings that are most meaningful and long lasting when disciplines are integrated and made relevant to their lives and when instructional techniques involve the learners in social interactive learning, such as cooperative learning, peer tutoring, and cross-age teaching.

Now, to finalize your understanding and your knowledge about unit and lesson planning, Chapter 8, the final chapter of Part One, addresses the *how well the children are learning* component of effective teaching; that is, the assessment component.

Questions for Class Discussion

1. Form teams of four, and have each team develop one interdisciplinary thematic unit with a science component for use at a specific grade level.
2. From a variety of sources, obtain current samples of science resource units, teaching units, and interdisciplinary thematic units and share and discuss them with your classmates.
3. Describe the characteristics of children who may be at-risk students. Describe what the classroom teacher can do to put these students at less academic risk. Is it possible that a student identified as being at risk is also one who is gifted and talented? Explain.
4. Explain what is meant by the term *developmentally appropriate practice*. Describe at least five instructional practices that are considered appropriate for teaching science to all K–8 students and explain why those practices are developmentally appropriate.

---

[23] See, for example, K. K. Sutton, "Curriculum Compacting: Teaching Science in a Heterogeneous Classroom," *Science Scope* 24(4):22–27 (January 2001).

5. The planning and structure of a lesson are often predictors of the success of its implementation. Consider this scenario of a real lesson that took place one spring semester in a middle school life science class. The class period ran from 1:12 to 2:07, immediately after lunch.

1:12	Tardy bell rings.
1:12–1:21	Teacher directs students to read from their textbooks, while the teacher takes attendance.
1:21–1:31	Teacher distributes a handout to each student; students are to label the parts of a flower shown on the handout.
1:31–1:37	Silent reading and labeling of the flower on the handout.
1:37–1:39	Teacher verbally gives instructions for working on a real flower (e.g., by comparing it with the drawing on the handout). Students may use the microscopes if they want.
1:39–1:45	Teacher walks around room, giving each student a real flower.
1:45–2:05	Chaos erupts. There is much confusion, with students wandering around, throwing flower parts at each other. Teacher begins writing referrals and sends two students to the office for their misbehavior. Teacher is flustered, directs students to spend remainder of period quietly reading from their textbooks. Two more referrals are written.
2:05–2:07	Several students begin meandering toward the classroom exit.
2:07	End of period (much to the delight of the teacher).

Answer the following questions and use your responses as a basis for class discussion about the lesson.

a. Do you think the teacher had a lesson plan? If so, what if any were its good points? Its problems?
b. If you believed that the teacher had a lesson plan, do you believe that it was written and detailed? Explain your response. What is your evidence?
c. How might the lesson have been prepared and implemented to avoid the chaos?
d. Was the format of the lesson traditional? Explain.
e. Have you experienced a class such as this? Explain.
f. Which teacher behaviors were probable causes of much of the chaos? (*Hint:* You might want to refer to Chapters 4 and 5.)
g. What might the teacher have done (teacher behaviors) to prevent the chaos and make the lesson more effective?
h. Within the 55-minute class period, students were expected to operate rather high on the Learning Experiences Ladder (see Figure 5.4). Consider this analysis: 9 minutes of silent reading; 10 minutes of listening; 6 minutes of silent reading and labeling; 2 minutes of listening; 6 minutes of active learning (the only direct experience); and an additional 22 minutes of silent reading. In all, there were approximately 49 minutes (89 percent of the class time) of abstract verbal and visual symbolization. Is this a problem?

6. Do you have questions generated by the content of this chapter? Where might answers be found?

Chapter **8**

Assessing and Reporting Student Achievement

Maria B. Vonada/Merrill

Teachers of science engage in ongoing assessment of their teaching and of student learning.

- Teachers systematically gather data on students and their development.
- Teachers analyze assessment data to guide teaching.
- Teachers guide students in self-assessment.[1]

It should be quite apparent to you by now that competent teaching is a kaleidoscopic, multifaceted, and eclectic process. When preparing and writing a book to use in one segment of a teacher preparation program one must separate that kaleidoscopic process into separate parts. It is not always possible to do this in a way that makes the most sense to everyone using the book. For the sake of clarity and sensible organization, this book is divided into two parts with numerous chapters in each part. While preceding chapters of this Part One addressed the *why* (Chapter 1), *what* (Chapters 2 and 3), and *how* (Chapters 4 through 7) of teaching and learning, the focus in this final chapter of Part One is on the fourth component—the *how well,* or assessment, component. Together, these four components are the essentials of effective instruction, regardless of subject or grade level. It is neither likely nor advisable that one should or could effectively learn about one part entirely exclusive of the others. The four parts are inextricably intertwined, each affected by and dependent upon the others. Therefore, the assessment component deals with both how well the students are learning and how well the teacher is teaching.

Assessment is addressed as the fourth and final component of effective instruction, but it is really an integral part of an ongoing process in the total educational arena. Curricula, buildings, materials, specific courses, teachers, supervisors, administrators, and equipment must all be periodically assessed in relation to student learning—the purpose of the school. When gaps between anticipated results and student achievement exist, efforts are made to eliminate the factors that seem to be limiting the educational output or, in some other way, to improve the situation. Thus, educational progress occurs.

Much concern today is expressed over what is referred to as *high-stakes assessments.* An assessment is called *high stakes* if use of the assessment's results carry serious consequences; for example, a student's grade level promotion or graduation from high school rests on the student's performance on a single test. We agree with the many educators who argue that important decisions that affect an individual student's educational career should not rest on just one test score but on multiple sources of data that accumulate over a period of time. Some fear that placing high reliance on a single source of data will cause an increase in the school dropout rate. In a recent joint announcement, Vincent Ferrandino and Gerald Tirozzi, executive directors of the National Association of Elementary School Principals (NAESP) and the National Association of Secondary School Principals (NASSP), respectively, said "Test results should not be used to reward or punish a school, a system, or a state, but instead should be used as diagnostic tools to improve teaching and learning. Tests should not be used for high-stakes purposes or as exit exams."[2]

To learn effectively, students need to know how they are doing and how they can improve. Similarly, to be an effective teacher, you must be informed about what the student knows, feels, and can do so that you can help the student build on her or his skills, knowledge, and attitudes. You and your students need continuous feedback on their progress and problems so you can plan appropriate learning activities and make adjustments to those already planned. If this feedback says that progress is slow, you can provide alternative activities; if it indicates that some or all of the students have already mastered the desired learning, you can eliminate unnecessary

[1]Reprinted from National Research Council, *National Science Education Standards,* © 1996 by the National Academy of Sciences, 37–38. Courtesy of the National Academy Press, Washington, DC.

[2]V. L. Ferrandino and G. N. Tirozzi, "Test Driven or Data Driven," *NAESP Principal Online,* June 15, 2001.

activities and practice for those students. In short, assessment provides a key for both competent teaching and effective learning.

The importance of continuous assessment mandates that you are knowledgeable about various principles and techniques of assessment. This chapter explains some of those and shows you how to construct and use assessment instruments. It defines terms related to assessment suggests procedures to use in the construction of assessment items, and identifies the advantages and disadvantages of different types of assessment items and procedures.

Anthony Magnacca/Merrill

There are many ways to assess student achievement. Children's developing abilities and skills in science can be assessed through direct observation made by the teacher to determine a child's thinking and how well the child can manipulate materials.

In addition, this chapter discusses grading (or marking) and reporting student achievement, two responsibilities that can consume much of a teacher's time and cause frustration for many teachers. What should be graded? Should grades or marks represent student growth, level of achievement in a group, effort, attitude, general behavior, or a combination of these? What should determine grades—homework, tests, projects, class participation and group work, or some combination of these? And what should be their relative weights? These are just a few of the questions that have plagued teachers, parents/guardians, and the profession in general and for a century or more of education in this nation.

The development of the student encompasses growth in the cognitive, affective, and psychomotor domains (discussed in Chapter 2). Traditional objective paper-and-pencil tests provide only a portion of the data needed to indicate student progress in those domains. Many experts have always questioned traditional sources of data and encourage the search for, development of, and use of alternative means to assess more authentically the students' development of thinking and higher-level learning. Although there are still many unknowns, it is clear that various techniques of assessment with the resultant multiple kinds of data must be used to determine how the student works, what the student is learning, and what the student can produce as a result of that learning. As a teacher, you must develop a repertoire of ways to assess learner behavior and academic progress. Be patient and kind to yourself; to become skilled in the practices of assessment will take considerable study, time, practice, and reflection.

Although marks and grades have been a part of school for more than a century, it is clear to many experts that the conventional report card with marks or grades falls short of being a developmentally appropriate procedure for reporting the academic performance or progress of learners. Some schools are experimenting with other ways of reporting student achievement in learning, but letter grades, especially for grades 4 and up, still seem firmly entrenched. Parents and guardians, students, colleges, and employers have come to expect grades as evaluations. Today's focus is (or should be) more on what the student can do (performance testing) as a result of learning than merely on what the student can recall (memory testing) from the experience.[3] This fact is reflected, for example, in the state curriculum standards that have been published in recent years.

In addition, there have been complaints about subjectivity and unfair practices. As a result of these concerns, various systems of assessment and reporting have evolved and are still evolving. They will likely continue to evolve throughout your professional career.

When teachers are aware of alternative systems, they are better prepared to develop assessment and reporting practices that are fair and effective for particular situations. So, after beginning with assessment, the final portion of this chapter considers briefly today's principles and practices in grading and reporting student achievement.

[3]See, for example, C. Demers, "Beyond Paper-and-Pencil Assessments," *Science and Children* 38(2):24–29, 60 (October 2000).

Purposes and Principles That Guide the Assessment Program

Assessment of achievement in student learning is designed to serve several purposes. These are as follows:

To *assist in student learning*. This is the purpose usually thought of first when speaking of assessment, and it is the principal topic of this chapter. For the classroom teacher, it is (or should be) the most important purpose.

To *identify students' strengths and weaknesses*. Identification and assessment of students' strengths and weaknesses are necessary for two reasons: to structure and restructure learning activities and to restructure the curriculum. Concerning the first, for example, data on student strengths and weaknesses in science content and process skills are important in planning activities appropriate for both skill development and intellectual development. This is *diagnostic assessment* (known also as preassessment). For the second, data on student strengths and weaknesses in content and skills are useful for making appropriate modifications to the curriculum.

To *assess the effectiveness of a particular instructional strategy*. It is important for you to know how well a particular strategy helped accomplish a specific goal or objective. Exemplary teachers continually reflect on and evaluate their strategy choices, using a number of sources: student achievement as measured by assessment instruments, their own intuition, informal feedback given by the students, and, sometimes, informal feedback given by colleagues, such as members of a teaching team or mentor teachers.

To *assess and improve the effectiveness of curriculum programs*. Committees composed of teachers and administrators and sometimes parents/guardians, students, and other members of the school and community continually assess components of the curriculum. The assessment is done while students are learning (formative assessment) and afterward (summative assessment).

To *assess and improve teaching effectiveness*. To improve student learning, teachers are periodically evaluated on the basis of (a) their commitment to working with students; (b) their ability to cope with students at a particular age, or developmental or grade level; (c) the achievement of subject matter knowledge by the students they teach; and (d) their ability to show mastery of appropriate instructional techniques articulated throughout this text.

To *provide data that assist in decision making about a student's future*. Assessment of student achievement in grades K–8 is important in guiding decision making about program placement, promotion, and school transfer.

To provide data in order to *communicate with and involve parents/guardians in their children's learning*. Parents/guardians, communities, and school boards all share in accountability for the effectiveness of the children's learning. Today's schools are reaching out, perhaps more than ever before, and engaging parents guardians and the community in their children's education. All teachers play an important role in the process of communicating with, reaching out to, and involving parents/guardians and the community.

Because the welfare and, indeed, the future of so many people depend on the outcomes of assessment, it is impossible to overemphasize its importance. For a learning endeavor to be successful, the learner must have answers to basic questions: Where am I going? Where am I now? How do I get where I am going? How will I know when I get there? Am I on the right track for getting there? These questions are integral to a good program of assessment. Of course, in the process of teaching and learning, the answers may be ever-changing. The teacher and students must continue to assess and adjust plans as appropriate and necessary. As you have been reminded many times in Part One of this book, the exemplary school is in a mode of continuous change and progress.

The following principles guide the assessment program and are reflected in the discussions in this chapter. They are based on the questions in the preceding paragraph.

- A teacher's responsibility is to facilitate student learning and to assess student progress in that learning. For that, the teacher should be held accountable.
- Assessment is a continuous process. The selection and implementation of plans and activities require continuous monitoring and assessment to check on progress and to change or adopt strategies to promote desired behavior.
- Assessment is a reciprocal process, which includes assessment of teacher performance as well as student achievement.
- Evidence and input data for knowing how well the teacher and students are doing should come from a variety of sources and types of data-collecting devices.
- Reflection and self-assessment are important components of any successful assessment program. Reflection and self-assessment are important if students are to develop the skills necessary for them to assume increasingly greater ownership of their own learning. Reflection and self-assessment are important for the continued and increasing effectiveness of a teacher.
- Students need to know how well they are doing.
- Teachers need to know how well they are doing.
- The program of assessment should aid teaching effectiveness and contribute to the intellectual, social, and psychological growth of students.

Terms Used in Assessment: A Clarification

When discussing the assessment component of teaching and learning, it is easy to be confused by the terminology used. The following clarification of terms is offered to aid your reading and comprehension.

Anthony Magnacca/Merrill

Assessment of student learning is an ongoing process that involves children in their own self-assessment.

Assessment and Evaluation

Although some authors distinguish between the terms *assessment* (the process of finding out what students are learning, a relatively neutral process) and *evaluation* (making sense of what was found out, a subjective process), for the purposes of this text we do not. We consider the difference to be too slight to matter and treat the terms as synonymous.

Measurement and Assessment

Measurement refers to quantifiable data about specific behaviors. Tests and the statistical procedures used to analyze the results are examples. Measurement is a descriptive and objective process; that is, it is relatively free from human value judgments.

Assessment includes objective data from measurement but also from other types of information. Some of this is more subjective, such as information from anecdotal records and teacher observations, and ratings of student performance. In addition to objective data (data from measurement), assessment also includes arriving at value judgments made on the basis of subjective information.

An example of the use of these terms is as follows. A teacher may share the information that Margo Black received a score in the 30th percentile on the eighth-grade statewide achievement test in science (a statement of measurement) but may add that "according to my assessment of her work in my science class, she has been an excellent student" (a statement of assessment).

Validity and Reliability

The degree to which an instrument actually measures what it is intended to measure is its validity. For example, when we ask if an instrument (such as a performance assessment instrument) has validity, key questions are: Does the instrument adequately sample the intended content? Does it measure the cognitive, affective, and psychomotor knowledge and skills that are important to the unit of content being tested? Does it sample all the instructional objectives of that unit?

The accuracy with which a technique consistently measures what it is intended to measure is its reliability. If, for example, you know that you weigh 114 pounds, and a scale consistently records 114 pounds when you stand on it, then that scale has reliability. However, if the same scale consistently records 105 pounds when you stand on it, we can still say the scale has reliability. An instrument can be reliable, producing similar results when used again and again, but not necessarily valid. The scale is not measuring what it is supposed to measure, so although it is reliable, it is not valid. *A technique might be reliable but not valid, but a technique must have reliability before it can have validity*. The greater the number of test items or situations on a particular content objective, the higher the reliability. The higher the reliability, the more consistency there will be in students' scores measuring their understanding of a particular objective.

Authentic Assessment

When assessing for student achievement, it is important that you use procedures that are compatible with the instructional objectives. This is referred to as authentic assessment. It is also called *accurate, active, aligned, alternative,* or *direct assessment*. The term *performance assessment* is sometimes used, but that refers to the type of student response being assessed, whereas authentic assessment refers to the assessment situation. Although not all performance assessments are authentic, assessments that are authentic are most assuredly performance assessments.[4]

[4]See, for example, the discussion on pp. 213–214 in A. Oosterhof, *Classroom Applications of Educational Measurement,* 3rd ed. (Upper Saddle River, NJ: Merrill/Prentice Hall, 2001).

"If students have been actively involved in classifying objects using multiple characteristics, it sends them a confusing message if they are then required to take a paper-and-pencil test that asks them to 'define classification' or recite a memorized list of characteristics of good classifications schemes."[5] An authentic assessment technique would be a performance item that actually involves the students in classifying objects. In other words, to obtain an accurate assessment of a student's learning, the teacher uses a performance-based assessment procedure, that is, a procedure that requires students to produce rather than to select a response.

Advantages claimed for the use of authentic assessment include the direct (also known as performance-based, criterion-referenced, outcome-based, standard-based) measurement of what students should know and can do, and an emphasis on higher-order thinking. Disadvantages of authentic assessment include a higher cost; difficulty in making results consistent and usable; and problems with validity, reliability, and comparability.

Unfortunately, a teacher may never see a particular student again after a given school semester or year is over, so the effect that teacher has had on a student's values and attitudes may never be observed by that teacher. In schools where groups or teams of teachers remain with the same cohort of students—as in the school-within-a-school and looping programs—those teachers often do have the opportunity to observe the positive changes in their students' values and attitudes.

Diagnostic, Formative, and Summative Assessment

Assessing a student's achievement is a three-stage process, involving the following:

1. *Diagnostic assessment* (sometimes called preassessment)—the assessment of the student's knowledge and skills *before* the new instruction
2. *Formative assessment*—the assessment of learning *during* the instruction
3. *Summative assessment*—the assessment of learning *after* the instruction, ultimately represented by the student's final term, semester, or year's achievement grade

Grades (or marks) shown on unit tests, progress reports, deficiency notices, and interim reports are examples of formative assessment reports. However, an end-of-chapter test or a unit test is summative when the test represents the absolute end of the student's learning of material for that instructional unit.

[5]S. J. Rakow, "Assessment: A Driving Force," *Science Scope* 15(6):3 (March 1992).

 Assessing Student Learning: Three Avenues

Three general avenues are available for assessing a student's achievement in learning. You can assess

1. What the student *says*—for example, the quantity and quality of a student's contributions to class discussions
2. What the student *does*—for example, a student's performance, such as the amount and quality of a student's participation in the learning activities
3. What the student *writes* (or *draws*)—for example, as shown by items in the student's portfolio, such as homework assignments, checklists, project work, and written tests

Although your own situation and personal philosophy will dictate the levels of importance and weight you give to each avenue of assessment, you should have a strong rationale if you value and weigh the three avenues for assessment differently than one-third each.

Assessing What a Student Says and Does

When evaluating what a student says, you should listen to the student's oral reports, questions, responses, and interactions with others, and observe the student's attentiveness, involvement in class activities, creativeness, and responses to challenges. Notice that we say you should *listen* and *observe*. While listening to what the student is saying, you should also be observing the student's nonverbal behaviors. For this you can use narrative observation forms (see Figure 8.1), observations with checklists and scoring rubrics (see sample checklists in Figures 8.2, 8.3, 8.5, and 8.6, and sample scoring rubrics in Figures 5.6, 8.3, 8.4, 8.12, and 8.13), and periodic conferences with the student.

Anthony Magnacca/Merrill

While listening to what the student says, the teacher also observes the student's nonverbal behaviors.

Student ______	Class ______	School ______
Observer ______	Date ______	Period ______
Objective	Desired behavior	What student did, said, or wrote
Teacher's (observer's) comments:		

FIGURE 8.1 Sample form for evaluating and recording student verbal and nonverbal behaviors.

Activity Number ______ Date ______ Student ______

Skills Record

Observe	Classify	Communicate	Measure	Predict	Infer	Other	Teacher comments

Attitude Record

Curious	Persistent	Open-Minded	Cooperative	Withholds Judgment	Other	Teacher comments

FIGURE 8.2 Checklist for recording students' sciencing process skills and attitudes development.

With each technique used, you must proceed from your awareness of anticipated learning outcomes (the instructional objectives), to assess a student's progress toward meeting those objectives. That is referred to as *criterion-referenced* assessment.

Observation Form

Figure 8.1 illustrates a sample generic form for recording and evaluating teacher observations of a student's verbal and nonverbal behaviors. With modern technology, such as that afforded by the software program

Sample Checklist for Assessing a Student's Skill in Map Work

Check each item if the map comes up to standard in this particular category.

_________ 1. Accuracy

_________ 2. Neatness

_________ 3. Attention to details

Sample Rubric for Assessing a Student's Skill in Listening

Score Point 3—Strong listener

Responds immediately to oral directions
Focuses on speaker
Maintains appropriate attention span
Listens to what others are saying
Is interactive

Score Point 2—Capable listener
Follows oral directions
Is usually attentive to speaker and to discussions
Listens to others without interrupting

Score Point 1—Developing listener
Has difficulty following directions
Relies on repetition
Is often inattentive
Has short attention span
Often interrupts the speaker

FIGURE 8.3 Checklist and rubric compared.

Score Point 4—correct purpose, mode, audience; effective elaboration; consistent organization; clear sense of order and completeness; fluent

Score Point 3—correct purpose, mode, audience; moderately well elaborated; organized but possible brief digressions; clear, effective language

Score Point 2—correct purpose, mode, audience; some elaboration; some specific details; gaps in organization; limited language control

Score Point 1—attempts to address audience; brief, vague, unelaborated; wanders off topic; lack of language control; little or no organization; wrong purpose and mode

FIGURE 8.4 Sample scoring rubric for assessing student writing. *Source:* Texas Education Agency, *Writing Inservice Guide for English Language Arts and TAAS* (Austin, TX: Author, 1993).

Learner Profile, a teacher can record observations electronically anywhere at any time.[6] Figure 8.2 is a checklist for recording students' science process skills and attitudes development.

Checklist versus Scoring Rubric

As you can see from the sample rubric and sample checklist shown in Figure 8.3, there is little difference between a checklist and a rubric. Rubrics show the degrees for the desired characteristics, and checklists usually show only the desired characteristics. The checklist could easily be made into a scoring rubric and the rubric could easily be made into a checklist.

Guidelines for Assessing What a Student Says and Does

When assessing a student's verbal and nonverbal behaviors in the classroom, you should

- Maintain an anecdotal record book (teacher's log) or folder, with a separate section for each student.
- List the desirable behaviors for a specific activity.
- Check the list against the specific instructional objectives.
- Record your observations as quickly as possible following your observation. Audio or video recordings and, of course, computer software programs can help you maintain records and check the accuracy of your memory. If this is inconvenient, you should spend time during school, immediately after school, or during the evening recording your observations while they are still fresh in your memory.
- Record your professional judgment about the student's progress toward the desired behavior, but think it through before transferring it to a permanent record.
- Write comments that are reminders to yourself, such as, "Discuss observation with the student," "Check validity of observation by further testing," and "Discuss observations with colleagues on the teaching team."

Assessing What a Student Writes

To assess what a student writes, you can use worksheets, written homework and papers, student journal writing, student writing projects, student portfolios, and tests (all discussed later in this chapter). In many schools, portfolios, worksheets, and homework assignments are the tools usually used for the formative evaluation of each student's achievement. Tests, too, should be a part of this evaluation, but tests are also used for summative evaluation at the end of a unit and for diagnostic purposes.

Guidelines for Assessing Student Writing

Use the following guidelines when assessing what a student writes.

Student writing assignments, test items, and scoring rubrics (see Figure 8.4) *should be criterion-referenced;* that

[6]For information about *Learner Profile,* see http://www.sunburst-store.com.

is, they should correlate with and be compatible with specific instructional objectives. Regardless of the avenue you choose and the relative weights you assign, you must evaluate against the instructional objectives. Any given objective may be checked by using more than one method and by using more than one instrument. Subjectivity, inherent in the assessment process, may be reduced as you check for validity—comparing results of one measuring strategy against those of another.

Read nearly everything a student writes. (Note: We are not talking here about student diaries and private journals, which are just that—private. In our opinion, they should be left at home, not brought to school.) Regarding schoolwork, if it is important for the student to do the work, then it is equally important that you give your professional attention to the product of the student's efforts. Of course, in deference to the teacher's productive and efficient use of valuable time, student papers can be read with varying degrees of intensity and scrutiny, depending on the purpose of the assignment.

Provide written or verbal comments about the student's work, and be positive in those comments. Rather than just writing "good" on a student's paper, briefly state what, in your opinion, made it good. Rather than simply saying or pointing out that the student didn't do it right, tell or show the student what is acceptable and how to achieve it. For reinforcement, use positive comments and encouragement as frequently as possible.

Think before writing a comment on a student's paper, asking yourself how you think the student (or a family member) will interpret and react to the comment, and whether that is a correct interpretation of or reaction to your intended meaning. (See "Teacher's Log with a Caution About Anecdotal Comments" later in this chapter.)

Avoid writing evaluative comments or grades in student journals.[7] Student journals are for encouraging students to write, to think about their thinking, and to record their creative thoughts. In journal writing, students should be encouraged to write about their experiences in school and out of school and especially about their experiences and feelings related to what is being learned and how they are learning it. Writing in journals gives them practice in expressing themselves in written form and in connecting their learning; it should provide nonthreatening freedom to do so. Comments and evaluations from teachers might discourage creative and spontaneous expression. You can write simple empathic comments such as "Thank you for sharing your thoughts," or "I think I understand what makes you feel that way."

When reading student journals, talk individually with students to seek clarification about their expressions. Student journals are useful to the teacher (of any subject) in understanding the student's thought processes and writing skills (diagnostic assessment), and should not be graded. For grading purposes, teachers may simply record whether students are maintaining journals and, perhaps, how much they are writing in them, but no judgment should be made about the quality. In the end, the only way to get better at writing is to actually write; student journals offer this outlet.

When reviewing student portfolios, discuss with students individually the progress in their learning as shown by the materials in their portfolios. As with student journals, the portfolio should not be graded or compared in any way with those of other students. Its purpose is for student self-assessment and to show progress in learning. For this to happen, students should keep in their portfolios all, or major samples of, papers related to the course. (Student portfolios are discussed later.)

Assessment for Affective and Psychomotor Domain Learning

While assessment of cognitive domain learning lends itself to traditional written tests of achievement, the assessment of learning within the affective and psychomotor domains is best accomplished by using performance checklists where student behaviors can be observed in action. However, many educators today are encouraging the use of alternative assessment procedures (i.e., alternatives to traditional paper-and-pencil written testing). After all, in learning what is most important to students and what has the most meaning to them, the domains are inextricably interconnected. Learning that is meaningful to students is not as easily compartmentalized as the taxonomies of educational objectives would imply. Alternative assessment strategies include the use of projects, portfolios, skits, papers, oral presentations, and performance tests.

Anthony Magnacca/Merrill

Portfolios can be used for instruction and as one means of assessing student learning.

[7] See, for example, A. Chandler, "Is This for a Grade? A Personal Look at Journals," *English Journal 86*(1):45–49 (January 1997).

Student Participation in Assessment

Students' continuous self-assessment should be planned as an important component of the assessment program. If students are to progress in their metacognition and in their intellectual development, they must receive instruction and guidance in how to become more responsible for their own learning. During that empowerment process, they learn to think better of themselves and of their individual capabilities. To achieve this self-understanding and improved self-esteem requires the experiences afforded by successes, along with guidance in self-understanding and self-assessment.

To meet these goals, teachers provide opportunities for students to think about what they are learning, how they are learning it, and how far they have progressed. Specifically, to engage students in the assessment process you can provide opportunities for the students to

- identify learning targets that they especially value
- help design assessment devices for the units of study
- evaluate the tests that are furnished by the textbook publisher in terms of how well they match the learning targets that you and the students have identified
- help interpret assessment results

To help interpret assessment results, students can maintain portfolios of their work, using rating scales or checklists periodically to self-assess their progress, and then discuss their self-assessments with their parents/guardians and teacher. Engaging students in assessment offers them some degree of control over their learning and performance.

Using Student Portfolios

Portfolios are used by teachers as a means of instruction and by teachers and students as one means of assessing student learning. Although there is little research evidence to support or refute the claim, educators believe that the instructional value comes from the process of the student's assembling and maintaining a personal portfolio. During that creative process, the student is expected to self-reflect, and to think critically about what has and is being learned. In addition, the student is assuming some responsibility for his or her own learning.

Student portfolios should be well organized and, depending on the purpose (or category), should contain assignment sheets, class worksheets, results of homework, project binders, forms for student self-assessment and reflection on their work, and other class materials that are thought to be important by the students and teacher.

Portfolio Assessment: Knowing and Dealing with Its Limitations

Before using portfolios as an alternative to traditional testing, you are advised to carefully consider and clearly understand the reasons for doing so, and its practicality in your situation. Then carefully decide the portfolio content, establish rubrics or expectation standards, anticipate grading problems, and consider and prepare for reactions from parents/guardians.

While emphasizing the criteria for assessment, rating scales and checklists provide students with the means to express their feelings and give the teacher still another source of input data for use in assessment. To provide students with reinforcement and guidance to improve their learning and development, teachers can meet with individual students to discuss their self-assessments. Such conferences should provide students with understandable and achievable short-term goals as well as help them develop and maintain adequate self-esteem.[8]

Although almost any instrument used for assessing student work can be used for student self-assessment, in some cases it might be better to construct specific instruments with the student's understanding of the instrument in mind. Student self-assessment and self-reflection should be done on a regular and continuing basis so comparisons can be made periodically by the student. You will need to help students learn how to analyze these comparisons. They should provide a student with information previously not recognized about his or her own progress and growth.

Using Checklists

One of the items that can be maintained by students in their portfolios is a series of checklists. Checklist items can be used easily by a student to compare with previous self-assessments. Items on the checklist will vary depending on your purpose, subject, and grade level. (See sample forms, Figures 8.5 and 8.6.) Open-ended questions allow the student to provide additional information and to do some expressive writing. After a student has demonstrated each of the skills satisfactorily, a check is made next to the student's name, either by the teacher alone or in conference with the student.

Guidelines for Using Portfolios for Assessment

Following are guidelines for using student portfolios in the assessment of learning.

- The portfolio should not be graded or compared in any way with those of other students. Its purpose is for student self-assessment and for showing progress in

[8] See, for example, R. Sylwester, "The Neurobiology of Self-Esteem and Aggression," *Educational Leadership* 54(5):75–79 (February 1997).

Oral Report Assessment

Student ______________________________ Date ______________

Teacher ______________________________ Time ______________

Did the student	*Yes*	*No*
1. Speak loud enough that everyone could hear?	________	________
Comment/evidence:		
2. Speak clearly enough that everyone could understand?	________	________
Comment/evidence:		
3. Finish sentences?	________	________
Comment/evidence:		
4. Give a good introduction?	________	________
Comment/evidence:		
5. Seem well informed about the topic?	________	________
Comment/evidence:		
6. Explain ideas clearly?	________	________
Comment/evidence:		
7. Stay on the topic?	________	________
Comment/evidence:		
8. Give a good conclusion?	________	________
Comment/evidence:		
9. Use effective visuals to support the presentation?	________	________
Comment/evidence:		
10. Give good answers to questions from the audience?	________	________
Comment/evidence:		

FIGURE 8.5 Checklist: Assessing an oral report.

Assessment Checklist: Interdisciplinary Thematic Unit Learning

Student ______________________ Date ____________

Teacher ______________________ Time ____________

The student	*Yes*	*No*	*Comments/Evidence*
1. Can identify theme, topic, main idea of the unit			
2. Can identify contributions of others to the theme			
3. Can identify problems related to the unit study			
4. Has developed skills in:			
Applying knowledge			
Assuming responsibility			
Categorizing			
Classifying			
Decision making			
Discussing			
Gathering resources			
Impulse control			
Inquiry			
Justifying choices			
Listening to others			
Locating information			
Metacognition			
Ordering			
Organizing information			
Problem recognition/identification			
Problem solving			
Reading maps and globes			
Reading text			
Reasoning			
Reflecting			
Reporting to others			
Self-assessing			
Sharing			
Studying			
Summarizing			
Thinking			
Using resources			
Working independently			
Working with others			
(Others unique to the unit)			

Additional teacher and student comments:

FIGURE 8.6 Checklist: Student learning assessment for use with interdisciplinary thematic instruction.

learning. For this to happen, students should keep all papers, or major papers, related to a course in their portfolios. For grading purposes, you can simply record whether or not the portfolio was maintained, and then use a checklist to determine whether all required items are in the portfolio.

- Determine what materials should be kept in the portfolio and announce clearly when (post schedule in room), how, and by what criteria portfolios will be reviewed.
- Contents of the portfolio should reflect course grade-level goals, learning standards, target objectives.
- Everything that goes into their portfolios should be dated by the students.
- Portfolio maintenance should be the students' responsibility.
- Portfolios should not leave the classroom.
- Students should be encouraged to personalize their portfolios, for example, with brightly decorated exteriors and the student's photo.

Maintaining Records of Student Achievement

You must maintain well-organized and complete records of student achievement. At the very least, the record book should include attendance records and all records of scores on tests, homework, projects, and other assignments. You may do this using either a written or an electronic record book. With electronic record keeping, the teacher can easily share achievement data for individual students with the school principal, a request that may become more frequent. As one intermediate school principal states, "If ever there was a time when principals needed to begin asking for, collecting, and compiling achievement data from classroom teachers on a regular basis, that time is now."[9]

Teacher's Log with a Caution about Anecdotal Comments

Daily interactions and events occur in the classroom that may provide informative data about a student's intellectual, emotional, and physical development. In addition to your formal record keeping, maintaining a dated log of your observations of these interactions and events can provide important information that might otherwise be forgotten. At the end of a unit and again at the conclusion of a grading term, you will want to review your records. During the course of the school year, your anecdotal records (and those of other members of your teaching team) will provide important information about the development of each child and ideas for attention to be given to individual students.

You must think carefully about any written comments that you intend to make about a student. Young people can be quite sensitive to what others say about them, and most particularly to comments about them made by a teacher.

Additionally, we have seen anecdotal comments in students' permanent records that said more about the teachers who made the comments than about the students. Comments that have been carelessly, hurriedly, and thoughtlessly made can be detrimental to a student's welfare and progress in school. Teacher comments must be professional; that is, they must be diagnostically useful to the continued intellectual and psychological development of the student. This is true for any comment you make or write, whether on a student's paper, on the student's permanent school record, or on a message sent to the student's home.

What separates the professional teacher from "anyone off the street" is the teacher's ability to go beyond mere description of behavior. Always keep that in mind when you write comments that will be read by students, by their parents/guardians, and by other teachers. Keep in mind that children are growing and changing every day with each event in their lives. Our assessments of their behavior reflect who they were and not necessarily who they are or who they may be.

Grading and Marking Student Achievement

If conditions were ideal (which they are not), and if teachers did their job perfectly well (which many of us do not), then all students would receive top marks (the ultimate in mastery or quality learning), and there would be less need to talk about grading and marking. Believing that letter grades do not reflect the nature of the developmental progress of young children, many school districts hold off using letter grades until children are in at least third grade; instead, they favor using developmental checklists and narrative statements.[10] Mastery learning implies that some end point of learning is attainable, but there probably isn't an end point. In any case, because conditions for teaching are never ideal and we teachers are mere humans, let us continue with this topic of grading that is undoubtedly of special interest to you, your students, their parents/guardians, and school counselors, administrators, and school boards.

The term *achievement* is used frequently throughout Part One of this text. What does it mean? Achievement

---

[9]M. A. Dubrovich, "Student Achievement Data: Holding Teachers Accountable," *Principal 81*(4):30–32, 34 (March 2002), 30.

[10]K. Lake and K. Kafka, "Reporting Methods in Grades K–8," Chapter 9 in T. R. Guskey, ed. *Communicating Student Learning* (Alexandria, VA: ASCD Yearbook, Association for Supervision and Curriculum Development, 1996).

means accomplishment, but is it accomplishment of the instructional objectives against preset standards, or is it simply accomplishment? Most teachers probably choose the former, where the teacher subjectively establishes a standard that must be met for a student to receive a certain grade for an assignment, project, test, quarter, semester, or course. Achievement, then, is decided by degrees of accomplishment.

Preset standards are usually expressed in percentages (degrees of accomplishment) needed for marks or *ABC* grades. If no student achieves the standard required for an *A* grade, for example, then no student receives an *A*. However, if all students meet the preset standard for the *A* grade, then all receive *A*s. Determining student grades on the basis of preset standards is referred to as *criterion-referenced* (or *competency-based*) *grading*.

Criterion-Referenced versus Norm-Referenced Grading

Unlike criterion-referenced grading, norm-referenced grading measures the relative accomplishment of individuals in the group (e.g., one classroom of fourth graders) or in a larger group (e.g., all fourth graders) by comparing and ranking students, and is commonly known as "grading on a [normal] curve." Because it encourages competition and discourages cooperative learning, *norm-referenced grading is not recommended.* It is educationally dysfunctional. For your personal interest, after several years of teaching, you can produce frequency-distribution studies of grades you have given over a period of time, but *do not* give students grades that are based on a curve. That grading and reporting should always be done in reference to learning criteria, and never on a curve is well supported by research studies and authorities on the matter.[11] Grades for student achievement should be tied to performance levels and determined on the basis of each student's achievement toward preset standards. As stated by Stiggins, "Teachers who develop success-oriented partnerships with students have no use for grading on a curve. They know they are not the best teacher they can be until every student attains an A—demonstrating the highest possible achievement on rigorous high-quality assessments."[12]

In criterion-referenced grading, the aim is to communicate information about an individual student's progress in knowledge and work skills compared with that student's previous attainment or the pursuit of an absolute, such as content mastery. Criterion-referenced grading is featured in continuous-progress curricula, competency-based curricula, and other programs that focus on quality learning and personalized education.

Criterion-referenced grading is based on the level at which each student meets the specified objectives (standards) for the subject or grade level. The objectives must be clearly stated to represent important student learning outcomes. This approach implies that effective teaching and learning result in high grades (*A*s) or marks for most students. In fact, when a mastery concept is used, the student must accomplish the objectives before being allowed to proceed to the next learning task. The philosophy of teachers who favor criterion-referenced procedures recognizes individual potential. Such teachers accept the challenge of finding teaching strategies to help students progress from where they are to the next designated level. Instead of wondering how Sally compares with Juanita, the comparison is between what Sally could do yesterday and what she can do today, and how well these performances compare to the preset standard.

Most school systems use a combination of norm-referenced and criterion-referenced data usage. Sometimes both kinds of information are useful. For example, a report card for a student in the eighth grade might indicate how that student is meeting certain criteria, such as receiving an *A* grade for addition of fractions. Another entry might show that this mastery is expected, however, in the sixth grade. Both criterion- and norm-referenced data may be communicated to the parents/guardians and the student. Appropriate procedures should be used: a criterion-referenced approach to show whether or not the student can accomplish the task, and if so, to what degree, and a norm-referenced approach to show how well that student performs compared with the larger group to which the child belongs.

Determining Grades

Once entered onto school transcripts, grades have significant impacts upon the futures of students. When determining achievement grades for student performance, you must make several important, professional decisions. In a few schools, and for certain classes or assignments, only marks such as *E, S,* and *I* or *pass/no pass,* are used, but percentages of accomplishment and letter grades are used for most middle and upper grade schools.[13] For determining student grades, consider the guidelines presented in the following paragraphs.

At the start of the school term, explain your marking and grading policies first to yourself, and then to your students and their parents/guardians at "back-to-school night." A written explanation might also be sent

[11] See, for example, T. R. Guskey, ed., *Communicating Student Learning,* 18–19; R. J. Stiggins, *Student-Involved Classroom Assessment,* 3rd ed. (Upper Saddle River, NJ: Prentice Hall, 2001), 443–444; and R. L. Linn and N. E. Gronlund, *Measurement and Assessment in Teaching,* 8th ed. (Upper Saddle River, NJ: Merrill/Prentice Hall, 2000), 392.

[12] Stiggins, *Student-Involved Classroom Assessment,* 444.

[13] For other methods being used to report student achievement, see K. Lake and K. Kafka, "Reporting Methods in Grades K–8," Chapter 9 in T. R. Guskey, *Communicating Student Learning.*

Valerie Schultz/Merrill

Competent planning, preparing, administering, and scoring of tests is an important professional skill.

home. Share sample scoring and grading rubrics with students and parents/guardians.

When converting your interpretation of a student's accomplishments to a letter grade, be as objective as possible. For *ABC* grades, select a percentage standard, such as 92% for an *A*, 85% for a *B*, 75% for a *C*, and 65% for a *D*. The cutoff percentages used are your decision, although the district, school, program area, grade-level team, or department may have established guidelines that you are expected to follow.[14]

To determine students' final grades, many teachers use a point system, in which things that students write, say, and do are given points (but not for journals or portfolios, except, perhaps, for whether the student does one or not); then the possible point total is the factor for grade determination. For example, if 92% is the cutoff for an *A* and 500 points are possible, then any student with 460 points or more (500 × .92) has achieved an *A*. Likewise, for a test or any other assignment, if the value is 100 points, the cutoff for an *A* is 92 (100 × .92). With a point system and preset standards, the teacher and students know the current points possible at any time during the grading period, and can easily calculate a student's current grade standing. Thus, students always know where they stand in the course.

Build your grading policy around degrees of accomplishment rather than failure, where students proceed from one accomplishment to the next. This is continuous promotion, not necessarily promotion of the student from one grade level to the next, but within the classroom. However, some schools have eliminated grade-level designation and use the concept of continuous promotion from the time a student enters the school until he or she graduates or exits from it.

Remember that *assessment* and *grading* are not synonymous. As discussed at the start of this chapter, assessment implies the collection of information from a variety of sources, including measurement techniques and subjective observations. These data, then, become the basis for arriving at a final grade, which in effect is a final value judgment. Grades are one aspect of evaluation and are intended to communicate educational progress to students and to their parents/guardians. To be valid as an indicator of that progress, you *must* use a variety of sources of data to determine of a student's final grade.

About Makeup Work

Decide your policy about makeup work beforehand. Students will be absent and will miss assignments and tests, so it is best that your policies about late assignments and missed tests be clearly communicated to students and to their parents/guardians. For makeup work, please consider the following.

Homework assignments. We recommend that, as a general policy, after due dates have been negotiated or set for assignments, no credit or reduced credit be given for work that is turned in late. Sometimes, however, a student has legitimate reasons for not being able to complete the assignment by the due date, and the teacher must exercise a professional judgment in each instance. Although it is important that teachers have rules and procedures—and that they consistently apply them—the teacher is a professional who must consider all aspects of a student's situation and, after doing so, show compassion, caring, and regard for the human situation.

Tests. If students are absent when tests are given, you have several options. Some teachers allow students to miss or discount one test per grading period. Another technique is to allow each student to substitute a written homework assignment or project for one missed test. Still another option is to give the absent student the choice of either taking a makeup test or having the next test count double. When makeup tests are given, in our opinion the makeup test should be taken within a week of the regular test unless there is a compelling reason (e.g., medical or family problem) why this cannot happen.

Sometimes students miss a testing period, not because of being absent from school but because of involvement in other school activities. In those instances, the student may be able to arrange to take the test during another of your class periods, or during your prep period, on that day or the next. If a student is absent during performance testing, the logistics and possible diminished reliability of having to re-administer the test for one student may necessitate giving the student an alternate paper-and-pencil test or some other option.

[14] See the discussion in T. R. Guskey, "High Percentages Are Not the Same as High Standards," *Phi Delta Kappan 82*(7):534–536 (March 2001).

Quizzes. Many teachers give frequent and brief quizzes, as often as several times a day in self-contained classrooms. As opposed to tests (see next section), quizzes are usually brief (perhaps taking only 5 minutes of class time) and intended to reinforce the importance of frequent study and review. (However, quizzes should be prepared using the same care and precision as presented in the guidelines that follow in the sections for testing and preparation of assessment items). When quizzes are given at frequent intervals, no single quiz should count very much toward the student's final grade; therefore, you will probably want to avoid having to schedule and give make-up quizzes for students who were absent when a quiz was given. The following are reasonable options to administering make-up quizzes, and are presented here in order of our preference, with *a* being our preferred choice. (a) Give a certain number of quizzes during a grading period, say 10, but allow a student to discount a few quiz scores, say two of the ten, thereby allowing the student to discount a low score or a missed quiz due to absence or both. (b) Count the next quiz double for a student who missed one due to absence. About the only problem with this option is when a student misses several quizzes. If that happens, (c) count the unit test a certain and relative percentage greater for any student who missed a quiz during that unit. By the way, we see absolutely no educational value in giving pop or unannounced graded quizzes.

Caution about assigning zero credit. Be very cautious about ever assigning a score of zero to a student for a missed or incomplete assignment, test, or quiz, or for cheating, especially when using a point system for grading. Depending on the weight of the assignment in relation to the total points possible for the grading period, assigning a zero grade can have an extremely negative effect on the student's total grade, thus becoming an act of punishment by the teacher rather than a fair representation of the grade earned (or, in this instance, not earned) by the student. This is another example where you, the teacher, must exercise your professional judgment. In addition to those just mentioned, alternatives to using a zero grade include ignoring the missing grade and calculating the student's final (quarter or semester) percentage grade using a lesser number of total points possible, or, if not counter to school policy, assigning a grade of "incomplete" that gives the student some additional time to complete the work.

 Testing for Achievement

One source of information for determining grades is data obtained from testing for student achievement. There are two kinds of tests—those that are standardized and those that are not.

Standardized and Nonstandardized Tests

Standardized tests are those constructed and published by commercial testing bureaus and used by states and districts to determine and compare student achievement, principally in the core subjects of reading, mathematics, and science. Usually on a state or national level, norms for particular age groups of children are established by administering it to large groups of children. Standardized norm-referenced tests are best for diagnostic purposes and should *not* be used for determining student grades.

The administration of standardized achievement tests and the use of their results are major concerns to classroom teachers and school administrators in particular. In some locales, for example, their salaries and indeed their jobs are contingent on the results of student scores on standardized achievement tests. It is not our purpose and space does not allow a consideration of standardized achievement testing in this text. Rather, the focus is on nonstandardized criterion-referenced tests, ones that you design (or collaboratively design) for your own unique group of students to determine their level of learning on particular instructional objectives. However we do not mean to devalue the concern that you will have for high-stakes standardized norm-referenced achievement testing as a classroom teacher. (For more on assessment, especially standardized testing, see the suggested readings at the end of this chapter.)

Competent planning, preparing, administering, and scoring of tests is an important professional skill. You may want to refer to the following guidelines while you are student teaching, and again, occasionally, during your initial years as an employed teacher.

Purposes for Testing

Tests can be designed for several purposes. A variety of kinds of tests and alternate test items will keep your testing program interesting, useful, and reliable. As a college student, you are probably most experienced with testing to measure for achievement, but as a classroom teacher you will use tests for other reasons as well. Tests are also used to assess and aid in curriculum development; to help determine teaching effectiveness; to help students develop positive attitudes, appreciations, and values; to help students increase their understanding and retention of facts, principles, skills, and concepts; to motivate students; to provide diagnostic information to plan for individualization of instruction; to provide review and drill to enhance teaching and learning; and to serve as informational data for students and parents/guardians.

Frequency for Testing

First of all, assessment for student learning should be continual; that is, it should be going on every minute of every school day. This is not to say that students are being graded at all times, but rather that they have the opportunity through their actions to show signs of growth and progress. For grading or marking purposes, it is difficult to generalize about how often to formally test for student achievement, but we believe that just as in reading or any other discipline, testing for achievement in science should be cumulative and frequent. By *cumulative*, we mean that each assessment should assess for the student's understanding of previously learned material as well as for the current unit of study; that is, it should assess for connected learning. By frequent, we mean as often as once a week for classes that meet daily. Advantages of cumulative assessment include the review, reinforcement, and articulation of old material with the most recent. Advantages of frequent assessment include a reduction in student anxiety over tests and an increase in the validity of the summative assessment.

Test Construction

After determining why you are designing and administering a test, you need to identify the specific instructional objectives the test is being designed to measure. As you learned in Chapter 2, your written instructional objectives are specific so that you can write assessment items to measure against those objectives. That is referred to as *criterion-referenced assessment.* When the objectives are aligned with specific curriculum standards, as they usually are or should be, then it can also be referred to as *standards-based assessment.*

Therefore, the first step in test construction is to identify the purpose(s) of the test. The second step is to identify the objectives to be measured, and the third step is to prepare the test items. The best time to prepare draft items is after you have prepared your instructional objectives—while the objectives are fresh in your mind, which means before the lessons are taught. After a lesson is taught, you will want to rework your first draft of the test items related to that lesson to make any modifications to the draft items as a result of the instruction that occurred.

Administering Tests

For many students, test taking can be a time of high anxiety. Children demonstrate test anxiety in various ways. Just before and during testing some are quiet and thoughtful, while others are noisy and disruptive. To more accurately measure student achievement, you will want to take steps to reduce their anxiety. To control or reduce student anxieties, consider the following guidelines for administering tests.

Since children respond best to familiar routine, plan your assessment program so tests are given at regular intervals and administered at the same time and in the same way. In some middle schools in particular, days of the week are assigned to departments for administering major tests. For example, Tuesdays might be for language arts and mathematics testing, and Wednesdays for social studies and science testing.

Avoid tests that are too long and that will take too much time. Sometimes beginning teachers have unreasonable expectations of children's attention spans during testing. Frequent testing with frequent sampling of student knowledge is preferred over infrequent and long tests that attempt to cover everything. This approach reduces the weight of each test, offering students more opportunities to succeed and reducing the effect of a bad day.

Attend to creature comforts. Try to arrange the classroom so it is well-ventilated, the temperature is comfortable, and, when giving paper-and-pencil tests individually, the seats are well-spaced. If spacing is a problem, consider using individual privacy providers made by the students (see Figure 8.7). Other possibilities are group testing or alternate forms of the test, where students seated adjacent to one another have different forms of the same test (for example, multiple choice answer alternatives are arranged in different order).

Before distributing the test, explain to students what they should do when finished, such as quietly begin an *anchor activity* (see Chapter 7), because not all of the students will finish at the same time. Sample anchor activities are portfolio work, writing in journal, learning center work, and work on an aspect of a long-term project. For most children, it is unreasonable to expect them to just sit quietly after finishing a test; they need something to do. Of course, like everything else that is classroom routine, children need to be trained in the way to perform their anchor activity work without disturbing children still testing.

When you are ready to test, don't drag it out. Distribute tests quickly and efficiently. Once testing has begun, avoid interrupting the students. (It is amazing how often teachers interrupt students once the students are at a task, and those same teachers resent being interrupted themselves.) Items or announcements of important information can be written on the board or, if unrelated to the test, held until all are finished with the test. Stay in the room and visually monitor the students. If the test is not going to take an entire instructional period (and most shouldn't) and it's a major test, then give it at the beginning of the period, if possible, unless you are planning a test review just prior to it. However, that is rather late to conduct a meaningful review, and a review just prior to giving the test is likely to upset children who discover they don't know the material as well as they thought they did). It's improbable that any teacher can effectively teach a lesson with a reasonable degree of student interest in it just prior to or immediately after a major test.

Space dividers provide privacy during testing and other independent activities. Attaching three approximately 8 × 10-inch rectangular sections of cardboard can make privacy providers or space dividers. The divider is placed, standing, in front of the student, making it impossible for neighboring students to see over or around. Dividers can be made from cardboard boxes or heavy folders of various sorts. It could be a project at the beginning of the year for each student to design and make an individual space divider that is then stored in the classroom for use on test days. Students enjoy being allowed to personalize their dividers.

FIGURE 8.7 Constructing individual privacy provider.

Controlling Cheating

Whatever the causes, some students will try to cheat on tests. There are steps you can take to discourage cheating or to reduce the opportunity and pressure that cause students to cheat on tests. Consider the following.

Preventing cheating. Space students or, as mentioned before, use alternate forms of the test, or use privacy protectors (see Figure 8.7). Frequent testing and not allowing a single test to count too much toward a term grade reduce test anxiety and the pressure that can cause cheating. Prepare test questions that are clear and unambiguous, thereby reducing student frustration caused by a question or instructions that students do not understand. Avoid tests that are too long and will take too much time. During long tests, some students get discouraged and restless, which is when classroom management problems can occur. Of course, we realize that children must learn to control their behavior but little is gained from pushing the envelope; that is, by expecting what is developmentally unreasonable to expect.

Consider using open-text and open-notebook tests or allowing each student to prepare a page of notes to use during the test. When students can use their books and notes, it not only reduces anxiety but it helps with their organization of information and their retention of what has been learned. The use of open notes and open book testing are useful adaptations that are appreciated by many students.[15]

Stopping cheating. The preceding paragraphs provide hints to prevent student cheating. If you suspect cheating is occurring, move and stand in the area of the suspected student. Usually that will stop it.

Dealing with cheating. When you suspect cheating has occurred, you are faced with a dilemma. Unless your suspicion is backed by solid proof, you are advised to forget it but to keep a close watch on the student the next time to prevent cheating from happening. Your job is not to catch students being dishonest, but to discourage dishonesty. If you have absolute proof that a student has cheated, then you are obligated to proceed with school policy on student cheating. That may call for a session with the counselor or the student and the student's parent/guardian, or perhaps an automatic *F* grade on the test.

Determining the Time Needed to Take a Test

Again, avoid giving tests that are too long and that will take too much time. As a general rule (and we are speaking of teacher-made tests, not standardized tests such as statewide achievement tests and other tests that are out of the teacher's control), testing duration should be limited to 10 to 20 minutes for most K–3 situations; 30 to 40 minutes should be long enough for grades 4–8. Preparing and administering good tests is a skill that you will develop over time. In the meantime, it is best to test frequently and to use tests that sample student achievement rather than try for a comprehensive measure of that achievement.

Some students take more time on a given test than do others. You want to avoid giving too much time, or classroom management problems will result. However, you don't want to cut short the time needed by students who can do well but need more time to think and to write. As a very general guide, use the table of time needed for different types of test items shown in Table 8.1. This is only a guide for determining the approximate amount of time to allow students to complete a test.

Preparing Assessment Items

Preparing and writing good assessment items is yet another professional skill, and to become proficient at

[15] J. S. Nelson et al., "Student Preferences for Adaptations in Classroom Testing," *Remedial and Special Education* *21*(1):41–52 (January/February 2000) and T. V. Eilertsen and O. Valdermo, "Open-Book Assessment: A Contribution to Improved Learning?" *Studies in Educational Evaluation* *26*(2):91–103 (2000).

TABLE 8.1 Approximate time to allow for testing as determined by the types of items. For example, for a test made up of ten multiple-choice items, five arrangement items, and two short-explanation items, you would want to plan for about 30 minutes for students to complete the test. Students with special needs or students with limited English proficiency, of course, may need more time per item. They might also need to have the test administered in briefer sessions, or they might need some other accommodation depending on their special needs.

Type of Test Item	Time Needed per Item
Matching	30 seconds per matching item
Completion	30 seconds
Multiple-choice	30–60 seconds
Completion drawing	2–3 minutes
Arrangement	2–3 minutes
Identification	2–3 minutes
Short explanation	2–3 minutes
Essay and performance	10 or more minutes

it takes study, time, practice, feedback, and reflection. Because of the importance of an assessment program, you should approach this task seriously and responsibly. Although poorly prepared items take no time at all to construct, they will cause you more trouble than you can ever imagine. As a professional, you should take time to study different types of assessment items and how best to write them, and then practice writing them. When preparing items, ensure that they match and sufficiently cover the instructional objectives. In addition, prepare each item carefully so that students will understand exactly what is being asked. With the diversity of students in today's school classroom, especially with respect to their proficiency in oral and written English language and the inclusion of students with exceptionalities, this is an especially important point. For your high-stakes tests, such as unit tests and semester exams, ask a trusted colleague or friend to read your test for clarity and errors and to check the test's key for accuracy. Finally, after administering a test, you must take time to analyze the results and reflect on the value of each item before ever using that item again.

Classification of Assessment Items

Assessment items can be classified as verbal (oral or written words), visual (pictures and diagrams), and manipulative or performance (handling of materials and equipment; performing). Written verbal items are the ones that have traditionally been used most frequently in testing. However, visual items and visual tests are useful, for example, when working with students who lack fluency with the written word or when testing students who have limited or no proficiency in English language.

Performance items and tests are useful when measuring for psychomotor skill development. Common examples are performance testing of a student's ability to carry a microscope or hold a jumping rope in place (gross motor skill) or to focus a microscope or to jump rope (fine motor skill). Performance testing also can and should be a part of a wider testing program that includes testing for higher-level thinking skills and knowledge. For example, a student or small group of students might be given the problem of creating a habitat for an imaginary animal from discarded materials and then displaying, writing about, and orally presenting their product to the rest of the class.

As we have noted before, educators have an interest in this last described form of performance testing as a means of assessing learning that is closer to measuring for the real thing—that is, authentic. In a program for teacher preparation, micro peer teaching and student teaching are examples of performance assessment; that is, assessment practices used to assess the teacher candidate's ability to teach (to perform). It seems axiomatic that assessment of student teaching is a more authentic assessment of a candidate's ability to teach than would be a written (paper-and-pencil test) or verbal (oral test) form of assessment. Although less direct and perhaps less reliable than a checklist observation and analysis of a student teacher actually teaching, an observation of a student teacher's analysis of a video recorded episode of another teacher's performance would be another way of more authentically assessing a teacher's ability to teach than would be a paper-and-pencil response item test.

Performance testing is usually more expensive and time-consuming than verbal testing, which in turn is more time demanding and expensive than written testing. However, a good program of assessment will use alternate forms of assessment and not rely solely on one form (such as written) and one type of written item (such as the multiple-choice question).

The type of test and items that you use depends upon your purpose and objectives. Carefully consider the alternatives within that framework. To provide validity checks and to account for the individual differences of students, a good assessment program should include items from all three types. That is what writers of articles in professional journals are referring to when they talk about *alternative assessment.* They are encouraging the use of multiple assessment items, as opposed to the traditional heavy reliance on objective items such as multiple-choice questions.

General Guidelines for Preparing for Assessment of Student Learning

Every test that you administer to your students should represent your best professional effort. It should be clean and sans spelling and grammar errors. One that was obviously prepared hurriedly and is wrought with spelling and grammar errors will be frowned upon by discerning parents/guardians. If you are a student teacher, such sloppiness and unprofessional output will certainly bring about an admonishment from your university supervisor and, if it continues, your speedy release from the teacher preparation program. Consider the following general guidelines when preparing to assess for student learning.

◆ Ensure that content coverage is complete (i.e., that all objectives or relevant standards are being measured).

◆ Ensure that each item is clear and unambiguous to all students.

◆ Ensure that each item is reliable—that it measures the intended objective. One way to check item reliability is to have more than one item measuring for the same objective.

◆ Because it is time-consuming to write good assessment items, you are advised to maintain a bank of items, with each item coded according to its matching instructional objective and its domain of learning (cognitive, affective, or psychomotor) and perhaps according to its level within the hierarchy of a particular domain. Another code could indicate whether the item requires thinking that is recall, processing, or application. Computer software programs are available for this. Ready-made test item banks are available on computer disks and accompany many programs or textbooks. If you use them, be certain that the items match your course objectives and that they are well written. It doesn't necessarily follow that because they were published they are well written or match what students were supposed to have learned. When preparing items for your test bank, use your creative thinking and best writing skills. Prepare items that match your objectives, put them aside, think about them, then work them over again.[16]

◆ Include several kinds of items and assessment instruments (see 12 types that follow).

◆ Plan each item to be difficult enough for the poorly prepared student but easy enough for the student who is well prepared.

Attaining Content Validity

To ensure that your test measures what is supposed to be measured, you can construct a table of specifications. A two-way grid indicates behavior in one dimension and content in the other (see Figures 8.8 and 8.9).

In this grid, behavior relates to the three domains: cognitive, affective, and psychomotor. In Figure 8.8, the cognitive domain is divided, according to Bloom's taxonomy (Chapter 2), into six categories: knowledge or simple recall, comprehension, application, analysis, synthesis (often involving an original product in oral or written form), and evaluation. The specifications table in Figure 8.8 does not specify levels within the affective and psychomotor domains.

To use a table of specifications, the teacher examining objectives for the unit decides what emphasis should be given to the behavior and to the content. For example, if vocabulary development is a concern for this sixth-grade study of matter and energy, then making 20% of the test on vocabulary would probably be appropriate, but 50% would be unsuitable. This planning enables the teacher to design a test that fits the situation rather than a haphazard test that does not correspond to the objectives either in content or behavior emphasis. Since this is to be an objective test and because it is so difficult to write objective items to test affective and psychomotor behaviors, this table of specifications calls for no test items in these areas. If these areas are included in the unit objectives, some other assessment devices must be used to test learning in these domains. The teacher could also show the objectives tested, as indicated within parentheses in Figure 8.8. Then, a later check on inclusion of all objectives is easy.

Some teachers prefer the alternative table shown in Figure 8.9. Rather than differentiating among all six of Bloom's cognitive levels, this table separates cognitive objectives into just three levels: those that require simple low-level recall of knowledge, those that require information processing, and those that require application of new knowledge. In addition, the affective and psychomotor domains are each divided into low- and high-level behaviors. A third alternative, not

[16] For additional guidelines, see L. Rudner, *Item Banking* (Washington, DC: ED42331098, ERIC Clearinghouse on Assessment and Evaluation, 1998).

Content	Behaviors								
Science (Grade 6)	Cognitive								
Matter and Energy	Knowledge	Comprehension	Application	Analysis	Synthesis	Evaluation	Affective	Psychomotor	TOTAL
I. Vocabulary development		2 (1, 2)	3 (2)						
II. Concepts		2	1 (3, 4)	1 (4)	(5)				
III. Applications	1 (5)	1 (5)		1 (5)		1 (5)			
IV. Problem solving	1 (6)	1 (6)			1 (6)	1 (6)			
Total	2	6	4	2	1	2		17	
Percentage	11.7	35	23.5	11.7	6	11.7		100%	

FIGURE 8.8 Table of specifications I. *Note:* Percentages do not equal 100 because of rounding.

	Behaviors							
	Cognitive			Affective		Psychomotor		
Content	Input	Processing	Application	Low	High	Low	High	TOTAL
I.								
II.								
III.								
IV.								
TOTAL								

FIGURE 8.9 Table of specifications II.

illustrated here, is a table of specifications that shows all levels of each of the three domains.

Types of Assessment Items: Descriptions, Examples, and Guidelines for Preparing and Using

This section presents descriptions, advantages and disadvantages, and guidelines for preparing and using 12 types of assessment items. When reading about the advantages and disadvantages of each, you will notice that some types are appropriate for use in direct or performance assessment, and others are not.

Arrangement

Description: Terms or real objects (realia) are presented and the student is to arrange them in a specified order.

Example: The assortment of balls on the table represents the planets in our solar system. (Note: The balls are of various sizes and include a marble, tennis ball, basketball, and so on, each labeled with a planetary name, with a large sphere in the center labeled the sun.) Arrange the balls in their proper order around the sun.

Advantages: This type of item tests for knowledge of sequence and order and is good for review, for starting discussions, and for performance assessment. The example given is also a performance test item.

Disadvantages: Scoring could be difficult, so be cautious and meticulous when using this type for grading purposes.

Guidelines for use: To enhance reliability, you may need to instruct students to give the rationale for their arrangement, making it a combined arrangement and short-explanation type of assessment. Be sure to allow space for explanations on an answer sheet. This is useful for small, heterogeneous group assessment to allow students to share and learn from their collaborative thinking and reasoning.

Completion Drawing

Description: An incomplete drawing is presented and the student is to complete it.

Example: Draw a line connecting the sun, the owl, the corn grains, and the field mice to show the direction in which energy travels through the food web.

Advantages: This type requires less time than would a complete drawing that might be required in an essay item. Scoring is relatively easy.

Disadvantages: Care needs to be exercised in the instructions so students do not misinterpret the expectation.

Guidelines for use: Use occasionally for diversion, but take care in preparing. This type can be instructive when assessing for student thinking and reasoning because it can measure conceptual knowledge. Consider making the item a combined completion-drawing and short-explanation type by having students give their rationales for the thinking behind their drawing completion. Be sure to allow space for their explanations. Useful for small, heterogeneous group assessment to allow students to share and learn from their collaborative thinking and reasoning.

Completion Statement

Description: Sometimes called a *fill-in* item, an incomplete sentence is presented and the student is to complete it by filling in the blank space or spaces.

Example: To test their hypotheses, scientists conduct ___________.

Advantages: This type is easy to devise, take, and score.

Disadvantages: There is a tendency to emphasize simple recall and to measure procedural knowledge only. Providing a word bank of possible answers is sometimes useful, especially with mainstreamed students, to reduce dependency on simple recall. It is difficult to write this type of item to measure for conceptual knowledge and higher levels of cognition. You must be alert for a correct response different from the expected. In the example, the teacher's key has *investigations* as the correct answer, but a student might answer the question with *experiments* or *tests* or *trials* or some other response that is equally valid.

Guidelines for use: Use occasionally for review or for preassessment of student knowledge. Avoid using this type for grading unless you can write items that extend student thinking beyond mere recall. In all instances, avoid copying items verbatim from the student book. As with all types, be sure to provide adequate space for students' answers, and large spaces for students with motor control difficulties. Try to use only one blank per item. Try also to keep the blanks equal in length. Useful for small, heterogeneous group assessment to allow students to share and learn from their collaborative thinking and reasoning.

Correction

Description: This is similar to the completion type except that sentences or paragraphs are complete but with italicized or underlined words that can be changed to make the sentences correct.

Example: Photosynthesis in *Arkansas* is the breakdown of *children* into hydrogen and oxygen, the release of *gold*, and then the combining of arms with carbon dioxide to make *Legos*.

Advantages: Writing this type can be fun for the teacher for preassessment of student knowledge or for review. Students may enjoy this type, especially when used only occasionally, for the tension relief afforded by the incorrect absurdities. This type can be useful for introducing words with multiple meanings.

Disadvantages: As with the completion type, the correction type tends to measure for low-level recall and rote memory. The underlined incorrect items could be so whimsical that they might cause more classroom disturbance than you want.

Guidelines for use: Use occasionally for diversion and discussion. Try to write items that measure for higher-level cognition. Consider making it a combined correction, short-explanation type. Be sure to allow space for student explanations.

Essay

Description: A question or problem is presented, and the student is to compose a response in the form of sustained prose using the student's own words, phrases, and ideas, within the limits of the question or problem.

Example: A healthy green coleus plant sitting in front of you has been planted in fertile soil and sealed in a glass jar. If we place the jar on the window sill where it will receive strong sunlight and the temperature inside the jar is maintained between 60 and 80 degrees Fahrenheit, how long do you predict the plant will live? Justify your prediction.

Advantages: This type measures conceptual knowledge and higher mental processes, such as the ability to synthesize material and to express ideas in clear and precise written language. It is especially useful in integrated thematic teaching. It provides practice in written expression and, as in the example, it can be used in performance assessment.

Disadvantages: Essay items require a good deal of time to read and to score. They tend to provide an unreliable sampling of achievement and are vulnerable to teacher subjectivity and unreliable scoring. Furthermore, they tend to punish the student who writes slowly and laboriously, or who has limited proficiency in the written language but may have achieved as well as a student who writes faster and is more proficient in the language. Essay items tend to favor students who have fluency with words but whose achievement may not necessarily be better. In addition, unless the students have been given instruction in the meaning of key directive verbs (such as *justify* in the example) and in how to respond to them, the teacher should not assume that all students understand them.

Guidelines for Using Essay Items

1. For an essay-only test, many questions that each require a relatively short prose response (see the short-explanation type), are preferable to a smaller number of questions requiring long prose responses. Briefer answers tend to be more precise, and the use of many items provides a more reliable sampling of student achievement. When preparing short-prose response, be sure to avoid using words verbatim from the student textbook.
2. Allow students adequate test time for full responses.
3. Different qualities of achievement are more likely comparable when all students must answer the same questions, as opposed to providing a list of essay items from which students may select those they answer.
4. After preparing essay items, make a tentative scoring key, deciding the major ideas you expect students to identify and how many points will be allotted to each.
5. Students should be informed about the relative test value for each item. Point values, if different for each item, can be listed in the margin of the test next to each item.
6. Inform students of the role of spelling, grammar, and sentence structure in your scoring of their essay items.
7. When reading student essay responses, read all student papers for one item at a time in one sitting, and, while doing that, make notes to yourself; then repeat and while reading that item again, score each student's paper for that item. Repeat the process for the next item but change the order of the pile of papers so you are not reading them in the same order by student. While scoring essay responses, keep in mind the nature of the objective being measured, which might or might not include the qualities of handwriting, grammar, spelling, punctuation, and neatness.
8. To nullify the "halo effect" that can occur when you know whose paper you are reading, have students put their name on the back of the paper or use a number code rather than names on essay papers, so while reading the papers, you are unaware of whose paper you are reading.
9. Although they have some understanding of a concept, many students are not yet facile with written expression, so you must remember to be patient, tolerant, positive, and prescriptive. Mark papers with positive and constructive comments, showing students how they could have explained or responded better.
10. Prior to using this type of test item, give instruction and practice to students in responding to key directive verbs that will be used (see Figure 8.10).

Grouping

Description: Several items are presented, and the student is to select and group those that are in some way related.

Example: Separate the following pictures of animals into two groups, one that consists of those that are mammals, the other of those that are not mammals. (Pictures not shown here.)

Advantages: This type of item tests knowledge of grouping and can be used to measure conceptual knowledge and higher levels of cognition, and to stimulate discussion.

Disadvantage: Remain alert for the student who has an alternative but valid rationale for his or her grouping.

Guideline for use: To allow for an alternative correct response, consider making the item a combined grouping and short-explanation type, being certain to allow adequate space to encourage student explanations.

Identification

Description: Unknown specimens are to be identified by name or some other criterion.

Compare asks for an analysis of similarity and difference, but with a greater emphasis on similarities or likenesses.
Contrast asks more for differences than for similarities.
Criticize asks for the good and bad of an idea or situation.
Define means to express clearly and concisely the meaning of a term, as from a dictionary or in the student's own words.
Diagram means to put quantities or numerical values into the form of a chart, graph, or drawing.
Discuss means to explain or argue, presenting various sides of events, ideas, or situations.
Enumerate means to name or list one after another, which is different from "explain briefly" or "tell in a few words."
Evaluate means to express worth, value, and judgment.
Explain means to describe, with emphasis on cause and effect.
Generalize means to arrive at a valid generalization from provided specific information.
Identify means to state recognizable characteristics.
Infer means to forecast what is likely to happen as a result of information provided.
Illustrate means to describe by means of examples, figures, pictures, or diagrams.
Interpret means to describe or explain a given fact, theory, principle, or doctrine within a specific context.
Justify means to show reasons, with an emphasis on correct, positive, and advantageous.
List means just that, to simply name items in a category without much description.
Outline means to give a short summary with headings and subheadings.
Prove means to present materials as witnesses, proof, and evidence.
Relate means to tell how specified things are connected or brought into some kind of relationship.
Summarize means to recapitulate the main points without examples or illustrations.
Trace means to follow a history or series of events, step by step, by going backward over the evidence.

FIGURE 8.10 Meaning of key directive verbs for essay item responses.

Example: With your dichotomous key to leaves of trees on our school campus, proceed outdoors and in pairs use the key to identify five different trees. The trees are marked with numbers; use those numbers to reference the name of each tree you identify.

Advantages: Verbalization (i.e., the use of abstract symbolization) is less significant, because the student is working with real materials. It should be measuring for higher level learning rather than simple recall. The item can also be written to measure for procedural understanding, such as for identification of steps in booting up a computer program. This is another useful type for authentic and performance assessments.

Disadvantages: Because of a special familiarity with the material, some students may have an advantage over others; to be fair, specimens used should be equally familiar or unfamiliar to all students. This type takes more time than many of the other types, both for the teacher to prepare and for students to do.

Guidelines for use: Whatever specimens are used, they must be familiar to all or to none of the students, and they must be clear, not confusing (e.g., fuzzy photographs or unclear photocopies, dried and incomplete plant specimens, and garbled music recordings can be confusing and frustrating to discern). Consider using dyad or team rather than individual testing.

Matching

Description: Students are to pair items from one list with items in a second list of choices or in some way connect items that are the same or related.

Example: Match items in Column A (stem column) to those of Column B (answer or response column) by drawing lines to the matched pairs.

Column A	Column B
snake	bird
eagle	insect
whale	mammal
praying mantis	reptile
	worm

Advantages: Matching items can measure for ability to judge relationships and to differentiate between similar facts, ideas, definitions, and concepts. They are easy to score and can test a broad range of content. They reduce guessing, especially if the answer column contains more items than the other, and they are interesting to students and adaptable for performance assessment.

Disadvantages: Although the matching item is adaptable for performance assessment, items are not easily adapted to measuring for higher cognition. Because all parts must be homogeneous, it is possible that clues will be given, thus reducing item validity.

Guidelines for use: The number of items in the response or answer column should exceed the number in the stem column. The number of items in the stem column to be matched should not exceed 10. Fewer is better. Matching sets should have high homogeneity (i.e., items in both columns or groups should be of the same general category; avoid, for example, mixing dates, events, and names). Answers in the response column should be kept short—one or two words each—and should be ordered logically, such as alphabetically. If answers from the response column can be used more than once—a tactic that is advised to avoid guessing by elimination—the directions should so state. Be prepared for the student who can legitimately defend an "incorrect" response. To eliminate the paper-and-pencil aspect and make it more direct, use an item such as "using the materials on the table, pair up those that are most alike."

Multiple Choice

Description: This type is similar to the completion item in that a statement is presented (the stem), sometimes in incomplete form, but with several options or alternatives requiring recognition or even higher cognitive processes rather than mere recall.

Example: Of four cylinders with the following dimensions, the one that would cause the highest-pitched sound would be

a. 4 inches long and 3 inches in diameter
b. 4 inches long and 1 inch in diameter
c. 8 inches long and 3 inches in diameter
d. 8 inches long and 1 inch in diameter

Advantages: Items can be answered and scored quickly. A wide range of content and higher levels of cognition can be tested in a relatively short time. This type is excellent for all testing purposes—motivation, review, and assessment of learning.

Disadvantages: Unfortunately, because multiple-choice items are relatively easy to write, there is a tendency to write items measuring only for low levels of cognition. Multiple-choice items are excellent for major testing, but it takes care and time to write good questions that measure higher levels of thinking and learning.

Anthony Magnacca/Merrill

Study after study shows that when parents/guardians are involved in their child's school and school work, students learn better and earn better grades, and teachers experience more positive feelings about teaching.

Guidelines for Using Multiple-Choice Items

1. If the item is in the form of an incomplete statement, it should be meaningful in itself and imply a direct question rather than merely lead into a collection of unrelated true and false statements.
2. Use a level of language that is easy enough for even the poorest readers and those with limited proficiency in English to understand; avoid unnecessary wordiness.
3. If there is much variation in length among the choices, arrange them in order from shortest phrase to longest. For single-word choices, use a consistent arrangement, such as by length of answer or alphabetically.
4. Arrangement of choices should be uniform throughout the test and listed vertically (in a column) rather than horizontally (in paragraph form).
5. Incorrect choices (distracters) should be plausible and related to the same concept as the correct choice. Although an occasional humorous distracter may help relieve text anxiety, along with absurd distracters they should generally be avoided. They offer no measuring value and increase the likelihood of the student's guessing the correct response.
6. It is not necessary to maintain a fixed number of choices for every item, but using fewer than three is not recommended. Although it is not always possible to come up with four or five plausible choices, the use of four or five reduces chance responses and guessing, thereby increasing reliability for the item. If you cannot think of enough plausible distracters, include the item on a test the first time as a completion item. As students respond, wrong answers will provide you with some plausible distracters that you can use the next time to make the item multiple-choice.
7. Some mainstreamed students may work better when allowed to circle their selected response rather than writing its letter or number in a blank space.
8. Responses such as "all of these" or "none of these" should be used only when they will contribute more than another plausible distracter. Care must be taken that such responses answer or complete the item. "All of the above" is a poorer choice than "none of the above" because items that use it as a correct response need to have four or five correct answers; also, if it is the right answer, knowledge of any two of the distracters will cue it.
9. All items should be grammatically consistent. For example, if the stem is in the form of an incomplete sentence, it should be possible to complete the sentence by attaching any of the alternatives to it.
10. The stem should state a single and specific point.
11. The stem must mean the same thing to every student.
12. The item should be expressed in positive form. A negative form can present a psychological disadvantage to students. Negative items are those that ask what is *not* characteristic of something, or what is the *least* useful. Discard the item if you cannot express it in positive terminology.

13. The stem must not include clues that would give away the correct choice. For example, "A four-sided figure whose opposite sides are parallel is called ___________."
    a. an octagon
    b. a parallelogram
    c. a trapezoid
    d. a triangle
14. There must be only one correct or best response. However, this is easier said than done (refer to guideline 19).
15. Measuring for understanding of definitions is better done by furnishing the name or word and requiring a choice from among several definitions than by presenting the definition and requiring a choice from among several words.
16. Avoid using choices that include absolute terms such as *never* and *always*.
17. Multiple-choice items need not be entirely verbal. Consider the use of realia, charts, diagrams, videos, and other visuals. They will make the test more interesting, especially to students with low verbal abilities or to those who have limited proficiency in English, and, consequently, they will make the assessment more direct.
18. Once you have composed a series of multiple-choice items or a test comprised completely of this item type, tally the position of answers to be sure they are evenly distributed to avoid the common psychological habit (when there are four choices) of having the correct choice in the third position. In other words, when the choices are A, B, C, and D, or 1, 2, 3, and 4, unless the test designer is aware and avoids it, more correct answers will be in the C or 3 position than in any other.
19. Consider providing space between test items for students to include their rationales for their response selections, thus making the test a combination multiple-choice and short-explanation type. This provides for the measurement of higher levels of cognition and encourages writing. It provides for the student who can rationalize a choice that you had not considered plausible, which is especially possible today with the diversity of cultural experiences represented by students. For example, we recall the story of the math question on a test that asked, "If a farmer saw 8 crows sitting on a fence and shot 3 of them, how many would be left?" Of course, the "correct" response on the answer key was "5." However, one critical-thinking student, who reasoned that the crows that were not shot would be frightened and would all fly away, chose "none" as his response, and his answer was marked wrong by the teacher.
20. While scoring, on a blank copy of the test, tally the incorrect responses for each item. Analyze incorrect responses for each item to discover potential errors in your scoring key. If, for example, many students select B for an item for which your key says the correct answer is A, you may have made a mistake on your scoring key or in teaching the lesson.
21. Sometimes teachers attempt to discourage cheating by preparing several versions of the multiple-choice exam with the questions in different order. This could give one group of students an unfair advantage if their questions are in the same sequence in which the information was originally presented and learned and for another group of students the questions are in a random order. To avoid this, questions should be in random order on every version of the exam.

Performance

Description: Provided with certain conditions or materials, the student solves a problem or accomplishes some other action.

Example: (As a culminating project for a unit on sound, groups of students are challenged to design and make their own musical instruments. The performance assessment includes five steps.)

Advantages: Performance-type test items come closer to direct measurement (authentic assessment) of certain expected outcomes than do most other types. As has been indicated in discussions of the preceding question types, other types of questions can actually be prepared as performance-type items; that is, where the student actually does what he or she is being tested for.

Disadvantages: This type can be difficult and time-consuming to administer to a group of students. Adequate supply of materials could be a problem. Scoring may tend to be subjective. It could be difficult to give make-up tests to students who were absent.

Guidelines for use: Use your creativity to design and use performance tests, because they tend to measure the important objectives well. To reduce subjectivity in scoring, prepare distinct scoring guidelines (rubrics), as was discussed in scoring essay-type items and as shown in Figures 8.11 and 8.12. To set up a performance assessment situation see Figure 8.13.

Short-Explanation

Description: The short-explanation question is like the essay type but requires a shorter answer.

Example: Explain what, if anything, is wrong with the science implied by the following drawing.

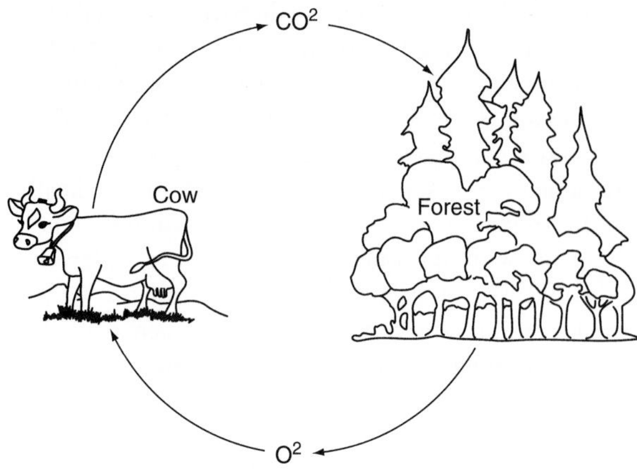

Advantages: As with the essay type, student understanding is assessed, but this type takes less time for the teacher to read and to score. In the example, the diagram of the cow and the forest, which is similar to drawings we have seen in some science textbooks, represents a misconception about our own place in nature. The intent of the authors of such a diagram is to illustrate the interdependence of animals and plants; the lesson frequently learned is that plants use carbon dioxide produced by animals and that animals use oxygen produced by plants. Following such a study, we interviewed teachers and their students, asking, "Do plants use oxygen?" The majority said no, revealing a misconception: The teachers and students did not understand that all living organisms need oxygen. The focus was on what humans gain from interdependence, rather than on the nature of interdependence. *Artificialism* is the term used by Jean Piaget to represent the tendency to believe that everything here on earth is for the benefit of humans. Although natural for students in early grades, it does represent a selfish, prejudiced, nonobjective misconception that should be corrected and avoided in teaching. Science teachers have an obligation and an opportunity to correct such misconceptions, providing they have correct understandings themselves.

By using several questions of this type, teachers can cover more content than with a few essay questions. This type of question is good practice for students to learn to express themselves succinctly in writing.

Disadvantages: Some students will have difficulty expressing themselves in a limited fashion or in writing. They need practice, coaching, and time.

Guidelines for use: This type is useful for occasional reviews and quizzes and as an alternative to other types of questions. For scoring, establish a scoring rubric and follow the same guidelines as for the essay-type item.

1. Specify the performance objective.
2. Specify the test conditions.
3. Establish the standards or criteria (scoring rubric) for judging the quality of the process and/or product.
4. Prepare directions in writing, outlining the situation, with instructions that the students are to follow.
5. Describe the procedure to a colleague for feedback before using it with students.

FIGURE 8.11 Sample of a scoring rubric for student research-project paper. Possible score = 100. Scorer marks a relevant square in each of the six categories (the horizontal rows), and the student's score for that category is the number within that square. For ranges (e.g., 1–10, 12–13, 20–22), the teacher makes a single number selection based on his or her judgment.
Source: Elk Grove School District, Elk Grove, California.

True-False

Description: A statement is presented that students are to judge as being accurate or not.

Example 1: Photosynthesis occurs only in green plants. T or F?

Example 2: Pluto is the outermost planet of our solar system. T or F?

Advantages: Many items can be answered in a relatively short time, making broad content coverage possible. Scoring is quick and simple. True-false items are good as discussion starters, for review, and for diagnostic assessment of what students already know or think they know.

Disadvantages: As illustrated by both examples, it is sometimes difficult to write true-false items that are purely true or false or without qualifying them in such a way that clues the answer.

Much of the content that most easily lends itself to the true-false type of test item is trivial. Students have a 50% chance of guessing the correct answer, thus giving this item type both *poor validity* and *poor reliability.* Scoring and grading give no clue about why the student missed an item. Consequently, the disadvantages of true-false items far outweigh the advantages; *pure true-false items should not be used for arriving at grades.* For grading purposes, you may use modified true-false items (see guideline 11 that follows), where space is provided between items for students to write in their explanations, thus making the item a combined true-false and short-explanation type.

Parenthetical References	14–15 All documented correctly. Paper's references document a wide variety of sources cited—at least five from bibliography.	12–13 Most documented correctly. Few minor errors. At least three sources from bibliography are cited.	11 Some documented correctly. Some show no documentation at all. May not correlate to the bibliography.	1–10 Few to none are documented. Does not correlate to the bibliography. May be totally absent.
Bibliography and Sources	14–15 Strong use of library research. Exceeds minimum of five sources. Bibliography is correctly formatted.	12–13 Good use of library research. Exceeds minimum of five sources. Bibliography has few or no errors in format.	11 Some use of library research. Meets minimum of five sources. Bibliography is present but may be problematic.	1–10 Fails to meet minimum standards for library research. Bibliography has major flaws or may be missing.
Mechanics/Format	14–15 Correct format and pagination. Neat title page, near-perfect spelling, punctuation, and grammar.	12–13 Mostly correct format and pagination. Neat. Few errors in title page, spellings, punctuation, and grammar.	11 Errors in format and pagination. Flawed title page. Distracting errors in spelling, punctuation, and grammar.	1–10 Incorrect format. Title page is flawed or missing. Many errors in spelling, punctuation, and grammar. Lack of planning is obvious. Paper is difficult to read.
Thesis	9–10 An original and comprehensive thesis that is clear and well thought out. All sections work to support it.	8 Comprehensive and well-focused thesis, which is clearly stated. All sections work to support it.	7 Adequate thesis that is understandable but may be neither clear nor focused. It covers the majority of the issues found in the sections.	1–6 Inadequate thesis that is disconnected from the research or may be too broad to support. May be convoluted, confusing, or absent.
Completeness/ Coherence	18–20 Paper reads as a unified whole. There is no repetition of information. All sections are in place, and transitions between them are clearly developed.	16–17 Paper reads as a unified whole with no repetition. All sections are in place, but transitions between them are not as smooth.	14–15 Paper has required sections. Repetitions may be evident. The paper does not present a unified whole. Transitions are missing or inadequate.	1–13 Paper lacks one or more sections and makes no attempt to connect sections as a whole unit. Sections may be grossly repetitive or contradictory.
Thinking/Analyzing	23–25 Strong understanding of the topic. Knowledge is factually relevant, accurate, and consistent. Solutions show analysis of research discussed in paper.	20–22 Good understanding of the topic. Uses main points of information researched. Solutions build on examination of research discussed in paper.	17–19 General understanding of topic. Uses research and attempts to add to it; solutions refer to some of the research discussed.	1–16 Little understanding of topic. Uses little basic information researched. Minimal examination of the topic. Solutions may be based solely on own opinions, without support.

FIGURE 8.12 Sample of a scoring rubric for student project presentation. Possible score = 100. Scorer marks a relevant square in each of the six categories (the horizontal rows), and the student's score for that category is the number within that square. For ranges (e.g., 1–10, 12–13, 20–22), the teacher makes a single number selection based on his or her judgment. *Source:* Elk Grove School District, Elk Grove, California.

Professional Presentation	14–15 Well organized; smooth transitions between sections; all enthusiastically participate and share responsibility.	12–13 Well organized with transitions, students confer/present ideas; group shows ability to interact; attentive discussion of research.	11 Shows basic organization; lacks transitions; some interaction; discussion focuses mostly on research.	1–10 Unorganized, lacks planning; no transitions; reliance on one spokesperson; little interaction; disinterest; too brief.
Engagement of Audience	14–15 Successfully and actively engages audience in more than one pertinent activity; maintains interest throughout.	12–13 Engages audience in at least one related activity; maintains attention through most of presentation.	11 Attempts to engage audience in at least one activity; no attempt to involve *entire* audience. May not relate in significant way.	1–10 Fails to involve audience; does not maintain audience's attention; no connection with audience. No relationship between activity and topic.
Use of Literature	18–20 Strong connection between literature and topic; significant, perceptive explanation of literature; pertinent to topic. At least two pieces used.	16–17 Clear connection between literature and topic; clear explanation; appropriate to topic. Two pieces used.	14–15 Weak connection to topic; unclear explanation; one genre; one piece used.	1–13 No connection to topic; no explanation; inappropriate literature; no literature.
Knowledge of Subject	18–20 Strong understanding of topic; knowledge factually relevant, accurate, and consistent; solution shows analysis of evidence.	16–17 Good understanding of topic; uses main points of information researched; builds solution on examination of major evidence.	14–15 Shows general understanding; focuses on one aspect, discusses at least one other idea; uses research, attempts to add to it; solution refers to evidence.	1–13 Little understanding or comprehension of topic; uses little basic information researched; forms minimal solution; relies on solely own opinions without support.
Use of Media	18–20 Effectively combines and integrates three distinct forms with one original piece; enhances understanding; offers insight into topic.	16–17 Combines two forms with one original piece; relates to topic; connection between media and topic is explained.	14–15 Includes two or three forms but no original piece; media relates to topic. Explanation may be vague or missing.	1–13 One form; no original piece; connection between media and topic is unclear.
Speaking Skills	9–10 Clear enunciation; strong projection; vocal variety; eye contact with entire audience; presentation posture; solid focus with no interruptions.	8 Good enunciation; adequate projection; partial audience eye contact; appropriate posture.	7 Inconsistent enunciation; low projection with little vocal variety; inconsistent posture.	1–6 Difficult to understand; inaudible; monotonous; no eye contact; inappropriate posture; interruptions and distractions.

FIGURE 8.13 Procedure for setting up a performance assessment situation.

Guidelines for Using True-False Items

1. For preparing a false statement, first write the statement as a true statement, then make it false by changing a word or phrase.
2. Try to avoid using negative statements, because they tend to confuse students.
3. A true-false statement should include only one idea. For example, "Spiders are animals that have six legs" would be a poor question because it measures for comprehension of two ideas—animals and number of legs.
4. Use close to an equal number of true and false items.
5. Try to avoid using specific determiners (e.g., "always," "all," or "none"), because they usually clue that the statement is false. Avoid also words that may clue that the statement is true (e.g., "often," "probably," and "sometimes").
6. Avoid words that may have different meanings for different students.
7. Avoid using verbatim language from the student textbook.
8. Avoid trick items, such as a slight reversal of numbers in a date.
9. Avoid using symbols for the words *true* and *false* (sometimes teachers use symbols such as 1 and 2) that might be confusing, or having students write the letters *T* and *F* (sometimes a student does not write the letters clearly enough for the teacher to be able to distinguish which it is). Instead, have students either write out the words *true* and *false* or, better yet, have students simply circle *T* or *F* in the margin of each item as indicated by the example.
10. Proofread your items (or have a friend do it) to be sure that the sentences are well constructed and are free from typographical errors.
11. To avoid "wrong" answers, caused by variations in thinking, and to make the item more valid and reliable, encourage students to write in their rationale for selecting true or false, making the item a *modified true-false* item. For instance

    Example 1: Photosynthesis occurs only in green plants. T or Ⓕ?

    Explanation: Many plants carry on photosynthesis although their predominant coloring is not always green. Brown kelp, for example, if considered to be a plant, is by sheer acreage perhaps the greatest photosynthesizing plant on the Earth.

    Example 2: Pluto is the outermost planet of our solar system. T or Ⓕ?

    Explanation: Sometimes it is; sometimes Neptune is. Some astronomers even question whether Pluto is in fact a planet.

As stated earlier, for grading purposes, you may use modified true-false items, thus making the item a combined true-false and short-explanation type and allowing for divergent and critical thinking. Another form of modified true-false item is the "sometimes-always-never" item, where a third choice, "sometimes," is introduced to reduce the chance for guessing.

Reporting Student Achievement

One of your responsibilities as a classroom teacher is to report student progress in achievement to parents/guardians as well as to the school administration for record keeping. In some schools, the reporting is of student progress and effort as well as achievement. As described in the discussions that follow, reporting is done in at least two, and sometimes more, ways.

The Grade Report

Periodically a grade report (report card) is issued (generally from four to six times a year, depending upon the school, its purpose, and its type of scheduling). Grade reports may be distributed during an advisory period, or they may be mailed to the student's home. This grade report represents an achievement grade (formative evaluation). The final report of the semester is also the semester grade, and for courses that are only one semester long it also is the final grade (summative evaluation). In essence, the first and sometimes second reports are progress notices; the semester grade is the one that is transferred to the student's transcript of records.

In addition to the student's academic achievement, you must report the student's social behaviors (classroom conduct) while in your classroom. Whichever reporting form is used, you must separate your assessments of a student's social behaviors from the student's academic achievement. Academic achievement (or accomplishment) is represented by a letter (or sometimes a number) grade (A through E or F; E, S, and U; or 1 to 5—sometimes with minuses and pluses). Social behavior is given a "satisfactory" or an "unsatisfactory" or a more specific evaluation, or is supplemented by teacher-written or computer-generated comments. There may also be a place on the reporting form for teachers to check whether basic grade-level standards have been met in the core subjects.

Teacher Parental/Guardian Connections

Study after study shows that when parents/guardians are involved in school and school work, students learn better and earn better grades, and teachers experience more positive feelings about teaching. As a result, schools and their teachers are constantly searching for new and better ways to communicate with and to involve parents/guardians. What follows are suggestions and resources.

Although it is not always obligatory, most K–8 teachers purposefully contact parents/guardians by telephone or by e-mail, especially when a student has shown a sudden turn for either the worse or the better in academic achievement or in classroom behavior. That initiative and contact by the teacher is usually welcomed by parents/guardians and can lead to productive conferences with the teacher. An electronic conference (telephone or e-mail) can save valuable time for both the teacher and the parent/guardian.

Another way of contacting parents/guardians is by letter. This gives you time to think and to make your thoughts and concerns clear to the parent/guardian and to invite them to respond at their convenience by letter, by phone, or by arranging to have a conference with you.

In the absence of a computer-link assignment/progress report hotline, or in addition to that, most schools have a progress report form that, upon request by a parent/guardian, can be sent home as often as agreed upon by the teacher and the parent/guardian.

You will meet some of the parents/guardians early in the school year during Back-to-School night (or Meet the Teacher or Curriculum night as it is variously called) and throughout the year in individual conferences and later in the year during spring open house. For the beginning teacher, these meetings with parents/guardians can be anxious times. The following paragraphs provide guidelines to help you with those experiences.[17]

Back-to-School night is the evening early in the school year when parents/guardians and other family members come to the school and meet their children's teachers. The parents/guardians arrive either at the student's homebase/homeroom or in the auditorium for a greeting and a few words from various school officials and then proceed through a simulation of their sons' or daughters' school day. As a group, they meet each class and each teacher for a few minutes. Later, in the spring, many schools host an open house where parents and guardians may have more time to talk individually with teachers, although the major purpose of the open house is for the school and teachers to celebrate and display the work and progress of the students. Spring open house is a grand time for your students to proudly share with their families and the rest of the school community what they have accomplished in their science learning.

At Back-to-School night, parents/guardians are anxious to learn as much as they can about their children's teachers. You will meet each group of parents/guardians for a brief time, usually about 10 minutes. During that meeting you will provide them with a copy of the course syllabus, make some straightforward remarks about yourself, and talk about the course, its requirements, your expectations of the students, and how they, the students' parents/guardians, might help.

Specifically, parents/guardians will expect to learn about your curriculum: goals and objectives, any long-term projects, class size, schedules for tests, and grading procedures. They will want to know what you expect of them: Will there be homework, and if so, should they help their children with it? (Note: The answer to the preceding question is in the nature of the help given; parents and other family members should encourage and help facilitate their children doing homework, but they "should be careful, however, not to solve content problems for students.")[18] How can parents/guardians contact you? Try to anticipate other questions. Your principal and colleagues can help you anticipate and prepare for these questions. Of course, you can never prepare for the question or comment that comes from left field. Just remain calm and avoid being flustered (or at least appear so). Ten minutes will fly by quickly, and parents and guardians will be reassured to know you are an in-control person.

When meeting parents/guardians for conferences, you should be as specific as possible when explaining the progress of their children in your class. And, again, express your appreciation for their interest. Be helpful to his or her understanding, and don't saturate the parent/guardian with more information than he or she needs. Resist any tendency to talk too much. Allow time for the parent or guardian to ask questions. Keep your answers succinct. Never compare one student with another or with the rest of the class. If the parent/guardian asks a question for which you do not have an answer, tell the person you will try to find an answer and will phone him or her as quickly as you can. And do it. Have the student's portfolio and other work with you during the conference so you can show the parent/guardian examples of what is being discussed. Also, have your grade book on hand, or a computer printout of it, but protect from the person the names and records of the other students.

Sometimes it is helpful to have a three-way conference with the parent/guardian, the student, and you, or a conference with the parent/guardian, the principal or counselor, and several or all of the student's teachers. If, especially as a beginning teacher, you would like an administrator to be present at a parent/guardian-teacher conference as backup, don't be hesitant to arrange that.

Some educators prefer a *student-led conference,* arguing that "placing students in charge of the conference makes them individually accountable, encourages them to take pride in their work, and encourages student-parent/guardian communication about school performance."[19] For example, from Derby Middle School (Derby, KS) a teacher reports that

[17] For suggestions from a school administrator for "delivering powerful presentations to parents," see W. B. Ribas, "Tips for Reaching Parents," *Educational Leadership* 56(1):83–85 (September 1998).

[18] R. J. Marzano, D. J. Pickering, and J. E. Pollock, *Classroom Instruction that Works* (Alexandria, VA: Association for Supervision and Curriculum Development, 2001), 63.

[19] D. W. Johnson and R. T. Johnson, "The Role of Cooperative Learning in Assessing and Communicating Student Learning," p. 43 in T. R. Guskey, *Communicating Student Learning.*

"I can't imagine going back to the previous way we met with parents. The preparatory time and work that this alternative takes is worth it, especially when you hear a struggling student explaining what he or she learned from an assignment, and taking responsibility for the score he or she achieved."[20] Another school reports that when students were put in charge of conferences, parent/ guardian attendance at conferences increased by as much as 95 percent.[21]

Summary

Whereas preceding chapters of this book addressed the *why, what,* and *how* components of teaching, this chapter has focused your attention on the fourth and final component—the *how well* component. Assessment is an integral and ongoing factor in the teaching-learning process; consequently, this chapter has emphasized the importance of your including the following in your teaching performance:

- Use a variety of instruments to collect a body of evidence to most reliably assess the learning of students that focus on their individual development.
- Involve students in the assessment process; keep students informed of their progress. Return tests promptly, review answers to all questions, and respond to inquiries about marks given.
- Consider your assessment and grading procedures carefully; plan them, and explain your policies to the students.
- Make sure to explain any ambiguities that result from the terminology used, and base your assessments on the target objectives and material that has been taught.
- Strive for objective and impartial assessment as you put your assessment plan into operation.
- Try to minimize arguments about grades, cheating, and teacher subjectivity by involving students in the planning; reinforcing individual student development; and providing an accepting, stimulating learning environment.
- Maintain accurate and clear records of assessment results so that you will have an adequate supply of data on which to base your decisions about achievement.

Because teaching and learning work hand in hand, and because they are reciprocal processes where one depends on and affects the other, the how well component deals with the assessment of both how well the students are learning and how well the teacher is teaching. Your skill development in teaching is just beginning. It will continue throughout your teaching career. As a teacher you are a learner among learners. We wish you the very best in your endeavor to become the best teacher you can be.

Questions for Class Discussion

1. For a particular grade level (your choice, K–8), describe in detail how you would assess whether the children understand the meaning of *sciencing*.
2. Other than a paper-and-pencil test, identify three alternative techniques for assessing student learning during or at completion of an instructional unit.
3. For a grade level of your choice (K–8), investigate various ways that schools are experimenting today with assessing and reporting student achievement in science. Share what you find with your classmates. With your classmates, discuss the pros and cons of various systems of assessing and reporting.
4. With today's emphasis on curriculum standards and high-stakes proficiency testing, the challenge is to design standards and achievement measures that are not so high that many students cannot reach them nor so low that they become meaningless and risk boring quicker learning children. The reality is, for example, that on any middle school campus there are students doing algebra and students who cannot do simple multiplication—and they are the same age. The question is this: For any area of the curriculum, is one set of standards sufficient or should there be multiple standards, such as a set of minimal standards and another set that will challenge the most capable students? Share your thoughts about this with your classmates.
5. Describe any student science learning activities or situations that you believe should *not* be graded but should or could be used for assessment of student learning.
6. Do you have questions generated by the content of this chapter? If you do, list them along with ways answers might be found.

[20] L. Hayden, "Letting Students Lead Parent Conferences," from *Middle Matters*, NAESP (National Association of Elementary School Principals) *Principal Online* [online 3/20/01 http://www.naesp.org/comm/mmf98b.htm], Fall 1998, 3.

[21] P. Farber, "Speak Up: Student-Led Conference Is a Real Conversation Piece," *Middle Ground* 2(4):21–24 (April 1999). For additional information about student-led conferences, see B. Cesarone, "Parent-Teacher Conferences," *Childhood Education* 76(3):180 (Spring 2000).

Part TWO

Basic Science Information, Learning Activities, and Other Resources: An Introduction to Inquiry

In Chapter 5, we introduced the concept of inquiry learning, along with a table outlining the levels of inquiry learning based on the National Science Education Standards. In Part Two of this book, occasionally, we provide an example of an Inquiry-based Learning Activity labeled as a "Modified" version of a preceding activity. These modified activities are intended to serve as a springboard for class discussion. The need to scaffold students into higher levels of inquiry learning is essential, since higher levels of inquiry require greater autonomy and self-direction on the part of the children. Teachers who offer students autonomous learning opportunities without proper guidance and practice, often discourage and confuse their students. We hope these examples will offer an entry into inquiry teaching that will allow you to carefully construct science lessons to scaffold your students into increasingly more self-directed learning with the goal of nurturing life-long science learning.

Each example of inquiry discusses the three components of inquiry learning: (a) problem identification, (b) process of solving the problem, and (c) identification of tentative solutions to problem.

The Universe and Earth

NSES Content Standard D[1]

Students in **grades K–4** should develop an understanding of

- Properties of Earth materials
- Objects in the sky
- Changes in Earth and sky

Students in **grades 5–8** should develop an understanding of

- Structure of the Earth system
- Earth's history
- Earth in the Solar System

[1]Reprinted from National Research Council, *National Science Education Standards,* © 1996 by the National Academy of Sciences, 130, 158. Courtesy of National Academy of Sciences, Washington, DC.

Chapter 9

The Universe

NASA Headquarters

The Sun

I. The Nature of the Sun

A. The stars that scientists formerly could study only with the aid of a telescope are no longer so mysterious. Massive computer programs now simulate the nuclear reactions at the stars' cores and follow the flow of energy by convection and radiation to the visible surfaces. These computer programs help scientists to understand and explain both the present appearance of stars and how they have evolved.

B. The Sun is a star.
   1. It is only one of billions of stars in the universe, but it is the star that is closest to Earth, about 300,000 times closer to the Earth than is the next nearest star, Proximal Centauri.
   2. It is an average size star. It looks larger than the other stars because it is relatively close to us on Earth, although it still is about 150 million kilometers (93 million mi) from the Earth.

C. The Sun is much larger than the Earth and contains about 99% of the mass of our entire solar system.
   1. The diameter of the Sun at its equator is about 1,380,000 kilometers (860,000 mi), about 109 times larger than the diameter of the Earth. If the Sun were a hollow ball, it could hold more than a million Earths.

D. Like all other stars, the Sun gives off a vast amount of energy, including light energy and solar wind.
   1. The Sun's energy comes from a series of nuclear reactions taking place inside the Sun. Hydrogen atoms in the Sun keep combining to form helium atoms. While the helium is being formed, some of the hydrogen is converted into tremendous amounts of energy.
   2. The nuclear reaction causes the Sun to be very hot. Its surface temperature is about 6,000°C (10,800°F), and the temperature at its center is estimated to be about 15 million degrees C (27 million degrees F).

II. The Parts of the Sun

A. Unlike the Earth, the Sun is not a solid body but a huge ball of several layers of very hot gases, including the core, the photosphere, and the Sun's atmosphere.

B. The layer of the Sun that emits the radiation that we see is called the **photosphere.**
   1. Its radius is the radius of the Sun, which is approximately 696,000 kilometers (435,000 mi).
   2. Deep within the Sun is its core of gases, the site of nuclear reactions that generate the Sun's gigantic energy output.
   3. Energy from the photosphere travels to Earth in the form of electromagnetic wave energy, in tiny units called **photons.**

C. Just above the photosphere is the Sun's lower atmosphere, the **chromosphere.** The chromosphere is pinkish red and can be seen only when the Sun is blotted out in a total eclipse. It rises about 3,200 kilometers (2,000 mi) above and beyond the photosphere.

D. Beyond the chromosphere and extending outward for up to 10,000 kilometers (6,200 mi) is a hotter layer of atmosphere called the **transition zone.**
   1. A silvery halo of gases, called the **corona,** surrounds the transition zone as the Sun's outer atmosphere.
   2. The corona is some 2,000 times hotter (1 million to 2 million degrees C or 1.8 million to 3.6 million degrees F) than the Sun's surface, the photosphere, which is about 6,000°C or 10,800°F. The energy source for heating the corona may be the solar flares feeding energy into the corona. (See section that follows.)
   3. The corona glows with a weak white light that reaches far in all directions from the Sun and can be seen from Earth during a solar eclipse.

III. Sunspots, Solar Prominences, and Solar Flare Activity

A. A **solar flare** is a tremendous explosion on the surface and in the atmosphere of the Sun that results in a bright cloud of gas leaping from the Sun's surface, emitting an extreme amount of ultraviolet and X-ray radiation.
   1. A flare may cover an area of 1 billion square kilometers (391 million square

LEARNING ACTIVITY 9.1

Comparing the Size of the Sun and the Earth

Draw two circles, one with a diameter of 54½ centimeters (21⅘ in.) and the other with a diameter of ½ centimeter (⅕ in.). The larger circle, labeled *Sun,* will be 109 times larger than the smaller circle, labeled *Earth.* Place the circles 150 centimeters (93 in.) apart. By letting 1 centimeter equal 1 million kilometers (or 1 in. equal 1 million mi), then the 150 centimeters (or 93 in.) would indicate the distance of the Earth from the Sun.

miles) and shoot up as high as 480,000 kilometers (300,000 mi). Typical small solar flares are about the size of the Earth. In their brief 5-minute lives each flare releases as much energy as 10 million hydrogen bombs.
2. A flare becomes 20 to 30 times brighter than other areas of the Sun and then fades away in a few hours.

B. Solar storms occur near **sunspots** on the Sun's surface.
1. Sunspots are dark spots that *seem* to move slowly from east to west across the Sun's surface. Actually, sunspots stand still while the Sun turns on its axis. The spots look dark because they are cooler than the surrounding glowing gases.
2. The spots most often appear in the photosphere near the Sun's equator, often as pairs, but sometimes in large groups.
3. Their size can vary from 800 kilometers (500 mi) in diameter to more than 80,000 kilometers (50,000 mi).
4. Sunspots usually appear in 11-year cycles; that is, they reach their greatest number every 11 years.
5. Sunspots are regions where magnetic fields have become concentrated, and are evidence of magnetic storms within the Sun.
6. These magnetic storms send out electrified particles, called **solar wind**, that affect the Earth.
7. When the particles strike the Earth's thermosphere, they interfere with radio, television, and telecommunication signals.
8. The particles also strike the Earth's lower thermosphere and produce the brilliant show of colored lights near the north pole (**northern lights**, or aurora borealis) and south pole (**southern lights**, or aurora australis).

C. When the Sun's rotation on its axis carries a sunspot to the edge of the Sun, solar **prominences** are sometimes formed. Although both are the result of the Sun's magnetic instabilities, prominences are not as violent as flares. They appear to move more gracefully, and an individual prominence may last for hours, days, or even weeks.
1. A typical prominence will measure 10 times the diameter of Earth.
2. Prominences send great streamers of bright gas far out into the Sun's atmosphere. Some prominences suddenly rush back to the Sun, whereas others seem to be blown off the Sun.

D. Because the Sun provides the energy that drives all weather systems, scientists have long believed that solar variations likely affect weather on Earth, although little is yet known about the mechanisms linking our Sun with Earth's weather.
1. Scientists have been able to demonstrate that winter storms follow an 11-year pattern of low-pressure systems over the North Atlantic Ocean, a pattern that matches the 11-year cycle of sunspots.
2. Evidence indicates that our troposphere, the dense bottom layer of the Earth's atmosphere, grows hotter and cooler in step with the solar cycle, in regions near the tropics.

E. Although it is obvious that great disturbances happen within the Sun, scientists do not yet know the exact reason for the appearance, or the exact effects here on Earth, of sunspots, solar flares, and prominences.
1. In 1992, the National Aeronautics and Space Administration (NASA) launched its Extreme Ultraviolet Explorer (EUVE) satellite. An hour after the launch, the EUVE was in orbit 550 kilometers (340 mi) above the Earth. The satellite has four telescopes that in 6 months can map the entire sky above the Earth.
2. High above the Earth's atmosphere, the telescopes are capable of detecting and measuring ultra-high-frequency radiation (extreme ultraviolet), undetectable by Earth-bound telescopes. Extreme ultraviolet radiation is emitted by stars and planetary objects from both within and outside our solar system. With new technology, such as extreme ultraviolet sensing telescopes and EUVE satellite, scientists are still learning about our Sun, planets, interstellar media, and other celestial bodies.

IV. The Life Span of the Sun

A. Like many other systems, stars have a beginning and an end—a life span.

B. Evidence indicates that matter, energy, space, and time began in a violent explosion, called the **Big Bang**, between 10 billion and 15 billion years ago.
1. The Sun resulted from the emergence of hydrogen and helium.

C. Scientists believe that a star that burns hydrogen, such as the Sun, has enough energy for a lifetime of about 10 billion years.
1. Scientists believe that the Sun has been producing energy for at least 5 billion years, which means the Sun will continue to produce energy for many billions of years to come.

D. It is believed that, eventually, when about 15 percent of its hydrogen atoms have been used up, the nuclear reaction inside the Sun will speed up, slowly at first, then faster and faster.
1. The inside of the Sun will get hotter, and the Sun will expand to about 100 times its size.
2. Meanwhile, the surface of the Sun will become cooler, and its color will change to orange and then to red (a **red star**).
3. When enough of the hydrogen has been consumed, the Sun will suddenly collapse and become so small (called a **white dwarf**) that both its size and its light will be only a small fraction of what they are today.
4. The Sun will become cooler and fainter until it becomes completely dark and cannot be seen at all.

LEARNING ACTIVITY 9.2

Solar Eclipse and Sunspots

Arrange a telescope or binoculars (at least six-power) so that it is pointing directly at the Sun (Figure 9.1). This arrangement can be made by getting a long, rectangular cardboard carton from the supermarket. One side of the carton should be open to allow the sunspots to be easily seen. Prop the carton on a box or another carton so that the rear end is facing the Sun's rays directly. In the front end of the carton make a hole large enough for the eyepiece end of the telescope or binoculars to be inserted.

If a telescope is used, make just one hole. Then make a large cardboard sunshade for the barrel of the telescope. If binoculars are used, make two holes and fasten the binoculars securely to the box with tape. Cover one of the outer binocular lenses with dark paper so that only one image of the Sun will be produced inside the carton. A sunshade is not necessary when binoculars are used.

Now adjust the eyepiece of the telescope or binoculars until there is a sharp, clear image of the sun on the inside rear end of the carton. A sheet of white paper taped there will make the image more easily visible. The sunspots will appear on the Sun's image as small, dark marks near the equator. Observe the sunspots every day at the same time. They will slowly move across the Sun as the Sun rotates. Note that they appear only on or near the Sun's equator and never at the poles. If the sunspots seem to be moving from west to east (instead of east to west), this is because of the way the astronomical telescope operates. Moreover, the sunspots will be upside down.

(*Note:* Do not look directly at the Sun through the telescope or binoculars! You can permanently damage your vision in this way.)

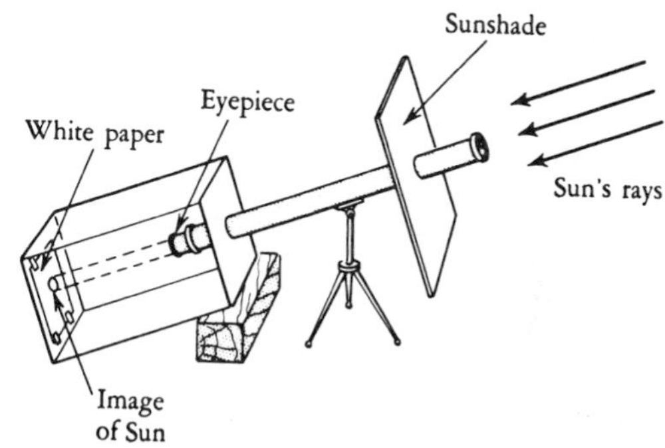

FIGURE 9.1 Arrangement for observing sunspots.

LEARNING ACTIVITY 9.3

Model Solar System

Compare the size of the planets with each other and with the Sun, and show their relative distances from the Sun. To get the correct relative sizes and distances, use a model of the Sun that is 27 inches in diameter, and let 1 inch represent 20 million miles. Using this scale, Table 9.1 shows the proper size and distance for each planet.

Cut out a large cardboard or paper circle that is 27 inches in diameter, and write the word *Sun* in large letters across its surface. Tape this circle to one end of the chalkboard. Now draw circles on the chalkboard, each representing a planet. Make each planet the proper size and place it at the correct distance from the Sun, as shown in Table 9.1. If the chalkboard is not wide enough, cut out paper circles and tape them on the wall adjacent to the chalkboard. Be sure to insert a large number of dots between Mars and Jupiter to show the presence of the asteroids. Write on the chalkboard, as close to the planets as possible, such pertinent information as the name of the planet, its actual size, its distance from the Sun, and the number of moons it has.

TABLE 9.1 Dimensions and Distances for a Chalkboard Diagram of the Sun and Planets

Body	Diameter in Inches	Distance
Sun	27	–
Mercury	⅛	1¾ inches
Venus	¼	3¼ inches
Earth	¼	4¾ inches
Mars	⅛	7 inches
Jupiter	2¾	2 feet
Saturn	2⅜	3 feet 8 inches
Uranus	1	7 feet 5 inches
Neptune	⅞	11 feet 8 inches
Pluto (dwarf planet)	⅜	15 feet 3 inches

Inquiry-Based Learning Activity 9.3.Modified

Let's make a model Solar System. Divide the students into working groups, and provide each group with the following items: (a) a copy of data from Table 9.1, (b) 1 roll of tape, (c) 10 sheets of paper, and (d) a pair of scissors for each student. Each working group's task is to make a model of the Solar System using the information on the data table you have given them. They may choose to make the Sun and planets any way they like, but they are only allowed to use the materials provided to them.

What level of inquiry is this modification?

The design of this activity offers students some degree of autonomy within a well-defined framework. Clearly, they are given the data to analyze and are provided guidelines and possible connections, rather than being asked to seek out information. These characteristics suggest that this activity is at ***Level II (Transition from Level I).*** **Some questions to consider**. What do students in the working groups need to understand about their roles? How would the students' work be assessed?

The Solar System

I. The Members of the Solar System

A. What is referred to as our Solar System is a group of bodies, called **satellites**, that move around our Sun. A satellite is any body that travels around another body. The principal members of the Solar System are eight satellites called **planets.**

1. The word *planet* means wanderer. Collectively, the planets were given this name because they seemed to wander over the sky instead of staying in a fixed position like the stars.
2. In 2006, the International Astronomical Union voted to change Pluto's status to dwarf planet. Despite the result of this vote, the debate continues at the time of the publication of this text. As a result, we have not chosen to eliminate Pluto from the list of planets at this time.
3. The names of the planets of the Solar System, in order of their increasing distance from our Sun, are Mercury, Venus, Earth, Mars, Jupiter, Saturn, Uranus, Neptune, and the dwarf planet, Pluto. Because of the extreme elliptical (oval) shape of their orbits, Pluto and Neptune alternate in their relative positions from the Sun. Once in every 248 years, for about 20 years, Pluto is closer to the Sun than Neptune. The next time period in which Pluto will be closer to the Sun is expected to begin in about the year 2247.
4. There could be other planets in our Solar System yet unconfirmed.
5. Scientists hypothesize that there may be billions of planets within our own galaxy alone.
6. To date, scientists have discovered at least 100 exo planets; that is, planets that are outside of our Solar System.
7. In the Solar System, billions of fast-moving rocks of all sizes, called **asteroids**, also move around the Sun. Between Mars and Jupiter is a belt of asteroids. (The difference between an asteriod and a **meteoroid** is only size; anything larger than 100 m [330 ft] in diameter is an asteroid, anything smaller is a meteoroid.)

B. Planets are not stars and stars are not planets.

1. Stars shine because they give off light, but planets shine because they reflect the light of the Sun or other stars.
2. Planets are much smaller than the Sun and are smaller than most of the other stars.
3. Unlike stars, planets do not appear to **twinkle.**
4. Although stars seem to twinkle, they really do not.
5. Stars are so far away from the Earth that they appear only as small dots of light when we look at them with the naked eye.

NASA Headquarters

Planets of the Solar System.

LEARNING ACTIVITY 9.4

Twinkling

To demonstrate the cause of the twinkling effect of stars, you can set up a demonstration similar to that shown in Figure 9.2, as follows. Establish a light image on a screen. This can be done by placing a light source on a pile of books. Place the handle of a magnifying glass (convex lens) in a small lump of clay so that the magnifying glass remains fixed in an upright position. Adjust the height of the magnifying glass so that the center of the lens is at the same height as the bulb. Place the magnifying glass in front of the bulb, between the bulb and the screen, and adjust the position of the glass and screen until a clear image of the bulb appears on the screen. Darken the room. Note that the image is fixed and does not move or twinkle. Now place a hot plate or other heat source close to the lens and below it. The image will tremble or twinkle, just as a star does, because heat energy from the heat source makes the air above move. This movement makes the light rays shift back and forth as well, making the light bulb appear to twinkle.

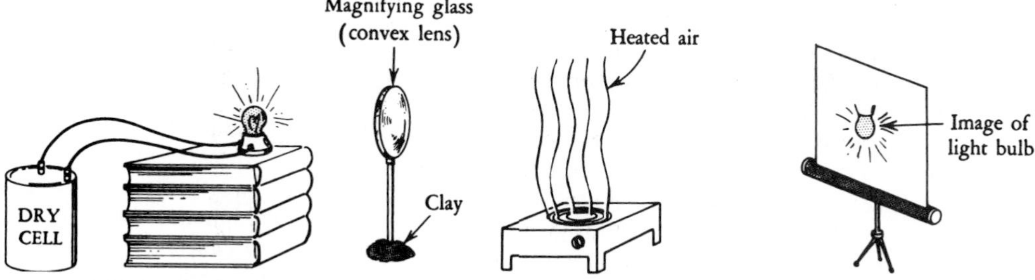

FIGURE 9.2 Moving air makes light rays shimmer and the bulb appear to twinkle.

LEARNING ACTIVITY 9.5

Planets Shine as the Result of Reflected Light

Use a playground ball, basketball, or globe to represent a planet. This planet can barely be seen in a darkened room. In a closet or completely darkened room it cannot be seen at all. If you use a flashlight (or a 35-mm projector, which will give a much brighter light) to represent the Sun and shine the light on the planet, it can be seen because the light from the Sun is reflected off the planet to your eyes.

LEARNING ACTIVITY 9.6

Elliptical Orbit

An elliptical orbit can be demonstrated by using a lighted lamp (without its shade) in a stationary position to represent the Sun. While walking an Earth globe counterclockwise (west to east) and elliptically (noncircularly) around the "Sun," point out that it takes the Earth 365.25 days to make this orbit. That is the Earth's year.

6. Movements of the Earth's atmosphere caused by heat make the thin rays of light from these distant stars seem to twinkle.
7. Planets, unlike stars, are not point sources of light; instead, they reflect light at different angles.
8. Movements of the Earth's atmosphere do not affect these thicker reflected rays of light, so there is no appearance of a twinkle when one is observing a planet with the naked eye.

C. The planets travel in an elliptical (oval) path around the Sun.

1. The invisible, noncircular path followed by orbiting planets (and moons, comets, and asteroids, as well) is called an **ellipse** or orbit.
2. Johann Kepler, in 1605, was the first to conclude that planets orbit the Sun in elliptical paths. Nearly blind himself, Kepler drew his conclusion from studying the reports made by naked-eye astronomer Tycho Brahe, to whom he was an assistant. It was not until several years later, about 1610, that Galileo became the first to use a telescope.
3. All the planets revolve in a counterclockwise elliptical path around the Sun.

LEARNING ACTIVITY 9.7

Planetary Spin on an Axis

If you do not have a large Earth globe, you can demonstrate planetary spin with a knitting needle and a grapefruit (or other large fruit) or a Styrofoam ball and skewer. Push the knitting needle through the grapefruit. The knitting needle represents the axis, or imaginary line, running through the Earth's north and south poles. Tilt the needle slightly and make the grapefruit, which represents the Earth, spin or rotate. Draw a line on the grapefruit with a felt-tip marker from top to bottom, to show the spin more clearly.

4. In 1619, Kepler, through his study of data recorded by other astronomers, concluded that the distance planets are from the Sun determines precisely how long they take to orbit the Sun. By demonstrating that there are distinct mathematical relationships that bind the solar system together, this conclusion helped separate astronomy from astrology.
5. The time needed for a planet to complete one revolution around the Sun is called the planet's **year.**

D. As the planets travel around the Sun, they also spin, or rotate, like tops around an imaginary line, called an **axis,** which runs through the north and south poles of the planet. The time needed for a planet to make one complete rotation on its axis is called the planet's **day.**

E. Most planets have their own smaller satellites that revolve around them. These satellites are called **moons.** In the Solar System, there are at least 94 moons: 1 for Earth, 2 for Mars, 39 for Jupiter, 22 for Saturn, 21 for Uranus, 8 for Neptune, and 1 for Pluto.

F. The planets are alike in certain ways.
1. They are satellites of the Sun.
2. They obtain energy from the Sun.
3. They rotate on their axes.
4. Although the proportions differ, they all contain the same basic chemical elements.

G. The planets differ in many ways.
1. They differ in distance from the Sun.
2. They differ in size and mass.
3. They differ in their atmospheres.
4. They differ in the time it takes them to revolve around the Sun, the planetary year.
5. They differ in the time it takes them to rotate once on their axis, the planetary day.
6. They differ in the number of moons each has.
7. They differ in chemical makeup.
8. They differ in the tilts of their axes.

H. In the Solar System, there are also bodies called **comets,** which have long oval-shaped orbits that bring the comets close to the Sun and then take them far out into the Solar System.

II. How the Solar System Was Formed

A. Over the centuries, many theories have been proposed to explain how the Solar System formed. The theory that is most widely accepted by scientists today is that the Solar System was formed from huge clouds of gases and dust that resulted from the Big Bang that occurred between 10 billion and 15 billion years ago. This seems to be able to explain not only the formation of the Sun and the Solar System but also the formation of the stars and their satellites. This theory or model is known as the **condensation theory.**
1. The light from the stars pushed atoms in these gases and dust toward one another and formed larger particles.
2. These larger particles were attracted to one another by their respective gravitational pulls and began to crowd together. Large numbers of these particles came together, then shrank (condensed), becoming more massive and dense. Eventually a huge ball of material was formed, with its particles packed closely together.
3. Hydrogen atoms in the center of the ball were pulled close together by gravity, causing them to become very hot. They began to collide with sufficient energy to change into helium, which in turn released radiant energy, including light. In this way, our Sun, a star, was formed.
4. Part of the cloud of dust and gases, from which the Sun was formed, remained around this new star and slowly rotated.
5. Later, huge whirlpools formed in the rotating cloud, creating smaller globes of gases and dust. Each globe eventually cooled into a planet, which still revolves around the Sun because of the original motion of the rotating cloud of gases and dust.
6. Planetary satellites were formed from this rotating cloud in the same way, by **accretion.** Cosmic dust that resulted from the Big Bang collided and gradually lumped together to form fine particles called particulates. Particulates became gravel, then small balls, then big balls, then tiny planets, or **planetesimals** (objects the size of small moons that have slight gravitational fields). Finally, what began as dust became the size of the planets and other planetary objects.

LEARNING ACTIVITY 9.8

Effects of Inertia and Gravity

Attach a string that is 1 meter (3 ft) long to a ball or a chalkboard eraser and, while holding one end of the string in your hand, whirl the ball around your head; then let go of the string suddenly and you will observe how the ball travels out in a straight line as it obeys Newton's first law of motion. Whirl the ball around your head again. Note how your hand must pull inward on the string so that the ball will travel around in a circle and not fly out. This pull corresponds to the pull or force of gravity, whereas the tendency of the ball to fly out and travel in a straight line corresponds to the movement due to inertia.

7. As the planetesimals became larger, their increasingly stronger gravitational fields produced high-speed collisions between them. The collisions caused **fragmentation** or the breaking of some of the objects into smaller chunks. Some of the chunks produced the concentrated meteoritic bombardment that occurred during the early evolution of the planets and moons, thereby adding even more mass to the planet or moon. Other chunks, escaping collision with a planet or moon, became asteroids and comets.
8. As their numbers decreased, collisions between them occurred less and less often.

III. The Cause of the Planets' Revolving around the Sun

A. Two simultaneous conditions keep planets in orbit around the sun—inertia of the moving planet and the Sun's gravitational pull.
   1. According to **Newton's first law of motion** (named for Isaac Newton, 1643–1727), a body at rest will remain at rest unless some force starts it moving, and a body that is moving will continue to move in the same direction and at the same speed unless some force acts on that body to change its direction and speed. We have all experienced inertia as passengers in a moving vehicle when brakes are applied. We continue to move forward as the vehicle stops. This is why seat belts are necessary. All planets would continue moving straight into space and away from the Sun if they were not affected by another force, gravity.
   2. According to **Newton's law of gravitation**, every body in the universe attracts or pulls on every other body. The more mass a body has, the greater its pull on another body. Because the Sun has more mass than any of its planets, its gravitational pull on any given planet is much more powerful than the planet's gravitational pull on the Sun. If only gravity were acting on the Sun and each planet, the more powerful pull of the Sun's gravity would cause the planet to rush into the Sun and burn up.
   3. Both inertia and gravity, however, affect each planet at the same time and in such a way that the planet travels neither straight into space nor toward the Sun; instead, it travels in orbit around the Sun.

IV. Mercury

A. Mercury is the planet nearest the Sun, about 58 million kilometers (36 million mi) from the Sun.
   1. Because it is so near the Sun, Mercury is visible to the naked eye but only when the Sun's light is blotted out—shortly after sunset or just before sunrise.
   2. Mercury revolves around the Sun once every 88 Earth days, so its year is much shorter than Earth's year.

B. Like Earth's Moon, Mercury is heavily cratered.

C. Mercury has no appreciable atmosphere or water.

D. Mercury has a magnetic field and is suspected to have a dense iron core.

E. Its diameter is approximately 4,800 kilometers (3,000 mi).

F. It rotates on its axis once in 59 Earth days, so it has long days and nights.

G. The side of Mercury that is facing the Sun is as hot as 467°C (872°F), and the side that faces away from the Sun is quite cold, as cold as −183°C (−300°F).

V. Venus

A. Venus is the next closest planet to the Sun, about 108 million kilometers (67 million mi) from the Sun.
   1. Venus revolves around the Sun once every 224.7 Earth days. It rotates on its axis only once in about 243 Earth days. Consequently, its day is longer than its year.
   2. Like Mercury, Venus can be seen near the horizon as an "evening star" just after sunset, and as a "morning star" just before sunrise.

B. Although Venus has an iron-rich core, because of its slow rotation it has no magnetic field.

C. With a diameter of about 12,100 kilometers (7,500 mi), Venus is slightly smaller than Earth.

D. The hottest part of the sunlit side of Venus is 500°C (900°F)—hot enough to melt lead—while the cool or dark side, the side facing away from the Sun, is about 200°C (360°F). The rocks on the surface of Venus are as hot as the rocks buried deep beneath Earth's surface.
   1. Strong winds on Venus transfer heat from the hot side (sunlit side) to the dark side.
   2. Seasons are absent on Venus.

LEARNING ACTIVITY 9.9

Comparing the Relative Sizes and Distances of the Earth, Moon, and Mars

Place a plain white sheet of paper at one end of a football or soccer field. On the paper place a green pea and write *Earth* next to the pea. Take a small stone that is about 1.5 millimeters across (half again the thickness of a dime or 1/16 inch) and lay it on the paper 17 centimeters (6.5 inches) away from the bean and mark *Moon* next to the stone.

Now at the opposite end of the playing field, about 100 meters (approximately 100 yards) away from the paper with the pea and stone on it, lay another plain white sheet of paper and place a seed, or "corn," of black pepper. Write *Mars* beside the peppercorn. You now have a scale model of the Earth, Moon, and Mars.

E. Thick, reflective clouds surround Venus.
   1. Because of its highly reflective cloud cover, Venus is the third brightest object in the sky as viewed by the naked eye from Earth and can even be seen in the daytime.
   2. Traditional optical telescopes are not able to penetrate through the thick cloud covering to the surface.
   3. The clouds are made of tiny droplets of sulfuric acid.
   4. Venus's barometric pressure is about 100 times higher than Earth's.
   5. Small-impact craters are missing on the surface of Venus, probably because only large bodies can penetrate its dense atmosphere of carbon dioxide to reach its surface.
   6. Evidence indicates active volcanic activity on the surface of Venus, which may explain the planet's thick cloud cover.

F. Using data derived from microwave radar when Venus is closest to Earth, visitations and probes by orbiting spacecraft, and probes by instruments dropped onto Venus, scientists are now beginning to understand more clearly our nearest planet neighbor.

VI. Earth

A. Earth, the next planet from the Sun after Venus, is about 150 million kilometers (93 million mi) from the Sun.
   1. It revolves around the Sun once every 365.25 days.

B. Earth has a diameter of about 12,600 kilometers (7,900 mi).
   1. It rotates on its axis once every 24 hours and a few seconds.
   2. At its equator, Earth rotates at a speed of about 1,600 kilometers (1,000 mi) an hour, but the speed decreases as you move from the equator toward the poles, because the distance decreases.

C. Earth has one moon.

D. Earth is the only planet whose surface temperature is usually between the boiling and freezing points of water. Consequently, much of the water on Earth is found in the liquid state, rather than in the solid (ice) or the gaseous (water vapor) state.
   1. This temperature stability has probably lasted for nearly 4 billion years.
   2. Earth is biologically active, with a vast variety of life forms spread widely over its surface.

VII. Mars

A. Mars, the next planet after Earth, is about 228 million kilometers (141 million mi) from the Sun.
   1. Every 15 years, as in 2003, the paths of Mars and Earth come to a point where there are only about 56 million kilometers (35 million mi) between them.

B. Mars is a small planet; with a diameter of about 6,700 kilometers (4,160 mi), it is about half the diameter of Earth. On Mars, you would weigh only one-third as much as on Earth.
   1. A curious aspect of the Martian topography is the striking difference between the planet's low, smooth northern hemisphere and its heavily cratered southern hemisphere.
   2. Rotating on its axis once every 24.5 hours, its day is about the same as Earth's.

C. Mars revolves around the Sun once every 687 Earth days, so its year is almost twice that of Earth.
   1. Unlike Earth, which stays in an almost circular orbit 93 million miles from the Sun, Mars travels in an elliptical orbit ranging from about 127 million to about 154 million miles from the Sun.

Courtesy of NASA/JPL/California Institute of Technology

Mars from Hubble Space Telescope in 1999.

D. The average temperature on Mars is about −250°C (−258°F). Compare this with an average temperature of about 15°C (59°F) on Earth.
   1. During the day the temperature at the Martian equator may be as warm as 20°C (68°F), but at night it drops to about −270°C (−294°F).
   2. When Mars is closest to the Sun, its surface gets as warm as 0°C (32°F), the sky turns pink, and windblown dust fills its atmosphere.
   3. About a year later, when Mars is 27 million miles farther from the Sun, the dust is swept away, the temperature plunges, and brilliant white ice clouds, like cirrus clouds on Earth, appear against its dark blue sky.
E. Mars has two small moons, named Phobos (Fear) and Deimos (Panic).
F. Like Earth, but unlike Venus, Mars has seasons.
   1. Frozen caps of carbon dioxide at its poles grow smaller in summer, exposing rings of sand, and larger in winter.
   2. In addition to carbon dioxide, the Martian south pole is believed to contain a significant water-ice component.
   3. Water-ice is also believed to be present in large quantities just below the planet's surface.
G. Mars has an atmosphere, but it is much thinner than that of Earth.
   1. The Martian atmosphere is mostly carbon dioxide, with only trace amounts of oxygen and water vapor.
H. Scientists believe that 4.5 billion years ago, both Earth and Mars were warm and wet, with thick atmospheres and heavy volcanic activity. While life formed on Earth, Mars cooled to a frozen planet. Scientists wonder whether life exists on Mars beneath its frozen surface.
I. Mars has the largest known volcanoes in the Solar System, one of which is about the size of Texas and rises to a height of 25 kilometers (16 mi)—nearly three times taller than Mount Everest on Earth—with a crater that measures 80 kilometers (50 mi) across. The volcanoes have long been extinct.
   1. Giant channels carved from the plains indicate that huge floods once gushed from volcanic fissures.
   2. Because these channels seem to have few impact craters, scientists believe the flooding occurred sometime during the last few million years, indicating that the interior of the Martian planet may still be geologically active.

VIII. The Asteroids

A. The asteroids (or planetoids) are a belt of thousands of bodies that circle the Sun between Mars and the next planet, Jupiter.
B. They are called asteroids because they look like small stars and planetoids because they are really like small planets.
   1. The asteroid Ida, a chunk of rock 50 kilometers (31 mi) across, has a small moon.
C. All asteroids revolve around the Sun in the same direction as the larger planets, although some may leave their orbits and cross the paths of planets or moons—and even crash into those bodies.
   1. Scientists at NASA's Jet Propulsion Laboratory and others around the world are aware of a small but significant chance that an asteroid will strike Earth in 2030. To date it is unknown whether this object, called 2000 SG344, is a sizable asteroid, perhaps as large as a tall office building, or merely a spent rocket booster.
D. Asteroids are irregular lumps of rock, perhaps mixed with metal such as iron, that differ in size and brightness.
   1. Only a few are larger than 160 kilometers (100 mi) in diameter.
   2. Ceres, the largest yet discovered, is more than 949 kilometers (588 mi) in diameter, about one-fourth the size of our Moon.
   3. A few hundred are 16 to 160 kilometers (10 to 100 mi) in diameter, and the rest are less than 16 kilometers—some perhaps only about the size of a soccer ball.
E. Scientists are not sure how asteroids were formed. They may have come from a planet that exploded or from two planets that collided and exploded, or they may be from a part of the solar system that never grew large enough to form one or more larger planets.

IX. Jupiter

A. Jupiter, the next planet after Mars, is about 778 million kilometers (484 million mi) from the Sun.
   1. To the naked eye, it looks like a very large star.
   2. It revolves around the Sun once in about 11.86 Earth years.
B. Jupiter is the largest planet, with a diameter of about 143,000 kilometers (89,000 mi), about 11 times that of Earth.
   1. It rotates on its axis once in about 10 hours, so it has a very short day.
   2. Its speed of rotation is very fast, about 40,000 kilometers (25,000 mi) an hour at its equator, or about 25 times faster than Earth's speed of rotation at the equator.
   3. This rapid rotation causes Jupiter to flatten at its poles and bulge at its equator, even more than Earth does.
   4. Jupiter creates a strong magnetic field.
C. Jupiter has at least 39 moons.
   1. Ganymede is Jupiter's largest moon, even larger than planets Mercury and Pluto, and more than three-fourths the size of Mars. If Ganymede orbited the Sun it would undoubtedly be considered a planet. Its surface is icy, with craters, basins, and mountains.
   2. A vast ocean once flowed beneath the icy surface of Europa and possibly flows still today.

D. Rather than a solid surface, Jupiter seems to consist of shifting belts of ammonia clouds that run parallel to its equator and are spread out in colored bands that, when observed by telescopes, keep changing their patterns and colors.
   1. Evidence indicates that Jupiter is a giant ball of gas with an atmosphere of nearly 90% hydrogen, 10% helium, and a trace amount of water.
E. Jupiter has a large **Red Spot** that moves around irregularly as it rotates counterclockwise in Jupiter's southern hemisphere. It is believed to be an Earth-sized hurricane that has persisted for hundreds of years, although scientists believe that it is gradually diminishing in size.
F. Three thin (about 100 feet thick), flat, faintly visible rings encircle Jupiter. They consist mostly of ice particles but one contains large boulder-size debris that sometimes extends up to 200,000 miles from the planet.
G. In 1994, scientists were able to predict and observe the crashing of a comet, Shoemaker-Levy 9, into Jupiter. The impact left a hole in Jupiter's atmosphere that is estimated to be about the size of Texas.
   1. From further study of the impact of this comet on Jupiter, scientists expect to learn more about how energy spreads after huge impacts such as this, including those that may have caused mass extinction of life on Earth.

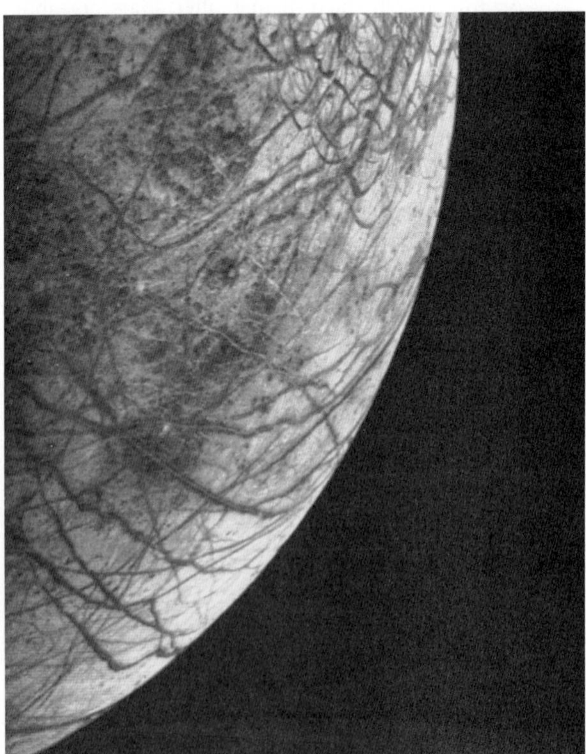
NASA Headquarters

Europa as seen from Voyager 2.

   2. From these studies, scientists also expect to learn more about the frequency at which large comets crash into Jupiter, and, by extension, into Earth. It has been hypothesized that such impacts on Jupiter or its moons occur about every 150 years.

X. Saturn

A. Saturn, the next planet after Jupiter, is about 1,430 million kilometers (890 million mi) from the Sun.
   1. It revolves once around the Sun in about 29.5 Earth years.
B. Saturn has a diameter of about 120,000 kilometers (75,000 mi).
   1. It rotates on its axis once in about 10 hours.
   2. Saturn produces a strong magnetic field.
C. Saturn has 22 known moons.
D. It is also surrounded by seven broad rings that revolve at different speeds around the planet. These rings are composed of ice and rock that range in size from tiny particles to boulders as large as tall buildings.

XI. Uranus

A. Uranus is the next planet after Saturn and is about 2,900 million kilometers (1,800 million mi) from the Sun.
   1. It revolves once around the Sun in about 84 Earth years.
B. Uranus has a diameter of about 50,000 kilometers (31,000 mi).
   1. It rotates on its axis once every 17 hours, but in a different position from all other planets.
   2. Whereas the other planets rotate on a vertical axis, like a top spinning upright, Uranus rotates on an almost horizontal axis, like a top spinning on its side.
C. Uranus has 21 known moons. At least 11 rings surround it, but unlike those of Saturn, the rings are narrow and faint.
D. Uranus seems to have a solid core that is surrounded by an icy layer, and a thick atmosphere of gases.

XII. Neptune

A. Neptune is usually the next planet after Uranus and is about 4,500 million kilometers (2,800 million mi) from the Sun.
   1. From 1990 to 2007, however, Neptune is in the part of its orbit that is farthest from the Sun, while Pluto is closer than usual to the Sun.
   2. Neptune revolves around the Sun once every 164.8 Earth years.
B. Neptune has a diameter of about 49,000 kilometers (30,000 mi).
   1. It rotates on its axis once in about 18 hours.

C. Neptune has eight known moons, and two narrow and two broader rings surrounding it.
D. It has a very dynamic atmosphere, with bright cloud-like covers and high-pressure systems appearing and disappearing in a matter of hours.

XIII. Pluto

A. Pluto was reclassified as a dwarf planet by an International Astronomical Union vote in September 2006.
   1. The size of Pluto led many to question its status as a planet since other recently discovered solar bodies are as big as or bigger than Pluto.
   2. These other dwarf planets are Eris, which is slightly larger than Pluto, and Ceres, pronounced like the word *series*. They both have highly elliptical orbits like Pluto.
   3. The debate regarding Pluto's status remains a controversial issue, and its status may change yet again.

B. Pluto is about 5,900 million kilometers (3,700 million mi) from the Sun.
   1. Pluto's elliptical orbit around the Sun is tilted 17 degrees from the orbits of the other planets.
   2. Because Pluto's and Neptune's elliptical orbits cross each other, Pluto is not always the planet that is farthest from the Sun.
   3. Pluto revolves around the Sun once in about 248.5 Earth years.

C. Its diameter is estimated to be about 2,300 kilometers (1,400 mi)—smaller than the Earth's Moon.
   1. It rotates on its axis once in about every 6 days.

D. Pluto has at least one moon.
E. The primary surface constituent of Pluto is frozen methane.
   1. The existence of frozen methane on Pluto implies a very cold surface temperature.
   2. Many astronomers today believe that Pluto is the largest or nearest member of a class of icy asteroids found in the outer Solar System. There are hundreds of chunks of rock and ice beyond Neptune, at least 70 of which share orbits similar to Pluto's.

XIV. Comets

A. Comets are bodies that revolve around the Sun in long, oval-shaped orbits (see Figure 9.3).
   1. The Sun is at one far end of the comet's orbit.
   2. The comet's orbit cuts across the paths of the planets' orbits.

B. A comet has a head and, as it nears the Sun, a tail.
   1. The head is made of small rocks and dust mixed with frozen gases; it is believed to contain ice.

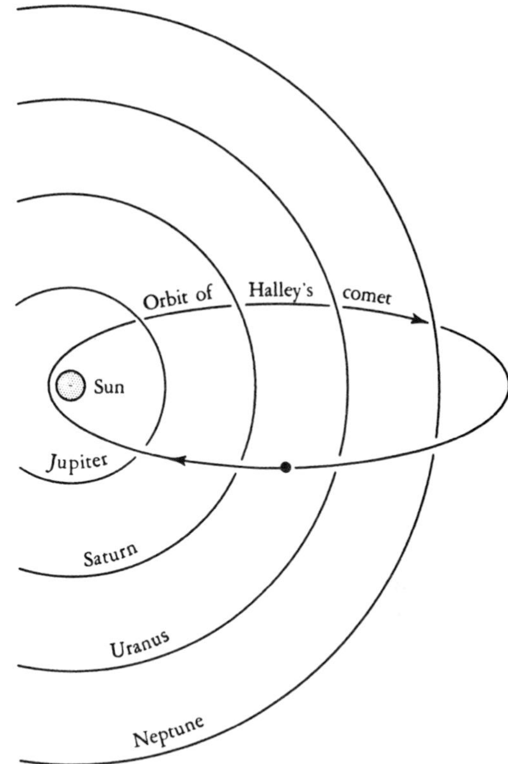

FIGURE 9.3 Orbit of Halley's comet.

   2. A comet does not have a tail until it nears the Sun, at which time the solid, frozen gases in the comet begin to vaporize. The tail is actually a thin stream of vapors that may be millions of kilometers long, and thin enough that stars can be seen through it. As the comet travels away from the Sun, the gases condense and freeze again and the tail disappears.
   3. The comet and its tail reflect the light of the Sun. The pressure of this light makes the tail point away from the Sun both when the comet approaches and when it leaves the Sun.

C. As a comet approaches the Sun it gains speed, and the Sun's pull of gravity on it becomes stronger; then it slows down again as it travels away from the Sun.
D. Some comets return to our view relatively quickly, but others take much longer. For example, Encke's comet returns every 3.5 years, whereas Halley's comet returns every 76 years.
   1. Some comets never return, either because they waste away as material is forced out of the head into the tail or because they are destroyed as they approach a large body.
   2. An example of a comet that was destroyed is the Shoemaker-Levy 9 comet that crashed into Jupiter in 1994.

E. It is not known how comets form.

XV. **Meteor and Meteorite**

A. A **meteor** is a sudden, brief streak of light in the night sky caused by friction between air molecules in Earth's atmosphere and an incoming piece of interplanetary matter—an asteroid, comet, or meteoroid—traveling about 160,000 kilometers (100,000 mi) an hour.

1. When the interplanetary matter is within about 80 kilometers (50 mi) of the Earth's surface, the friction caused by air rubbing against the object makes the object appear white hot. It begins to burn, creating a streak of light as it travels through Earth's atmosphere. These bright streaks are sometimes referred to as shooting stars. Most burn up in the atmosphere and therefore do not reach the Earth's surface.
2. Those that do strike the Earth's surface before they completely burn up are called **meteorites.**

B. Scientists believe that meteorites come from two sources.

1. Most are small bits of rocks, like those in the belt of asteroids between Mars and Jupiter, that are traveling through space.
2. Some meteorites come from comets. Swarms of meteors, called **meteor showers,** occur whenever the Earth crosses the path of a comet.
   a. Some meteor showers occur annually. These meteor showers are named after the constellations from whose direction they seem to come.
   b. Well-known among these are the Perseid shower, which occurs about August 10 to 14; the Orionid shower at about October 20 to 24; the Leonid shower at about November 15 to 19; and the Geminid shower at about December 10 to 14.

C. When a large meteorite or an asteroid strikes the Earth's surface, it can form an **impact crater** (which is not the same as craters like Crater Lake in Oregon that are formed from the eruption of a volcanic mountain).

1. The pressures and temperatures produced by the impact of large meteorites and asteroids are usually sufficient to melt and even vaporize them as well as the Earth material that is struck. Therefore, fragments of the incoming object are more likely to be found at the smaller craters, such as those caused by meteorites.
2. Approximately 150 impact craters have been identified on Earth. Scientists believe there have been many others that either have not yet been found or that were obliterated by changes in the Earth's topography, such as from erosion and flooding.
3. About 50,000 years ago, near Flagstaff, Arizona, an iron-nickel asteroid estimated to have been about 46 meters (150 ft) wide struck the Earth's surface and left a crater 1.2 kilometers (three-quarters of a mile) wide and 213 meters (700 feet) deep.
4. Created by an asteroid about 1.4 million years ago, the New Quebec Crater (also known as Chubb's Crater) is 3.5 kilometers (2.2 mi) wide and 430 meters (1,400 feet) deep.
5. Estimated to be 65 million years old, the Chicxulub Crater was discovered in 1981, completely hidden by sediments that formed the Yucatan Peninsula. It is 170 kilometers (110 mi) wide.
6. Large impacts like the one that caused the Chicxulub Crater have been hypothesized to be a cause of major extinctions of life on Earth.
7. Other large impact craters are the Vredefort Crater (South Africa), 300 kilometers (186 mi) wide; the Sudbury Crater (Ontario, Canada), 250 kilometers (155 mi) wide; the Popigai Crater (Russia) and the Manicouagan Crater (Quebec, Canada), each 100 kilometers (62 mi) wide; and the Chesapeake Bay Crater in Virginia, 85 kilometers (52 mi) wide.

The Effects of the Sun on the Earth

I. **The Sun Causes the Year on Earth**

A. The Earth travels in an elliptical (oval) path, called an **ellipse** or orbit, around the Sun.

1. It revolves in this orbit in a counterclockwise direction (from west to east).
2. The time needed for the Earth to make one complete revolution around the Sun is 365.25 days and is called the **Earth's year.**

II. **The Earth's Spin Causes Day and Night on Earth**

A. In addition to revolving around the Sun, the Earth spins or rotates like a top.

1. It spins around an imaginary line, called an axis, which runs through the Earth's north and south poles.
2. It rotates on its axis in a counterclockwise direction (from west to east).
3. The time needed for the Earth to make one complete turn on its axis is 24 hours and is called the **Earth's day.**

B. At the equator, the Earth rotates at a speed of about 1,600 kilometers (1,000 mi) an hour, but this speed diminishes as we move farther away from the equator toward the North and South Poles. Halfway between the equator and the North Pole, the speed is about 1,280 kilometers (800 mi) an hour.

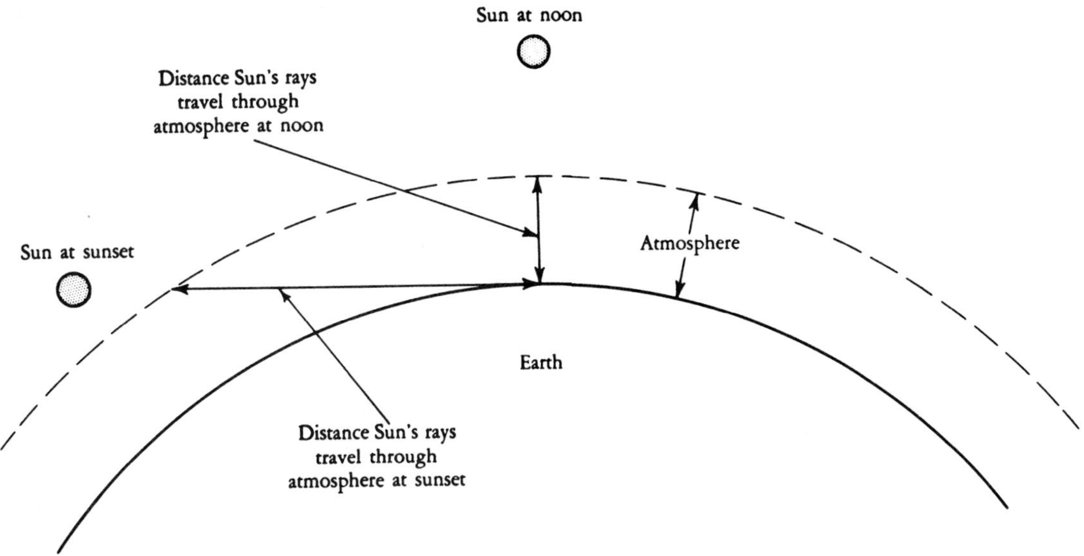

FIGURE 9.4 The distance that sunlight passes through the atmosphere at sunrise or sunset is greater than at noon.

C. The Earth gets its light from the Sun.
   1. Because of its spherical shape, only half of Earth can be lighted at one time. When one half is lighted by the Sun, that half is in daylight and the other half is in darkness (nighttime).
   2. Every 24 hours, as the Earth rotates once on its axis, any one part of the Earth will have had one period of daytime and one period of nighttime.
   3. Because the Earth turns from west to east, the Sun *seems* to move across the sky from east to west. The Sun is said to "rise" in the east and "set" in the west.

D. When the Sun (or the Moon) is just rising or just setting, it looks bigger than it does at any other time.
   1. This phenomenon is an optical illusion believed to be the result of viewing the Sun (or Moon) in relation to buildings or trees, when it is lower in the horizon. When it is higher in the horizon, there are no structures with which to compare it (see Figures 9.4 and 9.7).

E. Also at sunrise and at sunset, the Sun looks orange or reddish.
   1. This phenomenon happens because rays of red light can pass through a greater distance of the Earth's atmosphere more easily than rays of blue light, which are bent and scattered more than the red (see Figure 9.4).
   2. When the Sun is low on the horizon, as at sunrise or sunset, the light from the Sun must travel a much greater distance through the thicker part of the Earth's atmosphere than when the Sun is overhead.
   3. The blue rays in sunlight cannot get through this greater distance of air, so they are reflected and scattered by the dust particles in the air. The reflection and scattering of the blue light by the dust particles is what makes the sky appear blue.
   4. However, the red rays in sunlight can still pass through; the sunlight now has less blue in it, so the Sun looks orange or reddish.

LEARNING ACTIVITY 9.10

Day and Night

Use a globe of the Earth that rotates and a flashlight, slide projector, or lamp. Have a student find and mark on the globe with chalk or a piece of tape where you live. Darken the classroom and turn on the light source (which represents the Sun). Half the globe will be lighted (daytime) and half will be in darkness (nighttime). Now spin the globe slowly from west to east (counterclockwise when looking down from the north pole). Show the students that where they live goes from day to night and back to day again. Show also how the east will receive sunlight before the west, so that when it is dawn in New York, it is still dark in Chicago, Los Angeles, and Hawaii.

5. When the Sun is overhead, all the rays of light can get through this thinner and shorter distance of atmosphere, and so the Sun appears more white. Its rays are more concentrated, as demonstrated in Figure 9.5.

III. The Sun Causes the Seasons on Earth

A. The Earth's axis is tilted at an angle of 23.5 degrees and is always pointed toward Polaris, the North Star.

B. Because of this tilt and because of the Earth's revolution around the Sun, the Earth has different seasons of the year (see Figure 9.6).

C. When the northern hemisphere is tilted toward the Sun, the northern hemisphere has summer.
   1. Summer begins on June 21, which is called the **summer solstice.**
   2. In summer, the Sun's rays are shining directly on the northern hemisphere.
   3. The stronger, direct rays cover a smaller amount of the Earth's surface, and that surface becomes quite hot.
   4. Because of the tilt of the Earth's axis, the northern hemisphere also gets more daylight than darkness in the summer, so the days are longer than the nights.
   5. More daylight means that the northern hemisphere gets the Sun for a longer time, which also helps it become warmer in summer.
   6. When it is summer in the northern hemisphere, the North Pole has daylight all 24 hours.

D. When the northern hemisphere is tilted away from the Sun, it has winter.
   1. Winter begins on December 22, which is called the **winter solstice.**
   2. In winter, the Sun's rays are shining at a slant on the northern hemisphere.
   3. The weaker, slanted rays now cover a larger amount of the Earth's surface, and the surface is not heated as much as it was during summer.
   4. Because of the tilt of the Earth's axis, the northern hemisphere gets more darkness than daylight in the winter, so the nights are longer than the days.
   5. Longer nights mean that the northern hemisphere gets the Sun's rays for a shorter time, which also causes it to become much colder in the winter.
   6. When it is winter in the northern hemisphere, the North Pole is in darkness all 24 hours.

E. When it is summer in the northern hemisphere, the southern hemisphere is tilted away from the Sun and the southern hemisphere has winter; when it is winter in the northern hemisphere, the southern hemisphere is tilted toward the Sun and the southern hemisphere has summer.

F. At the beginning of spring and at the beginning of fall, the Earth is tilted neither toward nor away from the Sun.
   1. The direct rays of the Sun strike the Earth exactly on the equator.
   2. Days and nights are of equal length on the day of the **equinox.**
   3. The northern hemisphere spring begins March 21, the **vernal equinox,** at the precise moment when the Sun's direct rays hit the equator. After this moment, the direct rays of the Sun fall in the northern hemisphere until the time of the **autumnal equinox** on September 23.

IV. The Sun Is a Source of Energy for the Earth

A. The Sun sends out radiant energy in all directions, but only a fraction of the Sun's energy reaches the Earth. This energy heats the Earth and gives it light. Without the energy of sunlight, the Earth would be a frozen, lifeless wasteland.

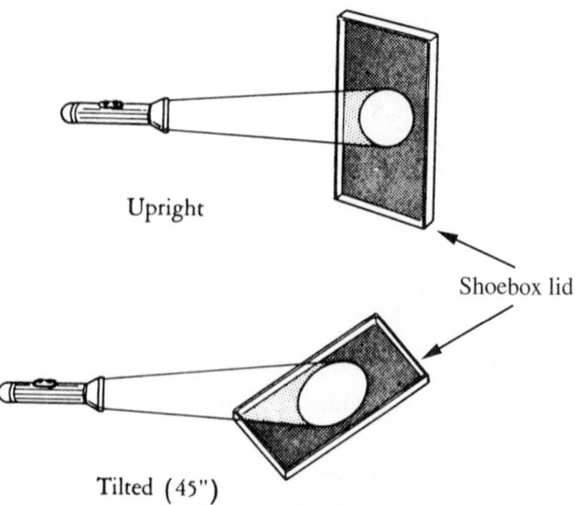

FIGURE 9.5 Direct rays are more concentrated than slanted rays.

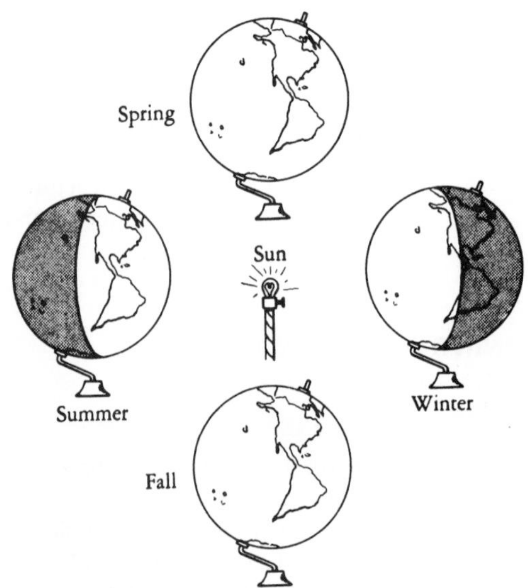

FIGURE 9.6 The tilt of the Earth's axis and the revolution of the Earth around the Sun together.

B. The Sun's energy makes it possible for some organisms to manufacture food by photosynthesis (see Chapter 12).
C. From the bodies of organisms that have died, the Sun's energy is stored in natural fuels such as wood, coal, oil, and gas.
   1. Coal is what remains of fernlike plants that died millions of years ago and were buried under masses of rock and soil and subjected to tremendous pressure and heat.
   2. Oil and gas are what remain of organisms that died and were buried under layers of mud and sand and subjected to tremendous pressure and heat.
   3. When natural fuels are burned, they give off energy in the form of heat and light—the same energy that originally came from the Sun and was stored in algae and plants through photosynthesis.

V. The Sun Causes the Weather

A. The Sun does not heat all parts of the Earth equally.
   1. The parts of the Earth near the equator are heated more than the parts of the Earth away from the equator, because the rays of light become more slanted farther away from the equator (see Figure 9.6).
   2. Because the Sun's rays heat only about one-half of the Earth at one time—during daytime—a daily heating and cooling cycle results.
   3. The land on the Earth is heated and cooled more quickly than is water.
   4. Dark-colored bodies of land absorb more heat than light-colored land bodies.
B. This unequal heating causes movements of great masses of air.
   1. Some air masses are cold, and others are warm.
   2. Cold air masses originate from the polar regions of the Earth, whereas warm air masses originate from the tropical or equatorial regions.
   3. The warmer, lighter air from the equator rises and moves toward the poles, and the colder, denser air from the poles moves toward the equator.
   4. Because gas expands when warm and contracts when cold, colder, denser air masses have greater pressure than warmer, less dense air masses.
C. The heat of the Sun also causes some of the water on the Earth to evaporate into the air and become a gas called **water vapor.**
   1. Warm air, because of the greater energy in its molecules, can hold more water vapor than cold air.
D. When a warm air mass and a cold air mass meet, the warm air mass is cooled and some of the water vapor **condenses** and falls out of the air as some form of **precipitation.**
E. The combination of moving air masses, differences in air pressure, and changing amounts of water vapor in the air—all caused by the Sun—are responsible for the different kinds of weather and changes in weather throughout the Earth.

Earth's Moon

I. The Nature of the Earth's Moon

A. The Earth's Moon is a large ball of rocky material that revolves around the Earth.
   1. It is about 3,500 kilometers (2,160 mi) in diameter; that is, about $\frac{1}{4}$ the diameter of the Earth.
   2. The volume of the Moon is about $\frac{1}{50}$ that of the Earth.
   3. Its mass is about $\frac{1}{80}$ that of the Earth.
B. The Moon's pull of gravity is only $\frac{1}{6}$ that of the Earth.
   1. A broad jumper who can jump 7 meters (23 ft) on Earth would jump 42 meters (138 ft) on the Moon; a high jumper who can jump 2 meters (6.5 ft) on Earth would jump 12 meters (39 ft) on the Moon.
   2. The high jumper would not fall any harder from the greater height, because his or her mass remains the same, but the jumper's weight would be only $\frac{1}{6}$ as much on the Moon as on Earth.
C. The Moon has no atmosphere. Without an atmosphere, there is no wind on the Moon, and sound cannot travel in that void.
D. Data indicate that there is water on the Moon.
   1. Research data from lunar spacecraft indicate that there are between 1 billion and 10 billion tons of water frozen near the Moon's poles. The water is believed to be frozen within craters that never receive sunlight.
   2. This could be enough water to supply a Moon colony or to fuel rocket ships on their way into deeper space.
   3. The water is believed to have come from comets that have smashed into the Moon over millions of years.
E. The temperature on the Moon's surface varies greatly, depending on whether it is day or night, from as high as 104°C (220°F) during the day to as low as −270°C (−294°F) at night.
F. The surface of the Moon consists of dark flat areas, lighter-colored areas, mountain ranges, and many craters.

1. The dark flat areas (called **maria**) cover about half the surface of the side we see; they are shaped like rough circles. The maria create the dark features in what some call "the man in the Moon."
2. The maria were caused by vast lava flows that leaked out onto the Moon's surface billions of years ago.
3. The largest maria is about 2,500 kilometers (1,500 mi) in diameter, about half the distance across the continental United States.
4. The lighter-colored areas are elevated several kilometers above the maria and are called the lunar **highlands.**
5. The highlands are made of rocks rich in aluminum, making them lighter in color and lower in density than the maria. The maria's basaltic matter contains more iron, giving it a darker color and greater density.
6. The surface of the Moon is covered with a layer of dust particles, pebbles, and stones—the Moon's version of soil—called **regolith.**
7. The regolith covers most of the Moon's surface at depths of up to 20 meters (approximately 66 ft). It is thicker on the highlands and thinnest on the maria.
8. Samples of the lunar regolith were brought back to Earth by U.S. astronauts Neil Armstrong and Buzz Aldrin from the voyage of the Eagle spaceship (flight of Apollo 11—see Figure 9.12) that landed on the Moon's surface in 1969 in a large maria called the Sea of Tranquility.
9. A person walking on the Moon kicks up a cloud of loose dust; the dust falls back to the surface just as quickly as heavy pieces of stone or iron, because there is no atmosphere of air to slow it down.

G. Most mountain ranges are concentrated in the Moon's southern hemisphere.

1. Some of these mountains soar 7,500 meters high (25,000 ft).
2. Because there are no forces of wind or water to wear them down to a smoother form, the mountains are very jagged.

H. There are also many rounded depressions called craters, spread over the Moon's surface.

1. Data indicate that the majority of the **lunar craters** were formed by impacts that occurred during the formation of the Moon about 3.9 billion years ago. A few were formed by volcanic activity.
2. It is estimated that in any one area of the Moon, within a radius of 100 kilometers (62 mi) there will be about 500 craters wider than one kilometer each (0.6 mi).
3. There are about 5,000 craters that are each larger than 5 kilometers (3 mi) in diameter.
4. More than 30,000 craters have been identified, the largest being about 240 kilometers (150 mi) in diameter.
5. In most craters, the floor is above the level of the surrounding basin.
6. Some craters have smooth floors; others have rough floors, often with smaller craters in them.
7. Some craters have light-colored streaks or rays radiating out in all directions. The most conspicuous rays come from the crater Tycho. It is believed that the rays were created by a lava flow that spread out over the moon's surface, caused by the impact of the object that made the crater.
8. The lunar surface also contains volcanic ditches where molten lava once flowed. These ditches are about 1 kilometer (0.6 mi) wide and of unknown depth. Some are crooked and others follow a straight line.

II. The Motion of the Moon around the Earth

A. The Moon revolves around the Earth in an elliptical orbit in a counterclockwise direction (from west to east)—the same direction that the Earth revolves around the Sun.

1. Because the Moon's orbit is elliptical, it approaches a little closer to the Earth on one side of its orbit.
2. The point of the Moon's orbit nearest the Earth is called its **perigee**, and the point farthest from the Earth is called its **apogee.**
3. Although the Moon's average distance from the Earth is 384,000 kilometers (240,000 mi), at perigee it is about 350,000 kilometers (220,000 mi) from Earth and at apogee it is about 400,000 kilometers (250,000 mi) from Earth.

B. The conditions that keep the Moon orbiting the Earth are the same ones that keep the planets in orbit around the Sun.

1. One condition is the pull of gravity, in this case the Earth's pull on the Moon. If this were the only condition, then the Earth's gravitational pull on the Moon would cause it to be pulled to the Earth.
2. The other condition that keeps the Moon from crashing into Earth (and the planets from crashing into the Sun) is inertia, in this case the Moon's own motion and tendency to continue in motion in a straight line. Were it not for the Earth's pull of gravity, the Moon's inertia would cause it to travel away from the Earth.
3. Because of the balance between inertia and gravity, the Moon travels neither straight into space nor toward the Earth, but instead in an orbit around the Earth.

C. The Moon revolves around the Earth at a speed of about 3,500 kilometers (2,200 mi) an hour. It takes about 27.3 days for the Moon to make one complete orbit around the Earth. This is called a **lunar month.**

1. However, because the Earth has, itself, been orbiting the Sun for this month, the Moon must orbit Earth for 2.2 more days before it is once again aligned straight out from the Sun and Earth. In other words, it takes 29.5 days for the Moon to go from one full Moon to the next (see "Phases of the Moon" and Figure 9.8). Calendars use 29.5 days as the time for one lunar month.

D. The Moon "rises" about 50 minutes later each day. The difference in rising time happens because the Moon moves in its orbit in the same direction (counterclockwise) as the Earth rotates. Therefore, it takes the Earth a little longer each day to turn around so that the Moon can next be seen as the Earth moves farther along its orbit.

E. The Moon rotates on its axis in a counterclockwise direction (west to east).

1. It takes the Moon just as long to rotate once on its axis as it does to revolve once around the Earth, which means that the Moon's day is the same length as its month. Thus, the Moon has about 2 weeks of daylight at one time, followed by about 2 weeks of nighttime.
2. Because the Earth rotates in a counterclockwise direction, the Moon seems to rise in the east, move across the sky, and set in the west. As with the Sun, an optical illusion causes the Moon to appear bigger when it is rising or setting (see Learning Activity 9.11).

F. Because of the Moon's rotation on its axis only once in a lunar month, all we ever see from the Earth is about half of the Moon's surface.

1. Actually, we see about 59% of the Moon's surface. Because its orbit is slightly tilted, we can see a little over the Moon's top and under its lower edge as it travels around.
2. We can also see a little more of each side of the Moon because it moves faster at perigee than at apogee. At perigee, when the Moon increases its speed, the Earth lags behind and we see a little more of one side of the Moon. At apogee, when the Moon decreases its speed, the Earth moves ahead and we see a little more of its other side.
3. Lunar space flights and Earth satellite pictures taken of the other side of the Moon indicate that its far side, the side we do not see, is different. It contains no major maria and is composed almost entirely of highlands.

NASA Headquarters

The far side of Earth's moon

LEARNING ACTIVITY 9.11

Optical Illusion of Moon's Size

To show the optical illusion of the size of the Moon (and the Sun) during rising and setting, bend a paper clip so that it fits a meter stick snugly, as shown in Figure 9.7. When there is a full Moon on the horizon, sight the Moon so that it fits exactly within the two ends of the paper clip, pinching or widening the ends if necessary. Look at the Moon again through the paper clip later when it is higher in the sky. Its size will not have changed at all.

Historically, the illusion of the size of the Moon (and the Sun) has inspired novelists, songwriters, artists, and the invention of myths and words (harvest moon, lunatic). Have your students research examples and share them with the class.

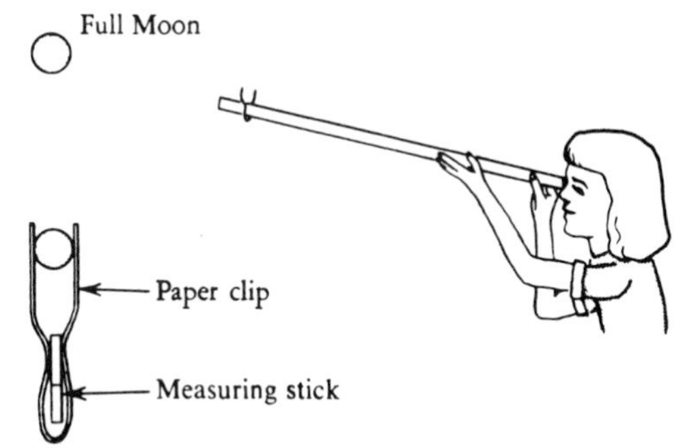

FIGURE 9.7 The apparent change in the Moon's size when it is rising or setting is an optical illusion.

LEARNING ACTIVITY 9.12

We See Only Half the Moon's Surface

To demonstrate this to students, make an *X* with chalk on a large ball that represents the Moon. Let one child represent the Earth and sit in the center of the classroom. Have a second child hold the ball and walk counterclockwise around the first child in a wide circle, always keeping the *X* facing the first child's head. It should be apparent to the students that the Moon rotates just once as it makes one revolution around the Earth. Therefore the Moon shows only one side to the Earth at all times.

III. Phases of the Moon

A. The Moon does not give off its own light but reflects the light of the Sun, just as the planets do.

  1. Because the Moon is so close to the Earth, to us on Earth it is the second brightest object in the sky.

B. As the Moon travels in its orbit around the Earth, we see different amounts of the Moon's lighted surface, as shown in Figure 9.8.

  1. These changes in the amount of lighted surface that we see are called the phases of the Moon (see Figure 9.8).
  2. During the calendar lunar month, when the Moon makes one complete revolution around the Earth in 29.5 days, the Moon passes through each of its phases, going from completely dark to completely bright and then back to completely dark again.
  3. When the Moon is between the Earth and the Sun, the dark side of the Moon is turned toward the Earth and we cannot see the Moon. This phase is called the **new Moon.**
  4. Sometimes the new Moon can be seen only faintly, because it is lighted by sunlight reflected from the Earth onto the Moon (earthshine).
  5. One or two days later, as the Moon continues to revolve from west to east around the Earth, a little of its lighted side can be seen from Earth. The part that can be seen is shaped like a thin crescent. The rest of the dark part can be seen faintly because of earthshine.
  6. About 1 week after the new Moon, half of the lighted side of the Moon is visible from Earth. This phase is called the **first quarter,** or **half Moon.**
  7. The first quarter rises at noon and sets at midnight.
  8. A few days later almost all of the Moon's lighted side is visible from Earth, a phase called the **gibbous Moon.**
  9. About 2 weeks after the new Moon, all of the lighted side is visible; this phase is called the **full Moon.**
  10. During full Moon, the Earth is between the Moon and the Sun.
  11. At full Moon, the Moon has made half of one complete revolution around the Earth.
  12. The full Moon appears to rise at sunset and set at sunrise.

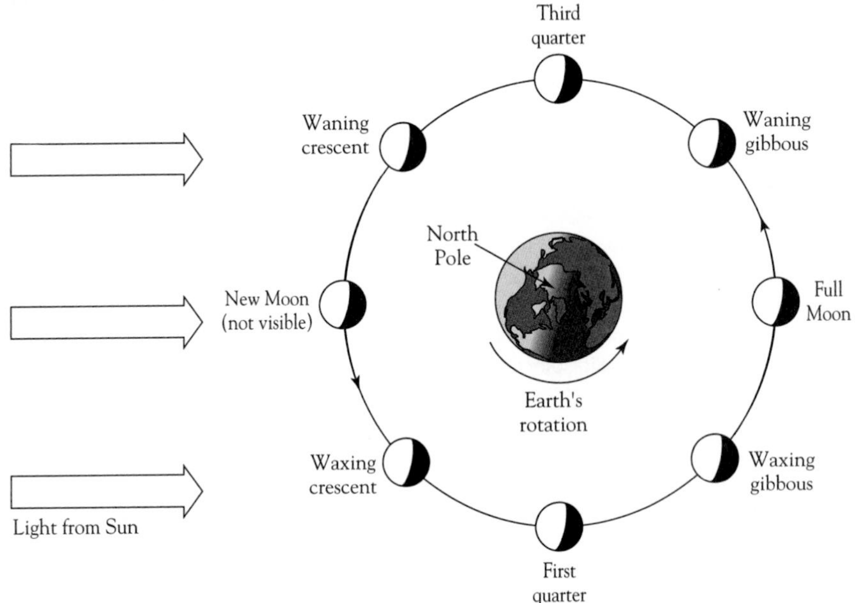

FIGURE 9.8 Phases of the Moon as seen from the Earth.

NASA Headquarters

Full moon as seen from Apollo 11 in 1969.

13. When it goes from new Moon to full Moon and the amount of lighted surface we see grows larger, we say the Moon is **waxing.**
14. When the Moon goes from full Moon to new Moon and the amount of lighted surface we see grows smaller, we say the Moon is **waning.**
15. One or two days after the full Moon, the amount of the lighted side that is visible from Earth grows smaller, or wanes, and we see a gibbous Moon again.
16. About one week after the full Moon, only half of the Moon's lighted side is visible from Earth. This phase is called the **last quarter,** or **half Moon.**
17. The last quarter rises at midnight and sets at noon.
18. After the last quarter, the Moon wanes even more until it is again crescent shaped.
19. About one week after the last quarter, the Moon has completed one revolution around the Earth and is back in its original position as a new Moon. The phases then start again, with the Moon waxing until it becomes a full Moon and then waning until it is a new Moon again.

C. The side of the Moon that faces the Sun is brightly lighted, but the side that is turned away from the Sun is in darkness.
   1. Because the Sun's light is very bright and because the Earth's atmosphere scatters the sunlight in all directions, the lighted side of the Moon is difficult to see in the daytime unless it is in a phase that is farthest from the Sun.
   2. A waxing Moon close to or past the first quarter phase may be seen in the late afternoon before the Sun has set.
   3. A waning Moon is visible in the early morning (after sunrise) until sometime past the last quarter, when it again moves closer to the Sun.

IV. The Moon Causes the Earth's Oceans to Rise and Fall

A. Tides are the rise and fall of the oceans on Earth, caused mainly by the Moon's gravitational pull on Earth.
   1. The Earth has a gravitational pull on the Moon, and at the same time the Moon has a pull of gravity on the Earth.
   2. Because the Earth is more massive than the Moon, its pull of gravity on the Moon is greater than the Moon's pull of gravity on the Earth.
   3. The Earth's stronger pull of gravity helps keep the Moon revolving around the Earth instead of going out into space away from Earth.
   4. The Moon's weaker pull of gravity affects the Earth by causing tides.

B. The Moon's pull of gravity on the side of the Earth facing the Moon makes the easily movable waters of the Earth on that side bulge out toward the Moon, and thus tides are formed. This watery bulge is called a **high tide** or **flood tide.** Because this tide is on the side of the Earth facing the Moon, it is also called a **direct tide.**

C. At the same time, another high tide is formed on the opposite side of the Earth by the pull of the Moon's gravity on the Earth itself.

D. The water that is drawn in to make bulges at these two points on Earth comes from the remaining water at the opposite two points on Earth. The water at the opposite two points now flattens out and forms lower levels, called **low tides.**

E. Because the Earth rotates on its axis once every 24 hours, it has two high tides and two low tides every 24 hours at different points on the Earth.
   1. The tide rises for about 6 hours; then it falls or ebbs for about 6 hours.
   2. Because the Moon rises about 50 minutes later each day, high tide and low tide also are approximately 50 minutes later each day, but with considerable variation.
   3. Knowing the timing of high and low tides is very important to people who work on or near the water. For example, in some channels, ships arrive and leave only at high tide when these channels are at their deepest and ships can come and go safely. Ship captains prefer to leave port when the tide is going out so that the ship does not have to fight an incoming tide. At low tide, people dig for clams.

F. The Moon's pull of gravity on the Earth becomes greater at its perigee, about 48,000 kilometers (30,000 mi) closer to the Earth than at apogee, so the tides then are higher and lower than usual.

G. The Sun's pull of gravity also affects tides on Earth. However, because the Sun is so much farther away from the Earth than is the Moon, tides caused by the Sun are less than half as strong as those caused by the Moon.

H. When the Sun is in line with the Moon, very high and very low tides are formed. These tides occur because the Sun and Moon combine their pull of gravity on the Earth. The Sun and Moon are in line with each other twice a month, at new Moon and at full Moon. These very high tides and very low tides are called **spring tides**, from the German word *springen*, meaning "to jump."

I. When the Sun and Moon are at right angles to each other, tides that are not as high or as low as usual are formed, because the Sun's pull of gravity and the Moon's pull of gravity are now working against each other. The Sun and Moon are at right angles to each other twice a month, at first quarter and at last quarter. These smaller high and low tides are called **neap tides**.

J. The rise in tides differs at different parts of the Earth, depending on the nature of the shoreline and the ocean floor at each location. For example, on the open sea the rise in tides is only about 1 meter (3 ft). At Cape Cod Bay (in Massachusetts) the rise in tides may be 3 meters (10 ft) at times. The narrow Bay of Fundy (in New Brunswick, Nova Scotia) can have tides that rise more than 15 meters (50 ft).

V. Eclipses

A. As the Sun shines on the Earth and the Moon, both throw a long shadow into space. Earth's shadow is about 1.4 million kilometers (866,000 mi) long. The Moon's shadow is about 384,000 kilometers (240,000 mi) long.

B. We experience night on Earth because we are carried by the Earth's rotation into the Earth's own shadow.

C. At certain times, the Moon passes between the Earth and the Sun in such a way that people on Earth cannot see the Sun. This phenomenon is called an **eclipse** of the Sun, or a **solar eclipse.** A solar eclipse happens only when there is a new Moon and the Moon is between the Earth and the Sun, blocking the Sun's light to Earth (see Figure 9.9).

1. In a solar eclipse, the Moon's shadow falls on the Earth.
2. The Moon's shadow on the Earth has two parts—a cone-shaped inner part called the **umbra**, which is completely dark, and a broader outer part, called the **penumbra**, where the light is only partially blocked.
3. The tip of the umbra covers only a small part of the Earth's surface, so only this small part is in complete shadow.
4. People within the umbra see the Sun become completely covered and blotted from view.
5. When the Sun's light is completely cut off, we say that a **total eclipse** of the Sun is taking place.
6. At any given spot on Earth a total eclipse lasts only about 8 minutes.
7. During a total eclipse, the Sun's corona can be seen without the use of special instruments, although one still needs to protect the eyes from damage. Even during a total solar eclipse, people should not look directly at the Sun.
8. The penumbra covers a larger part of the Earth's surface.
9. People within the penumbra see only part of the Sun as covered and blotted from view.
10. When the Sun's light is only partially blocked from view, we say a **partial eclipse** of the Sun is taking place.
11. Sometimes, especially if the Moon is near apogee and in position to produce a solar eclipse, the Moon's umbra may be too short to reach the Earth's surface.
12. When this phenomenon occurs, the Sun is still eclipsed but not completely; it shows a thin ring of light around the edges. This kind of eclipse is called an **annular** or **ring eclipse.**
13. Total eclipses of the Sun do not happen often. For a total eclipse of the Sun, the Moon must be in an exact line between the Sun and the Earth when the Moon reaches the new Moon phase.
14. This position is not reached often, because the Moon's orbit is tilted a little. Consequently, the Moon usually passes between the Earth and the Sun either too high or too low for its shadow to fall on the Earth. Therefore, we don't have an eclipse each month.

D. Sometimes the Earth passes between the Sun and the Moon so that the Earth blocks the sunlight that the Moon reflects, and the Moon cannot be seen. This phenomenon is called an eclipse of the Moon, or a **lunar eclipse**.

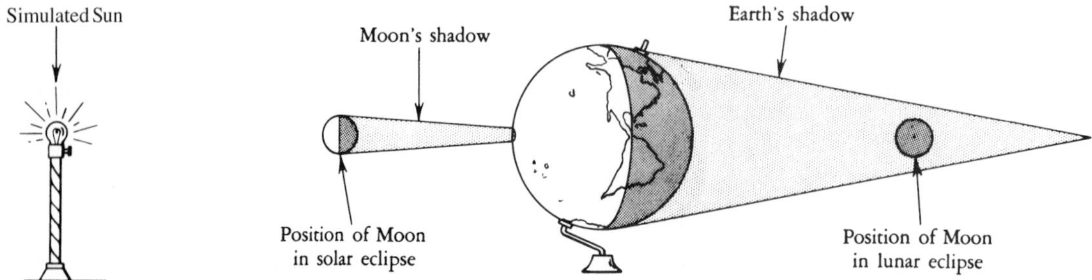

FIGURE 9.9 Solar and lunar eclipses.

1. An eclipse of the Moon occurs only when there is a full Moon, and the Earth is between the Moon and the Sun.
2. In a lunar eclipse, the Earth's shadow falls on the Moon.
3. The Moon frequently passes through the Earth's rather large penumbra, so a partial lunar eclipse happens rather often.
4. However, because the Moon's orbit is tilted, the Moon does not pass through the Earth's umbra very often and a total lunar eclipse is rare.
5. Again, because the Moon's orbit is tilted a little, the Earth's shadow does not always fall on the Moon; therefore, we do not have an eclipse every month.

 Beyond the Solar System

I. **How the Universe Is Studied**

A. The oldest instruments used in studying the universe were the **optical telescopes.**

1. An optical telescope is one designed to collect wavelengths that are visible to the human eye.
2. There are two categories of optical telescopes—the **refracting** and the **reflecting telescopes.** Refracting telescopes use a lens to focus the incoming light; reflecting telescopes use a curved mirror to gather and concentrate the incoming beam of light.
3. Both types have been around since the days of Galileo in the early 1600s.

B. Today, astronomers use not only sophisticated modern optical telescopes but also larger and more powerful telescopes designed to capture and analyze radiation in invisible regions of the electromagnetic spectrum (see Chapter 20).

1. Sophisticated electronic telescopes on spacecraft, such as the Space Radar Laboratory that flew on the space shuttle *Endeavor;* the radar system on board the *Magellan* spacecraft that mapped Venus; and satellites, such as NASA's Extreme Ultraviolet Explorer (EUVE) satellite and the satellite COBE (Cosmic Background Explorer), are providing ever more data about our Earth, Solar System, Galaxy, and universe. For example, in 1995 the **ultraviolet telescopes** aboard the spaceship *Endeavor* filmed what is thought to have been the collision of two galaxies that are approximately 90 million light years away from Earth. These two colliding galaxies involve as many as 20 billion stars, and their diameter is approximately 100,000 light years.
2. Astonomers believe that galaxy collisions today are less common than they were billions of years ago.
3. A collision of galaxies is an event that occurs over millions of years.
4. It is taking many years for scientists to scan and analyze all the pictures taken of the collision recorded in 1995.

C. The **radio telescope** is able to study distant objects by detecting the radio waves given off by these objects.

1. A large radio telescope built by the U.S. Navy in Sugar Grove, West Virginia, is about 185 meters (600 ft) across.
2. The Very Large Array (VLA) radio telescope network in New Mexico is equal to a single radio telescope about 30 kilometers (19 mi) in diameter.
3. At the top of Mauna Kea, on the Big Island of Hawaii, scientists and technicians assembled one end of one of the largest radio telescopes in the world. Called the Very Long Baseline Array (VLBA), it is more than 8,000 kilometers (5,000 mi) wide. Like an ant's eye, the VLBA is not just one viewer, but many. It consists of a string of 10 largeantennas that extend from Hawaii to the Virgin Islands and across the mainland in Washington, California, Arizona, New Mexico, Iowa, Texas, and New Hampshire.

LEARNING ACTIVITY 9.13

How Many Is a Billion? A Trillion?

Have the entire class count to 100 and see how long it takes to do so at the rate of one number per second. Multiply that by 10 to extrapolate the time it would take to count to 1,000 (probably about 16 minutes). If you wanted to count to 1 million (1,000,000), you would need more than 2 weeks of counting at the rate of one number per second, 16 hours per day (allowing 8 hours per day for sleep). To count to 1 billion (1,000,000,000) at the same rate of one number per second and 16 hours per day would take nearly 50 years. Counting to 1 trillion (1,000,000,000,000) would take more than 31,000 years even if you did not stop to sleep. Or consider that a stack of 1 trillion one-dollar bills would reach a height of 69,000 miles.

4. The VLBA system might be able to view details of an area 1,000 times greater than any previous optical telescope, and certain chemical compounds might become visible that have never before been seen with other telescopes.
5. Ultimately, the VLBA may be linked up with a European system. The linking of multiple, distant telescopes is called Very Long Baseline Interferometry (VLBI).

D. **Infrared telescopes** can penetrate dusty regions of interstellar space.

E. **High-energy telescopes** study the universe as it presents itself in X-rays and gamma rays.

II. How Distances in the Universe Are Measured

A. Until recently, scientists measured the vast distances in the universe by using a unit of measurement called the **light year.** Today they speak of the **parsec.**

1. Light travels through space at a speed of about 300,000 kilometers (186,000 mi) a second.
2. A **light year** is the distance that light travels at that speed in 1 year. It equals about 9,500 billion kilometers (6,000 billion mi). The distance light travels in 1 year is found by multiplying 300,000 kilometers by 60 seconds, then by 60 minutes, then by 24 hours, and then by 365.25 days.
3. By multiplying this answer by 3.26, the distance traveled in a parsec is obtained. A parsec is about 3.26 light years, or 31,000 trillion kilometers (19,000 billion mi).
4. A **megaparsec** is the distance light travels in 3.26 million years.

III. The Stars

A. Stars are suns in space; they produce their own light.

B. There are countless stars in the sky; about 3,000 are visible with the naked eye.

1. Proxima Centauri, the star nearest the Earth (excluding the Sun), is more than 4 light years (42 trillion kilometers or 26 trillion miles) away.

C. The stars in our galaxy, which are the only stars that can be seen with the naked eye, and most of those that can be seen with an ordinary telescope appear to be in fixed positions because, although they are moving, they do not have significant motion relative to our Sun.

D. Stars vary in size. Small stars, like our Sun, are called **dwarfs.** Large stars, such as Aldebaran and Pegasi, are called **giants.** Tremendously large stars, like Antares and Betelgeuse, are called **supergiants.**

E. Stars vary in color according to their age and temperature.

1. As stars grow older, their surfaces become cooler and they change color.
2. The youngest stars are blue-white to white, and their surface temperatures range from about 7,500°C to 30,000°C (13,500°F to 54,000°F).
3. Yellow star surfaces are about 6,000°C (10,800°F). Our Sun is a yellow star.
4. Orange star surfaces are about 4,000°C (7,200°F).
5. Red stars are the oldest stars, having surface temperatures of about 3,000°C (5,400°F).

F. Star brightness (**luminosity**) as observed from Earth depends on the star's temperature, size, and distance from Earth.

1. Astronomers call the apparent brightness of a star, as seen from Earth, its **magnitude.** The brighter the star, the lower its magnitude number.
2. First-magnitude stars are the brightest. A first-magnitude star is 2½ times brighter than a second-magnitude star; a second-magnitude star is 2½ times brighter than a third-magnitude star, and so on. The faintest stars the eye can see are sixth-magnitude stars. Stars of the twenty-third magnitude have been discovered with telescopes.

G. Double stars, also called binary stars, are two stars that are held closely together by their pull of gravity on each other.

1. The largest known binary star is Plaskett's star, comprised of two supergiants, each with a mass of 40 to 50 times our own sun.

H. **Variable stars** flare up and become brighter, then grow dimmer again.

1. For some stars, this happens because the star has exploded.
2. For others, this change in brightness occurs when they grow larger and shrink at intervals.
3. Astronomers can accurately measure distances to galaxies by monitoring a type of star referred to as a **Cepheid variable.** Cepheid variable stars are about 10,000 times brighter than our Sun.
   a. A Cepheid variable star changes in brightness in a periodic and distinctive way.
   b. During the first part of its cycle, the Cepheid's luminosity increases rapidly, whereas during the rest of the cycle, its luminosity decreases slowly.
   c. The distance to a Cepheid can be calculated from its period (the length of its cycle) and its average brightness. In 1908, Henrietta Leavitt discovered that the longer the period, the brighter the Cepheid, because the brightness of a Cepheid is proportional to its surface area.
   d. In the 1920s, using measurements taken by observing Cepheids, Edwin Hubble

established that other galaxies exist beyond the Milky Way Galaxy.

e. To observe and to calculate distances in the galaxy, astronomers use two devices together—light-measuring devices coupled to large reflecting telescopes such as those at Mauna Kea in Hawaii, Las Campanas in Chile, and Mount Palomar in California.

I. A **nova**, or new star, is a dim star that suddenly becomes thousands of times more brilliant than it had been previously.
   1. A nova is not really a new star; it only seems to be new because it has suddenly become so conspicuously bright.
   2. One type of nova is believed to occur in double star (binary) systems in which one of the stars is a very dense white dwarf. A white dwarf packs a mass roughly equal to the Sun's within a volume equal to the Earth's and therefore produces tremendous gravitational forces at its surface, typically 100,000 times the force of gravity on Earth.
   3. Because of its powerful gravity, the white dwarf draws matter from its companion star to itself, which triggers the resumption of thermonuclear fusion reactions on the white dwarf.
   4. Occasionally, an unusually bright nova, called a **supernova**, appears. This is a catastrophic explosion that marks the death of an extremely massive star (much larger than our Sun).
   5. Because supernovas release tremendous amounts of radiation, astronomers are hoping to be able to observe supernovas as far away as 5 billion light years.

J. **Star clusters** are groups of stars held together by their gravitational pull on one another.
   1. Some star clusters are made up of a few stars that are moving in parallel paths. Other star clusters are loose collections of stars called **open clusters.**
   2. **Globular clusters** are shaped like a ball or globe and may contain as many as 100,000 stars.
   3. Clusters that are so large and thick with stars that they look like shining clouds are called star **clouds.**

K. **Pulsars** are believed to be the dense remnants of collapsed stars, sometimes called **neutron stars.**
   1. Pulsars have very strong magnetic fields.
   2. A pulsar spins on its axis very rapidly, up to 1,000 revolutions per second.
   3. Because of a pulsar's rapid spin, the wave energy it emits is received on Earth as a pulsating beacon of energy.

L. **Black holes**, first discovered in 1972, are also believed to be the remnants of stars that have collapsed to a very dense state, with a resultant very strong gravitational field.
   1. The gravitational force of a black hole is so strong that until recently it was thought that no object or form of energy radiation could escape it.

M. Every fundamental particle of matter has a mirrored opposite partner, called **antimatter.**
   1. The antimatter partner of the negatively charged electron is the positively charged **positron.** In 1932, Carl Anderson discovered the positron in a device that captured cosmic rays from space.
   2. Today, scientists create antimatter in atomic accelerators.
   3. When an electron meets up with a positron, the two particles are annihilated instantly in an emission of pure gamma ray energy, with the energy of 511,000 electron volts, or 250,000 times the energy of visible light.

N. **Quasars** are very distant objects that emit immense amounts of light.
   1. Quasars are from 10 to 1,000 times more luminous than our entire galaxy.
   2. It is thought that a quasar represents the vast energy that is given off as matter spirals violently into a massive black hole.
   3. The objects providing fuel for the quasars appear to be giant galaxies.
   4. One of the many mysteries of quasars is the blobs bursting out of them, seemingly going faster than the speed of light, which is faster than is supposed to be possible.

IV. Constellations

A. Long ago astronomers divided the stars into groups, called **constellations**, which made it easier to describe the location of a given heavenly body. These constellations were named after Roman gods and legendary heroes and heroines, mythological animals, and objects. (Today the International Astronomical Union controls celestial naming.)

B. The movement of the Earth as it turns on its axis makes the constellations seem to move through the sky as if they were on a transparent globe surrounding the Earth.
   1. If the Earth's axis were extended into space, it would also become the axis for this imaginary globe.
   2. In the Earth's northern hemisphere, all the constellations seem to move around a point, called the **celestial north pole**, that is directly above the Earth's north pole.
   3. In the southern hemisphere, all the constellations seem to move around a point called the **celestial south pole**, which is directly above the Earth's south pole.

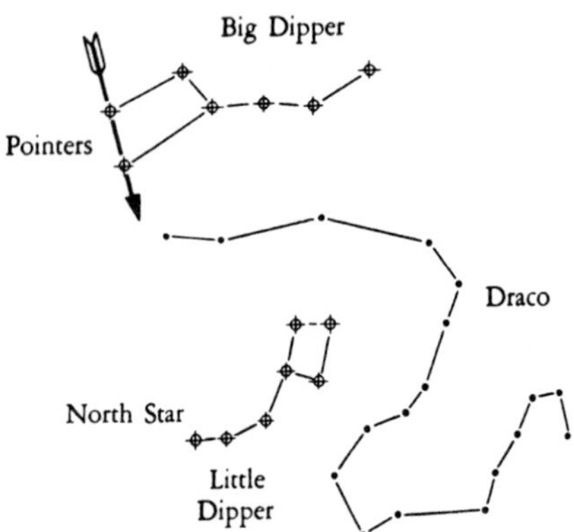

FIGURE 9.10 Finding the North Star.

4. A star located directly on the celestial north or south pole would not seem to move, so it would serve as an excellent signpost for navigation.
5. The **North Star**, called **Polaris**, is so close to the celestial north pole that it does not seem to move at all; therefore, Polaris has historically been used as a signpost for navigators. Polaris is the end star in the handle of the constellation known as the **Little Dipper** (see Figure 9.10). Constellations in the northern hemisphere appear to revolve around Polaris.

C. Because the Earth is in different positions as it revolves around the Sun, different constellations are seen at different times of the year and in varying positions. Moreover, persons living in the northern hemisphere see constellations that are different from those seen by persons living in the southern hemisphere.

D. The Sun's path among the constellations during one Earth-year is called the **ecliptic.** A strip of sky slightly above and below the Sun's path, or ecliptic, is called the **zodiac.** Special names, known as the signs of the zodiac, one for each month of the year, were given to 12 star formations in the zodiac.

V. Galaxies

A. A galaxy is a large collection of stars, dust, neutron stars, black holes, and gas, held together in a group by the pull of its own gravity.
1. There are literally millions of galaxies beyond our own.
2. Our Sun and the Solar System are part of one galaxy called the **Milky Way Galaxy**, or just *the Galaxy.*
3. There are at least 100 billion stars in the Galaxy, and their light gives the appearance of a milky band in the sky. Part of the Milky Way Galaxy can be seen any clear night as a broad band of light stretching across the sky.

B. With its billions of stars, the Galaxy forms a spiral shape that is somewhat like a flattened wheel.
1. The distance across the wheel is about 100,000 light years.
2. Three spiral arms curve out from the center of the Galaxy.
3. The entire Galaxy is rotating around its center at a tremendous speed. The Galaxy rotates once around its center in about 250 million years. All stars in the Galaxy revolve in the same direction but at different speeds.
4. One or more black holes are at or near the center of the Galaxy.
5. Recently, scientists discovered that a huge cloud of antimatter jets up (apparently) from somewhere near the center of the Milky Way Galaxy, reaching some 20,000 trillion miles high. The source and cause of the cloud is not yet known.
6. The Sun and our solar system are about 26,000 light years from the center of the Milky Way Galaxy, about halfway between the center of the Galaxy and its outer edge. The Sun and the solar system are moving at a speed of about 225 kilometers (140 mi) a second (504,000 mph) in a circular orbit around the center of the Galaxy.
7. The stars at the outer edge of the Galaxy are moving about four times as fast as our solar system.

C. A **nebula** is a great cloud of dust in a galaxy. In each galaxy, there are many nebulae.
1. Nebulae do not give off any, light of their own.
2. Some nebulae are easily seen because they reflect the light from nearby stars. Others are dark either because they cut off the light from stars behind them or because there are no stars nearby to light them.

D. Beyond the Milky Way Galaxy are more than a billion galaxies, all rotating at tremendous speeds.

E. Galaxies are usually found in three shapes: irregular, spiral, and elliptical.
1. **Irregular galaxies** have many blue-white stars in them and are probably young galaxies. Only about 10% of known galaxies are classed as irregular in shape.
2. **Spiral galaxies** have a number of spiral arms extending from their centers. In spiral galaxies, there are blue-white giant stars in the arms and red stars toward the center. Many astronomers believe that a spiral galaxy later becomes an irregular one. As the galaxy rotates, spiral arms form and direct the younger blue-white stars toward the center. Approximately 30% of known galaxies are of the spiral shape, including the Milky Way.

LEARNING ACTIVITY 9.14

The Expanding Universe and Hubble's Law

Before class: Take an ordinary balloon and blow enough air into it to begin its expansion (see Figure 9.11). Now tape several different-sized coins onto the balloon. The coins represent galaxies, and the two-dimensional surface of the balloon represents the "fabric" of our three-dimensional universe.

Demonstration: Ask the children to imagine themselves as a resident of one of the "galaxies" and to note their position relative to neighboring galaxies. Now start inflating the balloon more. Notice that as the balloon inflates (that is, as the universe expands), the other galaxies recede from you; more distant galaxies recede more rapidly. Note that the coins themselves do not expand along with the balloon, just as people, planets, stars, or galaxies—all of which are held together by their own internal forces—do not expand along with the universe.

As the coins recede, the distance between any two of them increases, and the rate of increase of this distance is proportional to the distance between them. Thus, the balloon expands according to Hubble's Law.

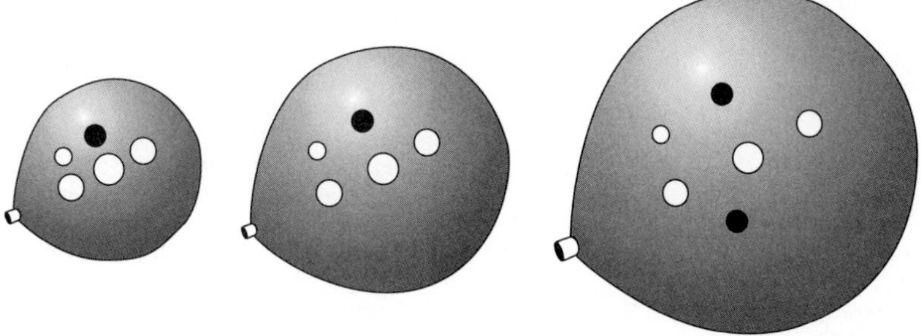

FIGURE 9.11 Coins taped to a balloon show a change in their relationship to one another as the balloon inflates; that is, the space between the coins steadily increases while the coins themselves remain the same size. *Source:* Demonstration and figure adapted from Eric Chaisson and Steve McMillan, *Astronomy Today,* 3d ed. (Upper Saddle River, NJ: Prentice Hall, 1999), 608–610. By permission of Pearson Education, Inc.

3. **Elliptical galaxies** are shaped like an oval or ellipse and are usually smaller than spiral galaxies, although the very largest known galaxies are also elliptical. Most of the stars of elliptical galaxies are older yellow and red stars. Many astronomers believe that an elliptical galaxy forms from a spiral one, when all the stars in the spiral arms have gathered into the main body of the galaxy. Sixty percent of all known galaxies are elliptical.

F. Galaxies are often grouped in **galactic clusters.**
   1. Some clusters contain thousands of galaxies.
   2. Our own, called the **Local Group,** contains at least 27 galaxies in addition to the Milky Way.
   3. Galactic clusters often reside in huge swarms called **superclusters.**

VI. The Expanding Universe and Hubble's Law

A. The universe seems to be a tremendous expanse of space that is at least 10 billion light years across. Scattered over this expanse of space are more than 1 billion galaxies.
   1. Most galaxies are separated from their neighbors by millions of light years of space.
   2. Evidence indicates that galaxies are moving away from one another at increasingly greater speed and will continue doing so indefinitely.
   3. It is believed that the galaxies are moving away from one another as a result of the Big Bang.
   4. Edwin Hubble, in 1929, made one of the most important discoveries of astronomy when he observed that galaxies are receding from us at a speed that is proportional to their distance. This is known as **Hubble's law.** The analogy frequently used is that of raisins in a loaf of raisin bread (the universe) that move apart as the bread expands during baking in an oven; the galaxies (raisins) are just along for the ride. The Hubble Space Telescope is named in honor of Hubble and his work.
   5. Some galaxies are moving through space at a speed of more than 48,000 kilometers (30,000 mi) a second.
   6. This high speed means that the space between galaxies is steadily increasing, while the galaxies themselves remain the same size.

- April 12, 1961: First person in Earth's orbit, Soviet cosmonaut Y. Gagarin in the Soviet Union's *Vostok 1* mission.
- May 5, 1961: First U.S. astronaut into space in a suborbital flight, A. Shepard, Jr., in *Mercury 3* mission.
- February 20, 1962: First U.S. astronaut in Earth's orbit, J. Glenn, Jr., in *Mercury 6* mission.
- June 16, 1963: First woman in space, cosmonaut V. Tereshkova, in the *Vostok 6* mission.
- March 18, 1965: First U.S. two-person space flight, V. Grissom and J. Young, in the *Gemini 3* mission.
- June 3, 1965: First U.S. spacewalk, E. White II, in *Gemini 4* mission with astronaut J. McDivitt.
- January 27, 1967: After astronauts V. Grissom, E. White, and R. Chaffee died in a launch-pad fire during a countdown dress rehearsal, the aborted mission of the *Apollo 204* spacecraft was later renamed *Apollo 1.*
- July 5, 1967: Unmanned *Apollo 2* mission.
- August 26, 1967: Unmanned *Apollo 3 Saturn 1-B* booster mission.
- November 9, 1967: First launch of 363-foot *Saturn V* launch vehicle, the unmanned *Apollo 4* mission.
- January 22, 1968: *Apollo 5,* the first Earth-orbit flight test of an unmanned lunar module.
- April 4, 1968: *Apollo 6,* an unmanned mission; engines of *Saturn V* either failed to ignite or shut down too early.
- October 11–21, 1968: *Apollo 7.* W. Schirra, D. Eisele, and W. Cunningham on board for the first test in orbit of a command module.
- December 21–27, 1968: *Apollo 8,* first manned flight to orbit the Moon. U.S. astronauts W. Anders, F. Borman, and J. Lovell, Jr., completed 10 lunar orbits.
- March 3–13, 1969: *Apollo 9.* Astronauts J. McDivitt, D. Scott, and R. Schweickart conduct first combined Earth-orbit test of the command and lunar modules.
- May 18–26, 1969: *Apollo 10.* Astronauts T. Stafford, J. Young, and G. Cernan are first to test both the command and lunar modules in orbit around the Moon.
- July 16–24, 1969: *Apollo 11,* first manned landing on the Moon. On July 20, U.S. astronauts N. Armstrong and E. Aldrin, Jr., land the lunar module *Eagle* on the Moon's surface and collect 48 pounds of lunar rock and soil samples while M. Collins orbits in the command module *Columbia.*
- November 14–24, 1969: *Apollo 12,* a second lunar landing. Astronauts C. Conrad, Jr., and A. Bean collect rocks while R. Gordon, Jr., orbits in the command module *Yankee Clipper.*
- April 11–17, 1970: *Apollo 13.* Plans for a third lunar landing are aborted when a cryogenic tank explodes. Astronauts J. Lovell, J. Swigert, and F. Haise are forced to use the lunar module *Aquarius* as a lifeboat.
- January 31–February 9, 1971: *Apollo 14.* A lunar landing in which A. Shephard and E. Mitchell touch down while S. Roosa orbits in the command module.
- June 7, 1971: First manned orbiting space station, cosmonauts G. Dobrovolsky, V. Patsayev, and V. Volkov.
- July 26–August 7, 1971: *Apollo 15.* Astronauts D. Scott and J. Irwin log 17.5 miles on the Moon's surface in the Lunar Rover on July 30 and collect approximately 170 pounds of lunar materials, while A. Worden orbits in the command module.
- April 16–27, 1972: Astronauts J. Young and C. Duke drive the Lunar Rover and collect 200 pounds of lunar samples, while K. Mattingly pilots the command module in orbit for this *Apollo 16* mission.
- December 7–19, 1972: *Apollo 17* mission. Astronaut G. Cernan returns to the Moon with scientist-astronaut H. Schmitt, collecting 250 pounds of lunar materials, then rejoins command module pilot R. Evans after leaving behind a plaque on the Moon that reads, "Here man completed his first explorations of the Moon."
- May 25, 1973: First manned U.S. space station, astronauts C. Conrad, Jr., J. Kerwin, and P. Weitz.
- July 15, 1975: First international space mission (*Apollo-Soyuz* Test Project), V. Brand, D. Slayton, and T. Stafford of the United States and A. Leonov and V. Kubasov of the Soviet Union.
- April 12, 1981: First space shuttle flight, U.S. astronauts J. Young and R. Crippen.
- June 18, 1983: First U.S. woman in space, astronaut S. Ride.
- August 30, 1983: First African American astronaut in space, G. Bluford, Jr.
- January 28, 1986: First loss of a U.S. spacecraft while in flight. The *Challenger* explodes 73 seconds after lift-off, killing all persons aboard—G. Jarvis, C. McAuliffe, R. McNair, E. Onizuka, J. Resnick, F. Scobee, and M. Smith.
- February 1986: Launch of Russian *Mir,* the first inhabited orbiting space station.
- December 21, 1988: Longest time spent in space, 366 days in a space station, cosmonauts M. Manarov and V. Titov.
- April 25, 1990: Crew of space shuttle *Discovery* places Hubble Space Telescope in Earth orbit.
- December 1993: Mission to repair the Hubble Space Telescope, astronauts R. Covey, K. Bowersox, K. Thornton, C. Nicollier, F. Musgrave, J. Hoffman, and T. Akers.
- February 1994: First Russian cosmonaut, S. Krikalev, flew on a U.S. space shuttle mission. Beginning of a newly inaugurated cooperation in space between Russia and the United States.
- February 1995: E. Collins becomes first woman to pilot a space shuttle; first flyby of the Russian *Mir* space station.
- March 14, 1995: N. Thagard becomes the first U.S. astronaut shot into space by the Russians, orbiting the Earth with two cosmonauts and then docking with the Russian space station *Mir,* then returning to Earth on the U.S. space shuttle *Atlantis.*
- March 1995–May 1998: NASA and Russian scientists conduct science experiments in space to include studies about human, animal, and plant functioning; the origin of the Solar System; building better technology in space; and how to build future space stations.
- October 1998: Senator J. Glenn, Jr., the first U.S. astronaut in orbit, in 1962, returns as an astronaut for a 10-day multipurpose mission.
- November 1998–2003: Construction of an orbiting international space station.

FIGURE 9.12 Chronological history of selected space exploration programs.

 Space Exploration Programs

I. **History of the U.S. and Russian Space Exploration Programs**

A. For a summary chronology of space exploration programs, from the first person to orbit the Earth in 1961 through 2003, see Figure 9.12. More detailed information can be obtained on NASA's Website given at end of this chapter.

II. NASA's Programs

A. The National Aeronautics and Space Administration (NASA) describes its spacecraft by groups or series, depending on their design and what they are supposed to do or find out.

1. **Scientific satellites** such as *Explorer, Vanguard, Discoverer, Landsat, Lageos,* Orbiting Astronomical Observatory, Orbiting Solar Observatory, and Orbiting Geophysical Observatory, all built and launched by the United States, carry instruments that supply information about radiation, Earth's magnetic field, Earth's shape, temperatures in space, micrometeoroids, and other conditions in the upper parts of the atmosphere and in outer space.
2. There are also joint projects between the United States and other countries.
3. **Weather satellites** such as the Tiros and the Nimbus series make weather observations, help scientists forecast the weather more accurately, and contribute to a better understanding of what causes weather.
4. **Communications satellites** such as *Echo, Telstar, Relay, Syncom, Intelsat, Oscar,* and *ATS-6* are used to send and reflect radio and television signals, telephotos, and telephone calls to all parts of the world.
5. **Navigation satellites** such as the Transit series help to guide aircraft and ships by transmitting special radio signals to them.
6. **Lunar and interplanetary spacecraft** are used to explore the moon and the planets.
7. The **Pioneer series** investigates interplanetary space to learn more about solar radiation, interplanetary magnetic fields, and micrometeoroids.
8. The **Ranger series** gathers information about the Moon to help pave the way for landing on the Moon.
9. The **Surveyor series** was designed to land gently on the Moon, send television pictures back to Earth, find suitable landing sites, analyze the Moon's crust, check the Moon's surface for strength and stability, and measure the bombardment of the Moon by meteorites.
10. The **Lunar Orbiter series** is designed to photograph suitable landing sites on the Moon and to learn more about the Moon's gravitational pull.
11. The **Mariner series** is designed to fly near Venus and Mars and to send back data about these planets.
12. The **Voyager series** is designed to fly near the planets beyond Mars and to send back information about them.
13. The purpose of **Project Mercury** was to investigate human reactions and abilities during space flight and to recover both personnel and spacecraft safely.
14. The purpose of **Project Gemini** was to determine human performance and behavior during prolonged space flight, develop techniques that would enable two or more spacecraft to rendezvous and couple together while in orbit, carry out space investigations that need human presence in the spacecraft, and demonstrate both controlled re-entry into the atmosphere and controlled landing at a specific site.
15. The purpose of **Project Apollo** was to land astronauts on the Moon and then return them to Earth.
16. After several successful Apollo missions, NASA's focus was on development of the **space shuttle** and an orbiting **space station.**
17. The shuttles carry into orbit such items as government and private communications satellites, military and weather surveillance hardware, scientific research laboratories, and a huge telescope for exploring space.

III. Space Station

A. A large artificial satellite revolving around the Earth is a space station with many uses.

1. The orbit of the satellite is almost circular, and well outside the Earth's atmosphere. Be-

NASA Headquarters

Full moon as seen from Apollo 11 in 1969.

cause there is no air resistance at such a high altitude, the station can stay in orbit for many years.
2. Multinational participation in the construction of a permanently inhabited space station began in 1998 and ended in 2003.
3. Shuttle flights ferried the materials for building the station and delivered supplies needed by the crew of astronauts who worked on the station.
4. From the space station, scientists can collect a vast amount of knowledge about the Earth, its atmosphere, its weather, and its fields of gravity and magnetism.
5. The space station can be used to reflect and send back radio, radar, and television signals all over the Earth.
6. It can be used to launch rockets easily into outer space, because the rockets will not have to overcome the Earth's pull of gravity to take off.

Exploratory Activities for "The Universe"

1. STUDYING THE ELLIPTICAL SHAPE OF A PLANET'S ORBIT (GRADES 3 AND UP)[2]

Overview Science and mathematics are partners in making discoveries about the universe. Orbiting planets, moons, comets, and asteroids follow invisible noncircular paths, called ellipses. Students can construct and examine the ellipse. A good way to begin studying the ellipse is for you to diagram one at the writing board while the students follow along with smaller versions at their desks.

Materials Needed Students: one set of two pushpins, string, paper, and cardboard for each pair of students. Teacher: two small sink plungers (suction cups sometimes known as "plumber's helpers") and some string.

Activity Wet the edge of one suction cup to form a seal and then "whap" it to the middle of the writing board—hard. From the handle, hang a loop of string that is shorter than the top and bottom limits of the board. Put a piece of chalk at the end of the loop and draw a circle on the board.

Then "whap" the other suction cup to the board, about 20 to 40 centimeters to the left or right of the first plunger. Stretch the string over the other handle and ask the students to guess what the "circle" will look like this time. Make the drawing with the chalk, but hold off naming the resultant figure. Students may call it "an egg," or "a circle that got sat on" (see Figure 9.13).

Pairs of students can then make smaller ovals at their desks. See Figure 9.14. What happens to the oval if the pins are moved farther apart? closer together?

Concept Introduction—Student Activity This shape is called an ellipse. Ellipses have a unique property that students can discover with a ruler. Have them make a new ellipse on a separate sheet of paper, then measure the line that passes through both push pins (line EF in Figure 9.13). This is the major axis, the longest line that can be drawn in an ellipse. Next ask the students to draw lines from any spot on the ellipse to each of the holes left by the pushpins. When they add the lengths of these two lines together, they'll find that the sum equals the length of the major axis. Have them try it again with two lines drawn from another point on the ellipse.

This discovery leads to the definition of an ellipse: a curved figure in which the sum of two lines, drawn from a point on the curve to the two points used to draw the ellipse, is a constant number.

Concept Application Ellipses, not circles, are the curved figures most commonly seen by people every day.

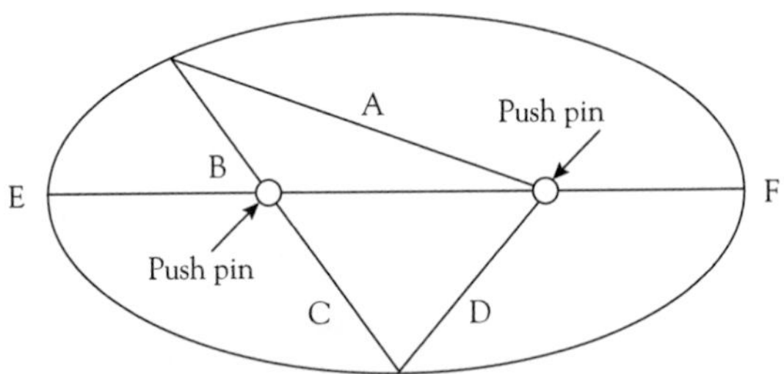

FIGURE 9.13 This diagram, which shows the A + B = C + D = EF, is a visual definition of an ellipse.

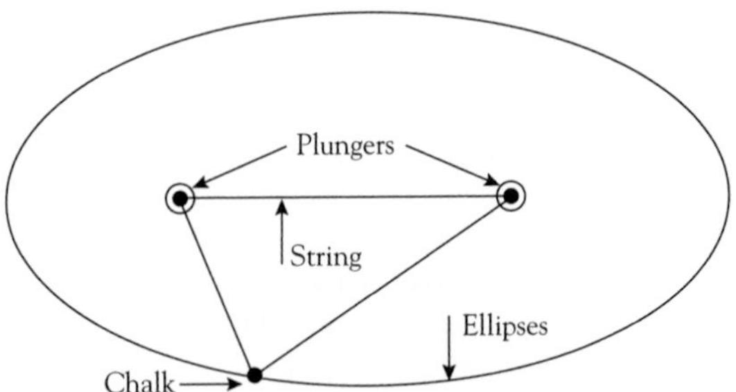

FIGURE 9.14 Two small plungers, string, chalk, and a chalkboard are all you need to draw an ellipse.

[2]From Michael B. Leyden, "Three Big Ideas Going Around and Around," *Teaching K–8*, 23(5):34–35 (February 1993). Reprinted with permission of the publisher, Early Years, Inc., Norwalk, CT. 06854.

Name ______________________________

My height ______________

	Length of shadow	*Direction the top is pointing*
Morning	______________	______________
Noon	______________	______________
Afternoon	______________	______________

My conclusions from this experiment:

My conclusions after sharing the results with others:

Questions I have as a result of this experiment and the sharing:

FIGURE 9.15 Student record sheet for the study of shadows.

Whenever a circle is viewed off-center, an ellipse is seen. Once people have been trained to look for non-circles, they see ellipses everywhere—even in cylindrical drinking glasses. Pour some water in a glass and have students tip the glass as if they were going to take a drink. The water's surface in a tipped cylindrical glass has an elliptical shape.

When the next space shuttle is launched, look in the newspaper for its orbital data. You'll find the astronaut's distance from the Earth reported as being anywhere from 356 to 563 kilometers (221 to 350 mi). The distance varies because even the shuttle's orbit is elliptical. If it were a circular orbit, the distance would be constant.

2. EXPLORING SHADOWS (ANY GRADE LEVEL)

Overview Incorporating several process skills (e.g., observing, measuring, recording, graphing) and integrating their learning of mathematics and science, the study of shadows is always of interest to students. Take students out on the school grounds to study their own shadows.

Procedure Have the students, working in pairs, stand with their backs to the Sun and observe their shadows. Have them do this three times during the day: once in the early morning, again at noon, and once again in the late afternoon.

- Young children can discover the kinds of shadows they can make with their bodies at these different times of the day; make shadows with different objects, such as umbrellas and boxes; outline shadows at different times of the day and compare their outlines; and play shadow tag.
- Older students can measure, record, and graph their own height, the lengths of their own shadows, and the direction in which their shadows are pointing (N, S, E, or W) for each of these three periods of time. Use record sheets as shown in Figure 9.15

Have students share their record sheets, first in their working pairs, then in groups of four, then as a whole class.

Students will note that the lengths of their shadows vary according to whether the Sun's light is striking their bodies at a slant or vertically. They will also note that the direction in which the top (head) of a shadow is pointing changes from morning to afternoon.

Follow-Up and Application Students can then be led into a discussion of what value this information might be.

Could their body heights be calculated according to the lengths of their shadows? Could the height of a tall object (tree or building or pole in the play yard) be determined as well? Is more heat generated from the more direct rays? Could the time of day be determined according to the lengths of their shadows? If lost in the wilderness, could a hiker determine direction and time of day by examining shadows? Would that information be of help to the hiker? Perhaps students would like to make a sundial to be used on the school grounds, or individual sundials so that each child can take one home to share with family members.

Chapter 10

The Earth

© Dorling Kindersley

The Composition of the Earth

I. How and When the Earth Was Formed

A. Evidence indicates that the Earth was formed from the same materials and in the same way as the Sun. An accumulation of materials that resulted from the Big Bang, which occurred between 10 billion and 15 billion years ago (bya) (see Chapter 9), indicates that the Earth's beginning occurred approximately 4.5 bya.

B. The Apollo's space program studies of Moon craters revealed that the craters were caused by the impact of objects that were in great abundance about 4.5 bya, after which the number of impacts quickly diminished.

1. In 1944, the Russian geophysicist Otto Schmidt postulated that planets grew in size gradually, by **accretion.**
2. According to the accretion theory, cosmic dust that resulted from the Big Bang lumped together to form fine particles called **particulates.**
3. Particulates became gravel; gravel became small balls, then big balls, then tiny planets; these became meteorites, or **planetesimals**; and, finally, what began as dust became the size of the Moon.
4. As the planetesimals became larger, their numbers became fewer and the number of collisions between planetesimals diminished.

C. Large meteorites, however, continued to slam into the new Earth, causing immense heat in the Earth's interior.

1. This heat caused a furnace effect deep in the Earth's interior, creating molten material called a **magma ocean.**
2. The magma ocean was active for millions of years, giving rise to volcanic eruptions.
3. Heat at the surface, caused by volcanism and lava flows from the interior of the Earth, was supplemented by a continuing bombardment of large meteorites, some of them thought to be as large as our Moon or even as large as Mars.
4. **Isotope geology**, the study of the radioisotopes found in rocks, is the primary tool that has permitted scientists to determine that the accretion of the Earth culminated in the differentiation of the Earth: the creation of the core, the source of the Earth's magnetic field, and the beginning of Earth's atmosphere.
5. Claire Patterson, in 1953, used the uranium-lead clock to establish an age of approximately 4.5 billion years for the Earth and many of the meteorites that formed it. Rock was found in Greenland that is about 3.75 billion years old, in North America that is about 4 billion years old, and in Western Australia that is about 4.2 billion years old, the oldest rock discovered yet.
6. More recently, scientists have concluded that the bombardment by meteorites continued for up to 150 million years. As the mass was heated by the radioactivity and energy released by the meteorites, dense materials such as iron and nickel sank to form the Earth's core. Lighter rocky material established the continental crust.
7. As the crust solidified, volatile gases escaped to form Earth's atmosphere.
8. Approximately 1.1 bya, the earliest supercontinent, Rodinia, formed, linking almost all of Earth's surface. Rain gradually filled the oceans.

II. Evolution of the Earth's Atmosphere and Early Life Forms

A. Evidence indicates that gases emerging from the planet's interior, similar to volcanic gases escaping today, created the Earth's terrestrial atmosphere.

1. The Earth's early atmosphere was mostly carbon dioxide, with nitrogen as the second most abundant gas.
2. The early atmosphere also contained sufficient quantities of ammonia and methane to give rise to organic matter, which in turn evolved into the earliest life forms on Earth.
3. Although records of early life would have been destroyed by early geologic activity, the earliest evidence of life on Earth consists of fossils of a cyanobacterium (also known as blue green algae), found in Australia and South Africa. These organisms lived about 3.5 bya.
4. To more fully understand the evolution of the Earth, scientists need to know more about our Sun's energy output during the Earth's early life. Evidence indicates that between 4.5 and 2.5 bya, the Sun's power output was just 75% of what it is today.
5. Although some aquatic microorganisms, such as chemosynthetic bacteria, can thrive in a carbon-dioxide-rich and oxygen-poor environment, the presence of oxygen in the atmosphere was necessary before life could begin to flourish on land.
6. Oxygen evolved when cyanobacteria in the oceans began producing it through photosynthesis. Evidence indicates that oxygen reached its present level in the Earth's atmosphere less than 2 bya.

B. The presence of atmospheric oxygen allows the formation of **ozone.**

1. Ozone forms when the Sun's ultraviolet (UV) radiation, which is deadly to life forms on land, splits oxygen molecules into the unstable atomic form O, which can combine

back into O_2 and into the very special molecule O_3, or ozone.

2. Ozone absorbs ultraviolet radiation, making it safe for life on land.

C. Although a fairly stable level of oxygen in the atmosphere was reached about 1 to 2 bya, the Earth's climate was not uniform.
   1. There were long stages of relative warmth and coolness.
   2. The composition of fossilized shells of plankton that lived near the ocean floor indicates that over the past 100 million years, bottom waters of the oceans have cooled by nearly 15°C (57°F).
   3. Sea levels dropped by hundreds of meters, and continents drifted apart.
   4. Inland seas mostly disappeared, and the climate cooled an average of 10°C to 15°C (50°F to 57°F).
   5. Approximately 20 million years ago (mya) permanent ice built up on Antarctica.
   6. Approximately 2 to 3 mya, there were significant expansions and contractions of warm and cold periods in cycles of about 40,000 years. The 40,000-year cycle or periodicity corresponds to the time it takes the Earth to complete an oscillation of the tilt of its axis of rotation.
   7. This change in the Earth's orbital geometry could alter the amount of sunlight and be responsible for starting or ending ice ages.
   8. Between 600,000 and 800,000 years ago this periodicity switched from 40,000-year to 100,000-year intervals between fluctuations.
   9. Ice sheets a mile thick at their peak 20,000 years ago, covered much of northern Europe and North America. These massive ice sheets revamped the face of the Earth, which was 5°C (41°F) cooler than it is today.

D. Scientists divide the Earth into **spheres.**
   1. The **atmosphere** is the sphere of gases that surround the Earth.
   2. The **hydrosphere** consists of the bodies of water, including not only the global ocean but the freshwater found in lakes, streams, glaciers, and underground.
   3. The **lithosphere** is the Earth's solid surface mass.
   4. The **biosphere** includes all life on Earth and consists of the parts of the lithosphere, hydrosphere, and atmosphere in which living organisms can be found.

III. Earth's Basic Structure

A. Earth's basic structure is a series of layers, starting in the center with a core, then a middle layer or mantle, and then an outer layer or crust (see Figure 10.1).
   1. The deeper we go toward the center of the Earth, the higher the temperature. In mines and oil wells, for example, the temperature rises about 1°C (2°F) for every 36 meters (120 ft) of depth.
   2. The temperature of the mantle may be as high as 1,600°C (2,880°F). The temperature of the core may be as high as 8,500°C (15,300°F).

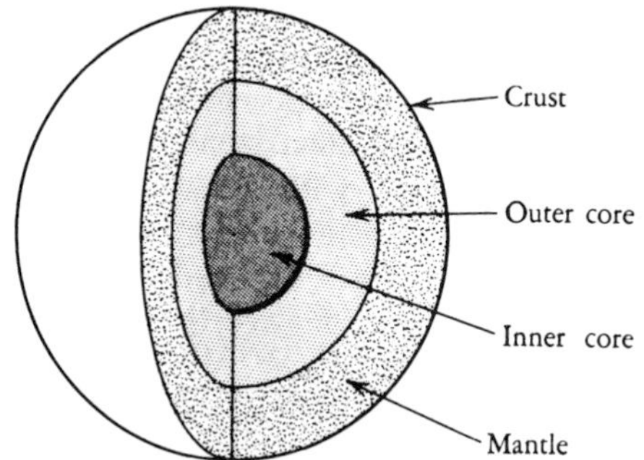

FIGURE 10.1 Model of the Earth's layers.

B. The **core**, believed to be a mixture of about 90% iron and 10% nickel, is actually divided into two layers, an inner core and an outer core.
   1. The **inner core** is believed to be a solid metallic sphere with a radius of about 1,280 kilometers (800 mi).
   2. The **outer core** is a layer of molten rock with a thickness of about 2,160 kilometers (1,350 mi).

C. The **mantle** is a rocky layer with a thickness of 2,885 kilometers (1,789 mi).
   1. The mantle is made of rock called **peridotite,** which is denser than the basalt and granite of the Earth's crust.
   2. An area of the upper or outer mantle, called the **asthenosphere**, which begins at around 100 kilometers (60 mi) and extends to a depth of about 350 kilometers (220 mi), is an area of rock that is hot and easily deformed because of pressures on it.
   3. This plastic characteristic of the asthenosphere allows the Earth's crust to migrate in pieces (called **plate tectonics**, discussed later in this chapter).

D. Outside the asthenosphere is the **lithosphere**, a cool and rigid layer of mostly granite (for the continental crust) and basalt (for the oceanic crust).
   1. The lithosphere averages about 100 kilometers (60 mi) thick and includes the entire crust as well as the uppermost mantle.
   2. Part of the lithosphere is the boundary that separates the crust from the underlying mantle, called the **moho.**

E. The **crust** is the thin outermost layer of Earth, varying between 5 and 40 kilometers (3 and 25 mi) thick. The crust is thickest beneath the continents and thinnest beneath the oceans.
   1. Tremendous forces inside the Earth continue to act on the crust, causing it to bend and crack, producing mountains, earthquakes, and volcanic activity.

2. In the Earth's crust are found soil, water, coal, oil, gas, and minerals.
3. Except for hydrogen and helium, which escape from the Earth's gravitational pull, the elements of the Earth are the elements of the universe, formed by stars and dispersed throughout the galaxy.
4. Although there are at least 90 chemical elements found in the Earth's crust, just five of these elements make up about 91% of the crust by weight.
   a. **Oxygen** makes up about 46.6 percent of the crust by weight. It is found in air, water, sand, quartz, limestone, clay, and other materials.
   b. **Silicon** makes up about 27.7% of the crust by weight. It is found in sand, quartz, clay, and other materials.
   c. **Aluminum** is the Earth's most abundant metal, making up slightly more than 8% of the crust by weight. It is found in clay and other materials.
   d. **Iron** makes up about 5% of the crust by weight. It is usually found combined with oxygen and sulfur.
   e. **Calcium** makes up about 4% of the crust by weight. It is found in limestone and other materials.

IV. Rock

A. The Earth's crust is made up of great masses of rock. Rock is a natural combination of two or more minerals into a solid mass called an **aggregate.** Large rock masses can be several miles thick. Smaller rocks and boulders are simply pieces that were broken off from the larger masses.
   1. Much of the rock on the Earth's surface is covered by soil.

B. According to how they are formed, rocks are divided into three categories—igneous, sedimentary, and metamorphic.

C. **Igneous** (formed from fire) **rock** is formed from molten material (**magma**) in or below the Earth's crust.
   1. Magma forms when pressure below the Earth's crust changes. When the pressure is reduced, the solid material in the Earth's mantle becomes liquid magma, which may then work its way upward through cracks or breaks in the layers of rock lying above it and flow out. Flowing magma on the Earth's surface is called **lava.**
   2. The heat and pressure of the flowing magma may also cause the rock above it to move, break up, or even melt, which makes room for the magma to rise.
   3. Rock formed from magma that reaches the Earth's surface and then cools is called **extrusive rock.** Extrusive rocks are either glassy or made up of very fine crystals. The lava cools so quickly that large crystals do not have opportunity to form.
   4. Rock formed from magma that could not reach the Earth's surface, and therefore cooled below the surface, is called **intrusive rock.** It is coarser than extrusive rock and may have large crystals because the magma cooled more slowly.

D. **Granite** is the most common igneous intrusive rock. El Capitan in Yosemite National Park is a massive granite rock.
   1. Granite is recognized by its speckled appearance, caused by the presence of three minerals—quartz, feldspar, and mica.
   2. Quartz has glass-like crystals that are usually colorless or milky.
   3. Feldspar can be most any color but most often is white.
   4. Mica can also be any color but most often is shiny brown or black.
   5. Granite rock is used in the construction of roads, buildings, and monuments.

E. **Basalt** is an igneous extrusive rock. It is dark colored and denser than granite. The Earth's continents consist of huge masses of granite lying on a foundation of basalt.

F. **Pumice** and **obsidian** are igneous extrusive rocks formed from magma or lava given off by erupting volcanoes.
   1. Pumice comes from lava that comprised many hot gases. The lava cooled so quickly that the gases did not have time to escape and were trapped inside the cooled lava, thus forming a light-colored spongy rock.

LEARNING ACTIVITY 10.1

Extrusive and Intrusive Crystals

Obtain alum in a drugstore. Dissolve as much alum as possible in each of two beakers almost full of hot water. Place one beaker in the refrigerator or surround it with ice so that the solution cools as quickly as possible. Place the other beaker in a quiet corner of the room and allow it to stand overnight. Examine the crystals from both solutions the next day. The crystals from the alum solution that was cooled quickly are rather fine and small, like extrusive crystals, because the solution was cooled so quickly that large crystals were unable to form. The crystals from the alum solution that was allowed to cool slowly are much coarser and larger, like intrusive crystals, because the solution cooled gradually and allowed large crystals to form.

Inquiry-Based Learning Activity 10.1.Modified

In nature, rocks are formed in many different ways. One way involves the cooling of magma that is underground and another the cooling of lava on the Earth's surface. Scientists believe that magma underground stays hotter longer as it cools down slowly, compared with lava on the surface of the Earth that cools down a lot faster. Let's do an experiment to study the difference between these two situations. You can make a liquid that acts like magma or lava by dissolving alum in hot water until no more alum will dissolve. Be sure to stir. In this activity, each of your students will have two containers. For the first container, ask them to come up with a plan for keeping it warm so that it can cool down slowly. For the second container, ask your students to come up with a plan for cooling it down quickly. Ask them to write down their ideas, so that they can share the ideas with the class. After sharing, have the class choose one or two plans for keeping containers warm and one or two plans for making them cool. Supply each student with the materials they need to make one warm container and one cool container. Then carefully fill them with the hot water and alum solution. Keep the containers in a safe place and have your students record what they see forming in their containers over the course of several days. Discuss with your students their ideas about what they see.

What level of inquiry is this modification? The design of this activity offers students some degree of autonomy within a well-defined framework. However, rather than providing students with data, students are asked to make observations without these observations being clearly defined by the teacher. In addition, rather than giving students evidence, they are guided in a process of formulating explanations from their observations. These characteristics suggest that this activity is at ***Level II (Mixing elements from both Transition from Level I and Transition to Level III).*** **Some questions to consider.** How should the students record their observations? Should students compare what they see in their own containers with what they see in their classmates' containers?

2. Because of the trapped gases, some samples of pumice have such a low density that they can float on water.
3. Obsidian, black and glassy with a chemical composition similar to that of glass, is another form of lava that cooled very quickly.

G. **Sedimentary rocks** were formed from different sediments that accumulated in water for thousands of years and then cemented tightly together.
1. Materials such as sand, clay, silt, pebbles, and gravel form from the weathering of igneous rock. Streams and rivers carry these sedimentary materials to lakes or oceans, where they settle to the bottom.
2. As the sediment accumulates, layers are formed that slowly change to solid rock as the weight of the upper layers presses the sediment of the lower layers tightly together.
3. At the same time, chemicals that are already dissolved in the water begin to deposit out again on and between the particles of sediment, filling in the tiny spaces between particles and cementing them together.
4. Conglomerate, sandstone, and shale are examples of sedimentary rock.
5. **Conglomerate** is made of pebbles and gravel that cemented together.
6. **Sandstone** is made of grains of sand that cemented together.
7. The material that cemented the sand determines the color and hardness of the sandstone. Sandstone may be red, brown, yellow, or light colored. It can be very soft, or it can be hard enough to use as a building material.
8. **Shale** is clay or mud that became sedimentary rock.
9. Because clay is made of fine, flaky material, shale usually can be split easily into flat, thin pieces. Shale is often gray or green but may also be red, blue, purple, or black.
10. Another kind of sediment that forms sedimentary rock includes the remains of organisms that live in the oceans and form shells or skeletons of calcium carbonate. As these organisms die, their shells and skeletons accumulate and then harden to form great beds of calcium carbonate, commonly called **limestone.** Limestone that is formed from the remains of coral and other tiny organisms that live in clear, warm, shallow water is fine, nearly pure, calcium carbonate.
11. Limestone has also formed from the shells of larger animals, such as clams, oysters, and mussels. This type of limestone is much coarser and may contain pieces of shell, as well as sand and clay.
12. **Chalk** is a soft, porous form of limestone, made of the shells of tiny organisms that lived millions of years ago.
13. Another kind of material that forms sedimentary rock includes chemicals that are dissolved in the ocean water, such as salt and calcium carbonate. Conditions in the oceans often change so that the water in certain parts of the ocean can no longer hold these chemicals. They deposit out and form accumulations that later harden into rock. **Rock salt** is formed from salt that once was dissolved in ocean water. A very pure and fine form of limestone is formed from calcium carbonate that has deposited out of ocean water.
14. Sedimentary rocks often have the fossil remains of early organisms embedded in them.

Test	*Hardness Number*	*Sample Mineral*
Mineral is scratched by fingernail	1	Talc
Mineral is scratched by fingernail	2	Gypsum
Mineral is scratched by a copper penny	3	Calcite
Mineral is scratched easily by a knife blade	4	Fluorite
Mineral is scratched by a knife blade	5	Apatite
Mineral will easily scratch glass	6	Orthoclase
Mineral will scratch glass	7	Quartz
Mineral will scratch most other minerals	8	Topaz
Mineral will scratch topaz	9	Corundum
Mineral will scratch all other minerals	10	Diamond

FIGURE 10.2 Classifying minerals by Moh's hardness scale.

15. Iron and other metal ores sometimes accumulate as sediment and are then found in sedimentary rock.
16. **Soft coal** is sedimentary rock formed from the remains of plants that died long ago and accumulated in a swamp. They were covered by other sediment to form layers, which were then changed by heat and pressure into a rocky material.

H. **Metamorphic** ("change in form") **rocks** are igneous and sedimentary rocks that were changed by heat and pressure.
   1. Some changes were physical, whereby the original materials in the rock were only rearranged. Other changes were chemical, whereby new materials were formed.
   2. Common metamorphic rocks are gneiss, quartzite, slate, marble, and hard coal.
   3. **Gneiss**, a coarse rock that contains parallel streaks or bands of minerals, is commonly formed from igneous granite and from many other kinds of igneous or sedimentary rocks.
   4. **Quartzite** is a very hard rock formed from sedimentary sandstone.
   5. **Slate**, formed from sedimentary shale, is a fine-grained rock that splits easily into thin sheets.
   6. **Marble** is a large-crystal rock formed from sedimentary limestone.
   7. **Hard coal**, formed from soft coal, contains much more carbon than soft coal.
   8. Hard coal is also changed by further heat and pressure to **graphite**. Graphite is pure carbon.
   9. **Diamond** is the final metamorphic form of graphite.

I. When metamorphic rock in the Earth is subjected to pressure changes, heat, or both, it will melt, creating magma, which will eventually crystallize into igneous rock, thus continuing what is known as the **rock cycle.**
   1. The rock cycle illustrates the origin of the three basic rock types and the interrelatedness of Earth materials and processes.

J. Although geologic activity, erosion, and metamorphism have destroyed almost all of the most ancient rocks, continents and their rock formations still provide much valuable data regarding the Earth's earliest history.
   1. Dating rocks using **radioactive clocks** allows isotope geochemists to study the most ancient rocks, those without fossil evidence.
   2. The "hands" of a radioactive clock are isotopes, atoms of the same element that have different atomic weights. Geologic time is measured by the rate of decay of one isotope into another (see Figure 10.2).

V. Minerals

A. Rocks are made up of two or more minerals. Minerals are solid materials made of one or more chemical elements, having an orderly arrangement of atoms and therefore a definite crystal structure.

B. Minerals are not made of organisms, nor do they come from organisms. Therefore, they are said to be **inorganic** substances.
   1. For this reason, **pearl**, even though it is a chemical compound, is not considered a mineral, because it was produced by an organism—the oyster.
   2. For the same reason, coal is not a mineral because it was formed from plant materials.

C. **Ore** is rock that contains enough of a particular mineral to make it economically worthwhile to mine.

D. Minerals are classified into groups according to the kinds of chemicals they contain and the structure of their crystals.
   1. One group of minerals includes those that contain the chemical element silicon. It makes up about 40% of the minerals on Earth. Members of this group, called the **silicate minerals**, include quartz, feldspar, mica, hornblende, augite, garnet, olivine, and talc. The minerals found in granite rock, which makes up 90% of the Earth's crust, are found in this group. **Olivine**, the most abundant mineral of the Earth's upper mantle, is important to scientists in the study of earthquakes.

2. Another group of minerals includes those considered to be nonmetallic—the **nonmetallic minerals.** Some members of this group contain elements such as calcium and magnesium that, chemically, are metals. Examples of nonmetallic minerals are calcite, dolomite, sulfur, rock salt, gypsum, apatite, fluorite, and graphite.
3. A third group of minerals contain the common metal ores; this group is called the **metal ore minerals.** It includes gold, silver, iron, copper, lead, zinc, tin, aluminum, mercury, titanium, and uranium.
4. A fourth group of minerals are those made into precious and semiprecious stones. These minerals, called the **gem minerals**, include opal, jade, garnet, topaz, tourmaline, emerald, aquamarine, ruby, amethyst, sapphire, zircon, and diamond. Because zircon is not dissolved during erosion but is deposited as sediment, it can survive for billions of years.
5. In recent years, zircon has become a signpost for better understanding the age of rocks and for determining when life first appeared on Earth. Scientists have been searching for the mineral and studying the continental rocks where it is found.

VI. Identification of Minerals

A. Many tests are used to absolutely identify a mineral. Only rarely can a mineral be identified by a single test.
   1. For the **color test**, the mineral is scratched, and the color of a fresh surface of the mineral is examined. Rather than a dull or tarnished surface that has been exposed to the air and soil, a fresh surface is more likely to display the true color of the mineral.
   2. Examining the color produced when the mineral is rubbed against a piece of unglazed porcelain tile is called a **streak test.** Nonmetallic minerals usually produce a colorless or a light-colored streak, whereas metallic minerals often produce a dark streak that may differ from the visible color of the mineral.
   3. Using such terms as *dull, pearly, silky, metallic, glassy,* and *brilliant* or *diamondlike,* scientists describe the **luster** of a mineral, that is, the shine the mineral has when light strikes it.
   4. Scientists also examine the **crystal form** of the mineral. Most minerals are made of crystals, showing that the atoms in the minerals are arranged in regular or definite patterns. These crystals have distinct forms, such as square, double triangle, cube, and pyramid.
   5. Minerals are also examined according to how they split or break when struck. This is referred to as the **cleavage test.** For example, some minerals may split into thin sheets (as does mica), into cubes (as does galena), or into an eight-sided cleavage (as does fluorite).
   6. Another test for minerals is the **hardness test.** Because there is such a wide difference in the hardness of minerals, certain minerals are used as standards of hardness. All others are then compared with these standards. The standard minerals are arranged on a scale in the order of their hardness, with the softest listed first. A commonly used scale of hardness is the **Mohs' scale of hardness.**
      a. Mohs' scale lists 10 minerals in the order of their hardness, with each mineral being harder than those with lower numbers that come before it (see Figure 10.2).
      b. Talc, one of the softest minerals, is first in the scale, and diamond, the hardest of all minerals, is last.
      c. Mineral hardness is determined by using one mineral to make scratches on another. For example, apatite, 5, is harder than fluorite, 4, but softer than orthoclase, 6. Any mineral that will scratch apatite, but not orthoclase, is said to have a Mohs' scale hardness between 5 and 6. The mineral would also scratch all minerals with hardness numbers lower than apatite, but none of those with hardness numbers higher than orthoclase.
   7. Minerals can also be determined by testing their **specific gravity,** or density. This is done by weighing a mineral in the air and then suspended in water. The weight in the air, divided by the difference in weight while in water, is called the specific gravity.

B. Many other tests are used for mineral identification.
   1. Some minerals, such as lodestone or magnetite, are magnetic and will be attracted by a magnet.
      a. Magnetite is found in the chitonous teeth on the radulla of chitons. The radulla is a tongue-like appendage of mollusks. The presence of magnetite causes a sensory response to magnetic fields in the animal's environment, thus enabling the chiton to leave its rock for night feeding and then return to exactly the same place when it is finished feeding. Serving a similar navigational function, magnetite is also found in the brain of at least some birds.
   2. Some minerals, such as sulfur, will become electrically charged when rubbed or squeezed.
   3. When exposed to ultraviolet light, some minerals give off a fluorescent glow.
   4. Many fluorescent minerals are also phosphorescent and will give off light after an ultraviolet light has been turned off.
   5. Some minerals, such as uranium, are radioactive; radioactivity is detected with a Geiger counter.

6. When a drop of dilute hydrochloric acid is placed on a mineral containing calcium carbonate, a chemical reaction occurs and bubbles of carbon dioxide gas are given off.
7. Some minerals give a special color to a flame when a bit of such a powdered mineral, which has been moistened with hydrochloric acid, is placed on one end of a clean platinum wire and thrust into a Bunsen burner flame.
8. Certain minerals will give a special color to powdered borax that has been put on one end of a clean platinum wire and heated to form a small glassy bead. The color changes when some of the powdered mineral is put on the bead and the bead is thrust into a flame that has been made hotter with a blowpipe.

VII. **Conservation of Mineral Resources**

A. Minerals are called fixed or nonrenewable resources because there is no regularly occurring natural process for recycling or replacing minerals that have been removed from the Earth. Only when an occasional meteorite strikes the Earth are any new mineral materials added to the lithosphere.
   1. Metals such as iron, aluminum, lead, zinc, copper, and silver must be used wisely and efficiently.
   2. Alternate materials must be developed.
   3. Economically effective ways are being found to extract metals from low-grade ores.
   4. New deposits of minerals are being searched for on Earth and eventually will be searched for on other celestial bodies.
   5. We must continue to recycle reclaimable materials such as glass and aluminum.
   6. Coal is still in ample supply to last many years, but alternate and cleaner fuels must be developed and used. Fossil fuels of coal, oil, and natural gas will not last forever.

B. Coal is our nation's primary energy source, accounting for one-third of total energy production.
   1. From 1970 through 1990, coal mining in the United States increased 72% and has more than doubled since 1980.
   2. The electric utility industry uses 80% of all coal mined.
   3. Satellites and the NAVSTAR (Navigation Satellite Timing and Ranging) Global Positioning System help locate potential coal-mining sites. With refined sensors and computers, satellites can measure distances of up to 25 miles to within an inch or less accuracy.
   4. Today's coal mining and use relies heavily on the concept of clean coal technology, which depends heavily on sophisticated machinery, including robotics, lasers, and computers.
   5. Surface mining accounts for more than half of U.S. coal mining. An important component of the surface mining industries is that of restoring the land that has been mined.

Air

I. **Where Air Is Found**

A. Air occupies the space all around the Earth. We live at the bottom of an ocean of air.

B. Air is also found in the tiny spaces between particles of materials, in soil, in water, and in such porous materials as sponges, bricks, wood, and bread.

II. **The Present Composition of Earth's Air**

A. Air is a mixture of many gases, but the two principal gases in the air are oxygen and nitrogen, making up about 99% of the air we breathe.

B. About 21% of air is oxygen.
   1. Oxygen is a very active gas and combines easily with many materials.
   2. Animals and plants need oxygen for metabolizing their food (that is, for cellular respiration).
   3. Homes and industries need oxygen to burn fuels.
   4. Plants are the major producers of atmospheric oxygen, releasing it into the atmosphere as a by-product of photosynthesis.

C. The most abundant gas in the air is nitrogen, making up about 78%.
   1. Nitrogen is not an active gas and does not help things burn, nor does it combine with other materials easily.
   2. If there were only oxygen in the air, without nitrogen, all burning would be very rapid and impossible to control. Nitrogen helps dilute the oxygen in the air and in this way controls burning.
   3. The amount of nitrogen in the air remains constant because of the **nitrogen cycle**, which is as follows.
      a. Most flora and fauna cannot use nitrogen in its atmospheric form.
      b. Lightning and some bacteria convert atmospheric nitrogen into nitrogen-containing compounds that can be used by plants and animals.
      c. Plants take up nitrates made by bacteria and lightning.
      d. Plant-eating animals (herbivores) eat plants and convert nitrogen-containing plant proteins into nitrogen-containing animal proteins.

LEARNING ACTIVITY 10.2

Percentage of Oxygen in Air

Obtain two test tubes of the same size. Insert a wad of steel wool into one of the test tubes and push it down to the bottom. Pour some water into each test tube, shake well, and then pour off the water. Put each test tube, mouth down, into a wide-mouthed jar or beaker of water and fasten each test tube with a clamp (Figure 10.3). Have the mouths of the test tubes the same distance (about 13 millimeters or 0.5 inch) below the surface of the water. Let the test tubes stand this way for 24 hours.

After 24 hours, water will have risen up the test tube containing the steel wool. Nothing will have happened in the empty test tube (the control). Measure the length of the test tube above the surface of the water, and then measure how high the water rose in the test tube. Compare these lengths: The water will have risen about one-fifth, or 20%, of the way up the test tube. Note the rusty appearance of the steel wool. The iron in the steel combined with the oxygen in the air inside the test tube to form iron oxide (rust). Because the water rose one-fifth of the way up the tube to replace the oxygen, it means that about one-fifth, or 20%, of the air in the tube was oxygen.

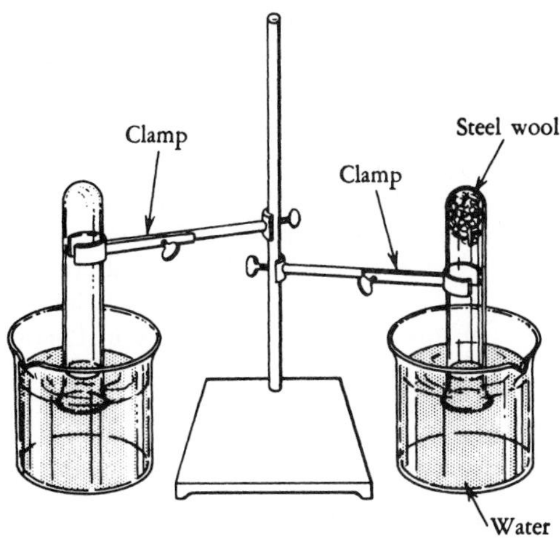

FIGURE 10.3 About 20% of the air in the test tube is oxygen.

Note: If you have difficulty getting this experiment to work, try washing the steel wool first in acetone, then in vinegar, and finally in vinegar diluted 1:10. The steel wool is swished around about 30 seconds in each wash and shaken out. It is important to keep the steel wool fluffy and to start the experiment quickly after the last wash.

e. During digestion, plant proteins and animal proteins convert to forms that combine to make human proteins.
f. When organisms die and decay, their decomposing bodies return nitrogen to the atmosphere, thus continuing the nitrogen cycle.

D. The remaining 1% of the air is made up of carbon dioxide gas, hydrogen gas, and a group of rare and inactive gases: helium, neon, argon, krypton, and xenon.
   1. Even though carbon dioxide is present in the air only in small quantities, it is an important gas.
   2. Through photosynthesis, plants with chlorophyll use carbon dioxide to make food, which is used not only by the plants themselves but by animals as well.
   3. If large quantities of plants were removed from the Earth by human intervention or by natural means, the amount of carbon dioxide in the air would increase, and the air in turn would retain more of the Sun's heat energy that would otherwise escape from the atmosphere into space. This phenomenon has been implicated in an increase in the normal *greenhouse effect* of our atmosphere and is believed to be the cause of a gradual global warming. Global warming could have serious effects, including flooding of coastal areas as a result of melting of polar ice caps.

E. The relative amounts of oxygen and carbon dioxide in the air remain nearly the same because of the **carbon dioxide-oxygen cycle.**
   1. In photosynthesis, algae and plants that contain chlorophyll take in carbon dioxide from the air and combine it with hydrogen taken from water to make food, such as carbohydrates; oxygen is given off by these organisms as a by-product of photosynthesis.
   2. Most organisms use oxygen to burn food in cellular respiration. Carbon dioxide is released as a waste product of this respiration.

F. Air also contains water in the form of an invisible gas called **water vapor.**
   1. Water vapor becomes part of the air through the evaporation of water occurring from the bodies of water on the Earth's surface.
   2. The amount of water vapor in the air differs from day to day and from place to place.

G. Air also carries changing amounts of dust, pollen, living spores, and waste gases given off by factories and the exhausts of vehicles.

III. Air Pollution

A. Atmospheric air is polluted every day by large quantities of gases and solids.
   1. These materials are given off by industrial furnaces, chemical plants, motor vehicles, and other sources.

2. Some impurities in the air are emitted directly from identifiable sources, and others are formed indirectly through photochemical reactions in the air.
3. Major air pollutants, their sources, and the problems they can cause in humans are illustrated in Table 10.1.
4. In addition to causing human health problems, pollutants in the air cause damage and death to plants, as well as irreversible damage from oxidation and acid erosion to cultural treasures of the world, such as the Parthenon in Athens; the Coliseum in Rome; Westminster Abbey in London; the Taj Mahal in Agra, India; the stained-glass windows of Chartres, France; and others throughout the cities of Europe.
5. As an example of the irreversibility of such effects, sulfur oxides in the smog over Athens chemically transform marble (of which the Parthenon is built) into gypsum, which in turn cracks and flakes off.

B. Air pollution becomes a serious problem when weather conditions are formed in which the polluted air cannot be blown away.
1. Such a condition occurs when there is a layer of cold air next to the ground with a layer of warm air lying on top of the cold air.
2. The upper layer of warm air acts as a cover and stops the cold air from being carried away. This condition is called a temperature inversion.

C. In the United States, attempts are being made to control air pollution.
1. Factories install equipment to remove the poisonous gases and smoke particles from their exhaust gases before they can escape into the air.
2. Automobiles come equipped with antismog devices to trap or burn the exhaust pollutants.

IV. The Earth's Atmosphere

A. The ocean of air around the Earth is called the **atmosphere.**
1. The Earth's pull of gravity holds the atmosphere close to the Earth's surface.
2. The atmosphere is important because all animals and most plants need air to live. The atmosphere also acts as a protective blanket to reduce the Sun's heat and to shield us from harmful rays that come from the Sun and outer space.

B. Although the atmosphere uniformly becomes thinner or less dense as altitude increases, temperature variations result in a division into five principal layers: the troposphere, the stratosphere, the mesosphere, the thermosphere (or ionosphere), and the exosphere.
1. The **troposphere** is the lowest layer of the atmosphere, the layer at the Earth's solid surface. It extends upward to a height of 6 kilometers (4 mi) at the poles and 16 kilometers (10 mi) at the equator, with an average of about 10 kilometers (6 mi) in the areas between these two. Because almost all water vapor in the atmosphere is in this layer, most weather conditions such as clouds and storms occur in the troposphere. The troposphere is warmest at the bottom, close to the Earth, where it is heated by the reradiation of solar energy from the Earth. The convection currents (see Chapter 9) that play an important role in weather are completely confined to the troposphere.
2. The next layer above the troposphere is the **stratosphere**. It extends upward from the top of the troposphere to a height of about 50 kilometers (30 mi). Air is much thinner in the stratosphere. The stratosphere contains only a few cirrus clouds and lacks the convective turbulence and wind of the troposphere. For this reason, pilots of commercial planes prefer flying in the stratosphere.
   a. A special form of oxygen, called **ozone**, is found in the stratosphere. Ozone absorbs most of the ultraviolet rays coming from the Sun, protecting organisms on Earth from severe damage.
3. Above the stratosphere is the **mesosphere**, which extends to a height of about 80 kilometers (50 mi). The coldest temperatures of the Earth's atmosphere are in the mesosphere.
4. The fourth layer of the atmosphere, the **thermosphere** (or **ionosphere**), extends to a height of about 640 to 800 kilometers (400 to 500 mi). The top of the thermosphere is the hottest part of the atmosphere because it is closest to the Sun. However, temperature is defined in terms of the average speed at which molecules move. Since the gases of the thermosphere are moving at very high speeds, the temperature is very high (approximately 1,000°C or 1,800°F). But the gases are so sparse that collectively, they possess only an insignificant quantity of heat. For this reason, the temperature of a satellite orbiting Earth in the thermosphere is determined primarily by the amount of solar radiation it absorbs and not by the high temperature of the nearly nonexistent surrounding air.
   a. Powerful ultraviolet rays from the Sun strike the particles of air in the thermosphere, causing them to be electrically charged. These electrically charged particles of air are called **ions**. The ionic (charged) particles of the thermosphere make worldwide radio reception possible.
   b. When radio waves, which travel in straight lines, travel out into space and reach the thermosphere, the waves bounce off the

TABLE 10.1 Major Air Pollutants, Their Sources, and Problems They Can Cause

Pollutant	Source	Problems
Arsenic	Fossil fuel furnaces and glass manufacturing	Can cause lung and skin cancer
Benzene	Refineries; motor vehicles	Can cause leukemia
Cadmium	Smelters; burning waste; fossil fuel furnaces	Can cause kidney and lung damage; weakened bones
Carbon monoxide	Motor vehicles; fossil fuel burning; smelters and steel plants	Prevents body from obtaining oxygen; damages heart
Chlorine	Chemical industries	Forms hydrochloric acid; irritates mucous membranes
Fluoride ions	Smelters; steel plants	Can mottle teeth
Formaldehyde	Motor vehicles; chemical plants	Irritates eyes and nose
Hydrocarbons	Unburned gasoline vapor	Combines with oxides of nitrogen to form smog
Hydrogen chloride	Incinerators	Irritates eyes and nose
Hydrogen fluoride	Fertilizer plants; smelters	Irritates skin, eyes, and mucous linings
Hydrogen sulfide	Refineries; sewage plants; pulp mills	Can cause nausea; eye irritation
Hydroxyl ion	Formed in sunlight from hydrocarbons and nitrogen oxides	Reacts with other gases to form acid droplets
Lead	Motor vehicles; smelters	Can cause brain damage; high blood pressure; impaired growth
Manganese	Steel and power plants	May contribute to Parkinson's disease
Mercury	Fossil fuel furnaces; smelters	Causes nerve disorders
Nickel	Smelters and fossil-fuel-burning furnaces	May cause lung cancer
Nitric acid	Forms from nitrous oxide, a major component of acid rain	Can cause respiratory problems
Nitric oxide	Motor vehicles; fossil fuel burning	Oxidizes to form nitrogen dioxide
Nitrogen dioxide	Formed in sunlight from nitrogen oxide	Produces ozone; causes bronchitis; lowers resistance to influenza
Nitrous acid	Forms from nitrous oxide and water vapor	Can cause respiratory problems
Ozone	Formed in sunlight from nitrogen oxides and oxygen	Irritates eyes; aggravates asthma
Peroxyacetyl nitrate	Formed in sunlight from nitrogen oxides and oxygen	Irritates eyes; aggravates asthma
Silicon tetrafluoride	Chemical plants	Irritates lungs
Sulfur dioxide	Fossil fuel burning	Restricts breathing; irritates eyes
Sulfuric acid	Forms in sunlight from sulfur dioxide and hydroxyl ions (from water vapor in air)	Can cause respiratory ailments

ions and are reflected back to a different place on Earth.

c. The northern lights (aurora borealis) and the southern lights (aurora australis) occur in the thermosphere. The northern and southern lights happen whenever particles from the Van Allen belts (see number 5.a) escape from the exosphere and collide with air molecules.

5. The fifth and final layer, the **exosphere**, begins at the outer limit of the thermosphere and extends upward, until it cannot be distinguished from outer space, about 500 kilometers (310 mi). There is almost no air at all in the exosphere.
   a. The exosphere contains an area of very intense radiation, called the **Van Allen radiation belt.** It is considered to consist of two rings or belts, something like a doughnut within a doughnut. The inner ring or belt begins about 1,280 kilometers (800 mi) above the Earth and extends to about 4,800 kilometers (3,000 mi). The outer belt begins about 12,800 kilometers (8,000 mi) above the Earth and extends to about 64,000 kilometers (40,000 mi). Here the charged particles from the solar wind are trapped in the Earth's magnetic field.

V. The Properties of Air

A. Air is composed of gases that are colorless, odorless, and tasteless.

B. Like all gases, air has no shape of its own; it assumes the shape of the container it is in.
   1. Although air is invisible, it takes up space and has weight. One liter of air weighs about 1 1/5 grams (1 cu ft weighs about 1 1/4 oz).

C. Because air has weight, it pushes or presses against other things.
   1. We live at the bottom of an ocean of air hundreds of kilometers or miles high.
   2. This air presses down on the Earth's surface and creates pressure on it; the pressure on the Earth's surface is called air pressure, or **atmospheric pressure.**
   3. As we go higher into the atmosphere, there is less air pressing down, so the air pressure decreases.
   4. Air presses in all directions—downward, upward, and sideways—on any exposed surface, and it presses just as hard upward and sideways as it does downward.
   5. Air presses on every square inch of the surface of our bodies, but we do not feel this pressure because air within our bodies pushes outward with the same pressure.

D. Moving air exerts pressure.
   1. When air moves, it pushes harder against other things.
   2. Wind is moving air, and the harder the wind blows, the greater its pressure.
   3. At sea level, the weight of the air pressing on 1 square centimeter of the Earth's surface is about 1 kilogram (or on 1 square inch it is about 15 lb).
   4. Air pressure is constantly changing from day to day.
   5. The barometer is an instrument used to measure air pressure.

E. An altimeter is an aneroid barometer that measures altitude, or height, above sea level.
   1. The higher in the atmosphere we go, the less air pressure there is and the lower the barometer reading.
   2. For every 305 meters (1,000 ft) up we go, atmospheric air pressure falls about 2 centimeters (1 in.).
   3. The dial of an altimeter is marked so that instead of giving the air pressure in centimeters or inches of mercury, it gives the number of meters or feet above sea level.

F. Air in a container pushes, or exerts pressure, on the walls of the container.
   1. Gases in the air are made up of molecules, which are moving rapidly.
   2. When fast-moving molecules hit the walls of a container, they push against the walls and exert pressure on them.
   3. Adding or removing air can change the air pressure in a closed container.
   4. If more air is added to the container, the air pressure inside increases because more molecules of air are now striking and pushing against the walls of the container. If air is removed from the container, the air pressure inside decreases, because fewer molecules of air are now striking and pushing against the walls of the container.
   5. If all the air is removed from a container, there will be no air pressure at all inside the container, because there are no molecules of air inside to strike the walls. An absence of all air inside a container is called a **vacuum.** When only part of the air is removed from the container, there is only a partial vacuum present.
   6. Changing the size of a closed container can change the air pressure inside it. If the size of a container is increased, air pressure inside is decreased. Because the air has spread out into a larger space, there are fewer molecules striking and pushing against each part of the container. If the size of a container is decreased, air pressure inside increases. Because the molecules of air have been squeezed into a smaller space, there are more of them striking and pushing against each part of the container.
   7. Heating or cooling the container can change air pressure inside a container.
   8. If a container is heated, the air pressure inside increases. Because the molecules of air

LEARNING ACTIVITY 10.3

Effect of Size of a Container on the Air Pressure Inside It

Hold a sturdy plastic bag halfway down its sides, blow up the bottom half of the bag, and twist the middle several times. Let a child squeeze the sides of the bag and note the pressure. Now twist the mouth of the bag several times, and then untwist the middle. The air inside will spread out through the increased space in the bag. Again note the pressure of the air inside the bag. (The air pressure decreases as the size of the container increases).

Blow a little air into the bag and note the small amount of air pressure inside. Now hold the mouth with one hand and use your other hand to push the air inside toward the bottom of the bag. (Note how, as the size of the part of the container that holds the air decreases, the air pressure increases.)

LEARNING ACTIVITY 10.4

The Effect of Heating and Cooling on the Air Pressure in a Container

A. Inflating a Balloon

Snap a balloon over a Pyrex flask or bottle. Place the flask on a hot plate and heat it for 1 minute (Figure 10.4). The air inside the flask and balloon expand when heated. This expanded air exerts pressure against the sides of the balloon and begins to inflate it. Now place the Pyrex flask into a pan of cold water containing ice cubes. The air inside the flask and balloon contract when cooled and exert less pressure. As a result, the balloon deflates and may even be drawn inside the flask because the decreased pressure inside the balloon is now so much less than the normal pressure of the air around the balloon.

B. Collapsing a Can

Pour into an empty soda can enough water to cover the bottom. Place the can on a hot plate and heat it until steam rises from its top. With a glove or hot pad, grasp the hot can and quickly invert it, inserting its top into a pan of water. You do not need to submerge the entire can. Under the force of atmospheric pressure the thin sides of the can will quickly collapse. Try to blow the can up again.

SAFETY NOTE: Use extreme caution for this demonstration.

1. Use extreme caution whenever using a hot plate (or any heat source) in the classroom, keeping curious or careless students protected from touching it.
2. Protect children from possible glass breakage (even when using Pyrex glassware) and from spattering of glass and boiling water.

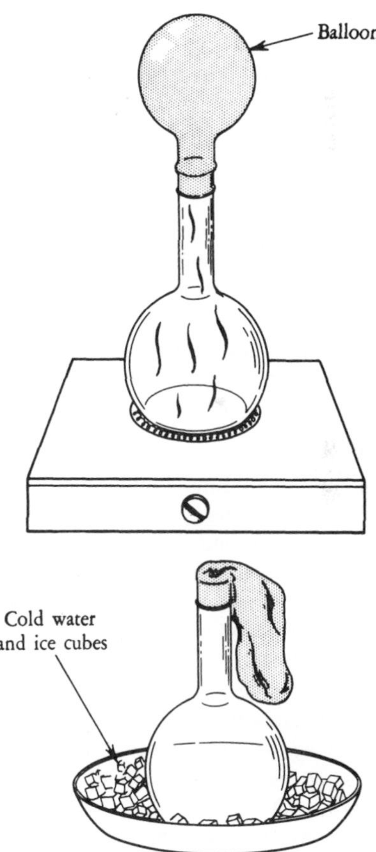

FIGURE 10.4 Air expands when heated and contracts when cooled.

inside the container gain more energy and move faster, they strike and push harder against the walls of the container.

9. If a container is cooled, air pressure inside the container decreases. Because the molecules of air inside the container lose energy and move more slowly, they strike and push less strongly against the walls of the container.

VI. Practical Applications of Air Pressure

A. The use of a soda straw depends on decreasing the air pressure inside the straw.
   1. When a straw is placed in a tumbler of soda, the soda rises up the straw to the level of the soda in the tumbler.
   2. The soda in the straw does not rise any higher because the air pressure on the soda

LEARNING ACTIVITY 10.5

Air Takes Up Space, Has Weight, and Exerts Pressure

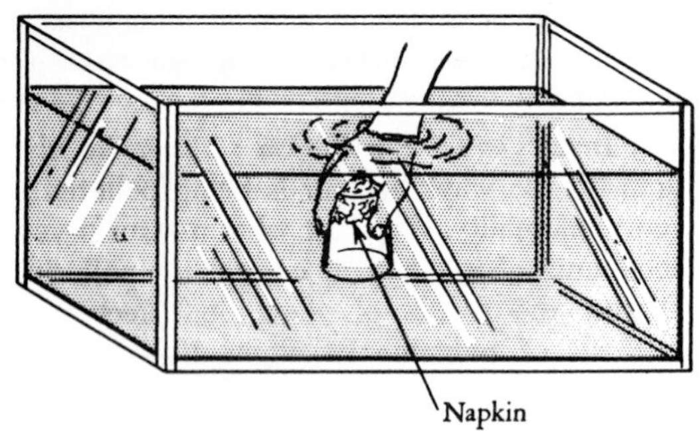

FIGURE 10.5 Because air occupies space, the napkin does not get wet.

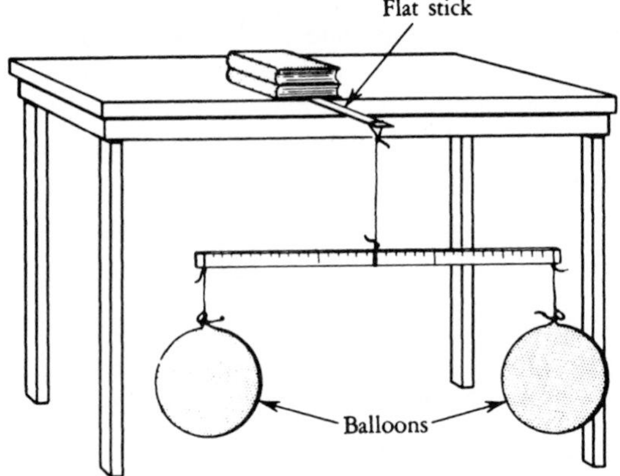

FIGURE 10.6 Air has weight.

A. Air Takes Up Space

Crumple a dry paper napkin and stuff it into a tumbler so that it will not fall out when the tumbler is held upside down. Now, while holding the tumbler upside down, push the tumbler straight down to the bottom of an aquarium or large glass jar that is filled with water (Figure 10.5). Note that the water does not fill the tumbler. The space in the tumbler is occupied by air. Tilt the tumbler slightly, and you will be able to see air escaping from the tumbler in the form of bubbles. Now lift the tumbler straight out of the water. Remove the paper napkin and note that it is still dry.

B. Air Has Weight

Place a pile of books at the edge of a table. Insert a flat stick about 30 centimeters (12 in.) long between the books and the table top. Tie one end of a string about 25 centimeters (10 in.) long to the stick, tie the other end to the middle of a meter stick or yardstick, and slide the meter stick back and forth until it balances (Figure 10.6). Obtain two large, round balloons of the same size, and blow them up so they are the same size when inflated. Tie a string about 15 centimeters (6 in.) long around the end of each balloon and hang the balloons near the ends of the meter stick at the same distance from the ends. Slide the balloons back and forth until the meter stick balances evenly. Puncture one balloon with a pin. The deflated balloon will not weigh as much as the balloon that still has air in it, and the meter stick will become unbalanced. (*Note:* When the balloon bursts, a piece or two of the rubber may be blown off. Be sure to collect these pieces and drape them around the deflated balloon. Otherwise the results will be inaccurate.)

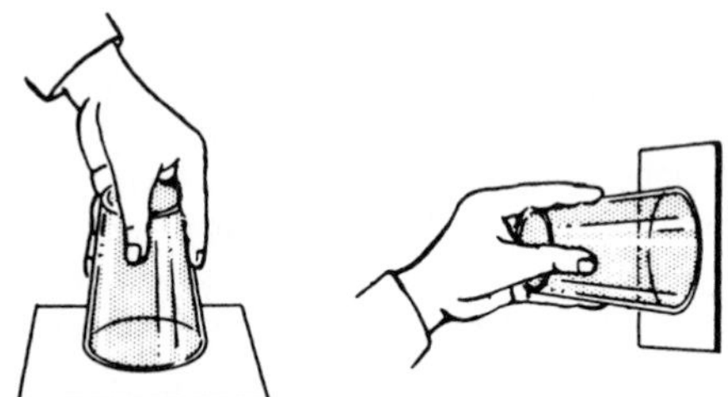

FIGURE 10.7 Air exerts pressure in all directions.

C. Air Exerts Pressure

Fill a tumbler with water. Put a piece of cardboard on top of the tumbler and hold it firmly against the tumbler with the palm of one hand. Grasp the base of the tumbler with the other hand and quickly turn it upside down (Figure 10.7). Remove the palm of your hand carefully from below the cardboard, being careful not to jar the cardboard or the tumbler. The cardboard and the water will remain in place. Point out that the water stays in the tumbler because air is exerting a pressure on the cardboard. The pressure of the air against the cardboard is greater than the pressure of the water against the cardboard.

Ask the students to predict what will happen when you turn the tumbler sideways. Turn the tumbler sideways and to many other positions. The water will still stay in the tumbler, showing that air exerts pressure in all directions. If a sensitive balance is available, weigh a basketball when it is deflated. Fill the ball with air and weigh it again. The difference in weights is the weight of the air in the ball.

---

inside the straw and the air pressure on the soda outside the straw are equal.

3. When the movement of the cheek muscles sucks some air out of the straw, there is a partial vacuum inside the straw, as the air pressure inside the straw is decreased.
4. Normal or regular air pressure on the soda outside the straw is now greater than the air pressure on the soda inside the straw.
5. The outside air pressure, because it is greater, forces the soda up the straw and into the mouth.

LEARNING ACTIVITY 10.6

Applications of Air Pressure

FIGURE 10.8 Using increased air pressure to lift a book.

A. Lifting with Air Pressure

Place a paper bag on a table so that its mouth extends beyond the table's edge. Put a book on top of at least half of the paper bag. Now hold the mouth of the bag closely against your mouth without letting in any air and blow hard into the bag (Figure 10.8). The increased air pressure will lift the book easily. Repeat the experiment, this time using two books.

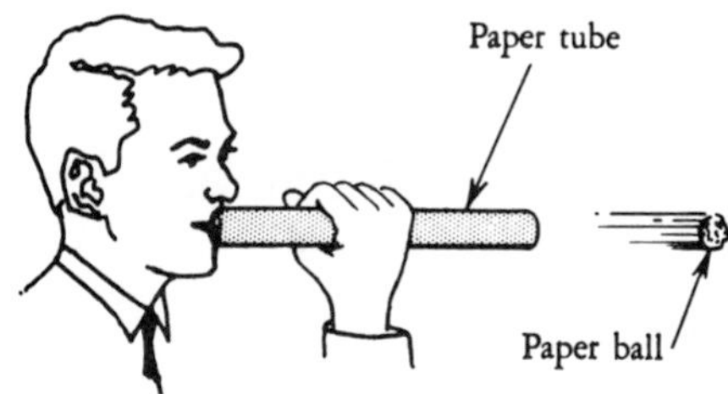

FIGURE 10.9 How an air gun works.

B. Pushing with Compressed Air

Roll up a sheet of paper so that it forms a tube. Crumple a piece of paper into a round ball that just fits inside the tube. Place the ball into one end of the tube and blow hard into this end (Figure 10.9). The ball will be shot out of the tube by the compressed air you created. Air guns and air hammers are common examples of this method of using compressed air.

B. The use of a medicine dropper depends on decreasing the air pressure inside the dropper.
   1. When the bulb is pressed, some of the air is forced out of the dropper.
   2. When the dropper end is then inserted in liquid and the pressure on the bulb released, this increases the volume of the air trapped in the dropper, which reduces its pressure, creating a partial vacuum.
   3. The regular air pressure on the liquid outside the dropper is now greater than the air pressure on the liquid inside the dropper.
   4. The outside air pressure, because it is greater, forces the liquid up into the dropper.
   5. The liquid will not flow out of the dropper because the pressure on the inside of the dropper is the same as the pressure outside.
   6. Pressing the bulb again increases the air pressure inside the dropper by decreasing the volume, and the liquid is forced out of the dropper.

C. Using a suction cup depends on decreasing the air pressure inside the cup.
   1. When a suction cup is pressed against a surface, some of the air is forced out of the cup, forming a partial vacuum and decreasing air pressure inside the cup.
   2. The outside air pressure is now greater and holds the cup firmly in place.
   3. If the cup is moistened first, a tighter seal is made, so outside air cannot get inside the cup and remove the partial vacuum.

D. Operating a vacuum cleaner depends on decreasing the air pressure inside the cleaner.
   1. An electrically driven fan drives air out of a compartment in the machine, forming a partial vacuum and decreasing air pressure inside the compartment.
   2. The outside air pressure is now greater than the air pressure inside the compartment, and the air rushes in through the nozzle, carrying dirt and lint with it.
   3. A bag or screen catches the dirt and lint, while the air passes through and out of the machine.

E. When a great deal of air is pumped into a container, the air is compressed and the air pressure inside the container is increased.
   1. The molecules of air are squeezed, or compressed, very close together, so there are many more of them striking and pushing against the walls of the container.
   2. The molecules are now striking with more force against the walls of the container, so the air pressure inside the container becomes greater.

F. Many devices make use of the increased pressure of compressed air.
   1. An air brake uses compressed air to stop trains, streetcars, buses, and heavy trucks. A motor-driven pump in the vehicle compresses the air, which is stored in a tank. When the brakes are applied, the compressed air passes into a cylinder, where the compressed air exerts pressure against a piston. The piston then forces the brake shoes tightly against a drum that is connected to the wheels, making the vehicle come to a stop.

2. A submarine sinks when tanks let in seawater and rises when compressed air forces the water out of the tanks.
3. Pneumatic drills and riveters operate with compressed air.
4. Automobile tires, footballs, basketballs, and volleyballs contain compressed air.
5. Many paint and garden spray machines are operated with compressed air.
6. Jet engines operate with compressed air.

 Forces that Shape and Change the Earth's Surface

I. Plate Tectonics

A. Above the Earth's metallic core lies a slowly churning mantle of rock kept in a plastic state by heat and pressure.

B. The cold, rigid crust of continents and ocean floors tops the mantle.

C. Mantle rock continuously rises toward the crust, cools, and then sinks.

1. This continuous motion has cracked the Earth's thick crust into about 20 rocky slabs, or plates.
2. These plates slowly drift on the mantle, causing the movement of continents.
3. Plates separate at rifts, where the plastic rock of the mantle, freed of overlying pressure, liquefies into magma and rises to the surface as lava.
4. A **subduction zone** results from a collision between an oceanic and a continental plate. The edge of the oceanic plate, since it is thinner and denser, is forced down into the mantle. At a subduction zone, the ocean floor dives under the edge of a continent and down toward the interior of the Earth. The subduction zone is the most important part of the system that causes plates to move. Ocean trenches, volcanic activity along the continental edge, and earthquakes result from this type of plate movement.
5. Plates may also slide past one another, causing earthquakes.
6. The crack or break in a plate is called a **fault** and the movement of the rock itself is called **faulting.**
7. This movement of plates, called **plate tectonics**, offers a theory about how continents have moved together and apart several times during Earth's history, and why similar fossils and related organisms can be found on continents that are today widely separated.

II. Earthquakes

A. Earthquakes may occur whenever any type of plate movement takes place.

1. The great plates of rock that lie next to a fault are pressed tightly together.
2. These plates are under great stress because one is usually being pushed in one direction while the other is pushed in the opposite direction.
3. After many years of increasing strain, there is a sudden movement as the plates slide and then come to rest in a new position that eases the pressure.
4. The plates may move up and down, sideways, or up and over one another, or they may even be pushed away from one another.
5. With this sudden movement, a series of violent vibrations occurs that can shake large landmasses for a period of many seconds.
6. The movement may be very slight, but it might set up earthquake vibrations that can destroy a city, as in the 1976 earthquake that killed a half million people and devastated the Chinese city of Tangshan.
7. The point on the Earth's surface above the place where the shifting takes place is called the earthquake's **epicenter.**

B. Sometimes earthquakes occur just below the surface, and sometimes they occur inside the Earth.

1. Most earthquakes occur within 70 kilometers (43 mi) of the Earth's surface as a result of the fracturing and sliding motions of plates.
2. The San Andreas fault in California is long but not deep. Earthquakes caused by it are within the upper 15 kilometers (9 mi) of the Earth's crust.
3. In 1994 a great earthquake rumbled through the Earth's mantle more than 600 kilometers (373 mi) below Bolivia. It was the largest earthquake ever recorded at such depths. The tremors of the Bolivian earthquake were felt as far away as Toronto, Canada. No other earthquake in history is known to have shaken the Earth at such a great distance from its epicenter.
4. Deep-focus earthquakes, those occurring 300 kilometers (186 mi) or more below the Earth's surface, may be caused by a different mechanism than earthquakes that are closer to the surface.

C. Although earthquakes may occur anywhere on Earth, they happen most often along two large areas of the Earth called **earthquake belts.**

1. Earthquake belts usually occur where tall mountain ranges are near deep ocean floors. These are zones where oceanic plates are subducting under continental plates.

2. The earthquake belts coincide with the edges of tectonic plates. The largest earthquake belt circles the Pacific Ocean, from Chile northward to Peru, Central America, Mexico, California, Puget Sound, the Aleutian Islands, and Japan, and southward to the Philippines, Indonesia, and New Zealand. The other large earthquake belt includes the mountainous areas next to the Mediterranean Sea, a section of northern Africa, Asia Minor, and southern Asia.

D. Earthquakes that begin under the ocean set up huge seismic sea waves, called a **tsunami**, sometimes mistakenly called "tidal waves." (See also Chapter 11.) Tsunamis can be more than 160 kilometers (100 mi) long, travel at speeds of up to 800 kilometers (500 mi) an hour, and travel through the entire depth of the ocean. Although barely detectable in the open ocean, as they reach the shallow shorelines they can build to 30 meters (100 ft) high.

E. An instrument called a **seismograph** detects earthquakes.
   1. Slippage along a fault that produces an earthquake, radiates vibrations or waves (called seismic waves) that travel through the Earth's crust.
   2. The seismograph detects and records these waves, and from the data it collects scientists can tell where an earthquake occurred and how strong it was.

F. The most widely recognized measure of the strength of an earthquake at its source is the scale of magnitudes developed in 1935 by Charles F. Richter and Beno Gutenberg, the **Richter scale.**
   1. Although the Richter scale has no limits, it is usually thought of in terms of numbers 1 to 10, each higher number representing an earthquake 10 times stronger than that of the preceding number. For example, an earthquake of magnitude 7 is 10 times stronger than one of magnitude 6.
   2. An earthquake registering 2 on the Richter scale is just strong enough to be felt. An earthquake with a rating of 5 can cause considerable damage; an earthquake with a rating of 7 or higher is a major earthquake. The 1906 San Francisco earthquake was a 7.7 quake.
   3. The smallest quakes recorded using the Richter scale have been at about minus 2. The largest have been between 8 and 9. A 1960 earthquake in Chile registered 9.5 on the Richter scale, the highest ever recorded. An earthquake with an 8 or 9 rating occurs somewhere on Earth about every 5 years.

G. Several other magnitude scales are also in use. One of the most recent measures of strength of an earthquake is a measure of the quake's **seismic moment**, rather than its seismic magnitude.
   1. Seismic moment is a measurement of the seismic energy emitted from the entire fault rather than from its epicenter.
   2. Using a scale based on a quake's seismic energy, rather than its strength at its epicenter, is thought to be a more useful and fundamental measure of the strength of an earthquake.

H. Many scientists are studying ways to reduce the hazards of earthquakes by learning how to predict their consequences.
   1. Equally important to the ability to predict the time, place, and magnitude of earthquakes is the ability to determine how the ground is likely to vibrate during a quake, how strong the quake will be, and how long it will last.
   2. Knowledge of the ground motion that can be expected during an earthquake makes it possible to design structures that are not unnecessarily strong, and thus uneconomical, but are still able to survive the shaking.
   3. To predict both the occurrence of an earthquake and its consequences, it is essential to understand the characteristics of the earthquake source. That is the direction of the research of many of today's seismologists.

III. Mountains

A. Mountains are great masses of rock pushed high by forces inside the Earth.

B. Mountains are formed in various ways, depending on whether the masses of rock have been folded, tilted, shaped into domes, built up from volcanic activity, or formed when wind and water erode the Earth material around a great mass of rock.

C. **Folded mountains** are formed when plates of rock are pushed into a series of wavelike folds by tremendous sideward forces that are produced by great pressure within the Earth.
   1. The **anticlines**, or crests of these waves, become mountain peaks; the **synclines**, or troughs of these waves, become valleys.
   2. Folded rocks can be uplifted many times over a long period, producing an entire region of long ridges that curve back and forth on each other.
   3. Parts of the Appalachian Mountains are folded mountains. The Himalayan range is a folded mountain that is still moving and growing today. Mt. Everest, currently an 8.8 km (29,035 foot) mountain, moves northeast at about 6 centimeters (2.4 inches) a year.

D. **Fault-block mountains** are formed when layers of rock break or crack, producing a fault.
   1. When faulting occurs, the layers of rock on one side of the fault are pushed up higher than are those on the other side.
   2. The layers of rock often tilt to one side after they have been pushed up.
   3. Mountains formed in this way look like huge blocks.

4. The Sierra Nevadas are fault-block mountains.
5. In some areas, block mountains are called **hogbacks**, because one side of the mountain is steep and nearly vertical and the other side has a gentler slope.

E. **Domed mountains** are formed either by folding or by the flow of magma (molten rock) up and between two layers of rock.
1. As the molten rock accumulates, it pushes up the layers of rock above it to form a large dome.
2. The Black Hills of South Dakota and Wyoming, and the Adirondacks of New York are domed mountains.

F. **Volcanic mountains** are formed by the gradual and periodic accumulation of lava and other materials that are thrown up when a volcano erupts. (See also V., Volcanoes.)
1. Mount Lassen, Mount St. Helens, and Mount Ranier in the United States; Mount Popocatepetl in Mexico; Mount Vesuvius in Italy; and Mount Fuji in Japan are volcanic mountains.
2. Occupying an area of 19,000 cubic miles, volcanic mountain Mauna Loa in Hawaii is the most massive mountain in the world. Measured from its base on the seafloor, it rises 56,000 feet, more than 27,000 feet higher than Mount Everest.

G. Mountains are often grouped together to form a mountain range, with a series of peaks of different heights. Ranges that are side by side, or parallel, are referred to as a chain of mountain ranges.

H. Like most systems, mountains have a life history, passing from youth to maturity to old age.
1. During their youth, mountains are still growing. Young mountains, such as the Tetons of Wyoming, are high and rugged, with steep slopes, rushing streams, and narrow valleys. Many young mountains have snow on their tops at all times. Snowslides and avalanches are common. The Rocky Mountains, Andes Mountains, Alps, and Himalaya Mountains are also examples of young mountains.
2. At maturity, the mountains have stopped growing, and the actions of water, ice, wind, and other elements of weather wear away the mountains, gradually lowering their peaks and making their slopes more gentle. Sometimes mature mountains become so much lower that trees grow all the way to their tops. Streams flow more slowly, and the valleys become wider. Examples of mature mountains are the Appalachian Mountains, the Adirondack Mountains, and the White Mountains.
3. At old age, the mountains have been worn down until almost level. The flat surface that is left is called a **peneplane**, which means "almost a level plane." Southern New England and the areas of Manhattan and Westchester County of New York are examples of peneplanes.
4. Sometimes a peneplane has low, rolling hills with an occasional high hill, called a **monadnock**, which is made of hard igneous rock that has resisted wearing, so it remains. Monadnock Mountain in New Hampshire and Pikes Peak in Colorado are monadnocks. Rivers of old mountain areas have low banks and move very slowly.
5. When mountains have passed through their life history and have been worn away, the process of mountain building will eventually begin again.

IV. Plains and Plateaus

A. Plains and plateaus are different from mountains, because they are made of rock layers that are in the very same horizontal position in which the layers originally formed.

B. Plains are low-level flat surfaces, and plateaus are high-level flat surfaces, as compared with the land around them.
1. **Coastal plains** are made of pieces of rock that either were worn away from rocks along the seashore by ocean waves, or were carried by rivers to the ocean. The wave motion of the ocean spread out the pieces of rock until a smooth, flat surface formed. Some coastal plains are very narrow, and others are quite broad.
2. A coastal plain extends into the ocean, sometimes for a great distance, forming what is called a **continental shelf.**
3. Sometimes forces inside the Earth will lift up all or part of a continental shelf so that it too becomes a coastal plain.
4. **Interior plains** were formed from large, shallow inland seas. Sediments filled these shallow seas until the water disappeared and flat plains formed. The Great Plains of the interior United States and the Argentine pampas are examples of interior marine plains.
5. **Lake plains** were formed from the bottom of large lakes.
6. Some lake plains formed when forces inside the Earth caused the lake floors to lift, and other lake plains formed when conditions caused all the water in the lakes to drain away.
7. The largest lake plain in North America includes a large part of Minnesota, North Dakota, and the provinces of Saskatchewan and Manitoba in Canada.

C. Most plateaus formed from forces beneath the Earth's surface that raised horizontal layers of rock straight up.
1. Some plateaus formed by lava flowing out of cracks in the Earth, spreading out over large areas, and forming level regions of layers of volcanic rock.
2. Like mountains, plateaus also have a life history, passing from youth to maturity to old age.

3. Young plateaus are very high and flat and have not been worn away much by rivers flowing through them.
4. Mature plateaus are frequently called mountains, even though they are not truly mountains, because many rivers and streams have cut wide valleys through their broad surfaces, giving the effect of a series of mountains.
5. The tops of these mountain-like plateaus are usually flat; the Catskill Mountains are an example of a mature plateau.
6. At old age, plateaus are worn almost level, with only a few parts of the original plateau still standing.
7. In dry areas the parts that remain have high walls and flat tops.
8. Large plateaus with broad tops are called **mesas**, and smaller plateaus with tops that are more rounded are called **buttes.**
9. Both mesas and buttes are found in New Mexico, Utah, and Arizona, whereas most of the plateaus in North Dakota, South Dakota, Montana, and Wyoming are buttes.
10. In humid areas, the remaining parts of a plateau are more rounded and look more like hills.

V. Volcanoes

A. A volcano is a mountain, hill, or vent formed around a crack in the Earth's crust, where tectonic plates have pulled apart, and through which molten rock and other hot materials exude.
   1. The rock inside the Earth's mantle is very hot, but it is solid because of the great pressures on it.
   2. When the pressure is reduced, as when a crack or fault forms in the Earth's crust, such as when tectonic plates move apart, the rock becomes liquid, or molten, rock called magma.
   3. The magma flows upward to the Earth's surface, either through a crack or through a weak spot in the Earth's crust.
   4. The initial opening at the top of the volcano is called a **vent**, which later may become a **crater.**
   5. Volcanic activity occurs in the oceans as well as on land. Thousands of active deep-sea vents exist in the Pacific Ocean, such as those off the coasts of Mexico and California, adding new sea floor to the area through the separation of tectonic plates.
   6. A crater is usually rather narrow, but sometimes it blows apart or collapses, forming a wide basinlike hollow, called a **caldera.** A caldera may fill with water and become a lake, such as Crater Lake in Oregon. The volcanoes of Yellowstone National Park are caldera volcanoes.

B. Some volcanoes, like those in Iceland, Yellowstone National Park, and the Pacific Ocean, erupt slowly and quietly, whereas others, like those in the East Indies and the Mediterranean area, erupt violently because of tremendous pressures inside. Some, like Stromboli in Italy, alternate between being quiet and being explosive. Depending on their eruption cycles, individual volcanoes are considered to be active, dormant, or extinct.
   1. Active volcanoes are erupting or have recently erupted.
   2. Dormant volcanoes have not erupted for some time but show signs of underground activity.
   3. Extinct volcanoes have not erupted for a long time and show no signs of underground activity.

C. When magma reaches the Earth's surface, it is called lava.
   1. Sometimes lava hardens to form a rough, jagged surface. Other times it forms a smooth, ropy surface.
   2. The tiniest drops of lava spray form fine **volcanic dust** that spreads out high into the atmosphere and is distributed in locations far from the volcano.
   3. Larger drops of lava become **volcanic cinders** (coarse) and **volcanic ash** (fine), which fall relatively close to the volcano.
   4. **Obsidian** is a dark glassy rock that forms from lava that cools quickly.
   5. **Pumice** and **scoria** are lightweight rocks, with holes in them, that form from lava that hardens while steam and other gases are still bubbling from it.
   6. **Tuff** is volcanic ash that becomes cemented to form a rock.

D.W. Peterson/U.S. Geological Survey, Denver

A shield volcano.

D. There are three categories or types of volcanoes: shield, cinder cone, and composite.
   1. **Shield volcanoes** are usually formed from quiet or oozing eruptions, from which the lava spreads out to form a broad base with gentle slopes. Two of the world's most active volcanoes, Mauna Loa and Kilauea in Hawaii, are shield volcanoes.
   2. **Cinder cone volcanoes** form from explosive eruptions, which create a fairly narrow base with steep slopes. Paricutin in Mexico is a cinder cone volcano.
   3. The difference between oozing and explosive volcanoes lies in the viscosity and gas content of the magma. Explosive volcanoes hold magma that is thick and sticky, with the gases under great pressure, so the magma explodes rather than oozes when released.
   4. **Composite volcanoes** usually form as a result of alternating explosive and quiet periods, which create alternate layers of lava and cinders or ash. Composite volcanoes have slopes that are steeper than those of shield volcanoes but gentler than those of cinder cone volcanoes. Fujiyama in Japan and Rainier in the United States are composite volcanoes.

E. Most volcanoes on Earth are located in the two earthquake belts.
   1. One belt circles the Pacific Ocean, and the other extends from the Mediterranean area eastward across southern Asia.
   2. In the areas around the Aleutian Islands and in the Pacific Ocean, volcanic mountain chains are being formed on the floor of the ocean.
   3. Most of the islands of the South Pacific are the tops of submerged and extinct volcanoes. The Philippines originated as huge volcanoes built up from the ocean floor. The island of Luzon alone has 13 active volcanoes.
   4. The pattern of volcanoes around the entire rim of the Pacific Ocean is called the **Ring of Fire**, and includes Washington's Mount St. Helens, Alaska's Katmai, Japan's Mount Fuji, and the Philippines' Mount Pinatubo.
   5. Volcanoes are also found in Iceland, the Azores, and some islands in the West Indies.

F. One of the most destructive forms of volcanic activity is the collapse of volcanic cones. The 1980 explosion of Mount St. Helens in Washington is an example.
   1. Earthquake activity often accompanies volcanic eruption; after centuries of sporadic eruptions of the lava and ash that built its cone, Mount St. Helens was jarred by earthquakes caused by magma moving upward. The north flank of its cone collapsed, and volcanic debris was scattered far in all directions.
   2. After an explosion and the eruption of ash, rather than a lava flow, some volcanoes produce what is known as a **pyroclastic flow.** This ground-hugging cloud of superheated gas and rock forces a cushion of air down the mountainside at up to 160 kilometers per hour (100 mph), incinerating anything in its path. Such was the case in the 1980 explosion of Mount St. Helens.

G. The effects of a single volcanic eruption can be felt and seen around the world.
   1. The lighter sulfur dioxides emitted can circle the Earth for years, lowering Earth's surface temperatures and damaging its ozone layer.
   2. Clouds of ash can pose a threat to aircraft, because the small pieces of volcanic glass can be sucked into jet engines, fuse into clumps, and destroy engine thrust.
   3. Volcanic eruptions beneath glaciers can melt the ice and cause flooding.

H. Using satellite imagery and analyzing for the kinds of gases rising from volcanoes, volcanologists are searching for ways of detecting signals of approaching eruptions. Their work is limited by finances available and the fact that there are more than 1,500 active volcanoes around the world.

VI. Hot Springs, Geysers, and Geothermal Energy

A. Hot springs and geysers are common wherever hot rock is present beneath the Earth's surface.

B. The Earth continuously produces heat, primarily by the decay of naturally radioactive chemical elements that occur in small amounts in all rocks.
   1. The annual heat loss from the Earth is enormous—equivalent to 10 times the annual energy consumption of the United States and more than what is needed to power all nations of the world, if it could be fully harnessed.
   2. If only 1% of the thermal energy contained within the uppermost 10 kilometers (62 mi) of the Earth's crust could be harnessed, it could replace 500 times the energy contained in all oil and natural gas resources of the world.
   3. The Earth's natural heat energy is cleaner than coal, oil, and gas, and there is less environmental impact associated with its use.
   4. Scientists and engineers are working on finding ways to utilize more fully the Earth's abundant thermal energy—commonly called **geothermal energy.**

C. **Hot springs** are formed when hot rock and gases beneath the Earth's surface heat the underground water, and the hot water then flows to the surface. Hot springs are common in regions where there is volcanic activity, because the heated rocks are very near the Earth's surface in these areas. In the United States, there are more than 1,000 such springs. About 95% of them are in the West.
   1. The passageway along which the hot water travels is wide and open, so the water reaches the surface quickly and easily.
   2. The water is heated either by contact with the hot, melted rock (magma), or by mixing

with steam and hot gases that are escaping from the magma.

3. The temperature of the water may range from warm to boiling. By definition, the water in hot springs is 6°C to 9°C (10°F to 15°F) warmer than the mean annual air temperature for the geographic region.
4. On its way to the surface, the hot water dissolves large amounts of minerals. Because hot water dissolves minerals better than cold water, most hot springs have a high mineral content.
5. These minerals, deposited around the mouth of the hot spring as the water evaporates, tend to build up colored layers or terraces.

D. A **geyser** is a hot spring that sprays its water into the air at intervals.

1. The eruption of water occurs because the geyser has to travel a narrow, twisted pathway rather than a wide pathway to reach the Earth's surface.
2. Heated water is often trapped in the passageway, where it continues to be heated far above its normal boiling point of 100°C (212°F) without being changed into steam.
3. This occurs because the water on top presses down on the water below, so the water under pressure can be superheated without boiling.
4. The superheated water expands and causes some of the water above it to overflow onto the Earth's surface.
5. The loss of water on top eases the pressure on the superheated water on the bottom. Some of it is suddenly changed to steam, which blows all the water above it high into the air as a geyser.
6. After the geyser erupts, some of the water flows back into the passageway, where it meets more underground water coming up, and the process repeats itself.
7. Some geysers, like Old Faithful in Yellowstone National Park, erupt at nearly regular intervals, whereas others erupt at irregular intervals.
8. Most geysers are found in three places in the world: Yellowstone National Park, Iceland, and New Zealand. However, geysers have also been found bursting through the ocean floor in the Atlantic and Pacific Oceans. While it was active in the early 1900s, the Waimangu Geyser, in New Zealand, was recorded to have spouted water to a height of more than 460 meters (1,500 feet).

E. In 1992, The Geysers, a hydrothermal system in northern California, became the world's largest development that uses geothermal energy to move large turbines to produce electricity.

1. Actually, The Geysers is not a spouting geyser or system of geysers but a field of slow-erupting vents, warm springs, and fumaroles.
2. Pipes set deep into ground wells carry steam to turbine generators that in turn generate electricity.

F. Other places using geothermal energy to create electrical energy are El Salvador, Nicaragua, Costa Rica, and France.

VII. Weathering and Erosion

A. Rocks that make up the Earth's surface are always being broken up by the process known as **weathering.**

1. The actions of the Sun, wind, and water cause weathering.
2. There are two types of weathering: mechanical and chemical.

B. Mechanical or physical weathering is the breakdown of rock into smaller pieces without causing any change in the chemical makeup of the rock.

1. Mechanical weathering can be caused by water seeping into cracks and pores of rocks and then freezing. When the water freezes, it expands, putting pressure on the rock and causing small pieces of rock to break off.
2. Another type of mechanical weathering is caused by water that has seeped into cracks and pores of rock when the temperature remains above freezing. When rocks are heated by sunlight during the day, the minerals in the rocks combine with the water and expand, causing cracks to occur in the rocks. At night the rocks cool and contract, and this eventually causes the outside of the rocks to peel off in thick layers or sheets, a process known as **exfoliation.** Examples are Stone Mountain in Georgia, and Half Dome and Liberty Cap in Yosemite National Park.
3. Plants can also cause mechanical weathering. As shrubs and trees grow, their roots work into small cracks in rock, eventually causing the rock to split or crumble.
4. Animals also play a part in mechanical weathering. Burrowing animals, such as gophers and prairie dogs, dig into the ground and expose rock surfaces to weathering. Earthworms bring fine particles of rock to the surface; they also make tiny passageways in the Earth that let air and water enter the soil and expose the rock surfaces to weathering.
5. Wind carries fine rock particles that, over time, can create friction on rock surfaces and weather them away.

C. Chemical weathering, caused by a chemical change in the rock's composition, is most likely to occur in damp areas.

1. Carbon dioxide in the air can produce chemical weathering. When dissolved in water, carbon dioxide forms carbonic acid, a relatively weak acid that can react with rocks such as limestone, breaking down the rock

LEARNING ACTIVITY 10.7

A Geyser

Put a funnel upside down in a Pyrex beaker and add water until the bowl of the funnel is covered and the water is level with the beginning of the stem (Figure 10.10). Heat the beaker on a hot plate. When the water begins to boil, the bubbles of steam expand and rise, pushing the water up the stem and making it spout like a geyser.

SAFETY NOTE: Use extreme caution for this demonstration.

1. Use extra caution whenever using a hot plate (or any heat source) in the classroom. Protect curious or careless students from touching it.
2. Protect students from possible glass breakage (even when using a Pyrex beaker) and spattering of glass and boiling water by placing the beaker into a baking pan (not shown here) that is in turn placed directly onto the hot plate.
3. If you use a glass funnel (a plastic funnel will work, too), the largest diameter of the funnel should be somewhat less than the diameter of the bottom of the inside of the beaker (as shown in the figure). The funnel should not fit so snugly into the beaker that problems are caused if the glass expands during heating and contracts when cool.
4. As with all demonstrations, practice this one in the absence of children. During the demonstration, the children should be protected from the hot water that spouts and sprays from the end of the funnel.

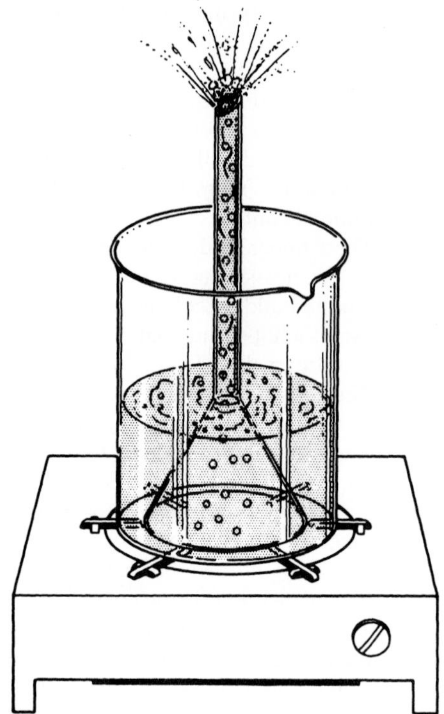

FIGURE 10.10 A funnel geyser.

into materials that easily dissolve and are then carried away by water and wind erosion.

2. Many rocks contain at least one mineral that is affected by carbonic acid. When that mineral is removed, the rest of the rock is exposed, making it easier for other forms of weathering to occur.
3. Oxygen in the air combines directly with many minerals in rocks, forming materials that crumble more easily.
4. Water, either in the air or on the ground, combines with many minerals, causing them to swell and form cracks in rock. This makes it easier for mechanical weathering to continue the process of breaking down the rock.
5. Lichens can grow on rocks, using the minerals of the rocks for their growth. This gives off an acid that causes the rock to break down and release its minerals, thereby causing chemical weathering.
6. When organisms die and decay, acids released in the decay process attack and break down rock material.

D. The process whereby the products of weathering by water, ice, and wind are carried away is called **erosion.**

E. Water is the greatest of all forces that produce erosion.
   1. Each year great quantities of water fall on the Earth's surface.
   2. Some of this water evaporates back into the air, and some seeps into the land and remains as groundwater. The rest flows over the Earth's surface in a huge number of streams and rivers.

F. Running water causes erosion of the Earth's surface.
   1. As rainwater runs off to join streams and rivers, it carries suspended particles of soil, rocks, and minerals with it.
   2. As the water flows in the streams and rivers, it wears away the streambeds and causes the sides to cave, making the streams and rivers wider.
   3. Particles of rock in the water also act as weathering forces to wear away more of the Earth's rock, carrying more suspended material to the lakes and oceans.
   4. Upon coming in contact with ocean salt water, particles that have remained suspended in a river for thousands of miles drop to the bottom immediately, forming sedimentary deposits called **deltas.** Ions in the saltwater

neutralize the electric charge that is responsible for suspending the particles in the fresh water. Upon becoming neutralized, the particles sink.

G. Groundwater causes erosion below the Earth's surface.
   1. Carbon dioxide in the air combines with water to form weak carbonic acid, which attacks limestone and forms materials that dissolve in the water and are eventually carried away.
   2. Where a great amount of limestone is present, large underground caverns and sinkholes may be formed by the action of carbonic acid on limestone.
   3. At times, the underground water, which has limestone dissolved in it, forms solid deposits inside the caves.
   4. The underground water forms these deposits by dripping so slowly through the roof of the cave that some of the water evaporates and the limestone deposits out again. This forms limestone "icicles," called **stalactites**, that hang from the cave ceiling. Columns of limestone, called **stalagmites**, may build upward on the cave floor.
   5. The Carlsbad Caverns in New Mexico and Mammoth Cave in Kentucky are caves with stalactites and stalagmites.

H. Oceans both erode and build up the Earth's surface.
   1. Waves, pounding against rocks and soil along a shore, wear them away and carry off particles of the rock and soil; at Cape Cod, for example, 1 to 2 meters (3 to 6 ft) of shoreline are worn away by the ocean each year.
   2. Current and waves also carry materials such as sand and pebbles to the shore and make beaches. Sometimes, however, storms and strong undercurrents carry beach materials away faster than the waves can deposit them.
   3. Sometimes waves deposit materials just off shore, forming sandbars and sandy islands.

I. **Glaciers** are huge masses of moving ice, formed where climate and weather are cold for much of the year.
   1. In these places, much snow falls each year, more than can melt or evaporate. Some of the snow remains year after year, accumulating layers that pile up into deep masses.
   2. The great weight of the snow presses on the layers beneath, causing these layers of snow to melt and refreeze as ice grains or pellets, called **neve**.
   3. In the deepest layers, the pressure is so great that the neve is recrystallized to form one solid mass of ice.
   4. Each winter more layers are added to the top, forming more ice below.
   5. Eventually the weight of this huge mass of snow and ice becomes so great that the whole mass slowly begins to move downhill because of the force of Earth's gravity.
   6. **Valley glaciers** are those that are formed in mountain valleys.
   7. Some valley glaciers are small, and others are quite large.
   8. As the valley glacier begins to move to lower levels, it gouges out the rock beneath it and carries the broken pieces along with it.
   9. As it moves forward, it picks up more rock that it wears away from the sides of the valley.
   10. These rocks, embedded in the ice, act as a huge file to wear away the Earth over which the glacier moves.
   11. This movement of the valley glacier tends to smooth out the valley floor. At the same time, the glacier grinds away the valley walls and straightens sharp bends, changing the V-shape of the valley to a broader U-shape.
   12. As the glacier moves, big cracks, called **crevasses**, form at the top and sides of the glacier.
   13. When the glacier meets warmer temperatures, it begins to melt and to drop the material it has been carrying or pushing along in front. The material that it drops is called **moraine.**
   14. **Continental glaciers** are found today only in the Earth's polar regions.
   15. In the polar regions, the average temperature is below freezing. Most of the snow that falls remains from year to year, although the South Pole gets less than 6 inches of new snow each year.
   16. The coldest temperature ever recorded on Earth was –288°C (–486°F), recorded in 1960 in Antarctica.
   17. The continental glacier at the North Pole, which also covers most of Greenland, is more than 2,440 meters (8,000 ft) thick. The glacier that covers the South Pole is more than 4,270 meters (14,000 ft) thick, deep enough to fit 14 Empire State Buildings on top of each other.
   18. These continental glaciers, covering Greenland and Antarctica, move outward toward the sea where the rise and fall of the ocean tides eventually snap off large pieces of the glaciers, which float off as **icebergs.**
   19. Continental glaciers smooth the surfaces over which they pass by grinding down the higher elevations and filling in the valleys.
   20. Where parts of the Earth's surface are softer, a glacier may gouge out huge depressions or basins.
   21. When the climate becomes warmer and the glacier retreats, these basins remain, filled with melted ice, as lakes. In summer, the continent of Antarctica is only half the size it is in winter when its ice pack includes more of the frozen surrounding sea.

J. The Earth has gone through four **glacial periods**, in which large parts of the Earth were covered by glaciers.
   1. These glacial periods followed a cycle.
   2. First the Earth's climate became colder and huge glaciers formed at the poles. The growing glaciers moved out from the poles in all directions to cover large parts of the Earth.
   3. Then the climate warmed, and the glaciers melted and retreated back toward the poles.
   4. The retreating glaciers left behind the moraines they brought, and also the grinding changes they made to the Earth's surface.
   5. The first glacial period occurred about 800 mya followed by a warm period of about 3 million years. The second period came about 500 mya, followed by a warm period of about 300 million years. The third period came about 200 mya, and the fourth period about 1 mya.
   6. The last major phase of glaciation ended about 10,000 years ago.
   7. At its height 20,000 years ago, ice sheets a mile thick covered much of northern Europe and North America.
   8. Enough ice was formed on land to cause sea levels to drop to more than 100 meters (nearly 330 ft) below where they are today.
   9. Evidence indicates that at present the Earth is in a period of glacial retreat.

K. The chief work of wind is to carry away loose bits of soil and rock.
   1. This erosion by wind is quite common in dry areas where there are few plants, shrubs, or trees to cover the ground and protect it.
   2. Even mild winds move fine particles of dust and rock, but strong winds create tremendous dust storms.
   3. Over a long time, wind can blow away all loose material from a desert floor, leaving behind only a floor of bare rock.
   4. Wind also deposits material. Hills of sand, called **dunes**, are wind deposits that are formed when there is something in the way of the wind, slowing it down and causing it to deposit the particles.
   5. As a mound of sand grows, it helps to slow the wind even more, allowing even more material to be deposited and the dune to grow even larger.
   6. Winds often move sand dunes from one place to another, unless grass and shrubs cover the sand sufficiently to hold it in place or fences are erected, which is often done to prevent dunes from covering highways, railroads, airplane runways, or even buildings.
   7. Another type of wind deposit is fine sediment called **loess**, which is composed of particles of earth. It is deposited over large areas of land and can become very thick. When water is available, loess makes very fertile soil.

L. Besides being an erosion agent, wind is also a weathering agent.
   1. As wind blows against solid rock, the particles of rock carried by the wind rub against the solid rock; this causes friction that wears the rock away.
   2. Beach cliffs and rocks are often made smooth in this way, as are desert rocks and boulders.

M. While the forces of weathering and erosion are constantly at work on the Earth's surface, as discussed earlier in this chapter, the forces inside the Earth continuously rebuild the surface.

Soil

I. The Formation of Soil

A. Although forces of mechanical and chemical weathering act on rock very slowly, over millions of years these forces have broken up almost all the rock on or near the Earth's surface.
   1. This is why the Earth's surface has a layer of pieces of rock on it.
   2. These pieces are of all sizes, ranging from microscopic pieces to massive boulders. This layer is called **mantle rock.**

B. The forces of weathering continue to act on the mantle rock until a layer of soil is formed.
   1. Soil is made of tiny grains of rock and minerals.
   2. Soil that has not moved from the original mantle rock from which it was formed is called **residual soil.**
   3. Soil that has been carried by erosion from one place to another is called **transported soil.**

C. Soil becomes fertile—that is, things will grow in it—when **humus** is added to it. Humus is the remains of dead organisms.

II. Types of Soil

A. Because humus is added only to the top portion of soil, there is a difference in the quality of soil layers. Soil scientists call the layers **horizons.** Five are identified. From the surface down, they are designated as O, A, E, B, and C.
   1. The **O horizon** consists mostly of loose and partly decayed organic material called **humus,** unlike the layers beneath it that consist mainly of mineral (inorganic) matter.

2. In addition to decaying plant material, the O horizon is rich in living organisms, including bacteria, fungi, algae, and insects, which contribute oxygen, carbon dioxide, and organic material to the soil.
3. Beneath the O horizon is the **A horizon**, a layer made up largely of mineral matter but still biologically active with some humus.
4. Together the O horizon and the A horizon make up what is called **topsoil**, which typically is about the first 20 centimeters (8 in.) of soil.
5. Topsoil has spaces filled with air or water or both.
6. It takes about 500 years for the Earth's weathering and erosion process to make 2.5 centimeters (1 in.) of topsoil.
7. Beneath the A horizon is the light-colored **E horizon**, which is mostly sand and silt.
8. Beneath the E horizon is the subsoil or **B horizon**. It is made mostly of minerals and clay and has little or no humus.
9. The O, A, E, and B horizons constitute the **solum**, or "true soil."
10. Beneath the B horizon is partially weathered bedrock (**C horizon**), then solid bedrock (sometimes referred to as the **R horizon**).

B. Soil scientists use vertical sections or **profiles** of soil to study it.
1. A soil profile shows each layer or horizon of the sample.
2. Soils can be classified according to the appearance and contents of the profile.

C. There are hundreds of soil types, with the characteristics of each type primarily reflecting climatic conditions. Three very general categories for classifying soils are pedalfers, pedocals, and laterites.
1. The term **pedalfer** is derived from *ped*, from the Greek word for soil, and the chemical symbols Al (aluminum) and Fe (iron).
2. Pedalfer soils are found where the annual rainfall is at least 63 centimeters (25 in.).
3. Because of the heavy rainfall, most of the soluble materials are leached from the topsoil, leaving it sandy, light-colored, and acid.
4. The iron oxides and aluminum-rich clays leached from the topsoil end up in the B horizon, giving that layer a brown to red-brown color.
5. Pedalfer soils are formed under forest vegetation. In the United States, pedalfers are found east of a line extending from northwestern Minnesota to south central Texas.
6. The term **pedocal** is derived from *ped*, the Greek word for soil, and the first three letters of *calcite* (calcium carbonate).
7. Pedocal soils are found where the annual rainfall is less than 63 centimeters (25 in.).
8. Pedocals are characterized by an accumulation of calcium carbonate, giving the soil a whitish color.
9. Vegetation is usually grass and brush.
10. Pedocal soils are typical of western United States.
11. **Laterite** soils develop in hot, wet tropical climates such as Hawaii and Puerto Rico.
12. Because of the heavy rainfall, there is considerable leaching of the layers, leaving a concentration of oxides of iron and aluminum, making the soil a brick red color.
13. Grass and trees are the typical vegetation of laterite soils.
14. Because of heavy bacterial activity in the tropics, laterite soils contain practically no humus, making laterites very poor for growing crops unless lime and fertilizers are added.

D. Soil contains different sizes and kinds of rocks and minerals, which include large pebbles or gravel, smaller particles of sand, tiny particles of clay, and sometimes particles of silt (which are smaller than grains of sand but larger than clay particles). Depending on the sizes and kinds of rocks and minerals, soil is also characterized as being sandy, clay, or loam.
1. **Sandy soil** is made mostly of sand, together with a little clay, but almost no humus. Sandy soil does not hold water well and contains very few minerals that plants can use to grow.
2. **Clay soil** contains mostly clay, with a little sand and a little humus. Clay soil holds water well, but becomes sticky when wet, almost as

LEARNING ACTIVITY 10.8

Examining a Soil Profile

Using sections of PVC pipe approximately 2.5 centimeters (1 in.) in diameter and 25 centimeters (10 in.) long, collect soil profile samples from a variety of places. Bring them to class, carefully remove them from the pipe sections, and have students in groups carefully and methodically investigate the profiles and their contents. Investigating their samples, students could chart their results and share the information with others. On the basis of information they obtain, ask students to predict where (for example, woods, prairie, wetland, yard, desert) each sample was obtained.

LEARNING ACTIVITY 10.9

Composition of Soil

Obtain a tall cylindrical jar, and fill half of it with garden soil. Add water until the jar is almost full and screw the cap on tightly. Shake the jar vigorously for a minute and then set it down. The soil will begin to settle in layers. The fine gravel sinks to the bottom immediately, followed by sand, and then by clay and silt. Particles of humus may float on top of the water. The muddy water may take days to become clear, because it takes time for the very fine particles of silt and clay to settle.

hard as rock when dry. A mixture of clay, sand, and water was used by the Romans to build dams.

3. **Loam soil** is a mixture of gravel, sand, clay, and humus, is dark in color, and is the best soil for most crops.
4. For growing crops, soil is *cultivated;* that is, the large clumps are broken up and the earth around the plant roots is loosened so the roots can grow and more easily obtain air and water.

III. Soil Erosion, the Loss of Fertile Topsoil

A. In areas of the Earth untroubled by humans, loss of fertile topsoil by erosion is a slow and natural process; it is part of the constant recycling of Earth materials that we call the *rock cycle.*
   1. Shrubs and trees above the ground level and roots below ground level help prevent soil from being washed away by water and wind.
   2. What little soil is lost is replaced by new soil formed over the years in the natural weathering processes.

B. When humans use soil to grow crops, erosion can occur very quickly, especially if the shrubs and trees that prevent soil loss have been removed.
   1. In many regions of the world, the rate of soil erosion is greater than the rate of soil formation.

C. The most powerful force causing soil erosion is the force of running water.
   1. Raindrops hit the soil and loosen it, causing it to be splashed away; this type of erosion is called **splash erosion.**
   2. When rain falls steadily, soil absorbs water until it is saturated and cannot hold any more; then the water runs off in broad sheets, carrying soil away with it, causing a type of erosion called **sheet erosion.**
   3. Sheet erosion can remove all the topsoil, leaving behind only the subsoil or even bare bedrock.
   4. As water runs off the soil, it eventually collects into small streams that flow to lower ground.
   5. As a stream flows, it may wash out some of the ground and form a small channel, called a **rille.**
   6. A rille is often formed when crops have been planted in rows that run up and down a sloping field.
   7. A rille can become deeper and wider with each rainfall, as the running water carries more soil away each time, eventually forming a larger channel, called a **gully.**
   8. This type of erosion is called gill or gully erosion.
   9. The small streams flow into larger streams, each taking away soil from the bottom and sides of the streambed.

IV. Preventing Soil Erosion

A. Farmers use **contour plowing** and planting on sloping land to slow the erosion of topsoil.
   1. This form of cultivation means that on hills the rows run sideways rather than up and down, thereby slowing soil runoff caused by rain.

B. Farmers use **terrace plowing** and planting when slopes are steep.
   1. The terraces follow the contours of the hill and run sideways, as in contour cultivation.

C. **Alternate strip cropping** is used on gentle slopes.
   1. In strip cropping, different crops are grown on the same piece of land, in alternating plots.
   2. One plot may contain row crops such as corn, and the adjacent plot may contain a ground-covering plant such as alfalfa or hay.
   3. The covering crops catch and prevent soil from being washed away.
   4. The following year the same crops are planted, but in opposite plots from the prior year; the covering crop is grown where the row crop was grown before, and vice versa.

D. Bare land, unsuitable for growing crops, is planted with trees and grass to help replenish lost soil.

E. In open land, or land bordering crop fields, trees can be planted in rows to provide a shelterbelt to slow erosion caused by wind.

F. Construction of catchment ponds to deter loss of soil into streams, maintenance of vegetation on agricultural lands and stream banks, and revegetation of construction and mining sites can also decrease the loss of fertile soils through erosion.

V. Enriching the Soil

A. There are many minerals in soil that plants need to grow and to make food through photosynthesis.

1. The most important of the needed minerals are those that contain nitrogen, phosphorus, potassium, calcium, and magnesium.
2. Plants remove large amounts of these minerals from soil, and the minerals must be replaced if the soil is to remain fertile.
3. One way to replace minerals is by using natural fertilizer, such as animal manure, which adds both minerals and humus to the soil.
4. Another way is to use commercial fertilizers that contain minerals in various quantities, depending on which minerals have been most depleted.
5. Yet another way is to rotate the kind of crop grown in a field from one year to the next. For example, if a field becomes low in nitrogen because it has been used to grow corn (which uses a lot of nitrogen), it might be planted next with a plant that helps return nitrogen to the soil, such as clover, alfalfa, beans, or peas.
   a. These plants have nodules on their roots—tiny but visible bumps where **nitrogen-fixing bacteria** live.
   b. Although 78% of air is nitrogen, crop plants cannot use this nitrogen in its gaseous state as found in the atmosphere. Nitrogen-fixing bacteria, however, can use this nitrogen, and they convert it to a form of nitrogen in the soil that crop plants can use.
   c. Soil can be tested to see how it can be improved to grow better crops. It can be tested for moisture content and its ability to retain water, for mineral content, to determine whether it is too acid or too alkaline, and for its humus content.

Geologic History of the Earth

I. **How Scientists Learn About the Earth's History**

A. The history of the Earth is recorded in the rocks.
   1. From Earth's rocks, we can learn about changes that have occurred in the Earth's surface, we can find evidence of changes in the Earth's climate, and we can find evidence of organisms of long ago.

B. **Stratigraphy** is the study of rock layers.
   1. The order in which rocks are layered is an important clue to the Earth's history.
   2. Layers are usually formed horizontally, with the oldest rock strata on the bottom and the youngest on top.
   3. Even when folding, faulting, and metamorphosis have changed rock formations, scientists can still identify them.
   4. Rock layers reveal data about the locations of earlier oceans, mountains, plains, and plateaus.

C. **Petrology** is the study of rocks themselves.
   1. Petrologists study rocks to learn how they were formed, what changes occurred, and what kinds of minerals they contain.
   2. Every rock tells a story through its structure, texture, and physical and chemical makeup, and through the traces of former life embedded in it.
   3. A piece of old sandstone may have ripple or wave marks, or it may contain seashells, indicating that the sandstone was formed in the ocean.
   4. A conglomerate rock may show evidence that it was made by a swiftly moving stream or by heavy ocean waves.
   5. The sediments left behind can reveal the earlier existence of shallow seas, lakes, deserts, glaciers, and other forms of the Earth's surface.
   6. Sediments can also reveal what kinds of rocks there were, the climate at the time, and other conditions on Earth a long time ago.

D. **Paleontology** is the study of fossils, the remains or traces in rock of early life forms.
   1. The remains may be skeletons, or they may be complete organisms.
   2. The traces may be footprints or body and tail marks.
   3. Fossils are rarely found in igneous rock.
   4. Fossils can be found in sedimentary rock that was changed to metamorphic rock, but most fossils were destroyed or damaged when the sedimentary rock changed.
   5. From sedimentary rock, scientists can learn many things about organisms of long ago, such as their development, body structure, habits, and the climate in which they lived.
   6. Fossils are formed in many different ways. Some were formed when life remains were covered by sediment. Animals that lived in or near bodies of water were sometimes buried by the mud, dirt, and gravel; then the sediment hardened into rock and the hard parts of the animals' bodies were preserved in their original form.
   7. Some animals fell into tar pits, swamps, or quicksand, which later hardened, preserving their bones and teeth.
   8. Some fossils were formed when animals were frozen in ice or mud and were preserved whole.
   9. Some insects became fossils when trapped by the sticky sap of trees, which then hardened. Then, later, oceans and their sediments covered the remains of the trees, changing the sap to a material called **amber**. While the insects dried inside the

amber, their bristles, wing scales, and thin exoskeletons were preserved.

10. Some organisms formed fossils by leaving behind a cast of their remains. When organisms were covered by sediment, water of the sediment dissolved the organisms' hard parts, leaving behind a hollow space that filled with minerals from the water, which hardened, forming a cast of the original organism.
11. Many organisms were preserved in great detail as fossils when they were petrified, or "turned into stone." This does not mean that the original material of the organism was really changed into stone. Rather, when the organism died and was buried by sediment, its body was replaced, particle by particle, with minerals, sometimes with such perfection that exceptionally clear and complete fossil specimens have been found.
12. Animals without hard parts, such as jellyfish and worms, and plants without woody parts often left fossil prints. When these soft living creatures were covered with sediment and the sediment hardened into rock, their parts were chemically changed into carbon, forming a detailed outline of the original organisms. Even the delicate outlines of fish scales and leaf veins can often be seen in these prints.
13. Fossils of footprints, outlines of body and tail marks, vein patterns of leaves, and imprints of stems and flowers have been found. These marks were first made in soft mud, and then soil or silt may have been blown or washed into the print. More layers of sediment were added, and eventually the sediment hardened into rock, preserving the marks and imprints in the original mud.
14. Fossils are often found in coal, especially soft coal. Coal itself is the fossil remains of plants that lived long ago in swampy land. The organisms were buried under layers of sediment and then, under heat and pressure, were changed and hardened into coal, with some of the original plant material found as fossils in the coal.

II. Using Radioactivity to Calculate the Age of the Earth

A. Dating rocks using **radioactive clocks** allows scientists to study the most ancient rocks, those without fossil evidence.
   1. The hands of a radioactive clock are **radioactive isotopes**, unstable atoms that become other elements as they decay (see Chapter 16, including Figure 16.2).
   2. Geologic time is measured by the rate of decay of one isotope into another.

B. One technique involves the study of uranium found in igneous and metamorphic rocks.
   1. Uranium is a radioactive element that slowly decays to form radium, which in turn breaks down into a number of other elements and finally becomes lead.
   2. Because uranium breaks down at a slow and steady rate, which is not altered by changes in temperature or pressure, it provides a reliable clock.
   3. It takes 4.5 billion years for half of the atoms of a piece of uranium to become lead. This is termed the **half-life**, the time it takes for one-half of the atoms of the element to break down into the simpler element.
   4. By examining a piece of rock that contains uranium and comparing the amount of uranium still present with the amount of lead that has formed from the uranium, scientists can calculate the age of the rock, and even the Earth, with considerable accuracy.
   5. By using this method, scientists estimate that the Earth is approximately 4.6 billion years old.

C. Another method involves the study of radioactive carbon-14, which is found in sedimentary rocks.
   1. All living things contain carbon-14, but when an organism dies, no more carbon-14 is produced; instead, the carbon-14 begins to break down at a slow and steady rate, just as uranium does.
   2. The half-life of carbon-14 is 5,700 years. The carbon-14 method is used to date the time of death of things that were once living. The actual method compares carbon-14 activity of the fossil with the carbon-14 activity of present day organisms to extrapolate back to the time of death.

D. The carbon-14 method is used to find the age of rocks up to 15,000 years old, and the uranium method is used to find the age of rocks that are older.

III. The Geologic Timetable and Life on Earth

A. Because the history of the Earth involves such a long time, when studying it, scientists refer to a geologic timetable.

B. The longest division of time in the timetable is an **eon**. The timetable is divided into three eons.
   1. The **Archean eon** and the **Proterozoic eon** are sometimes referred to as **Precambrian**, the time from the Earth's formation 4.6 bya until about 540 mya. Precambrian time, representing about four-fifths of the Earth's history, is the time of the Earth before complex life forms existed on it.
   2. The third eon is the **Phanerozoic.**

C. Each eon is divided into smaller units of time called **eras**. The earliest era is the **Azoic**. The most recent is the **Cenozoic.**
   1. Specific geologic changes took place on Earth during each era.
   2. New mountain ranges formed, shapes of continents changed, and shallow seas within the continents were either formed or drained.

3. Changes occurred in the atmosphere and in the oceans' circulations.
4. These changes brought about changes in climate, which in turn caused changes in the forms of life on Earth.
5. Some forms of life disappeared, and new forms developed that were better adapted to the new climate.
6. Each era usually had its distinctive kinds of organisms.

D. Each era is subdivided into units called **periods.** Periods are further divided into units of time called **epochs.** There were geologic changes characteristic of periods and of epochs, but these changes were not as great as those of eras.

IV. The Archean Eon

A. Beginning with the formation of the Earth about 4.6 bya, the Archean eon lasted until 2 bya.

B. At the end of the Archean eon, there was nothing on Earth but rocks, water, and air.

C. The **Azoic** era is the only era attributed to this eon. The word *azoic* means "without life."

V. The Proterozoic Eon

A. Lasting from about 2.5 bya until 570 mya, the **Proterozoic eon** is divided into two eras, the Archeozoic and the Proterozoic.

B. Lasting for 1 billion years, the **Archeozoic era** began about 2.5 bya.
1. During the Archeozoic era, there was much volcanic activity. Great mountain ranges formed, and the oceans alternated between covering the land areas and withdrawing.
2. Some Archeozoic rocks contain much graphite, a pure form of carbon.
3. Simple life forms may have existed, such as bacteria and algae.
4. Around 1.1 bya the earliest supercontinent, Rodinia, formed, linking nearly all of Earth's surfaces. About 350 million years later, Rodinia broke apart leaving ocean basins between landmasses.

C. The **Proterozoic era** began about 1 bya and lasted for approximately 450 million years.
1. During the Proterozoic era, the basic shapes of the Earth's continents as we know them to be today developed, vast masses of igneous rock formed, and glaciers may have been present.
2. Most life forms of this era were marine; that is, they lived in the oceans.
3. It was during this era that **invertebrates** (animals without backbones) first appeared. These organisms included the sponges, jellyfish, coral, and wormlike animals, and the more complex invertebrates, such as crabs, spiders, and insects.
4. Nonanimal life of this era was limited to the simplest forms of **protists**, including protozoa, bacteria, and algae.
5. The photosynthetic activity of algae was gradually increasing the amount of oxygen in the atmosphere.

VI. The Phanerozoic Eon

A. Starting about 570 mya, the Phanerozoic eon continues today. The Phanerozoic eon is divided into three eras—the Paleozoic, the Mesozoic, and the Cenozoic.

B. Beginning about 540 mya, the **Paleozoic era** lasted for about 330 million years.
1. Many geological developments occurred during this era, especially the movement and merging of great land masses, the continents.
2. The Paleozoic era was the age of the invertebrates, fishes, and amphibians.
3. It is divided into six periods—the Cambrian, Ordovician, Silurian, Devonian, Carboniferous, and Permian.

C. The **Cambrian period** lasted for about 70 million years.
1. Shallow seas covered large parts of the North American continent, and the Earth's climate was warm and wet.
2. Prevalent forms of life were blue-green bacteria, jellyfish, and **trilobites.**
3. An early ancestor of modern crabs and lobsters, the trilobite had a shell that was divided lengthwise in three clearly notched sections.
4. Trilobites had jointed legs that were used for walking on the ocean floor; some had eyes and feelers that helped them to find food, which was probably small organisms and decaying plants and animals.
5. Although some trilobites were more than 60 centimeters (2 ft) long and weighed as much as 7 kilograms (15 lb), most were less than 7.5 centimeters (3 in.) long.
6. By the end of the Paleozoic era, trilobites were extinct.

D. About 500 mya, the second period of the Paleozoic era, the **Ordovician period,** began and lasted about 65 million years.
1. During the Ordovician period, the continents of North America and Europe moved toward each other. The Appalachian Mountains resulted from that movement.
2. During the Ordovician, a great mass of ice covered South America, South Africa, India, and Australia.
3. Algae and invertebrate life flourished.

E. About 435 mya, the third period of the Paleozoic era, the **Silurian period,** began and lasted about 25 million years.
1. During this time, the continents of Europe and North America were one.
2. The Earth's climate was warm.
3. The first land plants appeared during this period, first beside oceans and lakes and then further inland. These earliest land plants were mosses, ferns, and early seed

plants. Some fernlike trees grew to heights of up to 12 meters (40 ft).
4. The first fish with jaws appeared. They included armored fish, the ancestors of modern-day sharks, and fish with lungs called lungfish.

F. About 410 mya, the fourth period of the Paleozoic era, the **Devonian period**, began and lasted for about 50 million years.
1. During the Devonian, the Earth had three large continents, called Euramerica, Asia, and Gondwana.
2. Earth's climate continued to be warm and dry. Forests appeared, and with the appearance of large plants on land, animals also began to live on land. These earliest land animals included amphibians and insects.

G. About 360 mya, the fifth period of the Paleozoic era, the **Carboniferous period**, began and lasted for about 70 million years.
1. During this period, the North American and African continents collided.
2. Swampy forests of giant mosses and ferns were abundant. Much of today's coal was formed during this period. Land in some of the forested areas sank slowly and gradually. Huge piles of dead plants accumulated.
3. The piles of plants were slowly covered by water, which helped to preserve them. The land areas continued to sink until they were far below sea level and eventually were covered by thick layers of sediment.
4. The weight of these layers produced much pressure and heat, which caused the plant material to change into coal.
5. The coal was soft coal, but because of the continued heat and pressure caused by the forces inside the Earth, some of it later became hard coal.
6. Insects and amphibians flourished during the Carboniferous period, and the first reptiles appeared.

H. About 280 mya, the sixth and final period of the Paleozoic era, the **Permian period**, began and lasted for about 50 million years.
1. During this period, continents had merged. There was now a new supercontinent, called **Pangaea.**
2. The climate was variable.
3. Many invertebrates became extinct, while reptiles flourished.
4. Mammal-like reptiles, which had teeth and skulls similar to those of today's mammals, were probably the ancestors of mammals that appeared later.
5. Seed plants appeared during this final period of the Paleozoic era.
6. Scientific evidence indicates that about 250 mya, the end of the Permian was marked by massive extinction of both flora and fauna, possibly caused or accelerated by an asteroid or comet that fell to Earth.

I. The second era of the Phanerozoic eon, the **Mesozoic era**, began about 180 mya and lasted about 140 million years.
1. During the Mesozoic, the Pangaea supercontinent broke into two major landmasses, Gondwana in the south and Laurasia in the north. Later splits separated North America from Europe, Africa from South America, and Antarctica and Australia from India.
2. The Mesozoic era, often called the **Age of Reptiles**, is divided into three periods: the Triassic, the Jurassic, and the Cretaceous.
3. During the **Triassic period**, dinosaurs and mammals first appeared.
4. The Triassic period lasted about 35 million years, during which the Pangaea supercontinent broke apart and the Atlantic Ocean formed.
5. Birds first appeared during the Triassic period, a time when dinosaurs were the dominant animals.

J. During the **Jurassic period**, lasting about 65 million years, dinosaurs and birds flourished.
1. One predator of dinosaurs during this period was a huge crocodile, *Sarcosuchus imperator.* The adult was longer than a school bus and weighed about 10 tons, with a jaw approximately 6 feet in length.

K. The **Cretaceous period** lasted about 138 million years, ending about 63 mya.
1. During the Cretaceous period the first snakes, marsupials, and flowering plants appeared.
2. Toward the end of the Cretaceous period, dinosaurs became extinct.
3. Several theories have been proposed to explain the rather sudden extinction of dinosaurs. The widely accepted theory today is that an asteroid crashed into the Earth on the Yucatan Peninsula (Mexico), causing cataclysmic damage, including the extinction of dinosaurs and many other species of flora and fauna. Another theory is that dinosaurs and many other organisms could not survive in the cold climate that occurred at the end of this era. Still another theory is that the dinosaurs and other animals succumbed to a global virus. Perhaps all of these theories played a role in two or more of the mass extinctions that have occurred throughout the history of life on Earth.

VII. The Mesozoic Era: The Age of Reptiles

A. Many land and water changes occurred during the Mesozoic era.
1. The shape of North America became much as we know it today. For the most part, the land was high and dry.
2. The Palisades Mountains were formed along the Hudson River but have been worn down over the many years since then.

Max Alexander © Dorling Kindersley
Interesting rock formations resulting from weathering.

3. The Sierra Nevada, the Rocky Mountains in North America, and the Andes Mountains in South America were formed during this era.
4. The Appalachian Mountains, an older mountain range that had formed millions of years earlier, during the Paleozoic era, were wearing down to a fairly level peneplane. Toward the end of the Mesozoic, they again were lifted by activity in the Earth, although not to their earlier height.

B. Marked changes in plants occurred during the Mesozoic era.
   1. Initially, in this era, land was covered with cycads, palmlike seed plants that produced flower-like structures, although not true flowers.
   2. Conifer trees were common in this era, including pine, cedar, spruce, juniper, and cypress.
   3. Also common were ginkgo trees, which have seeds but no flowers.
   4. During the Mesozoic, the giant mosses and ferns became extinct and were replaced by flowering plants, including oak, elm, maple, birch, and beech trees.
   5. Grasses and grain plants also made their appearance during the Mesozoic.

C. During the Mesozoic, reptiles flourished and became highly specialized. The best known of these were the huge **dinosaurs**, meaning "terrible lizards."
   1. They left behind many fossilized bones, teeth, and feces, which is why we have been able to learn so much about them.
   2. Approximately half of the 350 known dinosaur species have been identified only since 1970.

D. Over a period of 165 million years, many kinds of reptiles developed. They lived on land, in oceans, swamps, and in the air. Some were very large, and others were quite small. Some ate only plants (herbivorous), and others were meat eaters (carnivorous).
   1. **Eoraptor** is the oldest and one of the smallest known dinosaurs. It dates back to the beginning of the dinosaur age, about 225 mya. It grew to about 40 inches and 25 pounds, walked on two legs, and was a predator. Its remains have been found at the foot of the Andes in northwestern Argentina.
   2. **Plateosaurus** is the earliest known large dinosaur, measuring up to 8 meters (26 ft) from head to tail. It had a long neck and a long tail and browsed either on all fours or on hind legs. It lived in Europe and Greenland.
   3. **Baronyx** was a large swamp-dwelling, fish-eating dinosaur that could rear up on its hind legs and use its front, curved, 12-inch claws as hands, perhaps for grabbing fish. It had a long neck and a head that resembled a crocodile's head. Its standing height was 4.6 meters (15 ft). Its length was 9 meters (30 ft), and it weighed approximately 2 tons. It lived in England about 120 mya.
   4. **Apatosaurus** (formerly called **Brontosaurus**) was about 20 meters (65 ft) long and weighed about 27,000 kilograms (30 tons). It had a long, thin neck and a tiny head. Its legs were the size of thick tree trunks, and it had a very long tail and a very small brain. It walked on all four feet and was amphibious, living both on land and in water, where it fed on plants. It lived in western North America.
   5. **Diplodocus** resembled Apatosaurus but was longer. Its length was about 27 meters (88 ft), and it weighed about 88,000 kilograms (88 tons). It lived in western North America.
   6. **Stegosaurus** had a double row of triangular bony plates that ran from its small head almost to the end of its tail. The bony plates may have helped regulate body temperature. Its length was about 8 meters (25 ft). Near the end of its tail were two pairs of large, sharp, bony spikes. It had a heavy body with short, thick front legs. It was herbivorous and lived in western North America.

7. **Allosaurus** was a large predator with sharp, curved claws and long, serrated teeth. Evidence indicates that it hunted and killed in packs. Its length was about 9 meters (30 ft). It lived in western North America.
8. **Iguanodon** was a swamp dweller with teeth like an iguana's and a large thumb spike. Its length was about 10 meters (33 ft). It lived in western North America, northern Africa, and Asia.
9. **Sauropelta** was a broad-bodied plant eater with bony studs, pebbly plates, and fringes of spikes. It lived in western North America, where it grew to a length of about 5 meters (17 ft).
10. **Deinonychus** was an agile predator that may also have traveled and killed in packs. It had sickle-like claws. It grew to a length of about 3 meters (9 ft) and lived in western North America.
11. **Triceratops** was a plant eater with two sharp horns on top of its head and a third on its nose. Over its neck, there was a frill of strong bony plates connected to its head. Its length was about 9 meters (30 ft). It lived in western North America.
12. **Quetzalcoatlus** may have been the largest animal ever to fly. It had a standing height of about 3 meters (10 ft) and a wingspan of about 12 meters (40 ft). It was lightweight (about 68 kg or 150 lb), warm-blooded, and covered with fur. It lived in Texas about 75 mya and fed on fish.
13. **Giganotosaurus** was perhaps the largest of the carnivorous dinosaurs. It was approximately 12.5 meters (38 ft) long and weighed approximately 6.9 metric tons (7.5 U.S. tons). Its remains were discovered in 1993 in western Argentina, where it lived 100 mya. It had short front legs and could stand erect. Similar to Tyrannosaurus, which evolved approximately 35 million years later in North America, it had a large head filled with many short teeth set in powerful jaws.
14. **Tyrannosaurus** was about 11 meters (35 ft) long and weighed approximately 4.6 metric tons (5 U.S. tons). Although some scientists believe that it could move at a speed of up to 65 kph (40 mph), others believe that because of its heavy build it was too slow to catch live prey and therefore was a scavenger. It had short front legs and could stand erect, using its tail for balance. It had a large head that was roughly 1.2 meters (4 ft) long, filled with short teeth that were approximately 15 centimeters (6 in.) long. With its powerful jaws set with large saw-edged teeth, it tore apart its prey. It lived in western North America about 65 mya, during the close of the dinosaur age, the late Cretaceous era.
15. **Carcharodontosaurus**, or "shark-toothed reptile," was another large predatory dinosaur. Its remains have been found in Northern Africa, in what is now the Sahara Desert.
16. Recently found in Egypt are the skeletal remains of a giant alligator that preyed on the dinosaurs. At 24 to 30 meters (80 to 100 ft), **Paralititan stromeri** was longer than a modern-day school bus.
17. **Parasaurolophus** was a plant-eating reptile with a crest on its head that may have been used to resonate mating calls. It grew to a length of about 10 meters (33 ft) and lived in western North America.
18. In the sea there were crocodiles, turtles, and other kinds of reptiles.
19. The **Ichthyosaurs** were long, fishlike reptiles that used their feet and tails as paddles for swimming.
20. The **Plesiosaurs** were long, slender reptiles with necks that looked like snakes.
21. **Pterodactyls** were a group of carnivorous reptiles that glided, rather than flew, in the air. They were not true birds. They had a wide piece of skin connected from the very long joints of the fourth finger of each front leg to the body near the hip. They were of many sizes, some as small as a sparrow, and others with a wingspread of 6 meters (20 ft).

E. First discovered in Bavaria in 1861, the earliest bird, named **Archaeopteryx**, appeared during this era and was about the size of the modern-day pigeon.
   1. Most paleontologists today believe that modern birds evolved from the dinosaurs.
   2. Fossil remains of feathered dinosaurs that lived about 120 mya were recently discovered in China. They were about the size of a modern-day turkey and had feathers on their arms and tails. Scientists believe that they ran on their hind legs and did not fly.

F. Toward the end of this era, mammals appeared.
   1. The earliest mammals were small, about the size of modern rats, and had many of the same characteristics as the rodent.
   2. Although they bore a resemblance to reptiles, they were true mammals. They were warm-blooded and covered with hair, and the females had mammary glands to suckle their young.

G. At the end of the Mesozoic era, triggered by the arrival on Earth of an asteroid, dinosaurs and many other species of both flora and fauna became extinct; small mammals survived.

VIII. The Cenozoic Era: The Age of Mammals

A. Having its beginning about 60 mya, the Cenozoic era continues today. It is called the **Age of Mammals**.

B. Land changes took place during this era, giving rise to the landmasses we know today.
   1. The fourth and most recent glacial period carried over into this era. During this fourth glacial period, there were four separate ice ages.
   2. Areas along the Atlantic coast, the Gulf of Mexico, and parts of the Pacific coast, which had been under water, gradually became dry land during this era.
   3. Much volcanic activity took place in North America.
   4. The Colorado Plateau was lifted, and the Colorado River began cutting through to form the Grand Canyon.
   5. The Rocky Mountains and the Appalachian Mountains lifted, and forces of erosion began working on them. As erosion continued, great amounts of sediment were formed and deposited.
   6. The remains of many plants and animals were embedded in these sedimentary layers and became fossils.

C. Plants continued to evolve into the kinds we see today.

D. There was a tremendous increase in the number and species of insects.

E. Fishes developed into those we see today.

F. Reptiles left over from the Mesozoic era included crocodiles, alligators, turtles, lizards, and snakes.

G. Modern toothless birds with beaks appeared and grew in number and species.

H. Mammals became larger and flourished.
   1. At first there were two kinds of mammals—those that laid eggs from which their young were born and those that gave birth to their young alive, without laying eggs.
   2. Today only a few mammals, such as the duckbill and the spiny anteater, lay eggs.

I. Some mammals, called **marsupials**, developed pouches for their young. The kangaroo and opossum are marsupials. Young marsupials are born prematurely but remain in the mother's pouch where they get warmth, shelter, and milk.

J. One group of mammals returned to the sea to spend their lives. This group includes whales, porpoises, and dolphins. They have no hind legs, their forelegs are shaped into paddles, and their tails are like those of fish. Their young are born alive (not in egg shells) and are fed by their mother's milk, just like the young of land mammals.

K. Some mammals, such as the seal and the sea lion, spend most of their lives in the water.

L. Some mammals, such as the bat, developed flaps between their very long finger bones and are able to fly.

M. Many mammals of the early part of the Cenozoic era became extinct.
   1. The Smilodon, or saber-tooth tiger, had two large teeth, or fangs, in its upper jaw.
   2. The Megatherium was a giant sloth that stood about 6 meters (20 ft) high on its hind legs.
   3. The Mastodon looked like a large elephant, with woolly and coarse hair and large tusks.
   4. The Mammoth also looked like an elephant, but had such big teeth that there were never more than eight teeth in its mouth at a time.
   5. The 2 meter (6 ft) long *Canis diris* looked like a large wolf.

N. Mammals of this era that did not become extinct gradually developed into the mammals we see today. The horse is an example of a present-day mammal that developed from an earlier version in the Cenozoic era.
   1. The first horse was **Eohippus**, which appeared early in the Cenozoic era. Eohippus was about the size of a small dog, with a short neck, a few stiff hairs instead of a mane, and a short tail. Its teeth were not suited for eating grass, so it ate leaves and shrubs instead. Eohippus had four toes on each front foot and three toes on each hind foot.
   2. Eohippus evolved into **Mesohippus**, which was larger, about the size of a large dog. Mesohippus had a slightly longer neck, the beginning of a mane, and a longer tail. It had just three toes on each foot, with the middle toe larger than either of the other two, but when it walked or ran all three toes of each foot touched ground.
   3. Mesohippus evolved into **Meryohippus**, which was still larger, with a longer neck, mane, and tail. Meryohippus also had three toes on each foot, but only the longer middle toe touched ground.
   4. From Meryohippus evolved **Pliohippus**. Pliohippus was quite tall, with a good-sized mane and a long, flowing tail. Its teeth were specialized for biting and grinding the tough grass it ate. It had just one large toe on each foot, which helped it run more swiftly than its predecessors. The other two toes on each foot had become quite small and useless, that is, **vestigial**, and could no longer be seen because they were inside the foot. The nail of the large toe became the hoof. From Pliohippus evolved the modern-day horse, **Equus**.

IX. The Age of Humans

A. Although some scientists place the history of humans as beginning in the Cenozoic era, others put humans in an era called the **Psychozoic**. Whichever era, the Age of Humans began more than 1 mya, perhaps even 3 or 4 million years.
   1. From petrified bones, primitive tools, and fossil pollen; from studying the biochemistry and behavior of other animals; and from many other sources of evidence, scientists are gaining in their knowledge of early humans.

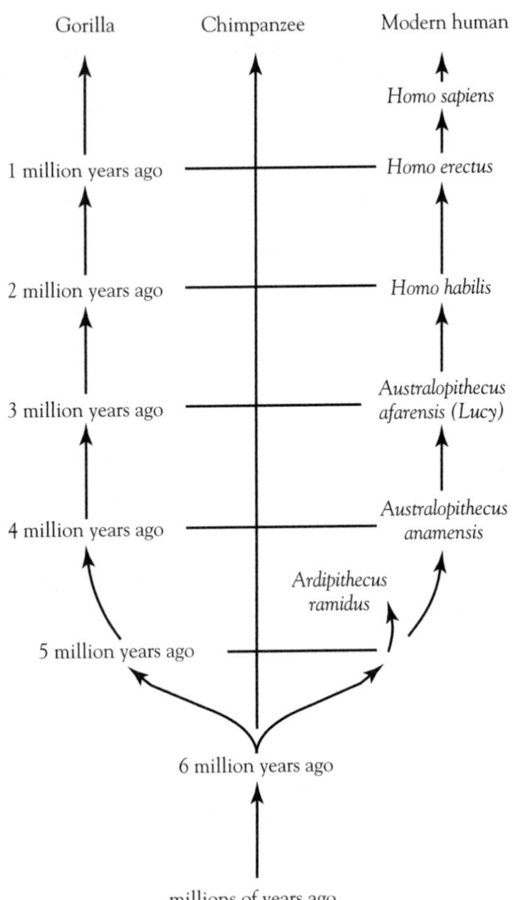

FIGURE 10.11 Common origin and parallel evolution of the hominids.

2. The evolution of humans appears to have begun in Africa. Tools, such as stone hand axes, have been found in Africa that date back about 1.5 million years.
3. Scientific evidence indicates that the branch of the animal kingdom that gave rise to humans emerged about 8 mya in eastern Africa. It indicates that hominids (chimps, gorillas, and humans) all descended from a single unknown species that lived 5 to 7 mya (see Figure 10.11).
4. The Earth's changing climate is believed to have played a role in two key events that led to the evolution of modern apes and humans (the hominids). The key events were a shift from living in trees to living on the ground and an increasing reliance on the brain.
5. Although apes and humans have a similar body structure, each species has developed different adaptations in response to its environment. Genetically, chimpanzees and bonobos are closest to humans. In fact, their DNA is so similar to that of humans that some scientists look at those two species for clues to the origin, evolution, and behavior of early humans.

B. A subfamily developed, the **australopithecines,** about three or four mya. They moved from eastern toward southern Africa as the forests retreated, and they were forced to adapt to dry and open land and to find other sources of food.
   1. As determined by the analysis of geographic strata where fossil remains have been found, evolution of the australopithecines begins with the *Australopithecus afarensis,* remains of which are found in the lower strata, evolving to several species in the upper strata, including *A. aethiopicus* and *Homo habilis.*
   2. In 1995, scientists unearthed 4-million-year-old bones that are believed to be of a previously unknown prehuman species, named *Australopithecus anamensis,* that lived between 3.9 and 4.2 mya in Kenya.
   3. *A. anamensis* is believed to be an intermediate step between the oldest known prehuman ancestor, called *Ardipithecus ramidus,* which lived 4.4 mya, and the short, apelike human ancestor called *Australopithecus afarensis,* whose most famous representative is a partial skeleton known as "Lucy."
   4. Found in Ethiopia in 1974, fossil remains of the 3-million-year-old hominid Lucy indicate that she was as adept at upright walking as people are today.

C. Beginning about 3 mya, the evolution continued with the emergence of another subfamily, the **hominines,** who moved extensively from eastern Africa around the entire planet. There is only one genus of hominines, and that is the genus *Homo.*
   1. It is believed that the last of the australopithecines coexisted for about 2 million years with the first of these hominines, *Homo habilis.*
   2. The remains of *Homo habilis* have been found in Africa in strata of the Earth that date back to between and 2.53 mya.
   3. *Homo erectus* first appeared in Africa about 1.8 mya and spread through Eurasia about 1 mya.
   4. *Homo erectus* is believed to have begun wandering off the African continent to other parts of the world about 1 mya.

D. **Neanderthals,** descendants of *Homo erectus,* flourished from western Europe to Central Asia between 75,000 and 35,000 years ago.
   1. Neanderthals lived in caves, hunted animals, used fire for cooking, and made fine tools.
   2. Neanderthals became extinct. It is not known why, although it is known that some Neanderthals coexisted with early Cro-Magnon people.

3. The differences between Neanderthal and early Cro-Magnon people was not as great as was once thought.

E. The **Cro-Magnon** is believed to be the immediate ancestor of *Homo sapiens*.
   1. Cro-Magnon lived during the Late Ice Age, from 40,000 to 12,000 years ago.
   2. Five skeletons of Cro-Magnon were discovered in about 1868 in the Cro-Magnon Cave in southern France. Since then, many more fossils have been found in caves in France, Spain, Italy, and other parts of southern Europe.
   3. Cro-Magnon did not have the low brow, thick brow ridges, protruding chin, and receding jaw of earlier species that are characteristic of the great apes.
   4. Cro-Magnon was tall, stood perfectly upright, and had a brain as large as that of modern humans.
   5. Cro-Magnon made excellent tools and stone weapons, hunted with a bow and arrow, and used animal skins for clothing.

F. The **Neolithic**, or the Recent Stone Age humans, followed Cro-Magnon.
   1. Neolithic humans knew how to grind and polish stone and bone to make smooth, sharp tools.
   2. They tamed wild animals and kept them in herds to be used for work, food, and clothing.
   3. They built their own shelters and joined with others in villages as protection from enemies and wild animals.

Exploratory Activities for "The Earth"

1. EXPLORING CRYSTAL FORMATION (ANY GRADE LEVEL)

Students are fascinated by crystal formation. Here is the procedure for the formation of various crystals.

Materials Needed

Sugar; hot water; alum; beakers or tumblers (plastic is okay); borax; cotton string; salt; saucer; hand lens, magnifying glass, or microscope

Procedure Dissolve as much sugar as possible in a tumbler half-filled with hot water, stirring vigorously as you add more sugar, a little at a time until no more will dissolve. Pour the sugar solution into a small, deep saucer and put a cotton string into the solution (see Figure 10.12). Place the saucer in a quiet corner of the room and allow it to evaporate for a day or two. Crystals will form on the string and at the bottom of the saucer. Pour off any solution that remains, allow the crystals to dry, and examine the crystal structure with a magnifying glass or through the low-powered lens of a microscope.

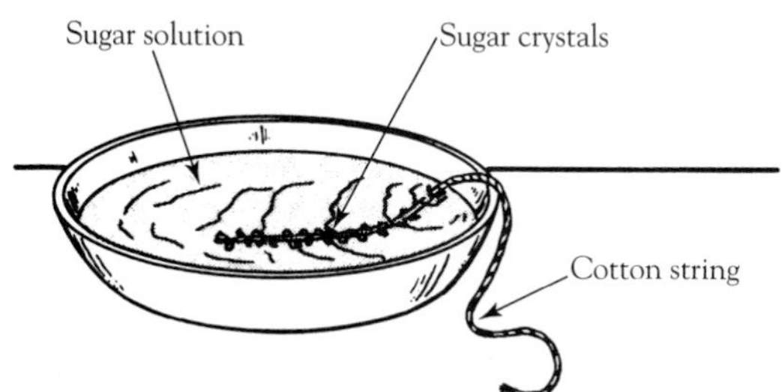

FIGURE 10.12 Forming sugar crystals.

You can divide your class into groups and have them repeat the experiment. Instead of sugar, one group uses salt, another uses borax, and another uses alum.

Closure and Application Once crystals have been formed, have the students sketch and compare the crystal structures of each type. Discuss the location and formation of Earth's crystals.

2. HISTORY OF THE EARTH: MAKING A LEAF OR A SHELL IMPRINT*

2.1 Make a Leaf or a Shell Imprint

Obtain a pie tin and coat the bottom and sides with a thin layer of petroleum jelly (Vaseline). Cover a leaf with petroleum jelly and place it on the bottom of the pie tin (Figure 10.13). Prepare a mixture of plaster of Paris in a large tin can by adding water to the plaster of Paris according to instructions on the package. Stir the mixture gently with a flat stick until it is smooth and has the consistency of pancake batter. Now pour the plaster of Paris slowly into the pie tin over the leaf until you have a layer 13 millimeters (1/2 in.) thick. Let the plaster of Paris set for 30 minutes and then remove the cast carefully. Wash

*To conserve space in this book, the activities that follow are written only as instructions on how to make leaf and shell imprints and not as detailed lessons. However, to the extent that materials and the maturity of your students allow, we encourage you to incorporate the activities into your own lesson plans in a way that your students are doing as much of the activity as possible, individually or in groups, rather than you doing them as teacher demonstrations.

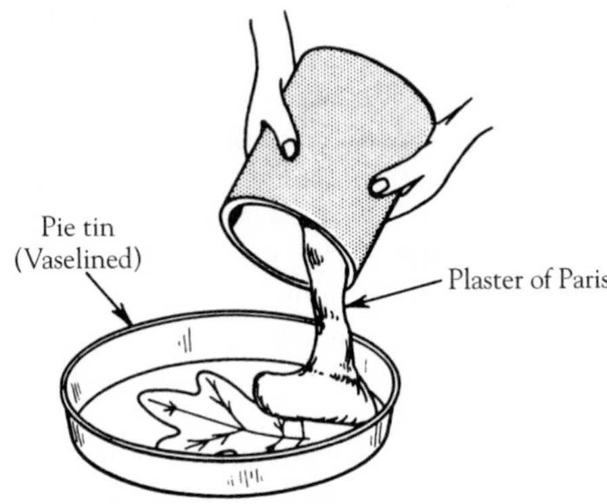

FIGURE 10.13 A plaster of Paris leaf imprint.

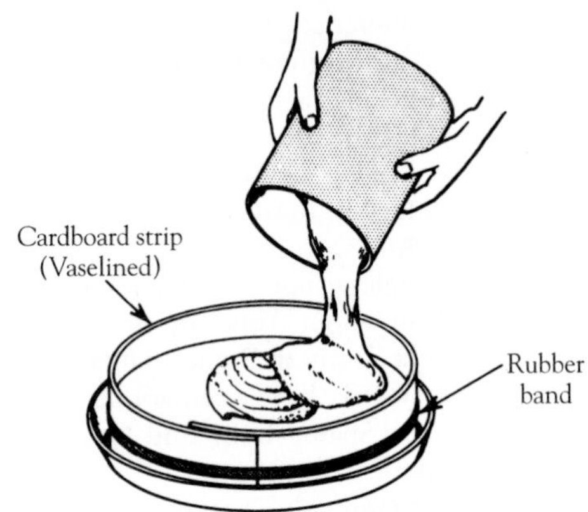

FIGURE 10.14 Making a negative and positive cast of an imprint.

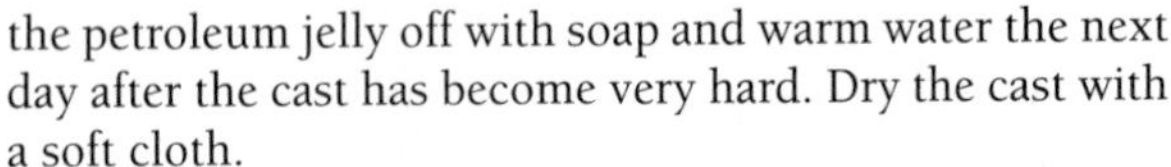

the petroleum jelly off with soap and warm water the next day after the cast has become very hard. Dry the cast with a soft cloth.

Repeat this activity, using a small seashell such as a clam or oyster shell. The cast you obtain will be a negative cast with a hollow imprint of the shell. To make a positive cast with a raised imprint, cover the negative cast with a thin coat of petroleum jelly. Coat one side of a strip of cardboard, 7.5 centimeters (3 in.) wide, with petroleum jelly, and wrap the cardboard around the cast, holding it firmly in place with a rubber band (Figure 10.14). Pour more plaster of Paris over the negative cast until you have a layer at least 2.5 centimeters (1 in.) thick. Let it set for 1 hour. Now remove the cardboard and, inserting a knife gently between the positive and negative casts, separate the two casts. Smooth the sides of the positive cast with sandpaper. The next day wash off the petroleum jelly with soap and warm water. Preserve the cast by giving it a coat of shellac.

2.2 Make a Carbon Imprint of a Leaf

Coat a leaf with a very thin layer of petroleum jelly, making sure to coat the side of the leaf where the veins are raised. Place the leaf, jellied side up, on some newspaper. Place a sheet of carbon paper, carbon side down, on the leaf. Cover the carbon paper with a sheet of white paper and rub the side of a round pencil or dowel back and forth many times on the white paper. The leaf will now be coated with carbon. Now place the leaf, carbon side down, between two fresh pieces of white paper, and rub the pencil or dowel back and forth on the top sheet several times. Remove the top sheet and the leaf. The bottom sheet will have a carbon imprint of the leaf, showing the size, shape, and vein formation. Draw in any gaps in the leaf's shape and vein pattern. Point out that you made an artificial coating of carbon on the leaf. What actually happens in nature is that the leaf itself carbonizes and forms an imprint on the top and underside of the rock.

Chapter 11

Water, Weather, and Climate

Brian Cosgrove © Dorling Kindersley

Water

I. The Water Table

A. When water falls to Earth as rain or other forms of precipitation, some of the water sinks into the Earth, sinking deeper until it reaches the nonporous (impermeable) rock layer beneath the soil.
   1. Porous rock is either loose (like gravel) or has spaces in it (like sandstone), allowing the water to enter and pass through it.
   2. Nonporous or impermeable rock (granite, for example) is solid and stops the water from sinking any deeper.
   3. The soil and rock above this nonporous layer then become soaked or saturated with water, which is called **groundwater.**
   4. The upper level of the groundwater in the soaked soil and rock is called the **water table,** the level or depth of which depends on the amount of rain that has recently fallen, how porous the soil and rock are, and how far down the porous layer goes before it meets a layer of impermeable rock.
   5. The level of the water table generally follows the contour of the land, sloping where the surface of the land slopes and rising where the surface rises.
   6. Groundwater can flow through a porous layer of soil and rock; thus it is possible for water to enter the ground at one place and to appear in another place later.

II. Spring

A. Whenever the land surface dips below the water table, the groundwater flows out to the surface of the land, forming a spring, joining with a river, or helping to feed a pond or lake.
   1. Springs may also form on hillsides where the water table cuts across the Earth's surface.
   2. Spring water usually has minerals dissolved in it. Spring water that comes from deep below the Earth's surface may have so many minerals dissolved in it that the water is not suitable for drinking.

B. Hot springs form when the groundwater is heated because of volcanic activity going on below the Earth's surface. (See "Hot Springs, Geysers, and Geothermal Energy" in Chapter 10.)

III. Well

A. A well is a hole that is dug or drilled deep enough into the ground to reach the water table.
   1. Water then flows into the hole, filling it and forming a well. When water is taken out of the well, the water that is flowing underground replaces it.
   2. Ideally a well is dug deep enough that when the level of the water table drops during dry weather, the well does not run dry.

B. An **artesian well** is one that is sunk deep into the Earth's surface. The water is obtained from a layer of porous rock, called an **aquifer.** The aquifer is sandwiched between two layers of nonporous rock.
   1. This layer of porous rock originally began at the Earth's surface and then slanted downward into the Earth. Water entering this layer can travel only through this porous layer. It cannot move up or down through the nonporous layers of rock above and below it.
   2. When a well is drilled deep enough to reach this porous layer, the water in it rises again, either to the land surface or to just below the surface, depending on the contour of the land. The water rises because the water at the beginning of the aquifer is higher and exerts pressure on water below it. Water in an artesian well is under pressure in exactly the same way as the water at the bottom of a long, slanting pipe would be under pressure.
   3. Water from artesian wells is usually pure, because it comes straight up the walls of the well and does not dissolve any minerals in other layers of rocks on its way up.
   4. About 60% of our nation's fresh water comes from aquifers.
   5. Many of the nation's aquifers are being depleted at alarming rates due to a number of factors. These include global warming and the concomitant increased evaporation rate of surface water and low mountain snowpack that supplies water to major rivers; urban sprawl; growing demands of agriculture; and the drying up of wetlands.

IV. Lakes, Wetlands, Swamps, Bogs, and Marshes

A. **Lakes** are large bodies of water, usually made up of a depression, called a basin, that is filled with water.
   1. Some lake basins were formed by faulting, in which layers of rock inside the Earth slipped over other layers of rock and were pushed up to form a hollow in the Earth's surface.
   2. Some basins were formed when forces within the Earth, acting in a sideways direction, pushed layers of rock into wavelike folds with crests and hollow troughs.
   3. Some basins were formed when glaciers gouged out deep hollows as they moved across the Earth's surface, leaving these hollows to fill with water as the glaciers later retreated.
   4. On Antarctica, there are about 70 known lakes lying beneath glaciers. The largest, Lake Vostok, lies nearly 4 kilometers (2.5 miles) below the ice surface and has a depth of about 460 meters (1,500 feet).

5. Some lakes were formed when lava from a volcano created a dam across a valley.
6. Some lakes were formed from rivers when trees, brush, rock, and other debris clogged the rivers, backing the water up to form a lake.

B. Lakes obtain their water in many ways.
1. Rain and other forms of precipitation fall directly into the lake.
2. Rain that falls on land around the lake runs off into the lake.
3. Rivers flow into the lake.
4. When the water table is above the surface of the lake basin, groundwater flows into the lake in the form of a spring.

C. Lakes do not exist for as long as hills or mountains do.
1. Some lakes become filled with sediment carried by streams.
2. Sometimes plants growing at the edge of a lake advance farther and farther into the lake until the lake becomes filled, and eventually disappears.
3. Some lakes disappear because the springs in their basins, or the rivers that fed the lakes, have dried up.

D. **Wetlands** is a term used for any natural land area that is wet for a portion of the year. This includes bogs, swamps, sloughs, flood plains, marshes, prairie potholes, and river bottomlands.
1. Found in every region and climate of the United States, wetlands are the special habitats for unique species of life.
2. Wetlands are producers of life, some being equal in output to the same size area of tropical rain forest.
3. Wetlands provide feeding, spawning, and nursery grounds for more than half the saltwater finfish and shellfish harvested annually in the United States, and for most of our freshwater game fish.
4. Wetlands are a habitat for a third of the nation's resident bird species, more than half of its migratory bird species, and a third of the plants and animals currently listed on the federal registry of endangered and threatened species.
5. Wetlands absorb and filter pollutants that would otherwise degrade lakes, rivers, reservoirs, and aquifers. Through photosynthesizing organisms, for example, wetlands bind large amounts of carbon, preventing it from entering the atmosphere as carbon dioxide.
6. Wetlands provide flood control, recharge groundwater aquifers, and help stabilize shorelines and riverbanks.
7. Because of their ecological value, it is illegal in the United States to drain wetlands to make more land available for farming and building construction.

E. **Swamps** and **marshes** are wetlands that are filled by small streams; they are partially or completely filled with live plants, dead plants, sediment, and water.
1. The plant life of a swamp consists largely of trees; that of a marsh consists primarily of grasses.
2. Some swamps and marshes are just beginning to become lakes, whereas others are slowly becoming dry land.

F. A **bog** is like a swamp, but smaller, and the water of a bog is almost completely covered by live plants, decaying plants, and sediment, so much so that you could walk on a bog. To do that is very dangerous, however, because the "ground" is plant life and sediment that is actually covering a small lake basin, and you could sink in and be unable to free yourself.
1. Unlike marshes and swamps, bogs receive rainwater as their primary source of water. The water of bogs has far fewer dissolved minerals.
2. The plants of a bog are often mosses, which can live in a less nourishing habitat than that of the mineral-rich swamps and marshes. For the same reason, bogs are often the habitat for insectivorous (insect-eating) plants such as the pitcher plant, sundew, and Venus flytrap.
3. Eventually a bog completely fills in and becomes land that can support grasses, shrubs, and trees.

V. Impurities in Water

A. Water is quite pure when it begins its descent from clouds.
1. As water falls through the air, it dissolves some of the gases in the air and collects dust and bacteria from the air.
2. In some heavily industrialized areas, the water also picks up sulfur and nitrogen compounds from the air put there by the burning of fossil fuels, such as coal and petroleum products, and forms of sulfuric acid and nitric acid. Precipitation containing these chemicals then kills plants and pollutes bodies of water. This form of contaminated precipitation is called **acid rain.**
3. Acid rain is believed to cause a decline in the population of amphibians, and is known to kill fish in lakes, damage crop plants, corrode metals, and damage stained glass windows and other works of art. It also contributes to the destruction of stone monuments and buildings.

B. When precipitation reaches the ground, it picks up other impurities. Many kinds of minerals dissolve in the water. Some sand, silt, mud, and other sediments are not dissolved but remain suspended in the water as very fine particles. When

LEARNING ACTIVITY 11.1

Testing Rainwater for Acidity

A. Teacher Demonstration Experiment

Collect rainwater in several plastic jars placed in various places on your school grounds. Mark the jars according to their location. After a rainstorm, collect the jars and test the water using a separate strip of litmus paper for each jar. Record the color change for each. (Litmus paper turns blue in basic solutions; that is, higher than pH 7. It turns red in acidic solutions; that is, less than pH 7.)

B. Individual Student Investigation

After discussing the results of the experiment, give each student one or several strips of litmus and have each student repeat the experiment at home and record the results.

C. Sharing Results

Finally, have students share their home experiments in class, perhaps marking a map of the city with a red or blue X and the date to indicate how the geographic area may or may not be affected by acid rain. Repeat the entire experiment several times during the year, maintaining a record with dates on the map.

---

it comes in contact with the wastes of organisms, it picks up bacteria. Some of the impurities in water are harmless to humans, plants, and animals, whereas others can be quite harmful.

1. Small amounts of minerals and gases in water give it a better taste; water would taste flat without them.
2. The mineral salt content of some bodies of water is nearly toxic to humans and other organisms and must be removed for the water to be potable (drinkable).
3. Some impurities in water make the water toxic to fish and other wildlife.
4. Certain bacteria in water cause diseases in humans and must be removed or killed; that is, the water must be purified to make it potable.

VI. Purification of Water

A. In the home, harmful bacteria in the water can be killed by boiling, and suspended material and gases that give the water a bad taste can be removed by passing the water through filters.

B. In the laboratory, water can be purified by **distillation.**

1. In distillation, the water is boiled, driving off the gases that are dissolved in the water, and the water vapor that forms is led through a tube that is surrounded by cold water, which condenses the water vapor back into liquid water.
2. The boiling water kills the bacteria.
3. Minerals and suspended materials such as the dead bacteria are left behind when the water is changed into water vapor.

C. City water goes through several steps to purify it for drinking.

1. First, the water is run into large basins, where the suspended particles of sediment settle to the bottom.
2. Because the very tiny particles settle very slowly, two chemicals—alum and lime—are added to the water, forming a jellylike material. The very fine particles of sediment stick to this material and settle to the bottom.
3. Some of the bacteria and other microorganisms in the water are also trapped by the material and are removed when the material settles.
4. The water is then run to another basin containing layers of sand and gravel. The water passes through these layers, which remove the rest of the suspended particles along with more of the microorganisms.
5. Sometimes a layer of charcoal is placed between the sand and the gravel to remove coloring matter and foul-tasting gases from the water.
6. To remove the remaining microorganisms, the water is sprayed into the air, a process called *aeration*. Aeration allows the oxygen in the air to kill the bacteria and other microorganisms and, at the same time, puts oxygen into the water to improve its taste. If there is a large amount of bacteria present, the water is treated with chlorine to kill the bacteria.
7. Most cities also add fluoride to the water. Fluoride is incorporated into growing teeth, which makes the teeth more resistant to bacterial decay.

VII. Soft and Hard Water

A. Water that has certain minerals dissolved in it, in the form of calcium and magnesium salts, is called **hard water.**

1. Rainwater that has not touched the ground is very soft water. It is excellent for washing purposes; however, once rainwater has hit the ground it begins to dissolve ground minerals with which it comes in contact and becomes harder. We call it *hard* because it is difficult to make a lather with it with soap.
2. Because hard water will not lather well with soap, it is difficult to use for washing; instead,

LEARNING ACTIVITY 11.2

Making Water Potable (Fit to Drink)

A. By Distillation

Fill a glass jar half full with water. To the water add some food coloring, a tablespoon of salt, and some soil. Shake the mixture well, then pour it into a teakettle. Obtain a long piece of rubber tubing. Place one end of the rubber tubing inside the spout of the teakettle and use modeling clay in and around the spout to hold the rubber tubing in place and to make sure that the steam will pass out only through the tubing (Figure 11.1). Put the other end of the rubber tubing into a glass tumbler that has been placed in a pan filled with ice cubes. Now place the teakettle on a hot plate. When the water boils, drops of water will condense in the tumbler or drip from the hose into the tumbler. This water will be clear and pure, and it will not taste salty. When the water in the teakettle boiled and changed into water vapor or steam, the impurities were left in the teakettle. Only pure, clean water condensed as the steam was cooled in the tumbler.

B. By Settling

Fill a glass jar about three-quarters full of water. Add a mixture of coarse and fine soil to the jar, shake the contents thoroughly, and then set the jar down, cover it, and allow the soil to settle. The coarse soil will quickly settle to the bottom, but it may take many days for the fine soil to settle completely, leaving the water free of sand and soil.

C. By Filtering

In a large plastic or glass funnel, place a layer of small pebbles, then a layer of gravel or coarse sand, and finally a layer of fine sand (Figure 11.2). First pour some clean water through the funnel to allow the layers to settle and pack together. Then place the funnel in a narrow-mouth glass jar and pour some muddy water into the funnel. The layers will filter the mud, and clear water will pass into the jar.

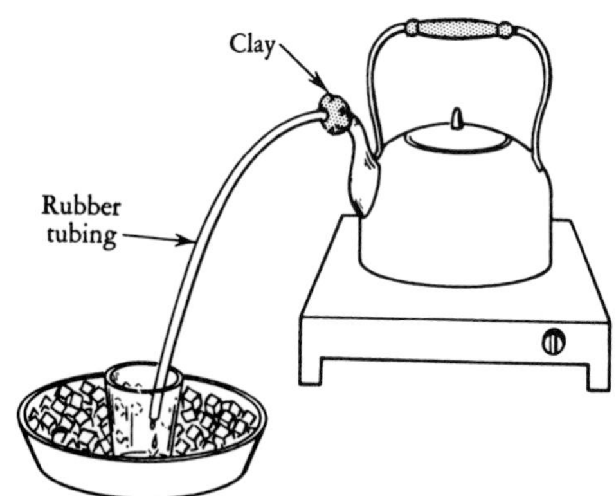

FIGURE 11.1 Distillation purifies water.

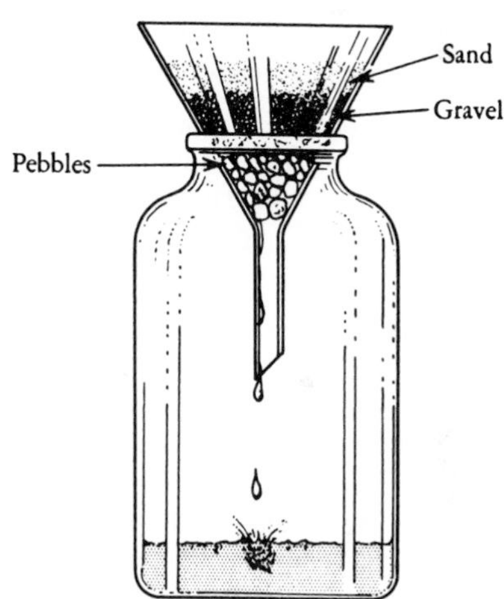

FIGURE 11.2 Filtering helps purify water.

it forms a scum, which is the product of the dissolved calcium and magnesium salts reacting with the soap.

3. Hard water leaves damaging mineral deposits inside steam furnaces, water heaters, hot water pipes, and tea and coffee pots.
4. Today, many people use **detergents** instead of soap. Although detergents are not soap, they are made of chemicals that have a cleaning action similar to that of soap. The calcium and magnesium salts in hard water do not affect the chemicals in solid and liquid detergents, so the detergents lather easily in hard water and do not form a scum.
   a. The earliest detergents were not biodegradable (did break down by natural processes), so they caused excessive suds in streams and lakes.
   b. Sometimes they would form so many suds that the surface of the body of water was covered with suds and the normal oxygen and gas exchange could not take place at the surface of the water. Fish and other aquatic organisms then died by suffocation.
   c. Modern-day detergents, however, are biodegradable and not harmful to natural waters and aquatic life.

B. Hard water can be softened by several methods.
   1. In the **lime-soda process** certain chemicals are added to the water, such as ammonia, washing soda, borax, or trisodium phosphate, which remove the calcium and magnesium by precipitating them out of the water.
   2. Another method is to use a chemical called **zeolite,** which removes the calcium and magnesium when hard water is passed through it, and replaces these minerals with sodium, which does not affect soap. Soaking it overnight in a strong saltwater solution, thereby replenishing the sodium, can restore used zeolite. Zeolite is a group of more

LEARNING ACTIVITY 11.3

Hard and Soft Water and the Action of a Detergent

A. Make and Soften Temporary Hard Water

Obtain some limewater from the drugstore. Pour limewater into a test tube until it is half full and, using a soda straw, bubble carbon dioxide from your breath through the limewater. At first the limewater will become milky, but continue the bubbling until the milkiness disappears. Pour an equal amount of distilled water or rainwater into a second test tube. Make a soap solution by dissolving soap shavings in warm water. Now add an equal number of drops of soap solution to each of the test tubes and, while holding a thumb over the mouth of each test tube, shake them vigorously. The soft water will make lots of suds, but the temporary hard water will make very few suds and form curds instead.

Make some more temporary hard water and boil it for a few minutes to remove the hardness. Add the same amount of soap solution you added to the other two test tubes, and note how the boiled water now makes lots of suds.

B. Make and Soften Permanent Hard Water

Obtain Epsom salts (magnesium sulfate) from a drugstore. To a test tube half full of water, add a small amount of Epsom salts, shaking the test tube until the salt dissolves. Pour the same number of drops of soap solution (as previously prepared) into the test tube containing the freshly prepared permanent hard water and into a test tube containing an equal amount of distilled water or rainwater. Shake both test tubes vigorously and note the difference in the amount of suds produced.

Soften the permanent hard water by adding some washing soda, borax, or ammonia. Now add the same number of drops of soap solution you added to the other test tubes and compare the increased amount of suds formed.

C. Test the Action of Detergent

Obtain some high-sudsing detergent. Prepare samples of temporary and permanent hard water (described in parts A and B). Obtain three test tubes. Pour some temporary hard water into one test tube, an equal amount of permanent hard water into the second test tube, and an equal amount of distilled water or rainwater into the third test tube. Now add the same amount of detergent to each test tube and shake them vigorously. Note that all three test tubes have lots of suds, showing that the sudsing (and cleaning) action of detergents is not affected by water hardness.

---

than 30 silicon-containing minerals naturally occurring in cavities and veins of volcanic and sedimentary rocks of arid regions and on the ocean floor. Zeolites have unusual properties that make them valuable as filtering agents. Synthetic zeolites have also been developed.

VIII. Water Conservation

A. Every year the need for freshwater becomes greater.
   1. Only a small percentage of the Earth's freshwater is available for immediate use.
   2. The Earth's total water distribution is shown in Table 11.1. The Earth's total freshwater distribution is shown in Table 11.2.

B. As the population of the world increases, the need for freshwater could become greater than the supply, so we must continue to take steps to conserve water.
   1. We should avoid needless use and waste of water.
   2. Soil and forest conservation practices help prevent water from running off quickly before it can be used.
   3. Dams hold back river water that is rushing to the sea.
   4. Scientists and engineers continue to explore economical ways to change seawater into usable freshwater.
   5. Through transpiration (the loss of water from plant surfaces, such as the leaves, by evaporation), plants of the tropical **rain forests** that encircle the earth near the equator play an important role in replenishing the earth's freshwater supply. There is concern among scientists and environmentalists about the effects of the destruction of the rain forests (for timber, agriculture, and development) on the global ecosystem.

TABLE 11.1 Earth's Total Water Distribution

Rivers, lakes, and shallow groundwater	0.3%
Deep groundwater	0.3%
Saltwater lakes, soil, atmospheric moisture, and glaciers	0.1%
Polar ice	2.2%
Oceans (saltwater)	97.1%

TABLE 11.2 Earth's Total Freshwater Distribution

Polar ice and glaciers	84.945%
Groundwater	14.158%
Lakes and reservoirs	0.549%
Soil moisture	0.294%
Atmospheric moisture	0.049%
River water	0.004%

C. Earth's freshwater supply continues to be polluted.
   1. Some factories still pour large amounts of pollutants into rivers, lakes, and oceans.
   2. Wastes and sewage from homes in some areas are also dumped into rivers, lakes, and oceans without first being treated so that the water will not be polluted.
   3. Sometimes waste materials accumulate or are so foul that, even after all regular methods of purifying water are used, the water is still unfit to use.

D. Because icebergs and polar icecaps consist of frozen freshwater and not ocean saltwater, they could become a future source of freshwater.

IX. Water Pressure

A. At any given point in a collection of water, because of its weight, the water will exert pressure downward, upward, and sideways, and the pressure is the same in all directions.
   1. At a deeper point in the water, the pressure will be greater, but this new and greater pressure will again be the same in all directions.

B. When water is in a container, its pressure is greatest at the bottom.
   1. The shape of the container does not affect the water pressure on the bottom, but the height of the container does. The taller the container, the deeper the water, and the greater the water pressure will be at the bottom.

C. When water is in a closed container, any pressure on the water will be sent or transmitted in all directions through the container. This pressure occurs because the molecules of water are so close together that the pressure is passed unchanged from molecule to molecule.
   1. Special machines, called hydraulic machines (such as the hydraulic lift for raising automobiles at service stations, and hydraulic brakes), make use of this property of water in a closed container, sending a small force elsewhere and, at the same time, changing the small force into a much larger force.

X. Water Can Be Used to Do Work

A. Because of the Earth's pull of gravity, when water moves from a higher level to a lower level it has a great deal of energy. This is called **kinetic energy**, the energy of motion.
   1. The faster the water moves the greater its kinetic energy.
   2. Moving water can be used to turn waterwheels. Waterwheels have been used to grind grain or run machines. In dams, for example, waterwheels, called **turbines**, are used to run large electric generators to convert kinetic energy into electricity.

B. When water is heated to a high enough temperature, it will boil, changing from a liquid to a gas, called **steam**, that expands tremendously and can exert a great deal of pressure and force.
   1. Steam can be used to run machines and engines and to turn large turbines, which can then run giant electric generators.

XI. Sinking and Floating

A. When a body is placed in water, two forces act on the body—the Earth's pull of gravity and the upward force of the water being displaced by the body.
   1. The first force, the Earth's pull of gravity, pulls downward on the body. The weight of the body determines the amount of downward force acting on it—the heavier the body, the greater the Earth's pull of gravity on it and the larger the downward force will be.
   2. The second force is the upward force of the water that has been displaced. The size of the body determines the amount of upward force of the displaced water—the larger the body, the more water it can displace, and the greater the upward force.

B. A small, heavy body usually sinks in water.
   1. Because it is small, such a body will displace a small amount of water, and a small, upward force will act on the body.
   2. Because the body is heavy, the downward force resulting from the pull of gravity will be great. Because the downward force acting on the body is greater than the upward force acting on the body, the body will sink.

C. A large, light body usually floats in water.
   1. Because it is large, such a body will displace a large amount of water, and a large, upward force will act on the body.
   2. Because the body is light, the downward force resulting from the pull of gravity will be small.
   3. A large, light body will sink in water only until the upward force of the displaced water equals the downward force of the object's weight, and then the object will float.

D. Although quite heavy, a ship made of iron or steel can float.
   1. The iron or steel is spread out over a large area to form a hollow shell that will displace a large amount of water, and a large upward force will act on the metal.
   2. The downward force, caused by the combined weight of metal, air, equipment, passengers, and cargo, is still less than the upward force caused by the displaced water, so the ship floats.
   3. When a ship is set afloat, it sinks until it displaces just enough water to create an upward force that equals the downward force produced by the ship's weight.

LEARNING ACTIVITY 11.4

Water Pressure

A. Demonstrate Water Pressure

Obtain a tall can. Place a piece of two-by-four wood, or any other wood of suitable thickness, in the can. Use a hammer and a large nail to punch a hole in one side of the can near the bottom (Figure 11.3).

Now take the can to a sink and, while keeping one finger over the hole, fill the can with water. Release your finger, and a stream of water will shoot out some distance from the hole, showing that water exerts pressure.

B. Demonstrate That Water Pressure Is the Same in All Directions

Use a hammer and large nail to punch holes around the sides of a tall can near the bottom (Figure 11.4). It may help to use a block of wood (as described in part A) when making the holes. Take the can to the sink and run water into it rapidly so that it stays full while water is escaping through the holes. Note how the water shoots out exactly the same distance from all the holes.

C. Demonstrate the Effect of Depth on Water Pressure

Use a hammer and large nail to punch three holes in one side of a tall can, using a block of wood (as described in part A) if necessary. One hole should be near the top of the can, another hole in the middle, and the third hole near the bottom (Figure 11.5). Take the can to the sink and run water into it rapidly so that it stays full while the water is escaping through the holes. The greater the depth of the water, the farther it will shoot out of the hole.

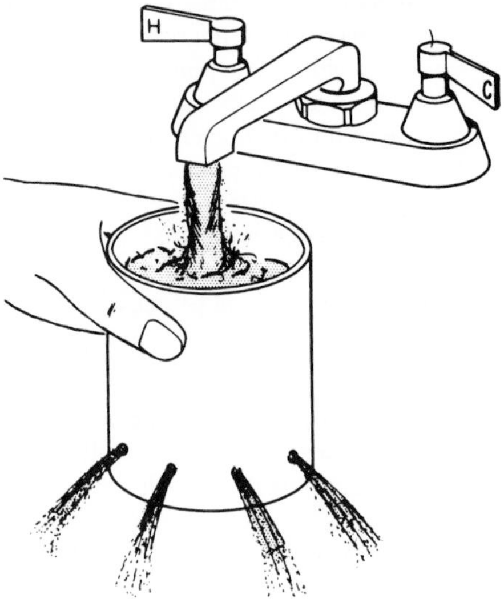

FIGURE 11.4 Water exerts the same pressure in all directions.

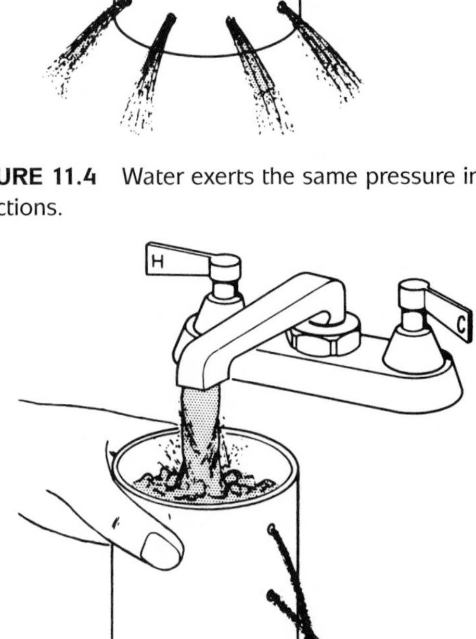

FIGURE 11.5 The deeper the water, the greater the water pressure will be.

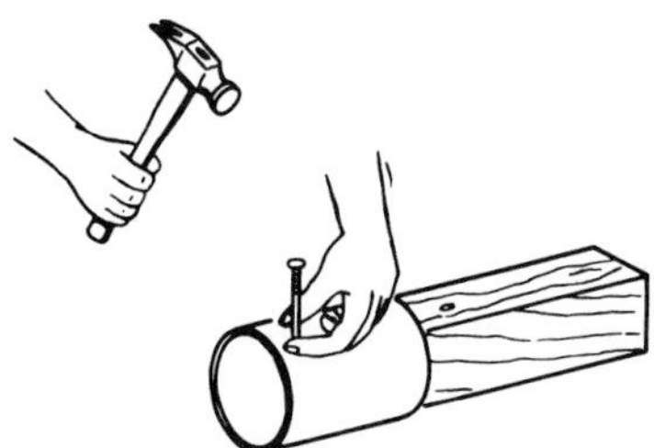

FIGURE 11.3 Using a piece of wood to punch a hole in one side of a can.

4. When the ship is loaded, it sinks deeper until enough water is displaced to produce an additional upward force to support the weight of the cargo.

E. A submarine floats for the same reason that an iron or steel ship floats.
   1. The submarine is able to sink because it has tanks that let in water and make it heavy enough (or increase the downward force) to sink.
   2. When the water is pumped out of the tanks, the submarine becomes lighter and rises to the surface.

F. A body floats more easily in saltwater than in freshwater.
   1. The same downward force of gravity acts on a body, whether it is in saltwater or freshwater.
   2. However, saltwater is denser than freshwater because it has more minerals dissolved in it and,

LEARNING ACTIVITY 11.5

Buoyancy and Displacement

A. A Body Appears to Lose Weight in Water

Tie a string around a stone, connect it to a spring balance, and note the weight of the stone in air (Figure 11.6). Now lower the stone into a large, wide-mouthed jar half filled with water. Observe the loss of weight caused by the upward buoyant force of the displaced water.

B. A Floating Body Displaces Its Own Weight of Water

Make an overflow cup. Obtain a large Styrofoam cup, and use a hole puncher to punch a hole near the top of the cup. Get a plastic straw with a diameter slightly larger than the hole, cut off a 5-centimeter (2-in.) piece of straw, and insert it into the hole (Figure 11.7). Seal the outside spot where the straw enters the cup with glue or chewing gum. Coat the underside of the end of the straw lightly with petroleum jelly. Pour water into the cup until it is just level with the straw. Get a block of wood that will fit inside the cup. Weigh the block. Get a small can and weigh it. Now place the can so that its center is beneath the end of the straw. Lower the block of wood gently into the cup of water. The displaced water will overflow into the empty can. When the water stops overflowing, weigh the can again. Subtract the weight of the can from the combined weight of the overflow water and the can. The difference will be the weight of the overflow water. Compare the weight of the overflow water with the weight of the block of wood. The weights should be just about the same.

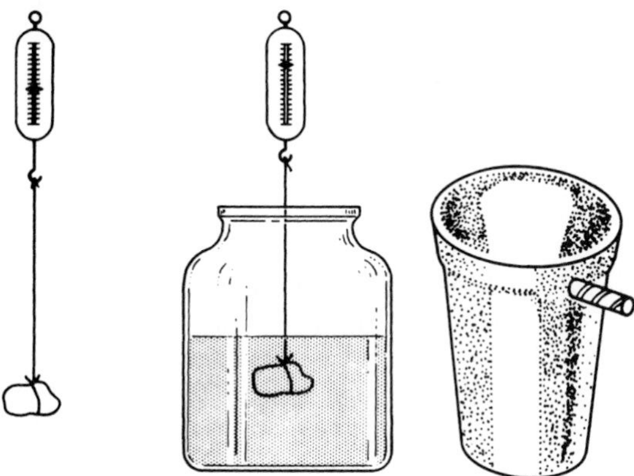

FIGURE 11.6 When lowered into water, the rock seems to lose weight.

FIGURE 11.7 An overflow cup.

C. A Steel Ship Floats

Cut out two pieces of aluminum foil 15 centimeters (6 in.) long and 10 centimeters (4 in.) wide. Fold one piece in half again and again, flattening the foil each time with your fingers to remove any trapped air, until you have a small, flat wad. Drop this wad into a pie tin full of water, and it will sink to the bottom because it displaces very little water, thus producing a small upward force. Fold the second piece of foil lengthwise and shape it with your fingers until you have a figure similar to a rectangular boat. Place this boat in the water. As with a steel ship, it will float because it displaces a large amount of water, producing a large upward buoyant force.

D. Demonstrate the Effect of More Cargo on a Ship

Place a small rectangular cake pan in a rectangular glass aquarium almost full of water. Measure how much of the sides of the pan sink below the level of the water. Now spread a few stones evenly along the bottom of the pan. Again measure how much of the sides of the pan sink. The pan sinks more deeply in the water, displacing enough water to support the added weight of the stones.

E. Compare the Buoyancy of Saltwater and Freshwater

Fill two identical large, wide-mouthed jars about three-quarters full of water. Add salt to the water in one jar, a tablespoon at a time, stirring vigorously, until no more salt will dissolve. Now place an egg first in the freshwater and then in the saltwater (Figure 11.8). The egg will float in the denser, more buoyant, saltwater. Get two large ice cubes of the same size, put one into each jar, and note which ice cube protrudes the most from the water.

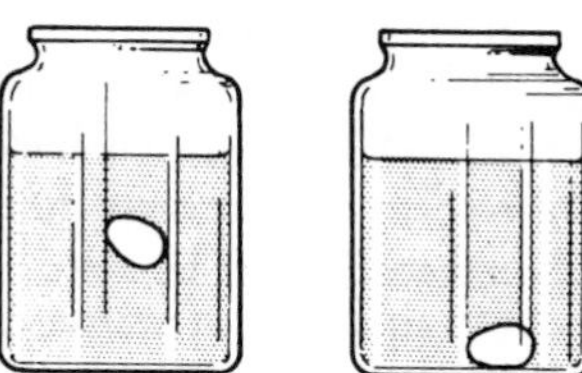

FIGURE 11.8 An egg will sink in freshwater and float in saltwater.

as a result, displaced saltwater has a greater upward force than displaced freshwater.

3. If a ship sails from freshwater into saltwater, it rises farther out of the water, because the salt water has a greater upward force than the freshwater.
4. If a ship sails from saltwater into freshwater, it sinks farther into the water, because the freshwater has a smaller upward force than the saltwater.

The Earth's Sea

I. Oceans of the Earth

A. Although oceans are sometimes thought of as separate bodies of water, all the oceans are part of one great sea that covers almost 71% of the Earth to an average depth of about 3,800 meters (12,500 ft). The deepest point ever measured, 11,022 meters (36,163 ft), is in the Mariana trench in the Pacific Ocean.

1. A larger portion of the Earth's sea is in the southern hemisphere. Approximately 61% of the surface of the northern hemisphere is water, while about 81% of the surface of the southern hemisphere is water.
2. The Earth's sea is divided into three great oceans—the Pacific, the Atlantic, and the Indian. Other oceans or seas are actually extensions, called **marginal seas,** of these three great oceans.
   a. The **Pacific Ocean** is the largest and the deepest, with an area of 165,250,000 square kilometers (102,703,543 sq. mi) and an average depth of 4,280 meters (14,040 ft). Marginal to the Pacific Ocean are the Bering Sea, the Coral Sea, the East and South China Seas, the Sea of Okhotsk, the Sea of Japan, the Yellow Sea, and the Philippine Sea.
   b. The **Atlantic Ocean** is the second largest with an area of 82,440,000 square kilometers (51,237,000 sq. mi) and an average depth of 3,330 meters (10,900 ft). Marginal to the Atlantic Ocean are the Arctic Ocean, the Scotia Sea, the North Sea, the Labrador Sea, the Weddell Sea, the Norwegian Sea, the Greenland Sea, the Mediterranean and Caribbean Seas, and the Gulf of Mexico.
   c. The **Indian Ocean** has an area of 73,440,000 square kilometers (45,900,000 sq. mi) and an average depth of 3,890 meters (12,700 ft). Marginal to the Indian Ocean are the Arabian Sea, the Red Sea, and the Bay of Bengal.
3. The **Antarctic Ocean,** a region of the south geographic pole that surrounds the Antarctic continent, is actually the southernmost extension of each of the three great oceans. In contrast to the Antarctic continent, where a bitter climate supports only a few species of life, the Antarctic Ocean is rich with organisms, especially where the cold Antarctic waters meet the warmer waters from northern latitudes, an area called the Antarctic convergence.

II. The Ocean Floor

A. The lower parts of the Earth's surface, where the oceans are located, are called **ocean basins.**

1. Ocean basins are the true surface of the Earth, whereas the continents are really huge islands that were raised above the ocean basins by forces acting inside the Earth.

B. Depths of the oceans vary.

1. Over the **continental shelf,** which is really the underwater edge of a continent, the ocean is shallow and rarely more than 180 meters (590 ft) deep.
2. Beyond the continental shelf, however, the ocean becomes much deeper very quickly, as the edge of the continent drops off sharply to the bottom of the ocean, forming a slope called the **continental slope.**
3. The deep **ocean floor** begins at the end of the continental slope.

C. The ocean floor is made up of many mountains, valleys, canyons, and trenches.

1. In the Atlantic Ocean floor, there is a tremendous mountain chain, called the Mid-Atlantic Ridge, that is about 320 kilometers (200 mi) wide and 3,050 meters (10,000 ft) high and stretches along the entire Atlantic Ocean to the southern tip of Africa.
2. Here the mountain chain joins with a similar mountain chain that runs through the Indian Ocean. This Indian Ocean chain then joins with many chains of mountains that stretch across the Pacific Ocean.
3. The tops of these Mid-Atlantic mountains are higher than many of those found on the continents, yet most of them are at least a mile below the surface of the ocean.
4. The Azores in the North Atlantic and Ascension Island in the South Atlantic are tops of the very high mountains in this chain. These mountains are believed to have formed from volcanic activity that took place millions of years ago.

D. Volcanic activity has also been responsible for forming mountains in other parts of the ocean floor. Ocean islands are the tops of these mountains.

1. The Aleutian Islands, West Indies, and South Sea Islands are tops of volcanic mountains rising from the ocean floor.
2. Near these islands are huge trenches and troughs, which may be as long as 1,600 kilometers (1,000 mi) and as wide as 160 kilometers (100 mi). They have been formed by cracks (faults) in the Earth's crust where the volcanic action that formed these islands took place.

E. In the continental slopes are deep canyons, some of which are deeper and wider than the Grand Canyon of the Colorado River and are believed to have been carved out of the slope by underwater ocean currents.

F. The entire ocean floor is covered with a layer of sediment.
   1. The continental shelf is covered with gravel, sand, clay, and shells.
   2. The ocean floor itself is covered with a soft, fine ooze, or mud, made up of volcanic dust and the remains of tiny marine organisms.
   3. Sometimes the sand and mud on the continental shelf and slope are dislodged and thrown into suspension. Since the mud-laden water is denser than normal seawater, gravity causes it to flow downslope, eroding and accumulating more sediment along the way, creating what is called a *turbidity current*. This downslope movement of dense, sediment-laden water is thought to be a major force in the excavation of most ocean floor canyons.

III. Exploring the Ocean

A. Oceanographers use a variety of instruments to explore the ocean.
   1. The deep-sea thermometer measures the temperature at different depths.
   2. Samplers can collect material from the bottom or from any level of the ocean.
   3. Corers and grabs bring sediments up from ocean bottoms.
   4. Ocean depth measurements are taken with various instruments.
   5. The *current meter* measures the speed and direction of the ocean currents.
   6. *Satellite imaging* is used to detect large features in the deepest parts of the ocean.
   7. The *deep-sea camera* can take pictures of sea life in the deep parts of the ocean and materials on the ocean floor.
   8. Wave data and sea temperatures are collected from aircraft, satellites, and buoys.
   9. Underwater vessels are used to explore the ocean and its bottom.

IV. Seawater

A. Oceanographers generally agree that the composition of seawater has been relatively constant throughout Earth's geologic time; that is, the sea has *not* become saltier over time as was once believed.

B. Every 45 kilograms (100 lb) of seawater contains about 1 kilogram (3 lb) of dissolved minerals.
   1. About three-fourths of this mineral material is sodium chloride, common table salt, while the rest is made up of salts of magnesium, calcium, and potassium. Since ancient times, the oceans have been a major source of salt for human consumption.
   2. Until recently, almost all the world's supply of magnesium and bromine was obtained from seawater. Magnesium is used in making aircraft and for other purposes. Bromine is used in making high-test gasoline and photographic film. Today, in the United States, those two chemicals are obtained from the water of the Great Salt Lake (Utah) and from brine wells and deposits in various areas.
   3. Although there is gold in seawater, 200,000 tons of seawater would have to be processed to extract a single ounce. That would yield 7,000 tons of solids from which the gold still would have to be extracted. So far the cost of recovering gold from seawater far exceeds its value.
   4. Recent discoveries of rich mineral deposits of copper, zinc, silver, gold, and other minerals in the sediment surrounding volcanic chimneys, called **seamounts**, of relatively shallow waters of the South Pacific have renewed interest in marine mineral mining.

C. Although the temperature of seawater varies, except around the seamounts, seawater is usually warmest at its surface.
   1. The warmest surface water is found in oceans near the equator.
   2. In the tropics, surface water is about 21°C (70°F), although in the Persian Gulf it has been as high as 35°C (95°F).
   3. In the polar regions, the average temperature of the surface water is about 2.2°C (28°F), which is the freezing point of saltwater. Marine vertebrate animals that live in polar waters have special body fluids, a kind of built-in "antifreeze," that keep them from freezing in the freezing waters.
   4. Most parts of the sea have surface temperatures between those of the tropical oceans and the polar oceans, depending on their location and on weather conditions.
   5. Deeper down in the ocean, the temperature of the water usually becomes colder. Even at the equator, the temperature of the deep ocean may be 2°C to 4°C (35°F to 40°F).

D. Two kinds of ice—icebergs and floes—are found floating in the sea.
   1. **Icebergs** are large freshwater blocks of ice that break off of glaciers and float in the sea.
   2. Icebergs that break off the Antarctic glaciers are huge; some may be more than 64 kilometers (40 mi) long.
   3. About 90% of an iceberg is below the surface of the water and the part below the surface is often spread far out in all directions, making icebergs very dangerous to ships. In the northern hemisphere, for example, the largest icebergs may be 1.6 kilometers (1 mi) long, with only 90 meters (295 ft) of ice showing above the water.
   4. Although icebergs seldom last more than a year, the glacial ice from which they formed may have been frozen for 15,000 years or more.

5. **Floes** are large pieces of frozen seawater that drift away from the Arctic Ocean.
6. In the Arctic Ocean, the temperature is cold enough for the surface water to freeze, and so the Arctic Ocean is always covered with an ice pack about 4 meters (13 ft) thick.
7. During the summer, some of this ice pack melts and breaks up, sending large pieces of ice floating southward.
8. Floes differ from icebergs in that they are smaller, have a flat shape, and are saltwater ice.

V. Wave Action

A. Most ocean waves are caused by winds. As the wind blows across the ocean, there is friction between the moving air and the surface of the water. This friction makes the water rise and fall in a regular rhythmic movement, called a *wave*.
   1. A wave has two parts: the highest point to which the water rises is called the *crest* of the wave; the lowest point to which the water falls is called the *trough* of the wave.
   2. The height of a wave is the vertical distance between its crest and its trough. The length of a wave is the horizontal distance from one crest to another or from one trough to another.
   3. The stronger the wind and the greater the distance over which the wind blows, the greater the waves will be. During a storm, waves may be more than 20 meters (65 ft) high and 150 meters (490 ft) long, and they may travel through the water at speeds of up to 96 kilometers an hour (60 mph).
   4. On windy days, waves may have foamy white tops, called *white caps*. White caps occur when strong winds push water off the tops of waves; they can be formed close to shore or far out at sea.
   5. When waves reach the shore, *breakers* are formed.
   6. A wave approaching the shore travels smoothly until its trough hits the bottom of the seashore.
   7. The trough of the wave is slowed down as it rubs against the bottom of the seashore.
   8. At the same time, the water in the wave piles up and the wave becomes higher and higher.
   9. Finally, the wave crest falls forward, and the wave breaks to form a breaker.
   10. At beaches where the seashore is steep, breakers form close to shore and do not last long. At beaches where the seashore is shallow, breakers form far out and can last for as long as a mile.

B. When a wave strikes the beach, the water immediately begins to move back along the ocean bottom as an *undertow*.
   1. The returning undertow moves beneath the waves that are coming in to shore.
   2. The stronger the waves, the more water they throw up on the beach and the stronger the returning undertows become.
   3. Undertows carry away sand from the beach to the deeper sea.

C. A **tsunami** is a series of waves spreading rapidly outward in all directions from a disturbance on the ocean floor. Sometimes tsunamis are mistakenly called *tidal waves*. A tsunami has no connection with tidal action caused by the Moon and the Sun.
   1. The usual cause of a tsunami is an earthquake, but volcanoes and landslides may also cause them.
   2. Because of so much tectonic plate activity beneath the Pacific Ocean, about 90% of the Earth's tsunamis occur in the Pacific Ocean.
   3. A tsunami can be more than 160 kilometers (100 mi) long, can move at speeds of 800 kilometers (500 mi) an hour, and can travel through the entire depth of the ocean.
   4. The individual waves that make up a tsunami are only several meters high and can pass under a ship in mid-ocean without being noticed. However, when a tsunami approaches shallow water, the waves slow down and their energy is compressed, generating surface waves up to 30 meters (100 ft) high.
   5. The individual waves of a tsunami are not always evenly spaced; as much as an hour can pass between the arrival of one wave and the next.
   6. Ocean floor activity is monitored by scientists, as is the up-and-down movements of the ocean. When a tsunami is expected, a warning is sent out to coastal communities so they can implement their tsunami-warning plan, which might mean the evacuation of low-lying areas.

LEARNING ACTIVITY 11.6

Water Displacement of an Iceberg

Place a square ice cube in a tumbler of water. Note how much (about 9/10) of the ice cube is below the surface of the water. Point out that although icebergs are huge, only about 1/10 of an iceberg can be seen above the surface of the water.

VI. Ocean Currents

A. The surface waters of the oceans are constantly moving in the form of currents.

1. The movement of these surface waters is caused mainly by the force of the winds blowing across the surface of the water. (See Figure 11.9.)
2. Because the Earth rotates, waters, which are flowing either north or south in the northern hemisphere, will move to their right (clockwise when looking from above) and the waters in the southern hemisphere move to their left (counterclockwise). (See Learning Activity 11.7.)
3. The outlines of the Earth's continents and other landmasses such as islands cause the currents to turn and change direction. The depth and shape of the ocean floor also affects the direction of currents.
4. Currents that flow away from the equator are warm currents, and currents that flow toward the equator are cold currents.

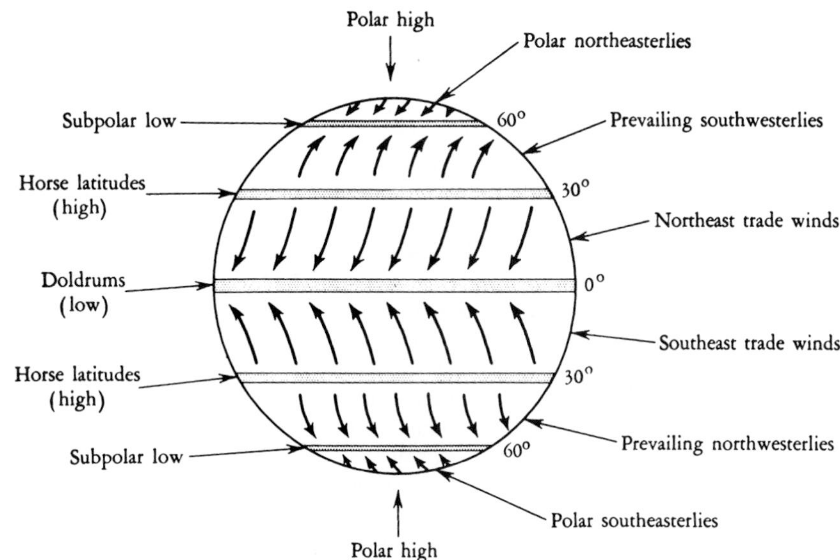

FIGURE 11.9 Diagram of the major wind belts on Earth.

B. In the oceans that lie along the equator, there are powerful currents just above and below the equator, called the **equatorial currents.**

1. The equatorial currents move toward the west, driven by the steady winds that are present in these regions.
2. If there were no continents, these currents would move in a continuous circle around the Earth. However, the continents make these currents turn to the north or the south, and they even make the currents turn back on themselves.
3. The current flowing just above the equator is called the North Equatorial Current, and the current flowing just below the equator is called the South Equatorial Current.

C. The **North Equatorial Current** of the Atlantic Ocean moves westward to the West Indies, where it branches.

1. One branch moves north along the east coast of the United States as the Gulf Stream, while the other branch goes into and around the Gulf of Mexico, where it becomes enlarged and warmer. Then it passes through the Straits of Florida and flows north, rejoining the first branch at Cape Hatteras and becoming part of the Gulf Stream.

D. The **Gulf Stream** is one of the strongest water currents on Earth, moving about 6 kilometers per hour (4 mph) in a path that is about 160 kilometers (100 mi) wide.

1. Because of the Earth's rotation, the Gulf Stream moves to the right, northeast toward Europe.

LEARNING ACTIVITY 11.7

Ocean Currents and the Earth's Rotation

Obtain a globe that can spin. Spin the globe very slowly in a counterclockwise direction (from west to east). At the same time pour a small amount of fairly thick blue washable paint in a thin stream onto the north pole. As the stream flows down the Northern Hemisphere, it is deflected to its right (to the west) by the earth's rotation. When the stream crosses the equator and enters the Southern Hemisphere, it is now deflected to its left (to the east). It can be made equally obvious that ocean currents moving to the north pole are deflected to their right, and currents moving to the south pole are deflected to their left. This demonstration will help to show students why the ocean currents have a clockwise circulation in the Northern Hemisphere and a counterclockwise circulation in the Southern Hemisphere.

2. When the Gulf Stream reaches the North Atlantic Ocean, it branches into two weaker currents.
3. The first branch moves directly toward Europe, where, as the **Norwegian Current,** it warms the shores of Iceland, the British Isles, Norway, and Sweden; the second branch turns south, as the **Canary Current,** and returns to the North Equatorial Current.
4. Thus, there is a complete circle of current in the North Atlantic Ocean. In the center of this circle is a very large, quiet area of water called the **Sargasso Sea,** where great masses of sargassum seaweed (kelp) accumulate. This area is sometimes remembered as the legendary graveyard of lost ships.
5. The **Labrador Current** flows out of the Arctic Ocean into the North Atlantic, carrying very cold water southward to the northeast coast of the United States as far as Cape Cod, where it then sinks below the surface.

E. South Atlantic Currents are similar to the North Atlantic Currents but flow in the opposite direction, moving from the equatorial zone westward, to the northern part of South America, where they turn south.

1. They move along the South American coast as the **Brazil Current,** then east as the South Atlantic Current to Africa, where they move north as the **Benguela Current,** and finally return to the **South Equatorial Current.**

F. The North Equatorial Current of the Pacific Ocean moves westward to the Philippines, where most of it turns northward as the **Japan Current** (called **Kuroshio** and the equivalent of the Atlantic Ocean's Gulf Stream).

1. The warm Japan Current then turns to the northeast as the **North Pacific Current.** It heads toward the Pacific coast of the United States and divides into two branches, the **Alaska Current,** which flows northward and warms the southern coast of Alaska, and the **California Current,** which flows southward, carrying cooler waters down the west coast of the United States. It then rejoins the North Equatorial Current off the coast of Mexico.

G. The **South Equatorial Current** of the Pacific moves westward across the Pacific Ocean.

1. The many islands in the South Pacific make it difficult to follow the direction of this current as it nears Asia and is turned southward. The islands weaken the current by dividing it into several smaller currents that branch off in different directions.
2. The only strong current in the South Pacific is the **Peru Current,** which carries cold water from the south polar region to the coast of South America and then rejoins the South Equatorial Current of the Pacific.
3. Generated by winds that are blowing to the west, the Antarctic Current is formed in the southernmost parts of the Atlantic and Pacific Oceans. Because there are no landmasses in this area, this current completely circles the Antarctic region and is called the **Antarctic Circumpolar Current.**
4. As the Antarctic Circumpolar Current approaches the western coast of Australia, a portion of it branches northward and helps to form the South Equatorial Current of the Indian Ocean, which, as it approaches Madagascar and the coast of Africa, branches into the southern-flowing **Agulhas Current** and the northern-flowing **Somali Current.** Circling eastward along the southern tip of India, the Somali Current becomes the **Southwest Monsoon Current,** which eventually branches, one branch flowing northward into the Bay of Bengal, the other southward along the western coast of Indonesia.

H. In addition to surface currents that are driven by the wind, there are also powerful currents that flow deep below the surface of the sea. These are called **deep-sea currents.**

1. Some deep-sea currents are caused by the slow movement of cold water from the polar regions to the equator. Because cold water is denser than warm water, the cold waters around the polar regions sink and travel along the ocean bottom to the equator.
2. In 1959, scientists found a deep current 2,750 meters (9,000 ft) below the Gulf Stream, going in the opposite direction of the Gulf Stream surface current at a speed of about 13 kilometers (8 mi) a day.
3. Other deep currents, also traveling in opposite directions from the surface currents, have been discovered in the South Atlantic Ocean and the Pacific Ocean.
4. Some deep currents are caused by a difference in concentration of salt in the seawater. The more salt in the seawater, the denser the water is.
5. Inasmuch as the **Mediterranean Sea** is shallow compared with the large oceans, a larger percentage of its water is exposed at its surface. As a result, evaporation of water from the surface causes a greater increase in salt concentration in the Mediterranean than it does in the Atlantic Ocean. For this reason, the waters of the Mediterranean Sea (like those of the Great Salt Lake in Utah) become saltier and denser.
6. At Gibraltar, where the Atlantic Ocean and the Mediterranean Sea meet, there is a strong, deep current of saltier and denser water that runs along the sea bottom past Gibraltar and into the Atlantic Ocean.

VII. Life in the Ocean

A. Ocean water has a tremendous amount of oxygen, minerals, and other chemicals dissolved in it—conditions necessary to support a wide variety of life.

B. The ocean contains tiny organisms, called **plankton**, that consist largely of diatoms (see Chapter 13) and other small organisms, which are the basic food for sea life. All forms of sea life either feed directly on plankton or eat animals that feed on plankton.

1. Plankton grow in tremendous numbers in the upper layers of the ocean, where sunlight is plentiful. Consequently, many organisms that live in the ocean are found either near the shore or in the surface waters.

C. In the middle and deepest parts of the ocean, there are also living things, but like the *coelacanth* fish, they often do not look at all like the living things found nearer the surface.

D. Small animals, called **corals** (see Chapter 14), affect shorelines in warm waters.

1. Corals live in colonies in clear, sunlit ocean water, where water temperature is at least 20°C (68°F), at a depth of no more than 30 meters (100 ft).
2. When young, the animals swim freely, but when they mature they permanently fasten to the sea floor, where they depend on the ocean waves and currents to deliver food to them.
3. Corals also remove calcium from the seawater to make the shells in which they live as adults. When the corals die, their shells remain. New colonies of corals grow on top of these shells. Eventually, the accumulation of shells forms a **coral reef**, which is separated from the mainland by a broad lagoon of calm water. Sometimes when there is a volcanic cone (a seamount) close to the surface of the water, corals form in a narrow, circular ring around that cone, called an **atoll.**
4. The coral reef is an important ecological habitat for many other organisms and also protects the shoreline from ocean storms.
5. Corals are sensitive to changes in ocean temperature. Global warming (the greenhouse effect discussed later in this chapter) results in an increase in ocean temperatures, which in turn can cause massive deaths of coral. Subsequent exposure to sunlight causes a bleaching out of the dead coral. This bleaching-out effect is hypothesized to be useful as an indicator of an increase in ocean temperatures due to global warming.

VIII. The Importance of the Oceans

A. Oceans have a tremendous effect on global weather and climate.

1. The slow heating and cooling properties of water have a moderating effect on Earth's temperature and help prevent extremes of hot and cold.
2. Temperature fluctuations in the ocean, such as those caused by the **El Niño,** can also have tremendous effect on the global weather and economy.
3. El Niño (Spanish for "The Little Boy," referring to the Baby Jesus because of the tendency of the phenomenon to arrive around Christmas) is a disruption of the ocean-atmosphere system in the Tropical Pacific along the coast of Ecuador and Peru. This is due to an unusual warming of the ocean temperatures in the Equatorial Pacific. For example, during the 1997–1998 El Niño the eastern Pacific had risen more than 6°C (43°F) from its temperature a year before.
4. **La Niña** (Spanish for "The Little Girl") is the opposite, characterized by unusually cold ocean temperatures in the Equatorial Pacific. Occurring between El Niños, La Niña occurs roughly half as often as does El Niño.
5. An El Niño occurs every 4 to 5 years, during which time unusual weather conditions occur around the globe, as jet streams, storm tracks, and monsoons are shifted. The El Niño event may last for a few months to a year or longer, having significant economic and atmospheric consequences worldwide.
6. Twenty-three El Niño events were recorded in the 20th century, the most damaging of which was the one in 1997–1998.
7. During non-El Niño years, in the Tropical Pacific, trade winds generally drive the surface waters westward. The surface water becomes progressively warmer going westward because of its longer exposure to solar heating. El Niño is observed when the easterly trade winds weaken, allowing warmer waters of the western Pacific to migrate eastward and eventually reach the South American Coast. The cool nutrient-rich seawater normally found along the coasts of Ecuador and Peru is replaced by warmer water depleted of nutrients, resulting in a dramatic reduction in ocean life.
8. To learn more about El Niño, a network of buoys has been established in the tropical Pacific to collect data on temperature, currents, and winds in the equatorial band. The data are available to researchers and forecasters around the world.

B. Oceans are like huge highways that ships use to bring food and supplies to all parts of the world.

C. The oceans supply a large amount of the food we eat. The farming and cultivation of materials from the ocean is called **mariculture.**

D. The oceans make it possible for us to grow things on land.

1. Water evaporates in tremendous amounts from the surface of the oceans, forming water vapor that rises into the air.
2. The air then moves across the land, and eventually the water vapor condenses into rain and other forms of precipitation, providing water for the soil.

E. Because our demand for freshwater may eventually become greater than the supply, scientists and engineers continue to look for inexpensive ways of changing salt seawater into freshwater.
1. The removal of salts and other chemicals from seawater is called **desalination.**
2. Although hundreds of desalination plants are now operating, the cost of operation is still high.

F. Ocean waves and tides can be harnessed to power turbines to generate electricity.

G. The oceans are far more delicate than people once believed, so today's scientists worldwide are cooperating to find ways to preserve and protect this vast natural resource.
1. Threats to ocean ecology include oil spills, destruction of estuaries, toxic dumping, and the introduction of nonindigenous species of plants and animals that outcompete the indigenous species.
2. Fishing is one of the greatest threats to marine diversity. For example, the population of swordfish in the Atlantic Ocean is estimated now to be only 50% of what it was in the 1970s. Seafloor trawling disrupts bottom communities and coral reefs. For example, sponges in the Gulf of Maine, which are believed to have been important nursery habitats for cod, have not been seen since 1987.

Winds

I. The Earth and Its Atmosphere Are Heated by the Sun

A. The radiant energy from the Sun passes through the air, causing little rise in temperature. Most of the Sun's radiant energy passes through the atmosphere and strikes the Earth's surface, which absorbs this energy and changes it into heat.
1. The heated Earth's surface then warms the air above it. It does this in two ways.
2. The warm Earth radiates some of its heat energy back into the air, which absorbs much of this heat energy and becomes warmer.
3. Although air is a poor conductor of heat, some of the Earth's heat is conducted into the air just above the Earth.

B. Every day the air goes through a cycle of heating and cooling.
1. When the Sun shines on the Earth, the air becomes warmer as the heated Earth radiates heat energy.
2. At night, the Earth cools and the air becomes cooler.
3. The air becomes much warmer in the summer, when the days are longer, than in the winter, when the nights are longer.
4. Cloudy nights are warmer than clear nights because the clouds act as a blanket to reflect and absorb the radiant energy given off by the Earth. In this way, they keep the heat within the air next to the Earth.

II. The Earth Is Heated Unequally

A. The Earth is heated unequally because of its shape.
1. Because the Earth's surface is curved, the Sun's rays strike different parts of the Earth at different angles.
2. The direct or vertical rays of the Sun are always striking the Earth fairly close to the equator.
3. Away from the equator, the Sun's rays strike the Earth's surface at a slant.
4. The closer we get to the polar regions, the more the Earth is curved, and the greater is the slant of the Sun's rays striking the Earth's surface.
5. Direct rays are warmer than slanted rays. With direct rays the Sun's energy is concentrated over a smaller area of the Earth's surface, whereas with slanted rays the same amount of energy is now spread out over a large area, making the energy less concentrated.
6. Because the Earth's surface that receives direct rays of the Sun becomes warmer than the surface that receives slanted rays, the air above this warmer surface becomes warmer as well.
7. When the northern hemisphere has spring and summer, the Earth is tilted so that the Sun's rays shine directly on the northern hemisphere somewhere between the equator and the Tropic of Cancer. This makes the northern hemisphere warmer during its spring and summer than it is during its fall and winter, when the Sun's rays are more slanted in the northern hemisphere and more direct in the southern hemisphere.

B. The different surfaces of the Earth are heated unequally.
1. Some surfaces of the Earth absorb and radiate heat faster than others.
2. Dark and rough land surfaces, such as rocks and soil, absorb heat quickly and radiate it just as quickly.
3. Bodies of water have clear, smooth surfaces. They absorb and radiate heat more slowly.
4. As a result, when the Sun shines directly on land and water surfaces, the land surfaces become warmer than the water surfaces, and the air above the land surfaces becomes warmer as well.

LEARNING ACTIVITY 11.8

Absorption of Radiant Energy by Dark and Light Surfaces

Obtain two cans exactly the same size. Paint the outside of one can with flat, black paint, and paint the outside of the other can with white paint. Now put equal amounts of water into each can so that the cans are about one-half to three-quarters full. Place a thermometer in each can (the thermometers must have the same reading), and place both cans in the sunlight (Figure 11.10). If no sunlight is available, use a hot plate placed on its side and equidistant from both containers. Record the temperature reading every 15 minutes for 1 hour. The water in the black can will become warmer than the water in the white can.

FIGURE 11.10 A black surface absorbs radiant energy more quickly than a white surface.

Inquiry-Based Learning Activity 11.8. Modified

Ask your students a question, "If you want to stay cool on a hot and sunny day, does the color of the clothes you wear make a difference? Let's do some experiments to find out if there is any difference in temperature between some different colored shirts." Ask your students to bring to class a colored t-shirt. If any of the shirts have a logo on them, simply turn them inside out. For this activity you will need some thermometers. Place each thermometer in a plastic ziplock bag, and place the bag into a shirt laying flat on the ground in the sunshine. Lay out an array of shirts with bagged thermometers inside of them. Wait 15 minutes and check the temperature on the thermometers. Record the data on a sheet of paper. Divide your students into groups of two or three, ask them to come up with a creative way to display the information to help people understand which colors are hotter and which colors are cooler to wear on a hot, sunny day. Provide each group with markers, crayons, and a poster board.

What level of inquiry is this modification? This activity begins with a question provided to them by you, the teacher. However, once the data is collected, they are given the freedom of creating a means of communicating the results of the experiment. In addition, they are responsible for collecting the data and recording it. This activity combines ***Level I with Level II (Transition from Level I).*** This type of activity offers students some initial structure to guide their thinking, but then provides them with some limited autonomy to express what they have learned. **Some questions to consider.** Should you as the teacher read and record the data from the thermometers to be more accurate? Should you measure the temperature of every t-shirt that the students bring in, or should you group them into colors and choose only one t-shirt from each group? How should this decision be made?

III. Unequal Heating of the Earth's Surface Causes Winds

A. Convection occurs when hot air rises because it has expanded and become less dense, and cool air falls because it has contracted and become more dense.

1. Convection causes vertical (up and down) winds.

B. Because cold air is denser than warm air, cold air exerts more pressure or force than warm air.

1. Winds are formed when cold air from high-pressure areas moves to low-pressure areas where the air is warmer.
2. In general, this type of wind blows from the poles toward the equator.
3. It might also blow from land to water or vice versa whenever there is a temperature difference between the air over the land and the air over the body of water.

IV. The Constant Movement of Air Over the Entire Earth Is Referred to as Wind Belts

A. If the Earth did not rotate on its axis, the movement of the air over the Earth would be simpler.

1. At the equator, the heated air would rise and flow toward the North and South Poles, and at the North and South Poles the colder air would move toward the equator. However, because the Earth does rotate, the movement of air over the Earth is more complicated.
2. Winds in the northern hemisphere are deflected to their right. Winds in the southern hemisphere are deflected to their left. As a result, a series of wind belts is produced around the Earth, with the winds in each belt moving in a definite direction (see Figure 11.9).
3. The sun's rays shine differently on the northern and southern hemispheres in the

LEARNING ACTIVITY 11.9

Land and Sea Breezes

Place sand in a beaker until it is half full. To another beaker add water until it is the same level as the sand. See Figure 11.11. Place a thermometer in each beaker and keep the beakers in a shady place until both thermometers read the same. Now place both beakers in direct sunlight (or if no sunlight is available, place them a few inches and equidistant from a hot plate lying on its side), and read the thermometers every 15 minutes for 1 hour. The temperature of the sand will be higher than the temperature of the water. Relate this difference in temperature to the formation of sea breezes and land breezes.

FIGURE 11.11 Soil heats up more quickly than water.

summer and winter, causing the wind belts to shift with the seasons.

B. The **doldrums** is an area of low pressure at the equator. Most of the air movement in the doldrums is upward, as the heated air rises. There are mostly calms in the doldrums, with occasional light breezes.

C. The heated air above the equator rises and moves toward the North and South Poles, cooling as it moves higher into the atmosphere. At about one-third of the distance from the equator to the poles (30-degrees latitude), the air has cooled enough to sink down toward the Earth's surface again. This belt of descending, high-pressure air is called the **horse latitudes.** The air is still warm, but not as warm as the air in the doldrums. There are also mostly calms in the horse latitudes, with occasional light, changeable winds.

D. The air sinking at the horse latitudes forms two wind belts. One flows back toward the equator, and the other flows toward the poles.
   1. The winds flowing back to the equator are called the **trade winds.**
   2. Because of the Earth's rotation, in the northern hemisphere the trade winds are deflected, or turned, to their right and become the northeast trade winds, and, in the southern hemisphere the trade winds are deflected to their left and become the southeast trade winds. The trade winds blow very steadily with respect to direction and speed.
   3. Winds that flow from the horse latitudes toward the poles are called the **prevailing westerlies.**
   4. Because of the Earth's rotation, in the northern hemisphere the prevailing westerlies are deflected to their right and become the southwesterlies, and in the southern hemisphere the prevailing westerlies are deflected to their left and become the northwesterlies.
   5. The prevailing westerlies are not as steady as the trade winds and vary more, both in direction and in speed.

E. At a little more than two-thirds of the distance from the equator to the poles (65 degrees latitude), there is a second belt of low-pressure area, called the **subpolar lows.** At this point, the warmer air that is still moving toward the poles is pushed up by the cold air moving down from the poles toward the equator. The upward movement of this warm air produces an area of low pressure.

F. At the poles, masses of cold air move down toward the equator, forming **polar easterlies.** They move to their right in the northern hemisphere to become the polar northeasterlies, and to their left in the southern hemisphere to become the polar southeasterlies. The polar easterlies move in the same direction as the trade winds, but are cold and violent.

G. In the northern hemisphere, there is a narrow band or river of high-speed winds, called the **jet stream,** that separates cold and warm air masses.
   1. These winds are located in the prevailing westerlies, but they are 8 to 16 kilometers (5 to 10 mi) above the surface of the Earth and travel at speeds as high as 640 kilometers per hour (400 mph).
   2. They move eastward around the Earth, but with some variation.
   3. The position and speed of the jet stream vary with the seasons, moving northward in the summer, and southward in the winter.
   4. The jet stream is about 13 to 16 kilometers (8 to 10 mi) high (above the Earth) in the summer, and 8 to 11 kilometers (5 to 7 mi) high in the winter.
   5. Its winds move faster in the summer.
   6. Besides the northern jet stream, there is a jet stream in the southern hemisphere similar to the stream in the northern hemisphere, another in the lower stratosphere of the Arctic Circle, and yet another in the lower stratosphere of the Antarctic Circle.

7. In the winter, when traveling in the same direction, jet airplanes take advantage of the jet stream, using it as a strong tailwind to reduce flying time and fuel consumption.

H. A **monsoon** is a seasonal wind that changes its direction in summer and in winter. A monsoon wind is produced by the difference in heating between continents and oceans during summer and winter.

1. In summer the land is heated more than the ocean, and so the cooler air over the ocean moves in across the land.
2. In winter the land becomes colder than the ocean, and so the cooler air over the land moves out toward the ocean.
3. The best example of a monsoon is found in India. In summer, the Indian Ocean is cooler than the hot land. The air above the hot land becomes hot and buoyant, forming a low-pressure area, and the cooler, moist air from the Indian Ocean blows across the land. This summer monsoon, also called a **wet monsoon,** brings India its rainy season from May through October. In winter, northern India becomes much colder than the Indian Ocean. The air above the cold land becomes cold and dense, forming a high-pressure area, and the cold, dry air blows from the land to the Indian Ocean. This winter monsoon, also called a **dry monsoon,** brings dry weather to India from November through April.
4. Australia, Spain, and Portugal also have monsoons.

I. The conditions that cause land and sea breezes are similar to those that create the monsoons.

1. Land and sea breezes are winds at the seashore that blow in one direction in the daytime and in the opposite direction at night.
2. During the day, the land and sea receive the same amount of heat from the sun. But land heats more quickly and becomes warmer than the sea.
3. The air over the land becomes warmer and more buoyant (less dense) than the air over the sea. The warmer air over the land is forced upward by the cooler air coming from the sea to produce a sea breeze.
4. At the seashore a sea breeze usually begins before noon and dies down at sunset.
5. At night the land loses its heat more quickly than the water, and the air over the land becomes cooler and denser than the air over the water. The cooler, heavier land air moves out to sea, forming a land breeze.
6. Land breezes blow during the night and die down at sunrise.
7. Land breezes are weaker than sea breezes.
8. Land and sea breezes can also be formed at large lakes.

J. Mountain and valley breezes are also a kind of daily monsoon.

1. During the day, the sunny, exposed mountain heats up more quickly than the sheltered, shady valley.
2. The air over the mountain becomes warmer and more buoyant than the air in the valley.
3. A cool valley breeze then blows up the mountain and pushes the warmer, less dense mountain air up and away.
4. At night the mountain cools more quickly than the valley, so the air over the mountain becomes cooler than the air in the valley. A cool mountain breeze then blows down the mountain into the valley, pushing the warmer, more buoyant valley air up and away.
5. The narrower the valley, the stronger the mountain and valley breezes. Because a valley breeze has to travel uphill, its speed is not as great as that of a mountain breeze.

Water in the Air

I. Evaporation

A. When water changes from a liquid into an invisible gas, called **water vapor,** this change is called **evaporation.** Evaporation takes place because of molecular motion within the water. Evaporation occurs at the surface of the water.

1. Water is made up of molecules that are constantly moving. Some of these molecules have more energy and move faster than others.
2. The faster-moving molecules near the surface of the water leave the surface and go off into the air, becoming molecules of water vapor.
3. Some solids, like mothballs and solid air deodorizers, can evaporate directly as a solid without first becoming a liquid.

B. Several factors affect the speed of the evaporation of water.

1. Heat makes water evaporate more quickly. It makes the molecules move faster, so more molecules can leave the water at one time.
2. The larger the surface, the more quickly evaporation will take place because more molecules can leave the water at one time.
3. The amount of water vapor already in the air affects the speed of evaporation. If the air already contains a lot of water vapor, there is less room in the air for more molecules of water vapor to enter, and the speed of evaporation is slow. If the air contains only a little water vapor, there is plenty of room in the air for more molecules to enter, and evaporation takes place more quickly.

4. Wind helps water evaporate more quickly. As molecules leave the water and become water vapor, the air above the water eventually becomes filled, or saturated, with water vapor. This saturation slows evaporation because there is no more room in the air for more molecules of water vapor to enter. Wind blows away the air that is saturated with water vapor and provides new air that can hold a fresh supply of water vapor.
5. The lower the air pressure above the surface of the water, the faster evaporation takes place. Lower air pressure means that the air is not pressing down as hard on the surface of the water. This lower air pressure makes it easier for the molecules to leave the water and go into the air as water vapor.
6. Warm, dry air can hold more water vapor than cold, moist air. Consequently, the warmer and drier the air above the water, the faster the water evaporates.

C. Liquids other than water also evaporate. At a given temperature, some liquids evaporate faster than others because of a weaker attractive force between molecules of the more volatile liquid.

D. Evaporation is a cooling process.
1. When a liquid evaporates, it takes in, or absorbs, heat from materials around it.
2. When a drop of liquid is placed on a person's skin, the liquid begins to evaporate, and because the evaporating liquid gets its heat from the skin, the skin becomes cooler. The quicker the liquid evaporates, the more heat it needs and the cooler the skin becomes.
3. This is why evaporation of perspiration, or water, on the skin cools the body.
4. When a liquid evaporates, the liquid itself becomes cooler.
5. The faster-moving molecules in the liquid have a higher temperature than the slower-moving molecules.
6. When the faster-moving molecules leave a liquid and become a vapor, the cooler, slower-moving molecules are left behind, making the liquid cooler.

LEARNING ACTIVITY 11.10

*Evaporation of Water**

A. The Effect of Heat on Evaporation

Put 10 drops of water in each of two pie tins the same size. Put one on the window sill where the sun can shine on it. Put the other tin in the coolest place in the classroom. The water will evaporate more quickly in the heated tin because the water molecules move faster, and thus the molecules can leave the water faster.

B. The Effect of Surface Area on Evaporation

Using a measuring cup, put equal amounts of water in a pie tin, a water tumbler, and a bottle. Set all three containers on a table where conditions such as temperature and air currents will be the same for each container. The next day, pour any water remaining in the containers back into the measuring cup, one at a time for each container, and measure each amount. The most water will have evaporated from the pie tin, which has the largest surface area, because more water molecules were able to leave the water at one time.

C. The Effect of Wind on Evaporation

Obtain two sponges of the same size and wet them. Make two spots of equal wetness on the chalkboard. Fan one of the spots vigorously with a piece of cardboard. The moisture on the fanned spot will evaporate more quickly because the fanning blows away the saturated air above the spot and provides a fresh supply of unsaturated air.

D. The Effect of Humidity on Evaporation

Compare the time it will take for water in a wet cloth (or in a pie tin) to evaporate on a dry day when the humidity is low, and on a damp or rainy day when the humidity is high. The greater the humidity, the more water vapor there will be in the air, and the less opportunity there will be for more molecules of water to go off into the air.

E. The Cooling Effect of Evaporation

Dip your forefinger into a tumbler of water. Keeping the wet forefinger and dry middle finger a slight distance apart, blow on both fingers at the same time. As the water evaporates from the forefinger, the heat needed for evaporation is taken from the finger, leaving the finger cooler. The middle finger, which serves as a control, does not become cooler.

F. The Rate of Evaporation of Different Liquids

Have a student extend both hands, palms down. Put one drop of rubbing alcohol on the back of one hand and a drop of water on the back of the other hand. Observe that the alcohol will evaporate more quickly because of the weaker attractive forces between its molecules. In addition, because the rubbing alcohol evaporates more quickly, it takes heat away from the hand more quickly, and the spot with the alcohol on it will feel cooler as well.

*To conserve space in this book, these activities are written only as instructions for studying the evaporation of water. To the extent that safety, availability of materials, and the maturity of your students allow, we encourage you to incorporate these activities into your own lesson plans in such a way that your students are doing as much of the activity as possible, individually or in groups, rather than you doing them as teacher demonstrations.

II. Humidity

A. Humidity refers to the water vapor content of the air.

1. **Absolute humidity** is the actual amount of water vapor present in the air at a certain temperature.
2. **Relative humidity** is the ratio between the actual amount of water vapor in the air (absolute humidity) at a certain temperature and the maximum amount of water vapor the air can hold at that temperature.
3. Relative humidity is multiplied by 100 to give the result in percentages. When the air contains as much water vapor as it can hold at a certain temperature, the air is considered saturated, and the relative humidity is 100%.

III. Condensation and Deposition

A. **Condensation** is the term referring to the change of water from a vapor to a liquid.

1. Condensation takes place because of a change in the molecular motion of the molecules of water vapor in the air. When air containing water vapor is cooled, the water vapor molecules move more slowly and come closer together, and if the air is cooled enough, the molecules come together closely enough to become liquid water.
2. Condensation also takes place because air contracts, or becomes smaller, when cooled. As air containing water vapor is cooled, the air will keep on contracting until it is saturated with water vapor and can hold no more. Any further cooling will make the air contract even more and cause some of the water vapor to liquefy.
3. The temperature below which air must be cooled for condensation to take place is called the **dew point.** The higher the dew point temperature, the higher the moisture content for air at a given temperature.
4. The same factors that affect the speed of evaporation also affect the speed of condensation, but in reverse. The condition that speeds evaporation slows the process of condensation, and vice versa.

B. **Deposition** is the term referring to the change of water from vapor to solid.

1. **Dew** and **frost** are forms of deposition that take place on surfaces at or near the Earth at night.
2. At night, the Earth's surface and solid objects on it give up their heat rather quickly and become cool. The air coming in contact with these surfaces is also cooled.
3. If the air is cooled below its dew point, the water vapor in the air deposits on these surfaces as water droplets, called dew.
4. If the dew point is below freezing (0°C, or 32°F), the water vapor deposits as crystals of ice, called frost. Frost is not frozen dew.
5. Dew and frost deposit on any surface that has a temperature lower than the dew point of the air that touches the surface.
6. Dew and frost form more easily on a clear night, when the surfaces can radiate their heat away more quickly through the air, whereas clouds act like a blanket to prevent the heat from radiating away.
7. Dew and frost form more easily on a calm night, because winds blow the air around and prevent the air next to the Earth from getting cold enough to cause deposition.

LEARNING ACTIVITY 11.11

*Condensation of Water**

A. Condensing Water Vapor

Add water to a shiny can until the can is half full. Add ice cubes and stir. Soon a thin film of tiny droplets of water will form on the sides of the can, as the air containing water vapor is cooled and the molecules of water vapor move more slowly and come close enough together to become water again. The thin film will gradually form large droplets. In summer the humidity may be so high that the water vapor condenses without the addition of ice cubes. In winter the humidity may be so low that salt has to be added to the cold water and ice cubes to get the water vapor to condense.

B. Factors Affecting Condensation

The same factors affecting the speed of evaporation also affect the speed of condensation, but in reverse. Repeat part A in (a) a cold and a warm location, (b) a windy and a calm location, and (c) a dry and a humid location.

C. Find the Dew Point

Repeat part A, and relate the results to the formation of dew and rain. Find the dew point by slowly adding small pieces of ice to a can half filled with water, stirring regularly with a thermometer. Measure the temperature at which a thin film of water appears on the sides of the can. Be careful not to breathe on the sides of the can when watching for dew to form, because the water vapor in your breath will condense on the cold sides of the can and produce inaccurate results.

*To conserve space in this book, these activities are written only as instructions for studying condensation of water. To the extent that safety, availability of materials, and the maturity of your students allow, we encourage you to incorporate these activities into your own lesson plans in such a way that your students are doing as much of the activity as possible, individually or in groups, rather than you doing them as teacher demonstrations.

IV. Fogs and Clouds

A. When a sizable layer of air next to the Earth's surface is cooled below its dew point, the water vapor in this layer condenses into tiny water droplets to form a fog.
   1. A fog is a cloud at or near ground level.
   2. The water droplets are heavier than air, but they are so small and fall so slowly that the slightest air movement is enough to keep them floating in the air.
   3. **Ground fog** forms under exactly the same conditions as dew and frost form.
   4. Ground fogs often form in valleys, which fill with cold, heavy air.
   5. In the morning, the sun warms the air, which expands and can then hold more water vapor. The water droplets in the fog evaporate and the fog disappears.
   6. An **advection fog** is formed when warm, moist air from one region blows over a cool surface.
   7. Advection fogs are quite common along the seacoast when warm, moist air from the sea blows over the cooler land. In the Grand Banks of Newfoundland, fogs are very common because the warm, moist air from the Gulf Stream blows constantly over the cold Labrador Current.

B. **Clouds,** like fogs, are formed when a mass of air is cooled.
   1. When warm air containing water vapor rises high in the air, it becomes colder.
   2. The warm, rising air reaches levels where the air pressure is less, and the air expands.
   3. When air expands by itself, it uses up some of its heat energy to make it expand, and the air becomes colder.
   4. If the air is cooled below its dew point, the water vapor in the air condenses as tiny droplets of water to form a cloud.
   5. The water vapor usually condenses around tiny bits of dust or other particles in the air.
   6. If the air is below freezing (0°C, or 32°F), the water vapor condenses directly as tiny ice crystals.
   7. Just as with fog, the droplets of water or ice crystals in the cloud are heavier than air, but they are so small and fall so slowly that the slightest air movement is enough to keep them floating in the air.
   8. A cloud on Earth would look like fog, and a fog high in the air would look like a cloud.

C. The shapes of clouds are determined by how they are formed.
   1. If the movement of the cooling air is vertical, clouds form in large, billowy masses.

LEARNING ACTIVITY 11.12

Fog

Fill a clean, dry soda bottle (or any narrow-necked bottle) with very hot water, adding the water slowly to prevent the glass from cracking. Now pour out most of the water, leaving about 5 centimeters (2 in.) at the bottom. Put an ice cube on the mouth of the bottle (Figure 11.12) and hold the bottle between you and the sunlight or the light of a lamp. A fog will form in the bottle as the warm, humid air is cooled by the ice cube and the cool air below the ice cube, and the water vapor condenses in tiny droplets that float in the air.

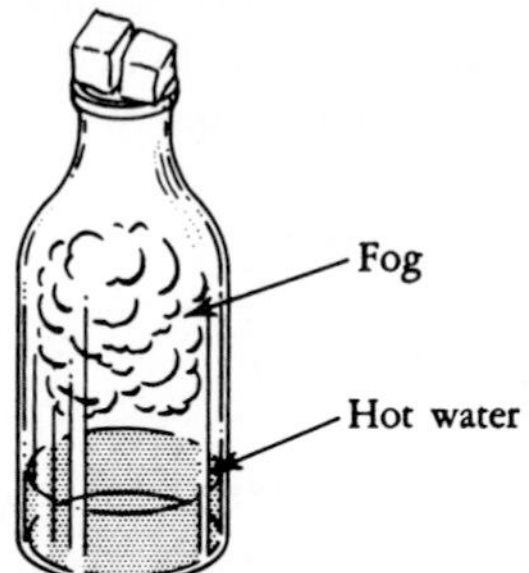

FIGURE 11.12 Condensation produces a fog in a bottle.

LEARNING ACTIVITY 11.13

Dust Particles Help in the Formation of Clouds

Take a clear, clean 2-liter plastic water bottle. Pour 2 or 3 centimeters (about 1 in.) of very hot water into the bottle. Put on the cap and swirl the water around inside the bottle so the inside of the bottle is wet throughout. Remove the cap and pour out the water. Light a match and blow it out. While the match is still smoking, squeeze the bottle, then hold its mouth near the match and let go, pulling smoke into the bottle. Put the cap on the bottle. When you squeeze the bottle, wispy clouds of water vapor will form. When the bottle is let go, the clouds disappear.

Explanation: The smoke is made of tiny particles, as are specks of dust. When you squeeze the bottle, you increase the pressure inside. Droplets of water form on the smoke particles and a cloud is formed.

2. If the movement of the cooling air is horizontal, clouds form in layers.

D. The three basic types of clouds are cirrus, cumulus, and stratus.
   1. **Cirrus** (meaning "curl") **clouds** are the highest clouds, from 6 to 13 kilometers (4 to 8 mi) high in the sky. They look like thin wisps of curls or like thin feathers. Because they are so high, they contain tiny ice crystals.
   2. **Cumulus** (meaning "heap") **clouds** look like large fluffs of cotton or wool and are below 1.8 kilometers (approximately 1 mi) in the sky. Although they are flat on the bottom, they can pile up quite high. They most often form in the afternoon, and they usually disappear toward evening. They are usually associated with fair weather. On hot summer days, cumulus clouds may grow very large and black, causing thunderstorms with heavy rain and sometimes hail.
   3. **Stratus** (meaning "layer") **clouds** are made up of low layers and are the clouds nearest (below 1.8 km, or about 1 mi) to the Earth. They usually cover the whole sky and blot out the Sun. They are usually associated with stormy weather.

E. Sometimes a cloud is given two names because it has the characteristics of two different cloud types.
   1. **Cirrostratus clouds** are high, thin, feathery layers of ice-crystal clouds that often produce the appearance of a halo or ring around the Moon or Sun, indicating the coming of rain or snow.
   2. **Stratocumulus clouds** are layers of cumulus clouds (below 3 km, or 3.3 mi) that cover the whole sky, especially in winter.
   3. **Cirrocumulus clouds** are a large group of small, round, high (above 5.5 km, or 3.5 mi) fluffy clouds that are made up of ice crystals.

F. Scientists also add prefixes to the names of clouds, which help them describe the clouds more accurately; prefixes include *alto* (high), *nimbus* or *nimbo* (rain), and *fracto* (broken).
   1. **Altostratus clouds** are high (1.8 to 6 km, or 1 to approximately 4 mi) stratus clouds, and **altocumulus clouds**, high (1.8 to 6 km, or 1 to approximately 4 mi) cumulus clouds.
   2. **Nimbostratus clouds** are rain clouds.
   3. **Cumulonimbus clouds** are thundershower clouds, also called thunderheads.
   4. **Fractocumulus** clouds are cumulus clouds that have been broken up into smaller masses.

V. Precipitation

A. *Precipitation* refers to all forms of moisture that fall to Earth from clouds in the upper atmosphere.
   1. Rain, drizzle, sleet, snow, and hail are forms of precipitation because they fall from the atmosphere.
   2. Fog and clouds are not forms of precipitation. They are forms of condensation.
   3. Dew and frost are not forms of precipitation. They are forms of deposition.

B. **Rain** is water that falls from a cloud. The droplets of water in a cloud are so small that the slightest air movement is enough to keep them floating in the air. These droplets come together and form larger drops, which in turn come together to form even larger drops. When the drops of water are large and heavy enough, they fall to the Earth as rain.

C. **Drizzle** is the only other form of precipitation that falls as a liquid. Drizzle is made up of very fine cloud (or fog) droplets that fall very slowly. Ordinarily, these water droplets would stay in the cloud or fog, but sometimes the air is so still that they fall to Earth.

D. **Snow** is the most common form of solid precipitation.
   1. Snow forms from water vapor that condenses when the temperature of the air is below freezing.
   2. The water vapor condenses directly into ice crystals, or snow.
   3. Snow, therefore, is frozen water vapor, not frozen rain.
   4. Every snow crystal has six sides to it, but no two snowflakes are exactly alike.
   5. When the air near the ground is cold, the snowflakes fall separately.
   6. When the air near the ground is warmer, the snowflakes melt together to form large clots of wet, sticky snow.

E. **Sleet** is frozen rain, usually formed during the winter when raindrops fall through a below-freezing layer of air near the ground.

F. **Glaze** is a coating of ice that forms when rain freezes after it reaches the ground.
   1. The rain forms a thick coating of ice on streets, trees, telephone and electric wires, and other objects.
   2. When this phenomenon occurs, it is called an **ice storm.**
   3. The coating of ice often becomes so heavy that it makes bushes and tree branches collapse, breaks telephone and electric wires, and makes traveling on highways dangerous or impossible.

G. **Hail** is formed mostly in the summer during a thunderstorm, when there are strong upward currents of air within a thundercloud.
   1. These currents carry the raindrops high into a layer of below-freezing air.
   2. The raindrops freeze and become pellets of ice.
   3. These pellets of ice then fall into warmer air, where they pick up another coating of water.
   4. Then the pellets, now coated with water, are blown up again into the colder air, where the coating of water freezes to form a second layer of ice.

LEARNING ACTIVITY 11.14

Frost, Snow, Sleet, and Glaze

Fill a tall can with alternate layers of cracked ice and table salt. Make each ice layer twice as thick as the salt layer. Pack the mixture down firmly. Put some drops of water on a piece of wax paper, and set the can on top of the water (Figure 11.13).

Use enough water to make one large drop high enough to touch the bottom of the can. Some dew may form on the sides of the can and then freeze, but frost will also form as the temperature of the air beside the can falls to below freezing.

When the sides of the can are well covered with frost, remove the can from the wax paper. The large drop of water will have frozen into ice. Point out that frost and snow are formed when water vapor condenses directly into ice crystals, whereas sleet and glaze are formed when raindrops freeze.

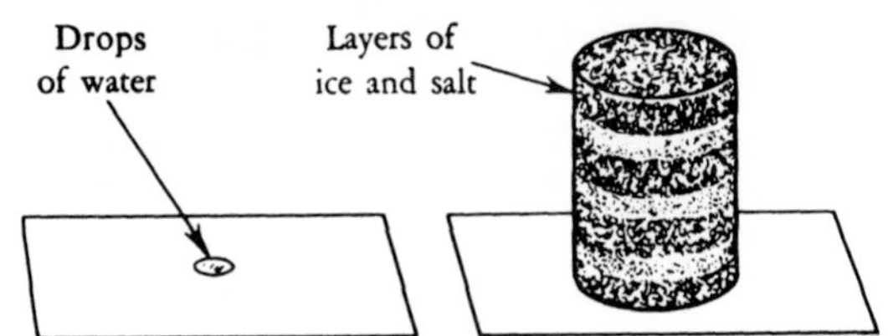

FIGURE 11.13 Frost, snow, sleet, and glaze are formed at temperatures that are below freezing.

LEARNING ACTIVITY 11.15

Model of the Hydrologic Cycle

Fill a Pyrex pot with water and heat it on a hot plate until the water is boiling. Fill a frying pan with ice cubes and hold the pan about 10 centimeters (4 in.) above the pot (Figure 11.14). A miniature water cycle will be produced as the water vapor from the boiling water is cooled by the cold bottom of the frying pan, causing droplets of water to condense on the bottom of the pan and then drop back into the water.

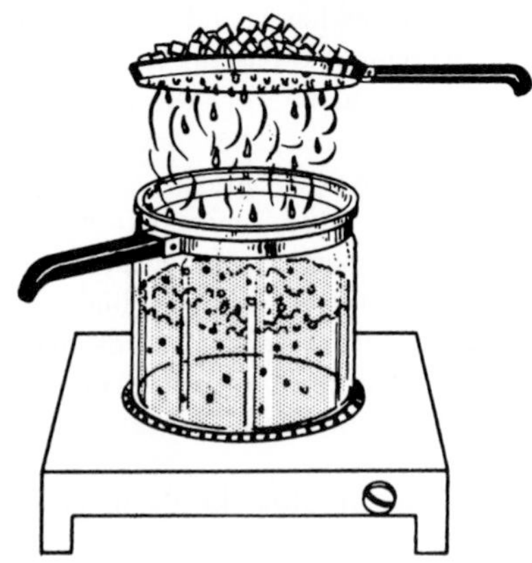

FIGURE 11.14 A model water cycle.

5. This process is repeated until the pellets of ice, now called hailstones, become too heavy for the upward air currents to lift, and the hailstones fall to Earth.
6. A hailstone is formed somewhat like an onion, with an ice pellet as its center and many layers of ice around this center.
7. Each layer shows one complete movement up into cold air and back down again into warmer air.
8. The more violent the thunderstorm, the more times the hailstones move up and down between the layers of cold and warm air and the larger the hailstones become, sometimes as large as a softball. When hailstones are large enough, they can cause great damage to crops and can even hurt small animals. The largest hailstone ever recorded in the United States fell on Coffeyville, Kansas, in September 1970. It weighed 757 grams (1.7 lb) and had a diameter of more than 14 centimeters (5.5 in.).

VI. The Water, or Hydrologic, Cycle

A. All the water on Earth is constantly evaporating to form water vapor.
   1. This evaporation takes place from the surfaces of the oceans, lakes, ponds, reservoirs, and rivers. Water also evaporates from the soil, and plants give off water vapor during transpiration.
   2. This water vapor is constantly condensing back into water again.
   3. On or near the ground, water vapor condenses as dew, frost, and fog.
   4. High in the air, water vapor condenses as clouds and finally falls back to Earth as precipitation.
   5. This process of evaporation and condensation goes on in a continuous cycle, called the water cycle or hydrologic cycle.

B. One aspect of the hydrologic cycle is that all water that evaporates from the ocean eventually returns to the ocean.
   1. Most water flowing in rivers and streams is eventually carried to the oceans.
   2. Groundwater also flows directly into the sea or into streams and lakes on the Earth's surface.
   3. Precipitation over the oceans may return water directly to the oceans.

Weather

I. Conditions and Changes in the Weather

A. When describing the weather at a certain time and place, a forecaster usually lists the conditions of the air at that time and place.
   1. These conditions include the temperature of the air, the air pressure, the amount of moisture in the air (humidity), the dew point, and the direction and speed of the wind.

B. When predicting or forecasting the weather, the weather forecaster looks at the kinds of air masses that are moving across the Earth.
   1. These air masses are responsible for changes in the weather.

II. Air Masses

A. An air mass is a huge body of air that may cover a vast portion of the Earth's surface and may be very wide and quite high.
   1. In any air mass, the temperature and humidity are about the same throughout.
   2. Air masses differ greatly from one another; the weather an air mass will bring depends mostly on its particular temperature and humidity.
   3. An air mass is formed when the atmosphere remains quietly over a certain part of the Earth's surface until it picks up the temperature and humidity of that part of the Earth's surface.
   4. An air mass formed over Canada is cold and dry. An air mass formed over the Gulf of Mexico is warm and humid.

B. Air masses are named according to the part of the Earth's surface over which they are formed.
   1. Those that are formed in the tropics are called **tropical** (T) and are warm.
   2. Those that are formed in the polar regions are called **polar** (P) and are cold.
   3. Air masses also come from continents and oceans. Air masses from continents are called **continental** (c) and are dry.
   4. Air masses from oceans are called **maritime** (m) and are humid.
   5. Consequently, there are four possible kinds of air masses (see Figure 11.15).
      a. The **continental tropical** (cT) air mass is dry and warm.
      b. The **maritime tropical** (mT) air mass is moist and warm.
      c. The **continental polar** (cP) air mass is dry and cold.
      d. The **maritime polar** (mP) air mass is moist and cool to cold.
   6. Once an air mass is formed, it is usually carried to another place by the general movements of the atmosphere.
   7. Air masses often change their conditions when they move from one place to another.
   8. A dry air mass can move out over the ocean and become moist.
   9. When a cold air mass moves over a warmer surface, the lower part of the air mass becomes warmer and rises, producing clouds and possibly precipitation.
   10. A warm air mass can become a cold air mass automatically, just by moving over a part of the Earth's surface that is colder than the air mass.
   11. In the same way, a cold air mass can become a warm air mass if it moves over a warmer part of the Earth's surface.

C. The air masses that affect the weather in North America come from six different areas.
   1. **Polar Canadian** (cP) air masses are formed over north-central Canada and move in a southeasterly direction across Canada and the northern United States. They are cold and dry. In the winter they bring the cold waves that sweep across the United States and sometimes move as far south as the Gulf coast; in the summer they bring cool, dry weather.
   2. **Polar Atlantic** (mP) air masses are formed over the northern Atlantic Ocean, and although they generally move eastward toward Europe, they can also move southward to affect the northeastern part of the United States. They are cold and moist, and in the winter they bring cold, cloudy weather and some form of light precipitation; in summer they bring cool weather with clouds and fogs.
   3. **Polar Pacific** (mP) air masses are formed over the northern Pacific Ocean, and although they usually travel southward along the Pacific coast, they sometimes move eastward across the United States. They are cool rather than cold and are very moist. In winter they bring rain and snow, and in summer they bring cool, foggy weather.
   4. **Tropical Continental** (cT) air masses are formed over Mexico and the southwestern United States and usually move in a northeasterly direction over the central part of the

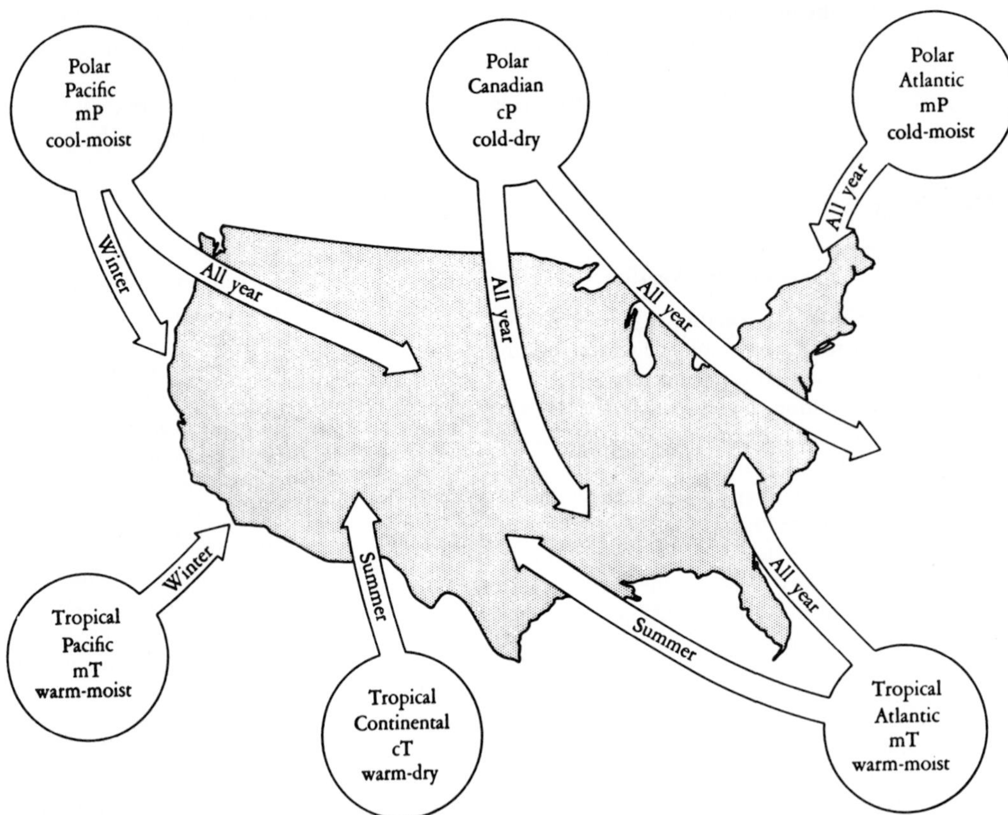

FIGURE 11.15 Diagram of the major North American air masses.

United States. They are warm and dry and affect North America only in the summer, bringing dry, clear, and very hot weather.

5. **Tropical Atlantic** (mT) air masses are formed over the tropical part of the Atlantic Ocean and the Gulf of Mexico and usually move in a northeasterly direction over the eastern part of the United States. They are warm and moist; in winter they bring mild weather, and in summer they bring hot, humid weather; thunderstorms; and hurricanes.
6. **Tropical Pacific** (mT) air masses are formed over the tropical part of the Pacific Ocean and usually move in a northeasterly direction across the Pacific coast. They are warm and moist and affect the Pacific coast only in winter, bringing cool, foggy weather.

III. Weather Fronts

A. When two air masses meet, the boundary between them is called a **front.** Along the front, there is almost always some form of precipitation. This precipitation occurs because a very large amount of warm, moist air is rising to great heights along the front, and rising, moist air means precipitation.

B. There are two common kinds of fronts—warm fronts and cold fronts.
   1. If warm air is pushing colder air ahead of it, the front is called a **warm front.** Because masses of warm tropical air usually come from the southwest, warm fronts in the United States generally move toward the northeast.
   2. If cold air is pushing warmer air ahead of it, the front is called a **cold front.** Because masses of cold polar air usually come from the northwest, cold fronts in the United States generally move toward the southeast.

C. In the Temperate Zones of both North and South America, the principal changes in weather are brought about by the passage of warm and cold fronts.
   1. When a warm front advances, warm air moves up over the retreating cold air. The slope of the warm front is very gradual, and the warm air may have to travel as much as 1,600 kilometers (1,000 mi) to rise 8 kilometers (5 mi).
   2. When the warm air rises, it becomes cooler and the water vapor in the air condenses to form large masses of clouds along the entire warm front.

3. Where the level of the warm air is highest, cirrus clouds form.
4. Behind the cirrus clouds are different forms of stratus clouds, each kind floating lower and lower, with nimbostratus or rain clouds last and nearest the ground.
5. The rains produced by a warm front cover a wide area, are usually steady, and last until the warm front passes.
6. When a cold front advances, the cold air pushes under the warm air that is retreating and lifts up this warm air.
7. A cold front moves more quickly than a warm front because the air in a cold front is colder and denser. Dense, cold air can push less dense, warm air out of the way more quickly than less dense, warm air can push more buoyant, cold air.
8. As the warm air is lifted up very quickly, it cools, and the water vapor in the air condenses to form different kinds of clouds, most typically cumulonimbus or thundershower clouds.
9. The rains produced by a cold front cover a smaller area, are rather violent, and last only a short time as the front passes.

D. A **stationary front** is the boundary line between a cold air mass and a warm air mass when both air masses stop and do not move for several days.
   1. When this stoppage occurs, the boundary between the two air masses becomes a slope that is as gentle as that of a warm front.
   2. As a result, the weather produced by a stationary front is about the same as that produced by a warm front.

E. Sometimes an **occluded front** is formed when a warm air mass, which lies between two cold air masses, is lifted up by the cold air mass behind it.
   1. To create an occluded front, both cold air masses and the warm air mass between them must all be moving in the same direction.
   2. Because cold fronts move faster than warm fronts, sometimes the second cold air mass at the rear catches up with the first cold air mass in front, and at the same time lifts the warm air mass completely off the ground.
   3. This condition—an occluded front—brings a combination of warm and cold front weather.
   4. Moreover, as the occluded front passes, there is no change in the temperature of the air, because there is only a change from one mass of cold air to another.

IV. Lows and Highs

A. The air masses that move across the Earth differ in air pressure.
   1. Cold air masses have higher pressures than warm air masses.
   2. This difference occurs because cold air is denser than warm air, and it can exert more pressure than warm air.

B. An area of low pressure is called a **low**, or a **cyclone.**
   1. The lowest air pressure in a low is at its center.
   2. As a result, air of higher pressure blows inward toward the center of the low.
   3. Because of the Earth's rotation, the air in the northern hemisphere is deflected to the right. In the southern hemisphere, it is deflected to the left.
   4. This deflection makes the air blowing toward the center of the low travel in a circular, counterclockwise direction in the northern hemisphere (see Figure 11.16).
   5. Lows, or cyclones, usually bring precipitation. This occurs because the warmer, buoyant air in a low pressure area is pushed up by the colder, denser air around it.
   6. The warmer air rises and becomes colder, so clouds and precipitation form.
   7. The precipitation caused by lows usually covers a wide area. The lows in the United States start in the northwest, southwest, and southeast, and then move toward the northeast and end in New England, bringing all kinds of weather changes. They travel about 1,100 kilometers (700 mi) a day in winter and 800 kilometers (500 mi) a day in summer.

C. An area of high pressure is called a **high** or an **anticyclone.**
   1. The highest air pressure in a high is at its center. As a result, air blows outward from the center of the high.
   2. Because of the Earth's rotation, the air blowing outward from the center of a high travels in a circular, clockwise direction in the northern hemisphere (see Figure 11.16).
   3. Highs, or anticyclones, usually bring fair weather. This weather occurs because the colder, denser air in a high-pressure area is falling toward the Earth. As the air falls, it becomes warmer.

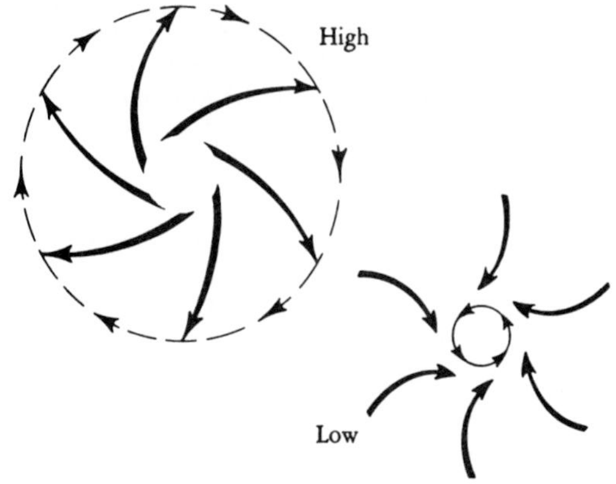

FIGURE 11.16 Highs travel in a clockwise direction, and lows travel in a counterclockwise direction.

4. Because warm air can hold more moisture, or water vapor, than cold air, no precipitation takes place and the weather is bright and clear.
5. Highs in the United States can start in either polar or tropical regions.
6. They also travel eastward across the United States, but more slowly than lows.
7. Highs from the polar regions bring extreme cold waves in winter, and cool, clear weather in summer. Highs from the tropical regions bring mild weather in winter, and hot, dry spells in the summer.

V. Hurricanes, Cyclones, and Typhoons

A. Hurricanes develop from thunderstorms that begin over warm water in the Atlantic Ocean or eastern Pacific Ocean.
   1. Ocean thunderstorms form as the warm, moist air of summer rises and hits cold air.
   2. The thunderstorms begin to merge into a cluster, which may reach from 161 to 483 kilometers (100 to 300 mi) in diameter.
   3. The thunderstorm cluster forms a center of low pressure, which is then classified as a **tropical depression.**
   4. Surface winds of a tropical depression reach 32 to 61 kilometers per hour (20 to 38 mph) as the storm drifts and begins to rotate.
   5. As evaporation and condensation intensify, rising warm air is trapped and spreads out in all directions, forming rain bands.
   6. Spinning, as a result of the Earth's rotation, increases, and winds reach 63 kilometers per hour (39 mph). The storm is now classified as a **tropical storm.**
   7. Billions of gallons of water evaporate and condense, fueling the storm.
   8. Warm air in the center loses its moisture, forming an **eye.**
   9. A calm area of about 32 kilometers (20 mi) across, the eye is surrounded by wall clouds where the strongest winds and heaviest rains are found. The winds of the wall clouds can cause a **storm surge,** where the ocean along a shoreline rises up to 5 meters (15 ft).
   10. In the Pacific Ocean, when winds reach 119 kilometers per hour (74 mph), with an average diameter of 483 kilometers (300 mi), a tropical storm is technically known as a **tropical cyclone.**
   11. A tropical cyclone formed west of the **International Date Line**—the 180th meridian—is called a **typhoon.** If it is east of the line, it is called a **hurricane.** All hurricanes formed in the western Atlantic Ocean are called hurricanes. All hurricane-force storms formed in the Indian Ocean are known as **cyclones.**

B. Hurricanes are classified according to the strength of their winds and their barometric pressure. There are five categories of hurricanes as designated by the Saffir-Simpson scale.
   1. A Category 1 hurricane produces winds of 119 to 154 kilometers per hour (74 to 95 mph). It can blow down signs, power lines, and tree branches but is unlikely to cause structural damage to buildings. It creates a barometric pressure of 28.94 or more.
   2. A Category 2 hurricane produces winds of 155 to 177 kph (96 to 110 mph) and is likely to cause greater damage to signs and trees. It creates a barometric pressure of 28.50 to 28.93.
   3. A Category 3 hurricane produces winds of 178 to 209 kph (111 to 130 mph) and can cause damage to signs, trees, and some buildings. It creates a barometric pressure of 27.91 to 28.49.
   4. A Category 4 hurricane produces winds of 210 to 250 kph (131 to 155 mph) and can cause great destruction to doors, windows, and roofs of buildings, and to utility poles, trees, and crops. It creates a barometric pressure of 27.17 to 27.90. In 1992, hurricane Andrew, which devastated south Florida, and hurricane Iniki, which hit the Hawaiian Island of Kauai, were both classified as Category 4 hurricanes.
   5. A Category 5 hurricane, the strongest type, produces winds greater than 250 kph (155 mph) and causes catastrophic damage to buildings, trees, crops, utility poles, and anything else in its wide path. It creates a barometric pressure of less than 27.17. According to the National Hurricane Center in Coral Gables, Florida, only two Category 5 hurricanes have hit upon United States soil during the modern era of record keeping: one in Florida in 1935 and one on Mississippi's Gulf Coast in 1969. However, it is possible that hurricanes Andrew and Iniki, in 1992, may have developed Category 5 winds. The sheer strength of the winds of Category 4 and 5 hurricanes makes wind measurements very difficult. Wind-speed measuring instruments often are literally blown away.

VI. Tornadoes

A. Tornadoes, also called **twisters,** are the smallest, most violent, and most short-lived of all storms.
   1. They occur almost exclusively in the United States. There are between 700 and 1,000 a year, chiefly in the Mississippi Valley and the eastern half of the Great Plains. The states where tornadoes commonly form are Iowa, Kansas, Texas, Arkansas, Oklahoma, Mississippi, Illinois, Indiana, Ohio, and Missouri. However, tornadoes may also occur in any level land area.
   2. They are most frequent during the spring and early summer, and they usually occur during the afternoon.

B. Tornadoes are formed under special conditions.
   1. Ordinarily cold, heavy air moves under warm, light air.

2. When a tornado is formed, a layer of cold, dry air is pushed over a layer of warm, moist air. The warm, moist air then quickly forces its way in a spiral movement through the layer of cold air.
3. Strong, whirling winds are formed around a center of low pressure, producing a tornado.

C. A tornado looks like a narrow, funnel-shaped, whirling cloud that is very thick and dark.
1. The funnel reaches down toward the Earth, and its tip may touch the Earth as it moves along. Sometimes the funnel rises for a while, and then it comes down again a short distance away. More than one funnel may emerge from a tornado cloud.
2. The vortex or tip of the funnel acts like a big vacuum cleaner, sucking in air from near the ground. The tornado funnel is usually dark because of dirt and debris that has been sucked up from the ground.
3. Tornadoes vary in size but can be as much as 1 kilometer (.6 mi) wide.
4. Although the tornado itself moves in a wandering path at a speed of about 40 to 64 kilometers (25 to 40 mi) an hour, the winds spin around like a top and can reach a speed of 800 kilometers (500 mi) an hour. When a tornado passes a particular point, a deafening roar is heard. Many people report that it sounds like a train passing through.
5. Lightning, thunder, and heavy rain usually accompany a tornado.
6. The tornado usually lasts about 8 minutes and travels about 24 kilometers (15 mi).

D. A tornado that passes over a body of water is called a **waterspout.**
1. In a waterspout the bottom part of the funnel is made of spray instead of the dust and other materials found in a tornado over land.
2. A waterspout has very little water in it. Most of its lower part is a fine mist or spray, with perhaps a few feet of water at the bottom.

E. A tornado can cause a tremendous amount of damage.
1. The strong winds blow away almost everything in their path. Strong tornadoes can lift an automobile.
2. The center of the tornado is also very destructive, because the air pressure within the funnel is very low.
3. Buildings within the center of the funnel often explode, because the normal air pressure inside a building becomes so much greater than the suddenly reduced air pressure outside.

VII. Thunderstorms and Lightning

A. Thunderstorms are strong, local storms formed from cumulonimbus clouds that involve heavy rain, accompanied by lightning, thunder, and strong gusts of wind.
1. Sometimes hail falls at the beginning of a thunderstorm.
2. A thunderstorm is short, rarely lasting more than 2 hours, but it is possible to have many thunderstorms in a day.

B. Thunderstorms are formed whenever warm, moist air is pushed upward rapidly, accompanied by equally rapid downdrafts of cool air.

C. An **air-mass thunderstorm**, usually called a summer thunderstorm, is formed within an air mass during hot, summer afternoons.
1. Summer thunderstorms are local storms that form over scattered areas.
2. This happens when hot, moist air above the Earth's surface rises, forming first cumulus and then cumulonimbus clouds.

D. A **frontal thunderstorm** is formed when a cold front arrives, pushing warmer air ahead of it.
1. This air movement forms a series or line of thunderstorms, which may be hundreds of miles long and up to 80 kilometers (50 mi) wide.
2. Frontal thunderstorms can occur at any time of day or year.

E. **Lightning** is a huge electrical flash produced in cumulonimbus clouds during a thunderstorm.
1. Worldwide, there are an estimated 100 lightning flashes every second, with more occurring over land than over water.
2. By the time you have read this second sentence about lightning, lightning will have struck more than 100 times across the Earth.
3. Each lightning flash delivers about 1 trillion watts of electricity in a matter of microseconds.
4. Lightning originates around 15,000 to 25,000 feet above sea level when raindrops are carried upward until some of them convert to ice. For reasons that are not yet agreed upon, a cloud-to-ground lightning flash originates in this area of mixed water and ice.
5. Lightning flashes that do not strike the ground are called **cloud flashes** and make up about 80% of all lightning. Cloud flashes can be inside a cloud or they can travel from one part of a cloud to another or from cloud to air.
6. Most of the lightning that we see is the single bolt of bright light. However, there are other types of lightning, including forked lightning, ribbon lightning, bead lightning, ball lightning, and sheet lightning. Heat lightning is lightning that has occurred too far away for us to hear the accompanying thunder.
7. The fast-rising air rubs against the water droplets in the cloud and charges them electrically. The top of the cloud becomes positively charged, while the bottom of the cloud becomes negatively charged.
8. Sometimes the fast-rising air is strong enough to rip the cloud in two, so that each half has a different electrical charge.

9. When the force of attraction between the positively and negatively charged parts of a cloud becomes great enough, a huge spark of electricity, called lightning, flows from the negatively charged part to the positively charged part.
10. Lightning heats air to more than 15,000°C (27,000°F), nearly three times hotter than the surface of the Sun, which is about 6,000°C (10,800°F).

F. **Thunder** is the sound produced by the rapid heating and expansion of the air through which lightning passes.
   1. The rumbling of thunder is a series of echoes produced when thunder is reflected many times by clouds.
   2. Lightning is seen first and thunder is heard next.
   3. This order occurs because lightning travels with the speed of light, which is about 300,000 kilometers per second (186,000 mps) whereas thunder travels with the speed of sound, which is about 0.3 kilometers per second (0.2 mps).
   4. Because it takes thunder about 3 seconds to travel 1 kilometer (5 seconds to travel 1 mi) and lightning is seen almost instantaneously, we can calculate how far away we are from the lightning of a thunderstorm. If you count the number of seconds that pass from the time the lightning is seen and the thunder is heard, and divide this number by 3, the answer will be the number of kilometers you are away from the lightning. (If you divide the number of seconds by 5, the answer will be the number of miles away from the lightning.)

G. Just as powerful and fascinating as what comes from the underside of storm clouds are the flashes of gamma-rays, called **terrestrial gamma-ray flashes** (or TGFs), that have been observed coming from the top. The flashes last only a few milliseconds and have been detected only recently by satellites orbiting the Earth.

Meteorology and Climatology

I. Meteorology

A. **Meteorology** is the science that deals with the study of the weather, which is the condition of the atmosphere at a particular time and place. (**Climatology** is the science that deals with climates over long periods.) A meteorologist is a professional who studies and forecasts the weather. Meteorologists can make fairly accurate weather forecasts by collecting data about the temperature, the air pressure, the direction and speed of the wind, the humidity, the kind and amount of precipitation, and the condition of the sky. To collect this information, the meteorologist uses a wide variety of weather instruments.

II. Instruments Used in Meteorology

A. **Air temperature** is measured using a **thermometer.**
   1. One kind of thermometer used is the **liquid thermometer.** It consists of a hollow glass tube with a liquid in it. The liquid expands and rises when heated, and it contracts and falls when cooled. The temperature scale on the weather thermometer is either the Fahrenheit (F) scale or the Celsius (C) scale, which is the scale used in science laboratories. Although the United States still uses the Fahrenheit scale, the rest of the world uses the Celsius scale.
   2. Meteorologists also use a **metal thermometer.** Rather than having a liquid in it, the metal thermometer uses a strip of metal made up of two different heat-sensitive metals that have been welded together.
   3. The two metals expand and contract differently when heated and cooled, and the unequal expansion and contraction make the metal strip bend or twist.
   4. The metal strip is wound into a coil, and a pointer is attached to the outside free end of the coil. When the metal strip bends or twists, a pointer moves across the temperature scale and shows the temperature.
   5. A **thermograph** is a metal thermometer that records the temperature continuously all day.
   6. Today's meteorologists use electronic computers rather than the mechanical thermograph to make continuous and permanent recordings. This permanent record also shows the maximum, or highest, and the minimum, or lowest, temperature for that day.

B. **Atmospheric pressure** is measured with the **barometer.** Two kinds of barometers are commonly used: the mercury barometer and the aneroid barometer.
   1. The **mercury barometer** is a narrow glass tube about 92 centimeters (36 in.) long, sealed at one end, that has been filled with mercury and then turned upside down into a dish of mercury.
   2. Some of the mercury runs out of the tube until the pressure of the air on the mercury in the dish just supports a column of about 76 centimeters (30 in.) of mercury in the tube.
   3. When the air pressure becomes greater, or increases, the air pushes harder on the mercury in the dish, making the mercury in the tube rise.

4. The mercury moves easily up the tube because there is no air in the space above the level of the mercury, so there is nothing to slow or stop its upward movement.
5. When the air pressure lessens, or decreases, the mercury moves down the tube. The height of the mercury in the tube is a measure of the pressure of the air at the time.
6. The **aneroid** (meaning without liquid) **barometer** does not use mercury. It is sturdier, safer, and less awkward to use than the mercury barometer.
7. It has a thin, hollow disc from which some of the air has been removed. The removal of air makes the disc sensitive to changes in air pressure.
8. When the air pressure increases, the disc is squeezed in; when the air pressure decreases, the disc expands. These minute changes in thickness of the disc are passed on to a pointer that moves across an air-pressure scale.
9. A **barograph** is an aneroid barometer that has a pen at the end of the pointer and uses a revolving sheet of paper with an air-pressure scale on it so that there is a continuous record of the changes in air pressure during the day. To make permanent and continuous records, today's meteorologists use computers rather than the mechanical barograph.
10. Air pressure can be expressed in two ways: in inches or millimeters of mercury, showing the height of a column of mercury that could be supported by a particular air pressure; and in millibars, which are the international air-pressure units.
11. On a weather map, air pressure is shown by isobars, which are solid, curving lines that join points throughout the United States or other parts of the world where the air pressure is the same.
12. Falling air pressure means a low is coming, bringing stormy weather with it, whereas rising air pressure means a high is coming, bringing fair weather with it.

C. **Wind direction** is measured using a wind vane.
   1. The wind vane that is commonly used looks like an arrow. This arrow is mounted on a pole in such a way that it can swing freely when the wind blows on it.
   2. The arrow has a broad tail, and the wind strikes this tail, making the arrow swing so that the head points to the direction from which the wind comes.
   3. Winds are named according to the direction from which they come; thus a south wind is one that comes from the south. A south wind strikes the tail of the wind vane and makes the head point toward the south.

D. An **anemometer** is used to measure **wind speed,** or velocity.
   1. Wind speed is measured in kilometers or miles per hour.
   2. The most common type of anemometer has three hollow cups, all facing the same way, that catch the wind and begin to move. The stronger the wind, the faster the cups move, recording the speed of movement on a meter.

E. **Relative humidity** is measured using a **hygrometer.**
   1. Relative humidity is determined by dividing the actual amount of water vapor in the air (absolute humidity) by the maximum amount of water vapor the air can hold at a certain temperature, and multiplying the result by 100 to express the relative humidity as a percentage.
   2. One common form of hygrometer is the **psychrometer**, or wet-and-dry-bulb thermometer. The psychrometer has two thermometers that are the same, except that one of them has a water-soaked cotton cloth or wick wrapped around its bulb.
      a. Air is made to pass across both thermometer bulbs, either by whirling the thermometers around or by fanning them with an electric fan.
      b. The moving air does not affect the dry thermometer bulb, and that thermometer shows the temperature of the air around it.
      c. However, the moving air causes the water in the wet cloth to evaporate, taking the heat it needs to evaporate from the thermometer bulb inside the cloth.
      d. This evaporation cools the thermometer bulb and makes the temperature fall.
      e. The drier the air, the faster the water in the cloth evaporates, the cooler the bulb becomes, and the lower the reading of the wet thermometer.
      f. When the temperature of the wet thermometer has reached its lowest point, the meteorologist finds the difference in temperature between the wet thermometer and dry thermometer, using this difference to find the relative humidity by consulting a relative humidity table.
      g. Another type of hygrometer, the **hair hygrometer**, uses a bundle of human hairs to find the relative humidity. Human hair is very sensitive to moisture, becoming longer when the air is humid and shorter when the air is dry. This change in the length of the bundle of human hairs makes a pointer move across a scale, from which the relative humidity can be read directly in percentages.

F. **Rainfall** is measured with the **rain gauge.**
   1. The most common form of rain gauge is a narrow cylinder with a funnel on top.

2. The area of the mouth of the funnel is exactly 10 times larger than the area of the mouth of the cylinder; therefore, the cylinder receives 10 times as much water when the funnel is in it than it would receive alone.
3. This larger amount of water is easier to measure, but the amount must be divided by 10 to find the correct amount of rainfall.
4. To measure the amount of rain collected in the cylinder, a marked stick is dipped into the cylinder.
5. Rainfall and snowfall are measured in centimeters or inches, and in tenths or hundredths of a centimeter or inch.

G. **Snowfall** can be measured with a rain gauge or by the depth of snow in an open location.
1. Meteorologists are also interested in how much rain a snowfall might have produced. To make this determination, they melt and weigh a certain number of centimeters or inches of snow.
2. Because snow can be light and fluffy, or heavy and wet, the amount of rainfall that snow may have produced varies. A light, fluffy snow may produce 2 centimeters (1 in.) of rain for every 50 centimeters (20 in.) of snow, but a heavy, wet snow may produce 2 centimeters (1 in.) of rain for every 15 centimeters (6 in.) of snow. As an average, 25 centimeters (10 in.) of snow will make 2 centimeters (1 in.) of rain.

H. The **radiosonde** is used to measure weather conditions at upper levels of the Earth's atmosphere.
1. It contains a small thermometer, a barometer, and a hygrometer. It also has a small radio transmitter that automatically sends out signals showing the temperature, pressure, and relative humidity of the air through which the radiosonde is passing.
2. The 1-kilogram (2-lb) radiosonde is attached to a 2-meter (6-ft) balloon filled with helium. This balloon can travel 16 to 24 kilometers (10 to 15 mi) into the stratosphere before the balloon bursts. A parachute opens when the balloon bursts. This allows the radiosonde to return undamaged to Earth.

I. **Radar** is also used to measure conditions and predict weather.
1. Cloud droplets and raindrops reflect the radar waves and show up on the radar screen.
2. Radar can also locate storms and show the extent of the areas they are covering.
3. It can detect how a storm forms and moves across the Earth.
4. It can measure the speed of high-altitude winds by tracking a balloon as it moves through the air at high levels.
5. It can track hurricanes, locate the eye of a hurricane, follow the movement of the hurricane, and predict its path.

J. **Artificial satellites** are also used to measure conditions and predict global weather, and to send back radar pictures to Earth that are then analyzed by meteorologists.
1. Because the atmosphere's density is altered by the air's temperature, pressure, and humidity, scientists use microsatellites and radio signals beamed from one satellite to another to measure atmospheric density. Orbiting pairs of weather surveillance satellites make it possible to detect weather systems the moment they begin.

III. Artificial Weather

A. Scientists are constantly trying to establish some control of the weather.
1. Scientists have been able to get supercooled clouds high in the sky to give up their moisture. By dropping small particles of dry ice, silver iodide, or other crystals into these clouds, scientists have caused some of the cloud droplets to become ice crystals that grow larger as the water vapor in the cloud condenses on them. When the ice crystals are large enough, they fall as precipitation.
2. Scientists have also invented devices that are able to reduce or eliminate fog on airport landing fields.

IV. Climatology

A. Where **weather** is the condition of the atmosphere at a particular time and place, **climate** is the average weather of a place over a period of years. Climatologists have discovered many factors that affect the kinds of climate found in different parts of the Earth. These factors of climate can be divided into two groups: factors that control the yearly temperature of a particular place, and factors that control the yearly rainfall of that place.

B. Affecting temperature more than any other single factor is a region's **latitude**, that is, its distance from the equator.
1. A region near the equator is said to have a low latitude, and a region near the poles is said to have a high latitude.
2. The higher the latitude, the colder the climate is.
3. Near the equator, where the sun's rays are direct almost all year and the days and nights are equally long, there is the same hot climate throughout the year.
4. Halfway between the equator and the north pole, the Sun's rays are more direct during the summer than in the winter, and the days are much longer than the nights. However, during the winter the Sun's rays are very slanted and the nights are longer than the days, so the winters are cold.

5. Near the poles, the Sun's rays are always very slanted. There, during the summer, the Sun shines all 24 hours of the day for months. The weather is still cold, but mild in comparison with the winter. During the winter near the poles, the Sun does not shine for months and the weather is bitterly cold.

C. Latitude also affects the amount of rainfall a region receives.
   1. The latitude determines in which wind belt a region will be located during the year.
   2. Places where warm, moist wind is rising will have rainy weather, and places where cool, dry air is falling will have dry weather.
   3. Places in the doldrums will have heavy rains all through the year.
   4. Places in the trade winds and horse latitudes will be mostly dry during the year.
   5. Places in the prevailing westerlies will have moderate rainfall all year.
   6. Places in the polar easterlies will have light snow all year.

D. The climate of a place or region is also affected by its **altitude**; that is, its height in relation to sea level.
   1. The higher the altitude of a place, the colder is its climate. Even near the equator, a city that is located at a high altitude experiences a much cooler climate than a city located at sea level.

E. **Land and water masses** affect the climate of a place. Landmasses heat up and cool down more quickly than water masses. As a result, land regions are more likely to have hot summers and cold winters. Sea regions in the same latitude are more likely to have cooler summers and milder winters.

F. **Winds** affect an area's climate.
   1. Because wind belts shift during the year as the Earth revolves around the Sun, some places may be in a rainy belt for part of the year and in a dry belt for the other part of the year.
   2. The direction of the prevailing winds affects the climate of a continent's seacoasts. On the northwest coast of the United States, the prevailing westerlies blow in from the warm Pacific Ocean, so the northwest coast has a cool summer and a mild winter. On the northeast coast of the United States, the prevailing westerlies blow from the land out to the ocean, so the northeast coast has a hot summer and a cold winter.
   3. When winds blow in from the ocean, the regions nearest the ocean get the most rainfall. This distribution occurs because the moisture condenses out of the ocean air as it blows across the land. The warmer the ocean, the heavier the rainfall will be.

G. **Mountains** affect a region's climate.
   1. Mountain ranges and plains determine the extent to which faraway winds affect a region's climate. For example, the high Rocky Mountains stop the mild west coast climate from extending any farther into the Great Plains. At the same time, the level Great Plains allow very cold winds to speed from the poles all the way to the Gulf of Mexico, and allow hot winds from the south to move north, thereby giving the Great Plains hot summers and cold winters.
   2. Mountains affect the amount of rainfall a region will receive. For example, when warm, moist wind strikes the windward side of a mountain and rises, there is much rainfall on that side. However, the leeward or protected side will have very little rain, because most of the water vapor already will have condensed from the air before the air passes over the mountain to the leeward side.

H. **Ocean currents** can make the climate of a region much warmer or colder than normal for the region's latitude.
   1. The prevailing westerlies, blowing from the warm Gulf Stream, give the British Isles and northwestern Europe climates that are just as warm as those of regions that are nearer the equator.
   2. At the same time, winds from the cold Labrador Current give northern Labrador a climate much colder than that of other regions, such as southern Sweden, that has the same latitude.
   3. When ocean currents are much warmer or colder than the land or water around them, much fog is formed. For example, the warm Gulf Stream air striking the cold British Isles causes a great amount of fog. In summer, New England has a lot of fog when the warm winds coming up from the south are cooled by the cold waters of the New England coast.

I. During the past two centuries, carbon dioxide in the atmosphere has increased, and there is worldwide concern that this increase may be warming the Earth's atmosphere. This warming is known as the **greenhouse effect.**
   1. The increase in carbon dioxide is caused mostly by the burning of fossil fuels and the clearing and burning of forests.
   2. An increase in carbon dioxide allows solar radiation to penetrate the Earth's atmosphere but prevents part of the heat reflected or reradiated by land and bodies of water from escaping into space.
   3. As carbon dioxide increases, enough heat may be trapped to cause an increased warming of the Earth's atmosphere, much like heat trapped in a greenhouse. This is where the term *greenhouse effect* originated.

4. Scientists are confident that over the past century, the global average temperature has increased by about half a degree Celsius. Because populations and the use of technology are growing, they hypothesize that the global temperature will increase an additional 1.0°C to 3.5°C by 2100, making the Earth's atmosphere warmer than at any time during the past 100,000 years.
5. The impact of such a change could include the following:

   Changes in intensity and direction of storm tracks.
   Droughts to currently productive farmlands, such as those in the U.S. Midwest.
   Global shifts in rainfall patterns, bringing heavy rains to previously arid areas.
   Increased frequency and occurrence of heat waves.
   Longer frost-free seasons in climates where crops are grown, resulting in more rapid growth and development of weeds and pests.
   Mass flooding of coastal cities and farmlands as a result of the melting of part of the Antarctic ice sheet.
   More severe storms, especially hurricanes.

V. Classification of Climates

A. Climatologists divide the Earth into **tropical**, **middle latitude**, and **polar** climates. Each of these climates is subdivided into various types of climates, depending on their temperature and rainfall.

B. Three different types of climates are included under the classification of tropical climates: the **tropical rainforest**, the **savanna**, and the **desert climates**, all of which are located within 30 degrees latitude above and below the equator.
   1. They all have an average yearly temperature of at least 20°C (68°F), but they differ in the amount of rainfall they get.

C. The **tropical rainforest climate** is found encircling the Earth in regions at or close to the equator. Central Africa, the Amazon Valley, the east coast of Central America, Madagascar, and Indonesia have this climate.
   1. These regions have heavy rainfall all year, averaging 200 centimeters (80 in.) per year.
   2. The temperature is always high, averaging 27°C (80°F).
   3. Because of the high temperature and heavy rainfall, there is a dense growth of plants, often forming a jungle.
   4. The relative humidity is always high, and there is a thundershower almost every afternoon.
   5. Although home to nearly half the Earth's plant and animal species, today the tropical rainforest covers less than 7% of the Earth's land surface. There is international concern today about the rapid destruction of tropical rainforest land for wood, farming, and development.

D. The **savanna climate** is found farther away from the equator. The Sudan of North Africa, the veldt of South Africa, the campos of Brazil, the llanos of Venezuela, the downes of Australia, and parts of India and Burma all have savanna climates.
   1. These regions have wet and dry seasons as the wind belts shift during the year. Mostly coarse grasses, spiny plants, and a few trees grow in the savanna climate.
   2. During the doldrums, there is heavy rainfall. When the wind belts shift, the regions are subjected to the trade winds and have little to no rain.

E. The **desert climate** is even farther away from the equator. The Sahara, Arabian, American, Kalahari (southern Africa), Australian, and Peruvian deserts are found in the desert climate. These are sandy deserts.
   1. The regions in this climate are always in the wind belt of the trade winds, so they get little to no rainfall. As a result, only a few plants grow in these regions.
   2. When rain does come, it falls as a thundershower or cloudburst.
   3. Because there is very little moisture in the air, the days are warm and the nights are cool.

F. Six different types of climate are included under the classification of middle latitude climates: **Mediterranean**, **humid subtropical**, **marine west coast**, **humid continental**, **dry continental**, and **subarctic.** All are located between 30 and 65 degrees latitude.
   1. Although there is a wide range of temperature in these climates, they all have at least 1 month where the average temperature is 10°C (50°F) or higher.
   2. The regions in these climates lie mostly in the wind belt of the prevailing westerlies, which produces all kinds of weather.

G. The regions in the **Mediterranean climate** lie between 30 and 40 degrees latitude in both the northern and southern hemispheres. Southern California, southern Australia, central Chile, and the areas around the Mediterranean Sea have the Mediterranean climate.
   1. These regions are all found on the western side of the continents.
   2. They lie in the path of trade winds or horse latitudes in the summer, and in the path of the prevailing westerlies in the winter.
   3. Summers are warm or hot and almost completely dry. Winters are mild and have some rainy months.
   4. Because the rainfall is only about 40 to 65 centimeters (16 to 26 in.) a year, this climate is also called the **dry subtropical climate.** Fruits, olives, grapes, and nuts grow well in this climate.

H. The regions in the **humid subtropical climate** also lie between 30 and 40 degrees latitude, but on the eastern side of the continents. The southeastern United States, eastern and southern Asia, northern Argentina, and southern Brazil have a humid subtropical climate.
   1. There is no dry season. Annual rainfall is between 90 and 150 centimeters (36 and 60 in.). Tall grasses and pine forests grow in this climate.
   2. Summers are warm and winters are mild, although there are often cold waves and frosts during the winter.
   3. The humidity is very high in the summer and can become uncomfortable.

I. The regions in the **marine west coast climate** lie between 40 degrees latitude and the edges of the polar regions. They lie on the western side of the continents. The northwest coast of the United States, the British Isles, Norway, western Australia, New Zealand, and southern Chile have a marine west coast climate.
   1. Regions with a marine west coast climate are in the prevailing westerlies most of the year, so they get a good supply of rain all year. Hardwood and evergreen trees grow well in these regions.
   2. Where mountains block the movement of the winds, the rainfall is heavy on the windward side of the mountains.
   3. Because the westerlies blow in from the ocean, summers are cool and winters are mild in these regions.
   4. They get more rain and fog in winter than in summer.

J. Regions with a **humid continental climate** are in the same latitude as those with a marine west coast climate, but on the east side of continents. The eastern United States, from the Great Plains to the coast, eastern Europe, and eastern Asia have this humid continental climate.
   1. These regions have hot summers and cold winters.
   2. The weather changes are sharp. These regions experience blizzards, very cold spells, heat waves, high humidity, thunderstorms, and tornadoes.
   3. More rain falls in the summer than in the winter, and rainfall is heavier at the coast. Where the rainfall is more than 76 centimeters (30 in.) a year, both deciduous and evergreen trees grow.
   4. Where the rainfall is less than 76 centimeters (30 in.) a year, tall grasses grow, forming prairies.

K. The regions with a **dry continental climate** are also in the same latitude as the humid continental and marine west coast climates, but in the interior of the continents.
   1. These regions have hot summers and very cold winters.
   2. Rainfall is light and usually heavier in summer than in winter.
   3. Regions of the dry continental climate where the rainfall is 25 to 50 centimeters (10 to 20 in.) a year are called **steppes.** Steppes are found in the midwestern states of the United States, in Argentina, and in Russia. Low grasses and sagebrush grow in the steppes.
   4. Regions where the rainfall is less than 25 centimeters (10 in.) a year are called **middle latitude deserts.** Middle latitude deserts are found in the western United States, western Argentina, and the interior of Asia. The prevalent plants growing in the middle latitude deserts are sagebrush and cactus.

L. Most of the regions in the **subarctic climate** lie between 50 and 65 degrees latitude. Most of northern Canada, Europe north of 60 degrees latitude, and most of Siberia have a subarctic climate. Mostly small evergreen trees grow in this climate.
   1. These regions have very long, cold winters and short, mildly warm summers.
   2. They have less than 40 centimeters (15 in.) of precipitation a year, most of which falls in the summer.
   3. In summer the days are very long, and in winter the nights are very long.

M. Two different types are included under the classification of **polar climates:** the **tundra** and the **icecap climates.** These climates begin where the middle latitude climates end and extend to the poles.
   1. These climates have no summer at all, because the Sun's rays are so slanted that they give very little heat.
   2. There is very little precipitation, because the air is too cold to hold much water vapor.
   3. The **tundra climate** is cold, beginning where the subarctic climate ends. The tundra climate exists only in the northern hemisphere, as there are no land areas in this latitude at the Antarctic.
   4. The average temperature of the warmest month is between 0°C and 10°C (32°F and 50°F). The average temperature of the coldest month is −240°C (−400°F).
   5. The light summer rains permit mosses and lichens to grow.
   6. The **icecap climate** is found near the poles, where the temperature is never higher than 0°C (32°F). There are always icecaps or glaciers in this climate. Precipitation is light and falls only as light snow.
   7. The average yearly temperature is between −224°C and −235°C (−371°F and −391°F). The lowest temperature ever recorded was −288°C (−486°F), in 1960, on the Antarctic icecap.

Exploratory Activities for "Water, Weather, and Climate"

1. WEATHER STATION PROJECT (GRADES 3 AND UP)

Overview

Weather is always an area of interest for student project work in science. After an initial period of data collection from newspaper and television weather reporting, ask the students whether they would like to build a weather station as a class project. Instructions for building the various data collection instruments follow. If they choose to do this, divide the class into groups of three or four students. Each group assumes partial responsibility for the class weather station project. Depending on the evolution of this project, the final product of the students' work can take many forms, such as the following:

- The class makes daily weather forecasts that are announced each day to the entire school.
- Groups assume partial responsibility for aspects of weather study, predicting, and reporting.
- Students post a chart comparing the accuracy of their predictions with those of official weather forecasts.

1.1 Initial Activity

Have the students cut out daily weather maps from the newspaper for two weeks. You can also obtain official weather maps by consulting your local weather station or by writing to the United States Weather Service at Asheville, North Carolina. Examine the weather maps closely. Note the presence and movement of cold and warm fronts across the country. List the kinds of weather changes each front might bring, and check your list with the actual weather conditions that took place in your area. Note the location of highs and lows on the weather map. Compare the kinds of weather found in parts of the country that had highs with those that had lows.

Watch for the appearance of fronts, using the weather forecast as a guide. Forecasts can be as found in the newspaper, on Cable TV's Weather Channel, or in the Blue Skies service on the Internet. When a front begins to move in, have the students keep a record of the weather conditions until the front has passed.

On the chalkboard, draw diagrams of the movement of a cold front and a warm front, showing the kinds of clouds and precipitation that are formed in each case (Figure 11.17).

1.2 Keep a Record of the Weather

Have the students keep a daily weather chart for a month. Make seven columns on a sheet of paper. In the first column, write the date and time the weather observations were made. The weather should be observed at about the same time each day. In the other columns, record the following information: temperature outdoors, air pressure, humidity, direction and speed of the wind, condition of the sky, and kind and amount of precipitation, if any. In the column describing the condition of the sky, make a small circle. Show how much of the sky is covered with clouds by filling in all, part, or none of the circle. While the students are keeping this chart, have them clip the weather forecast from the newspaper each day of the month. Then have them compare the actual weather for each day with the weather predicted for that day, to see how often the weather forecaster was correct.

1.3 Make a Barometer

Obtain a glass jar with a medium-to-narrow mouth. Cut out the dome-shaped end of a rubber balloon and stretch the rubber tightly across the mouth of the bottle or jar, fastening it securely with a rubber band (Figure 11.18). Flatten both ends of a soda straw and cut one of the ends to a sharp point. Place rubber cement or glue on the flattened end of the straw and attach that end to the middle of the rubber sheet. Cut a tiny piece of wood from a match and glue it at the edge of the rubber sheet so that the straw rests on top of the wood.

When the air pressure in the room increases, the rubber sheet is pushed down, making the straw move up. When the air pressure in the room decreases, the greater air pressure inside the bottle pushes the rubber sheet up, making the straw move down. A cardboard scale can help the students see the change in air pressure. Calibrate the marks on the cardboard scale with the readings on a standard barometer. Keep the homemade barometer in a place as free from temperature changes as possible. Otherwise, the air inside the jar will expand and contract, pushing the rubber sheet in and out. Have the students take barometer readings each day for 2 weeks or 1 month and predict the weather on the basis of rising or falling air pressure.

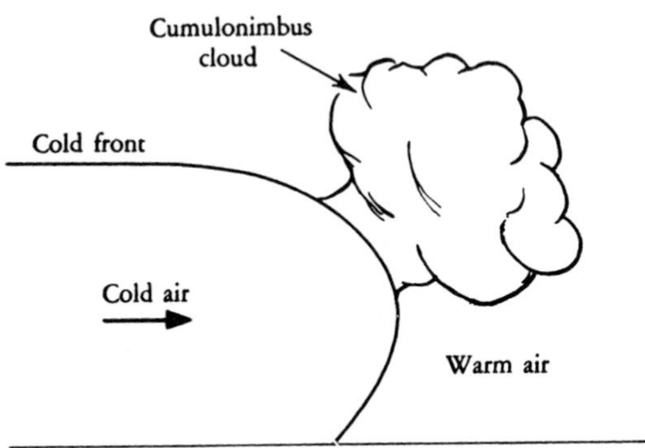

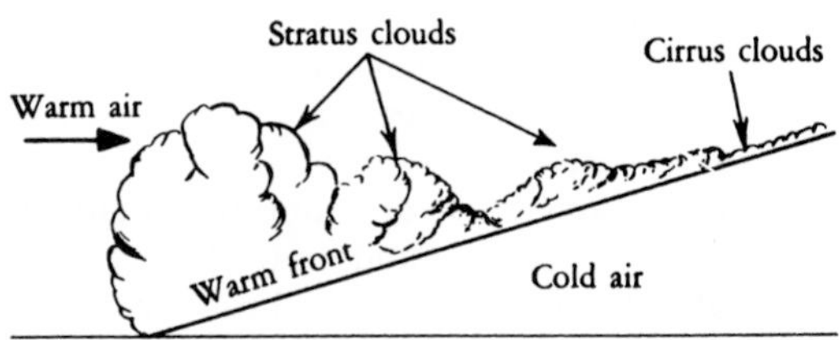

FIGURE 11.17 Diagrams of a cold front and a warm front.

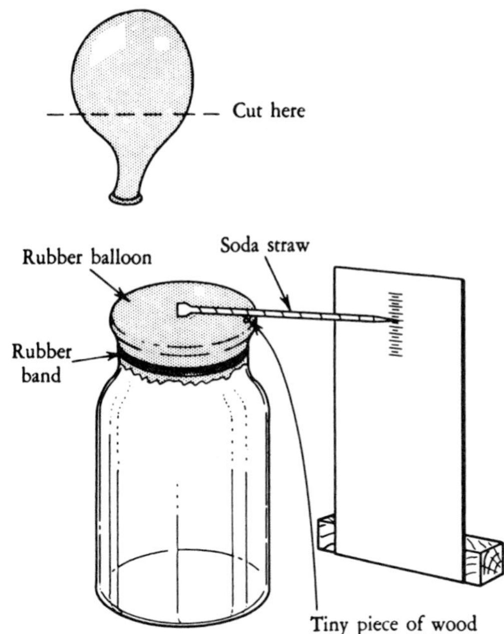

FIGURE 11.18 A homemade barometer.

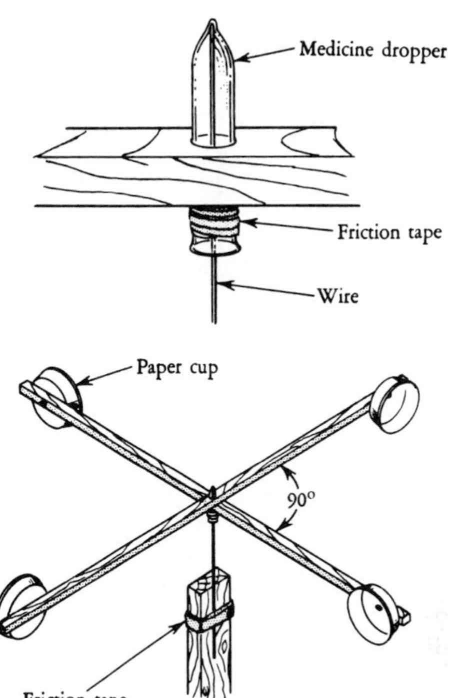

FIGURE 11.20 A homemade anemometer.

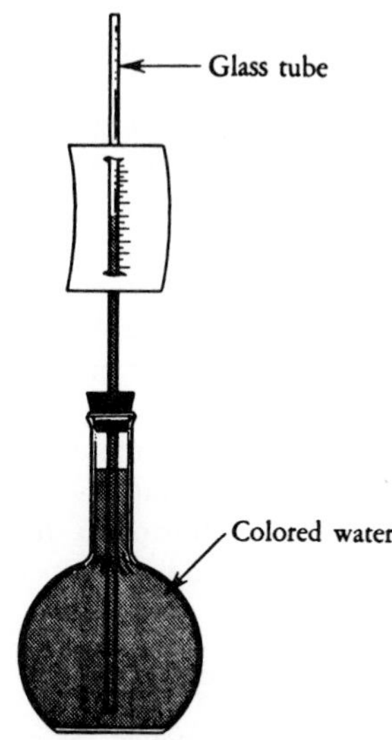

FIGURE 11.19 A homemade thermometer.

1.4 Make a Thermometer

Pour water that has been colored dark red with food coloring into a Pyrex flask until the flask is almost full. Insert a long glass or plastic tube into a one-hole rubber stopper and fit the stopper tightly into the mouth of the flask (Figure 11.19). The amount of water in the flask will have to be adjusted so that when the stopper is inserted, the colored water will rise about one-third to one-half of the distance of the part of the tube above the stopper. Make two slits in an unlined index card and slide the card over the tube. Mark the original height of the water in the tube.

When the temperature of the room becomes warmer, the water is heated; it expands and rises up the tube. When the temperature drops, the water is cooled; it contracts and falls down the tube. Calibrate the marks on the scale of the index card with the readings on a standard thermometer. Have the students take daily readings outdoors on a standard thermometer (placed away from direct sunlight) for an extended period. Keep a record of these readings and make a chart showing the changes in temperature during the year.

1.5 Make an Anemometer

Obtain two pieces of wood about 40 centimeters (16 in.) long, 2 centimeters (3/4 in.) wide, and 7 millimeters (1/4 in.) thick. Place one piece on top of the other so that they form four right angles. At the center, where the pieces meet, bore a hole just large enough for the glass part of a medicine dropper to pass through, so that both pieces of wood will rest on the lip of the medicine dropper (Figure 11.20). Now use small screws or nails to fasten the two pieces of wood together, leaving the hole free. Obtain four paper cups, paint one cup red, and tack a cup horizontally to each end of the pieces of wood.

Hold the medicine dropper by the rubber bulb and place the tip of the dropper in the edge of a gas flame or the flame of an alcohol lamp. Rotate the dropper slowly but steadily as you heat it, and continue heating until the tip of the dropper melts and the opening is closed. Make sure that the tip is completely closed before you remove it from the flame. Set the dropper to one side and allow the tip to cool for at least 5 minutes.

Use wire cutters to cut a straight piece of wire from a coat hanger. File one end of the wire to a sharp point. Fasten the wire upright with friction tape to a sturdy piece of wood. Now remove the rubber bulb from the medicine dropper and insert the dropper into the center hole of the two fastened pieces of wood. Use friction tape above and below the hole, if necessary, to prevent the pieces of wood from slipping off the medicine dropper. Place the medicine dropper over the sharp point of the wire; the anemometer is now ready to operate with a minimum of friction.

To calibrate the anemometer, hold it outside the window of a moving car on a calm day when there is no traffic and the road is smooth and level. With the car moving at a steady

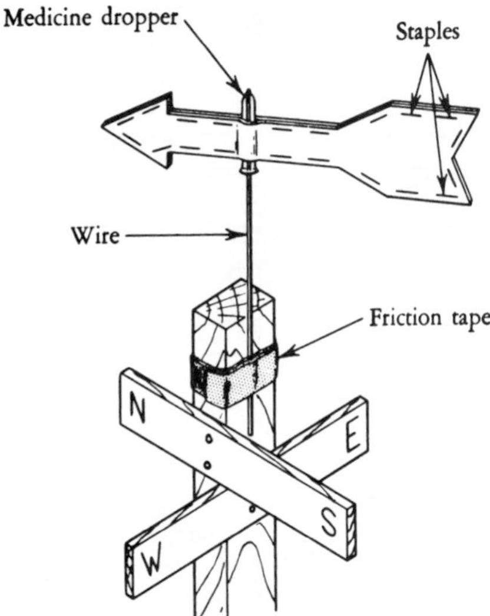

FIGURE 11.21 A homemade wind vane.

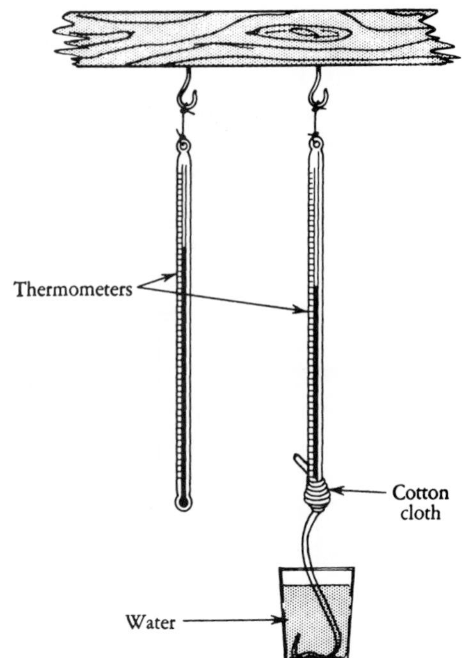

FIGURE 11.22 A wet-and-dry-bulb thermometer.

speed of 8 kilometers per hour (5 mph), use a watch with a second hand to count the number of turns the anemometer makes in 1 minute. The colored cup will make it easier to count the number of turns. Repeat the count at 16 kilometers per hour (10 mph) and again at 24 kilometers per hour (15 mph). From these three counts you can make a graph that will enable you to calculate the wind speed at any time. (A quick but rough method for finding the wind speed is to count the number of turns in 1 minute and then divide by 10. The result will be the wind speed in miles per hour.)

1.6 Make a Wind Vane

Cut two large identical arrows from a piece of heavy cardboard, making sure the tails are much larger than the heads. Staple or paper clip the two arrows together at the edges of the head and the tail (Figure 11.21). Seal the tip of a medicine dropper, as in, explained in "1.5 make an Anemometer." Place the arrow across the edge of a ruler and find the point where it best balances. Insert the medicine dropper between the two pieces of cardboard at this balancing point, and staple together the edges of the body of the arrow.

Use wire cutters to cut a straight piece of wire from a coat hanger, and file one end of the wire to a sharp point. Fasten the wire upright with friction tape to a sturdy piece of wood, and place the medicine dropper over the sharp point of the wire. Use a compass when mounting the wind vane to fix the direction of the wind vane properly. If small strips of wood with the compass directions on them are nailed onto the vane, the students will be able to determine the wind direction more quickly and easily.

Because the tail is larger than the head, it will catch more wind. As a result, when the wind blows, the vane will swing around until it points into the wind toward the direction from which the wind is blowing.

1.7 Make a Wet-and-Dry-Bulb Thermometer

Obtain two chemical thermometers with Fahrenheit scales and suspend them so that they hang side by side a few inches apart. If chemical thermometers are not available, use two identical wall thermometers, either suspended or strapped to a cardboard box with rubber bands.

Obtain a white woven cotton shoelace or a piece of soft cotton cloth. Fit a section of the shoelace snugly around one of the thermometer bulbs and insert the end of the shoelace into a tumbler of water (Figure 11.22). Now fan both thermometers, either by hand or with an electric fan, for a few minutes to blow away the air next to the cloth, so it is not surrounded by a layer of saturated air.

To find the relative humidity, read both thermometers and find the difference between the two temperatures. Use this temperature difference and the temperature of the dry-bulb thermometer to find the relative humidity (in percentages) in Table 11.3

1.8 Make a Hair Hygrometer

Obtain a blond human hair about 20 centimeters (8 in.) long. Wash it in hot, soapy water, rinse it in cold water, and let it dry. Obtain a piece of two-by-four lumber about 30 centimeters (12 in.) long. Use a razor blade to cut a piece about 2 centimeters (1 in.) long from a soda straw, making sure to preserve its round form. Obtain a broom straw 10 centimeters (4 in.) long, and glue one end to the piece of soda straw (Figure 11.23).

Obtain a long, narrow nail, put it through the piece of soda straw, and drive it into the center of the two-by-four lumber near one end. Fasten one end of the hair to a piece of cellophane tape 5 centimeters (2 in.) long, and glue the other end of the hair to the soda straw. When the glue has dried, turn the soda straw a few times to wrap the hair around the soda straw. Now attach the cellophane tape to the two-by-four lumber so that the

TABLE 11.3 Relative Humidity Index

Dry-Bulb Reading	Difference Between Wet- and Dry-Bulb Readings																													
↓	**1**	**2**	**3**	**4**	**5**	**6**	**7**	**8**	**9**	**10**	**11**	**12**	**13**	**14**	**15**	**16**	**17**	**18**	**19**	**20**	**21**	**22**	**23**	**24**	**25**	**26**	**27 . . .**			
65	95	90	85	80	75	70	66	62	57	53	48	44	40	36	32	28	25	21	17	13	10	7	3							
66	95	90	85	80	76	71	66	62	58	53	49	45	41	37	33	29	26	22	18	15	11	8	5	1						
67	95	90	85	80	76	71	67	62	58	54	50	46	42	38	34	30	27	23	20	16	13	9	6	3						
68	95	90	85	81	76	72	67	63	59	55	51	47	43	39	35	31	28	24	21	17	14	11	8	4	1					
69	95	90	86	81	77	72	68	64	59	55	51	47	44	40	36	32	29	25	22	19	15	12	9	6	3					
70	95	90	86	81	77	72	68	64	60	56	52	48	44	40	37	33	30	26	23	20	17	13	10	7	4	1				
71	95	90	86	82	77	73	69	64	60	56	53	49	45	41	38	34	31	27	24	21	18	15	11	8	5	3				
72	95	91	86	82	78	73	69	65	61	57	53	49	46	42	39	35	32	28	25	22	19	16	13	10	7	4	1			
73	95	91	86	82	78	73	69	65	61	58	54	50	46	43	40	36	33	29	26	23	20	17	14	11	8	5	2			
74	95	91	86	82	78	74	70	66	62	58	54	51	47	44	40	37	34	30	27	24	21	18	15	12	9	7	4			
75	96	91	87	82	78	74	70	66	63	59	55	52	48	44	41	38	34	31	28	25	22	19	16	13	11	8	5			
76	96	91	87	83	78	74	70	67	63	59	55	52	48	45	42	38	35	32	29	26	23	20	17	14	12	9	6			
77	96	91	87	83	79	75	71	67	63	60	56	52	49	46	42	39	36	33	30	27	24	21	18	15	13	10	7			
78	96	91	87	83	79	75	71	67	64	60	57	53	50	46	43	40	37	34	31	28	25	22	19	16	14	11	9			
79	96	91	87	83	79	75	71	68	64	60	57	54	50	47	44	41	37	34	31	29	26	23	20	17	15	12	10			
80	96	91	87	83	79	76	72	68	64	61	57	54	51	47	44	42	38	35	32	29	27	24	21	18	16	13	11			
82	96	92	88	84	80	76	72	69	65	62	58	55	52	49	46	43	40	37	34	31	28	25	23	20	18	15	13	10		
84	96	92	88	84	80	77	73	70	66	63	59	56	53	50	47	44	41	38	35	32	30	27	25	22	20	17	15	12		
86	96	92	88	85	81	77	74	70	67	63	60	57	54	51	48	45	42	39	37	34	31	29	26	24	21	19	17	14		
88	96	92	88	85	81	78	74	71	67	64	61	58	55	52	49	46	43	41	38	35	33	30	28	25	23	21	18	16		
90	96	92	89	85	81	78	75	71	68	65	62	59	56	53	50	47	44	42	39	37	34	32	29	27	24	22	20	18		
92	96	92	89	85	82	78	75	72	69	65	62	59	57	54	51	48	45	43	40	38	35	33	30	28	26	24	22	19		
94	96	93	89	86	82	79	75	72	69	66	63	60	57	54	52	49	46	44	41	39	36	34	32	29	27	25	23	21	19	17
96	96	93	89	86	82	79	76	73	70	67	64	61	58	55	53	50	47	45	42	40	37	35	33	31	29	26	24	22	20	18
98	96	93	89	86	83	79	76	73	70	67	64	61	59	56	53	51	48	46	43	41	39	36	34	32	30	28	26	24	22	20
100	96	93	90	86	83	80	77	74	71	68	65	62	59	57	54	52	49	47	44	42	40	37	35	33	31	29	27	25	23	21

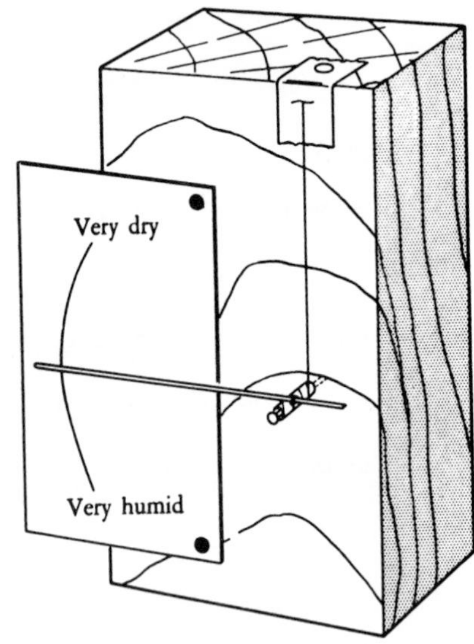

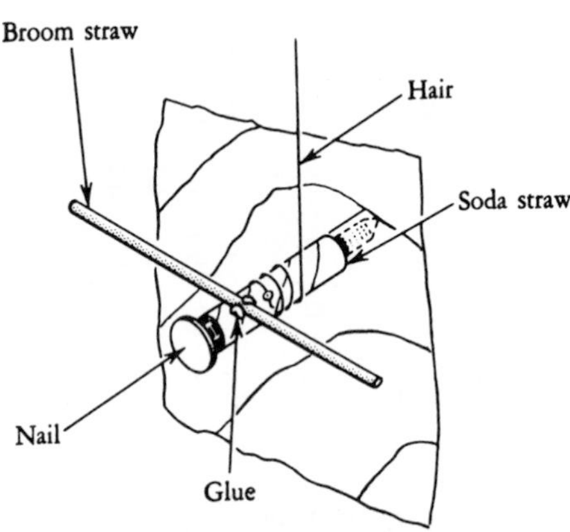

FIGURE 11.23 A homemade hair hygrometer.

hair is tight and the broom straw is in a horizontal position. Press the cellophane tape down firmly on top of the two-by-four lumber, inserting thumb tacks to prevent the tape from loosening. However, let the rest of the cellophane dangle loosely over the side to keep the hair from rubbing against the wood. Tack an index card to the two-by-four lumber on the side nearer the longer end of the broom straw.

When the air is dry, the hair contracts and the broom straw moves up. When the air is humid, the hair becomes moist and expands, making the broom straw move down. Calibrate the hygrometer by putting it into a pail and covering the pail with a towel that has been soaked in very hot water. The relative humidity in the pail will quickly reach 100 percent, and the broom straw will move down as the hair stretches. After 15 minutes, remove the hygrometer and mark the position of the broom straw as 100 percent relative humidity. Allow some time for the pointer to move back to a normal position, then calibrate other positions on the index card by using either a commercial hygrometer or a wet-and-dry-bulb thermometer.

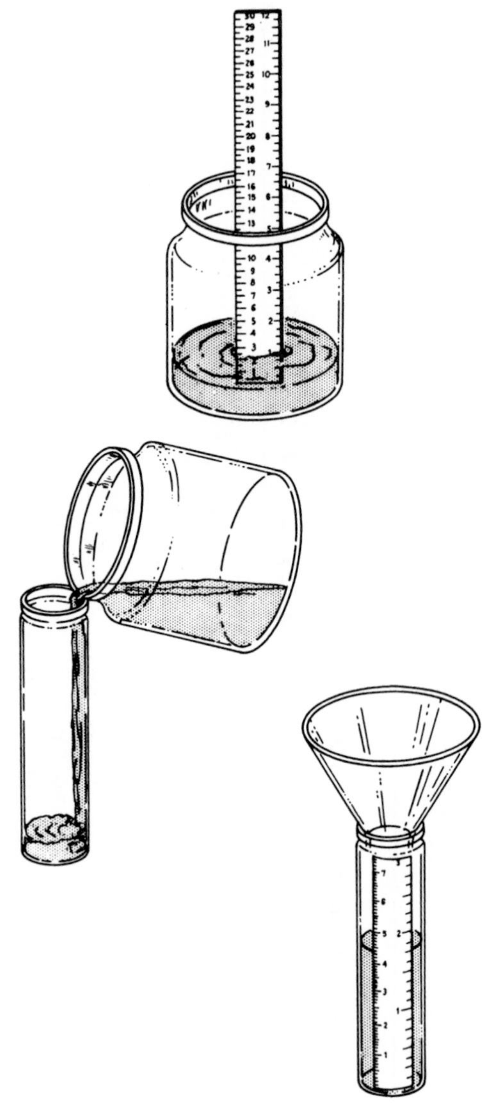

FIGURE 11.24 A homemade rain gauge.

1.9 Make a Rain Gauge

Obtain a large kitchen funnel and a glass jar whose mouth has exactly the same diameter as the rim of the funnel. Pour exactly 1 centimeter (or 1 inch) of water into the jar, using a ruler to get the exact depth (Figure 11.24). Pour this water into a narrow bottle, such as an olive jar. Place a strip of paper about 12 millimeters (or 12 inches) wide against the side of the narrow bottle, using strips of cellophane tape to hold the paper in place. With non-watersoluble ink, make a mark on the strip of paper to indicate the centimeter or inch of water, and label this mark "1 centimeter" or "1 inch." Measure the distance from this mark to the bottom of the water in the jar, and use this distance to make additional marks on the paper, each mark accounting for another centimeter or inch of water. Now divide the space between each mark into 10 smaller marks so that each smaller mark represents 1/10 centimeter or 1/10 inch of water. Empty the narrow bottle.

Put the narrow bottle in a large can so that the wind will not blow the bottle over during a rainstorm. Put the funnel in the neck of the narrow bottle, and place the can in an open area. The funnel will collect rain and send it into the narrow bottle, where the amount of rainfall can be measured.

2. OPENING THE OCEAN: AN INTERDISCIPLINARY THEMATIC UNIT (GRADE 5)[1]

Overview

Opening the Ocean is a 5-day unit designed for a fifth-grade classroom. Each day, the students focus on one aspect of the ocean: Water and Sound, Marine Life, People and the Ocean, and the Sandy Beach. For a culminating activity, we have suggested a field trip to the ocean. We have also included an anticipatory set for the unit—designing a class mural.

We have included a reference list to provide more activities and to help you individualize the unit for your class. Good luck and enjoy "Opening the Ocean" with your starved-for-knowledge students!

Opening the Ocean: Class Mural

1. Have the class brainstorm things that are needed for an ocean mural. Record the class suggestions on the overhead.
2. Your class may suggest sand, seaweed, boat, treasure chest, octopus, coral, fish, and so forth. If not, try to ask questions to stimulate discussion toward these ideas.
3. Have students select the items they would like to make. (Make sure you have at least two or three of each.)
4. Staple a 6′ × 5′ piece of dark blue butcher paper to the wall.
5. Have students, by groups, place their items on the wall. Because there are no specific instructions for where items should be placed, the mural will be very creative. (If you would rather give instructions, designate a "building engineer" to direct the placement of student work on the mural.)

2.1 Water and Sound

This section of the unit combines water and sound, two vital influences in the ocean. Each lesson relates sound in some way to the study of the ocean's water. Four lessons are represented in this section of an interdisciplinary unit. Specific materials as well as adjustments for needs of special and multicultural students are included in each lesson. This section can be taught as an entire day, since there are lessons involving language arts, science, math, and social studies. It can be divided into separate days, if desired, because the lessons do not directly depend on one another.

- Lesson 1: Language Arts. The Ocean: What Does It Say?
- Lesson 2: Math. Water and Sound: A Group Activity to Determine the Speed of Sound
- Lesson 3: Social Studies. The Ocean: A New-Found Planet
- Lesson 4: Science. Why Is the Ocean Salty? Myth and Fact

The Ocean: What Does It Say?

Objective After reading the children's book *Fish Eyes,* a counting book, the students may be inspired by the brilliant colors of the fish to be curious about the wonders and creatures of the ocean. Students will create an artistic representation of a sea creature. They may research the means by which this animal communicates or imagine how the fish or mammal sounds. Students will then write on the back of their creations how this animal contributes to the sounds of the ocean.

Materials *Fish Eyes* by Lois Ehlert or any other book that displays the brilliance and variety of sea life, construction paper of various colors, colored pens, pencils, white lined paper for the backs of the creatures, a set of encyclopedias for researchers, a list of ocean dwellers as possible art projects, and a tape of whale or ocean sounds. *Interludes* is a great CD of ocean sounds and can be ordered through Great American Audio, 33 Portman Road, New Rochelle, NY 10801.

Anticipatory Set Guide the students in their project somewhat like this: As you can hear, there is music of the ocean playing in the background. Close your eyes for a minute and listen to the sounds of the ocean. Because we have been studying marine life, you now know about the many types of creatures that inhabit the ocean. What do you know about how they sound and communicate? Imagine that you are a fish swimming through the waters of the ocean. What do you hear? You see the sea horses. What are they saying? How do they communicate with one another? I am going to show you the pictures in this book, *Fish Eyes.* Look at them and notice their colors. We are now going to pick an inhabitant of the ocean. You are each responsible for creating a sea dweller. We will then write about how you think the animal communicates, and this will be attached to your creation. You may be creative or you may use the encyclopedia or books from the library. These creations will be hanging in our classroom for everyone to enjoy and admire.

Procedures

1. Allow the students sufficient time to brainstorm and share ideas as well as ask questions. This assignment asks a lot of their creative juices.
2. Model both the creative choice and the factual.
3. Encourage the students to enjoy the art project and spend time designing their sea creatures. The writing will mean more to the students if they have a personal attachment to the creations.
4. Limit the time for creation and encourage writing.
5. Do one yourself to model procedure.

Closure Ask the students to share their writings or their drawings or both. Have the students talk about whether

[1]Courtesy of Chris Harrigan, Erika Yee, Deanne Sacchi, and Shannon Zundel.

they think that the ocean is quiet or loud. Collect the creatures and hang them from the ceiling or display them on a bulletin board.

Evaluation To determine the level of the children's thinking, study the outcomes. Also compare the number of students who selected the creative option with the number of those who selected the research option. Does this tell you anything about the individuals or your class? Special-needs students may need individual attention with this assignment. Match these students with a buddy in the class.

Assessment Ask the children what they learned and how they learned it. Use this as a quick writing assignment in a journal.

Water and Sound: A Group Activity to Determine the Speed of Sound

Objective Students will create mathematical problems using the equations for the speed of sound in water. This is a group activity in which the groups work together to create and solve math problems involving water and sound.

Materials Paper, pencils, at least one calculator per group, a chart with the equations and steps, and a map with mileage measurements.

Anticipatory Set Do you think sound travels faster in water or in air? Did you know that if you were a sound wave, you could travel five times faster in water than in air? That means if you were whispering to your friend in class and our classes were underwater, your friend would hear you five times faster than he or she would as you sit where you are right now. We are going to get into groups and create our own math problems using these equations. You may use any distance in the world you wish, as long as the distance is provided in your problem.

Procedures

1. Teach the math lesson that explains that the speed of sound is 5,000 feet per second in the water. One mile is equal to 5,280 feet. Therefore, to compute the amount of time it would take for sound to travel underwater from one town to another, assuming the distance is 30 miles, one would use the following procedure: 30 miles (the distance) times 5,280 feet (1 mile) = the distance in feet, which is 158,400 feet. You know that sound travels 5,000 feet each second; divide the 158,400 feet by 5,000 to reach the time in seconds. Answer: 31.68, or 32 seconds.
2. You will need a step-by-step chart for the students.
3. Have the students work in groups (incorporate strong math students).
4. Each student picks a distance for which he or she wants to measure the speed of sound underwater.
5. Each group writes its problem as a word problem on one paper and puts the solution on another.
6. The teacher then collects the groups' problems and passes out the problems for another group to solve.
7. Groups check their answers with the original group.
8. If a discrepancy exists, the class may work together, facilitated by the teacher, to solve the problem.
9. Each problem must include the distance from one location to a desired destination.

Conclusion Have students go over procedures for solving the problems with the teacher. Talk about problem solving and group work.

Evaluation Collect problems and work, to see how solutions were attempted and found.

Assessment Have the students write the steps needed to solve this equation, to be handed in to the teacher. Include why each step is necessary.

(Because this activity is group oriented, special-needs students should be able to participate without any problem.)

The Ocean: A Newfound Planet

Objective After discussing the combined size of the oceans, students will realize the vastness of the sea. Pose the question: Why not call this Planet Ocean inasmuch as 75% of our Earth is covered by water? Students will create posters displaying the new Planet Ocean.

Materials Posterboard or construction paper, pens, glue, and magazines if you wish.

Anticipatory Set Why do we call our planet *Earth* when 75% of it is covered with water? You have just been assigned to the committee to change the name of Earth to Planet Ocean. Your assignment is to create a poster, with a partner, that encourages us to change the name to Planet Ocean. The posters will be judged and given various prizes.

Procedures

1. Explain that the Earth is 75% water.
2. Have students work in pairs to create their posters.
3. Have other teachers and the principal select the most creative and influential poster. Tell students the judging criteria beforehand.
4. Award all posters a prize if you wish!

Closure Allow students to share posters and explain them to the class. Display them in the classroom.

Evaluation Check for understanding of surface area covered by water, by evaluating posters.

(Multicultural and special-needs students should have no problem with this activity if it is explained thoroughly.)

Why Is the Ocean Salty? Myth and Fact

Objective Students will discover why the ocean is salty. First, in groups, they will create their own myths to explain the salt in the ocean. Second, students will research and present the facts about the salt in the ocean.

Materials Paper, pencils, encyclopedia or science book that includes information on the ocean and a myth, such as that of Johnny Appleseed.

Anticipatory Set I am going to tell you why the ocean is salty today, class. In 1332, a gigantic ship was traveling from a faraway land carrying salt to sell to another nation. The ship hit a glacier and all the salt spilled into the ocean. The ship was so big that it made all the oceans in the world salty. Is that a fact or a myth? What do you think? Today you will be in groups to create your own myths about why the ocean is salty. We will then work together as a class to find out the facts about why the ocean is salty.

Procedures

1. Read a myth to the students so that they are clear as to what a myth is. Johnny Appleseed is a popular myth.
2. Place students in groups and ask them to brainstorm and create a reason or myth about why the ocean is salty.
3. Give the students ample time to work, and let them know their myths will be read aloud.
4. Have the students read their myths to the class.
5. Work together under teacher instruction to find the real answer. (Do you know? Work with your class to find out!)

Closure Ask the students what they learned about myths as well as about the ocean and its salt. Place their myths on the wall in your classroom.

Evaluate Read students' work. Determine whether they mastered the concept of *myth*. Because this is a group activity, all students should be able to participate.

Assessment Ask students the following day to define *myth* and explain the facts about why the ocean is salty.

2.2 Marine Life

The following lessons are about the kings of the ocean—the whales. The disciplines covered are art, language arts (writing), science, physical education, and mathematics. Each lesson's time will vary from class to class, but here are some estimates:

- Lesson 1: The Art of Scrimshaw (art and social science)—90 minutes. This activity requires drying time for the artwork. It may be beneficial to schedule this for a recess or natural scheduling break.
- Lesson 2: A Whale Story (language arts)—60 minutes. This activity should follow the Art of Scrimshaw lesson because there can be a natural transition from one to the other.
- Lesson 3: Blubber Is Beautiful (science)—45–75 minutes. Hands-on science. This activity may require a few minutes' setup by the instructor.
- Lesson 4: Migration Graph (math and physical education)—90 minutes. Time to exercise and think. Always a great wakening activity about distance; can also spruce up a slow afternoon.

Have a whale of a time!

The Art of Scrimshaw

Objective After learning about scrimshaw art (history, examples), students will create their own artwork and distinguish its history.

Materials Large, smooth white seashells; linseed oil; polish (light, clear cover-spray or paint); nails; superfine sandpaper; ink or watercolor

Anticipatory Set Show students scrimshaw art. Can they figure out what materials it would take to create such beauty? What do they figure the art means to the artist? Provide students with prompts. Could the artist be a recycler?

Procedures Share with students the history of the art of scrimshaw.

Provide students with the materials and necessary steps for their artwork: sand and polish the shell to be inscribed. Scratch with a nail, a marine-oriented scene using a nautical theme (for example, a whaler scene, harpooners, a battle scene, mermaids, or pirates). Cover the shell with ink and wipe with linseed oil. The inscribed design will be filled with ink.

Closure Explain to students that this art activity is going to be a transition to their language arts later in the day. During language arts, they will be writing or dictating their art's history. Discuss as a whole class their thoughts about scrimshaw.

Evaluation What was scrimshaw art used for? (trade)

Why don't we see much scrimshaw anymore? (few whales and even fewer whales' teeth are available)

A Whale Story

Objective Students will analyze and support their Art of Scrimshaw work through writing its history in the American whalers' setting.

Materials Completed student scrimshaw work; writing instruments; sand, seashells, other materials; paper cut in whale shapes; historical vocabulary journals; glue

Anticipatory Set Read students a teacher-written history of your scrimshaw work. Be creative here. Depending on your comfort level, try turning your history piece into a reader's theater or other dramatic presentation.

Procedure Remind students of the historical and cultural importance of scrimshaw art. Provide them with whale-shaped paper and materials for authentic writings. Have students write their short historical fiction (extensions for able students: dictate history into a tape recorder, do share-pair, write poetry, provide historical vocabulary journals). After writing, provide students with marine materials (sand, shells) to decorate their writing.

Closure In groups, have students share their historical fiction along with their scrimshaw artwork. Ask each group to choose one piece they thought was historically accurate, interesting, funny, exciting, and/or had a strong correspondence with the artwork. The chosen piece will then be shared with the entire class.

Evaluation After students have displayed their writing and artwork, evaluate their work based on their ability to connect the art and history. Did the students place their writing in American whaling history as asked to do?

Blubber Is Beautiful

Objective Students will investigate the beauty of whale blubber and compare and contrast blubber with plain body heat.

Materials Plastic gloves (2 pairs for every two students); crushed ice/ice cubes; laboratory thermometers (1 for every two students); buckets (1 for every two students); water; shortening; clock with second hand; recording sheet

Anticipatory Set BLUBBER. "Blubber Is Beautiful"—today on (your name) talk show. Many in the United States are lean and slick. Few in the world are blubbers and beautiful. It is a personal choice for some but a genetic makeup for others. Join us today on (your name) talk show to hear from and examine the truth—blubber or not?

Procedures Students are now the scientists testing the two opinions about blubber. In groups of two they will:

1. Fill a bucket with ice water. Measure and record the water temperature.
2. Student one will put on a pair of gloves. Student two will spread a thick layer of shortening over student one's right hand. Then student one will put the second pair of gloves over the first.
3. Have student one put both hands in the ice water, making sure that no water enters the top of the gloves.
4. Student one will keep hands immersed, sharing feelings with student two (recorder).
5. Student will remove each hand as soon as it becomes uncomfortable. Recorder will note how long he or she was able to keep each hand in the water.
6. Repeat the activity, changing roles of students. (Be sure to measure water temperature to ensure that it is the same each time.)
7. Each student-scientist pair will then answer the discussion questions on a record sheet (Fig. 11.25) and then record their findings on the class summary wall chart.

Closure Class discussion—review the class summary wall chart. Ask the following questions of (your name) talk show guests: Explain the scientific experiment to our audience. Which hand stayed in the water longer? Why? Discuss why shortening insulated these hands. How does shortening compare with blubber? Why do marine animals need blubber to keep warm? Close as host of the talk show: "As I promised, we have an answer to the Is Blubber Beautiful? debate. For the lean, slick fish, blubber is not so important. Yet for the survival of whales in our world's ocean, BLUBBER IS BEAUTIFUL!"

Related Activities To demonstrate how blubber helps prevent the loss of body heat, have students take their palm temperatures under the gloves directly before putting their hands in the water. For best results, use laboratory thermometers. After 1 minute, have them remove their hands from the ice water and immediately take their palm temperatures again. Subtract the end temperature from the start temperature. Repeat with other students. Compare temperature loss between the blubber and plain hands and analyze the results. What was the average heat loss for each hand?

Migration Graph

Objective Students will develop an appreciation and understanding of the gray whales' migration (problem solving, graphing, physical education).

Materials Example graphs; materials for graph making; exercise area for runner, swimmers, wheelchairs

Anticipatory Set Challenge students to make predictions about how many days it would take them to finish the 5,000-mile migration of the gray whale. Display various types of graphs and explain how predictions can be made from graphs.

Procedures Students will make their own predictions for the amount of time it would take them to complete a 5,000-mile migration. Then they will create their own graphs to illustrate their prediction and the distance per day using an equation: for example, 20 miles a day times number of days = migration distance.

Students will walk, run, or wheelchair a mile to determine the time. Then they will return to their graphs to reestimate the distance and days. (Students will realize the

Names: ______________________

	#1		#2	
Is blubber beautiful?				
Water temperature:				
Which hand was removed first?				
How long were you able to keep hands in the bucket?	R	L	R	L

On a separate piece of paper, answer the following:
Which hand stayed in the bucket longer?
Why?
Did the shortening make a difference?
Share your findings and conclusions.

FIGURE 11.25 Record sheet.

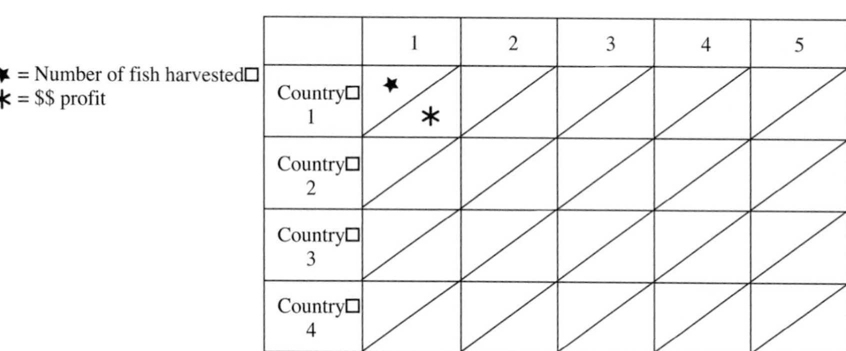

FIGURE 11.26 Gone Fishing chart.

distance and most likely adjust their prediction for days.) Redo estimated graphs and equations for distance.

Closure Hold a class discussion, sharing original estimations of distance and migration time. Graph student time estimates.

Evaluation Did the students finish the activity with a stronger sense of distance? Were the equations generated acceptable for finding solutions? Have the students write their final estimation of time needed to complete the distance.

Resources for Marine Life

The following resources provide ideas, guidelines, and information for these lessons.

The Art of Scrimshaw

The art of scrimshaw has been considered a very important indigenous folk art of the Indians and, later, early Americans. It involved the carving and decorating of whales' teeth, walrus tusks, or bone (usually whales' teeth). Whalers had a considerable amount of time on their hands and, with scant tools, etched whales' teeth to pass the time. A trophy of a whale hunt—a large tooth—was the measure of the whaler's success, and the carefully etched pictures expressed great individuality.

2.3 People and the Ocean

On this day, we will discuss how people use the oceans and how people affect the oceans. For a culminating activity, we will cook seafood recipes from different countries, using at least one of our senses—taste.

The day is divided by the different disciplines: math, language arts, social studies, and science. An approximate time line for each discipline and a day's schedule follow, for your use in completing all activities in one day.

Time Line

- Lesson 1: Gone Fishing (Sharing of Common Resources) (math)—45 minutes
- Lesson 2: Mini-Paper (language arts)—1 hour
- Lesson 3: Globetrotters (social studies)—45 minutes
- Lesson 4: Plastic in the Sea (science)—1 hour
- Lesson 5: Cooking—1 hour, 20 minutes

Sample day's schedule

8:00–8:45 Lesson 1
8:50–9:50 Lesson 2
10:05–10:50 Lesson 3
11:10–12:40 Lesson 5
11:45–12:45 Lesson 4
12:50–1:40 Eating

Most of the following activities contain cooperative group work, so you might want to preassign the groups to have some variety.[2]

Gone Fishing

Objective After simulation, students will be able to discuss the different scenarios that could occur with a large group of people fishing in the same waters.

Materials 600 paper clips, poster board, 50 square meters of area, marking pens, and small magnets.

Procedures

1. Randomly scatter paper clips within the 50 square meters.
2. Duplicate the chart in Figure 11.26 on poster board.
3. Divide the class into four groups, and have each group choose a name for its country.
4. Explain to students that they will be fishing in common waters, and each country depends on fishing for survival.
5. Each group is allowed one boat (one person) and 1 year (1 minute) to fish.
6. Each country sends out one boat, and they fish for 1 year using a magnet as a fishing pole. After 1 minute is up, have each group divide its fish into piles of 10.
7. Each group must have at least 10 fish a year to survive. Any extra fish can be used for profit.
8. Every 10 fish after the first 10 are worth $2. Groups can use the profit to purchase more boats for $20 each.

[2] Lessons 2–4 are omitted here to conserve space. The complete unit is available in Richard D. Kellough et al., *Integrating Mathematics and Science for Intermediate and Middle School Students* (Upper Saddle River, NJ: Merrill/Prentice Hall, 1996), 545–568.

9. Have countries record their catch on the chart on poster board (Figure 11.26).
10. Have groups do their buying at this time. Each group should also choose another person to be the boat.
11. After a round, have students figure out how many fish are left from the original 600.
    - If 400 or more remain, you can collect all the fish that were caught and replenish the ocean.
    - If 300-399 remain, only 150 may be returned.
    - If less than 299 remain, then the ocean is left as is.
12. Continue the same steps for the four countries for five rounds, or until all fish are caught.

Closure Ask the class to consider the following questions:

- Which country was most profitable in its fishing excursions?
- What happened to the number of paper clips students collected as fishing continued?
- If the goal was not to make money but to sustain themselves on Earth for the longest time, did anyone win?
- What could the students have done to sustain the fish population?

Evaluation Listen to discussion of closure questions to check for understanding of the topic: the positive and negative effects of sharing an area of water for fishing.

Cooking

1. Start cooking after you have finished three of your lessons.
2. Recipes have been included.
3. *Caution:* Seafood can be lethal if not stored or cooked properly.
4. Students can help by cutting the vegetables and putting together all the ingredients that are needed.
5. If you can obtain a crockpot and skillet, you can cook inside your classroom.
6. If timed properly, the food will be ready to eat after you finish your last lesson.

Note: You will need at least two parent volunteers to watch the food while it cooks and to help serve when it's finished.

2.4 The Sandy Beach

This unit introduces the sandy beach. It contains activities and information on sand and other related aspects of the beach. Each lesson, along with its incorporated discipline, follows. The time required for each lesson is specified.

- Lesson 1: The Facts About Sand (social studies)—approximately 1 to 1 1/2 hours
- Lesson 2: Sand Weight (math)—45–60 minutes
- Lesson 3: Strange Beginnings—A Creative Writing Activity (language arts)—1 hour.
- Lesson 4: What Is a Food Chain? (science)—approximately 1 hour

The Facts about Sand

Key Concept Sand grains can be made of many things and come in many different shapes, sizes, and colors. These differences can be clues about the material makeup and origin of sand.

Objective Students, using magnifiers and working in small groups, compare the color, size, and shape of several sand samples to determine their material makeup and origin.

Materials Magnifiers; ziplock bags, each containing a different type of sand; question work sheet; world map.

Background Information Nearly all solid materials in the world, both living and nonliving, will eventually be eroded into sand. Rocks, shells, corals, bones, metals, and glass are all worn in time by wind, waves, rivers, earthquakes, and other forces into smaller and smaller particles. For this reason, sand is often said to be the earth in miniature.

The sand of every beach has its own unique history. Detailed observations combined with some good detective work, however, often allow us to make some reasonable hypotheses about the material makeup and origin of the sand. Sand from the remains of plants or animals is referred to as *biogenic,* and sand from non-living sources is called *abiogenic.* A closer look at sand through a hand lens or microscope also reveals a lot about the sand's individual grains.

Some sand is produced right at the shore, where waves crash on rocks, headlands, and reefs. For example, black or red sand beaches in Hawaii and the Galapagos are found directly next to or on top of lava flows of the same color. White sand beaches in Florida and in the Caribbean are primarily made of eroded coral reefs. Parrot fish eat coral polyps, grinding up the corals with their sharp teeth and excreting up to 100 pounds of coral sand per year. Pink sand may be full of coralline algae fragments. Other sand comes from far inland. Mountains are weathered by freezing, wind, rain, and streams, and their fragments are carried down streams and rivers to the seashore. Quartz, a glass-like mineral, is often the most common component of these transported sands. Quartz is the most common mineral on earth and is nearly insoluble in water. Most light-colored sand beaches contain large amounts of quartz.

Anticipatory Set Today we will be working as geologists. We are going to try to figure out what sand is made of and where it came from. We will be doing some very interesting investigating.

Procedure

1. Divide students into groups of four. Give each group two bags of sand and a magnifier.
2. Each group selects a recorder to record the answers to the questions on the work sheet.
3. Each group will be given 5 minutes to inspect their two sand bags and record their observations. When time is called, groups will switch sand bags until all have been rotated around the room.
4. When all types of sand have been observed by each group, distribute the work sheet and allow about 10 minutes for its completion.

Work sheet questions

- What material do you think your sand is made of? (Small rocks? Shells? Wood? Glass? Plant material?)

- What do you think the source of your sand is? (A coral reef? A mountain? A lava flow? Clams or snail shells?)
- Do you think the material makeup of sand or its color can tell us anything about where it was produced? If yes, how?

5. Discuss the work sheets. Encourage students to share their answers.
6. Tell students that sand's makeup/color does give clues about where it came from. For example, black or red sandy beaches in Hawaii and the Galapagos are found directly next to or on top of lava flows of the same color. White sand beaches in Florida and in the Caribbean are primarily made up of eroded coral reefs.
7. Prepare an index card for each location mentioned in question 6. Draw the color of sand likely to be found there on each card.
8. Call on volunteers to locate each place on the map. Tape each index card on its proper location.
9. Collect all work sheets.

Closure Review the information about sand. Inform students that these were only a few of the many interesting facts to be learned about sand.

Evaluation Review the students' work sheets. The students' work should demonstrate an understanding of the task assigned.

Sand Weight

Key Concepts and Processes Measurement, patterns, functions, statistics, and probability

Objective After being introduced to sand and weight, students will work cooperatively in centers to estimate the weight of sand. Their results will be recorded and mapped out on a graph.

Materials Scale, teaspoon, weights, small cup, 1 cup of sand, and graph paper.

Demonstration

1. Show students 1/2 teaspoon of sand.
2. Have students estimate the weight of the sand in grams.
3. Place 1/2 teaspoon of sand in a small cup. Place the cup on a scale.
4. Place the smallest gram weight on the opposite side of the scale. Increase the weight until the scale is even.
5. Then tell students that they will be weighing sand in the same manner.

Procedure Tell each student which learning station he or she will be working at. List the following steps at each station.

1. Estimate how much 1 teaspoon of sand will weigh, and record your estimate on paper.
2. Put 1 teaspoon of sand in the cup and place it on the scale.
3. Put the smallest weight on the scale. Increase the weight until you discover the actual weight of the sand.
4. Record the weight on your paper.
5. Estimate how much 2 teaspoons of sand will weigh.
6. Weigh and record the weight of 2 teaspoons of sand.
7. Repeat for 3 teaspoons and 4 teaspoons.
8. Look for a pattern. Then estimate the weight of 10 teaspoons of sand.
9. Make a graph of your results.

Closure Review findings, asking students to share their results. Ask whether they had accurate estimations of how much the sand would weigh.

Evaluation Collect graphs. Check each graph for accuracy. The results of the graphs will determine the success or understanding of the lesson.

Strange Beginnings—A Creative Writing Activity

Objective After becoming familiar with animals from the beach and the ocean, students will practice creative writing skills by selecting one of the questions that follow and answering it as they choose.

Materials Paper, questions (included), pencils, drawing paper, and markers/crayons.

Anticipatory Set Today we will be having some fun with creative writing. I want everyone to get in a creative mood. On the board, I have written three questions. It is your job to choose the one you would like best to write on and go with it. Remember, creativity makes the most interesting reading.

Questions

- How did the octopus get its tentacles?
- How did the sea urchin get its spines?
- How did the eel get its electricity?

Procedure

1. Have students select a question to write about.
2. Tell them how much time they'll have to answer their questions.
3. Set expectations (at least one page).
4. Tell students when it is time to start wrapping up their writing.
5. Have students share their stories if they so choose.
6. (Optional) Have students draw a picture that corresponds with their stories.
7. Collect stories and drawings.
8. Display works on a bulletin board.

Closure Ask students if they enjoyed this assignment.

Evaluation Collect all writings and drawings, then determine by the outcome whether the assignment was a success.

Other Options

1. The class can vote on the best or most interesting creative writing/drawing. The winner's work can be displayed in a special place.
2. Rather than do this lesson on just one day, it can be spread out over a period of a week. This can be done by assigning one question a day.

For example, writing journals can be used. Time can be set aside (1/2 hour each day after lunch) for each question. The day's question may be on the board when students return from lunch. They are then given time to answer the question. Journals can be collected at the end of the week.

What Is a Food Chain?

Objective After reading *Life in the Oceans,* students should understand what a food chain is. To demonstrate understanding of a food chain, each student will complete a handout and construct her or his own food chain.

Materials Work sheet (not included), *Life in the Oceans* by Lucy Baker, and pencils.

Anticipatory Set Today we will be learning about food chains. First you will hear some important information about food chains, and then you will design your own food chain.

Procedure

1. Read *Life in the Oceans.*
2. Discuss the book and encourage students to ask questions.
3. Hand out a food chain work sheet and provide an example of a food chain.
4. Allow time for students to complete their food chain worksheets.
5. Encourage students to share their work.
6. Point out the importance of knowing how a food chain works.
7. Collect the students' work.

Closure Today we have learned that living things depend on each other for food and energy.

Evaluation Collect and assess students' work. Their food chains will reflect whether or not they grasped the concept.

Opening the Ocean: Culminating Activity Field Trip For a culminating activity, your students will enjoy a hands-on experience: a trip to the ocean. They can relate and apply everything they have acquired during the week to the real thing.

All you need to do is contact your local Department of Parks and Recreation or the tourist information bureau for an oceanside city near you. If an ocean is not available, an aquarium is also a worthwhile experience.

We hope you enjoy the ocean with your class!

Part THREE

Living Things

NSES Content Standards C and F[1]

Students in **grades K–4** should develop an understanding of

- The characteristics of organisms
- Life cycles of organisms
- Organisms and environments
- Personal health
- Characteristics and changes in populations
- Types of resources
- Changes in environments
- Science and technology in local challenges

Students in **grades 5–8** should develop an understanding of

- Structure and function in living systems
- Reproduction and heredity
- Regulation and behavior
- Populations and ecosystems
- Diversity and adaptations of organisms
- Personal health
- Populations, resources, and environments
- Natural hazards
- Risks and benefits
- Science and technology in society

[1]Reprinted from National Research Council, *National Science Education Standards*, © 1996 by the National Academy of Sciences, 127, 138, 155, 166. Courtesy of National Academy Press, Washington, DC.

Chapter 12

Plants

Bob Nichols/USDA/NRCS/Natural Resources Conservation Service

 Classification and Composition of Living Things

I. Classification of Living Things

A. All living things, called **organisms**, are grouped into main divisions, called **kingdoms.** Biologists place organisms into five or six kingdoms. For this book, we use a simpler classification: plants, animals, and those that are neither plant nor animal.

1. Kingdoms are subdivided into very large groups of organisms called **phyla** or **divisions** (sometimes used for plants). The further the phyla are subdivided into smaller groups, the greater similarity there is among members of each group.
2. Phyla are first subdivided into **classes.** Classes are subdivided into **orders**, orders into **families**, families into **genera** (plural of genus), genera into **species**, and species into **varieties** or **hybrids** (see Table 12.1).
3. A *species* is a group of closely related organisms that can interbreed in nature.
4. A variety or hybrid is an individual of a species that varies slightly from other individuals in the same species, but not enough to be considered a separate species.
5. The "neither plant nor animal" group, presented in Chapter 13, is divided into several kingdoms:
   a. The **Protista** (or **Protoctista) kingdom** (most algae and protozoans), which contains 15 phyla and up to 200,000 species.
   b. The **Monera kingdom** (including blue-green algae and bacteria), comprising at least two phyla and more than 40,000 species.
   c. The **Fungi kingdom**, which includes four phyla and approximately 100,000 species.
   d. The **viruses**, which are not included in any kingdom.
6. The plant kingdom, called the **Plantae** or **Metaphytae kingdom**, contains more than 265,000 species and is divided into eight phyla, but for the purposes of this book we divide the plants into two groups—the bryophytes and the tracheophytes.
7. The animal kingdom (Chapter 14), called the **Animalia kingdom**, is divided into 16 phyla and contains more than 1 million species.

B. When classifying organisms, scientists give each phylum and its subgroups scientific names that are Latin words or words that have been Latinized.

1. Because Latin is a universal and unchanging language, the names have and will continue to have the same meaning to scientists worldwide.
2. This scientific naming makes the classification of organisms definite, so there can be no duplication.
3. The **scientific name** of an organism is actually formed from two categories: the genus

TABLE 12.1 Classification tables for Cocker Spaniel and Red Delicious apple tree

Classification of the Cocker Spaniel Dog		Classification of Red Delicious Apple Tree	
Kingdom:	Animalia	Kingdom:	Plantae (Metaphytae)
Phylum:	Chordata (have a notochord)	Phylum:	Tracheophyta (have system of tubes)
Subphylum:	Vertebrata (have a backbone)		
Class:	Mammalia (are mammals)	Class:	Angiospermae (flowering plants with seeds inside the fruits)
		Subclass:	Dicotyledoneae (seeds have two cotyledons)
Order:	Carnivora (the flesh-eating mammals)	Order:	Rosales (roses and their relatives)
Family:	Canidae (including the foxes and the wolves)	Family:	Rosaceae (produce roselike flowers)
Genus:	*Canis* (includes the wolf, coyote, and dog)	Genus:	*Pyrus* (produce apple fruits)
Species:	*familiaris* (domestic dog)	Species:	*malus* (cultivated apple trees)
Variety:	Cocker Spaniel	Variety:	Red Delicious

and the species. For example, the scientific name for the domesticated dog is *Canis familiaris,* for the cultivated apple tree it is *Pyrus malus,* and for human beings it is *Homo sapiens.*

4. The scientific name is always italicized or underlined. The first letter of the genus name is always capitalized, and all letters of the species name are always lowercase.

II. Composition and Life Processes of Organisms

A. All organisms have **life cycles** that include being born, developing into adults, reproducing themselves, and dying. The details of this life cycle vary for different organisms.

B. The basic unit of structure and function for all organisms is the **cell.** This statement is known as the **cell theory.** The cell theory consists of three concepts.
   1. All organisms are composed of one or more cells.
   2. The cell is the basic unit of organization of organisms.
   3. All cells come from preexisting cells.

C. Depending on their internal organization, cells are of two types—prokaryotic and eukaryotic.
   1. A **prokaryote** is an organism with a cell that lacks internal structures and is surrounded by membranes. Most prokaryotes are unicellular (single-celled) organisms.
   2. A **eukaryote** is an organism that has cells containing internal membrane-bound structures, called **organelles.** The largest organelle is a membrane-bound nucleus that contains the cell's DNA and manages the cell's functions. Eukaryotes are either unicellular or multicellular (made of many cells).

D. All cells have an external boundary, called the **plasma (cell) membrane**, that separates the cell from its external environment.
   1. This plasma membrane controls what enters and exits the cell.
   2. Food and oxygen needed by the cell enter the cell through this membrane.
   3. Carbon dioxide and waste materials exit the cell through this membrane.

E. In addition to the plasma membrane, some cells have an outer rigid protective covering called the **cell wall.** It is made of different substances in different organisms. The cells of plants, fungi, most bacteria, and some protists have cell walls. Animal cells do *not* have cell walls.

F. The activities of a eukaryote cell are controlled by the **nucleus.** The nucleus can be anywhere inside the cell, but it is often found in the center.
   1. The nucleus is surrounded and held together by a **nuclear membrane** that controls what materials enter and leave the nucleus.
   2. The nucleus contains the cell's genetic material, called **deoxyribonucleic acid (DNA).**

G. The fluid part of the cell outside the nucleus and inside the cell membrane is called **cytoplasm** (meaning cell fluid), and the fluid part of the nucleus is called the **nucleoplasm.**
   1. The cytoplasm of eukaryotes contains many specialized structures called **organelles.** Each organelle has a role in the cell's functions.
   2. Much of the cytoplasm is occupied by a folded system of interconnected membranes, called the **endoplasmic reticulum (ER).**
   3. This system of membranes provides a large surface area on which chemical reactions can take place. For example, the ER contains the enzymes for almost all of the cell's lipid (fats and oils) synthesis. Therefore, membranes are the site of lipid synthesis in the cell.
   4. Some of the ER is coated with **ribosomes,** which are the sites of protein synthesis. In some cells, ribosomes may also be found free in the cytoplasm.
   5. **Vacuoles**—sacs of fluid surrounded by a membrane—store food, enzymes, water, and other materials needed by the cell. In some instances, vacuoles store waste products.
   6. Cytoplasm contains many other structures, each with important cellular functions. These include **mitochondria,** which play an important part in cellular respiration such as generating energy from the breakdown of food, and **chloroplasts,** which only appear in plant cells, and play an important role in photosynthesis.

H. Not all cells are alike.
   1. Many cells, especially those in the more complex plants and animals, have special functions. Consequently, they differ in size, shape, and cellular makeup.
   2. In more complex animals, examples of specialized cells are bone, muscle, egg and sperm, and red blood cells; in more complex plants, examples of specialized cells are root tip, egg and sperm, and guard cells in a leaf.

I. A group of specialized cells working together to perform a specific function is called a **tissue.**
   1. Examples of tissues in complex animals are blood, muscle, and nerve.
   2. Examples of tissues in complex plants are those of the xylem and phloem.

J. A group of two or more tissues working together for a common function make up what is called an **organ.**
   1. Examples of human organs are the skin, heart, and brain. The skin, for example, contains more than one kind of tissue: connective and nervous.
   2. Examples of organs of a tree are root, stem, and leaf. The stem, for example, contains more than one kind of tissue: xylem, phloem, and cambium.

K. A group of organs that work together for a common function are called an **organ system.**

LEARNING ACTIVITY 12.1

Examine Plant Cells

Slice an onion into rings. Discard the first two outer layers. Remove the thinnest possible piece of skin from the third layer. Have students place a portion of this skin on a microscope slide, add a drop of water and a drop of tincture of iodine, and cover with a cover glass. Soak up any excess liquid by placing the tip of a blotter against the edges of the cover glass. The iodine stains the onion cells and makes them stand out very clearly. Examine the onion cells under the microscope. The tip of the aquarium plant elodea can also be used to observe plant cells.

1. Organ systems of a body work together to maintain life and health.
2. An organ system in humans, for example, is the digestive system, which includes several organs: the esophagus, stomach, liver, and intestines.
3. The flower is an example of an organ system in some plants. It contains organs necessary for reproduction, organs that attract insects, and organs necessary for transporting materials to and from the flower and to other parts of the plant.

L. Cells exhibit the characteristic activities of life, called **life processes.**
   1. Life processes specific to plants include photosynthesis, transpiration, cellular respiration, digestion, circulation, assimilation, growth, excretion, reproduction, and tropisms.
   2. Disease can cause a breakdown in one or more of the life processes. Some diseases are the result of intrinsic failures of the system, whereas others are caused by infection by other organisms.

M. **Cellular respiration** is the breakdown of molecules of food to release energy used for building new cells.
   1. Cellular respiration is a biochemical process that occurs in all cells; it should not be confused with breathing, a mechanical process that occurs in higher animals.
   2. Cellular respiration is generally represented as the breakdown of carbohydrates into water and carbon dioxide. Some of the energy released during this process is captured by the cell in a molecule called **adenosine triphosphate (ATP).**
   3. The water and carbon dioxide are released by the cell as waste products, and the captured energy is used to carry on the activities of **assimilation** (building and repair of cells) and other processes (e.g., movement and osmosis).

N. **Digestion** is the mechanical and biochemical breakdown of food into molecules small enough for the body to absorb. These molecules are then used for cellular respiration and assimilation.
   1. Plants, like animals, digest their food so it can be absorbed by the cells.
   2. Since most plants manufacture their own food through photosynthesis and since this occurs mostly in the leaves, the food of plants is already inside the cells where it was manufactured.
   3. There the food is broken up into smaller molecules (digested) and then dissolved in the plant fluid, called **sap.** It is transported through the plant to the various cells, where it is used to supply energy and to repair tissues and build new cells.

O. At the cellular level, **excretion** is the process of eliminating waste products; it usually takes place when these substances are collected in vacuoles. In multicellular organisms, waste products are transported to other places where they are eliminated from the body.
   1. In some unicellular organisms, a specialized vacuole collects excess water and pumps it out of the cell. A plant cell has a single large vacuole that stores water and other substances.
   2. Some waste products are expelled from cells by **exocytosis** when vesicles or vacuoles fuse with the cell membranes and their contents are released outside the cell. Exocytosis is also the method used by cells to secrete substances produced by the cell, such as hormones.
   3. **Endocytosis,** the opposite of exocytosis, is a process in which a cell surrounds and takes in material from its environment. Instead of passing directly through the cell membrane, the material is engulfed and enclosed by a portion of the cell's membrane. That portion of the membrane then breaks away, and the resulting vacuole and its contents moves to the inside of the cell.
   4. Both endocytosis and exocytosis require energy and are therefore called **active transport processes.**
   5. Some substances, such as water and lipids, can pass directly through cell membranes by diffusion. Because the cell expends no energy when this occurs, it is referred to as **passive transport.**
   6. Active transport is an important means for the cell to expel or take in large molecules or substances that, for one reason or another, cannot pass through the cell membrane by simple diffusion.

P. **Motion** is the process of movement, either from one place to another or within a stationary location. Examples of moving from place to place include humans walking, fish swimming, birds flying, and protozoans swimming. Many other organisms move without changing location. Leaves of plants move with the wind and with respect to the Sun's location. Although sea anemones become stationary as adults, they still move their tentacles in search of food. When food is found the tentacles take it to their mouth openings.

1. Although plants cannot move from place to place, as many animals and protists (see Chapter 13) do, they can and do move. When an organism is affected by such things as light, water, heat, or gravity, it responds by moving either toward or away from the stimulus. This movement is called a **tropism.** If the organism moves toward the stimulus, it is called a positive tropism. If the organism moves away from the stimulus, it is called a negative tropism.
2. The response of an organism to light is called **phototropism.** Leaves and stems move toward light—a positive tropism; roots move away from light—a negative tropism. The movement of a stem toward light is due to a more rapid growth of cells on the side of the stem that is away from the light source.
3. The response of an organism to gravity is called **geotropism.** Roots grow downward because of the pull of gravity. This movement is a positive geotropism. Primary stems grow upward against the pull of gravity. This movement is a negative geotropism.
4. The response of organisms to water is called **hydrotropism.** Roots turn in any direction toward water. They can even grow upward against the force of gravity because of this strong hydrotropism.
5. The response of organisms to touch is called **thigmatropism.** The *Venus flytrap* has a leaf that quickly folds in half when touched by a fly or other insect. This is an example of thigmatropism. The leaves of the mimosa plant turn away from a tactile stimulus. As the result of thigmatropism, some vines, peas, and other climbing plants curl around any firm support.
6. The response of organisms to heat is called **thermotropism.** The leaves of certain plants, like the mimosa, turn away from strong heat.
7. The response of organisms to chemicals is called **chemotropism.** Most roots turn toward soil that has a good supply of the minerals that the plant needs.

LEARNING ACTIVITY 12.2

Tropisms

A. Hydrotropism

Cut off one side of a waterproof carton, such as a milk carton, to make a trough for holding soil. Cut a rectangular hole in one side of the trough and tape a piece of glass or some clear plastic wrap over the hole on the inside of the carton to produce a window (Figure 12.1). Punch a few holes in the bottom of the carton for drainage, cover the holes with flat rocks, and fill the carton with soil. Get some lima beans from a seed store and place them 2 to 5 centimeters (1 to 2 in.) deep in the soil beside the plastic wrap so that their germination and root growth will be visible. Place the carton in a shallow pan and water the soil regularly until the beans have germinated into growing plants. Now water the soil at one end of the carton only. In a week or two you will see the roots turned toward the direction of the water.

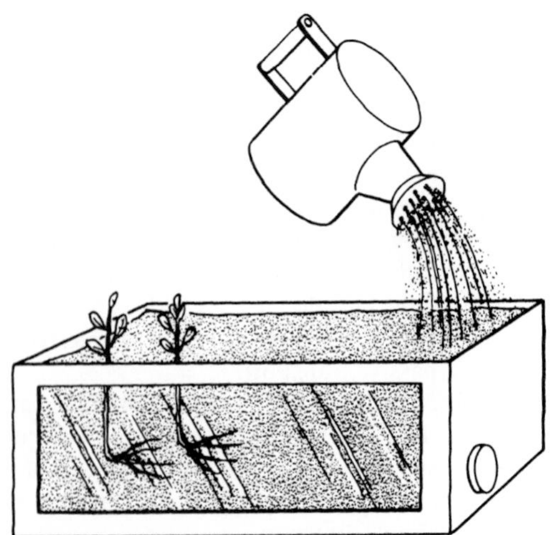

FIGURE 12.1 Roots turn toward water.

B. Climbing Plants Twist in a Counterclockwise Direction

Grow two twining plants, such as a morning glory or a pole bean plant. Insert a long, thin, round stick or dowel into each of the pots for the plants to twine around. Allow only one tendril in each plant to twine around the stick. The tendrils will twine in a counterclockwise direction. Try twining one of the tendrils around the stick in a clockwise direction. In a few hours the tendril will unwind itself.

C. Plants Sensitive to Touch and Heat

Obtain some mimosa seeds from a seed-order house, a scientific supply house, or someone who teaches in the South. Plant the seeds and cultivate them until they grow 15 centimeters (6 in.) high. Now pinch one of the top leaves, or stroke it gently a few times. The leaf will droop and will not regain its original shape for several hours.

Next, strike a match and let it burn for a second or two. Blow out the match and touch one of the leaves with the warm tip of the match. The leaf will droop and will not regain its original shape for several hours.

Inquiry-Based Learning Activity 12.2.Modified

Plants grow toward light, which is called phototropism. They turn their leaves to absorb as much light as they can. Plants also grow toward water, which is call hydrotropism. But can plants tell which way is up? How can we find this out? Have your students brainstorm about different ways they can experiment to see if plants can tell which way is up? Do they need to block out the light? How long do they think it will take for a plant to react to gravity? What do they think the plant will do? In this activity, your students will each need one bean plant to do their experiment. The plants will need about 4 to 7 days to germinate and grow. Have your students each fill a small cup with some potting soil. Wet the soil before the activity. Plant one seed in each cup and have a few extras in case some seeds don't grow properly. Discuss as a class the things they need to control for; specifically, light and water. This activity requires that each student design and build an experimental apparatus. In this case, they will most likely bring shoeboxes to class. This activity requires some preparation by you, the teacher. The plants will grow on their own, but they do need to be tended. Once they begin to grow, the experiment will only take a few minutes. Bean plants react very quickly to gravity and within 15 minutes the plants will begin to turn their tops away from the ground. This effect is called geotropism.

What level of inquiry is this modification? This activity offers students only a limited opportunity to design an experiment given the very limited parameters of the activity. Although they will actively participate by putting together a box to hold their plant in a dark place, the options are naturally very limited. These characteristics suggest that this activity is at ***Level I*.** **Some questions to consider.** How might you expand on this activity? Design an activity combining the three tropisms that would shift the inquiry to Level II or even Level III.

Q. **Reproduction** is the process of creating new individuals from existing ones. At the cellular level, this process is usually done by simple **cell division**; that is, without the involvement of the union of specialized cells called egg and sperm. Simple cell division is a method of **asexual reproduction.** The cell divides, forming two new cells.
   1. All cells experience a cycle of growth and division. This cycle is called the **cell cycle.** For unicellular organisms, such as bacteria and *Amoeba,* it is also the organism's **life cycle**; that is, the events in the life of an organism from one generation to the next.

R. The cell cycle consists of two steps or phases.
   1. The growth period of the cell cycle is known as the **interphase**, during which the cell grows in size, makes ATP, carries on metabolism, gets rid of wastes, and duplicates its chromosomes in preparation for the period of cell division.
   2. Following interphase, the cell enters its period of cell division. First its nucleus and then its cytoplasm divide to form two **daughter cells,** each containing a complete set of chromosomes. The process of simple cell division when chromosomes are distributed equally to daughter cells is known as **mitosis.**

S. **Mitosis** involves four phases or stages: the prophase, the metaphase, the anaphase, and the telophase. (See Figure 12.2.)
   1. **Prophase** is the visible beginning and longest lasting phase of mitosis. During prophase, the long stringy chromosome material (called **chromatin**) coils up into visible **chromosomes,** which were duplicated during interphase. Each duplicated chromosome is made up of two halves, called sister **chromatids.** Sister chromatids and the DNA they contain are normally exact copies of each other and are formed when DNA is copied during interphase. The sister chromatids are held together by a structure called a **centromere.**
   2. **Metaphase** is characterized by the alignment of the chromosomes in the center of the cell.
   3. **Anaphase** is characterized by the separation of sister chromatids toward opposite poles of the cell. Each chromatid has now become an independent chromosome.
   4. The fourth and final stage of mitosis is **telophase.** It is characterized by the formation of nuclear membranes around the two new daughter nuclei and the division of the original parent cytoplasm. That division is called **cytokinesis.** Each daughter cell has its

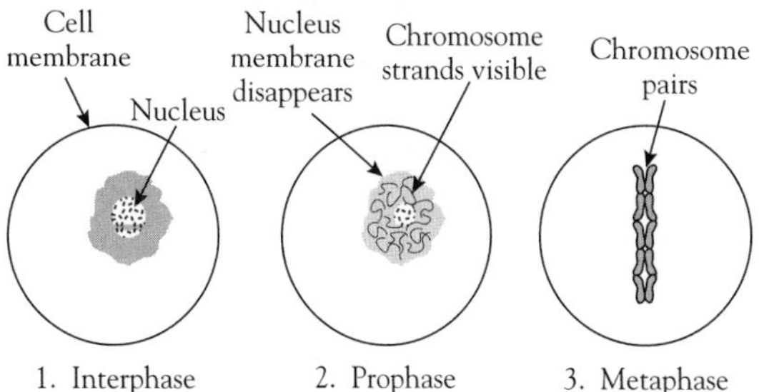

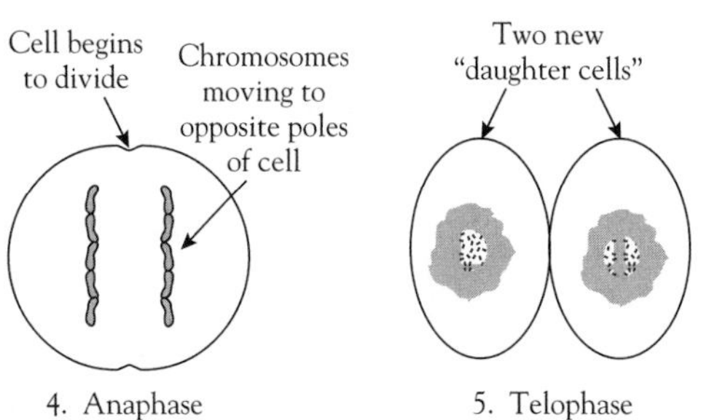

FIGURE 12.2 The cell cycle: interphase and mitosis, or cell division.

own cell membrane and the same number of chromosomes as in the original parent cell.

5. Cytokinesis in plant cells usually begins when membrane vesicles fuse to form an equatorial plate; cytokinesis in animals usually begins with the formation of a cleavage furrow, which constricts the cell around the outside cell membrane and pinches it in two. In other words, in plant cells cytokinesis starts from the inside and works outward, whereas in animal cells it starts from the outside and works inward.
6. The **resting stage** (or interphase) of the cell cycle occurs between telophase and the beginning of the next prophase. Although chromosomes are not visible during interphase, duplication of DNA in the chromosome takes place during interphase.

T. In contrast to asexual reproduction, which involves one parent cell giving rise to two new daughter cells, **sexual reproduction** involves the union of two cells to create a new individual.

1. Important to sexual reproduction is a unique process of nuclear division called **meiosis.**
2. Through meiosis, **sex cells**, or **gametes—egg** and **sperm** cells—are produced.
3. Meiosis consists of two separate divisions, called meiosis I and meiosis II. Meiosis I begins with one cell with the normal (called **diploid**) chromosome number, referred to as 2N. By the end of meiosis II, there are four cells (called **haploid** cells), each with one-half of the original chromosome number. This is the haploid chromosome number, referred to as 1N.
4. In animals and most plants, these haploid cells are called sex cells, or gametes.
5. When gametes unite in a process called **fertilization**, the cell that results from their union, called a **zygote**, is diploid (2N); that is, it has the same chromosome number as the original parent cells. In humans, for example, the diploid chromosome number is 46, but when meiosis occurs, each daughter cell receives only 23 chromosomes. This is the haploid or 1N number. When the egg and sperm unite, the 46 chromosomes (diploid number) characteristic of humans is maintained.

U. Mitotic cell division is the process by which multicellular organisms increase their number of cells for growth, healing, and maintenance.

1. Mitotic cell division is also the asexual method used to produce new organisms, such as in **budding**, which occurs in plants and in some animals.
2. An abnormally rapid rate of mitotic cell division can cause an enlargement of tissue, a **tumor**, which occurs in plants as well as animals. These abnormal growths in plants may be caused by the action of viruses, bacteria, or chemicals.

 The Plant Kingdom

I. The Plant Kingdom, Scientifically Called the Plantae Kingdom or Metaphytae Kingdom, Is Divided into as Many as 10 Divisions or Phyla:

Bryophyta, the mosses and liverworts
Psilophyta, the whisk ferns
Lycophyta, the club mosses
Sphenophyta, the horsetails
Pterophyta, the ferns
Cycadophyta, the cydads
Gnetophyta, certain highly specialized trees, shrubs, and climbing vines
Ginkgophyta, with only one living species, *Ginkgo biloba.*
Coniferophyta, the conifers
Anthophyta, the flowering plants

A. Members of the plant kingdom have chlorophyll and manufacture their own food by photosynthesis; that is, they are **autotrophic.**

B. The plant kingdom can be divided into two broad groups: the plants that have no vascular tissue (vessels for transport of plant fluids)—the **bryophytes**—and plants that do have vascular tissue—the **tracheophytes.**

 The Bryophytes

I. The Bryophytes Are Members of the Plant Phylum Bryophyta, which Includes the Mosses and Liverworts. (Liverworts Are Also Known as Hepatics Because of Their Liver-Shaped Leaf Structures.)

A. Members of the Bryophyta have simple leaves; that is, without the transport system of the more complex leaves of the tracheophytes. Although they do have rootlike and stemlike parts, these, too, are without the complex transportation system of tissues (xylem and phloem) of the tracheophytes.

B. Bryophytes do not produce flowers, fruits, or seeds.

C. Bryophytes reproduce both sexually (by meiosis and by the union of gametes) and asexually (by mitosis and by the production of spores).
   1. In mosses, spores are produced in tall structures called the spore capsules. These usually extend high above the miniature leaves of the moss (Figure 12.3.).
   2. Liverwort spores are produced in capsules that resemble little pits in their "leaves."
D. Bryophytes are small but ubiquitous plants; that is, they are found all over the world, although always on land areas and where it is damp with fresh water.
   1. There are no marine (saltwater) bryophytes and very few species that are aquatic. (Green, slimy plants frequently found growing on rocks in streams or along ocean shores are algae, not bryophytes.)
   2. Mosses commonly grow in places that stay moist, such as cracks of a sidewalk, wood shingle roofs, on the sides of trees (especially the northernmost sides, which remain moist because they get less direct sunlight), on the soil and clay pots in damp greenhouses, and on soil that remains moist much of the time.
E. Liverworts are flat, with broader "leaves." They are commonly found on the soil of moist and seldom-used pathways.
   1. Occurring about 470 million years ago, liverworts were the first land plants.
F. The term *moss* is frequently used incorrectly for plants that have no affiliation with a true bryophyte.

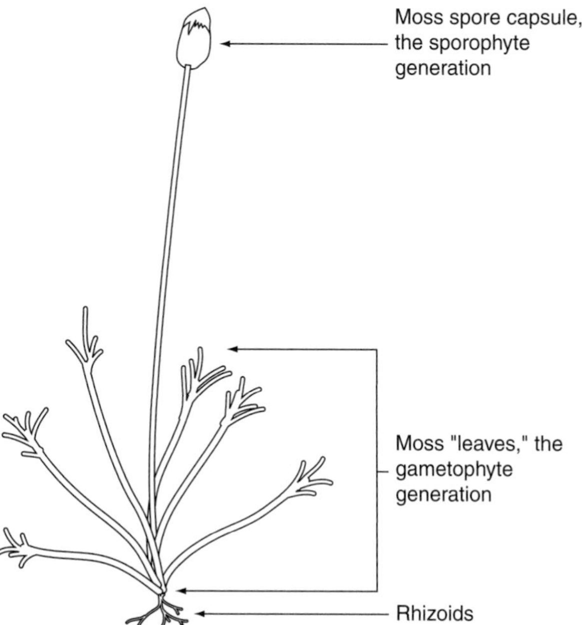

FIGURE 12.3 Moss II plant with both generations.

   1. *Spanish moss*, for example, is actually a member of the pineapple family of tracheophytes. The mossback turtle has an alga, not a moss, growing on its carapace. Mossy-looking plants that hang from the limbs of trees in forests are more likely lichens. Lichen is not a bryophyte but an organism consisting of an alga and a fungus growing together in a symbiotic relationship. There are many species of lichens.
G. Moss plants have cells that are capable of retaining large amounts of water. For that reason, **sphagnum moss** (peat moss) is used by plant nurseries for wrapping the roots of trees and shrubs for transplanting.
   1. Sphagnum moss grows in small lakes and ponds. It forms floating masses that eventually cover the water and form a bog. (See "Lakes, Wetlands, Swamp, Bogs, and Marshes" in Chapter 9.)
   2. The bog may thicken as grass, shrubs, and small trees become established and grow in it. Eventually the bog becomes solid land.
   3. Sphagnum moss and perhaps other bryophytes as well, have an antibiotic property. In an emergency situation, moss wrapped around an injury can absorb fluids from the injury and might even enhance the healing process.
H. Bryophytes play an important role in soil formation. Like lichens, bryophytes can grow in areas that have very little soil or minerals, and where more complex plants cannot become established. The metabolic activity of bryophytes and lichens growing on rock begins the breakdown of the rock into what ultimately will be soil.
   1. Because they can grow where more complex plants cannot, bryophytes are among the first organisms to inhabit devastated areas divested of plant life by fire, mudslide, or volcanic activity. They are important in initiating the rebuilding of the habitat that was destroyed. Bryophytes and other simple plants help to make and bind the soil so that larger and more complex plants can establish themselves and continue the process of rebuilding.
I. Bryophytes are of special interest to botanists, cellular biologists, and geneticists. In bryophytes the dominant generation (for example, the "leafy" moss plant that we are familiar with, and see growing on a tree or ground) is the gamete-producing generation known as the **gametophyte** (See Figure 12.3). It is the generation with the haploid (1N) chromosome number in each cell. However, in humans and other animals and in flowering plants, trees, and other tracheophytes, the dominant generation is that with the diploid

(2N) chromosome number in its cells. (When referring to plants, the diploid generation is referred to as the **sporophyte.**)

1. Sex cells, called gametes, which are the egg or sperm cells, always have the haploid (1N) number.
2. The dominant generation in bryophytes is the gametophyte (the haploid or 1N generation), and in higher plants, animals, and humans, the dominant generation is the diploid or 2N generation (called sporophyte when referring to plants).

 The Tracheophytes

I. The Tracheophytes Are Plants That Contain Vascular Tissue in Their Roots, Stems, and Leaves

A. Tracheophytes have vascular tissue, in which cells are specialized for the transport of materials throughout the organism. This vascular tissue is a continuous system of tubes running through the plants' roots, stems, and leaves; hence the name *tracheo* (tube) *phyte* (plant).

B. Tracheophytes usually have chlorophyll and are green in color. Most are autotrophic. (In the course of their evolution, a few species have lost their ability to manufacture food and have become parasitic to other plants.)

C. The tracheophytes are divided into those that have seeds and those that do not. Ferns, horsetails, and club mosses are tracheophytes that have roots, stems, and leaves but no flowers, fruits, or seeds.

D. Unlike that of bryophytes, the dominant generation of the reproductive cycle of tracheophytes is diploid; that is, the plant organism we see and are familiar with is the sporophyte generation.

E. Seed plants, which produce flowers, fruits, and seeds, include all trees, shrubs, crop plants and vegetables, garden and wild flowers, and grasses.
   1. Seed plants grow in soil and in fresh water.
   2. The smallest seed plants are the duckweeds, which grow floating on the surface of ponds and slow-moving streams. They are about 1 centimeter (0.3 in.) across.
   3. The largest are the giant sequoias and the redwoods of California, which can be more than 90 meters (300 ft) tall.

F. Depending on whether their seeds are covered or unprotected, scientists divide seed plants into two groups. **Angiosperms** have seed coverings. **Gymnosperms,** meaning "naked seed," are those without seed coverings.

G. In evolutionary history, gymnosperms are older seed plants than the angiosperms. Examples include pine, spruce, fir, cedar, bald cypress, redwood, hemlock, yew, and larch trees. It is believed that gymnosperms first appeared on Earth about 285 million years ago.
   1. They are also called **conifers,** because they produce woody cones.
   2. The cone, the "fruit" of the conifers, is made up of scales, wherein lie the "naked" or unprotected seeds.
   3. Conifer leaves are in the form of either needles or flat scales.
   4. Conifers keep their needles or scales for 2 to 5 years. The bald cypress and larch trees are exceptions, because they lose their needles each autumn.
   5. Because their "leaves" stay green all winter (actually, because they do not lose them all at one time), conifers are also called **evergreens.**
   6. When new needles or scales grow, they appear in the spring.
   7. The trunk of a conifer does not divide. It grows tall and straight, with most of the branches nearer the top of the trunk.
   8. Conifers produce a sticky substance called **resin.**
   9. The wood of conifers is usually softer than that of angiosperms. It is used for producing lumber and paper.

H. Angiosperms are seed plants that produce flowers that then form fruits with seeds. They include all garden and wild flowers, plants that produce crops and vegetables, grasses, cereal grains, and trees and shrubs that lose their leaves in the autumn. It is believed that angiosperms first appeared on Earth about 140 million years ago.
   1. Angiosperms have broad, flat leaves, which most species lose each year. For this reason, they are called **deciduous** (from the Latin *decidere*—to fall off) plants, rather than evergreens.
   2. Angiosperm trees have a main trunk that may divide in two. Branching begins rather low on the trunk.
   3. Depending on the nature of their seed coverings, the angiosperms are divided into two groups: the monocotyledons (meaning one cotyledon), or **monocots,** and the dicotyledons (meaning two cotyledons), or **dicots.**
   4. A **cotyledon** is a special kind of leaf found in the seed. It contains stored food that nourishes the tiny embryo plant inside the seed when the seed sprouts and grows into a new plant. Monocotyledon plants produce seeds that have just one leaf, and dicotyledon plants produce seeds with two seed leaves.
   5. Except for a few that are trees, monocotyledons are usually relatively small plants. They

include the lily, tulip, iris, onion, grasses and cereal grains, and coconut and date palms.
6. Dicotyledons include most flowers, vegetables, shrubs, and flowering trees.

I. The major organs of a flowering seed plant include the root, stem, leaves, and flowers. Each has special functions (discussed later in this chapter).

 Ferns, Horsetails, and Club Mosses

I. The Nature of Ferns, Horsetails, and Club Mosses

A. Ferns, horsetails, and club mosses are vascular plants (tracheophytes) without seeds.
B. Their size ranges from small moss-sized plants to large trees.
C. Although they all have true roots, stems, and leaves, they do not produce flowers, fruits, or seeds.
D. They are mostly land plants and grow best in cool, damp, shaded places where the soil is rich in humus. Some grow in the cracks of rocks and cliffs, and others grow in fields and open woods.
E. They all have chlorophyll, are green in color, and are autotrophic.
F. It is believed that earliest members of this group first appeared on Earth about 350 million years ago.

II. Ferns

A. Ferns were numerous millions of years ago, forming large forests in the wet and marshy land that was common at that time.
   1. Giant ferns as large as trees were common. Coal comes from the ferns that lived and died millions of years ago. Large masses of dead ferns accumulated in layers in the swampy areas where they grew; these layers turned into coal under the influence of great heat and pressure produced by strong upheavals and movements of the Earth's crust. Smaller ferns, much like those found today, also lived during that period. Today tree ferns are found only in the tropics, where they can be as much as 15 meters (49 ft) tall with leaves 4 meters (13 ft) long.
   2. Ferns are much smaller in the temperate zones.
B. The stems of ferns are underground, growing horizontally just below the surface. Such underground stems are called **rhizomes.**
   1. Each year these rhizomes put up new leaves.
   2. Fine roots also grow from the rhizomes.
C. In most ferns, the leaves, called **fronds**, are the only parts of the plant that appear above the ground.
   1. Fronds have many tiny leaflets arranged along one main vein, called the **midrib.**
   2. The other veins of fern fronds are forked, a characteristic of ferns.
   3. When the leaves appear in the spring, they are rolled up tight and are covered with a hairy growth at their base. This hairy covering is lost when the leaves unroll.
D. Ferns go through a reproductive cycle, having both a spore stage and a sexual stage.
   1. When the fronds are fully grown, spore cases form on their underside. Each spore case contains many tiny spores.
   2. When the spores become ripe, the spore case bursts open, and the spores are carried away by wind, water, or animals.
   3. If a spore falls on a moist place where conditions are right for growth, it develops into a threadlike chain or filament of cells.
   4. This chain or filament thickens and then broadens at the tip, which becomes a flat, heart-shaped green body, called a **prothallus,** that is notched on its upper side.
   5. On its underside, the prothallus has hairlike threads, called **rhizoids**, similar to the rootlike hairs of mosses and liverworts. The prothallus stage of the fern's life cycle is physically reminiscent of mosses. The rhizoids hold the prothallus to the ground and absorb moisture from the soil.
   6. Sex organs develop on the rhizoids. Male sexual organs, each containing several sperm cells, develop among the rhizoids. Female sexual organs, each containing one egg cell, develop on the underside of the prothallus near the notch.
   7. When the male organ is fully grown, it opens up and allows the sperm cells to escape. The sperm cells swim to the female organs after a rain or when the plant is covered with dew.
   8. A sperm cell enters a female organ and unites with the egg to form a fertilized egg, called a **zygote.**
   9. The zygote then grows into a fern plant with roots, stem, and leaves.
E. Ferns can also reproduce asexually.
   1. Some reproduce by budding. The leaves of some ferns form tiny buds, which break off and grow into new ferns.
   2. Some ferns can form new ferns from their leaves if the leaves bend down and touch the ground. When the tip of the leaf touches the ground, roots form at the tip. These roots then develop stems and leaves to become a new fern plant. The tip of the leaf dies, separating the new plant from the parent plant.

III. **Horsetails and Club Mosses**

A. Horsetails and club mosses are similar to ferns, especially in the way they reproduce. Also, like ferns, they were numerous millions of years ago. At that time, they were the size of trees. Most of them are now extinct, and their remains are seen as leaf and stem fossil imprints.
   1. There is only one living group of horsetails today, but they can be found nearly everywhere, especially in wet places such as drainage ditches and at the edges of lakes, ponds, and bogs.

B. Horsetails and club mosses have horizontal stems—underground for horsetails and just above or below the ground for club mosses—and upright branches grow from these stems.
   1. Some of their upright branches have bushy side branches.
   2. Other upright branches produce spores in cones that develop at their tips. There are small scale-like leaves in a circular pattern farther down the branches below the cones.

C. Club mosses are small, low-growing evergreen plants.
   1. They grow best in damp places, on the ground in temperate climates, and on tree trunks in tropical climates.
   2. Their upright branches look like the leaves of fir and spruce trees.
   3. They produce spores in cones (some of which are club-shaped) that grow at the tip of some of their branches.
   4. Because of their dainty beauty, some club mosses are used in making Christmas decorations and other ornamental arrangements.

Roots

I. **Definition and Kinds of Roots and Root Systems**

A. Roots are the part of a plant that anchors it by growing downward and outward in the ground.
   1. When a seed first begins to grow, the first root to appear, called the **primary root**, grows rapidly and pushes its way into the soil. The carrot and radish are examples.
   2. After a while, **secondary roots** branch out from the primary root, first near the top of the primary root and then farther down. The roots keep branching and rebranching until a complete root system is formed.

B. The two main kinds of root systems are the **taproot system** and the **diffuse root system.**
   1. In the taproot system, the primary root (the taproot) grows until it is the largest root in the root system. Smaller secondary roots grow from this large taproot. Examples are the carrot and the dandelion.
   2. In the diffuse root system, the primary root only lives for a short time, while the secondary roots continue to grow as a cluster at the base of the stem. The cluster becomes what is sometimes called a **fibrous root system.** Examples are corn and grass.
   3. Some taproots and fibrous roots become quite large, because of stored food, and are called **fleshy roots.** Beets, carrots, and radishes are examples of plants with fleshy

LEARNING ACTIVITY 12.3

Taproot and Diffuse Root Systems

Dig up a dandelion plant with the complete root. Also dig up a small clump of grass. Show students the long taproot of the dandelion and the many shorter diffuse roots of the clump of grass.

LEARNING ACTIVITY 12.4

Young Roots

Soak some radish seeds overnight. Put a dark-colored blotter on the bottom of a large saucer. Wet the blotter thoroughly with water, but do not have any excess water on the blotter. Scatter the seeds on the wet blotter and cover the saucer with a square, flat glass plate. Place the saucer in a darkened part of the room. The radish seeds will germinate in 2 or 3 days. Keep the blotter moist constantly. Examine the seeds each day. Note the primary root that grows directly from the seed, and the secondary roots that branch out from the primary root. Have the students, using hand lenses, look closely at the fuzzy outgrowths at the tips of the primary and secondary roots. These are the root hairs that absorb water and dissolved minerals from the soil.

taproots. Dahlias and sweet potatoes have fleshy fibrous roots.

C. Roots of some plants can grow from the stems or leaves of the plant, and are called **adventitious roots.**
   1. Tomato, cucumber, potato, and squash plants have adventitious roots. Leaves of the begonia, sedum, and sansevieria plants form adventitious roots when placed in soil.
   2. Some plants send out roots from their stems just above the ground. These roots are a special kind of adventitious root, called **prop roots** (as they help to prop or hold up the plant) or **brace roots.** They grow into the ground and help hold the plant upright. The corn plant is an example.
   3. Climbing plants, such as English ivy, poison ivy, and tropical orchids, send out roots from their stems. These roots are another special kind of adventitious root, called **aerial roots.** Aerial roots grow above the ground, clinging to a wall or tree, and hold the stem firmly in place.

II. The Structure and Growth of a Root

A. At the tip of the root is the **root cap**, which protects the delicate end of the root and contains most of the cells that by their rapid mitotic cell division add length and width to the root.
   1. The primary growth of a root occurs within this root cap.
   2. Although other cells of the root may grow in size, it is from the cell division within the root cap that new cells are added.

B. A short distance behind the tip of each root are many tiny, nearly microscopic, delicate **root hairs** that add immensely to the total surface area of the root system.
   1. In addition to helping to anchor the plant, by adding to the total surface area of the root system root hairs play a major role in absorbing water and dissolved minerals from the soil.
   2. As the root grows in the soil, new root hairs form near the tip, while the older root hairs wither and die from abrasion.

C. The length of a root varies, depending on the species of plant and the conditions of the environment. For example, the taproot of the mesquite plant can grow 12 meters (40 ft) down into the desert sand to reach a water supply, but the diffuse roots of a cactus plant cover large areas just beneath the surface of the ground to quickly absorb the surface water from infrequent rains. Roots of the eggplant and squash grow downward about 2 meters (7 ft) and then spread sideways from 1 to 6 meters (3 to 20 ft).

D. Roots do not necessarily grow down.
   1. Although it is true that roots tend to grow toward gravity, their primary response is to grow toward water. In other words, a root's positive hydrotropism (movement toward water) is stronger than its positive geotropism (movement toward gravity). See Figure 12.1.

E. A root grows toward water because of biochemical reactions taking place inside the root cells that cause cells of one side of the root to divide and to grow faster than cells on the other side of the root. Thus, the root bends toward or away from something.
   1. Because of a root's positive hydrotropism, the cells on the side away from the water source divide and grow faster than those on the side closest to the water source, thus causing the root to grow toward the water.
   2. The same cause-and-effect relationship applies to the growth movements of stems, leaves, and flowers.

III. The Functions of Roots

A. Roots serve several important functions for the plant system.
   1. Roots help anchor the plant.
   2. Root hairs give off an acid that helps dissolve minerals in the soil, thereby helping the roots grow through the soil and absorb needed water and minerals.
   3. Water and dissolved minerals absorbed by the root hairs are sent through the roots to the stem and leaves and other plant parts.

B. Through a history of genetic adaptation, roots of different species of plants have become specialized to the conditions of their environments.
   1. Some plants have developed fleshy roots in which to store food.
   2. By asexual reproduction (rather than union of gametes) some roots, such as those of the sweet potato and dahlia, can produce new plants.

LEARNING ACTIVITY 12.5

Roots Absorb Water and Dissolved Minerals

Dig up a dandelion plant with its roots, and gently wash the soil from the roots. If dandelions are unavailable, use plants grown from bean, radish, or tomato seeds instead. Place the roots in a glass jar containing water that has been colored a very deep red with food coloring. In a few hours, or by the next day, the veins of the dandelion leaves will be colored red, because the water and dissolved food coloring will have been absorbed by the roots and traveled up to the leaves.

IV. Use of Roots by Humans

A. Humans have many uses for roots: as food (e.g., carrot, turnip, parsnip, radish, beet, sweet potato), as seasoning (e.g., horseradish), as a source for medicines (e.g., sassafras, ginger, yew, Ginkgo, licorice, and mandrake), for making candy (e.g., licorice and ginger), and for making dyes (e.g., madder and yellowwood trees).

Stems

I. Definition and Kinds of Stems

A. A stem is the part of the plant located between the roots and the leaves.
   1. Stems may be found above the ground (aerial), below the ground (underground), or both above and below the ground.
   2. The trunk of a tree is actually the stem of the plant.
   3. The trunk of the palm tree is an example of a giant monocotyledon stem; the trunk of the oak or the elm tree is an example of a large dicotyledon stem.

B. Some stems are woody, and others are herbaceous (weedy).
   1. **Herbaceous stems** are usually soft and green. As they grow, they become longer, but not thicker, and they live for only one season. The stems of tomatoes, beans, peas, corn, grasses, and most annual flowers are herbaceous stems.
   2. **Woody stems** are brown and stiff and have woody tissue (stem tissue that contains dead and hardened cells). As they grow, they become both longer and thicker, and they form branches; they live season after season. The stems of trees and most shrubs are woody stems.

C. The four main groups of **aerial stems** are shortened stems, creeping stems, climbing stems, and erect stems.
   1. **Shortened stems** are very short stems, sometimes so short that they seem to be missing from the plant. Dandelion, primrose, and carrot all have shortened stems. Their very short, flat, circular stems can be seen growing just above the roots. Plants with shortened stems need open places to grow, where they can get lots of light.
   2. **Creeping stems,** also called runners or stolons, are long and slender and stay close to the ground, as exemplified by strawberry and bent grass. These stems do not have woody tissues and are weak, so they grow along the surface of the ground. Plants with creeping stems also need open places to grow, where they can get lots of light.
   3. **Climbing stems** are thin and very long; they include ivy, morning glory, and sweet potato. They do not have woody tissues and are weak, so they grow by wrapping themselves around a tall object.
   4. **Erect stems** stand above the ground by themselves, tall and erect, as exemplified by trees, shrubs, and many garden flowers. They may be either a few centimeters tall or very many meters high, and they may be either herbaceous or woody.

D. Stems that grow below the ground are called **underground stems.** The four main groups of underground stems are rhizomes, tubers, bulbs, and corms.
   1. **Rhizomes** are long underground stems that grow horizontally, close to the surface of the ground. Some rhizomes are thick and fleshy and filled with food. Examples are the rhizomes of the iris, the lily of the valley, and the trillium. Other rhizomes are thin, such as those of the grasses.
   2. **Tubers** are the enlarged tips of rhizomes with food stored in them, such as the white potato. The "eyes" of the potato are really buds on the stem from which new growth develops.
   3. A **bulb** is made up of a stem shortened to the size of a disk, surrounded by thick, fleshy, scalelike leaves that have food stored in them. Bulbs include the hyacinth, tulip, daffodil, and onion.
   4. A **corm** is different from a bulb only in that most of it is stem surrounded by thin scalelike leaves, as exemplified by the crocus and gladiolus.

II. Structure and Growth of Stems

A. The bare winter branch of a tree is an excellent example of a woody stem.
   1. The branch has buds on it. Each bud is a place on the branch where a new stem, leaves, and flowers can grow.
   2. As with the tips of roots, growth in length of a branch occurs because of rapid mitotic division of cells within the bud.
   3. In cold climates, overlapping bud scales protect the delicate cells within the buds.
   4. Each branch usually has a **terminal bud** at its tip; along the sides of a branch are **lateral buds,** from which other branches may grow.

LEARNING ACTIVITY 12.6

Stem Growth Occurs at the Tip, Not at the Bottom

Plant some zinnia seeds. When the plants are about 5 centimeters (2 in.) high, mark the stems with nail polish 2 centimeters (1 in.) from the soil. Have students check the height of the marks periodically.

5. Along the branch there are also oval, circular, or shield-shaped **leaf scars** that mark the spots where leaf stalks were attached during previous seasons.
6. A node is a point on the leaf scar where leaves or branches were produced by the stem.
7. Also along the branch are rings circling the branch, called **bud-scale scars**, which show the exact locations of the terminal buds during previous seasons. By starting at the present terminal bud and counting the number of bud-scale scars along the branch, one can find out the exact age of the branch.
8. Some branches have thorns, which help to protect the plant. Some thorns are short and broad, some are long and pointed, and others are branched.

B. Four distinct regions are located inside the branch or trunk of a **woody tree.** These regions are the bark, cambium, wood, and pith.

1. The **bark** is the outer covering of the stem and consists of two layers—an outer layer, which is mostly dead cells, and an inner layer made of mostly living cells. The outer bark protects the stem from injury, from disease, and from losing water. The inner part of the bark conducts the food made by the leaves downward to the roots, through the **phloem tissue.**
2. Sometimes bark-chewing animals, such as beavers, porcupines, deer, and horses, remove a circular section of the bark all the way around a tree. This is called **girdling,** and it will kill a tree because the tree's food transport system has been disrupted.
3. The wood of the stem consists of hollow tubes of specialized cells, the **xylem tissue,** that conduct water and dissolved minerals upward from the roots to the leaves.
4. In a mature stem there are often two kinds of wood: the **sapwood,** which is the living xylem tissue, and the **hardwood,** which is dead tissue whose only function is to provide support for the tree. Hardwood is the part of the tree used to make furniture.
5. The **pith** is in the center of the stem and serves as a place to store food. In an old, woody stem, the pith is hardly noticeable, but in a young stem, because there is still little wood in it, the pith seems to be quite large. However, the size of the pith is the same in both because the pith never grows beyond the size it reaches during the first year of the stem's growth.
6. Between the bark and the wood of a stem there is a fourth region, called the **cambium,** which is made up of a very thin layer of delicate tissue. The cambium tissue is made of cells that continue mitotic division to create new cells, adding to the diameter of the stem.
7. Each spring and summer the cambium forms new wood and new inner bark for the stem. As a result, each year a new layer of wood is added to the stem. This new layer of wood forms a circle or ring, called an **annual ring,** inside the stem. This formation of layers makes it possible to estimate the age of a tree by counting the number of annual rings in a cross-section of the tree's trunk.

C. A monocotyledon **herbaceous stem** has a hard outer covering called a rind, and a dicotyledon herbaceous stem has a thin skin called an epidermis.

1. The monocotyledon herbaceous stem does *not* have a cambium, but the dicotyledon herbaceous stem *does* have a cambium.
2. Because both types of herbaceous stems live only 1 year, they are usually long and thin.
3. The bundles of hollow tubes (xylem and phloem tissues) inside a monocotyledon herbaceous stem are scattered at random inside the stem, but in a dicotyledon herbaceous stem, the bundles of hollow tubes are arranged concentrically.

III. The Functions of Stems

A. In addition to providing support for the plant, stems serve several other functions.

1. Stems conduct water and dissolved minerals throughout the plant. They go upward from the roots to the leaves through the xylem tissue, and downward to the roots through the phloem tissue.
2. A stem produces and displays the leaves so they receive the sunlight they need.
3. Green herbaceous stems (those with chlorophyll) can manufacture food for the plant.
4. Some stems, like the potato, store food for the plant.
5. Some aerial stems, such as the coleus, philodendron, strawberry, and black raspberry,

LEARNING ACTIVITY 12.7

Stems Carry Water

A. Celery Stalk

Obtain a stalk of celery with some leaves still on it, and put it in a glass of water that has been colored a deep red with food coloring (Figure 12.4). With a sharp knife cut 2 centimeters (1 in.) off the bottom of the stalk while the stalk is under the colored water. Allow the celery stalk to stand overnight. Note that the colored water has moved up the stalk and into the leaves. Remove the stalk from the colored water and cut off a section of stalk from the bottom. Note the red color of the hollow tubes in the stem.

B. Make a Two-Colored Carnation

Obtain a white carnation with a long, thick stem. Split the stem in two parts for a distance of about 3 inches. Place one part in a test tube or glass of water that has been colored with red food coloring and the other part in a test tube that has been colored with blue or green food coloring (Figure 12.5). Allow the carnation to stand overnight. The flower will have two colors, the color of the various petals depending on which colored liquid reached them.

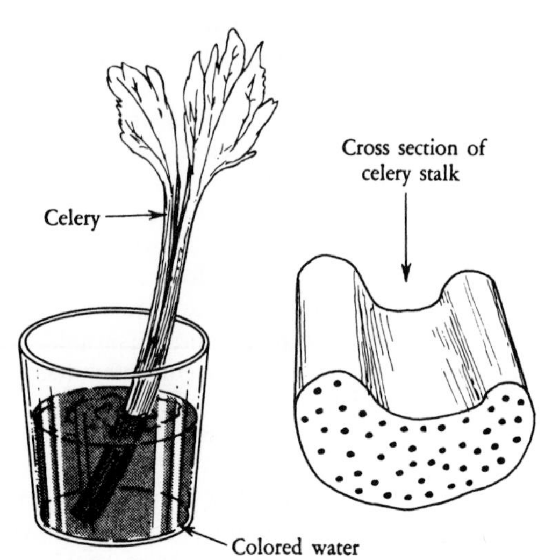

FIGURE 12.4 Colored water rises up the celery stalk.

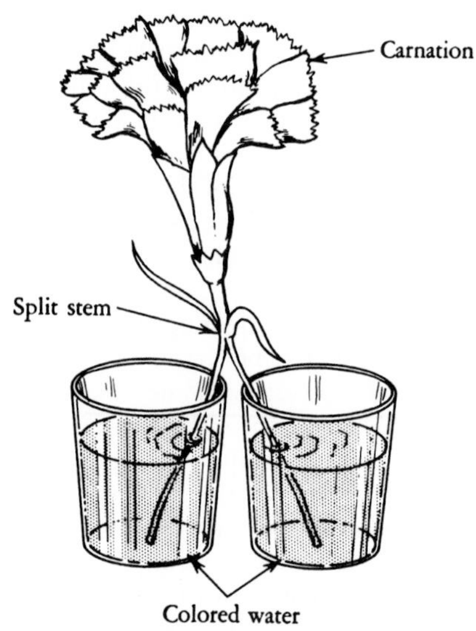

FIGURE 12.5 A two-colored carnation.

can grow new plants. Most underground stems can generate new plants.

6. Some stems have adaptations, such as thorns, that help protect the plant from animals or from dehydration during drought.

IV. Human Uses of Stems

A. Humans have found numerous uses for plant stems.

1. For many plant species, such as the potato, asparagus, and celery, the stem of the plant is used as a food source. The sap of the maple tree and the juice of the sugar cane are a source of sugar. Cinnamon bark is used to make spice for flavoring. The red, edible part of the strawberry plant that is usually referred to as the fruit is actually a modified extension of the plant's stem. Although not the most edible part of the plant, the true fruit of the strawberry is a small, yellow part that sticks to the side of the plant.
2. Rubber is made from the sap from the stem of rubber trees.
3. The stem of the flax plant is used to make linen.
4. The stems of many plants are sources of medicines. The cinchona bark produces quinine, used to treat malaria. The bark of the Pacific yew produces a cancer-fighting drug. The bark of the cherry tree is used for cough syrups. Camphor comes from the laurel tree, and witch hazel comes from the witch hazel shrub.
5. Ropes and various kinds of string are made from the fibers of hemp and other plants.
6. The bark of many trees is used to make dyes.
7. Turpentine from the pine tree is used in paint and varnish.
8. The wood of trees is used for heating and cooking, and for making lumber for building, furniture, paper, telephone poles, piles for piers, wooden boxes, baskets, and barrels.

Leaves

I. Leaf Structure

A. The main parts of a leaf are the blade, the petiole, and the leaf veins.

1. The **blade** is the flat, thin, green part of the leaf, with veins running through it.
2. The **petiole** is the stem of the leaf and is attached to the stem of the plant at a node. In some plants, the leaves do not have a petiole but are fastened directly to the plant's stem.
3. The **leaf veins** are tiny, hollow tubes, continuations of the xylem and phloem tissues that carry water, dissolved minerals, and food between the leaf and the stem. The veins also help to strengthen the leaf and make it firm.

B. There are three main patterns in which the veins of a leaf are arranged. These are called palmate, pinnate, and parallel patterns. The size and shape of a leaf are related to the arrangement of its veins. The type of vein pattern is one characteristic used in identifying flowering plants.

1. In the **palmate** pattern, there are a few large veins that start at the tip of the petiole and spread out very much like the outstretched fingers of your hand. Smaller veins, called veinlets, then branch out from these large veins. Leaves with palmate veins are usually broad. Examples are the leaves of geranium, maple, and sycamore plants.
2. In the **pinnate** pattern, one large vein, called a midrib, with smaller veins (veinlets) branching out on each side of the midrib, gives the same effect or appearance as the arrangement in a feather. Leaves with pinnate veins are shorter and wider than those with parallel veins. Elm and willow are examples of plants whose leaves display pinnate vein patterns.
3. In the **parallel** pattern, many large veins run parallel, or side by side, from the bottom of the leaf to its tip. Parallel veins are found mostly in the leaves of monocotyledon plants, whose seeds have only one seed leaf (cotyledon). Leaves with parallel veins are long and thin. Examples are the leaves of the lily, iris, and grasses.

C. Leaves have different kinds of edges.

1. Some edges are smooth, like the leaves of the willow, redbud, and magnolia. Some are toothed, or serrated, like the leaves of the elm. Some have lobes, or fingerlike projections, like the leaves of the maple.
2. If the blade of a leaf is all in one piece, it is called a **simple leaf**, but if the blade is divided into three or more separate parts, called leaflets, it is called a **compound leaf.** A leaf is still a simple leaf, even if it is lobed or greatly indented. Maple, oak, elm, and apple leaves are simple leaves. Clover, horse chestnut, locust, ash, and strawberry leaves are compound leaves.
3. When the leaflets spread out or radiate from a single common point, as in the horse chestnut and the clover, the leaf is called a palmately compound leaf. When the leaflets are arranged on each side of the midrib, or opposite one another, as in the ash and the pea, the leaf is called a pinnately compound leaf.

D. Leaves of the evergreens are different from those of other seed plants. In some evergreens, the leaves are thin and needle-like, such as the pine and the spruce. In others, such as the cedar, the leaves are overlapping scales.

II. Leaf Functions

A. The main function of a leaf is to make food for the plant. An important by-product of that is the release of oxygen into the atmosphere, which is the major source of oxygen for all living organisms on Earth.

1. Chlorophyll gives the leaf its green color and makes it possible for the plant to make food by the process of **photosynthesis.** *Photo* means light, and *synthesis* means putting together.
2. A plant part, such as a leaf, may contain chlorophyll but not be green in color because of the predominance of some other pigment, such as the carotenoid pigments, which are yellow and orange. These other pigments trap certain rays of sunlight and transfer that energy to help in the manufacture of food, usually in the form of carbohydrates.
3. Chlorophyll and the other pigments are located in the cytoplasm of leaf cells in organelles called **chloroplasts.**
4. Chloroplasts use two raw materials to manufacture carbohydrates: water and carbon dioxide.
5. Water, together with dissolved minerals, comes mostly from the ground, passing into roots, up the stem, and into the leaf.
6. Chloroplasts trap the energy of sunlight, convert it to chemical energy, and then store it.
7. The process of photosynthesis includes two main types of reactions. These are the **light reactions** and the **Calvin cycle.**
   a. In the light reactions, light energy is converted to chemical energy. They represent the "photo" part of *photosynthesis*. These reactions result in the splitting of water molecules, thereby providing hydrogen and an energy source for the Calvin cycle.
   b. The Calvin cycle is the series of reactions that forms carbohydrates (usually glucose) using carbon dioxide and the hydrogen that was released from water in

the light reaction. The Calvin cycle is the "synthesis" part of *photosynthesis*.

8. Carbon dioxide is a gas in the atmosphere that enters the leaf through its many tiny openings, called **stomata**, that are on the surface of the leaf—especially on the underside, which is more protected from sunlight.
9. The water-splitting reaction (called **photolysis**) constitutes the first series of reactions in photosynthesis and requires light energy. The Calvin cycle, the union of carbon dioxide and hydrogen from water, is the second series of reactions (sometimes called **catalysis**). It does not require light energy. For this reason, it is sometimes known as the dark reaction, although it occurs all the time, day or night.
10. Oxygen, released as a result of the light reactions, exits back into the surrounding atmosphere through the same stomata that allow the carbon dioxide to enter.
11. The leaf changes the sugar (glucose) to starch, either immediately or soon after photosynthesis has occurred. The leaf also changes some of the sugar into fats and proteins.

LEARNING ACTIVITY 12.8

Function of a Leaf and Its Stomata

A. Air Enters a Plant Through the Leaf

Fit a flask or jar with a two-hole rubber stopper. Into one hole insert a leaf with a long stem, such as the leaf of an African violet. Into the other hole insert a piece of glass tubing bent at a right angle or a plastic soda straw bent at an angle (Figure 12.6). Add enough water to the flask so that the stem of the leaf is below the level of the water, but the tubing or straw is not, when the cork is inserted. Now fit the stopper very tightly into the neck of the flask. Use drops of melted paraffin from a burning candle to seal the holes of the stopper containing the glass tubing and the stem of the leaf. Suck air from the glass tubing. Air bubbles will come from the end of the leaf stem, showing that air entered the leaf and traveled down its stem.

B. Stomata and Guard Cells

Select a leaf from a plant that has soft, tender leaves. *Geranium* and *Coleus* work well. If those are unavailable, fresh spinach leaves also work well. Tear a leaf at an angle to expose a thin section of epidermis. The epidermis will appear as a clear strip of leaf tissue at the jagged torn edge. Use tap water to make wet slide mounts of both the upper and lower epidermis sections. Cover each epidermis section with a cover glass. Have students observe both slides under a microscope and look for stomata and the surrounding guard cells. Notice that chloroplasts are seen only in guard cells. Epidermal cells contain no chloroplasts and are an irregular shape, while guard cells are sausage shaped. Also observe whether there are more, fewer, or the same number of stomata on the upper and lower epidermis sections.

C. Opened and Closed Stomata

Make another wet slide mount of the lower epidermis of a leaf, but rather than using tap water for the mount, use a 5% saltwater solution (5 gr of table salt in a graduated cylinder and enough water for the level to reach 100 ml). Have students observe this slide under a microscope and explain what they see and how it differs from the epidermal tissue in the tap water mount. In the saltwater solution, the guard cells will close because a higher water concentration inside cells compared with outside cells results in water moving out of guard cells, causing them to collapse and close the stomata.

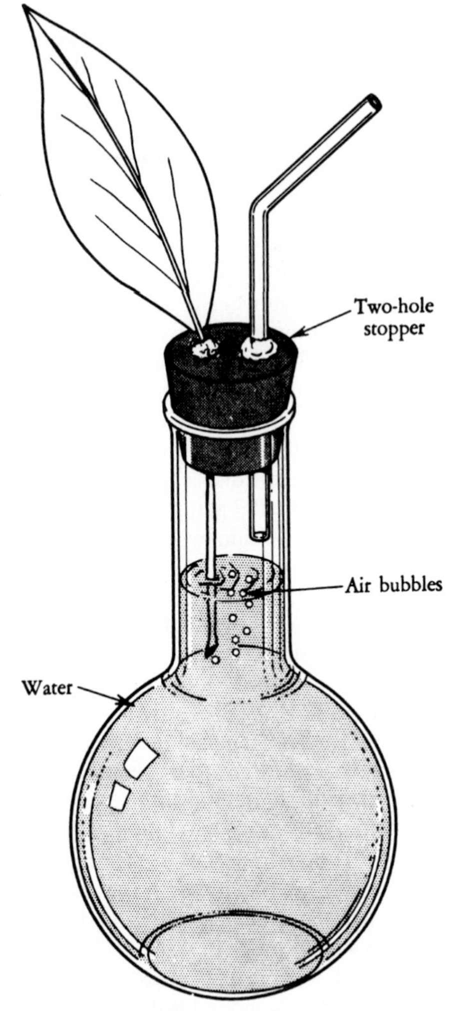

FIGURE 12.6 Air bubbles show that air enters the leaf and travels down the stem.

LEARNING ACTIVITY 12.9

Leaves, Chlorophyll, and Photosynthesis

A. Examining Chloroplasts

Obtain the water plant elodea from a store that sells aquarium supplies. Have students examine a leaf of elodea under the microscope and note the green chloroplasts that are present.

B. Extracting Chlorophyll from Leaves

You can extract chlorophyll from any green leaf by first boiling the leaf in water for several minutes to break down the plant cell walls. Frozen or fresh spinach leaves work nicely. Prepare a double boiler with water in the bottom section and rubbing alcohol in the upper section. Place the leaf in the alcohol and heat the double boiler until the water boils, then continue to boil for 10 to 15 minutes. The hot alcohol will extract the chlorophyll from the leaf and become dark green.

C. Leaves Need Carbon Dioxide for Photosynthesis

Obtain a geranium plant. Coat the top and bottom surfaces of one leaf with a thin layer of petroleum jelly. Keep the plant in a sunny location. In a few days the jelly-coated leaf will begin to turn yellow. Point out that the petroleum jelly prevented carbon dioxide in the air from entering the leaf's stomata, and this lack of carbon dioxide stopped the process of photosynthesis in the leaf.

D. Leaves Need Sunlight for Photosynthesis

Repeat demonstration C, but now cover one leaf completely with aluminum foil instead of petroleum jelly. The leaf will turn yellow because the aluminum foil prevents sunlight from reaching the leaf, and this stops the process of photosynthesis.

E. Leaves Produce Starch During Photosynthesis

Put a plant, such as a geranium, in the sun for several hours so that photosynthesis can take place. Pluck one of the leaves and boil it in water for several minutes to break down the cell walls in the leaf. Prepare a double boiler with water in the bottom section and rubbing alcohol in the top section. Place the leaf in the alcohol, heat the double boiler until the water boils, and continue to boil for 10 to 15 minutes (or longer if necessary) until the alcohol extracts most of the chlorophyll from the leaf.

Remove the leaf and rinse it in hot water. Place the leaf in a large, shallow saucer and dry it by blotting gently with cleansing tissue. Place a few drops of tincture of iodine on the leaf. A dark blue or purple color will appear after a few minutes, indicating the presence of starch in the leaf. Show that the blue color is a test for starch by adding a few drops of iodine to cornstarch or to a slice of potato. If you use a coleus leaf, only the green sections will test for starch.

F. Leaves Give Off Oxygen During Photosynthesis

Obtain a water plant, such as elodea or sagittaria, from an aquarium supply store. Put the plant in an aquarium filled with water and set a short-stemmed transparent funnel over the plant. Fill a test tube with water, making sure that there are no air bubbles in the water, then invert the test tube, still full of water, over the stem of the funnel (Figure 12.7). Now put the aquarium in a sunny place for several days. The plant will give off bubbles of oxygen, which will displace the water in the test tube. After most of the water is displaced, remove the test tube and hold it mouth upward. Blow out a burning wood splint and quickly put the glowing splint inside the test tube. The oxygen in the test tube makes the splint either glow more brightly or burst into flame.

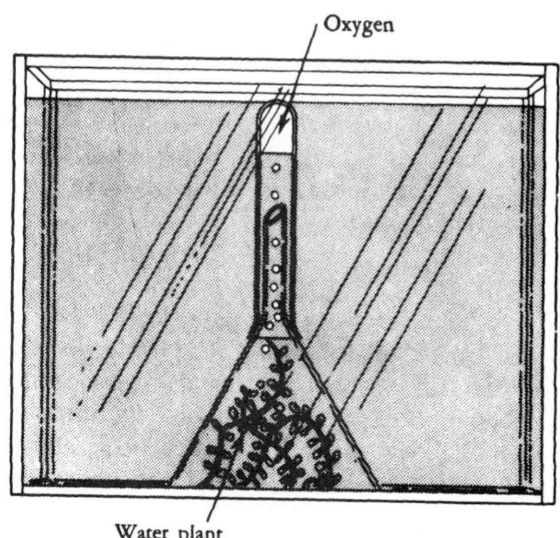

FIGURE 12.7 The water plant gives off bubbles of oxygen during photosynthesis.

G. Leaves Give Off Water

Obtain a potted geranium plant and a wooden stick about the same length as the flowerpot and plant combined. Place the stick in the soil of the pot so that the top of the stick extends slightly above the plant. Cover the soil and the sides of the flower pot with aluminum foil. Now place a plastic bag over the plant and tie the mouth of the bag securely around the stem (Figure 12.8). Prepare a control by duplicating every condition except the presence of the geranium plant. Such a control involves having the same size flower pot, same amount of soil and moisture in the soil, same size wooden stick, aluminum foil over the soil and sides of the pot, and the same size plastic bag over the stick and tied around the stick.

Now place both flower pots in the sun for a few hours. A large number of water droplets will appear on the inside of the plastic bag covering the geranium plant. Point out that covering the soil and the sides of the flowerpot eliminated the possibility of the water coming from the soil or through the porous pot. Because no water droplets appear in the control, the water cannot have come from the air, which usually

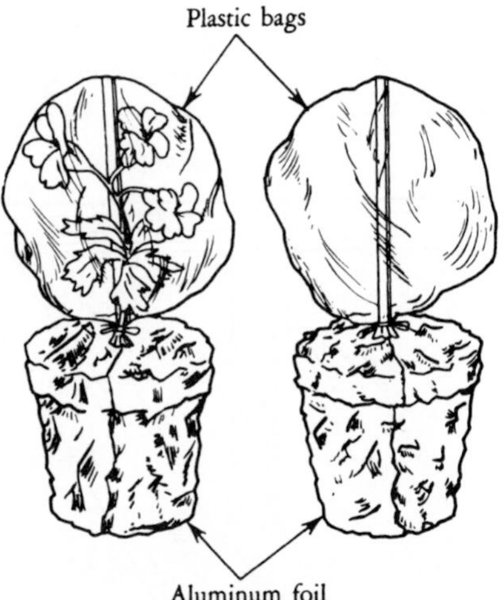

FIGURE 12.8 A controlled experiment to show that leaves give off water.

contains water vapor. Therefore, the water droplets can only have come from the plant itself.

H. Leaves Change Color in the Fall

Observe the changes in the color of leaves of various trees in the fall, and associate the change in color with the kind of tree. The colors appear when the leaves stop making chlorophyll. Obtain two plants of the same kind and size. Allow one plant to stay in the sunlight all day. Keep the other plant in a dark closet for half the day. After a few days, note the yellowish appearance of the leaves that had less sunlight. These leaves now have less chlorophyll in them, and the yellow pigment in the leaves has begun to show.

12. Food made by the leaf may then be carried to the stem and the roots, for use or for storage.
13. Any part of the plant that has chlorophyll can make food for the plant, but the plant's leaf predominates in photosynthesis.
14. Many factors influence the rate at which plants photosynthesize. These include the availability and quality of the light source, the availability of the raw materials water and carbon dioxide, and the environmental temperature.

B. Another important function of the leaf is **transpiration**, the loss of water from the leaf's surface by evaporation.

1. Although the plant needs water to make food and for other functions, it usually takes in more water than it uses. Excess water passes through the stomata, where it evaporates into the atmosphere as water vapor. This evaporation provides a cooling effect on the leaf.
2. Typically, plants give off a great amount of water by transpiration. A sunflower, for example, gives off 1 liter (approximately 1 qt) of water a day. During the summer months, an average-size tree can give off as much as 47 liters (50 qt) of water a day.
3. Specialized leaf cells, called **guard cells**, control the amount of water that passes out of the leaf. Each **stoma** (singular of *stomata*) is surrounded by two guard cells.
4. Guard cells usually keep the stomata wide open, allowing water to move out of the leaves freely. However, when the plant does not have enough water and is wilting, the guard cells make the stomata smaller, which slows the loss of water from the leaf.
5. Through transpiration, plants in the **tropical rainforests** that encircle the Earth near the equator play an important role in replenishing the Earth's freshwater supply. Some of the rainforest is being destroyed for development and agriculture. There is concern about the effects of this destruction on the global ecosystem. For example, it is estimated that because the rainforests hold approximately 10 million species of flora and fauna, the destruction of these forests is causing the extinction of about 50,000 species a year, many of which have never even been identified.

C. Other functions of the leaf are that it helps the plant digest food and change the food into the energy it needs to live and grow, and it helps the plant remove waste materials. Some leaves, such as those of sedum, sansevieria, and African violet, can produce new plants by budding.

III. Some Leaves Change Color, Especially in Fall

A. During late spring and summer the leaves keep making chlorophyll and stay green, but in fall, when the weather becomes colder, leaves of many plants stop making chlorophyll and the green color in the leaves disappears, giving way to other pigments that had been masked by the dominant chlorophyll pigments.

1. The hidden yellow and orange pigments in some of the leaves then appear.
2. Continuing decline in temperature and an increase in the amount of moisture in the air also reveal red colors in other leaves.
3. When the weather becomes still colder, the leaves die, turn brown, and fall to the ground.

IV. Use of Leaves by Humans

A. Many leaves are used for human food, such as the leaves of lettuce, cabbage, spinach, endive, parsley, and kale plants.
B. Tea leaves are used to make a beverage.
C. Spearmint, peppermint, sage, and thyme leaves are used for spices and flavoring.
D. Palm and grass leaves are sometimes used to cover the roofs of dwellings.
E. Leaves of some plants, or extracts from leaves, are used for medicinal purposes.

Flowers

I. Definition and Flower Structure

A. The flower is a special part of a plant that produces new plants by sexual reproduction; that is, by the union of sex cells. It is believed that the first plants with flowers appeared on Earth about 70 million years ago.
  1. The flower lives for a short time only, and then parts of the flower become a fruit.
  2. The fruit contains seeds, and the seeds produce the new plants.
  3. The fruit serves the function of dispersing or scattering the seeds, which helps to prevent overcrowding of individual plants.

B. The large, flattened part of the stalk that holds the flower is called the **receptacle.**

C. Most flowers have four kinds of organs: sepals, petals, stamens, and pistils.
  1. **Sepals** are the thin, usually green, leaflike parts on the outside of the flower. They cover and protect the young flower bud and the flowers that close at night. When the bud opens, the sepals separate and fold back in support and protection for the open flower. Collectively, the sepals are called the **calyx.**
  2. Inside the calyx are the **petals.** Petals are usually larger than the sepals, and often brightly colored, and they attract insects. Collectively, the petals are called the **corolla.**
  3. At the base of the petals are usually small pockets or cups of a sweet liquid, called **nectar**, which is attractive to hummingbirds, bees, and other insects. (Flowers that are pollinated by beetles and flies are often those that lack colorful petals and nectar but produce a strong scent. Examples include magnolias and skunk cabbage.)
  4. In some flowers, such as tulips and the lilies, the sepals and the petals are the same color.
  5. The calyx and the corolla are called the **accessory parts** of the flower, because they are not entirely needed for reproduction.
  6. The stamens and the pistil, in contrast, are essential for reproduction and therefore are referred to as the **essential parts.**
  7. The **stamens**, which constitute the male organ of the flower, are inside the petals and are usually grouped in a ring around the center of the flower.
  8. Each stamen has two parts: the filament and the anther. The **filament** is the thin stalk or stem of the stamen. The **anther** is at the top of the filament and is usually knobby or boxlike.
  9. The anther produces a yellow or reddish powdery substance called **pollen.** Inside the pollen are the **male gametes**, or sperm cells.
  10. The **pistil**, which is the female organ, is in the center of the flower, usually surrounded by the stamens. There are three parts to a pistil: the stigma, the style, and the ovary.
  11. The **stigma** is the sticky top of the pistil, the **style** is the thin stalk or stem of the pistil, and the **ovary** is the large or swollen base of the pistil, usually positioned on top of the receptacle.
  12. Inside the ovary are one or more **ovules**, which, if they become fertilized, develop into **seeds.**

D. There is such a variation in shapes, sizes, colors, and configurations of flower parts that these features are often used in plant identification.
  1. A flower, such as the rose or the lily, that has all four parts (sepals, petals, stamens, and pistil) is called a **complete flower.** A flower, such as the willow or the oat, that has one or more parts missing, is called an **incomplete flower.**
  2. An incomplete flower, such as the oat or wild ginger, that has both stamens and a pistil, even if its sepals and its petals are missing, is called a **perfect** flower. An incomplete flower, such as the pussy willow or cottonwood, that has only stamens or a pistil but not both is called an **imperfect flower.**
  3. Flowers that are a whole cluster of individual flowers on one stem rather than a single flower on one stem are called **composite flowers.** Examples include the zinnia, aster, daisy, chrysanthemum, marigold, and dandelion.

E. Flowers of monocotyledon plants are different from the flowers of dicotyledon plants.
  1. Monocotyledon flowers, such as the tulip and the lily, have their flower parts in threes or in multiples of three, like six or nine. The tulip has three sepals and three petals (both the same color), six stamens, and a pistil with three parts to its ovary.
  2. Dicotyledon flowers, such as the rose, buttercup, and columbine, usually have their flower parts in fours or fives, or in multiples of fours or fives.

II. Pollination and Fertilization: Two Separate Events

A. For seeds to be formed, the pollen from the anther of a stamen must be carried to the sticky stigma of the pistil. This transfer of pollen is called **pollination.**
  1. When the pollen is carried from the anther to the stigma in the same flower, or to the stigma of another flower on the same plant, it is called **self-pollination.**
  2. The process of self-pollination does not occur often. In some flowers, the stamens are too short for the pollen to fall and land on the pistil. In other flowers, the stamens lose their pollen before the pistil is mature enough to receive it. Imperfect flowers are lacking either stamens or a pistil.

LEARNING ACTIVITY 12.10

Flowers and Pollen

A. Examine a Flower

Obtain a large simple flower, such as a tulip, lily, gladiolus, petunia, or sweet pea. Examine the flower closely (Figure 12.9). Observe the flower stalk and its upper larger part, the receptacle. At the base of the receptacle, note the sepals that surround the petals. In the tulip and the lily, the sepals are the same color as the petals. Use tweezers to remove the sepals and petals, place them on separate pieces of paper, and label them appropriately. Count the number of sepals and petals.

Observe the stamens surrounding the pistil in the center of the flower. Count the number of stamens, remove them with the tweezers, and place them on a labeled piece of paper. Examine the stamens with a magnifying glass. Locate the filament and anther, and observe the pollen that may be present on the anther. Remove the pistil and observe the stigma, style, and ovary under the magnifying glass. With a razor blade or sharp knife cut through the ovary lengthwise. Observe the ovules with the magnifying glass and try to count the number present.

Have the students make a large drawing or diagram of the whole flower and its individual parts. Label the parts of the flower and the parts of the pistil and stamen.

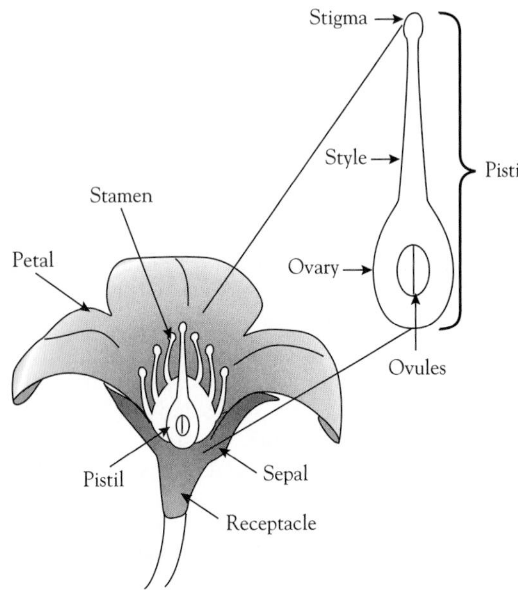

FIGURE 12.9 Diagram of the parts of a flower.

B. Compare Kinds of Flowers

Have the students observe examples of different kinds of flowers. Note the basic difference between complete and incomplete flowers, perfect and imperfect flowers, and monocotyledon and dicotyledon flowers. Point out that the flower parts of monocotyledon plants are in threes or multiples of three, whereas the flower parts of dicotyledon plants are in fours and fives or their multiples. Note also, that the sepals and petals of monocotyledon flowers are often the same color.

Obtain a composite flower such as a daisy, dandelion, chrysanthemum, zinnia, marigold, sunflower, or aster. Pull out a ray flower (petal) and a disk flower (little tube in the center), and examine them with a magnifying glass. Do the ray flower and disk flower have all the parts of a perfect flower? What parts, if any, are missing?

C. Germinate Pollen Grains

Place a drop of water on a microscope slide. Shake pollen from a flower onto the drop and cover with a cover glass. Examine the pollen under a microscope.

Pollen will germinate in a solution containing the right proportions of sugar in water. Fill three cups with boiled water. Add 1 teaspoon of sugar to one cup, 2 teaspoons of sugar to the second cup, and 3 teaspoons of sugar to the third cup. Stir the water in each cup until all the sugar is dissolved. Now pour a portion of each sugar solution into a clean, shallow saucer. Shake the pollen of a different kind of flower onto the surface of each sugar solution. Cover each saucer with a piece of glass and let the solutions stand at room temperature for several hours. Examine the pollen grains with a magnifying glass to see whether tubes are growing from them. If nothing is visible, place a drop of the sugar solution on a microscope, cover with a cover glass, and examine under the microscope.

3. When the pollen is carried from the anther of one flower on one plant to the stigma of a flower on another plant, it is called **cross-pollination.**
   a. Wind may blow pollen from flower to flower.
   b. Gymnosperms and many flowering plants depend on only the wind for pollination.
   c. Water may carry pollen from flower to flower of aquatic plants. As insects, like the bee, crawl into flowers to find nectar, they pick up pollen on their hairy bodies and coincidentally carry the pollen from flower to flower.
   d. Some flowers lack attractive coloration or nectar, but produce strong scents that attract certain insects such as beetles and flies, which, while looking for a place to deposit their eggs, inadvertently collect pollen on their bodies and transfer it to another flower.
   e. Hummingbirds inadvertently carry pollen from flower to flower on their beaks and long tongues.
   f. Humans perform pollination, called **artificial pollination**, to develop new kinds of flowers, fruits, vegetables, corn, and wheat.

LEARNING ACTIVITY 12.11

Exploring Developing Ovaries

Collect flowers at different stages in their growth, ranging from those with freshly opened buds to those whose petals have all fallen off. Cut open the ovary of each and observe the changes that have taken place. Two excellent flowers to observe are the iris, which has hundreds of ovules in its ovary, and the rose, which forms a sizable fruit after it has been fertilized.

Obtain a quantity of fresh string beans or peas, and open some of the pods that do not seem to be completely filled. The tiny, seedlike parts are the remains of ovules that were not fertilized by pollen and so did not develop into beans or peas.

B. The control of pollination by humans is also called **selective breeding.**
   1. Scientists use selective breeding to combine different qualities of two varieties of a flower into one new variety of the same flower. For example, the breeder may try to combine a large flower that has little fragrance with a small but fragrant flower to produce a large, fragrant flower.
   2. Plant breeders perform artificial pollination by carefully transferring pollen by hand from one flower to the stigma of another flower of the same kind.
   3. Usually, the flower with the stigma has had its stamens removed before the pollen was mature to ensure that no other pollen could be transferred to that stigma.
   4. After the flower has been artificially pollinated, it must be protected from visits by insects, which may inadvertently transfer pollen from their hairy bodies.
   5. Selective breeding through artificial pollination has produced many new varieties of flowers, especially of roses and corn. A new variety is called a **hybrid.**

C. When a grain of pollen from the right kind of flower falls on the stigma, it starts to form a **pollen tube,** which extends down the stigma and the style and into the ovary.
   1. From the pollen grain emerge sperm cells that swim down the pollen tube and enter the ovule through a small opening, called the **micropyle.** Inside the ovule is the female gametophyte, the embryo sac, which contains several cells surrounded by cytoplasm. One of the cells is the haploid egg cell. When the tube reaches the egg cell, the nucleus of one sperm cell unites with the nucleus of the egg cell to form a diploid zygote.
   2. This union of the sperm cell with the egg cell in an ovule is called **fertilization.**
   3. Although pollination must occur before fertilization can take place, fertilization is a separate process from pollination.
   4. Pollination starts the development of the ovary into a **fruit.** A fruit is a ripened ovary.
   5. If fertilization occurs, the ovule develops into a seed. If an ovule is not fertilized, a seed will not be formed in that ovule. Fertilization starts the development of the seed. A seed is a matured ovule.
   6. Pollination without fertilization results in a seedless fruit.

III. Use of Flowers by Humans

A. Because of their beauty, flowers are used for decoration.

B. Some flowers, such as buds of the cauliflower, are used for food; others are used in making dyes and perfumes.

C. Saffron, a yellow dye, comes from the stigmas of the saffron crocus.

D. Cloves are the dried flower buds of the myrtle tree, which grows in the tropics. The buds are used as a seasoning or spice and also produce oil that is used in medicines.

Fruits and Seeds

I. Definition and Function of Fruits

A. After the ovule in the ovary of a flower has been fertilized, seeds form and the ovary enlarges and ripens.
   1. A fruit is the ripened ovary of the flower, with or without the presence of other parts of the flower. It is the part of the plant that contains the seeds.
   2. To many persons, the word *fruit* means only tree fruits, such as the apple, pear, peach, orange, grape, and banana. To a botanist, however, fruit means the ripened ovary from any flowering plant.
   3. Garden flowers, wild flowers, grasses, shrubs, and flowering trees all produce fruits.
   4. Cereal grains such as corn, oats, and wheat are fruits. Nuts are fruits.
   5. Many "vegetables," such as the pea, bean, tomato, cucumber, pumpkin, and squash, are really fruits, not vegetables. True veg-

etables come from roots, stems, or leaves of plants.

B. A fruit has two main functions. One is to protect the seeds inside it; the other is to help scatter or disperse the seeds.

C. Fruits are classified in two main groups: fleshy fruits and dry fruits. Fleshy fruits, like the peach, are soft and fleshy when ripe. Dry fruits, like nuts, are dry when ripe.

1. Fleshy fruits are classified in three main groups: pomes, drupes, and berries.
2. In a **pome**, the fleshy part is formed by the sepals (calyx) and the large flattened end of the receptacle. The papery core of the pome is really the ovary, which contains the seeds. The apple, pear, and quince are examples of pomes.
   a. Pomes usually contain many seeds.
   b. The strawberry is a pome in which many tiny, hard fruits (ripened ovaries) are embedded in one fleshy receptacle. A strawberry is formed this way because its flower has many pistils inside it.
3. In a **drupe**, the ovary wall ripens into two layers. The outer layer becomes soft and fleshy, and the inner layer becomes very hard, usually containing one or two seeds. The plum, peach, apricot, cherry, and olive are examples of drupes.
   a. The almond comes from a drupe. We throw away the fleshy outer part and eat the seed of the hard inner part.
   b. The raspberry and blackberry are really collections of many tiny drupes clustered on one receptacle. The raspberry and blackberry are formed this way because their flowers have many pistils inside them.
4. In the **berry**, the whole ovary becomes fleshy. Some berries, such as the tomato, grape, and gooseberry, have rather soft, thin skins, whereas some other berries, such as the cantaloupe, watermelon, and cucumber, have hard skins. Still other berries, such as the orange, lemon, and grapefruit, have leathery skins.
   a. Berries usually contain many seeds.
   b. The pineapple is a fleshy fruit that is really made up of many fruits joined together, called a **multiple fruit**. A multiple fruit forms from many flowers that are clustered together. The mulberry is another example of a multiple fruit.
5. Dry fruits are classified as either dehiscent or indehiscent.
6. **Dehiscent fruits** are further divided into pod fruits and capsule fruits. Both pod and capsule fruits contain many seeds.
   a. Pod fruits, such as the bean, pea, and milkweed, split open along definite seams when ripe.
   b. Capsule fruits, such as the poppy, iris, and lily, crack open when they are ripe.
7. **Indehiscent fruits** do not split open along definite seams and do not open when they are ripe.
   a. Indehiscent fruits usually contain just one or two seeds.
   b. Some indehiscent fruits, such as the acorn, hazelnut, and chestnut, have a hard ovary wall covering the seed; others, such as corn, wheat, and oat, have a thin ovary wall fastened to the seed.
   c. In some indehiscent fruits, such as the sunflower, buttercup, and dandelion, the seed is not fastened to the ovary wall but is separated from it.
   d. In some other indehiscent fruits, such as the elm, maple, and ash, the seed is separated from the wall, but there are winglike growths attached to the ovary wall.

II. Definition and Structure of a Seed

A. A seed is a matured ovule whose egg cells have been fertilized by sperm cells from pollen grains. The seed can grow into a new plant of the same kind as the parent plants.

B. Seeds typically have three parts: a seed coat, stored food, and a tiny young plant called the **embryo**.

1. The **seed coat** is the covering of the seed that protects the embryo. Most seeds have two seed coats, but some have only one. The outer coat, which was the wall of the ovule, is usually thick and tough, and the inner coat is much thinner.
2. When the embryo begins to grow, it lives on the stored food until its own leaves are able to make food for the plant.
3. Some seeds store their food in thick seed leaves, called **cotyledons**. Cotyledons are a part of the young embryonic plant, and may appear as the first leaves of the young plant.
4. Monocotyledon plants, such as the corn plant, have only one cotyledon in their seeds. Dicotyledon plants, such as the bean plant, have two cotyledons.
5. The **embryo** is a tiny, young plant inside the seed that developed from the fertilized egg, the zygote. When mature, the embryo has tiny roots, stem, and leaves that will develop into the new plant.

C. Several conditions must exist for the embryo to develop into a new plant.

1. Seeds need water to grow. Water makes a seed swell and softens its outer coat.
2. Seeds need the right temperature to grow. Most seeds grow best when the temperature ranges between 16°C and 27°C (60°F and 80°F).

3. Seeds need oxygen to grow, and this is why the soil in a garden must be loose and the seeds must be planted close to the surface of the soil.
4. Seeds do *not* need sunlight because they live off the food stored within. When the new plant develops leaves, it then needs sunlight to make its own food.
5. When a seed begins to grow, we say that it is sprouting or **germinating.** First, the seed absorbs water. Water makes the seed swell and softens the seed coat. This softening of the seed coat allows the tiny plant (embryo) inside the seed to grow out through the seed coat.
6. In most seeds, the roots are the first part to grow; next, the primary stem grows upward; then the tiny leaves unfold, forming the first true leaves of the plant.
7. While the roots, stem, and true leaves are forming, the young plant lives on the stored food inside the seed. At this time it is called a **seedling.**
8. In the bean seed, which is a dicotyledon plant, the two cotyledons grow with the stem above the ground; in the corn seed, which is a monocotyledon plant, the single cotyledon stays below the ground.
9. By the time the young plant is able to make its own food and no longer needs the stored food in the cotyledons, the cotyledons have shriveled and will drop off. The true leaves of the plant then supply food for the plant through photosynthesis.

D. Seedlings grow best when they are scattered far away from the parent plant. When seeds fall to the ground only beside and beneath the parent plant, there is overcrowding of the young plants, all struggling for survival. The large number of seedlings depletes the minerals from the soil making the soil poor for growing. When there is a condition unfavorable for growing, the seedlings die, thus endangering the survival of that species. Many adaptations have occurred in the dispersal of seeds, which help to ensure species survival.
   1. Some fruits scatter their own seeds.
      a. Some fruits that grow in pods, such as the bean and the pea, twist when they ripen, so the pods break open and scatter the seeds.
      b. Some pods, such as those of the balsam and the touch-me-not, burst open at the slightest touch and propel their seeds some distance away.
      c. Tiny holes open in the fruit of the poppy, and, as the poppy stem moves back and forth in the wind, the seeds fly out through the holes.
   2. Many plants depend on wind to scatter their seeds.
      a. Some seeds, such as those of the milkweed, cottonwood, and dandelion, have fine hairs or tufts that act like parachutes to carry them far away on the wind.
      b. Other seeds, such as those of the maple, ash, elm, and pine, have wings that act like tiny propellers or sails and also carry them away on the wind.
      c. The tumbleweed scatters its seeds as the wind rolls it across the ground.
   3. Some seeds, such as the coconut, are carried away by water.
   4. Birds and other animals scatter seeds.
      a. A bird's feet accidentally pick up seeds in mud and then deposit the seeds elsewhere. Seeds may stick to a bird's bill or feathers and be carried to another place. Some birds eat fleshy fruits, such as the cherry, and then drop the seeds to the ground. Sometimes birds eat the whole fruit and pass the seeds as waste products, which fall to the ground.
      b. Squirrels bury nuts, such as the hickory and acorn, in the ground and may fail to dig up some of them.
      c. Many plants, such as the thistle and burdock, produce fruits with stickers that cling to the fur of animals and later come loose far from the parent plants.
   5. People help scatter seeds.
      a. When a vehicle drives through mud that has seeds in it, some of the mud might stick to the wheels and carry the seeds away.
      b. Burrs of the thistle and cocklebur cling to clothing and are carried away.
      c. Seed companies ship seeds to all parts of the world.

III. Use of Seeds by Humans

A. Seeds are used for food.
   1. The fruits and seeds of grasses like wheat, corn, oats, rice, and barley are among the most valuable sources of food in the world.
   2. Peas and beans are used throughout the world for food.
   3. The peanut is used as food, and its oil is used for cooking.
   4. Chocolate and cocoa are made from the cacao bean, and coffee is made from the coffee bean.
   5. The seeds of pepper, mustard, nutmeg, and celery are used as spices.

B. Cotton seeds are used to make cooking oil, and the fibers that stick to the seeds are used to make cotton cloth.

C. Oil from the seeds of the coconut tree is used to make soap, candles, and butter substitutes.

D. Seeds from the flax plant produce linseed oil, which is used to make paint, varnish, and other materials.
E. Soybeans are used as food and have many industrial uses as well.

IV. **Fruits Without Seeds**

A. Some fruits develop from the flower without forming seeds.
   1. The banana is a seedless fruit. The tiny black dots that look like seeds in the banana are really unfertilized ovules. Banana trees do not ordinarily produce seeds. Instead, new sprouts grow from the roots each season and their flowers produce more bananas without being fertilized.
B. Fruit growers produce seedless oranges, grapefruits, and grapes by grafting parts of seedless plants onto the roots and stems of ordinary plants that produce these fruits with seeds in them.
C. Through selective breeding, plant geneticists are steadily trying to improve the kinds of fruit we eat.
   1. Scientists try to make a fruit larger, give the fruit more flavor, make the skin smooth instead of hairy, get more seeds in the fruit, eliminate seeds from a fruit, make fruit mature earlier, or make a fruit sturdier and more resistant to disease.
   2. Sometimes plant geneticists create new fruits by transferring the pollen from a flower that produces one kind of fruit to the stigma of a flower that produces another kind of fruit. The tangelo is a fruit that is produced by crossing a tangerine with a grapefruit. The plumcot is a fruit produced by crossing a plum with an apricot.

Caring for Earth's Plants

I. **Understanding the Conditions Necessary for Plant Growth**

A. Like all organisms, plants need oxygen to metabolize their food and release energy by the process of cellular respiration.
B. Like all organisms, plants need water.
   1. They use water to make food through the process of photosynthesis.
   2. Water also contains dissolved minerals that plants need for maintenance and growth of tissues.
   3. Plants also use water to dissolve waste materials and to eliminate those materials.
C. Plants need the proper environmental temperature to grow.
   1. For each kind of plant there is an optimum temperature for growth and temperature limits beyond which it cannot live.
   2. Plants may die if the temperature rises and falls too quickly.
D. Plants need the energy of sunlight to make food and to grow.
E. Land plants need soil and minerals to grow.
   1. Plants need nitrogen, phosphorus, potassium, calcium, magnesium, and other chemical elements.
   2. Although some plants grow best in acid soil, most grow best in soil that is neutral or slightly alkaline.
F. Pruning, the cutting or trimming of dead or dying branches from trees and shrubs, helps keep the trees and shrubs healthy.
   1. In nature, pruning occurs naturally from forces such as wind and fire.
   2. Live branches are often pruned by humans to give a tree a certain shape or to make a tree produce more fruit and fewer leaves.
G. The climate has a great deal to do with the kinds and amounts of plants that will grow in a certain region.
   1. The **tropics** contain an abundance of plants because of the favorable temperature and heavy rainfall. A greater number and variety of plants grow in the tropics than anywhere else on Earth. The foliage is dense, and the leaves are broad. Plants grow continuously all year. Such plants as banana trees, date palms, bamboo, orchids, and large ferns grow in the tropics. Although the tropical rain forests cover less than 7% of the Earth's land surface, it is estimated that they contain about half of all the Earth's plant and animal species, many of which are still unidentified.
   2. Very few plants grow in the cold **Arctic** and **Antarctic** regions. There are almost no trees in these regions. A few dwarf willow trees can sometimes be found. Ferns, mosses, lichens, some flowering plants, and grass grow in the very short summer of these regions. Many of the plants are covered with a sort of hair, and the plants have thick seed coats. Plants in the polar regions have a very short growing season, because there may be only 10 weeks when the temperature is above freezing.
   3. A wide variety of plants grow in the **temperate climate** regions.
      a. Oranges, lemons, limes, grapefruit, and cotton grow in the mild temperate regions, where there is little or no frost.
      b. Many kinds of trees, shrubs, fruits, flowers, and cereal grasses grow in the moderate temperate regions.

c. Evergreens and hardy trees, shrubs, flowers, and grasses grow in cold temperate regions.

4. Most plants in the temperate regions grow only in the warm weather of spring, summer, and fall.
   a. Leafy trees, such as the oak and the maple, lose their leaves in fall and are inactive during winter.
   b. Evergreen trees, such as the pine and the spruce, do not lose their leaves in fall; they stay green all winter, but most of the activity in the tree stops.
   c. Some nonwoody plants, such as the peony and chrysanthemum, die to the ground in winter, but their roots stay alive and produce new growth in spring.
   d. Other nonwoody plants, such as the balsam and zinnia, die completely in winter, but the seeds they produce grow new plants in the spring.
5. Few plants grow in **warm desert** regions because there is so little rainfall.
   a. Desert plants have fewer leaves than other plants; consequently, the loss of water from such a plant is minimal. The leaves have a thick covering and are often relatively narrow, which also helps to minimize water loss.
   b. The mesquite plant sends long roots down to the water table many feet below the surface.
   c. The cactus plant has roots that cover a wide area just below the surface; these roots can quickly absorb any rain that falls.
   d. Desert plants bloom very quickly; their flowers have brilliant colors, which immediately attract insects for pollination before the flowers die from the hot sun.

II. Preserving Earth's Precious Forests and Wildflowers

A. It is estimated that the Earth has lost one-half of its original acreage of tropical rain forests, and that the United States has lost three-fourths of its original forests. Many efforts are being made to conserve the forests that are left.
   1. Lumbering companies are managing trees more wisely. They are removing weed trees, crowded trees, crooked trees, damaged trees, and diseased trees so the trees that will be used for timber can grow bigger and healthier. They are removing only part of the forest, then planting new trees that will eventually take the place of those cut down.
   2. The United States Forest Service, established in 1905, controls forest fires, develops and recommends improved lumbering practices, and finds ways to control harmful fungi and insects.
   3. Education programs lessen our carelessness in starting forest fires and improve our understanding of the importance of natural wild fires.
   4. Global organizations are attempting to arrest the removal of the remaining global rain forests.
   5. States protect wildflowers by passing laws that control or forbid the picking of wildflowers.
   6. Individuals and organizations protect endangered species of plants by maintaining populations and growing new plants.

Exploratory Activities for "Plants"

1. EXPLORING A BRYOPHYTE MICROHABITAT (ANY GRADE)

Overview

Small clumps of moss plants growing on the ground or at the base of a tree represent a habitat for many small organisms. Use the following interesting and motivating science learning activities to teach students about bryophytes, to introduce them to the concept of a microhabitat, and to help them gain an appreciation for the world of small organisms. The steps that follow are only suggestions and can be modified according to the maturity and interests of your students.

Initiating Activity Begin by putting on the writing board the word *habitat* and have students use the think-pair-write-share technique (discussed in Chapter 5) to clarify their understanding of the meaning of the word.

When there is a consensus on the meaning of the term, ask the students what they hypothesize are factors that determine an organism's habitat. Record on the board all the factors that students offer. During this brainstorming session, note these key factors: food source, shelter and protection, the organism's size, and its mobility.

Once students understand the concept of habitat and some of the factors that determine an organism's habitat, talk about types of habitats, leading students to understand that for very small creatures, a habitat may be quite small as well.

Exploratory Activity Show the students a clump of moss that you have collected (a fairly good-sized clump, perhaps nearly a foot square) from a damp area beneath a tree in a forest. Ask students if they know what the green plant is called and whether it would represent a habitat. Guide them to understand that this might well represent a habitat for some very small creatures.

Ask students to predict what kinds of creatures they think would make this clump of moss their habitat for all or a great portion of their lives, and which of these they think would dominate in numbers. Record their predictions on the board.

Divide the class into groups of three or four students. Give each group a portion of the moss clump on a paper towel and have them explore the moss for (a) moss plant structures (as noted in the preceding section "The Bryophytes") and (b) small animals that spend all or a great portion of their lives in moss (spiders, mites, insects). Each team should make its own prediction of the percentages of different kinds of creatures that make the moss their habitat; their predictions may differ from that made initially by the entire class.

For this exploratory portion of the study, each member of a group should be given a special task. For example, one student might be the official recorder and graphing specialist; another, the procurer of the scientific equipment needed, such as a hand lens and forceps; another, the chief scientist whose responsibility it is to identify the procedure and creatures found; and another, the reporter whose responsibility it will be to report the group's findings to the entire class.

Each group must decide how they are going to find the creatures that are living in their clumps of moss. One way to do this is to shake the clump onto a white paper towel. Another is to place the moss clump upside down on a fine mesh screen that is laid on top of a shallow pan and then shine a very bright and hot lamp above and down on the moss—the heat from the lamp will force tiny animals away from the heat and down through the screen, where they will be caught in the shallow pan (see Figure 12.10).

Members of each team record all organisms found and then plot their numbers on a graph. This graph is compared with their initial predictions and with the class prediction. A final report is made to the entire class regarding their findings and what they learned about their exploratory study of this microhabitat.

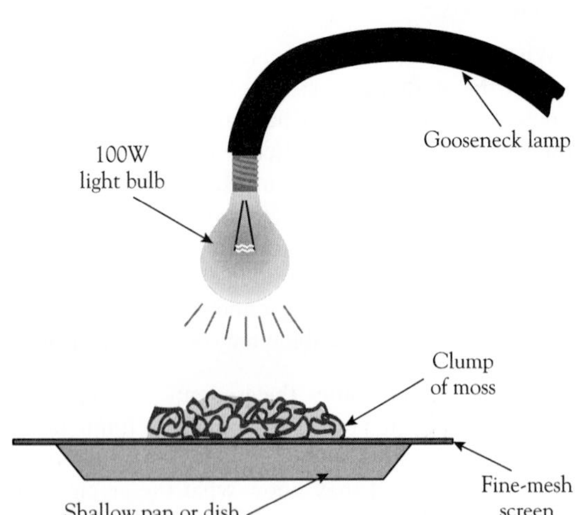

FIGURE 12.10 Forcing animals from their bryophyte microhabitat.

Application or Follow-up Activity A class discussion of group findings is held to discuss the features of habitats, factors that determine an organism's habitat, and what happens when habitats change or are modified.

2. EXPLORING LEAVES BY CLASSIFYING THEM AND BY MAKING LEAF COLLECTIONS AND LEAF PRINTS (ANY GRADE)

Overview

The following three exploratory activities may lead to students' questions and further study, as determined by the interest they generate.

2.1 Comparing Leaves

Have students collect a large variety of leaves (that have fallen from plants) to examine their parts, structure, similarities, and differences. Compare their sizes, shapes, edges, and different kinds of vein formation. Also distinguish between simple and compound leaves. Representative leaves may then be preserved by placing them on a large piece of blotting paper, arranging them so that they do not touch. Cover the leaves with another piece of blotting paper, then place a board on top of the blotting paper. Weight the board down with heavy books or stones, and let the leaves stay this way until they have dried out thoroughly. The leaves may then be removed and either placed in albums or taped to pieces of construction paper.

2.2 Classifying Leaves

Have the students collect autumn leaves and classify them by color. Let them explore other ways to classify the leaves. It may be appropriate for older students to practice using a key to classify the names of the plants from which the leaves come.

2.3 Making Blueprints of Leaves

From leaves that have been gathered, allow each student to select one, then proceed with the following directions. Cut a piece of blueprint paper larger than the leaf and put the paper, sensitive side up, on a piece of cardboard. Put the leaf on the blueprint paper and cover it with a pane of glass. Expose the leaf to sunlight for a few minutes until the paper darkens and turns blue. Dip the paper in a pan of cold water, rinse it well, then set it on a flat surface to dry. The paper will show a white print of the leaf's shape against a blue background.

3. EXPLORING SEED GERMINATION AND SEEDLING GROWTH (ANY GRADE)

Overview

The following exploratory activities may generate students' interest, leading to further questions and study. The procedures given here are only suggestions. After being given the initial idea, students should be allowed to hypothesize and design their own experimental procedures.

3.1 Germinating Seeds

Obtain lima beans and kernels of corn from a seed store. Do not use grocery store seeds, because they may be immature or heat-treated and may not germinate. Line a water tumbler with a rectangular piece of dark-colored blotter, and stuff absorbent cotton or peat moss into it to keep the blotter tight against its sides (Figure 12.11). Soak the lima beans and corn kernels overnight, then slip a few of each between the blotter and the sides of the tumbler. Moisten the cotton and keep it moist throughout the experiment to make sure the blotter is always moist. Place the tumbler in a warm place away from direct sunlight. Observe the tumbler each day and note the way the seeds germinate. Continue the germination until the seeds are well sprouted.

3.2 Exploring Conditions Necessary for Germination

Prepare eight tumbler germinators. Put one tumbler in the dark and one in the light (but not in direct sunlight). The seeds will germinate just as well in the dark as in the light. Students will learn that light is not necessary for germination and, in some cases, may even be harmful. However, once the plant has germinated and forms leaves, it needs light to grow.

Keep one tumbler watered regularly, and give the other tumbler no water at all. The seeds in the dry tumbler will not germinate.

Cover one tumbler tightly with plastic wrap and keep the other tumbler continually exposed to the air. The seeds in the covered tumbler will not sprout, because they need air to germinate.

Place one tumbler in a refrigerator and keep the other tumbler at room temperature. The seeds in the cold tumbler will not germinate, because they need warmth to germinate.

Obtain three flowerpots of the same size. Fill one pot with sand, the second with clay, and the third with rich soil containing humus. Soak some lima beans or radish seeds overnight, then plant two or three seeds in each pot. Keep all three pots at the same temperature and give all of them the same amount of water. Although the seeds in all three pots may germinate, the plants in the pot containing the rich soil will eventually be taller and sturdier.

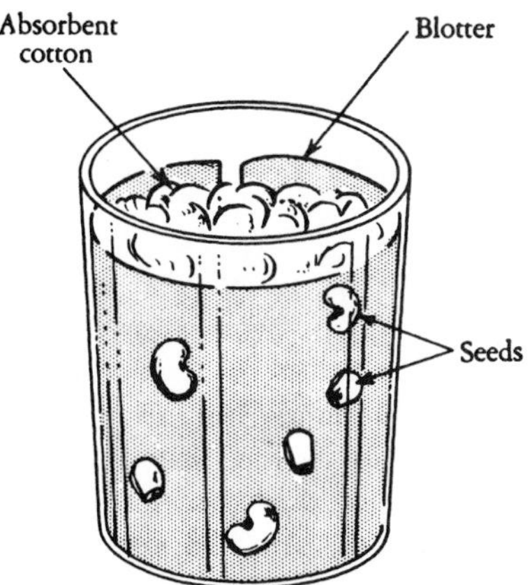

FIGURE 12.11 A tumbler seed germinator.

3.3 Test Seeds for Percentage of Germination

Obtain radish seeds from a seed store and soak 50 of them overnight. Obtain a piece of cotton flannel 30 centimeters (12 in.) square. Moisten the flannel cloth and place the radish seeds on it the flannel. Roll the flannel into a loose roll and place it in a shallow pan. Keep it moist and warm for a week, then unroll it carefully and count the number of seeds that have germinated. The number of germinated seeds divided by the total number of seeds (50), multiplied by 100, will give you the percentage of germination. Repeat the experiment using bean, corn, and tomato seeds.

3.4 Testing for Carbon Dioxide Given Off by Germinating Seeds

For a teacher or student demonstration: Obtain 20 to 30 lima beans from a seed store and soak them overnight. Put the seeds into a flask or jar and add enough water to cover about half the seeds. Fit the flask with a two-hole rubber stopper. Into one hole insert a thistle tube and let the tube extend to just above the bottom of the flask. Into the other hole insert a glass tube that leads to a water tumbler (Figure 12.12). Allow the beans to stay in the flask for a day or two. Then pour fresh limewater, which can be obtained from a drugstore, into the tumbler. Pour water slowly into the thistle tube until the flask is half filled. The water will force the carbon dioxide, which is now above the seeds, through the

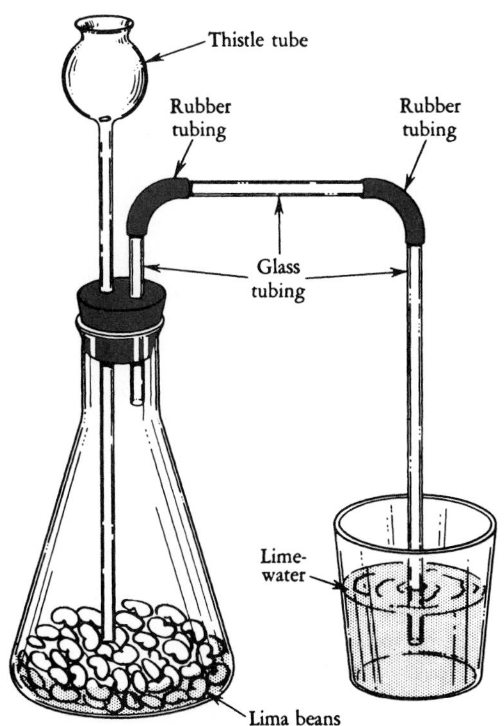

FIGURE 12.12 When seeds germinate, the carbon dioxide gas they give off causes limewater to become milky.

glass tubing and into the limewater, making the limewater turn milky. You can first show that carbon dioxide turns limewater milky by bubbling air from your lungs into limewater through a soda straw.

3.5 Exploring the Rate of Seed Growth

Obtain some radish seeds from a seed store, soak them overnight, and then plant them in a flowerpot filled with soil. Water the pot regularly and wait until the tiny plants begin to appear above the soil. Obtain two pieces of glass about 30 centimeters (12 in.) square, and insert a wet piece of dark-colored blotter between them. Each day, for 10 to 14 days, carefully remove one entire radish plant from the soil and place it on the moist blotter. You can keep the panes of glass together with string or rubber bands. Keep the blotter moist at all times. At the end of 2 weeks you will have a clear-cut record of the daily growth of the radish seeds.

Chapter 13

Neither Plant nor Animal

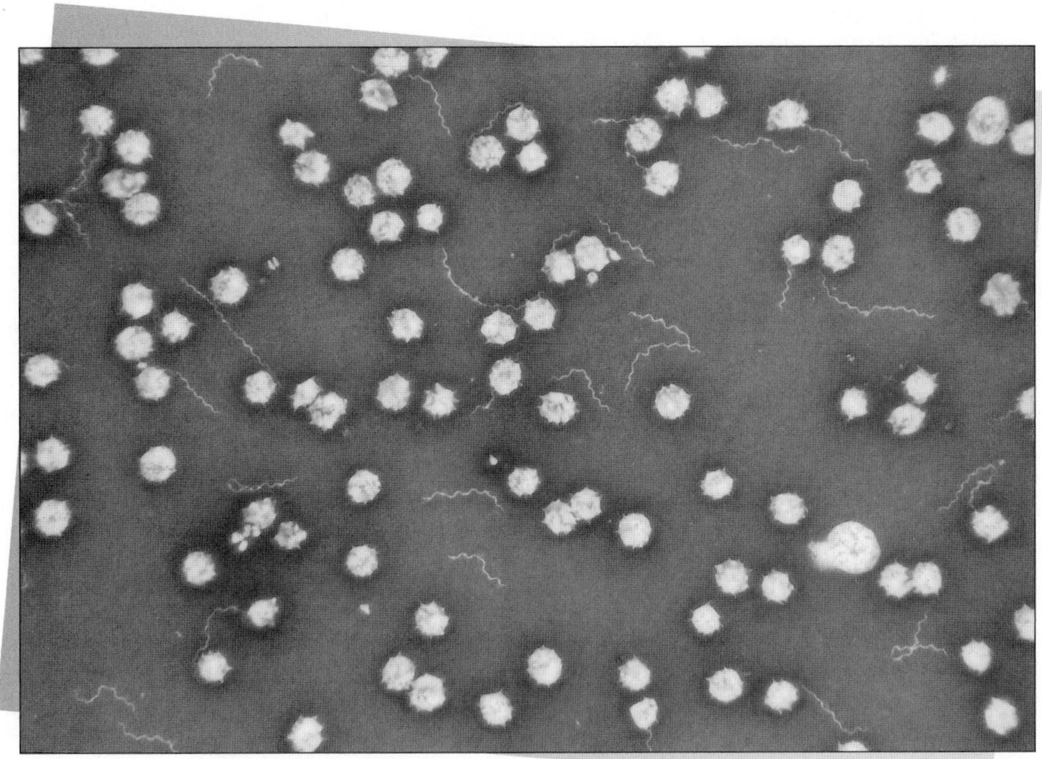

M. I. Walker © Dorling Kindersley

 Classification of Organisms That Are Neither Plant nor Animal

I. **The Nature of Science and Organisms That Are Neither Plant nor Animal**

A. Not all organisms fit neatly into schemes designed by humans to classify them.
   1. Schemes for classifying organisms are developed by scientists to help their understanding of, organization of, and communication about those organisms in an attempt to make order out of the millions of living things.
   2. Making sense and order out of what often first appears to be chaos is the nature of science. Specifically, in learning about and attempting to make sense out of the nature of organisms, scientists are always playing catch up. That is, nature leads and our understanding always lags behind.
   3. Organisms continue to adapt and change within their environments; therefore, systems that have been created in the past may not always accommodate all of the organisms that exist in the present or that will exist in the future.
   4. Human attempts to classify organisms are never perfect. As organisms change, new discoveries are made. Likewise, as the tools for learning become ever more sophisticated, more is learned about any group of organisms and about their unique characteristics. Classification systems are continually modified and changed by scientists.

B. As scientists learn more about the complexity of the living world, the system for classifying organisms increases in complexity.
   1. When we review ancient classification schemes, those systems appear to be quite uncomplicated. For example, depending on their size, plants were either trees, shrubs, or weedy. If an insect flew, it was probably called a fly. If not, it was likely called a bug. If an animal lived in the ocean, it was probably called a fish, and if it flew in the air, it was probably called a bird. For the time, such an uncomplicated system worked.
   2. Later, as tools for learning about creatures became more sophisticated and as what was learned revealed greater detail, classification systems became more extensive and detailed.
   3. For a long time organisms were divided into just two kingdoms—plant and animal.
   4. As biologists learned more about the similarities and differences between organisms, it became obvious that this two-kingdom approach did not always work. Certain organisms classified as plants did not fit well in the plant kingdom because of their own unique characteristics; likewise, certain organisms classified as animals did not fit well in the animal kingdom.
   5. Biologists invented a third kingdom, **Protista** (or **Protoctista**), which, because the definition is flexible, can include between 9 and 13 phyla.

C. The protists included the following groups: algae, bacteria, fungi, slime molds, mildew, and protozoans.
   1. The taxonomy (classification) of organisms is important to taxonomists (persons who study classification) but may not be very important to scientists who specialize in the study of certain groups of organisms.
   2. Students of **botany** (the study of plants), for example, probably include algae and even fungi. A general course in **zoology** (the study of animals) may include protozoans.
   3. **Virologists** investigate viruses, and **bacteriologists** study bacteria, without much concern about where these organisms most logically fit in today's overall scheme for the classification of living things.

D. Today both bacteria and the blue-green algae are usually classified in a separate kingdom, **Monera.** This kingdom, which may include both spirochetes and rickettsiae, includes more than 40,000 species.

E. Our study of organisms in this chapter begins with still another group, the **viruses,** which do not always fit into the generally accepted concept of what constitutes a living thing; that is, what an organism is.

 Viruses

I. **What Viruses Are**

A. It was easier to classify objects into either living things or nonliving things before the discovery of viruses.
   1. When scientists began to study viruses, they discovered that viruses seemed to be both living and nonliving things. Alone, they do not seem to be alive. Within the cells of hosts, they appear to be very much alive.

B. We usually think of a virus as something that has to do with a disease. As a matter of fact, the word *virus* comes from the Latin word meaning poison. There are hundreds of viruses that can produce diseases in different kinds of organisms, but there are also viruses that seem harmless.

C. Scientists classify viruses into four groups, based on the host cells they infect: **bacterial viruses** live in bacteria cells; **plant viruses** live in the cells of seed plants, especially flowering plants; **animal viruses** live in the cells of animals; and **human viruses** live in the cells of humans. However, humans are also susceptible to some animal viruses.
   1. It seems that unless a mutation occurs, each kind of virus enters only certain kinds of living cells. For example, a bacterial virus enters only a certain kind of bacterial cell; a plant virus may enter only the cells of the flowers, leaves, or stem of a certain plant; a human or animal virus may enter the cells of the nervous system, skin, or lungs of a human or animal.
   2. Unlike living organisms that are given Latin names, viruses are more often named for the diseases they cause, or for the tissue or organ they infect. Code names are sometimes used for several viruses that infect the same host.

II. Characteristics of Viruses

A. Viruses are particles of protein and nucleic acid, about one-half to one-hundredth the size of the smallest bacterium, which can be seen only with an electron microscope.
   1. One million of the smallest viruses can sit side by side and occupy only 2.5 centimeters (1 in.) of space.

B. Unlike plants, animals, and protists, viruses are not composed of cells. They are **acellular.**
   1. They are particles of **nucleic acid** (DNA or RNA, but never both) surrounded by one or two protein coats. (**Viroids**, the smallest known agents of infectious disease, are merely short strands of ribonucleic acid, or RNA. Viroids cause several plant diseases and have been implicated in certain diseases of humans and other animals.)
   2. The nucleic acid consists of genes that contain coded instructions for making copies of the virus. They code for nothing else.
   3. Viruses exist in a variety of shapes. Some are round and look like tiny golf balls, some are shaped like bricks or cubes, and some resemble needle-like rods. These shapes play a role in the infection process.

C. Viruses cannot manufacture their own food.
   1. They can live and grow only inside a living cell of a host.
   2. A virus is **parasitic**, living in an organism, called its host, and absorbing nutrients from it.

D. When outside a host cell, viruses do not demonstrate characteristics of living things.
   1. Scientists have been able to isolate viruses from living cells and obtain them in the form of crystals, similar to salt or sugar crystals. Virus crystals can be stored in a jar for long periods of time.
   2. When virus crystals are brought into contact with or put inside living host cells, the virus takes on the characteristics of a living organism, that is, to live, grow, and reproduce itself.

III. Bacterial Viruses

A. Much of what we know about viruses comes from the study of bacterial viruses, called bacteriophages or **phage viruses**, that in shape, resemble somewhat a miniature version of the lunar landing module.

B. By studying the action of these viruses on bacteria, scientists have learned how viruses reproduce to make new viruses.
   1. When a virus attaches to a bacterial cell, part of the virus enters the cell.
   2. Attachment is a very specific process. Most viruses can attach, enter, and reproduce in only a few kinds of host cells.
   3. Once attached, the virus must enter the host cell and take over that cell's metabolism.
   4. The method of entry varies, depending on the shape and structure of the virus. Some viruses are shaped so that they inject their nucleic acid into the host cell. Others make an indentation in the host cell's membrane and burst into the cell.
   5. Once inside, the virus quickly takes over the metabolic activity of the bacterial cell, destroys the host's DNA, and re-programs the cell to copy the viral genes and make new viruses.
   6. In a short time the bacterial cell bursts, allowing 200 to 300 newly formed viruses to escape.
   7. The new viruses are now free to enter and destroy other bacterial cells.
   8. If a bacterial cell survives the onslaught of a virus, the DNA of the original bacterial host may be mutated to a new form or strain of bacterium. Some microbiologists hypothesize that this is the cause of new outbreaks of certain types of bacterial infections in humans and other organisms.

IV. Plant Viruses

A. Several hundred viruses are known to infect plant cells, causing a thousand or more plant diseases that damage and even kill the plant hosts.
   1. Plant viruses are often named after the plant they enter (e.g., the American elm virus); the special part of the plant they damage (e.g., the tobacco leaf mosaic virus); or the appearance they produce in the plant (e.g., the Rembrandt tulip that has stripes in its petals caused by a virus).

B. Plant viruses can spread in many ways.
   1. Most plant viruses are spread by insects, such as the aphid and the leafhopper, that suck juices from leaves.
   2. Some viruses are spread when a leaf of an infected plant comes in contact with a leaf of a healthy plant.
   3. Some are spread when the roots of an infected plant grow and come into contact with the roots of a healthy plant.
   4. Sometimes gardeners spread them inadvertently when handling diseased plants.
   5. Sometimes a virus can be spread in multiple ways, such as by infected insects that feed on a plant, and then by roots that are infected, which in turn infect roots of other nearby trees or plants.

V. Human and Animal Viruses

A. Viruses cause many diseases in humans and animals. Some viral diseases in humans are shown in Table 13.1.
B. The virus that causes hantavirus pulmonary syndrome was first detected in the United States in a non–disease-related form more than 10 years before its virulent outbreak in 1993.
   1. By 1994 cases of hantavirus pulmonary syndrome had been reported in people in more than 20 states.
   2. Victims can become ill by simply inhaling dried urine or feces of infected deer mice, which are the primary vectors of the virus.
C. Human and animal viral diseases are spread in a number of ways.
   1. Coughing and sneezing spreads virus-caused diseases that infect the respiratory system, such as the common cold and influenza.
   2. Some viral diseases, such as yellow fever, are spread from one host to another by mosquitoes.
   3. Touching the sores spreads diseases that produce sores on the skin, such as chicken pox and cold sores.
   4. Viruses of diseases such as polio and infectious hepatitis are passed out in feces, which may then be touched by flies and carried to food and water that is consumed by humans.
   5. The human immunodeficiency virus (HIV) that causes acquired immunodeficiency syndrome (AIDS) is passed from one victim to another in body fluids that contain the virus. Body fluids of an infected person that can have a high concentration of the HIV virus are blood, semen, vaginal fluids, and breast milk.

      AIDS is an umbrella term for any or all of a number of viral-caused infections. A person having one of these infections who also tests positive for antibodies to HIV is then diagnosed as having AIDS.
D. Humans and animals often become immune to certain diseases after they have had those diseases. Becoming immune to a disease means never getting that disease again.
   1. When a person gets a viral disease, the body starts to make special proteins or molecules, called **antibodies.**
   2. The body makes a different kind of antibody for each virus.
   3. Normally, the body makes more antibodies than it needs, and these extra antibodies float around in the blood.
   4. Antibodies try to neutralize the viruses that have entered the body by covering the viruses and making them harmless.
   5. Sometimes a virus reproduces so fast it overpowers the antibodies; the victim's immune system begins to break down and the person is then susceptible to other diseases.
   6. Some antibodies stay in the blood for the rest of a person's life. This means that the antibodies will destroy a certain virus if it should ever enter the body again.
E. Not all virus infections are fatal to their host cells.
   1. Some types of viruses go through what is called a *lysogenic cycle,* a viral reproductive cycle in which the viral DNA becomes integrated into the host cell's chromosome.

TABLE 13.1 Diseases in Humans Caused by Viruses

AIDS	Infectious hepatitis	Polio
Chicken pox	Infectious mononucleosis	Rabies
Cold sores and fever blisters	Influenza	Shingles
Common cold	Janta fever	Smallpox
Cowpox	Lassa fever	Viral pneumonia
Ebola	Measles	Warts
Hantavirus pulmonary syndrome	Mumps	Yellow fever
Herpes	Parrot fever	

2. Once the viral DNA is inserted into the host cell chromosome, it is known as a *provirus*.
3. The provirus does not interfere with the normal functioning of the host cell, but every time the host cell reproduces, the provirus is replicated right along with the host cell's chromosome. This means that every descendant of the host cell will have a copy of the provirus in its own chromosome. This lysogenic phase can continue undetected for many years. For reasons and conditions not yet clearly understood, however, the provirus can exit the host cell's chromosome at any time and enter its normal destructive cycle.
4. The lysogenic process explains why cold sores recur. Once you have had a cold sore, the virus causing it—herpes simplex 1—remains as a provirus in one of the chromosomes in your cells. HIV, genital herpes, hepatitis B, and influenza virus can behave similarly. The virus that causes chicken pox in children gives life-long immunity to the return of chicken pox but can return later in life in the form of the disease known as *shingles*.

VI. The Control of Harmful Viruses

A. Some viral diseases can be controlled by using a **vaccine**.
   1. A vaccine has a small amount of weakened or dead viral particles in it.
   2. Some vaccines, such as smallpox and flu vaccine, are either scratched or injected into the arm or another part of the body. Giving a vaccine this way is called **vaccination**. Other vaccines, such as the polio vaccine, are given orally.
   3. When a person is given a vaccine, the body begins to make antibodies immediately. The antibodies remain in the blood for a long time. The person now is immune to the viral disease. If new viruses for the same disease should get into the body, the antibodies will destroy the viruses.

B. Some plant, animal, and human viruses mutate so rapidly that finding and developing drugs that are effective as treatment against them is a never-ending task.

C. Because viruses can transfer genetic material between different species of host, they are used extensively in genetic engineering studies, affording some promise for the future fight against viruses. For example, by manipulating plant genes, genetic engineers have been able to transfer a gene that expresses a hepatitis B antigen into potato plants. Mice eating these potatoes develop antibodies against the hepatitis virus.
   1. The U.S. Human Genome Project was started in 1990 and is coordinated by the U.S. Department of Energy and the National Institutes of Health. The goal was to identify all the estimated 80,000 genes in human DNA and to determine the sequences of the pairs of chemical bases that make up human DNA, store this information in databases, and develop tools for data analysis.
   2. A **genome** is the entire DNA in an organism, including its genes.
   3. DNA is composed of four similar chemicals (called bases and abbreviated A, T, C, and G) that are repeated millions or billions of times throughout a genome. The human genome, for example, has 3 billion pairs of bases.
   4. Researchers are also studying the genetic makeup of other organisms, including *E. coli*, the virus found in human intestines.

D. Antibiotics, such as penicillin, only work against bacterial infections and therefore *cannot* be used to stop virus infections.

E. However, the following precautions will help prevent the spread of viral diseases.
   1. Always cover your mouth when coughing or sneezing. Wash your hands frequently, especially when you cough or sneeze.
   2. Never touch virus-caused sores.
   3. Disinfect or burn things that have been touched by people who are sick with a viral disease.
   4. Be very careful when getting rid of body wastes from people who have the disease.
   5. Never touch dead or wild animals or their droppings.
   6. Protect yourself from inhaling dust particles that may carry a virus.
   7. Generally be knowledgeable about how particular viral infections are spread and avoid or take precautions in situations where you might become exposed or might expose others.

Bacteria

I. Classification, Structure, and Variety of Bacteria

A. Bacteria can be found everywhere—in the air; in the waters of streams, ponds, lakes, and oceans; in ice on the surface of ponds and lakes; in the soil; in other organisms; in dead plants and animals; on our skin and throughout our intestines; and in garbage.
   1. Because fossil remains of bacteria have been found in rock dating back more than

3.5 billion years, bacteria represent the oldest form of life that is still found on Earth today.
2. Bacteria have been revived and cultured after some 25 million years of encapsulation in the guts of a resin-trapped bee.
3. The study of both viruses and bacteria has been important to scientists in their formation of theories of how life began on Earth.

B. To live and thrive, bacteria need a suitable temperature, which varies among different bacteria.
1. Some bacteria grow well in high temperatures, and others grow well in low temperatures, but most bacteria grow best at temperatures ranging from 25°C to 40°C (77°F to 104°F).
2. Although very high temperatures kill many bacteria, low temperatures do not usually kill them but will slow their metabolic activity and growth.

C. Some species thrive at extreme temperatures.
1. Bacteria have been found thriving within the interior of an operating nuclear reactor. And perhaps most surprising yet, a species of *Streptococcus* bacteria survived for 3 years in a space camera left on the moon's surface. The cells survived space vacuum, 3 years of radiation exposure, deep-freeze temperatures, and no nutrient, water, or energy source.
2. Certain bacteria thrive on the ocean floor where deep-sea volcanic vents release very hot fluids (with temperatures as high as 400°C or 757°F), where the water pressure may be as high as 250 tons per square inch, and where there is little to no oxygen. Around such deep-sea vents, bacteria form the base of a food chain in that unusual environment, where energy is supplied not by sunlight but by hydrogen sulfide discharged from deep within the Earth. The bacteria are able to oxidize the hydrogen sulfide and convert carbon dioxide from seawater into organic compounds.
3. Colonies of anaerobic (not dependent upon oxygen) bacteria have recently been recovered from depths of 7 kilometers (4.2 mi) or more in the Earth's crust.
4. Colonies of cold-thriving bacteria have been found growing in an ice pond near the geographic South Pole.

D. Bacteria need water or moisture for growth.
1. Although lack of water does not kill most bacteria, it does stop or slow their activity and growth. That is why dehydrated foods can be stored for long periods of time without spoiling.

E. Bacteria are classified in two groups, the archaebacteria and eubacteria.

F. The **archaebacteria** are bacterial organisms that are able to live, or at least remain viable, under very extreme conditions and that may represent a separate kingdom. Although, like bacteria, the genetic material of archaebacteria floats freely throughout the cell rather than being enclosed in a cell nucleus, their DNA more closely resemble that of plants and animals than normal bacteria. Archaebacteria are considered to be one of the earliest forms of life to inhabit the Earth. Some scientists believe that if life is discovered elsewhere in our Solar System, such as on Jupiter's moon Europa, it may be similar to Earth's archaebacteria. Archaebacteria on Earth are divided into three groups.
1. One group lives in oxygen-free (anaerobic) environments and produces methane gas. Some members of this group live in the stomachs of cows, where the bacteria help to break down cellulose in the grass eaten by cows. Methane-producing bacteria are also found in sewage treatment plants, freshwater swamps, and deep-sea habitats. They get their energy from carbon dioxide and hydrogen gas, producing methane as a waste product.
2. Another group lives only in bodies of concentrated saltwater, such as the Great Salt Lake in Utah and the Dead Sea in the Middle East. These bacteria produce a purple pigment that enables them to photosynthesize.
3. A third group is found in the hot, acidic waters of sulfur springs, such as those in Yellowstone National Park. These bacteria grow best at temperatures of about 60°C (140°F) and at a pH of 1 to 2, which is the pH of full-strength sulfuric acid.

G. The **eubacteria** are the more diverse in terms of habitat and metabolism.
1. One group of eubacteria, the **heterotrophs,** are found everywhere. Heterotrophic bacteria need organic molecules as an energy source but are not adapted for trapping the food that contains these molecules. Therefore, some live as **parasites.** Others live as **saprobes,** organisms that feed on dead organisms or organic wastes. Saprobes help to recycle the nutrients contained in decomposing organisms.
2. A second group of eubacteria is **photosynthetic autotrophs.** They obtain their energy from light. These bacteria have a photosynthetic pigment that allows them to trap sunlight. Some are blue-green and others are red or yellow. The cyanobacteria (also called *blue-green algae*) are in this group. They are common in ponds, streams, and moist land areas. They are composed of chains of cells, rather than single cells. Cyanobacteria are often one component of lichens. The other component is a fungus.
3. A third group of eubacteria is **chemosynthetic autotrophs.** These bacteria obtain their energy from the breakdown of

inorganic substances such as sulfur and nitrogen compounds. Some of these bacteria, such as those living in nodules or swellings on the roots of plants called *legumes* (including soybeans, clover, and peas) are important in converting nitrogen in the atmosphere to forms that can be used readily by plants.

H. Bacteria are considered to be the smallest and simplest of living things, falling in complexity between the viruses and the cellular organisms.
   1. Bacterial cells have *no* membrane-bound organelles, such as a nucleus, mitochondria, or chloroplasts.
   2. Their cytoplasm is bound by a plasma membrane that regulates what enters and exits the cell.
   3. Around that is a cell wall that gives the cell its shape. However, the cell wall has a different chemical composition than the plant cells.
   4. In addition to the plasma membrane and the cell wall, some bacteria are coated with a gelatinous capsule and still others have yet another but thinner coating called a slime layer. These coatings help such bacteria to stick to the surface of a food supply, prevent them from drying out, and protect them from predators, such as a host animal's white blood cells.
   5. Their inherited information (DNA) is contained in a region in the cytoplasm called a *nucleoid.* There is extra chromosomal nucleic acid outside the nucleoid in circular arrangements called plasmids.
   6. Although larger than viruses, which can be seen only with an electron microscope, bacteria appear tiny under a light microscope. They are so small that hundreds of thousands of them can be placed on the period at the end of this sentence. Their size ranges from 0.5 to 2.0 micrometers in diameter for spherical bacteria, to 60 micrometers in length for some spiral bacteria.

I. Their shapes and the arrangements of their cells are used to classify bacteria.
   1. The three most common shapes are spherical (coccus), rods (bacillus), and spirals (spirillum). In addition, there are comma-shaped bacteria called vibria and flexible wavy-shaped bacteria called spirochetes.
   2. Although some bacterial cells live singly, others group together. When arranged in pairs of cells, the prefix *diplo-* is used. A diplococcus bacterium is one that exists as pairs of spherical cells. When cells arrange in grapelike clusters, the prefix *staphylo-* is used. A staphylococcus bacterium is one that exists as grapelike clusters of spherical cells. The prefix *strepto-* refers to long chains of cells. A streptococcus bacterium is one with long chains of spherical cells, like a necklace.
   3. Many bacilli and spirilli have tiny, thread-like structures called flagella protruding from their cells. Some have flagellae at one or both ends of the cell, and others have these structures distributed throughout the surface of the cell. These structures have a whip-like movement, which makes it possible for the bacteria to move about in water, blood, and other liquids.

II. How Bacteria Reproduce

A. Because they have no nuclei, bacteria *cannot* reproduce by mitosis or meiosis. Instead, they have evolved different methods of reproduction.
   1. They usually reproduce **asexually** by **binary fission.** This involves four steps.
      a. A cell grows in size.
      b. The cell duplicates its single chromosome.
      c. The pair of chromosomes separate and move to opposite sides of the enlarged cell.
      d. The cell then divides into two new daughter cells, each of which is genetically identical to the original parent cell.
   2. In some cases, the two new cells break apart, and in other cases they stay connected to form a chain of cells.
   3. When conditions for growth are just right, cells can mature in 20 to 30 minutes and start the process all over again. Under the right conditions, a few hundred bacteria can become millions in a very short time.
   4. Their ability to grow and reproduce quickly is what makes bacteria so important and what makes **pathogenic** (disease-causing) bacteria so dangerous.
   5. When conditions are unfavorable for growth, bacteria protect themselves by producing an **endospore.** An endospore is produced within a bacterial cell. Endospores have a hard outer covering and are resistant to drying out, boiling, and many chemicals. While in the endospore form, the bacterium is in a state of slow metabolism, and it does not reproduce. When it encounters more favorable conditions, the endospore germinates and gives rise to a bacterial cell that resumes growing and reproducing. Some endospores have been found to germinate after thousands of years. Because endospores can survive boiling, canned foods and medical instruments must be sterilized under high pressure. The greater heat can kill endospores.
   6. Endospore formation is especially common with bacilli, the rod-shaped bacteria.
   7. Some bacteria, such as the *E. coli* bacterium, have a simple form of sexual reproduction called **conjugation.** During conjugation,

LEARNING ACTIVITY 13.1

The Exponential Growth of Bacteria

Demonstration

Bring a checkerboard and $21.00 in pennies to class. Ask students to calculate how many squares you can cover on the board if you put one penny in the first square, two in the second, four in the third, and so on until you run out of pennies. (Eleven squares will be completely covered and $0.53 will remain.) Relate this demonstration to the way large populations of bacteria can be produced in just a few generations.

Problem

When living in a favorable environment, bacteria can reproduce every 20 minutes or so. As conditions become less ideal, the rate of cell division slows. Suppose you begin with a single bacterium, and it and its progeny reproduce once an hour. Ask students to set up a table to determine how many bacteria there would be at the end of 1 day (24 hours). To do this, they should set up a table listing hours 0 to 24. At hour 0, there would be one bacterium. After hour 1, the bacterium will have reproduced once, so there will be two bacteria. At hour 2, each of these bacteria will have reproduced once, giving a total of four. To find the number of bacteria after 24 hours, continue this doubling 24 times, once for each time the bacteria reproduce. (After 24 hours there will be 2^{24}, or 16,777,216 bacteria). Remind students that bacteria in food may double in number every 20 minutes. Food poisoning often results when foods are not properly refrigerated.

Source: Adapted from Alton Biggs et al., *Biology: The Dynamics of Life* (Westerville, OH: Glencoe/McGraw-Hill, 1995), 524. By permission of the publisher.

one bacterium cell transfers all or part of its chromosome material to another cell through a bridge formed to temporarily connect the two conjugating cells.

III. **Beneficial and Harmful Aspects of Bacteria**

A. Most bacteria are harmless, living in air, soil, and water; on our skin; and even in our bodies, without doing any harm.
   1. Even bacteria that are potentially pathogenic may not always cause disease. For example, the coccus bacterium that causes meningitis is often found in people who are healthy, never causing them harm. The meningitis-causing bacterium is found in the throat. Normally, the throat's epithelial lining is a barrier to the bacterium, keeping it from getting into the bloodstream and moving to the meninges—the membranes that surround the brain and spinal cord. But if the normal lining is broken down and the bacterium gains access to the bloodstream and finds its way to the cerebrospinal fluid that bathes the central nervous system, it can cause the disease meningitis, which is fatal if untreated.
   2. Recent studies indicate that an infection by one kind of nonpathogenic bacterium may sometimes protect against invasion by a similar but pathogenic strain. This might be one reason that some people seem more susceptible to certain diseases (both bacterial and viral) than others. Exposure to a strain of a similar but nonpathogenic bacteria or virus may provide immunity to a person later exposed to pathogenic strains.

B. Humans have found many uses for bacteria.
   1. One group of bacteria sours milk, which is important in the making of butter and cheese.
   2. Bacteria put the tang in yogurt and the sour in sourdough bread.
   3. Certain kinds of cheeses, such as Swiss cheese, get their flavor from the metabolic activity of bacteria.
   4. Another group of bacteria changes alcohol into vinegar.
   5. The action of bacteria on the stems of the flax plant loosens the plant fibers, which are then stripped and woven into linen.
   6. Bacteria live on our skin. The good ones prevent pathogenic bacteria and fungi from occupying space and causing skin diseases, unless we overwash.
   7. Bacteria help to separate the flesh from animal skins and, in a process called tanning, change the skin into soft leather.
   8. Bacteria are used in septic tanks and sewage treatment plants to get rid of sewage by changing the solid wastes into easily removable liquids.
   9. Bacteria act quickly on dead plant and animal matter, changing it into humus, which enriches the soil.
   10. Nitrogen-fixing bacteria, like those that live in the roots of legumes, take nitrogen gas from the air and change it into nitrogen materials that plants need to grow.
   11. An anaerobic bacterium that lives in the digestive tract of bowhead whales may eventually be used to help clean up oil spills by degrading key oil spill components, PCBs, and other carcinogenic compounds. Further study of this bacterium may also explain how whales can consume high levels of toxic compounds without getting cancer, as other animals would.
   12. Bacteria produce antibiotics such as streptomycin and nocardicin.

LEARNING ACTIVITY 13.2

Some Bacteria Are Helpful to Humans

Bring to class a bag full of groceries containing food items that could not be made without bacteria. Include Swiss cheese, pickles, vinegar, sauerkraut, yogurt, peas, beans, soybeans, peanuts, milk, and sour cream. Explain the importance of bacteria to the development of each product, including the role of nitrogen-fixing bacteria to the growth of certain kinds of plants.

Source: Alton Biggs, Chris Kapicka et al., *Biology: The Dynamics of Life* (Westerville, OH: Glencoe/McGraw-Hill, 1995), 524. By permission of the publisher.

Inquiry-Based Learning Activity 13.2. Modified

Sometimes bacteria can make us sick when we eat it, but sometimes it can be used to make things we eat. Show some pictures of cottage cheese, tofu, soy sauce, bleu cheese, vinegar, sour cream, yogurt, and ice cream. Ask your students, "Which of these foods do you think are made by using bacteria? Which of these foods do you think are not?" After making a list, put your students into groups of two or three and give them the resources (e.g. Internet access or time in the library) to research how each of these products are made. Assign each group two of the eight food products.

What level of inquiry is this modification? This activity offers a clear task, but does not give students direction on how to carry it out. They are not given any data to analyze, but they are asked to seek out information. These characteristics suggest that this activity is a mixture of **Level I problem identification** and ***Level III solutions to the problem.*** Many times, for students to gain the skills to do research for information, they need to be given a clear task. The search itself is not guided, but the objective of the search is. These types of activities may help scaffold students into **Level III inquiry activities** where they pose their own questions and design their own investigations. **Some questions to consider.** How could this activity be modified to be a **Level III problem identification activity**? What do you think the students should do to report the results of their research?

TABLE 13.2 Diseases in Humans Caused by Bacteria

Bacterial pneumonia	Ear infections	Rocky Mountain spotted fever	Tetanus
Boils	Gonorrhea	Scarlet fever	Tuberculosis
Botulism	Leptospirosis	Staph infections	Typhoid fever
Cholera	Lyme disease	Strep throat	
Diphtheria	Meningitis	Syphilis	

C. Some bacteria are harmful to humans.
   1. Some bacteria make food spoil, producing poisonous materials, called **toxins**, that can cause illness and even death to humans.
   2. Some bacteria are pathogens; that is, they cause disease (see Table 13.2).

D. Scientists have found ways to control harmful bacteria. Unfortunately, the means of controlling bacteria often affects the beneficial as well as the harmful forms.
   1. Ultraviolet rays can kill bacteria.
   2. Antibiotics can destroy many kinds of bacteria that are parasitic and that cause disease in the human body.
   3. Disinfectants, germicides, heat, filters, heavy metals, changes in pH, ionizing radiation, changes in osmotic pressure—all can kill bacteria outside the body.
   4. Heat, cold, and certain chemicals can stop the growth of many bacteria. For example, heating the milk to 60°C (140°F) for 20 to 30 minutes stops the growth of harmful bacteria in raw milk. Milk treated this way is said to be **pasteurized.**
   5. Quick-freezing can slow or stop the growth of bacteria.
   6. When food is canned, it is heated to stop the growth of harmful bacteria in the food and then sealed in airtight containers to prevent other harmful bacteria from getting into the containers.
   7. The removal of water from foods, a process called dehydration, stops the growth of bacteria. Salting, sugar curing, and pickling all preserve foods. Both the salt and sugar remove moisture from the bacteria cells and stop their growth. Smoking foods also removes moisture and stops the growth of bacteria.
   8. Antiseptics can stop the growth of bacteria.

Fungi

I. Characteristics, Structure, and Variety of Fungi

A. Fungi resemble viruses and bacteria in that they lack chlorophyll and cannot make their own food; that is, they are not autotrophic. Instead, fungi are **heterotrophic.**
   1. There are more than 77,000 kinds of fungi, including molds, mildews, yeasts, rusts, smuts, and mushrooms.
   2. Fungi vary in size. Some are so tiny that they can be seen only under a microscope; others combine to form large masses that make up mushrooms and puffballs. A mushroom is only an aboveground portion of an individual fungus that can be larger than a whale. In 1992 an enormous fungus specimen of *Armillaria bulbosa* was found on the border of Wisconsin and Michigan. It is estimated to weigh at least 220,000 pounds, to spread over more than 37 acres, and to be 1,500 years old. In 2000, an even larger fungus specimen of a different species, *Armillaria ostoyae,* was found in eastern Oregon. Covering 2,200 acres (3.5 miles across) and estimated to be 2,400 years old, this specimen may be the largest and oldest of all living organisms.

B. Most fungi are made up of threads, or filaments, called **hyphae.**
   1. Each hypha is made up of many cells, some with cell walls and some without cell walls.
   2. Unlike plants, which have cell walls made of cellulose, the cell walls of most fungi contain a complex carbohydrate called **chitin.** Chitin is also found in the external skeletons of some animals such as the arachnids.
   3. The whole mass of hyphae that make up the fungus is called the **mycelium.**
   4. The hyphae themselves are white or gray, but many fungi have red, orange, yellow, green, blue, or black pigments that give the fungi a special color.

C. Fungi grow best in conditions of moist and warm darkness.

D. Because fungi have no chlorophyll and consequently cannot produce their own food, they must get their food from other sources (that is, they are heterotrophic).
   1. Some fungi are parasites. Parasitic fungi invade the cells of their hosts with specialized hyphae called **haustoria,** which penetrate and grow into the host's cells without killing them.
   2. Other fungi are **saprobes,** getting their food from dead plants and animals, or from materials made from plants and animals, such as food products.
   3. Still other fungi live with other organisms in a mutual symbiotic relationship, called **mutualism.** For example, Douglas fir and western hemlock trees, in old-growth forests of the Pacific Northwest, depend on a fungus that lives on the logs of fallen trees. The fungus provides a shield around the trees' roots and secretes antibiotics into the soil that helps to prevent infection in the trees' roots. The fungus, in turn, depends on the sugar provided by the photosynthesis occurring in the trees.

E. Nearly all fungi are **aerobic**; that is, they are able to use the free oxygen in the air.

F. All fungi can reproduce asexually by forming tiny, round bodies called **spores.**
   1. Fungi produce tremendous numbers of spores. For example, a single puffball the size of a marble, or about 1-inch around, produces roughly 1 trillion spores.
   2. A protective cover or wall surrounds each spore.
   3. The spores are carried off in all directions by the wind and through other means. When they land on objects, if conditions are favorable for growth (moisture, warmth, darkness, and suitable food supply), the spores grow into fungi. For example, the fungus that causes Dutch elm disease is carried and spread by bark beetles. Spores of the fungus stick to the bodies of the beetles as they feed on infected trees.
   4. When conditions are unfavorable, the spores can live quietly without growing for long periods until conditions become favorable for growth.

G. Some fungi can reproduce sexually by forming gametes, by **meiosis.**
   1. The male haploid cell (with the 1N chromosome number) is called a sperm, and the female haploid cell is called an egg.
   2. The male and female cells unite (**fertilization**) to form a diploid cell (2N chromosome number), called a **zygote.**
   3. The zygotes form new parent fungi, which can then repeat the life cycle by reproducing either asexually—by forming spores—or sexually—by forming gametes that unite to form new zygotes.

II. Molds

A. Although most molds grow best in places that are dark, damp, and warm, some grow well at temperatures near freezing. They can grow on most foods, as well as on paper, leather, wood, and human skin.

B. Most molds are made up of tubular threads, or filaments, called **hyphae.**
   1. Some molds, such as bread mold, have three kinds of hyphae. Tiny, rootlike hyphae,

called **rhizoids**, grow downward into the bread, digest the food materials, and then take in, or absorb, the digested food.

2. Other hyphae, called **stolons**, spread out horizontally over the surface of the bread and then grow downward to form more rhizoids.
3. Some hyphae grow upright, and their function is to form spores. After a few days, round bodies or knobs appear on the ends of these hyphae.
4. Each knob is a spore case, called a **sporangium**, containing thousands of spores. It is these spores, which are colored, that give the molds their characteristic colors; for example, black bread mold has black spores.
5. When the spore cases (sporangia) are ripe, they split open and the spores float away in the air. Each spore can form a new hyphae, which will soon become a complete mold made up of many hyphae, thus starting the life cycle all over again.

C. Some fungi can also reproduce sexually.

1. Sometimes two hyphae of the same mold develop connecting branches that join together.
2. Where the branches join together, a cell from each branch acts as a sexual cell, and these cells unite to form a zygote, which then grows into a new mold.

D. Some molds are beneficial to humans; others are harmful.

1. Many molds spoil foods. Molds growing on fruit trees damage the fruit, and some parasitic water molds kill fish and other sea animals.
2. One mold, *Aspergillus flavus*, invades stored grains of soybean, wheat, corn, rice, barley, bran, and peanuts. It produces a chemical called aflatoxin, which is a known carcinogen, and can also destroy the human liver if ingested. One of the greatest dangers is from eating contaminated peanuts still in the shell. Do not eat any peanuts if their shells seem moldy.
3. Molds are used in making such cheeses as Roquefort, Camembert, and Limburger.
4. Molds are used in making antibiotics, such as penicillin, streptomycin, and aureomycin.

III. Mildews and Yeasts

A. **Mildews** are whitish or dark-colored fungi and are closely related to molds. They reproduce asexually by spore formation. Most are parasites; some are saprobes.

1. Some mildews have a downy texture and are parasitic on such plants as radishes, potatoes, cereal grains, sugar cane, and tobacco.
2. Some mildews are powdery and are parasitic on such plants as lilacs, roses, phlox, clover, grapes, and apples.
3. Black mildew is a saprobe found on clothes and shower stalls that have been exposed to dampness for a long time.

B. **Yeasts** are microscopic, one-celled fungi, usually oval in shape, that reproduce asexually by budding. They can also produce spores.

1. When conditions are favorable, a little knob or bud pushes out from one side of the yeast cell and breaks away to form a new yeast cell.
2. Sometimes many buds stay attached to the same yeast cell and form a chain.
3. When conditions are unfavorable for growth, a yeast cell may produce a spore case, usually containing four spores.

C. Yeasts are important to humans.

1. Yeasts break down sugar to form alcohol and carbon dioxide gas. This action is called **fermentation.** When yeast is used in making alcohol, the alcohol is saved, but the carbon dioxide is usually allowed to escape.
2. Yeast is used in making bread. Bubbles of carbon dioxide gas are formed, which swell and make the dough rise. This bubbling leaves many small spaces and makes the bread light and fluffy. As the bread is baked, the heat drives off the carbon dioxide and the alcohol that have been formed.
3. Fruits, such as grapes and apples, ferment when they are crushed. Their skins usually have wild yeast on them. When the skin of these fruits is broken, the yeast acts on the sugar in the fruit, turning the juice into wine or cider.
4. Yeasts are also helpful to humans as a source of vitamin B_2.
5. Some yeasts cause infections in humans.

IV. Rusts and Smuts

A. Rusts and smuts are parasitic fungi that thrive under moist, dark, and warm conditions.

1. Rusts produce reddish brown spores that look like rust. They can destroy such plants as wheat, apple trees, white pine trees, roses, oranges, and melons.
2. Smuts produce blackish spores and can destroy cereal grains, such as corn, oats, barley, and wheat.

V. Mushrooms

A. Mushrooms are the largest fungi.

B. They are saprobes, living on dead plant and animal matter in the soil.

C. They may grow underground for years, producing a large mass of tangled threads (hyphae) that eventually come together just below the surface of the ground to form a small cap.

D. When the weather is damp, especially in spring or fall, this closely packed mass pushes its way above the ground and the cap opens to form a mushroom.

1. The mushroom stalk is called the **stipe.**
2. The umbrella-shaped top of the mushroom is called the **cap** or pileus.
3. On the underside of the cap are fleshy plates, called gills, that contain the spores of the mushroom.

E. Some mushrooms have a ring around their stalk, which is the point where the cap was attached to the stalk before the mushroom moved above the ground and the cap spread open.
   1. Each fleshy gill contains hundreds of spore cases.
   2. Each spore case contains four spores.
   3. The spores may be black, white, pink, yellow, or brown.

F. Some mushrooms are edible, but others are very poisonous.
   1. Some mushrooms that are deadly to humans look very much like the edible kinds, but eating just one could be fatal. More than once, a person who considered himself or herself an expert on wild mushrooms has died from mushroom poisoning.

G. Puffballs are either round or pear-shaped balls, usually white in color.
   1. Full-grown puffballs can be as large as 1 meter (3 ft) across.
   2. When the puffballs are fully grown, they dry up and split open, sending all their spores out into the air.

H. Mycologists (biologists who specialize in fungi) are concerned about a seeming global decline in mushroom populations, possibly caused by air pollution.

Slime Molds

I. Characteristics of Slime Molds

A. Slime molds usually grow on damp, decaying leaves and other dead plant material. Their colonies can be orange, yellow, blue, violet, white, black, or colorless.

B. Slime molds are quite different from the true molds. During the slime mold's life cycle, it is both animal-like and plant-like.
   1. Slime molds reproduce from spores.
   2. At first they are one-celled and have thread-like hairs, called flagella. At this stage, they move around as they feed and grow.
   3. Individuals join to form a very large colony, which also moves as it feeds on bacteria, other protists, and dead plant or animal matter.
   4. Later the colony moves to a drier place, stops moving, and produces spore cases.

Lichens

I. Characteristics of Lichens

A. Although lichens are often grouped with fungi, a lichen is really two organisms—either a green alga or a cyanobacterium and a fungus—living together as one organism in the special form of symbiosis called **mutualism** where each benefits from the association. (In other forms of symbiosis, such as parasitism, only one benefits.)
   1. The fungus gets its food from the algal or the cyanobacterial component, which contains chlorophyll and makes food through photosynthesis. The fungus protects the photosynthesizing component with its hyphae (threads) and supplies it with the moisture needed for photosynthesis.
   2. Scientists have found some evidence that the fungus component actually consumes some of the algae or bacteria for food energy. Where this occurs, the relationship would be more parasitic than mutualistic.

B. Lichens are usually green because of the green algae they contain. Some have other pigments, too, that make them appear red, orange, yellow, or brown.

C. Lichens grow on the bark of trees, on the ground, and on rocks.
   1. Lichens that grow on rock eventually cause the rock to crumble. The lichen gives off carbon dioxide gas, which combines with water to form carbonic acid. The acid causes the rock to soften and to eventually crumble and become soil.

D. Although lichens can grow most anywhere, they cannot survive in polluted air; air pollution and acid rain quickly kill lichens. Some even grow in desert regions and near the north and south poles.
   1. Lichens grow very slowly. Very large lichens may be thousands of years old.
   2. Sometimes lichens are erroneously referred to as moss, but lichens can grow in a much drier habitat than can moss plants.
   3. Reindeer moss and Iceland moss, for example, are not mosses but lichens. (Spanish moss is neither a lichen or a moss but a flowering plant, a member of the pineapple family.)
   4. Reindeer and other animals use the lichens commonly called reindeer moss and Iceland moss as a source of winter food.

E. Lichens have been used in making dyes, in tanning hides for leather, and in making perfumes. Litmus paper, used to test acidity, can be made with a lichen dye. Navajo people used lichen dye to add color to their blankets. In some regions of China, Japan, and Iceland, some lichens are used as food, sometimes called *rock tripe*.

Algae

I. Classification of Algae

A. All algae contain chlorophyll. Therefore, algae are **autotrophs** that are capable of making their own food through photosynthesis.
   1. Although all algae contain green-colored chlorophyll, many algae also have other pigments that dominate or mask their green color.
   2. Algae are classified according to their dominant pigments.

B. Algae are classified into five (or six when euglenoids are included) phyla.

C. Euglenoids, diatoms, and dinoflagellates are composed of only unicellular species. The green, red, and brown algae may contain some unicellular members, but most are multicellular.

II. Structure of Algae

A. As already indicated, some algae have only one cell (unicellular) and others have many cells (multicellular). The multicellular forms are cells living together.
   1. Algae that form colonies are not truly multicellular organisms, but are made up of many one-celled organisms living together. The algae that make up a colony are attached to each other, yet each lives independently and does not have to depend on other algae.

B. Many algae are mobile.

C. All algae are aquatic or semiaquatic (living in very moist habitats).
   1. Some algae seem to swim around like animals, whereas others float in the water or settle to the bottom.

D. Many algae are shaped like threads and are called filaments. These may be attached to one another to form colonies.
   1. The world's largest and most differentiated single-celled organism is a tropical alga known as *Caulerpa*. More than 70 species exist around the world. One species, *C. prolifera,* thrives in the ocean waters off the Florida Keys. Another species is commercially grown for use in fresh green salads.
   2. *Caulerpa* is of special interest to biologists because it was long thought that no single cell could grow to a length of 2 or 3 feet like *Caulerpa* does, much less differentiate into separate organs, such as stem, roots, and leaves.

E. Many kinds of algae have a jelly-like cell covering.
   1. This covering protects the cell from dehydration, which would occur, for example, when a pond dries up.
   2. These coverings make the algal colony feel slimy and hard to grasp when in the water.

III. How Algae Reproduce

A. Algae can reproduce in several ways. All algae can reproduce asexually through mitotic cell division or fission.
   1. When the algae in a colony reproduce by fission, the colony becomes larger, because all the new algae cells are connected to the older ones and to each other.

B. Many algae reproduce asexually by forming spores.
   1. At first the spores swim around freely like tiny animals.
   2. Later, they settle against an object such as a pebble or rock in the stream or pond.
   3. Some spores form new algae immediately. Other spores remain dormant for weeks or months until environmental conditions are right, and then they quickly develop into new algae.

C. Some algae reproduce sexually through meiosis, which results in gametes.
   1. The male gamete, called a **sperm**, and the female cell, called an **egg**, unite to form the new diploid cell, called a fertilized egg or **zygote**.
   2. Some zygotes remain dormant for a time, but others grow into new algae immediately.

IV. The Euglenoids

A. Euglenoids belong to the phylum **Euglenophyta.** A commonly studied representative genus is *Euglena* (see Figure 13.1). (Euglena is likely to be studied both in general botany and in general zoology.)

B. Euglenoids are green, aquatic, unicellular, autotrophic/heterotrophic organisms that display traits of both plants and animals.
   1. They lack the cellulose wall that is characteristic of plant cells, but they do contain chlorophyll and can produce their own food through photosynthesis. They are autotrophic.
   2. Euglena has a bright red spot, called an eyespot, that is light sensitive and may help direct the cell toward sunlight.

C. When light is unavailable for photosynthesis, the euglenoid can ingest food from its

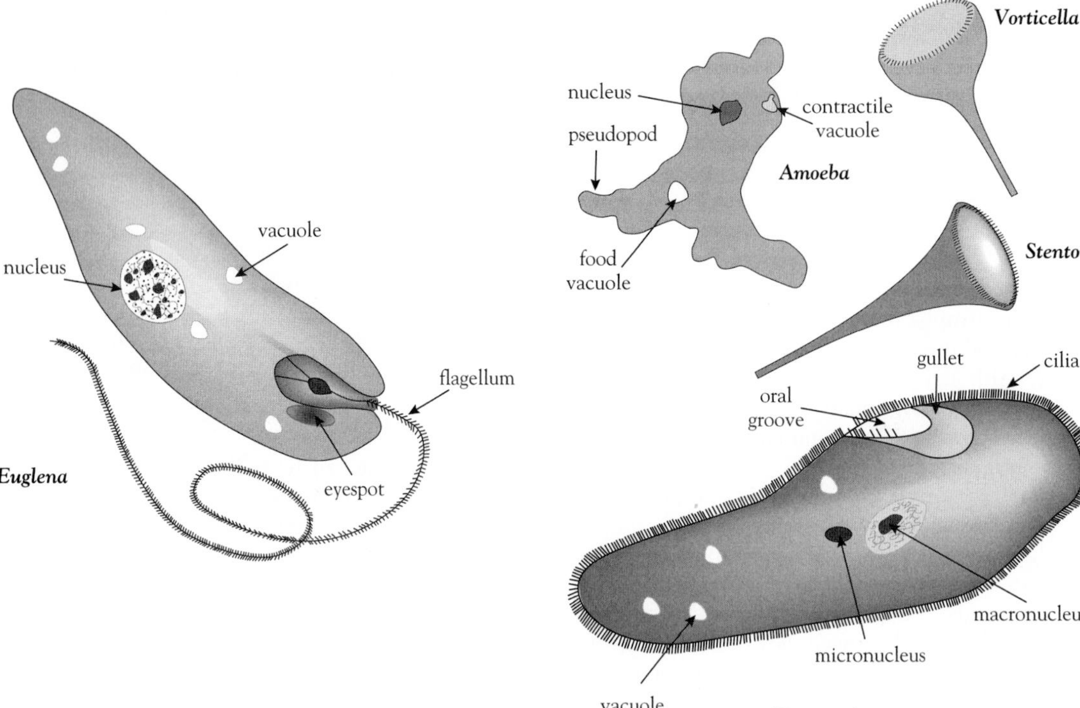

FIGURE 13.1 Some common protozoans (not to scale).

surroundings, much like protozoans do. Euglenoids can be heterotrophic.

D. Euglena is commonly found in freshwater ponds and streams. It is shaped like a pear, with one end rounded and the other pointed. It seems to be flexible and can change its shape, such as into a ball.

E. Euglena is quite mobile, moving about by using one or two flagella located at one end of the cell that turn in a spiral motion and drive the euglena through the water.

F. When environmental conditions become unfavorable, such as during a drying-out period, euglena forms a protective coating, called a cyst, around its cell and loses its flagellum. Inside this cyst, the euglena can live through periods of drought. When conditions become favorable, the cyst breaks open and the euglena again becomes an active organism. Many protozoans also have this ability to form cysts when environmental conditions are unfavorable.

V. Diatoms: The Golden-Brown Algae

A. Diatoms belong to the phylum **Bacillariophyta,** unicellular organisms with cell walls that create a shell made of silica.

B. Diatoms are unicellular algae that are usually golden-brown, although some are yellow-green. They contain chlorophyll, but their dominant pigments are carotenoids, which give the diatoms their characteristic coloring.

C. Diatoms are photosynthetic autotrophs. They are abundant in both marine and freshwater ecosystems, where they make up a large component of the phytoplankton.
   1. Diatoms are major players in the food chain of marine animals. They are the principal food of whales and other marine life.
   2. The food they manufacture photosynthetically is stored in the form of oils rather than starch. These oils give fish and other animals that feed on them the familiar fishy or oily taste.

D. Diatoms have distinctive shapes. They can be round, oval, triangular, rectangular, spindle-shaped, or boat-shaped.
   1. Because of their geometric shapes, intricate patterns, and interesting designs, artists and mathematicians have long been fascinated by them.

E. Diatoms have cell walls that are filled with a glass-like material called silica.
   1. The cell wall is composed of two parts that fit together, one over the other, like the lid on a shoebox.

F. Diatoms reproduce both asexually by mitotic cell division, and sexually by the production of gametes.
   1. When diatoms reproduce asexually, the two halves of the "box" separate; each half then produces a new part to fit inside itself. With each new generation, half of the offspring are always smaller than the parent cells. When asexually reproduced diatoms reach the point where they are roughly one-quarter of their original size, sexual reproduction occurs.
   2. Gametes are produced and released and fuse with those from another individual to produce a zygote. The zygote develops into a full-size diatom, which goes on to repeat the entire cycle again.

G. When diatoms die, their shell-like walls fall to the bottom of the ocean or pond and, over a long period of time, pile up into masses. These masses, called *diatomaceous earth,* are scooped up, cleaned, and refined by industry to be used in scouring powders, glass polish, toothpaste, air and water filters, and other materials.

VI. Dinoflagellates: The Spinning Algae

A. Dinoflagellates belong to the phylum **Dinophyta.**

B. Dinoflagellates are unicellular and have cell walls made of thick cellulose plates.

C. Dinoflagellates have two flagella. When these flagella beat, the cells spin, giving the group the common name of *spinning algae.*

D. With their chlorophyll, carotenoids, and red pigments, they are autotrophic.

E. They typically reproduce by mitotic cell division.

F. The dinoflagellates are mostly marine; that is, they are found in saltwater oceans.
   1. Many species live symbiotically with jellyfish, mollusks, and corals, giving those animals vivid coloration.
   2. Some free-living species are bioluminescent.
   3. Several species produce very poisonous neurotoxins. In the warm waters of the summer, they can reproduce in great numbers, causing the phenomenon known as the *red tide,* and killing fish and shrimp.

VII. The Red Algae

A. The red algae belong to the phylum **Rhodophyta.**

B. All red algae are marine. These are the red seaweeds, all of which are multicellular. Red algae grow attached to rocks along shorelines in both tropical and colder waters. Some species live in deep water.
   1. Some cells of a colony have become specialized to attach the colony to rocks by structures known as *holdfasts.*

C. Red algae reproduce sexually; that is, by producing gametes (egg and sperm that unite to form a zygote).

VIII. The Brown Algae

A. The brown algae constitute the phylum **Phaeophyta.**

B. Many of the brown algae live in saltwater along rocky coasts in cool seas. Some float free while others become attached to the sea bottom or to rocks along the coast.
   1. Some are very small, but giant brown algae, called **kelp,** of the eastern Pacific can grow as long as 60 meters (197 ft), forming dense marine forests called kelp beds.
   2. Kelp can grow fast, as much as a half meter a day.
   3. Kelp beds sometimes cover vast areas of water, as in the Sargasso Sea in the central North Atlantic Ocean.
   4. Kelp beds provide food and shelter for many kinds of marine animals.

C. Some cells of the colonial forms of brown algae have become specialized.
   1. Some cells have formed air bladders that help keep the colony afloat so that it is exposed to fresh oxygen and sunlight.
   2. A cuplike part, called a holdfast, similar to those of the red algae, holds some cells tightly to a rock.

D. The smaller forms of brown algae usually reproduce asexually by fission (mitotic cell division) or by spores. The larger forms reproduce sexually (gametes).

IX. The Green Algae

A. The green algae belong to the phylum **Chlorophyta.** Although the dominant pigment of members of the phylum is chlorophyll, their color ranges from bluish- to yellowish-green.

B. Although most species of green algae live in freshwater, some live in oceans; some on land on moist soil; and others on tree trunks, in snow, and even on the shell of turtles and the fur of sloths.

C. Of all the algae types, the green algae are the most diverse, with more than 7,000 species worldwide.

D. Some green algae are unicellular (single-celled), whereas others form large colonies of cells.

E. Some green algae reproduce asexually by mitotic cell division or by spores, and still others reproduce sexually.

F. Because they have a high protein content (higher in percentage than fish meal), unicellular forms of green algae, especially a genus known as *Chlorella,* have been grown hydroponically (in controlled liquid solutions) as a potential food source for humans either on Earth or in space. For example, *Chlorella* can be grown on rooftops of buildings in large, shallow hydroponic containers; harvested; dried; and made into a high-protein powder that can then be used in dough for baking.

X. Uses of Algae

A. Algae are the chief source of food for many aquatic animals.
B. Because of their ability to photosynthesize and their large numbers, algae are also a major source of the Earth's atmospheric oxygen. They are the primary source of oxygen for aquatic animals.
C. Algal blooms (massive and sudden growth) may deplete an aquatic oxygen supply, thereby contributing to a mass mortality of other aquatic organisms.
D. Because brown algae are rich in potassium, seaweed is sometimes used by coastal farmers for fertilizing the soil.
E. Alginic acid is obtained from brown algae and is used as a thickening agent. It is sometimes used in making ice cream and dairy products, shaving cream, rubber, and paint, and by dentists to make dental impressions of teeth.
F. In some parts of the world, algae are used to make soups, gelatins, and a variety of other foods: kombu, nori, and wakame (Japan); hai dai (China); limu (Hawaii); dulse (Scotland); dillisk (Ireland); sol (Iceland); Irish moss or Carraghean (Europe).
G. Red algae is used to make agar-agar, which forms a jellylike material good for growing bacteria (in agar plates) in hospitals and laboratories. Agar is also used in the manufacture of cosmetics, photographic film, shoe polish, and various body lotions.
H. In tropical regions, coralline algae can be as important as corals in the formation of reefs (see Chapter 14).

 Protozoans

I. Classification of Protozoans

A. Protozoans are tiny, one-celled, animal-like protists.
   1. Because they can eat, breathe, move, and reproduce, just like animals do, protozoans used to be considered members of the animal kingdom.
   2. Today, because they are unicellular, most classification schemes separate protozoans from the animal kingdom, which consists of multicellular animals.
   3. Most protozoans are so small that they can be seen only with a light microscope or hand lens. However, at least two kinds of sessile (attached to an object in the water) protozoans, *Vorticella* and *Stentor*, are large enough to be seen with the unaided eye.
B. Although most protozoans live independently, some live together in colonies. However, as with colonial forms of algae, each colony member usually lives independently of other members.
C. Protozoans live either in water or where conditions are moist.
   1. Aquatic protozoans are found in either freshwater or saltwater.
   2. Some protozoans live in damp soil; others live in decaying animal or plant matter.
   3. Some protozoans even live in the intestines of insects. Protozoans living in the termite gut are able to break down cellulose material, which permits the termite to feed on wood and other materials that have high cellulose content.
D. Most protozoans are not autotrophic and cannot manufacture their own food. They are heterotrophic.
E. Examples of well-studied and well-known protozoan genera include the *Amoeba, Paramecium, Vorticella, Stentor*, and *Euglena* (see Figure 13.1).

II. Amoebas

A. Amoebas belong to the phylum **Sarcodina.**
   1. Most of the hundreds of species in this phylum are marine amoebas, but there are freshwater amoebas that live in the slime on the bottom of ponds and rivers, in backyard puddles, in wet clumps of moss, and on the surface of the leaves of aquatic plants.
   2. Two forms of sarcodines have shells. These marine amoebas have a hard, outer shell of either calcium carbonate or silica. These sarcodines are so abundant that much of the bottom ooze that covers the sea floor is made up of their tiny shells.
B. Under a light microscope, an amoeba looks like a blob of grayish jelly with no definite shape.
   1. Because amoebas are nearly colorless, they are seen most readily under low power using minimum light levels. One species of amoeba, *Chaos chaos*, is almost large enough to be seen with the unaided eye.
   2. The shape of the amoeba keeps changing as it moves. Movement speeds up when the

temperature is warm and slows down when the temperature is cool.

3. As it moves, the amoeba sends out fingerlike projections called **pseudopodia** (false feet). The rest of the amoeba's body then flows in the direction of the false feet.
4. As the amoeba moves, it engulfs bits of food by flowing around and over them.
5. There are tiny spaces or cavities, called vacuoles, in the cell of the amoeba. Some vacuoles contain food. Freshwater amoebas must constantly take in water because they live in a hypotonic environment (where the concentration of dissolved substances is less than that of their cytoplasm). To counter this problem, they have contractile vacuoles that collect and pump out excess water from the cell.
6. Oxygen in the water enters the amoeba by diffusion through the cell membrane, and carbon dioxide produced by the cell's metabolism leaves in the same manner.

C. The amoeba reproduces asexually by simple mitotic cell division.

III. Paramecia

A. Paramecia are also unicellular. They are generally larger than amoebas.
   1. Unlike the amoeba, the paramecium has a definite shape, somewhat like a cigar (see Figure 13.1).

B. Paramecia belong to the phylum **Ciliophora**, known as ciliates.
   1. Paramecia move by the synchronized beating of the thousands of tiny hairlike cilia that emerge from their tough cell membranes to cover their cigar-shaped bodies. By coordinated movement of these cilia, paramecia can move forward or backward and can change directions quickly.

C. Paramecia can be found in every kind of aquatic habitat—from backyard ponds to streams, lakes, oceans, and sulfur springs.
   1. The paramecium feeds primarily on bacteria that are swept into the cell through an opening known as the **oral groove**, located on the side of the paramecium's cell.
   2. The food then passes into a narrow tube, called the gullet, which leads into the cytoplasm of the cell.
   3. The food is held in vacuoles, where it is digested.
   4. The paramecium also has two vacuoles, one at each end of the cell, that get rid of excess water and some of the waste products.
   5. Oxygen from the water enters by diffusion through the cell membrane, and carbon dioxide produced by metabolism leaves the same way.

D. There are two kinds of nuclei in the paramecium: large (macronucleus) and small (micronucleus).
   1. The large nucleus controls and directs the regular activities of the cell.
   2. The small nucleus functions in reproduction.

E. The paramecium reproduces like the amoeba does; that is, it splits in two.
   1. First the small nucleus splits, and each half moves to an end of the cell.
   2. Then the large nucleus splits.
   3. The cell narrows in the middle and separates, forming two new paramecia.

F. Occasionally, two paramecia come together and exchange nuclear material.
   1. This process of coming together is called *conjugation.*
   2. In conjugation, no new paramecia are formed as in true sexual reproduction, but from the exchange of nuclear material, the paramecia are given a new genetic makeup; they then continue reproducing asexually through mitotic cell division.

IV. Spore-Forming Protozoans

A. Some protozoans reproduce by forming tiny, round bodies, called spores. These belong to the phylum **Sporozoa**. They are all parasitic, nonmotile protozoans.
   1. They have no structures for moving but are carried along in water or in the blood of their host.

B. A spore is a reproductive cell that can produce a new organism asexually; that is, without fertilization or the union of gametes.
   1. The nucleus of the cell divides into many small nuclei.
   2. Parts of the cytoplasm around the nucleus then surround each of the new nuclei to form spores.
   3. Finally, the whole protozoan breaks up and releases these spores.
   4. The spores then become new protozoans.

C. Living as internal parasites in one or more hosts, sporozoans have complex life cycles.
   1. The life cycle includes a sexual stage, during which gametes are produced and fuse to form a zygote.
   2. The zygote then divides many times (by mitotic cell division) to form spores.
   3. Once inside a second host, each spore can divide many times to produce many more spores.

D. Among the best known sporozoans are members of the genus *Plasmodium.*
   1. Different species of *Plasmodium* cause malaria in humans, some mammals, and birds.
   2. Malaria is caused by sporozoans that are spread from host to host by female *Anopheles* mosquitoes.

3. In humans, the malaria cycle begins when a female mosquito bites an infected person.
4. It takes in the *Plasmodium* reproductive cells with its blood meal. Inside the mosquito, those cells fuse to form a zygote, which, in turn, divides many times to form many spore fragments. Eventually the zygote breaks open, releasing the spores.
5. These spores invade the mosquito's salivary glands. From there, they will be injected into a new host when the mosquito bites again. When the mosquito bites another human host, these spores are released into the victim's bloodstream. Through the bloodstream, the spores reach the victim's liver, where they form a second type of spore cell.
6. From the liver, they reenter the bloodstream, invade red blood cells, and multiply rapidly inside those red blood cells. Eventually, the blood cells rupture, releasing great numbers of spores, and the process of invading and destroying red blood cells continues.
7. If untreated, the victim can become anemic and die. Worldwide, several million people die each year from malaria.

V. Beneficial and Harmful Aspects of Protozoans

A. Protozoans are important members of the food chain for fish and other aquatic animals.
B. Protozoans are helpful because they eat large amounts of bacteria that may be harmful.
C. Some protozoans cause serious diseases, such as amoebic dysentery, African sleeping sickness, giardia, and malaria.

Exploratory Activities for "Neither Plant nor Animal"

1. EXPLORING FOR ALGAE AND PROTOZOANS (ANY GRADE LEVEL)

The following activities for exploring algae and protozoans contain general guidelines; specific procedures for student investigations will vary according to student maturity, grade level, availability of equipment and materials, and the interest that develops from these initiating activities.

Have students collect samples of pond water and water from backyard puddles to explore for living algae and protozoans. This activity can continue all year long.

1.1 Exploring Algae

Algae are easiest to collect during spring and summer. They may be found as a greenish scum in shallow or stagnant pools and lakes, as a greenish coating on moist stones and walkways, or on the damp bark of the shaded side of a tree. Collect the algae from pools and lakes in large wide-mouthed jars, taking along a good amount of the water in which the algae were found. Do not put too many algae in one jar. Collect algae from bark by prying off a few small pieces of the bark and soaking it in tap water that has been allowed to stand for 24 hours in a large, wide-mouthed, open jar (to allow any chlorine in the water to escape). Algae found on stones may be scraped off and placed in jars containing tap water that also has been allowed to stand for 24 hours. In addition, collect water from standing puddles, ditches, and so on.

Because algae and protozoans kept in containers die rather quickly, they should be examined as soon as possible. Keep the containers in strong light, but not in direct sunlight. Place a drop of the green material on a microscope slide, cover with a cover glass, and examine the algae under both the low and high powers of a microscope, watching for protozoans, too. In the cells of algae and euglena, look for the tiny bodies (chloroplasts) containing chlorophyll. See whether you can find examples of algae in different stages of reproduction. Find pictures of the common algae and use these to identify the specimens you have collected.

1.2 Investigating Conditions for Growth of Algae

Divide your class of students into investigatory teams. Have students hypothesize about the conditions necessary for algae to thrive. Place samples of algae in darkness, in medium to strong light, and in sunlight. Also keep samples of algae in the refrigerator, on or near a heated radiator, and at room temperature. This variation of conditions will help the students learn the optimum conditions of light and heat for the growth of algae.

1.3 Exploring Kelp

Look for rockweed, seaweed, or kelp along the seashore. If you live inland, obtain some from a fish store. Ask for the kind of seaweed or kelp that is used to pack lobsters, clams, and oysters that are flown or shipped from the seacoast to your city or town. Examine and cut open the air bladders. Look for the cuplike holdfasts and examine them. The larger specimens will have divisions that look like stems and leaves. Look for protozoans and other creatures that inhabit the kelp. Have the students read about and report on the Sargasso Sea and the sargassum (brown kelp) floating on its surface. (During the days of the early explorations, the Sargasso Sea was the legendary graveyard of lost ships.)

2. Exploring Fungi (Any Grade Level)

The following activities for exploring fungi are general guidelines; specific procedures for student investigations will vary according to student maturity, grade level, availability of equipment and materials, and the interest that develops from these initiating activities. When working with mushrooms, it is advisable to wear a mask and plastic gloves.

2.1 Grow and Examine Yeast Cells

Dissolve 1 teaspoon of sugar in a tumbler of warm (not hot) water. Add a quarter of a yeast cake or a package of dried yeast, then let the tumbler stand for 24 hours in a warm place. Place a drop of the yeast culture that has formed on a microscope slide, cover with a cover glass, and observe the yeast plants under both the low and high powers of a microscope. Look for cell shapes, special features of yeast cells, and evidence of budding.

2.2 Observe the Action of Yeast on Dough

Mix flour, water, and sugar in the proper proportions to make bread dough. Divide the dough into two equal parts, and mix one part with half of a yeast cake or package of dry yeast that has been dissolved in some water. Place each dough sample in a pan and set in a warm place for a few hours. The dough with the yeast will rise as the action of the yeast produces bubbles of carbon dioxide that expand in the dough.

2.3 Investigate the Effect of Temperature on Yeast

Prepare a batch of bread dough and yeast, as described in the preceding activity. Divide the dough into three equal parts and place each part in a pan. Put one pan in the refrigerator, another in a warm place, and the third in a hot place. Examine all three batches of dough after a few hours. The dough in the warm place will show the greatest action of the yeast.

2.4 Yeast Causes Fermentation

Dissolve a full tablespoon of sugar in a tumbler of warm water. Add a quarter of a yeast cake or package of dried yeast, and let the tumbler stand for several days in a warm place. Smell the yeast culture and note the odor of ethyl alcohol. Point out that the yeast causes the sugar solution to ferment, producing ethyl alcohol and carbon dioxide.

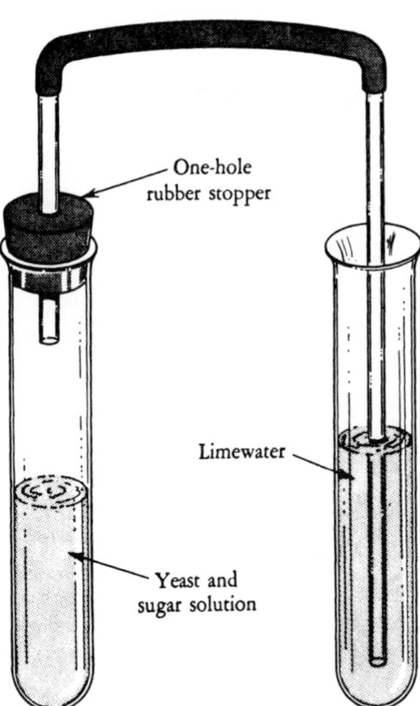

FIGURE 13.2 When yeast ferments, the carbon dioxide it gives off causes limewater to become milky.

2.5 Fermentation Produces Carbon Dioxide

For a teacher demonstration: Prepare a yeast and sugar solution, as described in activity 2.4. Pour some solution into a test tube or narrow-necked glass jar and fit tightly with a one-hole rubber stopper, or modeling clay. Insert a small glass or plastic tube into the hole of the stopper, and connect this tube to another tube with rubber tubing (Figure 13.2). Insert the second tube into a test tube or jar containing clear limewater, which can be obtained from a drugstore. Place the apparatus in a warm place. In a few hours the limewater will turn milky, showing the presence of carbon dioxide. Show that limewater is a test for carbon dioxide by bubbling your breath through a straw into a test tube containing a little limewater.

2.6 Exploring Mushrooms and Making Spore Prints

Collect full-grown mushrooms and examine the stalks, caps, and gills. Carefully and gently cut away the stalk of a mushroom. Coat a piece of smooth or shiny cardboard with egg white. If the gills of a mushroom are covered with light-colored spores, use dark cardboard. If the spores are

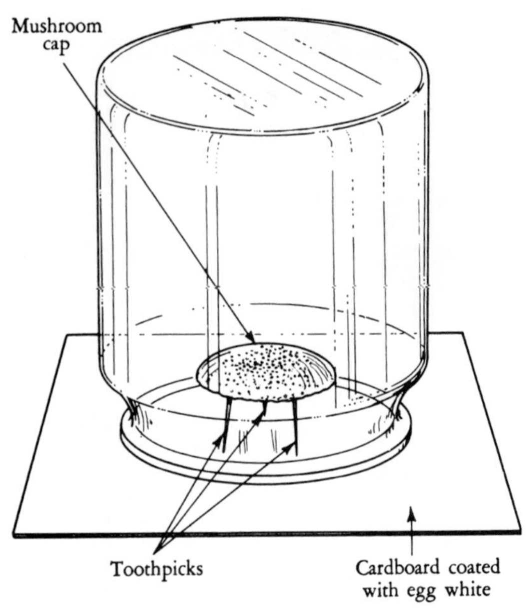

FIGURE 13.3 Obtaining spore prints from a mushroom.

dark, use light cardboard. Push three toothpicks vertically into the sides of the mushroom cap so that they hold the cap 13 millimeters (1–2 in.) above the cardboard (Figure 13.3). Place the cap on the cardboard and cover it with a wide-mouthed glass jar to prevent air currents from disturbing the spores. After 24 hours, remove the jar carefully; then remove the cap. The gills of the mushroom will be permanently outlined on the cardboard by the spores that have fallen on it.

Chapter 14

Animals

Barbara Schwartz/Merrill

LEARNING ACTIVITY 14.1

Examining Animal Cells

Obtain a toothpick with a blunt end. Gently scrape the inside of your cheek a few times with the blunt end of the toothpick. Spread the accumulated material on a microscope slide. Add a drop of water, stain with a drop of tincture of iodine, then cover the material with a cover glass. Examine the material carefully under the microscope until you find a clearly defined cell (that is, one that is very flat, polyhedral, and containing some small dark structures). Look for and identify the different parts of the cell. Compare this animal cell with a plant cell, such as an onion skin cell. Note both the similarities and the differences between the plant and the animal cells.

 Classification of Animals

I. The Animal Kingdom
   A. The animal kingdom, scientifically called the **Kingdom Animalia** (or the **metazoan kingdom**) is divided into 16 phyla that contain more than 1,200,000 known species.
      1. The kingdom comprises two broad groups: animals with backbones (**vertebrates**) and animals without backbones (**invertebrates**).
      2. Members of phylum Chordata are vertebrates. All other animal phyla are invertebrates.
   B. All animals are **multicellular** organisms. Their bodies are made of many cells with different functions.
   C. Unlike plant cells, animal cells do not have chlorophyll or walls made of cellulose.

 Sponges and Coelenterates

I. Phylum Porifera: The Sponge Animals
   A. All poriferans are aquatic. Some live in the saltwaters of oceans; others live in freshwater lakes and streams.
   B. Sponges have irregularly shaped bodies; that is, they are **asymmetrical** (without symmetry). Asymmetrical animals are often sessile organisms. *Sessile* means that they are fastened to something and generally do not move from place to place.
      1. The body of a poriferan is a hollow tube with many pores, or openings, in it. Water flows through the hollow tube, bringing food and dissolved oxygen to the sponge cells, and taking away carbon dioxide and other waste products.
      2. The body wall is made up of two layers of cells; that is, it is two cells thick.
   C. Poriferans are classified according to their types of skeleton, which may be made of calcium carbonate, silicon, or a soft and flexible material called spongin.
      1. Natural sponges (not synthetic) are the spongin skeletons of large sponges from warm waters, especially the Mediterranean Sea, the Red Sea, the waters around the West Indies, and the Florida Gulf Coast.
      2. In deep waters, the sponges are collected by divers; in shallow waters they are collected with hooks attached to the ends of long poles. The sponges are hung on the collectors' boats or piled on shore, where they are left until the living cells die. The skeletons that remain are then washed, dried, and sorted according to size.
   D. Sponges may be white, red, orange, yellow, green, purple, brown, or black.
      1. Some sponges look green because they are living with algae. The algae have chlorophyll and make their own food through photosynthesis, giving off oxygen that the sponges use.
      2. The sponges give off carbon dioxide as a waste product of metabolism, and the algae use the carbon dioxide for photosynthesis.
      3. This arrangement, whereby two organisms live together and help each other, is a form of **symbiosis** called **mutualism.** It is similar to the relationship of fungi and algae, or fungi and cyanobacteria, in lichen.
   E. Living either singly or in colonies, sponges also feed on tiny organisms.
   F. Sponges can reproduce asexually by **budding.**
      1. A bud develops near the base of the sponge and grows into a new sponge.
      2. Some grown buds stay attached to the parent sponge, but others break off, attach to an object, and live independently.
      3. As is true with many of the simpler animals, when a live sponge is cut up into many pieces, each piece can grow into a new sponge by **regenerating** the lost parts.

LEARNING ACTIVITY 14.2

Comparing a Natural Sponge with a Synthetic Sponge

Obtain a natural sponge and have the students observe the many holes in it. Let them feel the sponge; then point out that this soft, flexible material is the skeleton of the sponge. Compare a natural sponge and a synthetic sponge.

G. Sponges can also reproduce sexually by producing gametes via meiotic nuclear division. (See Chapter 12.)
   1. The gametes are either male cells (called sperm) or female cells (called eggs).
   2. A sperm cell unites with an egg cell (fertilization), producing a **zygote** that develops into a young sponge. The zygote can swim freely in the water by means of long whiplike threads called flagella. As young sponges grow older, they settle to the bottom of the sea and finally become sessile by attaching to a rock or another object.

II. **Phylum Coelenterata: Hydra, Jellyfish, Sea Anemone, and Coral**

A. The general characteristics of the coelenterates, also called **cnidarians**, are as follows:
   1. Like the poriferans, coelenterates have body walls that are two cells thick.
   2. Their bodies have only one opening, called the mouth, and all have tentacles that surround their mouths, radiating out regularly like the spokes of a wheel. Some have as few as six tentacles, but others may have hundreds.
   3. Circulation and digestion take place inside their hollow bodies.
   4. Unlike sponges, the coelenterate body demonstrates **radial symmetry**. This means that a line drawn through the body along *any* plane would divide the animal into roughly equal halves. Radial symmetry is an adaptation that enables the animal to detect and capture prey coming toward it from any direction.
   5. Coelenterates display two basic body forms at different stages of their life cycle, **polyp** and **medusa.** Polyps are typically sessile (attached), whereas medusa forms are free-swimming.
   6. Coelenterates can reproduce both sexually and asexually. Polyp forms reproduce asexually by budding. Medusa forms reproduce sexually, forming zygotes that grow into polyps. Polyps, in turn, reproduce asexually to form new medusae.

B. **Hydra** is a member of phylum Coelenterata.
   1. *Hydra* is a generic name. There may be several species of hydra, but here the name is used as if it is referring to one organism, as was done with other organisms such as euglena, paramecium, and amoeba in Chapter 13.
   2. Hydra is 3 to 6 millimeters (1/8 to 1/4 in.) long and lives only in fresh water.
   3. Hydra may be white, brown, or green. Some are green because they are living in symbiosis with green algae.
   4. Hydra has a round, tubular body with a mouth at one end. Surrounding the mouth are six to ten tentacles that radiate outward like wheel spokes. (See Figure 14.1.)
   5. The tentacles contain specialized stinging cells, called **nematocysts.** When small animals come into contact with the tentacles, the stinging cells shoot out tiny threads with poison that paralyzes or kills the prey. Then the tentacles bend inward and push the captured animals through the hydra's mouth and into its body cavity.
   6. Cells inside the hollow body digest the animals, and any waste products pass out through the mouth.
   7. The polyp form attaches itself to rocks or aquatic plants at its closed, base end. It can move by leaving the point where it is attached, floating in the water, then attaching itself at another point. It can also move by turning "cartwheels": The body bends over, the tentacles touch the ground, then the body releases the attachment and swings up and over.
   8. When hydra is disturbed or irritated, its tentacles and body quickly contract.

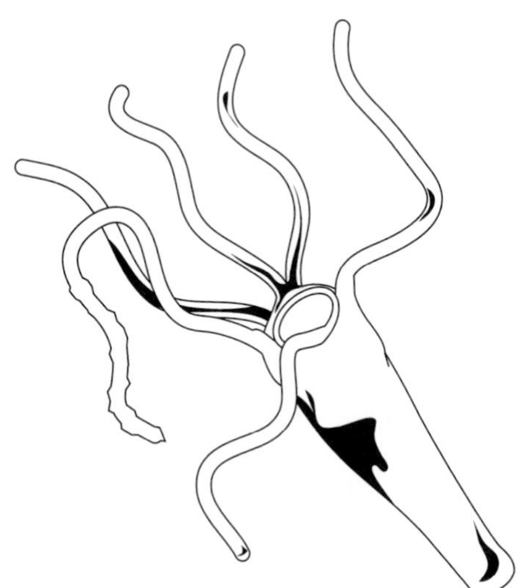

FIGURE 14.1 Hydra, a member of the Phylum Coelenterata.

9. Similar to poriferans, hydra can reproduce asexually by budding. A bud develops on the side of the body and forms a new hydra, which separates from its parent to live independently.
10. As with the sponge, when hydra is cut up into pieces, each piece can regenerate cells and grow into a new hydra.
11. Hydra can also reproduce sexually. Sexual reproduction usually occurs in the fall. The hydra develops a swelling, called a **testis**, in which sperm cells form. Another hydra, or sometimes the same individual, produces a different swelling, called an **ovary**, in which an egg cell forms. Sperm cells leave the testis and swim toward the ovary. When a sperm cell unites with the egg cell in an ovary, the fertilized egg cell (zygote) grows into a new hydra.
12. Some forms of hydrozoans form colonies. The **Portuguese man-of-war** is a colonial hydroid. Individual cells of colonial forms carry on specialized functions such as reproduction, feeding, or keeping the colony afloat.

C. The **jellyfish** is another member of the phylum Coelenterata.
   1. *Jellyfish* is the common name for a large number of species. All live in seawater and live their lives predominately as medusa forms. The body of the medusa form is shaped like an open umbrella.
   2. Many are transparent and difficult to see in the water.
   3. Some jellyfish are only 0.5 centimeters (about 0.2 in) across, whereas others can be as wide as 2 meters (6 ft).
   4. Between the two cell layers of the body wall, there is a gelatinous, or jelly-like, material that gives the jellyfish its name. In the evolutionary development of more complex body systems, this gelatinous material represents the beginning of what in higher animals is a third layer of cells in the body wall.
   5. The mouth of the jellyfish is on the underside of the body and is usually surrounded by tentacles. Each tentacle has thousands of stinging cells.
   6. In large jellyfish, the tentacles can be more than 15 meters (49 ft) long and, because of their sheer number and length, can entrap a swimmer or sea animal. One species of jellyfish with tentacles 40 meters (125 ft) long, is perhaps the longest animal in the world.
   7. Large jellyfish catch small fish and other sea animals that swim within range of its tentacles. They are stung and either paralyzed or killed by the poison secreted by the nematocysts. When the tentacles of a jellyfish come in contact with a swimmer's skin, the stinging cells can produce painful blisters—and even death. **Australian box jelly** is one of the most poisonous of all ocean animals.
   8. Jellyfish are usually found close to the surface of the water. The animal swims by taking some water into its umbrella-like body, then forcing the water out again. As the water is forced out, it makes the jellyfish move up and down with a jerking motion.

LEARNING ACTIVITY 14.3

Exploring Live Hydra

Hydras can be found attached to the submerged stems or undersides of floating leaves of water plants in ponds. They are large enough to be seen with the naked eye. Tear off bits of plants to which hydras are attached and place them in glass jars with some of the pond water. In the classroom, keep the jars in semidarkness and feed the hydras a few tiny bits of lean meat once or twice a week.

Transfer one or two hydras to a saucer using a medicine dropper with a wide tip. If necessary, break off part of the tip to make it wide enough to pick up a hydra without harming it. Place the tip of the medicine dropper directly over the hydra when sucking it up. After the hydra is in the saucer, add enough pond water to keep it covered.

Wait until the hydra has relaxed and stretched; then examine it with a magnifying glass. Note the movement of the tentacles. Tap the saucer with your finger. The startled hydra will contract to a tiny ball. The hydra will also contract if you touch it gently with a pin. Place one or two tiny bits of lean meat near the hydra and observe how the tentacles take the meat and bring it to the hydra's mouth. The tentacles will sting live tiny animals, such as water fleas or mosquito wigglers, that are placed near them. Look to see whether any of the hydras are reproducing by forming buds. Cut a hydra into two or more pieces with a razor blade and place the pieces and some pond water in a glass jar. In 2 or 3 weeks, each piece will have become a new hydra.

D. The **sea anemone** (of which there are many species) is also a coelenterate. Sea anemones attach to rocks and look like king-sized hydras. Their dominant stage is the polyp stage, as in the hydra. They have hundreds of short tentacles around their mouths. Many sea anemones are brightly colored and can often be seen alone or in great numbers along some seacoasts at low tide. Like all coelenterates, sea anemones reproduce both asexually and sexually.

E. **Coral** (of which there are many species) is a coelenterate that lives in large colonies in clear, sunlit ocean water that is at least 20° C (68° F) and at a depth of no more than 30 meters (100 ft).
   1. The coral animal looks like a large hydra.
   2. Each adult coral animal uses calcium from the seawater to build an external skeleton of calcium carbonate (limestone). Each skeleton is connected firmly to the skeletons around it, making one large colony. When corals die, their skeletons remain.
   3. The coral's body and tentacles usually extend beyond the skeleton, but when the coral is disturbed, it can withdraw its tentacles and shorten its body so that the entire body is contained inside its skeleton.
   4. Corals can reproduce by budding, but unlike new hydras, the new corals stay connected to the parents. This results in a mass of skeletons that becomes higher and wider until it forms a rocky ridge, termed a **reef**.
   5. Reefs are usually under water, but some protrude above water, either temporarily at low tide or permanently. Permanent protrusions occur if changes take place either in the Earth's climate (such as a colder world climate resulting in larger polar ice masses) or inside the Earth (resulting in deeper oceans or higher continental landmasses). Both changes result in a lowering of the sea level.
   6. Coral reefs are commonly formed near islands where the water is shallow; some reefs even circle small islands. Sometimes a circular reef is formed with open water in the center. This is called an **atoll**. Atolls accumulate soil and other particles from the air, eventually becoming islands.
   7. The coral reef is an important ecological habitat for many other organisms and also protects the shoreline from ocean storms.
   8. Because corals are sensitive to changes in ocean temperature, any increase in ocean temperature causes massive deaths of the animals. Subsequent exposure to sunlight causes a bleaching out of the dead coral. It has been hypothesized that this bleaching out effect is an indicator of an increase in ocean temperatures due to global warming, known as the greenhouse effect (see Chapter 10).
   9. Corals can also reproduce sexually. The zygote forms a young coral, which swims freely. When it gets older, it attaches to the sea bottom or to an object, and remains there until it dies.

Worms

I. Phylum Platyhelminthes: The Nonsegmented Flatworms

A. Zoologists have divided worms into three groups: flatworms, roundworms, and segmented worms. Each group constitutes a separate phylum. Flatworms belong to the phylum Platyhelminthes.

B. Platyhelminthes are flat and ribbonlike, with lengthwise (bilateral) symmetry but no rings or body divisions (segments).
   1. **Bilateral symmetry** is a body plan in which the right and left halves form mirror images when the animal is evenly divided down its length.
   2. In animals with bilateral symmetry, there is a distinct head, or **anterior end**, and a distinctly different tail, or **posterior end**. Moreover, the **dorsal**, or backside, looks different from the **ventral**, or belly side.
   3. Animals with bilateral symmetry have a distinct advantage over those that are radially symmetrical: They can find food and mates and avoid predators more efficiently because they have greater muscular control.

C. Like the coelenterates, flatworms have a digestive tube with an opening at only one end. Unlike the sponges and coelenterates, their body walls are three cell layers thick.

D. They have simple digestive and nervous systems.

E. Some flatworms move around freely in water and get their food from the water. Others live as parasites in larger animals, getting their food from the host animal.

F. Members of this phylum include the planarian, tapeworm, and fluke.

G. The **planarian** (a generic name that includes several species) is a flatworm that is free-living (not parasitic) in freshwater or very damp soil.

LEARNING ACTIVITY 14.4

Exploring Live Planarians

Planarians can be found in quiet ponds, either clinging to reeds or on the undersides of stones. You will have to look carefully, because they are only 3 to 13 millimeters (1/8 to 1/2 in.) long and they blend so well with their surroundings that they are difficult to see. Suck up the planarians with a medicine dropper and keep them in jars filled with pond water. Be sure to obtain an extra supply of pond water.

Planarians may also be obtained from scientific supply houses. Feed the planarians twice a week with a few tiny bits of lean beef or boiled egg yolk. It is wise to change the water shortly after each feeding, using either the additional pond water you collected or tap water that has been allowed to stand for 2 or 3 days.

Observe the planarians with a magnifying glass or under the low power of a microscope. Note their triangular heads and two dark eyespots.

Animals with very simple nervous systems have amazing regenerative abilities. Observe how planarians regenerate. Suck up three planarians with a medicine dropper and place them on a wet paper towel. With a sharp razor blade, cut one planarian horizontally in half, the second planarian horizontally in thirds, and the third planarian vertically in half (Figure 14.2). After each planarian is cut, wash the pieces in a saucer of pond water. Keep the saucers covered with glass squares to prevent evaporation. Feed and add water regularly. In about 2 weeks each piece will have become a new planarian.

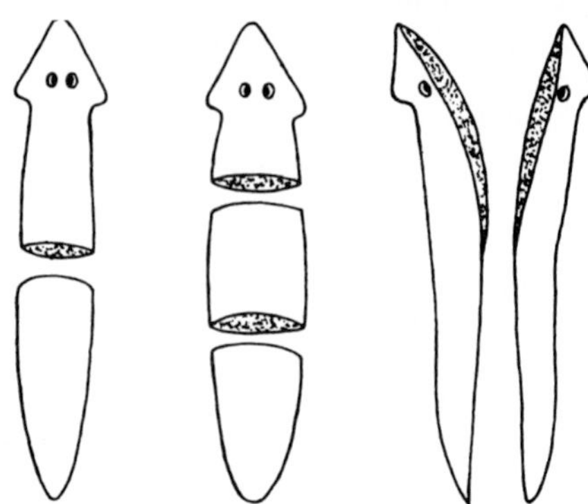

FIGURE 14.2 When planarians are cut into segments, each segment regenerates.

1. Planarian is usually found under stones in ponds and streams.
2. It is 3 to 13 millimeters (1/8 to 1/2 in.) long and can be brown, black, or white.
3. Planarian's head is triangular. There are two light-sensitive eyespots on the head, which give the animal the appearance of being cross-eyed.
4. Planarian's mouth is in the middle of the ventral surface of its body. An enzyme-releasing tube called the **pharynx** may protrude from the mouth when the planarian is searching for food or is feeding. Like the coelenterates, the planarian has a simple digestive system that is open at only one end, the mouth. Food enters and waste materials pass out from the same opening.
5. Planarian feeds on tiny aquatic animals and on dead plant and animal matter.
6. It moves both by means of muscles and by using many tiny hairlike cellular projections, called cilia, located on its underside.
7. Planarian can reproduce asexually by splitting in two. If a planarian is cut into many pieces, each piece can regenerate cells by cell division to form a new planarian.
8. It can also reproduce sexually, each planarian having both male sex cells (sperm) and female sex cells (eggs). That is, planaria are **hermaphroditic**.

H. The **tapeworm** is a flatworm.
   1. All tapeworms are parasitic, living off a host organism. During its life cycle, the tapeworm has two hosts. The host for the adult tapeworm is called the primary host, and the host for the young tapeworm is called the secondary host.
   2. A tapeworm has a knob-shaped head with suckers and sometimes hooks. Suckers and hooks help the tapeworm clamp itself to the wall of a host animal's intestine. People are sometimes infected with a tapeworm from meat that has not been cooked thoroughly.
   3. The tapeworm is a highly evolved and specialized parasite. It has no mouth or intestine. The digested food from the host's intestine diffuses directly into the tapeworm's head. The tapeworm has no eyes, and as an adult it does not move.
   4. Sections keep forming just behind the tapeworm's head. As new sections form, older sections are pushed farther away from the head. As a result, the worm eventually looks like a long piece of flat measuring tape. Sometimes there are more than 200 sections to a tapeworm's body, and the tapeworm can be more than 15 meters (50 feet) long. Each section behind the head of the tapeworm is specialized for reproduction.

5. The end sections of the tapeworm's body grow larger and older and then drop off and pass out of the primary host's body. These sections are filled with egg cells that have already been fertilized, because each section of the tapeworm is able to produce both male sex cells (sperm) and female sex cells (eggs). The tapeworm is hermaphroditic.
6. Sections that drop off soon decay, but the fertilized eggs remain alive. When eggs are eaten accidentally by an animal, such as a cow or pig, they develop into tiny young tapeworms. They remain in the cow or pig, the tapeworm's secondary host animal, where they work their way into tissue, such as that of the muscle or the liver. Once inside the tissue, each young tapeworm **encysts**; that is, it forms a capsule called a **cyst** around itself.
7. Inside the cyst, the tiny tapeworm forms a head (with suckers) and a few sections, then waits until a primary host eats the meat of the animal.
8. If the cow or pig meat is eaten raw or not thoroughly cooked, a young tapeworm that is still alive can come out of its cyst, clamp onto the new host's intestine, and grow into an adult tapeworm, living off the nutrients in the intestines of the new primary host.
9. A host with a tapeworm can become anemic, develop an ulcer, and lose weight, but the condition is curable and not usually fatal. Successful parasites, like the tapeworm, do not usually kill their hosts.
10. While in the primary host, each tapeworm produces thousands of fertile eggs. When segments from the new tapeworm drop off and pass out of the primary host's body, the life cycle of the tapeworm starts again.

I. The **fluke** is another highly successful parasitic flatworm.
1. In size and shape, many flukes resemble the planarian.
2. Flukes are very dangerous to many animals, including humans. Fluke infections in humans are most common in parts of Africa and Asia. Flukes live in organs such as the stomach, intestine, liver, or lung where they damage or destroy the lining tissues and cause ulcers and loss of blood.
3. Almost all flukes have more than one host during their life cycle. One of the fluke's secondary hosts is always a snail.

II. Phylum Nematoda: The Nonsegmented Roundworms

A. Each member of the phylum Nematoda has a round, unsegmented body.
1. A definite digestive tract extends the length of the body, with an opening at each end. At the anterior is the **mouth**; at the posterior is the **anus**.
2. Although some roundworms are free-living (nonparasitic) in soil, freshwater, and ocean water, many others are parasites.
3. Free-living roundworms are very small and are harmless. Some parasitic roundworms can be up to 1 meter (3 ft) long.
4. Many parasitize humans. Parasitic roundworms include the hookworm, pinworm, and trichinella.
5. Some nematodes parasitize plants, especially the roots of plants, causing damage to crops and horticultured plants.

B. A common parasitic roundworm is the **ascaris**, a relatively large worm that lives in the intestine of mammals such as the dog, pig, and horse, and sometimes humans. There it feeds on the partly digested food in the intestine.
1. Ascaris worms lay millions of eggs that pass out of the host's body with the waste products.
2. In regions lacking in sanitary sewage disposal, these eggs are deposited in water and soil, and in food grown on that soil. The eggs enter and infect other animal and human bodies through the contaminated food or water. In places that may be contaminated with ascarids, water should be boiled or purified before drinking. Vegetables should be washed thoroughly before they are eaten.
3. Although most ascaris infections are not serious, sometimes such large masses of these worms form that they block the intestine and death can result. Sometimes the adult worms bore through the intestine, travel through the body, and enter into vital organs such as the liver or heart where they can cause the host's death.

C. The **hookworm** is a parasitic roundworm that in some parts of the world is a serious health menace to humans, especially in tropical and semitropical regions that are lacking in sanitary sewage disposal.
1. Hookworms are quite small, less than 1.25 centimeters (1/2 in.) in length.
2. Adult hookworms attach themselves to the wall of the intestine with their hooklike teeth and suck the blood from the intestine wall. Thousands can live in the host's intestine at one time. This steady loss of blood makes the host anemic and tired.
3. In the intestines, the worms reproduce and lay eggs that pass out of the host's body with the feces. The eggs hatch in the soil and grow into young hookworms.
4. Young hookworms enter the bodies of animals and humans by boring through the skin, usually at the feet. This is a reason for

not going barefoot in areas where the soil could be contaminated with hookworms.

5. Once hookworms enter the body, they travel in the blood to the lungs. In the lungs, they pass through the air passages and move up the windpipe into the throat. In the throat, they are swallowed and pass through the stomach into the intestine, where they attach themselves and grow into adult hookworms, producing more eggs to continue their life cycle.

D. The **pinworm** is a parasite commonly found in young children.
   1. The pinworm invades and inhabits the human's intestinal tract.
   2. Children become infected when they eat something that has come into contact with contaminated soil and has not been thoroughly washed.
   3. While in the intestinal tract of the host, female pinworms lay eggs near the anus that hatch and cause itching.
   4. Reinfection commonly occurs in young children when they place their fingers into their mouth after scratching the infected area.

E. **Trichinella** is a parasitic roundworm that causes the disease trichinosis, which can cripple and kill its animal or human host.
   1. Trichinella lives in the intestine of its host, where each worm can produce as many as 2,000 eggs.
   2. These eggs hatch into young worms that travel in the blood or lymph vessels to muscles and other organs. The young worms bore into the muscles where they encyst.
   3. The young worms stay inside these cysts and cannot grow into adults until the flesh of the host is eaten by another animal or by a human. When animals or people eat raw or poorly cooked infected meat (usually pork), the young worms emerge from their cysts, grow into adult worms, and start producing their own young worms, continuing their life cycle.
   4. When a human is infected with trichinella, the muscles become inflamed and painful as the young worms bore their way into the muscles and form cysts. The disease can cripple the host and even cause death.

III. Phylum Annelida: The Segmented Roundworms

A. Members of the phylum Annelida, including the earthworm, sandworm, and leech, are worms whose bodies are divided into rings or body divisions called **segments.**
   1. Annelids can be found in aquatic, marine, and terrestrial habitats.
   2. Of all the worms, annelids are the most highly developed. They have many well-developed organ systems, including digestive, circulatory, excretory, reproductive, and nervous systems.

B. The **earthworm** is a common terrestrial annelid. One acre of fertile soil may be home for as many as 3 million earthworms.
   1. The earthworm eats soil, digesting the decayed plant and animal matter from the soil and eliminating the rest. Earthworms are valuable to humans because they bore holes and loosen and turn the soil, thus allowing air and water to enter the soil and help plant roots grow. One common earthworm can till, fertilize, drain, and aerate 0.2 kilogram (1/2 lb) of soil per day.
   2. The many species of earthworms range from as small as 1 millimeter (1/25 in.) long to as large as the **Giant South African earthworm** that can grow to a length of more than 7 meters (22 ft).
   3. The earthworm's head end is usually darker and more pointed than its tail.
   4. Four pairs of bristles, called **setae,** stick out from the sides and underside of each body segment except the first and the last segments. Setae help the earthworm anchor itself as it moves through the soil.
   5. The earthworm is able to move, because it has two sets of muscles. One set (circular muscles) is used to stretch the earthworm so it is long and thin. The other set (longitudinal muscles) is used to make the earthworm short and thick.
   6. The earthworm has no respiratory system. It absorbs oxygen and gives off carbon dioxide directly through its thin skin. To allow for this gaseous transfer, the skin of the worm must stay moist. Too much water, however, will drown the worm.
   7. The earthworm has as many as five pair of simple "hearts" in its circulatory system.
   8. The digestive system has a mouth, an esophagus, a crop, a gizzard for grinding food, an intestine, and an anus.
   9. If an earthworm is cut across in half, each half can regenerate into a new earthworm. If cut, but not in halves, only the portion or portions containing the vital organs will live and grow the lost portions.
   10. Each earthworm forms both sperm and eggs, so it is hermaphroditic. Two earthworms, however, will mate (copulate). Two earthworms come together and exchange sperm. After the exchange, the egg cells are fertilized by the sperm cells. This is done outside the body in the developing **cocoon** that the earthworm secretes from its specialized area, called the **clitellum.**

LEARNING ACTIVITY 14.5

Exploring Live Earthworms

The best place to find earthworms is in rich garden soil. Either dig them up or wait until after a heavy rain, when the worms come to the surface at night. Try to collect the large night crawlers. Keep the worms in a box containing equal parts of peat moss and rich garden soil. Cover the box with a damp piece of thick cloth towel. Keep the earth and towel damp, but not wet, at all times. About once a week, feed the worms a quarter cup of oatmeal or bread that has been softened in water.

Place an earthworm on a damp paper towel and see how it crawls by lengthening and then contracting its body. Find the head of the earthworm by watching closely for the lip or pharynx that the worm pushes out as it moves along. Touch the head and note how the worm contracts the front part of its body; it may even crawl backward.

Pass your fingertips gently along the underside of the earthworm and feel the bristle feet (setae). Observe these feet through a magnifying glass. See what happens when you place the earthworm on a damp, smooth glass surface, where there is nothing for these bristle feet to grip.

Place an earthworm on a piece of damp paper towel and cover it with a saucer so it cannot escape. Keep the worm in a dark room for about an hour, then shine a flashlight on the worm's head. Note how it quickly pulls its head away from the bright light.

Inquiry-Based Learning Activity 14.5. Modified

Begin the activity by asking your students some questions. How many of you have seen earthworms? How many of you have held an earthworm in your hands and taken a close look at one? Generally your students will have some direct experience with earthworms. The focus of this inquiry activity will be on three questions: (1) How do earthworms move through the dirt? (2) What do earthworms eat? (3) Since earthworms don't have eyes or ears like we do, can they tell dark from light and can they hear sounds? Divide students into groups of two or three. Ask each group member to choose one question that he or she will be responsible for answering for the group. Finally, inform your students that the next day each group will be given a large cup containing an earthworm in garden soil so they can carry out their investigations. None of the investigations should harm the earthworms during this activity. Your students will be responsible for devising strategies for studying the earthworms to discover how they move, what they eat, and if they respond to light or sound. Plan for this activity to take a week or more to complete, but each of the daily sessions should take only about 15 to 30 minutes to complete. Some days groups may plan their next investigation, and some days they might carry out their investigations after bringing the proper tools to class. See Learning Activity 14.5 for instructions on earthworm care.

What level of inquiry is this modification? This activity begins with questions asked by you, the teacher. However, once the questions have been posed, the students are responsible for designing and carrying out their investigations during daily sessions limited to 15-30 minutes. The activity begins with **problem identification** at ***Level II (Transition from Level I).*** However, after the initial assignment of the task, the students become responsible for carrying out the tasks. This shifts the activity to **Level II *(Transition to Level III)*** *and maybe even* ***Level III*** *for* ***processes of problem solving*** *and* ***identification of tentative solutions.*** **Some questions to consider.** How would the students' work be assessed? What would you have them produce to display the knowledge that they have gained through their investigations?

It then gradually slides out of it. As the earthworm slides out of the cocoon, first eggs are secreted into it and then sperm, to fertilize the eggs. Therefore although earthworms copulate, fertilization is external, taking place in the cocoon outside the worm. The earthworm deposits the cocoon in the soil and its ends close. The eggs soon hatch and emerge from the cocoon as young earthworms.

C. The **sandworm** is a segmented roundworm that lives in the ocean near the shore, where it feeds on tiny marine animals.
   1. The sandworm may burrow into the sand with only its head exposed to the water or swim around in the water, helped by little projections on each side of its body.
   2. On its head are four light-sensitive eyespots and a group of tentacles.

D. The **leech** is a segmented aquatic roundworm that is parasitic.
   1. Most leeches are found in freshwater; a few live in the ocean.
   2. They are commonly called *bloodsuckers* because they live by sucking the blood from larger animals such as fish and turtles—or even humans if they venture into the leech's habitat.
      a. A leech has two suckers, one at each end of its body, by which it clings to its host.
      b. It breaks the skin of the host with sharp jaws in its mouth. The bite of a leech is not painful, however, because the saliva

of the leech contains chemicals that act as an anesthetic. Other chemicals in its saliva prevent the blood from clotting and dilate blood vessels to increase blood flow. Because of these characteristics, leeches have many medical uses.

c. In one feeding, the leech may ingest up to five times its own weight. Once fed, it may not eat again for a year.

3. Leeches are hermaphroditic. However, during mating, one performs the male role and clings to the body of the one performing the female role, depositing a sac of sperm on "her" skin. The sac produces flesh-deteriorating enzymes that eat a hole into the skin and fertilize the eggs within the body.
4. Because of their unusual abilities, leeches are used in medical treatment and research. For example, they are sometimes used to help establish circulation after limb reattachments.

 Echinoderms and Mollusks

I. **Phylum Echinodermata: The Spiny-Skinned Animals**

A. Derived from the Greek words meaning *spiny skin,* echinoderm refers to a group of saltwater animals whose common characteristics include a five-part, radially symmetric anatomy and an internal skeleton (**endoskeleton**). Members of the phylum include the sea star (starfish), brittle star, sea urchin, sand dollar, sea cucumber, feather star, and sea lily.

1. All echinoderms are marine animals and are found in all oceans of the world; there are no freshwater or terrestrial species.
2. All echinoderms have a hard, spiny, or bumpy calcium carbonate endoskeleton covered by a thin layer of skin. Some of the spines of starfishes and sea urchins have become modified into pincerlike appendages termed pedicellarias that are used for protection.
3. For most adult members of the phylum, the parts of their bodies radiate out regularly from the center like the spokes of a wheel. This kind of symmetry is known as **radial symmetry** (as in the coelenterates) as opposed to the bilateral symmetry of planarians, earthworms, humans, and many other animal groups.
4. Prior to its development into an adult echinoderm, the echinoderm in the larval stage is a free-swimming, ciliated and bilaterally symmetrical form.

B. The **starfish** is *not* a fish.

1. It has no head but is made up of a circle of arms that come together at a central body disc, forming a star shape.
2. Most starfish have five arms, but some have six or more. At the end of each arm is a light-sensitive area called an eyespot.
3. There are spines all over the body and arms.
4. The stomach of the starfish is at the center of the body. Its mouth is on the ventral or underside of the central disc. Its anus is located dorsally.
5. On the underside of each arm are hundreds of little tubes called tube feet, each acting as a suction cup that can stick firmly to any object on which it is pressed.
6. A starfish is carnivorous, feeding on clams and oysters. It crawls over the top of a clam or oyster and presses its tube feet firmly on both sides of the shell. It pulls on the shell until the victim tires and relaxes its muscles and its shell opens. Then the starfish inverts its stomach so it extends through the mouth and into the opening in the clam or oyster shell, where it digests the victim's body.
7. A starfish can crawl in any direction. It is most active at night.
8. Starfish can regenerate lost parts. If a starfish loses an arm, it can grow a new one. If a starfish is chopped into three or four pieces, and if each piece has at least one arm and part of the central disc, each piece may grow into a new starfish.
9. The sexes are separate; starfish are either male or female. They discharge their sperm and eggs into the water, where fertilization takes place externally. A female starfish may lay more than 100 million eggs in one season. Eggs hatch into a larva that gradually grows and changes into an adult starfish.

C. The **brittle star** has long, flexible, snake-like arms (or rays); hides among sponges; and feeds on dead and decaying matter, termed detritus, that falls to the ocean floor. The arms easily break off if attacked by a predator; thus the name *brittle star.* Replacement arms are quickly regenerated.

D. The **sea urchin** is a globe-shaped echinoderm with very long spines that protect it from predators and make it resemble a pin cushion. In some species, the spines are poisonous. The sea urchin is herbivorous, feeding on algae.

E. The **sand dollar** is a flat echinoderm with short spines. It burrows into the sandy ocean floor and feeds on detritus.

F. The **sea cucumber** is long and soft-bodied, with very short spines. It feeds on detritus. An interesting and unusual behavior of the sea urchin is that of expelling a sticky mass of its intestines through the anus when disturbed. These internal organs are then regenerated.

G. Both the **feather star** and the **sea lily** are feather-shaped and are often found coexisting with coral. They feed principally on detritus. The sea lily is the only echinoderm that is sessile (attached) in the adult stage. The feather star is sessile in the larval stage and slow swimming as an adult.

II. Phylum Mollusca: The Shellfish

A. The phylum Mollusca comprises a large and varied group of animals including the chiton, oyster, snail, squid, and octopus. Some are terrestrial and many others are aquatic. Many different kinds of mollusks are used by humans as food.
   1. **Mollusks** have soft, fleshy bodies that are not segmented.
   2. Most have a protective shell made of calcium carbonate; hence, the name shellfish. As is often true with common names, shellfish is a poor name for the mollusks. They are *not* fish and not all have shells.
   3. Clam and oyster shells are used to make buttons and mother-of-pearl, which is then fashioned into buttons and other decorative items. Shells are also ground up and used in chicken feed to provide the calcium carbonate needed by chickens to make egg shells.
   4. A mollusk has a muscular **foot** and a special sheet of tissue called the **mantle**, which produces the shell.
   5. Within this large phylum are seven classes. The three classes that include the most common and well-known species are the bivalvia, gastropoda, and cephalopoda.
      a. Bivalved mollusks live inside two shells hinged at the mid-dorsal line. Powerful muscles hold the shell parts together. This group includes the clam, oyster, scallop, and mussel.
      b. Gastropods have just one spiral shell and seem to be moving on their bellies, carrying their shells on their backs. This group includes the snail, slug, conch, periwinkle, and abalone.
      c. Cephalopods have a definite head, surrounded by many arms, called tentacles. This group includes the chambered nautilus, octopus, cuttlefish, and squid.

B. The bivalved mollusks all live in the ocean, but some clams and mussels can also be found in freshwater habitats.
   1. Bivalves never shed their shells. The shells become larger and larger. Lines on the outside of a shell are an indication of the age of the animal, each line representing a year's growth.
   2. Bivalves exhibit a range of sizes. Some are less than 1 millimeter long (the thickness of a U.S. dime), and others, such as the giant clams found in the South Pacific Ocean, are as large as 2 meters (6 ft) across.
   3. They all have a tough muscular foot shaped somewhat like a hatchet that sticks out from the shells and is used for digging or anchoring. This class is sometimes referred to as the hatchet-footed mollusks.
   4. Two tubes, called siphons, direct the water flow through the animal. Water carrying oxygen and food flows into the animal through one siphon. Water carrying carbon dioxide and waste products flows out of the other siphon.
   5. Bivalves' respiratory organs, called gills, allow oxygen in the water to diffuse into the blood in the body and allow carbon dioxide to leave.
   6. Both the gills and the siphons are lined with cilia that beat to draw water in and to direct its flow. Cilia lining the gills filter and push food particles to the stomach.
   7. Bivalves have a well-developed digestive system, an excretory system, a nervous system, a reproductive system, and a circulatory system with a heart, blood, and blood vessels.
   8. They reproduce sexually, and the sexes are separate.
   9. In the ocean, the oyster and many kinds of clams permanently attach to a rock or some other object.
   10. Certain oysters make pearls. A **pearl** is formed when an irritating object, such as a parasitic worm, gets inside the flesh of an oyster and forms a tiny round capsule called a cyst. The mantle (shell-producing tissue) forms layers of shell material around the cyst, producing the pearl. The Japanese discovered a way of making a pearl from an oyster. They take a small round bead made from shell, cover the bead with living mantle cells, and push the bead inside the oyster. The oyster is then put into the ocean for a few years, and a pearl develops around the bead. This pearl, which is called a cultured pearl, looks just like a natural pearl.

C. Most **gastropods** are univalves; that is, they have one shell or valve, which is usually spiral shaped. The slug does not have a shell. It looks like a snail that has lost its shell. For protection, land slugs secrete a thick layer of mucus. Sea slugs, or nudibranchs, protect themselves in other ways. Some incorporate the poisonous nematocysts from jellyfish into their own bodies. Others secrete mucus that has a strong, unpleasant odor and may even be poisonous.
   1. Univalves have the same vital body organs as bivalves, except that land snails have lungs instead of gills for breathing.
   2. Univalves also have a much larger foot than the bivalves. This large foot looks like part of the univalve's body, causing it to appear to be crawling on its belly and carrying its shell

on its back. Hence the common name sometimes used for this class—stomach-footed mollusks.

3. When a univalve is attacked, it pulls its foot and head up inside its shell.
4. The snail has two tentacles on its head. Some snails have an eye on the tip of each tentacle. When the snail is touched, it draws in its tentacles.
5. The foot of a land snail or slug gives off a lubricating slime, and these animals move only on this slime.
6. Snails and slugs also have a straplike rasping organ called a radula, which acts as a file to scrape or rasp off bits of food from the surface of objects. Water snails help keep an aquarium clean by using their radulas to eat algae, bacteria, and detritus that collect on the glass sides of the aquarium.

D. The **cephalopods** (meaning "head-footed") are marine only.
   1. Cephalopods have most of the same parts as the other mollusks, but they are arranged differently. The chambered nautilus, however, is the only cephalopod that has an external shell.
   2. When attacking, attacked, or frightened, the squid and octopus shoot out an inky material that clouds the water and hides them. The secretion of another substance that dulls an attacker's sense of smell accompanies this expulsion of ink. The first ink used in writing came from the octopus's ink sac.
   3. Most cephalopods can change their skin coloration to camouflage themselves.
   4. They can also escape from predators by shooting a jet of water through their bodies to create a burst of jetlike speed.
   5. Squids, octopuses, and cuttlefish have beaklike jaws used to bite and to enter the hard shells of their prey.

E. The **squid** has a long, narrow, torpedo-like body and no external shell.
   1. Its foot is divided into two long and eight short tentacles that have double rows of suction cups for grasping objects.
   2. It has a large eye on each side of its head. The giant squid has eyes that can be up to 25 centimeters (10 inches) across—the largest eyes of any animal—giving it good vision for the darkness of the deep ocean water in which it resides.
   3. Although most squids are no more than 1 meter (3 ft) in length, giant squids may reach 20 meters (67 ft) in length.

F. The **octopus** is built much like the squid, but with a shorter, more rounded, bag-shaped body, which is the animal's mantle. Inside its body is only the vestige of a shell.
   1. It has only eight tentacles, all the same size, which it uses for swimming, crawling, fighting, building nests, holding prey, and mating. Its tentacles have nerve endings that help the octopus sense its surroundings. The tentacles also have many suction cups that help to hold prey. After capturing its prey, the octopus paralyzes its victim with a secretion of nerve poison. Some octopuses have tentacles 15 centimeters (6 in.) long, but others may have tentacles that are 4 meters (13 ft) long. If a tentacle is lost, a new one is regenerated.
   2. The largest octopus can grow to approximately 3 meters (10 ft) long and weigh up to 55 pounds, although most are smaller.

LEARNING ACTIVITY 14.6

Exploring Live Snails

A. Water Snails

Obtain some water snails from a pet shop or scientific supply house. Snails can also be found among the water plants in a pond that has a muddy bottom. Place two or three snails in an aquarium or large glass jar of tap water that has been allowed to stand for 2 or 3 days, making sure that there is a good supply of water plants in the container.

Note how the snail uses its foot to move along a surface. Use a magnifying glass to watch the snail's rough "tongue" scrape the algae from the aquarium walls. Touch the snails and see how they withdraw into their shells and fall to the bottom of the aquarium. The snails may lay masses of transparent eggs on the walls of the container. Examine these eggs periodically for 2 or 3 weeks and see them hatch.

B. Land Snails

Land snails are often found early in the morning feeding on plants in the garden. They can be kept in an aquarium or in a large glass jar containing damp garden soil. If you use a glass jar, keep the mouth covered, either with a wire screen or with a screw top that has been perforated several times by a nail. Keep the snail well supplied with soft, green leaves or lettuce.

Note how the snail's foot leaves a trail of slime, along which it travels. See how the snail quickly shreds the leaves and lettuce with its "tongue." Look for the eyes at the ends of the larger pair of feelers. Touch the feelers gently with a pencil and see how they retract. Touch the feelers more forcibly and make the snail withdraw into its shell. A snail mates only once in its entire life, but the act of copulation may last as long as 12 hours.

3. The octopus is nocturnal and a bottom feeder. During the day, it stays hidden in its nest, which is usually a hole or rock crevice or a nest dug in the sand, usually in fairly shallow waters.
4. The octopus has a well-developed brain and nervous system, making it a relatively intelligent animal. It is considered to be the most intelligent of all the invertebrates. Octopuses have been trained to distinguish among shapes and to recognize objects by touch. They are very clever and effective predators.
5. Like the squid, the octopus has eyes that can change position to focus, and it has a sharp beak.
6. When mating, the male sends sperm cells down one of its tentacles (called the hectocotylus) into the female to fertilize her eggs.
7. At maturity, about age 2, the female lays up to 150,000 eggs. The female octopus stays with her eggs to protect them and may even starve to death while doing so. Most young, however, are eaten by other animals before or soon after hatching into small larvae that look like the adult octopus.

 Arthropods

I. Phylum Arthropoda: Animals with Jointed Appendages

A. The bodies of members of the phylum Arthropoda are covered by the cuticle, an external skeleton (**exoskeleton**) made of a tough material called chitin. The cuticle is thick, hard armor over some parts of the body and thin and flexible over other parts, such as over joints that can bend.
   1. The muscles of the body are attached to the inside of the skeleton.
   2. Arthropods' bodies are segmented and organized into distinct body regions.

B. Arthropods' legs and other attached body parts are called appendages. The appendages are jointed and can bend.
   1. All appendages are paired. They are arranged on the right and left sides of the body in such a way that one side of the body is a mirror image of the other. This is bilateral symmetry.
   2. The number of paired legs is used to divide the phylum into its classes.

II. The Crustaceans

A. The crayfish, the lobster, the crab, the shrimp, the tiny water flea, and the pill bug are members of the class **Crustacea**, one of the classes within the phylum Arthropoda. Except for the pill bug, which lives on land, all are aquatic, living in saltwater or freshwater. Many crustaceans are used by humans as food.
   1. In addition to having the characteristics common to arthropods, the crustaceans have unique characteristics that distinguish them as a class within the phylum Arthropoda.
   2. The class Crustacea is sometimes called Decapoda, because they have 10 legs (five pairs).
   3. They have two pairs of feelers, called antennae.
   4. Their external skeletons contain calcium carbonate.
   5. They have two distinct body regions—the cephalothorax and the abdomen.
   6. Most have special breathing organs called gills that allow oxygen to enter their bodies and carbon dioxide to leave as water passes over the gills.

B. The **crayfish** exemplifies a typical crustacean.
   1. It has a dark outer skeleton containing calcium carbonate.
   2. It has two distinct body regions—the cephalothorax and the abdomen.
   3. The cephalothorax is really made up of two regions, the head and the thorax, grown together to look like one region.
   4. A hard, thick cuticle called the carapace that gives the crayfish extra protection covers the cephalothorax.
   5. The abdomen, commonly called the tail, consists of seven movable segments.
   6. The crayfish has two eyes, each on the end of a short, movable stalk on each side of the front end of the cephalothorax. Each eye consists of many lenses and, for this reason, is called a compound eye.
   7. The crayfish has two pairs of long feelers, called antennae, and several smaller feelers, called antennules.
   8. It has six pairs of mouthparts. Three pairs are connected to the head, and three pairs are connected to the thorax. All are used for holding food, cutting and grinding it, and pushing it into the mouth.
   9. Its five pairs of legs are all connected to the thorax. The first pair, called the chelipeds, are much larger than the other four pairs. The chelipeds have large pincers that are used for grabbing and holding food. One cheliped is larger than the other.
   10. The remaining four pairs of legs are used mostly for walking. Two pairs of these walking legs end in tiny pincers, and two pairs end in tiny claws.

11. On its abdomen are six pairs of appendages, called swimmerets. Each segment of the abdomen has a pair of swimmerets, except for the last segment, which has none.
12. The first five pairs of swimmerets are quite small and are used by the female for carrying her eggs until they are hatched. Both males and females use these pairs for slow, forward swimming.
13. The sixth pair of swimmerets is large and paddle-like. These swimmerets are called uropods. The uropods and the seventh segment of the abdomen, called the telson, together constitute the tail fan of the crayfish.
14. The crayfish usually moves backward, using its sixth and seventh abdominal segments and its four walking legs. The crayfish also uses its four walking legs to travel forward and sideways.
15. The crayfish breathes through feathery organs called gills, which are attached to the five pairs of legs, and through the three pairs of mouthparts that are connected to the thorax. The gills allow oxygen in the water to diffuse into blood in the body of the crayfish, and carbon dioxide to diffuse out.
16. The crayfish is a freshwater animal living at the bottom of lakes, ponds, and streams, where it eats plants and any live or dead animal material it can grasp.
17. Crayfish breed once a year, usually in fall. In spring the female lays about 100 eggs, which are attached to the first five pairs of swimmerets on her abdomen. They are carried there until they hatch.
    a. The young crayfish stay attached to the swimmerets for about 2 weeks, holding onto the hairs of the swimmerets with their pincers. During this time, the young crayfish feed on the yolk in the eggs.
    b. After 2 weeks, the young crayfish let go of the swimmerets and become independent.
18. Crayfish grow larger by shedding their exoskeletons, a process called **molting.** Most crayfish molt about seven times the first year and once or twice a year thereafter. While a crayfish is molting, it is defenseless, so it usually goes into hiding until the new skeleton

LEARNING ACTIVITY 14.7

Exploring Live Crustaceans: Crayfish or Lobsters

The freshwater crayfish and the ocean lobster are highly similar, and either is quite suitable for the study of crustaceans. Crayfish are found in ponds and streams, hiding under rocks and logs. You can catch one by tying one end of a string around a small piece of meat and dangling the meat near a rock at the bottom of the pond or stream. When the crayfish seizes the meat with its claws, pull up the string with a slow steady movement. If you are quick, you can also catch a crayfish by lifting up its rock and grabbing it as it swims backward. Keep the crayfish you collect in large glass jars filled with pond water or with tap water that has been allowed to stand for 2 or 3 days to allow any chlorine in the water to escape.

Observe the crayfish carefully. Note how the outside skeleton forms a hard, protective shield for the crayfish, especially over the head and chest area. Note the segments of the abdomen and the paddles of the tail. Count the number of jointed walking legs and examine the large pair of front claws. Feed the crayfish earthworms or small pieces of raw meat and see how it uses its claws and mouth parts. Locate the feelers and count them. Observe the eyes and see how they move around on their stalks.

If one cheliped is always larger than the other, is there a way to predict whether the left or the right side is the larger one? Is it possible a crayfish is left- or right-cheliped dominant?

Turn a crayfish on its back. Lift up the free, lower edge of the skeleton that covers the chest region and observe the gills. Find the mouth parts. Examine the swimmerets and see how the crayfish uses them. Note how the crayfish uses its abdomen to swim backward quickly.

LEARNING ACTIVITY 14.8

Exploring Live Crustaceans: Water Fleas (Daphnia)

Water fleas are tiny, transparent crustaceans that can be found during the spring and summer in almost any quiet pool or stream. Because they eat algae, water fleas are easiest to find in ponds that are covered with green scum. A good way to catch them is to use a sieve or tea strainer that has been lined with cheesecloth. Use needle and thread to hold the cheesecloth against the sides of the sieve or strainer. Place the water fleas in glass jars containing pond water and a good supply of green algae, and keep the jars in sunlight. When you finish examining the water fleas, use them as food for fish, tadpoles, and hydra. They can also be placed in aquariums to remove excessive algae in the water.

Use a medicine dropper to suck up a water flea, then place it on a slide and examine it under the low power of a microscope. Because it is transparent, you will see not only the outer skeleton and the appendages but also the inner organs. Notice the rapidly beating heart. Look for the intestine and trace it from the mouth to the anus.

is formed. The term *soft-shell* is used when referring to crayfish (and lobsters and crabs) just after they have molted and before they have grown a new hard exoskeleton.

19. If the crayfish should lose one or more of its appendages during molting or in a battle, new appendages can be regenerated to replace the lost ones.

C. The **lobster** is built like the crayfish, but the lobster is larger and lives in a marine habitat. One kind is found in the North Atlantic Ocean. Another kind of lobster, found in the coastal waters of Florida, California, and the West Indies, does not have the enlarged first pair of legs, the chelipeds.

D. The body of a **crab** is wide and round, rather than long and narrow like that of the crayfish and the lobster. The crab's abdomen is very small and folds under the broad shell (cephalothorax). Crabs move by walking sideways.

E. **Shrimp** have a large muscular abdomen. They can swim very fast, moving backward like the crayfish and the lobster. When the shrimp is threatened, it buries itself in the sand, exposing only its antennae and eyes.

III. The Insects

A. Insects belong to the class of arthropods called **Insecta** (or **Hexapoda**). This is the largest single class of animals in terms of number of species, number of individuals, and total biomass. There are more than a million known species of insects, which may be less than half the total number of insect species on Earth. In other words, there are many species yet unidentified.

B. The characteristics of the class Insecta are as follows.
   1. Insects have three separate and distinct body regions—head, thorax, and abdomen.
   2. They have one pair of feelers, called antennae, attached to their heads.
   3. They have three pairs of legs, all attached to the thorax. The class Insecta is sometimes called Hexapoda because insects all have six legs (three pairs).
   4. Most insects have one or two pairs of wings, also attached to the thorax.
   5. Most adult insects have both simple eyes, which are made up of just one lens, and compound eyes, which are made up of many single lenses.
   6. In their adult stage, most insects live on land.
   7. They breathe through branching tubes called tracheae that are connected to tiny outside openings, called spiracles, located on each side of the abdomen and thorax.
   8. Insects are able to adjust to their environment well. They have been very successful in their struggle for existence and as an animal group have lived on Earth for a long time.

C. From the time their eggs hatch until the young insects become fully grown adults, most insects pass through a series of forms or stages, a process called **metamorphosis**.
   1. There are three kinds of insect metamorphosis: gradual metamorphosis, incomplete metamorphosis, and complete metamorphosis.
   2. Insects such as the grasshopper, cricket, dragonfly, true bug, aphid, and termite undergo gradual metamorphosis. Gradual metamorphosis has three stages: egg, nymph, and adult.
   3. The nymph hatches from the egg and looks just like the adult, except that it does not have wings or mature sex organs. When it hatches, the nymph is only as large as the egg and its head is much larger than its body.
   4. The nymph eats and grows, but its exoskeleton does not grow as fast as the rest of the nymph. As a result, from time to time the nymph rests, splits and sheds its exoskeleton, and then continues to grow a new, larger one.
   5. The shedding of the exoskeleton is called molting, which usually takes place about five times before the nymph becomes an adult insect. After each molting, the nymph looks and becomes more like the adult insect. After the final molting, the nymph is a fully grown and fully functioning adult.
   6. The metamorphosis of the dragonfly and the damselfly is similar to gradual metamorphosis, except that the second stage, called a naiad, is an aquatic stage in the insect's life cycle. The naiad looks nothing like the adult. This is called **incomplete metamorphosis** and includes three states: egg, naiad, and adult. Fishermen sometimes use naiads as bait for freshwater fishing.
   7. Insects such as the butterfly, moth, bee, ant, beetle, fly, and mosquito undergo **complete metamorphosis**, in which there are four stages: egg, larva, pupa, and adult.
   8. The larva hatches from the egg and looks like a segmented worm. It eats and grows, stopping from time to time to shed its skin (to molt). After each molting, the larva does not change in form but continues to eat and become larger.
   9. After several moltings, the larva enters the pupa stage. Although there are no apparent changes during the pupa stage, an extraordinary transformation nevertheless is taking place. During the pupa stage, all the tissues of the larva change into those of an adult insect. When the change is complete, a fully grown adult insect emerges by biting its way out of the pupa case.
   10. In many insects that undergo complete metamorphosis, the larva has a voracious appetite, whereas the adult form may have incomplete mouthparts and not eat at all.

D. Entomologists divide the class of insects into approximately 26 orders, based largely on the types of metamorphosis and the kinds of mouthparts and wings of the adults. The orders discussed next are perhaps the most common and the most relevant to teaching elementary and middle school children.

E. The grasshopper, cricket (including the Jerusalem cricket or "potato bug"), praying mantis, katydid, walking stick, locust, and cockroach belong to the order **Orthoptera** (which means "straight-winged").

1. Orthopterans undergo gradual metamorphosis.
2. Orthopterans have mouthparts designed for chewing, with jaws that move from side to side.
3. They have two pairs of wings. The front wings are long, narrow, and leathery, and the hind wings look like cellophane and are wide, thin, and veined. When not in use, the hind wings fold up lengthwise like a fan and are protected under the front wings.
4. In some, such as the grasshopper, the rear legs are large and developed for jumping. For its size, the grasshopper has perhaps the greatest jumping ability of any animal on Earth. It can leap a vertical distance of approximately 500 times its own height and it can jump horizontal distances about 20 times its own length.
5. The grasshopper makes sounds by rubbing a row of spines on its rear leg against a wing vein.
6. The grasshopper and cricket eat pasture and grain crops. The praying mantis eats other insects (even its own kind).

F. The dragonfly and damselfly belong to the order **Odonata.**

1. They have long, thin bodies. One of the largest odanates is the **Borneo dragonfly,** which can measure nearly 10 centimeters (4.24 in.) long and have a wingspan of 20 centimeters (7.5 in).
2. Members of this order have chewing mouthparts.
3. They have two pairs of wings; both pairs are thin, like cellophane. The wings do not fold but stick straight out from the body.
4. Odonates undergo incomplete metamorphosis. The larval form is aquatic and feeds on the aquatic larvae of other insects.
5. Adult odonates eat mosquitoes, gnats, and other insects.

G. The Japanese beetle, bark beetle, potato beetle, wood boring beetle, boll weevil, ladybird (sometimes called the "ladybug"; see next section), and carrion beetle belong to the order **Coleoptera,** the order of insects known as beetles.

1. The name Coleoptera means "sheath-winged." Beetles have two pairs of wings. The forward wings are very hard and meet in a straight line down the back, fitting closely over the body and resembling a shell. The rear wings are thin or membranous and fold beneath the front wings when the insect is not in flight. The hard forward wings cause these insects to make a whirring sound when flying.
2. Beetles undergo complete metamorphosis; their larvae are called grubs.
3. Adult beetles have chewing or sucking mouthparts.
4. The potato beetle feeds on potato plants, the boll weevil feeds on grain and cotton, and the Japanese beetle feeds on the fruit and leaves of trees, shrubs, and grasses.
5. The ladybird beetle (sometimes called the "ladybug") feeds on other insects, mainly

LEARNING ACTIVITY 14.9

Exploring Live Insects: Grasshoppers

A. Observing the Grasshopper's Habits

Catch a live grasshopper and put it in a large glass jar along with some twigs, leaves, and blades of grass. Keep the jar covered with a lid that has several holes punched in it. Notice the division of the body into three regions. Locate and identify the parts attached to the head and the thorax. Point out the difference in size of the legs. Watch the grasshopper eat and observe how it chews its food. See how the color of the grasshopper blends in with the color of the leaves and grass. When you hold the grasshopper between your finger and thumb, it will "spit molasses." This brown liquid is partially digested food from the grasshopper's crop. Examine the grasshopper with a magnifying glass. Look at the eyes and the antennae. Find out how many mouth parts it has. Spread out and observe the outer and inner wings. Examine the sides of the abdomen and find the holes that are the openings of the grasshopper's breathing tubes. Trace the life cycle of the grasshopper, using appropriate pictures or drawings. Note that the very young grasshopper has no wings but develops them after it has molted a few times.

B. Organize a Grasshopper Jumping Contest

Divide your class of students into groups, and give each group an adult grasshopper. Hold a grasshopper jumping contest. Have groups predict, observe, measure, and graph how far their grasshoppers jump.

aphids. The carrion beetle acts as a scavenger by feeding on dead animals.

6. The European elm bark beetle is the carrier of a fungus that can kill elm trees (the Dutch elm disease). The fungus blocks the water transfer system of the tree. Once the fungus infects the elm tree, the tree will die. Another beetle lives on the leaves of elm trees and, when not checked by treatment, will quickly defoliate and eventually kill a tree. Other beetles infect still other kinds of trees.

H. Often people use the word *bug* to mean almost any insect, but to entomologists bug refers to just one order of insects, the Hemiptera. The bedbug, stinkbug, squash bug, and water bug belong to this order, but the ladybug and the potato bug do not.

1. In their adult stage true bugs, the hemipterans, have sucking mouthparts and feed by sticking these parts into plants and sucking the plant juices. The bedbug sucks the blood of humans and is a carrier of disease as well.
2. Although a few kinds of bugs have no wings, most have two pairs of wings. Both the front and back wings are thin. The edges of the wings overlap and one-half of the wing is thicker than the other. Hemiptera means "half-winged."
3. Members of this order undergo gradual metamorphosis.

I. The aphid or plant louse, scale insect, mealy bug, leaf hopper, and cicada belong to the order **Homoptera.**

1. Homopterans have sucking mouthparts and feed on the juice of plants. Many do great damage to crop plants; some carry disease. The lac insect, however, is a source of shellac that is used in making lacquers and wood finishes.
2. Some have two pairs of wings, but others are wingless. Those that have wings hold them over their bodies like an upside-down V. Both pairs of wings are thin. The name Homoptera means "like wing."
3. Homopterans undergo gradual metamorphosis.

J. Moths and butterflies belong to the order **Lepidoptera.**

1. Lepidopterans have sucking mouthparts, although some adult moths have no mouthparts at all. Other moths and all butterflies have a long, coiled tube that they use to sip nectar from inside flowers.
2. They have two pairs of wings that are covered with tiny scales. Lepidoptera means "scale-wing." These scales produce the often brilliant and beautiful colors in their wings. Most butterflies and some moths have colorful wings, but the wings of many moths are more subdued in hue.
3. Butterflies and moths undergo complete metamorphosis. Their larvae are called caterpillars or worms, such as the tomato worm and tent caterpillar. The moth larva usually spins a strong silk case, called a cocoon, when it goes into the pupa stage. The butterfly pupa, however, rests in a hardened case called a chrysalis.
4. Many people have difficulty distinguishing between butterflies and moths, especially if both have colorful wings. Here are ways to distinguish between them.

Butterfly Characteristics	Moth Characteristics
Thin abdomen	Thicker abdomen
Antennae usually knobbed on ends	Antennae usually feathery
Flies more commonly during the day	Flies more commonly at night
Wings usually vertical at rest	Wings horizontal at rest
Pupa in a hard chrysalis	Pupa usually in a spun cocoon

5. Some butterflies and moths migrate, traveling to different parts of the country or world

LEARNING ACTIVITY 14.10

Caterpillars, Chrysalids, and Cocoons

Collect some caterpillars and place them in glass jars containing moist soil and some of the leaves on which they were found. Each jar should also have a twig to support the chrysalids or cocoons when they are formed. Cover the mouth of each jar with either fine screen wire or with the jar's lid after it has been perforated several times with a small nail. Put only one caterpillar in a jar to determine whether the caterpillar is a butterfly or moth larva. Continue feeding the caterpillar until it passes into the pupa stage. If the caterpillar is a butterfly larva, it will form the hardened case called a chrysalis. If the caterpillar is a moth, it will spin a cocoon.

Additional chrysalids and cocoons may be collected in the garden and woods. You will have to look carefully, because they often resemble dead leaves or twigs. Place each chrysalis or cocoon in a glass jar with a perforated cover or fine screen wire over the mouth. Each jar should contain some moist soil and a twig for the adult moth or butterfly to stand on when it comes out of its container. Keep the jars in a warm place and examine the chrysalids and cocoons regularly until the adult moths and butterflies emerge. Eventually, turn them loose.

LEARNING ACTIVITY 14.11

Fruit Flies

You can easily collect fruit flies most of the year. Peel a ripe banana and leave the skin, soft side up, on a saucer. Tiny fruit flies will soon gather on the skin. Collect some of the flies and put them in a glass or plastic jar. Put a small piece of banana peel or a thin slice of ripe banana in the jar to keep the fruit flies alive. Plug the mouth of the jar with a wad of cotton. The cotton will keep the fruit flies from escaping but still supply them with air.

Study the behavior of the flies and observe them with a magnifying glass. If the flies mate and lay tiny eggs, observe their life cycle as larvae, pupae, and then adult flies appear. How long does it take for the rapid life cycle to occur? Try to distinguish the male from the female flies. The male fruit fly is a little smaller than the female, and its abdomen tends to be more strongly colored than the female's.

during different seasons of the year. For example, monarch butterflies live in the northern United States during summer. In late summer, they fly away in very large groups, some going to the Gulf states and others to the Pacific Coast, where they remain until winter is over. In spring they fly northward again.

6. The larvae of butterflies and especially moths can be very destructive to plants. The apple worm, tomato worm, corn borer, cabbage worm, cotton boll weevil, and tobacco worm all eat and destroy vegetables and crops. The larvae of the gypsy moth and browntail moth destroy forest and orchard trees by eating their leaves. The larvae of the clothes moth feed on clothing, especially wool.
7. The silkworm moth larva spins a cocoon of silk threads, which people use to make silk cloth.
8. All butterflies and many moths play an important role in the cross-pollination of flowers as they travel from flower to flower in their search for nectar.

K. The housefly, tsetse fly, stable fly, and mosquito belong to the order **Diptera.**

1. Diptera usually have mouthparts specialized for sucking. Mosquitoes, for example, do not bite. They stab their hosts and then suck up to three times their own weight in blood in one feeding.
2. Except for some fruit flies that only have rudimentary wings and cannot fly, members of this order have just one pair of thin but highly developed wings with veins. The name Diptera means "two-wing."
3. Members of this order undergo complete metamorphosis.
4. The housefly has large eyes, short antennae, and a baseball-bat-shaped sucking tube. The housefly does not bite. Other flies, such as the horsefly and the tsetse fly, do bite.
5. The housefly's feet have suction pads and sticky hairs, which help it attach securely to walls, windows, and ceilings. The sticky hairs work well only if they are free from dust. The fly seems to always be cleaning its feet.
6. The female housefly lays its eggs in manure or decaying organic matter. Its larvae that hatch are commonly called maggots.
7. The fly carries many kinds of bacteria on its hairy feet and body. When a fly lands on food, it can leave bacteria that cause serious human diseases, such as typhoid fever, dysentery, and cholera.
8. The female mosquito lays its eggs in water. Larvae that hatch are commonly called wigglers. The pupa stage of the mosquito is different from most insect pupa stages in that mosquito pupae are mobile.
9. The adult mosquito has mouthparts that are designed for stabbing and sucking. The mosquito (only the female) usually feeds on the blood of people and other animals. To make it easier to suck blood and to prevent the blood from clotting, the mosquito injects a little of its saliva into the host. The saliva contains a chemical that prevents blood from clotting and causes the irritation and swelling that we know as a mosquito bite.
10. Some female mosquitoes carry the organisms that cause diseases, such as malaria (caused by a protozoan) and yellow fever (caused by a virus), and spread these diseases from person to person as they bite and suck blood.

L. Bees, hornets, wasps, and ants belong to the order **Hymenoptera.**

1. Hymenopterans usually have two pairs of thin, veined wings, with the front pair much larger than the back pair. The name Hymenoptera means "membrane wing."
2. They have biting, sucking, or lapping mouthparts.
3. They undergo complete metamorphosis.
4. There is a defined narrowing, or constriction, between the thorax and the abdomen.
5. Although most insects live alone, some live together in large groups or communities, called colonies. These insects are called **social insects** because different members of the

colony have special jobs that help the colony. Most hymenopterans are social insects.

M. In a **bee colony**, there are three kinds of bees—the queen, the drones, and the workers.
   1. The **queen** is the only egg-laying bee. Although one colony may contain 50,000 individual bees, there is only one queen.
   2. The queen is the largest bee in the colony. She has a long, pointed abdomen with an egg-laying organ at the tip of the last abdominal segment. Her only function is to lay eggs so that the colony can continue to exist. She can lay about 1,500 eggs a day. She usually lives 5 or 6 years, although some queen bees have been known to live for 10 years.
   3. The queen is mated just once, by a drone, while in flight. From that mating, she will receive several million sperm cells that she keeps in a pouch in her body and uses to fertilize eggs for the rest of her life.
   4. She can lay both fertilized and unfertilized eggs. Fertilized eggs develop into non-egg-laying females, which become the workers. Unfertilized eggs develop into males, called drones.
   5. Drones are smaller than the queen bee, but larger than the female workers. There are hundreds of drones in a colony. They have fat bodies, large eyes, and powerful wings, but no stinger.
   6. Drones do no work. Worker bees care for them. Their mouthparts are not long enough to suck up nectar, so the workers must feed them. The drones' only function is to mate with the queen. Their big eyes help them find her as she flies.
   7. During summer there are usually a few hundred drones around the beehive, but only one of them mates with the queen. Soon after mating with the queen, the drone dies. In fall, when the supply of honey is low, the workers refuse to feed the drones and sting them to death.
   8. The workers are infertile female bees, developed from fertilized eggs. Workers are the smallest bees in the colony and the most numerous. There are thousands of workers in each colony.
   9. Worker bees have a stinger at the tip of their last abdominal segment, which is connected to a gland that produces a poison. Drones do not have stingers. When a worker bee stings a person or animal, usually the stinger and parts of the bee's internal organs are pulled out and the bee dies.
   10. Although workers are infertile and, therefore, cannot lay eggs, they carry on all the other duties of the colony. They bring in the nectar and pollen from flowers. Most bees we see flying around are worker bees.
   11. Workers prepare the materials and build the honeycomb that makes up the hive. They collect and prepare food for members of the colony. Some feed and groom the queen, others feed the drones, and still others nurse feeding larvae that hatch from the eggs laid by the queen.
   12. Some workers guard the hive and keep it clean. Others fan the hive, either to keep it airy and cool or to help speed evaporation that thickens the honey. Indeed, worker bees are "busy little bees" during their brief 6-week life in the summer working season. Worker bees that hatch in fall or winter may live for as long as 6 months.
   13. Worker bees learn by early adulthood to recognize certain scents carried by bees of their colony. They reject or accept other bees depending on their scents.
   14. Their mouthparts form a long tube (called the proboscis), that makes it possible for the bee to suck up nectar from flowers. The nectar is sucked into the bee's honey stomach, or crop, where it remains until it is taken to the hive to be used as food.
   15. Although pollen collects on all parts of a bee's hairy body and legs, much of it is deposited in a hairy cavity, called a pollen basket, located on its hind legs. Pollen brought back to the hive is made into food.
   16. The workers make three kinds of material for use in the hive: wax, honey, and propolis. The wax oozes out of the segments of a worker's abdomen. It usually is produced after the worker has eaten a lot of honey. Other workers remove the wax that forms, chew it to make it soft, and then take it to still other workers who use the wax to make the honeycomb of the hive—a structure made of six-sided cells.
   17. The honeycomb is used for storing honey and a special food, called beebread, that is made by the bees from pollen and bee saliva.
   18. The queen also puts eggs into the honeycomb, one to a cell, where they hatch into larvae that, in turn, are cared for by the worker bees.
   19. Honey is made from flower nectar that the bees have collected in their stomachs (crops). In their stomachs, the nectar is changed into honey, which is then emptied into the cells of the honeycomb. The honey thickens as the water it contains evaporates. When the honey is thick enough, the bees seal the cell.
   20. Propolis is bee glue. It is a brown material collected from the sticky leaf buds of certain plants. The workers use propolis to hold the honeycomb together, to patch up holes and cracks, to make the inside of the cells smooth, and sometimes to cover the body of a small, dead animal that has died inside the hive.

21. A worker bee can handle 300 times its own weight, the equivalent of a human moving a 10-ton object.
22. Bees communicate with one another by doing different kinds of dances. In this way, they are able to tell other workers in their colony where they have found pollen and nectar.
23. Occasionally, during early spring or summer, a large group of bees may swarm; that is, they leave the hive to look for location to start a new home. Bees may swarm because the colony has become too big or because food in the vicinity has become scarce. Sometimes they leave if another queen is developed in the colony.
24. A queen develops when the workers give a fertilized egg special treatment. The workers make one cell of the honeycomb larger, and when the egg hatches, the workers feed the larva a substance called royal jelly, which is a special mixture of honey and pollen. The larva is fed this royal jelly until it spins a cocoon and enters the pupa stage. Later, when it emerges from this pupa stage, it is an adult queen bee.
25. The new queen bee will try to kill the old one. If workers prevent this action, the new queen bee, many workers, and some drones swarm from the hive.
26. After a new colony is established, the queen bee flies into the air and is followed by the drones. One drone mates with the queen, after which the drone dies and the queen returns to the hive to lay eggs for the rest of her life.

N. **Ants**, too, are social insects.
1. There are many different species of ants, some large and others quite small.
2. It has been estimated that ants constitute a greater biomass than any other single group of organisms on Earth.
3. Some ant species live in tunnels in the ground. Others build large mounds, called anthills. Still others live in decaying trees.
4. Ants cannot sting like bees, but they have a strong bite and powerful jaws.
5. Like a bee colony, an ant colony has many workers but relatively fewer males. An ant colony also has many queens, living peacefully together.
6. Both queens and males have wings, but workers do not.
7. During the mating season, the females fly high into the air, followed by the males.
8. The males mate with the females, depositing a huge number of sperm cells. The males die soon after mating with the females.
9. The females return to Earth, bite off their own wings, and begin laying eggs.
10. Many species of ants also have soldiers in their colonies. They have larger heads and powerful biting jaws. Soldiers do the fighting for a colony.
11. Soldier ants sometimes attack another ant colony. If they defeat the other colony, they carry away the larvae and pupae of the conquered ants. When these captured larvae and pupae become mature ants, they become slave workers for the colony.
12. All ants undergo complete metamorphosis. Their eggs are tiny and generally can be seen only with the aid of a magnifying glass. Their larvae are usually white and have no legs.
13. When the larvae go into the pupa stage, they usually spin white cocoons, sometimes mistakenly called "ant eggs."
14. With an ability to lift 50 times their own body weight, the workers in an ant colony have many duties. They take care of and protect the larvae and pupae, gather food for the colony, build the anthill, and keep the colony clean.
15. Many species of ants keep their own "cows," which are aphids. During the winter the ants carry these aphids into their colony and care for them. In spring the ants set the aphids on plants, where the aphids feed. The ants then stroke the bodies of the aphids with their antennae, which causes the aphids to give off a sweet liquid that the ants drink.

O. Over the course of their evolutionary development many insects have developed a means of camouflage, which protects them from their enemies.
1. Some insects have developed protective coloration that causes them to blend with their environment. The grasshopper's wings and upper parts are green, blending with the grass so that it is not easily seen. The praying mantis is the same color as a green leaf and so is not easily detected.
2. Some insects have adapted their appearances and look like the objects on which they rest. The walking stick, a relative of the grasshopper and member of the order Orthoptera, looks like a twig. The walking-leaf butterfly looks like a large green leaf. The dead-leaf butterfly looks like a dead leaf.
3. Some insects look like other, more annoying insects. The robber fly looks like a bumblebee, but it is a fly, not a bee. The viceroy butterfly looks very much like the monarch butterfly, which apparently tastes bad to birds.
4. The harvestman, or daddy longlegs, looks very much like a long-legged spider, but with its long, segmented abdomen and three pairs of legs, it is an insect, *not* a spider. When irritated, it will vibrate its body causing the entire web to vibrate, which probably confuses its enemies into believing it is larger than it is. It is found in gardens, fields,

and woods, where it feeds on aphids, and sometimes in human dwellings, where it feeds on mites.

P. Some insects are beneficial to humans, and others are detrimental to human interests.
   1. Many insects, such as bees, wasps, butterflies, moths, beetles, bugs, and certain kinds of flies, play an important part in the pollination of plants. Also, bees produce honey and beeswax. The silk moth gives us silk. The lac insect gives us shellac. The bodies of some insects, such as the cochineal insect, are ground up to produce dyes. Some insects, such as the dragonfly, praying mantis, and ladybug, prey on harmful insects. Others, such as the carrion beetle, are scavengers that feed on the dead bodies of animals.
   2. Many insects, including the grasshopper, cricket, boll weevil, fruit fly, and Japanese beetle, destroy grain crops, vegetables, and fruits. Some insects, especially certain kinds of moths and beetles, destroy entire forests of trees. Other insects, such as the termite, damage wooden buildings and foundations. Certain moths and beetles destroy clothes and carpets. Others, such as the mosquito, flea, louse, and fly, carry disease-causing microorganisms to humans and animals. Some insects, like the flea, louse, and bedbug, are parasites on humans and pet animals.

Q. Scientists have devised many methods for controlling harmful insects.
   1. One method is habitat control. For example, draining ditches and ponds where mosquitoes breed breaks the life cycle of these insects. Changing or rotating crops that certain insects depend on for food eliminates their food supply.
   2. Another method is the enforcement of quarantine laws to prevent the intentional or inadvertent importing of insects into a state or country. Sometimes the eggs or larvae of insects are inadvertently brought into an area because they are hidden on plants or fruit. These insects can destroy the balance of nature in the area if there are no natural predators of the insects to hold them in check. The insects can quickly become numerous and highly destructive. Agricultural inspectors at seaports, state lines, and airline terminals inspect plants and fruit coming into the area and take away and destroy those suspected of carrying harmful insects.
   3. A third method of controlling harmful insects is chemical control. Stomach poisons can be sprayed on plants that are attacked by chewing insects. Contact poisons, sprayed on plants that are attacked by insects that suck rather than chew leaves, kill as they come in contact with an insect's body. Poison gases that enter an insect's body through the tiny openings (spiracles) on each side of the thorax and abdomen kill insects instantly. Some gases, like the vapor used for controlling the clothes moth, do not kill adult insects but do discourage them.
      a. Many people, scientists included, are concerned about the use of chemical insecticides. Insecticides can have detrimental effects. They can enter plants and be eaten by humans; they can pollute streams and kill life in the streams; and they can kill valuable birds, animals, and insects.
      b. Many insect species build up a resistance to chemical poisons, with a larger percentage of each subsequent generation resistant to the chemical. This can render insecticides ineffective, unless their concentrations of poisonous ingredients are increased. But increases in the concentration of poisonous ingredients makes the insecticides more and more unsafe to use.
   4. Another method is biological control.
      a. One form of biological control is to import natural enemies of the insects or to make use of local natural enemies. Birds are among the best natural enemies of insects. Other natural enemies are spiders, frogs, toads, and snakes. Importing a natural enemy can become a problem if the balance of nature is upset and the natural enemy becomes too numerous and becomes destructive itself.
      b. Another form of biological control is sterilization. A large number of insects are exposed to X-rays, radioactive materials, or chemicals to make them sterile and thereby reduce the population.

IV. Spiders, Ticks, Mites, and Scorpions

A. **Arachnida** is the class of arthropods that consists of spiders and their close relatives, the ticks, mites, and scorpions. Arachnids are not insects. Their characteristics are different from those of insects and other arthropods, which place them in their separate class.
   1. Whereas most arthropods have three body regions—head, thorax, and abdomen—arachnids have no distinct thorax.
   2. Arachnids have six pairs of jointed appendages. The first pair, called chelicerae, are located near the mouth. In arachnids, chelicerae are usually modified as pincers to hold food, or as fangs that can inject prey with poison.
   3. Arachnids do not have antennae. Their second pair of appendages, called the pedipalps, are adapted for handling food and for sensing.
   4. The two remaining pairs of appendages are legs used for locomotion.

B. A **spider's** head and thorax are joined together, whereas an insect's head and thorax are separate from each other.
   1. Spiders have only simple eyes, each made of just one lens. Nearly all insects have compound eyes made up of many lenses.
   2. Spiders have two pairs of appendages attached to their heads. One pair, the chelicerae, are hollow and have small openings in their tips, through which poison from glands in the spider's head can be injected into a victim. The other pair, the pedipalps, are used as feelers. They also are used by the male spider to hold sperm cells during union with a female.
   3. A spider usually has eight eyes, arranged in a definite pattern on its head. This pattern varies among the different kinds of spiders and is used in classifying spiders.
   4. The breathing organs of spiders are called book lungs, because their folds look like pages of a book. Spiders usually have either two or four of these book lungs. Air enters the book lungs from a slit in the spider's abdomen.
   5. Many spiders have three pairs of appendages called spinnerets on the tip of the underside of the abdomen. Each spinneret contains hundreds of tubes. Liquid silk from the spider's silk glands flows through these tubes out into the air, where it hardens to form a thread. This thread is used to spin a web and to build cocoons or nests for eggs.
   6. In fall, the young of some spiders spin long threads. When wind catches the thread, it carries the young far away.
   7. Spiders bite but do not sting. When they bite, they inject poison into the victim. In humans, this can cause pain and swelling.
   8. Spiders usually mate in late summer or early fall. The female spider is usually larger than the male. In many species, the female eats the male after mating.
   9. The female lays a large batch of eggs, around which she spins a cocoon or nest. Some females die soon after laying their eggs. The eggs hatch in winter, and the young stay inside the cocoon or nest. Young spiders often are cannibalistic. In spring the spiders that have survived leave the cocoon or nest.
   10. Spiders feed mostly on insects by sucking the juices from them.

C. The tarantula, or banana spider, can measure as much as 15 to 20 centimeters (6 to 8 in.) across when its legs are spread. The cane spider, which lives in sugar cane fields, is similar in size. One of the largest spiders is the South American bird-eating spider, which has a body about 9 centimeters (3.5 in.) long and a leg span up to 25 centimeters (10 in.).
   1. These spiders are found mostly in the tropics, where they eat insects but sometimes attack small mammals and birds.
   2. Their bite is painful, but not deadly, to humans.

D. The black widow spider is found mostly in warm, temperate climates.
   1. Its most distinguishing physical characteristic is its round, black abdomen with a red hourglass-shaped spot on the underside.
   2. The female is vicious. After mating, she kills the male, unless he is able to protect himself by binding her with web silk.
   3. To humans, a black widow bite is painful and poisonous, sometimes causing death. This is especially true of the Australian black widow spider.
   4. Because the thread of the black widow spider is so fine and strong, and will stretch about 30% before breaking, it has been used in marking lenses of gunsights; bombsights; and surveying, navigational, and astronomical instruments. Its use is now giving way to synthetic materials.

E. The brown recluse spider has a violin-shaped figure on the underside of its abdomen. It is found in temperate climates and has a poison that can be fatal to humans.

F. Trap-door spiders are found in the southeastern and western United States. Instead of spinning webs to catch insects, they build a kind of trapdoor. They dig a tubelike hole in the ground, line it with silk, and fasten a hinged "door" over the hole. When an insect prey comes into the hole, the open door is shut tight, trapping the insect.

G. The **scorpion** is found in all tropical countries and in the southern and southwestern United States. It has many abdominal segments and large pincers.
   1. In addition to its four pairs of walking legs, a scorpion has a large pair of appendages attached to its head, with a large pincer at the end of each appendage.
   2. It has a long, segmented abdomen that forms a tail at the end. At the tip of the tail is a poisonous stinger that the scorpion uses to kill insects and spiders. The scorpion's sting is very painful, but seldom fatal, to humans.

H. Related to the scorpion is the horseshoe or king crab (which is not a crab). This marine animal is considered to be a living fossil because it has remained relatively unchanged since it first appeared on Earth some 500 million years ago. It lives on the ocean floor.

I. **Mites** and **ticks** are small arachnids with only a single body section—the head, thorax, and abdomen are completely fused.
   1. They live mostly as parasites on the bodies of humans and other animals. They can carry

germs from one host to the next. Mites carry the diseases that cause sheep and dog mange.
2. Ticks carry Rocky Mountain spotted fever, Texas cattle fever, and Lyme disease.
3. Lyme disease, so-called because it was first discovered in Lyme, Connecticut, in 1975, is a disease caused by a corkscrew-shaped bacterium that is transmitted to humans through the bite of certain ticks. The ticks pick up the bacteria by sucking the blood of infected deer and white-footed mice. Lyme disease is a crippling disease but if diagnosed and treated early, it can be arrested with antibiotics.
4. Chiggers are mites that bore into the skin, causing itchiness and pain. The "red spider" that feeds on apple leaves and fruit is a mite, not a spider.

V. **Centipedes and Millipedes**

A. Centipedes and millipedes belong to the class **Myriapoda**, which means "many feet."
   1. They both have bodies composed of many segments.
   2. The head of each has its antennae and mouthparts.

B. The centipede's first body segment has a pair of poison claws. Because of their poison, centipedes are dangerous.
   1. All other segments, except the last two, have one pair of legs each.
   2. The centipede moves relatively fast.

C. The millipede's body segments, except the last two, have two pairs of legs each.
   1. It moves slowly and may curl up when disturbed.
   2. Millipedes are not poisonous.

Vertebrates

I. **Phylum Chordata**

A. Characteristics of this phylum are as follows.
   1. All chordates have a dorsal hollow nerve cord.
   2. In their embryonic state, they have an anterior-posterior axis that provides a support structure. This structure is called the notochord.
   3. Most adult chordates have a backbone, which develops around the notochord. These chordates comprise the subphylum called Vertebrata—the vertebrates.
   4. At some point during their development, chordates have pharyngeal gill slits and a muscular post-anal tail.
   5. Most chordates have an internal skeleton, called an endoskeleton.
   6. Most have two pairs of limbs attached to their bodies.

B. The major classes of chordates are Osteichthyes and Chondrichthyes (collectively referred to as fish), Amphibia, Reptilia, Aves, and Mammalia.

C. Both fish and amphibians evolved from a primitive fish called the lobefin, which lived from about 380 million to 80 million years ago. Lobefins had both fins and a primitive lung.
   1. The coelacanth is a lobefin that was thought to be extinct until it was discovered in 1938 in waters off the coast of South Africa. More recently, coelacanths have also been found living in Indonesian waters 6,000 miles from Africa.

Fish

I. **Classification and Location of Fish**

A. Fish are members of the phylum Chordata and share the characteristics common to that phylum. Fish are grouped into three classes: bony fish (Osteichthyes), lampreys (Agnatha), and sharks and rays (Chondrichthyes).
   1. The Osteichthyes have skeletons of bone.
   2. The skeletons of the Agnatha and Chondrichthyes are made of a tough tissue called cartilage.

B. Fish only live in water—in the ocean, lakes, ponds, rivers, and brooks. Some live near the surface of the water; others live closer to the bottom. Mudskippers that live in the mangrove swamps of Malaysia can use their specialized fins to climb on the exposed roots and branches of the mangrove trees. Some fish live alone; others travel in large groups, called schools.

C. Fish eat a variety of foods.
   1. Some fish eat only algae and aquatic plants.
   2. Many are carnivorous, eating foods such as insects, worms, crayfish, snails, and other fish.
   3. Fish that are carnivorous have many sharp teeth. The teeth slant backward toward the throat, making it easy for a fish to swallow the prey and making it hard for the prey to escape. Fish can use their teeth to seize, tear, and hold food, but they cannot chew.

II. **Physical Characteristics of Fish**

A. Fish range in size from less than 2.5 centimeters (1 in.) long to as much as 15 meters (49 ft) long. Most fish are less than 1 meter (3 ft) long.

LEARNING ACTIVITY 14.12

The Classroom Aquarium

A rectangular tank that holds 23 liters (6 gal) is an excellent size for classrooms. Clean the tank thoroughly with detergent and water and rinse it several times. Obtain enough aquarium gravel from a pet shop to cover the bottom of the tank 5 centimeters (2 in.) deep. Before adding it to the tank, place the gravel in a large pan, tilt the pan to one side, and allow running water to flow in and then overflow the pan. Continue running the water into the pan until the gravel is quite clean.

Place the gravel evenly in the tank, add one or two colored rocks, and put a few clam or oyster shells in the gravel. The shells will slowly dissolve in the water and provide the calcium that the growing snails will need for their shells.

Lay a piece of paper over the gravel so that when water is poured into the tank, the water will not become cloudy (cloudiness usually lasts a long time). Use either clear pond water or tap water that has been allowed to stand for two days so that the chlorine dissolved in it can escape. Pour the water into the tank almost to the top.

Place the tank in north or east light, but not in direct sunlight. From the pet shop, obtain some rooted plants, such as sagittaria or valisneria, and some floating plants, such as elodea or cabomba. Place the plants toward the back of the tank so you will have a clear view of the fish. The water plants will take in the carbon dioxide given off by the fish and give off oxygen that the fish will need. Remove any dead leaves. Allow the aquarium to stand for about a week until the water is clear and the plants are growing.

Now you are ready to add the fish. Do not overcrowd the aquarium. About one 2-centimeter (3/4 in.) fish to every 3 liters (1 gal) of water is recommended. The 23-liter (6-gal) tank will hold either six 2-centimeter (3/4-in.) fish or three 5-centimeter (2-in.) fish. Obtain small, active fish, such as guppies, rather than goldfish, which tend to be sluggish.

Add about six to twelve snails, also obtained from the pet shop, and then place a glass cover over the tank. Do not overfeed the fish; uneaten food causes the water to become foul, and the fish may die. Fish will eat prepared fish food, bread crumbs, bits of egg yolk, and oatmeal. Occasionally, give them small amounts of chopped earth worms or meal worms.

Observe the fish in your aquarium. Compare shapes and sizes of the head, trunk, and tail regions. Identify the fins, and see which fins are paired. Observe how the fish use their fins and tails. Watch the eyes and see whether they move. Note how the fish take in water through their mouths and then force the water out through their gill covers. See how easily the fish can rise or sink in the water without using their fins very much. This movement is made possible by the inflation or deflation of the air bladder inside the fish.

Remove a small fish from the aquarium and wrap it in wet absorbent cotton, leaving only the tail exposed. Place the fish on a flat glass dish and observe the tail. You will see the arteries, veins, and capillaries. Note the blood cells moving through the blood vessels—quickly through the arteries and slowly through the veins. In the small capillaries, the blood cells move almost in single file. Switch to the high power of the microscope and observe the blood cells. Do not keep the fish out of water this way for more than 15 minutes.

B. There are three parts to the body of a fish—head, body, and tail.
   1. The head has no neck and is attached directly to the body.
   2. The body is the largest part of a fish. The body is streamlined and tapers at both ends.
   3. The tail is narrow and immediately behind the body. It is often confused with the tail fin.

C. The bodies of most fish are covered with scales that grow from pockets in the skin and overlap one another like the shingles on the roof of a house.
   1. The skin of a fish secretes mucus that oozes between the scales and covers the body, lubricating the body and making it easier for the fish to swim.
   2. The mucus also protects the fish from being attacked by small parasites in the water.

D. Some fish are brightly colored, either partially or completely. The colors are often arranged in spots, lines, or bars.
   1. Many fish are dark-colored on top and light-colored beneath, a camouflage pattern that helps them to avoid being seen by their enemies from either above or below.

E. Most fish have large eyes that are partially movable. They have no eyelids.
   1. Compared with pupils in the eyes of other vertebrates, the pupil of the fish eye is large and can admit a large amount of light.

F. The body of a fish has several appendages called fins.
   1. Each fin is made of many bony spines called rays, which are covered by a thin fold of skin.
   2. Corresponding to the front legs of land vertebrates, a pair of fins called the pectoral fins is located near the head.
   3. Posterior to the pectoral fins is a second pair of fins called the pelvic fins, which correspond to the rear legs of land vertebrates.
   4. Along the dorsal (back) side of the body are one or two dorsal fins.
   5. Along the ventral (front) side of the body, toward the tail, there is a caudal fin, which is the end of the fish's tail.

G. Fish are ectothermic animals, meaning that the temperature of their blood is approximately the same as that of the surrounding water. Consequently, the blood temperature varies with the seasons.

III. How Fish Breathe

A. Located on each side of the head are the respiratory organs, called gills.
   1. The gills are made of many small, threadlike filaments, giving them a feathery appearance. Each filament contains tiny, thin-walled blood vessels.
   2. Most fish obtain oxygen from water by opening and closing their mouths. When a fish opens its mouth, water rushes in. When the fish closes its mouth, the water is forced out through two openings on each side of the back of the head. A movable external flap called an operculum covers each opening.
   3. There are four or five gills in each gill chamber located just in front of the opening. As water is forced out over the gills, dissolved oxygen in the water passes through the thin walls of the blood vessels and is picked up by the blood. The blood exchanges its carbon dioxide for the fresh oxygen.
   4. Because cold water holds more oxygen than warm water, fish are more active in cool water than in warm water.

IV. How Fish Move

A. A fish swims forward rapidly by moving its tail and tail fin from side to side.
B. Dorsal fins are used mostly for balance.
C. The paired pectoral and pelvic fins have several functions.
   1. They help a fish maintain its balance when it is resting.
   2. They help the fish steer to the right or left when it is swimming.
   3. When spread out at right angles, they act as brakes to help the fish come to a stop.
   4. A fish also uses its fins to swim backward.
D. In shallow waters off the southernmost coast of Australia, scientists have found a fish, called the handfish, whose pectoral and pelvic fins look and act more like legs with feet. The handfish tends to walk rather than swim.
E. Most fish have a swim bladder inside their bodies, located beneath the backbone and surrounded by the ribs.
   1. The swim bladder makes it possible for the fish to rise, sink, or stay at a particular depth.
   2. Fish sink as more air is taken into the swim bladder and rise as air is released from it. The overall volume of the fish remains fairly constant while the amount of air taken into the swim bladder from the gills increases or decreases. As the swim bladder takes in more air, the overall density (specific gravity) of the fish increases to more than 1 (the specific gravity of freshwater is approximately 1) and the fish sinks in the water.

V. How Fish Reproduce

A. Most fish develop from eggs that the female deposits outside her body.
   1. At a certain time of the year, a female fish lays a large number of eggs. This process is called spawning.
   2. Shortly after spawning, the male swims over the eggs and secretes a liquid called milt that contains large numbers of sperm cells.
   3. The sperm cells swim to the eggs and fertilize them by uniting with them. When fertilization takes place outside the female's body, it is called external fertilization.
   4. The fertilized eggs develop and hatch into tiny fish, usually from 10 to 40 days later, depending on the kind of fish and the temperature of the water.
   5. While the fish are developing from the egg, the yolk of the egg feeds them.
   6. The yolk is contained within the yolk sac, which remains attached to the newborn fish for some time after they hatch, supplying them with food.
B. The young of some freshwater tropical fish, like the guppy, molly, and swordtail, develop inside the female's body and are born alive.
   1. The female of these fish keeps her eggs inside her body and receives the sperm of the male when he mates with her, in a process called internal fertilization.
   2. The sperm fertilize the eggs, which develop inside the female's body and then are brought forth alive.
C. As a rule, most freshwater fish either spawn where they live or travel a short distance to shallower water for spawning. The eel, however, has an unusual spawning habit.
   1. Eels live in rivers and streams that flow into the ocean.
   2. At spawning time, eels that live in rivers flowing into the Atlantic Ocean and the Gulf of Mexico swim far out into the Atlantic Ocean.
   3. The female lays her eggs and the male deposits his sperm on the eggs. Then both adult eels die.
   4. When the young eels that hatch are about 5 centimeters (2 in.) long, they return to the rivers and streams from which their parents came.
   5. After 3 to 8 years, the adult eels return to the same part of the Atlantic Ocean for spawning.
   6. Although both North American and European eels spawn in the same part of the Atlantic

Ocean, the young eels never make a mistake and go to the wrong continent.

D. The **Pacific salmon** also has unusual spawning habits.
   1. The adult fish live in the ocean along the north Pacific coast.
   2. At spawning time, they swim up the Columbia River to the streams where they hatched 3 or 4 years earlier.
   3. The females spawn, and the males deposit their sperm to fertilize the eggs. Both adults soon die.
   4. The young salmon that hatch from the eggs swim to the ocean and live there for 3 or 4 years until it is time for them to spawn.

VI. The Conservation of Fish

A. Fish are an important source of food for humans.
   1. Common saltwater food fish include tuna, herring, sardine, swordfish, halibut, cod, mackerel, haddock, sole, flounder, and sea perch.
   2. Common freshwater food fish include trout, salmon, pike, whitefish, perch, buffalo carp, and catfish.
   3. The eggs of sturgeon, commonly called caviar, and of the shad roe are eaten as food.
   4. Oil from the liver of the codfish, halibut, and shark is rich in vitamins A and D.

B. Ground fish, called fishmeal, is used in making foods for cats, dogs, and chickens.

C. Many people catch fish for sport and recreation, as well as for food.

D. Fish oil is used in making certain paints.

E. The bones and other body parts of fish are used to make glue.

F. Fish are sometimes lost from bodies of water, usually because of human interference.
   1. The water level of a lake may become lower during hot, dry spells or because of unwise treatment of the land around the lake. This lowering of the water level may destroy spawning areas or areas where the food supplies are rich.
   2. Sometimes humans straighten river channels, which can discourage the breeding of fish; fish live better in rivers that have bends, rapids, and quiet pools.
   3. Dams across rivers prevent fish from traveling upstream to spawn.
   4. Lakes and streams are sometimes contaminated by sewage and chemical wastes that can poison and kill the fish.
   5. Sometimes too many adult fish are caught during the spawning season, or too many young fish are caught before they can become adults and have the opportunity to breed new fish.

G. To protect and conserve fish, states have passed many laws.
   1. There are restrictions regarding the catching of fish. Fish under a certain length cannot be kept; they must be thrown back. One person may catch only a certain number of fish in one day. Certain fish may not be caught during their spawning season.
   2. Sewage and chemical wastes cannot be dumped in certain lakes and streams that have been set aside for fishing.
   3. Dams that interfere with the travel of fish upstream to spawn must have fish ladders beside them, a series of small pools, one higher than the other, connected by small waterfalls that the fish can leap.

H. Both the federal and the state governments have established fish hatcheries to breed and raise fish for lakes and streams. In a hatchery, eggs are taken from the female and put into a tank; then milt, containing the sperm of the male, is poured over the eggs. In this way, almost all the eggs are fertilized and hatch. When the young fish are old enough to take care of themselves, they are released into lakes and streams.

I. Scientists constantly monitor diseases, fungus infections, and natural enemies of fish in an effort to maintain a balance in nature.

VII. The Cartilaginous Fish

A. The **lamprey** belongs to the class **Agnatha.**
   1. Some kinds of lampreys live in saltwater, and others in freshwater.
   2. With its long, thin body the lamprey resembles an eel.
   3. Its skeleton is made of cartilage rather than bone.
   4. It has a soft, slimy skin.
   5. Its only fins are two fins along its back and a tail fin.
   6. It has no jaws, but it does have a round sucking mouth lined with sharp teeth.
   7. Its tongue is hard and rough, with teeth on it.
   8. The lamprey is a parasite, living on the blood of other fish. Its sucking mouth clamps onto the side of a fish, and its teeth and tongue rip through the scales and flesh of the victim. The lamprey then sucks out the blood, and sometimes even the internal organs.

B. The **shark** belongs to the class **Chondrichthyes.**
   1. Sharks live only in saltwater.
   2. Depending on the species, sharks range in size from about two-thirds of a meter (2 ft) long to 20 meters (60 ft) or longer.
   3. A shark's scales lie side by side rather than overlapping like those of bony fish.
   4. Its fins are very much like those of a bony fish, but the dorsal surface of its tail fin is longer than the ventral (lower) surface.
   5. Its mouth, on the lower side of its head, is lined with rows of very sharp teeth.
   6. Sharks feed on other fish and sea animals, dead or alive.

7. The **tiger shark** is a deadly predator that will eat most anything that is dead or alive.
   a. Tiger sharks average about 4 meters (13 ft) in length, but can be twice that length.
   b. Tiger sharks live mainly in tropical, coastal waters throughout the world. They spread north and south during summer months, frequently inhabiting deep waters on the fringe of reefs. Occasionally they will move into the channels of the reef and up to within a few feet of shorelines in search of prey.
   c. The small pits on each side of its head are electrical sensors that allow the tiger shark to sense even the tiniest muscle movement of other animals, so it can find prey even in dark waters.
   d. In addition, the tiger shark has an acute sense of smell that enables it to sense even the faintest traces of blood in the water and follow them to their source.
   e. The wedge-shaped head of the tiger shark gives it minimum side resistance in the water, allowing it to make quick turns. Its pectoral fins act like wings, providing lift as the shark swims. The long upper lobe on its tail fin provides thrust for sudden bursts of speed.
8. The **great white shark** is the largest predatory shark, reaching a length of more than 7 meters (23 ft) and weighing 3,175 kilograms (7,000 lb) or more. An individual shark may live for as long as 50 years.
   a. The great white is found in temperate oceans, mainly in the shallow coastal waters of North America, southern Africa, Australia, New Zealand, Japan, and the Mediterranean.
   b. The spindle-shaped, streamlined body of the great white helps make it one of the fastest and most dangerous predators in the sea.

C. The **ray** is also known as the devilfish, sting ray, or blanket fish.
   1. It has a large, flat body that looks like a blanket.
   2. The ray lives only in saltwater and often lies half buried in the sand.
   3. When it swims, the sides of its body look somewhat like moving wings.
   4. It has a long, whiplike tail with a sharp spine that can penetrate its victim and cause tissue damage, infection, swelling, and severe pain. The ray's spine is a skin-covered cartilage bone located at the base of the tail, near the anus, not at the end of its tail. There is no poisonous secretion, but the skin on the spine is covered with bacteria that can cause an infection in the punctured victim. The ray uses this spine to wound its prey.

Amphibians

I. The Classification of Amphibians

A. Amphibians are members of the animal phylum **Chordata** and share the characteristics of this phylum with other classes of chordates.
   1. Common amphibians include frogs, toads, and salamanders. Caecilians are a less-common group of amphibians that live in burrows in damp ground of tropical regions. Without limbs or a pelvis, and ranging in length from 10 to 127 centimeters (8 to 50 in.), caecilians have a worm-like appearance.
   2. Most frogs and toads are from 5 to 15 centimeters (2 to 6 in.) long, although the African frog is about 30 centimeters (12 in.) long; salamanders are 5 centimeters (2 in.) to 2/3 meter (2 ft) long, but there is a giant salamander in Japan that is 1.5 meters (5 ft) long.

B. Amphibians also have their own special characteristics that separate them from other groups in the phylum and place them in their own class, Amphibia.
   1. Young amphibians live in water, but adult amphibians live mostly on land (amphibia means "double life").
   2. Young amphibians look different from adult amphibians, which means that a change, or metamorphosis, takes place as the young amphibian becomes an adult.
   3. Their bodies are covered with a thin, loose skin that is usually moist.
   4. Their feet are often webbed, and they have no claws on their toes.
   5. Their eggs are fertilized externally.
   6. Like fish, amphibians are ectothermic. However, through muscular contractions and increased breathing, they can raise their body temperature above their surroundings for short periods.

II. The Frog, the Toad, and the Salamander

A. Frogs and toads are members of the order Anura. Worldwide, members of this order exhibit an extensive variety of sizes and colors and can be found in many different types of habitats.
   1. The frog has a short, broad body covered by a thin, loose, moist skin that is colored very much like the surroundings the frog lives in. Glands in the skin secrete mucus that keeps the skin moist and makes the skin feel slippery.
   2. On land, the adult frog breathes through its lungs; in water it breathes through its skin.

Oxygen dissolved in the water passes directly through the skin into the blood, while carbon dioxide leaves the blood and passes out through the skin. This breathing through the skin makes it possible for the frog to stay under water or to bury itself in mud for long periods, such as during a drought.

3. The skin glands of some frogs secrete toxins, making these frogs poisonous. Some of the most colorful frogs in the world are found in South and Central America, including more than 130 species that are poisonous.
4. The frog has large, bulging eyes with upper and lower lids. There is also a third eyelid, called the nictitating membrane, joined to the lower eyelid. This extra lid protects the eye when the frog is underwater and keeps the eye moist when the frog is on land.
5. The frog has a large mouth with a long, sticky tongue that is attached anteriorly and lies on the floor of the mouth. When a frog catches its prey, the mouth opens wide and the sticky tongue shoots out and catches the prey, throwing the prey against the roof of the mouth.
6. The frog has two short, weak front legs, each with four toes. The front legs are used to support the frog and to break the force of its fall after it has made a leap.
7. The frog has two highly developed hind legs, which are used for swimming and leaping, each with five long toes with webbing between them. When the frog is resting on land, the rear legs fold together along the body in a position that makes it possible for the frog to make a sudden leap.
8. The heart of the frog is three-chambered; it mixes oxygen-rich blood with oxygen-poor blood.
9. Frogs and toads have vocal cords capable of producing a wide range of sounds. In many male frogs, air passes over the vocal cords, then into a pair of vocal sacs lying beneath the throat. Male frogs use their distinct sounds to attract female frogs. Females make sounds to indicate whether they are willing to mate.
10. Most frogs breed in water. The female lays her eggs, which are usually black and white. As the eggs pass out of the female, the male immediately spreads sperm over them. The sperm enter the eggs and fertilize them. Thus, fertilization is external.
11. The white part of the egg is the yolk, which contains stored food for the young frog when it first hatches from the egg. The black part of the frog egg is the living embryo. The young frog that hatches from the egg is called a tadpole.
12. The young tadpole immediately attaches itself to water plants and feeds on the yolk of the egg and on the jellylike material that surrounds the egg.
13. A mouth and horny jaws quickly develop, and the tadpole begins to feed on tiny aquatic plants.
14. The body and tail lengthen and gills form at the sides of the head but are enclosed in an atrial chamber. The tadpole is now a freely swimming fish-shaped animal.
15. Depending on the species, development and metamorphosis into an adult frog can take anywhere from 3 weeks to as long as 28 years.
    a. First the hind legs appear, and then the front legs form. As the legs develop, the tail is absorbed into the body and disappears.
    b. Internal body changes occur, gills are reabsorbed, and lungs form. The tadpole is now completely changed, or has undergone metamorphosis, into a frog.
16. As winter approaches in temperate climates, the body temperature of the frog becomes so low that it cannot remain active. The frog buries itself in the mud at the bottom of a pond and stays quiet all winter; this period of inactivity is called hibernation. In spring the days become warmer, and the frog becomes active again.
17. During the hottest summer days, the frog may bury itself in the cool mud and again become inactive. This period of summer inactivity is called estivation.

B. The **leopard frog** is one of the most common frogs in the United States, living in damp places near ponds, marshes, and ditches where it feeds on insects, worms, and crayfish.
   1. Its back is covered with dark spots surrounded by white or yellow rings, a protective coloration that allows it to blend in with the grass and rocks among which it lives.
   2. Its underside is a creamy white.
   3. With a favorable water temperature, the tadpoles of leopard frogs become adults in a single summer.

C. The **bullfrog**, a large frog with legs as much as 25 centimeters (10 in.) long, lives mostly in water, where it feeds on insects, worms, crayfish, and small fish.
   1. Most bullfrogs range in color from greenish yellow to greenish brown.
   2. Their undersides are a grayish white mixed with dark splotches.
   3. With favorable water temperatures, it takes two summers for the tadpole of the North American bullfrog to develop into an adult.
   4. The large legs of the bullfrog are sometimes used by humans as food.
   5. The African bullfrog takes nearly 28 years to reach full adult size. Canine-teeth-like projections on this bullfrog's lower jaw enable it to catch and feed on larger animals, such as rodents.

LEARNING ACTIVITY 14.13

The Classroom Terrarium

Set up a terrarium as a home for frogs, toads, salamanders, turtles, and lizards.

A. Keep, Observe, and Compare Frogs and Toads

Frogs and toads live very well in a terrarium. Put a frog and a toad in separate cartons and watch them closely. Compare their appearance, skin, and color. Touch their skin to see if it is wet or dry. Compare the way they hop. Count the number of toes on each foot and see if the frog and toad have the same amount of webbing between their toes. Bring your finger very near their eyes and see if they can wink. Locate their large tympanic membranes, which correspond to a human's eardrum.

Place the frog and toad in separate, covered glass jars for a few minutes. Introduce some live houseflies or fruit flies into each jar and see how the frog and toad use their tongues to catch and eat the flies. Note how the eyes move inward to help the frog and toad swallow their food. Frogs and toads eat only living insects, such as flies, grasshoppers, caterpillars, June beetles, roaches, and meal worms. However, they can be trained to eat bits of lean beef and liver if the meat is dangled in front of them with a string.

Place a frog in a large aquarium containing about 15 centimeters (6 in.) of water. Watch how the frog swims. Note that when the frog is resting, it keeps its eyes and nostrils above the water. If you hold the frog under water and gently rub its sides, it will usually croak. Replace the water in the aquarium with very cold water, and see how the frog becomes motionless, as if it is ready to go into hibernation.

B. Raise Tadpoles

Frogs and toads lay their eggs in spring. The eggs are found in shallow, quiet pond water, floating at or just beneath the surface near water plants. Frogs' eggs are found in clumps, whereas toads' eggs are found in strings. Both kinds of eggs are embedded in a jellylike material. Collect the eggs with a cup and pour them into a glass jar containing some of the pond water.

Place the eggs in an aquarium or in a terrarium pond that has water plants growing in it. If possible, add some of the green scum (algae) that is often found floating on top of ponds. Have the aquarium only partly full of water, and put a large rock in the aquarium that juts above the water. This rock will allow the tadpoles to leave the water and crawl around.

Watch the eggs each day with a magnifying glass. After a few days, tiny tadpoles will appear. Observe their growth and accompanying changes. Note that the toad's tadpole stage does not last as long as the frog's tadpole stage. Feed the tadpoles algae (green pond scum), small living insects, and dried fish food.

C. Keep and Observe Salamanders

Land salamanders can be kept very well in a woodland terrarium. Water salamanders can be kept in your classroom aquarium. They both can be fed earthworms, meal worms, ground lean beef, and liver cut into small pieces. It is better to feed the water salamander in a shallow pan of water outside the aquarium to avoid contamination of the water in the aquarium.

Observe the salamander closely. Although it may look like a reptile, it is really an amphibian and has all the characteristics of an amphibian. Touch the salamander's body gently with the palm of your hand and see how smooth and moist the skin is. Observe how small and weak the legs are. Count the number of toes on the front and hind legs, and see whether the toes are webbed and have claws. Watch how the water salamander uses its tail for swimming. See how the salamander seizes and eats its food. Find out whether salamanders are attracted or repelled by strong light. Compare the salamander with other amphibians, such as the frog and toad, and note the similarities and differences. Contrast their living, feeding, and breeding habits as well.

D. Keep and Observe Turtles

The box turtle, which is mostly a land turtle, can be kept in a classroom terrarium. Water turtles can be kept in an aquarium tank containing about 7 centimeters (3 in.) of water, with a few flat stones jutting above the water. Feed the turtles earthworms, meal worms, tadpoles, snails, bits of raw hamburger, slices of apple and banana, berries, and small pieces of lettuce. Because water turtles only eat underwater, be sure to throw the food directly into the water. Do not become alarmed if water or land turtles refuse to eat for long periods of time and become sluggish. This inactivity is quite usual, so let them alone.

Observe the turtle closely. Examine the top and bottom shells and see how the shells form an excellent means of protecting the turtle from enemies and injury. Poke the turtle's head gently with a stick and watch the turtle pull its head, neck, legs, and tail inside its shell. Bring the stick near the turtle's eyes and see whether they can blink. Observe how the turtle seizes and eats its food. Try to find out if the mouth contains any teeth. Also note how the flexible neck can turn in all directions. Examine the short legs and count the number of toes on the front and hind legs. See whether the toes are webbed and have claws. Observe how the water turtle swims. Review the characteristics of a reptile and see whether the turtle has all these characteristics. Have the students find out how to distinguish among a turtle, a tortoise, and a terrapin. Compare the turtle with other reptiles, such as the lizard and snake, and note the similarities and differences. Contrast their living, feeding, and breeding habits as well.

D. The **tree frog** is very small, about 2.5 centimeters (1 in.) long and spends most of its life in trees.
   1. Its body and coloration makes it look very much like the bark of a tree.
   2. Its toes have sticky pads that make it possible for this frog to climb trees easily.
   3. For its size, it makes a very loud sound.

E. All members of the order Anura are frogs. However, some frogs bear the common name **toad.** Frog species that are called toads usually have a drier, bumpier skin. Other characteristics of toads include the following:
   1. The toad has shorter legs than the frog.
   2. The toad lives on land all the time, returning to the water only to lay eggs.
   3. The toad's eggs are laid in strings instead of masses.
   4. The toad has no teeth.
   5. The toad cannot swim as well as other frog species.
   6. The rounded bumps on its back, sides, and legs contain poison glands that help protect the toad from its enemies.
   7. The toad sleeps most of the day under rocks and logs and becomes active at night.
   8. Toads feed on insects and slugs.

F. The **salamander** looks more like a lizard than a frog.
   1. It has a long, slender body and a long tail.
   2. Its short legs are all about the same size. Some species have no legs at all.
   3. Its skin is soft and moist, and its legs have no claws.
   4. Some salamanders live in water, and others live in damp places on land.
   5. The mudpuppy or necturus, common in the Midwest, has a pair of red gills around its head just above its front legs that it keeps throughout its life.
   6. The tiger salamander has yellow bars on a brown body, whereas the spotted salamander has yellow spots on a black body. The tiger salamander has a flat tail, and the spotted salamander has a round tail. Both live in water the first three months of their lives, then on land the rest of their lives.
   7. Reaching a length of nearly 1.5 meters (5 feet), the Japanese salamander is the world's largest salamander.
   8. The **newt** is a salamander with a "triple life." For the first 2 months of its life it lives in the water and breathes only through its gills. During the next 1 or 2 years it lives on land and breathes through lungs. Then it returns to the water for the rest of its life, breathing through its lungs when on the surface of the water and through its skin when underwater.

Reptiles

I. The Characteristics of Reptiles

A. Reptiles are members of the animal phylum Chordata, with characteristics common to all members of that phylum. Together with fish, amphibians, birds, and mammals, they make up a special group of animals called vertebrates.
   1. As vertebrates, reptiles have a backbone, their skeletons are inside their bodies, and most of them have two pairs of appendages attached to their bodies at the shoulder and hip.

B. Reptiles also have their own special characteristics, which gives them their own class, Reptilia. This class includes snakes, turtles, lizards, and alligators.
   1. Reptiles have a rough, thick, dry skin covered with scales. This dry scaly skin has provided the key to the success of reptiles on Earth.
   2. Reptiles with feet have claws on their toes.
   3. Both young and adult reptiles breathe only through lungs.
   4. Reptiles have a breastbone called the sternum that protects the heart and lungs.
   5. Fertilization is internal, that is, the female's eggs are fertilized by the male's sperm, which is deposited inside her body during mating.
   6. The eggs, which are laid on the ground (not in water, as with amphibians), have a protective shell or membrane around them.
   7. Like fish and amphibians, reptiles are ectothermic. However, by regulating their behavioral activity (such as sunning to get warm on a cool morning or lying in the shade of a rock during a hot afternoon), snakes and lizards can maintain body temperatures quite different from those of their surrounding environments. Nevertheless, because they are still dependent on the temperatures of their environment, reptiles are not found in extremely cold climates.
   8. Most reptiles, like amphibians, have three-chambered hearts. The crocodile and the alligator, however, have four-chambered hearts. Only with a four-chambered heart is there a complete separation of the supply of oxygen-enriched blood from oxygen-depleted blood.

II. The Turtle

A. Some turtles live in saltwater, others live in freshwater, and still others live on land. Land turtles are often called tortoises.
   1. Some turtles are quite small, but others, especially the sea turtles and the tortoises found on the Galapagos Islands off the coast

of Ecuador, can be 2 meters (7 ft) long and weigh 450 kilograms (1,000 lb).

B. All turtles have an upper and lower shell; the body is located between these shells.
   1. The shells protect the turtle. Most turtles can withdraw into their shells. Some can even close their shells tightly.
   2. The shells have plates that are of different colors and markings—differences that are used in identifying species of turtles.

C. A turtle has either a pointed or triangular head.
   1. It has no teeth, but it does have horny jaws that form a sharp beak, which the turtle uses to bite off pieces of food.
   2. It has well-developed eyes and eyesight, with upper and lower eyelids.
   3. There is also a third eyelid, called the nictitating membrane, which is transparent and moves from the front corner of the eye to cover and protect the eyeball.

D. A turtle's legs are quite short, and it walks slowly.
   1. The skin on a turtle's legs is scaly and tough.
   2. Most turtles have five toes on each leg, and the toes have claws.
   3. Some turtle species have completely webbed toes, but others have very little webbing between the toes. Aquatic turtles use their webbed feet for swimming.

E. Some turtles have fairly good-sized tails while others have short tails or no tail.

F. Turtles mate and fertilization of the eggs is internal. The females of all species, even sea turtles, lay their eggs on land in shallow holes. They cover them with sand or dirt. The heat of the sun helps incubate the eggs.

G. Land turtles eat insects, earthworms, and plants. Aquatic turtles eat fish, frogs, and birds that live near the water.

H. Turtles constitute a major protein food source for humans in many parts of the world.

III. The Lizard

A. Lizards have adapted to many types of habitats and can be found all over the world except in regions of extreme cold.

B. Some lizards, like the skink or swift, are small, but the Komodo dragon lizard of the East Indies is 4 meters (15 ft) long and weighs almost 115 kilograms (250 lb). The Komodo dragon will prey on animals as large as water buffalo.

C. Most lizards have four legs; some can run quite swiftly.
   1. A few lizards, such as the "glass snake," have no legs and, as the common name implies, are sometimes mistaken for snakes.
   2. The basilisk lizard of Central and South America can stand and run on its hind legs, even across a body of water, because of its long toes.

D. Lizards have distinct eyelids.

E. If their tails break off between the caudal vertebrae, many lizards can regenerate new ones.

F. **Chameleons** are tree-dwelling lizards that can change their color repeatedly in response to light, heat, and emotional states. There are approximately 80 species of chameleons, most of which live in Africa. One species lives in Hawaii.

G. The **horned "toad"** is really a lizard and is found in the western United States.
   1. It has scales of different lengths that give it a horny appearance.
   2. Some horned "toads" lay their eggs (oviparous), but others keep the eggs inside their bodies and bear their young alive (ovoviparous), especially those that live in the colder climates.
   3. The horned toad can squirt blood from its eyes to surprise or frighten its enemy.

H. The only poisonous lizards are the **Gila monster** and the **beaded lizard.**
   1. Found in Arizona, New Mexico, and Mexico, the Gila monster grows to approximately two-thirds of a meter (2 ft) long.
   2. Its skin is brown or black and covered with blotches of orange or pink.
   3. Like a mad dog, it bites hard and ferociously, twisting its head from side to side.
   4. Its poison, seldom fatal to humans, is secreted from glands at the rear of its lower jaw.
   5. The beaded lizard is found in Mexico.

I. Iguanas are a large family of lizards, found primarily in the tropics.
   1. The **green iguana** of Central America lives in the treetops of tropical rainforests. Because it has been considered a delicacy and has been hunted by humans for many years, it is endangered and faces extinction.
   2. Grazing on shoreline seaweed, the Galapagos marine iguanas are the only lizards in the world that feed in the ocean.

J. **Geckos** are small nocturnal lizards that live in warm, tropical climates. The toe pads of some geckos enable them to walk across walls and ceilings. With the aid of flaps of skin that flare out from its abdomen, and webbed feet that spread out to catch air, flying geckos of Southeast Asia can leap and glide through the air.

IV. The Snake

A. Snakes have long, round bodies that are covered with scales and are often quite colorful.
   1. Clear scales cover their eyes, which are always open.
   2. Unlike lizards, if a snake's tail breaks off it cannot generate a replacement tail.

B. Snakes may shed (molt) their outer layer of scales several times during a single season. When the thin layer becomes loose, the snake hooks a loose part over a twig or stone edge and then works its way out of this old layer of "skin."

1. The frequency with which a snake sheds its skin depends on several factors, including how much food is eaten. On average, a snake sheds its skin from two to four times a year. Rattlesnakes add a new segment onto the tail each time the skin is shed.

C. Although snakes have no legs, some can swim and climb trees.
   1. Most snakes move slowly and even the fastest, the black mamba of Africa, cannot travel faster than 3.5 meters per second (8 miles an hour). (See "black mamba" in G6 that follows.)
   2. The snake moves by using the broad scales, called scutes, on the underside of its body and a large number of muscles.
   3. Snakes commonly move by winding from side to side and forming curves.
   4. Some snakes move up and down slowly in a straight line, like a caterpillar.
   5. Some snakes that live in the desert have a side-winding movement, whereby the body is raised and twisted into S-shaped loops, moving across the ground touching it at only two or three points.

D. Unlike lizards, snakes have no external ears, only inner ears. Only vibrations that reach the bones of the inner ears detect sound. Snakes have developed other specialized sense organs that enable them to detect prey or danger in their environment.
   1. Snakes (and lizards) have a specialized sense organ in the roof of the mouth for detecting airborne chemicals.
   2. Rattlesnakes have heat-sensitive pits below their eyes that enable them to detect prey, and the distance and direction of the prey, even in total darkness.

E. The snake has a large mouth with a double row of teeth on each side of its upper jaw and a single row of teeth in its lower jaw.
   1. The teeth all slant backward toward the throat.
   2. The snake swallows its food whole, using its teeth only to hold and pull the food while it is swallowing.
   3. The snake's jaws are flexible and can dislocate, allowing it to swallow victims that are thicker than its own body.
   4. There is a long, forked tongue in the snake's (and in the lizard's) mouth, which the snake thrusts out to capture airborne molecules that it then transfers to the organ in the roof of its mouth for analysis.
   5. Snakes can go for long periods, sometimes up to a year, without eating.

F. The snake has no eyelids, which makes it different from other reptiles. There is a protective transparent scale, however, that covers the eye.

G. All snakes eat only animals, and they use different methods for getting their food.
   1. Most snakes, such as the garter snake, hognosed snake, and milk snake, simply grab victims with their mouths and swallow them alive. These snakes eat insects, frogs, toads, lizards, rats, mice, squirrels, and other small animals.
   2. Some snakes, such as the boa, python, king snake, and bull snake, first wrap their bodies around the victim's chest and squeeze hard so that the animal cannot breathe and it dies. Usually, these snakes are quite long and have fairly thick bodies. The king snake eats other snakes, even poisonous ones.
   3. Snakes such as the rattlesnake, water moccasin, copperhead, coral snake, and cobra first poison their prey and then swallow it. Such a snake has poison fangs in the roof of its mouth. The fangs are hollow, and when the snake strikes the animal, poison from the glands flows through the fangs into the victim and kills it.
   4. A spitting cobra spits its poison into the eye of its victim.
   5. The most poisonous snake in the United States is the coral snake of the Southeast. People sometimes confuse the venomous coral snake and the nonvenomous scarlet king snake because both snakes are ringed with red, black, and yellow.
   6. Other poisonous snakes include Africa's black mamba, which grows to about 4.3 meters (14 ft). The black mamba travels with a third of its body off the ground, which can quickly put the snake head-high to a human. A bite to the face or torso can bring death from paralysis within 20 minutes. In addition, it tends to bite many times in rapid succession. Other mambas include the green, western green, and Jameson's mambas—all poisonous.
   7. The world's longest poisonous snake is Asia's king cobra, which is about 5 meters long (16.5 ft). Other poisonous snakes include Australia's taipan, king brown, western brown, tiger, and death adder, and South America's bushmaster.

H. Most snakes lay eggs that have a tough, leathery white shell.
   1. Each egg contains stored food for the young snake that is developing within.
   2. The heat of the Sun helps incubate the egg.
   3. A few snakes, like the garter snake, rattlesnake, and copperhead, keep the eggs inside their bodies, and the young snakes are born alive (as opposed to being hatched from eggs outside the mother's body).

V. The Alligator and the Crocodile

A. The alligator and the crocodile are large reptiles that live mostly in tropical and semitropical climates, usually in swamps and along the banks of

LEARNING ACTIVITY 14.14

Keep and Observe Nonpoisonous Snakes

Garter snakes are easily found and are very safe to keep and observe. When lifting the snake, hold it just behind the head with one hand and support the rest of the body with the other hand. When first captured, the frightened garter snake may void feces and expel musk from its anal scent glands. This expelled material is not harmful and washes off easily. Take the snake back to the classroom in a cloth bag or pillow case with the mouth of the bag or pillow case tied securely.

Keep the snake in a large aquarium tank covered by zinc mesh (hardware cloth), which can be obtained from a hardware store. Get enough zinc mesh to bend the edges down snugly against the sides of the tank (Figure 14.3). Then place at least two heavy bricks on opposite corners of the top frame of the tank. The mesh and the bricks will ensure that the snake does not escape. Place some rocks, one or two forked branches, and a pan of water in the aquarium. Clean the cage once a week by flushing the cage well with water. Wash the snake with water at the same time. Feed the snake small living animals, such as frogs, mice, lizards, tadpoles, earthworms, and large insects. Snakes are especially hungry after they shed their skins, so have plenty of food on hand at that time.

Observe the snake closely. Note how it moves. Locate the eyes and see whether they blink. See whether you can find any ears. Watch how and why the snake uses its forked tongue. Observe how the snake seizes and eats its food. See whether the snake has all the general characteristics of a reptile. Compare the snake with other reptiles, such as the lizard and the turtle, and note the similarities and differences. Compare their living, feeding, and breeding habits as well.

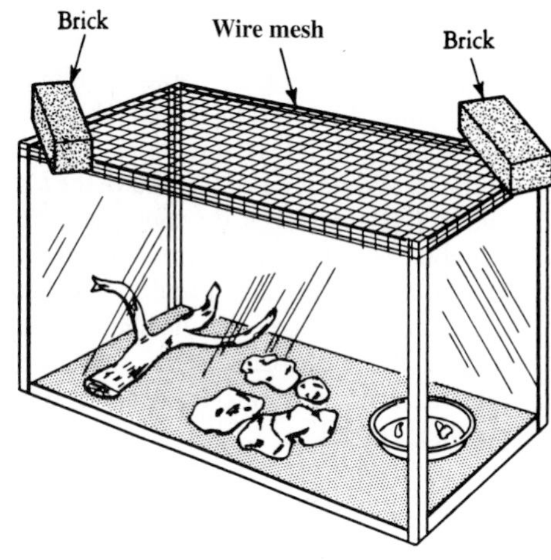

FIGURE 14.3 A prepared cage for a snake.

rivers. With a true cerebral cortex and a four-chambered heart, they are the most advanced of today's reptiles.

1. Alligators are found in the southeastern United States, mainly in Alabama, Florida, and Georgia.
2. Crocodiles are found largely in Africa and India, but there are also some crocodiles in the southeastern United States, China, and Central and South America.

B. The American alligator and the American crocodile are similar but with clear differences.

1. The crocodile has a narrower and more triangular head, and its snout is more pointed.
2. The crocodile is slightly smaller than the alligator and less bulky.
3. The alligator is brown, whereas the crocodile is a grayish green.
4. The alligator is sluggish, especially on land; the crocodile is more active.
5. In the alligator, all teeth in the upper jaw overlap with those in the lower jaw, whereas the crocodile has a pair of enlarged teeth in the lower jaw that fit into a notch on each side of its snout. Those enlarged teeth can be seen even when the crocodile's mouth is closed.
6. The crocodile spends more time in the water than does the alligator.

C. These reptiles are covered with large, bony scales, and their legs have toes that are partly webbed.

D. The alligator and the crocodile eat fish and any land animals that come near them.

1. They do not chew food but swallow it whole. Small stones in their stomachs help grind the food. Similarly, birds, lacking teeth, routinely swallow gravel that grinds food when agitated in the bird's stomach.
2. Both alligators and crocodiles attack humans, but the crocodile, especially the Nile crocodile, is more likely to do so than the alligator.
3. The Nile crocodile, found in Africa south of the Sahara, along the River Nile and in Madagascar, can reach a length of 20 feet (64 meters) and have an estimated lifespan of up to 100 years.

E. Adult alligators and crocodiles mate at night in shallow water during the spring.

1. The male (bull) roars loudly to attract females and to warn off other males.
2. After choosing a mate, the bull swims around her in circles a few times before mating.
3. The female lays her eggs in a nest of mud and vegetation.
4. The young hatch a few months later and are protected for a while by the mother. The young hatchlings, only about 20 centimeters (8 in.) long, are completely independent at birth, and grow to maturity in about 6 years.

Birds

I. Characteristics of Birds

A. As members of the phylum Chordata, birds demonstrate the characteristics of members of that phylum. They belong to the subphylum Vertebrata, along with fish, amphibians, reptiles, and mammals. As vertebrates, birds have the following general characteristics in addition to those common to all chordates: vertebral column; endoskeleton; two pairs of limbs, or appendages, attached to their bodies at the shoulder and hip; one pair of eyes; separate sexes; developed cerebral cortex; ventral heart and a dorsal aorta; and paired kidneys.

B. Birds have their own special characteristics that place them in the class Aves.
   1. Their bodies are covered with feathers.
   2. They have light, compact skeletons with porous or hollow bones containing air spaces. This characteristic of their skeletons makes it easier for birds to fly.
   3. Instead of front legs, birds have wings, which they use only for flying.
   4. They stand and perch on two legs.
   5. They have horny beaks and no teeth in their mouths.
   6. The female's eggs are fertilized by the male's sperm inside her body.
   7. The females lay eggs that have a protective shell.
   8. Birds are endothermic, meaning that they can regulate their body temperature to keep it constant, regardless of the temperature of their environment.

C. Birds vary greatly in size and shape. The smallest is the hummingbird, which is a little more than 5 centimeters (2 in.) long and weighs about 3 grams (1/10 oz). The largest bird is the ostrich, which can be as much as 2 meters (6 ft) tall and can weigh 115 kilograms (250 lb).
   1. The bald eagle, the national bird of the United States since 1782, is as much as one meter in length (3 feet) with a wingspan of up to 2.4 meters (8 feet).

D. The feathers of birds are modified scales. Their form has changed through the course of evolution, although scientists still do not agree on the evolutionary origin of birds; that is, whether they evolved directly from the dinosaurs. (Birds, for example, lack an embryonic thumb that would tie them more closely to the dinosaurs.)
   1. The feathers grow from little pits in the skin.
   2. They grow only on certain parts of the skin, but they spread out to cover those parts that are featherless.
   3. There are four kinds of feathers.
      a. Soft down feathers, plainly seen on young birds, are close to the skin and help keep both young and adult birds warm. Baby birds have mostly down feathers, which helps to make them look different from their parents.
      b. Filoplumes are thin, almost hairlike, feathers with a tuft on the end.
      c. Contour feathers cover and protect the body, and give the adult bird its characteristic color.
      d. Large, strong quill feathers are in the wings and tails and are used mostly for flying.
   4. The feathers of birds are widely different in color. In some species, the males have brilliantly colored feathers, whereas the females have very little color. In other species, the feathers of both the male and female are of the same colors.
   5. Birds shed, or molt, their feathers at least once a year. New feathers replace those that have fallen out or that have been broken.

E. Birds have keen hearing and eyesight and a good sense of balance, and are excellent at remembering how to get from place to place. Vultures and some ocean birds also have a good sense of smell. Birds have large eyes that not only give them sharp eyesight but also make them adept at judging distances.

F. Most birds have a small, horny tongue that they use to sense things by touch.

G. Most birds have a voice. About half of the known species actually sing.
   1. Some species of birds have a larger repertoire of songs than others. Sparrows, meadowlarks, and cardinals each have about eight songs in their individual repertoires, while a starling may have as many as 67, a mockingbird 150, and a brown thrasher more than 2,000.
   2. Recent technology, using advanced recording equipment, sonograms (which put bird sounds on a graph), and computers, has led to the discovery that bird songs communicate much more than was formerly thought. Bird songs are used, for example, to establish territorial rights, to indicate a change in aggression, and to direct their communication to one another.
   3. Like human language, bird songs are composed of phrases made up of smaller units called syllables.
   4. Birds are among the world's fastest animals. Geese and ducks often travel straight at 96 kilometers per hour (60 mph). Peregrine falcons can dive through the air at more than 320 kilometers (200 mi) per hour.

II. Where Birds Live

A. Birds live in all parts of the world, from the polar regions to the tropics. Many species of birds live in woodlands and in open fields and meadows. Other species live near oceans, lakes, swamps, and marshlands. Some, such as the pigeon and the starling, live in the city.

B. Many birds migrate, or move from one home to another, during spring and fall.
   1. Scientists offer various reasons to explain why birds migrate.
      a. The climate changes.
      b. Their food supply is gone.
      c. They are accustomed to breeding in certain parts of the world.
   2. Most birds that live in the north fly south for the winter. For example, the bobolink spends its winter in Argentina, the wood thrush in southern Mexico, and the house wren in Florida.
   3. Some birds have very long migration flights. The arctic tern holds the record for distance—22,000 miles per year for its seasonal round trip from the Arctic to the Antarctic. The golden plover summers in northern Canada and winters in Brazil and Argentina. The ruddy turnstone summers in Alaska and winters in Hawaii. Despite its small size, the ruby-throated hummingbird migrates more than 1,850 miles from the eastern United States, crossing 600 miles of the Gulf of Mexico, to spend the winter in Central America. Before embarking on its migration, this hummingbird stores food as a layer of fat equal to half its body weight.

III. What Birds Eat

A. Because they are so active, birds need large amounts of food. They seem to eat all the time, which helps maintain their internal body temperature.
   1. The hummingbird uses so much energy that it must eat twice its body weight in food every day. Humans, by contrast, consume about 1/50 their body weight in food each day.

B. Two main foods of birds are insects and seeds. However, many birds eat other foods.
   1. Some birds, like the crow, bluejay, and red-winged blackbird, also eat corn, grain, rice, and peas.
   2. Some birds, such as the bluebird, robin, cedar waxwing, and wren, also eat fruit and berries.
   3. Some large birds, for example the owl and the hawk, eat small animals, such as rats, field mice, and rabbits.
   4. Other birds, like the pelican, kingfisher, and loon, eat mostly fish.
   5. Birds such as the vulture and buzzard eat dead animals.
   6. Although flower nectar is its main food, the hummingbird also eats small insects and spiders.

C. Most birds drink by taking a beak full of water, then tilting their heads back to let the water run down their throats.

IV. How Birds Reproduce

A. Birds display elaborate pre-mating courtship rituals and patterns.

B. When the male and female bird finally mate, the male deposits sperm inside the female.
   1. The female's egg cells are fertilized internally.
   2. The female lays a number of eggs with hard shells around them.
   3. Each egg contains a tiny fertilized egg cell.
   4. The egg also contains yolk that serves as a food source for the young bird developing inside the egg.
   5. Some birds, such as the owl and hawk, may lay just one egg. Others, like the chicken, duck, goose, and turkey, may lay two or more eggs at a time.
   6. As soon as the female bird lays her eggs, she sits on them to keep them warm. Most birds have a patch of bare skin, called a brooding patch, that transmits heat from the bird's body to the eggs. This process of sitting on the eggs and keeping them warm until they hatch is called incubation. The time needed to incubate the eggs varies from about 10 days for smaller birds to as much as 50 days for large birds.
   7. Usually the female sits on the eggs while the male gets food, but the habit of some birds, like the ostrich, is for the male bird to take turns with the female bird in sitting on the eggs.
   8. When the egg is ready to hatch, the baby bird pecks the shell until it splits open and then works its way out of the shell.

C. Baby robins and cardinals, which hatch in 10 to 14 days, are quite helpless.
   1. They are weak, almost blind, and covered with very few down feathers.
   2. They must be fed and attended to for many days before they become feathered, are able to fly, and can obtain food for themselves.
   3. Other birds, for example the chicken and the quail, which hatch in 3 to 6 weeks, are well formed and can run around and look for food within a few hours after hatching.

V. The Nesting Habits of Birds

A. Choosing sites that are as safe as possible from their enemies and from heavy rains and strong winds, birds build nests to provide a place for incubating and hatching their eggs and for protecting the baby birds after their birth.

B. Nests vary in size and shape, in the materials used to build them, and in how well they are constructed. All birds within a certain species build their nests by the same method, with the same kinds of materials, and in the same sort of location.

1. Birds use such materials as soil, clay, twigs, grass, stems, leaves, bark, hair, feathers, and even string to build their nests.
2. Some birds build large nests with materials only loosely put together. Other birds build small nests that are beautifully constructed with twigs and other rough materials and then lined with leaves, grass, and other soft materials.
3. Shore birds, such as the penguin and the Arctic tern, lay their eggs on rocks or pebbles that are arranged on the ground to keep the eggs from rolling.
4. The whippoorwill lays its eggs on dead leaves in a small hole in the ground.
5. The kingfisher lays its eggs in a hole that has been dug in a clay bank. The eggs rest either on the bare ground or on feathers.
6. A duck builds an uncomplicated grass nest.
7. The oriole builds a long, baglike nest made of grass, string, and hair on the branch of a tree.
8. The owl and woodpecker live in holes cut out of hollow or dead trees.
9. The bluejay builds a bulky, rough nest on a tree branch.
10. The robin builds a heavy, bulky nest either on a tree branch or in the crotch of a tree. The nest is made of twigs and mud and then lined with grass.
11. The meadowlark and quail build grassy nests in underbrush.
12. The barn swallow builds its nest in hollow trees or in the eaves of a house. It uses straw and mud and lines the nest with hay or feathers.
13. The hummingbird builds a tiny, basketlike nest on the branches of a tree.
14. Some hawks and eagles build their nests up high in very tall trees.
15. Flamingoes use mud to build nests shaped into volcano-like cones.

VI. Bird Bills, Feet, Wings, and Tails

A. Over the course of time much adaptation of the feet, bills, wings, and tails of birds has occurred. As a result, various forms and structures have developed for special functions, such as perching, swimming, catching food, eating, and flying.

B. Birds have developed different kinds of feet, depending on whether they are adapted for perching, climbing, swimming, wading, or grasping.

1. Seed-eating birds, such as the robin and bluebird, have three toes in front and one in back, which are used for perching on branches.
2. The duck and the goose have long, webbed toes for swimming.
3. The crane and the heron have long legs and toes for wading.
4. The duck and the loon have short legs, set far back on their bodies, for diving.
5. The woodpecker has two toes in front and two toes in back, an arrangement that helps it climb tree trunks.
6. The owl, hawk, and eagle have powerful claws called talons on their toes that are used for grabbing and holding small animals.

C. Birds have bills that are adapted for gathering food and eating.

1. The duck has a wide, flat, notched bill that is used for scooping and straining food.
2. The booby has a tapered, pointed bill with serrated edges, ideal for grasping fish out of ocean water.
3. The owl, hawk, and eagle have the upper jaw curved over the lower jaw, making the bill hooked so that it is easy to tear flesh.
4. The heron and snipe have a long, pointed bill for searching for food in mud.
5. The sparrow and finch have a short, straight, stout bill for crushing seeds and other hard foods.
6. The hummingbird has a long, thin bill, curved in some cases, for reaching deep into flowers and obtaining nectar. In addition, the ability of the hummingbird to hover and to fly backward and upside down is unique.

D. The shape of a bird's wing is adapted for the kind of flying the bird does.

1. Soaring birds, like the hawk, have long, broad wings.
2. Sailing or gliding birds, such as the gull, have long, slender wings.
3. Birds that maneuver quickly, like the robin, have short, broad wings.
4. Ground birds, such as the pheasant and the partridge, have short wings that can furnish only short, quick flights.
5. Domesticated chickens do not fly much and have underdeveloped wings.
6. The penguin has wings that are paddle-shaped for swimming.
7. Because flying can ruffle a bird's feathers, when it stops, the bird often preens its feathers by pulling them through its beak, making them smooth again.

E. A bird's tail acts as a rudder in flying and as a balance in perching.

1. The woodpecker has a stiff tail that supports it when it is climbing a tree trunk.
2. The bluejay has a long tail for balancing itself on tree branches.

VII. Conservation and Protection of Birds

A. Large numbers of song birds and game birds have been wantonly destroyed by human civi-

LEARNING ACTIVITY 14.15

Flap Your Wings

Ask students how many times they believe they can flap their arms up and down in 10 seconds. After recording their guesses on the chalkboard, have them stand in dyads and find out, one person at a time while the other counts. Record all student results. Compare their results with the following chart of how rapidly certain birds flap their wings in the same amount of time.

heron	20	starling	70	hummingbird	700
pigeon	60	chickadee	270		

lizations through the destruction of nesting sites when forests are cut, underbrush is cleared, and fields are burned; by the drainage of marshes and wetlands and the lowering of the water level in lakes and ponds that removes the food supply and nesting sites of water fowl; and by the vast numbers of birds that are killed for sport or for food.

B. Both state and national governments pass laws to protect and conserve bird wildlife.

Mammals

I. **Characteristics of Mammals**

A. As members of the phylum Chordata, mammals demonstrate the characteristics of members of that phylum. They belong to the subphylum Vertebrata along with fish, amphibians, reptiles, and birds. As vertebrates, mammals have the general characteristics of vertebrates in addition to the characteristics common to all chordates.

B. Mammals also have their own special characteristics that distinguish their class, Mammalia.

C. All mammals have hair on their bodies. Hair grows from follicles—tiny epidermal pits in the skin.

1. While most mammals have much hair on their bodies, whales have almost no body hair, only a few bristles.
2. Some mammals, such as the mink, seal, beaver, and muskrat, grow thick coats of hair in winter.
3. The hair of some mammals, such as the weasel, arctic fox, and snowshoe rabbit, changes color in different seasons of the year. In late spring, summer, and early fall the hair of these animals is brown. In late fall, they shed their brown coats of hair and grow white coats that stay white all winter.
4. Some mammals have hair that has become highly specialized in form and structure. The porcupine's hair is in the form of quills. The armadillo's hair has evolved into horny plates that overlap and act like a coat of armor. The horns of the rhinoceros are made of masses of hair.

D. Many mammals have fingernails and toenails growing from their skin.

E. All mammals have lungs for breathing.

1. When a dolphin, an aquatic mammal, is in deep sleep, half of its brain remains alert enough to signal the animal when it is time to resurface to breathe.

F. All mammals are endothermic, able to regulate their body temperature to keep it constant regardless of the temperature of their environment.

G. All mammals have seven neck bones (cervical vertebrae), although these are not the same size for all mammals.

H. Most mammals have two pairs of limbs.

1. The whale and the manatee have lost their hind limbs, and their front limbs look like fins.
2. The seal and the walrus have limbs in the form of flippers.
3. The front limbs of the bat have long finger bones with webbed skin between them, enabling it to fly.

I. Mammals have different numbers of toes on their legs, but there are rarely more than five toes on one leg. Most smaller animals have separate toes, which help them walk and run.

1. The horse walks and runs on one toe that has developed into a hoof. (See Chapter 10 for the evolution of the horse).
2. The cow walks on a hoof that formed from two toes.
3. Some animals, such as the lion and the tiger, have powerful nails or claws on their toes, which are used for catching and injuring smaller animals.
4. Some animals, such as the squirrel and raccoon, have claws that can bend and are used for climbing trees.

J. The young of mammals are, with very few exceptions, born alive; that is, mammals are viviparous. They are not born from shelled eggs that hatch either outside (oviparous) or inside (ovoviviparous) the mother's body.

1. Fertilization is internal. When mammals mate, the male deposits sperm inside the female to fertilize the female's eggs.
2. The female's eggs are very small and do not have enough yolk to feed the developing baby mammals. Consequently, each egg attaches to the wall of the uterus in the female reproductive system. While in the uterus, the young developing mammal receives food and oxygen from the mother's blood.
3. It takes various periods of time for different mammals to develop from a fertilized egg to birth. This period of time is called gestation. Gestation is about 21 days for a mouse, 30 days for a rabbit, 63 days for a cat or dog, 40 weeks for a human, 48 weeks for a horse, and 20 to 22 months for an elephant.

K. All mammals care for their young after birth. The female parent nurses the young by giving them milk that comes from special glands called mammary glands. The presence of mammary glands in both males and females gives this class of animals its name, Mammalia.

L. Adult mammals vary in size. Some mice and shrews are about 5 centimeters (2 in.) long and weigh less than 28 grams (1 oz). In contrast, the largest mammal, the blue whale, can be more than 30 meters (100 ft) long and weigh more than 136,000 kilograms (150 tons).

M. Mammals are ubiquitous, living all over the world. Many mammals live on land. Whales and porpoises live in the ocean. Seals and walruses live in saltwater and on land. The beaver, muskrat, and hippopotamus live in freshwater and on land. The mole and shrew live mostly underground. The monkey and squirrel live mostly in trees. Mountain sheep and mountain goats live on high mountains. Bats live in caves and cavelike places. Polar bears and reindeer live in polar climates. The lion and tiger live in hot, dry climates. A large number of mammals live in the temperate climates.

N. In eating habits, mammals may be herbivorous, carnivorous, or omnivorous.
   1. Some mammals, such as the cow and the horse, are herbivorous, eating only vegetation.
   2. Some mammals, such as the lion and the tiger, are carnivorous, eating only meat (other animals).
   3. Other mammals, such as the bear and the raccoon, are omnivorous, eating both meat and vegetation.

O. Some mammals move to different locations (migrate) at different seasons of the year.
   1. Seals spend the winter in the Pacific Ocean between Alaska and California. In spring they travel north of the Aleutian Islands to the Pribilof Islands. Here, the adult seals breed and new seals are born.
   2. Elk live high in the mountains during summer and in the valleys in winter.

P. Some mammals are inactive all winter. Winter inactivity may be the result of hibernation or it may be the result of winter sleep. In both, the inactive animal lives on food that has been stored in its body.
   1. In hibernation, the animal's heartbeat slows, the body temperature drops, breathing slows to as little as once in 5 minutes, and the animal *cannot* be wakened. Animals in hibernation do not waken until spring. Woodchucks and ground squirrels hibernate.
   2. Rather than hibernating, some mammals, such as the bear, skunk, and raccoon, go into what is termed winter sleep. During this time, the heartbeat and breathing rate slow, but the animals can wake up on mild-temperature days, feed, and then go back to sleep again.

II. Egg-Laying Mammals

A. The Australian duck-billed platypus and the spiny anteater are mammals that lay eggs (are oviparous).
   1. The duck-billed platypus has fur like a beaver's, webbed feet like a muskrat's, and a

LEARNING ACTIVITY 14.16

Keep and Observe Small Mammals

CAUTION: When keeping live animals in the classroom, always be sure that the animals were not brought in from the wild. Live mammals and live birds in particular may have diseases that can be passed to humans. (See "safety guidelines" in Figure 5.5 in Chapter 5.)

White mice, guinea pigs, gerbils, and hamsters are excellent small mammals to observe in the classroom. Although different kinds of homemade animal cages can be built, it may be more expedient to purchase sturdy, well-built animal cages made of metal that are the proper size. The animals, along with suitable food and books on their care, can be obtained at a pet shop. There are also many reference books available on the care of pet mammals. When purchasing these animals, try to get young ones. They quickly become accustomed to being around students and to being handled by them. Faithfully follow instructions for the care of these animals. Have the students note the physical characteristics and the living and feeding habits of each animal.

A frequent problem for the teacher who wishes to keep live organisms in the classroom, especially animals, is how to care for the organisms on weekends and during vacation periods when the heat for the building might be turned off. Be sure to consider such potential problems and plan accordingly.

horny bill like a duck's. It lays two or three eggs that resemble reptile eggs. When the eggs hatch, the young lap up a kind of milk given off by mammary glands on the mother's abdomen.
2. The spiny anteater is covered with long spines that resemble porcupine quills. It has a tubelike bill and a long tongue, which it uses to catch ants. It lays two eggs, which it places into a special pouch on its ventral side.

III. Pouched Mammals

A. Pouched mammals, the marsupials, include the kangaroo, opossum, koala, numbat, spotted cuscus, sugar glider, wombat, and wallaby. Most live in Australia.
   1. The average koala sleeps about 22 hours a day, perhaps more than any other mammal. For comparison, the average per night sleep time for various other animals is: 20 hours for bat; 14 hours for chimpanzee; 12 hours for cat; 8 hours for human; 4 hours for cow; 3 hours for horse; 2 hours for giraffe.

B. Young marsupials are helpless when they are born. Immediately after birth they enter into a special body pouch near the mother's mammary glands, which have nipples. The young feed on milk from the mammary glands until they are developed enough to leave the pouch.

IV. "Toothless Mammals"

A. These animals are not completely toothless, but have no teeth at all in front. The sloth, armadillo, and great anteater are members of this group.
   1. The sloth is a bearlike animal that hangs upside down from trees and moves slowly. It feeds chiefly on leaves. The hair of some kinds of sloths appears to be green because of green algae growing in it.
   2. The armadillo has a body covered with heavy, overlapping, bony scales. It feeds chiefly on insects. Its young are born as either identical twins or quadruplets.

V. Insect-Eating Mammals

A. This group includes the mole, the shrew, and the hedgehog.

B. The **mole** has soft fur and uses its sharp front legs to dig long burrows just beneath the surface of the ground. It has a long, sharp nose, which it uses for digging insect grubs and worms out of the soil. It lives underground and is blind.

C. The tiny **shrew** looks both like a mouse and like a mole. It eats not only grubs and worms but also mice and other shrews.

D. **Tree shrews**, not true shrews, represent a separate order of 16 species of small shrew-like mammals found in eastern Asia from India to the Philippines. The largest is only 20 centimeters long (about 8 in.). They feed on insects and fruit.

E. The **hedgehog** has long, quill-like hair, looks like a porcupine, and eats only insects.

VI. Flesh-Eating Mammals: The Carnivores

A. Members of this group have large, well-developed canine teeth located near the corners of the mouth, and strong jaws for tearing flesh. Their other teeth are pointed and help cut up the flesh. They are referred to as the carnivores.

B. Sea members of this group include the seal, walrus, and sea lion.

C. Land members of this group are divided into three subgroups, according to how they walk.
   1. One subgroup, which includes the bear and raccoon, walk flat-footed on the soles of their feet.
   2. Another subgroup, which includes the cat, fox, dog, lion, tiger, wolf, and coyote, walk only on their toes.
   3. A third subgroup, which includes the skunk, weasel, mink, and otter, walk partly on their toes and partly on the soles of their feet.

D. The bear family is made up of seven species, including the American black bear, the brown bear, the polar bear, the grizzly (which some scientists classify as a member of the brown bear group), and the Kodiak bear.
   1. Having evolved from dog-like, carnivorous ancestors, bears today are omnivorous, claiming a varied diet of nuts, berries, plant roots, insects, small vertebrates, carrion, and fish.
   2. Found across Europe, Asia, and North America, brown bears increase in size from east to west. For example, the subspecies of brown bears living in the European Alps and Apennines of western Europe weigh only about one-fourth as much as the grizzly. The grizzly can weigh up to 320 kilograms (700 lb) and has a shoulder height of about 1 meter (3.5 ft). When standing on its hind legs, the grizzly can measure more than 2.5 meters tall (8 ft).
   3. The largest members of the bear family are the polar bear and the Kodiak bear. When on all fours, a polar bear can be about 1.5 meters (5 ft) tall, but when standing on its hind legs, it can measure as much as 3.3 meters (11 ft). The male can weigh more than 700 kg (1,500 lb). Although the polar and Kodiak bears are mainly carnivorous, preying on seals and their young pups, they will also feed on vegetation.
   4. Conservation projects and regulated hunting have allowed the world population of polar bears to increase to about 40,000 animals, whereas just a few years ago it had declined to less than 10,000.
   5. Outside of Alaska, the grizzly is listed as an endangered species. In recent years, however, the Grizzly population has increased in Yellowstone National Park.

E. Most of the 37 species of feral cats, large and small, are in decline, largely because of poaching for medicines, hunting for the fur, and habitat degradation. Larger than its relative the Bengal tiger (found in India, Nepal, Bangladesh, Bhutan, and Burma), the largest living cat is the Siberian tiger, found today in Siberia, China, and Korea. It is estimated that only about 400 individual Siberian tigers remain in the world today.
   1. A male Siberian tiger can measure up to 3.7 meters (12 ft) from its head to the tip of its tail and can weigh more than 270 kilograms (600 lb).
   2. Siberian tigers feed principally on wild pig.
   3. The Siberian tiger lives for about 25 years.
F. Other large cats in danger of extinction are the closely related lion, which can weigh as much as 225 kilograms (500 lb), and the leopard (also called panther) and jaguar, each of which can weigh nearly 90 kilograms (200 lb).
   1. While the lion once roamed every continent but Australia and Antarctica, it is now found only in Africa and western India.
   2. Leopards have the widest distribution of any large cat, ranging from Africa to Southeast Asia and Siberia. Both black and spotted leopards can be born in the same litter.
   3. The jaguar is the only large cat that does not roar. Jaguars are found in Central and South America.
G. Another large cat, which belongs to a genus separate from that containing the lion, tiger, leopard, and jaguar, is the **cheetah**, found in Africa and Asia. The cheetah is the fastest land mammal. In just 3 seconds, it can reach a maximum speed of nearly 100 kilometers per hour (60 mph).

VII. Gnawing Mammals: The Rodents

A. The group referred to as rodents includes the rat, mouse, squirrel, chipmunk, prairie dog, woodchuck, rabbit, hare, muskrat, and beaver. Most members of this group do a great deal of damage eating grain and crops. The rat spreads disease as well.
B. All but the rabbit and the hare have two large, chisel-like front incisor teeth on each jaw. The rabbit and hare have four of these teeth on each jaw.
   1. These incisor teeth have sharp edges that stay sharp because the front edge is harder than the back edge so the biting surface always wears out at an angle. The teeth themselves do not wear out because they keep growing.
   2. All rodents have strong grinding teeth behind their sharp front incisors.

VIII. Hoofed Mammals

A. This group is divided into two large subgroups: the odd-toed and the even-toed hoofed animals. The odd-toed hoofed group includes such animals as the horse and the rhinoceros; the even-toed group is further divided into two smaller groups: the cud-chewers and the non–cud-chewers.
B. The even-toed cud-chewers include the cow, sheep, goat, camel, giraffe, and deer.
   1. These animals' stomachs have four divisions.
   2. These animals usually swallow large amounts of food quickly. This food passes into the first stomach division, where it is stored temporarily.
   3. Later, the food is forced back into the mouth and chewed thoroughly as a cud.
   4. The cud then passes into the second stomach division, where it begins to be digested.
C. The even-toed non–cud-chewers include the pig and the hippopotamus.
D. Some hoofed mammals have horns.
   1. The cow, ox, and bison have hollow horns, which are never shed.
   2. The deer, elk, caribou, and moose have solid horns with many branches. These horns are shed each year.
E. Some hoofed mammals can survive a long time without drinking water.
   1. Water is essential to all living organisms. Humans cannot survive if water is withheld for about 10 days.
   2. The camel can survive without drinking water for up to 2 weeks. However, it then may drink as much as 106 liters (28 gal) in 10 minutes.
   3. A giraffe can go without water even longer than a camel can—for up to several weeks.
F. The giraffe is the tallest animal on Earth today; males may be as tall as 6 meters (20 ft). Its habitat is limited to the tropical grasslands (the savannas) of Africa.
   1. Because it is so tall, the giraffe must spread its forelegs very wide and then bend its knees to be able to drink from a watering hole. When doing this, the giraffe is especially vulnerable to its predators, such as the lion.
   2. To keep out dust, giraffes can close their nostrils completely.
   3. The giraffe uses its long upper lip and its dark gray tongue, which can extend outward more than 54 centimeters (21 in.), to forage food from tall trees.
   4. The giraffe's tongue has a built-in sunscreen that protects it from the hot African sun.
   5. Because the giraffe cannot swim, rivers are barriers to its roaming.
   6. Much of the habitat of giraffes has become land for cattle farms. People have hunted the giraffe for food and have used the hide for making sandals and the tail to make ornaments, string, and fly swatters.
G. Poachers in Africa, seeking the horn of the rhinoceros to sell for use in Middle Eastern daggers and Asian folk medicine, have slaughtered both black and white rhinos. In the 1960s, approximately 100,000 black rhinos roamed the savannas of

sub-Saharan Africa, but fewer than 2,500 survive today. Today's population of white rhinos is about 7,000, almost all of which are in protective care in southern Africa.

IX. Trunk-Nosed Mammals

A. The African and the Asian elephants are the only trunk-nosed animals alive today.
   1. As recently as 10,000 years ago, however, the hairy mammoth, the ancestor to today's elephants, roamed the Earth in large numbers.
   2. Remains of the hairy mammoth have been found in Siberia, northern Europe, northern Eurasia, and North America. Complete specimens have been discovered deep-frozen in the ice of the Arctic tundra.
   3. With no tusks or trunks, predecessors of the hairy mammoth and today's elephants were more like hippopotamuses than today's elephants.

B. Weighing 6,350 kilograms (7 tons) or more, elephants are the largest land mammals living today.
   1. The elephant's trunk is a stretched-out upper lip and nose.
   2. Elephants are entirely vegetarian, eating a wide range of grasses, foliage, and fruit.
   3. Elephants are intelligent animals with very elaborate means of communication.
   4. Because of their heavy exploitation by humans and our encroachment upon their habitats, the few remaining herds of elephants today are protected by most of the nations who are party to the Convention on International Trade in Endangered Species.
   5. At present there are two kinds of elephants—the Asian elephant and the African elephant.

C. The **Asian elephant** is found only in India, Sri Lanka, and Southeast Asia.
   1. Scientists estimate that there are only 50,000 individual Asian elephants in the wild.
   2. The Asian elephant has an arched back, an enormous domed head with relatively small ears, and a single protuberance, or "finger," at the tip of its trunk.
   3. Only the male has tusks.

D. The **African elephant** is only found south of the Sahara Desert in Africa. It is slightly larger than the Asian elephant.
   1. The total population of African elephants is estimated to be 600,000.
   2. The African elephant has a swayed back, a tapering head with large ears, and two trunk "fingers."
   3. Its large ears are used as fans to cool the body. Heat loss in animals occurs mainly through surface area, whereas heat production occurs in all cells and varies in proportion to an animal's volume. Because volume (proportional to the cube of average length) increases faster than surface area (proportional to the square of average length), as the size of an animal decreases, heat loss increases. In proportion to body weight, small animals lose more heat than humans and so need extra calories to maintain body temperature. This is why the hummingbird, for example, consumes such a large quantity of food daily. However, the African elephant, living in a hot climate, needs the larger surface area provided by its large ears to get rid of extra body heat through radiation and evaporation.
   4. In the African elephant, both sexes have tusks, which are elongated incisor teeth that continue to grow throughout the elephant's lifetime, about 70 years.

X. Flying Mammals

A. Bats are mammals that fly.
   1. The toe bones of their front legs are very long and have skin stretched over and between them.
   2. The skin is also attached to the side of the body, the back legs, and the tail.
   3. This gives the bat a large wingspread.
   4. Because skin covers the bat's front and back legs, bats cannot walk very well. They usually drink and feed while in flight.
   5. The bat flies at night. During the day it stays in a cave or another dark place, where it hangs upside down by the claws of its back legs.

B. Most bats eat insects, but the vampire bat feeds exclusively on the blood of large animals, such as cows, pigs, and horses.
   1. The vampire bat is found in Central and South America. Its range includes tropical and subtropical regions from Mexico to northern Chile and Argentina. It is also found on the Caribbean islands of Trinidad and Margarita.
   2. The vampire bat does not suck blood like a mosquito but laps it up with its long tongue. It can take up to its own weight (about 28 g) in one feeding.
   3. Although no larger than a mouse, the vampire bat is a threat to domestic animals because it can infect its host with disease organisms, such as the virus that causes rabies.

C. Contrary to the myths about bats, they are not blind and they will not tangle in people's hair. Bats are very adept at flying in complete darkness without bumping into things.
   1. Because of the myths about bats, they have been extensively killed by humans, and many of their habitats have been destroyed. In some locations today, their habitats are protected.
   2. Bats can hear very well; they listen to the echoes of their own very high-pitched voices as the echos bounce back from objects around them. This is called echolocation.

3. Bats can also see very well and often fly without engaging their echolocation signals.

D. Bats in the deserts of the southwestern United States play an important role in pollinating cactus plants and dispersing their seeds. The desert-inhabiting bats feed on the plant's nectar and transfer pollen from plant to plant. They also feed on the cactus fruits, thereby inadvertently aiding in seed dispersal.

E. Bats feed on countless mosquitoes and on beetles and moths that can destroy farm crops and forest trees. Some farmers have built bat houses and placed them strategically on their farms to attract and keep bats to eradicate destructive crop-eating insects.

F. Most North American bats use caves to sleep in winter and to raise their young during summer. Sleeping and nursing bats should not be awakened or disturbed. If awakened from winter sleep, a bat can quickly consume its stored food and then may not survive until spring.

XI. Marine Mammals

A. The whale, dolphin, and porpoise are mammals that, although they have lungs and breathe air, spend their lives in the ocean, where they feed on plankton, fish, and other marine life.
   1. They use their tails for swimming and their finlike front limbs for balance.
   2. They usually have one or two young at a time, which are fed by their milk just like other mammals.

B. The fast swimming "killer whale," or **Orca**, has the most varied diet of any large ocean predator and is the most feared of all the toothed whales. It is the only whale to hunt other warm-blooded animals.
   1. With the widest distribution of all whales, the Orca is found in every ocean.
   2. Although the Orca is surviving well, some are captured for display in theme parks.

C. At 30 meters (100 ft) and 138 metric tons (154 short or U.S. tons), the **blue whale** is perhaps the largest animal ever to live on Earth.
   1. In comparison, a full-grown African elephant is about the same weight as a newborn baby blue whale.
   2. The blue whale has a very slow metabolism with a heartbeat of only about nine times a minute. A toothless whale, the blue whale feeds almost solely on sea plankton, which consists largely of diatoms and other small organisms.
   3. Like the dinosaurs before them, both the blue whale and the elephant are threatened by extinction. Unlike that of the dinosaurs, however, their extinction is human-induced.

D. Because the whale, dolphin, and porpoise have been exploited in the past, the endangered populations of these intelligent animals are now protected by international agreements, although enforcement of the agreements is an ongoing problem.

XII. Flexible-Fingered Mammals: The Primates

A. Members of this group include the lemur, monkey, gibbon, orangutan, bonobo, chimpanzee, gorilla, and human. The group is referred to as the primates. Despite their diversity of sizes and shapes, all primates share certain characteristics.
   1. A distinctive characteristic of primates is the shape of the head. It is relatively rounded and the face is flattened. This is due, in part, to the size of the brain in primates. Only marine mammals have larger brains. However, the brains of primates are much more complex than are those of other animals. This complexity is reflected in their diverse behaviors and social interactions.
   2. All primates have a highly developed sense of vision. The position of their eyes on their heads permits them to perceive depth and to gauge distance. They also have color vision.
   3. Most primates are tree dwellers. Primates have thumbs that enable them to grasp objects, and many have feet that are also constructed for grasping.
   4. Both hands and feet have flexible joints, and nails rather than claws.
   5. The ability to oppose the thumb with the fingers allows primates to make finer manipulations with their hands.
   6. The shoulder and hip joints of primates are adapted for flexible movement in varying directions. Primates can walk on just their hind legs or move about on all four legs.

B. Many members of this group are endangered or potentially endangered animals.
   1. Their habitats have become highly limited, primarily to Africa and Southeast Asia. Many suffer from habitat destruction.
   2. Many members of this group have been and continue to be killed by humans—for sport, for trophy, for medical purposes, and for food. For example, central African people, who do little cattle farming, historically have depended on ape meat as a primary source of protein.
   3. Some members of this group are now being protected by national parks and preserves and through international agreements. Money to keep up these parks and preserves, to educate people, and to enforce

international agreements continues to be a problem.
4. The rare bonobo (known also as the pygmy chimpanzee) has almost no protected habitat. This animal's total population in the wild is estimated to be no more than 20,000 individuals, all living within the country of Zaire.
5. The worldwide chimpanzee population is about 200,000 individuals.
6. First seen in 1901, only about 100 years ago, the mountain gorilla is in serious danger of extinction. Today there are only about 300 mountain gorillas living in the wild, all in central Africa, near Lake Victoria.
7. Today's population of lowland gorillas is about 50,000 individuals, found in several countries of central Africa, including Zaire, Gabon, Congo, and Nigeria.
8. With their habitats suffering from degradation, orangutans now are found only in Southeast Asia—in Sumatra and Borneo—and number only about 20,000 individuals.
9. The chimpanzee and the bonobo have genetic configurations nearly identical to those of humans.

XIII. Conservation of Wild Mammals

A. Historically, humans have killed many mammals without giving any thought to protecting and conserving them.
   1. Fur-bearing animals have been tortured and slaughtered in huge numbers.
   2. The bison of the Great Plains were nearly made extinct because of the earlier demand for their fur and meat.

B. Mammals are among the world's great natural resources and, like our forests, deserve to be protected and preserved by the world community. State, federal, and international laws are now in force for the purpose of protecting and conserving wildlife. Enforcement of the laws is a continuing problem.

Exploratory Activities for "Animals"

1. EXPLORING THE QUESTION: WHAT IS AN ANIMAL? (ANY GRADE LEVEL)[1]

Overview

The object of this exploration is to facilitate students' understanding of the common characteristics of animals. During this study, students will hypothesize, design an experiment, compare and contrast, and observe and infer. Older students should be expected to make and use tables.

Materials Needed Live animals (e.g., mouse, earthworm, crayfish, frog, crab, sea urchin, cricket, lizard, planarian, snail, starfish, spider, beetle) that are safe and common to your location; suitable containers for each animal; rulers.

Procedure

Whole Class

1. Display a large goldfish in a bowl. Ask students how they can tell that the goldfish is an animal. (Most suggestions will deal with moving and breathing.)
2. Feed the goldfish. Instruct students to time how long it takes the fish to swim to the food. As they watch the fish eat, ask how this behavior is important in identifying the goldfish as an animal. (All animals obtain food from their environments.)
3. Ask students what the fish does with the food. (It uses the food for energy or as raw material for building tissue.)
4. Ask how the fish is different from a protist that might move around to get food. (The fish is multicellular and has tissues and organs.)
5. Ask how they can tell the animal is a fish. (Swimming, backbone, scales, and gills.)

Small Group Exploratory Investigations: Part I

Students should wash their hands before and after handling the animals.

1. Divide the students into groups of four, and give each group its own animal to observe and study. Explain to the students that they are to develop ways of identifying their organisms first as animals, and next as part of a particular animal group. It is not important that their answers are correct, but it is important that students think critically about their animals and their unique traits. As in previous explorations, each member of a group should assume certain responsibilities, such as those of chief scientist, recorder, and materials engineer.
2. First, students brainstorm in their groups a list of possible characteristics that could be used to categorize and identify their animal.
3. Students next construct a data table for the features that identify the organism as an animal.

[1] *Source:* Adapted from Alton Biggs, Chris Kapicka, et al., *Biology: The Dynamics of Life* (Westerville, OH: Glencoe/ McGraw-Hill, 1995), 696–697. By permission of the publisher.

4. They then give reasons for constructing their table as they did.
5. Ask, "What data do you plan to collect?" (The students' tables may include the following types of data: type of movement toward food, reaction to touch stimulus, structural adaptations that enable the animal to get food or escape predators, time spent in lighted part of container. The tables should also include some quantitative data, structural features, and behavioral data.)
6. Check each group's data table before the group continues with its exploration.
7. Each group then carries out its investigation.
8. Each group records measurements and observations in its data table.

Small Group Exploratory Investigations: Part II

1. After Part I of the investigation has been done, have groups trade animals and repeat steps 6 through 13.

Culminating Activity and Assessment

1. As a conclusion to this activity, have groups share and compare their completed data tables and summarize what they learned about how organisms are identified as animals and how animals are classified. The following are questions that groups should address (science process skills are given in parentheses):
   a. On what basis did you identify your animals both generally and specifically? (identifying variables)
   b. Did your results confirm your hypothesis? Why or why not? (checking a hypothesis)
   c. When you compared your table with that of another group, how were the tables the same, and how were they different? (comparing and contrasting)
   d. What did you learn in this exploration about animals that you did not know before? (drawing conclusions)
   e. How are animals identified? (thinking critically)

2. EXPLORING AN OWL PELLET (ADAPTABLE TO ANY GRADE)[2]

Rationale

Owl pellets can be collected from around the nests of owls or purchased from science supply companies. Careful opening and sorting of material in the pellets reveals interesting information about the eating habits of owls. The contents of the pellets can be the inspiration for an interesting discussion and informative study of

- how aspects of the environment are interrelated and that changes to one aspect affect other aspects
- the concept of interdependence
- food chains
- skeletal anatomy

[2] Portions of this investigation were provided by Charles R. Downing, © 1993–1994 by Charles R. Downing. By permission of Charles R. Downing.

Disciplines Involved in This Study

Science and mathematics.

Skills Involved

Fine locomotor control, sketching, comparing and contrasting, observing, calculating, writing, sorting and classifying, basic calculations.

Instructional Procedures

Read the entire exploration and then adapt it according to your own needs, or present it to your class of students as it is here.

Background Information

Owls, as birds of prey, eat small rodents (such as mice and shrews) as a major part of their diet. They do not rip the prey apart, they swallow them whole. Since the stomach muscles and stomach acid in an owl are not very strong, all of the bones and fur of a mouse or shrew cannot be completely digested. If a bone were to accidentally start to move through the intestine, it could poke a hole in the intestine and cause serious problems for the owl. Faced with this problem, nature has supplied the owl with a solution that allows the owl to continue its regular diet of rodents without worrying about the weak stomach or the possibility of intestinal poking. The solution is the owl pellet.

Owl pellets are balls of fur and bones that the owl regurgitates (spits up) after the meat is digested from its prey. This process is similar to the way a cat makes fur balls to keep the fur it licks off its own coat from clogging its intestines. An owl will produce one pellet about every 12 hours. (Have students now answer questions 1 and 2 shown at the end of this exploration.)

Investigatory Procedures

1. Divide your class of students into groups of four. One person in each group is the "materials manager" and will obtain the pellet and other materials needed by the group. From each group, children are to select two people to be "hunters." The hunters will divide the pellet in half, locate bones, and place the bones in the team's Petri dish. The fourth person is the "sorter."
2. *Materials needed:* The materials manager should now obtain the following materials for the group exploration: owl pellet, Petri dish, sheet of plain white paper, pair of scissors, metric ruler, tweezers, dissecting needles, bone sorting sheet (showing major types of rodent bones).
3. The sorter outlines the bottom (small half) of the Petri dish on a sheet of paper, cuts out the circle, writes the names of the four group members on the paper, and pushes the paper up into the top of the Petri dish with the names showing. Later, the sorter will take each of the bones placed in the Petri dish bottom by the hunters, decide what kind of bone it is, and place it on the bone sorting sheet provided with the team owl pellet.
4. Students now answer questions 3 and 4 listed at the end of the exploration.

5. Students place the owl pellet on the table in front of them and unwrap it. Using the metric ruler, they measure the length and width of the pellet.
6. Group members very carefully use the tweezers and dissecting needles to split the pellet into two approximately equal parts. Each hunter gets one part.
7. Hunters now use the tweezers and needles to gently pull the pellet apart and locate bones. They remove fur from the bone (if necessary) to be sure that each bone has as little fur on it as possible before placing it into the Petri dish.
8. The sorter takes the bones, checks them against the bone sorting sheet, and places them on the correct space on the sorting sheet.
9. Students continue to locate, clean, identify, and sort bones until all of the bones are removed from the pellet. Each group member is responsible for checking the accuracy of the sorting.
10. Students now answer questions 5, 6, 7, and 8.
11. The entire group now takes their completed chart (question 6) to the teacher. The teacher gives the sorter a "skeleton page" and a bottle of glue. Both hunters copy the group data onto the Entire Class Bone Chart either on the board or the overhead projector.
12. They glue the bones on the skeleton page to form their own rodent skeleton.
13. Students then copy the class data from the Entire Class Bone Chart onto their own chart.
14. They turn in their group skeleton page.
15. Students take their own chart and answer sheet home and total the number of bones of each type from the entire class data.
16. Students now answer questions 9 through 12.

Questions (to be duplicated for students)

1. How many pellets would an owl produce in each of the following lengths of time? Show your work.
   a. 1 day
   b. 1 week
   c. 1 month
   d. 1 year
2. Imagine that you live on a farm. You clean your barn each Saturday, picking up everything on the concrete floor of the barn and washing the floor off with water from a hose. When you clean one week you find 42 owl pellets. How many owls are living in your barn?
3. Who is your group's materials manager?
   Sorter?
   Hunters?
4. Why does the sorter need a sheet of paper?
5. How long was your pellet (in millimeters)? How wide was it?
6. Make a chart on your paper. Put the type of bone across the top and the number of bones your pellet contained under each type of bone.
7. What type of bone did you have the most of?
   a. How many were there?
   b. Why do you think there were so many?
8. What type of bone did you have the least of?
   a. How many were there?
   b. Is this type of bone the same as your group's highest number? If it is not, why do you believe this to be so?
9. What type of bone did the class have the most of?
   a. How many were there?
   b. Is this type of bone the same as your group's highest number? If it is not, why do you think this is so?
10. What type of bone did the class have the least number of?
   a. How many were there?
   b. Is this type of bone the same as your group's lowest number? If it is not, why not?
11. What is the total number of rodent skulls found by your class?
   a. How many femurs should the class have? Did they have that many? If not, why not?
   b. How many humerus bones should the class have? Did they have that many? If not, why not?
12. Assume that all the rodent skulls found by your class were from the pellets of a single owl.
   a. How many days of eating did this sample cover?
   b. If the number of rodents eaten in 1 day equals 0.5% of the total rodent population, what is the rodent population in this owl's hunting territory?

Chapter 15

The Human Body

Scott Cunningham/Merrill

Makeup of the Human Body

I. Cells of the Human Body

A. The human body is made up of millions of tiny cells. Many cells have specific functions, so they differ in size and shape and may even contain special materials. All of this makes it possible for them to perform their particular kinds of work. Examples of specialized cells include blood, epithelial, muscle, nerve, and bone cells.

B. A group of specialized cells working together to perform a specific function is called a **tissue.** There are four major types of tissue in the human body.
   1. **Epithelial** tissue covers exposed surfaces, lines internal passageways and chambers, and forms glands.
   2. **Connective** tissue fills internal spaces, provides structural support for other tissues, transports materials within the body, and stores energy reserves.
   3. **Muscle** tissue contracts to perform specific movements and in the process generates heat that keeps the body warm.
   4. **Nerve** tissue allows information to travel from one part of the body to another in the form of electrical impulses.

C. A group of different tissues working together in a common function is called an **organ.** An organ carries out a special activity or group of activities in the body. Examples of organs are the heart, lungs, liver, stomach, eyes, and brain.

D. A group of organs working together in a special body activity is called an **organ system.**

II. The Organ Systems

A. There are 11 organ systems in the human body.
   1. The **integumentary system** covers and protects the body, helps maintain body temperature, and eliminates wastes. It includes the skin, hair, sweat glands, and nails.
   2. The **skeletal system** supports the body. It also provides protection to internal organs, stores minerals, and produces blood. It includes the bones, cartilage, tendons, and ligaments.
   3. The **muscular system** makes it possible for the body and its parts to move. It also helps to protect internal organs and produces body heat. It includes the muscles.
   4. The **digestive system** makes possible the digestion and absorption of the food we eat. It includes the mouth, esophagus, stomach, liver, and intestines.
   5. The **cardiovascular system** moves the materials needed by cells and carries away wastes. It includes the blood, heart, arteries, veins, and tiny blood vessels called capillaries.
   6. The **respiratory system** takes in oxygen and eliminates carbon dioxide; it includes the nose, windpipe (trachea), larynx (voice box), bronchi, and lungs.
   7. The **urinary system** helps to eliminate the excess water, salt, and waste products formed in the body. It includes the kidneys, ureters, urinary bladder, and urethra.
   8. The **nervous system** makes it possible for the body to respond to stimuli. It includes the nerves, brain, sensory organs, and spinal cord.
   9. The **reproductive system** includes the organs that affect sex characteristics and allows the body to produce offspring. It includes the male penis and testes and the female vagina, uterus, and ovaries.
   10. The **endocrine system** consists of various glands that produce chemicals that control and regulate body functions.
   11. The **lymphatic system** provides defense against infection and disease. The system consists of lymph, lymphatic vessels, lymphocytes, spleen, appendix, and lymphatic nodules scattered throughout the body.

Integumentary System

I. Functions of the Integumentary System

A. The skin has many important functions.
   1. It acts as a protective covering to prevent harmful bacteria from entering the body.
   2. It forms a waterproof covering, preventing water and other liquids from leaving the inner tissues.
   3. It protects the inner parts of the body from such injuries as scratches, bruises, bumps, and cuts.

B. When the skin is injured, many of its cells are damaged or killed. However, the skin is able to repair itself and regenerate new skin.

C. **Melanin,** a pigment in the skin, helps protect the skin from the Sun's rays. A person with a large amount of melanin pigment (whose skin is dark) is better protected from the Sun's ultraviolet rays than is a person whose skin is much lighter or an albino person (one who has no melanin). Changes in melanin allow animals like the chameleon to change colors.

D. The skin has many nerve endings, which give it protective sensitivity to touch, pressure, pain, heat, and cold.

E. Certain features of the skin help the body to maintain **homeostasis;** that is, the equilibrium of the body's internal conditions necessary to remain alive and healthy.

1. The sweat glands open through pores on the surface of the skin, allowing the escape of body wastes (sweat). Like urine filtered from the blood by the kidneys, sweat is a mixture of water, salt, sugar, lactic and ascorbic acids, and small amounts of organic wastes.
2. Each sweat gland has a tiny tube leading from the surface of the skin to the lower part of the dermis, where the tube winds around and around to form a coil.
3. Tiny blood vessels surround the cells of the sweat glands. The cells of the sweat glands filter saltwater, minerals, and other waste products from the blood. The sweat mixture then flows up the tube and out onto the skin, where the water component evaporates from the skin.
4. There are more than a million sweat glands in the skin. These are spread out over the entire body but are most numerous in the palm of the hand, the sole of the foot, and the armpit.
5. In very warm environments, sweat glands give off large amounts of sweat, which evaporates on the surface of the skin.
6. Water needs heat to evaporate; it takes this heat from the surface of the skin, thus cooling the body.
7. In cold environments, sweat glands give off very little sweat; thus, less evaporation and heat loss occur.
8. Blood vessels in the skin also help to control or regulate body temperature; that is, to maintain homeostasis. When the body is warmer than normal, blood vessels in the dermis open wider (dilate), and body heat is lost by radiation through the skin. When the body is colder than normal, the vessels constrict and heat is conserved. In addition, when the body is warmer than normal, body heat is lost during the evaporation of sweat from the skin's surface. In these ways, the skin helps maintain body temperature.

F. Oil glands are connected to the cells that produce hair. Oil that is secreted by these glands helps keep hair from drying out, keeps the skin elastic, and retards the growth of certain bacteria found on skin.

G. When exposed to ultraviolet rays from sunlight, cells in the dermis convert carotene to vitamin D, a nutrient that aids the absorption of calcium and phosphorus in the small intestine, into the bloodstream.
   1. Children who live in areas with overcast skies and whose diets lack vitamin D can have retarded bone development (rickets), a condition that has been eliminated in the United States because dairy companies add the vitamin to milk that is sold in grocery stores.

II. Structure of Skin

A. The skin is an organ, about 3 millimeters (1/8 inch) thick, that covers and protects the body. The average adult's skin occupies approximately 7 square meters (approximately 23 sq. ft), making it the largest organ of the body.
   1. The skin is made up of two layers: a thin outer layer, called the epidermis; and a thicker inner layer, called the dermis.

B. The **epidermis** consists of many layers of cells, with more layers in the thick skin of the palms of the hands and the soles of the feet than in the skin that covers the rest of the body.
   1. The outer cells are flat, scaly, and horny and are constantly being shed or rubbed off as dead cells. As these dead cells are lost, new living cells from the living layers beneath push up and take their place. As these new cells come closer to the surface of the skin, they become harder and flatter.
   2. If a spot on the skin, such as the side of the large toe, is rubbed extensively, a large number of living cells may push up quickly and form an extra-thick layer of dead cells, called a callous.
   3. When minor injuries occur to the epidermis, living epidermal cells divide by mitotic cell division to quickly replace the damaged cells. Damage to dermal cells takes longer to repair.
   4. The living cells of the epidermis contain two color pigments—orange-yellow carotene and brown, yellow-brown, or black melanin—that gives the skin its characteristic color.
   5. Continued damage to the epidermis from overexposure to UV radiation can cause premature wrinkling of the skin and skin cancer.

LEARNING ACTIVITY 15.1

Skin Helps to Regulate Body Temperature, Thereby Helping the Body to Maintain Homeostasis

Have students wet a finger and blow on it. The finger feels cool as the moisture evaporates; that is, as heat energy is taken away from the finger to produce evaporation. Point out that the evaporation of perspiration produces the same cooling effect.

Have the students recall how flushed their faces become when they are hot. Point out that this flushing occurs because the blood vessels expand and allow more of the heated blood to flow into the skin. Now have the students recall the "goose bumps" that form on their arms when they become cold. The reason for this phenomenon is that the blood vessels contract and the pores close tightly to prevent body heat from escaping. As a result, tiny bumps are formed all over the surface of the skin.

LEARNING ACTIVITY 15.2

Compare Fingerprints

Have the students make and compare fingerprints. Obtain an ink stamp pad. Let each student pick up ink on his or her right forefinger by pressing the right side of the fingertip against the pad and rolling the finger from right to left. Then have the student roll the inked fingertip from right to left on a small piece of white paper with the student's name on it. Let the students compare fingerprints, using a magnifying glass, and note that no two prints are exactly the same. Common patterns, however, are the arch, the whorl, the loop, and combinations of these.

Inquiry-Based Learning Activity 15.2. Modified

Every person is a little bit different from everyone else. One of these differences can be found in our fingerprints, but just how different are our fingerprints? Let's begin by placing your students in groups of 3 or 4. Have them make a set of fingerprints by coloring their fingertips with washable colored markers and then stamping them onto index cards. Avoid using yellow, but green, blue, red, black, and orange work well. After writing their names next to the appropriate fingerprints, have your students investigate them using a magnifier to see how many different kinds they can find. What are the different groupings?

What level of inquiry is this modification? In this activity, the students are provided with a question. However, they are only given direction on the data collection. Also, the students working in groups work independently of you, their teacher, to uncover the various connections among their fingerprints. These characteristics suggest that this activity mixes three different levels. Beginning with the **problem identification,** the activity starts at **Level I** with you, the teacher, clearly providing your students with the question they will be investigating. Next, the **problem solving process** shifts the inquiry to **Level II (Transition to Level III)** since the students are only given direction on the data to collect and not given the actual data. Finally, for the **identification of the solution,** the activity shifts to **Level III.** Here the students are allowed to develop their own ideas about how to group the different fingerprints they will see. **Some questions to consider.** What are some advantages to mixing inquiry levels in a single activity? What are some of the disadvantages? What do you think this approach will help students understand about carrying out their own independent investigations?

C. Beneath the epidermis is the thicker **dermis**.
   1. The dermis is made of tough connective tissues that allow the skin to stretch and then return to its original shape.
   2. In the dermis are blood vessels, nerves, oil glands, sweat glands, muscles, and cells that produce hair.

D. Beneath the dermis is the **subcutaneous** layer of fatty tissue that attaches the skin to the rest of the body.

III. **Hair and Nails**

A. **Hair** is a thread of horny material produced by special cells in the dermis. It is made of the same material as that found in the dead cells of the epidermis.
   1. As newly formed hair grows, it passes up a tube through both the dermis and epidermis and then moves out beyond the surface of the skin. Hair can be coarse or fine, straight or curly.
   2. Although the root of the hair is alive, the rest of the hair is dead.
   3. The hair grows until it reaches a certain length and then falls out. When a hair falls out, a new one may grow in its place. The length of a hair depends on whether it is body, head, eyebrow, or eyelash hair.
   4. Inside the hair is a pigment that gives it its special color. When people become older, the hair pigment disappears and the hair grows in white.

B. Hair serves several important functions.
   1. Hair protects the body from ultraviolet radiation.
   2. Hair on the skull helps to insulate the skull and to cushion blows to the head.
   3. Hairs guard openings to the body from foreign bodies and insects.
   4. Sensory nerve endings around each hair follicle provide an early warning system to movement in that area.

C. **Nails** are also made of a horny material produced in the skin. This material is the same as that found in the dead cells of the epidermis. The root of the nail is alive, but the rest is dead. The primary function of nails is to protect the tips of fingers and toes.
   1. Fingernails grow about three times faster than toenails.

LEARNING ACTIVITY 15.3

Exploring Human Hair and Nails

A. Compare Color and Texture of Various Hairs Under a Microscope

Take a hair from your own body. See whether you can find three layers of cells. The middle layer is the one that contains the pigment that gives the hair color. Look at various hairs from your body and note any difference in appearance and quality of the hairs. Compare human hair with hair from various animals such as cat and dog hairs.

B. Measure the Rate of Growth of Nails

With a permanent marker, draw a narrow line across the nail close to the base of one fingernail and one toenail. Measure the greatest distance between the outer edge of each nail and the line. Repeat the measurement each week until the line is cut off. Plot the measurements on graph paper. Determine and compare the rates of growth of the nails. Compare your results with those of your classmates.

Skeletal System

I. Functions of the Skeletal System

A. The skeleton holds the body erect and gives the body its shape.

B. Muscles attach to the skeleton, making it possible for the body to walk, breathe, and eat.

C. Many bones function as levers that can change the magnitude and direction of the forces generated by skeletal muscle.

D. The skeleton provides protection to body organs.

E. Some bones are responsible for producing blood cells and storing fat and minerals.

F. Specialized bones of the middle ear function in hearing.

II. Structure of the Skeleton

A. The 206 bones that comprise the human skeleton can be divided into two groups.
   1. The **axial skeleton** includes the skull (cranium) and the bones that support it.
   2. The **appendicular skeleton** includes the bones of the arms and legs and the structures associated with them.

B. **Cranial bones** form a case that surrounds the brain.
   1. In children, the joints between these bones are movable, allowing the bones to grow. In adults, the bones have grown together to form a solid case, and the joints are no longer movable.
   2. Other bones in the skull include the cheek, nose, and jaw bones.

C. The spinal (or vertebral) column consists of 33 bones, called **vertebrae**, stacked on top of one another with discs of cartilage between them.
   1. These vertebrae and their structure provide a strong support for the weight of the body and the head, and make it possible for the head and trunk of the body to turn and bend in different directions.
   2. The spinal column also protects a large bundle or network of nerves, called the spinal cord.

D. In both males and females, the skeleton has 12 pairs of ribs that form a **rib cage** protecting the heart and lungs. All 12 pairs are connected in back, by hinge joints, to the vertebrae of the spinal column. The upper seven pairs of ribs are connected in front to the breastbone, or sternum, by cartilage.

E. The arm is made up of a long bone that runs from the shoulder to the elbow, the two bones of the forearm, the wrist bones, the hand bones, and the finger bones.

F. A pair of bones joins each arm at the shoulder. A long, narrow collarbone connects the upper end of the breastbone with each shoulder. A large, flat shoulder blade is at the back of each shoulder.

G. The leg is made up of a long bone that runs from the hip to the knee, a kneecap that protects the knee joint, the two bones that go from the knee to the ankle, the ankle bones, the foot bones, and the toe bones.

H. Several hip bones together form the pelvis and are connected to the vertebrae near the bottom (above the coccyx vertebrae or tailbone) of the spinal column.
   1. The pelvis provides a firm circular support, called the pelvic girdle, for the body.
   2. The pelvis allows the legs to move freely.
   3. In females, the pelvic girdle can expand at its joints to allow for childbirth.

I. The place where two bones meet is called a **joint**.
   1. Some joints, called immovable joints, do not allow movement. This lack of mobility occurs because the bones have grown together to form a solid mass. Examples of immovable joints include the cranial bones, the breastbone, and the tailbone.
   2. Some joints, like the joint between the ribs and the backbone, as well as the female pelvis, are partially movable.
   3. Joints that can move quite freely are referred to as movable joints.
      a. One type of movable joint is called a hinge joint. Similar to a door hinge that allows a door to swing back and forth, a hinge joint allows a bone to move back

and forth easily. Joints of the elbows, knees, fingers, and toes are hinge joints.

b. Another type of movable joint is the ball-and-socket joint, where the end of one bone forms a ball that fits into a hollow, or socket, of another bone. A ball-and-socket joint makes it possible for a bone to move in many directions. The shoulder and hip joints are examples.

c. Another type of movable joint is the pivot joint, which works like a pivot to allow the bones to move around and back. The lower arm bones and the head on the spine move on pivot joints.

J. Bones that come together at movable joints are all held together by strong bands of connective tissue called *ligaments*.

III. Materials in the Skeleton

A. Bone and cartilage are types of connective tissue.

1. In **bone**, a large amount of hard mineral matter, especially calcium phosphate, is deposited between the cells making the outer part of the bone hard.
2. **Cartilage** has a soft, smooth material that is tough and flexible between its cells.
3. When a baby first begins to form inside its mother's womb, its skeleton is mostly cartilage. Bone cells soon replace many of the cartilage cells.
4. Long bones in young people have cartilage **growth plates** near each end of the bones. Bone cells are produced in this area. The change from cartilage to bone tissue, which continues until the child grows into an adult, requires calcium. This is a major reason why nutritionists recommend that children drink milk and consume other foods rich in calcium. Eventually, the growth plates fill in with bone cells and growth ceases.
5. The adult skeleton still contains some cartilage. The ears and the end of the nose are made of cartilage. There is a disc of cartilage between each of the vertebrae of the spinal column, and the ends of the long bones are covered with cartilage. Ribs are connected to the breastbone by strips of cartilage.

B. Many bones have a center cavity containing a soft, spongy tissue called *marrow*. Bones that contain a center cavity of marrow include the ribs, sternum, vertebrae, and skull, and the long bones of the arms and legs. There are two kinds of marrow—red and yellow.

1. **Red marrow** is found in the ends of long bones, in the vertebrae, and in flat bones such as the ribs, breastbone, and shoulder bones. Red and white blood cells are made in the red marrow, giving red marrow its reddish color and name.
2. **Yellow marrow** is found in the shafts of the long bones. Yellow marrow stores fat for energy, which gives the marrow a yellowish color and its name.

Muscular system

I. Functions and Kinds of Muscles

A. The human body contains more than 700 muscles.

1. A primary function of muscles is to provide movement. The muscles contract and cause other parts of the body to move. Muscles cause every movement the body makes.
2. There are two types of muscles—voluntary and involuntary. Both are controlled by the nervous system.

B. **Voluntary muscles** are muscles we can consciously control.

1. These muscles move whenever we want them to move.
2. The muscles that move the bones of the skeleton are voluntary muscles.
3. Some voluntary muscles, such as the arm muscles, are connected to bones by tough white cords of connective tissue called *tendons*.
4. Other voluntary muscles are connected directly to the bones.
5. Some voluntary muscles, such as the lip muscles, are connected to other muscles.
6. The cells of voluntary muscles are long and round and are bound together by connective tissue into small bundles.
7. These voluntary muscle cells have cross-stripes, and the muscles are called *striated muscles*.

C. **Involuntary muscles** are muscles that we cannot consciously control.

1. The action of involuntary muscles is controlled by the nervous system.
2. These muscles produce the movements needed to keep us alive by moving food through the digestive system, by moving blood through the body, and by controlling breathing.
3. The cells of involuntary muscles are spindle-shaped and are found in layers in the walls of the digestive system, blood vessels, and other organs.
4. These cells do not have any cross-stripes, so involuntary muscles are called *smooth muscles*.
5. Contraction of smooth muscle is slower and more prolonged than that of heart or skeletal muscle.

6. The **heart muscles** consist of a special kind of involuntary muscle that is branched. Heart muscles are found only in the heart.

D. Some muscles are both voluntary and involuntary. They operate automatically, without our control, but also can be partially controlled. Muscles that operate the eyelid and the diaphragm are both voluntary and involuntary. We can consciously control the action of those muscles but, because of muscle fatigue, conscious control is limited.

II. How Muscles Work

A. Muscles work in only one way: by contracting. When muscles contract, they become shorter

LEARNING ACTIVITY 15.4

Exploring Bones, Joints, Muscles, Ligaments, and Tendons

A. Examine an Animal Bone

Obtain the leg bone of a lamb, calf, or pig from a meat market. Ask for a bone that has the end of a joint still on it, and have the bone split lengthwise in half. Examine the joint and distinguish between the cartilage and the bone. Identify the ligaments holding the joint together. Look for bits of tendon tissue that hold the muscles to the bone. Locate the yellow, fatty marrow in the center of the long part of the bone.

B. Determine the Composition of Bone

Put a chicken bone in a metal pie tin and heat it over a hot plate or in the oven until the bone is covered with a grayish-white ash. Let the bone cool, and note how light and brittle the bone is now. Point out that the heat has burned away all the animal matter in the bone, leaving only the mineral matter. If you have an accurate balance, weigh the bone both before and after heating, and determine the percentages of animal and mineral matter in the bone.

Soak the leg or thigh bone from a chicken in a jar of strong vinegar for 4 or 5 days. Remove the bone and wash it in water. Now bend the bone. The vinegar has dissolved and removed the mineral matter from the bone, leaving the soft, flexible animal matter. Although the bone still has its original shape and appearance, it will now be soft and flexible enough that you can very easily tie it into a knot.

C. Examine a Ligament

Obtain a joint from a calf, lamb, or pig shoulder from a meat market. Move the joint and examine the ligament that holds the ends of the bones together.

D. Examine X-rays of Broken Bones

Obtain X-rays of broken bones and point out the different kinds of breaks. Point out the need for a cast or splint in helping a broken bone to mend. Discuss what might happen if an unqualified person moves a person who may have broken bones in an accident.

E. Locate Body Tendons

Have students move the fingers of both hands up and down rapidly, as if they were playing the piano. Notice the movement of the tendons on the back of the hand. The tendons are being moved by muscles in the forearm. Continue the movement for a full minute or two, and notice the forearm muscles becoming tired.

Place the fingers of the left hand on the inside of the elbow of the right hand, just above the joint, and flex the right forearm a few times. You will feel the tendons moving. Grasp the back of one ankle and move your foot up and down. The large tendon that you feel moving is the Achilles tendon.

F. Explore the Tendons of a Chicken's Foot

Obtain a chicken's foot from a meat market. Cut away some of the skin and flesh to expose the strong, white tendons. Pull the tendons one at a time. Some tendons will make the toes bend; whereas others will straighten the toes. Because the tendons are attached to muscles, note that the muscles only pull, and never push, regardless of how the toes move.

G. Observe How Voluntary Muscles Work

Double your arm and feel your muscle. This muscle is the biceps muscle. Now grasp the outside of your upper arm near the elbow and straighten the arm. You will feel the pull of your triceps muscle. Note that muscles work in pairs. When you bend your arm, the biceps muscle contracts while the triceps muscle relaxes. When you straighten your arm, the biceps muscle relaxes and the triceps muscle contracts. Point out that when a muscle contracts, it becomes shorter and thicker, producing a pull on the bones.

Grip the back of your thigh and bend your leg at the knee, bringing your heel up toward the thigh. Note how the thigh muscle thickens as it contracts and pulls on the bone.

H. See the Action of Involuntary Muscles

Look in a mirror. Watch your eyelid close automatically. This demonstration shows that involuntary muscles are working. Now use voluntary muscles to close the eyelid yourself. This phenomenon can also be observed in the movement of your diaphragm. Note how involuntary muscles make the diaphragm move automatically as you breathe. Now use voluntary muscles to raise and lower the diaphragm muscles yourself.

I. Observe the Action of the Lip Muscles

Purse your lips tightly, just as if you were whistling, and feel the ring of muscles around the lips. Point out that these lip muscles are unusual in that they are attached to other muscles rather than to tendons or bones.

and thicker and in this way exert a pull. Muscles can exert only a pull, never a push.

B. Voluntary skeletal muscles that move joints always work in pairs.
   1. When one muscle contracts, the other muscle relaxes.
   2. The muscle that bends a joint is called a *flexor*, and the muscle that straightens the joint is called an *extensor*.
   3. The flexor biceps muscle on the top of our upper arm makes the forearm move upward, and the extensor triceps muscle beneath our upper arm makes the forearm move down again. When the biceps contracts and works, the triceps rests and relaxes.

C. Involuntary muscles usually work singly, by contracting and relaxing.

Nutrients

I. **The Body's Need for Nutrients**

A. A nutrient is any substance acquired from the environment and needed by the body for homeostasis; that is, for growth, maintenance, and repair. The absorption of nutrients from foods is called **nutrition.**
   1. Nutrients are divided into five categories: carbohydrates, lipids, proteins, vitamins, and minerals.
   2. Carbohydrates, lipids, vitamins, and proteins are made of molecules that contain carbon and hydrogen and thus are categorized as **organic molecules.** Minerals are inorganic.

B. Some individuals are allergic to certain foods. **Food allergies** occur when the body reacts negatively to a particular food.
   1. Although a person could be allergic to any food, eight foods account for almost all allergic reactions: peanuts, tree nuts (e.g., pecans, walnuts), milk, eggs, wheat, soy, fish, and shellfish).
   2. Food-allergic symptoms usually appear within minutes to 2 hours after the food has been ingested. Food-allergic reactions are due to an overactive immune system producing histamines to counter the harmful food.
   3. The most common symptom of a food-allergic reaction is hives. Other symptoms include tingling in the mouth, swelling of the tongue and throat, difficulty breathing, abdominal cramps, vomiting, diarrhea, and eczema. Anaphylaxis is a sudden, severe allergic reaction that involves several of these symptoms, as well as a drop in blood pressure and loss of consciousness.

C. **Carbohydrates** are used in the body as the primary source of quick energy for all bodily functions.
   1. Carbohydrates are compounds of carbon, hydrogen, and oxygen, with the general chemical formula of $(CH_2O)_x$.
   2. The carbohydrates include the sugars and the starches. Honey, candy, and pastry are foods that are rich in sugar. Bread, potatoes, rice, cereals, spaghetti, and macaroni are rich in starches.
   3. Body energy must be obtained from a simple sugar called **glucose**, which has the formula $C_6H_{12}O_6$.
   4. Complex carbohydrates must be broken down early in digestion to be absorbed into the bloodstream and used in the body as glucose.
   5. When a person eats more carbohydrates than the body needs, a small amount of the extra carbohydrates are stored in the liver and muscles in the form of a carbohydrate known as **glycogen.** A larger amount of the excess carbohydrates is changed into fat and then stored throughout the body.

D. **Lipids** are also used to supply energy. They are necessary for building cell membranes, for synthesizing hormones, for protecting the body against injury, and for insulating the body against cold.
   1. Lipids are a diverse group of complex organic molecules that are insoluble in water. Lipids include fats (or triglycerides), oils, phospholipids, and cholesterol. Butter, shortening, oils, salad dressing, bacon, and nuts are foods that are rich in fats.
   2. Compared with a portion of equal weight, fats are capable of producing more than twice as much energy as carbohydrates.
   3. Unused fats are stored as fat deposits throughout the body.

E. The major role of dietary **protein** is to provide organic compounds known as **amino acids** that are used by the body to make new molecules for the repair and growth of cells, tissues, and organs.
   1. In the digestive tract, dietary protein is broken down into its amino acids. Then, when transported by the blood to body cells, the amino acids are reunited as necessary to form various proteins.
   2. The body can synthesize some amino acids from other amino acids. For example, the liver can synthesize from other amino acids nearly half of all amino acids used in building proteins. Amino acids that cannot be synthesized, but that must be supplied directly by foods, are called essential amino acids.
   3. Meat, milk, eggs, corn, beans, and soybeans are foods rich in essential amino acids.

F. **Vitamins** are complex organic compounds that control or regulate certain activities in the body and are important for body growth. In general, vitamins cannot be synthesized by the body (or cannot be synthesized in sufficient amounts) and must be obtained from dietary food sources.
   1. Vitamins required by humans are usually grouped into two categories, those that are water-soluble and those that are fat-soluble.
   2. Water-soluble vitamins dissolve in the water of the blood plasma and are excreted by the kidneys.
   3. Fat-soluble vitamins can be stored in body fat and can accumulate, with the potential of becoming toxic to the body.

G. Water soluble vitamins include the following.
   1. **Vitamin B1** (also called thiamine) helps to control the digestion and use of carbohydrates in the body and plays an important role in the transmission of nerve impulses. A mild deficiency of vitamin B1 causes loss of appetite, poor digestion, headaches, tiredness, and irritability. A severe lack of vitamin B1 can cause a serious nerve disorder called beriberi, as well as edema and heart failure. Vitamin B1 is found in milk, meat, and bread. Also, it is synthesized by bacteria in the large intestine where it is then absorbed into the bloodstream.
   2. **Vitamin B2** (also called riboflavin) is needed in energy processes, wound healing, and the activation of other vitamins. A deficiency of vitamin B2 causes stunted growth, lesions of the eye, reddened and cracked lips, and scaly skin. Vitamin B2 is found in green leafy vegetables, eggs, and organ meats. Also, it is synthesized by bacteria in the large intestine where it is then absorbed into the bloodstream.
   3. **Vitamin B3** (also called niacin) helps the digestive and nervous systems function properly and is needed for the digestion and use of fats. A deficiency of vitamin B3 causes a disease called pellagra, which results in skin rashes, a smooth tongue, digestive disturbances, mental problems, and paralysis. Vitamin B3 is found in liver, lean meats, grains, and legumes.
   4. **Vitamin B5** (known also as pantothenic acid) is important in metabolism and the synthesis of hormones and is found in milk, eggs, yeast, and liver. Vitamin B5 deficiency can cause allergies, morning stiffness, muscle cramps, fatigue, and impaired coordination.
   5. **Vitamin B6** (also known as pyridoxine) is important in the metabolism of fats and in antibody formation. It is found in meats, wheat germ, yeast, and whole grains. A deficiency can cause insomnia, muscular twitching, irritability, dermatitis, artherosclerosis, and kidney stones.
   6. **Vitamin B12** (also known as cobalamin) is important in the development of red blood cells and in the metabolism of amino acids. It is found in milk, meat, eggs, root vegetables, and fermented soy products. Also, it is synthesized by bacteria in the large intestine where it is then absorbed into the blood stream. A deficiency can cause atherosclerosis, memory loss, gastrointestinal problems, and pernicious anemia.
   7. **Biotin**, important in metabolism, is found in legumes, vegetables, and meat. A deficiency can cause fatigue, depression, muscle pain, dermatitis, and nausea.
   8. **Vitamin C** (also called ascorbic acid) regulates the use of calcium and phosphorus, helps build and maintain healthy teeth and gums, and functions in protein metabolism and wound healing. A mild lack of vitamin C produces sore gums, soft teeth, and weak blood vessels. A severe lack results in a disease called scurvy, which causes bleeding gums, a swollen tongue, a tendency to bruise easily, bleeding around the bones, and sometimes loss of teeth. Vitamin C is found in citrus fruits, cabbage, red pepper, and broccoli.
   9. **Folic acid** (known also as folacin) is important in the synthesis of RNA and DNA and in the production of blood cells. It is found in beans, green leafy vegetables, and whole wheat. A deficiency can cause red tongue, anemia, fatigue, and gastrointestinal disorders.

H. **Fat soluble vitamins** are vitamins A, D, E, and K.
   1. **Vitamin A** (also known as retinol) keeps the lining of the nose, throat, and eyelids healthy. A deficiency of vitamin A causes problems with night vision and can decrease the body's resistance to colds and other infections. A severe deficiency may result in blindness. Vitamin A is found in red, yellow, and green vegetables. In the United States it is also a frequent additive to dairy products.
   2. **Vitamin D** helps in the absorption of calcium and phosphorus into the blood stream. A deficiency can cause bone deformities and skeletal deterioration. Vitamin D is found in shrimp, liver, egg yolk, and fortified milk. The skin produces it when exposed to ultraviolet radiation in sunlight.
   3. **Vitamin E** (also known as tocopherol) is important in cellular respiration and as an antioxidant. A deficiency may cause heart disease, anemia, and neurological aging. It is found in seeds, leafy green vegetables, margarines, and shortenings.
   4. **Vitamin K** (also called menadione) helps the blood to clot. A deficiency can cause bleeding. Vitamin K is found in tomatoes, broccoli, spinach, green tea, and green cabbage.

Also, it is synthesized by bacteria in the large intestine where it is then absorbed into the blood stream.

I. **Minerals** are inorganic substances needed for body growth, for the repair of body tissues, and for regulating some activities of the body. The functions and sources of major minerals are shown in Table 15.1.
   1. In addition to the minerals shown in Table 15.1, other minerals are needed by the body in trace amounts. Some are used in conjunction with the work of specific enzymes; for others, their exact function is not known. Minerals needed in trace amounts include copper, manganese, nickel, selenium, tin, and vanadium.

J. **Water** is a mineral and is the most abundant substance in the body. It is so important to the body that a person will die more quickly from lack of water than from lack of any nutrient. All cells in the body need water to function properly. The body needs water to digest food, absorb it, carry it to all parts of the body, and get rid of the waste materials that are formed.
   1. The body loses about 2.5 liters of water per day through exhalation during breathing and through the elimination of sweat and urine. Consequently, water must be replaced constantly to prevent the serious problems caused by dehydration.
   2. Water for the body comes from three sources. Most foods contain water; some water is formed when the food is burned in the body; and water is taken into the body as drinking water or in other liquids.

II. Amount of Energy the Body Needs

A. The human body uses food as its source of energy. The amount of energy a person needs depends on many factors, such as size, age, level of activity, and metabolic rate.
   1. The amount of energy a food releases when it is metabolized in the body is measured in units called **calories.**
   2. The calorie is the amount of heat needed to raise the temperature of 1 milliliter (1 gram, or about 0.03 ounce by weight) of water 1° Celsius.
   3. Every bit of food is the source of a certain number of calories. Some foods are richer in calories than others. The amount of heat energy available in foods is represented in Calories, which is *calories* spelled with a capital C. A **Calorie** (spelled with a capital C) is equal to 1,000 calories (spelled with a lowercase *c*). The numbers in a dieting guide that give the caloric value of various foods indicate Calories, not calories.
   4. If a person takes in more Calories a day than the body can use, the extra energy is stored in the body as fat, and the person gains weight. If a person takes in fewer Calories a day than the body needs, the body burns the stored fat, and the person loses weight.

TABLE 15.1 Major Minerals Important for Growth and Maintenance

Mineral	Function	Source
Calcium	Bone and tooth formation; blood clotting; nerve impulse function	Milk, green vegetables, cheese, legumes
Chlorine	Gastric juice formation; acid-base balance	Table salt
Fluorine	Bone and tooth formation and protection	Tea, seafood, treated drinking water
Iodine	Constituent of thyroid hormones	Seafish and shellfish, dairy products, vegetables, iodized salt
Iron	Constituent of hemoglobin and of enzymes involved in metabolism	Eggs, meats, legumes, whole grains, green vegetables
Magnesium	Muscle nerve function; bone formation; enzyme function	Whole grains, leafy green vegetables
Phosphorus	Bone and tooth strengthening; energy production	Milk, cheese, meats, poultry, grains
Potassium	Nerve function; acid-base balance	Meats, milk, fruits
Sodium	Regulation of body pH; transmission of nerve impulses	Okra, celery, black mission figs, table salt
Sulfur	Component of insulin; hair, nails, and skin building	Nuts, dried fruits, barley, oatmeal, eggs, beans, cheese
Water	Transport of nutrients; temperature regulation; metabolic reactions	Solid foods, liquids, drinking water
Zinc	Metabolic processes	Wheat germ, wheat bran, pumpkin seeds, seafood, avocado

III. Balanced and Healthy Diet

A. Food experts have divided the foods that we need to grow and to keep healthy into groups (see Exploratory Activity 1.10). A person who eats the proper amounts of food from each food group every day has a balanced and healthy diet.

B. A balanced and healthy diet is one that helps a person grow normally, helps to keep the body free of excessive and harmful fat, and provides the body with the energy it needs. About four-sixths of the diet should be carbohydrates, one-sixth fats, and one-sixth proteins. The diet should also contain the proper amounts of minerals and vitamins the body needs.

Digestive System

I. Digestion

A. The changing of foods into a simpler, dissolved form that can enter and be used by the cells is called digestion.
   1. For food to be used by the body, it must enter the bloodstream, where it is carried to the cells of the body.
   2. The foods we eat are chemically too complicated, and usually in pieces too large, to be sent directly into the bloodstream for use by the cells.
   3. Moreover, because some of the foods we eat are insoluble in water they could not enter the cells even if they reached the cells.
   4. Therefore, the foods are broken down, simplified, and changed into soluble forms that the cells can use.
   5. Special organs that make up the digestive system in the body carry on digestion.
   6. There are two parts to the digestive system: the alimentary canal and the digestive glands.

B. The **alimentary canal** is the food tube, or digestive tract or passageway, through which the food moves in the body.
   1. About 9 meters long (nearly 30 ft), it includes all the organs that act on the food and digest it—the mouth, pharynx, esophagus, stomach, small intestine, large intestine, rectum, and anus.

C. The **digestive glands** include salivary glands, liver, pancreas, gastric glands of the stomach, and glands of the small intestine.
   1. These glands give off juices that enter the alimentary canal through small tubes called **ducts**.
   2. These juices contain powerful chemicals, called **enzymes**, that act on the foods and break them up into simpler, dissolved forms that can then be digested.

II. Digestion in the Mouth

A. The function of the mouth is to start the preparation of food for digestion.

B. The **teeth** break up the food to start the release of its nutrients.
   1. A child first grows a temporary set of 20 baby teeth, 10 in each jaw.
   2. As the jaws grow larger, the child loses these baby teeth and grows a permanent set of 32 teeth, 16 in each jaw.
   3. The four flat, sharp-edged front teeth in each jaw are called incisors and are used for biting and cutting (see Figure 15.1).
   4. The two long, pointed teeth, one on each side of the incisors, are called canine teeth and are used for tearing.
   5. On each side of the canine teeth are two premolars and three molars (10 in each jaw), that have large surfaces and are used for grinding and chewing.

C. Most of the tooth is made of a hard, bonelike material called dentine.
   1. The part of the tooth beyond the gum is called the crown and is covered with a very hard white material called enamel.
   2. The root of the tooth fits into a socket in the jawbone.
   3. Incisor and canine teeth usually have one root, and premolar and molar teeth have two, three, or even four roots.
   4. Blood vessels and nerves run from the root into the hollow center of the tooth.

D. While food is being chewed, it is mixed with saliva. **Saliva** moistens and softens the food, making it easier to swallow.
   1. Saliva comes from three pairs of glands, located in the sides of the face and lower jaw.

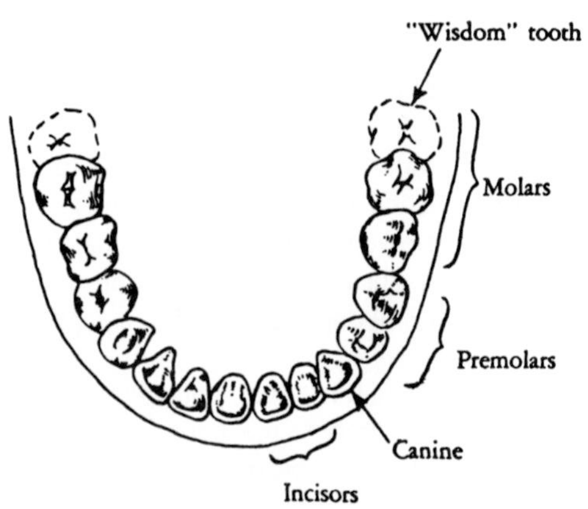

FIGURE 15.1 Diagram of the teeth in a jaw.

LEARNING ACTIVITY 15.5

Digestion in the Mouth

Have the students chew a soda cracker or saltine and note how the cracker tastes sweeter after it has been chewed for some time and the saliva has had a chance to act on the starch in the cracker. Place some of this chewed cracker-saliva mixture in a test tube and test with Benedict's solution (available from a pharmacy or scientific supply house) for the presence of simple sugars. As a control, test some saliva alone for the presence of simple sugars.

2. Saliva also contains an enzyme (amylase) that digests starch, changing it into sugars that can dissolve in water.

E. The **tongue** helps in chewing the food by keeping it between the teeth, and helps in swallowing by pushing the food to the back of the mouth.

F. Food stays in the mouth for a short time, is swallowed, and then is moved by muscles down the throat and esophagus into the stomach.

1. The action of involuntary muscles moving food in one direction through the esophagus is called peristalsis. Peristalsis occurs also in the stomach and intestines where it helps move food along the digestive tract.

III. Digestion in the Stomach

A. The stomach is a pear-shaped pouch located on the left side of the body below the lower ribs.

1. The stomach is elastic and can expand to hold food. Its main function is to hold food while it is being prepared for digestion in the small intestine.
2. Food usually remains in the stomach for 2 to 4 hours.

B. The lining of the stomach has many glands, called **gastric glands.**

1. These glands secrete gastric juice, which flows through tiny tubes (ducts) into the stomach, where it mixes with food.
2. Gastric juice contains an enzyme (pepsin) that breaks some proteins down into simpler materials. It also contains a hormone, gastrin, that stimulates the secretion of hydrochloric acid, which dissolves minerals in the food and kills bacteria that enter the stomach with the food.
3. To prevent the stomach from digesting itself, which it does to some extent, the lining of the stomach also secretes a protective layer of mucus. Stomach lining cells that are damaged by digestion are constantly being replaced with new cells. If this replacement or the mucus lining is insufficient, a person may develop an ulcer, which in effect is the result of the stomach's self-digestion.

C. The stomach has powerful muscles that keep contracting and relaxing, churning the food.

1. This churning action breaks the food into small pieces and mixes these tiny pieces with the gastric juice.
2. Only a few substances, including water, some drugs, and alcohol, can enter the bloodstream through the stomach wall.

D. The food, now a thick, acidic liquid called chyme, passes from the stomach into the small intestine, a little at a time, through a valve that opens and closes regularly about every 20 seconds.

IV. Digestion in the Small Intestine

A. The small intestine is the main organ for digesting food. In an adult living human, it is about 3 meters (10 ft) long and 2–5 centimeters (1–2 in.) in diameter. Because it is so long, it coils back and forth many times inside the body. It is called small because its diameter is small relative to the diameter of the large intestine.

B. While food is in the small intestine, juices from three digestive glands pour into the small intestine.

1. Glands in the lining of the small intestine produce **intestinal juice.**
2. The **pancreas,** a long gland that lies just behind the stomach, produces pancreatic juice. The juice flows through a duct (tube) into the duodenum, which is the upper end of the small intestine.
3. Bile is a brownish-green liquid produced in the **liver,** a large gland located in the upper right part of the abdomen. Bile flows from the liver into the gallbladder, where it is stored until needed.
4. When food leaves the stomach and enters the small intestine, the bile flows into the bile duct, which joins with the pancreatic duct just as they both reach the duodenum and enter the small intestine.
5. An enzyme in bile breaks the fat into simpler materials, and at the same time the bile separates the fat into tiny droplets, which can be more easily attacked by enzymes from the pancreatic juice.
6. Both pancreatic and intestinal juices contain various enzymes that collectively digest carbohydrates, fats, and proteins, changing them into simpler, dissolved molecules that can enter and be used by the cells in the body.

C. After food has been digested in the small intestine, it is absorbed into the bloodstream through the walls of the small intestine.

1. The inside of the small intestine has many ridges and fingerlike bulges, called villi, that absorb the simple, dissolved forms of digested food.
2. The ridges and villi contain blood vessels that absorb the dissolved nutrients, and the bloodstream carries the nutrients away to cells throughout the body, where they are absorbed by osmosis.

D. **Osmosis** is the movement of water molecules through a cell membrane, either out of a cell or into a cell. Water will diffuse through a cell membrane from an area of higher water concentration to an area of lower water concentration.
1. The movement of dissolved materials into or out of any living cell is partly due to this process of osmosis. Sometimes materials dissolved in the water simply pass through the membrane with the water. Requiring no consumption of cellular energy, this process is referred to as **passive transport.**
2. For other nutrients, such as minerals, to move across a cell membrane, the cell may have to expend energy. This is **active transport.** In this process, a cell protein binds with the particle of the substance to be transported. Chemical energy from the cell is then used to change the shape of the proteins so that the particle to be moved is released on the other side of the cell membrane. Once the particle is released, the protein's original shape is restored. Thus, a substance can be transported into or out of a cell, moving from an area where there is less of the substance (a lesser concentration) to a region where there is more of it (greater concentration).

E. The process of changing digested food into cellular material is called **assimilation.**

V. Actions of the Large Intestine

A. The large intestine, about 1.5 meters (5 ft) long and 7.5 centimeters (3 in) in diameter, begins below the small intestine.
1. For most of its length, the large intestine is called the **colon.** The final 15 centimeters (6 in.) is called the **rectum.**

B. Food that cannot be digested or used by the body passes from the small intestine into the colon as waste material.
1. Initially, the waste materials are quite watery.
2. They pass through the large intestine very slowly while the water and salts are absorbed back into the bloodstream through the walls of the large intestine.
3. Waste materials also contain large amounts of bacteria that normally live in the large intestine. These bacteria synthesize vitamins B1, B2, B12, and K, which would otherwise be deficient in a normal diet. Cells lining the colon absorb these vitamins into the bloodstream.
4. The removal of the water gives the waste material a more solid form, called **feces** (fecal matter), which consists of indigestible wastes and the remains of dead bacteria.

C. The fecal matter passes into the rectum for temporary storage—18 to 24 hours—and then out through an opening, called the **anus.** This act of eliminating feces is called defecation.
1. Defecation is a reflex action that becomes voluntary from about the age of 2.

D. The entire journey from the time food enters the mouth until the defecation of waste materials takes from 24 to 33 hours.

Cardiovascular System

I. Function of the Cardiovascular (Circulatory) System

A. The cardiovascular system, consisting of the blood, blood vessels, and heart, has four major functions.
1. It carries digested and dissolved food to the cells of the body.
2. It brings oxygen to the cells for burning the food and producing heat and energy.
3. It takes away the waste materials produced by the cells and carries the materials to organs that remove them from the body.
4. It carries germ-fighting blood cells.

II. Blood

A. Blood is a liquid tissue. There are about 5 liters (6 qt) of blood in the human body. The liquid part of blood is called **plasma** and represents about 55% to 60% of the blood.
1. Plasma is about 90% water, with many substances dissolved in it.
2. Plasma contains salts of sodium, calcium, potassium, and magnesium.
3. Plasma contains a special protein called fibrinogen that helps blood clot to reduce blood loss from an injury.
4. It also contains other proteins, such as albumins that help maintain the blood's osmotic pressure, and globulins that transport nutrients and play a role in the immune system.
5. Plasma contains antibodies, which fight disease.
6. Plasma contains hormones, which are given off by ductless (tubeless) glands in the body and help control the activities of the body.
7. Plasma also carries away waste materials, such as carbon dioxide and solid wastes of amino acid decomposition called urea.

B. Blood consists of three kinds of solid materials: red cells (or erythrocytes), white cells (or leucocytes), and platelets.

C. **Red blood cells** (RBC) are the most numerous cells in the body. Red blood cells are produced in bone marrow at the rate of about 2,000 per second. They live for only a few months, and are eventually destroyed in the liver.
   1. They have no nucleus. From a side view, they look like biconcave discs, that is, discs with both sides caved in. Their shape and lack of a nucleus gives each RBC a relatively large surface area through which gases may be exchanged between the cell and the surrounding blood plasma.
   2. They contain an iron compound called hemoglobin that gives them their red color and can bind with oxygen or carbon dioxide.
   3. The hemoglobin of the RBCs picks up oxygen from the lungs and carries it to the cells in the body.
   4. The cells use the oxygen to burn food, and carbon dioxide is produced as a waste material.
   5. The hemoglobin of the RBCs pick up the carbon dioxide and carry it to the lungs; from there the carbon dioxide exits the bloodstream and body via the tracheal passage.
   6. Blood type is determined by proteins on the surface of RBCs, which differ among individuals.

D. **White blood cells** (WBC) are larger than red cells but are less numerous: There is about one white cell to every 600 red cells. They, too, are produced in bone marrow.
   1. Although there are five different types of white blood cells, their function generally is to engulf pathogens or debris in tissues, thereby protecting the body against germs, or toxins.
   2. They are clear, colorless, and irregularly shaped, but they do have a nucleus.
   3. With an amoeboid-like movement, some can leave the walls of the blood vessels and move among the cells in the body.

E. **Platelets**, which also are produced in bone marrow, are much smaller than the red blood cells. They are not cells but only cytoplasmic fragments of cells that contain enzymes.
   1. Platelets are irregularly shaped and colorless.
   2. Their function is to aid in the process of clotting to prevent excessive blood loss from an injury.
   3. When a blood vessel breaks and bleeds, platelets stick to the edges of the wound and begin to contract.
   4. Platelets give off a chemical that unites with the calcium salts and fibrinogen in the plasma to form threadlike fibers called fibrin.
   5. Fibrin form a net that slows the flow of blood, traps the blood cells, and forms a clot that prevents the blood from escaping.

F. The average normal temperature of an adult's blood is about 38°C (100.4°F).
   1. Some persons have a normal blood temperature a little above or below this average.
   2. When ill, the temperature will be elevated a bit. However, a blood temperature above 40°C (104°F) or below 36°C (97°F) can cause disorientation, and a temperature above 42°C (108°F) can cause convulsions and permanent damage to the brain and other body cells.

G. Harmful bacteria, disease germs, and worn-out blood cells in the blood are filtered and removed by the liver and the spleen. The spleen also stores a reserve of red blood cells.
   1. The **liver** is a large organ, located in the upper right part of the abdomen.
   2. The **spleen** is much smaller and is located in the upper left part of the abdomen behind the stomach.

III. Blood Vessels

A. The blood moves throughout the body in closed tubes called blood vessels. There are three kinds of blood vessels in the body: arteries, veins, and capillaries.

B. **Arteries** are blood vessels that carry blood away from the heart.
   1. A large artery leaves the heart and keeps branching into smaller and smaller arteries (called arterioles) that spread throughout the body.
   2. The smallest branches lead to every part of the body.
   3. The walls of arteries are made of involuntary muscle, which contracts in much the same manner as the heart muscles contract.

C. **Veins** are blood vessels that carry blood back to the heart.
   1. There are tiny veins (called venules) throughout the body.
   2. These tiny veins come together, joining to form larger and larger veins, until a large vein that enters the heart is formed.
   3. Veins are wider than arteries, and their walls are thinner and less elastic; therefore, the flow of blood in the veins is slower than the flow in the arteries.
   4. The larger veins have cuplike valves that keep the blood from flowing backward.
   5. Veins do not contract, as do the large arteries.

D. **Capillaries** are very tiny blood vessels connecting the smallest arteries (arterioles) and the smallest veins (venules).
   1. Some are so small that blood cells must go through them in single file.
   2. Blood from the smallest arteries (arterioles) flows into the capillaries, travels through the capillaries, and then flows into the smallest veins (venules).

LEARNING ACTIVITY 15.6

Valves in the Veins

Ask students to stand; then ask each to let an arm hang down until the large veins on the hand become quite visible. Give the following instructions: Make a fist, place a fingertip on one vein, and push firmly downward toward the knuckles. While holding the finger in place, note how smooth the vein becomes as your finger presses on the valve and prevents blood from flowing into that portion of the vein. Now take away your finger. The vein will fill up with blood again.

3. All cells in the body are adjacent to a capillary.
4. Capillaries are the blood vessels that actually supply the cells of the body with the materials they need.
5. The walls of the capillaries are so thin that molecules of materials in the blood can pass into the cells, and molecules of materials in the cells can pass into the blood of the capillaries. The blood gives the cells nutrients and oxygen, whereas the cells give the blood carbon dioxide and other waste materials to carry away.
6. The total capillary surface area for this exchange is immense, averaging in an adult about 6,300 square meters—about half the area of a football or soccer field.

IV. Heart

A. The heart is a strong muscle, shaped like a pear and about as big as a human fist, that slants downward and is located to the left of the middle of the chest.

B. It acts as a pump by contracting and relaxing. When it contracts, blood is pumped out of it into the arteries, which also contract. When it relaxes, blood flows into the heart from the veins. The heart pumps the blood through the blood vessels to every part of the body and back again, all in about 30 seconds.

C. The heart has two sides: a right side and a left side.
   1. The two sides are completely separated by a wall called the septum.
   2. Each side pumps blood separately from the other.
   3. The blood in the two sides does not mix while it is in the heart.

D. The heart is also divided into four chambers, or compartments.
   1. The top two chambers are called atria, and the bottom two chambers are called ventricles.
   2. Thus, the heart has a right atria and a left atria at the top, separated from each other by the septum, and a right ventricle and a left ventricle at the bottom, also separated by the septum.
   3. The atria receive blood from the veins in the body and pump it down into the ventricles.
   4. The ventricles pump the blood into the arteries in the body.
   5. Both atria contract or pump at the same time, followed quickly by both ventricles contracting or pumping at the same time.

E. The heart has valves that prevent the blood from flowing back into the atria when the ventricles are contracting.
   1. There is a flap of connective tissue between the opening of the right atrium and the right ventricle, and between the opening of the left atrium and the left ventricle.
   2. When an atrium contracts, the flap is pushed aside, allowing the blood to move down into the ventricle.
   3. When a ventricle contracts, the flap is pushed upward and closes the opening so that the blood cannot flow up into the atrium.

F. Where the arteries leave the heart, there are also valves.
   1. These valves are pushed aside when the blood leaves the heart and enters the arteries.
   2. If the blood tries to flow back into the heart, it pushes the valve shut, stopping the blood from flowing back.

G. Veins also have valves located all through the body that prevent the blood from flowing back and force the blood to move toward the heart.
   1. Varicose veins are dilated superficial veins that are visible at the skin surface and are caused when venous valves malfunction.

H. The closing of the heart valves causes the sound of the beating heart.

I. A pulse is the beat that can be felt in the arteries every time the heart beats.
   1. The surge of blood through the arteries makes the artery walls expand and also produces a beat.
   2. This pulse can be felt by placing the finger (not the thumb) over an artery in the wrist or neck.
   3. The number of pulse beats in a minute indicates how fast the heart is beating, or contracting.

V. Circulation of the Blood

A. Blood flows through two large circulatory systems in the body that are connected to and controlled by the heart: the pulmonary system and the systemic system.

B. In the **pulmonary system**, blood flows from the heart to the lungs and returns.

LEARNING ACTIVITY 15.7

Examine an Animal Heart

Obtain the heart of a calf, sheep, or pig from a meat market. Pare away any fatty material present, and note how muscular the heart walls are. Try to identify the ventricles and atria before you begin to cut the heart open. Make incisions on either side of the lower narrow end of the wall. When you enter the ventricle, cut away more material so that you may see the cavities more clearly. Note how thick the walls are, especially those of the left ventricle.

Use a probe to find the main artery leading from the left ventricle to the body, and the pulmonary artery leading from the right ventricle to the lungs. Also probe for the flabbier veins entering the right and left atria. Look for the valves between the atria and ventricles. Slit the artery walls lengthwise and look for the valves that prevent blood from flowing back into the heart.

LEARNING ACTIVITY 15.8

Exploring Heartbeat and Pulse Rate

A. Explore with a Stethoscope

Make a stethoscope from three funnels, a glass Y-tube or T-tube, and two long plus one short pieces of rubber or plastic tubing (Figure 15.2). Have the students take turns listening to heartbeats. Compare the heartbeats when they are quiet with their heartbeats after they have jumped up and down 15 to 20 times or in some other way exercised vigorously.

B. Explore Your Pulse

Using the first two fingers of the right hand, feel for the pulse on the left hand at the base of the thumb where the left hand joins the wrist (Figure 15.3). Count the number of pulse beats in 1 minute. Now jump up and down 15 to 20 times, or in some other way exercise vigorously, and take your pulse beat for 1 minute again. Note how much stronger and faster the pulse beat has become.

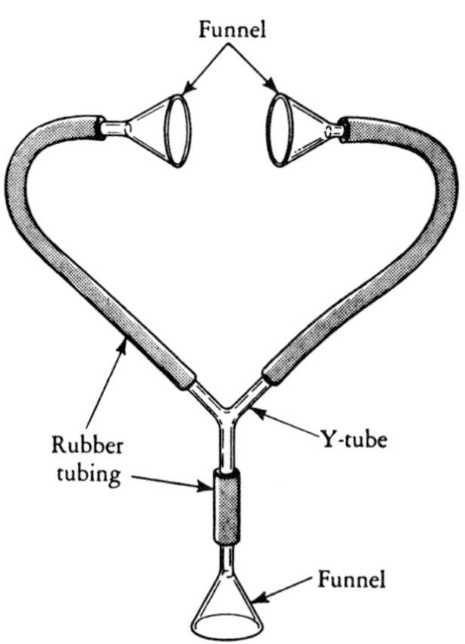

FIGURE 15.2 A homemade stethoscope.

FIGURE 15.3 Taking a pulse beat.

1. Blood coming from all over the body enters the right atrium of the heart.
2. The right atrium pumps the blood down to the right ventricle.
3. The right ventricle then pumps the blood to the lungs.
4. In this system the blood contains carbon dioxide; when the blood is sent to the lungs, it gives up the carbon dioxide and picks up oxygen.

C. In the **systemic system**, blood flows from the heart throughout the body and returns.

1. Blood coming from the lungs enters the left atrium of the heart.
2. The left atrium pumps the blood down to the left ventricle.
3. The left ventricle then pumps the blood to the body.
4. In this system, the blood brings fresh oxygen to the cells in the body, gives up the oxygen to the cells, and at the same time picks up carbon dioxide, which it brings back to the heart.

D. Each ventricle has one artery leading from it.

   1. The artery leading to the lungs branches about 1 inch above the heart, each branch going to one of the lungs.
   2. The other large artery passes to various parts of the body with branches going to the brain, arms, rib areas, body organs, and legs.

E. More than one vein returns blood to the atria.
   1. Four veins return blood from the lungs to the left atrium.
   2. Two veins return blood from the body to the right atrium, one vein coming from the head and arms, and the other vein coming from the lower part of the body.

F. In each system, the large arteries branch again and again into smaller arteries and finally lead into capillaries; then the capillaries lead into small veins (venules) that come together again and again to form the large veins.

 Lymphatic System

I. Function

A. The lymphatic system protects the body against infection and disease.

II. Structure

A. The lymphatic system consists of the fluid lymph, a network of lymphatic vessels, specialized cells called lymphocytes, and tissue and organ components integrated with other body systems.
   1. The **appendix**, for example, located at the top of the large intestine, functions as an organ of the lymphatic system.
   2. The appendix produces hormones necessary for regulating growth and development of the human fetus and young children during their early years, especially in strengthening the immune system.
   3. The function of the appendix diminishes with increasing age.

B. As blood flows through the capillaries, some of the plasma passes through the thin capillary walls and fills the spaces between the cells of the body. This liquid, called **lymph**, is the clear liquid that fills blisters and appears when the skin is scraped and bruised.
   1. Lymph contains digested food, water, salts, and other materials.
   2. The lymph bathes the cells and supplies digested food, and the cells give the lymph the waste products from the cells.

C. The lymph returns to the bloodstream through special lymph vessels.
   1. The lymph collects in tiny tubes that join again and again to form larger tubes.
   2. These lymph vessels have valves, just as veins do.
   3. The contraction of muscles, such as during exercise, moves lymph through the lymph vessels.
   4. The lymph finally collects in two large vessels that open into two large veins just above the heart.

D. Enlarged lymph vessels are called **lymph nodes.**
   1. Lymph nodes are scattered throughout the body, but many are concentrated in the neck, armpit, and groin. During an infection, nodes may swell and become painful.
   2. In the lymph nodes the lymph tubes break up into many smaller tubes again.
   3. The nodes contain large numbers of special white blood cells (lymphocytes) that are produced in the thymus and whose function is to kill bacteria and other disease germs that may have entered the lymph from the cells in the body.
   4. The function of the lymph nodes, then, is to filter and purify the lymph before it returns to the blood.
   5. The spleen also helps to filter blood by removing foreign matter and aged RBCs from plasma.

 Respiratory System

I. Function of the Respiratory System

A. The breakdown of carbohydrates in the cells that produces energy is called **cellular respiration.** In cellular respiration the cells of the body take in oxygen, use the oxygen to burn the digested food and produce heat and energy, and then give off carbon dioxide.

B. The function of the respiratory system is to bring oxygen into the body and to get rid of the waste carbon dioxide.

II. Structure of the Respiratory System

A. The respiratory system includes the nose and nasal passages; the throat, or pharynx; the windpipe, or trachea; the voice box, or larynx; the bronchi; the bronchial tubes; and the lungs.

B. Air enters the nose through two nostrils, which are separated by a wall called the septum.
   1. The air then passes through the nasal passages, which are spaces that lie above the mouth.

2. In the nostrils and the front part of the nasal passages are hairs that trap dust and germs.
3. In the rear part of the nasal passages are hairlike projections, called cilia, that steadily beat back and forth.
4. The cilia trap dust and other materials and carry them toward the mouth, where they are either swallowed or coughed up. Nicotine and tars from tobacco paralyze these cilia, prohibiting their removal of foreign materials, which then build and cause irritation of the cells that line the passageways. This irritation can result in cancer.
5. The nasal passages have a soft lining that gives off a liquid called mucus that also helps trap dust and germs.
6. As the air passes through the nasal passages, it becomes warm and moist.

C. The air passes from the nasal passages to the throat, or pharynx.
1. In the back of the throat are two tubes. The gullet, or esophagus, leads to the stomach. The windpipe, or trachea, which is in front of the esophagus, leads to the lungs.
2. At the top of the windpipe is a flap or lid of tissue called the epiglottis. When food and water are being swallowed, the epiglottis covers and closes the windpipe, preventing the food and water from going down the windpipe and causing choking.
3. The epiglottis is raised during breathing, allowing air to enter the windpipe freely.

D. At the top of the windpipe, above the epiglottis, is the voice box, or larynx. The voice box, which is really shaped like a box, is made of cartilage.
1. The "Adam's apple" is a strip of cartilage that sticks out in front of the voice box.
2. Inside the voice box are two strips of elastic tissue called the vocal cords. Tiny muscles can pull the vocal cords, making them tight.
3. When the vocal cords are tight and air passes between them, they vibrate, thereby producing sound.
4. The tighter the vocal cords, the faster the cords vibrate and the higher is the pitch of the sound produced. The looser the vocal cords, the slower they vibrate, and the lower the pitch of the sound.
5. Because men's voice boxes are larger than women's and their vocal cords are longer and thicker, men's vocal cords vibrate more slowly and the pitch of their voices is lower.

E. The arrangement of the trachea, esophagus, and larnyx in humans is different from that of any other animal or primate; this difference is what allowed humans to develop speech. This particular arrangement is also what prevents humans from speaking, breathing, and eating (or drinking) simultaneously (or causes choking if they should occur simultaneously).

F. The bottom of the windpipe divides into two branches, called bronchi. Each bronchus enters one of the lungs, where it divides into smaller branches called bronchial tubes.

G. The bronchial tubes branch again and again until the smallest tubes end in clusters of little air sacs called alveoli (plural for alveolus). The alveoli look like tiny clusters of grapes. Each lung is one great mass of these clusters of air sacs.

III. How We Breathe

A. Breathing is the mechanical process of getting air containing oxygen into the lungs and getting air containing carbon dioxide out of the lungs. Although breathing is a function of our respiratory system, it is only one function.
1. The actual exchange of these two gases takes place at the cellular level. The chemical process of breaking down food to release energy is called cellular respiration (discussed in the next section).
2. What is commonly referred to as artificial respiration would be more correctly called *artificial breathing*.

B. There is a common belief that in breathing the lungs draw in air, expand, and make the chest bulge. In fact, air is inhaled by being forced into the lungs *because* of changes in the size of the chest cavity and changes in the air pressure of the chest cavity.
1. The **diaphragm**, a strong sheet of muscle between the chest and the abdomen, plays an important function in breathing.
2. When muscles in the diaphragm contract, the diaphragm is pulled downward.
3. At the same time, the rib muscles contract and lift the ribs upward and outward.
4. This action of the diaphragm and ribs increases the size of the chest cavity, and the elastic lungs expand and become larger.
5. The increased lung size reduces the pressure of the air already in the lungs.
6. The air outside the body now exerts greater pressure than the air inside the lungs, so it rushes into the nose, nasal passage, windpipe, and lungs to these areas of lesser pressure.

C. Air is exhaled when the chest cavity becomes smaller.
1. The muscles in the diaphragm relax, and the diaphragm moves upward again.
2. The muscles in the ribs relax, and the ribs move downward and inward.
3. The chest cavity now becomes smaller, making the lungs smaller, so that air is forced out of the lungs and the body.

D. Breathing is an activity of the body that can take place involuntarily or voluntarily. In involuntary breathing, nerves in the brain control the muscles of the diaphragm and the ribs so that breathing takes place automatically. Although we can hold our breath and stop breathing, we cannot do it for very long before the involuntary action takes over and we breathe again.

IV. Process of Gas Exchange

A. The alveoli of the lungs are surrounded by millions of capillaries.
B. The oxygen that comes with the air into the lungs passes through the thin walls of the alveoli and through the thin walls of the capillaries into the blood.
C. Red blood cells pick up the oxygen by osmotic diffusion of oxygen into the cells, and the blood becomes bright red because of the oxygenated hemoglobin.
D. The blood passes from the lungs to the heart, which pumps it through the arteries and capillaries to every part of the body.
E. The cells in the body use the oxygen to burn glucose, thereby producing heat and energy and giving off carbon dioxide.
    1. The chemical process of breaking down food to release energy is called **cellular respiration.**
    2. Oxygen is required for this process to occur; oxygen is the catalyst that speeds up the process.
    3. The breakdown of a carbohydrate, for example, in the presence of oxygen, is shown by the following chemical equation:

$$O_2 + CH_2O \rightarrow H_2O + CO_2 + \text{energy}$$

LEARNING ACTIVITY 15.9

Exploring the Respiratory System

A. Examining Animal Lung Tissue

Obtain a portion of the lung of a calf, sheep, or pig from a meat market. Note how spongy the lung tissue is. Examine a section of this lung tissue under the low power of a microscope and locate a cluster of the many air sacs that are found throughout the tissue. Note that each air sac is surrounded by a fleshy wall. Change to the high power of the microscope, and you will be able to see capillaries in the wall.

B. Exploring How We Breathe

Obtain a lamp chimney and a one-hole rubber stopper to fit the top opening of the chimney. Insert a glass or plastic tube through the hole of the stopper. Use a rubber band to fasten a small rubber balloon to the bottom end of the glass tubing, then insert the stopper into the top of the chimney (Figure 15.4). Cut a piece of rubber from a large rubber balloon and use a rubber band to fasten this piece of rubber firmly to the bottom opening of the chimney. The chimney will represent the chest cavity, the balloon will represent one of your lungs, and the large piece of rubber will represent your diaphragm.

Pull the piece of rubber (diaphragm) downward. The air in the chimney (chest cavity) expands, reducing the air pressure in the chimney. Air from outside the chimney is forced in, inflating the balloon (lung). Now push the piece of rubber (diaphragm) upward. The air in the chimney (chest cavity) is compressed and contracts, increasing the air pressure in the chimney. Air will be forced out of the chimney through the glass tubing, causing the balloon (lung) to deflate. Repeat this procedure several times to simulate the steady action of inhaling and exhaling.

C. Exploring the Effect of Exercise on the Rate of Breathing

Have one student place a hand on another student's chest and count the number of times the student is breathing in 1 minute. Let one inhalation and one exhalation together count as just one breath. Now have the second student jump up and down 15 to 20 times or in some other way exercise until he or she is breathing quite heavily; then let the first student count the number of breaths in 1 minute again.

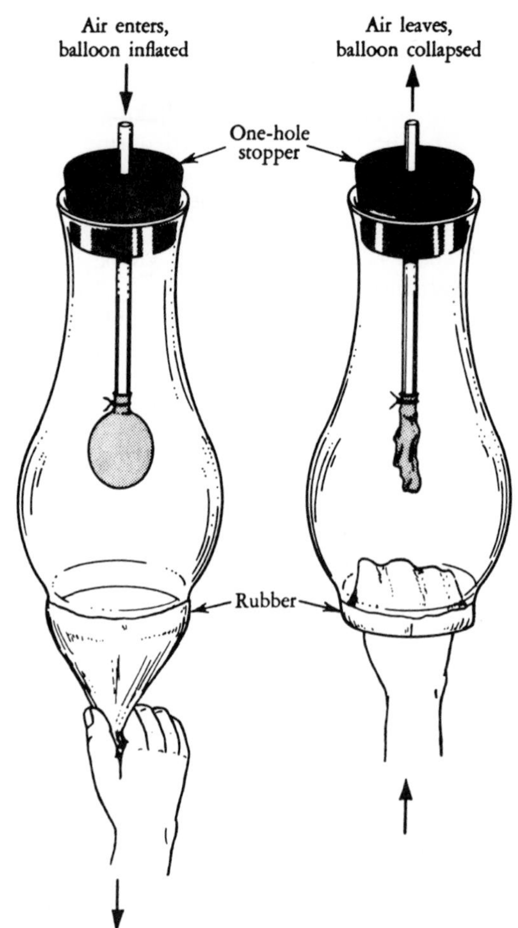

FIGURE 15.4 Simulating the operation of the diaphragm and lungs during breathing.

LEARNING ACTIVITY 15.10

Products of Respiration

A. Excretion of Carbon Dioxide

Obtain some limewater from a drugstore and pour a little into a test tube. Have one or all of the students bubble the limewater with a soda straw until the limewater becomes milky, showing the presence of carbon dioxide. The carbon dioxide comes from the air inside the students' lungs.

B. Excretion of Mineral Salts

Have the students lick their wrists after they return from a recess period where they have been playing actively. Point out that the salty taste is caused by the presence of mineral salts, which were dissolved in their perspiration and left behind when the perspiration evaporated.

4. The products of this breakdown of a carbohydrate are water, carbon dioxide, and energy.
5. The energy is in the form of heat energy and chemical energy; the chemical energy is a compound called adenosine triphosphate (ATP).
6. Some water is released with the exhaled air, and some of it is recycled by the blood and used elsewhere in the body.
7. The rate at which cellular respiration occurs is referred to as the metabolic rate. It is defined as the amount of energy (Calories) burned per hour per body surface area. Metabolic rate is affected by gender (males generally have a higher rate than females), age (rate decreases with age), and level of activity.
8. The basal metabolic rate (BMR) is a person's metabolic rate when at rest.

F. The red blood cells pick up the carbon dioxide, and the blood becomes dark red.

G. The blood passes through the capillaries and veins back to the heart.

H. The heart sends the blood containing the carbon dioxide to the lungs.

I. In the lungs, the carbon dioxide leaves the blood by passing through the thin walls of the capillaries and the thin walls of the air sacs into the lungs.

J. The air containing carbon dioxide is forced out of the lungs, and fresh air containing oxygen is forced into the lungs.

K. This action—getting oxygen into the body, using oxygen to produce heat and energy, and getting waste carbon dioxide out of the body—goes on continuously.

L. People yawn when the brain has received the message that the carbon dioxide content of the blood is getting high. A yawn is the body's way of inhaling a larger than normal quantity of fresh air to exchange oxygen for the carbon dioxide.

M. At higher altitudes, there is less oxygen than there is at sea level. To compensate, people who live at very high altitudes have larger lungs and more red blood cells per cubic centimeter of blood.

V. Cell Energy Cycle

A. Cells obtain the energy to do work through a special energy process.

B. All cells—plant, animal, and human—contain high-energy ATP (adenosine triphosphate) molecules that result from the breakdown of food.

C. The cell breaks the ATP down into ADP (adenosine diphosphate) and P (phosphate), and energy is given off for the cell to do its work.

D. The ATP is replenished when the cell receives glucose (a simple sugar) from digested food.
1. The glucose combines with oxygen, giving off energy.
2. This energy changes ADP and P back into ATP again.

E. Thus, there is a continuous cycle, called the **cell energy cycle.** ATP is broken down into ADP and P to provide energy, then energy obtained from glucose and oxygen changes the ADP and P back to ATP again.
1. It is estimated that the average adult uses more than 45 kilograms (100 pounds) of ATP every day.

Urinary System

I. Body Wastes and Their Elimination from the Body

A. The human body produces various kinds of waste materials.
1. Carbon dioxide and water, produced by the cells, are waste materials, although some of the water may be used elsewhere in the body.
2. The used digestive juices that remain after digestion are waste materials.
3. When cells, tissues, and muscles wear out or break down, mineral salts and nitrogen compounds are formed as waste materials.
4. Undigested and unused foods are waste materials.

B. The body gets rid of the various waste materials in different ways.
1. The lungs give off carbon dioxide and some water in the form of water vapor.

LEARNING ACTIVITY 15.11

Examine an Animal's Kidney

Obtain the kidney of a calf, sheep, or pig from a meat market. Note the size and shape of the kidney. Observe where a large artery and a large vein enter the kidney. Cut the kidney lengthwise in half with a sharp knife. Note the many tubes in the tissue near the surface of the kidney and the large chamber where the urine collects. Point out that the urine leaves this chamber and travels through a duct that empties into the bladder.

2. The skin gives off perspiration, which contains water and dissolved mineral salts.
3. Solid undigested wastes are passed through the digestive tract and eliminated as feces during defecation.
4. Some liquid and dissolved solid wastes are filtered from the bloodstream and eliminated through the urinary system.

II. **Kidneys and the Structure of the Urinary System**

A. The **kidneys** play an important part in the removal of waste materials.

1. The kidneys are two dark-red, bean-shaped organs located in the lower part of the back.
2. Each kidney is packed with millions of tiny tubes, called nephrons, which are the functioning filtering units of kidneys.
3. Nephrons filter from the blood such waste materials as mineral salts and protein compounds.
4. Along with excess water, these wastes form the liquid called **urine.**
5. The urine flows from each kidney through a tube, called a ureter, to a storage organ called the urinary bladder.
6. From the urinary bladder, urine is voluntarily eliminated from the body through a tube called the urethra, located in the penis of males and in front of the vagina in females.

Nervous System

I. **Function and Parts of the Nervous System**

A. The nervous system has several functions. It controls the action of the muscles and other tissues; the actions of the sense organs; and thinking, learning, memory, and many human behaviors.

B. The central part of the nervous system consists of the brain and the spinal cord. The rest of the nervous system is made up of nerves, which spread out from the brain and spinal cord through the body.

II. **Brain**

A. Located inside the skull, where it is protected, the brain is the most highly specialized organ in the human body. It is the control center of the body, receiving messages from all parts of the body and sending out orders in return. It has a wrinkled appearance because its surface has many folds. There are three main parts to the brain: the cerebrum, the cerebellum, and the medulla.

B. The **cerebrum,** the largest part of the brain, located at the front and top, is made up of two halves that are firmly joined together.

1. Generally, the left side of the cerebrum controls movement of the right side of the body, and the right side of the cerebrum controls movement of the left side of the body.
2. The cerebrum has many functions. It controls thinking, reasoning, learning, memory, and imagination. It receives messages from the sense organs and recognizes them as smell, taste, touch, pressure, sight, hearing, heat, cold, and pain. It also controls the voluntary movement of the muscles in the body.

C. The much smaller **cerebellum** is located below and behind the cerebrum. It coordinates the movements of the muscles so that they operate together smoothly, as in walking. It also helps the body to keep its sense of balance.

D. The **medulla** is located at the base of the brain, where it joins the top of the spinal cord. It controls the operation of the involuntary muscles. This means that it controls such vital functions as heart action, breathing, digestion, coughing, and sneezing.

III. **Spinal Cord**

A. Connecting with the brain's medulla, the spinal cord is a long rod of nerve tissue going down almost the whole length of the backbone.

B. Thirty-one pairs of nerves branch off the spinal cord and connect the brain with the rest of the body.

C. If the spinal cord is cut, none of the nerves operate below the point of the cut (that is, on the opposite end from the brain), and all parts of the body controlled by these nerves are paralyzed.

LEARNING ACTIVITY 15.12

Examine an Animal's Brain

Obtain a fresh, undamaged brain of a calf, sheep, or pig from a meat market. Locate and identify the cerebrum, cerebellum, and medulla. Note how large the cerebrum is and how its surface is folded in many places. Cut into the gray matter of the cerebrum and note the white matter beneath. See how the cerebellum is attached to the rest of the brain. Observe how the medulla connects with the other parts of the brain and with the spinal cord.

IV. Nerves

A. The cells of the nervous system are called **neurons.** Neurons vary in size and shape, but all are designed to carry messages called nerve impulses through the body.

B. Every neuron has a cell body and many fine threads called nerve fibers that spread out through the body.
   1. One of these nerve fibers, called an axon, is long and carries messages away from the cell body.
   2. All the other nerve fibers, called dendrites, are shorter and carry messages to the cell body.
   3. The axon and dendrites branch many times at their tips, making the tips look like tiny brushes.

C. The bodies of the nerve cells usually lie in the brain and spinal cord, and the nerve fibers run to the head, trunk, feet, and other parts of the body.

D. There are three kinds of neurons: sensory, motor, and associative.
   1. **Sensory neurons** carry impulses for feelings or sensations.
      a. Their cell bodies usually lie in the brain and spinal cord, and their nerve fibers spread out to sense organs all over the body.
      b. The nerve fibers carry messages (nerve impulses) from the sense organs to the cell bodies.
      c. A nerve impulse flows somewhat like an electrical current does but is actually a process of biochemical reactions.
   2. **Motor neurons** carry impulses that produce motion in the body.
      a. Their cell bodies also usually lie in the brain and spinal cord, and their nerve fibers spread out to the muscles, tissues, and organs of the body.
      b. The nerve fibers carry messages from the cell bodies to the muscles, tissues, and organs.
   3. **Associative neurons,** sometimes also called central neurons, are located between the cell bodies of the sensory and motor neurons, where they act as go-betweens in receiving and sending messages. Both the cell bodies and the nerve fibers of associative neurons are usually located in the brain and the spinal cord.

E. All three kinds of neurons are involved in receiving and sending messages (nerve impulses).
   1. Nerve fibers in the sense organs all over the body carry messages to the cell bodies of the sensory neurons.
   2. The sensory neurons send these messages through nerve fibers to the cell bodies of the associative neurons, which immediately transfer these messages through nerve fibers to the cell bodies of the motor neurons.
   3. The cell bodies of the motor neurons then send messages through nerve fibers to the muscles, tissues, and organs of the body.

V. Reflex Action

A. A reflex action is an action of the body that takes place automatically or involuntarily without a person's thinking about it.
   1. In most reflex actions, the nerve impulses travel only to the spinal cord and then back to the area involved, without going to the brain.
   2. An example of a simple reflex action is the behavior that takes place when a person touches something hot. The person pulls the fingers away almost immediately, even before pain is felt.
   3. This action occurs because the skin sends a message to sensory nerve cells in the spinal cord.
   4. The sensory nerve cells transfer the message to nearby associative nerve cells that transfer the message to motor nerve cells.
   5. The motor nerve cells then send a message to the muscles in the person's arm, and the muscles contract, pulling the arm and fingers away.
   6. Meanwhile, the spinal cord also sends a message to the brain, which then recognizes the sensations of both heat and pain.
   7. The extra time saved by the reflex action, which takes place before the brain is able to learn what is happening, prevents the finger from becoming badly burned.

B. Other reflex actions include jumping when frightened, blinking when objects suddenly come near, and laughing when tickled.

C. The medulla of the brain controls such reflex actions as swallowing, coughing, and sneezing.

LEARNING ACTIVITY 15.13

Exploring a Reflex Action

Have one student sit with his or her legs crossed so that one leg swings freely. Strike the leg just below the knee with the side of your hand. The leg will kick out immediately in a simple reflex action. Other simple reflex actions that can be demonstrated include a person blinking his or her eyes when an object suddenly comes near them, laughing when tickled, yawning, sneezing, and shivering.

VI. Special Senses

A. The nervous system makes it possible for the human body to have many sensations.
   1. Different sensory nerves located in special sense organs send nerve impulses (messages to the brain, which recognizes these impulses as sensations). Such sensations include touch, pressure, heat, cold, pain, smell, taste, sight, hearing, and balance.
   2. These sensations come from five sense organs: skin, nose, tongue, eyes, and ears.

B. The skin has five kinds of sensory nerve endings, each responsible for a different type of sensation. These sensations are touch, pressure, heat, cold, and pain.
   1. Because sensory nerves are not spread out evenly over the skin, the skin is more sensitive in some places than in others.
   2. The fingertips and the forehead have a great many nerve endings that are sensitive to touch.
   3. The nerve endings sensitive to touch are near the surface of the skin; those sensitive to pressure are located deeper.

C. The sense of smell is located in the nose. In humans, the sense of smell is poor compared with that of many other animals, such as the deer or dog.
   1. Nerve endings in the nose are sensitive to chemicals in the air.
   2. When inhaled, these chemicals dissolve in the liquid (mucus) that covers the lining of the nasal passages.
   3. When the nose smells the same odor for a long time, the nerve endings become accustomed or sensitized to that particular odor, and sensation of smell for that odor ceases.

D. The sensation of taste is located in clusters of cells, called taste buds, that are spread unevenly over the tongue. The taste comes from chemicals in the food, which must first be dissolved in the saliva before the tastes of sweet, sour, salty, and bitter can be sensed.
   1. The taste buds at the tip of the tongue are sensitive to sweet and salty flavors.
   2. The taste buds along the sides of the tongue are sensitive to sour flavors.
   3. The taste buds at the back of the tongue are sensitive to bitter flavors.
   4. Many foods include more than one flavor.
   5. Much of what we may think is taste is really smell. While a food is being chewed, odors are given off that enter the nasal passages and reach the nerve endings that are sensitive to smell. The combination of taste and smell gives the food its complete flavor.

E. The sense of sight is located in the eye. The eye is protected by the bones of the skull on all sides except the front. Eyelids protect the front of the eye.
   1. They close, or blink, to protect the front of the eye.
   2. They help spread a watery liquid across the surface of the eye that keeps the eye surface moist, protects the eyes against germs, and washes out dirt. When drops of this watery liquid come out of the eye, they are called tears.

F. Because the entire human eye is shaped like a ball, it is sometimes called the eyeball.
   1. Most of the eyeball has a tight, white cover around it. The part of that covering we see is called the white of the eye. A small part of this covering, called the cornea, is transparent; that is, light can pass through it.
   2. The cornea covers a dark opening in the eye, called the pupil, which appears black because of the darkness from inside the eye. The pupil is the opening that allows light to pass into the eyeball.
   3. The colored circle around the pupil is the iris. The iris controls the amount of light that enters the eye. Muscles of the iris change the size of the pupil, depending on the intensity of light reaching the eye. When the light is bright, the iris enlarges, making the opening of the pupil smaller and thereby reducing the amount of light entering the eye. When the light is dim, the iris narrows, making the pupil larger to allow more light to enter the eye.
   4. Inside the eye are a convex lens and two liquids. The watery liquid in front of the lens is called aqueous humor. Behind the lens is a jellylike liquid called vitreous humor.
   5. With the help of these two liquids, the lens bends the rays of light as they enter the eye and causes the rays of light to come together to focus on the sensitive lining, the retina, at the back of the eye. The retina has sensitive nerve endings that lead to the optic nerve.

LEARNING ACTIVITY 15.14

Exploring the Senses of Touch, Taste, and Smell

A. The Sense of Touch in the Hand

Touch the point of a thin, sharp nail to different spots, front and back, of a student's fingers. In some spots, the student will feel only a sense of pressure. In other spots that are more sensitive, there will also be a feeling of pain.

Spread a hairpin or paper clip until the points are about 5 centimeters (2 in.) apart. Blindfold a student and touch the palm of the student's hand with both ends of the hairpin. The student will feel both points. Repeat the procedure several times, bringing the points a little closer each time. Eventually the student will say that she feels just one point. At this stage, both points of the hairpin are touching just one nerve ending.

B. The Sense of Touch in the Hand Versus the Upper Arm

Spread points of the paper clip (or hairpin) and begin on the back of the hand, moving gradually up the forearm, to the back of the neck, touching with one and sometimes two points, asking each time for the student to tell you how many points he feels. As you do this, hold one or two fingers up to let the rest of the class know how many points are actually touching the skin each time. As you move upward, the student's skin will show less sensitivity to the touch of the points, and the student will be less able to tell how many points his skin is being touched with. Have the rest of the class keep data on correct/incorrect responses as you move up the student's arm.

C. Diffusion and the Sense of Smell

Have the students sit quietly in various parts of the classroom. Pour some strong perfume on a handkerchief and wave the handkerchief in the air. Ask the students to raise their hands as soon as they smell the perfume. Call their attention to the way the odor diffuses progressively to all parts of the classroom.

D. The Sense of Taste

Blindfold a student and have her stick out her tongue. Dip an absorbent cotton stick into a solution of sugar and water. Touch the cotton to the tip, sides, and back of the tongue. Have the student identify the taste as sweet, sour, salty, or bitter in each case. Make sure the student's tongue is moist with saliva. Repeat, using a salt solution, lemon juice, and a bitter solution of an aspirin tablet in a small amount of water, with the student rinsing her mouth after each test. The student will detect sweet flavors mostly at the tip of her tongue, salt flavors at the tip, sour flavors along the sides, and bitter flavors at the back of the tongue.

Have students repeat the experiments in groups of two or four.

E. Smell and Taste

Point out that smell has a lot to do with taste. Blindfold a student and have him hold his nose tightly. Give him raw mashed apple, then pear, then potato to eat and have him try to identify which he is eating. Now let the student eat a piece of apple while you hold a piece of pear under his nose. The student will think he is eating a pear. Reverse the procedure, and the student will now think he is eating an apple. After the demonstration, you may want to have groups of students repeat the experiments.

---

6. When light strikes the retina, the nerves send impulses through the optic nerve to the brain, where the impulses are interpreted as the sensation of sight.
7. In the retina, there are two types of neurons, called the cones and the rods. The cones allow us to see objects in bright light and to recognize colors. The rods allow us to see objects in dim light and to detect brightness. Many other animals see better than humans at night because their retinas contain more rods and fewer or no cones. Squirrels and deer, for example, see only in black and white but see very well even in dim light. A cat's eye has a maximum density of 400,000 rods per square millimeter, as opposed to 175,000 rods per square millimeter in the human eye. Also, some animal eyes, such as the cat's, have a tapetum, an extra layer next to the retina that intensifies and reflects light. This is why a cat's or deer's eyes sometimes seem to glow in the dark.

G. Due to the round shape of the eye, adjustments must be made to allow a clear focus at varying distances.

1. Muscles attached to the lens can make the lens more convex or less convex.
2. These muscles allow the rays of light reflected from objects to come together, that is, to focus, at the retina.
3. When an object is far away, the lens becomes thinner or less convex because the rays of light from the distant object do not have to be bent as much to focus at the retina. When an object is near, the lens becomes thicker or more convex because the rays of light from the nearer object must be bent more to focus at the retina.
4. In humans, the eye must make adjustments for clear focus at varying distances, but this is not true for all animals. Squirrels and many birds of prey, for example, have perfect focus for their entire field of vision.

H. Since the lens of the eye is a convex lens, the image formed on the retina is upside down, but the brain is able to invert the image or to interpret this message as right side up.

1. Furthermore, because we have two eyes, we get two images, which the brain is able to put together as one image.

2. The advantage of having two eyes is that it provides depth perception.

I. The eye is able to retain the image of an object for a little while after light from the object is no longer entering the eye. This effect is called persistence of vision.
   1. Motion pictures use persistence of vision to give a series of still pictures the effect of motion. A series of still pictures, each a little different from the last, is shown on a screen so quickly that we continue to see one picture while the next is being shown. Persistence of vision allows the series of still pictures to blend together, and our brain creates the impression of movement.

J. Most animals, including humans, can hear a much broader frequency range than they can produce.
   1. For example, humans can receive between 20 and 20,000 Hz (cycles per second) but can emit sounds ranging only from 80 to 1,100 Hz. Dolphins can receive from 150 to 150,000 Hz but can emit only 7,000 to 120,000 Hz. Bats can receive 1,000 to 120,000 Hz but can emit only 10,000 to 120,000 Hz.
   2. A wider range of hearing likely has a survival advantage in the wild.
   3. For humans, the sense of hearing is located in the ear, of which there are three parts: the outer ear, the middle ear, and the inner ear.
   4. The outer ear collects the sound waves and sends them through a tube to the middle ear.
   5. A thin piece of tissue (membrane), commonly called the tympanum or eardrum, is stretched across the end of the tube.
   6. When sound waves strike the eardrum, they make it move back and forth rapidly, or vibrate.
   7. The higher the sounds, the faster the eardrum vibrates.
   8. The louder the sound's frequency, the more strongly the eardrum vibrates.
   9. The middle ear passes the vibrations of the eardrum to the inner ear.
   10. The middle ear has three small bones that are joined together. Because of their shapes, they are called the hammer, the anvil, and the stirrup.
   11. The first bone, the hammer, is connected to the eardrum.
   12. The second bone, the anvil, connects the hammer to the stirrup.
   13. The third bone, the stirrup, is connected to the inner ear by another membrane called the oval window.
   14. As these three bones vibrate, they cause the oval window to vibrate.
   15. The inner ear consists of a spiral passage, called the cochlea, which is shaped like a snail's shell and is filled with a liquid.
   16. Inside the liquid, and attached to the cochlea, are thousands of tiny nerve endings.
   17. When the oval window of the inner ear vibrates, the liquid inside the cochlea also begins to vibrate.
   18. The tiny nerve endings receive the vibrations of the liquid and send nerve impulses to the auditory nerve, which, in turn, relays these to the brain where they are translated as sounds.
   19. The inner ear helps to control our sense of balance.
   20. The inner ear contains three tubes that curve around in half circles called the semicircular canals.
   21. The semicircular canals are laid out in the three directions in which the head can move: up, down, and sideways.
   22. The canals are filled with a watery liquid that moves whenever the head moves.
   23. Nerve endings line the walls of the canals, and when the head moves, the liquid in one of the canals rushes to one end and presses on the nerve endings.
   24. This pressure on the nerve endings causes nerve impulses to travel through a branch of the auditory nerve to the cerebellum of the brain.
   25. The cerebellum then sends a message to the muscles that help us keep our balance.
   26. Any whirling movement, or a steady up and down movement like that produced in a boat, makes the liquid in the canals move continuously from one side to the other, causing dizziness and sometimes a feeling of nausea.

LEARNING ACTIVITY 15.15

Exploring Vision

A. Examine an Animal's Eye

Obtain the eye of a cow, sheep, or pig from a meat market. Use a single-edge razor to slice the eye in half length-wise. The aqueous and vitreous humors will flow out. Examine the rest of the eye closely and identify each of the parts. If you can obtain another eye, dissect it carefully and remove the lens. Note that the lens is convex.

B. A Convex Lens Produces an Image

Tape a sheet of paper on a wall opposite a window. Draw the shades on all the windows in the room except the one facing the paper. Hold a magnifying glass close to the paper, and move it back and forth until you see a clear image on the paper (Figure 15.5). The convex lens of the magnifying glass will form a smaller inverted image of the window, of whatever is on the window sill, and of objects that are outside the window at the time.

C. Effect of Light on the Size of the Pupil

Have a student sit in a dark part of the room for 5 minutes. Let the other students note how large the pupil of the eye has become to admit as much light as possible into the eye. Now shine a flashlight into the student's eye. Note how quickly the pupil becomes smaller to cut down the amount of light entering the eye.

D. The Blind Spot

Make a square and a circle 10 centimeters (4 in.) apart on a white card (Figure 15.6). Hold the card at arm's length. Close your left eye and look at the square with your right eye. Slowly bring the card toward you, staring at the square, but looking at the circle from the corner of your eye. At a certain position, the circle will disappear. Point out that the image of the circle has fallen on that spot of the retina where all the nerves come together and go to the brain through the optic nerve. No image can form at this spot, making it a blind spot for the eye. When you continue to bring the card closer, the circle reappears.

E. Each Eye Produces a Separate Image

Bring the forefingers of both hands together 30 centimeters (12 in.) in front of you, at eye level (Figure 15.7). First look at both fingertips, then look just over the fingertips at the wall across the room. You will see a tiny third finger appear between your two fingers. Point out that each eye sees both fingers, but the images from both eyes overlap to produce the third finger.

F. The Retina Holds an Image for a Short Time

Obtain a sturdy piece of white cardboard about 7 centimeters (3 in.) long and 5 centimeters (2 in.) wide. Draw a fish bowl on one side and a goldfish on the other side (Figure 15.8). Make a small hole at each corner of the cardboard and thread a 30-centimeter (12-in.) piece of fine, strong string through two holes on each side of the card, as shown in Figure 15.8. Twist each string as much as you can, then insert a finger in each of the loops and twirl the card rapidly by pulling the two loops hard sideways. When the card twirls, the goldfish will seem to be inside the bowl. Point out that the eye holds an image for a short time after the object has disappeared. When the card twirls, the pictures follow each other so rapidly that you see one picture before the image of the other has had time to disappear. As a result, you see both pictures at the same time.

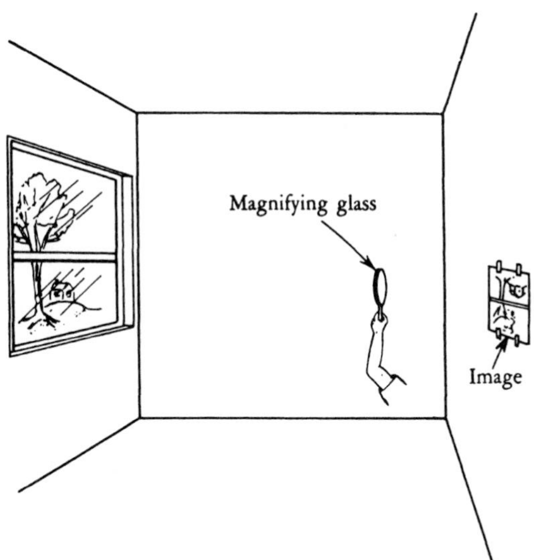

FIGURE 15.5 A convex lens produces a small inverted image.

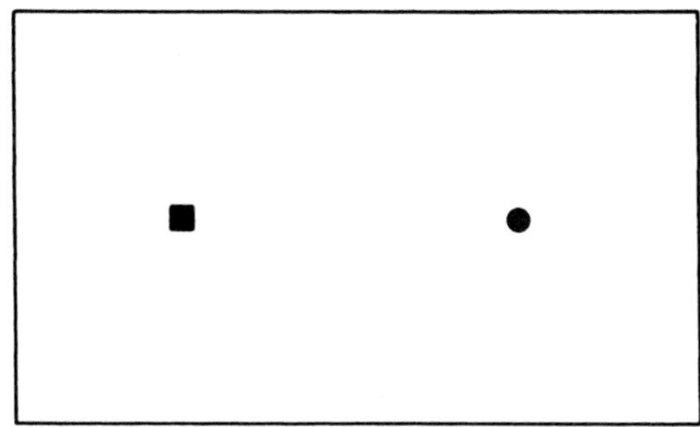

FIGURE 15.6 Find the blind spot of your eye.

FIGURE 15.7 Images from both eyes overlap to produce a tiny third finger.

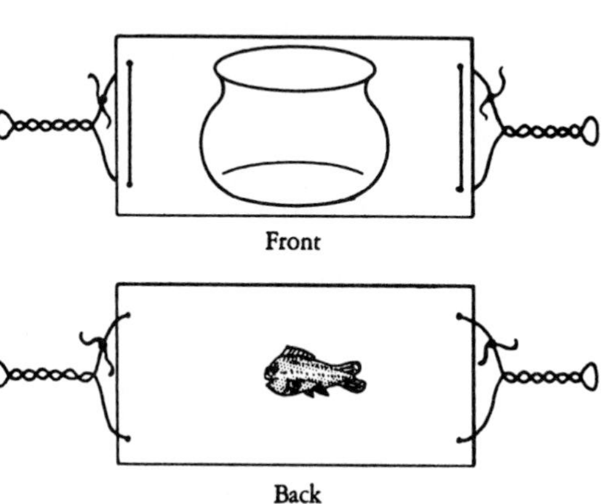

FIGURE 15.8 Persistence of vision puts the goldfish inside the bowl.

LEARNING ACTIVITY 15.16

The Ear

A. Locating the Direction of Sounds

Blindfold a student and have her sit in the center of the room. Stand at different locations in the room and strike two pencils together. She will be able to tell from what direction the sound is coming, because sound usually reaches one ear sooner than the other. Now have the student place a wad of cotton in one ear. Repeat the procedure. This time she will have difficulty telling the direction from which the sound is coming.

B. The Sense of Balance

Have a student spin around for a short while. After stopping, the student will continue to have a spinning sensation because the liquid in the semicircular canals of the inner ear is still whirling around.

Reproductive System

I. **Function and Parts of the Reproductive System**

A. The primary function of the reproductive system is to continue the species by producing offspring.

B. The male reproductive system has two functions. It produces sperm and delivers these cells to the reproductive tract of the female. It produces the male sex hormones, called androgens.
1. The androgens are responsible for the development of the male secondary sex characteristics, which are facial axillary and pubic hair, lower voice, broad shoulders, narrow hips, and growth of the penis and testes.
2. The sperm cells, or spermatozoa, are produced continuously in the coiled tubules in the two testes.
3. The testes lie outside the pelvic cavity in a sac called the scrotum.
4. Upon leaving the testes, the sperm cells pass through a sperm duct, the vas deferens.
5. In the vas deferens, secretions are added to the sperm cells from four glands—the seminal vesicles, the prostate, the ampulla, and the bulbourethral gland. This fluid makes up what is known as semen.
6. Mucous membranes line the urethral canal, adding lubricant to the semen.
7. Semen is passed through the urethra and out of the body via the penis.

C. The female reproductive system has three functions. It produces egg cells, called ova. It secretes the female sex hormones, called estrogens and progesterones. It protects and nourishes the developing embryo from fertilization (union of egg and sperm that results in a zygote) until birth.
1. The egg cells are developed in the ovaries; one is located on each side of the lower part of the abdominal cavity.
2. The ovaries are surrounded by funnel-like extensions of the oviducts, or fallopian tubes.
3. The oviducts are connected posteriorly to a pear-shaped organ called the uterus.
4. The embryo grows in the uterus.
5. The lower part of the uterus is a thick muscular ring called the cervix.
6. The cervix extends partially into the birth canal, the vagina.
7. The vagina opens to the exterior of the body.

D. Beginning with puberty, eggs are released from the ovaries, usually one egg from one ovary about every 28 days. This release of eggs continues for about 35 years.
1. At the onset of release of an egg, the uterine lining thickens, readying for an egg, if fertilized, to implant and grow. If no egg implants, the uterine lining sheds.
2. This pattern is known as the menstrual cycle, which is interrupted if pregnancy occurs.

E. The release of an egg cell from the ovary is controlled by hormones released from the pituitary gland in the brain.
1. The pituitary hormones also control the release of other hormones by the ovary.
2. In turn, the hormones released by the ovary regulate the release of pituitary gland hormones.
3. The pituitary gland secretes a follicle-stimulating hormone (FSH) that is carried to the ovary in the blood.
4. FSH causes cells around the egg to develop a fluid-filled sac or follicle. The follicle then begins to produce estrogen.
5. FSH is also produced in males, where it stimulates the formation of sperm in the testes.

F. Estrogen serves several functions.
1. It causes the development of the primary and secondary female sex characteristics. The primary sex characteristics are the sex organs.
2. In females, the secondary sex characteristics are a wider pelvis, smoother skin, breasts, and a thicker layer of fat beneath the skin.
3. Estrogen also regulates FSH production by the pituitary.
4. Another function of estrogen is to stimulate the pituitary to release luteinizing hormone (LH), which helps to break the follicle and release the egg, a process called ovulation.

5. At ovulation, the remaining cells of the broken follicle develop into a new and temporary gland, the corpus luteum.
6. The corpus luteum produces another female hormone called progesterone, which helps to prepare the lining of the uterus for the embryo if the egg is fertilized.
7. If fertilization does not occur, after about 10 days the corpus luteum breaks down. This causes a drop in the level of progesterone and the beginning of the menstrual flow, the discarding of the lining of the uterus.
8. Menstrual flow lasts about 5 days, at which time estrogen levels are high enough to stimulate rebuilding of the uterine lining.

G. Fertilization usually takes place in the upper third of the oviduct.
1. Sperm cells are deposited into the vagina by the penis.
2. Helped along by contractions of the uterus and oviduct, they swim to the oviduct.
3. Sperm cells move along quickly, entering the oviducts within 15 minutes after semen has been introduced into the vagina.
4. The egg cell lives for only about 1 day after emerging from the ovaries. Sperm cells may live for about 2 days in the oviducts.
5. If fertilized, the egg, now called a zygote, moves down the oviduct to the uterus, where it attaches to the uterine lining and becomes a developing embryo.
6. Once it is attached, a new organ, the placenta, forms. The placenta is composed of tissue from both the mother and the embryo. The placenta allows for the exchange of nutrients and wastes between the mother and the baby.
7. The placenta produces several hormones, including human chorionic gonadotropin (HCG), which stimulates the production of progesterone to keep the lining of the uterus from being shed. HCG will appear in the blood and urine of the mother. Its detection in the urine is used as a test for pregnancy.

II. Our Inheritance

A. Like other plant and animal organisms, we resemble our biological parents.
1. Many of our characteristics (both physical and behavioral) are inherited from our biological parents.

B. Reproduction is characteristic of all living organisms. Because no individual organism lives forever, reproduction is essential to the continuation of the species.
1. In many species of plants and animals, including humans, females produce eggs and males produce sperm.
2. An egg and sperm unite, beginning the development of a new individual, the zygote. (Meiosis, the cell division process that results in egg and sperm cells with haploid chromosome numbers, is discussed in Chapter 12.)
3. The zygote has an equal contribution of genetic information from each of its parents, contributed by the egg and the sperm.
4. Sexually produced offspring are never identical to either parent.

C. Each organism requires a set of instructions for specifying its traits.
1. Heredity is the passage of these instructions from one generation to the next.
2. Hereditary (genetic) information is contained in genes, located in the chromosomes of each cell.
3. Each gene carries a single unit of instruction. One or many genes can determine an inherited trait of an individual.
4. A human cell contains many thousands of different genes.
5. Genes are small sections of deoxyribonucleic acid (DNA), which itself is a large molecule.
6. A mutation is a change in the DNA code. Mutations may affect one gene or entire chromosomes.

D. Gender is determined by just two chromosomes, named for their shapes—the X chromosome and the Y chromosome.
1. A female contains a pair of X chromosomes, one inherited from each parent, whereas a male contains an X chromosome inherited from the mother and a Y chromosome inherited from the father. Again, one is inherited from each parent.
2. If the zygote receives an X chromosome from the egg and an X chromosome from the sperm, then the offspring is a female. If, however, an X chromosome is inherited from the egg and a Y chromosome from the sperm, then it is a male.
3. The mathematical probability of the offspring being a male or a female is 50 percent.

E. Some inherited traits are dominant and others are recessive. If a trait is dominant, the offspring needs only one chromosome to inherit that trait. To inherit a recessive trait, the offspring needs two chromosomes, one from each parent.
1. Some dominant traits in humans are tongue curling, free-hanging earlobes (which is dominant over attached earlobes), and Huntington's disease (a genetic disorder that leads to early death caused by a rare dominant chromosome).
2. Unlike Huntington's disease, most genetic disorders are recessive traits, meaning that genes for the disease must be inherited from both parents.

F. The **International Human Genome Project** is nearing completion of the mapping of the genetic makeup of human chromosomes.
1. The identification of genes and genetic tests for disease susceptibility offers a chance for preventive action, which can extend life expectancy.

Endocrine System

I. Structure and Function of the Endocrine System

A. The endocrine system directs changes in the other organ systems.
   1. The endocrine system carries out this function by producing chemical secretions from various glands that make up the system and that are then carried by the blood to other parts of the body.
   2. Glands are organs whose cells give off secretions that have special uses in the body. There are two kinds of glands: those with ducts (tubes) and those without ducts.

B. Glands with ducts, called duct glands, or **exocrine glands**, give off secretions that travel through the ducts to the body parts they affect.
   1. Examples of duct glands are the salivary glands in the mouth and the sweat and oil glands in the skin.
   2. The digestive juices that help digest foods in the body are given off by duct glands in the stomach, the intestine, the pancreas, and the liver.

C. Glands without ducts, called ductless glands, or **endocrine glands**, give off secretions called *hormones.*
   1. Hormones pass directly through the walls of the capillaries into the blood and travel to different parts of the body.
   2. Their function is to regulate the body's activities.
   3. Some hormones affect every part of the body, but others affect only certain parts.
   4. Organs included in the endocrine system because of their production of hormones are the pituitary gland, hypothalamus, thyroid gland, parathyroid glands, pancreas, adrenal glands, thymus gland, heart, kidney, digestive tract, and male testes and female ovaries.

II. Pituitary Gland and Hypothalamus

A. The pituitary gland (also known as the hypophysis) is a tiny gland, about the size of a cherry, attached to the base of the brain. It secretes at least 10 different hormones and is sometimes referred to as the master gland.
   1. Some of these hormones affect or regulate the activity of almost all the other ductless glands.
   2. Other hormones affect the activity of the kidneys and blood vessels.
   3. One hormone, commonly called *growth hormone,* regulates the growth of the skeleton and the body.
   4. If the pituitary gland is overactive during childhood, the child will grow up to be well beyond average size. If it is overactive in an adult, the adult's jaws, nose, hands, and fingers will become very large. If it is underactive during childhood, the child will be well below average size.

B. Also located in the brain, and close to the pituitary, the hypothalamus secretes hormones that regulate and integrate the nervous and endocrine systems.

III. Thyroid and Parathyroid Glands

A. The thyroid gland looks like a butterfly with its wings spread and is located below the voice box on the windpipe. It gives off a hormone, called *thyroxine,* that controls the speed or rate of metabolism.

B. The parathyroids are four small glands on the back of the thyroid gland. They secrete *parathormone,* which controls the use of calcium in the body.

IV. Pancreas

A. The pancreas is both a duct gland and a ductless gland and is located just behind the stomach, adjacent to the duodenum.
   1. As a duct gland, it gives off pancreatic juice, which helps in the digestion of food in the small intestine.
   2. Scattered throughout the pancreas are small groups of cells called the islets of Langerhans, which are ductless glands that produce the hormone insulin.

B. Insulin regulates the use and storage of sugar in the body.
   1. When the body digests food, the carbohydrates are broken down into simple sugars, mainly one called glucose.
   2. The cells in the body use oxygen to burn some of this glucose, producing heat and energy in the form of adenosine triphosphate (ATP).
   3. Whatever glucose the body does not use at the moment is stored in the liver until needed by the cells.
   4. When the pancreas does not produce enough insulin, a person develops a disease called diabetes.
   5. The liver then cannot store the sugar, and the cells cannot use it efficiently.
   6. The muscles and tissues cannot get the sugar they need, and the blood becomes flooded with sugar.
   7. The person loses weight, urinates often, and is very thirsty.
   8. Some of the excess sugar in the blood passes out through the urine.
   9. Persons with diabetes are given insulin regularly by injection. They are given pills to help their bodies release more of their own insulin if their pancreas is still producing it. They are also put on a special diet.

C. Diabetes can occur in young children.
   1. When it does, it is probably due to a viral infection or to an autoimmune reaction in a person with a genetic predisposition.
   2. An autoimmune reaction is one in which the body's immune system attacks its own tissue—in this case the islet cells of the pancreas—as if they were a foreign substance.

D. Diabetes can also affect adults in their middle years.
   1. In the adult form of diabetes, the adult has a higher than normal amount of insulin as well as sugar in the blood because the pancreas is producing insulin normally, but the body cells are resistant to the insulin.

V. Adrenal Glands

A. The adrenal glands are two small glands located on top of the kidneys.

B. The outer layer of the adrenal glands gives off many hormones that control the digestion of food and regulate the balance of salt and water in the body.

C. The inner layer gives off a hormone called *adrenaline*.
   1. When a person becomes angry or frightened, the adrenal glands respond quickly and pour adrenaline into the blood.
   2. Adrenaline makes the heart beat faster, makes blood pressure rise, and makes digestion slow down. Adrenaline also causes breathing to become faster and deeper; it causes the liver to send more of its stored sugar to the blood; and it drives more blood into vessels in the deeper muscles.
   3. In addition, adrenaline makes blood clot more easily and quickly.

Exploratory Activities for "The Human Body"

1. EXPLORING THE CONTENT OF FOODS: BEING A NUTRITION DETECTIVE (ANY GRADE LEVEL)

Overview

Students enjoy and learn when they are active participants in learning. In this series of exploratory studies, students participate as chemists and nutrition detectives, exploring (by hypothesizing and testing their hypotheses) various foods for their sugar, starch, fat, protein, mineral, water, and energy content.

Connections with Other Disciplines Students will do reporting, writing, and graphing. Art activities include the creation of posters and charts. Extension activities may include the study of food marketing and supermarket shelving practices. Students may want to investigate careers in nutrition, chemistry, and others, as related to this study.

Initiating Activity Have students keep a record of what they eat each day for a week, being quite specific about the size of the portions and the number of helpings. Have them put their records on individual poster charts that they each create. At the end of the week of record keeping, either as a whole class or in groups of four, have students select sample foods from the charts that are most prevalent in their weekly diets.

Student Exploratory Learning Activities Have students bring in sample foods that represent their weekly diets as shown by their records. Divide the class into groups of four, assign responsibilities to the members of each group, and then have the groups test the food samples. In all tests, students should hypothesize about the content of material being tested for in each food and plot their results on a table of their own making.

Individual titles and roles within each group might include the following:

Materials, Equipment, and Safety Manager: monitors group safety and sees that the group has the materials needed for the test
Record Keeper: maintains records of the experiment
Chief chemist: performs the actual test
Reporter: works with the record keeper and prepares a group report on the results of the test

Classroom Management Suggestions Ten exploratory activities follow. All groups could do each of the 10 activities, or groups could be divided so that all activities are completed, but not by all groups. Because of safety hazards and depending on the maturity of your students (as noted in the individual activities) some of the tests might better be done as demonstrations by the teacher.

1.1 Testing Foods for the Presence of Simple Sugars

Materials Test tubes, corn syrup, water, Tes-Tape or Clinitest tablets (available from drugstores), assorted fruit juices, various solid foods, soda crackers, table sugar, raisins, onion.

Control Test Pour 10 drops of corn syrup into a test tube. Add water until the test tube is half full, then shake to dissolve the syrup in the water. Follow instructions carefully for Tes-Tape, Clinitest tablets, or another similar material used to test for the presence of sugar. Observe the change in color that shows the presence of sugar.

Exploratory Tests Repeat the test, using different amounts of syrup. Repeat the test, using various fruit juices. Try using small amounts of solid foods mixed with water, including soda crackers or saltines, raisins, table sugar, and a bit of onion. Students should hypothesize about the content of simple sugar in each food and plot their results on a table that they devise. (The students will be surprised to learn that the onion is rich in simple sugars, whereas the table sugar is not. In this test, students are testing for simple sugars, or monosaccharides; sucrose [found in table sugar] is a complex sugar, a disaccharide.)

1.2 Testing Foods for the Presence of Starch

MATERIALS Test tubes, cornstarch, water, tincture of iodine, various foods.

SAFETY NOTE: tincture of iodine is poisonous and so should be handled only by the teacher or by mature students under the careful guidance of the teacher.

Control Test Place a small amount of cornstarch in a test tube half filled with water. Add one or two drops of tincture of iodine to the solution and stir. A blue-black color will form, showing the presence of starch. Place a drop or two of the iodine on a slice of raw potato and on a slice of bread. The blue-black color will again show the presence of starch.

Exploratory Tests Repeat the test using a variety of both starchy and nonstarchy foods, such as soda crackers or saltines, boiled macaroni or spaghetti, boiled rice, a lump of table sugar, cooked egg white, cheese, bacon, and meat. Students should hypothesize about the content of starch in each food and plot their results on a table that they devise.

1.3 Testing Foods for the Presence of Fats

Materials Butter, brown wrapping paper or lunch bag paper, hot plate, water, various foods.

SAFETY NOTE: The hot plate should be used only by the teacher or by mature students under the careful guidance of the teacher.

Control Test Rub a bit of butter on a piece of brown paper bag, and warm the paper gently over a hot plate (use caution). Put two or three drops of water on a second piece of brown paper. Now hold both pieces of paper up to sunlight or a bright light. Both spots will be translucent; that is, they will allow light to pass through. However, the water spot will dry and will no longer be translucent, but the grease spot will continue to be translucent.

Exploratory Tests Try this test for the presence of fats with such foods as bacon, nuts, the white and the yolk of a boiled egg, olive oil, mayonnaise, beef, bread, and leafy vegetables. Note which foods produce a permanent grease spot on the brown paper. Students should hypothesize about the content of fat in each food and plot their results on a table that they devise.

1.4 Testing Foods for the Presence of Proteins

Materials Test tube, hard-boiled eggs, dilute nitric acid, alcohol burner, test tube clamp or holder, household ammonia, various foods.

SAFETY NOTE: This testing should be done as a demonstration by the teacher if students are not mature enough to work with heat and nitric acid.

Control Test Place a small piece of the white of a boiled egg in a test tube. Add enough nitric acid to cover the piece of egg white. Holding the test tube with a test tube holder, heat the test tube gently over the flame of an alcohol lamp. Shake the test tube to keep the egg white moving, while keeping the mouth of the test tube pointed away from yourself and others. Remove the test tube as soon as the nitric acid begins to boil. Pour off the nitric acid into a plastic tub (to be discarded later). Note that the egg white has turned yellow. Now pour a little ammonia into the test tube. An orange color will form on the egg white, showing the presence of proteins.

Exploratory Tests Repeat the test, using a variety of foods, such as bread, cheese, boiled spaghetti or macaroni, lean meat, and lima beans.

1.5 Testing Foods for the Presence of Minerals

Materials Alcohol burner, bread, metal spoon, burner mitt, various foods.

SAFETY NOTE: This testing should be done as a demonstration by the teacher if students are not mature enough to work with an alcohol burner.

Control Test Place a small piece of bread on an old metal spoon and, holding the spoon with a mitt, heat well over an alcohol burner flame. The bread will burn, turn black, and finally become a small amount of gray-white ash. This ash shows the presence of minerals.

Exploratory Tests Repeat the test, using a variety of foods.

1.6 Testing Foods for the Presence of Water

Materials Bread, test tubes, alcohol burner, various foods.

SAFETY NOTE: This testing should be done as a demonstration by the teacher if students are not mature enough to work with an alcohol burner.

Control Test Place a few small pieces of bread in a dry test tube and heat the tube gently over the flame of an alcohol lamp. Tiny droplets of water will appear on the upper part of the test tube. The water was driven out of the heated bread in the form of steam, and it then condensed on the cool upper part of the test tube.

Exploratory Tests Repeat the test, using a variety of foods.

1.7 Investigating the Vitamin Content of Foods

Have the students make a chart listing foods that are good sources of vitamins. Let them check the foods in their daily diets to see whether they appear on the chart. There are more than 25 vitamins that our bodies need. Have the students read about and report on the diseases caused by vitamin deficiencies.

1.8 Discovering That Foods Release Heat Energy When Digested

Materials Paper clip; peanut, brazil nut, or cashew; matches; butter or cooking oil; saucer; string.

SAFETY NOTE: This test should be done as a demonstration by the teacher.

Demonstration Put a straightened paper clip through a peanut, brazil nut, or cashew. Apply a lighted match to the nut. The nut will burn, giving off heat energy.

Pour some melted butter or cooking oil into a small saucer and place a piece of soft string in the butter or oil, with one end of the string protruding above the liquid and hanging over the side of the saucer. After the string has become saturated with the butter or oil, apply a lighted match to the end of the string. The string will act as a wick, and the butter or oil will burn for some time. Point out that when foods are digested in the body, they give off heat energy.

1.9 Investigating the Calorie Value of Food

Using their individual records of their diets for a week, have the students consult a chart of the Calorie values for common foods, to find out how many Calories they took in each day, and then find an average for the week. Let them compare their average daily Caloric intake with the value suggested in the Calorie chart. (Most life insurance companies have booklets available including calorie charts and other pertinent information.)

1.10 Checking Diets for the Basic Food Groups

Using their individual records of their diets for a week, have the students check each day's diet to see whether the following food groups were represented and whether the recommended number of servings for each group was consumed.

Food groups

Milk group: 2–3 servings; provides carbohydrate, calcium, vitamin B2, protein, fat

Meat group: 2–3 servings; provides protein, niacin, iron, vitamin B1, fat

Vegetable group: 3–5 servings; provides vitamins A and C, carbohydrate, fiber

Fruit group: 3–5 servings; provides vitamins A and C, carbohydrate, fiber

Grain group: 6–11 servings; provides carbohydrate, vitamin B1, iron, niacin

Conclusion of Study and Assessment of Student Learning

Groups should make their reports to the entire class about their findings on the nutritional content of the various foods and their diets for the week. The following key questions should be answered:

1. What did you learn from this study?
2. What conclusions have you made about your diet for the week?
3. Will you make any changes in what you eat as a result of what you have learned? Why?
4. What did you learn about scientific research?

Part FOUR

Matter, Energy, and Technology

NSES Content Standards B and E[1]

Students in **grades K–4** should develop an understanding of

- Properties of objects and materials
- Position and motion of objects
- Light, heat, electricity, and magnetism
- Types of resources
- Changes in environments
- Science and technology in local challenges

Students in **grades 5–8** should develop an understanding of

- Properties and changes of properties in matter
- Motions and forces
- Transformations of energy
- Natural hazards
- Risks and benefits
- Science and technology in society

[1]Reprinted from National Research Council, *National Science Education Standards*, © 1996 by the National Academy of Sciences, 123, 138, 149, 166. Courtesy of National Academy of Sciences, Washington, D.C.

Chapter 16

Changes in Matter and Energy

Laima Druskis/PH College

The Structure of Matter

I. Matter

A. Matter is anything that occupies space and has weight. Air, water, wood, stones, and metals are examples of matter. People, plants, animals, the Sun, stars, and the planets are also examples of matter.

B. Some materials are made up of only one particular kind of matter, and others are made up of more than one kind of matter.

1. A material that is made up of only one particular kind of matter is called a pure substance. Water, salt, sugar, silver, and oxygen are examples of pure substances.
2. Air is matter that is made up of many substances. Air consists of oxygen, nitrogen, carbon dioxide, and other substances.

C. Matter is found in four states: solid, liquid, gas, and plasma.

1. A **solid** has a definite size and shape. Solids can be hard or soft. Wood, iron, glass, ice, rubber, wool, and butter are examples of solids.
2. A **liquid** has a definite size, but it does not have a definite shape. A liquid's shape depends on the shape of its container. Water, milk, alcohol, blood, oil, and gasoline are examples of liquids.
3. A **gas** has neither a definite size nor a definite shape. In a container, a gas spreads out until it has the same size and shape as the container. Air, oxygen, carbon dioxide, and ammonia are examples of gases.
4. If a gas is heated to many thousands of degrees or if it is bombarded by other forms of energy, such as ultraviolet or gamma rays, electrons are knocked free from the atoms. The gas is then said to be in a highly ionized state (it consists of positively charged ions and free, negatively charged electrons). The gas is then called a **plasma.** Plasma is a fourth state of matter. It is estimated that 99% of the matter in the universe is in the plasma state. This is the material in and around the stars and throughout interstellar space.

D. Matter can be changed from one state to another by heating or cooling it, there by adding or removing energy. For example, when liquid water is cooled until it freezes, it becomes a solid—ice. When liquid water is heated until it boils, it becomes a gas called steam.

II. Gravity, Weight, and Mass

A. Every body in the universe attracts, or pulls on, every other body. This attraction or pull is called **gravity.**

1. The more massive a body, the greater its pull of gravity.
2. The farther away two bodies are from each other, the lesser their pull of gravity on each other.

B. The Earth's gravity pulls on every body at or near the Earth's surface. This pull is always directed down toward the center, no matter where on the Earth the body is located. This downward pull of the Earth's gravity keeps people from falling off the Earth and holds the air and water on the Earth as well.

1. The measure of the Earth's pull of gravity on a body is called the **weight** of that body.
2. The weight of a body changes depending on its distance from the center of the Earth. The nearer a body is to the center of the Earth, the greater the downward pull of the Earth's gravity on the body, and the more the body will weigh.

C. Every body has a **center of gravity**, the point at which all of the weight of the body seems to be located.

D. The actual amount of matter in a body is called its **mass**. Although the force of gravity on an object is determined by the mass of the object, the mass of the object is completely independent of the Earth's gravitational pull. A body has the same mass whether it is on the Earth's surface or far out in space.

1. The mass of a body is also a measure of the body's inertia. All objects have inertia. **Inertia** is the tendency of a body at rest to stay at rest, and a body in motion to stay in motion.
2. A force is needed to overcome the inertia of a body and change its motion (speed or direction). The greater a body's mass, the more force is needed to overcome its inertia.
3. **Newton's second law of motion** states that force is equal to mass times acceleration, where acceleration is defined as a change in speed or direction.

LEARNING ACTIVITY 16.1

The Definition of Matter

Show that solids, liquids, and gases are matter because they occupy space and have weight. A book or block of wood is a solid that can be measured and weighed easily. Pouring water into a glass jar can show that a liquid occupies space, and weighing the jar before and after pouring can show that the liquid has weight.

LEARNING ACTIVITY 16.2

The Center of Gravity

Have a student balance a uniform object, such as a meterstick or a yardstick, on the end of one finger. The point at which the meterstick balances is where the center of gravity is located. Now make the meterstick unsymmetrical by putting some modeling clay at one end. Balance the meterstick again, and note that the center of gravity has shifted toward the thicker, and heavier, part of the meterstick.

III. **Physical and Chemical Properties of Matter**

A. All matter has certain qualities or characteristics, called properties. The properties of a substance help us to distinguish one substance from another and to determine the purposes for which various substances can be used. These properties are divided into two main groups: physical properties and chemical properties.

1. The **physical properties** of a substance are the qualities or characteristics that we can readily observe with our five senses. Physical properties include the characteristics of color, odor, taste, density, hardness, brittleness, elasticity, melting and boiling temperatures, solubility in water and other liquids, conductivity of heat and electricity, ductility, and malleability.
2. The **chemical properties** of a substance are the qualities or characteristics that have to do with its tendency to undergo chemical change (either by reacting with other substances or by itself). We observe chemical properties when we see air and moisture act on iron to make rust, when vinegar acts on baking soda to produce bubbles of carbon dioxide gas, and when a fuel uses the oxygen in the air to burn. In each case, a new substance is formed.
3. A substance that reacts readily with other substances is called chemically active; a substance that does not react readily with other substances is called chemically inert.

IV. **Physical and Chemical Changes**

A. There are two kinds of changes that can happen to matter: physical changes and chemical changes. For either to occur, energy—such as heat, light, or electricity—is either needed or given off or both.

1. In a **physical change**, only the physical properties or characteristics of a substance are changed. It remains the same substance. A physical change takes place when a substance changes in size or shape, such as when wood is chopped, paper is torn, or glass is broken. A physical change takes place when a substance is heated and expands or is cooled and contracts. A physical change takes place when a substance changes its form, or state, such as when a solid is changed into a liquid, or a liquid is changed into a gas.
2. In a **chemical change**, the new substance has different physical and chemical properties than the original substance. Examples of chemical change include the burning of wood, rusting of iron, tarnishing of silver, souring of milk, and digesting of food.

V. **Molecules**

A. Substances are made up of tiny particles called molecules. A **molecule** is defined as being the smallest particle of a substance that is still that substance, having all the properties of that substance.

1. Molecules are so small that only the largest of them can be seen by an electron microscope. One drop of water is made up of more than a sextillion molecules.
2. A lump of sugar can be crushed and broken up into many particles of sugar. These particles can be ground into a fine powder, but each tiny particle of powder is still a particle of sugar. If we could keep breaking up a particle of sugar again and again into smaller and smaller particles, we would finally end up with the smallest possible particle of sugar, which would be one molecule of sugar.

B. All the molecules of a substance are alike, but the molecules of one substance are different from the molecules of another substance. For example, all the molecules of table salt in a container are alike, but molecules of salt are different from molecules of sugar.

C. Molecules are always moving rapidly, striking other molecules and then bouncing off in different directions.

1. In a gas, the molecules move very fast and are far apart.
2. In a liquid, the molecules move more slowly and are closer together.
3. In a solid, the molecules are very close together, and each molecule seems to be moving back and forth, or vibrating, in one fixed position rather than moving about freely.

D. Molecules attract each other. The attraction that molecules of the same substance have for each other is called **cohesion**. The attraction that molecules of different substances have for each other is called **adhesion**.

E. Cohesion makes it possible for molecules to come together to form the physical states of matter.
   1. In a solid, the attraction between molecules is very strong, so the solid holds its shape.
   2. In a liquid, the attraction between molecules is weaker. Although the molecules still stick together, the liquid does not hold its shape but takes the shape of its container.
   3. In a gas, there is very little attraction between molecules, so the molecules move away from each other, and spread (diffuse) throughout the container.

F. Adhesion makes it possible for two different substances to stick together.
   1. Because of the attraction of molecules of different substances for each other, paint sticks to wood.
   2. Because of adhesion, water sticks to other materials, making them wet.
   3. The action of glue, cement, and paste also depends on adhesion.
   4. The adhesive and cohesive properties of water in a drinking glass make it possible to overfill a glass of water without the water overflowing the sides of the glass.

VI. Atoms

A. Molecules are made up of even smaller particles called atoms.
   1. Some molecules are made up of just one atom. For example, a molecule of neon is made up of just one atom of neon.
   2. Most molecules are made up of more than one atom. A molecule of oxygen is made up of two atoms of oxygen. A molecule of water is made up of two atoms of hydrogen and one atom of oxygen.

B. Atoms are made up of even smaller particles: electrons, protons, and neutrons.
   1. The particle of an atom with a negative electrical charge (−) is called an **electron.** Although an electron has a very small mass, it usually has a great deal of energy and moves around quickly. Because all electrons have the same negative charge, they repel each other.
   2. The particle of an atom with a positive electrical charge (+) is called a **proton.** A proton's mass is about 1,836 times greater than that of an electron. A proton has about the same amount of energy as an electron, but because its mass is greater, it moves more slowly than an electron.
   3. Because the electrical charges of the proton and the electron are opposite, these two particles attract each other.
   4. The **neutron** is a particle of the atom that has neither a positive nor a negative electrical charge. As a result, the neutron does not attract or repel other neutrons, protons, or electrons.
   5. The energy of a neutron is slightly greater than the combined energies of one electron and one proton. Evidence indicates that a neutron is made up of an electron and a proton held together by a particle of energy, called a **neutrino**, which has no mass or electrical charge.

LEARNING ACTIVITY 16.3

Cohesion and Adhesion

Using a medicine dropper, allow a drop of water to fall on a penny. Point out that the drop of water remains intact because of the cohesion of the water molecules, and that the water sticks to the coin because of adhesion.

Ask students to predict how many drops of water they think the penny will hold before the water overflows the sides of the penny. Write their guesses on the board and then test. Many of the children will be surprised at the number of drops that it will hold.

Follow with questions about how the principles of cohesion and adhesion are used in nature and in technology.

Inquiry-Based Learning Activity 16.3. Modified

Water has some very interesting properties that are not shared with other fluids. Present to your students three liquids: water, rubbing alcohol, and cooking oil. Focusing on water, ask your students, "How many drops of water do you think you can put onto a penny before it spills off?" After writing down the guesses of a few volunteers, group the students into twos or threes and give them a dropper, a small cup of water, a plastic lid, and a penny. Have the students count the number of drops they can fit on a penny. Now ask your students the same question about alcohol and about oil. What do they see happening with alcohol? What do they see happening with oil? Have them record their thoughts about why they think this is happening.

What level of inquiry is this modification? This activity is highly managed and directed by you, the teacher. The students are given instructions each step of the way. Though the students are also allowed to perform their own experiments, the degree of teacher guidance indicates that this is a ***Level I activity*** across all three aspects of inquiry. However, Level I activities are very useful in establishing the ground rules for student behavior during an inquiry-based lesson. **Some questions to consider.** What sort of student behaviors might be modeled during this activity? What would you want your students to do in terms of forming groups, reporting their observations, or cleaning up after they are done with their work?

C. In an atom, the protons and neutrons, which are heavier than electrons, are closely packed together in the center of the atom, which is called the **nucleus**.
   1. Because protons all have the same positive (+) charge, and because like charges always repel each other, the protons in the nucleus should also repel each other rather than stay close together.
   2. Evidence indicates, however, that there is a strong force that holds or binds the protons and neutrons closely together in the nucleus of an atom. This is called the **binding energy** of the nucleus.
   3. The neutrons interspersed between the protons in a nucleus overcome the repulsion that exists between the protons and thus stabilize the nucleus. Every nucleus that has more than one proton must have at least the same number of neutrons (or more).

D. Electrons are spaced around the nucleus in well-defined regions, called shells or **energy levels**.
   1. Electrons do not move around the nucleus in smooth circular paths as illustrated in Figure 16.1, but are more like bees swarming around a hive in a sort of hazy "electron cloud."
   2. All the electrons in a particular energy level have approximately the same energy and the same average distance from the nucleus.
   3. Sometimes the electrons are near the nucleus and sometimes they are farther away, depending on how much energy they have at the moment.

E. Because every atom is made up of electrons, protons, and neutrons, matter is electrical in nature. Typically, an atom is electrically neutral because it contains the same number of electrons and protons.

F. The difference between the atoms of different substances lies principally in the number of electrons, protons, and neutrons contained in the atoms of these substances.

G. Although an atom may have many electrons, protons, and neutrons, it is mostly empty space.
   1. The nucleus is small compared with the rest of the atom, and all the protons and neutrons in the nucleus are packed very tightly together.
   2. The electrons, however, in their different shells, or energy levels, are spread out so that there is a relatively vast amount of space between the nucleus and the electrons.

VII. Elements

A. Although all atoms are made up of electrons, protons, and neutrons, they are not all alike. Atoms differ in their number of electrons, protons, and neutrons, and because of this difference, there are different kinds of atoms.

B. There are 92 naturally occurring kinds of atoms found in or on Earth. Each different kind of atom is called an **element**. Elements have been called the building blocks of matter. Each element has its own particular number of protons in the nucleus and electrons outside the nucleus. In addition to the 92 natural elements, scientists have made at least 17 other elements, bringing the total number of known elements to at least 109.
   1. An element is defined as the simplest form of a substance that cannot be broken up into anything simpler by ordinary chemical reactions.
   2. Elements can combine with each other to form new substances.

LEARNING ACTIVITY 16.4

Models of Atoms

Tape a sheet of paper on a piece of corrugated cardboard. Draw a small circle to represent the nucleus of an atom. Draw concentric circles to represent the shells or energy levels of the electrons outside the nucleus. Now use thumbtacks of three different colors to represent the number of electrons, protons, and neutrons in an atom of aluminum. Place 13 protons and 14 neutrons in the nucleus, and position 13 electrons in the concentric circles as shown in Figure 16.1.

Have the students make similar representations for other common atoms. Point out that an atom is really three-dimensional.

Have the students look at a table that provides the atomic numbers and atomic weights of several or all of the elements. Let the students use these values to determine the number of electrons, protons, and neutrons in atoms of some of the well-known elements.

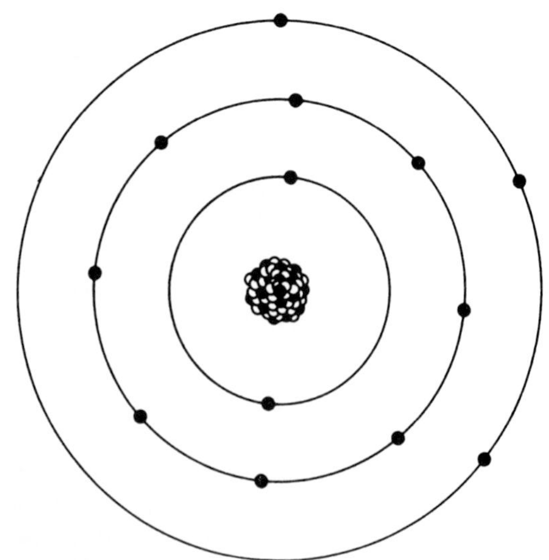

FIGURE 16.1 Atomic structure of an aluminum atom.

3. All the substances on Earth are made up of different combinations of these 92 natural elements.

C. The elements can be divided into two main groups—**metals** and **nonmetals**—according to certain properties they share.
   1. Most metals have a special shiny surface called a metallic luster, and they conduct electricity and heat very well. Many metals are ductile, which means they can be drawn out into wire, and malleable, which means they can be hammered into thin sheets. Examples of metals are gold, silver, copper, iron, and aluminum.
   2. Most nonmetals conduct electricity and heat very poorly, and the solid nonmetals cannot be drawn into wire or hammered into sheets. Examples of nonmetals are sulfur, carbon, oxygen, hydrogen, and nitrogen.
   3. Some elements have certain properties of both metals and nonmetals. These elements are called **metalloids**. Examples of metalloids are arsenic and silicon.

TABLE 16.1 Some Common Elements and Their Symbols

Element	Symbol	Element	Symbol
Aluminum	Al	Nickel	Ni
Arsenic	As	Nitrogen	N
Calcium	Ca	Oxygen	O
Carbon	C	Phosphorus	P
Chlorine	Cl	Platinum	Pt
Copper	Cu	Potassium	K
Fluorine	F	Selenium	Se
Gold	Au	Silicon	Si
Helium	He	Silver	Ag
Hydrogen	H	Sodium	Na
Iodine	I	Sulfur	S
Iron	Fe	Tin	Sn
Lead	Pb	Tungsten	W
Magnesium	Mg	Radium	Ra
Mercury	Hg	Uranium	U
Neon	Ne	Zinc	Zn

VIII. Symbols of the Chemical Elements

A. Instead of writing the whole word, chemists use a symbol for the name of an element.
   1. Sometimes the symbol is just one letter of the alphabet. In this case we use the first letter of the name of the element as the symbol. Examples of symbols using one letter are C for carbon and H for hydrogen.
   2. Two letters are used when we have two or more elements whose names begin with the same letter. In this case, the symbol is made up of the first letter of the name of the element together with another letter that helps identify the element. Examples of symbols with two letters are Ca for calcium, Co for cobalt, and Cr for chromium. The first letter of a symbol is always a capital letter, and the second letter, if needed, is always lowercase.

B. Many symbols are taken from the Latin name for the element. For example, the symbol for iron is Fe, from the Latin word *ferrum*. Some common elements and their symbols are shown in Table 16.1.

IX. The Atomic Structure of the Elements

A. The difference between the atoms of the various elements is the result of the number of electrons, protons, and neutrons contained in the atoms.

B. There is also a definite arrangement for the electrons, protons, and neutrons in the atoms of each element.

C. In all atoms, the protons and neutrons are located in the nucleus, and the electrons are located in shells, or energy levels, outside the nucleus.

D. The number of protons in the nucleus of an atom is the **atomic number** of the element. It is also equal to the number of electrons outside the nucleus. This number is distinct for the atoms of each element. For example, an atom of oxygen has 8 protons in its nucleus and its atomic number is 8. An atom of iron has 26 protons in its nucleus and its atomic number is 26. The atomic number of an element identifies the element and determines its chemical properties.

E. It is possible to arrange all 109 elements in a table of atomic numbers that range from 1 to 109.
   1. In this table the first element has an atomic number of 1, the second an atomic number of 2, the third an atomic number of 3, and so on until the last element, which has an atomic number of 109.
   2. Each element in the table has an atomic number that is one number higher (one more proton) than the element before it, and one number lower (one less proton) than the element after it.

F. When atoms are electrically neutral, there are the same number of negatively charged (–) electrons outside the nucleus as there are positively charged (+) protons inside the nucleus. An atom of hydrogen, for example, with an atomic number of 1, has one proton in its nucleus and one electron outside the nucleus. An atom of uranium, with an atomic number of 92, has 92 protons in its nucleus and 92 electrons outside the nucleus.

G. There are seven shells, or energy levels, that electrons may occupy.
   1. There is a definite limit to the number of electrons that can occupy each energy level. There can be no more than 2 electrons in the first energy level, the one nearest the nucleus; 8 electrons in the second; 18 electrons in the third; and 32 electrons in the fourth energy level.

2. Generally, the farther away the energy levels are from the nucleus, the more energy the electrons in these energy levels will demonstrate.
3. When chemical changes take place, it is caused by an action between the electrons in the outermost energy levels of the atoms of two or more different elements.

H. The mass of an atom is called its **atomic mass**, or its atomic weight. It is the mass of all the electrons, protons, and neutrons in the atom.
1. Because electrons have so little weight, for all practical purposes the weight of the atom can be said to be the weight of the protons and neutrons in the nucleus.
2. A neutron has a weight of 1 atomic mass unit.
3. A proton, which weighs about the same as a neutron, also has a weight of 1 atomic mass unit.
4. Because a proton and a neutron have just about the same atomic weight, the number of neutrons in a nucleus can be found by subtracting the atomic number from the atomic weight. For example, if the atomic number of the element aluminum is 13 and its atomic weight is 27 mass units, that means there are 13 protons and 27 minus 13, or 14, neutrons in the nucleus.
5. In general, as the atomic numbers of the various atoms increase, the atomic weights increase as well.

I. The atomic structure of the simplest element, hydrogen, is as follows.
1. The hydrogen atom has an atomic number of 1 and an atomic weight of 1.
2. The atomic number of 1 means that there is 1 proton in the nucleus and 1 electron in the first shell, or energy level, outside the nucleus.
3. The 1 proton in the nucleus makes up the atomic weight of 1.

J. The atomic structure of the next simplest element, helium, is as follows.
1. The helium atom has an atomic number of 2 and an atomic weight of 4.
2. The atomic number of 2 means that there are 2 protons in the nucleus and 2 electrons in the first shell, or energy level, outside the nucleus.
3. There are 4 minus 2, or 2, neutrons in the nucleus, which together with the 2 protons make up the atomic weight of 4.

K. The atomic structure for the first 24 elements is given in Table 16.2.

TABLE 16.2 Atomic Structure of the First 24 Elements

Element	Atomic Number	Atomic Weight	Number of Protons	Number of Neutrons	Arrangement of Electrons by Energy Levels
Hydrogen	1	1.00794	1	0	1
Helium	2	4.002602	2	2	2
Lithium	3	6.941	3	4	2,1
Beryllium	4	9.01218	4	5	2,2
Boron	5	10.811	5	6	2,3
Carbon	6	12.011	6	6	2,4
Nitrogen	7	14.0067	7	7	2,5
Oxygen	8	15.9994	8	8	2,6
Fluorine	9	18.998403	9	10	2,7
Neon	10	20.179	10	10	2,8
Sodium	11	22.98977	11	12	2,8,1
Magnesium	12	24.305	12	12	2,8,2
Aluminum	13	26.98154	13	14	2,8,3
Silicon	14	28.0855	14	14	2,8,4
Phosphorus	15	30.97376	15	16	2,8,5
Sulfur	16	32.06	16	16	2,8,6
Chlorine	17	35.453	17	18	2,8,7
Argon	18	39.948	18	22	2,8,8
Potassium	19	39.0983	19	20	2,8,8,1
Calcium	20	40.078	20	20	2,8,8,2
Scandium	21	44.95591	21	24	2,8,9,2
Titanium	22	47.88	22	26	2,8,10,2
Vanadium	23	50.9415	23	28	2,8,11,2
Chromium	24	51.9961	24	28	2,8,13,1

L. Not all atoms of the same element have the same weight. Atoms of an element that have the same atomic number but a different atomic weight are called **isotopes** of that element. Isotopes can occur naturally or they can be produced artificially.
   1. Some atoms of an element have a slightly different number of neutrons than other atoms of the same element.
   2. Because of this difference in the number of neutrons, some atoms of an element have a different atomic weight than other atoms of the same element.
   3. This partially explains why atomic weights are not expressed as whole numbers only.
   4. However, even though these atoms of the same element differ in atomic weight, they all still have the same atomic number, so they are all the same element and have the same chemical properties of that element.
   5. Isotopes of the same element have the same number of protons and electrons but a slightly different number of neutrons. Some isotopes, but not all, have more neutrons than a stable nucleus can support. These isotopes decay after a period of time into other isotopes of the same element or into other elements (see, for example, Figure 16.2).

uranium-238
(4.5 billion years)
↓
radium-226
(1,622 years)
↓
radon-222
(3.8 days)
↓
polonium-218
(3 minutes)
↓
lead-214
(26.8 minutes)
↓
bismuth-214
(19.9 minutes)
↓
polonium-214
(1.6 × 10 seconds)
↓
lead-206
stable

FIGURE 16.2 Uranium to stable lead decay series, showing half-lives.

M. The element hydrogen has three known isotopes.
   1. Hydrogen has an atomic number of 1, which means that all three isotopes have one proton in the nucleus and one electron outside the nucleus.
   2. The most common isotope has just one proton in the nucleus, so its atomic weight is 1. A second isotope, called **deuterium,** has a neutron in the nucleus, in addition to 1 proton, so its atomic weight is 2. A third isotope, called **tritium,** the heaviest isotope of hydrogen and the only radioactive form of hydrogen, has 2 neutrons and 1 proton in the nucleus, so its atomic weight is 3.
   3. The mass of an average hydrogen atom is called the **atomic weight** of hydrogen. Since more than 99.9% of hydrogen atoms have a mass number of 1, the average atomic weight is only slightly greater than 1, or 1.0079.

N. A radioactive isotope of carbon is used to estimate the age of rocks, fossils, and minerals. (See Chapter 10.)
   1. Carbon has an atomic number of 6, which means that all isotopes of carbon have 6 protons in the nucleus and 6 electrons outside the nucleus.
   2. The common isotope of carbon has an atomic weight of 12; so there are 12 minus 6, or 6, neutrons in the carbon-12 atom.
   3. The radioactive isotope of carbon has an atomic weight of 14; so there are 14 minus 6, or 8, neutrons in the carbon-14 atom.

O. Two of uranium's many isotopes have atomic weights of 238 and 235.
   1. Both of these isotopes have the atomic number of 92, so there are 92 protons in the nucleus and 92 electrons outside the nucleus.
   2. In the uranium-238 isotope, there are 238 minus 92, or 146, neutrons in the nucleus.
   3. The uranium-235 isotope has 235 minus 92, or 143, neutrons in the nucleus.

P. Only a few of the 92 elements found on Earth are naturally radioactive. However, scientists discovered that when they bombarded the other natural elements with neutrons or deuterons (the nuclei of hydrogen atoms containing a proton and a neutron), radioactive isotopes of these elements were formed.
   1. Using a nuclear reactor, a **cyclotron,** or other "atom smashers," radioactive isotopes of practically all the elements have been prepared.
   2. These artificial radioactive isotopes are more commonly called **radioisotopes.**

Q. Radioisotopes have been most helpful in medicine, industry, agriculture, and research.
   1. Because they all give off radiation that can be detected by instruments, they can be used as tracers in many different ways.

2. They can be traced as they move through pipelines to detect leaks in the pipes; and they can be used to study the wear of machine parts or automobile treads, to study refining processes in oil refineries, to detect flaws in metal parts, and to gauge the thickness of sheets of metal, rubber, plastic, cloth, and paper.
3. Radioactive carbon can be used to show how the leaves of green plants make food for a plant by photosynthesis.
4. Radioisotopes are used to tell how well a plant is making use of fertilizers that have been added to the soil.
5. The exposure of seeds and plants to radiation from radioisotopes is producing new and better varieties of plants.
6. Radioactive cobalt is used instead of radium to treat cancer because it is easily made, less expensive, and more satisfactory. Radioactive phosphorus, boron, and arsenic are used to detect brain tumors.
7. Radioactive iodine is used to detect and treat diseases of the thyroid gland.
8. Chemists use radioisotopes to discover how chemical changes take place and to learn more about the structure and properties of matter.

R. Scientists have also been able to use the nuclear reactor and the "atom smasher" to create entirely new elements.
1. All of these new elements have a higher atomic number than uranium, the 92nd natural element.
2. They are all radioactive. Some of them have a long half-life, but others have a half-life that lasts for just a few seconds or considerably less. (See discussion of *half-life* later in this chapter.)

X. Compounds and Mixtures

A. All substances that make up matter can be divided into three main classes: elements, compounds, and mixtures.
1. Because there are only 92 naturally occurring elements on Earth, most substances are either compounds or mixtures.

B. A **compound** is a substance made up of two or more elements that have combined in such a way that each element has lost its own special physical and chemical properties.
1. As a result, the compound is a new substance with physical and chemical properties different from those of the elements that formed the compound.
2. This means that when a compound is formed, a chemical change takes place. Energy is either required for the process to occur or released as a result of the process.
3. Every compound has its own special properties, so it is possible to distinguish one compound from another.
4. A compound is always made up of the same elements, and the number of atoms of each element that combine to form one molecule of the compound is always the same. For example, water is a compound made from the elements hydrogen and oxygen; there are always two atoms of hydrogen and one atom of oxygen in one molecule of water. Ammonia is a gaseous compound made of the elements nitrogen and hydrogen; there are always one atom of nitrogen and three atoms of hydrogen in one molecule of ammonia.
5. The elements in a compound cannot be separated easily. For the separation to take place, some form of energy, such as electricity or heat, is required.
6. With 92 natural elements, it is possible to make hundreds of thousands of compounds by using different combinations of elements.
7. Some elements, such as gold and platinum, do not combine easily to form compounds. A few elements, helium and neon, for example, never form compounds.

C. A **mixture** is a substance made up of two or more elements or compounds that have combined in such a way that each element or compound has not lost its own special physical and chemical properties. As a result, no new substance has been formed.
1. The amounts of the different substances that make up a mixture are not fixed. In a mixture, any amount of one substance can be combined with any amount of an other substance.
2. The air we breathe is an example of a mixture. Air is made up of many gases, including oxygen, nitrogen, carbon dioxide, and water vapor. None of these gases has combined with the others; each gas still retains its own special physical and chemical properties. The amounts of the gases in the air are not fixed, and therefore they change from time to time.
3. The substances in a mixture can be separated by making use of differences in their physical properties, such as density, color, solubility in water or other liquids, or boiling point. For example, when a strong magnet is stirred in a mixture of iron powder and sulfur powder, the magnet picks up all the iron powder, thus separating the iron from the sulfur.

XI. Formulas

A. Chemists use symbols and, where necessary, small numbers beside the symbols to show the makeup of a compound. This combination of symbols and small numbers is called a **formula.** A chemical formula tells us two things.
1. It tells us what elements are in the compound.
2. It tells us how many atoms of each element are in a molecule of the compound. For example, the formula for water is H_2O, illustrating that water is made up of the elements hydrogen and oxygen and that a

molecule of water contains two atoms of hydrogen and one atom of oxygen. The formula for cane sugar is $C_{12}H_{22}O_{11}$, illustrating that sugar is made up of the elements carbon, hydrogen, and oxygen and that a molecule of cane sugar contains 12 atoms of carbon, 22 atoms of hydrogen, and 11 atoms of oxygen. A list of some common compounds and their formulas is shown in Table 16.3.

XII. Types of Chemical Changes or Reactions

A. Chemical changes are also called chemical reactions. Many chemical changes or reactions can be grouped according to four types: combination, decomposition, simple replacement, and double replacement reactions.

B. In **combination reactions**, two or more elements or compounds combine to form a larger and more complicated compound.

1. For example, the elements carbon and oxygen combine to form carbon dioxide, and the compounds water and carbon dioxide combine to form carbonic acid.

C. **Equations** describe what happens during a chemical change or reaction.

1. Equations use formulas to show what materials take part in the chemical change or reaction and what new materials are formed.
2. For the two combination reactions described in section B, the equations are as follows:

$$C + O_2 \rightarrow CO_2$$

$$H_2O + CO_2 \rightarrow H_2CO_3$$

D. In **decomposition reactions**, a compound is broken up into the elements that formed it, or into simpler compounds.

1. For example, the breakdown of iron sulfide into iron and sulfur is shown by this equation:

$$FeS \rightarrow Fe + S$$

2. The breakdown of limestone (calcium carbonate) into lime (calcium oxide) and carbon dioxide is shown by this equation:

$$CaCO_3 \rightarrow CaO + CO_2$$

E. In a **simple replacement reaction**, a free element replaces another element from a compound.

1. For example, free iron replaces copper sulfate to form free copper and the compound iron sulfate, shown in this equation:

$$Fe + CuSO_4 \rightarrow Cu + FeSO_4$$

2. Free zinc replaces hydrogen from sulfuric acid to form free hydrogen gas and the compound zinc sulfate. That replacement reaction is shown by this equation:

$$Zn + H_2SO_4 \rightarrow H_2 + ZnSO_4$$

F. In a **double replacement reaction**, an element in one compound trades places with an element in another compound, and the result is two new compounds.

1. For example, silver in silver nitrate trades places with sodium in sodium chloride when both chemicals are first dissolved in water and then mixed together. Two new compounds, silver chloride and sodium nitrate, are formed. The equation for this reaction is as follows:

$$AgNO_3 + NaCl \rightarrow AgCl + NaNO_3$$

2. In another example, when equal amounts of hydrochloric acid (a strong acid) and sodium hydroxide (a strong base) are mixed, the hydrogen in the hydrochloric acid trades places with the sodium in the sodium hydroxide, and common table salt (NaCl) and water are formed, as shown in the following equation:

$$HCl + NaOH \rightarrow H_2O + NaCl$$

TABLE 16.3 Some Common Compounds and Their Formulas

Compounds	Formulas
Ammonia	NH_3
Baking soda (sodium bicarbonate)	$NaHCO_3$
Carbon dioxide	CO_2
Carbon monoxide	CO
Lime (calcium oxide)	CaO
Limestone (calcium carbonate)	$CaCO_3$
Salt (sodium chloride)	$NaCl$
Sand (silicon dioxide)	SiO_2
Sugar (sucrose)	$C_{12}H_{22}O_{11}$
Sulfuric acid	H_2SO_4
Vinegar (acetic acid)	$HC_2H_3O_2$
Water	H_2O

XIII. Solutions

A. When a lump of sugar is added to a glass of water, the sugar gradually disappears. By tasting the water, however, we can tell that there is still sugar in the water even though we may no longer see it.

1. The molecules of sugar have spread out and spaced themselves among the molecules of water.
2. The water has the same amount of sweetness throughout, because the molecules of sugar have spread evenly and equally among the water molecules.
3. We say that the sugar has dissolved in the water to form a solution.
4. A **solution** is any mixture of two substances or materials in which the molecules of one substance are spread evenly and equally between the molecules of the other substance.

LEARNING ACTIVITY 16.5

Types of Chemical Reactions

A. To Demonstrate Combination

Place some steel wool in water and allow it to rust. Remove the steel wool and examine the rust under a magnifying glass. Notice how the dark, metallic iron threads have been changed into the reddish-orange, powdery iron oxide. Soak another wad of steel wool in water and leave it exposed to the air for a few days until it has become quite rusty. Scrape off some of the rust and see whether it can be attracted by a magnet.

B. To Demonstrate Decomposition

Pour some 3% hydrogen peroxide (available from a drugstore) into a glass jar. Add a piece of liver the size of a half dollar, then cover the jar with a piece of cardboard. (Keep the liver cool, but do not freeze, until 1 hour before using.) The bubbling shows that a liver enzyme, called catalase, decomposes the hydrogen peroxide into water and oxygen gas. When the bubbling subsides, insert a glowing wood splint into the jar. The splint will burst into flame, showing the presence of oxygen.

C. To Demonstrate Simple Replacement

Dissolve some copper sulfate crystals (available from a plant nursery) in a tumbler of water and stir until the crystals dissolve completely. Place a small wad of steel wool into the solution for a few minutes. Remove the steel wool and examine the coating of copper that has formed on it. Note that some iron from the steel wool has replaced the copper from the solution of copper sulfate.

D. To Demonstrate Double Replacement

Obtain a small amount of dilute silver nitrate solution from a drugstore. Dissolve some table salt (sodium chloride) in a glass tumbler or beaker half filled with water. Pour the clear silver nitrate solution into the equally clear salt solution. A white solid, or precipitate, forms immediately. Point out that the silver nitrate and sodium chloride interact to form silver chloride and sodium nitrate. The sodium nitrate remains in solution, whereas the silver chloride comes out of solution as the insoluble white solid.

---

5. The substance that dissolves is called the **solute**, which, in our example, is the sugar. The solute can be a solid, a liquid, or a gas.
6. The substance that does the dissolving, which in our example is the water, is called the **solvent.**
7. A solvent is usually a liquid, such as water, although it can also be a gas or a solid.
8. So many substances can dissolve in water that water is referred to as the **universal solvent.**

B. A **dilute solution** is one in which only a small amount of solute is dissolved in the solvent.

C. A **concentrated solution** is one in which a large amount of solute is dissolved in the solvent.

D. A **saturated solution** is one in which as much solute as possible is dissolved in the solvent at a certain temperature and pressure.

E. The most common type of solution is one in which a solid dissolves in a liquid. Other common types of solutions are as follows:
1. A solution of a gas in a liquid, such as carbon dioxide gas dissolved under pressure in water to form soda water.
2. A solution of a gas in a gas, such as air, where the several gases in the air are spread evenly and equally among one another.
3. A solution of a liquid in a liquid, such as alcohol and water.

F. Special words are used to describe substances that will or will not dissolve.
1. For example, when a solid can dissolve in a liquid, we say that the solid is **soluble** in the liquid.
2. A solid that does not dissolve in a liquid is said to be **insoluble.**
3. When two liquids mix to form a solution, we say that the two liquids are **miscible.**
4. Two liquids that will not mix to form a solution are said to be **immiscible** or nonmiscible.

G. Usually solids dissolve better in hot liquids than in cold liquids. Consequently, more solid will usually dissolve in a liquid when it is hot than when it is cold.
1. More sugar can dissolve in hot water than in cold water.
2. Some solids, such as salt, are almost as soluble in cold liquids as in hot liquids. Almost as much salt will dissolve in cold water as in hot water.
3. Some solids, such as calcium sulfate, are less soluble in hot liquids than in cold liquids, which means that less calcium sulfate will dissolve in hot water than in cold water.

H. Gases dissolve better in cold liquids than in hot liquids. Consequently, less gas will dissolve in a hot liquid than in a cold liquid.
1. When a glass of cold water is allowed to stand in a warm room for a while, bubbles of air collect on the sides of the glass.
2. As the water becomes warmer, it cannot hold as much of the air that is dissolved in it, so some of the air comes out of the water.

I. An increase in pressure makes a gas more soluble in a liquid.
   1. Soda water is water in which much carbon dioxide has been made to dissolve by using great pressure.
   2. When the cap is removed from a bottle of soda water, the pressure is lessened or reduced, and carbon dioxide escapes from the solution in the form of gas bubbles.

J. There are three ways to make solids dissolve more quickly in a liquid.
   1. Stirring can help the molecules of the solid spread quickly throughout the molecules of the liquid while bringing fresh parts of the liquid into contact with particles of the solid that have not yet dissolved.
   2. Powdering the solid can allow more of the liquid to come in contact with the solid at one time. This increased contact will help the solid dissolve more quickly.
   3. Heating the liquid will make the molecules of the liquid move more quickly so that the particles of solute are spread more quickly throughout the molecules of the solvent. At the same time, fresh parts of the liquid will come in contact more quickly with particles of still undissolved solid.

XIV. **The Law of Conservation of Matter**

A. In many chemical changes, such as when hydrogen gas and oxygen gas combine to form water, it seems as though new matter has been created. In other chemical changes, such as when a candle burns, matter seems to disappear, and we get the impression that matter has been destroyed. However, the **law of conservation of matter** tells us that, in ordinary chemical reactions, matter is neither created nor destroyed but only changed from one form to another.
   1. When wood is burned in air, gases are formed and ashes are left, and it can be shown that the combined weight of the wood and the air that was used to burn the wood are exactly equal to the combined weight of the ashes and gases that are formed.
   2. So, in this chemical change, the matter changes from one form to another, but the amount of matter itself does not change.

Energy

I. **Definition and Kinds of Energy**

A. Energy is the ability of matter to move other matter or to produce a chemical change in other matter. When talking about machines, scientists define energy as the ability to do work (discussed Chapter 17).

B. The movement of energy from one place to another is called **radiation.**

C. There are two kinds of energy: kinetic energy and potential energy.
   1. **Kinetic energy** is the energy a body has when it is in motion. Therefore, it is the energy of motion, an active energy. A moving automobile, falling water, a strong wind, and expanding gas are all examples of kinetic energy.
   2. **Potential energy** is the energy a body has because of its position or condition. Potential energy is stored-up energy that will not do any work until it is set free or released.
      a. A rock balanced on a cliff has potential energy because it is in a position to do work when it is released. Water at the top of a dam or waterfall also has potential energy because of its position.
      b. A stretched rubber band and a wound-up spring both have potential energy, because they are in a condition to do work when they are released.
      c. A chemical, such as gunpowder, also has potential energy because it is in a condition to do work when it ignites and explodes.
      d. The chemicals in a dry cell battery have potential energy because they are in a condition to do work when the dry cell is connected to an appliance.
   3. When potential energy is set free, it is changed to kinetic energy. For example, when water at the top of a dam or waterfall is released, it moves faster and faster, gaining more and more kinetic energy; when the water hits the bottom, its potential energy has been changed to kinetic energy. The potential energy of a stretched rubber band or wound-up spring is changed to kinetic energy when the band or the spring is released. The potential energy of gunpowder is changed to kinetic energy when the gunpowder explodes.

II. **Forms of Energy**

A. There are six major forms of energy: mechanical, thermal, electrical, wave, chemical, and nuclear.

B. **Mechanical energy** is the form we see most often around us—the energy of machinery in motion. All moving bodies produce mechanical energy. The energy produced from most kinds of machines is mechanical energy.

C. **Thermal energy** is the energy produced by the kinetic energy of molecules. The faster its molecules move, the more energy a substance has and the hotter it becomes. This form of energy heats our homes, dries our clothes, cooks our food, and runs power plants.

D. **Electrical energy** is the energy of electrons as they transfer energy through a substance. A transfer of energy from one electron to the next through a substance is called an electrical current. **Electrical current** is the flow of electrical charge, not the flow of electrons. It can be compared to a bucket brigade, where the individuals of the brigade passing the bucket stand in one place but the water moves at the rate at which the bucket is being passed. Electrical energy lights our homes, runs motors, and makes our telephones, radios, and television sets operable.

E. **Wave energy** travels in waves.
   1. One kind of wave energy is **sound energy,** which is produced when matter moves back and forth, or vibrates, rapidly.
   2. Another kind of wave energy is **radiant energy.** There are many different forms of radiant energy, including light rays, X-rays, radio waves, infrared rays, and ultraviolet rays.

F. **Chemical energy** is really a form of potential energy, because the energy is stored in substances. Chemical energy is released when a chemical reaction takes place and new substances are formed. The new substances are formed because of the action between the electrons in the outermost shells, or energy levels, in atoms of the different substances.

G. **Nuclear energy** comes from the nucleus of an atom when the atom splits in two or when the nuclei of atoms fuse together.

III. The Transformation and Conservation of Energy

A. Energy can be changed from one form to another.
   1. The production of electricity in a power plant illustrates how energy can be changed from one form to another.
   2. When coal or another fuel is burned, the chemical energy in the fuel is released and changed into heat energy.
   3. The heat energy changes water into steam, and the steam then turns a turbine to produce mechanical energy.
   4. The turbine runs an electric generator, or dynamo, which changes mechanical energy into electrical energy.
   5. The electrical energy may then be changed into light energy in a light bulb, or sound energy in a doorbell.

B. In all these changes, energy is not destroyed but changed in form. The **law of conservation of energy** says that energy is neither created nor destroyed but only changed from one form to another. When energy is changed from one form to another, other forms of energy are also produced. Usually these other forms of energy are not wanted and are wasted because we have not found a use for them. For example, when we get light energy from an electric light bulb, unwanted and unused heat energy is produced at the same time.

IV. The Law of Conservation of Matter and Energy

A. In 1905, using mathematics, Albert Einstein explained the relationship between matter and energy. According to Einstein, energy and matter are equivalent, meaning that energy can be transformed to matter and, conversely, matter can be transformed into energy. Matter can be destroyed, but it reappears as newly created energy. Energy can be destroyed, but it reappears as newly created matter.
   1. Einstein's theory is usually expressed by the mathematical formula $E = mc^2$, where E represents the amount of energy, m represents the mass (amount of matter) and c represents the speed of light in a vacuum; c^2 means that this value for the speed of light is multiplied by itself. Thus, the formula reads: energy equals mass times the speed of light times the speed of light.

B. Einstein's theory was verified when scientists began to study the atom.
   1. They discovered that when certain atoms break up into simpler atoms, the simpler atoms together weigh less than the original atom from which they came.
   2. However, when atoms do break up into simpler atoms, a tremendous amount of energy is also given off, which means that some of the matter in the atoms turns into energy.

C. Scientists also found that when energy is used to make an electron move faster, the mass of the electron becomes greater. Supplying energy to the electron increases not only its speed but its mass as well. Some of that added energy turns into matter.

D. These findings showed that the law of conservation of matter and the law of conservation of energy do not always hold true. Now both laws are combined into a single law, the **law of conservation of matter and energy.** According to this law, neither matter nor energy can be destroyed, but either can be changed into other forms of matter or energy. Matter can be changed into energy, and energy can be changed into matter. As a result, the total amount of matter and energy in the universe remains constant.

Nuclear Energy

I. Natural Radioactivity

A. Certain elements, such as radium and uranium, give off invisible radiations, or rays, that have peculiar properties.
1. They can penetrate solid materials such as paper, wood, thin sheets of metal, and flesh.
2. They affect a photographic negative in exactly the same way visible light affects the negative when it is exposed to light.
3. They can stop seeds from germinating, kill bacteria, and destroy small animals.
4. A person exposed to these rays for some time will receive severe burns, which take a long time to heal and might even be fatal.
5. When compounds of these elements are added to certain other compounds, the mixture will become fluorescent, or glow in the dark.

B. These elements and their compounds also give off heat, visible light, and invisible radiations.

C. Elements that give off these invisible radiations are said to be radioactive; this highly unusual property is called **radioactivity.** Elements that are naturally radioactive include uranium, thorium, carbon-14, potassium-40, radon, and radium.

D. These radiations are produced because the radioactive elements are breaking up; that is, they are giving up matter and energy.
1. In all cases, it has been found that the breakup takes place in the nucleus.
2. While the breakup is going on, three different kinds of invisible radiations are given off.
3. Two of these radiation types are really particles of matter, called alpha particles and beta particles. The third radiation type is an energy wave, called a gamma ray.

E. **Alpha particles** are the nuclei of helium atoms.
1. Each helium nucleus has two protons and two neutrons and is about four times as heavy as a hydrogen atom.
2. Because of the positively charged protons in the helium nucleus, an alpha particle is positively charged.
3. When an alpha particle, or helium nucleus, gains two electrons, it becomes a helium atom.
4. Alpha particles have a speed of about 16,000 to 32,000 kilometers per second (10,000 to 20,000 miles per second).
5. They have the least penetrating power of the three invisible radiation types given off by radioactive elements and can be stopped by a thin sheet of paper.

F. **Beta particles** are electrons traveling at high speeds.
1. These electrons are given off when neutrons in the nucleus of the radioactive element decompose.
2. They are negatively charged and travel 96,000 to 256,000 kilometers per second (60,000 to 160,000 miles per second).
3. Because of their high speed, beta particles have high penetrating power. A fairly thick sheet of aluminum metal is needed to stop them.

G. **Gamma rays** are high-energy electromagnetic radiation.
1. They have more penetrating power than the other two radiation types.
2. Very thick layers of lead or concrete are required to stop them.

H. Radioactive elements break up because the nuclei of their atoms are unstable. These unstable atoms are known as **radionuclides.**
1. The nuclei of radionuclides give off either alpha or beta particles.
2. New nuclei are formed, which are a little lighter and more stable than the original nuclei.
3. Gamma rays are produced because changes in energy levels take place in the nucleus when the new nuclei are formed.
4. At the same time, while the radioactive elements are breaking up, a small amount of their matter is changed into tremendous amounts of energy.

I. When the unstable nuclei of radioactive elements give off alpha particles, new elements are formed.
1. An alpha particle is a helium nucleus, containing two protons and two neutrons.
2. When an atom of a radioactive element loses an alpha particle from its nucleus, this means that the nucleus has lost two protons, so the atomic number (number of protons in the nucleus) is now two less than it was previously.
3. Because the atomic number has changed, an atom of a new element has been formed.
4. Moreover, because the two protons and two neutrons in the alpha particle give it an atomic weight of four, the loss of an alpha particle from the nucleus means that the atomic weight of the new element is four less than the atomic weight of the original element. An example of how the loss of an alpha particle produces a change in atomic number and atomic weight is shown by the radioactive element radium, which has an atomic number of 88 and an atomic mass number of 226. When the nucleus of a

radium atom loses an alpha particle, an atom of the gaseous element **radon** is formed, with an atomic number of 86 and an atomic mass number of 222.

5. Radon is an odorless, colorless, and tasteless radioactive gas formed by the natural radioactive decay of uranium, which is found in minute amounts throughout the Earth's crust. From the Earth, radon seeps into homes and other buildings through fissures in foundations. It can accumulate in homes to create much higher concentrations than those measured outdoors. Radon can also enter homes through groundwater supplies.
6. Radon itself is radioactive because it also decays, losing an alpha particle and forming the element **polonium** (see Figure 16.2). Polonium, produced by the decay of radon in the air and in people's lungs, can cause lung cancer.

J. When the unstable nuclei of radioactive elements give off **beta particles**, new elements are also formed.
   1. A beta particle is an electron given off by a neutron in a nucleus.
   2. When a neutron gives off an electron, the neutron becomes a proton.
   3. As a result, there is now one more proton in the nucleus than there was previously, so the atomic number has been increased by 1. This means that a new element has been formed.
   4. Because an electron has little or no weight, the loss of a beta particle does not change the weight (mass) of the new element that has been formed. An example of how the loss of a beta particle produces a change in atomic number but not in atomic weight is shown by the radioactive element thorium, which has an atomic number of 90 and an atomic weight of 234. When an atom of thorium loses a beta particle, an atom of the element protoactinium is formed, with an atomic number of 91 and an atomic weight of 234.

K. The unstable nucleus of a radioactive element continues to give off either alpha or beta particles, accompanied by gamma rays in each case, forming lighter and more stable nuclei until a nucleus is finally formed that is completely stable.
   1. When this condition results, radioactivity stops and no more alpha or beta particles or gamma rays are given off.
   2. For example, the radioactive element uranium goes through a series of breakups, giving off either alpha or beta particles and forming new radioactive elements with each breakup, until it finally becomes lead, which is nonradioactive and stable (see Figure 16.2).

II. The Breakup of Radioactive Elements

A. Radioactivity is very different from ordinary chemical changes.
   1. Ordinary changes can be speeded up or slowed down by changes in heat or pressure or by other means.
   2. Radioactive elements, in contrast, break up at a steady rate of speed that cannot be changed.

B. Different radioactive elements break up at different rates.
   1. Some elements take billions of years to break up into simpler elements, whereas others take days, hours, minutes, seconds, or fractions of seconds to break up.
   2. The time required for one-half of the atoms in a piece of a radioactive element to break up into simpler atoms is called the **half-life** of that element. Each radioactive element has its own half-life (see Figure 16.2).
   3. Radium, for example, has a half-life of 1,622 years, which means that half the atoms in a piece of radium will break up into simpler atoms in 1,622 years. Half of the radium atoms that remain, or one-fourth of the original number, will break up in the next 1,622 years. Half of the remaining radium atoms, or one-eighth of the original number, will break up in the next 1,622 years. The radium atoms will keep on breaking up this way as long as there are radium atoms present. The half-life of uranium-238 is about 4.5 billion years.

III. Detecting and Measuring Radioactivity

A. Because radiations from radioactive elements are invisible, special instruments are necessary to detect and measure them.

B. One simple method of detecting radiations is to observe their action on special, highly sensitive photographic film.
   1. Radiations from radioactive materials affect photographic film even though the film has not been exposed to ordinary light.
   2. For safety, persons who work with or near radiations wear film badges to detect the amount of radiation present.
   3. Each of these badges contains a small piece of special, highly sensitive photographic film, which is removed and developed to show the amount of radiation that has been absorbed by the person.

C. Another instrument used to detect and measure radiation is the **electroscope**.
   1. An electroscope is an instrument that is commonly used to detect and measure small electrical charges.
   2. When radiations from radioactive materials pass through air, they cause the particles of air to become electrically charged.
   3. The electroscope detects and measures these electrically charged particles of air, and in this way also detects and measures radiations.
   4. One type of electroscope, called a **dosimeter**, looks like a pencil and is clipped to a person's lapel or shirt pocket.

D. Another instrument used to detect and measure radiations is the **Geiger counter.**
   1. This instrument is a cigar-shaped tube made of glass and metal, with a wire running through it, connected to a storage battery and a loudspeaker or amplifier.
   2. When a Geiger counter is brought near a radioactive material, the radiations cause a small pulselike flow of electricity to take place inside the tube.
   3. This tiny electric current is amplified and either produces a series of "clicks" or makes a light flash on and off.
   4. Normally, a Geiger counter produces 25 to 50 clicks a minute even without being near a radioactive material. These clicks come from cosmic rays passing through the air and from natural radioactivity in the ground.
   5. However, when a radioactive material is present, a Geiger counter clicks very rapidly and produces a "machine gun" effect.
   6. Geiger counters are used to hunt for uranium ore and are also used in laboratories where radioactivity is being studied.

E. The particles that make up radiations are invisible, but their paths can be seen and photographed in a **cloud chamber.**
   1. The cloud chamber is filled with air that is saturated with water vapor.
   2. When the particles pass through the chamber, the water vapor condenses.
   3. Although the particles themselves are still invisible, the paths of the condensed moisture, called fog tracks, are visible and can be photographed.
   4. A fog track is very much like the vapor trail made by a jet plane flying so high that it is invisible to the unaided eye.

IV. Nuclear Fission

A. As a result of learning how uranium, radium, and other radioactive elements break up naturally to form new, lighter elements, scientists decided to try to break up atoms.
   1. They began by bombarding atoms of simpler elements with all kinds of high-speed particles, including protons, electrons, alpha particles (the nuclei of helium atoms), and **deuterons** (the nuclei of hydrogen atoms containing a proton and a neutron).
   2. With the exception of the electrons, all these highspeed particles are positively charged.
   3. The high speeds are given to these particles by instruments commonly called "atom smashers" or atomic accelerators.
   4. Atomic accelerators are able to give the particles speeds as high as 240,000 kilometers per second (150,000 mps) and tremendous amounts of energy.
   5. In the atomic accelerator, called the cyclotron, protons or deuterons are made to whirl around faster and faster in a spiral path until they finally shoot out of the cyclotron at tremendous speed. Other accelerators that are used to give high speeds to positively charged particles include the cosmotron, the synchrotron, and the linear speed accelerator.

B. When scientists bombarded the nuclei of atoms of simple elements with the high-speed particles, new elements were formed.
   1. A particle entered the nucleus of an atom and made the nucleus unstable.
   2. The unstable nucleus then rearranged itself by giving off a proton or a neutron, forming a new element and releasing much energy.
   3. This nuclear energy is produced when a small amount of an element's matter is changed into large amounts of energy, in accordance with Einstein's formula $e = mc^2$.
   4. When scientists bombarded nitrogen with high-speed alpha particles (helium nuclei), oxygen and neutrons were formed.
   5. When lithium was bombarded with high-speed protons, two alpha particles (helium nuclei) were formed.
   6. When beryllium was bombarded with high-speed alpha particles, carbon and neutrons were formed.
   7. Scientists had finally found a way to change one element into another.

C. However, scientists were not completely satisfied with these high-speed particles.
   1. The protons, deuterons, and alpha particles had to be given tremendous amounts of energy before they could enter the nucleus of an atom.
   2. This high energy was necessary because these particles were all positively charged. When they came near the nucleus of an atom, they were repelled by the same kind of positive charges that the protons in the nucleus had.
   3. However, the electrons were negatively charged and were attracted to the positively charged protons in the nucleus, but the electrons were so light that it was hard for them to break up the atom.

D. As a result, as soon as scientists learned how to obtain neutrons by bombarding beryllium with high-speed alpha particles, they began to use neutrons to bombard the nuclei of atoms of other elements.
   1. The neutrons were much better particles to use, because they were neutral and would not be repelled by the positively charged nucleus of an atom.
   2. At first scientists used high-speed neutrons.
   3. However, they soon learned that because atoms were mostly empty space and because the nucleus is very small compared with the rest of an atom, too often these high-speed neutrons went right through the atom without striking the tiny nucleus.

4. They discovered that when they slowed the neutrons, the neutrons were more likely to hit and be captured by the nucleus.
5. In fact, the slowed-down neutrons seemed to behave as if they were attracted to the nucleus, going straight to the nucleus.
6. One of the ways commonly used to slow neutrons is to allow them to pass through graphite, a pure form of carbon. The graphite in this case is called a moderator, because it slows or moderates the speed of the neutrons.

E. When scientists began to bombard the atoms of heavy elements with neutrons, a surprise occurred.
1. When they bombarded uranium with slowed-down neutrons, it did not break up like the lighter elements did, giving off a proton or a neutron and forming a new element.
2. Sometimes the uranium atom split into two parts, forming an atom of barium and an atom of krypton, both having medium-high atomic weights.
3. Two or three slow-moving neutrons were also given off, together with radiations in the form of gamma rays.
4. In addition, more energy was given off than had ever before been released.
5. This energy was formed when a small amount of the matter in the nucleus of the uranium atom was changed into large amounts of energy.
6. Scientists called this splitting of the nucleus of the atom **nuclear fission.**

F. The products of uranium fission are not always barium and krypton. Sometimes they are strontium and xenon, and still other elements can also be produced.

G. Because the uranium atom released two or three slow-moving neutrons, scientists hoped that a continuous splitting up of uranium atoms would be possible.
1. These slow-moving neutrons could split more uranium atoms, which would release more neutrons, which could split even more uranium atoms.
2. In this way, a continuous splitting, called a chain reaction, would take place until all the atoms split.

H. However, the scientists found that only a few uranium atoms would split.
1. One reason for the failure to produce a chain reaction was the nature of uranium itself.
2. The uranium used had two isotopes: uranium-235, with 143 neutrons in its nucleus; and uranium-238, with 146 neutrons in its nucleus.
3. The uranium-235 isotope splits very easily, but the uranium-238 isotope does not.
4. More than 99% of the element uranium is made up of the uranium-238 isotope, and less than 1% is made up of the uranium-235 isotope.
5. So, for a chain reaction to take place, the uranium-235 isotope must be separated from the uranium-238 isotope, and only the uranium-235 isotope used.
6. A second reason for the failure of a chain reaction to take place had to do with the amount of uranium being used in the reaction.
7. If too small an amount of uranium is used, the released neutrons from the fission of one of the uranium atoms will be emitted without striking any other uranium atoms, and the reaction stops.
8. Enough uranium must be present to allow the neutrons to strike other uranium atoms and keep the chain reaction going.
9. The smallest amount of uranium needed to keep a chain reaction going is called the critical size.
10. Because so little uranium-235 is available, scientists began looking for other, more easily available elements that could be split by neutrons.
11. They discovered that they could change the more common uranium-238 isotope into a new element that could be split by neutrons.
12. When uranium-238 atoms were bombarded with neutrons, each nucleus kept a neutron and became unstable, giving off a beta particle (an electron) and forming a new artificial element called neptunium with an atomic number of 93.
13. Neptunium is an unstable element. It gives off a beta particle, too, forming a second artificial element called plutonium with an atomic number of 94.
14. Plutonium is comparatively stable, but when bombarded by neutrons it splits up just as easily as uranium-235 to produce a chain reaction.

V. Controlling and Using Nuclear Energy

A. It is possible to control nuclear energy with a device called a **nuclear reactor**, which is sometimes also called an atomic pile.
1. A nuclear reactor helps to keep a chain reaction under control and makes use of the energy produced as a result of this reaction.
2. The reactor acts somewhat like a large oven or furnace.
3. In the reactor is a large block of graphite serving as a moderator to slow down the neutrons so they can enter the nuclei of the uranium-235 and produce a chain reaction.
4. Rods of uranium-235, sealed in aluminum cans for protection, are put into holes running horizontally through the graphite block from one end to the other.
5. Boron-steel or cadmium-steel rods are inserted into holes at the top of the reactor and run vertically through the graphite block.

6. These steel rods, called control rods, can be moved in and out of the reactor to control the speed of the chain reaction.
7. The control rods absorb any neutrons that hit them.
8. If the chain reaction is going too fast, the control rods are lowered farther into the reactor so they can absorb more neutrons and thus slow down the reaction. If the reaction is going too slow, the rods are lifted farther out of the reactor so that fewer neutrons are absorbed and the reaction can accelerate.
9. In some reactors, the tremendous amount of heat produced is removed by blowing air through circulating tubes in the reactor; in other reactors, the heat is removed by water or another liquid passing through the circulation tubes in the reactor.
10. The entire reactor is enclosed in a thick layer of solid concrete, which absorbs any dangerous radiations and therefore helps to protect the people operating the nuclear reactor.

B. The heat produced from the nuclear reaction is used to boil water and to change it into steam.
   1. The steam then turns a turbine that runs an electric generator that produces electricity.
   2. After the steam passes through the turbines, it is condensed and returned to the boilers to be changed back into steam again.

C. Nuclear reactors are used to run submarines and ships.
   1. Vessels driven by the power from nuclear reactors can sail for long distances without the need to refuel.
   2. The first nuclear submarine, the *Nautilus,* traveled almost 96,000 kilometers (60,000 mi) before it had to refuel.

D. Disposal of nuclear waste material is an environmental problem that has not been satisfactorily resolved.

E. On April 26, 1986, in what was then the Soviet Union, a nuclear power plant at Chernobyl, said to be one of the most powerful in the world, exploded and became the worst accident reported in the history of controlled nuclear reactions.
   1. The cause of this explosion was a series of errors by the power plant operators that caused a power surge.
   2. Tons of the uranium dioxide fuel and fission products such as cesium-137 and iodine-131 were thrown into the air.
   3. Explosion and heat sent up a 5-kilometer (3-mi) plume full of radioactive contaminants.
   4. Although the complete toll of damage and deaths resulting from the accident at Chernobyl is yet unclear, of the 116,000 people immediately evacuated, 24,000 received serious radiation doses of 45 rem. Five rem is considered acceptable for a nuclear power plant employee for 1 year.
   5. Children of the village of Lelev, 9 kilometers (5.6 mi) away, have been found to have thyroid radiation as high as 250 rem, the result of ingesting iodine-131.
   6. Scientists have estimated that as many as 280,000 deaths may ultimately result from the accident at Chernobyl.
   7. Soil and water contamination may make the immediate area uninhabitable for a long time.
   8. In 1995, it was reported that the sarcophagus that had been built over the explosion site to encase the high radiation was decaying, cracking, and leaking. It is likely that the environmental, health, and economic effects of the accident at Chernobyl will be experienced for decades to come.

Exploratory Activities for "Changes in Matter and Energy"

1. Exploring the Properties of Mixtures and Compounds (Grades 3–8)

The activities of this exploration should be performed by the teacher, but with student input responding to teacher questioning.

Overview

These activities are designed to facilitate student understanding of the nature of the properties of mixtures and compounds.

1.1 Exploring the Properties of Mixtures

Mix fine sand, sugar, iron filings, bits of cork filed from a stopper, and small marbles. Now ask students to hypothesize about ways of separating the components of the mixture. Then test their hypotheses. Conclusions should be something like the following. The marbles can be removed by hand or by pouring the mixture through a kitchen strainer. The iron filings can be removed with a strong magnet. Adding water to the remaining part of the mixture and then stirring causes the sugar to dissolve and the bits of cork to float on top of the solution. The bits of cork can be removed with a large spoon. The solution can then be poured off, leaving the sand behind. The solution can be allowed to evaporate in a pie tin or other shallow container, which will cause the sugar to be left behind.

1.2 Exploring the Properties of Compounds

Physical change only: Mix three parts sulfur powder and one part iron powder by weight. Stir until the mixture is uniform and the ingredients are indistinguishable. Ask

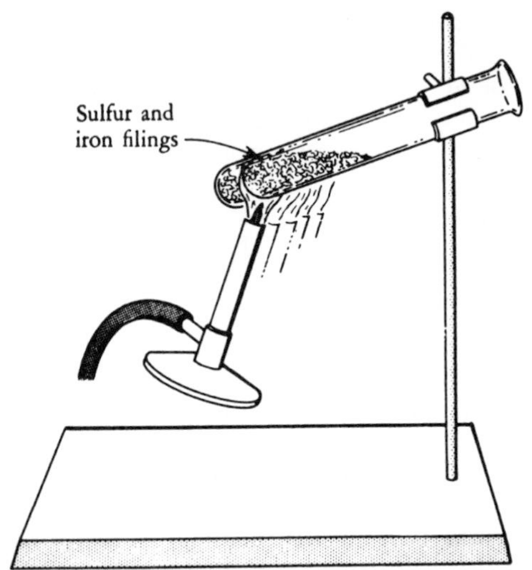

FIGURE 16.3 Heating sulfur and iron will produce a compound.

students to hypothesize ways of separating the substances that you mixed together. Test their hypotheses. Conclusions should be as follows.

Place one-half of the mixture in a shallow dish, and use a strong magnet to separate the iron from the sulfur, thus showing that the materials in a mixture retain their own special properties and can usually be separated by very simple means. Pass the magnet over the sulfur several times to pick up all the iron powder.

Chemical change: Now pour the second half of this mixture of sulfur and iron powder into a Pyrex tube that is supported on a ring stand with a clamp (Figure 16.3). Heat the test tube with a Bunsen burner, first gently and then strongly. Keep moving the flame up and down the lower half of the test tube to make sure the contents are being heated uniformly. Soon the contents will begin to glow, showing that a chemical change is taking place. Remove the flame and observe that the chemical change continues to take place, with the contents glowing strongly. Allow the test tube to cool to room temperature, wrap it in a piece of cloth or toweling, and break the end of the test tube gently with a hammer. Remove the contents with tweezers and place the material in a shallow dish. Try to separate the iron powder with a magnet. Ask students to hypothesize about what has happened. Nothing will happen because a new substance, called iron sulfide, has been formed, and it is not magnetic.

2. What's the Matter? Exploring the Properties of Density (grades 5–8)

(See Figure 7.4 in Chapter 7.)

3. Exploring the Properties of Solutions (Grades 4–8)

Set up six stations, with instructions at each station as follows.

3.1 Exploring Solutions

Obtain three tumblers the same size. Fill each tumbler threequarters full of tap water of the same temperature. To one tumbler add 1/4 teaspoon of sugar and stir until all the sugar is dissolved. To the second tumbler add 2 teaspoons of sugar and stir until all the sugar is dissolved. This can be set up as a blind test for students. Let them taste both solutions and predict which is dilute and which is concentrated.

To the third tumbler add 1/2 teaspoon of sugar and stir until all the sugar is dissolved. Continue adding sugar, a teaspoon at a time and stirring after each addition, until no more sugar will dissolve and a small pile of undissolved sugar remains at the bottom of the tumbler. Total the number of teaspoons of sugar you added to obtain a saturated sugar solution. Graph the results.

3.2 Some Substances Are More Soluble in Water Than Others

Add equal amounts of water at room temperature to three test tubes. Add a level teaspoon of sugar to one test tube, a level teaspoon of salt to the second test tube, and a level teaspoon of sodium bicarbonate to the third test tube. Placing your thumb over its mouth, shake each test tube vigorously 10 times; then place the test tubes upright and allow any undissolved material to settle. Record your conclusions about the degree of solubility of the three different materials.

3.3 Some Substances Are Insoluble in Water

Place a small stone in a test tube of water. Place your thumb over the mouth of the test tube and shake the tube vigorously. Record your conclusion. (No dissolving will take place.)

Add a few drops of oil to a test tube containing water. Record what happens. (The oil floats on top of the water.) Shake the test tube vigorously. Although the oil may break up into small drops, the drops will reassemble and the oil will continue to float undissolved on top of the water. Repeat the experiment, using a commercial "spot remover" instead of water. Record your conclusion. (The oil will be dissolved.)

3.4 The Effect of Temperature on the Solubility of Solids in Liquids

Pour a measured amount of water at room temperature into a tumbler. Add sugar, a teaspoon at a time, stirring after each addition until no more will dissolve. Repeat the experiment, using an equal amount of hot water this time. Compare the number of teaspoons of sugar that dissolved in the cold water with the number that dissolved in the hot water. Write your conclusions.

3.5 The Effect of Temperature on the Solubility of Gases in Liquids

(Possibly as a teacher demonstration.) Obtain two identical bottles of soda. Put one in the refrigerator and allow it to stand overnight. Keep the other bottle at room temperature. The next day remove the caps from both bottles. Place the cold, open bottle back in the refrigerator, and let the warm, open bottle stand again at room temperature. At the end of an hour pour the contents of each bottle into a tumbler. Observe and record your conclusion. (The soda from the cold bottle will fizz fairly vigorously, showing the presence of dissolved gas. The soda from the warm bottle will fizz weakly, if at all, showing that most of the dissolved gas has been driven from the soda at the warmer temperature.)

3.6 Making Solids Dissolve More Quickly in Water

Pour equal amounts of water at the same temperature in two tumblers. Record the temperature of each. Obtain two cubes of sugar and crush one of the cubes into small crystals. Put the lump of sugar into one tumbler and the crushed sugar into the second tumbler. Stir the water in each tumbler vigorously. Observe and record your conclusion. (The crushed sugar dissolves more quickly, because more of the water can come in contact with the sugar at one time.)

Pour equal amounts of water at the same temperature into two tumblers. Record the temperature of each. Add a level teaspoon of sugar to each of the tumblers. Stir the water in one of the tumblers, but not the other. Observe and note the result. (The sugar in the stirred water dissolves more quickly, because the stirring helps spread the sugar more quickly throughout the water and at the same time brings fresh parts of the water in contact with particles of sugar that have not yet dissolved.)

Pour a measured amount of water at room temperature into a tumbler. Pour an equal amount of hot water into a second tumbler. Record the temperature of each. Drop a sugar cube into each tumbler and note the results. (The sugar dissolves in the hot water more quickly.)

Chapter 17

Friction and Machines

Anthony Magnacca/Merril

 Friction

I. The Nature of Friction

A. Friction is the force that resists the movement of one material over another material. Whenever the surfaces of two materials rub against each other, friction is produced.
   1. Friction, caused by irregularities in the surfaces of materials, can make it difficult to push one material across another material.
   2. Every surface contains little bumps and hollows. On rough surfaces these bumps and hollows can be seen or felt, but on smooth surfaces the bumps and hollows can be seen only with the aid of magnification.
   3. When two surfaces are rubbed together, the bumps and hollows catch and stick and resist the movement of the surfaces over each other.
   4. Friction is also caused by the attraction (adhesion) of the molecules of one surface to the molecules of another surface as the surfaces rub against each other.

B. Friction causes heat. The greater the friction, the more heat produced.

II. Kinds of Friction and the Factors Affecting Friction

A. There are three major kinds of friction: sliding, rolling, and fluid.
   1. **Sliding** or **kinetic friction** is the resistance produced by two surfaces sliding across each other. In sliding friction, the bumps and hollows catch against each other.
   2. **Rolling friction** is the resistance produced when a rolling body moves over a surface. In rolling friction, the roller or wheel lifts up over the bumps and hollows instead of sliding and catching against them. The resistance or rolling friction is less than that caused by sliding friction.
   3. **Fluid friction** or viscosity is the resistance produced between moving fluids or between fluids and a solid. Generally, the resistance between two fluids will be less than that between a fluid and a solid or between two solids.

B. Several factors affect friction.
   1. Firm, hard materials produce less friction than materials that are soft and sticky.
   2. The nature of the surfaces affects friction. Smooth surfaces produce less friction than rough surfaces.
   3. For a given force, an increase or decrease in area of contact affects friction. For example, the larger the area of disc pads on automobile brakes, the greater the friction and the braking force.
   4. The force of the two surfaces against each other affects friction. The greater the force pressing the surfaces against each other, the greater the friction.

III. Advantages and Disadvantages of Friction

A. Friction provides many advantages.
   1. Without friction, we could not walk, because our feet would slip; we could not write with a pencil, pen, or chalk, or hold a baseball and bat.
   2. Sand or cinders are dropped in front of an automobile's rear wheels to increase friction and stop the wheels from spinning on icy roads.
   3. Vehicle brakes use friction to slow or stop the moving vehicle.
   4. Friction helps hold nails and screws in wood, and it helps us unscrew the tops of bottles or jars, and open cans.
   5. In industry, friction helps a conveyor belt move things along.
   6. Friction is useful in making things smoother, as in sanding wood or grinding lenses.
   7. The heat caused by friction can be useful, such as when striking a match to make a flame.

B. Friction can be a disadvantage.
   1. Friction wears away materials, such as automobile tires, shoes, and clothing.
   2. The moving parts of machines rub against each other and wear away.
   3. Because extra force must be used to overcome friction, friction makes work harder.
   4. Friction resists the movement of objects, making sliding parts stick.
   5. Friction between air and moving objects hinders the speed of these objects.
   6. Friction produces heat, which can start a fire or cause machine parts to melt or bend. At high speed, the friction between the air and a plane, spacecraft, or rocket may cause parts of the craft to become so hot that they will melt, bend, or ignite.
   7. If a person falls and slides across a gymnasium floor, the heat produced by the friction between a part of the body and the floor may cause a painful burn.

LEARNING ACTIVITY 17.1

Friction Produces Heat

Have the students rub the palms of their hands together briskly and note the heat produced by the resulting friction. The more briskly the hands are rubbed, the greater the friction and the hotter the hands become.

LEARNING ACTIVITY 17.2

Sliding, Rolling, and Starting Friction

A. Comparing Starting Friction and Sliding Friction

Slip a loop of string inside a large book and place the book on a table. Attach the string to a spring balance (Figure 17.1). Pull on the scale (making sure to hold it horizontally) until the book begins to move. Note the reading on the scale just before the book moves. Now pull the scale and book together along the table and note the reduced reading on the scale while the book is moving.

B. Comparing Rolling Friction and Starting Friction

Slip a loop of string inside a large book and attach the string to a spring balance, as described in part A. Pull the scale and book together along the table and note the reading on the scale while the book is moving. Now place about a dozen round pencils beneath and beside the book, and pull the book along the table again (Figure 17.2). Note the reduced reading on the scale as the book moves along the rollers.

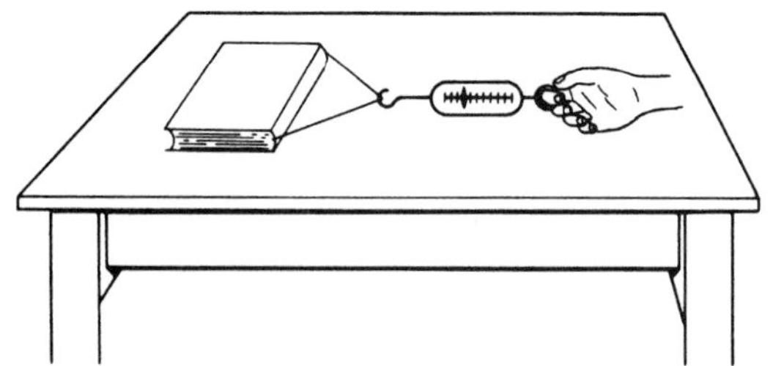

FIGURE 17.1 Sliding friction is less than starting friction.

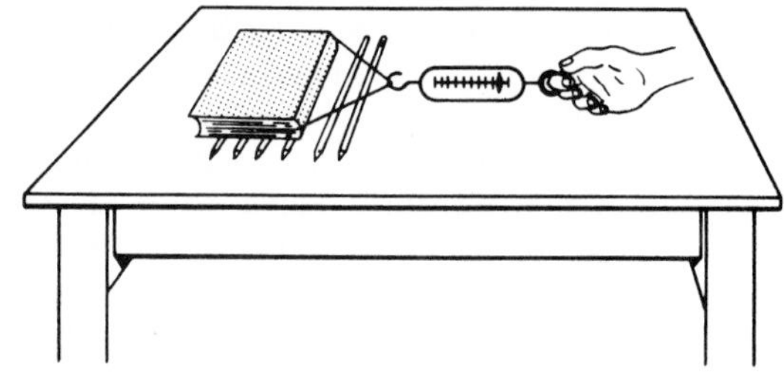

FIGURE 17.2 Rollers can reduce friction.

LEARNING ACTIVITY 17.3

Lubricants Reduce Friction

Rub two pieces of dry toast together. Note the amount of friction and the wearing away of bits of toast. Now spread some jam thickly across each piece of toast and rub the pieces together again. The pieces will now slide smoothly over each other because the jam has filled the hollows and covered the bumps, thus reducing the friction.

IV. Methods of Reducing Unwanted Friction

A. Making surfaces smoother levels out the bumps and hollows and reduces the friction between them.

B. A slippery material, called a **lubricant**, can be applied to reduce friction.

1. The lubricant is placed between the two surfaces, filling up the hollows and covering the bumps; in effect, making the surfaces seem smoother.
2. In this way, the lubricant prevents the two surfaces from rubbing directly against each other.
3. Oil is a lubricant used to reduce friction between parts of machines; grease is used to lubricate parts of an automobile; glycerin and water can be used as lubricants to reduce the friction between rubber and glass; soap and candle wax are used as lubricants to reduce friction between two pieces of wood, or between wood and metal; graphite (a form of pure carbon) can be used to reduce friction between two metals, or between wood and metal.

C. Rollers, wheels, and ball bearings reduce friction by changing sliding friction to rolling friction.

D. Streamlining reduces the friction of automobiles and airplanes moving through air, and the friction of a boat moving through water.

Machines

I. What Machines Do

A. Machines are devices that help make our work easier.

B. A **force**, which is a push or a pull, must be applied to make a machine work. A force can be produced by any of the following: Earth's gravity, electricity, falling water, gasoline, muscles, springs and weights, steam, the Sun's rays, and wind.

C. Machines can help do work in four ways.

1. Machines can transfer a force from one place to another.

LEARNING ACTIVITY 17.4

Machines Can Increase the Distance and Speed of a Force

Let a student sweep with a kitchen broom. As the student sweeps, point out that the upper part of the broom handle is moving just a short distance back and forth. However, the lower and bottom parts of the broom are moving faster and farther.

Inquiry-Based Learning Activity 17.4. Modified

Sweeping the floor using a regular kitchen broom is a very common thing to do, but does where you put your hands on the handle when you sweep make the job harder or easier? Put students into groups of 3 or 4, and give them the task of determining if where they place their hands on the handle of a broom makes it easier or harder to sweep. Give each group a broom to perform their experiments. Ask them to record their observations on a poster that they will use to explain what they did in their experiment and what they concluded. A broom is actually a simple machine—it is a lever.

What level of inquiry is this modification? This activity begins with you, the teacher, presenting a task to your students, so problem identification is at **Level I**. However, the task gets turned over very quickly to the students, who are given the task of designing, performing, and reporting on their research efforts, **Level III process and solution identification**. The shift here is quite dramatic. **Some questions to consider**. What prior work must be done to establish the expectations for designing and performing experiments, collecting data, and reporting results? How will each student be assessed on their work and contribution to the group effort?

2. Some machines can increase the amount of force so that we can lift heavier things or exert more force with the machine than we can alone.
3. Some machines can change the direction of a force so that we can make things move in different directions.
4. Some machines can increase the distance and speed of a force so that we can move things farther or faster.

D. No machine can increase both force and distance moved at the same time. If only a small force is needed to move or lift a heavy object, there is a gain in force; however, the heavy object will now move or be lifted through a shorter distance. So, although there is a gain in force, there is a loss in distance.

II. Work

A. Machines help make work easier, but machines do *not* save work.

B. Work is done only when an effort or a resistance moves through a distance.

1. The force exerted on a machine is called the **effort**.
2. The force that the machine exerts, or the object that the machine lifts or moves, is called the **resistance**.
3. No matter how much effort or resistance is exerted, if neither the machine nor the object has moved through a distance, no work has been done. For example, if you are standing and pushing on a brick wall but the wall is not moving, then you are doing no work (although your muscles may be using up energy and will fatigue).
4. To find out how much work has been done, the force is multiplied by the distance through which the force moves, which can be stated as a formula:

   Work = (force used) × (distance moved)
5. In the **English system** of measurement, force is usually stated in pounds, distance in feet, and work done in **foot-pounds**.
6. To calculate the work that is put into a machine, multiply the effort times the distance the effort moves. For example, if an effort of 2 pounds is exerted over a distance of 5 feet, 2 × 5, or 10 foot-pounds of work is done.
7. To calculate the work that a machine does, or puts out, multiply the resistance times the distance the resistance moves. For example, if a machine lifts an object weighing 5 pounds through a distance of 2 feet, the machine has done 2 × 5, or 10 foot-pounds of work.
8. In the **metric system**, force is stated in newtons, distance in meters, and work done in **newton-meters** (more commonly called **joules**). For example, if you move a body 5 meters with a force of 2 newtons, you do 10 joules (or newton-meters) of work.

C. The speed with which the effort or resistance moves will make no difference in the amount of work done.

D. It is impossible for a machine to produce more work than the work that was put into the machine.

E. If there were no friction, the amount of work a machine could do, or put out, would be equal to the amount of work put into the machine. This concept is the **principle of work**.

1. The principle of work helps explain why a small force must move through a longer distance to make a heavy object move through a shorter distance.
2. Because of friction, however, the amount of work put out by a machine is less than the work put into the machine.
3. Extra effort, which means more work, must be used to overcome friction; the amount of extra effort involved in overcoming friction affects the efficiency of a machine.

III. Mechanical Advantage and Simple Machines

A. When we apply a small force on a machine and the machine gives us more force, or lifts or moves a heavy object, we say that we get a **mechanical advantage** (M.A.) **of force**. If, for example, a machine produces a force that is 5 times as great as the force that is acting on the machine, we say that the mechanical advantage of force is 5.
   1. There are two ways of finding the mechanical advantage of force of a simple machine. One way is to divide the resistance, or weight, by the effort that is exerted. This can be stated as a formula:

      M.A. = Resistance/Effort

   2. If the effort is 2 pounds, and the resistance 8 pounds, the mechanical advantage is 8/2, or 4.
   3. This mechanical advantage is called the **actual mechanical advantage** (A.M.A.) because extra effort had to be exerted in overcoming friction. Therefore, this mechanical advantage is the advantage of force that you actually get when you use the machine.
   4. The second way is to divide the distance the effort moves by the distance the resistance moves. This can be stated as a formula, too:

      M.A. = Effort distance/Resistance distance

   5. If the effort moves 10 feet while the resistance moves 2 feet, the mechanical advantage is 10/2, or 5.
   6. This mechanical advantage is called the **ideal mechanical advantage** (I.M.A.), because friction is not involved in this calculation.
   7. For many simple machines there are also special, and usually easier, ways to find the ideal mechanical advantage.
   8. If extra effort were not needed to overcome friction, the A.M.A. and the I.M.A. would be exactly the same.
   9. However, because extra effort is needed to overcome friction, the A.M.A. is smaller than the I.M.A.
   10. The I.M.A. then tells us the highest possible mechanical advantage we can get from a machine, whereas the A.M.A. tells us the actual or real mechanical advantage we get when we use the machine.

B. A machine can also give us a **mechanical advantage of speed**. When a machine makes an object move faster, we get a mechanical advantage of speed. If, for example, a machine makes an object move five times as fast as the force that is acting on the machine, we would say that its mechanical advantage of speed is 5.

C. No matter how many parts they have, all machines are made up of one or more of **six simple machines:** the lever, the wheel and axle, the pulley, the inclined plane, the wedge, and the screw.
   1. The wheel-and-axle and the pulley are different forms of the lever.
   2. The wedge and the screw are different forms of the inclined plane.

IV. The Lever

A. A lever is a rigid bar, straight or curved, that rests on a fixed point called the **fulcrum**.

B. The force exerted on the lever is called the **effort**.

C. The force that the lever exerts, or the object that the lever lifts or moves, is called the **resistance**.

D. The distance from the fulcrum to the point where the effort is exerted is called the **effort arm**, and the distance from the fulcrum to the point where the resistance is exerted or lifted is called the **resistance arm**.

E. The closer the fulcrum is to the resistance, the less effort is needed to move or lift the resistance; the effort, however, will move a longer distance and the resistance will move a shorter distance.
   1. There will be a gain in force, but a loss in distance and speed.
   2. This action follows the principle of work.

F. The closer the fulcrum is to the effort, the greater the force needed to move or lift the resistance; but now the effort will move a shorter distance and the resistance will move a longer distance.
   1. There will be a loss in force, but a gain in distance and speed.
   2. This action also follows the principle of work.

G. The A.M.A. of the lever is found by dividing the resistance or weight by the effort.

H. The I.M.A. can be found in two ways:
   1. Dividing the distance the effort moves by the distance the resistance moves.
   2. Dividing the length of the effort arm by the length of the resistance arm.

I. Levers are divided into three classes, depending on the positions of the effort, resistance, and fulcrum.

J. A **first-class lever** is one in which the fulcrum is located anywhere between the effort (or force) and the resistance (or weight) (see Figure 17.3).

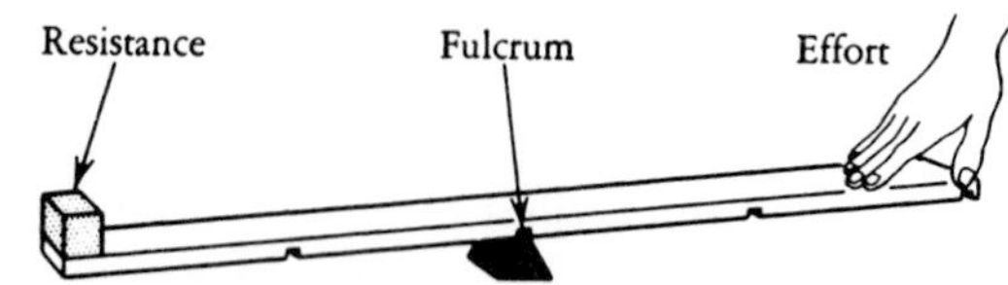

FIGURE 17.3 A first-class lever.

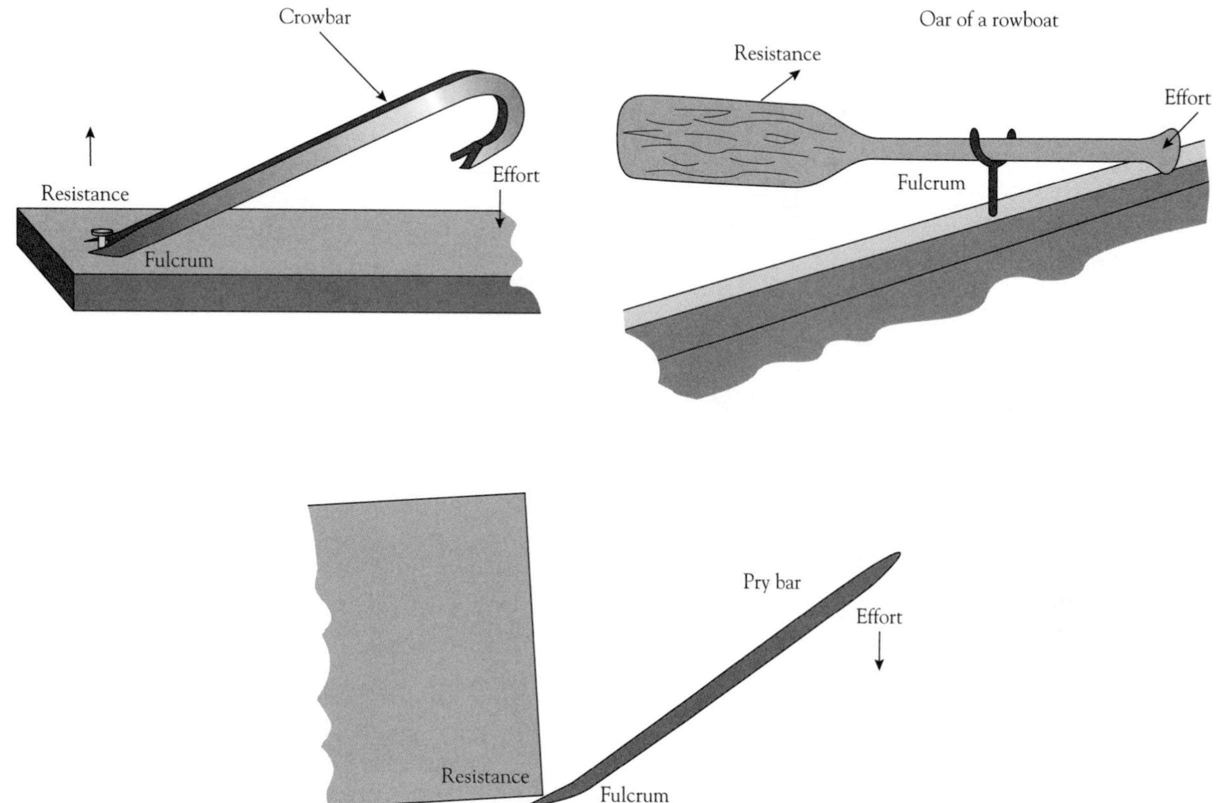

FIGURE 17.4 Crowbar, oar of a rowboat, and pry bar as first-class levers.

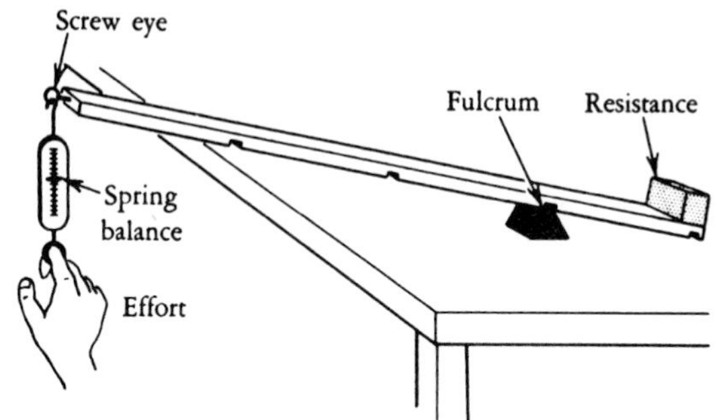

FIGURE 17.5 Less effort is needed when the fulcrum is nearer the resistance.

1. Examples of first-class levers include the crowbar, scissors, pliers, tin snips, tack puller, pry bar, oar of a rowboat, and seesaw.
2. A first-class lever changes the direction of a force, so the effort pushes in one direction while the resistance moves in the opposite direction (see Figure 17.4).
3. When the fulcrum is closer to the resistance than to the effort, we gain in force but get less speed and distance (see Figure 17.5).
4. When the fulcrum is closer to the effort than to the resistance, we get more speed and distance but lose force.
5. When the fulcrum is exactly between the effort and the resistance, there is no change in force, speed, or distance, but there is a change in direction.

K. A **second-class lever** is one in which the resistance is between the effort and the fulcrum (see Figure 17.6).
   1. Examples of second-class levers include the wheelbarrow, nutcracker, crowbar, and bottle opener (see Figure 17.7).
   2. A second-class lever does not change the direction of a force, so the effort and resistance move in the same direction.
   3. In a second-class lever, the fulcrum is usually closer to the resistance, so there is a gain in force.

L. A **third-class lever** is one in which the effort is between the resistance and the fulcrum (see Figure 17.8).
   1. Examples of third-class levers include the broom, shovel, sugar tongs, tweezers, and fishing pole.
   2. A third-class lever does not change the direction of the force.
   3. In a third-class lever, there is always a gain in speed and distance and a loss in force.

V. The Wheel and Axle

A. A simple wheel-and-axle machine is one in which a large wheel is connected to a smaller wheel or shaft, called an axle (see Figure 17.9).

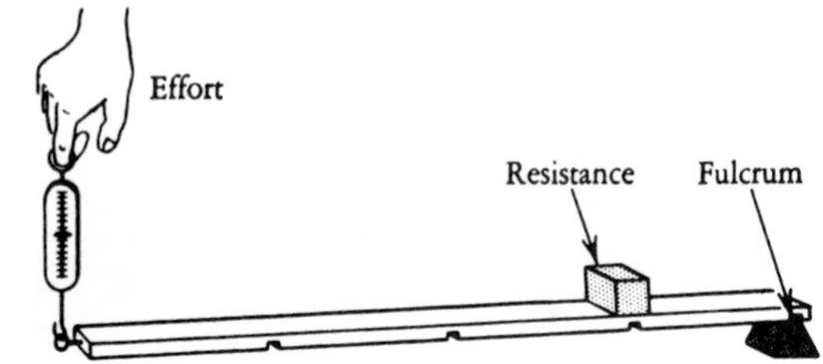

FIGURE 17.6 A second-class lever.

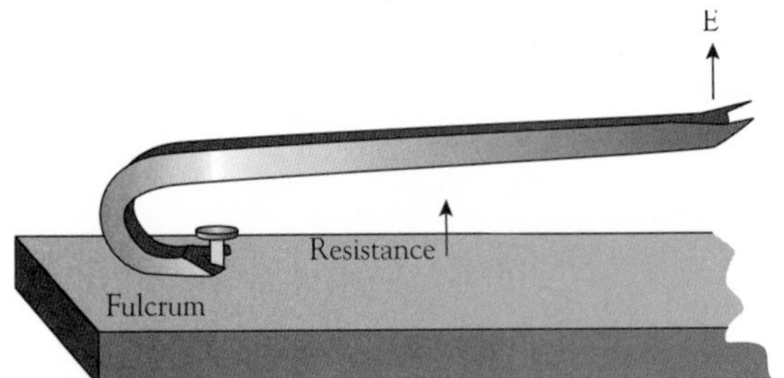

FIGURE 17.7 A crowbar used as a second-class lever.

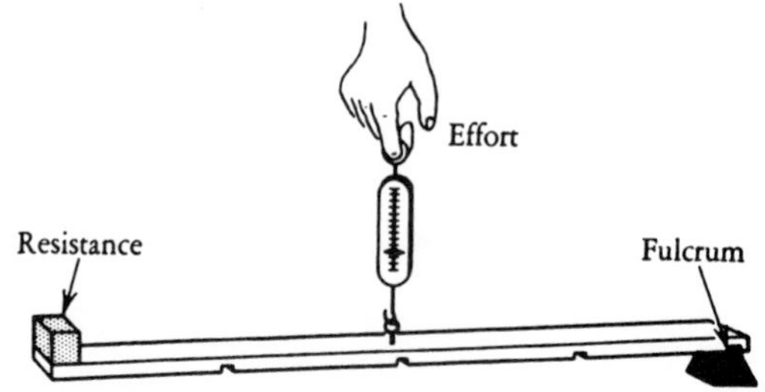

FIGURE 17.8 A third-class lever.

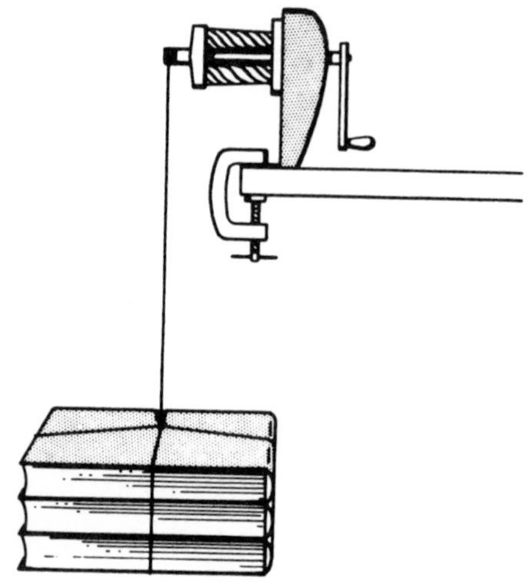
FIGURE 17.9 The pencil sharpener acts as a wheel and axle.

1. When either the wheel or the axle turns, the other part also turns.
2. One complete turn of the wheel produces one complete turn of the axle.
3. If the wheel turns but the axle does not, the device is not a wheel-and-axle machine.
4. The wheel does not have to be a complete wheel; instead, there may be a crank that turns.
5. When the crank is turned, it makes a complete circle, just as though it were a complete wheel.

B. A wheel and axle is really a form of the lever; it is a rotating lever.
   1. The spinning lever can be seen very clearly when a crank is used instead of a wheel.
   2. The fulcrum is at the center of the axle and the wheel (or crank).
   3. The radius of the wheel is the effort arm, and the radius of the axle is the resistance arm of the lever.

C. A wheel and axle can change the direction of a force.

D. When the wheel turns the axle, there is a gain in force.
   1. A smaller force, or effort, at the wheel will move a larger weight, or resistance, at the axle.
   2. The weight, or resistance, will not move as far or as fast as the force, or effort, because the wheel is larger than the axle.
   3. The larger the wheel, as compared with the axle, the greater the gain in force will be.

E. When the axle turns the wheel, there is a loss in force and a gain in distance and speed.
   1. With a greater force exerted at the axle, the wheel (the resistance) will turn faster and farther.
   2. The smaller the axle compared with the wheel, the greater the gain in speed and distance.

F. The A.M.A. of the wheel and axle is found by dividing the weight or resistance lifted by the effort exerted.

G. The ideal mechanical advantage (I.M.A.) can be found in the following ways:
   1. Divide the distance the effort moves by the distance the weight or resistance moves.
   2. Divide the circumference of the wheel by the circumference of the axle.
   3. Divide the diameter of the wheel by the diameter of the axle.
   4. Divide the radius of the wheel by the radius of the axle.

H. Examples of wheel-and-axle machines containing complete wheels include an automobile steering wheel, gear wheels of a bicycle, a doorknob, and a screwdriver.

I. Examples of wheel-and-axle machines containing a crank rather than a complete wheel can be found in a pencil sharpener, a meat grinder, and an eggbeater.

VI. The Pulley

A. A pulley is a wheel that turns around a stationary axle.
   1. There is usually a groove in the rim of the pulley so that the rope around it will not slip off.

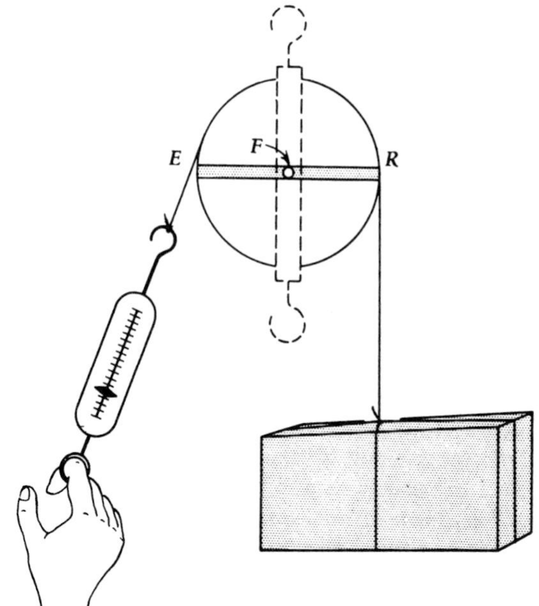

FIGURE 17.10 A fixed pulley is a spinning first-class lever.

2. Sometimes two or more wheels are placed side by side on the same axle.

B. There are two types of pulley: the fixed pulley and the movable pulley.
   1. A fixed pulley does not move from its location but will rotate.
   2. It helps by changing the direction of the force.
   3. It gives no gain in force, speed, or distance.
   4. Fixed pulleys are used with flagpoles, clotheslines, curtain rods, and venetian blinds.
   5. The fixed pulley acts like a turning first-class lever, with the fulcrum at the center of the axle, the effort at one rim of the pulley wheel, and the resistance at the other rim (see Figure 17.10).
   6. A movable pulley moves along a rope.
   7. It helps us gain in force, but we lose in distance.
   8. In a single movable pulley, two sections of rope support the pulley so that only half as much effort is needed to raise a resistance.
   9. However, the effort must now move about twice as far as the resistance.
   10. A movable pulley does not change the direction of the force.
   11. A movable pulley acts like a turning second-class lever, with the fulcrum at one rim of the pulley wheel, the resistance at the center of the axle, and the effort at the other rim of the pulley wheel (see Figure 17.11).

C. A single pulley may be combined with a movable pulley to change direction and gain force at the same time (see Figure 17.12).
   1. Such a combination is called a **block and tackle**.
   2. Several fixed and movable pulleys can be used in a block and tackle.

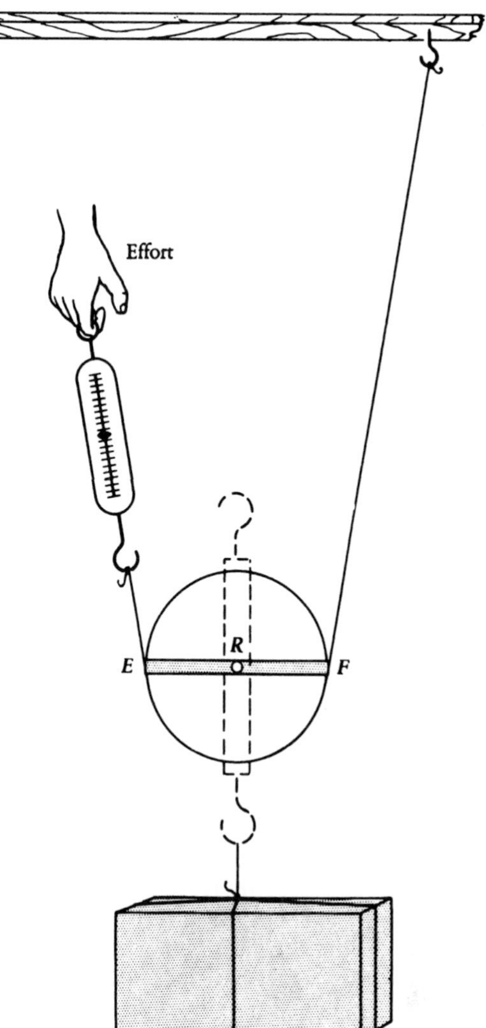

FIGURE 17.11 A movable pulley is a spinning second-class lever.

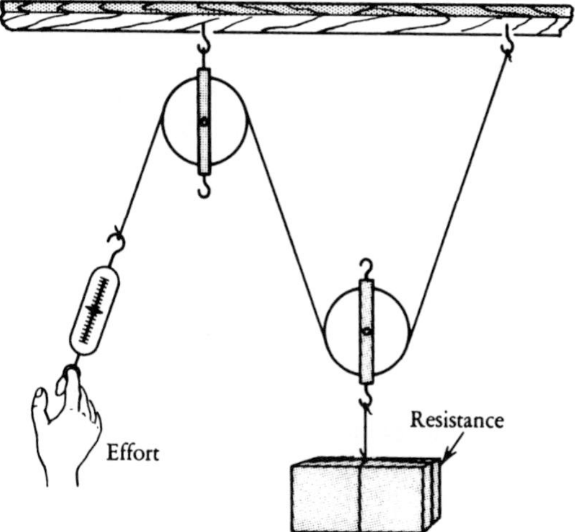

FIGURE 17.12 A block and tackle is a combination of a fixed and a movable pulley.

3. Each fixed pulley changes the direction of the force, and each movable pulley changes the amount of the force.
4. The more movable pulleys used, the less force will be needed.
5. A block and tackle is used in scaffolds for painters and billboard workers.

D. The A.M.A. of a pulley, or set of pulleys, is found by dividing the resistance by the effort.

E. The I.M.A. can be found in two ways:
1. Divide the distance the effort moves by the distance the resistance moves.
2. Count the number of sections of rope that support the movable pulleys.

VII. The Inclined Plane

A. An inclined plane is a slanting surface that connects one level to a higher level, thereby requiring less force to lift an object.
1. By moving an object up an inclined plane, we use less effort in getting the object to the higher level than if we had to lift the object directly from the lower to the higher level.
2. We gain lifting power at the expense of distance. The object must be moved a longer distance as it travels up the inclined plane to reach the desired higher level.
3. The longer the inclined plane, the more gradual the slope and the less the effort needed to move the body up the incline. The shorter the inclined plane, the steeper the slope and the greater the effort needed to move the body up the inclined plane.

B. The A.M.A. of an inclined plane is found by dividing the resistance by the effort. The I.M.A. is found by dividing the length of the inclined plane by the height.

C. Examples of the inclined plane include a plank, a ramp, the sloping floor of a theater or auditorium, a straight road up a hill, an escalator, and a stairway.

VIII. The Wedge

A. A wedge is a simple machine used either to spread an object apart or to raise an object. A wedge has a sloping or slanting side, like an inclined plane.
1. A single wedge looks like an inclined plane and has one sloping side.
2. A double wedge looks like two inclined planes that have been joined together with their sloping sides facing outward.

B. A wedge is a form of inclined plane with only one difference.
1. With an inclined plane, an object moves up the incline, but with a wedge, the incline moves into or under the object.
2. The gain in effort is obtained at the expense of distance, because the effort moves over a longer distance than the resistance.
3. The farthest the resistance can be moved is the thickness of the large end of the wedge.

C. The A.M.A. of a wedge is found by dividing the resistance by the effort. The I.M.A. is found by dividing the length of the wedge by the thickness of its large end.
1. The A.M.A. of a wedge is always much less than the I.M.A. because of the friction between the wedge and the object.
2. Friction is helpful in this case, because it keeps the wedge from slipping out.

D. Examples of the wedge include an ax, knife blade, scissors blade, chisel, pin, nail, and plow.

IX. The Screw

A. A screw is an inclined plane that winds around and around in a spiral.
1. The spiral ridge of the screw is called the thread.
2. One complete turn of the screw moves the screw into the object the same distance as from one thread to another.
3. The distance between two threads is called the pitch of the screw.
4. The screw gives a gain in force, but at the expense of distance.
5. The effort distance of one complete turn of the screw is larger than the resistance distance of one pitch.
6. The closer together the threads are, the smaller the pitch becomes and the greater the gain in force.

B. The A.M.A. of the screw is found by dividing the resistance by the effort. The I.M.A. is found by dividing the circumference of the screw (distance of one complete turn) by the pitch.

C. Because of friction, the A.M.A. is much less than the I.M.A. However, friction helps keep the screw from turning backward or pulling out.
1. We can make up for the loss of effort caused by friction by using another machine, such as the lever or wheel and axle, to turn the head of the screw.
2. Using another machine to turn the head of the screw produces a great gain in effort.

D. Examples of the screw are found in a wood screw, bolt, cap of a jar or bottle, base of an electric light bulb, monkey wrench, clamp, and vise.

X. Efficiency of Machines

A. There are two ways of finding out how efficient a machine is.
1. One way is to divide the A.M.A. by the I.M.A., then multiply by 100. This can be stated as a formula:

Efficiency = A.M.A/I.M.A. × 100

2. We multiply by 100 so that we can describe the efficiency of a machine as a percentage.
3. If the A.M.A. of a machine is 4, and its I.M.A. is 5, the efficiency of the machine is $\frac{4}{5} \times 100$, or 80%.

4. The second way to find the efficiency is to divide the amount of work put out by the machine by the amount of work put into the machine, then multiply by 100. This can be stated as a formula:

Efficiency = Work put out/Work put in × 100

5. The work put out can be found by multiplying the resistance by the distance the resistance moves, and the work put in can be found by multiplying the effort by the distance the effort moves.
6. If a machine puts out 30 foot-pounds of work and the work put into the machine is 50 foot-pounds, the efficiency of the machine is 30/50 × 100, or 60%.

B. Because extra force, or effort, is needed to overcome friction, the A.M.A. is always less than the I.M.A. and the work put out is always less than the work put in, so the efficiency of a machine is always less than 100%.

XI. Power

A. Power is the rate of doing work. When one machine can do the same or more work than another in a shorter time, we say that the first machine provides more power than the second machine.
1. The unit of power is the **horsepower**, which is 33,000 foot-pounds of work in 1 minute (or 550 foot-pounds of work in 1 second).
2. To find the horsepower of a machine, the foot-pounds of work done is divided by 33,000 times the number of minutes it takes to do the work. This can be stated as a formula:

Horsepower = Work done (in foot-pounds)/33,000 × number of minutes

XII. Compound Machines and Gears

A. Many machines, called **compound machines**, are made up of two or more simple machines.
1. There are many examples of compound machines. The handle of an ax is a lever, and the blade is a wedge; a pair of scissors has two levers and blades that are wedges; the handle of a pencil sharpener is part of a wheel and axle that turns two screws with sharp wedge-shaped edges that act like blades to sharpen a pencil; a rotary can opener is made up of a wheel and axle and a circular wedge.

B. Sometimes, in compound machines, one wheel is used to turn another wheel.
1. Each wheel is connected to an axle that also turns, making a wheel-and-axle machine.
2. One way to cause a wheel to turn another wheel is to put a tight belt around both wheels. When one wheel is turned, it makes the belt move and turn the other wheel. The second wheel moves in the same direction as the first wheel.
3. If we want the second wheel to turn in the opposite direction of the first wheel, we cross (in a figure 8) the belt that goes around the wheels.
4. When the first wheel—the driving wheel—is larger than the second wheel—the driven wheel—we get a gain in speed, but we lose in force. When the driving wheel is smaller than the driven wheel, we get a gain in force and a loss in speed.
5. A second way to cause wheels to turn is to put teeth on the wheels and slip a chain around both wheels. The teeth fit into the open places in the chain, and the cross-pieces of the chain fit into the notches between the teeth. The teeth and notches of the wheels stop the chain from slipping.
6. Wheels with teeth and notches are called gears or gear wheels.
7. A bicycle is a machine that uses gears and a chain. The gears are part of a wheel-and-axle machine. The pedal turns a crank that turns a large gear. A chain connected from the large gear to the smaller gear on the rear wheel turns the smaller gear. The smaller gear then turns the rear wheel, which drives the bicycle forward. Each time the pedals turn the larger gear around once, the smaller gear turns the rear wheel around many times. In this way, the gears of a bicycle give up force but gain in speed and distance.
8. A third way to make wheels turn is to fit two gears together without a chain. The teeth of one gear fit into the notches of the second gear and make the second gear turn. Each gear is part of a wheel and axle. When one gear makes another gear move this way, the second gear moves in a direction opposite to the first gear. If a large gear turns a small gear, there is a gain in speed and distance but a loss in force. If a small gear turns a larger gear, there is a gain in force but a loss in speed and distance.
9. To make two gears move in the same direction, a third gear must be placed between them.
10. The A.M.A. of two gears may be found by comparing the forces that both gears exert.
11. The I.M.A. can be found by either comparing the number of teeth that each gear has or comparing the speeds of both gears.

XIII. Complex Machines

A. The **windmill** is a machine that uses wind as the force to run the machine and do the work.
1. The windmill has blades, or propellers, connected to a shaft that runs through the center of the blades.
2. The blades are set at an angle and slope backward so when the wind hits the blades, it makes them turn around and around.

3. The turning blades make the shaft turn, so together they act like a wheel-and-axle machine.
4. A windmill can be used to pump water and to run an electric generator to produce electricity.

B. The **water wheel** uses the force of falling or moving water to run machines.
1. It has many blades that make the wheel turn quickly when the water strikes them.
2. A shaft in the center of the wheel turns as the wheel turns, forming a wheel-and-axle machine.
3. Water wheels called **turbines** use the tremendous force of falling or moving water from huge dams, such as the Grand Coulee Dam on the Columbia River or the Norris Dam on the Tennessee River. Turbines are used to run giant electric generators, producing large amounts of electricity.

C. The **steam engine** uses the heat of burning fuels to run machines.
1. The heat of the burning fuel changes water into steam.
2. When water changes into steam, it expands about 1,700 times, and the expanding steam provides the energy to operate the engine.
3. The steam engine is called an **external combustion machine**, because the fuel is burned outside the engine.
4. Steam is produced by making water boil in a boiler outside the engine.
5. The steam then passes through a pipe into a cylinder inside the engine.
6. In the cylinder, the expanding steam pushes a sliding piston back and forth.
7. The piston is attached to a wheel with a lever called a connecting rod.
8. As the piston moves back and forth in the cylinder, the attached connecting rod makes the wheel turn.
9. Every movement of the piston is useful, producing power that makes the wheel turn.
10. The steam engine has been used to pull trains, push boats, saw wood, spin thread, and weave cloth.
11. The **steam turbine** also uses steam to run machines. It works very much like the water turbine, except that it is run by steam that comes from a boiler.
12. Most steam turbines have many curved blades arranged in rows so that a row of movable blades is followed by a row of fixed blades.
13. The expanding steam is shot through nozzles at a slant or angle against the movable blades, making the blades spin at a very high speed.
14. After the steam has passed a row of movable blades, it is then directed by a row of fixed blades to the next row of movable blades.
15. Each row of movable blades is larger than the row before it, because the steam expands as it travels through the turbine and can make good use of the larger space to get more power from the turbine.
16. The spinning movable blades turn a long rod that can run a large electric generator or turn the propellers of a large ship.

D. **Gasoline and alcohol engines** use hot, expanding gases, produced by burning gasoline or alcohol, to run machines.
1. These are called **internal combustion engines**, because the fuel is burned inside the cylinder of the engine.
2. Outside the engine either a carburetor or a fuel injector changes the liquid fuel into a vapor and mixes this vapor with the proper amount of air to make the fuel burn properly.
3. Fitted into the top or head of the cylinder is a spark plug, which has a small space or gap between its two metal tips so that at the right moment a hot electric spark can jump across the gap and make the mixture of fuel vapor and air in the cylinder burn.
4. A piston in the cylinder moves up and down when the engine is running.
5. In the most common gasoline engine—the automobile engine—the piston has to move four times, or make four strokes, inside the cylinder to get just one stroke that will produce power to run the machine.
6. In the first stroke or movement, called the intake stroke, the piston moves down, allowing a valve at the top of the cylinder to open and let the mixture of gasoline vapor and air enter the cylinder.
7. Then the piston moves up for its second stroke, called the compression stroke, compressing or squeezing the mixture of gasoline and air into a very small space.
8. Just when the mixture of gasoline and air is compressed the right amount, an electric spark from the spark plug sets the mixture on fire.
9. The mixture burns quickly, almost explosively, producing very hot, expanding gases, which give the piston a tremendous downward push.
10. This third downward stroke, called the power stroke, provides the power that runs the machine.
11. The piston then moves up again for its fourth stroke, called the exhaust stroke, pushing out the waste gases through another valve at the top of the cylinder.
12. Now the same series, or cycle, of four strokes starts all over again and continues in this way as long as the engine is running.
13. The piston is attached to a connecting rod, which turns the crankshaft of the engine.
14. The crankshaft is connected to the drive shaft, which is then connected to the axle of

the machine (for example, in an automobile) and makes the machine run.

15. Because only one piston stroke in every four is a power stroke, the more cylinders a gasoline engine has, the more smoothly it will run.
16. An automobile has at least four cylinders in its engine, so there will be one power stroke taking place at all times.
17. Compact automobiles usually have four-cylinder gasoline engines, but larger automobiles may have six, eight, or more cylinders.
18. Gasoline engines are also used to run small airplanes, motorcycles, motorbikes, outboard motors, lawn mowers, and power saws.

E. The **diesel engine** also uses hot, expanding gases to run machines.
   1. Machines that use diesel engines do not use a carburetor or spark plugs.
   2. A simple diesel engine uses a cycle of two strokes to produce one power stroke.
   3. The first stroke is a combustion intake-compression-exhaust stroke.
   4. During the first stroke, air is blown in at one side of the cylinder while waste gases are being forced out through two valves at the top of the cylinder.
   5. Then the piston moves up, compressing the air a great deal more than in the cylinder of a gasoline engine, making the air very hot.
   6. When the piston nears the top of the cylinder, the fuel oil is sprayed into the cylinder through a nozzle at the top, and the hot air makes the oil catch fire immediately and burn very quickly.
   7. The hot, expanding gases push the piston down with great force for its second, or power, stroke.
   8. When the piston nears the bottom of the cylinder, the waste gases are pushed out through the valves and more air enters the cylinder.
   9. Great pressure is produced in the cylinders, so they must be made of thick metal.
   10. Because the diesel engine is so much more powerful and efficient than the gasoline engine, it is commonly used to drive trucks, buses, tractors, power shovels and bulldozers, locomotives, ships, submarines, and electric generators. The diesel engine also burns a special fuel oil that is usually cheaper than gasoline.

F. The **ramjet engine** is the simplest type of jet engine. It has no moving parts.
   1. It is a hollow tube with nozzles inside to spray the fuel.
   2. When the ramjet travels forward at great speed, air is packed or "rammed" into the front of the engine. The ramming of the air into the engine helps to compress it.
   3. Jet fuel is sprayed into the compressed air by the nozzles, and burns. The hot gases expand and rush out through the rear of the engine with great speed.
   4. These hot gases, escaping from the rear of the engine, produce the forward thrust needed to move the plane.
   5. The ramjet plane cannot start from the ground but must be moving at high speed to ram air into the engine. Usually a ramjet plane is carried into the air under another plane, which cuts the ramjet loose when it has achieved enough speed.

G. The **turbojet engine** is the engine used most often by commercial and military aircraft.
   1. The turbojet engine has three main parts: a compressor, a combustion chamber, and a turbine.
   2. The compressor compresses the air that enters the engine, then feeds the compressed air to the combustion chamber.
   3. In the combustion chamber, a fuel such as kerosene is sprayed into the compressed air.
   4. The mixture of kerosene and compressed air burns, giving off hot gases that expand and shoot out the rear of the engine.
   5. Before the gases can leave the engine, they must first turn the blades of the turbine.
   6. A shaft connects the turbine to the compressor so the escaping gases turn the turbine, which then operates the compressor.
   7. When the turbojet plane is on the ground, a small engine starts the shaft turning and operates the compressor.
   8. After the aircraft has reached sufficient speed, the jet engine itself takes over and operates the turbine and the compressor.

H. The **turboprop engine** is like a turbojet engine except that it has a propeller in front.
   1. The propeller is attached to the same shaft that connects the turbine and the compressor.
   2. Thus, both the propeller and the escaping gases from the rear of the engine produce the thrust that moves the turboprop aircraft forward.
   3. Unlike the turbojet aircraft, the turboprop aircraft operates very well at low speeds or low altitudes because of the added thrust from the propeller.

I. **Rockets**, like jet engines, burn fuels that produce hot, expanding gases that blast from the tail of the rocket and give it the thrust required to climb into space.
   1. The main difference between a rocket and a jet is the source of oxygen needed to burn the fuel.
   2. Whereas a jet engine gets its oxygen from the air, a rocket carries its own oxygen supply, called the **oxidizer**, either as liquid oxygen (LOX) or as a solid or liquid fuel chemical that contains oxygen and gives it up readily.

3. The fuel and oxidizer together are called the **propellant**.
4. Because a rocket carries its own oxygen, its flight is not limited to the Earth's atmosphere; it can travel in space where there is little or no oxygen.

J. The simplest rockets are the solid fuel, or solid propellant, rockets.
   1. The solid fuel is really a mixture of a fuel and a chemical that contains oxygen.
   2. These rockets are used to help launch planes, and also in fireworks and as signal rockets.

K. High-altitude rockets are usually liquid fuel, or liquid propellant, rockets.
   1. These rockets use both a liquid fuel and liquid oxygen.
   2. These two liquids are stored in separate tanks in the rocket and are pumped into the combustion, or burning, chamber at the same time.
   3. High-altitude rockets do not have wings because they travel where there is no air to provide lift.
   4. The intercontinental ballistic missile (ICBM) is a high-altitude rocket. The missile can travel far into outer space and then return to Earth a great distance from the point where it was launched.

L. Rockets can be made to travel faster and farther when two or more rockets are connected to form a **multistage rocket**.
   1. A three-stage rocket has three rockets, one mounted on top of the other, each with its own fuel and combustion chamber.
   2. On top of the rocket is the **payload**, which in peacetime may be a satellite or a spacecraft. It is covered with a nose cone to protect it from the heat produced by friction as the rocket moves through the air.
   3. At the bottom is the first stage, which is the largest rocket. When the first stage is fired, it launches all three rockets and the payload.
   4. The rocket climbs until all the fuel in the first stage is depleted.
   5. Then the first stage drops off, and the second stage is fired. The second and third stages together climb faster and higher until all the fuel in the second stage is depleted. Then the second stage falls off, and the third stage is ignited.
   6. The third stage fires and directs the payload either into orbit around the Earth, or deeper into space.

M. The **electric motor** (discussed in Chapter 21) uses electricity to run machines and do work.

Exploratory Activities for "Friction and Machines"

1. EXPLORING WITH SIMPLE MACHINES (ANY GRADE LEVEL)

Overview

As stated by James Kirkwood, "Children are intrigued by the functions of objects, but they're not much interested in the abstract construct of 'simple machines.'"[1] Kirkwood suggests that the study of simple machines begin with asking students questions such as, Why is a steering wheel round? How does it steer the car? How does a teeter-totter work? Where do you sit on a teeter-totter when you try to balance with an adult? Why is there no curb at a driveway? Or why is it not as tall? How can it be possible to pull down to lift something up? The following set of 14 separate exploratory activities supply the basics for making and scientifically exploring simple machines. Depending on the age and maturity of your students, you may want to supplement these activities with student-found and student-built simple machines.

1.1 Exploring with the First-Class Lever

Obtain a piece of wood 92 centimeters (36 in.) long, 7½ centimeters (3 in.) wide, and about 13 millimeters (½ in.) thick. Use a triangular block of wood about 5 centimeters (2 in.) wide and 2½ centimeters (1 in.) high as a fulcrum. Cut grooves on the underside of the board at each end and at the quarter, midway, and three-quarter marks.

For all students. Rest the center of the board (at the midway groove) on the fulcrum. Put a weight or brick at one end of the board and push down at the other end (see Figure 17.3). Note the force you have to exert to lift the weight. Also note that you push down while the weight moves up, so that there is a change in direction, and your hand moves just as far down as the weight moves up.

Move the fulcrum nearer the weight and push down on the board again. This time less force is needed to lift the weight, but now the weight moves up a little, while your hand moves down a lot. Now move the fulcrum so that it is near your hand. You will have to use a lot of force to lift the weight, but the weight will now move up a lot while your hand moves down just a little.

For older students. Repeat this activity, this time using quantitative techniques. Insert a screw eye into one end of the board and have this end extend a little beyond the edge of the table (see Figure 17.5). For the resistance, use a known weight or a brick whose weight you have determined. Attach a spring balance to the screw eye to measure the effort needed to lift the weight. Now place the fulcrum at different positions under the board and measure the force necessary to lift the weight in each case.

[1] James J. Kirkwood, "Simple Machines Simply Put," *Science and Children 31*(7):15, 40 (April 1994).

Measure the lengths of the effort arm and the resistance arm. Also measure the distances that both the resistance and the effort move. Find the ideal and actual mechanical advantage (refer to page 000). Calculate the amount of work done, both input and output, and determine the efficiency of the lever. (Keep in mind that you will obtain only approximate results, because the weight of the board will not have been taken into consideration in the calculations. Moreover, when the spring balance is held upside down, its position affects the reading of the balance.)

1.2 Exploring with the Second-Class Lever

Repeat activity 1.1, but now position the board as a second-class lever, with the resistance between the effort and the fulcrum (see Figure 17.6), as in a wheelbarrow or bottle opener). Depending on the age and maturity of your students, conduct both qualitative and quantitative measurements. (Note that the second-class lever does not change the direction of the force, because both the effort and the resistance move upward.)

1.3 Exploring with Third-Class Levers

Repeat activity 1.1, now positioning the board as a third-class lever, with the effort between the resistance and the fulcrum (see Figure 17.8), as exemplified by a hammer and a fishing pole. You will have to insert a second screw eye into the board, this time into the top surface. In addition, you will have to press down on the board to keep it from being lifted into the air when you pull up on the spring balance. Depending on the age and maturity of your students, conduct both qualitative and quantitative measurements. (Note that the third-class lever does not change the direction of the force, because both the effort and the resistance move upward.)

For all students. Ask students to enlist parents or guardians in locating and identifying other examples of levers at home. Ask them to bring their finds to class, if permitted. Repeat these exploratory activities using some of their examples.

1.4 Exploring the Wheel and Axle

Clamp a pencil sharpener, with its cover removed, to the edge of a table, as shown in Figure 17.9. Turn the handle of the sharpener and point out that when the handle is turned, it makes a complete circle, just as though it were a complete wheel. The shaft of the sharpener is the axle. When the handle (wheel) is turned, the shaft (axle) is turned.

Tie three books together with a string and have the students lift the books by the string, noting the force needed to do this. Tie the other end of the string firmly around the shaft of the sharpener, using cellophane tape, if necessary, to keep the string from slipping. Now turn the handle and lift the books. (Holding your forefinger lightly against the string while you turn the handle will keep the string from slipping off the shaft.)

Note that much less force is needed to lift the books, using the handle. This gain in force is accompanied by a loss in distance and speed, because the handle must move many times to raise the books a short distance. Older students can find the ideal mechanical advantage of the pencil sharpener.

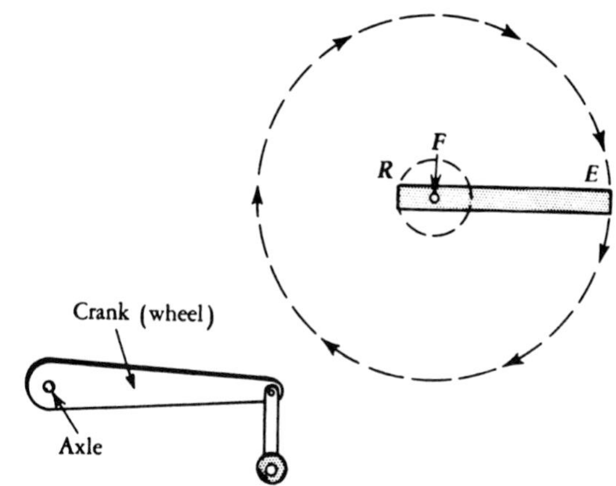

FIGURE 17.13 The wheel and axle is a spinning first-class lever.

(The radius of the wheel is the length of the handle, and the radius of the axle is one-half the diameter of the shaft.)

Turn the handle of the pencil sharpener until the books are close to the shaft, then let go of the handle and allow the books to move downward. Now the axle is turning the wheel. Note the loss in force, but the large gain in distance and speed, as the handle spins rapidly.

Draw a diagram to show that the wheel and axle is a form of spinning first-class lever (Figure 17.13). Its fulcrum is always at the center of the axle and the wheel. The radius of the wheel and the radius of the axle are the two arms of the lever. Have the students locate and identify other examples of wheel-and-axle machines. Let them repeat the experiment, using some of their examples.

1.5 Exploring the Fixed Pulley

Screw two cup hooks about 10 centimeters (4 in.) apart into a long, rectangular wood board about 13 millimeters ($^1/_2$ in.) thick. Rest the board on the backs of two chairs placed a short distance apart (Figure 17.14). Tie a string around a brick or book and weigh it with a spring balance. Attach a pulley to one cup hook and pass a string around the groove of the pulley. Connect one end of the string to the brick and the other end to a spring balance.

Pull down on the spring balance. Note that the force needed to raise the brick is just about equal to the weight of the brick, so all you have done is change the direction of your force. Older students can calculate the amount of work done, both input and output. Find the mechanical advantage and determine the efficiency of the fixed pulley.

Draw a diagram to show that the fixed pulley is a form of spinning first-class lever (Figure 17.15). Its fulcrum (*F*) is at the center of the axle, with the effort (*E*) and resistance (*R*) at opposite ends of the wheel. Note that the effort arm and the resistance arm are equal.

1.6 Exploring the Movable Pulley

For older students: Rearrange the pulley as shown in the diagram (Figure 17.16). Pull up on the balance and note that only half as much force is needed as was used with the

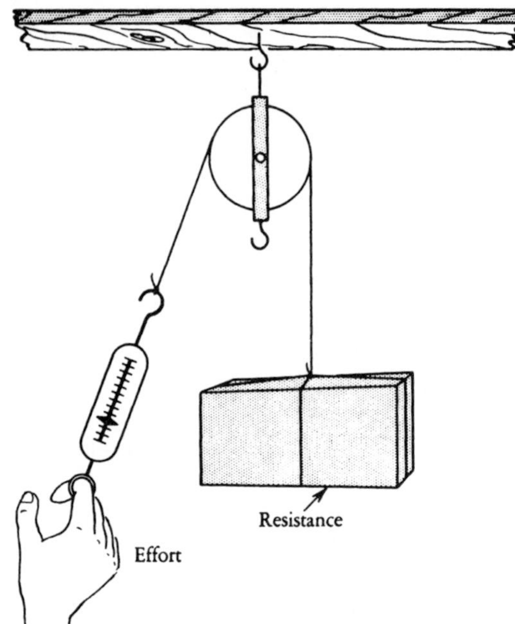

FIGURE 17.14 A fixed pulley changes direction.

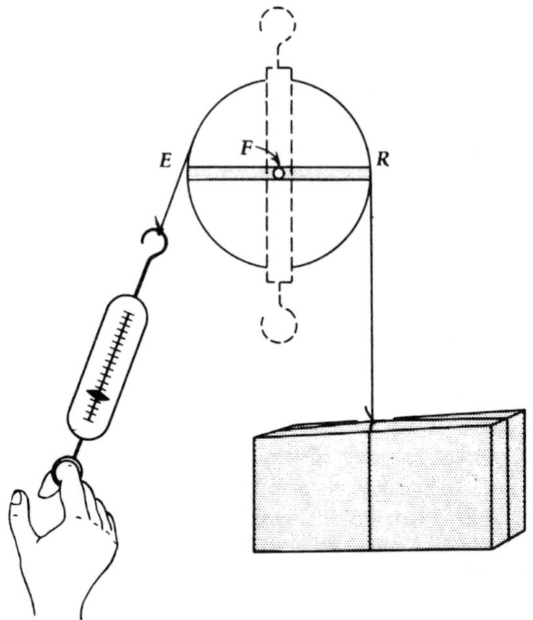

FIGURE 17.15 A fixed pulley is a spinning first-class lever.

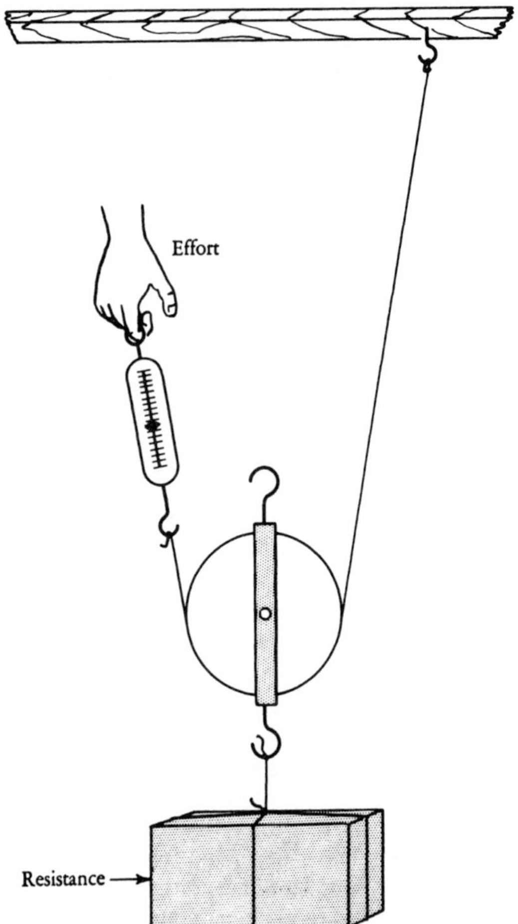

FIGURE 17.16 A movable pulley requires half as much force as a fixed pulley.

fixed pulley. However, your effort must move twice as far as the distance the brick is lifted. Note that there is now no change in the direction of your force. Calculate the amount of work done, both input and output. Find the ideal and actual mechanical advantage, and determine the efficiency of the movable pulley.

Draw a diagram to show that the movable pulley is a form of spinning second-class lever (Figure 17.17). Its fulcrum (*F*) is at one end of the wheel, the effort (*E*) at the opposite end, and the resistance (*R*) at the center of the axle. The effort arm is twice as long as the resistance arm.

1.7 Exploring the Block and Tackle

Use two pulleys to form a combination fixed and movable pulley, as shown in the diagram (Figure 17.18). Note that there is no difference between this block and tackle and the movable pulley shown in Figure 17.17, regarding increase in force, work done, mechanical advantage, and efficiency. The block and tackle allows increasing force and changing direction at the same time. If possible, repeat, using a double fixed and a double movable pulley.

1.8 Exploring the Inclined Plane

Rest one end of a long wood board at least 13 millimeters (½ in.) thick on a pile of books so that the board makes an inclined plane. Obtain a toy cart and place some stones in it to give added weight. Tape the stones to the cart so they will not fall out, and then weigh the cart and stones with a spring balance.

Now attach the spring balance to the cart and pull it slowly up the board, keeping the balance horizontal with the board while you are pulling (Figure 17.19). Note that much less force is needed to pull the cart up the incline than to lift it straight up into the air, but the cart must now be moved a longer distance to reach the same height. Find the height of the inclined plane by measuring the vertical distance from the

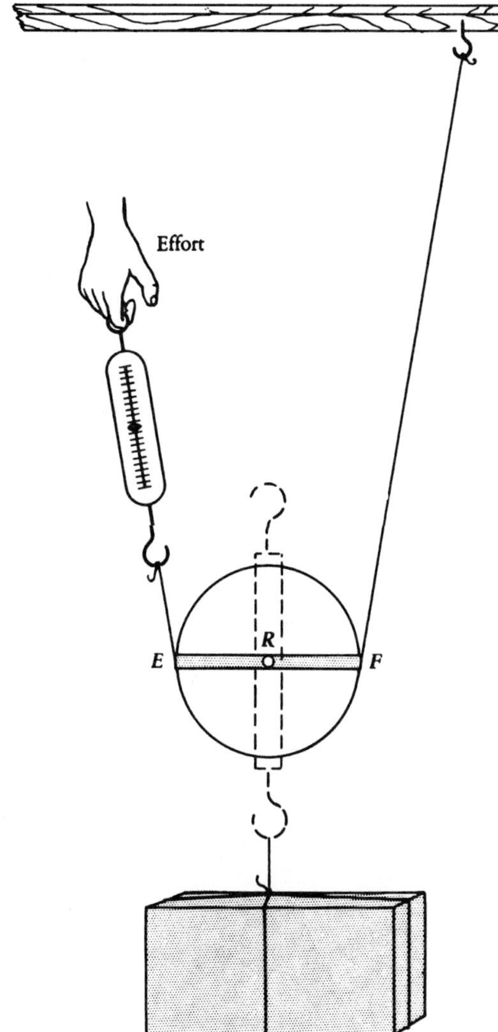

FIGURE 17.17 A movable pulley is a spinning second-class lever.

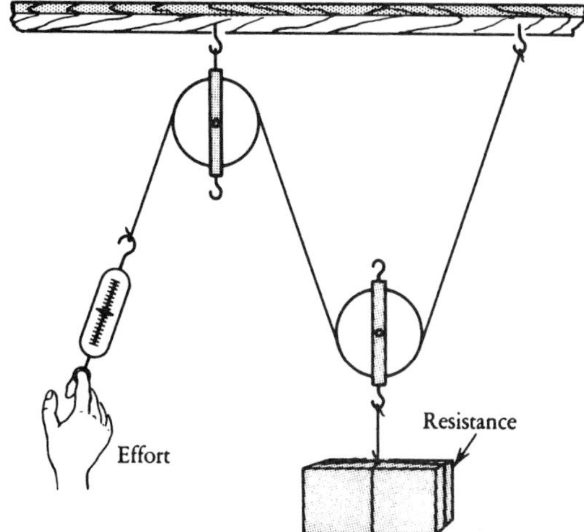

FIGURE 17.18 A block and tackle is a combination of a fixed and a movable pulley.

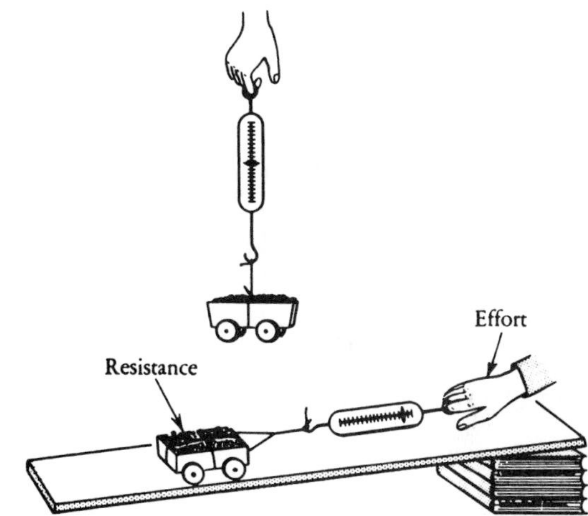

FIGURE 17.19 Less force is needed with an inclined plane.

higher end of the board to the surface upon which the books are resting. Calculate the amount of work done, both input and output. Find the ideal and actual mechanical advantage, and determine the efficiency of the inclined plane.

Make the slope of the inclined plane steeper, either by using a shorter board or by adding more books to the pile. Note the increase in force needed to pull the cart up the incline. Have the students locate and identify examples of inclined planes in their everyday world.

1.9 Exploring the Wedge

Make two wedges by sawing diagonally a block of wood 20 centimeters (8 in.) long, 10 centimeters (4 in.) wide, and 5 centimeters (2 in.) thick (Figure 17.20). Hold up one wedge to show that it really is an inclined plane. Place both wedges back to back and form a double inclined plane. Measure the length of the wedge and the thickness of the large end, and then calculate the ideal mechanical advantage. Insert the sharp end of the wedge a short distance under a pile of books and tap the thick end with a hammer, driving the wedge under the books and lifting them. Have the students locate examples of wedges.

1.10 Exploring the Screw

Cut out a right triangle from a sheet of white paper. Make the base of the triangle 20 centimeters (8 in.) and the height 10 centimeters (4 in.). Hold up the triangle and show that the hypotenuse, or diagonal side, is an inclined plane. Make a heavy black line along the hypotenuse. Starting with the 10-centimeter (4-in.) side, wrap the paper around a pencil so that the black line shows up clearly as a spiral (Figure 17.21). Hold up a large wood screw beside the pencil and show the similarity between the spiral and the screw. Point out the thread of the screw, and then find the pitch by measuring the distance between two threads. With the students, locate and identify examples of screws.

1.11 A Hunt for Compound Machines

Ask students to search at home, with a parent or guardian, to find pictures of and identify the simple machines in such

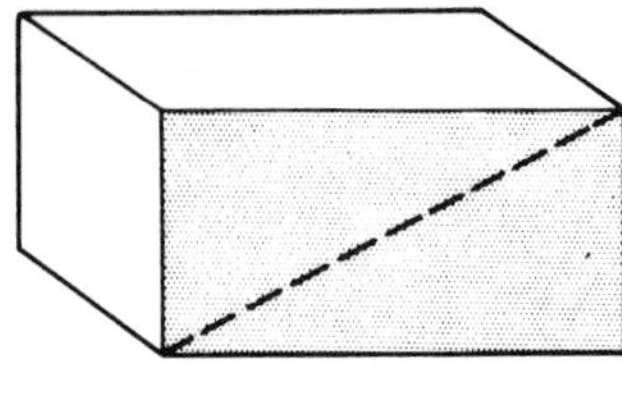

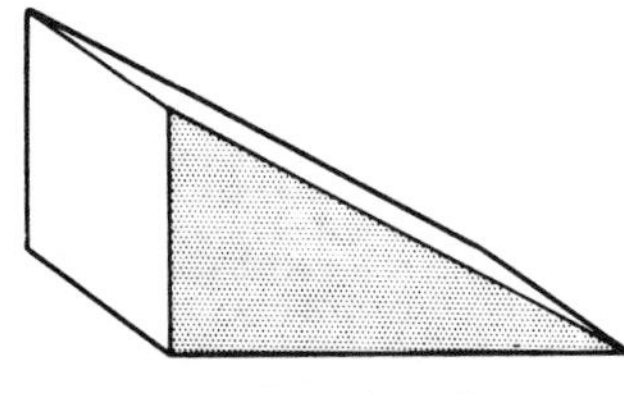

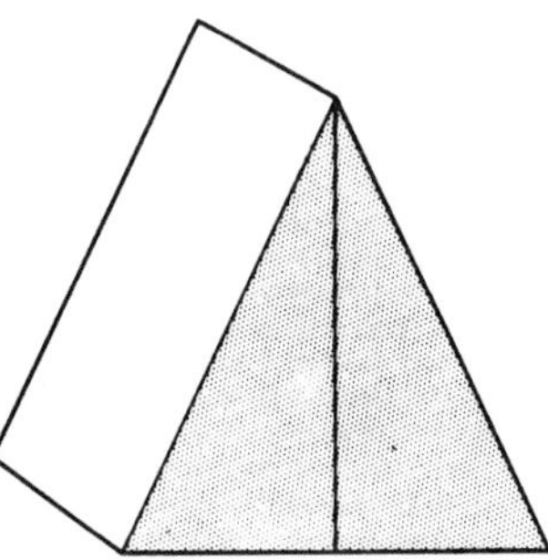

FIGURE 17.20 Making a single and a double wedge.

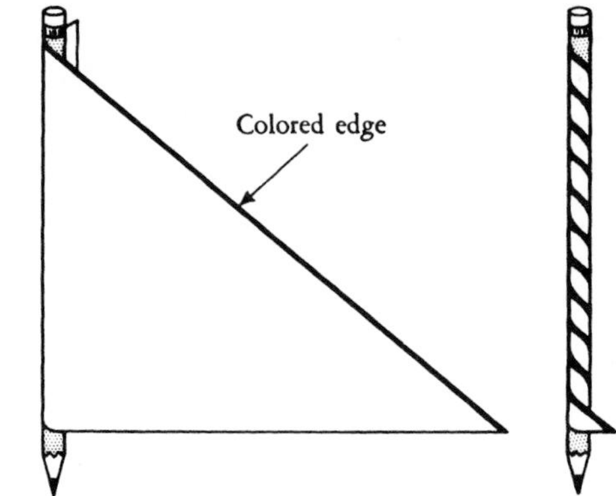

FIGURE 17.21 A screw is a spiral inclined plane.

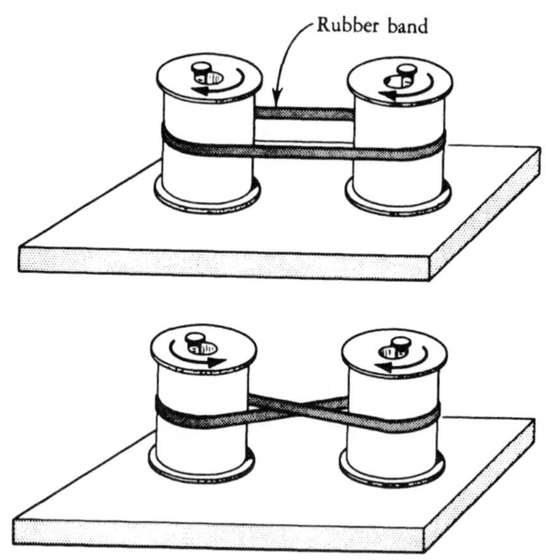

FIGURE 17.22 A belt makes it possible for one wheel to turn another wheel.

everyday compound machines as scissors, playground equipment, a can opener, a pencil sharpener, various toys, water faucets, a piano, a bicycle, and wrenches. Have the students make collages and report to their classmates on their discoveries.

1.12 Exploring Wheels and Belts

Obtain a thick rectangular block of wood and two spools of the same size. Place the spools a short distance apart on the wood, insert loose-fitting nails into the holes of the spools, and drive the nails into the wood. Slip a wide rubber band over both spools (Figure 17.22). Have a student give one spool a complete turn and report his or her observations. (Note that the other spool also makes a complete turn, moves at the same speed, and turns in the same direction.)

Now cross the rubber band so that it makes a figure 8, and have the student give one spool a complete turn again. Ask the student to explain what happens. (This time the driven spool will turn in the opposite direction.)

Repeat both activities, using a smaller and a larger spool this time. Have students explain their observations. (When the larger spool drives the smaller spool and makes one complete turn, the smaller spool turns more than once and moves faster. When the smaller spool drives the larger spool and makes one complete turn, the larger spool turns less than once and moves more slowly. Point out that the fan belt in an automobile is an example of a belt turning a wheel.)

1.13 Finding Gears with Chains

Turn a bicycle upside down. Push the pedal with your hand and see how it turns the large gear wheel, which turns the chain, which turns the small gear wheel, which then turns the rear bicycle wheel. One turn of the large gear wheel makes the small gear wheel turn more than once and move faster. Compare the number of teeth in each gear and find the ideal mechanical advantage.

Use black crayon to place a mark on each gear. Make one complete turn of the large gear and see how many turns the smaller gear makes. Count the number of teeth on the large and small gears, and find the ideal mechanical advantage of the bicycle.

1.14 Make a Pinwheel Windmill

For older students: Have enough supplies so that each student can make his or her own pinwheel windmill. Use these instructions: Cut out a sheet of paper 15 centimeters

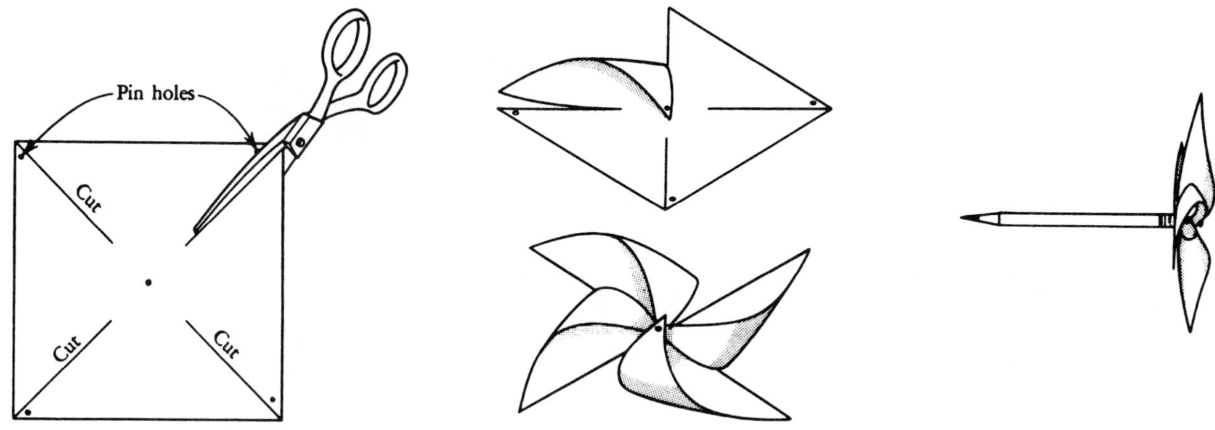

FIGURE 17.23 Making a windmill.

(6 in.) square and make lines and pinholes as shown in Figure 17.23. Cut each line, and then bend in the corners to bring the pinholes in line with the center hole of the paper. Run a pin through the pinholes, and then push the pin into the eraser on a pencil or into a cork stopper. Blow on the pinwheel or hold it in front of an electric fan. Ask students to explain their observations. (The air turns the pinwheel because the air strikes the curved blades at a slant. A windmill operates in much the same way.) Ask students which type of simple machine is represented by a windmill (wheel-and-axle machine).

Have the students read about and report on windmills and their uses and how they are used today to convert energy from wind into electrical energy.

Chapter 18

Heat, Fire, and Fuels

Anthony Magnacca/Merrill

The Nature of Heat

I. Kinetic Theory of Heat

A. All materials, or substances, are made of **molecules.**

1. The energy that molecules have is called **kinetic energy** (energy of motion).
2. The faster the molecules of a material are made to move, the more kinetic energy they have, and the hotter the material becomes; the slower the molecules of a material move, the less kinetic energy they have, and the cooler the material becomes.

B. **Heat**, then, is the energy of moving molecules.

II. Sources of Heat Energy

A. Heat energy can be produced from the **mechanical energy** of friction, compression, or percussion.

1. When two surfaces rub together, friction makes the molecules move faster and the materials become hotter.
2. When molecules of gas are crowded together, or compressed, heat is produced.
3. When a hammer pounds a piece of iron, the molecules of iron move faster and have more kinetic energy, so the iron becomes warmer.

B. Heat energy can be produced from **chemical energy.**

1. When two materials react chemically, often the chemical energy that is released is changed, or transformed, into heat.
2. The burning of a fuel such as oil, gas, coal, or wood is a chemical action that produces heat.

C. Heat energy can be produced from **electrical energy.**

1. When an electric current flows through a thin wire of a light bulb or a toaster, heat is given off.
2. The resistance of the wire to the flow of electric current produces heat.

D. Heat energy can be produced from the **radiant energy** of the Sun or other glowing materials.

1. The Sun is our chief source of heat, obtained either directly from the Sun itself or indirectly from the Sun's energy stored in fuels.
2. Radiant energy, then, is our chief source of heat energy on Earth.

E. Heat energy can be produced from **nuclear energy.**

1. When the nucleus of an atom is split, either naturally or artificially, the nuclear energy produced can be transformed into vast amounts of heat energy.

III. Effect of Heat on Changes in the State of Matter

A. All materials on Earth are found in any one of three forms, or states, of matter: **solid, liquid,** or **gas. Plasma,** which is gas that is electrically charged, is a fourth state of matter (see Chapter 16). The discussion that follows, however, is limited to the three states—solid, liquid, and gas.

LEARNING ACTIVITY 18.1

Heat Is the Energy of Moving Molecules

Place tumblers of cold water and hot water side by side, and add two drops of red food coloring to each tumbler. Point out that the molecules of hot water have more kinetic energy and are moving more quickly than the molecules of cold water. The faster-moving molecules of hot water disperse the food coloring more quickly than the slower-moving molecules of cold water.

Inquiry-Based Learning Activity 18.1. Modified

Place clear tumblers of cool water and warm water side by side and add one drop of food coloring to each tumbler. Ask your students, "Which tumbler has the warmer water and which one has the cooler water?" Allow your class to observe the glasses for a few minutes and then say, "Take a few minutes and explain your reasons for your choices. You may draw pictures if it will help you explain your ideas." This activity begins in precisely the same manner as the unmodified activity, but using cool and warm water so that condensation and evaporation will not be evident. **What level of inquiry is this modification?** This activity begins at ***Level I,*** but shifts from a more didactic approach to an approach that relies on students' observations, ***Level III.*** The shift from ***Level I*** at the **Problem Identification** stage to ***Level III*** at both the **Process and Solution** stages offers an example of the flexibility of inquiry-based lesson designs. **Some questions to consider.** Since students are not told what to specifically observe, would they need prompting to offer reasonable explanations? If students offer incorrect responses, how will you as the teacher handle these ideas?

LEARNING ACTIVITY 18.2

Sources of Heat Energy

A. Friction as a Source of Heat

Have the students rub the palms of their hands together briskly and note the heat produced by the resulting friction.

B. Compression as a Source of Heat

Use a pump to inflate a tire or a ball. Point out that the barrel of the pump becomes warm because the air inside has been compressed.

C. Percussion as a Source of Heat

Pound a block of iron with a hammer several times. The continued percussion makes the molecules of iron move faster, and the block becomes warmer.

D. Chemical Energy as a Source of Heat

Strike a match and note that the friction of the match head rubbing against a rough surface produces enough heat to cause a chemical reaction to take place. The match head bursts into flame, and the chemical energy of the burning match is the source of heat.

E. Electrical Energy as a Source of Heat

Turn on a hot plate or electric toaster. Electrical energy is being converted to heat energy.

F. Radiant Energy as a Source of Heat

Put a match head on a pie tin. Use a magnifying glass to focus the Sun's rays on the match head. The match head will burst into flame.

---

1. In gases, the molecules have a great amount of energy. They usually move very fast and are far apart.
2. In liquids, the molecules have less energy. They move less quickly and are closer together.
3. In solids, the molecules have even less energy. They are very close together, and each molecule seems to vibrate at one spot rather than move about.

B. Water is a material found in all three forms, or states. As ice, it is in the form of a solid; as water, it is in the form of a liquid; and as water vapor, it is in the form of a gas called steam.

C. A change in the state of a material can be brought about by heating or cooling the material.

D. If enough heat energy is added to a solid, the solid becomes a liquid.
   1. The added heat energy makes the molecules in the solid vibrate more and more quickly until they finally break away, move about freely, and are farther apart, as in a liquid.
   2. When this condition occurs, we say the solid melts. The temperature at which melting takes place is called the **melting point.** Each solid has its own melting point.

E. If enough heat energy is removed from a liquid, the liquid becomes a solid.
   1. Removing heat energy causes the molecules to move more slowly and come closer together, until they are very close together and each molecule vibrates at one spot and does not move about.
   2. When this condition occurs, we say the liquid freezes. The temperature at which freezing takes place is called the **freezing point.** Each liquid has its own freezing point.

F. If enough heat energy is added to a liquid, the liquid becomes a gas.
   1. The added heat energy causes the molecules in the liquid to move more quickly and to stay farther apart until they are moving very quickly and are very far apart.
   2. When this condition occurs, we say that the liquid has **evaporated**, or turned into a gas or vapor.
   3. Evaporation takes place at all temperatures, but if a liquid is heated sufficiently, at a certain temperature bubbles of gas form that rise to the surface of the liquid.
   4. When bubbles form in this way, we say that the liquid boils. The temperature at which this occurs is called the **boiling point**. Each liquid has its own boiling point.

G. Removing enough heat energy from a gas causes gas to become a liquid.
   1. Removing heat energy causes the gas molecules to move more slowly and come closer together until the gas condenses, or turns into a liquid.
   2. For each gas, there is a certain temperature at which it will condense, or become a liquid.

IV. Expansion and Contraction

A. When materials are heated, the molecules move faster and spread farther apart so the materials expand in volume. When materials are cooled, the molecules move more slowly and come closer together, so the materials become smaller in volume, or contract.

B. The rates of expansion and contraction are different for solids, liquids, and gases.
   1. In solids, the molecules are very close together and seem to vibrate rather than move, so in relation to liquids and gases, solids expand and contract less.

LEARNING ACTIVITY 18.3

Expansion and Contraction

A. Solids Expand When Heated and Contract When Cooled

Wrap one end of a wire around a nail and attach the other end to a clamp, covered with rubber or cloth, on a ringstand (Figure 18.1). Adjust the length of the wire so that the tip of the nail just clears the table and can swing freely. Now heat the wire with a Bunsen burner or alcohol lamp, moving the flame up and down the wire. The wire expands, causing the tip of the nail to touch the table, so the nail can no longer swing freely. Remove the flame and let the wire cool. The wire contracts, letting the nail swing freely again.

B. Liquids Expand When Heated and Contract When Cooled

Color water dark red with food coloring and pour it into a Pyrex flask until the flask is almost full. Insert a long glass or plastic tube into a one-hole rubber stopper and fit the stopper tightly into the mouth of the flask. The amount of water in the flask will have to be adjusted so that when the stopper is inserted, the colored water will rise about one-half the distance of the part of the tube above the stopper (Figure 18.2).

Place a small rubber band around the tube at the level of the liquid. Heat the flask on a hot plate just long enough to show the water expanding and rising up the tube. Transfer the flask to a pan of cold water and note that the water contracts and falls within the tube.

SAFETY NOTE: Use caution for this demonstration.

1. Use extra caution whenever using a hotplate, Bunsen burner, or any other heat source in the classroom, keeping curious or careless children protected from touching it.
2. Protect children from possible glass breakage (even when using Pyrex glassware) and from the spattering of glass and boiling water.
3. Use care whenever pushing glass tubing through a rubber stopper. It should be done only by the teacher and after lubricating the glass rod by wetting it with water and slowly twisting the rod through.

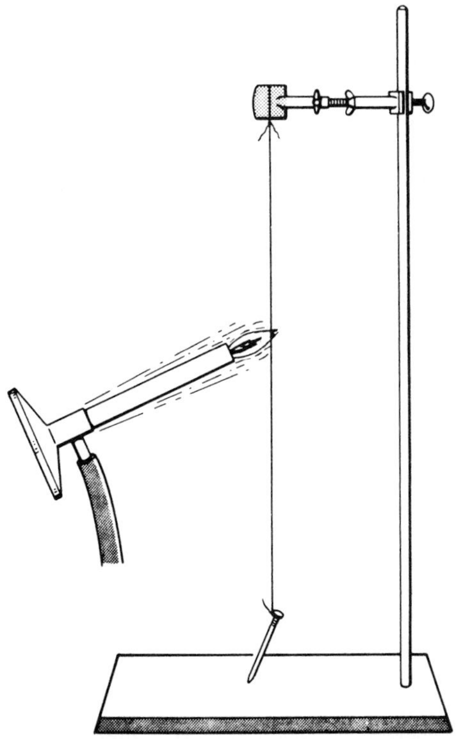

FIGURE 18.1 The wire expands when heated and contracts when cooled.

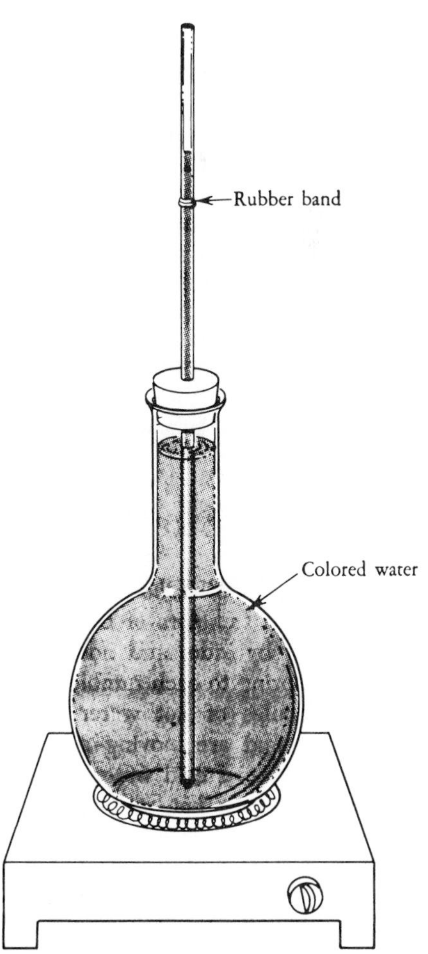

FIGURE 18.2 The water expands and rises when heated and contracts and falls when cooled.

LEARNING ACTIVITY 18.4

Exceptions to the Contraction and Expansion Rule

A. Water Is an Exception to the Rule of Expansion and Contraction

Fill a plastic bottle with water and screw the cap on tightly. Allow the bottle to stand overnight in the freezer of a refrigerator. Remove the bottle the next day and note how it bulges because the water expanded when it was cooled below 4°C (39°F) and then froze.

B. Rubber Is Also an Exception to the Rule of Expansion and Contraction

Cut a long rubber band. Tie one end of the band around the head of a nail and attach the other end to a ringstand, as described and pictured in Figure 18.1. Now move a candle flame quickly up and down the rubber band several times, being careful not to hold the flame too close to the rubber band. The rubber band will contract when heated and will pull up the nail.

2. In liquids, the molecules move about quickly and are farther apart, so liquids can expand and contract more than solids.
3. In gases, the molecules move about quickly and are quite far apart, so gases expand and contract most.

V. Exceptions to the Rule of Expansion and Contraction

A. While most materials expand when heated and contract when cooled, water is an exception to this rule.
   1. When water is cooled, it contracts until its temperature reaches 4°C (39°F).
   2. When it is cooled from 4°C (39°F) to the freezing point of water, 0°C (32°F), it expands slightly. Because water expands as it freezes, ice is less dense than water and therefore can float in water.

B. This unusual characteristic of water explains some of the other special characteristics of water.
   1. It explains why the water in a lake freezes from the top down rather than from the bottom up.
   2. It explains why water pipes burst when the temperature is below freezing.
   3. It also explains why huge icebergs float.

VI. Utilization of the Concept of Expansion and Contraction in Our Daily Lives

A. When the metal lid of a glass jar is stuck tight, hot water will cause the lid to expand more rapidly than the jar, allowing the lid to be unscrewed easily.

B. When two glass tumblers are stuck, one inside the other, they can be loosened by pouring hot water on the outside tumbler while filling the inside tumbler with cold water, using caution against breakage.

C. When baking powder is used in baking a cake, carbon dioxide gas forms inside the dough and expands when heated, causing the cake to rise.

D. Telephone wires that are strung in summer are allowed to sag a little so they can contract without breaking in winter.

E. Engineers place one end of a bridge on rollers to allow for expansion and contraction of the bridge in summer and winter.

F. Concrete workers leave spaces between slabs of concrete road and sidewalk so that the concrete will not bulge and buckle in summer, or contract and crack in winter.

G. Metal rivets used in construction are hammered into place while red-hot so that when they cool, they will contract and pull the parts together with great force.

H. Thermostats and metallic thermometers contain a bar or coil made of strips of two different metals that expand at different rates, causing the bar or coil to turn when heated or cooled.

Temperature

I. Definition of *Temperature*

A. Temperature is a measure of the motion (the heat) of the individual atoms and molecules in a gas, liquid, or solid.
   1. Temperature describes in degrees how hot or cold a substance is.
   2. Temperature depends on the speed of movement of the molecules in a substance. The faster the molecules are moving, the higher the temperature of the substance; the slower the molecules move, the lower its temperature.
   3. There is an **absolute zero temperature** at which the motions of atoms and molecules almost stop.

II. Measurement of Temperature

A. A thermometer is used to measure temperature.
   1. The operation of a thermometer depends on the principle that materials expand when heated and contract when cooled.

B. The thermometer commonly used to measure temperature is a sealed glass tube containing a liquid, such as mercury or colored alcohol.
   1. There is a very narrow, hollow passageway or bore running through the tube.
   2. At the bottom of the bore is a bulb that contains the liquid.
   3. The liquid is also part of the way up the bore.
   4. When the liquid inside the bulb is heated, it expands and rises up the bore. When the liquid is cooled, it contracts and goes down the bore.

C. A scale on the thermometer tells us just how high the liquid is in the thermometer, and gives us the temperature of whatever is around the bulb.
   1. The scale on a thermometer is divided into many equal lines, or divisions, called degrees. The **degree** (°) is the unit of measurement of temperature.
   2. Two common temperature scales are the Fahrenheit scale and the Celsius (or centigrade) scale.

D. In the **Fahrenheit scale**, developed by the German physicist Gabriel Fahrenheit (1685–1736), the freezing point of water registers at 32° and the boiling point of water registers at 212°. There are 180 lines, or divisions, between the freezing point and the boiling point of water.
   1. Zero on the Fahrenheit scale is the lowest temperature that Fahrenheit could get from a mixture of salt and ice in water.
   2. Absolute zero on the Fahrenheit scale is −459°.

E. On the **Celsius scale**, also called the **centigrade scale**, the freezing point of water is at 0° and the boiling point of water is at 100°. There are 100 lines, or divisions, between the freezing point and boiling point of water.
   1. The Celsius scale is named after the Swedish scientist Anders Celsius (1701–1744).
   2. Absolute zero in the Celsius scale is −273°
   3. Scientists, and most of the world, use the Celsius scale.

F. It is easy to convert from the Fahrenheit scale to the Celsius scale, and vice versa.
   1. Because there are 180 Fahrenheit degrees and 100 Celsius degrees between the freezing and boiling points of water, 1°F is equal to 100/180, or 5/9°C; and 1°C is equal to 180/100, or 9/5°F.
   2. Moreover, because 0° on the Celsius scale is the same as 32° on the Fahrenheit scale, we must always subtract 32° when changing from the Fahrenheit to the Celsius scale, and always add 32° when changing from the Celsius to the Fahrenheit scale.
   3. So, to change from °F to °C, subtract 32° from the Fahrenheit reading and multiply the result by 5/9:

$$°C = (°F - 32) \times 5/9$$

   4. To change from °C to °F, multiply the Celsius reading by 9/5 and add 32°

$$°F = 9/5\ °C + 32$$

G. The **Kelvin scale**, used often by astronomers and physicists, sets zero at the absolute zero of temperature and uses degrees that are the same size as in the Celsius system. Whereas room temperature in the Celsius scale is 20°, room temperature is 293° in Kelvin. To convert to Kelvin from Celsius, use the formula:

$$°K = °C + 273.15$$

H. The **Rankine scale** is sometimes used in manufacturing. Use this equation to convert to Rankine from Fahrenheit:

$$°R = °F + 459.67$$

I. Another scale, rarely used today, is the **Reamur scale.** It sets 0° at the freezing point of water and 80° at the boiling point.

J. There are several kinds of thermometers.
   1. A **mercury thermometer** contains mercury, the only metal that is liquid at room temperature.
   2. Because mercury has a high boiling point (about 357°C or 675°F), the mercury thermometer can be used to measure fairly high temperatures. However, because mercury freezes at −39°C (−38°F), it cannot be used to measure very low temperatures.
   3. Because mercury is a very toxic metal, mercury thermometers are no longer used in public school classrooms.
   4. Most indoor and outdoor household thermometers and those used today by public schools are **alcohol thermometers.** An alcohol thermometer looks and operates like a mercury thermometer, but alcohol—colored red or blue—is used in the bulb and tube.
   5. Because alcohol has a boiling point lower than that of water (about 78°C or 172°F), an alcohol thermometer cannot be used to measure high temperatures. However, because alcohol has a very low freezing point (about −130°C or −202°F), the alcohol thermometer is used in polar regions.
   6. The **clinical thermometer** is a mercury thermometer, but it is short and has a scale that runs only from 33°C to 43°C (92°F to 110°F).

7. The bore of this thermometer is very narrow. Even one-tenth of a degree will make a big difference in the level of the mercury, and it can easily be read.
8. At one spot inside the bore, there is a narrow bend or pinch. When the clinical thermometer is placed inside a person's mouth, the mercury is heated and expands, pushing its way up and beyond this pinch to give the proper temperature reading. When the thermometer is removed, however, the mercury cannot fall back through the pinch, so the level of the mercury remains at the temperature of the person's body. This stationary position allows an accurate reading of the person's body temperature. To force the mercury down the tube again, past the pinch, one has to shake the thermometer quite vigorously a few times.
9. A **metal thermometer** does not use a glass tube, bulb, or liquid. It has a small coil made of two strips of metal welded together along their lengths. The inside strip of metal is usually brass, and the outside strip is steel.
10. When the coil is heated or cooled, the brass strip expands and contracts more than the steel strip, making the coil twist. As the coil twists, a pointer connected to one end of the coil moves across a scale that is marked in degrees.
11. The metal thermometer is used for obtaining temperature readings in home ovens and refrigerators.
12. **Digital thermometers** are usually highly sensitive thermometers that give accurate readings on electronic meters.
13. The **strip thermometer** is a celluloid tape made with heat-sensitive liquid crystal chemicals that cause a change in the color of the tape according to the temperature. Strip thermometers are useful in taking the temperature of infants because one needs only to place the strip on a baby's forehead for a few seconds to obtain a fairly precise temperature reading.

III. **Measure of the Amount of Heat**

A. Two units commonly used to measure the amount of heat are the British thermal unit (BTU) and the calorie.
   1. **British thermal unit** (BTU) is the amount of heat energy needed to raise the temperature of 1 pound (16 ounces by weight) of water 1°F.
   2. The **calorie** is the amount of heat energy needed to raise the temperature of 1 gram (about 3/100 of an ounce by weight) of water 1°C.
   3. This calorie is called the small calorie and is spelled with a lowercase *c*. The large **Calorie**, spelled with a capital *C*, is equal to 1,000 small calories. The large Calorie is used to determine how much heat energy is available from different foods.

Methods of Heat Travel and Their Effects

I. **Heat Can Travel by Conduction**

A. When a material such as a metal rod is heated, molecules nearest to the source of the heat move faster.
   1. The molecules bump into other molecules, making them move faster.
   2. These molecules then bump into still other molecules, making them move faster too.
   3. In this way, all the molecules in the material are made to move faster and have more kinetic energy, so the material becomes hotter.
   4. The heat energy has been passed, or conducted, from molecule to molecule within the material, yet the material itself does not move.
   5. This method of heat travel, whereby energy is passed along from molecule to molecule by bumping, or collision, is called *conduction*.

B. Material through which heat travels is called a **conductor**.
   1. Metals are good heat conductors.
   2. Good heat conductors are also good conductors of electricity.
   3. In good heat conductors, the molecules are very close together and conduct the heat energy from molecule to molecule very quickly and easily.
   4. Some metals, such as silver and copper, are better heat conductors than other metals.

C. Materials that do not conduct heat very well are called nonconductors, or poor conductors.
   1. Most nonmetals, liquids, and gases are poor conductors of heat.
   2. In poor heat conductors, the molecules are farther apart and do not conduct the heat energy from molecule to molecule quickly or easily.

D. A vacuum cannot conduct heat because there are no molecules to pass along the heat energy.

E. When a nonconductor is used to stop the conduction of heat, it is called an **insulator**.

LEARNING ACTIVITY 18.5

Heat Travels in Water by Convection

Fill a Pyrex container almost full of water. Shred a blotter with a food grater and place the fine particles in the water. Muddle the bits of blotting paper until they become thoroughly soaked and sink to the bottom of the beaker. Now place the container on one side of a hot plate and heat the container (Figure 18.3). The blotting paper will indicate the path of the convection current produced in the water. The bits of blotting paper will move up the side of the beaker resting on the hot coils, and travel down on the cooler side of the Pyrex container.

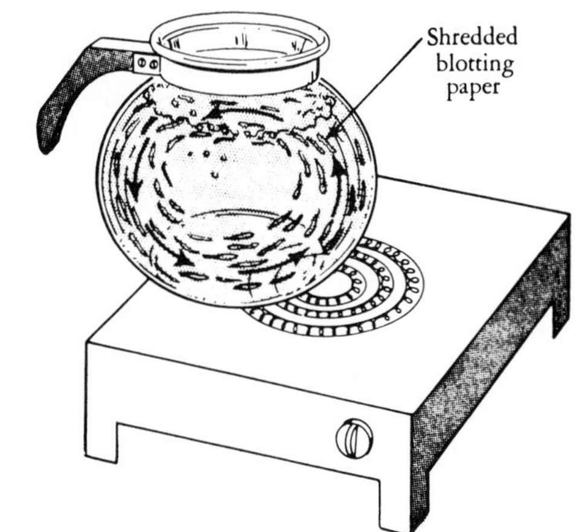

FIGURE 18.3 A convection water current.

1. Pot and pan handles are covered with insulators made of wood or plastic.
2. Rubber and cloth are also used as insulators.
3. Because air is a very poor heat conductor, anything with air spaces in it, such as wool or cork, is a good insulator.

II. Heat Can Travel by Convection

A. Convection is a method of heat travel that takes place only in gases and liquids, both of which scientists refer to as **fluids.**
   1. When a fluid such as air is heated, the molecules move faster and spread farther apart so the air expands.
   2. When air expands, it becomes less dense.
   3. The colder air above is denser, and gravity pulls down harder on the colder, heavier air than on the warmer, less dense air.
   4. Because of this greater pull of gravity, the cold air moves down and pushes the warm air upward.
   5. The cold air in turn is heated, expands, becomes less dense, and is pushed upward by colder, denser air above it.
   6. In this way, continuous currents of rising and falling air are produced.
   7. The same currents are produced with a liquid fluid such as water.

B. **Convection,** then, is a method of heat travel whereby the molecules of a heated gas or liquid actually move from one place to another.
   1. The heat is carried from a place of higher temperature to a place of lower temperature by the molecules of a moving gas or liquid.
   2. The movement of the gas or liquid is called a *convection current.*
   3. There can be no convection current in a vacuum.
   4. Some ovens are convection ovens. For example, solar ovens heat by creating convection waves from the energy of sunlight.

III. Heat Can Travel by Radiation

A. Radiation as a method of heat travel is very different from conduction and convection, because it has nothing to do with the transfer of heat by moving molecules.

B. The Sun and other glowing bodies give off, or radiate, energy in the form of invisible waves.
   1. These radiant energy waves travel out into space without the help of molecules.
   2. When radiant energy strikes a solid, opaque material, some of the energy is absorbed. This makes the molecules in the material move faster, so the material becomes hotter.

C. Radiant energy is not heat, but becomes heat when it is absorbed.
   1. The Sun heats the Earth, 150 million kilometers (93 million mi) away, in this way.
   2. This method of passing along heat by radiant energy waves is called radiation.

D. The kind of material determines how much radiant energy is changed into heat.
   1. Dark, rough materials are good absorbers of radiant energy and produce much heat.
   2. Light, smooth materials reflect most of the radiant energy that strikes them and do not produce much heat at all.
   3. Transparent materials, such as air and glass, allow almost all of the radiant energy to pass through them, so they produce little or no heat.

E. Some modern cooking ovens are designed to heat either by radiant energy or by convection.
F. Radiant heat waves are part of a family of radiant energy waves called **electromagnetic waves** (see Chapter 20). This family includes radio waves, infrared rays or heat waves, light rays, ultraviolet rays, X-rays, gamma rays, and cosmic rays.
 1. Microwave ovens, for instance, heat food with electromagnetic radiation at a special frequency that excites vibrations in water molecules.

IV. Heating the Home

A. Heating with a **fireplace.**
 1. When a fire is started in a fireplace, the heat of the fire warms the air in the fireplace and the air in the chimney.
 2. A convection current is produced that moves through the fireplace and up the chimney.
 3. This convection current removes cold air from the floor, but the current also carries much of the heat of the fire up the chimney.
 4. The heat that warms the room is mostly radiant heat, whereby the radiant energy from the fire is absorbed by the walls, furniture, and other materials in the room.

B. Heating with a **stove.**
 1. The heat from the fire in a stove passes through its metal walls by conduction, and into the air next to the walls by conduction as well.
 2. The heated air sets up a convection current that heats the whole room.
 3. The hot walls of the stove radiate some heat too.
 4. Gas, oil, kerosene, coal, and wood can be used as fuel for a stove.

C. Heating with **central heating systems.**
 1. Many homes and buildings are heated by central heating systems, with a stove or furnace located in the basement or utility room.
 2. The heat is conducted from the furnace to the rooms by pipes or ducts.
 3. The most commonly used central heating systems today are the hot-air, hot-water, steam, and radiant heating systems.

D. In a **hot-air heating system**, the furnace is surrounded by a brick or iron jacket filled with air.
 1. The furnace heats the jacket by conduction, and the jacket heats the air by conduction.
 2. The hot air inside the jacket is pushed up, either by cold air entering at the bottom of the furnace or by a fan.
 3. The hot air goes up the pipes into the different rooms in the house.
 4. It goes into each room through a metal grating, or register, in the floor, walls, or ceiling.
 5. The air circulates through the rooms and heats them by convection.
 6. The air is then either carried back to the furnace through a cold-air return so that it can be reheated, or it is allowed to escape and is replaced by fresh air from outdoors.

E. In a **hot-water heating system**, the furnace is surrounded by a boiler filled with water.
 1. When the water is heated, it is pushed up by cold water entering the bottom of the boiler.
 2. The hot water goes up the pipes into the different rooms in the house.
 3. It then goes into a metal radiator in each room.
 4. The radiator is divided into many sections of hollow pipe so it exposes a great deal of its surface to the air.
 5. The hot water heats the walls of the radiator by conduction.
 6. The radiator walls heat the air next to them by conduction.
 7. The hot air then heats the room by convection.
 8. At the same time, the radiator radiates some heat as well.
 9. After the hot water in the radiator gives up its heat and becomes cooler, it goes back to the boiler through return pipes and is reheated.
 10. The same water is used over and over again.

F. A **steam heating system** works very much like a hot-water heating system, but steam is used instead of hot water.
 1. The boiler is only partly filled with water.
 2. When the water is heated, it is changed into water vapor or steam.
 3. The steam has great pressure and is forced up the pipes into the radiators.
 4. When the steam gives up its heat to the radiators, it condenses back into water and returns to the boiler where it is reheated.

G. In a **radiant heating system**, hot water is circulated through copper pipes located in the floor or in the walls.
 1. The hot water heats the pipes by conduction.
 2. The pipes heat the floors and walls by conduction.
 3. The floors and walls radiate heat energy, which warms the rooms.

H. In **solar heating systems**, the Sun provides some of the heat. Solar heating systems work best on clear days when it is not too cold or windy.
 1. The sides of the building facing the Sun are mostly large glass windows.
 2. Radiant energy from the Sun passes through the windows into the rooms, where it is absorbed and changed into heat.
 3. Using the Sun's rays to heat space, materials such as masonry, or containers that hold water is called **passive solar heating.** Greenhouses and home greenhouse window boxes usually rely on passive solar heating.

4. Some people use solar collector panels to heat water that is then pumped into the house to provide hot water and home heating. This type of heating is called **active solar heating.**
5. Some homes, vehicles, and spacecraft use photovoltaic cells on their roofs that collect the Sun's energy and then cause an electric current to flow or to be stored for later electrical use. The system of creating electricity from the Sun's energy is called a **photovoltaic system.**

I. The **heat pump system** takes heat from the outside air, working like an air conditioner in reverse.
   1. A heat pump is not energy efficient at below-freezing temperatures, but in milder climates it is efficient and economical.
   2. In summer a heat pump operates as a conventional air conditioner.

V. Preventing Heat Loss

A. There are three ways in which heat may be lost in the home.
   1. Heat is conducted through the windows, walls, and roof.
   2. Heat is radiated through the windows.
   3. Heat escapes by convection through cracks around doors and windows.

B. This heat loss can be prevented or reduced in many ways by using insulation.
   1. Insulating materials can be used in the walls and under the roof.
   2. These materials, such as rock wool or glass wool, contain many air spaces and are nonconductors. They are insulators.
   3. Insulators stop heat from being conducted out through the walls and roof.
   4. Storm windows, when fitted over regular windows, create an air space between the two windows.
   5. Air is a poor conductor of heat and acts as an insulator (which is why glass wool and rock wool are such good insulators).
   6. This insulation prevents the windows from conducting heat out of the house.
   7. Permanent double-paned windows work according to the same principle as storm windows.
   8. Weather strips or special materials, when placed around windows and doors, stop heat from escaping through any cracks that may be present.

C. Insulation not only stops heat from leaving a house in winter, but helps keep heat from getting into the house in summer.

VI. Cooling in the Home

A. The refrigerator cools by taking heat away from materials.
   1. A refrigerator has a pipe running through it, and inside the pipe is a gas that is changed into a liquid when compressed.
   2. In an electric refrigerator, a motor runs a compressor, which compresses the gas and takes heat away from it until the gas becomes a liquid.
   3. The heat that is taken away from the gas passes out into the air of the room.
   4. The liquid gas then flows under pressure through the pipe in the refrigerator until it reaches a place that is to be cooled.
   5. Here the pressure is taken away from the liquid gas so the liquid evaporates into a gas again.
   6. When a liquid evaporates, it needs heat. It takes this heat from the space surrounding the liquid.
   7. Taking heat away cools the materials in the space surrounding the liquid that is evaporating.
   8. The gas then continues to the motor and compressor, where it is turned into a liquid again.

B. The deep freeze or freezer is a special refrigeration machine that freezes food quickly, until the temperature of the food in the machine is −10°F to −20°F.
   1. The freezing must be quick, or the food will lose much of its flavor and consistency.
   2. When food is frozen, the water in the food freezes and forms ice crystals.
   3. When food, especially fruits and vegetables, is frozen slowly, the ice crystals are large and can break the cells of the food, killing their taste and flavor.
   4. When food is frozen quickly, the ice crystals are very small and do not break the food cells.

C. The air conditioner in a home or in an automobile has a cooling unit that works like a refrigerator.
   1. An efficient air conditioner accomplishes three things: it cools the air in a room; it lowers the amount of water vapor (humidity) in the air; and it supplies fresh air and removes stale air.
   2. Warm air passes through the cooling unit, and heat is taken away from the air.
   3. The heat is passed on to the air outdoors, which carries it away.
   4. A dehumidifier helps the excess water vapor in the air condense as the air is cooled.
   5. A fan blows the air through a filter, which removes dust and pollen.
   6. An air conditioner usually has a fresh-air connection, which provides the conditioner with fresh outdoor air.

Fire

I. The Nature of Fire

A. Fire, the burning of a material, is also called **combustion.**

1. Combustion is a chemical change that takes place when certain materials combine rapidly with oxygen to give off heat and light.
2. This chemical reaction, which takes place when a material combines with oxygen, is called **oxidation.**

B. Materials can also combine with oxygen (oxidize) slowly and produce some heat, but no light.

1. This combination is oxidation, too, but it is a slow oxidation and is not called burning or combustion.
2. The rusting of iron is an example of slow oxidation.

C. To be called burning, the oxidation must be fast enough to produce both heat and light.

II. Factors Necessary for Fire

A. For burning to take place, three things are needed: fuel, oxygen, and heat for ignition.

1. A fire needs a material that will burn, which is called a fuel.
2. The more oxygen a fuel gets, the faster the oxidation will take place, and the hotter the fire will become.
3. Supplying the fire with more air will give the fuel more oxygen.
4. Breaking the fuel into small pieces will expose more of the fuel's surface to the air and, in this way, give the fuel more oxygen.
5. If a fuel is broken into pieces so small that they look like particles of dust, the fuel may combine with the oxygen so quickly that it will produce an explosion.
6. A fire needs a sufficient amount of heat to get the fuel hot enough to burn.

B. Some materials burn more easily than others.

1. We say that these materials have a lower **kindling temperature**, which is the lowest temperature at which a material will ignite and burn.
2. At this temperature, oxygen combines quickly enough with the fuel to keep the chemical reaction going steadily.

LEARNING ACTIVITY 18.6

Slow Oxidation Produces Heat

Soak a wad of steel wool thoroughly in water, remove the wad, allow it to drain, and then stuff it into a Thermos bottle. Obtain a one-hole rubber stopper large enough to fit the mouth of the Thermos bottle, and insert a thermometer into the hole. After the steel wool has been in the Thermos for about 10 minutes, insert the stopper and the thermometer (Figure 18.4). The temperature will soon rise, showing that heat is being produced as oxidation takes place. The temperature will stop rising after about 20 minutes, because all the oxygen present in the air inside the Thermos will be used up. When the temperature has stopped rising, remove the stopper, allow fresh air to enter, and then replace the stopper. The temperature will begin to rise again.

Ask children to suggest safety tips for home that are related to this demonstration of slow oxidation. (For example, slow oxidation of oily rags in a garage or of moist hay in a barn can start a fire.) Have them list things they could do at home to prevent fires that can occur from slow oxidation. (See Figure 18.8 for additional safety tips.)

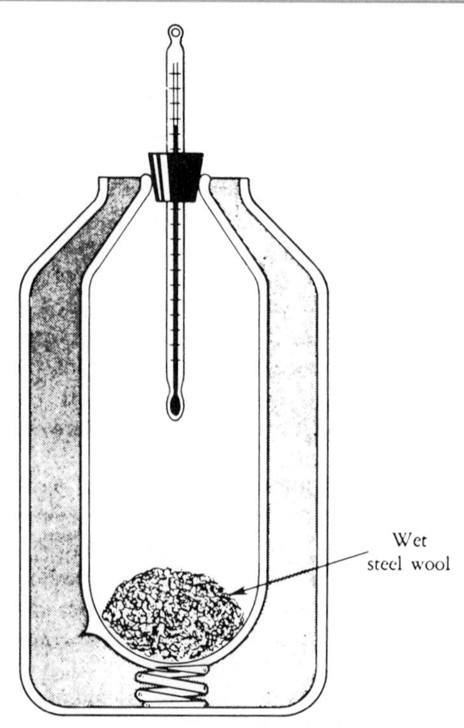

FIGURE 18.4 Wet steel wool oxidizes slowly and gives off heat.

LEARNING ACTIVITY 18.7

The Effect of the Amount of Oxygen on Burning

Prepare pure oxygen by pouring some 3% hydrogen peroxide into a glass jar. Add a piece of liver about the size of a half dollar, then cover the top of the jar with an index card or piece of cardboard. (Keep the liver cool, but do not freeze, until 1 hour before using.) An enzyme in the liver, called catalase, makes the hydrogen peroxide decompose, bubbling vigorously, to produce oxygen gas and water.

Untwist one end of a piece of thick picture wire or steel wool and hold this end in a flame until the wire begins to glow. Then quickly insert the glowing wire or steel wool into the jar of pure oxygen (Figure 18.5). The wire will burn like a Fourth of July sparkler in the pure oxygen.

Flames and sparks are very dangerous in the presence of high concentrations of oxygen. Ask the students to research and report their findings to the class about where high concentrations of oxygen are used, such as in industry and in medicine, and the safety measures that are in effect in those situations.

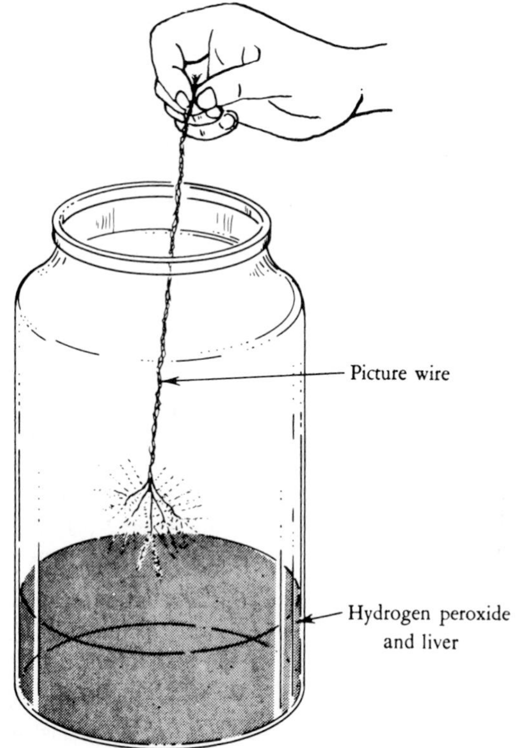

FIGURE 18.5 Picture wire burns vigorously in pure oxygen.

LEARNING ACTIVITY 18.8

The Concept of Kindling Temperature

Attempt to light a sugar cube with a match. Then, after failing to ignite the sugar cube, rub it in some ashes that you prepared earlier (by burning a piece of paper and crushing the ash) and try again to light the sugar cube. Ask your students why the sugar cube ignited when it was covered with ash but not before. Ask students to identify practical applications of this concept.

LEARNING ACTIVITY 18.9

Combustible Won't Burn

Do this as a teacher's demonstration of a discrepant event, but practice it first. Wrap a dollar bill (or a $20 if you are confident) around a drinking glass. While holding the bill tightly around the glass, try to ignite the bill with a match or lighter. The paper bill will not ignite because the glass conducts the heat away too rapidly, maintaining the paper below its kindling point. After removing the bill from the glass, you may (if you wish and are wealthy) ignite the bill for a moment to prove to the students that the bill will indeed burn.

3. Materials such as phosphorus, sulfur, and paper have low kindling temperatures and burst into flame easily.
4. When exposed to oxygen, such as in the air, pure phosphorus will ignite at room temperature; therefore, in the laboratory, this material must be kept in water in a tightly sealed container.
5. Materials such as wood and coal have high kindling temperatures and must be quite hot before they will ignite and burn.

III. The Products of Fire

A. Fire produces a flame, which is a mass of burning gas.
1. Some fuels produce a flame directly, but other fuels must be partially changed into a gas before they can burn with a flame.
2. A gaseous fuel, such as natural gas, burns directly to produce a flame.
3. A liquid fuel, such as gasoline or kerosene, must be heated until it turns into a gas before it will burn.
4. Some solid fuels, such as paraffin, first melt and then turn into a gas before they can burn.
5. Other solid fuels, such as wood and coal, when heated will give off gases that burn.

B. The color of a flame depends on how much oxygen the fuel is getting.
1. When a fuel gets all the oxygen it needs and burns completely, the flame is blue, or nearly colorless, and is very hot.
2. When a fuel does not get enough oxygen to burn completely, the flame is yellow or orange and is not as hot as a blue flame.
3. A flame is yellow because the particles of unburned fuel are glowing.

C. A candle's flame, for example, has three parts.
1. The center of the flame around the wick is dark, showing the presence of unburned gas.
2. Almost all the rest of the flame is yellow, which shows that the gas is burning but not getting all the oxygen it needs.
3. Around the edges, the flame is blue or colorless, which shows that here the gas is getting all the oxygen it needs and is burning completely.

D. Fire produces water vapor and carbon dioxide or carbon monoxide gas.
1. Most common fuels contain the chemical elements carbon and hydrogen.
2. When a fuel burns, the hydrogen combines with the oxygen to form water vapor.
3. Water vapor instead of liquid water forms because so much heat is given off during the burning.
4. When a fuel has all the oxygen it needs and burns completely, the carbon combines with the oxygen to form carbon dioxide gas.
5. When a fuel does not get enough oxygen, the carbon combines with the oxygen to form carbon monoxide gas instead.
6. Carbon monoxide gas is made up of less oxygen than carbon dioxide gas.

E. Smoke is unburned fuel.
1. Smoke is made up of particles of carbon that did not receive enough oxygen to make them burn completely.
2. When smoke collects on walls or in chimneys, it is called soot.

F. Some fuels leave behind an ash, which is a part of the fuel that does not ordinarily burn.

IV. Spontaneous Combustion

A. Sometimes materials burst into flame all by themselves, a phenomenon called **spontaneous combustion.**
1. Spontaneous combustion takes place when slow oxidation happens in a closed space where the air cannot circulate or escape.
2. An oily rag in a closed closet or garage can burst into flame through spontaneous combustion, as can dust and lint caught in a hose leading from a clothes dryer.
3. The oil, or dust and lint, combines with oxygen, or oxidizes, slowly and gives off a small amount of heat.
4. This heat cannot escape because there is no movement of air to carry it away.

LEARNING ACTIVITY 18.10

Flame Is a Burning Gas

Light a candle and allow it to burn for a few minutes. Tilt the candle and note the liquid paraffin that drips down. Point out that when the wick first began to burn, it melted the paraffin, which rose up into the wick and was changed to a gas by the heat of the flame. The gas burned, giving off heat and light.

Snuff out the candle flame with a test tube, then immediately light a match and lower it toward the wick (Figure 18.6). You will light the candle before you touch the wick. Point out that when the candle was snuffed, the wick was still hot and continued to change the liquid paraffin to a gas for a short time. The burning match set fire to this gas, which then set fire to the wick.

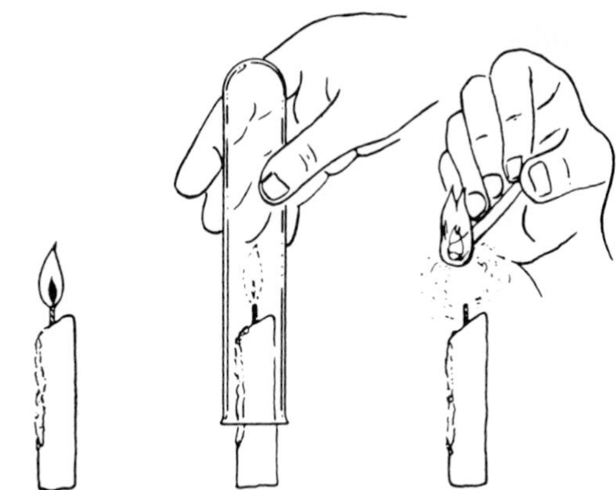

FIGURE 18.6 A flame is a mass of burning gas.

5. The heat makes the oil (or lint and dust) combine with oxygen more quickly, which produces more heat that cannot escape, making the fuel combine with oxygen even more quickly.
6. This process continues, producing more and more heat, until the kindling point of the cloth rag (or the dust and lint) is reached, and the material bursts into flame.

B. If green or wet hay is stored in a barn, spontaneous combustion may take place, because damp hay ferments and gives off heat.

V. Factors Necessary to Extinguish Fire

A. To extinguish a fire, we must take away one or more of the three things needed to make a fire—remove the fuel, cut off the supply of oxygen, or cool the burning fuel, making its temperature lower than the kindling point.
1. The most common methods of putting out fires are to cut off the supply of oxygen and to lower the temperature.
2. Removing the fuel is practical only with a small fire, such as a campfire or a fire in a wastebasket.
3. Using sand, soil, a heavy wool blanket or coat, water, carbon dioxide gas, or any other material that will not burn can cut off the supply of oxygen.
4. Using water or any other cool material that will not burn can lower the temperature.

B. A **fire extinguisher** is a storage container for an extinguishing agent such as water or chemicals.
1. The fire extinguisher is designed to extinguish small fires, not large ones.
2. Fire extinguishers contain chemical agents that extinguish fires by cutting off the supply of oxygen and lowering the temperature of the burning fuel.
3. Although there are many different agents, they can be classified generally as dry chemicals, foams, liquids, and compressed gases.
4. Dry chemical agents include monoammonium phosphate, a multipurpose agent for fighting Class (or Type) A, B, and C fires, and sodium or potassium bicarbonate-based agents for fighting Class B and C fires.
5. The oldest liquid agent is water.
6. Various complex foam agents have been developed for fighting various kinds of Class (or Type) A and B fires.
7. Compressed gases are also known as *clean extinguishing agents* because they leave no residue, like water, foam, or dry chemicals do. The oldest is carbon dioxide, which extinguishes a fire by diluting the oxygen in the area. More recently developed clean agents include inert gases and evaporating liquids that are especially useful for extinguishing fires in aircraft, boats, computer rooms, electronic equipment, and vehicles.
8. Depending upon the type of fire for which it is designed, fire extinguishers are labeled with one or more of four letters, A, B, C, or D, representing the four classes of fires. Color-coded symbols are also used with a

TABLE 18.1 Classes of Fires, Occurrences, and Extinguishing Options

Class and Symbol	Occurrences/Burning Material/(Mnemonic)	Extinguishing Options/Agents
A in a green triangle A	Paper, cloth, wood, rubber, many plastics (These materials usually leave ashes after burning; Type A for Ashes.)	Dry chemicals, foams, water, carbon dioxide
B in a red square B	The vapor-air mixture over the surfaces of flammable and combustible liquids, such as gasoline, grease, lubricating oils, alcohol (These materials often come in barrels; Type B for Barrels.)	Dry chemicals, foams, carbon dioxide, water fog
C in a blue circle C	Electrical equipment, such as wiring, fuse boxes, circuit breakers, machinery, and appliances (Type C for Currents.)	Dry chemicals, carbon dioxide
D in a yellow star D	Combustible metals, such as lithium, magnesium, potassium, sodium, titanium, and zirconium (Type D for Don't get involved.)	Special dry powders and special application techniques

LEARNING ACTIVITY 18.11

Fire Extinguishers

A. Carbon Dioxide Puts Out Fire

Place three candles of different lengths on a piece of cardboard. Prepare a cardboard trough with three holes, each hole just large enough to fit snugly over one of the candles. Fit the trough over the candles so that it is just below the top of each candle (Figure 18.7), and then light them.

Obtain a large glass jar or beaker. Prepare carbon dioxide by pouring some baking soda (sodium bicarbonate) into the jar, adding vinegar, and then covering the jar with a piece of cardboard or an index card until the bubbling subsides. Remove the cardboard and tilt the jar over the higher end of the trough, allowing just the invisible carbon dioxide to flow into the trough and put out the candle flames.

B. Making a Foam Fire Extinguisher

Put 2 tablespoons of baking soda into a tumbler of water, stir, and then pour into a quart-size glass jar. Break an egg and pour the contents into the jar. Cap the jar and shake the contents thoroughly. Obtain a large pie tin and place it on a fireproof mat. Pour some alcohol or lighter fluid into the tin and set fire to the alcohol with a lighted match (be very careful not to spread the fire). Place the jar in the center of the tin and immediately pour a cup of vinegar into the jar. A foam will form, which will overflow the jar, pour down the sides, and put out the fire. Point out that the egg made it possible for the bubbles of carbon dioxide to cling together and form a foamy mass.

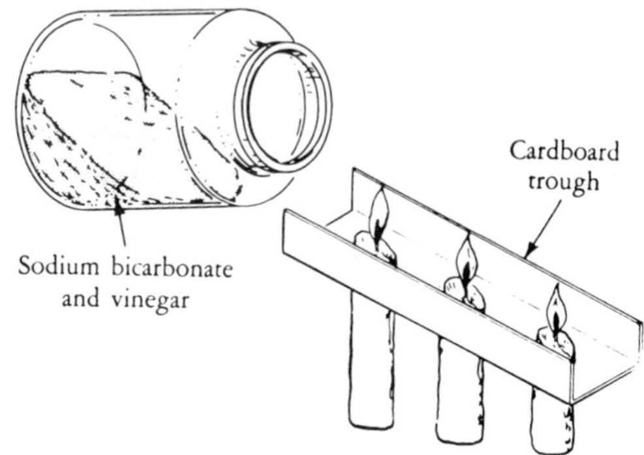

FIGURE 18.7 Carbon dioxide puts out the candle flames.

1. Keep matches and lighters away from heat.
2. Keep matches and lighters away from small children.
3. If you have to strike a match or a lighter, strike away from you and not toward you.
4. Be sure the flame is out when you throw a match away.
5. Surround a campfire with nonporous stones, bricks, or bare earth; porous materials can explode when they get too hot.
6. Be especially careful when making a campfire on a windy day.
7. Put out the campfire thoroughly with sand or soil when you do not want it any more.
8. Never use gasoline to start a fire of any kind.
9. Put a metal screen in front of a fireplace.
10. Put hot ashes in nonflammable containers only.
11. Do not allow trash that will burn to pile up in the basement or attic.
12. Do not put oily rags in closets or other places where there is no circulation of air.
13. Keep the lint traps and hoses of clothes dryers cleaned out.
14. If a container has materials in it that will burn, keep it away from heat or an open flame.
15. Keep a carbon dioxide fire extinguisher in the home, where it can be quickly reached.
16. If your clothes catch on fire, do not run: running supplies the fire with more oxygen, allowing it to burn faster. Roll on the floor or wrap up in a rug, coat, or blanket.
17. Learn how to telephone the fire department and turn in an alarm using a fire alarm box.
18. You can put yourself at risk by fighting a house fire. If at all in doubt, leave the house at once. Close the door to the room where the fire is, to cut down the supply of air in the room. Go to the nearest alarm box or telephone the fire department. Stay out of the house.
19. Keep chimneys clean.
20. In fireplaces, burn only those fuels recommended for the specific type or make of fireplace.
21. Do not use a home fireplace as a trash bin.

FIGURE 18.8 Fire safety precautions.

different color and symbol for each type of fire. See Table 18.1.

9. Fire extinguishers can be made to extinguish more than one type of fire. A recommended extinguisher to have in the home is the ABC type, designed to extinguish fires of Types A, B, and C. Type D fires must be left to the professionals.
10. Fire extinguishers may also be labeled with pictograms showing the type of fire on which the extinguisher is to be or not to be used. For example, the Type A extinguisher may show burning wood, and an electrical cord and outlet with a big slash through it. In other words, don't use it on an electrical fire.
11. Fire extinguishers also have a number rating that indicates the strength of that particular extinguisher; the higher the number, the larger the fire it can extinguish.
12. When an extinguisher is needed, there is no time to read directions. To remember how to use an extinguisher, use the mnemonic **PASS.**

    Pull the safety pin. Some units may require releasing a lock latch, pressing a punch lever, twisting to break a plastic tie, or carrying out some other motion to release a tamper indicator.

    Aim the extinguisher nozzle (horn or hose) at the base of the flames and remain at least 6 feet away from the flames—between the fire and an exit.

    Squeeze or press the handle.

    Sweep from side to side at the base of the flames until the fire is extinguished. Shut off the extinguisher and watch to be sure that the fire does not rekindle.
13. Most portable extinguishers discharge completely in as few as 8 seconds. Extinguishers must be recharged after every use.

Fuels

I. Definition and Classes of Fuel

A. A **fuel** is any material that is burned to produce heat for use in the home or in industry. There are three classes of fuels: solid, liquid, and gas.

B. To be considered a good fuel, the material should fit the following criteria: is inexpensive and easily obtained; is safe to store, ship, and use; is easy to ignite; produces a relatively large amount of heat and little smoke.

II. Solid Fuels

A. Solid fuels include wood, charcoal, coal, coke, peat, and lignite.
1. Wood has a low kindling temperature and gives a great amount of heat.
2. However, wood gives off much smoke and leaves a lot of ash.
3. Chimneys of wood-burning fireplaces must be cleaned out frequently; otherwise, a chimney, roof, and attic fire can result because of the buildup of soot and creosote.
4. When metal chimneys get too hot, they can melt, creating a serious fire hazard.

B. **Charcoal** is wood that is heated in the absence of air. It is an artificial fuel.
1. The liquid and gas impurities in the wood are driven off, leaving mostly burnable carbon.
2. Charcoal burns with a great deal of heat, gives off no smoke, and leaves very little ash.

C. **Coal** consists of the remains of plants and ferns that covered the Earth millions of years ago.
1. Because of the action of high temperatures and tremendous pressures in the Earth, the liquid and gas impurities were driven off, leaving mostly burnable carbon.
2. Soft coal contains about 70% carbon and burns with a great deal of heat, but it gives off much smoke and leaves quite a bit of ash.
3. Hard coal contains almost 90% carbon, burns with a great deal of heat, gives off much less smoke, and leaves little ash.

D. **Coke** is soft coal that is heated in the absence of air.
1. Gas impurities in soft coal are driven off, leaving mostly burnable carbon.
2. Coke burns with a great deal of heat, gives off no smoke, and leaves very little ash.

E. **Peat** and **lignite** are coal in its early stages of formation; they do not give very much heat.

III. Liquid Fuels

A. **Petroleum**, also known as crude oil, was formed from the remains of organisms that died millions of years ago.
1. These remains were buried in mud and rock beneath shallow seas.
2. Today most petroleum is found deep below the Earth's surface in certain kinds of rock formations.
3. In some areas, petroleum is also found below the Earth's surface a short distance from the seashore.
4. Raw petroleum is not used as a fuel but is broken up into different materials and refined. From petroleum we get such liquid fuels as fuel oil, diesel oil, gasoline, and kerosene. From petroleum we also get such commercially important materials as naphtha, benzene, lubricating oil, grease, and paraffin.

IV. Gas Fuels

A. Gas fuels include natural gas and artificial gases.

B. Natural gas is found together with petroleum deposits and near coalfields.

  1. Because it is denser than air, natural gas can be stored in underground caves.

C. Artificial gases are made from soft coal, coke, and petroleum.

D. All gas fuels have an advantage over both solid and liquid fuels in that they burn instantly.

  1. Moreover, gas fuels are clean and easy to handle and can be piped all over the country.
  2. Gas fuels also give much heat, produce no smoke, and leave no ash.

V. Alternative Fuels

A. Scientists and engineers search for energy alternatives.

B. The Earth continuously produces heat, primarily by the decay of naturally radioactive chemical elements that occur in small amounts in all rocks.

  1. The annual heat loss from the Earth is enormous—equivalent to 10 times the annual energy consumption of the United States—and more than enough to power all nations of the world if it could be fully harnessed.
  2. If only 1% of the thermal energy contained within the uppermost 10 kilometers (62 mi) of the Earth's crust could be harnessed, it could replace 500 times that contained in all oil and natural gas resources of the world.

C. **Hot springs** are formed when underground water is heated by hot rock and gases beneath the Earth's surface. The heated water then flows to the surface.

  1. The passageway along which the hot water travels is wide and open, so the water reaches the surface quickly and easily.
  2. The temperature of the water may range from just warm to boiling.
  3. On its way to the surface, the hot water dissolves large amounts of minerals.
  4. As the water evaporates, these minerals are deposited around the mouth of the hot spring and tend to build up colored layers or terraces.

D. A **geyser** is a hot spring that sprays its water high into the air at intervals.

  1. This eruption of water occurs because the geyser has to travel a narrow, twisted pathway, rather than a wide passage, to reach the Earth's surface.
  2. Heated water is often trapped in the passageway, where it continues to be heated far above its boiling point of 100°C (212°F) without being changed into steam.
  3. The reason for such superheating is that at higher than atmospheric pressure, the boiling point of water increases as well. Water heated above its boiling point without turning to steam is called superheated water.
  4. The superheated water expands and causes some of the water above it to overflow onto the Earth's surface.
  5. The loss of water above eases the pressure on the superheated water below, so that some of it is suddenly changed to steam, which blows all the water above it high into the air as a geyser.
  6. After the geyser erupts, some of the water flows back into the passageway, where it meets more underground water coming up, and the process repeats itself.

E. The Geysers, a hydrothermal system in northern California, uses geothermal (Earth's heat) energy to move large turbines to produce electricity.

  1. Actually, "The Geysers" is not a spouting geyser or system of geysers but a field of slow erupting vents, warm springs, and fumaroles.
  2. Pipes set deep into ground wells carry steam to turbine generators that, in turn, generate electricity.
  3. Other countries using geothermal energy to create electrical energy are El Salvador, Nicaragua, and Costa Rica. In Iceland and in some areas around Paris, France, geothermal energy is used to heat water and buildings.

F. The **fuel cell** was first discovered in 1839, when Sir William Grove of England discovered that electricity can be generated by supplying hydrogen and oxygen to two separate electrodes immersed in dilute sulfuric acid.

  1. Today, the fuel cell is a form of continuously operating battery, able to transform the chemical energy of various fuels into a flow of electrons—electricity.
  2. The U.S. space shuttles use alkaline potassium hydroxide fuel cells to supply electricity and drinking water.
  3. Buses driven by methanol fuel cells are in use in urban transit systems.
  4. The Southern California Gas Company has several phosphoric acid fuel cell plants on line.

Exploratory Activities for "Heat, Fire, and Fuels"

1. AN EXPLORATORY STUDY OF TEMPERATURE SCALES (ANY GRADE LEVEL)

Modify the activities that follow according to the interests, age, and maturity of your students.

1.1 Make Ribbon Temperature Scales

Teacher Preparatory Activity

Obtain some sturdy white cardboard about 76 centimeters (30 in.) long and 25 centimeters (10 in.) wide. Cut slits 2 centimeters (3/4 in.) wide in the center of the cardboard near the top and the bottom (Figure 18.9). Obtain pieces of red ribbon and white ribbon, each about 13 millimeters (1/2 in.) wide. Sew one end of the red ribbon neatly and firmly to one end of the white ribbon. Slip the loose ends of the red and the white ribbon through the slits, as shown in the diagram. Cut off any excess ribbon and sew the other two ribbon ends together. Now, by pulling the ribbon at the back, you can make the red ribbon (which represents the mercury or alcohol in a thermometer) rise or fall. Use felt-tip marker to mark the distance between both slits in equal divisions to produce an accurate representation of the Fahrenheit scale.

Prepare a second ribbon thermometer illustrating the Celsius (centigrade) scale. Then prepare a third thermometer showing a Fahrenheit scale on one side of the ribbon and a Celsius scale on the other side.

Student Activity

Have the students study each scale separately. Let them take readings with actual thermometers of the temperature of the room, hot and cold liquids, and other materials for which they are interested in finding temperatures. Find the boiling point and the freezing point of water on each thermometer and scale (using a mixture of ice and water for the freezing point). Point out that the boiling point and freezing point vary, depending on how far above sea level you are located.

After the students have mastered reading each scale separately, show them the ribbon thermometer containing both scales. Compare such fixed points as the boiling and freezing points of water on both scales. Show the students how to convert temperatures from one scale to another, checking the results on the ribbon thermometer.

1.2 Making an Air Thermometer

For older students or as a teacher demonstration: Obtain a small flask or bottle, a one-hole rubber stopper, and a narrow glass or plastic tube 45 centimeters (18 in.) long. Insert the tube into the stopper and fit the stopper tightly into the neck of the flask. Support the flask with an iron ring attached to a ringstand, as shown in Figure 18.10.

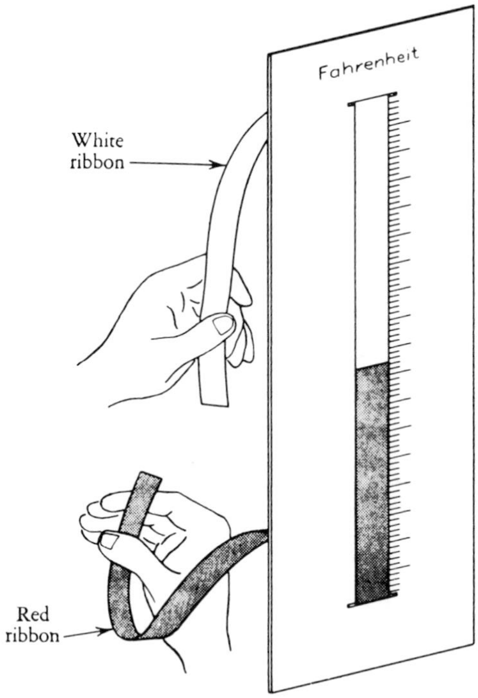

FIGURE 18.9 A red and white ribbon thermometer.

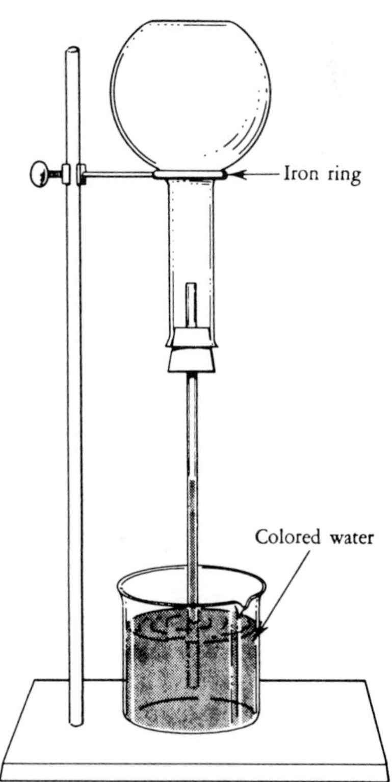

FIGURE 18.10 An air thermometer works differently from a liquid thermometer.

Place the end of the tube in a beaker or tumbler of water colored very deep red with food coloring.

Heat the flask very gently with a small Bunsen burner flame or with an alcohol lamp, moving the flame back and forth along the flask. The heat will cause the air inside the flask to expand, and bubbles of air will leave the bottom of the tube. Drive out enough air so that when the flame is removed and the air inside the flask cools and contracts, the colored water rises a sizable distance up the tube. Point out that the air pressure on the surface of the colored water forced the water up the tube, taking the place of the air that was driven out of the flask.

Now put your hands in hot water, dry them, and place them around the flask. The colored water will be driven down the tube as the air inside becomes warm and expands. Cool your hands and place them around the flask. This time the colored water will rise up the tube, as the air inside the flask cools and contracts. If you like, prepare a cardboard temperature scale behind the air thermometer and let the students take daily room temperature readings.

2. AN EXPLORATORY STUDY OF HEAT CONDUCTORS (GRADES 4–8)

2.1 Exploring Metals as Conductors

Into a cup of hot water, put a sterling silver spoon, a silver-plated spoon, and a stainless steel spoon. Note which spoon handle becomes the hottest. Repeat the learning activity, using rods of different materials such as brass, iron, and copper.

2.2 Exploring Other Materials as Conductors

Into a cup of hot water, put rods of such materials as wood, glass, and plastic. Use rods of equal length and thickness. Note that the parts above the surface of the water do not become hot, or even warm. Put a piece of rubber tubing in the hot water. The end outside the water will not become hot.

2.3 Exploring the Use of Nonconductors

Wrap some cloth around one end of a metal rod and place the other end into the flame of a Bunsen burner or alcohol lamp. Because the cloth is a poor conductor of heat, you will not burn your hand even though the metal rod becomes very hot. Repeat this learning activity, using some thicknesses of paper wrapped around the metal rod.

2.4 Exploring Water as a Conductor

Fill a Pyrex test tube almost full of cold water and clamp the test tube to a ringstand (Figure 18.11). Have the clamp nearer to the bottom of the test tube. Now heat the top of the test tube with the flame of a Bunsen burner or alcohol lamp, moving the flame back and forth, until the water boils. Carefully feel the bottom of the test tube. The water will still be cold.

2.5 Exploring Air as a Conductor of Heat

Hold one end of a short metal rod and place the other end in the flame of a Bunsen burner or alcohol lamp. In a very short time, the end of the rod you are holding will become hot, as the heat travels along the rod by conduction.

Let the metal rod become cool and repeat the learning activity, this time holding the end of the rod with a heat-proof mitt. At the same time, hold with your bare hand one end of a second short rod about 2 centimeters (1 in.) away from the end of the first rod (Figure 18.12).

The second rod will remain cool because air is a poor conductor of heat.

3. AN EXPERIMENTAL STUDY: CHANGING SYSTEMS (GRADES 4–8)

Overview

This investigation will help students understand what a system is and how energy affects it.

Materials Needed (One set of the following for each group of about four students): beaker, thermometer, ring stand, clamp, test tube, aluminum foil, cork, straight pins,

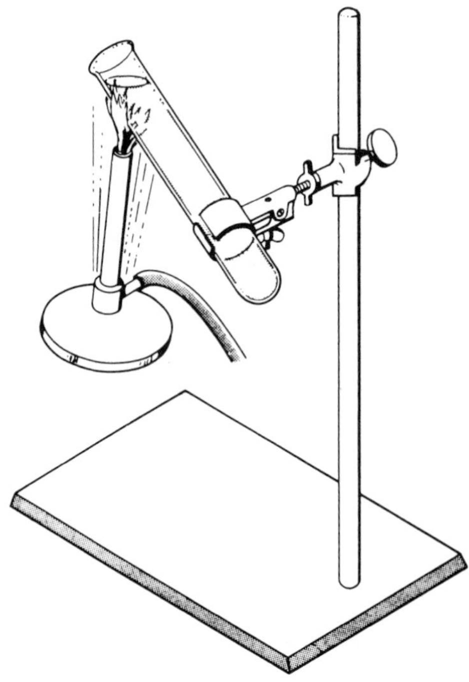

FIGURE 18.11 The water at the top of the test tube will boil while the water at the bottom is still cold.

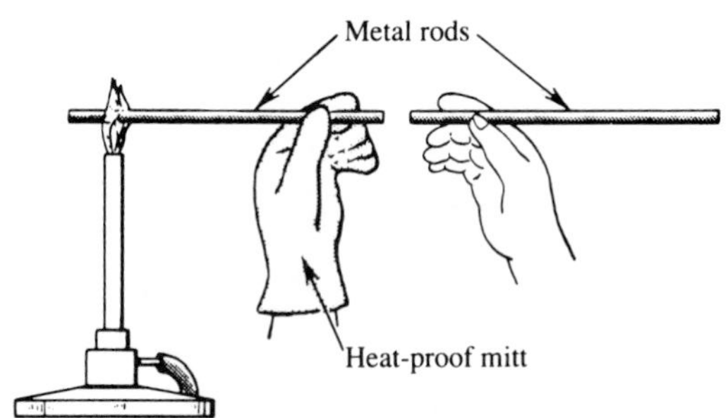

FIGURE 18.12 Because air is a poor heat conductor, the second rod remains cool.

various kinds of nuts (almond, walnut, peanut), water, scales (suitable for weighing a nut).

Focusing Questions

1. What is a system?
2. Can you name some examples of systems?
3. Do systems ever change?
4. We are going to test nuts for their energy content by burning them. Which nut do you predict will cause the greatest change in the temperature of the water?

Procedure

1. Add 25 ml of water to your test tube.
2. Suspend the test tube with a clamp to the ring stand.
3. Cover a cork with aluminum foil and stick a pin in it, then place the cork beneath the test tube.
4. Select a nut and weigh it.
5. Stick one of the nuts onto the pin.
6. Record the temperature of the water in the test tube.
7. Ignite the nut with a match.
8. Record the temperature of the water every 30 seconds for 4 minutes even if the nut burns out.
9. Record the temperatures on the chart to the right.
10. Weigh the cooled nut after burning.
11. Graph your results.

Temperature	*Peanut*	*Walnut*	*Almond*
Start: 0 sec.			
30 sec.			
1 min.			
90 sec.			
2 min.			
2.5 min.			
3 min.			
3.5 min.			
4 min.			

Closing Questions

1. While the nut was burning, in what way did the water system change?
2. Is the amount of change in the water system related to the amount of change in the nut system? Is there a way you can test this?
3. As the nut and water systems changed, what other system changed?
4. Which nut produced the greatest amount of heat energy? Why do you suppose this was so?

Chapter 19

Sound

Anthony Magnacca/Merrill

Producing and Transmitting Sound

I. **Sound and Its Characteristics**

A. Sound is an effect of mechanical radiation.

1. **Radiation** is the movement of energy from one place to another.
2. There are three general categories of radiation: mechanical, electromagnetic (Chapter 20), and particle (Chapter 16).
3. Mechanical radiation requires a material medium to proliferate energy from one place to another.

B. As an effect of mechanical radiation, sound is caused by an object that is moving back and forth, or vibrating.

1. Vibrations from the source disturb the molecules in the surrounding air and establish radiating waves of sound energy.
2. Plucking, stroking, blowing, and hitting can produce sound vibrations.
3. Sound cannot travel at all in a vacuum, where there are no molecules to vibrate and transmit the sound energy.
4. If there is a medium, such as air, vibrating waves move out in all directions from the vibrating source.
5. Perception of sound depends on three factors: a vibrating source that sets up the sound waves, a medium such as air to carry the waves, and a receiver to detect them.
6. Pleasant sounds, produced by regular vibrations, are called **music.** Harsh or unpleasant sounds, produced by irregular vibrations, are known as **noise.**

II. **How Sound Travels**

A. When an object, such as a violin string or a tuning fork, is made to vibrate, the sound energy travels out as waves in all directions.

1. When the string vibrates, it moves back and forth very rapidly. As it moves forward, it pushes against the molecules of air in front of it and presses them closer together. The space in which the molecules are pressed closer together is called a **compression.**
2. As the string moves backward, it leaves a space with fewer molecules in it, and these molecules spread farther apart. The space in which the molecules are spread farther apart is called a **rarefaction.**
3. One compression and one rarefaction together make up one complete **sound wave,** or **vibration,** or **cycle.** As an object vibrates back and forth, it produces cycles of compression and rarefaction, one after another.
4. Sound is measured by the number of cycles produced per second. This number is referred to as the **frequency** of the sound. Frequency is measured in units called **hertz** (Hz). One hertz is one complete cycle, or vibration back and forth.

LEARNING ACTIVITY 19.1

A Visual Simulation of Sound Vibrations

Although sound waves and water waves are quite different kinds of waves, water waves can be used to simulate sound waves. Strike a tuning fork with a soft mallet and touch the tip of the vibrating fork into the surface of a beaker of water. Ask students to describe what they see. Ask students whether effects of sound can be felt as well as heard and seen. Very low frequency sounds can sometimes be felt. (Students have probably felt the low frequency sounds that come from some car radios as they pass on the street. You can touch a radio speaker and feel the vibrations. Likewise, you can touch your throat and feel the vibrations of your vocal cords when you speak in low tones.)

Inquiry-Based Learning Activity 19.1. Modified

Sound is something we hear, but it is possible to see what sound can do. This activity will require three tuning forks of different sizes. Set up three stations each with a bowl of water and a tuning fork. Have students tap the tuning forks and touch the base of the tuning fork to the side of the bowl of water and observe vibrations in the water. Which tuning fork makes the smallest waves? Which tuning fork makes the biggest waves? Why do they think this is the case? The students should each write a short paragraph discussing their thoughts and ideas. **What level of inquiry is this modification?** This activity does not give students data, but the limitations of their actions and the observations the students will make is highly structured. As a result, the activity resides at ***Level I*** across all three segments (**Problem Identification, Process,** and **Solutions**). **Some questions to consider.** Are highly structured ***Level I*** activities as useful as ***Level III*** activities for helping students learn science? How may highly structured activities be used to help students to become more independent over time?

5. The presence of cycles of alternating compression and rarefaction means that the molecules of air have also been made to move back and forth, or vibrate.
6. As the molecules of air vibrate, they bump into other molecules and cause these molecules to vibrate, which then causes still other molecules to vibrate.
7. No single vibrating molecule travels very far. Each moves back and forth, pushing against other molecules, as the sound waves radiate out in all directions.

B. Most sounds come to us through the atmosphere, which is composed of gases.
   1. The speed of sound in air at sea level is about 336 meters per second (1,100 fps), or about 1 kilometer in 3 seconds (1 mi in 5 secs).
   2. The warmer the air, the greater the speed of sound will be. The speed of sound in air increases about 30 centimeters per second (1 fps) for every degree rise in Fahrenheit temperature, or about 60 centimeters per second (2 fps) for every degree rise in Celsius temperature.
   3. High on a mountain, the air is thinner and does not contain as many molecules as the air in a valley. Therefore, in the upper atmosphere sound does not travel as fast as it does at lower elevations.

C. Sound travels faster and farther through liquids than through gases. It travels about 1,464 meters per second (4,800 fps) in water, or about four times as fast as in air.

D. Sound travels faster and farther through hard solids than through liquids or gases.
   1. Sound travels more than 3,000 meters per second (10,000 fps) through wood, or about nine times as fast as in air.
   2. Sound travels more than 5,000 meters per second (16,500 fps) through steel, or 15 times as fast as in air.

E. Soft solids, such as cork, rubber, felt, and cotton, are poor conductors of sound because they tend to absorb sound waves rather than to conduct them. Therefore, soft solids that are poor conductors are used for soundproofing.

III. Differences in Sound

A. Humans perceive differences in sound. These differences are pitch, intensity, and quality (or timbre).

B. **Pitch** is related to a sound's frequency.
   1. When a body is vibrating, it produces a certain number of vibrations, or sound wave cycles, per second.
   2. The faster a body vibrates, the more vibrations it produces per second, and the higher the sound's frequency, or pitch. The slower a body vibrates, the fewer vibrations it produces per second, and the lower the sound's frequency, or pitch.
   3. The human ear cannot hear all possible frequencies, only those within a range of about 20 cycles per second to 20,000 cycles per second.
   4. Frequencies lower than the human ear can hear are called **subsonic**, and frequencies higher than the human ear can hear are called **supersonic** or **ultrasonic.** Because dogs can hear sounds above the human maximum range of 20,000 cycles per second, whistles that are pitched at supersonic frequencies are used to call dogs.
   5. Extremely low frequencies (below 10 Hz) and extremely high frequencies (of 100,000 to 500,000 Hz) can cause physical and chemical reactions. Ultrasonic sound waves can kill bacteria, insects, and pests; control and operate automatic garage doors; clean clothes by shaking the dirt out of them; and cause water and oil to form an emulsion.

C. A sound's **wavelength** is the distance between its compressions (or between its rarefactions), which is another way to define the pitch of a tone.
   1. The wavelength of a particular sound is equal to the velocity (*V*) of sound divided by the frequency (*f*) of the sound. The formula is

$$\lambda = \frac{V}{f}$$

   Because in air, sound travels at about 336 meters per second (1,100 fps), to find the wavelength for a particular sound you would divide 336 by that sound's frequency.
   2. If the source of a sound is moving, such as a car's horn while the car is speeding by, the distance between the crests of the sound waves is compressed in one direction and lengthened in the opposite direction. This compression and lengthening of a sound wave will change the frequency of the sound, a phenomenon known as the **Doppler effect.**

D. **Intensity** is the loudness or softness of a sound. It has nothing to do with the pitch.
   1. The loudness or softness of a sound depends on the distance the object is vibrating, which is known as **amplitude.** The greater the amplitude, the more energy the sound wave has. The more energy put into making a sound, the louder the sound will be.
   2. The farther sound waves travel, the softer the sound becomes, because as the waves move away from the source of the sound, they lose energy and decrease in amplitude.
   3. The unit of measurement of sound intensity is the **decibel.** A machine called the sound-level or decibel meter measures decibels. Whispering produces 10 to 20 decibels of sound. Talking rather loudly produces about 60 decibels. Heavy traffic noises produce about 70 to 80 decibels. Thunder produces about 110 decibels. The threshold

of human pain caused by sound is 120 decibels. The loudest automobile stereos have been measured at 154 decibels.

E. The **quality** of a sound tells us the difference between various musical instruments, or between different persons who are producing a similar sound.
   1. Even though sounds have the same pitch and intensity, they can appear different.
   2. This occurs because, when an object vibrates, it produces a fundamental frequency and overtones, or multiples of the fundamental tone.
   3. When this multiple vibration takes place, sounds of different frequencies are heard at the same time.
   4. The lowest sound a vibrating body produces is called the **fundamental tone.**
   5. The other sounds that the vibrating body produces simultaneously, but that have different frequencies, are called **overtones.**
   6. The quality of a sound depends on the number and strength of the various overtones that are produced.

IV. Hearing Sound

A. When sound waves reach the ear, they are changed to electrical signals that are carried by the auditory nerve to the brain, where they are then translated into what we know as sound.

B. Most animals, including humans, can hear a much broader frequency range than they can produce (see Chapter 14). This wider range of hearing likely provides a survival advantage in the wild.

C. Animals have adapted hearing mechanisms in different ways.
   1. Cicadas have hearing organs at the base of the abdomen, in their stomachs. Crickets have hearing organs in the oval slits of their forelegs. The cockroach hears with hairs on its abdomen. A caterpillar hears with the hairs all over its body.
   2. A snake picks up sound waves with its tongue.
   3. Bats and dolphins use echolocation, picking up the reflection of their own high-pitched squeaks.
   4. Some moths have developed a defensive mechanism against the bat by producing sounds that mimic the bat's, thereby jamming the bat's signal. Others alter the frequency by which they beat their own wings, thereby confusing the predator bat.
   5. In humans, the sense of hearing is located in the ear (discussed in Chapter 15).

D. An **echo** is a sound wave that bounces back, or is reflected, from a hard surface such as a cliff or a wall of a building.
   1. To hear an echo we must be at least 17 meters (56 ft) away from the reflecting surface.
   2. The farther away the reflecting surface is, the longer it will take to hear the echo. If we are too far away, of course, no echo will be heard.
   3. Sometimes a sound wave bounces off many surfaces and produces a series of echoes.
   4. Unwanted echoes can be prevented or reduced in several ways.
      a. Soft drapes on walls and window frames, and rugs on the floor can be used to absorb sound waves and prevent echoes.
      b. Covering the ceilings and the walls with rough materials or materials with many little holes in them can break up sound waves so that few reflect back to cause echoes.
      c. Sound waves are also absorbed by people present in an auditorium, thus reducing the echo effect.

V. The Voice

A. At the top of the windpipe, or trachea, in your throat is the voice box, or **larynx.**
   1. Stretched over the top of the larynx are two thin but strong bands of tissue called the vocal cords.
   2. When air from the lungs is blown through a narrow slit (the glottis) between these two cords, the cords are made to vibrate by the moving air and sound is produced.

B. Muscles attached to the vocal cords make the cords tight or loose and this controls the pitch of your voice.
   1. The tighter the vocal cords, the faster they vibrate and the higher the pitch.
   2. The greater the force with which air is blown between the vocal cords, the louder the sound.

C. Men's vocal cords are usually longer and thicker than those of women and so do not vibrate as fast. This difference explains why men have lower or deeper voices than women. A young male's vocal cords become longer and thicker as he gets older. As a result, his voice changes from a relatively high pitch to a lower one.

D. The quality of a person's voice depends on several factors.
   1. The strength and control of the vocal cords affect the quality of a person's voice. The muscles that control our vocal cords can be strengthened and controlled through practice.
   2. Air passages in the throat, mouth, and nose, as well as the sinuses of the head, also affect the quality of the voice. Passages that are opened wide and are free of mucus give a better voice quality than passages that are occluded and less open.
   3. The position of the lips, tongue, and teeth also functions in determining the kind and quality of sounds produced.

Musical Instruments

I. Musical Instruments

A. Musical instruments are devices used to produce pleasant sounds of different pitch, intensity, and quality.
   1. There are three categories of musical instruments: stringed instruments, wind instruments, and percussion instruments.

B. **Stringed instruments** contain one or more strings that are made vibrate in different ways to produce musical sounds.
   1. Some strings are stroked or rubbed with a bow, as in the violin, cello, and bass viol. Some strings are plucked either with the fingers or with a pick, as in the ukulele, guitar, banjo, and harp. In the piano, small hammers strike the strings.
   2. The pitch, or frequency, of all the musical sounds produced by stringed instruments can be changed in three different ways.
      a. The looser the string, the lower the pitch; the tighter the string, the higher the pitch.
      b. The longer the string, the lower the pitch; the shorter the string, the higher the pitch.
      c. The thicker the string, the lower the pitch; the thinner the string, the higher the pitch.
   3. Stringed instruments, including the violin, cello, and banjo, have just a few strings that are attached to pegs. The strings are of different thickness that produce sounds of higher or lower pitch. Pegs can be used to tighten or loosen the strings and make the pitch higher or lower. When these instruments are played, the fingers move up and down the vibrating strings, making them longer and shorter, thus producing lower and higher musical sounds.
   4. Instruments such as the harp and the piano have a great many strings. Their strings differ in length, thickness, and tightness to produce sounds of different pitch. The harp also has pedals that can pull the strings tighter and make them produce sounds with a higher pitch.
   5. Sounds from stringed instruments can be made louder or softer. The harder a string is bowed or plucked, the more strongly it vibrates and the louder the sound. The more gently a string is bowed or plucked, the more weakly it vibrates and the softer the sound. Furthermore, when a string vibrates, it makes the entire instrument vibrate at the same frequency, or pitch.
   6. The vibrating instrument makes the air surrounding the instrument vibrate at the same frequency as well. The large amount of vibrating air reinforces the original vibrations of the string and makes them stronger, which means the sound will be louder. In the piano, a sounding board above the strings vibrates, rather than the entire piano.
   7. Some instruments, such as the violin and the guitar, have openings to airspace within them. Not only does the instrument vibrate, but because the sound waves enter the instrument, the air inside it vibrates at the same pitch, or frequency. The vibrating air joins and reinforces the original vibrations, making them stronger and producing a louder sound. Reinforcement of the original vibrations to make the sound louder is called **resonance.**
   8. Sounds made by stringed instruments differ in quality.
   9. When a string vibrates, the whole string vibrates. The tone produced is called the **fundamental tone.**
   10. A vibrating string can vibrate not only as a whole but also in parts at the same time. When a string vibrates in two parts, it is just as if two shorter strings were vibrating, with each part just half as long as the original string. These shorter strings vibrate twice as fast, producing a tone called an **overtone.**
   11. Vibrating as a whole, the string produces its fundamental tone, which is the lowest tone it can produce. Vibrating in parts, the string produces overtones, which are higher than the fundamental tone.
   12. The quality of the sound depends on the number and strength of the overtones that are produced. The quality also depends on the size, shape, and material of the instrument, because these factors help to determine how many overtones will be produced.

C. **Wind instruments** contain a column of air that is made to vibrate to produce musical sounds.
   1. The air column can be made to vibrate either by blowing into it, as is done with the clarinet, saxophone, and trumpet, or by blowing across it, as is done with the flute and piccolo.
   2. Wind instruments are divided into two main classes: woodwind and brass.
   3. In all **woodwind instruments**, except the flute and the piccolo, a thin piece of wood or plastic, called a reed, is used to make the air column vibrate. The reed is in the mouthpiece of the instrument.
   4. Blowing into the mouthpiece makes the reed vibrate, which then makes the air column vibrate.
   5. In the flute and the piccolo, we blow across a hole to start the air column vibrating.
   6. Examples of woodwind instruments include the flute, piccolo, clarinet, oboe, bassoon, and English horn. The saxophone uses a reed but is made of brass, so it belongs partly to the brass family.

7. **Brass instruments** are made of brass and are played by vibrating the lips while they are pressed against the mouthpiece of the instrument. Examples of brass instruments are the saxophone, trumpet, cornet, bugle, trombone, French horn, and tuba.
8. The vibration of the lips starts the air column vibrating.
9. Making the air column longer or shorter can change the pitch or frequency of the vibrating air column. The longer the air column, the lower the pitch; the shorter the air column, the higher the pitch.
10. Woodwind instruments have a series of holes, usually covered by pads called keys. Pressing or releasing the keys opens or closes the holes, making the length of the air column inside the instrument longer or shorter.
11. Some brass instruments, such as the trumpet and the tuba, have valves that control the length of the air column.
12. The slide trombone has a slide that moves in and out to control the length of the air column. The valve trombone has valves; it works like a trumpet but sounds like a trombone.
13. Because it has no valves or slide to move in and out, there is no way to change the length of the air column in the bugle, so the different notes are produced by changing both the tightness of the lips and the force of the air blown into the instrument.
14. Many wind instruments, especially brass instruments with valves or a slide, also depend on the tightness of the lips and the force of the breath to produce notes of different pitch.
15. Sounds from wind instruments differ in quality. An air column not only vibrates as a whole but also vibrates in parts at the same time, producing overtones. The quality of the sound depends on the number and strength of overtones produced. The quality also depends on the size, shape, and material of the instrument, because these factors help to determine how many overtones will be produced.
16. Blowing harder into a wind instrument will make the air column inside the instrument vibrate more strongly and produce a louder sound. At the same time, the air column vibrates in parts. These new vibrations join and reinforce the original vibrations produced by the air column vibrating as a whole. This combination of vibrations makes the air column vibrate more strongly and produces a louder sound. In most wind instruments, blowing harder can make the sound not only louder but higher as well.

D. **Percussion instruments** are made of either solid materials, such as wood and metal, or materials stretched over a hollow container.
   1. The solid or stretched materials are struck by mallets, hammers, or the hands, which makes the materials vibrate and produce sounds.
   2. Percussion instruments made of solid materials include the xylophone, glockenspiel, triangle, cymbals, chimes, bells, castanets, and wood block.
   3. Percussion instruments made of material stretched over a hollow container include the bongo drum, snare drum, bass drum, kettledrum, and tambourine.
   4. In percussion instruments made of solid materials, the longer the material, the lower the pitch; the shorter the material, the higher the pitch.
   5. In percussion instruments made of a material stretched over a hollow container, the pitch can be changed in different ways.
      a. The tighter the covering, the higher the pitch; the looser the covering, the lower the pitch.
      b. The thinner the covering, the higher the pitch; the thicker the covering, the lower the pitch.
      c. The smaller the diameter of the instrument, the higher the pitch; the larger the diameter, the lower the pitch.
   6. Striking percussion instruments harder will make them vibrate more strongly and produce louder sounds. At the same time, the vibrating materials make the air around them vibrate at the same frequency. The large amount of vibrating air reinforces the original vibrations and makes them stronger, producing louder sounds.
   7. The hollow containers of percussion instruments like the drum, the marimba, and the chimes also help produce louder sounds. The column of air inside the container vibrates at the same frequency as the original sound, reinforcing the original vibrations and making them much stronger, thus producing a louder sound.

LEARNING ACTIVITY 19.2

Sounds Produced by Musical Instruments

Obtain, or have students bring to class, a variety of instruments, making sure you have adequate representation of stringed, wind, and percussion instruments. For each instrument, show how sounds are produced, made higher or lower, and made louder or softer. Have the students produce sounds of the same pitch and intensity from various instruments and note the difference in the quality of the sounds. Discuss the formation of overtones in each instrument and their relationship to the quality of the musical sounds produced.

Exploratory Activities for "Sound"

1. EXPLORING THE PRODUCTION AND TRANSMISSION OF SOUND (ANY GRADE LEVEL)

Review the following set of 11 activities and, depending on the age and maturity of your students, decide the best approach for involving them in the activities. One approach is to establish several learning stations, each with complete instructions for doing one of the activities, and have the students take turns visiting the stations in groups of three or four. Instructions given here for each activity may have to be rewritten, depending on how it is to be used.

1.1 Sound is Produced by Vibrating Objects

Give students the following instructions: Hold one end of a rubber band in your teeth and stretch the band. Pluck the band, noting the vibration and the sound produced. What do you notice? (The vibration is so rapid that it produces a blur. Note that when the vibration stops, the sound stops.) Now set a tuning fork vibrating by striking one prong sharply against your kneecap or the rubber heel of your shoe. (Never strike a tuning fork against a hard object.) Hold one end of a sheet of paper and touch one prong lightly to the other end of the paper. What do you conclude? (The vibrating prong will make the paper rattle, showing that the prong is, indeed, vibrating.) Feel the vibrations by touching the vibrating prongs lightly with the fingertips. Now place tissue paper against the teeth of a comb and hum a tune. What do you feel? (Students will feel the vibrations as a ticklish sensation on their lips.)

1.2 How Sound Travels

Pour some water into a tub or basin. Dip your finger quickly into the water and then pull it out. Draw a diagram of what you observe. How do you think this relates to the way sound travels? (Waves are produced and spread out in concentric spheres. Point out that sound waves themselves are not like water waves, but their methods of travel are somewhat alike.)

1.3 Sound Travels in All Directions

Place students in four corners of the room, facing the wall. Have one student in the middle of the room produce a sound. Let the students raise their hands as soon as they hear the sound. Have the students write down their tentative conclusion about the direction in which sound travels. Now place one student at the top of the stairs, a second student half-way down, and a third student at the foot of the stairs. Have the student half-way down the stairs make a sound. Have students check their original conclusion and modify it if necessary. (The sound will travel up and down, as well as in all horizontal directions.) Now fill a large beaker or tumbler with water. Strike the prongs of a tuning fork very sharply against your kneecap or the rubber heel of your shoe, and then quickly place the ends of the prongs in the center of the water (Figure 19.1). Write down what you observed. (The vibrating prongs will make the water splash out of the beaker in all directions.) Again, what do you conclude about the direction that sound travels?

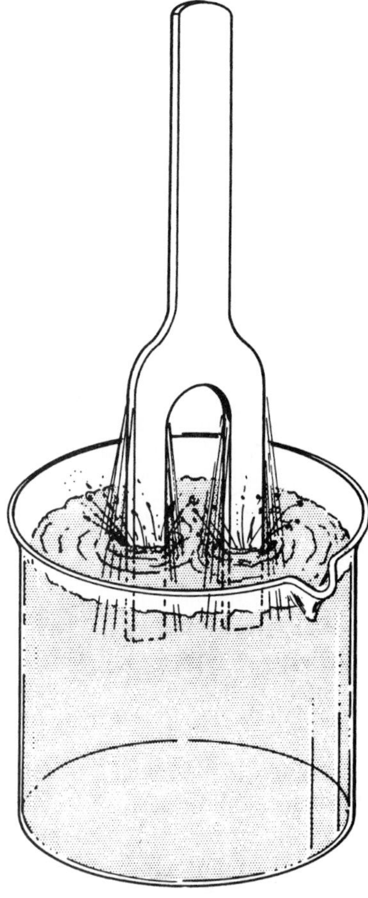

FIGURE 19.1 The vibrating tuning fork scatters water in all directions.

1.4 Sound Travels by Means of Compression and Rarefaction of Molecules

Obtain a Slinky (a walking spring coil) from a toy store. Attach one end to a hook, high off the floor, and allow the rest of the Slinky to stretch to the floor (Figure 19.2). Instruct students as follows: Press together two of the stretched coils close to the floor, and then release these coils suddenly. What do you observe? (An impulse, consisting of a series of compressions and rarefactions, will travel the length of the Slinky.) Compare this movement with the way sound travels by means of compressions and rarefactions of molecules. (Point out that each coil—and molecule—moves back and forth just a little, yet the result is an extensive movement and travel of the impulse.)

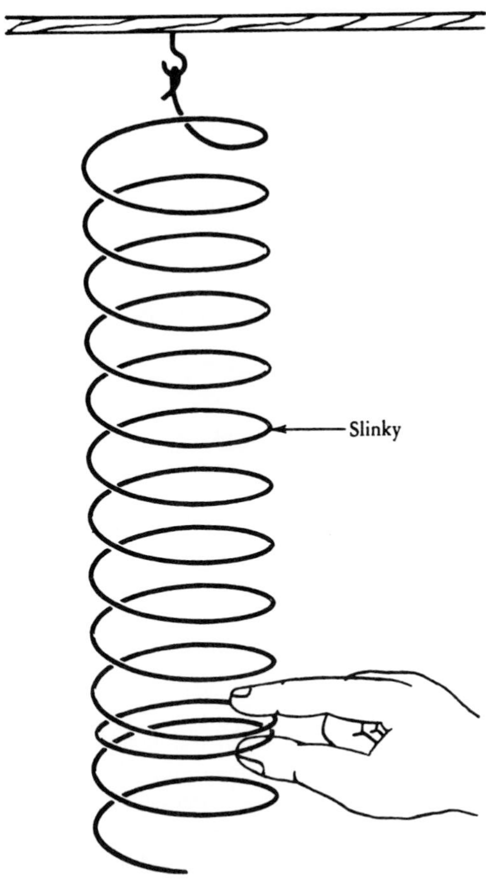

FIGURE 19.2 A Slinky shows how sound travels by compression and rarefaction of molecules.

1.5 Sound Travels Through Solids

Position two students at opposite ends of a table. Have one student scratch the table top so lightly with a fingernail that the other student cannot hear the sound. Now have the second student place one ear against the end of the table, and have the first student scratch the table top again. Ask, What do you observe? (The second student will hear the scratching sound very clearly, because sound travels faster through solids than through air.)

1.6 Sound Travels Through Liquids

Fill a large aquarium with water. Click two spoons together about 15 centimeters (6 in.) from a student's ear. Have the student put his or her ear against one end of the aquarium. Click the spoons again, this time under water in the aquarium. Ask, What do you conclude about sound traveling through water? (The student will hear the sound.)

1.7 Sound Travels Through Gases

Send one student out of the room with one end of a garden hose, and have another student speak softly into the other end. Ask, What do you observe? (The student outside will be able to hear the words very clearly. This activity also shows that sounds can be directed.) Students may want to make their own "phones," using a long piece of string with Styrofoam or paper cups or aluminum soft drink cans. The string can be connected through a hole in the bottom of each cup or can and tied off inside. Let students experiment with different kinds of containers and string to see which "phone systems" work best.

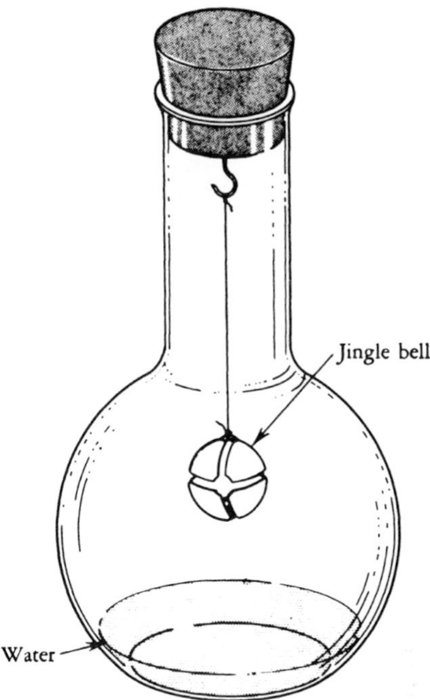

FIGURE 19.3 The sound of the bell cannot be heard in a vacuum.

1.8 Sound Does Not Travel Through a Vacuum (Probably Best as a Teacher Demonstration)

Obtain a large Pyrex flask and a solid rubber stopper that fits the flask. Push a small hook into the underside of the stopper. From the hook, suspend a string that is attached to a small jingle bell so that the bell will hang freely inside the flask when the stopper is inserted (Figure 19.3). Place a small amount of water in the flask, set the flask on a hot plate, and boil the water until almost all the air inside the flask has been driven off and there is mostly steam inside the flask. Remove the flask, insert the stopper, and allow the flask to cool. The steam will condense, leaving a partial vacuum in the flask.

Set up a second (control) flask exactly like the first, but do not boil the water, so the second flask is full of air. Now shake both flasks gently. Compare the loudness of the bell in the partial vacuum with that of the bell in air.

1.9 Investigate Pitch

Have a student draw the edge of an index card over a comb at different speeds. Ask, What do you observe? (The faster the index card moves against the teeth, the faster it vibrates and the higher the sound becomes.)

1.10 Sound Quality

Engage students in the following activity: Push a table against a wall. Attach an electric bell to a piece of wood and

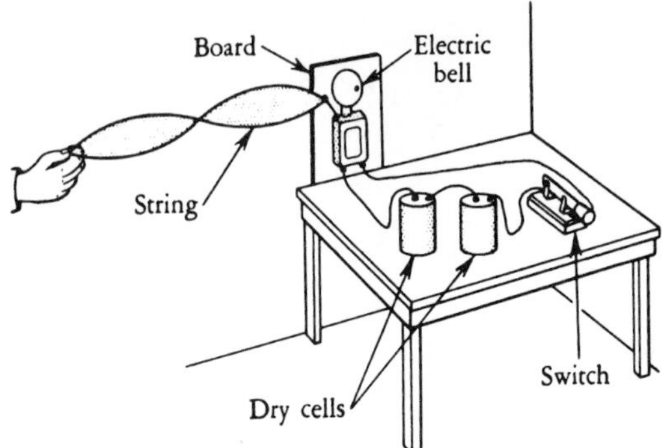

FIGURE 19.4 Forming loops to illustrate fundamental tone and overtones.

bend the clapper so that it will not strike the gong when it is moving back and forth. Connect the bell to two dry cells and a switch, as shown in Figure 19.4. Obtain 3 meters (10 ft) of thin, soft string and attach one end of the string to the clapper. Push down the switch to complete the electric circuit and set the clapper moving back and forth.

Stand some distance away and pull on the string as the clapper vibrates. By experimenting with the amount of pull on the string, you will be able to make the string vibrate as a whole to form just one loop, and then vibrate in parts to form two, three, or even four loops. Compare this formation of loops with the formation of the fundamental tone and overtones in vibrating objects to produce sounds of different quality.

1.11 Exploring the Voice

Have students feel their windpipes while humming or making low sounds. They will feel the vibrations of their vocal cords. Have them make loud and soft sounds, noting the greater force with which air is blown between the vocal cords to produce louder sounds. Let one student say something normally, and then repeat it while pinching his or her nostrils shut. Ask, What do you observe? (Students will note the change in quality of the sounds produced.) Inflate a balloon and allow the air to escape while you pinch and stretch both sides of the neck of the balloon. The more you pinch and stretch the rubber, the higher the sound becomes. Ask, How does this compare with your own ability to make sounds? (This effect compares with the tightening of the vocal cords to produce higher sounds.)

2. EXPLORING MUSIC AND MUSICAL INSTRUMENTS (ANY GRADE LEVEL)

2.1 Comparing Music and Noise

Begin by having the students list unpleasant noises they have heard. Ask them why each was unpleasant. Relate noise with irregular vibrations and music with regular vibrations. Draw a diagram of both regular and irregular vibrations on the chalkboard (Figure 19.5).

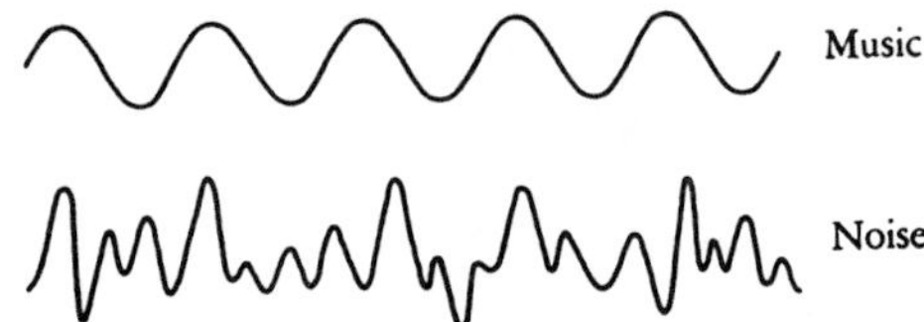

FIGURE 19.5 Diagram showing the difference between music and noise.

2.2 Forced Vibrations Increase the Intensity of Sounds

Strike a tuning fork, hold it up, and have the students listen to the sound produced. Strike the tuning fork again, but this time touch the handle of the tuning fork to a table top or the chalkboard. The vibrating tuning fork will force the table top to vibrate with the same frequency, and the vibrating table top will now force the air around it to vibrate with the same frequency too. This large amount of vibrating air reinforces the original vibrations of the tuning fork, making them stronger so that the sound becomes louder. Show how this same effect is produced with musical instruments.

Now review the following four activities and, depending on the age and maturity of your students, decide the best approach for involving them in these activities. One approach is to divide the class into groups and have each group do one of the activities as a project and then show and report their finished work to the rest of the class. Instructions for each activity will have to be rewritten, depending on how it is used.

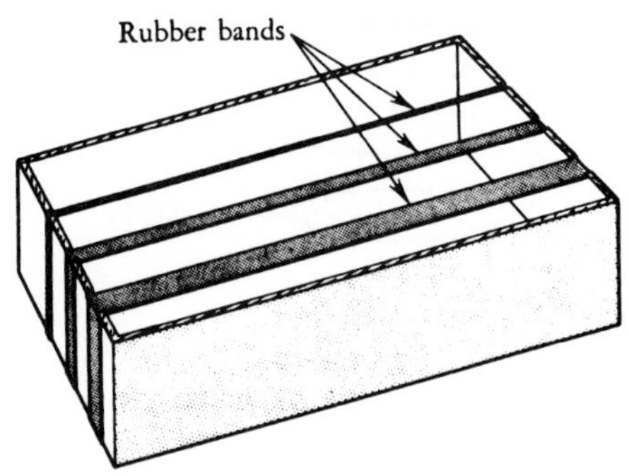

FIGURE 19.6 A stringed instrument made from a cigar box.

2.3 How the Pitch Is Changed in Stringed Instruments

Obtain a cigar box, remove the cover, and cut three grooves on opposite edges of the box. Stretch three rubber bands of equal length, but different thicknesses, lengthwise around the box, placing them in the grooves to keep them in place (Figure 19.6). Give students the following instructions: Pluck each band and note that the thinner the band, the higher the sound will be.

Pluck one band and note the sound produced. Hold the middle of the band with your fingers and pluck either portion of the band that extends from your fingers to one edge of the box. Note that only half of the rubber band now vibrates and the sound is higher. In fact, the sound is now an octave higher than the original sound. Hold the band at different positions. The shorter the length of the vibrating band, the higher the sound will be.

Pluck one rubber band and listen to the note produced. Now pull the band at one end, making it tighter.

FIGURE 19.7 Producing air columns of different sizes in soda bottles.

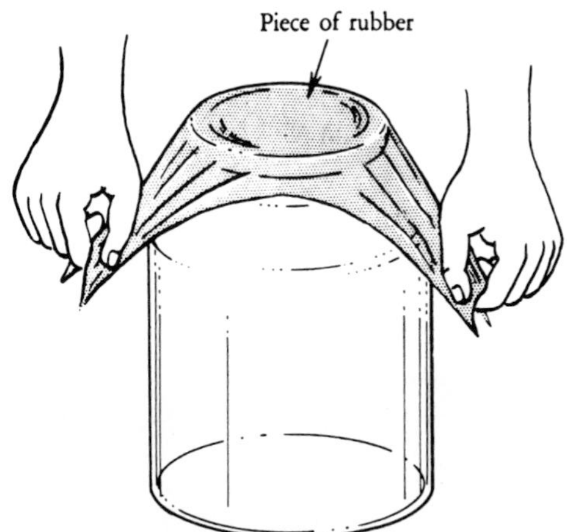

FIGURE 19.8 The tighter the drum head, the higher the sound will become.

Note that the tighter the band becomes, the higher the sound will be.

2.4 Changing the Pitch in Wind Instruments

Give the following instructions: Blow across an empty soda bottle. The sound is produced by the column of vibrating air inside the bottle. Repeat the activity, using bottles of different sizes. The smaller the bottle, the shorter the air column will be and the higher the sound will become.

Obtain eight soda bottles of the same size and line them up in a row. Pour different amounts of water in them, adding or taking away water as needed, until you can produce the eight notes of the scale when you blow across their mouths (Figure 19.7). Note the relationship between the length of the air column in each bottle and the pitch of the sound produced. Prepare a tune to play for the class.

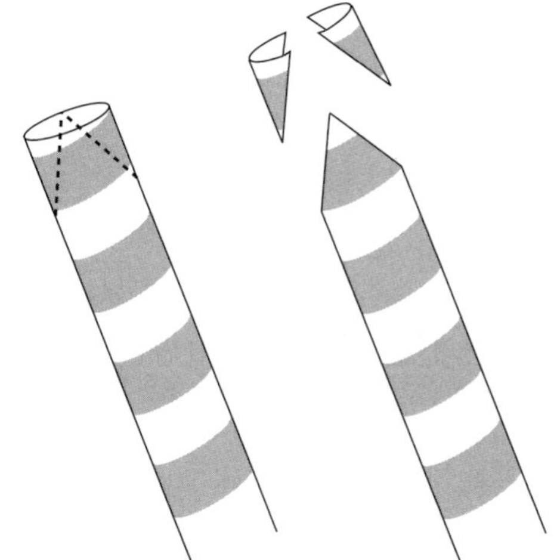

FIGURE 19.9 Making a straw instrument.

2.5 Changing the Pitch of Percussion Instruments

Give students the following instructions: Use a toy xylophone to show that the shorter the bar, the higher the sound. Cut a piece of rubber from a large balloon or an old inner tube and place it over the mouth of a glass jar. Grasp the rubber with both hands and pull it downward while a student strikes the rubber repeatedly with the eraser end of a pencil (Figure 19.8). Note that the tighter the rubber drum head becomes as it is pulled farther downward, the higher the sound will become. Repeat this activity with jars of the same size, but having mouths of different widths. The narrower the mouth of the jar, the higher the sound that is produced. Using rubber pieces of different thicknesses over the mouth of the jar will show that the thinner the rubber, the higher the sound that is produced.

2.6 Make a Musical Instrument

Give students the following instructions: Crease the ends of two straws so they are flattened. Snip off the corners at the tops of the flattened ends to form points, as shown in Figure 19.9. Cut off the bottom of one straw so it is 5 cm long. Predict which straw will have the higher pitch. Blow into the straws like a clarinet player would blow through a reed mouthpiece. Explain why the two straw sounds differ in pitch.

Chapter 20

Light

Pearson Learning Photo Studio

The Nature of Light

I. Visible Light Is a Form of Electromagnetic Radiation

A. Radiation is the movement of energy from one place to another.
   1. There are three general types of radiation: particle radiation (Chapter 16), mechanical radiation (Chapter 19), and electromagnetic radiation.

B. Electromagnetic radiation is classified according to the amount of energy being moved. Starting with lowest energy (longest wavelength) and moving up to highest energy (shortest wavelength), the **electromagnetic spectrum** includes radio waves, microwaves, infrared rays, visible light, ultraviolet rays, X-rays, and gamma rays (see Figure 20.1).
   1. At one end of this spectrum are waves with long wavelengths and low frequencies, and at the other end are waves with short wavelengths and high frequencies.
   2. Except for visible light, all of these electromagnetic waves are invisible to the human eye. We recognize the other waves by using detectors and observing the effects caused by the waves. Most detectors of electromagnetic radiation are antennas or telescopes.
   3. Electromagnetic radiation consists of both electric and magnetic fields; hence the name electromagnetic.
   4. Unlike mechanical energy (sound), electromagnetic radiation can travel through a vacuum as easily as it can through air. It can also pass through liquids and some solid materials.

II. Electromagnetic Waves Travel at the Same Speed but Differ in Wavelength and in Frequency

A. All electromagnetic waves, including light rays, travel in a vacuum at a speed of 299,743 kilometers per second (186,282 mps).

B. **Wavelength** is the distance between corresponding parts of two waves with the same motion.

C. **Frequency** is the number of waves that pass by a point in a specified amount of time, such as one second.
   1. Electromagnetic waves with long wavelengths, such as radio waves, have a low frequency. Electromagnetic waves with short wavelengths, such as X-rays, have a high frequency. The shorter the wavelength of the electromagnetic wave, the greater its energy and the higher its frequency.
   2. A **cycle** is one complete up-and-down movement of a wave. The frequency of a wave, then, is also the number of cycles that happen in 1 second. In a 60-cycle wave, for example, the wave moves up and down 60 times in 1 second. That means that in 1 second, 60 complete waves pass by a given point.
   3. Because electromagnetic waves have very high frequencies, their frequencies are usually given in kilocycles (thousands of cycles) or megacycles (millions of cycles). Because 1 **hertz** is one cycle, other terms used to express frequency are kilohertz and megahertz.

D. **Speed**, then, equals the wavelength times the frequency.

III. Waves with Long Wavelengths and Low Frequencies

A. Waves with long wavelengths and low frequencies include infrared rays and radio waves.
   1. **Infrared rays** are a band of invisible waves that we perceive as heat. Much of the Sun's energy comes to us as infrared rays.
   2. *Infra* means "below." Infrared rays are the first band of rays below visible red light rays.
   3. Infrared rays are used to take pictures in the dark, because all objects radiate heat; to obtain special photographic effects; in remote sensing imagery; to detect fingerprints or changes in documents and paintings; in night-vision goggles; and in medicine.

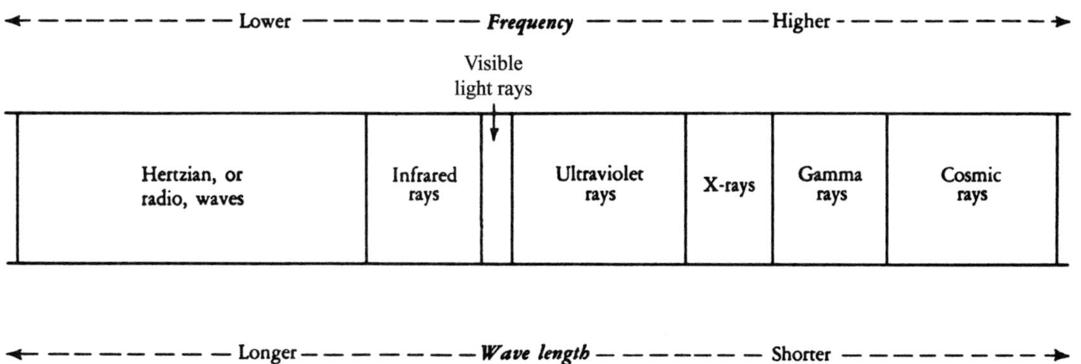

FIGURE 20.1 Diagram of the electromagnetic spectrum.

4. **Microwaves** are high-energy waves that are close in frequency to the infrared band. Microwave energy is produced by **masers**, which is an acronym for "*m*icrowave *a*mplification by *s*timulated *e*mission of *r*adiation."
5. Natural masers have been found in the atmospheres of both Earth and Mars as well as in interstellar space.
6. Depending on their wavelengths, some microwaves are reflected or absorbed by water. Microwave energy that is reflected by water is used in short-term weather forecasting. Microwaves that are absorbed by water are used for cooking in microwave ovens; this energy can be dangerous to living tissue, so persons must be shielded from it.
7. Because the energy can be focused into a narrow beam, microwave energy is useful in telephone and computer-data transmission.
8. **Radio waves** make up a very wide band of invisible rays that are found below the infrared rays; that is, they are longer wavelengths than infrared.
9. Radio waves are used in various kinds of communication. The band is so wide that it is further divided into smaller bands or channels. Separate channels are used for AM radio, FM radio, television, police calls, military communications, radar, amateur broadcasting, aviation, and distress signals. The waves in each band or channel are often identified by their frequencies (kilocycles and megacycles) rather than by their wavelengths.
10. Natural radio waves are produced by astrophysical processes in the star systems and in interstellar clouds of gas. Astrophysicists learn about these systems from studying the energy produced by them.

IV. Waves with Short Wavelengths and High Frequencies

A. Waves with short wavelengths and high frequencies include ultraviolet (UV) rays, X-rays, and gamma rays.

1. *Ultra* means "beyond." **Ultraviolet rays** are the first band of rays beyond visible blue light rays.
2. Ultraviolet radiation comes from the Sun and causes our skin to tan and burn. It is necessary for the production of vitamin D in our skin. UV radiation is also responsible for genetic mutation of skin cells and skin cancer. The Earth's atmospheric layer of ozone absorbs much of the Sun's UV energy.
3. Ultraviolet rays can be produced when an electric current flows through mercury vapor. When the invisible ultraviolet rays strike certain chemicals, called phosphors, the chemicals glow and give off visible light. This effect is used in fluorescent lamps and in identifying marks made on clothing by a laundry.
4. UV energy is also used for high-energy microscopy in scientific research, to kill harmful microscopic organisms, in advertising, and in safety-warning devices.
5. **X-rays** constitute a band of waves found beyond the ultraviolet rays. They have a shorter wavelength and higher frequency than ultraviolet rays.
6. Because of their high energy, X-rays can pass through nonmetals and through thin sheets of most metals. The radiation is stopped by thicker sheets of metals and by certain metallic salts, such as barium sulfate.
7. X-rays emanating from space are absorbed by the Earth's atmosphere. The process creates large numbers of ions; hence the Earth's ionosphere. Orbiting satellites allow space scientists to study this high-energy radiation coming from space.
8. X-rays are used to take pictures of the bones and organs in the body, detect cracks in metals, detect weapons on persons and in luggage, and inspect fruits for frost damage.
9. **Gamma rays** are high-energy electromagnetic waves found beyond the band of X-rays. Materials that are radioactive give off gamma rays. (See Chapter 16).

Visible Light

I. Magnetic Characteristic

A. Although scientists know much about light and the other electromagnetic waves, they do not fully understand the exact nature of electromagnetic waves.

1. Scientists know that, although light travels in waves, it has certain behaviors that are better explained by assuming that light acts like a particle.
2. When light is emitted or absorbed by atoms, it behaves as though it were composed of particles, or packets of energy, called **photons**. When light travels, however, it acts like an electromagnetic wave.
3. When light passes through a strong magnetic field, the lines that make up the light spectrum are split into two or more lines. This influence of magnetism on light is named the *Zeeman effect*.

II. Light Travels in Straight Lines

A. Even when light is made to change direction, it continues to travel in straight lines.
   1. A thin line of light is called a **ray**.
   2. A **beam** of light is made up of many rays.

B. Light travels at a speed of 299,743 kilometers per second (186,282 mps), or more than 1,060 million kilometers per hour (660 million mph). It takes about 8 minutes for light to travel from the Sun to the Earth. Light traveling faster than sound waves explains why we sometimes see things before we hear them, such as a batter hitting a ball or a train coming down the track.

C. Because the stars and planets are so far away from the Earth, astronomers use the speed of light as a unit for measuring these great distances.

III. Transparent, Translucent, and Opaque Materials

A. Light can pass through some materials but is stopped by other materials.
   1. Materials such as air, plastic wrap, water, and clear glass are called **transparent**. When light strikes transparent materials, almost all of the light passes directly through them. We can see clearly through transparent materials.
   2. Materials such as frosted glass and some plastics are called **translucent**. When light strikes translucent materials, only some of the light passes through them, while most is scattered. Because light is scattered as it passes through translucent materials, we cannot see clearly through them. Objects on the other side of a mildly translucent material are unclear. Through strongly translucent materials, we can see only light and shadow.

LEARNING ACTIVITY 20.1

Light Travels in Straight Lines

Obtain four index cards and find their center by drawing diagonals on each card. Make a good-sized hole at this center, and then attach each card with thumb tacks to a small block of wood (Figure 20.2). Place the index cards one in front of the other, some distance apart, making sure that the holes are in a straight line. Rest a flashlight on some books set 1 meter (3 ft) from the first card, making sure that the height is just right for the flashlight to shine directly through the holes.

Turn on the flashlight and darken the room. Have a student look through the holes and see the light of the flashlight. Imply that the light can be seen only because it is passing through each hole in a straight line. (If you clap two chalkboard erasers repeatedly along the path of the light, the student can see a beam of light in a straight line.) Now move one card so that it is out of line. The student cannot see the light because it travels in a straight line but is stopped by the card.

Obtain a large rectangular cardboard carton and remove the flaps to create an open side. Put the carton down so that the open side is at the back. Remove most of the top and front side of the carton and replace these pieces with plastic wrap, pressing the plastic wrap firmly to the carton (Figure 20.3). Paint the inside cardboard of the carton with flat black paint.

Obtain two pieces of black cloth, each slightly larger than half the length of the carton, and tack them to the open back so that they overlap at the middle. You can now put your hand inside the carton without permitting any light to enter. Halfway down one end of the carton, cut a window 7 centimeters (3 in.) long and 5 centimeters (2 in.) wide. Obtain a piece of black construction paper slightly larger than the window. Punch out three holes, one beneath the other, and then tape the paper over the window. Tape a small white index card on the inside of the other end of the carton, directly opposite the black paper. The card will act as a screen.

Fill the carton with smoke by burning a rope, damp paper, or incense in an ash tray. Obtain a three-cell focusing flashlight and rest it on some books set 1 meter (3 ft) away from the carton. Make sure the height is such that light from the flashlight will shine directly through the holes. Turn on the flashlight, then darken the room. Three rays of light will be visible inside the carton. The rays are parallel, showing that light travels in straight lines.

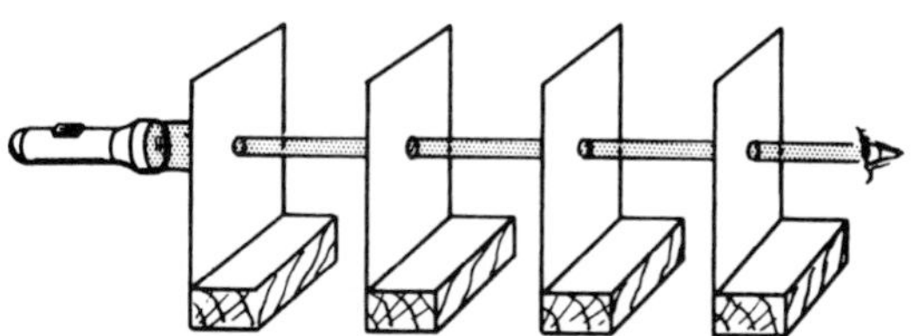

FIGURE 20.2 Light travels in a straight line through the holes in the index cards.

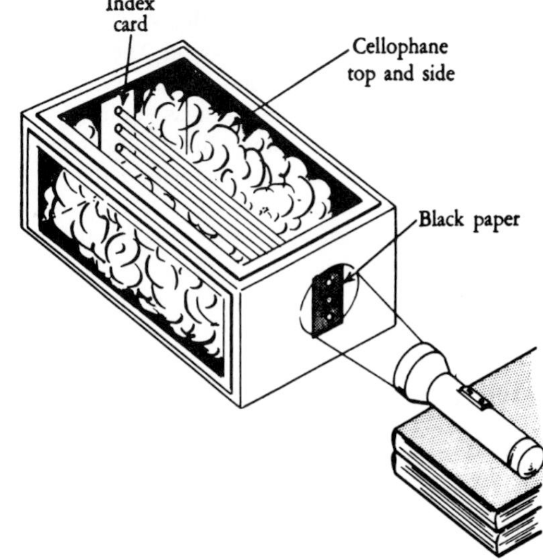

FIGURE 20.3 A light-ray box.

3. Most materials are **opaque**. When light strikes an opaque material, none of the light passes through the material. We cannot see through opaque materials. All of the light is either reflected by the opaque material or absorbed and converted into heat.
4. Even with transparent and translucent materials, some of the light is absorbed and converted into heat.

B. Because light travels in straight lines, shadows are formed when an opaque material is placed in the path of rays of light.

IV. Sources of Light

A. Materials that emit light are called **luminous** materials.

B. The Sun is a natural source of light and our chief source of light.
   1. Light energy from the Sun is produced when changes take place in the nuclei of atoms that make up the Sun (see Chapter 9).

C. Stars are also a natural source of light.

D. The Moon and the planets do not produce their own light but shine because sunlight strikes them and is reflected from their surfaces.

E. Some organisms, the firefly, for example, and certain marine animals and some fungi, can produce their own light through a biochemical process known as **bioluminescence**. The result of the special biochemical process is the production of light without producing any heat. The effect of bioluminescence in these living organisms is for communication, camouflage, or to attract prey.

F. Common artificial sources of light include the candle, kerosene lamp, gasoline lamp, electric light, fluorescent light, neon light, sulfur lamp, and laser light.

G. The **sulfur lamp** uses microwave energy on sulfur gas to create a bright, cool, energy-efficient source of light. A bulb is filled with a small amount of sulfur in an inert gas compound. The sulfur is agitated when bombarded by microwaves. The light given off is nearly the same as sunlight, except there is little heat and very little ultraviolet emission. The bulb has no metal wire parts but does contain a small microwave generator.

H. **Laser light** does not spread out as do other forms of light energy but travels in a narrow beam that spreads very little. It is made of only one wavelength or color (i.e., it is monochromatic).
   1. Laser light is produced by a laser, which is an acronym for "Light Amplification by Stimulated Emission of Radiation."
   2. Laser light can be concentrated into beams powerful enough to drill holes in a diamond, to be used as a cutting tool for surgical operations, and to be used to accurately measure lines and movements.

V. Measurement of Light

A. The intensity of a light source is measured in **candles** (or candelas in the international system).
   1. Long ago a candle was defined as the amount of light given off by a standard candle of precise construction. We spoke of candle power.
   2. Today a candle is defined as one-sixtieth of the light intensity of one square centimeter of a perfectly black object at the freezing point of platinum.

B. In determining the amount of light illuminated from a surface, given that the distance from the light source to the illuminated surface is measured in feet, the intensity of that illumination is measured in **footcandles**. At a distance of 1 foot, the illumination provided by a light source of 100 candles is 100 footcandles.
   1. The amount of light that is illuminated from a surface depends on several factors, including the intensity of the light source, the angle at which the light hits the surface from the source, and the distance of the surface from the source.
   2. The greater the distance from the light source, the weaker the illumination from the lighted surface. The distance versus illumination follows an inverse-square law. For example, if the distance from the source is doubled, the amount of light falling on a given area is reduced to one-fourth, the inverse of 2 squared. If the distance is tripled, the surface receives only one-ninth of the original illumination, and so on.

C. Another unit of light power, called the **luminous flux** of a light source, is also used today. Luminous flux is measured in **lumens**. An ideal one-candle source gives off 4 lumens. One footcandle is equal to 1 lumen per square foot. A **photometer** (or light meter) is used to measure the amount of light given off by a source.

The Reflection of Light

I. Light Can Be Reflected

A. To enable us to see an object that does not produce its own light, three things must happen.
   1. There must be a source of light.
   2. The light must strike the object.
   3. The light must be reflected from the object and then travel to the eye.

B. When light is reflected, it changes direction, but it still travels in straight lines.

C. Transparent and translucent materials allow most of the light striking them to pass through, but some light is absorbed and some light is reflected.
D. Opaque materials do not allow any light to pass through but absorb and reflect the light instead. Materials differ greatly in how much light they absorb and reflect. Dark-colored, rough, opaque materials absorb more light than they reflect. Light-colored, smooth, opaque objects reflect more light than they absorb.

II. Law of Reflection

A. When a ray of light strikes a mirror perpendicular to the surface of the mirror, the ray is reflected directly back. A perpendicular line has an angle of 90 degrees to the surface and is called the normal (see Figure 20.4).
B. When a ray of light strikes a mirror at a slant, or angle, the ray is reflected at a slant, or angle, in another direction.
   1. The ray that strikes the mirror is called the **incident**, or striking, ray.
   2. The ray that is reflected by the mirror is called the **reflected** ray.
   3. The angle between the ray of light that strikes the surface and the normal is called the **angle of incidence.**
   4. The angle between the reflected ray and the normal is called the **angle of reflection.**
   5. The law, or principle, of reflection states that the angle of incidence is equal to the angle of reflection (see Figure 20.4).
C. The law of reflection holds true for all smooth, polished surfaces.
   1. When a beam of light strikes a mirror, each ray in the beam is reflected regularly.
   2. Each ray has the same angle of incidence and angle of reflection, so the rays change direction, but they all do so the same amount, and in this way continue to form a beam. This means that parallel rays of light will reflect off the mirror and remain parallel.
   3. When a beam of light strikes a rough surface, each ray is reflected irregularly but still obeys the law of reflection. The rays hit the surface irregularities, which are oriented at different angles to each other, so the rays reflect at different angles.
   4. When light strikes a sheet of very smooth paper, the light is reflected regularly to the eye, producing a glare. When light strikes a sheet of coarse paper, the uneven surface reflects the light irregularly and scatters it, so very little glare is produced.

III. Mirrors

A. Some mirrors are flat or plane, and others are curved.
B. A **plane mirror** is usually made of a flat piece of clear glass. The back of the glass has a thin coating of silver or another shiny metal.
   1. The light striking the mirror passes through the transparent glass; then almost all the light is reflected back by the shiny, but opaque, silver.
   2. Unbreakable mirrors can be made from highly polished steel, but they do not reflect light as well as glass mirrors.
   3. Objects that you see in a mirror seem to be behind the mirror, but they are not. What you really see is the reflection of objects in front of the mirror. This reflection is called an **image.**
   4. When you look into a mirror, you see a reversed image of yourself. The image in a mirror seems to face you so that everything is reversed.
   5. The image in a mirror is just as large as the object in front of it.
   6. The image in a mirror also appears to be just as far behind the mirror as the object is in front of it.
C. **Curved mirrors** that are curved either inward or outward give different kinds of images than plane or flat mirrors.
   1. Mirrors that curve inward are called **concave mirrors.** A concave mirror causes rays of light to converge at a point called the focus (see Figure 20.6).
   2. Concave mirrors are used in some telescopes to gather the light from a distant star and concentrate the light so that the star may be examined. The important job of any telescope is to gather as much light as possible, not to magnify the image.
   3. Flashlights, automobile headlights, and spotlights also use concave mirrors made of shiny metal. However, in these instruments the mirrors work just the opposite as the mirrors used in telescopes. The light source, the light bulb, is placed at the focus of the mirror. The rays of light coming from the bulb are reflected by the mirror to throw a beam, instead of being scattered in all directions.

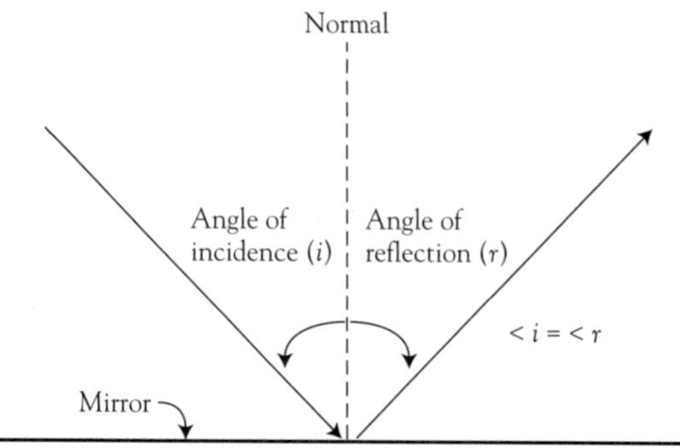

FIGURE 20.4 Angle of incidence is equal to the angle of reflection.

LEARNING ACTIVITY 20.2

The Law of Reflection

Place a mirror at the center of a table. Darken the room, and then turn on a focusing flashlight and aim it at an angle at the mirror. The light will be reflected and appear on the wall. Have a student clap two chalkboard erasers over the mirror and on each side of the mirror (Figure 20.5). Two rays of light, an incident ray and a reflected ray, will appear. Change the angle at which the ray strikes the mirror and note how the angle of the reflected ray changes accordingly. Point out that the angle of incidence and angle of reflection are always equal.

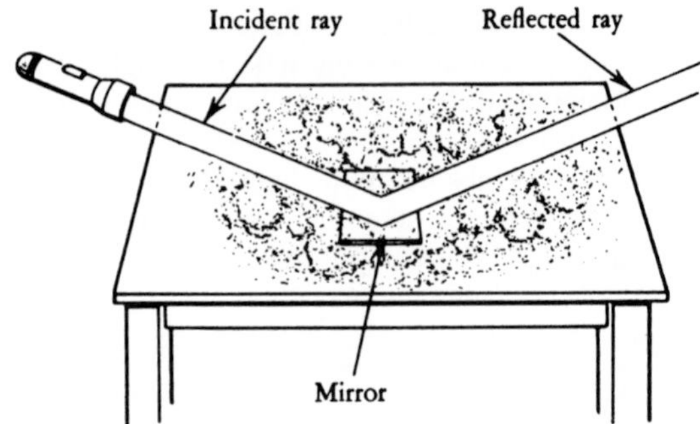

FIGURE 20.5 Illustrating the law of reflection.

Inquiry-Based Learning Activity 20.2. Modified

This activity will require several small aquariums and the same number of small flashlights, mirrors, and a small amount of milk or cream. Fill each aquarium with water and distribute your students into small groups at each aquarium. Ask them to shine the flashlight into the tank on the mirror at the bottom. In the clear water, the light rays will not be visible. Pour a small amount of milk or cream into the water of the aquariums. The milk will mix with the water and leave small particles suspended in the solution. These small particles will reflect light and allow the path of the light to be visible in a darkened room. Now, ask your students to describe what they see when they shine the flashlight on the mirror. What happens to the light bouncing off the mirror when they change the angle of the light going into the mirror? What level of inquiry is this modification? This activity spans Level I and Level II (Transition from Level I and Transition to Level III). The students are given a task to perform and they are allowed to explore their ideas within the limitations of the activity. The activity stops short of Level III since the students are asked only to report on observations rather than to make independent observations. The activity is designed to produce only one clear conclusion. Some questions to consider. How might this activity be changed to shift it to a Level III activity? What impact would this shift have on students' learning and on how the results might be reported?

4. Mirrors that curve outward are called **convex mirrors.**
5. A convex mirror does not bring rays of light together at one spot but spreads them out in all directions.
6. Although images from a convex mirror are erect and smaller, the convex mirror gives an image that covers a larger area. Some rear-view side-installed automobile mirrors are convex mirrors. These are often marked with a caution to the driver that the image seen in the mirror may actually be closer than it appears.

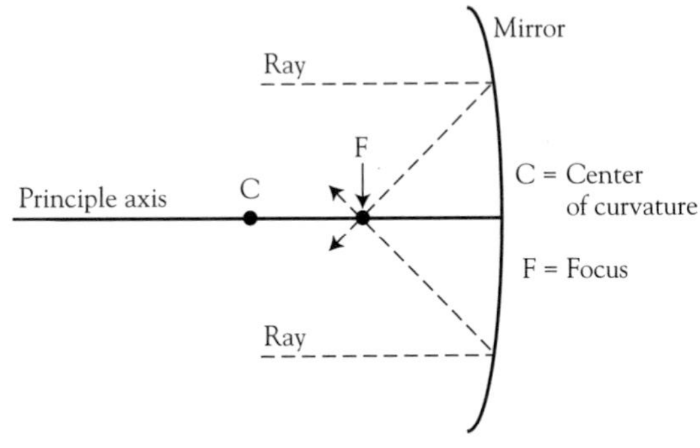

FIGURE 20.6 The point of focus of a concave mirror.

The Refraction of Light

I. The Nature of Refraction

   A. When light rays strike a transparent material at an angle of 90 degrees, they travel in a straight line and gradually slow down.

   B. When light rays pass at a slant, or angle, from one transparent material (such as air) into another transparent material (such as water), they are bent, or **refracted,** so they travel in a different direction.

      1. Although the rays are now traveling in a different direction, they still travel in a straight line.
      2. The light rays must pass at a slant, or angle, from one transparent material into another; otherwise, they will not be bent.
      3. If light rays pass from one material into another in a perpendicular line (at an angle of 90 degrees), they pass straight through without being bent, and there is no refraction.

C. Light is bent because there is a change in the speed of the light as it passes from one transparent material into another.
  1. Light passes at different speeds through different kinds of transparent materials.
  2. The difference in speed depends on the **optical density** of the material.
  3. The greater the optical density of a material, the more slowly light passes through it.

D. When light rays pass into an optically denser material at an angle, they are slowed down and bent toward the normal, but when light rays pass into a less optically dense material at an angle, they speed up and bend outward.
  1. The amount of refraction depends on the optical density of the material.
  2. The greater the optical density of the material, the more the light rays will be bent inward (the greater the angle of refraction).

II. Lenses

A. A lens is a piece of glass, or other transparent material, that is either curved on one side and flat on the other, or curved on both sides.
  1. Lenses are used to bend, or refract, light rays. Because the surface of the lens is curved, light rays strike the lens at a slant.
  2. The curvature of the lens makes the rays of light bend as they pass through it.
  3. When light rays pass through a lens, they are always bent toward the thickest part of the lens.

B. On one or both sides, lenses are curved either inward (concave) or outward (convex).

C. A **convex lens** is thicker in the middle than it is at its edges.
  1. When passing through a convex lens, light rays are bent toward the thicker middle of the lens. Thus, after passing through the lens, the rays come together and meet at a point.
  2. The point at which the rays meet is called the **focal point.** We say that the convex lens brings the rays into focus at this point.
  3. The thicker the middle of the lens is compared with its edges, the more the rays of light are bent and the shorter the focal length.
  4. By bending the rays of light and bringing them together, the convex lens can produce a real image.
  5. When a convex lens is placed between an object and a screen, an inverted, or upside down, image can be formed on the screen. This is called a **real image.**
  6. When a convex lens is placed between your eyes and an object, the object appears larger. It is magnified; that is, an erect, or right side up, image that is larger than the object is formed. This is called a **virtual image.**
  7. The lens of the human eye is a convex lens (see Chapter 15).

D. A **concave lens** is thinner in the middle than at its edges.
  1. Light rays passing through a concave lens are bent toward the thicker edges. After passing through the lens, the rays are spread apart.
  2. The rays seem to be coming from an imaginary point behind the lens.
  3. The thicker the edges of the lens, the wider apart the rays are spread.
  4. A concave lens produces only one kind of image—a virtual image. It is smaller than the object and is not inverted.

LEARNING ACTIVITY 20.3

Light Can Be Refracted

Fill a rectangular aquarium three-quarters full of water and add drops of milk until the water has a cloudy appearance. Darken the room, and then turn on a focusing flashlight and aim it at an angle at the aquarium (Figure 20.7). At the same time, have a student clap two chalkboard erasers over the aquarium to outline the path of the beam of light coming from the flashlight. The beam of light will be bent inward as it passes from the air into the water. Now hold the flashlight so that the beam of light enters the water vertically (at an angle of 90 degrees). The beam will pass from the air into the water without being refracted.

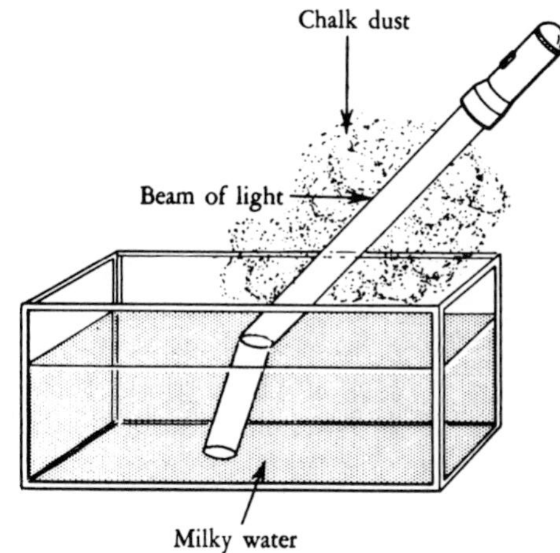

FIGURE 20.7 The light is refracted when it enters the water.

E. Lenses are used in many kinds of instruments, such as cameras, microscopes, telescopes, binoculars, eye glasses, and projectors. In most instances, the instruments use complex systems of lenses, that is, more than one lens.
   1. The basic parts of a **camera** are a lightproof box, an opening in the front of the camera, a shutter over the opening, a convex lens behind the opening, a film at the back of the camera, and a device to hold and turn the film.
   2. The shutter allows light to enter the camera and strike the lens, which bends the light rays so they come together; that is, they are brought into focus on the film.
   3. The film is coated with chemicals that are affected by light. When light rays focus on the film, a chemical change occurs. The film is then treated with chemicals and becomes a "negative," where the dark parts of the object appear light and the light parts appear dark. When light is then passed through the negative to light-sensitive paper, a "positive" is produced; the dark parts of the negative now become light and the light parts become dark, just as they were in the original object.
   4. In inexpensive cameras, the lens is fixed so that it can bring into sharp focus only light rays coming from objects that are more than 2 meters (6 ft) away from the camera. In more expensive cameras, the lens can be moved back and forth to bring into sharp focus light rays coming from both near and far objects.
   5. A **light microscope** has two convex lenses, one at each end of a lightproof tube. The upper lens is called the eyepiece, and the lower lens the objective. Rays of light from an object pass through the lens of the objective and are bent, producing an enlarged image of the object inside the tube. The lens of the eyepiece acts like a magnifying glass and magnifies this image even more, making it much larger than the object. To focus the microscope, one part of the tube is made to slide up or down inside another part.
   6. Based on the lens types and placements, there are two basic kinds of light **telescopes.** The reflecting telescope has a large concave mirror at one end, and a small convex lens at the other end that magnifies the image produced by the mirror. The refracting telescope works similarly to the microscope, with an objective and an eyepiece. A very large convex lens in the objective collects all the light it can from a distant object and bends the light rays to produce an image, which is magnified by the smaller convex lens in the eyepiece. One part of the tube slides in and out of another part of the tube to bring objects located at different distances into focus.
   7. **Binoculars** are two refracting telescopes connected side by side, one for each eye. Prisms in the binoculars reflect the light rays so the image is not inverted.
   8. **Projectors** use one or more convex lenses to project an enlarged image onto a screen. A strong beam of light passes through the object (in opaque projectors it reflects from the surface of the object), and a convex lens bends the rays of light coming from the object to produce an enlarged image on the screen.

Color

I. The Spectrum

A. When a narrow beam of sunlight passes at a slant into a triangular transparent material, called a **prism**, the sunlight is separated into a band of colored lights, called the **spectrum**, which can be seen on a white wall or screen (see Figure 20.8).
   1. This separation of sunlight into its component colors is called dispersion.
   2. Dispersion can be observed in a **rainbow**, which is the result of sunlight refracted and dispersed by water droplets in the atmosphere.
   3. There are six component colors in the spectrum: red, orange, yellow, green, blue, and violet. A long-used mnemonic for remembering this order is ROY G BIV. However, that mnemonic was created when seven colors of the visible spectrum were identified. Today, blue and indigo are considered one color.

B. When a second prism (or a convex lens) is placed at just the right position in front of the rays of colored light coming from a prism, the rays of colored light combine to form white light again.
   1. White light, then, is really a mixture of the six colors of the spectrum.
   2. These colors are called pure colored light, because none of them can be divided further by another prism.

C. A prism breaks up white light into a spectrum because the colors that make up the spectrum all have different wavelengths.
   1. Blue light has the shortest wavelength, red light the longest wavelength, and the others have wavelengths between those of blue and red.
   2. When white light enters a prism at a slant, the prism bends—or refracts—the different colors in different amounts.

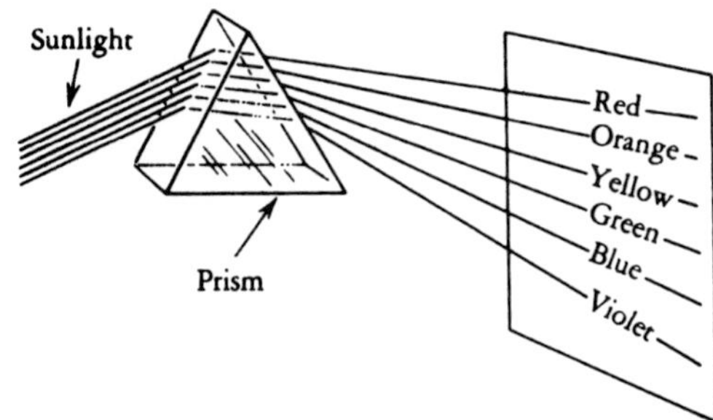

FIGURE 20.8 A prism produces a band of colored lights.

3. The colors with the shortest waves are bent more than those with the longest waves.
4. Blue light has the shortest waves and is bent most, and red light has the longest wave and is bent least.
5. The other colors are bent in different amounts, so all six colors that make up white light are separated as they pass through the prism and strike a screen at different places to form a band of colors.

II. Primary and Complementary Colors

A. A colored light is only a part of white light.
   1. To get a single colored light from white light, all colored lights other than the one you want must be taken away, or absorbed.
   2. When white light is passed through a transparent colored material, such as red cellophane, all the colors in white light are absorbed except the red light, which is allowed to pass through the cellophane.
   3. The lights that have been absorbed are converted into heat.

B. Red, green, and blue are the **primary additive colors** of light. (As discussed later, these primary additive colors of light are different from the primary colors of paint pigments.) Every shade of colored light can be made by mixing or forming different combinations of these colored lights. Together, the three primary additive colors produce white light.

C. Any two colors that, when mixed together, produce white light are called **complementary colors.** The following pairs of colors are complementary colors.

   Red and cyan (bluish green)
   Yellow and blue
   Green and magenta (purplish red)

III. Colored Materials

A. A material looks a certain color because, when white light strikes the material, some colors are absorbed and others are reflected to the eye. For example, a red dress looks red because the material absorbs all the colors of white light except red, which is reflected to the eye. Grass appears green because it absorbs all colors except green, which is reflected to the eye. The colors that have been absorbed are converted into heat.

B. A white material appears white because all the colors are reflected equally to the eye.

C. A black material appears black because all the colored lights are absorbed, so no light is reflected to the eye.

D. The color of a material also depends on the color of light shining on it. When red light shines on a white material, the material appears red; the red light is the only color striking the white material, so red is the only color that can be reflected to the eye. When blue light shines on a red material, the material appears black because the material can reflect only red light, and there is no red in the blue light shining on the material.

E. Colors may seem different in artificial light because artificial light may have less blue and more red in it than does natural sunlight. This is why, when buying clothes, some people like to take an article outdoors and away from the store's artificial lighting. In some sources of artificial light, blue may seem almost black because there is so little blue to be reflected. At the same time, red seems to be much brighter because some sources of artificial light have so much red, which is reflected.

F. Cyan, yellow, and magenta are called the **primary colors of paints**, or **subtractive colors** (not to be confused with the primary colors of light discussed earlier). Every other color can be produced by mixing different combinations of these pigments, such as:

   Magenta and yellow paints make orange.
   Magenta and cyan paints make purple.
   Yellow and cyan paints make green.
   Black and white paints make gray.

G. Mixing colored paints produces effects entirely different from those produced by mixing colors of light. Mixing paints is called a subtractive process, whereas mixing colors of light is an additive process.

IV. The Colors of the Sky and the Sun

A. During the day the sky appears blue and the Sun yellowish white. These effects are caused by the presence of dust in the atmosphere.
   1. The sky appears blue because blue light is scattered by the dust and reflected to the eye much more than are the other colors.
   2. The yellow and red colors of sunlight are not scattered but instead pass straight through, so that the loss of some of the blue color of sunlight makes the Sun appear yellowish white.

B. At sunrise and sunset, sunlight must travel at a greater slant, or angle, and thus passes through more of Earth's atmosphere containing particles of dust.

1. The blue color of sunlight is now scattered much more by the dust in the atmosphere, so that there is even less blue passing straight through.
2. The loss of more of the blue color of sunlight now causes the Sun to appear reddish or orange.
3. In addition, moisture in clouds absorbs green and blue from the sunlight; this causes a still greater appearance of reds, oranges, and yellows at sunrise and sunset.
4. These same principles hold for the Moon when it is just rising or setting and can appear quite reddish-orange.

Exploratory Activities for "Light"

1. EXPLORING WITH MIRRORS (ANY GRADE LEVEL)

Review the following four activities and, depending on the age and maturity of your students, determine the best approach for involving the students in these activities. One approach is to divide the class into groups and have each group do one of the activities as a project, then show and report their results to the rest of the class. Instructions for each activity will have to be rewritten, depending on how it is used.

1.1 Light Can Be Reflected Again and Again by Mirrors

First, have a student sit or crouch next to a wall with a window. Give the student two mirrors and have the student hold them in the position shown in Figure 20.9. By tilting the mirrors at the proper angles, the student will be able to see objects outside the window. Draw a diagram on the chalkboard to show how the light from the window strikes the top mirror, is reflected to the lower mirror, and then is reflected again to the student's eye. Point out that this is how a periscope works.

1.2 Pane Glass as a Mirror

Obtain a pane of glass and tape a piece of white paper over one side. Turn on a table lamp and darken the room. Give these instructions: Stand with your back to the lamp and hold up the glass and look at it, keeping the white paper behind the glass. Record what you see. (You will see a very faint reflection because most of the light passing through the glass and striking the white paper is reflected irregularly and scattered.) Now replace the white paper with a piece of black paper. What do you see now? (You will see a very clear reflection because the black paper absorbs the light striking it, allowing a small amount of light to be reflected regularly from the surface of the glass.)

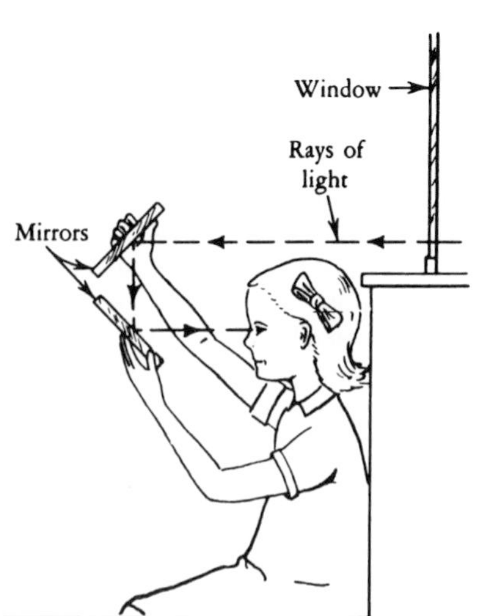

FIGURE 20.9 A periscope works by reflecting light more than once.

1.3 Reflection from a Concave Mirror

Have the students look into a magnifying mirror. Point out that the mirror is a concave mirror that curves inward just a little. This is the reason that the image is right side up and magnified.

Obtain a large, highly polished silver tablespoon. Ask a student to look at the concave (hollow) side of the bowl, then record and explain what he or she observes. (This concave mirror curves inward a lot, so the image is upside down and smaller.)

1.4 Reflection from a Convex Mirror

Obtain a large, polished silver tablespoon. Give these instructions: Hold the spoon vertically and look at the convex (bulging) side of the bowl. Record and explain your observations. (You will see a long, thin image of yourself that is smaller and right side up.) Now hold the spoon horizontally and look again. What do you observe now? (The image becomes short and fat, but still is small and right side up.)

2. EXPLORING WITH LENSES AND PRISMS (ANY GRADE LEVEL)

Review the following five activities and, depending on the age and maturity of your students, decide the best approach for involving the students in these activities. One approach is to divide the class into groups and have each group do one of the activities as a project, then show and report their finished work to the rest of the class. Instructions for each activity will have to be rewritten, depending on how it is used.

2.1 Images Formed by a Convex Lens

Give students the following instructions: Use a spring-type clothespin to hold a large piece of white cardboard vertically on a table. Place a lit candle about 1 meter (3 ft) away from the cardboard. Hold a magnifying glass near the cardboard

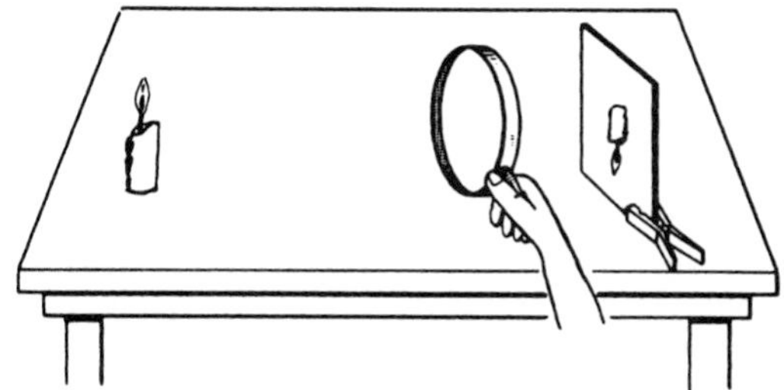

FIGURE 20.10 A convex lens held far from an object will produce an inverted, smaller image.

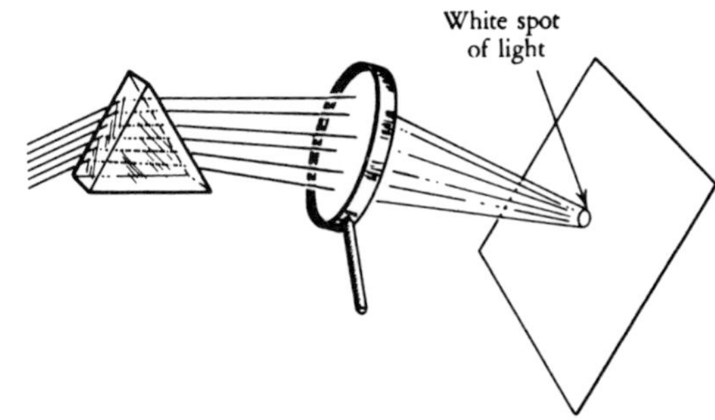

FIGURE 20.11 A convex lens recombines a spectrum to form white light again.

and move the magnifying glass slowly toward the flame until a clear, inverted, smaller image of the candle appears on the cardboard (Figure 20.10).

Now hold the magnifying glass close to the candle and move it slowly toward the cardboard until a clear, inverted, larger image of the candle appears on the cardboard. You may have to push the cardboard farther back to obtain this image. Point out that when the object is close to the lens, a large image appears. When the object is far from the lens, a small image appears. Both images are upside down.

Now use the glass as a magnifying instrument by placing the glass between your eyes and an object. Record and explain your observations. (The image produced is larger and right side up.)

2.2 Make a Spectrum

On a sunny day, when the Sun's rays are coming through the window into the classroom, hold a prism (or a wedge of lucite or any other clear plastic) in the path of the sunlight. Roll the prism around until you are able to throw a rainbow on the wall (see Figure 20.8). Have a student tape a piece of white cardboard to the wall so the spectrum will show up more clearly. Ask the students to locate and identify the different colors of the spectrum.

2.3 Colored Lights of a Spectrum Can Be Recombined

Repeat activity 2.2, but now place a magnifying glass between the prism and the cardboard (Figure 20.11). Move the magnifying glass back and forth until you make the spectrum disappear and there is only a spot of white light on the cardboard. Ask students, How can you explain this observation? (The convex lens of the magnifying glass caused the colored lights of the spectrum to converge and combine, forming white light again.)

2.4 Make a Soap Bubble Rainbow

Give students the following instructions: Punch a hole near the base of a Styrofoam cup and insert a soda straw slightly larger than the hole. Make a bubble solution by thoroughly mixing 2 cups of water, 1 to 2 tablespoons of liquid soap, and 1 cup of glycerin. Pour the solution into a soup bowl; put the mouth of the cup in the solution and shake. Lift the cup gently, upside down, and, blowing through the straw, blow a bubble. What do you see? How can this phenomenon be explained? (The thin soap film breaks up light rays to form rainbows.)

2.5 Produce Colored Lights

Turn on a focusing flashlight and darken the room. Have a student clap two chalkboard erasers together in front of the flashlight. Have students record their observations. Then ask them to note the beam of white light coming from the flashlight. Now wrap a piece of red cellophane smoothly around the glass of the flashlight. Ask, What do you observe and how can it be explained? (The beam of light is colored red because the cellophane absorbs all the colors of the spectrum except the red light, which is allowed to pass through.) Produce other beams of colored light by using pieces of cellophane of different colors.

3. EXPLORING WITH COLORS (ANY GRADE LEVEL)

Review the following two activities and, depending on the age and maturity of your students, decide the best approach for involving the students in these activities. One approach is to divide the class into groups and have each group do one of the activities as a project, then show and report their finished work to the rest of the class. Instructions for each activity will have to be rewritten, depending on how it is used.

3.1 Combine Primary and Complementary Colors

Give students the following instructions: Draw a circle about 10 centimeters (4 in.) in diameter on a piece of white cardboard, and cut out the circle. Mark three equal sections on the cardboard and color them red, green, and blue with wax crayons. Make two small holes near the center of the circle and pass a loop of string through them (Figure 20.12). Now make the circle spin rapidly by twisting the string, stretching it, and then allowing it to rewind. Continue stretching and rewinding to keep the card spinning constantly. What do you observe, and how can it be explained? (When the card is spinning, the primary colors will blend together to form a grayish white. If one color shows up predominantly, scrape a little of it off and replace it with more of the other two colors. Usually more blue is needed. To prevent the string from cutting through the holes, glue the cardboard circle to a large button, lining up the holes of the cardboard with those of the button.)

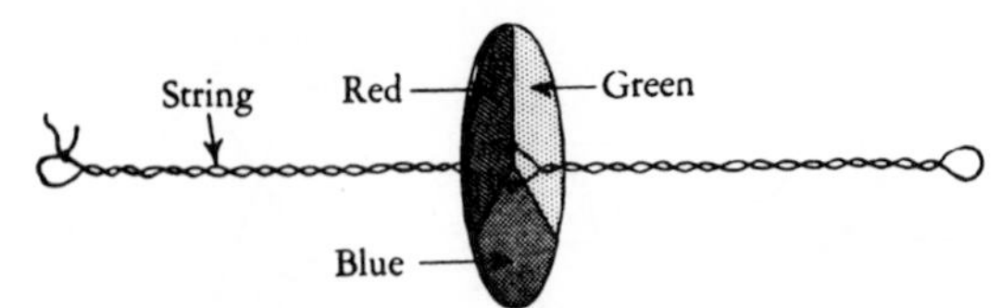

FIGURE 20.12 Combining primary colored lights produces white light.

Repeat the activity, using another cardboard circle containing just two complementary colors, such as yellow and blue. What do you observe, and how can it be explained? (The complementary colors will blend together when the circle is spinning, forming grayish white again.)

3.2 Combine Colored Pigments

Give the following instructions: Draw some streaks of yellow and blue tempera paints separately on a piece of white cardboard. Now mix these colors and explain why the green color results. Repeat, using such combinations as red and yellow, red and blue, and black and orange. Mix the six spectrum colors together (or just red, yellow, and blue paints) and record your observations. (The resulting mixture is black because it absorbs all the colors of the white light striking it and reflects none.)

Chapter 21

Magnetism and Electricity

Anthony Magnacca/Merrill

Magnetism

I. Magnets: Natural and Artificial

A. Only magnetic materials (such as iron, steel, cobalt, nickel, and a few rare Earth elements such as dysprosium and gadolinium) can be made into magnets.

1. These materials are termed **ferromagnetic** substances, which means that spontaneous magnetism exists in the substance even in the absence of a magnetic field. They are naturally magnetic.
2. However, at certain high temperatures (specific for each type of material) even ferromagnetic materials will lose their magnetism.
3. Artificial magnets can be made from ferromagnetic substances. Sometimes aluminum is used to make lightweight but strong magnets, called alnico magnets. These are made of aluminum, nickel, and cobalt, from which the name "alnico" is derived.
4. Magnets are given names according to their shapes: bar magnets, rod magnets, and horseshoe or U-shaped magnets.

B. It is possible to make both temporary and permanent magnets.

1. Ferromagnetic materials are put in two categories: those with high magnetic retention and those with low magnetic retention.
2. Ferromagnetic materials with high retention—that is, that tend to hold onto their magnetism for an indefinite period—are called hard magnets, or more popularly, permanent magnets.
3. Ferromagnetic materials with low retention—that is, that tend to lose their magnetism easily—are called soft, or temporary, magnets. Iron-silicon alloys are an example.
4. One way of making a magnet is to place a ferromagnetic material in a magnetic field. This way of making temporary magnets is called induced magnetism. The material now becomes a magnet but perhaps only temporarily. If it is made of a soft magnet material, the magnetism will be lost once the material is removed from the magnetic field.
5. Another way to make a magnet is to stroke a piece of ferromagnetic material (such as a nail) many times with a permanent magnet, but only in one direction. Stroking in one direction lines up the domains (or molecules) in the nail so that all the north-seeking poles are facing one direction and all the south-seeking poles are facing the opposite direction. The nail is only a temporary magnet; the domains will eventually lose their arrangement.
6. Still another way of making a temporary magnet is to wrap an insulated wire many times around a nail, or other soft ferromagnetic material, and connect the bare ends of the wire to the posts of a dry cell. This kind of temporary magnet is called an **electromagnet.** An electromagnet is magnetic only as long as the electric current flows through the wire. (See discussion about electromagnets that follows in Section VII "Magnetism Can Be Obtained from Electricity" of this chapter.)

C. Permanent magnets are often made from steel (an iron-carbon alloy). Needles, knives, scissors, and screwdrivers are usually made of steel.

1. Materials made of hard steel (high concentration, up to 2%, of carbon) are difficult to magnetize, but once achieved, their magnetism is more permanent; that is, they do not easily lose their magnetism. Their domains are harder to line up, but, once alignment is done, it is just as hard to throw them out of line. A permanent magnet may be made by stroking a steel knitting needle, or by using a piece of steel rather than a nail (soft iron) in an electromagnet.

D. There are three common ways that magnets can lose their magnetism: by dropping or striking them; by heating them; and by placing the north-seeking poles of two magnets side by side or on top of each other. In each case the domains (or molecules) will be thrown out of line.

E. There are ways to keep magnets strong.

1. One way is to put a piece of soft iron, commonly called a keeper, across the poles of a U-shaped magnet when the magnet is not in use. If the original keeper has been lost, any piece of soft iron will serve the purpose, or the magnet can be stored by attaching it to the side of a metal file cabinet.
2. Bar magnets should be stored in pairs with the north-seeking pole of one magnet beside or on top of the south-seeking pole of the other magnet but separated by a nonmagnetic divider (such as a wooden stirring stick or a piece of plastic) with a keeper at each end.
3. Disk and ring magnets should be stored in pairs with opposite poles together.

F. There are ways to rejuvenate weak magnets.

1. A weak bar magnet can be rejuvenated by dragging it lengthwise across one pole of a powerful magnet, such as a large horseshoe magnet. Repeat this several times, moving the weak magnet in the same direction and across the same pole of the stronger magnet.
2. To test the poles, bring the magnet to be tested near a magnet known to be correctly marked to see that opposite poles attract and like poles repel. A bar magnet may be suspended from a string so that it swings freely. When the magnet stops swinging, its north-seeking pole should be pointed in a

northerly direction. You can also test poles with a compass. The end of the compass that normally points north should point to the south-seeking pole of a bar magnet.

3. If the poles of the rejuvenated magnet are opposite to their markings, you can repeat the process of rejuvenating. This time drag the bar magnet across the same pole of the stronger magnet, but in the opposite direction, or drag the bar magnet in the same direction, but across the opposite pole of the stronger magnet.
4. A weak bar magnet can also be rejuvenated by wrapping insulated wire around its full length (up to 100 or more windings) and momentarily touching the ends of the wire to the terminals of a 6-volt battery. If the magnet's poles are then opposite to the markings on the magnet, repeat the procedure but reverse the ends of the wire that touch the battery.

II. The Law of Magnetic Attraction

A. The force (push or pull) of a magnet is strongest at its ends, which are called **poles.**
   1. All magnets have two poles: a north-seeking pole and a south-seeking pole.
   2. When a magnet is allowed to swing freely, its north-seeking pole points toward the Earth's north magnetic pole and its south-seeking pole points toward the Earth's south magnetic pole.
   3. A natural magnet (lodestone) has many poles, but there are always just as many north-seeking poles as there are south-seeking poles.

B. When the poles of two magnets are brought near each other, they obey the **law of magnetic attraction,** which states that two unlike poles attract each other and two like poles repel each other.

III. Magnetic Field

A. The space around a magnet also acts like a magnet. This space, within which the force of a magnet acts, is called the **magnetic field.**
   1. Magnetic fields are present wherever electricity flows, such as near electrical appliances and power lines. When associated with electricity they are called electromagnetic fields (EMF).

B. When iron filings are sprinkled around a magnet, the filings will arrange themselves into a pattern of parallel lines, called **lines of force.**
   1. At the ends of a magnet, where the magnetic force is strongest, the lines of force bunch closely together.

IV. The Force and Nature of Magnetism

A. A magnet can attract magnetic materials (iron, steel, cobalt, nickel) without touching them. The force of a magnet can pass through nonmagnetic material, such as air, paper, wood, glass, aluminum, and brass. The nearer the magnetic material is to the magnet, the more strongly the magnet will attract it.

B. Scientists attribute the magnetism of magnetic materials to the spinning movement of the electrons as they revolve or travel around the nucleus of an atom.
   1. In atoms of nonmagnetic materials, half their electrons spin in one direction and half spin in the opposite direction, which cancels their magnetic effects.
   2. In atoms of magnetic materials, more electrons spin in one direction than the other, making each atom a tiny electromagnet.

C. Magnetized atoms group together in large clusters, called **domains,** that line up in such a way that all the north-seeking poles face one direction and all south-facing poles face the opposite direction.

LEARNING ACTIVITY 21.1

The Law of Magnetic Attraction

Let a magnet swing freely by cradling it in a piece of copper wire and connecting the wire with string to a ruler inserted into a pile of books (Figure 21.1). Bring the north-seeking pole of another magnet near the north-seeking pole of the suspended magnet. Bring the two south-seeking poles together. Now bring the north-seeking pole of the magnet in your hand near the south-seeking pole of the suspended magnet. Note that like poles repel each other and unlike poles attract each other.

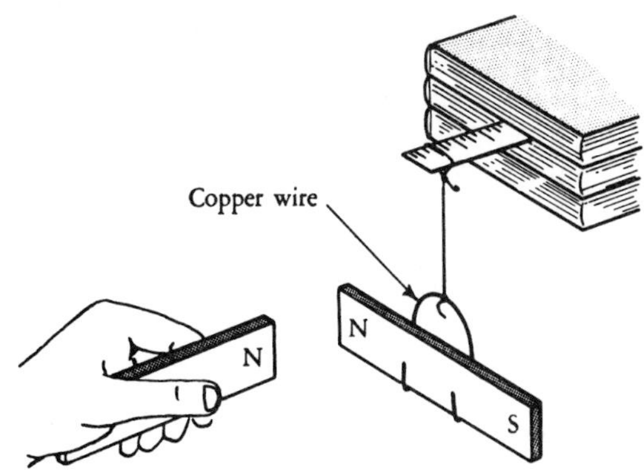

FIGURE 21.1 Like poles repel each other and unlike poles attract each other.

1. This arrangement leaves free north-seeking poles at one end of a magnet and free south-seeking poles at the other end.
2. A magnetized bar or rod, when cut in half, produces two new magnets even though the middle of the magnetized bar originally had little or no magnetic force.
3. Each of the two new magnets now has a free north-seeking pole at one end and a free south-seeking pole at the other end.

V. The Earth Behaves as a Magnet

A. If a magnet is suspended so that it can swing freely, the magnet will move until it is in a north-south position, with the north-seeking pole of the magnet pointing to the north. This movement occurs because the Earth behaves as if it were a huge magnet, with a north magnetic pole, a south magnetic pole, and a magnetic field.
   1. The **north and south magnetic poles** are not located at the same points as the **north and south geographic poles.** The magnetic poles are about 1,700 kilometers (1,100 mi) from the geographic poles. The poles drift about 10 kilometers per year. At present, Earth's magnetic north pole lies in northern Canada, at a latitude of about 80 degrees north, almost due north of the center of North America. The magnetic south pole lies at a latitude of about 60 degrees south, just off the coast of Antarctica south of Adelaide, Australia.

B. A compass tells us where the direction North is, because it contains a magnetized needle whose north-seeking pole is affected by the Earth's magnetic field. It points in the direction of the north magnetic pole, aligning itself with the Earth's magnetic field. A compass needle always points to the north unless it is brought near magnetic materials or a magnet, which then affects its position.

VI. Uses of Magnets and Magnetism

A. Magnets are used to pick up pins and needles, to keep cabinet and refrigerator doors closed, to hold the lids of cans after a can opener has removed them, and to hold pieces of paper and other objects to bulletin boards.

B. Although it has long been known that the bodies or brains of certain organisms and animals, such as bacteria, birds, and whales, contain small amounts of ferromagnetic material that help them navigate, scientists discovered and reported in 1992 that the human brain also contains small amounts of magnetic material, although its value in human brains is not known.

C. Magnets are used in electric motors and generators, in compasses, and in toys and games.

D. Maglev (magnetic levitation) vehicles are trains that are lifted, propelled, and guided by fast-moving magnetic fields. Suspended on strong magnetic field, they can easily move at a speed of more than 400 kilometers per hour (248 mph). Although not yet widely used, there are two types of Maglev vehicles, those built on the principle of magnetic attraction and those that use the principle of magnetic repulsion.
   1. EMS (or electromagnetic suspension) is based on the principle of magnetic attraction. The vehicle wraps around the steel track, leaving a gap around the sides and bottom of the track, or guideway. Electromagnets mounted in the gap are attracted to the bottom of the guideway, levitating the vehicle. Electromagnets mounted in the gap between the vehicle and the side of the guideway are attracted to the side of the guideway, keeping the train laterally on track.
   2. EDS is based on the principle of magnetic repulsion. In the EDS train, the vehicle does not wrap around the track. Instead, electromagnets mounted to the bottom of the vehicle repulse the flat steel guideway, thus levitating the train above the track.
   3. For propulsion, Maglev trains use linear electric motors built into the guideway to generate a magnetic field that attracts the vehicle, allowing the train to move.

VII. Magnetism Can Be Obtained from Electricity

A. Passing an electric current through a wire creates a magnetic field around the wire. When a wire carrying an electric current is placed over a compass, the compass needle turns away from its north-seeking position, seeking a position perpendicular to the wire.

B. If a wire carrying an electric current is wound into a coil, the coil acts just like a magnet, with north- and south-seeking poles. Placing a bar of soft iron in the center of the coil greatly increases the strength of this magnet. A magnet of this kind, made from electricity passing through a wire, is called an electromagnet.
   1. Three things are needed to make a strong electromagnet: a bar of soft iron, such as a large iron nail, which is called the core; a coil of insulated wire wrapped around the core; and a source of electric current, such as a dry cell.
   2. When the ends of the coil of wire are connected to the dry cell, the core and coil act like a magnet. The magnetism will continue as long as an electric current passes through the coil.
   3. Soft iron is almost always used as the core of an electromagnet because it demagnetizes quickly.

4. The poles of an electromagnet can be determined simply by bringing a compass near it. If the north-seeking part of the compass needle swings toward one end of the electromagnet, this end is the south-seeking pole of the electromagnet. If the north-seeking part of the compass needle swings away from one end of the electromagnet, this end is the north-seeking pole of the electromagnet.
5. When the connections of the wire to the dry cell, or other source of electric current, are reversed, the poles of the electromagnet are also reversed.
6. Commercial electromagnets use yards of wire, one or more large cores, and a strong electric current.
7. Any electromagnet can be made stronger by
   a. Increasing the number of turns of wire around the core.
   b. Increasing the electric current. (If either the number of turns of wire is doubled, or the strength of the current is doubled, the electromagnet is made twice as strong.)
   c. Using a U-shaped core.

C. An early use of the electromagnet was in the telegraph. Electromagnets today are used in other forms of communication, like the telephone, radio, and television. They are used in industry in such devices as the motor, generator, transformer, and crane. In the home, electromagnets are found in bells, buzzers, chimes, circuit breakers, VCRs, stereo speakers, and electric toys.

 Static Electricity

I. Static Electricity and How It Is Produced

A. Static electricity is produced by friction.
1. When two different materials, especially nonmetals, are rubbed together, they each attract light objects, such as small bits of paper and cotton thread, to themselves. We say that these materials have become electrically charged.
2. The kind of electricity that is produced in these materials does not move and is called static electricity, as opposed to electricity that does move and is called current electricity.

II. The Nature of Static Electricity

A. All matter is made up of atoms, inside of which are protons, neutrons, and electrons.
1. The protons and neutrons, which are much heavier than the electrons, are located in the center, or nucleus, of an atom.
2. The much lighter electrons are outside the nucleus and move rapidly around the nucleus.
3. The electrons move freely around the nucleus, whereas the protons are packed closely together with the neutrons in the nucleus.

LEARNING ACTIVITY 21.2

Friction Produces Static Electricity

Rub a hard rubber comb briskly with wool cloth. The comb will pick up small bits of paper. Rub a blown-up balloon with the wool and put the balloon against the wall. It will stick to the wall. In each case, electrons are rubbed off the wool onto the objects, charging the objects negatively and the wool positively. Hold the balloon over very fine sand. You will hear and see the sand being attracted to the balloon.

Inquiry-Based Learning Activity 21.2. Modified

Let's explore static electricity. Divide the students into groups of 2 or 3. For each of the groups, provide two inflated balloons, each tied with string. Have the students take each balloon, rub it with a wool cloth, and then hold it near small bits of torn paper. The small pieces of paper are attracted to the balloons. Now, allow the balloons to hang vertically from the strings as the students hold them above the floor. Have the students bring the balloons near each other. What happens? Why do the balloons appear to repel each other? Ask students to write down their ideas and draw pictures on poster boards to explain in their own words what they have just seen. **What level of inquiry is this modification?** This activity begins with ***Level I Problem Identification*** and ***Level I Process*** segments, but the ***Solutions*** segment of the lesson is at ***Level III.*** **Some questions to consider.** What would be some possible reasons for having a highly structured activity up to the **Solutions** segment? What would the students learn from such an approach? About their roles? How would the students' work be assessed?

LEARNING ACTIVITY 21.3

The Law of Electrostatic Attraction and Repulsion

Blow up two balloons to the same size and suspend each balloon from a string so that they are 2 centimeters (1 in.) apart. Rub each balloon briskly with a wool cloth. The balloons will become negatively charged and repel each other (Figure 21.2). Now rub a narrow glass jar or a test tube with nylon or a plastic bag and bring the jar near each of the balloons. The jar, having become positively charged, will attract the negatively charged balloons.

Ask students to share their experiences with electrostatic attraction and repulsion. Record their experiences on the board. After recording their ideas, with their help try to arrange the ideas into categories.

Have students brainstorm in class how knowledge of the law of electrostatic attraction and repulsion is used in technology. Record all their ideas on the board and then have students try to arrange the ideas into categories.

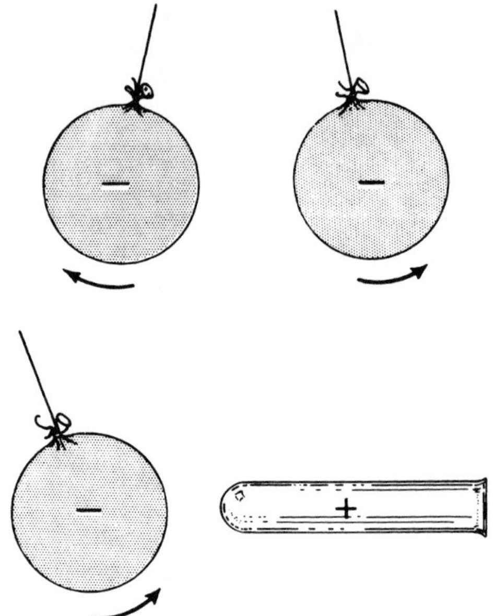

FIGURE 21.2 Like charges repel each other; unlike charges attract each other.

4. Each proton has a positive (+) electrical charge, and each electron has a negative (−) electrical charge.
5. The neutron is neither positively nor negatively charged. It is said to be neutral.
6. Ordinarily, there are the same number of positively charged protons and negatively charged electrons in an atom. As a result, an atom is electrically neutral, neither positively nor negatively charged.
7. However, it is possible to remove electrons from the atoms in a material by rubbing the material with another material. When two materials are rubbed together, electrons pass from one material to the other.
8. The material that loses electrons now has more positively charged (+) protons than negatively charged (−) electrons, so this material becomes positively charged. The material that gains electrons now has more negatively charged (−) electrons than positively charged (+) protons, so it becomes negatively charged.
9. Protons cannot be removed from an atom by rubbing.
10. When a hard rubber rod is rubbed with wool or fur, some electrons are rubbed off the wool or fur and onto the rubber. The rubber has gained electrons and now has more electrons than protons, so it becomes negatively charged. The wool or fur has lost electrons and now has more protons than electrons, so it becomes positively charged.
11. However, when the rubber rod is rubbed with a plastic bag, electrons are rubbed off the rubber and onto the plastic. The rubber has lost electrons, so it is now positively charged. The plastic has gained electrons, so it is now negatively charged.
12. When a glass rod is rubbed with a piece of nylon, some of the electrons are rubbed off the glass and onto the nylon. The glass has lost electrons and becomes positively charged because it now has more protons than electrons. The nylon has gained electrons and becomes negatively charged because it now has more electrons than protons.
13. Materials will stay charged only as long as electrons have no way of entering or leaving the materials.

B. Static electricity is most easily produced in winter, when it is very cold outside and warm and dry inside (low humidity). In summer there is more water in the air, making air a better conductor. As a result, the electric charges leak away almost as soon as they are formed, so it is very hard to give the materials an electric charge that will last very long.

III. The Law of Electrostatic Attraction and Repulsion

A. When two negatively charged materials are brought close to each other, they will repel, or move away from, each other.

B. The same thing happens when two positively charged materials are brought close together.

LEARNING ACTIVITY 21.4

Some Effects of Static Electricity

A. Charge a comb by rubbing it briskly with a wool cloth. Allow a thin stream of water to flow from a faucet, and then hold the comb near the water. The stream will be attracted by the comb and will bend toward it.

B. Charge a balloon by rubbing it briskly with a wool cloth. Pass the balloon over a student's head and cause the hair to stand on end.

C. Rub a fluorescent light tube briskly with a piece of nylon or silk in a completely darkened room or closet. The fluorescent tube will glow faintly.

C. But when a positively charged material is brought close to a negatively charged material, they will be attracted and will move closer to each other.

D. These behaviors can be stated as a law of electrostatic attraction and repulsion: Like electrical charges repel each other, and unlike charges attract each other.

IV. Why Electrically Charged Materials Attract Materials That Are Not Charged

A. Materials that are either positively or negatively charged will attract materials that are not charged.
   1. Materials that are not electrically charged are said to be neutral.
   2. Neutral materials have neither lost nor gained electrons.

B. When a negatively charged hard rubber rod is brought close to a small piece of paper, the paper is attracted to the rod.
   1. The negatively charged rubber rod repels electrons from the side of the paper nearest the rod.
   2. These electrons move to the other side of the paper, as far away from the rod as possible.
   3. The side of the paper nearest the rod is now positively charged, because it has more positive protons than negative electrons, so it is attracted to the negatively charged rod.
   4. When the paper touches the rod, some of the excess electrons from the rod flow into the paper, and the paper becomes negatively charged too.
   5. The paper then drops off the rod because it now has the same electrical charge (negative) as the rod and is repelled.

C. When a positively charged glass rod is brought close to a small piece of paper, the paper is attracted to the rod.
   1. The positively charged glass rod attracts electrons, and they accumulate on the side of the paper nearest the rod.
   2. The side of the paper nearest the glass rod is now negatively charged, because it has more negative electrons than positive protons, so it is attracted to the positively charged rod.
   3. When the paper touches the rod, some of the electrons from the paper flow into the rod, leaving the entire piece of paper positively charged, too.
   4. The paper then drops off the rod. Because it now has the same electrical charge (positive) as the rod, it is repelled.

V. Conductors and Nonconductors

A. Some materials allow an electric current to flow through them easily. Such materials are called **conductors.**
   1. The atoms in a good conductor of electricity do not have a very tight hold on some of their electrons, so an electric charge can flow freely through the material.
   2. Most metals are good conductors of electricity, including gold, copper, silver, aluminum, iron, and zinc.
   3. Carbon, although a nonmetal, can also conduct electricity.
   4. When certain chemicals known as acids, bases, and salts (ionic compounds) are dissolved in water, their solutions will conduct an electric current.
   5. Materials that are able to carry electricity with virtually no resistance at relatively warm temperatures are known as **superconductors.** Although the physics of how superconductors work is not yet clear, high-temperature superconductors are used today to improve signal reception in cell phone towers and for sensitive magnetic probes in scientific equipment.

B. Materials that do not allow an electric charge to flow through them easily, if at all, are called nonconductors or **insulators.**
   1. The atoms in a nonconductor of electricity have such a tight hold on their electrons that few, if any, flow through the material.
   2. Examples of insulators (nonconductors) are paper, wood, glass, porcelain, cloth, dry air, rubber, and many plastics.

LEARNING ACTIVITY 21.5

The Effect of Charged Materials on Uncharged Materials

A. Initial Demonstration

From a piece of Styrofoam, cut out a piece approximately 6 millimeters (1/4 in.) in diameter and form a Styrofoam ball. (A ball of that size can be obtained from a scientific supply house.) Suspend the ball from a silk or nylon thread. Charge a comb negatively by rubbing it briskly with a wool cloth, and then bring the comb near the ball (Figure 21.3). The ball will be attracted to the comb, because the negatively charged comb repels electrons from the side of the ball nearest the comb, leaving this side positively charged. Now touch the Styrofoam ball with the negatively charged comb. Electrons will flow into the Styrofoam, making it negatively charged, and the Styrofoam will be repelled by the comb.

B. Second Demonstration

Charge a glass test tube positively by rubbing it with a plastic bag or nylon. Make the Styrofoam ball neutral again by touching it with your fingers. Bring the positively charged test tube near the neutral ball. The ball will be attracted to the test tube because the positively charged test tube attracts electrons to the side of the ball nearest the test tube, making this side negatively charged. Now touch the ball with the positively charged test tube. Electrons will flow from the ball onto the test tube, leaving the ball positively charged, and the Styrofoam ball will be repelled by the test tube.

C. Third Demonstration: Make an Electroscope (Electrical-Charge Detector)

Obtain a bottle with a narrow neck and a cork stopper to fit. Obtain some insulated copper bell wire (No. 20) from a hardware store. Use an ice pick to make a small hole through the stopper. Force a piece of the bell wire, with all its insulation removed, through the stopper. Make an angular bend at the lower end of the wire and wind the upper end into a close circular coil (Figure 21.4). Hang a strip of thin aluminum foil about 7 centimeters (3 in.) long and 5 millimeters (1/4 in.) wide over the angular bend of wire. Press the cork firmly into the neck of the bottle.

Now charge a comb negatively by rubbing it briskly with a wool cloth. Touch the comb to the wire coil on top, rubbing it back and forth a few times. Electrons will leave the comb and flow down the wire into the aluminum halves, charging them negatively and causing them to spread apart because they repel each other. Remove the comb.

The electroscope is now charged and can be used to direct and determine the unknown charges on other objects. Bring a charged object near (but not touching) the wire coil at the top. If the charged object is negative, more electrons will be repelled from the coil down into the aluminum halves. The aluminum halves will become more negatively charged and will spread farther apart. However, if the charged object is positive, some electrons from the aluminum halves will be attracted up to the coil on top. The aluminum halves will now become less negatively charged and will come closer together.

To discharge the electroscope, touch the wire coil at the top with your fingers. Touching the coil allows electrons to leave the aluminum halves and travel through the wire, into your body, and then to the ground. The aluminum halves become neutral and collapse together.

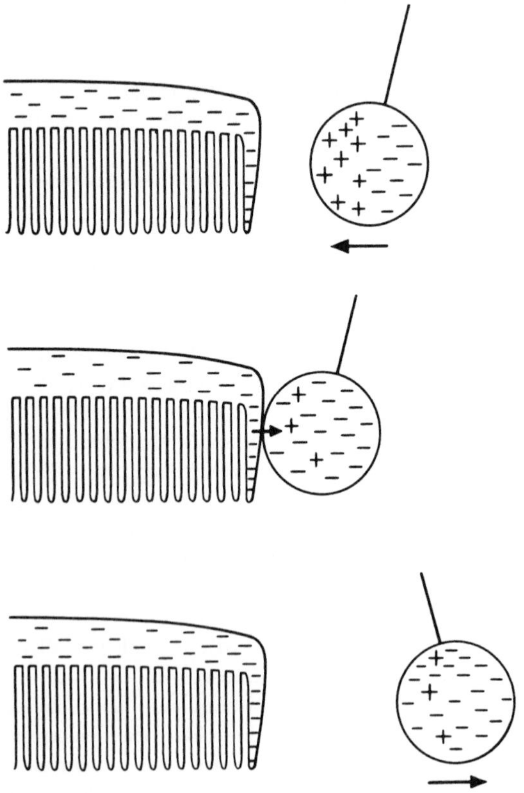

FIGURE 21.3 A charged body first attracts, then repels, an uncharged body.

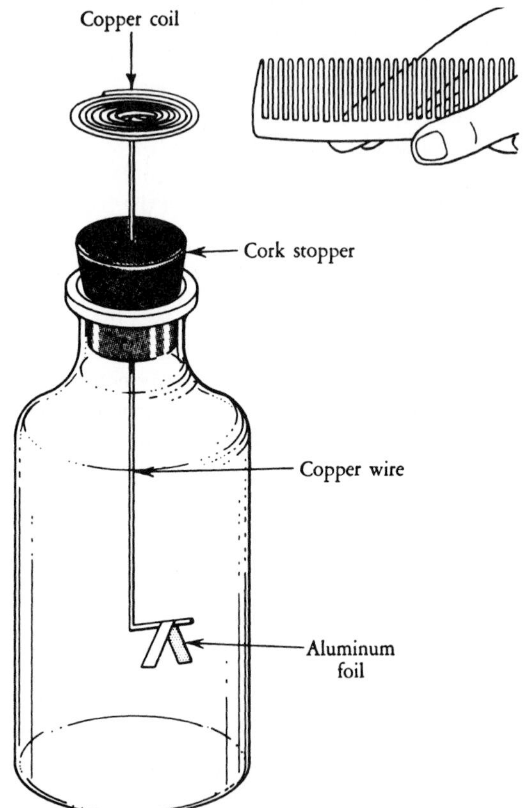

FIGURE 21.4 An electrical charge detector (electroscope).

C. Whenever necessary, conductors are covered with or supported by insulators.
   1. An insulator protects you against receiving an electric shock should you happen to touch the conductor.
   2. Insulators also prevent an electric current from leaving the conductor and taking an unwanted path.

D. Pure water is a nonconductor of electricity, but most water is not pure and contains ions. Even pure water has a concentration of hydrogen ions. These ions make water a good enough conductor that wet insulators can allow electricity to flow. Therefore, it is never safe to touch electrical appliances or electrical wiring with wet hands or when standing on a wet floor.

VI. Electric Sparks

A. Ordinarily, electrons do not flow very easily through the air, because air is an insulator.

B. Under certain conditions, however, electrons can be made to flow through the air.
   1. This flow may occur when a highly charged material is brought near an oppositely charged material, or even a neutral material.
   2. The electrostatic force of attraction between positively and negatively charged materials is very great.
   3. If the force of attraction is greater than the resistance of the air to the flow of electrons, a flow of electrons takes place between the two materials.
   4. This rapid movement of electrons through the air appears as a spark and is actually a flow of current electricity.

VII. Lightning and Thunder

A. **Lightning** is a huge electrical flash produced in cumulonimbus clouds during a thunderstorm (see also Chapter 11).
   1. Lightning originates about 15,000 to 25,000 feet above sea level when raindrops are carried upward until some of them convert to ice. For reasons that are not yet agreed upon, a cloud-to-ground lightning flash originates in this area of mixed water and ice.
   2. Lightning flashes that do not strike the ground are called **cloud flashes** and make up about 80% of all lightning. Cloud flashes may be inside a cloud, or they might travel from one part of a cloud to another or from cloud to air.
   3. Most of the lightning that we see is the single bolt of bright light. However, there are several other types of lightning, including forked lightning, ribbon lightning, bead lightning, ball lightning, and sheet lightning. Heat lightning is lightning that has occurred too far away for us to hear the accompanying thunder.
   4. The fast-rising air rubs against the water droplets in the cloud and charges them electrically. The top of the cloud becomes positively charged, while the bottom of the cloud becomes negatively charged.
   5. Sometimes the fast-rising air is strong enough to rip the cloud in two, so that each half has a different electrical charge.
   6. When the force of attraction between the positively and negatively charged parts of a cloud becomes great enough, a huge spark of electricity, called lightning, flows from the negatively charged part to the positively charged part.

B. When lightning strikes the Earth, it usually strikes an object located at a high point on the Earth's surface, such as the top of a tall tree. Lightning strikes this object because electrons flow more easily through solid objects than through a gas, such as air. Therefore, it is a good idea to stay away from trees and other tall objects during a thunderstorm.
   1. Lightning rods are used to protect buildings from damage by lightning.
   2. A lightning rod is made of a metal such as copper, which is a good conductor of electricity.
   3. A lightning rod's highest point is kept higher than the building, so lightning will be attracted to the rod and not the building.
   4. The lowest point of the rod goes deep into the ground so that lightning can be conducted quickly and harmlessly to the ground.

C. **Thunder** is the sound produced by the rapid heating and expansion of the air through which lightning passes.
   1. The rumbling of thunder is a series of echoes produced when thunder is reflected many times by clouds.
   2. Lightning is seen first, and thunder is heard next.
   3. This order occurs because lightning travels with the speed of light, which is about 300,000 kilometers per second (186,000 mps), whereas thunder travels with the speed of sound, which is about 1/3 kilometer per second (1/5 mps).
   4. Because it takes thunder about 3 seconds to travel 1 kilometer (5 seconds to travel 1 mi) and lightning is seen almost instantaneously, you can calculate how far away you are from the lightning of a thunderstorm. If you count the number of seconds that pass from the time you see the lightning to the time you hear the thunder, and divide this number by 3, the answer will be the number of kilometers you are from the lightning. (If you divide the number of seconds by 5, the answer will be the number of miles away from the lightning.)

5. Because it takes longer for sound to travel from the farther end of the lightning than from the nearer end, we hear the thunder as a long, rolling sound. Many flashes of lightning at one time also produce thunder with a long, rolling sound.
6. Sometimes lightning is too far away for us to hear the accompanying thunder.

VIII. Other Common Occurrences of Static Electricity

A. Scuffing or even just walking across a rug on a very cold day, when it is warm and dry indoors, can produce a shock or a spark when your finger touches a metal object. The body picks up negative electrons through the shoes and releases these electrons upon contact with the metal object. The same thing happens when you slide across the nylon seat of a car and touch the door handle.

B. Combing your dry hair with a rubber comb will charge the hair and cause it to stand on end.
1. The comb removes electrons from the hair, leaving the hair positively charged.
2. Because all strands of hair have the same positive charge, they repel one another and your hair tends to stand on end.
3. The same phenomenon is evident when you stroke a cat's fur.

C. Nylon sweaters and undergarments can become charged as they move against a person's body and often crackle and spark when they are removed.

D. Trucks containing gasoline and other flammable liquids can build up a large electric charge as the liquid sloshes inside the tank.
1. If there were no way to stop the charge from building up, a spark might be produced that would make the gasoline explode.
2. Attaching a metal chain to the tank and letting the chain dangle to the ground prevents the buildup of an electric charge.
3. As soon as an electric charge is formed in the tank, the charge is allowed to escape through the chain and into the ground.

Current Electricity

I. The Nature of Current Electricity and the Simple Electric Circuit

A. A transfer of energy from one electron to the next through a substance is called current electricity. An **electrical current** is the flow of electrical charge, not the flow of electrons as once believed. As stated in Chapter 16, it can be compared with a bucket brigade, where the individuals passing the bucket stand in one place but the water moves at the rate at which the bucket is being passed. The word *electricity* is used to describe a flow of electrical charge.
1. In response to an electric field, the electrons in a conductor "flow" very slowly through the conductor, less than 2.5 centimeters (1 in.) per second. It might be better to say that electrons "migrate."
2. However, the force due to electrical charge moves along at the speed at which electrons repel one another, about 1% the speed of light.

B. In an electric circuit, the electric current flows from the source of electricity along one path to the appliance, passes through the appliance, and then returns through a second path to the source of electricity.
1. There are three parts to a simple electric circuit: a source of electricity; a path, such as a copper wire; and an appliance that uses the electricity, such as a bell or a light bulb.
2. When all three parts of a circuit are connected so that an electric current can flow, the circuit is said to be completed or **closed.** When any of the three parts of the circuit is disconnected so that an electric current cannot flow, the circuit is said to be incomplete or **open.**

II. Switches

A. We control electricity with on-and-off switches, devices that make it easy and convenient to close or open an electric circuit. When the switch is turned or pushed one way, it completes the electric circuit and the electric current will flow. When the switch is turned or pushed the opposite way, it opens or breaks the circuit and the electric current stops flowing.

B. Four common types of switches are the knife, pushbutton, snap, and mercury (silent) switches.
1. The knife switch has a metallic, movable blade that moves in and out of metallic "jaws" to close or open an electric circuit.
2. The pushbutton switch, used with doorbells, has a flat, coil-like spring that pushes forward to close a circuit and then flies back to open the circuit.
3. The snap switch, used on walls, moves one way to close a circuit and the opposite way to open the circuit.
4. Mercury switches use a drop of mercury to establish the electrical connection. Because mercury is a toxic heavy metal, mercury switches are not as popular as they were when first marketed.

III. Series and Parallel Circuits

A. If more than one battery is used in an electric circuit, the batteries are usually connected in series. When batteries are connected in series, the wires run from the outside, or negative, terminal of one battery to the center, or positive, terminal of another battery.

1. Connecting batteries in series increases the amount of electrical force produced.
2. An example of appliances connected in series is a single strand of Christmas tree lights. If one light goes out in a set of this type, the circuit is broken and all the lights go out. These are no longer commonly found on the market.
3. Because all the electricity flows through each light, the more lights that are added, the more resistance the electricity meets, and the less current flows through the lamps.
4. Because the brightness of the lights depends on the amount of current flowing through them, the lights will become dimmer.

B. When appliances are connected in parallel, the electric current flows across each appliance.
1. The appliances are connected in such a way that the electric current branches off, with only part of the current going through each appliance.
2. Each appliance can operate independently of the other; if one appliance fails to function, the circuit is not broken and the other appliances continue to function.
3. The electric current flowing through each appliance is completely separate from the current flowing through the others.
4. An example of appliances connected in parallel is a set of double-strand Christmas tree lights. If one light goes out in this set of lights, there is still a complete circuit through the rest of the lights, and they stay lit. Because the electricity flowing through each light is separate from the electricity flowing through the others, the addition of more lights to the set will not affect their brightness. These are the type of Christmas tree light strands that are common today.
5. In most houses, the main circuit has branches, connected in parallel, carrying electricity to different parts of the house.

IV. Overloading an Electric Circuit

A. Whenever there is a flow of electrons (electric current) in a wire, heat is produced. Heat is formed because the metal of the wire resists the flow of electrons through the wire. The more current there is flowing through a wire, the hotter the wire becomes.

B. In a house, each branch circuit is designed to carry only so much current.
1. As appliances are connected into the circuit, each uses a certain amount of current.
2. If too many appliances are connected into a circuit at one time, the circuit becomes overloaded.
3. The combined current needed by all the appliances may be more than the circuit can carry.
4. This large amount of current may make the wires so hot that they burn away the insulation and can even start a fire.
5. A circuit can also become overloaded when a short circuit occurs.
6. Electricity always takes the shortest and easiest path back to its source.
7. The insulation on the wires of an electric circuit may wear off and expose the bare wires.
8. If the bare wires touch, the electric current takes a shortcut, or circuit, back to its source without first flowing through an appliance that is supposed to use the electrical energy.
9. A large amount of electricity will now flow quickly through the wires, making them very hot.

C. Fuses and circuit breakers are safety devices used to prevent wires from becoming too hot when an overload takes place. They are connected in series with the circuit so that the current must pass through them on its way to the appliances. They act like emergency switches to open the circuit if too much current is flowing through it.
1. A **fuse** contains a strip of metal that melts easily when heated.
2. The metal melts more easily than the wires in a circuit.
3. When a circuit becomes overloaded, either because of too many appliances in the circuit or because of a short circuit, the wires become very hot.
4. But the metal strip in the fuse also becomes hot and melts, or "blows," before the wires do, thus breaking the circuit before any damage is done.
5. A fuse is usually enclosed in a tube or socket to prevent the melted metal from spattering and causing a fire.
6. No current will flow through the circuit until the blown fuse is replaced.
7. A **circuit breaker** has a bar, made up of two strips of metal connected together.
8. One metal strip expands more than the other strip when heated, causing the bar to curve.
9. When a normal amount of electric current flows through the circuit and the circuit breaker, the bar remains flat and keeps the circuit closed.
10. When there is an overload, the bar becomes hot and begins to curve, thus opening the circuit.
11. A circuit breaker does not have to be replaced but can be pushed back into place after the cause of the overloading is removed.
12. When the bar of a circuit breaker has cooled and straightened, the circuit breaker is once again ready to do its job.
13. A more common type of circuit breaker is electromagnetic. If too much current flows through a circuit, the strength of the electromagnet overcomes a spring, pulling away a metal strip in the circuit and breaking the circuit.

LEARNING ACTIVITY 21.6

Short Circuit and Fuse

A. A Short Circuit

To make a simple circuit, obtain some electrical wire and cut it into two pieces (see Figure 21.5). Remove some insulation from the middle of each wire so that the bare wires are exposed. Place the blade of a screwdriver across both bare wires, *only for a second or two,* and the bulb will go out (Figure 21.5). On paper, show by lines the shorter path (or circuit) that the electric current now travels. Produce a short circuit again by pressing the bare wires together with your fingers, and feel how hot the wires become.

B. How a Fuse Works

Make a short circuit setup. Using two dry cells in series, place a two-cell flashlight bulb in the socket, and insert a homemade fuse (Figure 21.6). To make a homemade fuse, obtain two thumbtacks and two paper clips, and press them into one end of a small wood board so that the clips are upright and 2 centimeters (1 in.) apart. Cut a narrow strip of aluminum foil and insert it between the paper clips. When you produce a short circuit by placing the blade of a screwdriver across the bare wires, the aluminum foil will melt and break the circuit. (If the room is darkened, you may see the aluminum glow as it becomes hot and melts.)

Have the students examine a screw-type house fuse and note the short strip of easily melted metal in the fuse. Compare the appearance of a fresh fuse with that of a burned-out fuse.

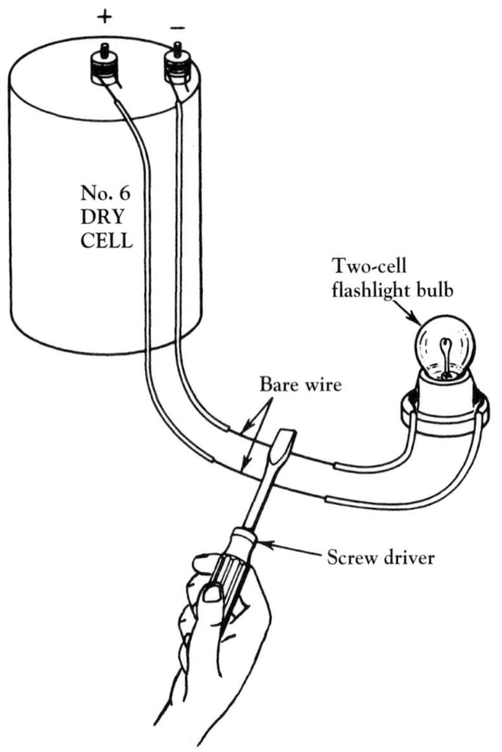

FIGURE 21.5 The blade of the screwdriver produces a short circuit.

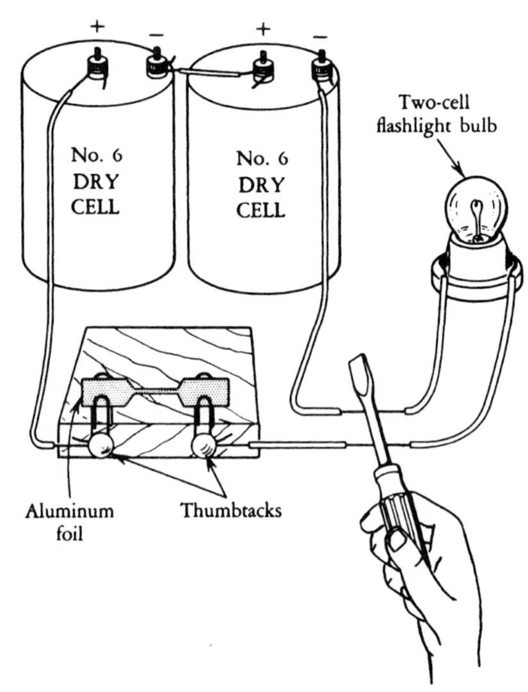

FIGURE 21.6 A simulated fuse.

V. Electrical Units of Measure

A. A **volt** is a unit of electrical pressure. It is a measure of the push of electrons through a conductor, overcoming the resistance of the conductor.

B. An **ampere** is a unit of the rate of flow of electric current. It is a measure of the number of electrons flowing per second, or the amount of current.

C. An **ohm** is a unit of electrical resistance. It is a measure of the resistance a conductor offers to the flow of electric current.

D. There is a relationship between electrical pressure, rate of flow of current, and electrical resistance.

1. The greater the electrical pressure (number of volts), the greater the current (number of amperes), and vice versa.
2. The greater the electrical resistance (number of ohms), the lesser the current (number of amperes), and vice versa.
3. This relationship, called **Ohm's law**, is expressed as follows: $I = V/R$, or Amount of Current = Electrical pressure/Electrical resistance.
4. Ohm's law is more commonly stated in electrical units, as follows:

Amperes = Volts/Ohms

E. A **watt** is a unit of electrical power.
   1. It is the measure of the rate, or how fast, electrical energy is being used.
   2. Watts can be found by multiplying the number of volts by the number of amperes. The formula is $P = IV$.

F. A **watt-hour** is a unit of electrical energy.
   1. It is the amount of energy used at the rate of 1 watt for 1 hour.
   2. We are charged for our use of electrical energy by the number of kilowatt-hours used. A kilowatt is 1,000 watts.

VI. Sources of Electricity

A. Electricity is a form of energy and therefore can be produced from other forms of energy. The following forms of energy can be changed, or transformed, into electrical energy:
   1. **Chemical energy**, using the wet cell, dry cell, storage battery, or fuel cell.
   2. **Mechanical energy**, using the generator or the piezoelectric cell.
   3. **Light energy**, using the photoelectric cell or the solar battery.
   4. **Heat energy**, using the thermocouple.

B. The **wet cell**, also known as the voltaic cell, consists of two different metals placed in a chemical solution that will conduct an electric current.
   1. The metals selected must be such that one will react faster with the solution than the other.
   2. When the metals are in the solution, they must be kept apart.
   3. A solution of an acid, a base, or a salt in water is able to conduct an electric current.
   4. A wet cell is commonly demonstrated by partially inserting a strip of zinc and a strip of copper in a glass of water containing a little sulfuric acid.
   5. The sulfuric acid acts chemically on the atoms of zinc, leaving many electrons behind on the zinc that remains.
   6. As the negative electrons accumulate on the zinc, the strip becomes negatively charged.
   7. The zinc strip is called the negative pole of the cell.
   8. At the same time, the copper strip loses electrons to the sulfuric acid.
   9. The copper strip now becomes positively charged because it has lost negative electrons.
   10. The copper strip is called the positive pole of the cell.
   11. In this way, an electrical pressure is built up between the two strips.
   12. When a wire is connected to the dry ends of the strips, there is a flow of electrons from the negatively charged zinc to the positively charged copper, and an electric current has been produced.
   13. The electric current flows in one direction only, from the zinc to the copper, and is called **direct current** (DC).

C. The **dry cell**, commonly called a battery, is a more convenient source of chemical energy.
   1. The materials of a dry cell are placed in a sealed container, so nothing can spill when the dry cell is carried or tipped.
   2. The chemicals inside must be kept moist; if the inside of the dry cell becomes dry, the cell will no longer operate.
   3. The older form of dry cell is the carbon-zinc battery.
   4. It includes a zinc can, which serves as the negative pole, as well as a container for the rest of the chemicals in the cell.
   5. A carbon rod in the middle of the can serves as the positive pole.
   6. The can is filled with a wet paste of ammonium chloride that has been mixed with particles of manganese dioxide and powdered carbon.
   7. Metal posts, or terminals, are on top of the can: one is attached to the carbon rod, the other to one end of the can.
   8. The chemical action in a carbon-zinc cell is much like that in a wet cell.
   9. The zinc reacts with the moist ammonium chloride and accumulates electrons, becoming negatively charged.
   10. The carbon rod loses electrons and becomes positively charged.
   11. An electrical pressure is built up between the zinc and the carbon.
   12. When a wire is connected to the two terminals of the dry cell, an electric current flows from the zinc to the carbon terminal.
   13. The zinc-chloride battery, commonly called a heavy duty battery, lasts 50% longer than the carbon-zinc battery and works better at lower temperatures.
   14. It has a steel can filled with moist potassium hydroxide.
   15. The positive pole is manganese dioxide; the negative pole is granulated zinc.
   16. The alkaline battery outperforms both carbon-zinc and zinc-chloride batteries. The newest forms of common batteries use lithium.
   17. Dry cells cannot give a strong, steady electric current for a long period of time.
   18. Dry cells are used in flashlights, portable radios, cameras, and doorbell circuits.

D. The common storage battery produces electricity, just as the wet and dry cells do, from chemical energy.
   1. A storage battery has lead as the negative pole, lead dioxide as the positive pole, and a solution of sulfuric acid.
   2. When the two terminals are connected, an electric current flows.

3. As the battery is used, both the lead and lead dioxide poles become covered with a chemical called lead sulfate.
4. When enough lead sulfate covers the poles, the storage battery will not operate, and we say that it has lost its charge.
5. But the storage battery is different from the wet and dry cell batteries because it can be recharged and used again and again.
6. Its terminals can be connected to a source of direct electric current, which changes the lead sulfate on the poles back into lead and lead dioxide.
7. In this way, electrical energy gives its chemical energy back to the storage battery.
8. Most storage batteries contain at least six cells connected in series.
9. Each cell has an electrical pressure of 2.1 volts.
10. Each cell adds its voltage to the others, so if there are six cells we get a 12-volt battery.
11. The most common use of the storage battery is in an automobile, to start the motor and to run appliances if the engine is not running.
12. A storage battery is recharged while the car is running.
13. Every car has an **alternator,** which is a machine for producing electricity once the engine is running.
14. The alternator is driven by the motor of the car. When the car is running, the electricity produced by the alternator flows into the storage battery and recharges it. In this way, the alternator resupplies the battery with the electrical energy that was used to start the car.
15. When the car engine is running, electricity to run lights, radio, and other appliances is provided by the alternator, not the battery.

E. The **nickel-cadmium battery** (nicad) is a small, efficient battery that performs like the storage battery.
1. A nickel-cadmium cell has a positive pole of nickel oxide, a negative pole of cadmium, and a solution of potassium hydroxide.
2. Like the storage battery, the nickel-cadmium battery can be recharged repeatedly with a recharger that plugs into an electrical outlet and changes alternating current (AC) into direct current (DC).
3. The nickel-cadmium battery is used in cordless electrical appliances and toys.

F. The **fuel cell,** discussed in Chapter 18, may be a chemical source of energy for the future.

G. The **generator** produces electricity from mechanical energy.
1. When a wire is moved up and down between poles of a U-shaped magnet so the wire cuts across the lines of force in the magnetic field, an electric voltage is produced.
2. The electric current can be detected by connecting the ends of the wire to the terminals of a sensitive instrument called a galvanometer, which is used to measure or detect weak electric currents.
3. When the wire is moved down, the needle of the galvanometer moves in one direction; when the wire is moved up, the needle moves in the opposite direction.
4. The movement of the needle shows that the electric current produced changes direction.
5. This kind of current is called **alternating current** (AC), because it alternates by first flowing in one direction, then in the opposite direction.
6. An alternating electric current is also produced if the wire is held stationary and the magnet is moved; if the wire or the magnet does not move, no current is produced.
7. Thus, the mechanical energy of motion needed to move the wire or the magnet is changed to electrical energy by means of magnetism.
8. A generator is simply a machine that makes wires cut magnetic field lines very quickly.
9. A simple alternating current generator has four necessary parts: a coil of many turns of wire, called an armature; a U-shaped magnet, with the armature placed between the poles of the magnet; two metal rings, called slip rings, each connected to an end of the coil to collect the current produced in the armature; and brushes, made of metal or carbon, to lead the current out of the generator.
10. In small generators and many large generators, the coil moves and the magnet remains stationary; in some large generators, the magnet moves and the coil remains stationary.
11. The amount of current produced by a generator depends on how many magnetic field lines are cut and how quickly they are cut.
12. There are several ways to increase the number of field lines to be cut: using more magnets, making the magnets stronger by using electromagnets instead of permanent magnets, using more turns of wire in the coil of wire, and inserting an iron core inside the coil.
13. Increasing the speed with which the field lines are cut can be done by moving either the coil or the magnet faster.
14. At **hydroelectric power stations,** falling water is used to turn large wheels, called turbines, that turn the coils or magnets of the generator and produce electric current.
15. Trains and ships burn fuel to run engines or turbines, which operate generators that supply the electricity needed to drive the wheels or propellers.

H. The alternating electric current produced at power plants has a high electrical pressure or voltage.
   1. This high electrical pressure is necessary to send the electricity over long distances and to overcome the resistance of miles and miles of wire.
   2. Sometimes the electrical pressure in the wires amounts to several thousand volts.
   3. Appliances in the home, however, use only 110 volts or 220 volts; several thousand volts in the home would be dangerous.
   4. Just before the wires that branch off the main wires enter the home, the high voltage is stepped down to 110 or 220 volts by a device called a **transformer.**
   5. Transformers are voltage changers. They can either step down or step up voltage, as needed.

I. Alternating current changes its direction many times each second.
   1. Two changes in direction are called a cycle.
   2. In the home, a 60-cycle alternating current is used.
   3. This means that in 1 second the current flows 60 times in one direction and 60 times in the opposite direction.

J. Sometimes generators are needed that will produce direct current instead of alternating current.
   1. Direct current over long periods of time is needed to charge storage batteries and to put metal plate on materials.
   2. To produce direct current, a generator uses a commutator instead of slip rings.
   3. A commutator is a single ring that is split in half.
   4. The commutator automatically reverses the flow of alternating current just as the current changes direction.
   5. As a result, the current flows in only one direction and so becomes a direct current.

K. The **piezoelectric cell** is another means of producing electrical energy from mechanical energy.
   1. When certain crystals, such as quartz and Rochelle salt, are squeezed mechanically, an electric current is produced.
   2. Piezoelectric cells containing such crystals are used in the cartridges of record players to pick up the sound as the needle moves along the groove of the record. The wiggles in the groove put pressure on the crystal, causing a voltage.
   3. They are also used in systems ignition for propane gas, such as that found in some recreational vehicles and outdoor gas barbecues.

L. Both the photoelectric cell and the photoresistive cell contain a light-sensitive metal and are able to change light energy into electrical energy.
   1. Certain metals, such as potassium, selenium, and cadmium, are sensitive to light.
   2. When light strikes such a metal, electrons flow from the metal and produce a weak electric current.
   3. The stronger the light, the stronger the electric current.
   4. These cells are used in camera light meters to measure the amount of light that strikes the film.
   5. The electricity produced by photoresistive cells is also used to open doors and operate burglar alarms.

M. The **solar battery** is used to produce and store electricity from sunlight.
   1. A solar battery contains many plates made from silicon doped with impurities such as germanium and gallium.
   2. When the plates are exposed to sunlight, an electrical current is produced.
   3. The solar battery is valuable because it needs nothing other than the silicon wafers. There are no parts to wear out.

N. The **thermocouple** makes it possible to change heat energy into electrical energy.
   1. A thermocouple can be made by twisting together an end of each of two wires of different metals and heating the twisted ends.
   2. Because the two metals expand at different rates when heated, a current flows in the direction of least resistance.
   3. When the free ends of the metal wires are connected to a galvanometer, the needle of the galvanometer moves, showing that a weak electric current has been produced.
   4. Thermocouples are used as delicate thermometers to measure very small differences in temperature.
   5. Several or many thermocouples connected together form a thermopile, an instrument sensitive enough to measure the temperature on distant solar bodies when connected to a telescope.

VII. Uses of Electricity

A. Electricity can be used to produce heat.
   1. Every electrical heating appliance has a conductor that gets hot when an electric current flows through it.
   2. The conductor can be a coil of wire or a solid rod.
   3. Heat is produced by the high resistance the conductor offers to the flow of electricity through it.

4. The greater the resistance, the hotter the conductor becomes.
5. Resistance can be increased either by making the wires thinner or by using a material, such as nichrome metal, that has a high resistance to the flow of electric current.
6. Furthermore, the greater the electric current, the hotter the conductor becomes.
7. Electrical appliances that produce heat include toasters, irons, coffee percolators, hot plates, roasters, stoves, water heaters, and blankets.

B. Electricity can be used to produce light (see Chapter 20).

C. Electricity can be used to produce motion and power to run motors.

D. The parts of a motor are exactly the same as the parts of a direct current (DC) generator but basically work just the opposite of generators.
1. Most motors have an armature, a magnet, a commutator, and brushes.
2. A generator changes mechanical energy to electrical energy; a motor changes electrical energy to mechanical energy.
3. A generator uses magnetism to produce electricity; a motor uses electricity to produce magnetism.
4. A motor uses the law of attraction between unlike poles, and of repulsion between like poles of magnets, to make the armature move.
5. When an electric current passes from the brushes and commutator into the armature of a motor, the armature becomes an electromagnet.
6. The north-seeking pole of the electromagnetic armature is attracted by the south-seeking pole of the permanent magnet, and the south-seeking pole of the electromagnet is attracted by the north-seeking pole of the permanent magnet, so the electromagnetic armature moves.
7. As the armature turns, it reaches a position at which the unlike poles of the armature and the permanent magnet face each other.
8. At this point, the commutator reverses the direction of the current flowing into the electromagnetic armature, which automatically reverses the poles of the electromagnetic armature.
9. Now like poles of the armature and the permanent magnet are facing each other.
10. These like poles repel each other, and the armature moves again.
11. As a result, there is continuous motion of the armature from the attraction of unlike poles and the subsequent repulsion of like poles.
12. The commutator keeps reversing the current regularly to change the poles of the electromagnetic armature.

E. Making the magnetic fields of the armature and the permanent magnets stronger can increase the power of a motor.
1. The magnetic field of the armature can be increased by using more turns of wire around the core and by sending more current through the armature.
2. The magnetic field of the permanent magnet can be increased by using more magnets and by converting the permanent magnets to electromagnets.

F. Some motors are built to run on alternating current only, whereas others run on direct current only. Still others can run on either alternating or direct current and are called universal motors. There are many, many uses for motors in modern society.

G. Electricity can be used to plate metals.
1. Using electricity, metals can be coated, or plated, with other metals, in a process called **electroplating.**
2. Only direct current can be used for electroplating.
3. To copper plate an object, the object to be plated and a bar of copper are placed in a solution containing copper sulfate.
4. This arrangement is very much like that of the wet cell, except that in the wet cell a chemical action produces electricity, whereas in electroplating, electricity produces a chemical action.
5. The object and the bar of copper are connected to a source of direct current.
6. The object to be plated acts as the negative pole and is connected to the negative terminal, or connection, of the source of direct current.
7. The copper bar acts as the positive pole and is connected to the positive terminal, or connection, of the source of direct current.
8. When a direct current flows, the copper in the solution is plated onto the object.
9. At the same time, copper from the bar replaces the copper in the solution.
10. The longer the current flows and the stronger the electric current used, the thicker the plate becomes.
11. Electroplating is used to plate silverware and to put chromium on automobile trimmings and zinc on the sheetmetal of cars.

H. Electricity is used in many forms of communication, such as the telephone, radio, television, computers, fax machines, and motion pictures.

LEARNING ACTIVITY 21.7

Electroplating

Obtain some copper sulfate crystals, some dilute sulfuric acid, and a copper strip. Put a heaping tablespoon of copper sulfate into a glass tumbler of warm water and stir vigorously until the copper sulfate dissolves. Then add a few drops of the sulfuric acid. Obtain two pieces of copper bell wire (No. 20), each piece 2/3 meter (26 in.) long. Remove quite a bit of the insulation from the end of one piece of wire and wrap a few turns of bare wire around one end of the copper strip, making sure you have a good contact between the strip and the wire. Bend the copper strip so it will hang over a pencil placed across the rim of the tumbler (Figure 21.7).

Wrap the bare end of the second piece of wire around a house key and suspend the key in the copper sulfate solution by wrapping the wire around the pencil. Now connect the other bare ends of both wires to two dry cells connected in series, as shown in the diagram, making sure that the key is connected to a negative terminal and the copper strip is connected to a positive terminal. Allow the current to flow for 15 minutes, then disconnect the wires and remove the key. The key will be coated with copper.

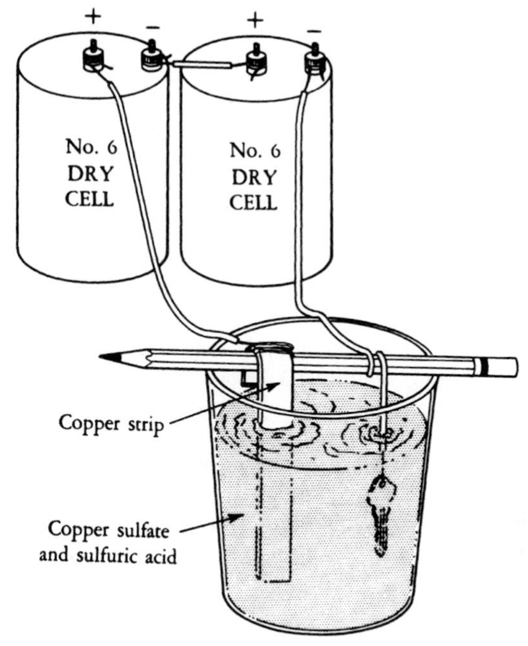

FIGURE 21.7 Coating a key with copper.

 Electronics and Integrated Circuits

I. Electronics

A. Electronics is the branch of engineering and technology that deals with the design and manufacture of devices such as radios, television sets, computers, and CD-ROM players that contain electron tubes, transistors, and related components.

B. An **electron tube** is a device in which conduction by electrons takes place through a vacuum or an inert gas, in a gas-tight container, with operation controlled by the voltage applied at the electrodes.

C. The history of electronics began in 1883 when Thomas Edison discovered that the heated filament in an incandescent bulb gave off material that darkened the inside of the bulb. This darkening of the inside of the bulb is called the **Edison Effect**, and its principle gave rise to the **vacuum tube** that paved the way for the development of radio, television, and computers.

D. The invention of the **transistor** in 1948 allowed for tremendous reduction in the size of electronic circuits and in their power requirements.

E. The later development of the **integrated circuit**, which is thousands of tiny circuits with thousands of transistors, resistors, diodes, and conductors imbedded in a single tiny piece of silicon, paved the way for the continued miniaturization of electronic devices and the increase in speed with which they can operate.

1. An integrated circuit is a complete, although miniature, circuit in itself.
2. It can be one part of an entire circuit board that may contain integrated circuits working together, as in a computer.
3. To place such a miniature, although complex, circuit on a tiny silicon chip (called a **microchip**), a process known as photolithography is used. Some microchips are small enough to pass through the eye of a needle.

F. A **circuit board** is a thin board that all of the silicon chips and integrated circuits in a computer, for example, rest on. In one computer there may be several circuit boards, including memory boards and a board for the processor, all connected by the main data path called a bus.

II. Optoelectronics

A. Conventional electronics is supplemented in communications by optoelectronics, the use of laser light carried by optical fibers to transmit information at high speed.

B. Laser pulses are effected by electronic signals, and the light at the other end of the fiber many kilometers away is converted back into electronic signals.

Exploratory Activities for "Magnetism and Electricity"

Before having children do any work with magnetism and electricity, be sure you and the children understand the safety rules displayed in Figure 21.8.

1. EXPLORING WITH MAGNETS (ANY GRADE LEVEL)

Review the following activities and, depending on the age and maturity of your students, decide the best approach for involving students in these activities. Instructions for each activity will have to be rewritten, depending on how it is used. One approach is to divide the class into groups and have each group do one of the activities as a project, then show and report their finished work to the rest of the class. Another approach is to set up the activities as learning stations around the classroom. Divide the students into groups and allow them to work at each station in turn.

1.1 Determining Which Materials a Magnet Will Attract

Have the students collect a variety of materials, such as tacks, nails, paper clips, pins, needles, coins, rubber bands, pebbles, sand, and small pieces of chalk, crayon, wood, paper, glass, cloth, leather, and aluminum foil. Let the students try to pick up or attract each object with a magnet. Put to one side all those objects that are attracted by the magnet, and ask students to explain why they are attracted. (These objects are all made of iron or steel.)

1.2 A Discrepant Event with Nickels

Give the students a handful of nickels to try to pick up with a magnet. Be sure that these coins include one Canadian nickel. Students will recognize the discrepancy: The magnet will pick up the Canadian nickel but not the American nickels. Have the students try to hypothesize an explanation. (Cobalt and nickel are also attracted by magnets. If the students comment that the U.S. nickels are not attracted by the magnet, explain that U.S. nickels contain mostly copper. Canadian nickels contain more nickel metal and therefore are attracted by the magnet.)

1.3 The Attraction of a Magnet: Strongest at Its Poles

Make a pile of tacks or iron filings. Obtain iron filings from a scientific supply house, or make your own filings by cutting fine steel wool into very small pieces with scissors. Now ask students to try to pick up the tacks or filings with a bar magnet, using different parts of the magnet each time. Ask, What do you observe? (The tacks or filings will be attracted most strongly to the poles of the magnet.) Repeat the activity, using a U-shaped magnet. Have students record and explain their observations.

1.4 Lodestone: A Natural Magnet

Obtain a lodestone and some iron filings from a scientific supply house. You can make your own iron filings by cutting fine steel wool into very small pieces with scissors. Have students dip the lodestone into a pile of iron filings. The filings will cling in bunches at the various poles of the lodestone. Have students count the number of poles in the lodestone. Ask, What do you observe? (There should be an even number, with just as many north-seeking as south-seeking poles.)

1.5 Exploring Magnetic Fields and Lines of Force

Place a sheet of cardboard or window glass over a bar magnet. Then give students the following instructions: Sprinkle iron filings or tiny bits of cut-up steel wool all over the cardboard, and then tap the cardboard gently a few times

1. Disconnect electrical appliances, especially heating appliances, when they are not being used.
2. Never touch a switch or electrical appliance when your hands are wet.
3. Never touch a switch, electrical appliance, radio, or telephone when you are in the bathtub.
4. Make sure the switch is turned off whenever you disconnect or connect an electrical appliance.
5. Do not overload your home circuit by plugging too many appliances into one wall receptacle.
6. Never touch a bare wire that is carrying an electric current.
7. Never poke around the back of a radio, television set, or computer when these appliances are plugged in.
8. Never put your finger into an open electric socket.
9. Replace electric cords when the insulation is cracked or worn thin.
10. Never touch an electric cord with wet hands.
11. Do not touch an electric cord with one hand and a water pipe, faucet, or radiator with the other hand.
12. When a fuse "blows," first find out what made it blow and correct the condition before resetting or putting in a new fuse. Always replace a blown fuse with a new one that will carry the same amount of current, never with a fuse of a higher amperage. Never put a penny in the fuse box instead of a new fuse.
13. Do not wrap or coil the cords of electric appliances that are in use.
14. Keep magnets away from computers and other electronic appliances; the magnetic field can damage the computer circuitry.

FIGURE 21.8 Safety rules for electricity and magnetism.

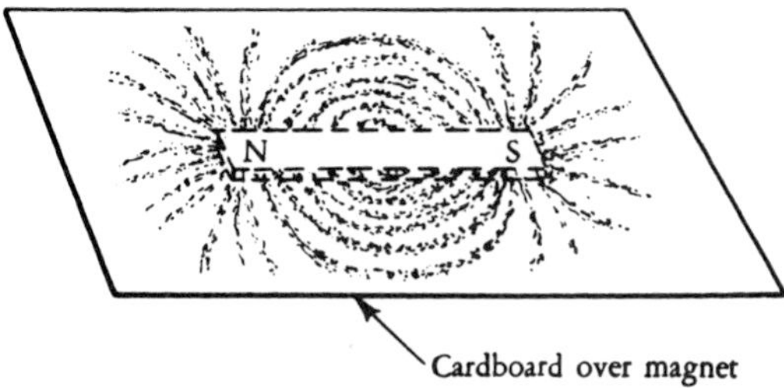

FIGURE 21.9 Lines of force in a magnetic field.

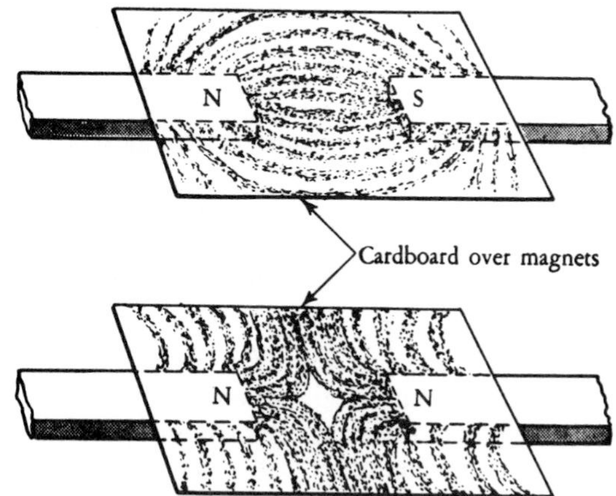

FIGURE 21.10 Lines of force between unlike and like poles.

(Figure 21.9). Diagram and explain your observations. (The filings will rearrange themselves to form a definite pattern, showing the magnetic field and the lines of force located within the field. Note how the lines of force are concentrated at the poles.)

Repeat the activity, having students use two bar magnets with the north-seeking pole of one bar magnet 5 centimeters (2 in.) from the south-seeking pole of the other bar magnet (Figure 21.10). Again, ask students to diagram and explain their observations. (The lines of force seem to attract each other.) Repeat the activity, this time having students place two like poles near each other. Ask them to diagram and explain their observations. (The lines of force show the repulsion between like poles.)

1.6 Magnets Attracting Through Nonmagnetic Materials

Give students the following instructions: Place a piece of cardboard on two piles of books set a short distance apart. Put some thumbtacks on the cardboard, and then slide a magnet along the underside of the cardboard (Figure 21.11). What do you observe? (The magnet will attract the tacks and make them move.) Repeat the activity, using other materials (sheets of glass, wood, aluminum foil, and cloth), and record your observations on a data table that you devise. Now use a sheet of iron, cut from a large "tin" can with tin snips. Explain your observation. (The tacks will not move because the force of the magnet passes into the iron, making it a magnet that attracts the tacks and holds them fast.)

FIGURE 21.11 The force of a magnet passes through nonmagnetic materials.

1.7 A Compass Needle Is a Magnet

Give students the following instructions: Examine a compass. The end of the needle that points to the north is usually colored blue, black, or red and is called the north-seeking pole. Bring the north-seeking pole of a bar magnet near the compass. Record your observations. (The north-seeking pole of the compass needle will be repelled, while the south-seeking pole of the needle will be attracted. Point out that a compass needle can be used to determine the poles of an unmarked magnet.)

1.8 The Nature of Magnetism

Give students the following instructions: Fill a test tube half full of iron filings and stopper it. Stroke the test tube from end to end with one pole of a strong bar magnet about 20 times. Stroke slowly and gently in one direction only, being sure to lift your hand up in the air before coming down for another stroke. The test tube will now act like a magnet, because you have lined up all the filings so that they behave just as the molecules in them would behave, with their north-seeking poles pointing in one direction and their south-seeking poles pointing in the opposite direction. Bring a compass near the test tube and determine the poles of this test-tube magnet.

Now shake the test tube vigorously for some time, and then test with the compass again. What do you observe? (Mixing up the filings causes the test tube to lose its ability to behave like a magnet.)

1.9 Making a Temporary Magnet by Induction

Give students the following instructions: Plunge one pole of a bar magnet into a pile of small tacks, and then lift up the magnet. What do you observe? (There will be a cluster of tacks around the pole.) How do you explain this? Do you observe anything else? (Each tack becomes a magnet by induction and attracts other tacks. This induced magnetism is temporary because as soon as the bar magnet is taken away, the tacks do not attract each other anymore.)

Hold a large iron nail or spike quite close to one pole of a strong bar magnet. Keeping the nail and magnet in this position, dip the nail into a pile of small tacks, and then lift up the nail (Figure 21.12). What do you observe and how do you explain it? (The nail has been magnetized by

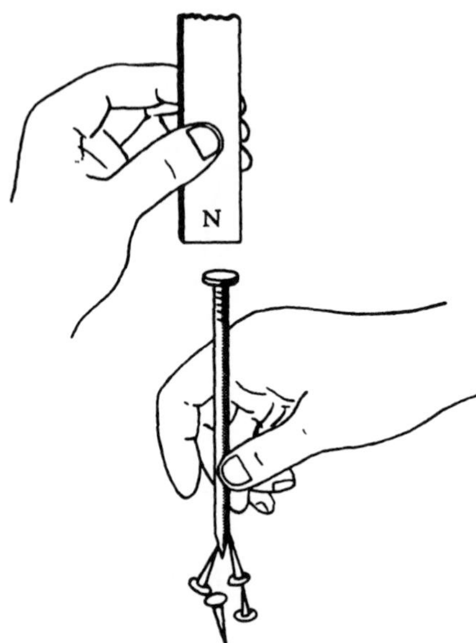

FIGURE 21.12 The nail attracts the tacks because of induced magnetism.

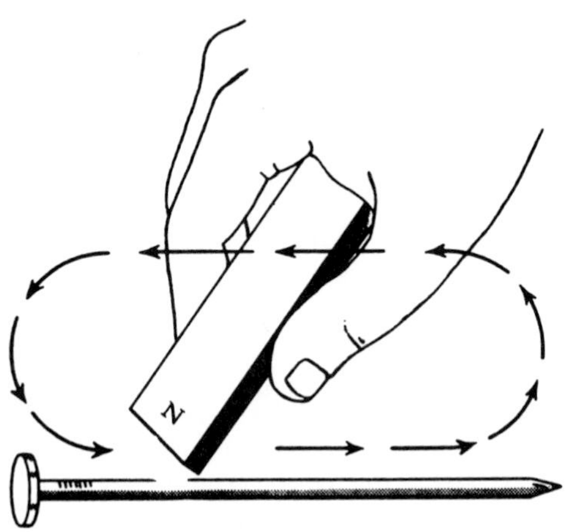

FIGURE 21.13 A nail becomes a temporary magnet when stroked with one pole of a bar magnet.

induction, without even touching the magnet, and attracts the tacks. The tacks in turn are also magnetized by induction. When the bar magnet is removed, the nail loses its magnetism and the tacks fall off.)

1.10 Making a Temporary Magnet by Stroking

Give students the following instructions: Stroke a large iron nail or spike from end to end with one pole of a strong bar magnet about 20 times. Stroke slowly and gently in one direction only, being sure to lift your hand up in the air before coming down for another stroke (Figure 21.13). Test the nail by dipping it into a pile of iron filings or tacks. What do you observe? (The nail will become a magnet and pick up iron filings or tacks.) Set the nail aside for 3 to 4 days, and then test it again. What do you observe? (Because the nail is made of soft iron, it will have lost most of its magnetism and it will pick up very few filings or tacks.)

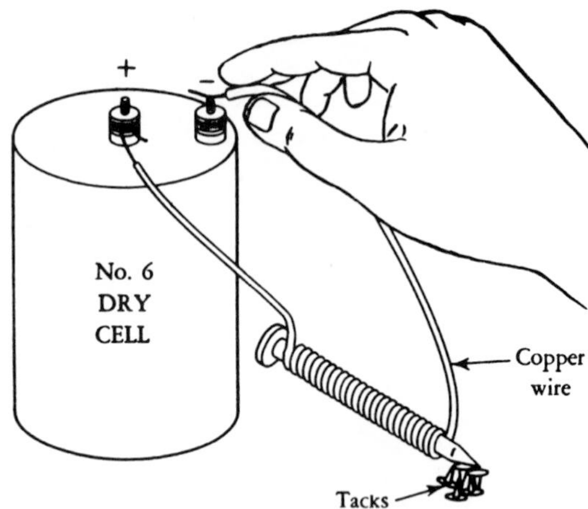

FIGURE 21.14 An electromagnet is a temporary magnet.

1.12 Making a Temporary Magnet with Electricity

Obtain some insulated copper bell wire (No. 20) from a hardware store. Give students the following instructions: Wind the wire in a coil around a large iron nail or spike about 15 to 20 times. Remove the insulation from both ends of the wire, connect one end to a terminal of a dry cell, and touch the other end to the second terminal for a few seconds (Figure 21.14). The nail will now pick up tacks and other objects made of iron or steel. It is called an electromagnet. When you remove the wire from one of the terminals, what do you observe and how do you explain it? (The electric current stops flowing and the nail loses its magnetism.) (Note: Keep the wires connected to the dry cell for as short a time as possible. Otherwise, the dry cell will be used up very quickly.)

1.13 Making a Permanent Magnet by Stroking

Repeat activity 1.11, having students use a steel knitting needle instead of an iron nail. Ask, What do you observe from this experiment? (The needle retains most of its magnetism after it has been set aside for 3 to 4 days.)

Have students determine the poles of this magnetized needle by bringing a compass near it. Then cut the needle in half with cutting pliers. Ask students, What do you observe and how can it be explained? (Each half will become a new magnet, with poles.)

1.14 Making a Permanent Magnet with Electricity

Obtain a cardboard tube, such as a mailing tube, about 25 centimeters (10 in.) long and 2 centimeters (1 in.) in diameter. Obtain some insulated thin copper wire (No. 26 or 28) from a hardware store. Give students the following instructions: Wind the wire around the tube, covering almost all of the tube, leaving about 45 centimeters (18 in.) of wire free at each end. Connect two dry cells in series, as shown in Figure 21.15. Place a steel knitting needle all the way into the cardboard tube. Now touch the two end wires to the terminals of the dry cells, as shown in the diagram, for 2 to 3 seconds only. Remove the needle and test it for magnetism on tacks and other iron or steel objects.

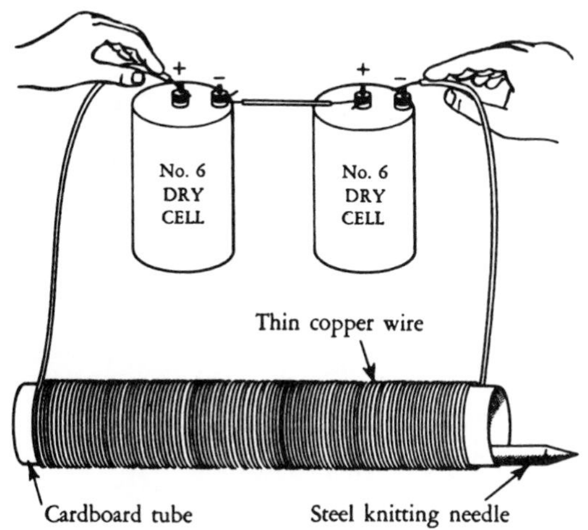

FIGURE 21.15 Making a steel knitting needle become a permanent magnet.

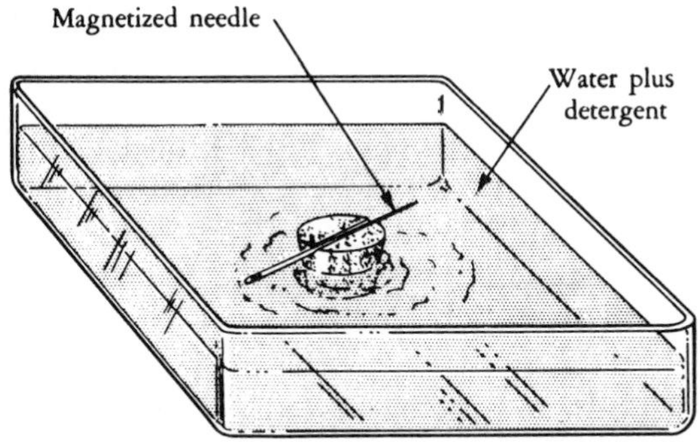

FIGURE 21.16 A floating, magnetized needle compass.

1.14 Observing Magnets Lose Their Magnetism

Have students magnetize two large, steel sewing needles by stroking them with one pole of a strong bar magnet. Let them see how many iron filings or small tacks each needle will attract. Now hold one needle with forceps or pliers in the flame of a Bunsen burner or alcohol lamp for about 3 minutes. At the same time, have one of the students pound the other needle repeatedly with a hammer. Now test both needles again to see how many iron filings each needle will attract. What do you observe? (Heating and striking or jarring a magnet will disarrange the molecules, causing the magnet to lose its magnetism.)

1.15 A Floating Compass

Give students the following instructions: Magnetize a steel sewing needle by stroking it with one pole of a strong bar magnet. Slice a round piece, 13 millimeters (1/2 in.) thick, from a cork stopper. Cut a groove across the center of the top of the cork slice. Put the needle into the groove and place the cork slice in a glass, china, or aluminum dish filled with water (Figure 21.16). (A teaspoon of detergent in the water will lower the surface tension of the water and prevent the cork from moving to one side of the dish and staying there. The needle will soon behave like a compass needle by assuming a north-south position because of the Earth's magnetic field.)

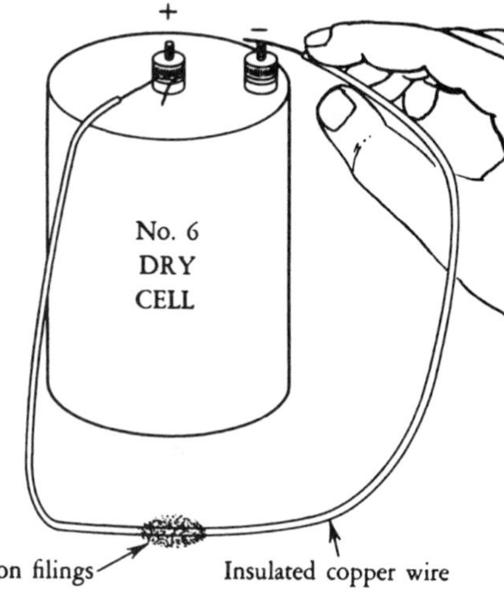

FIGURE 21.17 Wire carrying electric current acts like a magnet.

2. EXPLORING WITH ELECTROMAGNETS (GRADES 4–8)

Review the following three activities and, depending on the age and maturity of your students, decide the best approach for involving the students in these activities. Instructions for each activity will have to be rewritten, depending on how it is used.

Note: Electromagnets draw a great amount of current and can use up dry cells very quickly. When working with electromagnets, keep the wires connected to the dry cells for as short a time as possible.

2.1 Testing for Magnetism in a Wire Carrying an Electric Current

Obtain some copper bell wire (No. 20) from a hardware store. Give students the following instructions: Remove the insulation from both ends of the wire and connect one end to a terminal of a dry cell. Now touch the other bare end of the wire to the second terminal of the dry cell for a few seconds and try to pick up some iron filings or finely cut-up steel wool with the middle part of the wire (Figure 21.17). (The wire will attract the filings, showing that a wire carrying an electric current has a magnetic field around it.) Place a compass beside the wire, and then touch the bare end of the wire to the terminal of the dry cell again. (The compass needle will move, showing that the magnetic field around the wire affects the magnetized needle.)

2.2 Testing for Magnetism in a Coil of Wire Carrying an Electric Current

Give students the following instructions: Wrap the bell wire (No. 20) about 15 to 20 times around a pencil to form a coil, and then remove the pencil. Remove the insulation from both ends of the wire, connect one end to a terminal of a dry cell, and touch the other end to the second terminal for a few seconds (Figure 21.18). The coil will act like a magnet, picking up tacks and other objects made of iron or steel.

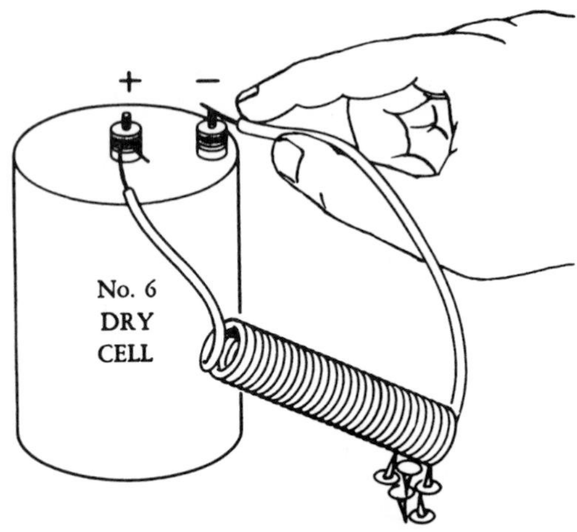

FIGURE 21.18 A wire coil carrying electric current acts like a magnet.

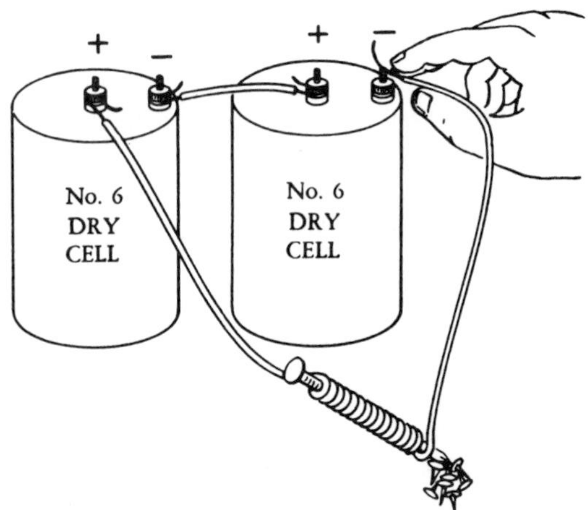

FIGURE 21.19 Increasing the strength of the electric current makes the electromagnet stronger.

Determine the poles of this coil magnet by bringing a compass near it. The blue or black end of the magnetized compass needle is a north-seeking pole, so it will be attracted to the coil magnet's south-seeking pole and repelled by the north-seeking pole.

2.3 Making an Electromagnet Stronger

Give students the following instructions: Make an electromagnet as described in activity 2.2, winding the wire around the nail exactly 20 times. Count the number of tacks the electromagnet will attract. Now wind 20 more turns of wire around the same nail, and again count the number of tacks the electromagnet will pick up. (Doubling the number of turns will double the strength of the electromagnet.)

Make another electromagnet with just 20 turns of wire, and count the number of tacks it will pick up. Now connect the electromagnet to two dry cells arranged in series (Figure 21.19), and again count the number of tacks that will be attracted. (Doubling the strength of the electric current will double the strength of the electromagnet.)

Have the students predict (and test) what will happen when both the number of turns and the strength of the electric current are doubled.

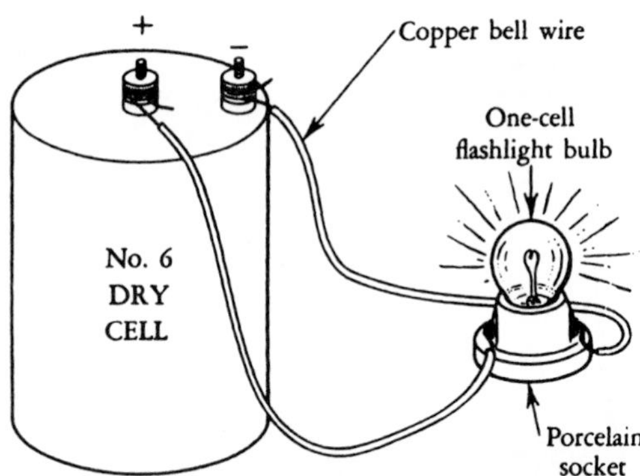

FIGURE 21.20 A simple electric circuit.

3. EXPLORING CURRENT ELECTRICITY (GRADES 4–8)

Review the following eight activities and, depending on the age and maturity of your students, decide the best approach for involving the students in these activities. As a result of these experiments, your students may want to design their own—to be done under your guidance.

One approach is to divide the class into groups and have each group do one of the activities as a project, then show and report their finished work to the rest of the class. Instructions for each activity will have to be rewritten, depending on how it is used.

3.1 Making a Simple Electric Circuit

Obtain a No. 6 dry cell, some insulated copper bell wire (No. 20), a one-cell flashlight bulb, and a small porcelain socket to hold the bulb from a scientific supply house or a hardware store. Instruct students as follows: Set up a simple electric circuit, as shown in Figure 21.20, being sure to remove the insulation from the ends of the wires. Trace the flow of current through the completed circuit. Now break the circuit by disconnecting one of the wires attached to the dry cell or porcelain socket.

3.2 Comparing Conductors and Nonconductors

Give students the following instructions: Connect a dry cell, some copper bell wire (No. 20), a one-cell flashlight bulb, and a porcelain socket as shown in Figure 21.21, being sure to remove the insulation from the ends of the wires. Touch the bare ends of the two wires to a nail, the metal part of a pen or pencil, various coins, aluminum foil, and pieces of wood, rubber, cloth, and glass. Note which kinds of materials do and do not conduct electricity. Establish the relationship between electrical conductivity and how tightly or loosely the atoms hold some of their electrons.

3.3 Including a Switch

Obtain a knife switch from a hardware store or scientific supply house. Give students the following instructions: Insert the switch into the simple electric circuit described in activity 3.2 (Figure 21.22). Operate the switch and show how it closes and opens the circuit. Replace the knife switch with a pushbutton switch, and then a snap switch.

Make your own switch. Using tin snips, cut a strip of metal, 10 centimeters (4 in.) long and 2 centimeters (1 in.)

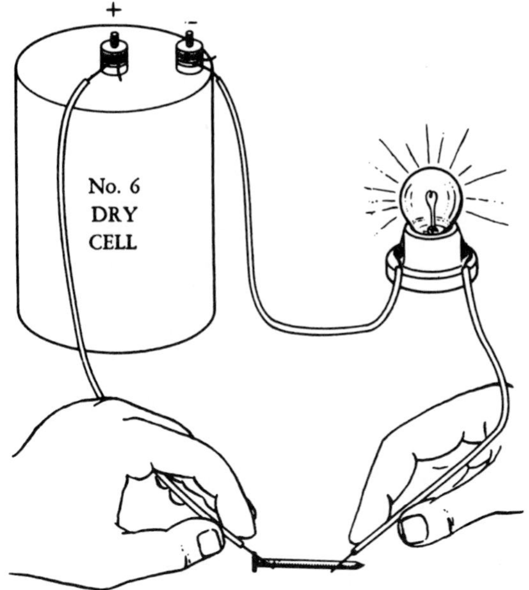

FIGURE 21.21 A nail is a good conductor of electricity.

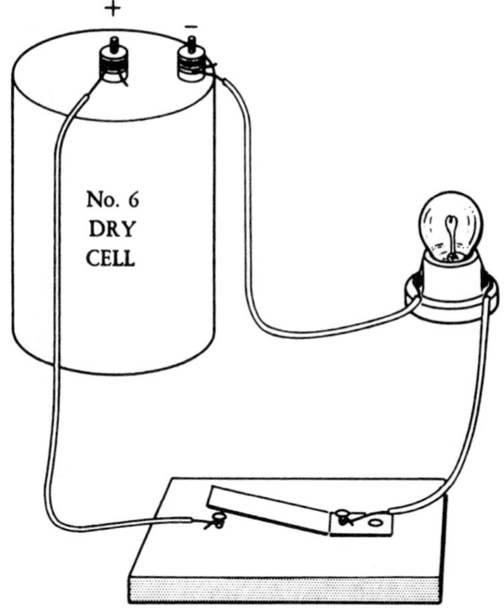

FIGURE 21.23 A homemade switch.

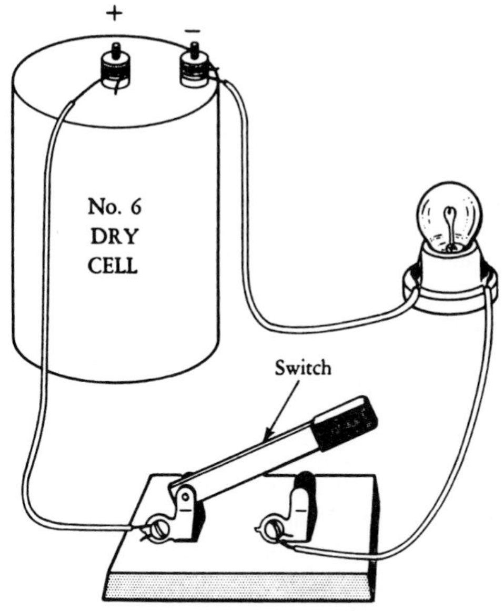

FIGURE 21.22 A knife switch can open and close an electric circuit.

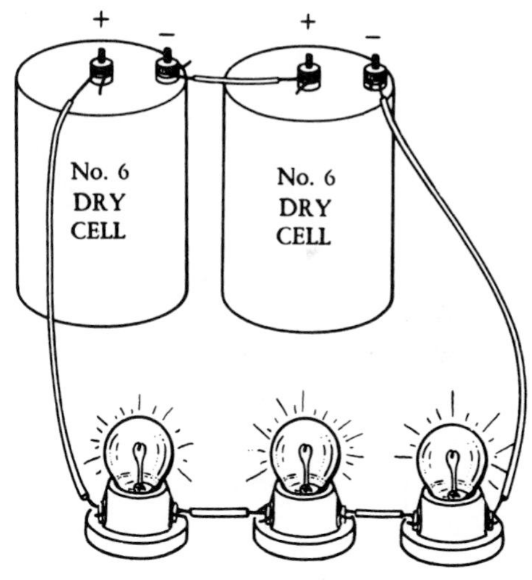

FIGURE 21.24 Flashlight bulbs connected in series.

wide, from a can. Nail one end to a small board. Use two nails, but drive one only partially into the board. Bend the strip back so that it angles away from the board. Drive a small roofing nail partially into the board so that its head is under the metal strip. Now insert this homemade switch into your simple circuit, as shown in Figure 21.23. Operate the switch to open and close the circuit.

3.4 Series and Parallel Circuits

Give students the following instructions: Connect three porcelain sockets and three one-cell flashlight bulbs in series, as shown in Figure 21.24. Note that the electric current flows through each bulb, one after the other, and the bulbs light up dimly. Note the relative brightness of the bulbs. The bulb closest to the positive side of the battery will be the brightest. Each succeeding bulb will be dimmer. Unscrewing one of the bulbs will break the complete circuit, and then the other bulbs go out.

Now connect the sockets and bulbs in parallel as shown in Figure 21.25. Point out that the current branches off, so part of the current goes through one socket and part goes on to the next socket. Note how brightly lighted all the bulbs are. Unscrewing one of the bulbs will break only the part of the circuit that flows through that bulb, so the remaining two bulbs continue to stay lighted. If you unscrew a second bulb, the third bulb will continue to burn. Hypothesize as to which type of circuit will run the battery down quickest. (The parallel circuit will.)

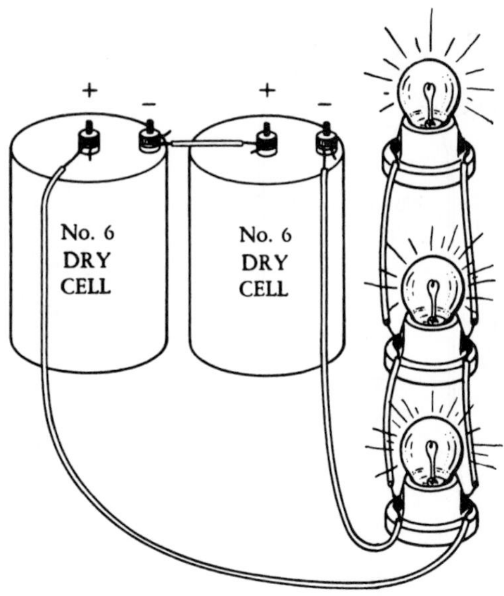

FIGURE 21.25 Flashlight bulbs connected in parallel.

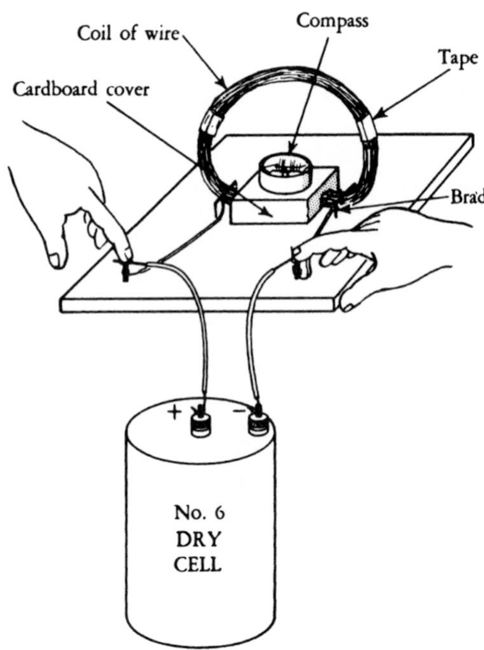

FIGURE 21.26 A current detector (galvanometer).

3.5 Making a Galvanometer (Current Detector)

Obtain insulated thin copper wire (No. 26 or 28) from a scientific supply house or hardware store. Give the following instructions: Wind about 100 turns of the wire around a glass jar, about 7 centimeters (3 in.) in diameter, to form a narrow coil. Slip the coil off the jar and tape it at two or three points to hold the wires neatly in place. Leave some wire free at each end of the coil, and remove 2 centimeters (1 in.) of insulation from each end of the wire. Use two brads to attach the coil to a small wood board and to hold the coil upright (Figure 21.26). Place the cover of a small cardboard box inside the coil, first cutting grooves on each side of the cover so it will rest in a stable and even position on the board. Drive two small nails almost all the way into the board and wrap the bare end of each wire around a nail.

Now rest a compass on top of the cardboard cover, and turn the board until the compass needle is parallel with the direction of the coil. Then turn the compass until the letters N and S are under the needle. Your galvanometer is now ready to operate. Connect a dry cell to the galvanometer by touching the bare ends of the wires from the dry cell to the nails of the galvanometer. The compass needle will be deflected, showing the presence of an electric current. (Point out that when an electric current flows through the galvanometer coil, a magnetic field is formed that affects the magnetized compass needle. The greater the current flowing through the coil, the stronger the magnetic field will be, and the more the compass needle will be deflected.)

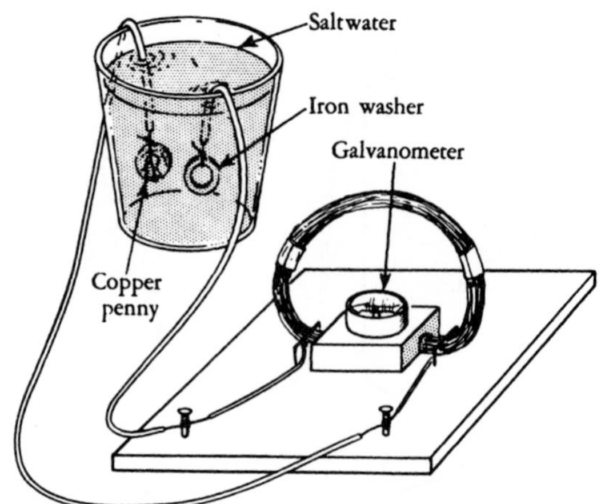

FIGURE 21.27 A simple electric wet cell.

3.6 Make a Simple Electric Cell

Give students the following instructions: Dissolve a tablespoon of common table salt in a glass tumbler of warm water. Obtain an iron washer, a penny, and two lengths of insulated copper bell wire (No. 20). Strip 7 centimeters (3 in.) of insulation from one end of each wire and 2 centimeters (0.75 in.) from the other end. Wrap the penny and the washer separately with the longer bare end of the wire and suspend them in the saltwater by bending the wires tightly over the edge of the tumbler (Figure 21.27). Make sure the coin and the washer are not touching each other. Now touch the other ends of the wires to the nails of the galvanometer described in activity 3.5. The compass needle will be deflected, showing the presence of an electric current. Repeat the activity, using other combinations of two different metals. (Point out that chemical energy has been changed into electrical energy.)

3.7 Generating Electricity with a Magnet and a Coil of Wire

Give students the following instructions: Wind about 50 turns of insulated copper bell wire (No. 20) around a glass jar, about 5 to 7.5 centimeters (2 to 3 in.) in diameter, to form a coil. Slip the coil off the jar and tape it at a

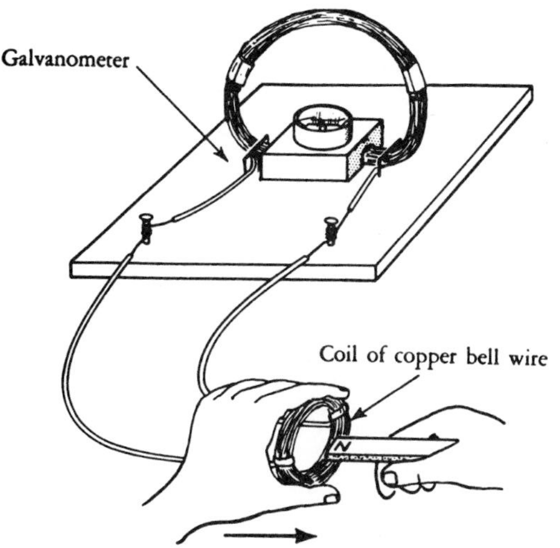

FIGURE 21.28 Generating electricity with a magnet and a coil of wire.

few points to hold the wires neatly in place. Leave 1 meter (3 ft) of wire free at each end of the coil. Remove the insulation from the end of the coil and from the end of each wire. Connect the coil to a galvanometer as shown in Figure 21.28. Hold the coil as far away from the galvanometer as possible and move the center of the coil across a bar magnet. The compass needle of the galvanometer will be deflected, showing the presence of an electric current. When you move the coil in the opposite direction, the needle is also deflected in the opposite direction. When you hold the coil stationary, there is no deflection because no lines of force in the magnetic field are being cut. When you move the coil continuously back and forth across the magnet, a continuous alternating current is produced. Repeat the learning activity, this time holding the coil stationary and moving the magnet. Point out that mechanical energy is being changed into electrical energy.

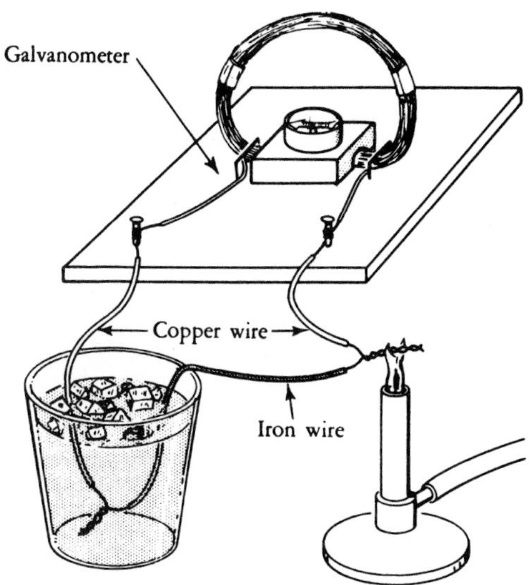

FIGURE 21.29 Generating electricity with a thermocouple.

3.8 Using a Thermocouple

Give students the following instructions: Cut a piece of wire from a coat hanger and scrape the paint away from both ends. Obtain two pieces of copper bell wire (No. 20) and remove the insulation from the ends of both wires. Tightly twist one end of a copper wire to each end of the coat hanger wire and connect the other free end of each copper wire to a galvanometer. Now place one of the twisted ends into a glass tumbler containing cold water and ice cubes, and heat the other twisted end with the flame of a Bunsen burner (Figure 21.29). The compass needle of the galvanometer will be deflected, showing the presence of an electric current. Heat energy has been changed into electrical energy.

Bibliography

 Chapter 1

Allen, E. E., and Lederman, L. "Lessons Learned: The Teachers Academy for Mathematics and Science." *Phi Delta Kappan 80*(2):158, 160, 162–164 (October 1998).

Anderson, O. R. "A Neurocognitive Perspective on Current Learning and Science Instructional Strategies." *Science Education 81*(1):67–89 (January 1997).

Bybee, R. W. W. *Achieving Scientific Literacy: From Purposes to Practices.* Crystal Lake, IL: Heinemann, 1997.

Craig, G. S. "Elementary School Science in the Past Century." *Science Education 24*(4):11–14 (February 1957).

Hurd, P. D. *Inventing Science Education for the New Millennium.* New York: Teachers College Press, 1997.

Kellough, R. D., Cangelosi, J. S., Collette, A. T., Chiappetta, E. L., Souviney, R. J., Trowbridge, L. W., and Bybee, R. W. *Integrating Mathematics and Science for Intermediate and Middle School Students.* Englewood Cliffs, NJ: Merrill/Prentice Hall, 1996.

Kellough, R. D., Carin, A., Seefeldt, C., Barbour, N., and Souviney, R. J. *Integrating Mathematics and Science for Kindergarten and Primary Children.* Upper Saddle River, NJ: Merrill/Prentice Hall, 1996.

Lopez, R., and Schultz, T. "Two Revolutions in K–8 Science Education." *Physics Today 54*(9) (September 2001). Accessed online January 28, 2002, at http://www.physicstoday.org/pt/vol-54/iss-9/p44.html.

National Research Council. *Inquiry and the National Science Education Standards: A Guide for Teaching and Learning.* Washington, DC: National Academy Press, 2000.

Newman, J. M., et al. *Tensions of Teaching: Beyond Tips to Critical Reflection.* New York: Teachers College Press, 1998.

Underhill, O. E. *The Origins and Development of Elementary School Science.* New York: Scott Foresman, 1941.

 Chapter 2

American Association for the Advancement of Science. *Atlas of Science Literacy.* Arlington, VA: NSTA Press, 2001.

Baxter, L. M., and Kurtz, M. J. "When a Hypothesis Is NOT an Educated Guess." *Science and Children 38*(7):18–20 (April 2001).

Bybee, R. W. W. *Achieving Scientific Literacy: From Purposes to Practices.* Crystal Lake, IL: Heinemann, 1997.

DeBacker, T., and Nelson, R. "Motivation to Learn Science: Difference Related to Gender, Class Type, and Ability." *The Journal of Educational Research 93*(4):245–254 (March/April 2000).

Decker, K. A. "Meeting State Standards through Integration." *Science and Children 36*(6):28–32, 69 (March 1999).

Hinman, R. L. "Who Is Scientifically Literate, Anyway?" *Phi Delta Kappan 79*(7):540–542 (March 1998).

National Research Council. *Linking Science and Technology to Society's Environmental Goals.* Washington, DC: National Academy Press, 1996.

Newman, J. M., et al. *Tensions of Teaching: Beyond Tips to Critical Reflection.* New York: Teachers College Press, 1998.

Phillips, M. N. "Science at Sea." *Science Scope 24*(6):16–19 (March 2001).

 Chapter 3

Armstrong, T. *Awakening Genius in the Classroom.* Alexandria, VA: Association for Supervision and Curriculum Development, 1998.

Beisenherz, P. C., Dantonio, M., and Richardson, L. "The Learning Cycle and Instructional Conversations," *Science Scope 24*(4):34–38 (January 2001).

Bruner, J. S. *Acts of Meaning.* Cambridge, MA: Harvard University Press, 1990.

Cavallo, A. M. L. "Convection Connections: Integrated Learning Cycle Investigations." *Science and Children* 38(8):20–25 (May 2001).

Colburn, A. *Constructivism and Science Teaching*. Bloomington, IN: Fastback 435, Phi Delta Kappa International, 1998.

Dunn, R., and Dunn, K. *Teaching Elementary Students Through Their Individual Learning Styles*. Boston: Allyn & Bacon, 1992.

Glock, J., Wertz, S., and Meyer, M. *Discovering the Naturalist Intelligence: Science in the School Yard*. Brookline, MA: Zephyr, 1999.

Holloway, J. H. "How Does the Brain Learn Science?" *Educational Leadership 58*(3):85–86 (November 2000).

Jensen, E. *Teaching with the Brain in Mind*. Alexandria, VA: Association for Supervision and Curriculum Development, 1998.

Lowery, L. "How New Science Curriculums Reflect Brain Research." *Educational Leadership 56*(3):26–30 (November 1998).

Marek, E. A., and Cavallo, A. M. L. *The Learning Cycle: Elementary School Science and Beyond*. Portsmouth, NH: Heinemann, 1997.

McDuffie, T. E, Jr. "Scientists—Geeks & Nerds?" *Science and Children 38*(8):16–19 (May 2001).

Minstrell, J., and van Zee, E. H., eds. *Inquiring into Inquiry Learning and Teaching in Science*. Washington, DC: American Association for the Advancement of Science, 2000.

National Research Council. *Inquiry and the National Science Education Standards*. Washington, DC: National Academy Press, 2000.

National Science Foundation. *Inquiry: Thoughts, Views, and Strategies for the K–5 Classroom*. Foundations, Volume 2. Arlington, VA: Author, 1999.

Piaget, J. *The Development of Thought: Elaboration of Cognitive Structures*. New York: Viking, 1977.

Searson, R., and Dunn, R. "The Learning-Style Teaching Model." *Science and Children* 38(5):22–26 (February 2001).

Sinclair, A., and Coates, L. "Teaching Multiple Intelligences." *Science Scope* 22(5):17–21 (February 1999).

Varelas, M., Pappas, C., Barry, A., and O'Neill, A. "Examining Language to Capture Scientific Understandings: The Case of the Water Cycle." *Science and Children* 38(7):26–29 (April 2001).

 Chapter 4

Anderson, O. R. "A Neurocognitive Perspective on Current Learning Theory and Science Instructional Strategies." *Science Education 81*(1):67–89 (January 1997).

Becker, R. R. "The Critical Role of Students' Questions in Literacy Development." *Educational Forum 64*(3):261–271 (Spring 2000).

Blosser, P. E. *How to Ask the Right Questions*. Arlington, VA: National Science Teachers Association, 1991.

Brualdi, A. C. *Classroom Questions*. ERIC/AE Digest 422407 (Washington, DC: ERIC Clearinghouse on Assessment and Evaluation, 1998).

Ciardiello, A. V. "Student Questioning and Multidimensional Literacy in the 21st Century." *Educational Forum 64*(3):215–222 (Spring 2000).

Eisner, E. W. "The Kind of Schools We Need." *Phi Delta Kappan 83*(8):576–583 (April 2002).

Gasparich, G., Cole, L., and Bell, R. "Who, Besides Marie Curie?" *Science Scope 24*(8):49–51 (May 2001).

Gauthier, L. R. "The Role of Questioning: Beyond Comprehension's Front Door." *Reading Horizons 40*(4):239–252 (2000).

Harpaz, Y., and Lefstein, A. "Communities of Thinking." *Educational Leadership 58*(3):54–57 (November 2000).

Harris, R. L. "Batting 1,000: Questioning Techniques in Student-Centered Classrooms." *Clearing House 74*(1):25–26 (September/October 2000).

Iwasyk, M. "Kids Questioning Kids: 'Experts' Sharing'." *Science and Children 35*(1):42–46, 80 (September 1997).

King, A. "Guiding Knowledge Construction in the Classroom: Effects of Teaching Children How to Question and How to Explain." *American Educational Research Journal 31*(2):358–368 (Summer 1994).

Koufetta-Menicou, C., and Scaife, J. "Teachers' Questions—Types and Significance in Science Education." *School Science Review 81*(296):79–84 (March 2000).

Kurose, A. "Eyes on Science: Asking Questions about the Moon on the Playground, in Class, and at Home." In J. Minstrell and E. H. van Zee, *Inquiring into Inquiry Learning and Teaching in Science* (Washington, DC: American Association for the Advancement of Science, 2000), 139–147.

MacKenzie, A. H. "The Role of Teacher Stance When Infusing Inquiry Questioning into Middle School Science Classrooms." *School Science and Mathematics 101*(3):143–153 (March 2001).

Martinello, M. L. "Learning to Question for Inquiry." *Educational Forum 62*(2):164–171 (Winter 1998).

Maxim, G. "When to Answer the Question 'Why?'" *Science and Children 35*(3):41–45 (November/December 1997).

National Research Council. *Inquiry and the National Science Education Standards*. Washington, DC: National Academy Press, 2000.

Shepardson, D. P., and Britsch, S. J. "Children's Science Journals: Tools for Teaching, Learning, and Assessing." *Science and Children 34*(5):12–17, 46–47 (February 1997).

Spargo, P. E., and Enderstein, L. G. "What Questions Do They Ask? Ausubel Rephrased." *Science and Children 34*(6):43–45 (March 1997).

Tower, C. "Questions That Matter: Preparing Elementary Students for the Inquiry Process." *Reading Teacher 53*(7):550–557 (April 2000).

Traver, R. "What Is a Good Guiding Question?" *Educational Leadership 55*(6):70–73 (March 1998).

Ward, C. "Never Give 'Em a Straight Answer." *Science and Children 35*(3):46–49 (November/December 1997).

Wilson-Sadler, D. "Using Effective Praise to Produce Positive Results in the Classroom." *Teaching and Change 4*(4):338–357 (Summer 1997).

Chapter 5

Anderson, O. R. "A Neurocognitive Perspective on Current Learning Theory and Science Instructional Strategies." *Science Education 81*(1):67–89 (January 1997).

Barak, M., and Raz, E. "Hot-Air Balloons: Project-Centered Study as a Bridge between Science and Technology." *Science Education 84*(1):27–42 (January 2000).

Beamon, G. W. "Guiding the Inquiry of Young Adolescent Minds." *Middle School Journal 33*(2):19–27 (January 2002).

Beisenherz, P. C., Dantonio, M., and Richardson, L. "The Learning Cycle and Instructional Conversations." *Science Scope 24*(4):34–38 (January 2001).

Brown, S. W. "A Human Systems Debate." *Science Scope 23*(5):37–41 (February 2000).

Buck, G. A. "Teaching Science to English-as-Second-Language Learners." *Science and Children 38*(3):38–41 (November/December 2000).

Byrnie, F. H. *Painless Science Projects.* Hauppauge, NY: Barron's Educational Series, 1998.

Checkovich, B. H., and Sterling, D. R. "Oh Say Can You See." *Science and Children 38*(4):32–35 (January 2001).

Colburn, A. "An Inquiry Primer." *Science Scope 23*(6):42–44 (March 2000).

Compton-Lilly, C. "An Award-Winning Approach to Lead Safety." *Science and Children 39*(4):26–30 (January 2002).

DeVore, E., and O'Sullivan, K. A. "Evolution: Fundamental Theme for Integrated Science." *California Journal of Science Education 1*(2):101–116 (Spring 2001).

Diffily, D. "Project Reptile!" *Science and Children 38*(7):30–35 (April 2001).

Downing, J. E. "How Animals Play Hide and Seek: A Game of Survival." *Science Activities 37*(4):15–17 (Winter 2001).

Fischer, D. "Time-Out for Science." *Science Scope 23*(3):20–22 (November/December 1999).

Gasparich, G., Cole, L., and Bell, M. "Who, Besides Marie Curie?" *Science Scope 24*(8):49–51 (May 2001).

Goldson, J. M., Marlette, S., and Pennington, A. "Centimeters, Millimeters, and Monsters." *Science and Children 39*(2):42–47 (October 2001).

Hand, B., et al. "Writing to Learn." *Science Scope 23*(1): 21–23 (October 1999).

Hinman, L. A. "What's the Buzz? A Classroom Simulation." *Science and Children 37*(5):24–27 (February 2000).

Holliday, W. G. "Integrating Writing with Science." *Science Scope 24*(1):72–74 (September 2000).

Holliday, W. G. "Scaffolding in Science." *Science Scope 25*(1):68, 70–71 (September 2001).

Jones, G., Carter, G., and Rua, M. "Children's Concepts: Tools for Transforming Science Teachers' Knowledge." *Science Education 83*(5):545–557 (September 1999).

Jones, I. "A Workshop Approach." *Science and Children 37*(3):26–30, 55 (November/December 1999).

Kaser, S. "Searching the Heavens with Children's Literature: A Design for Teaching Science." *Language Arts 78*(4):348–356 (March 2001).

Koenig, M. "Debating Real-World Issues." *Science Scope 24*(5):19–23 (February 2001).

Kolbe, T. "Community Investigations: Looking at Uncertainty." *Primary Voices K–6 8*(2):20–26 (October 1999).

Kwan, T., and Texley, T. *Exploring Safety: A Guide for Elementary Teachers.* Arlington, VA: National Science Teachers Association Press, 2002.

Laboratory Safety Institute. *Safety Is Elementary: The New Standard for Safety in the Elementary Science Classroom.* Natick, MA: Author, 2000.

Laplante, B. "Teachers' Beliefs and Instructional Strategies in Science: Pushing Analysis Further." *Science Education 81*(3):277–294 (June 1997).

Lee, M., Lostoski, M., and Williams, K. "Diving into a Schoolwide Science Theme: Interdisciplinary Lessons for an All-School Theme in Science, Art, and Music Classes." *Science and Children 38*(1):31–35 (September 2000).

Lindgren, J., and Cushall, M. "You Can Always Tell a Dancer by Her Feet: Integrating Science and Math Through Pressure Investigations." *Science Scope 24*(4):12–15 (January 2001).

Lowe, J. L., and Matthew, K. I. "Puppets & Prose." *Science and Children 37*(8):41–45 (May 2000).

Lowry, P. K., and McCrary, J. H. "Someone's in the Kitchen with Science." *Science and Children 39*(2):22–27 (October 2001).

McLeod, J., and Kilpatrick, K. M. "Exploring Science at the Museum." *Educational Leadership 68*(7):59–63 (April 2001).

Melancon, M. "Nature Transects: Examining Outdoor Habitats to Assess Students' Science-Process Skills." *Science and Children 38*(3):34–37 (November/December 2000).

Milbourne, L. A., and Haury, D. L. *Helping Your Child with Science.* ED432447. Columbus, OH: ERIC Clearinghouse for Science, Mathematics, and Environmental Education, 1999.

Mills, M., and Tunstall, C. "Celtic Science." *Science Scope 23*(1): 27–29 (October 1999).

Minstrell, J., and van Zee, E. H., eds., *Inquiring into Inquiry Learning and Teaching in Science.* Washington, DC: American Association for the Advancement of Science, 2000.

Misiti, F. L., Jr. "The Pressure's On." *Science Scope 24*(1):34–38 (September 2000).

Misiti, F. L., Jr. "Standardizing the Language of Inquiry." *Science and Children 38*(5):38–40 (February 2001).

Moscovici, H., and Carty, C. "Developing Inquiring Minds." *Science and Children 37*(1):38–43, 74 (September 1999).

National Research Council. *Inquiry and the National Science Education Standards.* Washington, DC: National Academy Press, 2000.

Pierce, W. "Inquiry Made Easy." *Science and Children 38*(8):39–41 (May 2001).

Pliske, C. "Natural Cycles: Coming Full Circle." *Science and Children 37*(6): 35–39, 60 (March 2000).

Pratt, H., and Hackett, J. "Teaching Science: The Inquiry Approach." *Principal 78*(2):20–22 (November 1998).

Quiry, I. "In Search of Science for All." *Science and Children 37*(1):8–9 (September 1999).

Rios, J. M. "Teaching Inquiry Skills Using Rainsticks." *Science Scope 24*(3):20–25 (November/December 2000).

Rud, A. G., Jr., and Beck, A. M. "Kids and Critters in Class Together." *Phi Delta Kappan 82*(4):313–315 (December 2000).

Shepardson, D. P., and Britsch, S. J. "Analyzing Children's Science Journals." *Science and Children 38*(3):29–33 (November/December 2000).

Smith, D. C., and Wesley, A. "Teaching for Understanding." *Science and Children 38*(1):36–41 (September 2000).

Stout, B. "Tools for Scientific Inquiry in a Fifth-Grade Classroom." *Primary Voices K–6 10*(1):23–27 (August 2001).

Suchman, R. *Developing Inquiry.* Chicago: Science Research Associates, 1966.

Tanner, C. K. "Into the Woods, Wetlands, and Prairies." *Educational Leadership 68*(7):64–66 (April 2001).

Tower, C. "Questions that Matter: Preparing Elementary Students for the Inquiry Process." *The Reading Teacher 53*(7):550–557 (April 2000).

Wafler, E. S. "Inspired Inquiry." *Science and Children 38*(4):28–31 (January 2001).

Warger, C. *Five Homework Strategies for Teaching Students with Disabilities.* ERIC/OSEP Digest E608. Arlington, VA: ERIC Clearinghouse on Disabilities and Gifted Education, 2001.

Welch, W., Klofer, L., Aikenhead, G., and Robinson, J. T. "The Role of Inquiry in Science Education: Analysis and Recommendations," *Science Education 65*(1):33–50 (1981).

Wittrock, C. A., and Barrow, L. H. "Blow-by-Blow Inquiry." *Science and Children 37*(5):34–38 (February 2000).

Yockey, J. A. "A Key to Science Learning." *Science and Children 38*(7):36–41 (April 2001).

Young-Soo, K., and Barrow, L. H. "Designing a Fair Test with Valentine Candy to Teach Scientific Inquiry." *Science Activities 35*(4):24–25 (Winter 1999).

Chapter 6

Andrews, K., and Marshall, K. "Making Learning Connections Through Telelearning." *Educational Leadership 58*(2):53–56 (October 2000).

Ashby, S. "NASA Quest." *Science Scope 24*(1):40–43 (September 2000).

Brogan, P. "The Good, the Bad, and the Useless: Recognizing the Signs of Quality in Educational Software." From the *American School Board Journal* [Online 3/26/01, http://www.electronic-school.com/2001/03/0301f3.html] Website.

Ertmer, P. A., Hruskocy, C., and Woods, D. M. *Education on the Internet.* Upper Saddle River, NJ: Merrill/Prentice Hall, 2000.

Foshay, J. D. *Project-Based Multimedia Instruction.* Fastback 445. Bloomington, IN: Phi Delta Kappa Educational Foundation, 1999.

Fredericks, A. D. *Science Discoveries on the Net: An Integrated Approach.* Westport, CT: Libraries Unlimited, 2000.

Gruber, S., ed., *Weaving a Virtual Web: Practical Approaches to New Information Technologies.* Urbana, IL: National Council of Teachers of English, 2000.

International Society for Technology in Education. *National Educational Technology Standards for Students: Connecting Curriculum and Technology.* Eugene, OR: Author, 2000.

Jehlen, A. "Science Texts Flunk the Test." *NEA Today 18*(7):29 (April 2000).

Kawka, B., and Burgess, B. *V-Trip Travel Guide—Classroom Strategies for Virtual Field Trips.* Eugene, OR: International Society for Technology in Education, 2001.

Labbo, L. D. "Twelve Things Young Children Can Do with a Talking Book in a Classroom Computer Center." *Reading Teacher 53*(7):542–546 (April 2000).

Levine, E. "A Web Policy Primer." *American School Board Journal 188*(7):20–23 (July 2001).

Melber, L. M. "Tap Into Informal Science Learning." *Science Scope 23*(6):28–31 (March 2000).

Newby, T. J., Stepich, D. A., Lehman, J. D., and Russell, J. D. *Instructional Technology for Teaching and Learning,* 2nd ed. Upper Saddle River, NJ: Merrill/Prentice Hall, 2000.

Renard, L. "Cut and Paste 101: Plagiarism and the Net." *Educational Leadership 57*(4):38–42 (December 1999/January 2000).

Rice, D. C., Dudley, A. P., and Williams, C. S. "How Do You Choose Science Trade Books?" *Science and Children 38*(6):18–22 (March 2001).

Roblyer, M. D., and Edwards, J. *Integrating Educational Technology into Teaching,* 2nd ed. Upper Saddle River, NJ: Merrill/Prentice Hall, 2000.

Russell, H. R. *Ten-Minute Field Trips: A Teacher's Guide to Using the School Grounds for Environmental Studies,* 2nd ed. Arlington, VA: National Science Teachers Association, 1990.

Sharp, R. M., Sharp, V. F., and Levine, M. G. *The Best Web Sites for Teachers,* 4th ed. Eugene, OR: International Society for Technology in Education, 2001.

Smith, S. W. "Getting Connected to Science." *Science and Children 37*(7):22–25 (April 2000).

Varelas, M., Pappas, C., Barry, A., and O'Neill, A. "Examining Language to Capture Scientific Understandings." *Science and Children 38*(7):26–29 (April 2001).

 Chapter 7

Akerson, V. L. "Teaching Science When Your Principal Says 'Teach Language Arts'." *Science and Children* *38*(7):42–47 (April 2001).

Butzow, C. M., and Butzow, J. W. *More Science through Children's Literature: An Integrated Approach.* Englewood, CO: Teacher Ideas Press, 1998.

Cassano, P., and Antol, R. A. "Integration Integrity." *Science Scope 24*(7):18–21 (April 2001).

Decker, K. A. "Meeting State Standards through Integration." *Science and Children 36*(6):28–32, 69 (March 1999).

Diffily, D. "Project Reptile!" *Science and Children* *38*(7):30–35 (April 2001).

Fioranelli, D. "Recycling into Art: Integrating Science and Art." *Science and Children 38*(2):30–33 (October 2000).

Hamm, M., and Adams, D. "Reaching across Disciplines." *Science and Children 36*(1):45–49 (September 1998).

Harms, J. M., and Lettow, L. J. "Poetry and the Environment." *Science and Children 37*(6):30–34 (March 2000).

Howe, A. C., and Bell, J. "Factors Associated with Successful Implementation of Interdisciplinary Curriculum Units." *Research in Middle Level Education Quarterly* *21*(2):39–52 (Winter 1998).

Kellough, R. D., Cangelosi, J. S., Collette, A. T., Chiappetta, E. L., Souviney, R. J., Trowbridge, L. W., and Bybee, R. W. *Integrating Mathematics and Science for Intermediate and Middle School Students.* Englewood Cliffs, NJ: Merrill/Prentice Hall, 1996.

Kellough, R. D., Carin, A., Seefeldt, C., Barbour, N., and Souviney, R. J. *Integrating Mathematics and Science for Kindergarten and Primary Children.* Englewood Cliffs, NJ: Merrill/Prentice Hall, 1996.

Keys, C. W. "Investigating the Thinking Processes of Eighth Grade Writers during the Composition of a Scientific Laboratory Report." *Journal of Research in Science Teaching 37*(7):676–690 (September 2000).

Lener, E. "Our Growing Planet: Interdisciplinary Population Activities for Elementary Students." *Science and Children 38*(8):26–30 (May 2001).

MacKinnon, G. R., and Yetman, K. "The Acadian Dikes." *Science and Children 38*(7):21–25 (April 2001).

Madrazo, G. M., Jr., and Rhoton, J. "Classroom Meets Real World." *Science Scope 22*(4):26–28 (January 1999).

McGinnis, J. R. "Teaching Science as Inquiry for Students with Disabilities." In J. Minstrell and E. H. van Zee, eds., *Inquiring into Inquiry Learning and Teaching in Science* (Washington, DC: American Association for the Advancement of Science, 2000), 425–433.

McMahon, M. M., et al., "Curriculum with a Common Thread." *Science and Children 37*(7):30–35, 57 (April 2000).

Merino, B. J., and Hammond, L. "Family Gardens and Solar Ovens: Making Science Education Accessible to Culturally and Linguistically Diverse Students." *Multicultural Education 5*(3):34–37 (Spring 1998).

Myers, R. E. *Mind Sparklers. Fireworks for Igniting Creativity in Young Minds.* Book 1 for Grades K–3 [and] Book 2 for Grades 4–8. Waco, TX: Prufrock Press, 1998.

Nuthall, G. "The Way Students Learn: Acquiring Knowledge from an Integrated Science and Social Studies Unit." *Elementary School Journal 99*(4):303–341 (March 1999).

Pottle, J. L. "Something to Crow About." *Science Scope* *22*(4):14–18 (January 1999).

Proctor, W., et al., "Cross-Curriculum Planning—It Works!" *Science Scope 23*(5):35 (February 2000).

Rakow, S. J., and Vasquez, J. "Integrated Instruction: A Trio of Strategies." *Science and Children 35*(6):18–22 (March 1998).

Rice, D. C., Dudley, A. P., and Williams, C. S. "How Do You Choose Science Trade Books?" *Science and Children* *38*(6):18–22 (March 2001).

Roberts, P. L., and Kellough, R. D. *A Guide to Developing an Interdisciplinary Thematic Unit,* 3rd ed. Upper Saddle River, NJ: Prentice Hall, 2004.

Rodger, D., and Ryan, A. G. "Sign On the Dotted Line." *Science Scope 21*(5):22–24 (February 1998).

Skehan, J. W., and Nelson, C. E. *Creation Controversy and the Science Classroom.* Arlington, VA: National Science Teachers Association, 2000.

Snyder, R. C. "'Scrounging' in Support of the Standards." *Science and Children 35*(4):18–20 (January 1998).

Stallings, L., and Wimpey, K. "Blowing Bubbles: An Interdisciplinary Science and Mathematics Lab." *Science Scope* *23*(5):24–27 (February 2000).

Tevebaugh, T. "Welcome to Our Web: Integrating Subjects through Entomology." *Language Arts 78*(4):343–347 (March 2001).

Varelas, M., Pappas, C., Barry, A., and O'Neill, A. "Examining Language to Capture Scientific Understandings: The Case of the Water Cycle." *Science and Children* *38*(7):26–29 (April 2001).

Warger, C. *Five Homework Strategies for Teaching Students with Disabilities.* ERIC/OSEP Digest E608. Arlington, VA: ERIC Clearinghouse on Disabilities and Gifted Education, 2001.

Williams, C. W., and Hounshell, P. B. "Enabling the Learning Disabled." *Science Teacher 65*(1):29–31 (January 1998).

 Chapter 8

Arter, J., and McTighe, J. *Scoring Rubrics in the Classroom: Using Performance Criteria for Assessing and Improving Student Performances.* Thousand Oaks, CA: Corwin Press, 2001.

Black, P., and Harrison, C. "Feedback in Questioning and Marking: The Science Teacher's Role in Formative Assessment." *School Science Review 82*(301):55–61 (June 2001).

Bond, B. "Using Standards-Based Performance Assessment with At-Risk Students."*Middle Ground 4*(3):36–39 (February 2001).

Bracey, G. W. *A Short Guide to Standardized Testing.* Fastback 459. Bloomington, IN: Phi Delta Kappa Educational Foundation, 2000.

Carr, J. F., and Harris, D. E. *Succeeding with Standards: Linking Curriculum, Assessment, and Action Planning.* Alexandria, VA: Association of Supervision and Curriculum Development, 2001.

Champagne, A. B., Kouba, V. L., and Hurley, M. "Assessing Inquiry." In J. Minstrell and E. H. van Zee, eds., *Inquiring into Inquiry Learning and Teaching in Science.* Washington, DC: American Association for the Advancement of Science, 2000, 447–470.

Chen, Y., and Martin, M. A. "Using Performance Assessment and Portfolio Assessment Together in the Elementary Classroom." *Reading Improvement* 37(1):32–38 (Spring 2000).

Coray, G. "Rubrics Made Simple." *Science Scope* 23(6):38–40 (March 2000).

Craven, J. A., III, and Hogan, T. "Assessing Student Participation in the Classroom." *Science Scope* 25(1):36–40 (September 2001).

Demers, C. "Beyond Paper & Pencil Assessments." *Science and Children* 38(2):24–29, 60 (October 2000).

Doran, R., et al. *Science Educator's Guide to Assessment.* Arlington, VA: National Science Teachers Association, 1998.

Enger, S. K., and Yager, R. E. *Assessing Student Understanding in Science.* Thousands Oaks, CA: Corwin Press, 2001.

Jorgenson, O., and Vanosdall, R. "The Death of Science? What We Risk in Our Rush Toward Standardized Testing and the Three R's." *Phi Delta Kappan* 83(8):601–605 (April 2002).

Kinney, P., Munroe, M. B., and Sessions, P. *A School-Wide Approach to Student-Led Conferences: A Practitioner's Guide.* Columbus, OH: National Middle School Association, 2000.

Melancon, M. "Nature Transects: Examining Outdoor Habitats to Assess Students" Science-Process Skills. *Science and Children* 38(3):34–37 (November/December 2000).

Oosterhof, A. *Classroom Applications of Educational Measurement,* 3rd ed. Upper Saddle River, NJ: Merrill/Prentice Hall, 2001.

Parker, V. A., and Gerber, B. L. "Performance-Based Assessment, Science Festival Exhibit Presentations, and Elementary Science Achievement." *Journal of Elementary Science Education* 14(1):59–67 (Spring 2002).

Popham, W. J. *The Truth About Testing.* Alexandria, VA: Association for Supervision and Curriculum Development, 2001.

Quellmalz, E., Schank, P., Hinojosa, T., and Padilla, C. *Performance Assessment Links in Science (PALS).* ED435708. College Park, MD: ERIC Clearinghouse on Assessment and Evaluation, 1999.

Rearden, K. T. "Who Wants to Make Assessment Fair?" *Science Scope* 25(2):22–25 (October 2001).

Ronis, D. *Brain Compatible Assessments.* Arlington Heights, IL: Skyline, 2000.

Shepardson, D. P., and Britsch, S. J. "Analyzing Children's Science Journals." *Science and Children* 38(3):29–33 (November/December 2000).

Skillings, M. J., and Ferrell, R. "Student-Generated Rubrics: Bring Students into the Assessment Process." *Reading Teacher* 53(6):452–455 (March 2000).

Stiggins, R. J. *Student-Involved Classroom Assessment,* 3rd ed. Upper Saddle River, NJ: Merrill/Prentice Hall, 2001.

Treagust, D. F., Jacobowitz, R., Gallagher, J. L., and Parker, J. "Using Assessment as a Guide in Teaching for Understanding: A Case Study of a Middle School Science Class Learning about Sound." *Science Education* 85(2):137–157 (March 2001).

Chapter 9

INTERNET

- Astronomy Picture of the Day's Educational Links, http://antwrp.gsfc.nasa.gov/apod/lib/edlinks.html
- Classifying Galaxies, http://www.smv.org/hastings/galaxy.htm
- Educational Space Simulations, http://chico.rice.edu/armadillo/Simulations/simserver.html
- International Space Station, http://spaceflight1.nasa.gov/station
- Jet Propulsion Laboratory, http://www.jpl.nasa.gov/index.cf
- Kennedy Space Center, http://www.nasa.gov/centers/kennedy/home/index.html
- Lunar Prospector, http://lunar.arc.nasa.gov
- Moon Fact Sheet, http://nssdc.gsfc.nasa.gov/planetary/factsheet/moonfact.html
- National Aeronautics and Space Administration, http://www. nasa.gov
- Overview of Solar System, http://seds.lpl.arizona.edu/nineplanets/nineplanets/overview.html
- Sky, The, http://www.seasky.org/sky.html
- Space News, http://www.spacenews.com
- Space Telescope Science Institute, http://www.stsci.edu/hst
- Windows to the Universe, http://www.windows.umich.edu

BOOKS AND PERIODICALS

Achenbach, J. "Life Beyond Earth," *National Geographic.* Special Millennium Issue, pp. 24–51 (January 2000).

Baxter, J. H., and Preece, P. F. W. "A Comparison of Dome and Computer Planetaria in the Teaching of Astronomy," *Research in Science and Technological Education* 18(1):63–69 (May 2000).

Beck, C. "Lunar Review Game," *Science Scope* 22(8):28–29 (May 1999).

Bond, P. *DK Guide to Space: A Photographic Journey Through the Universe* (New York: DK Publishing, 1999).

Branley, F. M. *Let's-Read-and-Find-Out Science: The International Space Station* (New York: HarperCollins, 2000).

Burnham, R. *The Reader's Digest Children's Atlas of the Universe.* (Pleasantville, NY: Reader's Digest Children's Books, 2000).

Christian, C. A., Eisenhamer, B., Eisenhamer, J., and Teays, T. " 'Amazing Space': Creating Educational Resources from Current Scientific Research Results from the Hubble Space Telescope," *Journal of Science Education and Technology* 19(1):31–38 (March 2001).

Cole, M. D. *Countdown to Space: Hubble Space Telescope* (Springfield, NJ: Enslow, 1999).

Dyson, M. J. *Space Station Science: Life in Free Fall* (New York: Scholastic Reference, 1999).

Fredericks, A. D. *Exploring the Universe: Science Activities for Kids* (Golden, CO: Fulcrum, 2000).

Hemenway, M. L. "Our Star, the Sun," *Science and Children 38*(1):48–51 (September 2000).

Kane, E. J. "Bringing Back the Analemma," *Science Scope 25*(1):26–29 (September 2001).

Kaser, S. "Searching the Heavens with Children's Literature: A Design for Teaching Science," *Language Arts 78*(4):348–356 (March 2001).

Langley, A. *The Oxford First Book of Space* (Cambridge, MA: Oxford University Press, 2001).

Letwinch, J. C. *Soaring through the Universe: Astronomy through Children's Literature* (Englewood, CO: Teacher Ideas Press, 1999).

Loeschnig, L. V. *Simple Space & Flight Experiments* (New York: Sterling, 2000).

Matthews, C. E., et al. "Planetary Paths," *Science Scope 22*(8):10–14 (May 1999).

Mohler, R. "More Space Shuttle Experiments," *Science and Children 38*(2):39–43 (October 2000).

Muirden, J. *Seeing Stars* (Cambridge, MA: Candlewick, 1999).

National Aeronautics and Space Administration, *NASA's Space Environments and Effects (SEE) Program: Meteoroid and Orbital Debris Lesson Plan* (Washington, DC: Author, 1999).

Newhouse, K. B. "What Lies in the Stars?" *Science and Children 39*(6):16–21 (March 2002).

Riddle, B. "Peeking at the Planets." *Science Scope 25*(4):12, 14 (January 2002).

Rillero, P., Gonzalez-Jensen, M., and Moy, T. "Moon Watch: A Parental-Involvement Homework Activity," *Science Activities 36*(4):11–15 (Winter 2000).

Roberts, D. "The Sky's the Limit," *Science and Children 37*(1):33–37 (September 1999).

Rommel-Esham, K., and Souhrada, C. "Mission to Mars: A Classroom Simulation," *Science and Children 39*(5):16–21 (February 2002).

Sawyer, K. "A Mars Never Dreamed Of," *National Geographic 199*(2):31–51 (February 2001).

Simon, S. *Destination: Mars* (New York: HarperCollins, 2000).

Wiley, D. A., and Royce, C. A. "Crash into Meteorite Learning," *Science and Children 37*(8):16–19 (May 2000).

Zimmer, C. "How Old Is . . .?" *National Geographic 200*(3):77–101 (September 2001).

Chapter 10

INTERNET

- Arctic Circle, http://arcticcircle.uconn.edu
- The British Natural History Museum, http://www.nhm.ac.uk
- The Dinosauria, http://www.ucmp.berkeley.edu/diapsids/dinosaur.html
- Environmental Literacy Council, resources for environmental education, http://www.enviroliteracy.org
- NASA's Earth Science Enterprise, http://www.earth.nasa.gov
- SeaWiFS, http://oceancolor.gsfc.nasa.gov/SeaWIFS.html
- University of California, Museum of Paleontology, http://www.ucmp.berkeley.edu
- World Bank's site on population growth and safe water, http://www.worldbank.org/depweb
- World Resources Institute site on global resources, http://www.wri.org

BOOKS AND PERIODICALS

Arnosky, J. *Wild and Swampy* (New York: HarperCollins, 2000).

Atkins, J. *Girls Who Looked Under Rocks: The Lives of Six Pioneering Naturalists* (Nevada City, CA: Dawn Publications, 2000).

Aulenbach, N. H., Barton, H. A., and Delano, M. F. *Exploring Caves: Journeys into the Earth* (Washington, DC: National Geographic Society, 2001).

Bial, R. *A Handful of Dirt* (New York, NY: Walker, 2000).

Booth, B., Brook, R., Rieben, E., and Wooster, E. "A Place in the Sun," *Science and Children 38*(5):27–34 (February 2001).

Cherry, L. *The Great Kapok Tree: A Tale of the Amazon Rain Forest* (New York: Harcourt General, 2000).

Cole, S. "Take a Risk with Earth Science Inquiry." *Science Scope 25*(4):48–51 (January 2002).

Collard, S. B., III. *The Forest in the Clouds* (Watertown, MA: Charlesbridge, 2000).

Conn, K. "A Beach in Your Classroom," *Science Scope 24*(8):12–17 (May 2001).

Dewey, J. O. *Antarctic Journal: Four Months at the Bottom of the World* (New York: HarperCollins, 2001).

Downs, S. *Earth's Fiery Fury* (Brookfield, CT: Twenty-First Century Books/Millbrook Press 2000).

Earle, S. A. *Dive! My Adventures in the Deep Frontier* (Washington, DC: National Geographic, 1999).

Eliot, J. L. "Deadly Haven: Mexico's Poisonous Cave," *National Geographic 199*(5):70–85 (May 2001).

Franklin, S. "Celebrations of Earth," *National Geographic*. Special Millennium Issue, pp. 2–23 (January 2000).

Gardner, R. *Science Projects about the Environment and Ecology* (Springfield, NJ: Enslow, 1999).

Gates, J. M. *Consider the Earth: Environmental Activities for Grades 4–8*, 2nd ed. (Englewood, CO: Teacher Ideas Press/Libraries Unlimited, 1999).

Gibb, L. "Second-Grade Soil Scientists," *Science and Children 38*(3):24–28 (November/December 2000).

Gibson, B. O. "The Building Blocks of Geology," *Science and Children 39*(1):38–41 (September 2001).

Girod, M. "Rocks as Windows into the Past," *Science and Children 37*(6):40–43 (March 2000).

Glaser, L. *Our Big Home: An Earth Poem* (Brookfield, CT: Millbrook Press, 2000).

Heinz, B. J. *Butternut Hollow Pond* (Brookfield, CT: Millbrook Press, 2000).

Hoare, S. *The World of Caves, Mines, and Tunnels* (New York: Peter Bedrick, 1999).

Hurst, C. O. *Rocks in His Head* (New York: Greenwillow, 2001).

Jackson, J. A., Zokaites, C., Smith, M. J., Crum, E., and Callahan, C. "An In-Depth Exploration of Karst," *Science Scope 24*(8):36–39 (May 2001).

Johnson, R. L. *A Walk in the Deciduous Forest* (Minneapolis: Lerner, 2001).

Johnson, R. L. *A Walk in the Desert* (Minneapolis: Lerner, 2001).

Johnson, R. L. *A Walk in the Prairie* (Minneapolis: Lerner, 2001).

Johnson, R. L. *A Walk in the Rain Forest* (Minneapolis: Lerner, 2001).

Jones, T. G., and Jones, L. C. "Digging Science," *Science and Children 37*(8):28–32 (May 2000).

Kelly, C. "The Diminishing Apple," *Science and Children 39*(5):26–30 (February 2002).

Laman, T. "Night Shift in the Rain Forest," *National Geographic 200*(4):32–47 (October 2001).

Lindgren, J., and Cushall, M. "You Can Always Tell a Dancer By Her Feet: Integrating Science and Math Through Pressure Investigations," *Science Scope 24*(4):12–15 (January 2001).

Livo, N. J. *Celebrating the Earth: Stories, Experiences, and Activities* (Englewood, CO: Teacher Ideas Press/Libraries Unlimited, 2000).

Locker, T. *Cloud Dance* (New York: Silver Whistle/Harcourt, 2000).

Lutz, R. A. "Deep Sea Vents," *National Geographic 198*(4):116–127 (October 2000).

May, K. "Bartering for Minerals." *Science Scope 25*(4):28–33 (January 2002).

Miller, D. S. *River of Life* (New York: Clarion, 2000).

Monastersky, R. "Pterosaurs," *National Geographic 199*(5):86–105 (May 2001).

Moss, M. *This Is the Tree* (La Jolla, CA: Kane/Miller, 2000).

Nagda, A. W. *World Above the Clouds: A Story of a Himalayan Ecosystem* (Norwalk, CT: Soundprints, 2000).

National Science Teachers Association. *Dig In! Hands-On Soil Investigations* (Arlington, VA: NSTA Press, 2001).

Newton, D. M. "Pressure, Pressure Everywhere," *Science and Children 36*(5):34–37 (February 1999).

Paty, A. H. "Rocks and Minerals—Foundations of Society," *Science Scope 23*(8):30–31 (May 2000).

Perry, L. "MultiMedia Rocks," *Science and Children 37*(8):24–27 (May 2000).

Philipek, F., Smith, S., and Brook, R. "Green Mansions," *Science and Children 37*(8):33–40 (May 2000).

Rockwell, R. E., Sherwood, E. A., Williams, R. A., and Winnett, D. A. *Caring for Our Planet* (White Plains, NY: Dale Seymour, 2001).

Ross, M. E. *Exploring the Earth with John Wesley Powell* (Minneapolis, MN: Carolrhoda Books/Lerner, 2000).

Ross, M. E. *Pond Watching with Ann Morgan* (Minneapolis, MN: Carolrhoda Books/Lerner, 2000).

Schmidt, J. "Journey to Shipton's Lost Arch," *National Geographic 198*(6):110–124 (December 2000).

Seibert, P. *Discovering El Niño: How Fable and Fact Together Help Explain the Weather* (Brookfield, CT: Millbrook, 1999).

Simon, S. *Tornadoes* (New York: Morrow/HarperCollins, 1999).

Smith, M. J., and Southard, J. B. "Exploring the Evolution of Plate Tectonics," *Science Scope 25*(1):46–49 (September 2001).

Smith, S. "Turning Bread into Rocks: A Multisensory Unit Opener," *Science Scope 24*(2):20–23 (October 2000).

Snedden, R. *Science Projects: Rocks and Soil* (Austin, TX: Steck-Vaughn, 1999).

Sussman, A. *Dr. Art's Guide to Planet Earth: For Earthlings Ages 12 to 120* (White River Junction, VT: Chelsea Green, 2000).

Suzuki, D., and Vanderlinden, K. *You Are the Earth* (New York: Sterling, 2000).

Tagliaferro, L. *Galápagos Islands: Nature's Delicate Balance at Risk* (Minneapolis: Lerner, 2001).

Taylor, K. "Auroras: Earth's Grandshow of Lights," *National Geographic 200*(5):48–63 (November 2001).

Theodorou, R. *From the Arctic to the Antarctica* (Crystal Lake, IL: Heinemann, 2000).

Tucker, R. H. "What a Relief!" *Science and Children 39*(2):38–41 (October 2001).

Van Cleef, C., Olivolo, B., and Shearer, C. "A New Way of Looking at the World," *Science Scope 24*(5):30–36 (February 2001).

Winner, S. *Erosion* (Minneapolis, MN: Carolrhoda/Lerner, 1999).

Zimmer, C. "How Old Is . . . ?" *National Geographic 200*(3):77–101 (September 2001).

 Chapter 11

INTERNET

- Aquarius Undersea Habitat, http://www.uncwil.edu/nurc/aquarius
- Environmental Literacy Council, resources for environmental education, http://www.enviroliteracy.org
- GLOBE (Global Learning and Observations to Benefit the Environment), http://www.globe.gov
- MARE (Marine Activities, Resources and Education), http://www.lhs.berkeley.edu/mare
- NASA's SeaWiFS Project, http://oceancolor.gsfc.nasa.gov/seaWIFS/
- National Marine Sanctuaries, http://www.sanctuaries.nos.noaa.gov
- National Oceanic and Atmospheric Administration (NOAA), http://www.noaa.gov
- Pacific Marine Environmental Laboratory, http://www.pmel.noaa.gov
- Reef Education Guide, http://www.reef.org
- Scripps Institute of Oceanography Library, http://scilib.ucsd.edu/sio
- Sea Education Association, http://www.sea.edu
- University of Illinois at Urbana-Champaign's Department of Atmospheric Sciences WW2010, http://ww2010.atmos.uiuc.edu/(GH)/home.rxml

BOOKS AND PERIODICALS

Ackerman, J. "New Eyes on the Oceans," *National Geographic 198*(4):86–115 (October 2000).

Baldwin, R. F. *This Is the Sea That Feeds Us* (Nevada City, CA: Dawn Publications, 1999).

Beard, D. B. *Twister* (New York: Farrar Straus Giroux, 1999).

Bradley, K. B. *Pop! A Book About Bubbles* (New York: HarperCollins, 2001).

Brown, S. W., and Hansen, T. M. "Connecting Middle School, Oceanography, and the Real World," *Science Scope 24*(3):16–19 (November/December 2000).

Cavallo, A. M. L. "Convection Connections," *Science and Children 38*(8):20–25 (May 2001).

Cody, C. "Clean Stream Program," *Science Scope 23*(1):26–31 (September 1999).

Conniff, R. "Swamps of Jersey," *National Geographic 199*(2):62–81 (February 2001).

Crawford, J. B. *Ocean Life* (Alexandria, VA: Time Life Education, 2000).

DeYonge, S. C. "Project Wet," *Science Scope 23*(4):22–28 (January 2000).

DuTemple, L. A. *Jacques Cousteau* (Minneapolis, MN: Lerner, 2000).

Earle, S. A. *Dive! My Adventures in the Deep Frontier* (Washington, DC: National Geographic, 1999).

Franks, L. "Charcoal Clouds and Weather Writing: Inviting Science to a Middle School Language Arts Classroom," *Language Arts 78*(4):319–324 (March 2001).

Heiligman, D. *Ocean Pilot: The Mysterious Ocean Highway, Benjamin Franklin and the Gulf Stream* (Austin, TX: Steck-Vaughn, 2000).

Henriques, L. "Children's Ideas about Weather: A Review of the Literature," *School Science and Mathematics 102*(5):202–215 (May 2002).

Konvicka, T. *Teacher's Weather Sourcebook: Information, Ideas, and Activities* (Englewood, CO: Teacher Ideas Press/Libraries Unlimited, 1999).

Leonard, J. "Taking Science Dialogue by Storm," *Science and Children 39*(4):31–35 (January 2002).

McCarty, R. V. "Water: A Sticky Subject?" *Science and Children 37*(6):44–47, 60–61 (March 2000).

Palmer, M. H. "Hands-On Thunderstorms," *Science and Children 37*(7):40–44 (April 2000).

Pratt-Serafini, K. J. *Salamander Rain: A Lake & Pond Journal* (Nevada City, CA: Dawn, 2001).

Royston, A. *Water* (Crystal Lake, IL: Heinemann, 2001).

Sconyers, J., and Trautwein, C. "Putting a Spring in Archimedes' Step," *Science Scope 23*(5):14–16 (February 2000).

Simon, S. *Tornadoes* (New York: Morrow/HarperCollins, 1999).

Sobey, E. *Wacky Water Fun with Science* (New York: McGraw-Hill, 2000).

Suplee, C. "El Niño/La Niña," *National Geographic 195*(3):72–95 (March 1999).

Theodorou, R. *To the Depths of the Ocean* (Crystal Lake, IL: Heinemann, 2000).

Thomas, J. A. "How Deep Is the Water?" *Science and Children 40*(2):28–32 (October 2002).

Varelas, M., Pappas, C., Barry, A., and O'Neill, A. "Examining Language to Capture Scientific Understandings: The Case of the Water Cycle," *Science and Children 38*(7):26–29 (April 2001).

Wiemann, K. "Blue Solids, Red Liquids, & Yellow Gases" *Science Scope 23*(5):17–19 (February 2000).

Woodman, N. *Sea-fari Deep* (Washington, DC: National Geographic, 1999).

Yolen, J. *Welcome to the River of Grass* (New York: Putnam, 2001).

Young, R., Virmani, J., and Kusek, K. M. "Creative Writing and the Water Cycle," *Science Scope 25*(1):30–35 (September 2001).

Chapter 12

INTERNET

- British Natural History Museum, http://www.nhm.ac.uk
- CELLs Alive! http://www.cellsalive.com
- Herb Research Foundation, http://www.herbs.org
- Internet Directory for Botany, http://www.botany.net/IDB
- Lady Bird Johnson Wildflower Center, http://www.wildflower.org
- Missouri Botanical Garden, http://www.mobot.org/welcome.html
- Project Learning Tree, a program of educational materials and teachers workshops by the American Forest Foundation, http://www.plt.org
- U.S. Department of Agriculture, National Agricultural Library, http://www.nal.usda.gov/fnic
- World Resources Institute site on global resources, http://www.wri.org

BOOKS AND PERIODICALS

Brown, R. *Ten Seeds* (New York: Alfred A. Knopf/Random House, 2001).

Cassie, B. *National Audubon Society First Field Guide: Trees* (New York: Scholastic Reference, 1999).

Castner, J. L. *Rainforest Researchers* (Tarrytown, NY: Benchmark/Marshall Cavendish, 2001).

Farmer, J. *Bananas!* (Watertown, MA: Charlesbridge, 1999).

Gibbons, G. *The Pumpkin Book* (New York: Holiday House, 1999).

Goodman, S. E. *Seeds, Stems, and Stamens: The Ways Plants Fit into Their World* (Brookfield, CT: Millbrook, 2001).

Hargis, J., and Houston, C. "Electronic Leaf Project," *Science and Children 37*(8):20–23 (May 2000).

Hickman, P. *Starting with Nature: Tree Book* (Tonawanda, NY: Kids Can Press, 1999).

Hickman, P. *The Plant Book* (Tonawanda, NY: Kids Can Press, 2000).

Horrigan, S. W. "The Big Picture," *Science Scope 23*(5):32–34 (February 2000).

Kudlinski, K. *Dandelions* (Minneapolis, MN: Lerner, 1999).

Levenson, G. *Pumpkin Circle: The Story of a Garden* (Berkeley, CA Tricycle/Ten Speed, 1999).

McLaughlin, C. W., et al. "Shining Light on Photosynthesis: Teaching About Photosynthesis and Plant Growth in the Primary Classroom," *Science and Children* *36*(5):26–31 (February 1999).

Moscovici, H., and Carty, C. "Developing Inquiring Minds," *Science and Children 37*(1): 38–43, 74 (September 1999).

Philipek, F., Smith, S., and Brook, R. "Green Mansions," *Science and Children 37*(8):33–40 (May 2000).

Pirotta, S. *Deep in the Rain Forest: Trees and Plants in the Rain Forest* (Austin, TX: Steck-Vaughn, 1999).

Posada, M. *Dandelions: Stars in the Grass* (Minneapolis: Carolrhoda, 2000).

Ruiz, A. L. *Cycles of Life: The Life of a Cell* (New York: Sterling, 1997).

Ryden, H. *Wildflowers Around the Year* (New York: Clarion, 2001).

Tolman, M. N., and Hardy, G. R. "Teaching Tropisms," *Science and Children 37*(3):14–17 (November/December 1999).

 Chapter 13

INTERNET

- Cells Alive, http://www.cellsalive.com
- Fungi, http://www.ucmp.berkeley.edu/fungi/fungi.html
- Human Genome Project, http://www.ornl.gov/TechResources/Human_Genome/home.html
- Link to Life on Earth by Teresa Audesirk and Gerald Audesirk (Prentice Hall) and additional content information, http://www.aw-bc.com/audesirk
- Viruses, http://www.ucmp.berkeley.edu/alllife/virus.html

BOOKS AND PERIODICALS

Anderson, O. R., and Druger, M., eds. *Explore the World Using Protozoa* (Arlington, VA: National Science Teachers Association, 1997).

Baker, W. P., Leyva, K. J., Lang, M., and Goodmanis, B. "Classifying Microorganisms." *Science Scope* 25(4):40–44 (January 2002).

Cerullo, M. M. *Sea Soup: Zooplankton* (Gardiner, ME: Tilbury House, 2001).

Chadwick, D. H. "Coral in Peril," *National Geographic* *195*(1):30–37 (January 1999).

Conn, K. "A Beach in Your Classroom," *Science Scope* *24*(8):12–17 (May 2001).

Darling, D. *There's a Zoo on You* (Brookfield, CT: Millbrook, 2000).

Doubliet, D. "Coral Eden," *National Geographic 195*(1):2–29 (January 1999).

Genthe, H. "The Sargasso Sea," *Smithsonian 29*(8):82–86, 88, 90, 92–93 (November 1998).

Murawski, D. A. "Diatoms," *National Geographic 195*(2): 114–121 (February 1999).

Murphy, A. P. "Students and Scientists Take a 'Lichen' to Air Quality Assessment in Ireland," *Journal of Science Education and Technology* 7(1):107–113 (March 1998).

Pascoe, E. *Nature Close-Up: Slime Molds and Fungi* (Woodbridge, CT: Blackbirch, 1999).

Sharnoff, S. D. "Lichens: More Than Meets the Eye," *National Geographic 191*(2):58–71 (February 1997).

Silverstein, A., and Silverstein, V. *A World in a Drop of Water: Exploring with a Microscope* (Mineola, NY: Dover, 1998).

 Chapter 14

INTERNET

- Animals of the Arctic, http://tqjunior.thinkquest.org/3500/index.htm
- Audubon Online, http://www.audubon.org
- Bats, http://intergate.cccoe.k12.ca.us/bats
- BIOSIS, http://www.biosis.org
- BirdSource, http://www.birdsource.org
- British Natural History Museum, http://www.nhm.ac.uk
- Dinosaurs, http://www.dinosauria.com
- Iowa State University Index of Internet Resources, http://www.ent.iastate.edu/List
- Link to Life on Earth by T. Audesirk and G. Audesirk, http://www.aw-bc.com/audesirk
- Marine mammals and aquariums, http://www.ammpa.org
- Partners in Flight, http://www.pwrc.nbs.gov/pif
- Yuckiest Site on the Internet: Bug World, Worm World, http://yucky.kids.discovery.com

BOOKS AND PERIODICALS

Allen, J., and Humphries, T. *Are You a Ladybug?* (New York: Kingfisher, 2000).

Allen, J., and Humphries, T. *Are You a Snail?* (New York: Kingfisher, 2000).

Aram, R. J., Whitson, S., and Dieckhoff, R. "Habitat Sweet Habitat," *Science and Children 38*(4):23–27 (January 2001).

Barman, C. R., Barman, N. S., Cox, M. L., Newhouse, K. B., and Goldston, M. J. "Students' Ideas About Animals; Results from a National Study," *Science and Children* *38*(1):42–47 (September 2000).

Barrett, P. *National Geographic Dinosaurs* (Washington, DC: National Geographic Society, 2001).

Bell, R. *Horses* (Crystal Lake, NY: Heinemann, 2000).

Bernard, R. *Insects* (Washington, DC: National Geographic Society, 2001).

Booth, B., Brook, R., Tisdale, M., and Wooster, E. "Wild Bunch," *Science and Children 38*(8):31–38 (May 2001).

Burke, M. C. "Animals in Disguise," *Science and Children* *38*(5):35–37 (February 2001).

Cave, R. "Jewel Scarabs," *National Geographic 199*(2):52–61 (February 2001).

Chadwick, D. H. "Evolution of Whales," *National Geographic 200*(5):64–77 (November 2001).

Chadwick, D. H. "Grizzlies," *National Geographic* *200*(1):2–25 (July 2001).

Chadwick, D. H. "Kingdom of Coral," *National Geographic 199*(1):30–57 (January 2001).

Chadwick, D. H. "Phantom of the Night," *National Geographic 199*(5):32–51 (May 2001).

Chorlton, W. *Woolly Mammoth: Life, Death, and Rediscovery* (New York: Scholastic, 2001).

Coehfeld, K. W. *Dinosaur Parents, Dinosaur Young: Uncovering the Mystery of Dinosaur Families* (New York: Clarion, 2001).

Conover, A. "The Little Foxes," *Smithsonian 32*(5):42–50 (August 2001).

Costello, E. *Realm of the Panther* (Norwalk, CT: Soundprints, 2000).

Darling, K. *Lions* (Minneapolis, MN: Lerner, 2000).

Dennard, D. *Koala Country: A Story of an Australian Eucalyptus Forest* (Norwalk, CT: Soundprints, 2000).

Denward, D. *Lemur Landing: A Story of a Madagascan Tropical Dry Forest* (Norwalk, CT: Soundprints, 2001).

DeVore, E., and O'Sullivan, K. A. "Evolution: Fundamental Theme for Integrated Science," *California Journal of Science Education 1*(2):101–116 (Spring 2001).

Dobey, D. C., and Springer, H. S. "Simply Butterflies," *Science and Children 40*(3):16–21 (November/December 2002).

Downing, J. E. "How Animals Play Hide and Seek: A Game of Survival," *Science Activities 37*(4):15–17 (Winter 2001).

Dudzinski, K. *Meeting Dolphins: My Adventures in the Sea* (Washington, DC: National Geographic Society, 2000).

DuTemple, L. A. *North American Moose* (Minneapolis: Lerner, 2000).

Earle, S. A. *Sea Critters* (Washington, DC: National Geographic Society, 2000).

Edwards, L. C., Nabors, M. L., and Camacho, C. S. "The Dirt on Worms," *Science and Children 40*(1):42–46 (September 2002).

Fay, J. "Investigation—Insects!" *Science and Children 38*(1):26–30 (September 2000).

Foote, T. "Where the Gooney Birds Are," *Smithsonian 32*(6):88–98 (September 2001).

Fredericks, A. D. *Slugs* (Minneapolis, MN: Lerner, 2000).

Froman, N. *What's That Bug?* (Boston, MA: Madison Press/Little, Brown, 2001).

Gallagher, K. E. *The Cottontail Rabbits* (Minneapolis, MN: Lerner, 2001).

George, T. C. *Jellies: The Life of Jellyfish* (Brookfield, CT: Millbrook, 2000).

Goodall, J. *The Chimpanzees I Love: Saving Their World and Ours* (New York: Scholastic Press, 2001).

Goodman, S. E. *Claws, Coats and Camouflage: The Ways Animals Fit into Their World* (Brookfield, CT: Millbrook, 2001).

Hickman, P. *Starting with Nature Bird Book* (Tonawanda, NY: Kids Can Press, 2000).

Hickman, P., and Stephens, P. *Animals in Motion: How Animals Swim, Jump, Slither, and Glide* (Tonawanda, NY: Kids Can Press, 2000).

Hiscock, B. *Coyote and Badger: Desert Hunters of the Southwest* (Honesdale, PA: Boyds Mills, 2001).

Horowitz, R. *Crab Moon* (Cambridge, MA: Candlewick, 2000).

Jango-Cohen, J. *Clinging Sea Horses* (Minneapolis, MN: Lerner, 2000).

Johnson, J. *National Geographic Animal Encyclopedia* (Washington, DC: National Geographic Society, 2000).

Kerley, B. *The Dinosaurs of Waterhouse Hawkings* (New York: Scholastic Press, 2001).

Klum, M. "King Cobra," *National Geographic 200*(5):100–113 (November 2001).

Kneidel, S. *Stinkbugs, Stick Insects, & Stag Beetles and 18 More of the Strangest Insects on Earth* (New York: John Wiley and Sons, 2000).

Laman, T. "Night Shift in the Rain Forest," *National Geographic 200*(4):32–47 (October 2001).

Laman, T. "Wild Gliders," *National Geographic 198*(4):68–85 (October 2000).

Lasky, K. *Interrupted Journey: Saving Endangered Sea Turtles* (Cambridge, MA: Candlewick, 2001).

Lewin, T., and Lewin, B. *Elephant Quest* (New York: Harper/Collins, 2000).

Mannesto, J. "The Truth About Wolves," *Science and Children 39*(8):24–29 (May 2002).

Matthews, C. E. "The Cormorant Controversy," *Science Scope 23*(7):17–21 (April 2000).

McGinnis, P. "Dissect Your Squid and Eat it Too!" *Science Scope 24*(7):12–17 (April 2001).

McLure, J. W. "Animal Watching: Outdoors and In," *Science Activities 37*(4):24–27 (Winter 2001).

Morell, V. "The Fragile World of Frogs," *National Geographic 199*(5):106–123 (May 2001).

Netherton, J. *Red-Eyed Tree Frogs* (Minneapolis: Lerner, 2000).

Orenstein, R. *New Animal Discoveries* (Brookfield, CT: Millbrook, 2001).

Parfit, M. "Hunt for the First Americans," *National Geographic 198*(6):40–67 (December 2000).

Patent, D. H. *Polar Bears* (Minneapolis: Lerner, 2000).

Patent, D. H. *Slinky Scaly Slithery Snakes* (New York: Walker, 2000).

Penny, M. *Giant Panda* (Milwaukee: Raintree, 2000).

Redmond, I. *The Elephant Book: For the Elefriends Campaign* (Cambridge, MA: Candlewick, 2001).

Reed-Jones C. *Salmon Stream* (New York: Dawn, 2001).

Rockwell, A. *Bugs Are Insects* (New York: HarperCollins, 2001).

Rosing, N. "Polar Bears," *National Geographic 198*(6):30–39 (December 2000).

Rosing, N. "Walrus," *National Geographic 200*(3):62–77 (September 2001).

Ross, M. E. *Fish Watching with Eugenie Clark* (Minneapolis: Lerner, 2000).

Ross, M. E. *Millipodedeology* (Minneapolis: Lerner, 2000).

Ross, M. E. *Spiderology* (Minneapolis: Lerner, 2000).

Ruggiero, L. "Shrimp Farming in the Classroom," *Science Scope 23*(4):18–21 (January 2000).

Savage, S. *What's the Difference?: Birds* (Austin, TX: Steck-Vaughn, 2000).

Sayre, A. P. *Dig, Wait, Listen: A Desert Toad's Tale* (New York: Greenwillow, 2001).

Simon, S. *Gorillas* (New York: HarperCollins, 2000).

Tagholm, S. *Animal Lives: The Frog* (New York: Kingfisher, 2000).

Tagholm, S. *Animal Lives: The Rabbit* (New York: Kingfisher, 2000).

Theodorou, R. *To the Depths of the Ocean* (New York: Heinemann, 2000).

Thomas, P. *Marine Mammal Preservation* (Brookfield, CT: Twenty-First Century Books/Millbrook, 2000).

Vancleave, J. *Teaching the Fun of Science* (New York: Wiley, 2001).

Walker, S. M. *Fireflies* (Minneapolis: Lerner, 2001).

Webb, S. *My Season with Penguins: An Antarctic Journal* (Boston, MA: Houghton Mifflin, 2000).

Whitin, P. "First Flight," *Science and Children* 39(4):16–21 (January 2002).

Wolhuter, K. "Tracking the Leopard," *National Geographic* 200(4):90–103 (October 2001).

Zuchora-Walske, C. *Leaping Grasshoppers* (Minneapolis, MN: Lerner, 2000).

Chapter 15

INTERNET

- A.D.A.M., http://www.adam.com
- CELLS ALIVE!, http://www.cellsalive.com
- Health Information A to Z, http://www.cdc.gov/health
- Healthfinder, http://www.healthfinder.com
- Human Genome Project, http://www.genomics.energy.gov
- Inner Learning Online, http://www.innerbody.com
- MedicineNet, http://www.medicinenet.com
- National Institutes of Health, http://www.nih.gov/health
- Quackwatch, www.quackwatch.com
- U.S. National Library of Medicine, http://www.nlm.nih.gov

BOOKS AND PERIODICALS

Alameida, C. C. P. "Skeletons in Your Classroom," *Science Scope* 25(2):18–21 (October 2001).

Ballard, C. *The Human Body: The Skeleton and Muscular System* (Austin, TX: Steck-Vaughn, 1998).

Beckelman, L. *Reader's Digest Pathfinders: The Human Body* (Pleasantville, NY: Reader's Digest Books for Children, 1999).

Berglund, K. "Thought for Food," *Science and Children* 36(4):38–42 (January 1999).

Bradway, H. A. "You Make the Diagnosis," *Science Scope* 24(8):23–27 (May 2001).

Brown, S. W. "A Human Systems Debate," *Science Scope* 23(5):37–41 (February 2000).

Cole, J. *The Magic Schoolbus Explores the Senses* (New York: Scholastic, 1999).

Grambo, G. "Vision and Motion Pictures," *Science Scope* 21(4):24–27 (January 1998).

Jackson, D. M. *Twin Tales: The Magic and Mystery of Multiple Births* (Boston, MA: Megan Tingley Books/Little, Brown, 2001).

Judson, K. *Medical Ethics: Life and Death Issues* (Berkeley Heights, NJ: Enslow, 2001).

Keller, J. D., and Berry, K. A. "Burning Questions About Calories," *Science Scope* 24(7):28–32 (April 2001).

Latta, S. L. *Disease and People: Food Poisoning and Foodborne Diseases* (Springfield, NJ: Enslow Publishers, 1999).

Morris, J., Neustadter, A., and Zidenberg-Cherr, S. "First-Grade Gardeners More Likely to Taste Vegetables," *California Agriculture* 55(1):43–46 (January/February 2001).

Pringle, L. *Everybody Has a Bellybutton: Your Life Before You Were Born* (Honesdale, PA: Boyds Mills Press, 1997).

Raye, S. "Genetics of Sesame Street Characters," *Science Scope* 24(5):12–17 (February 2001).

Simon, S. *Bones: Our Skeletal System* (New York: Morrow, 1998).

Simon, S. *Muscles: Our Muscular System* (New York: Morrow, 1998).

Walker, R. *DK Guide to the Human Body* (New York: DK, 2001).

Walpole, B. *See for Yourself: Hearing, Seeing, Touch, Smell and Taste* (Austin, TX: Raintree/Steck-Vaughn, 1997).

Walters, J. J., and Sunal, C. S. "Studying Our Skin," *Science and Children* 37(3):36–39, 54 (November/December 1999).

Webster, S. *The Kingfisher Book of Evolution* (New York: Kingfisher, 2000).

Wiese, J. *Head to Toe Science* (New York: John Wiley & Sons, 2000).

Zardetto-Smith, A., Houtz, L. E., Brown, G. L., Hanson, J. C., and Nieslanik, L. R. "Brain Attack," *Science Scope* 25(2):32–37 (October 2001).

Zimmer, C. "How Old Is . . .?" *National Geographic* 200(3):77–101 (September 2001).

Chapter 16

INTERNET

- California Energy Commission, The Energy Story, http://www.energyquest.ca.gov and Energy Quest,
- Chemistry Resources, http://www.thecatalyst.org
- Eric's Treasure Trove of Chemistry, http://www.treasuretroves.com
- Periodical Table of the Elements, http://periodictable.com
- Physical Science Resource Center, http://www.psrc-online.org
- University of Oregon Resources for Energy and the Environment, http://zebu.uoregon.edu/energy.html

BOOKS AND PERIODICALS

Allen, B. "Atoms Made from Marshmallows," *Science Scope* 24(2):38–39 (October 2000).

Beven, R. Q. *Move with Science: Energy, Force, and Motion. An Activities-Based Teacher's Guide* (Arlington, VA: National Science Teachers Association, 1998).

Booth, B., Fischman, S., and Wooster, B. "Energy Fuel for Thought," *Science and Children* 39(8):35–42 (May 2002).

Bracikowski, C. et al. "Getting a Feel for Newton's Laws of Motion," *Science and Children* 35(7):26–30, 58 (April 1998).

Burns, J. et al. "Solving Solutions: Exploring Unknowns through Chemistry," *Science Scope* 24(2):30–33 (October 2000).

Chahrour, J. "Conversion Contraption," *Science Scope* 24(1):26–29 (September 2000).

Commo, E., and Matthews, C. E. "The Atomic Dating Game," *Science Scope* 25(4):46–47 (January 2002).

Gartrell, J. E., Jr., *Methods of Motion* (Arlington, VA: National Science Teachers Association, 1998).

Goates, W. "Lavosier Measures with Polymers," *Science Scope* 24(1):30–33 (September 2000).

Hall, S., and Hall, D. "Packing Peanut Properties," *Science and Children* 39(5):31–35 (February 2002).

Hermann, C. K. F. "Beads + String = Atoms You Can See," *Science Scope* 21(8):24–26 (May 1998).

Hodge, D. *Starting with Science: Solids, Liquids, and Gases* (Buffalo, NY: Kids Can Press, 1998).

Iijima, R., and Rubeck, M. "Breakfast Density," *Science and Children* 36(2):22–25 (October 1998).

Ontario Science Centre. *Starting with Science Series: Solids, Liquids, and Gases* (Tonawanda, NY: Kids Can Press, 2000).

Royston, A. *Solids, Liquids, and Gases* (Crystal Lakes, NY: Heinemann, 2001).

Shaw, M. I. "Diving into Density," *Science Scope* 22(3):24–26 (November 1998).

Streitberger, H. E., and Burns, J. "The Versatile Armchair Penny Balance," *Science Scope* 22(4):22–25 (January 1999).

Taylor, B. *Exploring Energy with Toys* (Arlington, VA: National Science Teachers Association, 1998).

Varelas, M., Pappas, C., Barry, A., and O'Neill, A. "Examining Language to Capture Scientific Understandings: The Case of the Water Cycle," *Science and Children* 38(7):26–29 (April 2001).

Vasquez, V. A. "Sumos and the Center of Mass," *Science Scope* 22(6):11–14 (March 1999).

Zimmer, C. "How Old Is_?" *National Geographic* 200(3):77–101 (September 2001).

 Chapter 17

INTERNET

- Physical Science Resource Center, http://www.psrc-online.org

BOOKS AND PERIODICALS

Cronn, K. "Flinging into Science," *Science Scope* 22(2):24–29 (October 1998).

Desouza, J. M. S., and Jereb, J. "Gravitating Toward Reggio," *Science and Children* 37(7):26–29 (April 2000).

Fowler, A. *Simple Machines* (New York: Children's Press, 2001).

Fox, J. E. "Swinging: What Young Children Begin to Learn about Physics During Outdoor Play," *Journal of Elementary Science Education* 9(1):1–14 (Spring 1997).

Gartrell, J. E., Jr. *Methods of Motion* (Arlington, VA: National Science Teachers Association, 1998).

Herald, C. "Toys that Teach," *Science Scope* 25(2):26–30 (October 2001).

Hodge, D. *Simple Machines* (Tonawanda, NY: Kids Can Press, 2000).

Ibarra, H. "Balloon-Powered Racers," *Science Scope* 22(3):21–23 (November 1998).

Lesky, I. "Learn with Levers," *Science Scope* 23(3):18–19 (November/December 1999).

Royston, A. *Forces and Motion* (Crystal Lake, IL: Heinemann Library, 2001).

Sigford, A., and Nelson, N. "What's Inside?" *Science and Children* 35(6):47–49 (March 1998).

Sumrall, W. J. "Trash or Treasure," *Science Scope* 24(8):28–33 (May 2001).

Suplee, C. "Robot Revolution," *National Geographic* 192(1):76–95 (July 1997).

Taylor, A. P. "Push-no-Go: A Dynamic Energy Conversion Lesson," *Science Scope* 21(4):28–31 (January 1998).

Thompson, W. J. "A Moving Science Lesson," *Science and Children* 36(3):24–27, 70. (November/December 1998).

Wetzel, D. R. "Fan Car Physics," *Science Scope* 23(4):29–31 (January 2000).

 Chapter 18

INTERNET

- Physical Science Resource Center, http://www.psrc-online.org

BOOKS AND PERIODICALS

Gabel, D. L., Stockton, J. D., Monaghan, D. L., and MaKinster, J. G. "Changing Children's Conceptions of Burning," *School Science and Mathematics* 101(8):439–454 (December 2001).

Gardner, R. *Science Projects About Temperature and Heat* (Hillside, CA: Enslow, 1994).

Marstall, B. *Fire in the Forest: A Cycle of Growth and Renewal* (New York: Atheneum, 1995).

Royston, A. *Hot and Cold* (Crystal Lake, NY: Heinemann, 2001).

United States Department of Energy. *Fuel Cells for Transportation* (Washington, DC: Author, 1992).

Vogel, C. and Goldner, C., *The Great Yellowstone Fire* (Boston: Little, Brown, 1990).

 Chapter 19

INTERNET

- Physical Science Resource Center, http://www.psrc-online.org

BOOKS AND PERIODICALS

DiSpezio, M. *Awesome Experiments in Light and Sound* (New York: Sterling, 1999).

Farenga, S. J., Joyce, B. A., and Ness, D. "Science of the Symphony: Part I," *Science Scope* 25(4):60–64 (January 2002).

Fox, J. E. "Swinging: What Young Children Begin to Learn about Physics during Outdoor Play," *Journal of Elementary Science Education* 9(1):1–14 (Spring 1997).

Huetinck, L. "Physics to Beat the Band," *Science and Children* 32(3):27–30 (November/December 1994).

Kaner, E. *Sound Science* (Arlington, VA: National Science Teachers Association, 1991).

Levine, S., and Johnstone, L. *The Science of Sound and Music* (Sterling, 2000).

Royston, A. *Sound and Hearing*. Crystal Lake, IL: Heinemann Library, 2001.

Senior, T. "Head Noises," *Physics Teacher* 38(1):30 (January 2000).

Stevens, A. C., Sharp, J. M., and Nelson, B. "The Intersection of Two Unlikely Worlds: Ratios and Drums," *Teaching Children Mathematics* 7(6):376–383 (February 2001).

Thompson, S. "Super Ears," *Science and Children* 32(8):19–21, 50 (May 1995).

Treagust, D. F., Jacobowitz, R., Gallagher, J. L., and Parker, J. "Using Assessment as a Guide in Teaching for Understanding: A Case Study of Middle School Science Class Learning about Sound," *Science Education* 85(2):137–157 (March 2001).

 Chapter 20

INTERNET

- Optics for Kids, http://www.opticalres.com/kidoptx.html
- Physical Science Resource Center, http://www.psrc-online.org
- Rainbows, http://www.unidata.ucar.edu/staff/blynds/rnbw.html

BOOKS AND PERIODICALS

Achenbach, J. "The Power of Light," *National Geographic 200*(4) 2–31 (October 2001).

Branley, F. M. *Let's-Read-and-Find-Out Science: DayLight, Night Light* (New York: HarperCollins, 1998).

DiSpezio, M. A. *Awesome Experiments in Light and Sound* (New York: Sterling, 1999).

DiSpezio, M. A. "Motivation with Depth," *Science Scope 24*(1):20–25 (September 2000).

Famiglieti, M. C. "The EM Spectrum Is Everywhere," *Science Scope 24*(8):46, 48 (May 2001).

Fiarotta, P., and Fiarotta, N. *Great Experiments with Light* (New York: Sterling, 2000).

Graham, J. B. *Flicker Flash* (Boston, MA: Houghton Mifflin, 1999).

Grambo, G. "Vision and Motion Pictures," *Science Scope 21*(4):24–27 (January 1998).

Janes, P. "Kaleidoscope Science," *Instructor 111*(5):40–41 (January/February 2002).

Killough, C. *The Head Bone's Connected to the Neck Bone: The Weird, Wacky, and Wonderful X-ray* (New York: Farrar, Straus and Giroux, 2001).

Krupp, E. C. *The Rainbow and You* (New York: Harper-Collins, 2000).

Kubinec, W. R., and Van Sickle, M. "The Fifty-Cent Optics Lab," *Science Scope 23*(1):16–20 (October 1999).

Levine, S., and Johnstone, L. *The Optics Book: Fun Experiments with Light, Vision, and Color* (New York: Sterling, 1998).

Marshall, J. "Why Are Reef Fish So Colorful?" *Scientific American Presents 9*(3):54–57 (Fall 1998).

Proto, C., and Marek, D. A. "Dissecting Light," *Science Scope 23*(7):14–16 (April 2000).

Royston, A. *Color* (Crystal Lake, IL: Heinemann Library, 2001).

Royston, A. *Light and Dark* (Crystal Lake, IL: Heinemann Library, 2001).

Thomson, N. "Mystery Boxes, X-Rays, and Radiology," *Science Scope 23*(8):26–29 (May 2000).

Tiburzi, B., Tamborino, L., and Parker, G. A. "Light, Color, and Mirrors," *Science Activities 36*(4):25–28 (Winter 2000).

 Chapter 21

INTERNET

- Physical Science Resource Center, http://www.psrc-online.org
- Physics Internet Resources, http://www.het.brown.edu/physics/index.html

BOOKS AND PERIODICALS

Bombaugh, R. "Blast Off into Space Science with Fuses," *Science Scope 23*(5):28–30 (February 2000).

De Pinna, S. *Science Projects: Electricity* (Austin, TX: Steck-Vaughn, 1998).

Hoffman, J., and Stong, J. "Electric Connections." *Science and Children 40*(3):22–25 (November/December 2002).

Royston, A. *Magnets* (Crystal Lake, IL: Heinemann Library, 2001.)

Royston, A. *Using Electricity* (Crystal Lake, IL: Heinemann Library, 2001).

Sapp, L. "Teaching Circuits Is Child's Play," *Science Scope 22*(6):64–65 (March 1999).

Stein, M. "Toying with Science," *Science and Children 36*(1):35–39 (September 1998).

Stewart, G., and Gallai, D. "Build Your Own Motor," *Science Scope* 22(5):12–16 (February 1999).

Stewart, G., and Gallai, D. "Electrostatic Explorations," *Science Scope 21*(5):11–13 (February 1998).

Sunal, D. W. et al. "Semiconductive Science," *Science Scope* 22(1):22–26 (September 1998).

Wilson, A. *How the Future Began: Communications* (New York: Kingfisher, 1999).

Index